The **Rough Guide** to

The Caribbean

written and researched by

**J.P. Anderson, Undeleeb Din, Natalie Folster,
Sean Harvey, S.E. Kramer, Emma Lozman,
Benedict Mander, Fiona McAuslan,
Matt Norman, Kevin Revolinski,
Lesley Anne Rose, Polly Thomas,
Adam Vaitilingam**

D1009199

NEW YORK • LONDON • DELHI

www.roughguides.com

Contents

3

◄◄ Tobago parrot, Pigeon Point ◄ Diving in the Cayman Islands

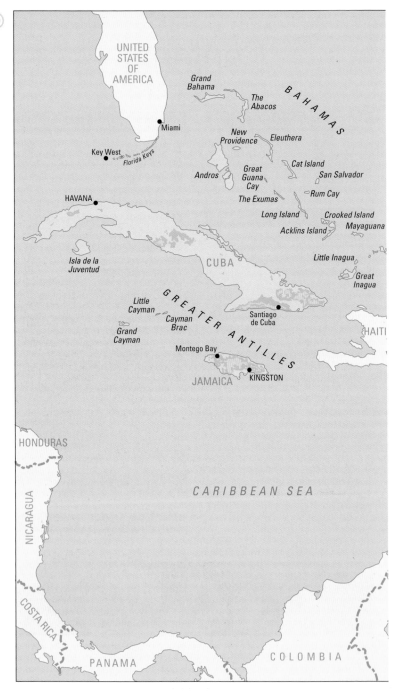

Metres

3000
2000
1000
500
200
0

N

0   200km

ATLANTIC OCEAN

Turks and
Caicos

Puerto Plata

LEEWARD ISLANDS

Virgin
Islands

SAN JUAN   Anguilla
                St Martin/   St Barthélemy
                St Maarten   Saba
SANTO DOMINGO   Barbuda
                St Croix   St Eustatius   St Kitts
DOMINICAN   PUERTO   Antigua
REPUBLIC   RICO   Nevis
                        Montserrat   Guadeloupe

                                      Dominica

WINDWARD ISLANDS   Martinique

                                      St Lucia
                                St Vincent
LESSER ANTILLES   Barbados

Aruba   Curaçao   Bonaire
                    Los Roques   Grenada
                            Isla de
                            Margarita   PORT OF   Tobago
                                        SPAIN
                                              Trinidad
            CARACAS

VENEZUELA

Introduction to

The Caribbean

Palm trees swaying over white-sand beaches, pellucid waters with teeming reefs just a flipper kick from the shore and killer rum cocktails brought right to your lounge chair – this is the Caribbean, everyone's favourite tropical fantasy. The ultimate place to lie on the beach and unwind, the region offers sun, sand and corporeal comforts aplenty, and has long seduced those after life's sybaritic pleasures.

Given these obvious draws, a holiday in the Caribbean – anywhere in the Caribbean – is commonly proffered as the ultimate getaway. But buying into this postcard-perfect stereotype – and failing to recognize the individual idiosyncrasies of the islands that make up the archipelago – is the biggest mistake a visitor can make. Drawing on the collective traditions of Africa and those brought here by Spain, Britain, France, the Netherlands and India, no other area in the Americas exhibits such a diverse range of cultural patterns and social and political institutions; there's a lot more on offer here than sun, sea, sand and learning to limbo.

Culturally, this relatively small, relatively impoverished collection of islands has had an impact quite out of tune with its size, from the Jamaican sound-system DJs who inspired hip-hop, to the pre-Lenten bacchanalia that has come to define carnivals worldwide. Over the last five hundred years, each country or territory has carved out and maintained its own identity (some much more recently than others, with the onset of mass tourism and the advent of the all-inclusive resort), and it's hard to think of worlds so near and yet so disparate as the sensual *son* and *salsa* of Cuba compared to the dancehall and Rasta militancy of neighbouring Jamaica or the poppy *zouk* of Martinique and Guadeloupe. **Sport** rivals music as a Caribbean obsession, and though golf is well represented by the scores of world-class courses, the region's game of choice has traditionally been cricket, introduced by the Brits and raised to great heights by the West Indies team, which led the world for much of the 1970s and 1980s. Wins are rather less common these days, but cricket remains central to the Caribbean psyche, with international matches known to bring their host islands to a complete standstill. Other popular spectator sports include soccer and baseball, firmly entrenched in the Dominican Republic, Puerto Rico and Cuba.

Each island has a strong **culinary** tradition, too, and while you might come here to sample Caribbean classics such as Trinidadian roti, Grenadian "oil-down" or Dominican mountain chicken (actually a very big frog), you can also enjoy croissants and gourmet dinners in the French islands, Dutch delicacies in the Netherlands Antilles and piles of good ol' burgers and fries in Puerto Rico and the Bahamas – and on every island with a fair-sized tourism industry you'll find

Fact file

• The combined **population** of the Caribbean islands is just over 38 million; Great Inagua in the Bahamas has a population of less than 1000 people but is home to 60,000 pink flamingos, spoonbills and ducks.

• **Tourism** is by far the region's biggest business, with between fifteen and twenty million visitors each year. With over two million visitors annually, the Dominican Republic is the most popular destination; Saba, with around 9000, is the least visited.

• The Caribbean Sea is the **fifth largest body of water** in the world, with a total area of 2.5 million square kilometres (slightly bigger than the Mediterranean).

• The **highest point** in the region is the Dominican Republic's Pico Duarte, at 3125m above sea level – it even gets some snow in winter. The DR also holds the Caribbean's **lowest point**: Lago Enriquillo, some 39m below sea level.

• With an estimated 390,000 people diagnosed HIV-positive, **HIV/AIDS infection rates** in the Caribbean are among the highest in the world, second only to sub-Saharan Africa.

• St Lucia has produced two **Nobel Prize winners**, the poet Derek Walcott and the economist Sir Arthur Lewis.

▲ Coconuts in Trinidad

"international" restaurants of every ilk alongside hole-in-the-wall shacks selling local specialities.

The Caribbean's natural attractions are equally compelling, its **landscapes** ranging from teeming rainforest, mist-swathed mountains and volcanic peaks to lowland mangrove swamps, lush pastureland and savannah plains. The entire region is incredibly abundant in its **flora**, despite the sometimes volcanic or scrubby interiors on certain islands. Heliconias and orchids flower almost everywhere, while hibiscus and ixoras brighten up the hedgerows, and the forest greens are enlivened by flowering trees such as poinsettia and poui. Not surprisingly eco-tourism abounds, whether it be hiking through the waterfall-studded rainforest of Dominica or St Lucia, high-mountain treks in Jamaica or birding in Trinidad, which has one of the highest concentrations of **bird species** in the world. The sea here is as bountiful as the land; besides taking in superlative **diving** and **snorkelling** around multicoloured reefs and sunken ships that play host to technicolour marine life, you can turtle-watch on innumerable beaches that see nesting leatherbacks and hawksbills, go whale-spotting from St Lucia, Dominica and the Dominican Republic or frolic with giant manta rays offshore from Tobago and stingrays in the Caymans.

Beyond their cultural and physical richness, the Caribbean islands share a similar history of **colonization**. The first known inhabitants, farming and fishing Amerindians who travelled from South America by way of dugout canoes around 500 BC, were swiftly displaced by **Christopher Columbus**, the Italian explorer who "discovered" the region for Spain in the late fifteenth century, touching down on the Bahamas, Cuba, Hispaniola (modern-day Haiti and the Dominican Republic) and Jamaica, and mistakenly assuming that he had found the outlying islands of India, bestowing

Rum

Tipple of choice for the region, **rum** is an integral part of Caribbean life – even the smallest village has a rum shop where old men nurse glasses of overproof "whites" and water and put the world to rights. Everyone has their favourite brew, ranging from home-brewed firewaters such as Tobago's babash or Jamaica's jancro batty (strictly for masochists), to weaker, cocktail-friendly whites from Trinidad and Tobago or sweet, rich, oak-aged concoctions like Cuba's Matusalem – best drunk after dinner, and never to be adulterated with a mixer.

Rum-making has remained much the same over the centuries. Yeast is added to sugar cane juice or molasses to kick-start fermentation (which converts the sucrose to alcohol); this "dead wash" is then boiled, and the evaporating alcohol is collected. After a little blending and the addition of water, the white rums are ready to bottle; smoother brown rums are aged in oak barrels, which colour the spirit to varying shades of brown. It's a simple process, but consider that it takes some ten to twelve tonnes of cane to produce half a bottle of pure alcohol, and you'll understand the prevalence of those endless fields of swaying cane.

the title "West Indies" to the region. Seduced by fantasies of innumerable riches, other European countries soon jumped on the bandwagon. The Spanish were followed by the **British**, **French** and **Dutch**, who squabbled over their various territories for most of the sixteenth century, their colonization of the islands hindered by **pirates** and state-licensed **privateers** who plundered settlements and vessels without mercy.

Nonetheless, European colonies were planted throughout the region, and by the seventeenth century, the islands had begun to be developed in earnest. The British proved most adept at establishing huge plantations of **sugar cane** – estates which required far more labour than the colonists themselves could provide, and which gave rise to the appalling tragedy of the **slave trade**, which saw some twelve million people transported to the region from Africa, many of whom died during the passage over. Plantation life for slaves was one of unimaginable barbarity, and eighteenth-century **rebellions**, combined with Christian tenets of humanity and charity, engendered the first moves toward emancipation – between 1833 and 1888 slavery was abolished in the Caribbean.

9

Haiti

Though we've not covered **Haiti** in this edition of the guide, out of **safety concerns** for travellers – kidnappings and assault are rife – its longtime spell over foreigners is hard to deny. One of the more culturally fascinating destinations in the Caribbean, Haiti is known for its African-derived artistic traditions, its common practice of voodoo religion and as the site of a successful slave rebellion, which overthrew the colonial government some two centuries ago. Not that that solved everything politically; military dictatorships and "presidents-for-life" have followed, as has the occasional contested election. The country remains, too, in the economic doldrums, its teeming capital **Port-au-Prince** comprised of many depressed neighbourhoods, and much of its green and lovely countryside not at all set up for the casual traveller. Furthermore, flood damage wrought by Hurricane Jean in September 2004 and flash floods in May 2005 have left the country in even deeper chaos. Prospective visitors to Haiti are strongly encouraged to consult recent **travel advisories** put out by the British Foreign Office (ⓦ www.fco.gov.uk) and the US State Department (ⓦ travel.state .gov/travel/warnings.html).

After emancipation, conditions for all but the planter elites remained abysmal, and the formation of unions and subsequent labour strikes led, by the 1930s, to the creation of political parties throughout the region. This in turn nudged the islands to call for **independence** from their colonial rulers, increasingly so after World War II. The early twentieth century also saw **tourism** start to take root. Wealthy Brits and North Americans had patronized palatial resorts here since the late nineteenth century, and the glitterati followed in the footsteps of Errol Flynn to Jamaica and Ernest Hemingway to Cuba, thus creating the air of exclusivity that remains inextricably tied to the Caribbean today. But with the introduction of long-haul air travel in the 1960s, tourists began to arrive en masse. While the fenced-off all-inclusive enclave is still going strong today, the region now has as many budget-oriented bolt holes as it does luxury resorts, and as many possibilities for adventurous travel as it does for staid beach holidays.

Where to go

Spanning an arc from southern Florida to Venezuela on the South American coast, the islands of the Caribbean are made up of two main chains which form a 3200 kilometre breakwater between the Caribbean Sea to the south and the Atlantic Ocean to the north. Running south from Florida, the mostly limestone **Greater Antilles** (Cuba,

Jamaica, Cayman Islands, Dominican Republic and Haiti, Puerto Rico and the Virgin Islands) comprise the largest and most geographically varied of the two chains, with white-sand beaches aplenty as well as rainforest-smothered peaks, remnants of submerged ranges related to the Central and South American mountain systems. Drier, somewhat flatter and boasting as many black-sand beaches as white, the volcanic **Lesser Antilles** can be further subdivided into the **Leeward Islands** (Anguilla, St Martin/St Maarten, St Barts, Saba, St Eustatius, St Kitts, Nevis, Antigua, Barbuda, Montserrat and Guadeloupe) and **Windward Islands** (Dominica, Martinique, St Lucia, Barbados, St Vincent,

Carnival knowledge

Balmy temperatures, stunning outdoor venues and a bacchanalian worldview – the Caribbean is a fabulous place to **party**, and there's an extensive programme of annual events that cater to the hedonistic urge. The festival calendar may kick off with Christmas **Junkanoo** parades throughout the region, but the real deal is **Carnival**, of which Trinidad's is the highlight, bursting with pure, unbridled energy and with the emphasis on participation. Buy a costume and "play mas" in a costume band with five thousand revellers, or get coated in mud, paint or oil at the rawer, early-hours Jouvert parade. Carnival culture runs pretty much year-round, too, with substantial events in March (Jamaica, St Thomas), July (St Lucia, Barbados, St Vincent, Cuba, Antigua and Barbuda) and August (Grenada).

Other major happenings with a uniquely Caribbean flavour include Jamaica's **Reggae Sumfest** (Aug), held next to the sea and under the stars – the ultimate way to enjoy the cream of reggae performers on their home turf. Caribbean scenery provides the perfect backdrop for other music, too, and there are major **jazz** festivals featuring international performers in Barbados (Jan), St Lucia (May), Jamaica and Aruba (both June), while Dominica stages the World Creole Music Festival every October. Although you may not be here for the big events listed above, rest assured that, as every island has its own sizeable roster, there'll be something going on whenever you visit; see individual chapters for lists of major festivals and events.

How to pick a beach

Finding a beach that suits your tastes shouldn't be hard, given that Caribbean beaches can be as varied as the islands themselves. Spectacular swathes of sand are ten-a-penny here, but for the archetypal stretch of powdery white sand, lapped by warm clear water and generously endowed with coconut palms, you'll want to head to low-lying coraline islands such as Antigua (said to boast 365 beaches – one for every day of the year), the Bahamas (which has pink sand as well as white) or, in no particular order, Barbados, Aruba, Cayman Islands, Virgin Islands, Anguilla and the Turks and Caicos. If you're after desert-island solitude, you'll be hard-pressed to find any: the best spots were snapped up long ago by developers who've added everything from hotels, bars and restaurants to watersports, and usually charge a fee for use of the facilities.

Those willing to travel off the beaten path might consider checking out the Caribbean's stunning grey- or black-sand beaches (the happy result of age-old volcanic activity), many of which are relatively undeveloped and surrounded by lush tropical foliage – St Lucia, Grenada, St Vincent, Guadeloupe and Martinique are all solid contenders, while the larger of the Windward Islands have all the types of beaches.

Remember that many islands have coastline on the Atlantic Ocean as well as the Caribbean Sea; beaches on the Atlantic side typically have rougher waves and cooler, green-tinged depths, while those on the Caribbean are usually calmer, warmer and properly conform to the classic "white-sand-and-palms" image.

the Grenadines and Grenada). North of the Greater Antilles, the Bahamas and Turks and Caicos Islands sit alone, as do Trinidad and Tobago and the "ABC islands" (Aruba, Bonaire and Curaçao) in the south, just off the Venezuelan coast, though the latter are also an autonomous part of the Kingdom of the Netherlands. Together with Saba, St Eustatius and St Maarten, these islands are collectively known as the **Netherlands Antilles**.

Deciding which of the islands to visit, however, is the fifty-million-dollar question. Obviously, you'll need to consider what you want from your holiday. If you're after two weeks of sunbathing and swimming and don't plan on doing any exploring, then you've the freedom to allow a travel agent to pick the cheapest deal available – or just flip through this guide and pick which sounds the most appealing. If variety is on your agenda, bigger islands which boast a diversity of landscapes – Cuba, Jamaica and the Dominican Republic – offer more scope for adventurous travel, with possibilities for hiking, rafting, eco-pursuits and cultural tours as well as beachlife; these probably demand a single-island trip. However, as **island-hopping** can be relatively easy, either by short plane trips or the occasional ferry, it's well worth seeing more than one island, especially if you've picked a destination in the close-set Lesser Antilles.

When to go

A s visitors mainly flock to the Caribbean to swap snow, rain and wind back home for the sun and warm waters of the tropics, it should come as no surprise to find that the region's busiest time is the northern hemisphere's **winter** (roughly Nov–Feb). During this high season, the daytime heat doesn't reach blistering proportions, and is tempered by cool breezes and balmy evenings, while rain is generally restricted to brief early-afternoon showers. The downside to this, however, is that the beaches and attractions are busy, hotels are often full and flights can get overbooked, with fares at a premium. Prices for almost everything may decrease in the slow **summer** season, but it's not an ideal time to visit the Caribbean: days are oppressively hot and humid and nights are muggy. Late summer also sees the start of the **hurricane season** (for more on which, see p.42), which runs

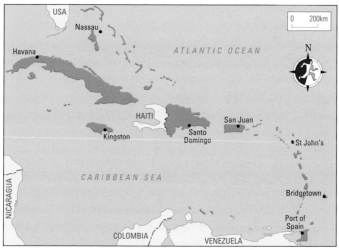

See overleaf for corresponding climate chart

roughly from July to November, and even if there's no big blow, this usually means a lot of **rain**. While there's never really a bad time to holiday in the region, the Caribbean is best enjoyed in the **shoulder seasons** (early Nov and Feb through June), when flights and hotels are plentiful (and less expensive) and the weather dependable. **Spring** is also the season for catching one of the Caribbean's many pre-Lenten carnivals.

Average daily temperatures and monthly rainfall

	Jan	Feb	Mar	Apr	May	June	July	Aug	Sept	Oct	Nov	Dec
San Juan, Puerto Rico												
Max °C	27	27	27	28	29	29	29	29	30	29	29	27
Min °C	21	21	21	22	23	24	24	24	24	24	23	22
Rain (mm)	109	69	74	104	150	137	145	160	158	142	160	137
Nassau, Bahamas												
Max °C	25	25	26	27	29	31	31	32	31	29	27	26
Min °C	18	18	19	21	22	23	24	24	24	23	21	19
Rain (mm)	36	38	36	64	117	163	147	135	175	165	71	33
Havana, Cuba												
Max °C	25	25	27	29	29	30	32	32	30	29	27	25
Min °C	19	19	20	21	22	23	24	24	24	23	21	20
Rain (mm)	71	46	46	58	119	165	125	135	150	173	79	58
Kingston, Jamaica												
Max °C	30	30	30	31	31	32	32	32	32	31	31	31
Min °C	19	19	20	21	22	23	23	23	23	23	22	19
Rain (mm)	23	15	23	20	102	86	86	89	97	178	76	36
Bridgetown, Barbados												
Max °C	28	28	29	30	31	31	30	31	31	30	29	28
Min °C	21	21	21	22	23	23	23	23	23	23	23	22
Rain (mm)	66	28	33	36	58	112	147	147	170	178	206	97
Port of Spain, Trinidad .												
Max °C	31	31	32	32	32	32	31	31	32	32	32	31
Min °C	21	20	20	21	22	22	22	22	22	22	22	21
Rain (mm)	69	41	46	53	94	193	218	246	193	170	183	125
St John's, Antigua												
Max °C	28	28	29	30	31	31	31	31	32	31	29	28
Min °C	21	21	21	22	23	24	24	24	23	23	23	22
Rain (mm)	122	86	112	89	97	112	155	183	168	196	180	140
Santo Domingo, Dominican Republic												
Max °C	29	29	29	30	30	31	31	31	31	31	30	29
Min °C	19	19	20	21	22	23	23	23	23	22	21	20
Rain (mm)	51	44	44	68	187	152	179	157	165	170	96	70

26

things not to miss

It's not possible to see everything that the Caribbean has to offer in one trip – and we don't suggest you try. What follows is a selective and subjective taste of the islands' highlights: spectacular natural attractions, thrilling ocean activities and rich cultural traditions. They're arranged in five colour-coded categories to help you find the very best things to see, do, eat and experience. All highlights have a page reference to take you straight into the guide, where you can find out more.

01 **Swimming with dolphins, the Bahamas** Page **89** • Swim, feed and frolic among dolphins off the coast of Grand Bahama.

03 The Pitons, St Lucia

Page **701** • Towering over Soufrière, St Lucia's oldest town, these distinctive twin peaks are, rightfully, the island's most photographed sight.

02 Trinidad Carnival Page **808**

• The original Caribbean Carnival, easily the biggest and best in the islands, culminates in two days of fabulous costumed parades.

04 Willemstad, Curaçao Page **886** • One of the Caribbean's most colourful capitals, Willemstad's Dutch heritage is apparent along its narrow winding streets and attractive waterfront.

05 **Street food** Page **807** • Be sure to visit food stalls in places like Trinidad and Tobago for *roti* and the like – they're often the top spots to sample local cuisine and rub elbows with the islanders.

06 **Cuban music** Page **172** • The sounds of the Caribbean are every bit as important as the sights – be sure to check out some *salsa* and *son* in Cuba's dance halls, or even on its streets.

07 **Bonaire Marine Park** Page **881** • Home to everything from angelfish to moray eels, and just one of the Caribbean's spectacular marine habitats.

17

08 **Places you've never heard of** Page **538** • Far off the beaten track lie islands like tranquil Saba, one of the unspoiled gems of the Caribbean.

09 **Jamaican nightlife** Page **271** • From sweaty dance halls to laid-back jam sessions or star-studded stage shows, the island's phenomenal music scene is bound to keep you busy night after night.

11 **Barbados surf** Page **731**
Though treacherous to swim in, the Atlantic waves along the island's little-explored east coast make it a popular surfing destination.

12 **Fresh seafood** Page **58**
Don't miss the region's countless seafood options, including succulent fresh lobster, a mainstay of menus everywhere from high-end restaurants to charming beachside shacks.

10 **Beach bumming** Page **634**
Flop down on your own patch of sand, like these sun-worshippers in Martinique, and savour the freedom of not having to do anything at all.

19

13 Soufrière Hills Page **575** • Witness first-hand the terrible power of Montserrat's active volcano, which erupted in 1995 and destroyed half the island, including the now-abandoned capital of Plymouth.

14 Scuba diving Pages **126, 242 & 881** • While most of the Caribbean isles boast sunken wrecks, reefs and colourful ocean creatures in spades, the Bahamas, the Cayman Islands and Bonaire are the highpoints for in-the-know diving enthusiasts.

16 Boiling Lake, Dominica Page **667** • If the island's ultimate hike leading to the lake fails to impress, the eerie sight of its steam-enshrouded waters most certainly will.

15 El Yunque, Puerto Rico Page **408** • There's great rainforest scenery on islands like Grenada, St Lucia and Puerto Rico. The latter is home to El Yunque, the largest rainforest in the US and excellent for birdwatching opportunities.

18 Snorkelling Page **62** • Often as rewarding as diving, snorkelling through the Caribbean's underwater world can be far cheaper, especially if you bring your own gear.

17 Old San Juan, Puerto Rico Page **394** • The preserved colonial buildings of the city make for excellent wandering, amid old fortresses, convents and the odd historic museum.

21

19 Sea kayaking in the Exumas Page **126** • Kayaking around this island chain – stopping off at whichever deserted beach strikes your fancy – is a compelling adventure for first-time paddlers and experienced explorers alike.

20 Seven Mile Beach, Grand Cayman Page **248** • Lovely strands of coast like this lengthy one help make the Cayman Islands known for more than just offshore banking.

21 Bomba's shack, Virgin Islands Page **480** • Quiet and unassuming most of the time, this ramshackle bar comes alive every full moon to host an all-out bash.

22 **The Baths, Virgin Islands** Page **487** • Clamber about in this otherworldly landscape, where gigantic boulders form striking grottoes, pools and underwater caves.

23 **Habana Vieja, Cuba** Page **183** • Untouched for years by tourism, the faded grandeur of Havana's old town is unmatched in the region.

24 Windsurfing at Cabarete, Dominican Republic Page 372 •

The world-class conditions, along with a plethora of schools and rental centres, make this lively coastal town the best place to windsurf in the Western Hemisphere.

25 Bonefishing in the Bahamas Page 115

• Enjoy some of the best fishing in the Caribbean at welcoming lodges on Andros, the archipelago's "big back yard".

26

Plantation inns, St Kitts
Page **558** • Exuding old-world ambience, inventive inns like *Rawlins* – housed in a former sugar cane plantation – are a refreshing break from the usual beachside accommodations.

Basics

Basics

Getting there

Given the ocean-bound nature of the Caribbean, **flying** is the only viable option for many visitors. Flights to the Caribbean tend to operate through a major US East Coast hub: Miami, say, or New York, though San Juan, Puerto Rico, is also well connected. Similarly, most **cruises** to the region depart from the US East Coast, making a flight to the US an inevitable part of the itinerary for those from outside America.

Air fares always depend on the season. In the Caribbean, **high season** is from mid-December to April, with fares peaking during the holiday season. Fares drop during the "**shoulder**" **seasons** – May to July – and you'll get the best prices during the **low**, **wet season**, which runs from August to November (though from the UK, prices during the school summer holidays can be high). Of course, prices vary wildly depending on your destination and it is inevitably much cheaper to vacation in countries hosting the transit hubs of major airlines, such as Puerto Rico, Jamaica, Trinidad and Barbados. Note also that flying at weekends is more expensive; price ranges quoted below assume midweek travel.

You can often cut costs by going through a **specialist flight agent** – either a **consolidator**, who buys up blocks of tickets from the airlines and sells them at a discount, or a **discount agent**, who in addition to dealing with discounted flights may also offer special student and youth fares and a range of other travel-related services such as travel insurance, car rentals, tours and the like. Some agents specialize in **charter flights**, which may be cheaper than any available scheduled flight, but departure dates are fixed and withdrawal penalties are high. Booking flights well in advance, or taking advantage of Web-only offers and airline frequent-flyer programmes, can often knock a couple of hundred dollars off the price of your flight. Another way to vastly reduce the price of your Caribbean holiday – especially if you book last-minute, accept charter flights and don't insist upon particular accommodation – is to book with a tour operator who can put together a **package deal** including flights and accommodation at an especially arranged price, and perhaps tours of the island or even a wedding ceremony as well.

Booking flights online

Booking tickets **online** can often save you money, cutting out the costs of agents and middlemen. Good deals can often be found through **discount** or **auction sites**, as well as through the airlines' own websites.

Useful websites

travel.yahoo.co.uk Incorporates a lot of Rough Guides material in its coverage of destination countries and cities across the world, with information about places to eat, sleep and etc.

www.cheapflights.co.uk Bookings from the UK and Ireland only; for the US, visit www. cheapflights.com; for Canada, www.cheapflights. ca; for Australia, www.cheapflights.com.au. All the sites offer flight deals, details of travel agents and links to other travel sites.

www.cheaptickets.com Hawaii-based discount flight specialists (US only) whose search engine claims to dig up the lowest possible fares worldwide, though the one drawback is its cumbersome log-in procedure.

www.counciltravel.com If your journey originates in the US and you've some flexibility, this site can come up with competitive deals.

www.etn.nl/discount.htm A hub of consolidator and discount agent Web links, maintained by the nonprofit European Travel Network.

www.expedia.com Discount air fares, all-airline search engine and daily deals (US only; for the UK www.expedia.co.uk; for Canada www.expedia. ca).

www.flights4less.co.uk Does just what it says on the tin.

www.flynow.com Simple to use independent travel site offering good-value fares.

ⓦ **www.hotwire.com** Bookings from the US only. Last-minute savings of up to forty percent on regular published fares. Travellers must be at least 18 and there are no refunds, transfers or changes allowed. Log-in required. If you're looking for the cheapest possible scheduled flight, this is probably your best bet.

ⓦ **www.lastminute.com** Offers good last-minute holiday package and flight-only deals (UK only; for Australia ⓦ www.lastminute.com.au).

ⓦ **www.qixo.com** A comparison search that trawls through other ticket sites – including agencies and airlines – to find the best deals.

ⓦ **www.skyauction.com** Bookings from the US only. Auctions tickets and travel packages using a "second bid" scheme, just like eBay. You state the maximum you're willing to pay, and the system will bid only as much as it takes to outbid others, up to your stated limit.

ⓦ **www.ticketplanet.com** California-based site that claims to be the first to sell consolidator fares over the web. Especially good for circle-Pacific and round-the-world fares.

ⓦ **www.travelocity.com** and ⓦ **www.travelocity.co.uk** Destination guides, hot Web fares and best deals for car hire, accommodation and lodging. Provides access to the travel agent system SABRE, the most comprehensive central reservations system in the US.

ⓦ **www.travelshop.com.au** Australian website offering discounted flights, packages, insurance and online bookings.

Flights from the US and Canada

Most American airlines operate their Caribbean flights from the **East Coast** of the US and from **Toronto**, except for American Airlines, which flies from most major US cities to their Caribbean hub in San Juan. Additional direct flights include a US Airways Saturday service to St Lucia from Philadelphia and Northwest's once-weekly summer service from Detroit to San Juan and Montego Bay; in Canada you can fly direct from Toronto to Grand Cayman, Barbados, Antigua and San Juan. Flights from New York and Toronto average around five hours, while flights from Miami are about three hours.

Air fares peak around Christmas and New Year, when they can reach US$900–1000/Can$1380–1535 from the East Coast of the US and Toronto, and from **January to April** when you can expect to pay up to US$800/

Can$1230, more for some flights from Canada – but for which you'll get the best weather. Amounts drop during **shoulder season**, when you'll pay around US$700/Can$1125, and the best prices are available during the (**wet**) **low season**, from August to November – you should be able to get a regular fare for around US$650/Can$1000. Count on paying an extra US$300 or so to fly from the **West Coast** of the US. Note also that flying at weekends ordinarily adds at least US$50 to the round-trip fare.

Package tours can often be the most economical option and range from combined flight and accommodation deals to specialist tours. For details on **scuba-diving** tours see p.63.

Airlines

Unless otherwise specified all phone numbers work in both the US and Canada.

Aeroflot US ☎1-888/340-6400, Canada ☎416/642-1653, ⓦwww.aeroflot.com.

Air Canada ☎1-888/247-2262, ⓦwww.aircanada.ca.

Air France US ☎1-800/237-2747, ⓦwww.airfrance.com, Canada ☎1-800/667-2747, ⓦwww.airfrance.ca.

Air Jamaica US ☎1-800/523-5585, Canada ☎416/229-6024, ⓦwww.airjamaica.com.

Air Sunshine US ☎1-800/327-8900, ⓦwww.airsunshine.com.

AirTran Airways ☎1-800/247-8726, ⓦwww.airtran.com.

American Airlines ☎1-800/433-7300, ⓦwww.aa.com.

Bahamas Air US ☎1-800/222-4262, ⓦwww.bahamasair.com.

British Airways ☎1-800/247-9297, ⓦwww.ba.com.

BWIA International ☎1-800/538-2942, ⓦwww.bwee.com.

Cayman Airways US ☎1-800/422-9626 or 345/949-2311, ⓦwww.caymanairways.com.

Chalk's Ocean Airways US ☎1-800/424-2775, ⓦwww.chalksoceanairways.com.

Continental Airlines domestic ☎1-800/523-3279, international ☎1-800/231-0856, ⓦwww.continental.com.

Delta Air Lines domestic ☎1-800/221-1212, international ☎1-800/241-4141, ⓦwww.delta.com.

Gulfstream International Airlines ☎954/226-3000 or 1-800/231-0856, ⓦwww.gulfstreamair.

com.

JetBlue ☎1-800/538-2583, ⊛www.jetblue.com.
Lynx Air International US ☎1-888/596-9247 or
954/772-9808, ⊛www.lynxair.com.
Mexicana ☎1-800/531-7921, ⊛www.mexicana.
com.
North American Airlines ☎718/656-6250 or 1-
800/359-6222, ⊛www.northamair.com.
Northwest/KLM Royal Dutch Airlines domestic
☎1-800/225-2525, international ☎1-800/447-
4747, ⊛www.nwa.com, ⊛ww.klm.com.
Pan American Airways ☎ 1-800/FLY-PANAM,
⊛www.flypanam.com.
Spirit Airlines ☎1-800/772-7117, ⊛www.
spiritair.com.
United Airlines domestic ☎1-800/241-6522,
international ☎1-800/538-2929, ⊛www.ual.com.
Virgin Atlantic Airways ☎1-800/862-8621,
⊛www.virgins-atlantic.com.

Travel agents

Air Brokers International ☎1-800/883-3273,
⊛www.airbrokers.com. Consolidator.
Airtech ☎212/219-7000, ⊛www.airtech.com.
Standby seat broker; also deals in consolidator fares
and courier flights.
Educational Travel Center ☎1-800/747-5551
or 608/256-5551, ⊛www.edtrav.com. Student/
youth discount agent.
STA Travel US ☎1-800/781-4040, Canada 1-
888/427-5639, ⊛www.statravel.com. Worldwide
specialists in independent travel; also student IDs,
travel insurance, car rental, rail passes etc.
Student Flights ☎1-800/255-8000 or 480/951-
1177, ⊛www.isecard.com. Student/youth fares,
student IDs.
TFI Tours ☎1-800/745-8000 or 212/736-1140,
⊛www.lowestairprice.com. Consolidator.
Travelers Advantage ☎1-877/259-2691,
⊛www.travelersadvantage.com. Discount travel
club; annual membership fee required (currently $1
for three months' trial).
Travel Cuts Canada ☎1-866/246-9762, US ☎1-
800/952-2887, ⊛www.travelcuts.com. Canadian
student-travel organization.
Worldtek Travel ☎1-800/243-1723, ⊛www.
worldtek.com. Comparison site.

Specialist tour operators

American Express Vacations ☎1-800/335-
3342, ⊛www.americanexpressvacations.com.
Luxury vacations to various Caribbean islands.
Caribbean Concepts ☎206/575-0907 or 1-
800/777-0977, ⊛www.caribbeanconcepts.com.
Caribbean specialists offering tours and packages all

over the region.
Caribbean Journey ☎1-888/236-1924,
⊛www.caribbeanjourney.com. Personalized trips
to most Caribbean islands, with all categories of
accommodation, as well as trips built around festivals
and weddings/honeymoons.
Cheap Caribbean ☎1-800/915-2322, ⊛www.
cheapcaribbean.com. Flight and accommodation
deals throughout the Caribbean.
Delta Vacations ☎1-800/654-6559, ⊛www.
deltavacations.com. Vacations in most Caribbean
islands from major US cities.
Ecosummer Expeditions ☎1-800/465-8884
or 250/674-0102, ⊛www.ecosummer.com. Sea
kayaking trips in the Bahamian Exumas.
Free Spirit Travel ☎201/845-5313, ⊛www.
freespirittravel.com. Small operator offering cruises
and flight/accommodation packages to various
Caribbean islands.
Global Exchange ☎415/225-7296, ⊛www.
globalexchange.org. Cultural and eco-tours to Cuba
and Jamaica.
Leisure Time Travel ☎352/795-3474 or 1-
800/771-2202, ⊛www.leisuretimetravel.com. Tour
operator specializing in fly fishing and light tackle
vacations to the Bahamas, Cayman Islands and Costa
Rica.
TourScan Inc ☎1-800/962 2080, ⊛www.
tourscan.com. This Caribbean specialist offers
discounted vacations all over the region.
Tradewind Tours ☎1-800/860-8013, ⊛www.
tradewindtours.net. A small, specialist travel
agency offering in-depth local knowledge as well as
skilled and personal service. Trips to Antigua, Aruba,
Bahamas, Barbados, Curacao, Jamaica, St Lucia and
the Turks and Caicos islands.

Cruises from the US

Cruises are a popular way to visit multiple
islands in a very short time – trips can last
anywhere from a few days up to a week or
more and ships usually stop for a day at each
port. Plenty of corporate cruise lines ply the
Caribbean, offering **all-inclusive** cruises that
can scale the heights of luxury (and costs)
but can also be relatively affordable: a seven-
day spin on a not-so-swanky ship in the
region could set you back just US$700–900.
One drawback of choosing a cruise is that
you only get to visit the tourist ports, making it difficult to know what the island is like
in anything more than a superficial sense.
Cruises can, however, be more reasonably
priced than their package tour counterparts

– **prices** for cruises from Florida for seven nights range from US$600 for the Western Caribbean, US$700 for the Eastern region and slightly more for the southern islands.

The **Internet** is a good place to start your research. Websites such as ⓦ www.cruise. com and ⓦ www.cruisereviews.com are helpful resources for deciding which cruise is best for you, taking into account price range, size of boat and length of trip; **Cruise Discounters** (☎ 1-800/268-0854, ⓦ www. cruisediscounters.com) are a specialist agent that offer discounts with all the lines offering Caribbean itineraries. While some companies offer cruises only, there are still many others that negotiate rates with major airlines allowing for fly/cruise options from most major airports in the US and the rest of the world.

Cruise lines

The **fares** quoted are for single person/double occupancy "inside" (no ocean views) cabins, outside of the high season, when prices can jump by US$300–500. Prices given are also exclusive of **port charges**, which add an extra US$200 or so.

Carnival ☎ 1-866/299-5968, ⓦ www.carnival. com. A youthful cruise line with a big emphasis on fun, offering seven nights from Miami, Orlando or Fort Lauderdale from US$549 in the eastern Caribbean, $519 in the western Caribbean and $499 in the southern Caribbean.

Disney ☎ 1-800/951-3532, ⓦ disneycruise.disney. go.com/disneycruiseline/index. Packages include seven nights from Key West from US$799, including a trip to Disney's own Bahamian island. Other ports of call include St Maarten, Grand Cayman, St Thomas/St John and Nassau.

Holland America ☎ 1-877/724-5425, ⓦ www. hollandamerica.com. Family cruise line, with hefty scheduled entertainment for both adults and kids. Weeklong cruises from Fort Lauderdale from around US$600.

Norwegian ☎ 1-800/327-7030, ⓦ www.ncl.com. Top-quality luxury fleet offering seven-day cruises from Florida to the western Caribbean from $879.

Princess ☎ 1-800/PRINCESS, ⓦ www. princesscruises.com. Seven-day luxury cruises (including spas and scuba diving) from Florida for upwards of US$649.

Radisson Seven Seas ☎ 1-877/505-5370, ⓦ www.rssc.com. Seven-day cruises from Florida to LA via the Caribbean and South America, starting at US$4496 for two people.

Royal Caribbean ☎ 1-800/389-9819 ⓦ www. royalcaribbean.com. Caribbean specialists offering great deals for trips from Florida to destinations all over the region, from as little as $409, and ships with such facilities as rock-climbing walls.

Silversea ☎ 1-877/760-9052, ⓦ www.silversea. com. Top-notch cruises and fly/cruise options from all over the world – nine-day all-inclusive packages start at around US$4339.

Flights from the UK and Ireland

The majority of **British** and **Irish** visitors to many Caribbean islands, such as Barbados, Jamaica and Trinidad and Tobago, are on some form of **package tour**. This is usually the simplest way of going about things, and even if you plan to travel independently and organize your own accommodation, a seat on a charter can be the cheapest way to reach your destination. But charters do have their drawbacks, especially if your plans don't fit exactly into their usual two-week straitjacket. As an alternative, several airlines fly direct scheduled **flights** from London to many Caribbean destinations, and you can find comparable fares with other carriers that require a stopover in the US. For former **Dutch colonies** like Aruba, Bonaire, Curaçao, Saba, St Eustatius and St Maarten, try KLM via Amsterdam, or for Guadeloupe and Martinique – both former **colonies of France** – you can fly from London with Air France via Paris, depending on the time of year.

There are **no direct flights** from Ireland to a number of islands, including Antigua and Barbados, but there are good connections via London, New York or Miami (see "Flights from the US and Canada").

Many islands in the Caribbean are popular **package tour** destinations, and as such there are legions of operators to choose from. If you're planning to do little more than stay in one place and soak in the sun, then a package holiday might be your best option. There are many specialist companies that can arrange flights as well as accommodation ranging from self-catering apartments to all-inclusive hotels (meals and drinks are included in the room price). Many operators offer specialized tours geared towards a wide range of interests: from couples wishing to

get married in the Caribbean to diving enthusiasts and spa-seekers.

Airlines

Unless otherwise specified all phone numbers work within the UK only.

Air France UK ☎0870/142 4343, ☜www.
airfrance.co.uk, Republic of Ireland ☎01/605
0383, ☜www.airfrance.ie.

British Airways UK ☎0870/850 9850, Republic
of Ireland ☎1800/626747, ☜www.ba.com.

BWIA International ☎0870/499 2942, ☜www.
bwee.com.

Continental UK ☎0845/607 6760, Republic of
Ireland ☎1890/925 252, ☜www.flycontinental.
com.

KLM Royal Dutch Airlines ☎08705/074074,
☜www.klm.com.

Lufthansa UK ☎0845/7737 747, Republic of
Ireland ☎01/844 5544, ☜www.lufthansa.co.uk.

United Airlines UK ☎0845/8444 777, ☜www.
unitedairlines.co.uk.

Virgin Atlantic Airways UK ☎01293/747747,
☜www.virgin.com/atlantic.

Charter flight operators

BMI ☎0870/6070 222, ☜www.flybmi.com.

Britannia Airways ☎0870/607 6757, ☜www.
britanniaairways.com.

First Choice ☎0870/850 3999, ☜www.
firstchoice.co.uk.

My Travel ☎0870/238 7777, ☜www.mytravel.
com.

Travel agents

Apex Travel Republic of Ireland ☎01/241 8000,
☜www.apextravel.ie. Specialists in flights to
Australia, Africa, Far East, US and Canada.

Aran Travel International Republic of Ireland
☎091/562 595, ☜homepages.iol.ie/~arantvl/
aranmain.htm. Good-value flights to all parts of
the world.

CIE Tours International Republic of Ireland
☎01/703 1888, ☜www.cietours.ie. General flight
and tour agent.

Flightbookers UK ☎0870/010 7000, ☜www.
ebookers.com. Low fares on an extensive selection
of scheduled flights.

Joe Walsh Tours Republic of Ireland ☎01/241
0888, ☜www.joewalshtours.ie. General budget
fares agent.

Lee Travel Republic of Ireland ☎021/277 111,
☜www.leetravel.ie. Flights and holidays worldwide.

McCarthy's Travel Republic of Ireland ☎021/427

0127, ☜www.mccarthystravel.ie. General flight
agent.

North South Travel UK ☎ & ☎01245/608 291,
☜www.northsouthtravel.co.uk. Friendly, competitive
travel agency, offering discounted fares worldwide.
Profits are used to support projects in the developing
world, especially the promotion of sustainable tourism.

Premier Travel Derry ☎028/7126 3333, ☜www.
premiertravel.uk.com. Discount flight specialists.

Rosetta Travel Northern Ireland ☎028/9064 4996,
☜www.rosettatravel.com. Flight and holiday agent.

STA Travel UK ☎0870/1600 599, ☜www.
statravel.co.uk. Worldwide specialists in low-cost
flights and tours for students and under-26s, though
other customers are welcome.

Trailfinders UK ☎0845/0585 858, ☜www.
trailfinders.co.uk, Republic of Ireland ☎01/677
7888, ☜www.trailfinders.ie. One of the best-
informed and most efficient agents for independent
travellers.

usit NOW Republic of Ireland ☎01/602 1600,
Northern Ireland ☎028/9032 7111, ☜www.
usitnow.ie. Student and youth specialists for flights
and trains.

Specialist tour operators

British Airways Holidays ☎0870/850 2145,
☜www.baholidays.co.uk. Using British Airways and
other quality international airlines, offers an exhaustive
range of package and tailor-made holidays.

Caribbean Expressions ☎020/7433 2610,
☜www.expressionsholidays.co.uk. Specializing in
hotel holidays to most Caribbean islands, including
diving packages to St Lucia, Tobago and the Cayman
Islands, and yacht charters in the Virgin Islands.

Caribtours ☎020/7751 0660, ☜www.caribtours.
co.uk. Long-established operator offering tailor-made
breaks – including trips designed for families, spa-
seekers, island hoppers and honeymooners – using
scheduled flights to the Caribbean.

Complete Caribbean ☎01423/531031, ☜www.
completecaribbean.co.uk. Tailor-made holidays on
most islands for families, couples and adventure
seekers, with accommodation in villas and hotels.

Hayes & Jarvis UK ☎0870/366 1636, ☜www.
hayes-jarvis.com. Specialists in long-haul holidays,
particularly with diving destinations. Exotic weddings
organized.

Journey Latin America UK ☎020/8747 3108,
☜www.journeylatinamerica.co.uk. Specialists in
flights, packages and tailor-made trips all over the
Caribbean.

Just Grenada ☎01373/814214, ☜www.
justgrenada.co.uk. The only company focusing
exclusively on holidays in Grenada, with

knowledgeable staff who have stayed at most properties and know the area well.

Kuoni Travel UK ☎01306/744 442, ☻www. kuoni.co.uk. Flexible package holidays with extensive presence in the Caribbean and good family offers.

Thomas Cook UK ☎0870/750 5711, ☻www. thomascook.co.uk. Long-established one-stop 24hr travel agency for package holidays or scheduled flights.

Trips Worldwide ☎0117/311 4400, ☻www. tripsworldwide.co.uk. Tailor-made holidays to the "alternative Caribbean" include rainforests, culture, birdwatching and plenty of activities. Website lets you create your own itinerary.

Tropic Breeze ☎01752/873 377, ☻www. tropicbreeze.co.uk. Holidays ashore and afloat in St Kitts and Nevis, Antigua, the Grenadines, Tobago, Barbados, St Lucia and the British Virgin Islands. Two-week yacht charters from £900 per person, including flight, in the low season, to £1500 per person at peak times.

Cruises from the UK and Ireland

Cruises aren't as good value an option from outside of the US, as you will have to **fly stateside** before getting on a boat, but there are several cruise operators that work with major airlines to give you an all-in **package deal**.

Celebrity UK ☎0800/018 2525, US ☎1-800/722-5941, ☻www.celebritycruises.com. Cruises with an emphasis on high-end pampering, including spas and art classes. Seven nights from Fort Lauderdale, Baltimore or San Juan from £550 (cruise only).

Fred Olsen UK ☎01473/742 424, ☻www. fredolsencaribbean.co.uk. An extensive range of Caribbean cruises; fourteen nights from £2265, including a flight from London or Manchester.

Flights from Australia and New Zealand

There are **no direct flights** from Australasia to the Caribbean, and the best option for travellers is to fly to the US, the UK or the Netherlands – all of which have interests in the Caribbean – in order to avail themselves of the best possible selection of routes and fares. The most straightforward routes involve flying to the US – usually the West Coast or Canada – and then transferring to an East Coast hub such as Miami, or to the American Airlines hub in San Juan, for onward transportation to the Caribbean islands. **Fares** tend not to vary much year-round, so expect to pay up to Aus\$2000/NZ\$2173 from Sydney to Miami, more at Christmas and New Year; add around Aus\$500/NZ\$590 to fly from Darwin or Perth. A viable alternative, if you have the time, is to buy a **Round-the-World ticket** (**RTW**) – though a sample itinerary leaving from Sydney and stopping in the US, Venezuela, Trinidad, Jamaica, England, Greece and Thailand before returning to Sydney could set you back around Aus\$6000/NZ\$7055. For RTW travel specialists, see "Specialist agents", opposite.

Cruising from Australia is not really an option, and travellers wishing to sail the Caribbean will have to book with a specialist travel agent in their home country and fly to meet the cruise ship, usually to Florida – for more on cruises from the US, see p.29.

Airlines

Air Canada Australia ☎1300/655 767 or 02/9248 5757, New Zealand ☎0508/747 767, ☻www. aircanada.ca.

Air France Australia ☎02/9244 2100, New Zealand ☎09/308 3352, ☻www.airfrance.com.au.

Air New Zealand Australia ☎13 24 76, New Zealand ☎0800 247 764, ☻www.airnewzealand.com.

Air Pacific Australia ☎1800/230 150, New Zealand ☎0800/800 178, ☻www.airpacific.com,

Alitalia Australia ☎1300/0361 400, ☻www. alitalia.com,

America West Airlines Australia ☎02/9810 7400, New Zealand ☎0800/866 000, ☻www. americawest.com.

American Airlines Australia ☎1300/650 747, New Zealand ☎09/309 0735 or 0800/887 997, ☻www.aa.com.

British Airways Australia ☎1300/767 177, New Zealand ☎09/966 9777, ☻www.ba.com.

BWIA International Australia ☎02/8080 5666, ☻www.bwee.com.

Cathay Pacific Australia ☎13 17 47, New Zealand ☎09/379 0861, ☻www.cathaypacific. com.

Continental Airlines Australia ☎02/9244 2242, New Zealand ☎09/308 3350, ☻www. flycontinental.com.

Delta Air Lines Australia ☎1-300/302 849, New Zealand ☎09/379 3370, ☻www.delta-air.com.

KLM Royal Dutch Australia ☎1300/303 747, New Zealand ☎09/302 1792, ☻www.klm.com.

Northwest Airlines Australia ☎1300/767 310, ☻www.nwa.com.

Qantas Australia ☎13 13 13, New Zealand ☎0800/808 767, ⦿www.qantas.com.au. United Airlines Australia ☎13 17 77, New Zealand ☎0800/508 648, ⦿www.ual.com. Virgin Atlantic Airways Australia ☎1300/727 340, ⦿www.virgin-atlantic.com.

Travel agents

Flight Centre Australia ☎13 31 33, ⦿www.flightcentre.com.au, New Zealand ☎0800 243 544, ⦿www.flightcentre.co.nz. Long-established independent travel agent that books everything from cheap flights to cruise ship specials.
STA Travel Australia ☎1300/733 035 or 02/9212 1255, ⦿www.statravel.com.au, New Zealand ☎0508/782 872 or 09/309 9273, ⦿www.statravel.co.nz. Student/youth travel agent offering discounted fares.

Trailfinders Australia ☎/9247 7666 or ☎1300/780 212, ⦿www.trailfinders.com.au. Discount flights, car rental, tailor-made tours, rail passes and RTW tours, especially for the independent traveller.

Specialist agents

Caribbean Bound Australia ☎02/9267 2555 or 1300/786 637, ⦿www.caribbean.com.au. Flights and packages to all the Caribbean islands, plus specialized honeymoon and wedding trips.
Caribbean Destinations Australia ☎03/9813 5258, ⦿www.caribbeanislands.com.au. Specializing in hotel accommodation throughout the Caribbean, as well as holidays geared towards festivals and cricket.
Cruiseworld ☎08/9322 2914, ⦿www.cruiseworld.com.au. Agents for the American Express range of cruise holidays.

Red tape and visas

Island-specific advice about **visas** and **entry requirements** is covered at the beginning of each chapter, where necessary. As a broad guide, citizens of the **US**, **Canada** and **Great Britain** do not need a visa for stays of less than thirty days; however, nearly every country requires that your passport be valid for at least six months from your date of entry.

Some countries demand proof of onward travel (such as an air ticket) or sufficient funds to buy a ticket; others will require the address of wherever you're staying. As all visa requirements, prices and processing times are subject to change, it's always worth double-checking with the embassies before you leave home.

Caribbean embassies and consulates abroad

Anguilla

The UK handles consular responsibilities.
Australia British High Commission, Commonwealth Ave, Yarralumla, ACT 2600 ☎02/6270 6666, ⦿www.uk.emb.gov.au.
Canada British High Commission, 80 Elgin St,

Ottawa ON K1P 5K7 ☎613/237-1530, ⦿www.britainincanada.org.
Ireland British Embassy, 29 Merrion Rd, Ballsbridge, Dublin 4 ☎01/205 3822, ⦿www.britishembassy.ie.
New Zealand British High Commission, 44 Hill St, Thorndon, Wellington ☎04/924 2888, ⦿www.britain.org.nz/general/ukterra.html.
UK Foreign and Commonwealth Office, Old Admiralty Building, London SW1A 2PA ☎020/7008 1500, ⦿www.fco.gov.uk.
US British Embassy, 3100 Massachusetts Ave, Washington DC 20008 ☎202/588-6500, ⦿www.britainusa.com.

Antigua and Barbuda

Australia handles consular responsibilities.
Canada Embassy of Antigua and Barbuda, 112

Kent St, Ottawa ON K1P 5P2 ☎613/236-8952,
✉info@antigua-barbuda-ca.com.
UK and Ireland Antigua and Barbuda Diplomatic
Mission, 15 Thayer St, London W1U 3JT
☎020/7486 7073, ⌨www.antigua-barbuda.com.
US Embassy of Antigua and Barbuda, 3216 New
Mexico Ave NW, Washington DC 20016, ☎202/362-
5122, ✉embantbar@aol.com.

Aruba

The Netherlands handles consular respon-
sibilities.
Australia Consulate General of the Netherlands,
PO Box 261, Bondi Junction NSW 1355 ☎02/9837
6644, ⌨www.netherlands.org.au.
Canada Royal Netherlands Embassy, Constitution
Square Building, 350 Albert St, Suite 2020,
Ottawa ON K1R 1A4 ☎613/237-5030, ⌨www.
netherlandsembassy.ca.
Ireland Royal Netherlands Embassy, 160
Merrion Rd, Dublin 4 ☎01/269 3444, ⌨www.
netherlandsembassy.ie.
New Zealand Royal Netherlands Embassy, PO Box
840, Ballance at Fetherston St, Wellington ☎04/471
6390, ⌨www.netherlandsembassy.co.nz.
UK Netherlands Diplomatic Mission, 38 Hyde Park
Gate, London SW7 5DP ☎020/7590 3200, ⌨www.
netherlands-embassy.org.uk.
US Netherlands Embassy, 4200 Linnean Ave,
Washington DC 20008 ☎202/244-5300, ⌨www.
netherlands-embassy.org.

Bahamas

Canada Bahamas High Commission, Metropolitan
Life Centre, 50 O'Connor St, suite 1313, Ottawa
ON K1P 6L2 ☎613/232-1724, ✉ottawa-
mission@bahighco.com.
UK and Ireland Bahamas High Commission, 10
Chesterfield St, London W1X 8AH ☎7408 4488,
⌨www.bahamashclondon.net/index(1).html.
US The Embassy of the Commonwealth of the
Bahamas, 2220 Massachusetts Ave NW, Washington
DC 20008 ☎202/319-2667, ☏319-2668.

Barbados

Australia Consulate-General, 4 Warren Rd, Double
Bay NSW 2028 ☎02/9327 7009.
Canada High Commission for Barbados, 130 Albert
St, Suite 1204, Ottawa ON K1P 5G4 ☎03/236-
9517, ☏230-4362.
UK and Ireland Barbados High Commission, 1
Great Russell St, London WC1B 3ND ☎020/7631
4975, ✉london@foreign.gov.bb.

US Consulate General, 150 Alhambra Circle, suite
1000, Coral Gables, Florida 33178 ☎305/442-
1994, ⌨barbados.diplomacy.edu/miami-consulate.

British Virgin Islands

The UK handles consular responsibilities.
Australia British High Commission,
Commonwealth Ave, Yarralumla ACT 2600
☎02/6270 6666, ⌨www.uk.emb.gov.au.
Canada British High Commission, 80 Elgin St,
Ottawa ON K1P 5K7 ☎613/237-1530, ⌨www.
britainincanada.org.
Ireland British Embassy, 29 Merrion Rd,
Ballsbridge, Dublin 4 ☎01/205 3822, ⌨www.
britishembassy.ie.
New Zealand British High Commission, 44 Hill
St, Thorndon, Wellington ☎04/924 2888, ⌨www.
britain.org.nz/general/ukterra.html.
UK Foreign and Commonwealth Office, Old
Admiralty Building, London SW1A 2PA ☎020/7008
1500, ⌨www.fco.gov.uk.
US British Embassy, 3100 Massachusetts Ave,
Washington DC 20008 ☎202/588-6500, ⌨www.
britainusa.com.

Cayman Islands

The UK handles consular responsibilities.
Australia British High Commission,
Commonwealth Ave, Yarralumla, ACT 2600
☎02/6270 6666, ⌨www.uk.emb.gov.au.
Canada British High Commission, 80 Elgin St,
Ottawa ON K1P 5K7 ☎613/237-1542, ⌨www.
britainincanada.org.
Ireland British Embassy, 29 Merrion Rd,
Ballsbridge, Dublin 4 ☎01/205 3822, ⌨www.
britishembassy.ie.
New Zealand British High Commission, 44 Hill
St, Thorndon, Wellington ☎04/924 3888, ⌨www.
brithighcomm.org.nz.
UK Foreign and Commonwealth Office, Old
Admiralty Building, London SW1A 2PA ☎020/7008
0232 or 0233, ⌨www.fco.gov.uk.
US British Embassy, 3100 Massachusetts Ave,
Washington DC 20008 ☎202/588-6500, ⌨www.
brit-info.org.

Cuba

Australia Consulate General of the Republic of
Cuba, IPI House, ground floor, 128 Chalmers St,
Surrey Hills NSW 2010 ☎02/9698 9797, ⌨www.
users.bigpond.net.au/conscuba.
Canada Embassy of the Republic of Cuba, 388
Main St, Ottawa ON K1S 1E3 ☎613/563-0141,
⌨www.embacuba.ca.

UK Embassy of the Republic of Cuba, 167 High Holborn, London WC1V 6PA ☎020/7240 2488, @cuba.embassyhomepage.com.
US Cuban Interests Section, 2630 16th St NW, Washington DC 20009 ☎202/797-8518, @cubaseccion@igc.apc.org.

Dominica

Australia handles consular responsibilities.
Australia Department of Foreign Affairs and Trade, R.G. Casey Building, John McEwen Crescent, Barton ACT 0221 ☎02 6261 1111, @www.dfat.gov.au.
UK and Ireland Dominican High Commission, 1 Collingham Gardens, London SW5 0HW ☎020/7370 5194, @www.dominica.co.uk.
US Embassy of the Commonwealth of Dominica, 3216 New Mexico Ave NW, Washington DC 20016 ☎202/364-6781, @embdomdc@aol.com.

Dominican Republic

Australia Consulate of the Dominican Republic, 343A Edgecliff Rd, Edgecliff NSW 2027 ☎02/9363 5891, @consudom@bigpond.net.au.
Canada Embassy of the Dominican Republic, 2727 Steeles Ave W, suite 301, Toronto, ON M3J 3G9 ☎416/739-1237, @www.dominicanrepublic services.com.
UK and Ireland Embassy of the Dominican Republic, 139 Inverness Terrace, Bayswater, London W2 6JF ☎020/7727 6285, @dominicanrepublic.embassyhomepage.com.
US Embassy of the Dominican Republic, 1715 22nd St NW, Washington DC 20008 ☎202/332-6280, @www.domrep.org.

Grenada

Canada Consulate of Grenada, 439 University Ave, suite 930, Toronto, ON M5G 1Y8 ☎416/595-1339, @www.grenadaconsulate.com.
UK and Ireland Grenada High Commission, 5 Chandos St, London W1G 9DG ☎020/7631 4277, @grenada@high-commission.freeserve.co.uk.
US Embassy of Grenada, 1701 New Hampshire Ave NW, Washington DC 20009 ☎265-2561, @www.grenadaembassyusa.org.

Guadeloupe

France handles consular responsibilities.
Australia Embassy of France, 6 Perth Ave, Yarralumla, ACT 2600 ☎02/6216 0100, @www.france.net.au.
Canada Embassy of France, 42 Promenade St,

Sussex, Ottawa, ON K1M 2C9 ☎613/789-1795, @www.ambafrance-ca.org.
Ireland Chancery, 36 Ailesbury Rd, Dublin 4 ☎01/277 5000, @www.ambafrance.ie.
New Zealand Embassy of France, 34-42 Manners St, Wellington ☎04/802 1590, @www.ambafrance-nz.org.
UK Embassy of France, 58 Knightsbridge, London SW1X 7JT ☎020/7201 1000, @www.ambafrance.org.uk.
US Embassy of France, 4101 Reservoir Rd NW, Washington DC 20007-2172 ☎202/944-6200 or 6187, @www.ambafrance-us.org.

Jamaica

Canada Jamaican High Commission, Standard Life Building, 275 Slater St, suite 402, Ottawa, ON KIP 5H9 ☎613/233-9311, @jhcott@comnet.ca.
UK and Ireland Jamaica High Commission, 1-2 Prince Consort Rd, London SW7 2BQ ☎020/7823 9911, @www.jhcuk.com.
US Embassy of Jamaica, 1520 New Hampshire Ave NW, Washington DC 20036 ☎202/452-0660, @www.emjamusa.com.

Martinique

France handles consular responsibilities.
Australia Embassy of France, 6 Perth Ave, Yarralumla, ACT 2600 ☎02/6216 0100, @www.france.net.au.
Canada Embassy of France, 42 Promenade St, Sussex, Ottawa, ON K1M 2C9 ☎613/789-1795, @www.ambafrance-ca.org.
Ireland Chancery, 36 Ailesbury Rd, Dublin 4 ☎01/277 5000, @www.ambafrance.ie.
New Zealand Embassy of France, 34-42 Manners St, Wellington ☎04/802 1590, @www.ambafrance-nz.org.
UK Embassy of France, 58 Knightsbridge, London SW1X 7JT ☎020/7201 1000, @www.ambafrance.org.uk.
US Embassy of France, 4101 Reservoir Rd NW, Washington DC 20007-2172 ☎202/944-6200 or 6187, @www.ambafrance-us.org.

Puerto Rico

The US handles consular responsibilities.
Australia US Embassy, Moonah Place, Yarralumla ACT 2600 ☎02/6214 5970, @canberra.usembassy.gov.
Canada Embassy of the United States of America, 490 Sussex Drive, Ottawa, ON K1N 1G8 ☎613/238-5335, @www.usembassycanada.gov.
Ireland US Embassy, 42 Elgin Rd, Ballsbridge, Dublin

4 ☎01/668 8777, ✉dublin.usembassy.gov.
New Zealand US Embassy, 29 Fitzherbert Terrace,
Thorndon, Wellington ☎04/462 6000, ✉usembassy.
org.nz
UK US Embassy, 24 Grosvenor St, London W1A 1AE
☎020/7499 9000, ✉www.usembassy.org.uk
US US Department of State, 2201 C St NW,
Washington DC 20520 ☎202/647-4000, ✉www.
state.gov.

Saba

Same as Anguilla (see p.33).

St Barts

France handles consular responsibilities.
Australia Embassy of France, 6 Perth Ave, Yarralumla,
ACT 2600 ☎02/6216 0100, ✉www.france.net.au.
Canada Embassy of France, 42 Promenade St,
Sussex, Ottawa, ON K1M 2C9 ☎613/789-1795,
✉www.ambafrance-ca.org.
Ireland Chancery, 36 Ailesbury Rd, Dublin 4 ☎01/277
5000, ✉www.ambafrance.ie.
New Zealand Embassy of France, 34-42 Manners
St, Wellington ☎04/802 1590, ✉www.ambafrance-
nz.org.
UK Embassy of France, 58 Knightsbridge, London
SW1X 7JT ☎020/7201 1000, ✉www.ambafrance.
org.uk.
US Embassy of France, 4101 Reservoir Rd NW,
Washington DC 20007-2172 ☎202/944-6200 or
6187, ✉www.ambafrance-us.org.

St Eustatius

Same as Anguilla (see p.33).

St Kitts And Nevis

Australia handles consular responsibilities.
Australia Australian Department of Foreign Affairs
and Trade, R.G. Casey Building, John McEwen
Crescent, Barton ACT 0221 ☎02/6261 1111, ✉www.
dfat.gov.au.
Canada Honorary Consulate of St Kitts and Nevis,
133 Richmond St W, suite 311, Toronto, ON M5H 2L3
☎416/368-7319, ✉consulatestkittsnevis@rogers.
com.
UK and Ireland St Kitts and Nevis High Commission,
10 Kensington Court, London W8 5DL ☎020/7460
6500, ✉sknhighcom@aol.com.uk.
US Embassy of St Kitts and Nevis, 3216 New
Mexico Ave NW, Washington DC 20016 ☎202/686-
2636, ✉www.stkittsnevis.org.

St Lucia

Australia handles consular responsibilities.
Australia Australian Department of Foreign Affairs
and Trade, R.G. Casey Building, John McEwen
Crescent, Barton ACT 0221 ☎02/6261 1111,
✉www.dfat.gov.au.
Canada Consulate General for St Lucia, 8 King E,
suite 700, Toronto, ON M5C 1B ☎416/203-8400,
✉can@sluconsulate.com.
UK and Ireland 1 Collingham Gardens, London SW5
0HW ☎020/7370 7123, ✉hcslu@btconnect.com.
US Embassy of St Lucia, 3216 New Mexico Ave NW,
Washington DC 20016 ☎202/364-6792, ✉364-
6723.

St Vincent And The Grenadines

Australia handles consular responsibilities.
Australia Australian Department of Foreign Affairs
and Trade, R.G. Casey Building,
John McEwen Crescent, Barton ACT 0221 ☎02/6261
1111, ✉www.dfat.gov.au.
Canada Consulate of St Vincent and the Grenadines,
333 Wilson Ave, suite 601, Toronto, ON M3H 1T2
☎416/398-4277, ✉ebjohn@svgconsulate.org.
UK and Ireland St Vincent Diplomatic Mission, 10
Kensington Ct, London W8 5DL ☎020/7937 2874,
✉highcommission.svg.uk@cwcom.net.
US Embassy of St Vincent and the Grenadines,
3216 New Mexico Ave NW, Washington DC 20016
☎202/364-6730, ✉www.embsvg.com.

Trinidad And Tobago

Australia Consulate-General of the Republic
of Trinidad and Tobago, unit 2, 72 New South
Head Rd, Vaucluse NSW 2030 ☎02/9327 8468,
✉consgett@aol.com.
Canada Trinidad and Tobago High Commission, 200
First Ave, 3rd level, Ottawa, ON K1S 2G6 ☎613/232-
2418, ✉www.ttmissions.com.
New Zealand Honorary Consul of Trinidad and
Tobago, level 26, 151 Queen St, PO Box 105-042,
Auckland ☎09/302 1860, ✉wifacon@xtra.co.nz.
UK and Ireland Trinidad & Tobago High Commission,
42 Belgrave Sq, London SW1X 8NT ☎020/7245
9351, ✉trinidad.embassyhomepage.com.
US Embassy of Trinidad and Tobago, 1708
Massachusetts Ave NW, Washington DC 20036
☎202/467-6490, ✉ttembassy.cjb.net.

Turks And Caicos

The UK handles consular responsibilities.
Australia British High Commission, Commonwealth
Ave, Yarralumla, ACT 2600 ☎02/6270 6666, ✉www.
uk.emb.gov.au.
Canada British High Commission, 80 Elgin St,

Ottawa, ON K1P 5K7 ☎613/237-1530, ✆www.
britainincanada.org.
Ireland British Embassy, 29 Merrion Rd, Ballsbridge,
Dublin 4 ☎01/205 3822, ✆www.britishembassy.ie.
New Zealand British High Commission, 44 Hill St,
Thorndon, Wellington ☎04/924 2888, ✆www.britain.
org.nz/general/ukterra.html.
UK Foreign and Commonwealth Office, Old Admiralty
Building, London SW1A 2PA ☎020/7008 1500,
✆www.fco.gov.uk.
US British Embassy, 3100 Massachusetts Ave,
Washington DC 20008 ☎202/588-6500, ✆www.
britainusa.com.

US Virgin Islands

The US handles consular responsibilities.
Australia US Embassy, Moonah Place, Yarralumla
ACT 2600 ☎02/6214 5970, ✆canberra.
usembassy.gov.

Canada Embassy of the United States of America,
490 Sussex Drive, Ottawa, ON K1N 1G8 ☎613/238-
5335, ✆www.usembassycanada.gov.
Ireland US Embassy, 42 Elgin Rd, Ballsbridge,
Dublin 4 ☎01/668 8777, ✆dublin.usembassy.gov.
New Zealand US Embassy, 29 Fitzherbert Terrace,
Thorndon, Wellington ☎04/462 6000, ✆usembassy.
org.nz.
UK US Embassy, 24 Grosvenor St, London W1A 1AE
☎020/7499 9000, ✆www.usembassy.org.uk.
US US Department of State, 2201 C St NW,
Washington DC 20520 ☎202/647-4000, ✆www.
state.gov.

Health

In general, travelling in the more developed areas of the Caribbean won't raise many
health concerns. You can count on food being well and hygienically prepared, and
tap water in hotels and restaurants that's safe to drink (if heavily chlorinated and not
very palatable). The preventive measures you need to take elsewhere will depend
on the areas you visit but some general advice is given below.

Note, however, that the quality of medical
care and facilities varies widely throughout
the Caribbean. While it is excellent and
readily available in places such as Aruba,
the Bahamas, Barbados, the Cayman
Islands, Martinique and Guadeloupe, others
– particularly in rural areas on islands like the
Dominican Republic – may consist of only a
small, poorly equipped clinic. In any event,
it's a good idea to make sure that your medical insurance covers you abroad or else take
out an insurance policy that includes medical
coverage (see p.41 for more on insurance).

Inoculations

No specific **inoculations** are required to enter
any of the Caribbean islands, unless you're
arriving from a country where yellow fever is

endemic, in which case you'll need a vaccina-
tion certificate. (Consult your doctor or a travel
clinic for advice on specific shots.) Islands
that require yellow fever inoculations include
Antigua, Bahamas, Cayman Islands, Cuba,
Grenada, Guadeloupe, Jamaica, St Kitts and
Nevis, St Lucia, St Vincent, and Trinidad and
Tobago.

It's also worth making sure that you're up to
date with **polio**, **tetanus** and **typhoid** protection; the latter is particularly recommended for
those planning to visit rural areas of Puerto
Rico, Cuba, Dominica and the Dominican
Republic. Inoculations against **hepatitis A
and B** are also strongly advised.

Malaria and dengue fever

The Caribbean is not a malarial zone, but

cases of **malaria** have been reported in the Dominican Republic, mainly along the Haitian border. While the risk to travellers is small, if you intend to travel in this area it's a good idea to take a course of prophylactics (usually **chloroquine**), available from a doctor or travel clinic.

There are slightly higher rates of **dengue fever**, another mosquito-borne illness whose symptoms resemble those of malaria but include extreme aches and pains in the bones and joints, along with fever and dizziness. The only cure for dengue fever is rest and painkillers, and the only precaution you can take is to avoid mosquito bites (for details, see below).

Stomach problems

The most common food-related illness for travellers is **diarrhoea**, possibly accompanied by **vomiting** or a **mild fever**. Its main cause is a change in diet, whereby bacteria you're not used to are introduced into your system. In many cases, the condition will pass within a few days without treatment. In the meantime, rest up and replace the fluids you've lost by drinking plenty of water or – for persistent diarrhoea – an oral rehydration solution, readily available from your home pharmacy, should do the trick. Barring that, you can make a home-made solution by dissolving half a teaspoon of salt and eight teaspoons of sugar in a litre of boiling water. If symptoms last more than four or five days, or if you are too ill to drink, seek medical help immediately.

Travellers should note that dairy products aggravate diarrhoea and should be avoided.

Food and water

While stomach disorders aren't likely to be a big problem in the Caribbean, taking a few **common-sense precautions** will lessen the chances greatly. Steer clear of unpasteurized dairy products and unrefrigerated food, and wash and peel fresh fruit and vegetables. When buying street food, stick to obviously popular food vendors and restaurants, and wash your hands well before you eat.

Although tap water is generally safe to drink (one main exception is the Dominican Republic), locals tend to boil it before drinking to get rid of the taste of chlorine – you may prefer to stick to bottled water for this reason. You should be wary of drinking tap water after heavy rain (when supplies can become contaminated), or in remote areas; you can make water safer by both passing it through an "absolute 1-micron or less" filter as well as adding iodine tablets to the filtered water. Filters and tablets are available from travel clinics and good outdoor equipment stores.

Swimming or bathing in rivers and lakes has risks as well, particularly **giardia**, a bacterium that causes stomach upset, fever and diarrhoea, and **schistosomiasis**, a freshwater flatworm found in parts of Antigua, the Dominican Republic, Guadeloupe, Martinique, Puerto Rico and St Lucia that can penetrate unbroken skin; both are treatable with **antibiotics**. If you suspect that you have either of these, seek medical help.

Ciguatera

Ciguatera is a form of poisoning caused by eating infected reef fish, and sporadic outbreaks have been reported throughout the Caribbean. Symptoms include nausea, numbness, diarrhoea, abdominal pains, muscular weakness and vomiting, and can last up to two weeks. As infected fish are indistinguishable from healthy ones, the only way to reduce most of the risk is by avoiding commonly affected fish such as grouper, amberjack, snapper, and barracuda in particular. Travellers who suspect that they have ciguatera should seek immediate medical assistance.

Bites and stings

Bites and **stings** can lead to infection, so keep wounds clean and wash with antiseptic soap. It's inevitable that you will get some bites, but there are steps you can take to avoid them. Use a heavy-duty **insect repellent** (preferably containing **DEET**) on exposed areas of skin at all times, though especially from dusk until dawn, when mosquitoes are most active. Try to ensure that your hotel room has **screened windows** or a **mosquito net** over the bed; if you don't have either, sleep in clothes that cover as much of your body as possible, or cocoon yourself in your sheets; constant air from a fan will also keep the bugs at bay.

Often present on beaches at dusk and so small that they're practically impossible to see, **sand flies** are possessed of a painful, incredibly itchy and long-lasting bite; they ignore most repellents but can typically be avoided if you use Avon Skin-so-Soft, a moisturizer that's renowned for its unintentional bug-repelling power.

There are some **snakes** in the Caribbean, but very few are poisonous. One notable exception is the **fer-de-lance**, found in Martinique, St Lucia and Trinidad, and identifiable by its pointed head, yellow underside and chin, and orangish-brown triangular markings. Fortunately, most snakes, including the fer-de-lance, will slither away before you know they are there. However, to be safe you should wear thick socks and boots when hiking through undergrowth or rainforest. If you do get bitten, note the snake's appearance, immobilize the bitten limb as much as possible and seek medical help immediately.

You're more likely to encounter the many spiny black **sea urchins** that inhabit reefs and bays; if you tread on one, remove as much of the spine as possible, douse the area in vinegar (or even urine) and see a doctor. Take care to avoid the purple **Portuguese man o' war**, a rare but toxic jellyfish whose trailing tendrils leave red welts. Similarly, **never touch coral**; you'll kill the organism on contact and come away with a painful, slow-healing rash. In both instances, washing with vinegar or iodine will help; again urine can be used if nothing else is available. Should pain persist in the event you come in contact with any of the above, consult a doctor. For **stingray** and **stonefish stings**, alleviate the pain by immersing the wound in very hot water – just under 50ºC – while waiting for medical help.

Manchineel trees

Take care to avoid **manchineel trees**, which grow to around twelve metres tall and are recognizable by their small dark green leaves and tiny apple-like fruit. Both the fruit and its milky sap are **poisonous**. Don't touch any part of the tree and avoid taking shelter under its boughs in the rain: the sap will cause blisters if it drips on you. On the more popular beaches manchineel trees have notices nailed to their trunks warning visitors of the potential danger. However, caution is advised on quieter beaches where these trees are less likely to be identified.

Heat trouble

The Caribbean's position near the **equator** means that the sun's rays here are very strong – use a good **sunblock** (minimum SPF 15) and apply it liberally at least every two hours and after swimming or exercise. Keep sun exposure to a minimum, especially between the hours of 11am and 4pm; wear a hat and a shirt, drink plenty of water and make sure children are well covered up. If you do **burn**, it's well worth getting hold of a couple of leaves of **aloe vera**, which grows throughout the region and is incredibly soothing; it also reduces the likelihood of peeling. To use it, split open the leaf and spread the gel liberally over your skin, taking care not to let it touch your clothes until dry (it leaves a marked yellow or purple stain).

Dizziness, headache and nausea are symptoms of **dehydration** and should be treated by lying down in a shaded place and sipping water or other hydrating fluids. Should symptoms persist, or if you are suffering from hot, dry (but not sweaty) skin – potentially a sign of **heatstroke** – seek medical assistance immediately.

AIDS and HIV

The Caribbean has the highest regional prevalence of **AIDS** and **HIV** outside of sub-Saharan Africa. Haiti is the worst-afflicted area, with the Bahamas and the Dominican Republic close behind. With regard to sex, the same common-sense rule applies here as anywhere else; condomless sex is a serious health risk, and it's worth **bringing condoms** from home as those sold in some areas (eg Cuba and the Dominican Republic) are of poor quality.

Prescriptions

Be aware that even on islands with good medical facilities and well-stocked pharmacies you may not be able to find the exact **medication** that you take at home, or even a viable alternative. To be safe, bring any prescribed medicine in its original container and make sure you have enough for the length of your trip, as well as a copy of the prescription itself. The US State Department also advises bringing a letter from the prescribing doctor explaining why the drugs are needed.

Medical resources for travellers

Websites

ⓦ **www.cdc.gov/travel** US Department of Health and Human Services travel health and disease control department, listing precautions, diseases and preventive measures by region, as well as a summary of cruise ship sanitation levels.
ⓦ **www.fitfortravel.scot.nhs.uk** UK NHS website carrying information about travel-related diseases and how to avoid them.
ⓦ **www.istm.org** The website of the International Society for Travel Medicine, with a full list of clinics specializing in international travel health.
ⓦ **www.masta.org** Comprehensive website for Medical Advisory service for travellers abroad (see also listing in next column).
ⓦ **www.tmvc.com.au** Contains a list of all Travellers' Medical and Vaccination Centres throughout Australia, New Zealand and Southeast Asia, plus general information on travel health.
ⓦ **www.travelvax.net** Everything you could ever want to know about diseases and travel vaccines.
ⓦ **www.tripprep.com** Travel Health Online provides a comprehensive database of necessary vaccinations for most countries, as well as destination and medical service provider information.

In the US and Canada

Canadian Society for International Health 1 Nicholas St, suite 1105, Ottawa, ON K1N 7B7 ☎613/241-5785, ⓦwww.csih.org. Contains an extensive list of travel health centres in Canada.
Centers for Disease Control 1600 Clifton Rd NE, Atlanta, GA 30333 ☎1-800/311-3435, ⓦwww. cdc.gov. Publishes outbreak warnings, suggested inoculations, precautions and other background information for travellers. Useful website plus International Travelers Hotline on ☎1-877/FYI-TRIP.
International Association for Medical Assistance to Travellers (IAMAT) 1623 Military Rd, #279, Niagara Falls, NY 14302, ☎716/754-

4883, ⓦwww.iamat.org, and 1287 St Clair Ave W, suite #1, Toronto, ON M6E 1B8 ☎416/652-0137. A non profit organization supported by donations, it can provide a list of English-speaking doctors in the Caribbean, climate charts and leaflets on various diseases and inoculations.
International SOS Assistance 3600 Horizon Blvd, suite 300, Trevose, PA 19053 ☎1-800/523-8930, ⓦwww.intsos.com. Members receive pre-trip medical referral info, as well as overseas emergency services designed to complement travel insurance coverage.
Travel Medicine ☎1-800/872-8633, ⓦwww. travmed.com. Sells first-aid kits, mosquito netting, water filters, reference books and other health-related travel products; there's a travel clinic directory, too.

In the UK and Ireland

British Airways Travel Clinics 213 Piccadilly, London W1G 9HQ (Mon–Fri 9.30am–5.30pm, Sat 10am–4pm, no appointment necessary); 101 Cheapside, London EC2 (Mon–Fri 9am–4.30pm, appointment required; ☎0845/600 2236); ⓦwww.britishairways.com/travel/healthclinintro. Vaccinations, tailored advice from an online database and a complete range of travel healthcare products.
Communicable Diseases Unit Brownlee Centre, Glasgow G12 0YN ☎0141/211 1074. Travel vaccinations including yellow fever.
Dun Laoghaire Medical Centre 5 Northumberland Ave, Dun Laoghaire, Co. Dublin ☎01/280 4996, ⓟ01/280 5603. Advice on medical matters abroad.
Glasgow Travel Clinic 3rd floor, 90 Mitchell St, Glasgow G1 3NQ ☎0141/221 4224. Advice and vaccinations; walk-in clinics Wed–Fri 10am–6pm, otherwise appointments.
Hospital for Tropical Diseases Travel Clinic 2nd floor, Mortimer Market Centre, off Capper St, London WC1E 6AU (Mon–Fri 9am–5pm by appointment only; ☎020/7388 9600; a consultation costs £15 which is waived if you have your injections here) ⓦwww.uclh.org/services/htd. A recorded Health Line (☎0906/133 7733; 50p per min; fax-back service ☎0906/991 992; £1.50 per min) gives tips on hygiene and illness prevention as well as listing appropriate immunizations.
Liverpool School of Tropical Medicine Pembroke Place, Liverpool L3 5QA ☎0151/708 9393 or premium-rate helpline ☎09067/010 095, ⓦwww.liv.ac.uk/lstm. Walk-in clinic (Mon–Fri 9am–noon); appointment required at other times.
MASTA (Medical Advisory Service for Travellers Abroad) London School of Hygiene

and Tropical Medicine. Operates a recorded 24hr Travellers' Health Line (UK ☎0906/550 1402, £1 per min), giving written information tailored to your journey by return of post; you get the same info online. Database of UK travel clinics, too.

Nomad Pharmacy surgeries 52 Grosvenor Gdns, Victoria, London SW1W 0AG ☎020/78323/5823; 43 Bernard St, London, WC1N 1LE ☎020/7833 4114; and 3-4 Wellington Terrace, Turnpike Lane, London N8 0PX ☎020/8889 7014. All have walk-in and appointment clinics from Monday to Saturday.

Travel Medicine Services 16 College St, Belfast 1 ☎028/9031 5220. Offers medical advice before a trip and help afterwards in the event of a tropical disease.

Tropical Medical Bureau Grafton Buildings, 34 Grafton St, Dublin 2 ☎01/671 9200, plus locations all around Ireland; call ☎1850/487 674 or visit ⊛tmb.exodus.ie for details. Advice and vaccinations.

In Australia and New Zealand

Travellers' Medical and Vaccination Centres ⊛www.tmvc.com.au. Vaccination and general travel health advice, and disease alerts; call ☎1300/658 844 for details of travel clinics countrywide.

Insurance

It is always sensible, and often necessary, to take out an **insurance** policy before travelling to cover against theft, loss and illness or injury. Before buying a new policy, however, it's worth checking whether you are already covered: some all-risks home insurance policies may cover your possessions when overseas, and many private medical schemes include cover when abroad.

In **Canada**, provincial health plans usually provide partial cover for medical mishaps overseas, while holders of official **student/teacher/youth cards** in Canada and the US are entitled to meagre accident coverage and hospital in-patient benefits. Students will often find that their student health coverage extends during the vacations and for one term beyond the date of last enrolment.

After exhausting the possibilities above, you might want to contact a **specialist travel insurance company**, or consider the travel insurance deal we offer (see box below). A typical travel insurance policy usually provides cover for the loss of baggage, tickets and – up to a certain limit – cash or cheques, as well

Rough Guides Travel Insurance

Rough Guides has teamed up with Columbus Direct to offer you travel insurance that can be tailored to suit your needs.

Readers can choose from many different travel insurance products, including a low-cost **backpacker** option for long stays, a **short break** option for city getaways, a typical **holiday package** option and many others. There are also annual **multi-trip** policies for those who travel regularly, with variable levels of cover available. Different sports and activities (trekking, skiing, etc) can be covered if required on most policies. Rough Guides travel insurance is available to the residents of 36 different countries with different language options to choose from via our website – ⊛www.roughguidesinsurance.com – where you can also purchase the insurance.

Alternatively, UK residents should call ☎0800/083 9507, US citizens should call ☎1-800/749-4922 and Australians should call ☎1-300/669 999. All other nationalities should call ☎+44 870/890 2843.

as cancellation or curtailment of your journey. Most of them exclude so-called **dangerous sports** unless an extra premium is paid: in the Caribbean this can mean scuba diving, whitewater rafting, windsurfing and trekking, though probably not kayaking or jeep safaris. Many policies can be chopped and changed to exclude coverage you don't need – for example, sickness and accident benefits can often be excluded or included at will. If you do take medical coverage, ascertain whether benefits will be paid as treatment proceeds or only after return home, and whether there is a 24hr medical emergency number.

When securing **baggage cover**, make sure that the per-article limit – typically under US$730/£500 – will cover your most valuable possession. If you need to make a claim, you should **keep receipts** for medicines and medical treatment, and in the event that you have anything **stolen**, you must obtain an official statement from the police.

Information, websites and maps

Advance **information** on many of the Caribbean islands can be obtained from the tourist information offices listed below. Once you've arrived at your destination, you'll find most major towns have visitor centres of some description that will give out detailed information on the local area and can often help with finding accommodation. Free newspapers in many areas carry news of events and entertainment.

Recommended **maps** of individual islands are detailed at the beginning of each chapter where appropriate. The most detailed map of the Caribbean is the *World Map: Caribbean*, published by GeoCenter International.

Tourist offices abroad

Local tourist information offices are discussed in the individual chapters. Note that in some cases public relations firms handle tourist requests from abroad.

Hurricane watch

Though **hurricanes** are a rather nasty fact of life for residents of the Caribbean, relatively few big blows have swept through the region in the last few decades. 2004, however, was an exception, when the deadliest season in fifty years saw no less than four hurricanes batter the region. Packing windspeeds of up to 200mph, category 5 **Ivan** pretty much obliterated the Cayman Islands and Grenada, destroying 90 percent of homes in the latter, while less than two weeks later, flooding as a result of **Jeanne** led to the deaths of more than 3000 people in Haiti; Charley and Frances, meanwhile, pummelled the Bahamas, Cuba and Jamaica. Assisted by emergency relief funds from all over the world, the Caribbean recovered remarkably quickly, however – by the start of the 2004 winter tourist season, many hotels in even the worst affected islands were open for business. For more on hurricanes, visit the sites below.

ⓦ**www.nhc.noaa.gov** The US's main hurricane site, with info on ongoing storms as well as tracking charts and satellite images.

ⓦ**ww2010.atmos.uiuc.edu/(Gh)/guides/mtr/hurr/home.rxml** Easy-to-follow background on hurricanes, from how they get their names to forecasts of current conditions, including a great tropical storm tracker.

Caribbean Tourism Organisation

A useful general resource is the **Caribbean Tourism Organisation** (CTO; @www. doitcaribbean.com), an international development agency that promotes tourism throughout the Caribbean with an eye towards sustainable tourism and preserving local culture and the environment.

Caribbean Tourism Organisation offices
Barbados One Financial Place, Collymore Rock, St Michael, Barbados ☎246/427 5242, @ctobar@caribsurf.com.
Canada 512 Duplex Ave, Toronto, ON M4R 2E3 ☎416/485-8724, @485-8256.
UK 422 The Quadrant, Richmond, Surrey TW9 1BP ☎020/8948 0057, @ctolondon@caribtourism.com.
US 80 Broad St, 32nd floor, New York, NY 10004 ☎212/635-9530, @ctony@caribtourism.com.

Anguilla

@www.anguilla-vacation.com
Canada William & Sari Marshalls, 116C Hazelton Ave, Toronto, Canada M5R 2E4 ☎416/944-8105, @xybermedia@aol.com.
UK Anguilla Tourist Board, 7a Crealock St, London SW18 2BS ☎020/8871 0012, @anguilla@tiscali.co.uk.
US 246 Central Ave, White Plains, NY 10606 ☎914/287-2400, @mwturnstyle@aol.com.

Antigua and Barbuda

@www.antigua-barbuda.org
Canada 60 St Claire Ave E, suite 304, Toronto, ON M4T 1N5 ☎416/961-3085, @info@antigua-barbuda-ca.com.
UK 15 Thayer St, London W1U 3JT ☎020/7486 7073, @antbar@msn.com.
US 610 Fifth Ave, suite 311, New York, NY 10020 ☎212/541-4117 or 1-888/268-4227, @info@antigua-barbuda.org.

Aruba

@www.aruba.com
Canada 5875 Highway #7, suite 201, Woodbridge, ON L4L 1T9 ☎905/264-3434 or 1-800/268-3042, @ata.canada@aruba.com.
UK The Copperfields, 25 Copperfield St, London SE1 0EN ☎020/7928 1600, @geoff@saltmarshpr.co.uk.
US 1200 Harbor Blvd, Weehawken, NJ 07087 ☎201/330-0800 or 1-800/TO-ARUBA, @ata.newjersey@aruba.com.

Bahamas

@www.bahamas.com
Canada 121 Bloor St E, suite #1101, Toronto, ON M4W 3M5 ☎416/968-2999, @BMOTCA@bahamas.com.
UK and Ireland Bahamas House, 10 Chesterfield St, London W1J 5JL ☎020/7355-0800, @info@bahamas.co.uk.
US 1200 Cornerstone, South Pine Island Rd, suite 770, Plantation, FL 33324 ☎954/236-9292, @bking@bahamas.com.

Barbados

@www.barbados.org
Canada suite 1010, 105 Adelaide St W, Toronto, ON M5H 1P9 ☎416/214-9880, @barbados.org/canada.
UK 263 Tottenham Court Rd, London W1P 9AA ☎020/7636 9448, @www.barbados.org/uk.
US 800 Second Ave, New York, NY 10017 ☎212/986-6516 or 1-800/221-9831, @www.barbados.org/usa.

Bonaire

@www.infobonaire.com
Europe Basis Communicatie BV, Wagenweg 252, PO Box 472, NL-2000 AL Haarlem, The Netherlands ☎23/5430 704, @europe@tourismbonaire.com.
US and Canada Adams Unlimited, 10 Rockefeller Plaza, suite 900, New York, NY 10020 ☎212/956-5912 or 1-800/266-2473, @usa@tourismbonaire.com.

British Virgin islands

@bvitouristboard.com
UK BVI Tourist Board, 15 Upper Grosvenor St, London W1K 7PS ☎020/7355 9587, @infouk@bvi.org.uk.
US BVI Tourist Board, 1270 Broadway, New York, NY 10001 ☎212/696-0400 or 1-800/835-8530, @ny@bvitouristboard.com.

Cayman Islands

ⓦ www.caymanislands.ky
Canada 234 Eglinton Ave E, suite 306, Toronto, ON
M4P 1K5 ⓣ 416/485-1550 or 1-800/263-5805,
ⓕ 416/485-7578.
UK 6 Arlington St, London SW1 1RE ⓣ 020/7491
7771, ⓦ www.caymanislands.co.uk.
US 3 Park Ave, 39th floor, New York, NY 10170
ⓣ 212/889-9009, ⓕ 986-5123.

Cuba

ⓦ www.cubatravel.cu
Canada Cuba Tourist Board, 1200 Bay St, suite
305, Toronto ON M5R 2A5 ⓣ 416/362-0700,
ⓦ www.gocuba.ca.
UK Cuba Tourism Office, 154 Shaftesbury
Ave, London WC2H 8JT ⓣ 020/7240 6655
ⓔ tourism@cubasi.info.

Curaçao

ⓦ www.curacao-tourism.com
Europe Curaçao Tourist Board, Vastland 82–84,
3011 BP Rotterdam, The Netherlands ⓣ 10 414
2639, ⓦ www.ctbe.nl.
UK Axis Sales & Marketing Ltd, Curaçao
Representation UK, 421a Finchley Rd, London NW3
6HJ ⓣ 020/7431 4045, ⓔ destinations@axissm.com.
US Curaçao Tourist Board 7591 SW 6th St,
Plantation, FL 33324, ⓣ 1-800/328-7222,
ⓔ jbgrossman@aol.com.

Dominica

ⓦ www.ndcdominica.dm
UK Morris Kevan International, Mitre House, 66
Abbey Rd, Bush Hill Park, Middlesex EN1 2QE
ⓣ 020/8350 1000, ⓔ mki@ttq.co.uk.
US Dominica Tourist Office, 110-164 Queens
Blvd, PO Box 427, Forest Hills, New York, NY
11375 ⓣ 718/261-9615 or 1-888/645-5637,
ⓔ dominicany@dominica.dm.

Dominican Republic

ⓦ www.dominicanrepublic.com
Canada 35 Church St, unit 53, Toronto, ON M5E
1T3 ⓣ 416/361-2126/27 or 1-888/494-5050,
ⓔ toronto@sectur.gov.do.
UK 18-22 Hand Court, High Holborn, London
WC1V 6JF ⓣ 020/7242 7778, ⓔ domrep.
touristboard@virgin.net.
US 2355 Salzedo St, suite 307, Coral Gables,
Miami, FL 3313 ⓣ 305/444-4593 or 1-888/358-
9594, ⓔ domrep@herald.infi.net.

Grenada

ⓦ www.grenada.org
Canada Grenada Board of Tourism, Phoenix
House, 439 University Ave, suite 930, Toronto ON
M5G 1Y8 ⓣ 416/595-1339, ⓔ tourism@grenadac
onsulate.com.
UK Grenada Board of Tourism, 1 Battersea Church
Rd, London SW11 3LY ⓣ 020/7771 7016, ⓦ www.
grenadagrenadines.com.
US Grenada Board of Tourism, 317 Madison Ave,
suite 1704, New York, NY 10017 ⓣ 212/687-9554
or 1-800/927-9554, ⓔ noel@rfcp.com.

Guadeloupe

ⓦ www.antilles-info-tourisme.com/guad-
eloupe/p2-in-gb.htm
Canada Maison de la France, 1981 Ave McGill
College, suite 490, Montreal PQ 3A2 2W9
ⓣ 514/288-4264, ⓕ 514/845-4868.
UK Maison de la France, 187 Piccadilly, London
W1V 0AL ⓣ 020/7493-6694, ⓕ 020/7493-6594.
US Guadeloupe Tourist Office, 161 Washington
Valley Rd, suite 205, Warren, NJ 07059 ⓣ 1-
888/448-2335.

Jamaica

ⓦ www.jamaicatravel.com
Canada 303 Eglinton Ave E, suite 200, Toronto,
ON M4P 1L3 ⓣ 416/482-7850 or 1-800/465-2624,
ⓔ jtb@jtbcanada.com.
UK 1–2 Prince Consort Rd, London SW7 2BZ
ⓣ 020/7224 0505, ⓔ jamaicatravel@btconnect.com.
US 1320 Dixie Highway, suite 1101, Coral Gables
FL 33146 ⓣ 305/665-0557 or 1-800/233-4582,
ⓔ jamaicatrv1@aol.com.

Martinique

ⓦ www.martinique.org
Canada Martinique Tourist Office, French Tourist
Office, 444 Madison Ave, 16th floor, New York, NY
10022 ⓣ 212/838-7800, ⓕ 212/838-7855.
UK Maison de la France, 178 Piccadilly, London
WIJ 9AL ⓣ 020/7399 3500, ⓕ 020/7493-6594.
US Martinique Promotion Bureau, 444 Madison
Ave, 16th floor, New York, NY 10022 ⓣ 212/838-
7800 or 1-800/391-4909, ⓔ info@martinique.org.

Puerto Rico

ⓦ www.gotopuertorico.com
Canada 41–43 Colbourne St, suite 301,
Toronto, ON M5E 1E3 ⓣ 416/368-2680 or 1-

800/667-0394, ☎416/368-5350.
UK 2nd floor, 67a High St, Walton-on-Thames, Surrey KT12 1DJ ☎01932/253 302, ✉puertoricouh@aol.com.
US 666 Fifth Ave, 15th floor, New York, NY 10003 ☎212/586-6262 or 1-800/223-6530, 🖷212/586-1212.

Saba

☻www.sabatourism.com
Netherlands Netherlands Kabinet van de Gevolmachtigde Minister van de Nederlandse Antillen, Badhuisweg 173–175, 2597 JP's-Gravenhage ☎70/351-2811, 🖷70/351-2722.

St Barts

☻www.st-barths.com
For all enquiries, contact your country's French Tourist Board office via ☻ www.franceguide.com.

St Eustatius

☻www.statiatourism.com
See under St Maarten.

St Kitts and Nevis

☻www.stkitts-tourism.com
Canada St Kitts Tourism Authority, 133 Richmond St W, suite 311, Toronto, ON M5H 2L3 ☎416/368-6707 or 1-888/395-4887, ✉canada.office@stkittstourism.kn.
UK St Kitts Tourism Authority, 10 Kensington Ct, London W8 5DL ☎020/7376 0881, ✉uk-europe.office@stkittstourism.com.
US 414 E 75th St, suite 5, New York, NY 10021 ☎212/535-1234 or 1-800/582-6208, ✉nyoffice@stkittstourism.kn.

St Lucia

☻www.stlucia.org
Canada 8 King St E, suite 700, Toronto, ON M5C 1B5 ☎416/362-4242 or 1-800/869 0377, 🖷416/362-7832.
UK 1 Collington Gardens, London SW5 0HW ☎0870/900 7697, ✉stlbinfo@stluciauk.org.
US 800 Second Ave, 9th floor, New York, NY 10017 ☎212/867-2950 or 1-800/456-3984, ✉stluciatourism@aol.com.

St Maarten

☻www.st-maarten.com
Canada 703 Evans Ave, suite 106, Toronto, ON

M9C 5E9 ☎416/622-4300, 🖷416/622-3431.
US 675 Third Ave, suite 1806, New York, NY 10017 ☎212/953-2084 or 1-800/786-2278, 🖷212/953-2145.

St Martin

☻www.st-martin.org
Canada Maison de la France, 1981 Ave McGill College, suite 490, Montreal PQ 3A2 2W9 ☎514/288-4264, 🖷514/845-4868.
US St Martin Tourist Office, 675 Third Ave, suite 1807, New York, NY 10017 ☎212/475-8970, ✉sxmtony@msn.com.

St Vincent and the Grenadines

☻www.svgtourism.com
UK 10 Kensington Ct, London W8 5DL ☎020/7937 6570, ✉svgtourismeurope@aol.com.
US 801 Second Ave, 21st floor, New York, NY 10017 ☎212/687-4981 or 1-800/729-1726, ✉svgtony@aol.com.

Trinidad and Tobago

☻www.visittnt.com
Canada The RMR Group, Taurus House, 512 Duplex Ave, Toronto, ON M4R 2E3 ☎416/485-7827 or 1-888/535-5617, ✉andy@thearmgroup.ca.
UK Mitre House, 66 Abbey Rd, Bush Hill Park, Enfield, Middlesex EN1 2QE ☎020/8350 1000.
US Cheryl Andrews Marketing Inc, 311 Almeria Ave, Coral Gables, FL 33144 ☎305/444-7827 or 1-888/595-4868, ✉cheryl@cherylandrewsmarketing.com.

Turks and Caicos

☻www.turksandcaicostourism.com
Canada RR# 2 Bancroft, Ontario KOL 1CO ☎613/332-6472 or 1-866/413-8875, 🖷613/332-6473.
UK Mitre House, 66 Abbey Rd, Bush Hill, Enfield, Middlesex EN1 2QE ☎020/8350 1000, 🖷020/8350 1011.
US 2715 East Oakland Park Blvd, suite 101, Fort Lauderdale, FL 33306 ☎954/568-6588 or 1-800/241-0824, ✉tcitrsm@bellsouth.net.

US Virgin Islands

☻www.usvi.net
Canada 703 Evans Ave, suite 106, Toronto, ON M9C 5E9 ☎416/622-7600, 🖷416/622-3431.
UK Molasses House, Clove Hitch Quay, Plantation Wharf, London SW11 3TW ☎020/7978 5262, ✉usvi@destination-marketing.co.uk.

US 1270 Avenue of the Americas, suite 2108, New York, NY 10020 ☎212/332-2222 or 1-800/372-USVI, ℗212/332-2223.

Websites

There is a wealth of information about the Caribbean on the **Web**. For the latest information on **safety issues** in the region, check out either the British Foreign & Commonwealth Office website (⊛www.fco.gov.uk) or the US State Department Travel Advisories (⊛travel. state.gov/travel_warnings.html). For details of **Internet access** within the region, see each country's individual basics section.

BBC Caribbean ⊛www.bbc.co.uk/caribbean. Essential site with Caribbean news reports (audio and online), including the week's highlights, plus arts, entertainment and sports coverage.

CANA On-Line ⊛www.cananews.com. Daily sports, news, business and features stories on the English Caribbean.

Caribbean Aviation ⊛www.caribbeanaviation.com. Very up-to-date and comprehensive website detailing charter and scheduled airlines serving the Caribbean.

Caribbean Information Office ⊛www. caribbeans.com. Information on travelling to the region (including advice on weddings), as well as accommodation, packages and airlines.

Caribbean On Line ⊛www.caribbean-on-line.com. Extensive coverage of airlines, car rental, restaurant reviews and accommodation throughout the islands.

Caribbean Travel and Life ⊛www. caribbeantravelmag.com. Comprehensive Web version of the print magazine, with reader forums, custom trip planning, classifieds and resort information.

Cruise Critic ⊛www.cruisecritic.com. Detailed reviews of cruise ships serving the Caribbean.

First Magazine ⊛www.first-jamaica.com/ magazine. Out of Jamaica, this is a stylishly produced 'zine concentrating on the more underground aspects of Caribbean culture.

Sunhead magazine ⊛www.tribelife.com. Excellent politics/arts/youth culture 'zine for young people in the Caribbean.

Turquoise Net ⊛www.turq.com. In-depth site covering everything from maps to hotel listings, weather, books and travel tips.

Travel bookshops and map outlets

In the US and Canada

Book Passage 51 Tamal Vista Blvd, Corte Madera, CA 94925 ☎1-800/999-7909, ⊛www. bookpassage.com.

Complete Traveller Bookstore 199 Madison Ave, New York, NY ☎212/685-9007, ⊛www. completetravellerbooks.com.

Distant Lands 56 S Raymond Ave, Pasadena, CA 91105 ☎1-800/310-3220, ⊛www.distantlands. com.

Elliot Bay Book Company 101 S Main St, Seattle, WA 98104 ☎1-800/962-5311, ⊛www. elliotbaybook.com.

Globe Corner Bookstore 28 Church St, Cambridge, MA 02138 ☎1-800/358-6013, ⊛www.globecorner.com.

Map Link 30 S La Patera Lane, unit 5, Santa Barbara, CA 93117 ☎805/692-6777 or 1-800/962-1394, ⊛www.maplink.com.

Rand McNally ☎1-800/333-0136, ⊛www. randmcnally.com.Three US stores; check the website for the nearest location.

The Travel Bug Bookstore 3065 W Broadway, Vancouver V6K 2G2 ☎604/737-1122, ⊛www. travelbugbooks.ca.

World of Maps 1235 Wellington St, Ottawa, ON K1Y 3A3 ☎1-800/214-8524, ⊛www. worldofmaps.com.

In the UK and Ireland

Blackwell's Map and Travel Shop ⊛maps. blackwell.co.uk/index.html. Branches all over the UK; check the website for details.

Easons Bookshop 40 Lower O'Connell St, Dublin 1 ☎01/858 3800, ⊛www.eason.ie. Call or check the website for details of other branches around Ireland.

John Smith & Son Glasgow Caledonian University Bookshop, 70 Cowcaddens Rd, Glasgow G4 0BA ☎0141/332 8173, ⊛www.johnsmith.co.uk. For details of other branches in Scotland and England, call or check the website.

The Map Shop 30a Belvoir St, Leicester LE1 6QH ☎0116/247 1400, ⊛www.mapshopleicester.co.uk.

National Map Centre 22–24 Caxton St, London SW1H 0QU ☎020/7222 2466, ⊛www.mapstore. co.uk.

Ordnance Survey Ireland Phoenix Park, Dublin 8 ☎01/8025 300, ⊛www.irlgov.ie/osi.

Ordnance Survey of Northern Ireland Colby House, Stranmillis Ct, Belfast BT9 5BJ ☎028/9025 5755, ⊛www.osni.gov.uk.

Stanfords 12–14 Long Acre, London WC2E 9LP ☎020/7836 1321, ⊛www.stanfords.co.uk. For details of branches in Manchester and Bristol, call or check the website.

The Travel Bookshop 13–15 Blenheim Crescent,

London W11 2EE ☎020/7229 5260, ⌨www.
thetravelbookshop.co.uk.

The Map Shop 6–10 Peel St, Adelaide, SA 5000
☎08/8231 2033, ⌨www.mapshop.net.au.

Mapland 372 Little Bourke St, Melbourne, Victoria
3000, ☎03/9670 4383, ⌨www.mapland.com.au.
MapWorld 173 Gloucester St, Christchurch
☎03/374 5399 or 0800/627 967, ⌨www.mapworld.
co.nz.

Money and costs

The **US dollar** is widely accepted in the Caribbean along with local currency – albeit at a less-than-favourable exchange rate. In fact, the US dollar is the official currency in the Virgin Islands, Turks and Caicos and Puerto Rico. The **British pound**, however, is not used in the former British colonies, and while French islands such as Guadeloupe and Martinique do accept US dollars, the **euro** is the preferred currency.

As the majority of Caribbean islands are fairly developed, at least in the touristed areas, **travellers' cheques** and **credit cards** are accepted. **ATMs** accept debit and credit cards linked to the Cirrus, Plus and Visa networks (cash is given in local currency), while most hotels will change money, though at less favourable rates than banks. In less developed areas, it's best to carry local currency as few establishments will take credit cards and ATMs are rare. (See individual chapters for information specific to the islands.)

Cash and travellers' cheques

If you are going to be away from urban or tourist centres or shopping in local markets and stalls, **cash** is a necessity – preferably in small denominations of local currency.

As a general rule, US or UK pound **travellers' cheques** are accepted in lieu of cash in resorts – those issued by Visa or American Express are best; in countries where the euro is used (Martinique, Guadeloupe, Curaçao, Saba, St Barts, St Martin/St Maarten and St Eustatius) you might be better off using cheques in euro denominations.

You can cash travellers' cheques in **banks** and **bureaux de change** in city centres and airports, as well as in resorts. It's a good idea to get your cheques in small denominations so that you don't end up carrying a large amount of cash on your person once you've cashed them.

The usual **fee** for travellers' cheque sales is one or two percent, though this fee may be waived if you buy the cheques through your bank. Some outlets, particularly banks, offer better rates for cheques than for cash and most charge a commission. Keep the purchase agreement and a record of cheque serial numbers safe and separate from the cheques themselves. In the event that they're lost or stolen, you'll need to **report the loss** to the issuing company; refer to the list of phone numbers provided with the cheques; most companies claim to replace lost or stolen cheques within 24 hours.

Credit and debit cards

Credit cards are a handy back-up and can be used to get cash advances at ATMs and over the counter at banks as well as to pay for goods and services. MasterCard and Visa are the most commonly accepted in the Caribbean; other cards may not be recognized and US-issued cards are not accepted in Cuba at all. Remember that if you use your credit card to obtain cash advances, you'll pay credit-card rates of interest on the cash from the date of withdrawal; there may be a transaction fee on top of this.

If you want the security of travellers' cheques without the hassle of carrying large amounts of cash or waiting for exchange offices to open, consider using your **ATM card** – many ATMs in the region now take US and European debit cards (linked to Cirrus, Plus or Maestro) at a minimal fee – check with your bank for details. Make sure you have a personal identification number (PIN) that lets you access your account from overseas. A complete list of ATMs on the Cirrus and Maestro networks can be found at ⓦ www.mastercard.com/atmlocator/index.jsp; for those on the Visa Plus network, log on to ⓦ visa.via.infonow.net/locator/eur/jsp/SearchPage.jsp.

A compromise between travellers' cheques and plastic is **Visa TravelMoney**, a disposable prepaid debit card with a PIN which works in all ATMs that take Visa cards. You load up your account with funds before leaving home, and when they run out, you simply throw the card away. Up to nine cards can be purchased to access the same funds – useful for couples or families travelling together – and it's a good idea to buy at least one extra as a backup in case of loss or theft. The card is available in most countries from branches of Thomas Cook and Citicorp. For more information, check the Visa TravelMoney website at ⓦ www.usa.visa.com/personal/cards/prepaid/visa_travel_money.html.

Wiring money

Having money **wired** from home using one of the companies listed below can be convenient, in that funds can be collected within minutes of the transaction being made in your home country, but hefty commissions (at the time of writing roughly £14/$21 on top of the first £100/$150 sent, with larger sums charged according to a sliding scale) slapped on top of the amount sent means that the amount you eventually receive may be considerably less than originally paid in.

It's possible to have money wired directly from a bank in your home country to a bank

in the Caribbean, although this is somewhat less reliable because it involves two separate institutions. If you go this route, your home bank will need the address of the branch bank where you want to pick up the money and the address and telex number of its main island office. Money wired this way normally takes two working days to arrive, and costs around US$40/£25 per transaction.

Money-wiring companies

Moneygram
ⓦ www.moneygram.com
Australia ☎ 1800/666 3947
Canada ☎ 1800/933 3278
Ireland ☎ 0800/666 3947
New Zealand ☎ 0800/666 3947
UK ☎ 0800/8971 8971
US ☎ 1-800/926-9400

Thomas Cook
ⓦ www.thomascook.com
US ☎ 1-800/287-7362
Canada ☎ 1-888/823-4732
Great Britain ☎ 01733/318922
Northern Ireland ☎ 028/9055 0030
Republic of Ireland ☎ 01/677 1721

Western Union
Australia ☎ 1800/173 833, ⓦ www.westernunion.com.au.
Canada ☎ 1-800/325-6000, ⓦ www.westernunioncanada.ca.
New Zealand ☎ 09/270 0050, ⓦ www.westernunion.com.
Republic of Ireland ☎ 1800/395 395, ⓦ www.westernunion.com.
UK ☎ 0800/833 833, ⓦ www.westernunion.co.uk.
US ☎ 1-800/325-6000, ⓦ www.westernunion.com.

Costs

Your **daily budget** in the Caribbean depends, of course, on where you are travelling and how comfortable you want to be. The **cheapest destinations** are likely to be Dominica, Trinidad and Tobago and the Dominican Republic, where you can get by sleeping in the cheapest accommodation, travelling by bus and eating food from street stalls and supermarkets on about US$30/day, possibly less. A couple of other islands, such as Barbados and Jamaica, can be visited on around US$50/day, or US$100/day with a little luxury; however, most Caribbean islands will be around US$125/day, with a few – such as Bonaire – setting you back US$150/day or more. Remember that **incidentals** such as car rental, room and departure tax, local driving permits and guides – never mind island-hopping, whale-watching, fancy dinners or scuba diving – really add up, though these are some of the most enjoyable facets of a Caribbean holiday.

Island transport

Public transport on the larger Caribbean islands is generally cheap, though not wholly reliable in many cases. Most tourists tend to travel in taxis or rental cars – sometimes a hair-raising experience given the erratic nature of Caribbean driving, but worth it for the independence granted. Those unprepared to risk the roads themselves might consider taking the **bus** – routes usually cover all main destinations on most islands, and many minor ones besides, and are much used by the locals. Be aware, though, that many bus drivers don't adhere to a timetable and will leave only when the bus is full. For island-specific details, see individual chapters.

Buses and taxis

Buses tend to operate a frequent, if erratic, service between 6am and 8pm on the more populated islands of the Caribbean, stretching to 10pm or even midnight in more developed locales. There is often limited or no service on a Sunday. The buses themselves are usually small minivans which the drivers like to pack to the gills before departure, and fares are invariably low – rarely more than US$3, usually closer to 50¢.

Taxis are plentiful throughout the Caribbean; drivers are often very knowledgeable and act as tour guides and advisers, even accompanying single women to street parties and the like (for a fee), as well as serving as chauffeurs. Sometimes the only way to identify a taxi is by checking the number plate for a designated letter or colour. Usually taxis are not metered and **fares** are regulated by the various island governments (although some taxi drivers may ignore the official rates and set their own, especially for longer trips). Lists of sample taxi fares are available from tourist offices, but you should always agree to a rate before you start your journey. Don't be afraid to negotiate, either, as this is often customary.

Measurements and distances

You'll notice that there's a kind of schizophrenia when it comes to **measurements** in many Caribbean islands; Jamaica, for example, officially uses imperial measurements, but all of the country's road signs are metric, giving distances in kilometres rather than miles, and speed limits in KPH rather than MPH. The table below lists a few helpful conversions.

1 mile = 1.6093 kilometres
1 metre = 1.0936 yards

Car rental

Car rental is straightforward on most Caribbean islands, with major companies vying with local outfits in terms of price. On many of the islands you will need to buy a local, temporary **driving permit**, usually valid for three to six months and costing US$15–25 (see box below). Car rental will cost on average US$200–350 per week for a compact automatic with air conditioning. Be prepared to be refused, or at least charged a hefty surcharge – sometimes as much as the regular rate again – if you are under 25. On most Caribbean islands vehicles drive on the left, with the exceptions being Aruba, Cuba, the Dominican Republic, Guadeloupe, Martinique, Bonaire, Curaçao, Saba and St Eustatius.

Driving conditions and local driving patterns vary widely. Many roads are narrow or winding, signs may not be in English or not there at all, some routes may be little more than dust tracks and inaccessible after rain or without a four-wheel-drive vehicle, and in some places domestic animals roam freely. Defensive driving, therefore, is a must. Be prepared to use your horn – and hand gestures – liberally.

Car rental companies

In North America
Avis US ☎1-800/331-1084, Canada ☎1-800/272-5871, ⊛www.avis.com.

Budget US ☎1-800/527-0700, ⊛www.budgetrentacar.com.
Dollar US ☎1-800/800-4000, ⊛www.dollar.com.
Hertz US ☎1-800/654-3001, Canada ☎1-800/623-0600, ⊛www.hertz.com.
Thrifty ☎1-800/367-2277, ⊛www.thrifty.com.

In Britain and Ireland
Autobookers UK ☎ 020/8878 8333, ⊛www.autobookers.com.
Avis UK ☎0870/606 0100, ⊛www.avis.co.uk, Republic of Ireland ☎01/605 7500, ⊛www.avis.ie.
Budget UK ☎0800/181 181, ⊛www.budget.co.uk, Republic of Ireland ☎0903/27711, ⊛www.budget.ie,
Hertz UK ☎0870/844 8844, ⊛www.hertz.co.uk, Republic of Ireland ☎01/676 7476, ⊛www.hertz.ie,

In Australia and New Zealand
Avis Australia ☎13 63 33, ⊛www.avis.co.au, New Zealand ☎0800/655 111, ⊛www.avis.co.nz.
Budget Australia ☎1300/362 848, ⊛www.budget.com.au, New Zealand ☎09/976 2222, ⊛www.budget.co.nz.
Hertz Australia ☎13 30 39, ⊛www.hertz.com.au, New Zealand ☎0800/654 321, ⊛www.hertz.co.nz.
Thrifty Australia ☎1300/367 227, ⊛www.thrifty.com.au; New Zealand ☎09/309 0111, ⊛www.thrifty.co.nz.

Bicycles, motorbikes and scooters

Many hotels and resorts will either rent **bicycles** to guests or have a company nearby

---

Local driving permits

Visitors planning to drive in the Caribbean will need to obtain a **local driving permit** on the following islands. You'll need to show a current driver's licence, and often an international driver's licence as well.

Anguilla Available from car rental companies for US$20.

Antigua and Barbuda Available from car rental companies for US$20. Valid for three months.

Barbados Required only if you do not have an international licence. Available from the airport, local police stations and car rental companies for US$5.

British Virgin Islands Available from car rental companies or Police Headquarters for US$10.

Grenada Available from the police at La Carenage or at car rental companies for EC$30.

St Kitts and Nevis Available from the Police Traffic Department for EC$50. Valid for one year.

with whom they can arrange preferential rates (US$10–25/day with discounts for weeklong rentals). Similarly, **scooters** and **motorbikes** are available; some local car rental agencies have motorbikes and scoot-

ers for hire. Count on paying around US$30 per day or US$150 per week for a scooter; US$40 per day or US$180 per week for a motorbike.

Inter-island transport

One of the joys of Caribbean travel is the ease with which travellers can journey between islands, taking in two or three different cultures in one trip. Most islands are well connected by local and international airlines, although some – Cuba, for example, or Dominica – are less well served than most. Many of the bigger airlines offer **airpasses** costing from US$300 for three stopovers to US$600 for unlimited Caribbean travel within an airline's range – see overleaf for details of specific deals.

If you plan simply to travel between groups of islands – the Caymans, for example, the Virgin Islands or the Grenadines, the many small airline companies operating there run a regular and reasonable service. Alternatively, you might consider travelling by **ferry**: there is a high-speed service between St Lucia, Martinique, Dominica and Guadeloupe and another between St Barts, Saba and St Maarten. Full details of inter-island ferry services are given on p.52-53.

Airlines

Abaco Air ☎242/367-2266, ⊛www.go-abacos. com/news/conian/6-1-2/abacoair.html. Flights between the Bahamian islands; scheduled seats cost US$44–90 each way.
Air Caraïbes ☎0820/835 835, US ☎1-877/722-1005, ⊛www.aircaraibes.com. Serves St Barts, St Maarten, St Lucia, Dominica, the Dominican Republic, San Juan, Guadeloupe and Martinique.
Air Culebra ☎787/268-6951, ⊛www.airculebra. com. Operates flights between Puerto Rico and most Caribbean islands.
Air Jamaica ⊛www.airjamaica.com. Scheduled flights to Barbados, Bonaire, Turks and Caicos, Curaçao, Grand Cayman, Grenada, Cuba, Jamaica, the Bahamas, the Dominican Republic and St Lucia.
Air St Thomas ☎340/776-2722 or 1-800/522-3084, ⊛www.airstthomas.com. Service between

St Barts, St Thomas, San Juan, Fajardo, Culebra and Virgin Gorda.
Air Sunshine ☎954/434-8900, North America ☎1-800/327-8900, ⊛www.airsunshine.com. Fort Lauderdale to the Bahamas, Puerto Rico, US and British Virgin Islands, Turks and Caicos, Dominican Republic and Jamaica, and flights between the above islands.
Air Turks and Caicos ☎649/941-5481 or 646/946-1777, ⊛www.airturksandcaicos.com. Flights throughout Turks and Caicos, and the Dominican Republic.
BWIA International ☎868/627-2942, ⊛www. bwee.com. Regular service throughout the Caribbean.
American Eagle ☎1-800/433-7300, ⊛www.aa.com. Service between American Airlines' San Juan hub and most Caribbean destinations.
Bahamasair ☎242/377-8451, ⊛www. bahamasair.com/online. Flights between several American cities and the Bahamas.
Caribbean Star ☎268/480-2561, ⊛www. flycaribbeanstar.com. Operates between Antigua, Anguilla, Barbados, Grenada, Dominica, Nevis, St Kitts, St Lucia, St Maarten, St Vincent, Trinidad, Tobago and Tortola.
Carib Aviation ☎268/462-3147, UK ☎01895/450 710, ⊛www.candoo.com/carib/index.html. Charter flights between Antigua, St Kitts and Nevis.
Cayman Airways US ☎1-800/422-9626 or 345/949-2311. Scheduled flights between several US cities and the Cayman Islands, Cuba and Jamaica.

Cubana ☎05/255-3776, ⊛www.cubana.cu. Major Cuban airline flying inter-island and to Canada.

Dutch Caribbean Excel ☎297/588-1900. Scheduled flights between Amsterdam and the Dutch Caribbean.

Fly BVI ☎284/495-1747, US ☎1-866/819-3146, Canada ☎1-800/465-5955, ⊛www.fly-bvi.com. Operates charter flights between most eastern Caribbean islands and Puerto Rico.

Gulfstream International Airlines US ☎1-800/231-0856, Bahamas ☎242/394 6019, ⊛www.gulfstreamair.com. Scheduled flights between Miami, Fort Lauderdale and the Bahamas.

Inter Island Express San Juan ☎787/253-1400, US ☎1-866/747-5263, ⊛www.interislandexpress.com. San Juan-based airline offering charter and scheduled flights to most islands in the region.

LIAT in the Caribbean ☎1-888/844-5428, elsewhere ☎868/624-4727, ⊛www.liatairline.com. Services Anguilla, Antigua, Barbados, Dominica, Nevis, Mustique, Grenada, Bequia, San Juan, St Croix, St Kitts, St Lucia, St Maarten, St Thomas, St Vincent, Trinidad, Tobago, Union Island and Tortola.

Lynx Air International ☎954/772-9808, US ☎1-888/596-9247, ⊛www.lynxair.com. Flights between Fort Lauderdale and the Bahamas, Turks and Caicos and Cuba.

Mustique Air ☎784/458-4380, US ☎1-800/526-4789, Canada ☎416/352-5379, UK ☎0845/127 4857, ⊛www.mustique.com. Scheduled flights between Barbados, the Grenadines and Grenada. Charters also available.

Sky King Air ☎649/941-3136, ⊛www.skyking.tc. Scheduled services between the Bahamas, Cuba, Turks and Caicos and the Dominican Republic.

SVG Air ☎784/457-5124, ⊛www.svgair.com. Offers service between St Vincent and the Grenadines, St Barts, Grenada, Barbados, Martinique, Dominica, St Vincent and St Lucia.

Trans Island Air 2000 ☎246/418-1650, ⊛www.tia2000.com. Barbados-based airline with scheduled services between most eastern Caribbean islands.

Windward Express Airlines ☎599/545-2001, ⊛www.windwardexpress.com. Charter airline serving St Barts, Anguilla, Saba, St Eustatius and St Maarten.

Airpasses

BWIA airpass

For passengers whose international flights are booked with BWIA, the airline offers a **pass** for travel between Antigua, Barbados, Cuba, Grenada, Jamaica, Trinidad and Tobago, the Dominican Republic, St Lucia, St Vincent and St Maarten. For US$450, you can fly to any of the above destinations in any 30-day period (except from Dec 19 to Jan 6); for US$350, you can fly to any of them excluding Jamaica, Cuba and the Dominican Republic. If you don't fly to the region with BWIA, the same packages cost US$550 and US$450 respectively. All itineraries must be booked in advance (though you can make changes for US$25); no open returns and no backtracking is allowed (though you can backtrack for connections only).

LIAT airpass

LIAT operates between Anguilla, Antigua, Barbados, Dominica, Martinique, Grenada, Guadeloupe, Nevis, Trinidad, St Croix, St Kitts, St Lucia, St Thomas, St Vincent and the Grenadines, St Maarten, Tobago, the British Virgin Islands, San Juan and Puerto Rico, and offers three **passes**, valid only on their flights (not codeshares), all of which must have an itinerary booked in advance, with no open returns and no backtracking. The passes are valid year-round and can be booked with Caribjet in the UK.

Mini Explorer Allows a maximum of four stopovers in 21 days, returning to the originating destination to connect with the international flight. US$300.

Super Explorer Unlimited travel to all of LIAT's destinations for 30 days. US$525.

Airpass European travellers buying this airpass in conjunction with their international ticket can avail themselves of three to six stopovers in 21 days. US$100 per segment.

Ferries

While there is no **ferry** service that covers the entire Caribbean, there are a number of ferries that run between certain islands. We've listed some of the more useful lines below.

Between Bonaire and Curaçao

There is a twice-daily ferry service operated by **Flamingo Fast Ferries** (Bonaire ☎599/717-7001); there is no service between Curaçao or Bonaire and Aruba.

Between St Maarten, Saba and St Barts

The Edge (☎599/514-2640) is a high-speed ferry leaving Wed–Sun; the crossing takes one hour and costs US$40 one-way or US$60 return.

The Voyager (☎590/87 10 68, ⊛www.voyager-st-barths.com) travels between the islands every day. The round-trip fare is US$69 (one-way US$49) and the journey takes 14min–1hr 15min.

Between the Dominican Republic and Puerto Rico

Ferias del Caribe (DR ☎809/433-7300, San Juan ☎809/832-4800) connects Mayaguez, Puerto Rico and Santo Dominigo, departs Mon, Wed & Fri from Mayaguez and Tues, Thurs & Sun from Santo Domingo. It costs US$144.

Between Guadeloupe, Martinique, Marie Galante and the lesser French West Indies

Brudey Frères (Guadeloupe ☎502/90 04 48, Martinique ☎596/70 08 50, Marie Galante ☎590/97 77 82, ⊛www.brudey-freres.fr) and **Deher Frères** (Guadeloupe ☎502/99 50 68) operate a regular service between the islands.

Between Guadeloupe, Marie Galante, Les Saintes, Dominica, Martinique and St Lucia

Express-des-Isles (☎0825/359 000, ⊛www .express-des-iles.com) is a high-speed catamaran operating daily in the Southern Caribbean.

Between Anguilla and St Martin

Ferries depart daily from Anguilla beginning at 7.30am approximately at regular half-hour intervals. The last day ferry departs Marigot Bay, St Martin at 5.40pm. The day ferry costs US$10 plus US$2 departure tax. There is one evening ferry that departs Anguilla at 6.15pm. The return ferry departs St Martin at 7pm. Evening fare is US$12 plus US$2 departure tax.

Phones, post and email

What follows is general advice about **communications** across the Caribbean region; island-specific information on phone, mail and Internet facilities is given at the beginning of each chapter.

Post

Post offices in cities and major towns offer a wide range of services; those in villages are much more basic, with shorter opening hours and often slow service. Most resorts and hotels sell stamps and have a postbox – if you are staying in such an establishment, this can often be the most convenient way to send a letter home. **Mail** to Europe and North America normally takes from one to two weeks, but it can take up to one month depending on the departure and destination points. Travellers can receive mail via **poste restante** in any Caribbean country except Dominica. The system is universally fairly efficient (if you're going to be abroad for a while) but tends to be available only at the main post office in cities, not in small towns and villages. Most post offices hold letters for a maximum of one month, though some hold them for up to three.

Phones

You should be able to **phone home** from most islands in the Caribbean without any problems. Islands usually have both payphones that accept coins and those that require phone cards, which are usually available from shops everywhere.

Local calls in the Caribbean are usually very cheap, while many tour companies, hotels and activity providers will have free call numbers that you can dial from any public or private phone.

Avoid calling **long-distance** from hotels unless you have a cheap long-distance phone card with a free or local access number; even then check to see if the establishment charges for such calls. Some larger resorts have been known to charge upwards of US$1 per minute for local dialling.

Calling home from abroad

One of the most convenient ways of phoning home from abroad is via a **telephone charge card** from your phone company back home. Using a PIN number, you can make calls from most public and private phones (including in-room hotel phones) that will be charged to the telephone card account. Since most major charge cards are free to obtain, it's certainly worth getting one at least for emergencies; enquire first, though, whether your destination is covered, and bear in mind that rates aren't necessarily cheaper than calling from a public phone.

In the **UK and Ireland**, British Telecom (☎ 0800/345 144, ⊕ www.chargecard. bt.com) will issue free to all BT customers the BT Charge Card, which can be used in 116 countries; AT&T (☎ 1-800/222-0300 in the US, ⊕ www.consumer.att.com/global/english/away/callingcard.html) has the similar International Calling Card.

In the **US and Canada**, AT&T, MCI, Sprint, Canada Direct and other North American long-distance companies all allow their customers to make credit-card calls while overseas, which are then billed to their home

number. Check with your phone company to see if they provide service from the Caribbean; If they do, remember to ask for the toll-free access code.

To call **Australia and New Zealand** from overseas, telephone charge cards such as Telstra Telecard or Optus Calling Card in Australia and Telecom NZ's Calling Card, can be used to make calls abroad, which are charged back to a domestic account or credit card. Apply to Telstra (☎1800/038 000, ⊕www.telstra.com), Optus (☎1300/300 937, ⊕www.optus.com.au) or Telecom NZ (☎04/801 9000, ⊕www.telecom.co.nz).

In many islands, you can also purchase **prepaid cards** which allow you to make international calls at a discounted rate; you dial an access number, key in the PIN from the card and then the number you want to reach. Cards are usually widely available; see individual chapters for details.

Mobile phones

If you want to use your **mobile phone** abroad, you'll need to check with your phone provider to see whether it will work there, and what the call charges will be. However,

Codes needed to call home from abroad

To **phone abroad** from the following islands, you must first dial the international direct dialling or IDD code, followed by the country code, the area code and then the phone number.

International direct dialling codes

Anguilla ☎011
Antigua ☎011
Aruba ☎00
Bahamas ☎011
Barbados ☎011
Bonaire ☎00
British Virgin Islands ☎011
Cayman Islands ☎011
Cuba ☎119
Curaçao ☎00
Dominica ☎011
Dominican Republic ☎011
Grenada ☎011
Guadeloupe ☎00
Jamaica ☎011
Martinique ☎00
Nevis ☎011

Puerto Rico ☎011
Saba ☎00
St Barts ☎00
St Eustatius ☎00
St Kitts ☎011
St Lucia ☎011
St Maarten/St Martin ☎00
St Vincent and the Grenadines ☎011
Trinidad and Tobago ☎011
Turks and Caicos ☎011
US Virgin Islands ☎011

International country codes
Australia ☎61
New Zealand ☎64
Republic of Ireland ☎353
UK ☎44
US and Canada ☎1

any dual-band digital mobile phone with an 800MHz band that is primed for roaming can work on most Caribbean mobile networks. If you do have a phone that works in the region, the cheapest way to make mobile calls is to pay a nominal fee (around US$25) for a local SIM card (or "chip") which you can insert into a phone brought from home and use to make local and international calls; you add credit by way of a pay-as-you-go system. SIM cards are widely available from independent mobile phone shops and Cable and Wireless/Digicel outlets throughout the region. The main **service providers** in the Caribbean are Cable and Wireless (@ www. cwmobile.com; Antigua and Barbuda, Anguilla, Barbados, the Cayman Islands, Dominica, Grenada, Jamaica, St Kitts and Nevis, Turks and Caicos, Montserrat, St Lucia, and St Vincent and the Grenadines) and Digicel (@ www.digicelgroup.com; Jamaica, Cayman Islands, Aruba, Barbados, Grenada, St Lucia, Curaçao, St Vincent and the Grenadines). Phones from either network roam in all of the countries served by the company.

Email

One of the best ways to keep in touch while travelling is using a free Internet **email address** that can be accessed from anywhere, such as Yahoo (@www.yahoo.com) or Hotmail (@www.hotmail.com). If you're taking a laptop with you, @www.kropla.com is a useful website giving details of how to plug your laptop in when abroad and information about electrical systems in different countries.

Accommodation

Accommodation choices in the Caribbean range from basic guesthouses with no hot water through genteel bed and breakfasts and boutique hotels – usually slightly away from the cruise ship ports and main tourist drag – to moderately priced family resorts, all-inclusives for couples or families set right on the beach, all the way up to luxury hotels with spa facilities and ultra-exclusive remote eco-resorts serving five-star cuisine.

True **budget** accommodation in much of the Caribbean is hard to come by, especially in the more exclusive islands. If most of your budget will go towards getting to the Caribbean, then Cuba, the Dominican Republic and the rural parts of Jamaica and Trinidad and Tobago have some of the lowest costs of living and accommodation in the region, as tourism is still developing. Be aware, though, that **hostels** and **camping** facilities are few and far between, and private rooms in local houses are usually not an option, except in places like Cuba and the Dominican Republic.

Most **tourist offices** will happily provide a list of accommodations, but bear in mind that establishments often have to pay to be included on these lists. Generally, however, tourist boards will not recommend specific accommodation, nor will they book it – for this, you either have to go through a travel agent or do it yourself. The Web is a great place to look for accommodation choices, as you can often check out rates, photographs of properties and rooms, and special offers and amenities before you decide on a place. The website of the **Caribbean Tourism Organisation**, @ www.doitcaribbean.com/accommodation/index.html, is a good place to start your independent search.

Prices are much cheaper off-season, and many establishments will give a reduced

55

Ⓑ Accommodation price codes

All accommodation listed in this guide has been graded according to the following **price categories**. Rates are generally for the least expensive double or twin room in high season, and do not include tax, except where this is explicitly stated. For islands that quote prices in currencies other than US dollars, we've converted the local price to US dollars, unless we've stated otherwise.

❶ up to US$25	❹ US$75–100	❼ US$160–200
❷ US$25–50	❺ US$100–130	❽ US$200–250
❸ US$50–75	❻ US$130–160	❾ US$250+

price for longer stays in the low season. It's worth asking around and bargaining a little, as desperate hoteliers will sometimes upgrade rooms or drop the hefty accommodation tax in order to get tourist custom. The more popular destinations may, however, have a seven-night minimum stay, especially in the high season.

Hotels

The range of Caribbean **hotel accommodation** is astounding, not only within islands but often within resorts themselves. Be aware that if you seem to be getting an extraordinary deal for a top-name resort, you may well end up in a small room far from the beach and other amenities – ask to see the room, or at least ask for a description in writing, before you sign anything or pay. Hotel buildings themselves range from modern, purpose-built resorts to old plantation mansions, and the most basic hotel rooms will usually have a mosquito net and possibly a sink; prices increase with minor amenities such as a bathroom, air-conditioning, or cable TV and a phone, and increase exponentially with the range of extras available: plunge pools, fridges stocked with drinks, mountain or sea views, beachfront access and outdoor showers and hammocks. Whatever your preference, there's probably a hotel in the Caribbean that has what you're after.

All-inclusives

Pioneered in Jamaica, **all-inclusive hotels** are resorts where a single price covers the room, all meals, snacks and tips, and often all drinks and non-motorized sports (though scuba diving can be an exception). The advantages of staying at an all-inclusive are the product offered, which can be excellent value, along with the convenience of not having to reach for your wallet all the time. The main disadvantage is that there's not much incentive for guests to get out and sample the wide variety of local restaurants and bars – or get a feel for the islands themselves. At the smaller resorts, especially, the appeal of having everything provided in one place can wear off quickly. It's also worth bearing in mind that all-inclusives do little for the local economy: the chains are invariably foreign, much of the food they serve is imported and guests don't frequent local businesses.

Apartments and villas

One of the best ways to save money if you're travelling as a family or in a group is to rent a **villa** or **apartment** for the length of your stay. Accommodation ranges from secluded one-bedroom apartments on a remote stretch of beach to palatial villas built for parties and group weekends. They are typically self-catering, with well-equipped kitchens or kitchenettes (though a cook can almost always be supplied), and can stand alone or as part of a "holiday village" where you share amenities such as a laundry, restaurant and shop with other holiday-makers but retain the privacy and independence of your own cottage. Independently leased apartments – as opposed to those which form part of a "village" – can **cost** anything from US$250 per week for a beachfront one-bedroom in the Dominican Republic to US$1500 per week for a two-bedroom, two-bathroom property on St Lucia or US$1500 per night for a five-bedroom waterfront estate with decks and a huge pool in Barbados.

Property owners tend to stipulate the maximum number of guests allowed (reckon on two per room) but are sometimes flexible, allowing additional people to stay for a fee. Extras can include anything from a maid who cleans daily or weekly (often included in the price of the more exclusive places) to free use of a car, or at least discounted car rental.

Caribbean villa rental agencies

Caribbean Way 740 Notre Dame W, suite 1305, Montreal, Quebec H3C 3X6 ☎514/393-3003 or 1-877/953-7400, ✆www.caribbeanway.com. Representing over 800 villa properties, some on private islands, with photos, information and booking available online.

Island Hideaways ☎212/663-9222 or 1-800/832-2302, ✆www.islandhideaways.com. Agents representing private island hideaways throughout the Caribbean with an emphasis on luxurious, unique properties.

The Owners' Syndicate 3 Calico Row, Plantation Wharf, Battersea, London SW11 3TY ☎020/7801 9801, ✆www.ownerssyndicate.com. Villa specialists with properties on Anguilla, Antigua, Barbados, Grenada, Jamaica, Nevis, St Lucia, Tobago and the Virgin Islands.

Villa Connections ☎01625/858 158, ✆www.prestburytravelgroup.co.uk. Established for fifteen years and offering a choice of over 300 villas all over the Caribbean. Several properties are available on private islands.

Guesthouses

Guesthouses, usually with basic rooms and shared bathrooms, and rarely on the beach, can nonetheless be a welcome bargain option for Caribbean travellers on a budget and usually cost no more than US$30/night. In areas where there are no campsites and little choice of private rooms in family homes, these locally owned places often work out to be the least expensive places to stay.

In recent years, a number of boutique guesthouses, or **bed and breakfast** operations – small, intimate and luxurious, operating more along the lines of miniature hotels – have been cropping up on some of the more exclusive islands. They make a lovely alternative to large-scale resorts and, while they might not be the most private places in the region, they are often friendly, accommodating and very stylish.

Alternative accommodation

Unregulated **camping** is illegal, or else strictly controlled on many Caribbean islands, in an effort to protect the beauty and wildlife of the region's indigenous rainforests. The few regulated campsites in existence are covered in the individual country chapters.

In **Cuba**, visitors have the option of "camping" in rudimentary cabins set in countryside areas called *campisimos*; there is at least one in every province, and at little more than US$5 per cabin they are excellent value.

Food and drink

Caribbean food and drink can be a delight and a shock to the Western palate, with its polar extremes of heavily fried foods and fresh fruit, but it's a varied cuisine that's well worth seeking out. A blend of African, Indian, Arab, Chinese, Spanish, French, Dutch and British influences, Caribbean cooking draws on a wide range of ingredients: African groundnuts, yams, okra and oxtail; East Indian curries and rotis; French Creole and bouillabaisse; and Spanish sofritos and citrus fruits.

Fruits and vegetables

Amongst the many **fruits** on offer, some of the best are the familiar favourites: bananas, grapefruits and oranges all tasting more sweet, juicy and flavoursome than their imported equivalents. Juices made from citrus fruits, and fresh-baked banana breads are available everywhere. More exotic fruits include the milky white pulp of the soursop, from which a refreshing juice is made; the carambola or star fruit, which is de-seeded and then eaten whole or sliced in salads or as a garnish for drinks and meat dishes; guava – often used to make breakfast jelly – and coconuts, which produce milk when ripe and a refreshing, extremely healthy coconut-flavoured water when green.

Vegetables tend to be versatile and filling, like the yucca, breadfruit or callaloo – a spinach-type vegetable in Jamaica, where it is used like greens, and the leaves of the dasheen tuber in the Eastern Caribbean, where they are often cooked with okra. Plantains, sweet when ripe and mealy when green, are prepared as a side dish to rice and beans or fried and made into chips, a delicious accompaniment to a beer or a cocktail at sunset. Also popular is christophene, whose pale green and crisp flesh is much used in Chinese, Latin American and West Indian cooking; calabaza, a generic term for West Indian pumpkins, which are often similar in texture to butternut squash; cassava, a root vegetable that comes in bitter and sweet forms; and okra, a finger-shaped vegetable that is often added to soups and stews.

Meat, seafood and stews

Meat – with the exception of goat – is expensive and most islanders survive on vegetables and delicious variations of chicken and fish; in Cuba, however, pork is a major feature of most cooking.

Unsurprisingly, the region's **seafood** is excellent, cheap and easy to come by. Popular Caribbean fruits of the sea include lobster, crab, shrimp, blue marlin, kingfish red snapper and flying fish – all of which should be sampled at a local weekend **fish fry**, which is a great opportunity to fill up on the freshest fish for very little money, while soaking up the atmosphere, music and some local rum. The fish is cooked by the road, barbecued, fried or grilled and served with hot cakes – heavy, grilled patties of unleavened bread.

By and large, **soups** and **stews** are variations on a theme, based on what's available at the local market on a given day – spiked with onions and peppers and bulked out with "hard food" or root vegetables. No stew would be complete without a bottle of Caribbean **pepper sauce**, developed by the Carib and Arawak Indians who combined hot peppers, cassava juice, brown sugar, cloves and cinnamon to produce a thick, tangy sauce for sprinkling over barbecued fish, chicken and the like.

Cooking styles

Cooking styles in the Caribbean islands are as diverse and heterogeneous as the various nations that have populated the region over the years. Generally, French and Spanish styles predominate, with lots of garlicky, tomato sauces served over fish, and meat cooked very simply in an oven or on an open grill. Vegetables usually come on the side, as do rice and beans.

Yet despite similarities in cuisine, most of the islands have distinct leanings that show through in the most local of dishes and from top-notch restaurants to street-side stalls. **Criollo** cooking is popular on Spanish-speaking islands such as Puerto Rico, Cuba and the Dominican Republic, and makes liberal use of cilantro and mixed seasonings like *adobo*. Chefs in the Netherlands Antilles add **Indonesian** touches such as soy sauce, satay and nasi goreng, while old **French** colonies in particular have a tendency to cook in a Creole style, in which chives, bouquet garni and tomato are made into a delicious, thick sauce and applied liberally to fish and chicken.

Jerk cooking is also common throughout the Caribbean, and originated with the African slaves who came to Jamaica in the 1600s and began to coat meat in spice mixtures (jerk) using island-grown ingredients – such as ginger, thyme, pimento, hot peppers and green onion – before cooking it very slowly in a pit, smoker or on a barbecue grill.

Drinking

Rum is the liquor of choice in the Caribbean, and most islands distil their own brand. You'll find rum distilleries, factories and museums all over the islands, from Jamaica and Barbados to Trinidad and Tobago, with the most famous brand, Bacardi, being made in Puerto Rico. Rum comes in three distinct varieties: **white** rum, a sweet, fruity drink used as the base for the popular Caribbean cocktail Ti-Punch; **ambered** rum, which is white rum aged in barrels of oak, from which it gets its darker colour and slightly more dense flavour; and the richest rum of all – **old** rum, aged for three to six years in barrels of oak from North America that once contained bourbon or whisky. Most islands also produce overproof white rum, the base of many a lethal cocktail.

Caribbean **beers** are refreshing and moderately light, somewhere between their European and American counterparts. Particularly good are Jamaica's Red Stripe, St Lucia's Piton lager and ubiquitous regional favourite Carib, which is brewed on Trinidad and Tobago. Others include Antigua's pale lager Wadadli, the Barbadian and Bahamian Banks Beer and Kalik, and the Dominican Kubuli, made with the island's springwater.

Fantastic **fruit juice** concoctions are a great alcohol-free alternative: the quality of Caribbean citrus fruits is very high, and limes, lemons, oranges and grapefruits are available freshly squeezed in most cafés and restaurants, as well as by the side of the road. The roadside is also the place to buy delicious coconut water – vendors chop off the outer layer from the top of the nut with a machete to allow you to get to the delicious sweet water inside – ask for a straw, and avoid letting the hull touch your clothes, as it leaves a persistent stain. Tropical fruit juices such as pineapple, mango and papaya are also widely available, as is a delicious cranberry-coloured beverage made from the flowers of the slightly sour sorrel plant, and the almost creamy, milky-white juice of the prickly and dark-skinned soursop.

Tea and **coffee** are readily available but – with the exception of strong, rich roasts from Jamaica and Dominica – tend to be of negligible quality; instead, many islanders will drink a cup of milky hot chocolate made from the shavings of a locally grown cocoa stick with their breakfast.

There are also some local forms of **soda**: the ubiquitous Tang, which comes in various different flavours, Jamaican grapefruit soda (Ting) and home-made ginger beer, for which the island is justly famous. Carbonated malt drinks are also sold throughout the region, and are surprisingly good.

Opening hours, public holidays and festivals

Each island has its own unique **holidays**, saints days, constitution, independence and **festival** or carnival days during which nobody works – except for employees of specific tourism enterprises, such as hotel workers and resort staff. For island-specific information refer to individual chapters.

Opening hours for most tourist attractions are daily 9am to 4 or 5pm, although some businesses close early on Saturday – specific opening hours vary from place to place and island to island. Caribbean **banks** are usually open from 8 or 9am to 2 or 3pm Monday to Thursday, with extended hours (often until 5pm) on Fridays. Weekend banking is practically nonexistent.

Public holidays

The main **public holidays** celebrated throughout the Caribbean, during which virtually all shops and offices close, are:

January 1 New Year's Day
Good Friday
Easter Monday
May 1 Labour Day
Whit Monday
Dec 25 Christmas Day
Dec 26 Boxing Day

Bear in mind that islands ruled by European countries will celebrate the national holidays of the governing country; for example, Bastille Day is celebrated in Guadeloupe and Queen's Day in the Netherlands Antilles.

Carnival

Celebrated throughout the region, Caribbean **carnival** is an elaborate spectacle, when your senses are assaulted by the best in Caribbean culture and camaraderie. It has its roots in the pre-Lenten *carnevale* of early Italian Roman Catholicism, a time when Catholics were meant to finish up the meat in their pantries in preparation for the fasting period of Lent. The Italians chose to go out in style with a wild costume festival (*carne vale*, which literally means "farewell to flesh"), and the practice soon spread to France, Spain and Portugal and then to the Americas as they were colonized by Catholic Europe. In the Caribbean itself, carnival has grown from a two-day festival into a season of hedonism and debauchery stretching from February to August. These days more than ever it's all about spectacle, and with each passing year costumes are more flamboyant, dance routines more daring and headdresses more precariously balanced as each island seeks to throw the ultimate Caribbean carnival, at its peak in **Trinidad and Tobago**. Unlike Carnival in Brazil, Caribbean carnival is a participatory celebration that anyone can become a part of simply by signing up to "play mas" with a costume band. This can often be arranged online before you arrive (see individual chapters for details) and is a great way to fully experience the exuberance and joy of the festivities.

Sports and outdoor activities

The biggest **spectator sports** down this way are cricket, soccer and, in certain cases like Cuba, Puerto Rico and the Dominican Republic, baseball. If you're looking to participate, there's plenty of resort space with top-notch golf courses, tennis and other leisure activities. More actively, numerous islands have, if not mountainous and/or rainforested interiors, at least a few good areas to explore on **hikes**; bike trips and horse riding are other enjoyable options.

Cricket

Cricket is respected and exalted throughout parts of the Caribbean, and despite their declining fortunes these days, the West Indies team was the very best on the planet during the 1970s and 1980s. Those interested in the game as it is played here should check out ⓦ www.caribbeancricket. com for details of players, match play and an excellent news section. Another good source of information is the official site of the West Indies cricket board, ⓦ www.windiescricket. com; check there, or visit ⓦ ww.icc-cricket. com/events/worldcup, for details of the Cricket World Cup, which is being staged in

The rules of cricket

The **rules of cricket** are so complex that the official rule book runs to twenty pages. The basics, however, are by no means as byzantine as the game's detractors make out. There are two teams of eleven players. A team wins by scoring more **runs** than the other team and dismissing the opposition – in other words, a team could score many runs more than the opposition, but still not win if the last enemy **batsman** doggedly stays "in" (hence ensuring a draw). The match is divided into innings, when one team **bats** and the other team **fields**. The number of innings varies depending on the type of competition: one-day matches have one per team, Test matches have two.

The aim of the fielding side is to limit the runs scored and get the batsman "out". Two players from the batting side are on the pitch at any one time. The bowling side has a **bowler**, a **wicketkeeper** and nine **fielders**. Two umpires, one standing behind the stumps at the bowler's end and one square on to the play, are responsible for adjudicating whether a batsman is out. Each innings is divided into **overs**, consisting of six deliveries, after which the wicketkeeper changes ends, the bowler is changed and the fielders move positions. The batsmen score runs either by running up and down from wicket to wicket (one length = one run), or by hitting the ball over the boundary rope, scoring four runs if it crosses the boundary having touched the ground, and six runs if it flies over. The main ways a batsman can be dismissed are: by being "clean bowled", where the bowler dislodges the bails of the **wicket** (the horizontal pieces of wood resting on the stumps); by being "run out", which is when one of the fielding side dislodges the bails with the ball while the batsman is running between the wickets; by being caught, which is when any of the fielding side catches the ball after the batsman has hit it and before it touches the ground; or "LBW" (leg before wicket), where the batsman blocks with his leg a delivery that would otherwise have hit the stumps.

the Caribbean in 2007. The top islands for watching the sport are Jamaica, Trinidad, Antigua and Barbados, and even if you're not a fan of the game, a day watching cricket can be tremendous fun, with music pumping from speakers between overs, free-flowing rum and a real party atmosphere.

Baseball

In the **Dominican Republic** baseball is the national spectator sport. Many of the top American major league players have come from here, including Alex Rodríguez, Sammy Sosa and Pedro Martínez. A professional winter season runs from mid-November to mid-February, after which the winner goes on to compete in the Caribbean Series. In addition to the professional season, amateur winter seasons take place in San Francisco de Macorís, San Juan de la Maguana, San Cristóbal and a few other towns.

The **Cuban** national league, the Serie Nacional de Beisbol, takes place over a regular season that usually begins in October and finishes with the playoffs in March and April. Every provincial capital has a baseball stadium and, during the season, teams play five times a week, so there's a good chance of catching a game if you're in the country during the summer months.

Like the Dominican Republic, **Puerto Rico** has produced many ballplayers who've succeeded in the US major leagues, among them the great Roberto Clemente. The island competes in the Caribbean Series against teams from Venezuela, Mexico and the Dominican Republic, and the season runs from November to March.

Hiking

An excellent way to see some untouched, and often protected, indigenous wildlife, as well as enjoying the fresh air and sunshine, is to go **hiking**. The lush rainforests of Puerto Rico, Dominica, Antigua, Trinidad and Tobago, the Dominican Republic, Jamaica and St Lucia, the coastal hikes of St Croix or the huge national park that constitutes most of St John in the US Virgin Islands, are all highly recommended. For more detailed information about hiking, see the individual island chapters.

The best plan is to start very early in the morning and cover plenty of distance before the midday heat sets in, or else choose a hike that goes through forest. Some of the mountain trails in the Caribbean are badly marked and even dangerous; check with the relevant tourist authority about conditions before you head off, and be sure to tell someone where you are going if you are planning to hike alone. There are also plenty of **tour companies** that offer private hiking trips if you'd prefer to travel with a group.

Remember to bring plenty of water, a hat, a spare pair of socks, a jumper, a map, compass and first-aid kit, sunblock, a sandwich and some high-energy snack foods, insect repellent, sunglasses and a camera. Many Caribbean trails have waterfalls and swimming holes along the way, so bring a bathing suit if a dip might be on the agenda.

Camping is illegal on many Caribbean islands; on the few where it is allowed, permission is usually required in advance from the relevant government department and a fee must be paid.

Ocean activities

The Caribbean's vast, clear waters make the region a veritable playground for **watersports**. The quality of diving and snorkelling in many places is superb, thanks to the sheer abundance of marine life, and there are excellent opportunities for sport fishing, waterskiing, windsurfing, parasailing, jet-skiing, kayaking, glass-bottomed boat trips and sailing, most of which are usually offered by the major resorts for free. Resorts are also packed with operators offering dive trips and snorkelling excursions; the most reputable are listed throughout the Guide.

Scuba diving and snorkelling

Wall dives, wreck dives, under-mountain dives, coral gardens, pinnacles, muck dives, drift dives and slopes all await the scuba diver in the Caribbean. The most famous site of all is off **Virgin Gorda**, where the wreck of the HMS *Rhone* has lain since 1867. Other famous **wrecks** are to be found off St Croix and St Lucia; Stingray City on Grand Cayman is renowned for the scores of ray fish that populate the site and are willing to be fed by hand; while Speyside in Tobago is known for its population of friendly giant manta rays. Also highly regarded are Saba's underwater lava flows and black sand, or the amazingly accessible **reefs** of Bonaire and St Lucia. **Bonaire** is perhaps the finest of all the dive islands, as its entire perimeter has

been protected as a marine park since 1979 and eco-friendly regulation is very much enforced.

Each of the islands famous for diving is well equipped in terms of **instruction courses** and diving **package deals** and many people choose to become certified as divers on their Caribbean holiday. Instruction ranges from resort courses for beginners that last a day (US$50–150) to the more advanced open-water certification, which can take three to five days and varies more in price (starting around US$300). You'll need a clean bill of health and at least a week where you can dive every day; remember you cannot fly until 24 hours after your last dive, due to the difference in air pressure.

If you want to go out to sea, check with dive operators as they often take **snorkellers** on their trips. Most resorts provide free snorkelling gear; if yours doesn't it's worth bringing your own as buying equipment in the Caribbean can be expensive.

Scuba holiday operators

Scuba Safari PO Box 8, Edenbridge, Kent TN9 7ZS, ☎01342/851 196, ⊛www.scuba-safaris. com. UK-based company offering diving holidays to Turks and Caicos, Saba, St Kitts and the Cayman Islands.

Scuba Voyages 595 Fairbanks St, Corona, CA 92879 ☎951/204-2987 or 1-800/544-7631, ⊛www.scubavoyages.com. All-inclusive diving packages to Bonaire, Dominica, Saba, St Lucia, St Vincent and Tobago.

Snooba Travel Ltd PO Box 31487, London W4 2QW ☎0870/162 0767, ⊛www.snooba.com. Snorkelling and diving trips all over the Caribbean.

US Dive Travel ☎1-888/741-3483, ⊛www. caribbeandivetravel.com. Family-run operation offering Caribbean-wide diving holidays.

Fishing

The Caribbean boasts some good **sport fishing**, an expensive though potentially dramatic pastime. The waters around the Bahamas and the Turks and Caicos especially offer countless fishing opportunities, among them deep-sea fishing for wahoo, tuna and marlin and shark; bottom-fishing for reef fish such as grouper, snapper and parrotfish; and fly-fishing for bonefish. Also recommended is big-game fishing along the southern coast of the Dominican Republic, around Trinidad and Tobago, and off the northern coast of Cuba. Throughout these islands you'll find plenty of charter boat operators offering **fishing excursions** as well as fully equipped boats for rent. Most boats take groups of up to six in number, and can cost anywhere from US$400 to 1000/day.

Sailing

Needless to say, the Caribbean is a major **sailing** destination. Those not fortunate enough to visit the region on their own sailing boats will find a slew of **charter operators** offering all manner of trips, from rum-soaked party cruises and luxurious yacht charters to relaxed day-trips of island-hopping. Resorts, too, often rent out small sailing boats for use close to shore. For details on specific islands refer to the individual chapters.

Crime and personal safety

With a total of 35 countries making up the region, each with different levels of population, development and standards of living, it's difficult to do anything but generalize about safety standards in the Caribbean. On the whole, though, the region is **politically stable** and **safe**, and not troubled by the potential for terrorist acts. If you don't venture outside the resorts and heavily touristed areas, you might believe that it is also economically prosperous – though this is not necessarily the case, as the region is heavily reliant on tourist trade for survival and large pockets of poverty do exist.

Certain common-sense measures should be observed when travelling in the Caribbean. For tourists, the most common hazards are **bag-snatching** and **pickpocketing**, so always make sure you sling bags across your body rather than letting them dangle from one shoulder; keep cameras concealed whenever possible; don't carry valuables in easy-to-reach places or wear heaps of expensive jewellery; and always take a minimum of cash out with you. Needless to say, don't leave bags and possessions unattended anywhere, especially at the beach. Most resorts and hotels in the Caribbean are very safe; guests should nonetheless use room safes when they're available. Also avoid leaving personal possessions on view in a rental car, even in the boot, as these are also a prime target, and think twice before venturing out for that romantic moonlit walk on an undeveloped beach.

Violent street crime – such as tourist assault and even rape – while rare on most islands has been reported throughout the region. Incidents tend to take place at weekend "jump-ups" or street parties, where locals and tourists mingle freely and many visitors make the mistake of ostentatiously displaying their wealth or make themselves vulnerable via their rum- or ganja-induced inebriation. Visitors should take extra care at street parties and during carnival time, when everything seems like one big heady mix of music, alcohol and people.

That said, criminals can attack at any time, and are more likely to do so at night: women especially should take care after dusk and try not to wander through unpopulated areas alone at any time. Avoid deserted beaches or poorly lit areas at night, and make sure that any taxi you take is officially licensed – look for identification, take down the licence number and check the plates for the identifying "H"

symbol (if there is one – see individual chapter entries for details of taxi travel). For advice for **women travellers**, see p.68.

As an additional precaution, visitors should know that **car theft** has been on the increase, so be sure to check all documentation carefully – sometimes vehicle leases or rentals may not be fully covered by local insurance, and car thieves often target rental cars. If you are unlucky enough to be the victim of theft or other offences, report the incident immediately as you'll need a police report to make any insurance claim.

Visitors should also be aware that heavy **drug trafficking** and production is a major problem in many Caribbean countries – the Bahamas and the Dominican Republic have been included on the US government's list of major narcotics producers. Penalties for committing a crime in the Caribbean can be extremely harsh, and those for drug use, possession and trafficking are severe and usually include jail sentences and heavy fines.

Certain islands in the Caribbean – especially Cuba, Jamaica and the Dominican Republic – are known for both their potent **marijuana** and the lax attitude of the authorities regarding recreational marijuana use. However, the consumption or possession of marijuana is not legal on any of the islands, and as governments of individual countries try to crack down on drug trafficking in general, penalties are likely to be harsh.

Gay and lesbian travellers

Like any other large region, attitudes towards homosexuality in the Caribbean differ from place to place. The Bahamas take the lead in terms of positive attitude, with the government openly condemning homophobia, although there still isn't much of a gay scene. Trinidad and Tobago has had a gay rights group since 1994, and the fairly sizeable community is quite visible, especially during Carnival; in Puerto Rico, gay and lesbian visitors are not only accepted but sustained by a lively gay social scene. On many islands, such as Aruba, Bonaire and Curaçao, there is no organized gay life as such, but because of the free-thinking Dutch influence on these islands, a live-and-let-live attitude prevails. Barbados, the British Virgin Islands and Saba operate in a similar fashion. Martinique has an emergent and fairly open gay community and St Lucia has several gay-friendly resorts, though attitudes in towns and cities may be less friendly.

Other islands, however, are much **less tolerant**: in the Cayman Islands, a gay cruise ship was turned away from the port; attitudes in the US Virgin Islands – with the exception of St John's nude beach – and in Dominica are fairly intolerant. In Cuba and Jamaica, public displays of affection between gays are very much frowned upon, although there are nascent gay scenes, albeit pretty underground.

Contacts for gay and lesbian travellers

On the Web

Gay and Lesbian Travel ⊛ www.galta.com.au. Directory and links for gay and lesbian travel in Australia and worldwide.

Gay Dive ⊛ www.gaydive.com/home.htm. Provides summaries about attitudes on individual islands as well as information on dive sites and gay-friendly accommodation.

Gay Places to Stay ⊛ www.gayplaces2stay.com /caribbean.html. Information about accommodation in Bonaire, the Cayman Islands, St Croix, Jamaica, St Kitts, Puerto Rico, Saba and St Martin.

Gay Travel ⊛ www.gaytravel.com. *The* site for trip planning, bookings and general information about gay and lesbian international travel.

In the US and Canada

Alyson Adventures PO Box 180129, Boston, MA 02118 ☏ 1800/825-9766, ⊛ www.alysonadventures .com. Adventure holidays all over the world, including gay scuba diving packages to the Caribbean.

Damron Company PO Box 422458, San Francisco, CA 94142 ☏ 415/255-0404 or 1-800/462-6654, ⊛ www.damron.com. Publisher of the *Men's Travel Guide*, a pocket-sized yearbook full of listings of hotels, bars, clubs and resources for gay men; the *Women's Traveler*, which provides similar listings for lesbians; and *Damron Accommodations*, which lists over 1000 accommodations for gays and lesbians worldwide.

Envoy Resorts and Tours 1649 N Wells St, suite 201, Chicago, IL 60614 ☏ 312/787-2400 or 1-800/44-ENVOY, ⊛ www.envoytravel.com/rainbow. html. Gay-specific information and travel services, including gay cruise ship bookings.

Ferrari Publications PO Box 37887, Phoenix, AZ 85069 ☏ 602/863-2408 or 1-800/962-2912, ⊛ www.ferrariguides.com. Publishes *Ferrari Gay Travel A to Z*, a gay and lesbian guide to international travel; *Inn Places*, a worldwide accommodation guide; the guides *Men's Travel in Your Pocket* and *Women's Travel in Your Pocket*; and the quarterly *Ferrari Travel Report*.

International Gay & Lesbian Travel Association 4331 N Federal Hwy, suite 304, Ft Lauderdale, FL 33308 ☏ 1-800/448-8550, ⊛ www.iglta.org. Trade group that can provide a list of gay- and lesbian-owned or -friendly travel agents, accommodation and other travel businesses.

Out and About Travel ☏ 1-800/842-4753, ⊛ www.outandabouttravel.com. Gay- and lesbian-oriented cruises, tours and travel packages.

In the UK

⊛ www.gaytravel.co.uk Online gay and lesbian travel agent, offering good deals on all types of holidays. Also lists gay- and lesbian-friendly hotels around the world.

Dream Waves Redcot High St, Child Okeford, Blandford DT22 8ET ☏ 01258/861 149, ✉ dreamwaves@aol.com. Specializes in exclusively gay holidays, including skiing trips and summer sun packages.

Madison Travel 118 Western Rd, Hove, East Sussex BN3 1DB ☏ 01273/202 532, ⊛ www.madisontravel.co.uk. Established travel agents specializing in packages to gay- and lesbian-friendly mainstream destinations.

In Australia and New Zealand

Gay and Lesbian Travel PO Box 208, Darlinghurst, NSW 1300 ☏ 02/9380 4115, ⊛ www.galta.com.au. Directory and links for gay and lesbian travel worldwide.

Parkside Travel 70 Glen Osmond Rd, Parkside, SA 5063 ☏ 08/8274 1222 or 1800/888 501, ✉ hwtravel@senet.com.au. Gay travel agent associated with local branch of Hervey World Travel; covers all aspects of gay and lesbian travel.

Silke's Travel 263 Oxford St, Darlinghurst, NSW 2010 ☏ 02/9380 6244 or 1800/807 860, ✉ silba@magna.com.au. Long-established gay and lesbian specialist, with the emphasis on women's travel.

Tearaway Travel 52 Porter St, Prahan, VIC 3181 ☏ 03/9510 6344, ✉ tearaway@bigpond.com. Gay-specific business dealing with international and domestic travel.

Travellers with disabilities

Cruise lines and top Caribbean resorts have made big steps over the course of the last decade towards catering for disabled travellers, with many cruise ships now offering cabins that have been fitted out for wheelchairs and the number of wheelchair-accessible cabins having increased by 60 percent between 1999 and 2002.

Of course, a lot remains to be done, and some islands, such as Dominica, have virtually no facilities, accommodation or restaurants that cater to travellers with disabilities, save in the top resorts. Remember that while Caribbean **legislation** is nowhere near as stringent as American or European law when it comes to accessibility for all, tourism has taken a downturn in recent years and many of the larger resorts are ensuring that their premises can cater for most special needs in order to fill beds. Especially at the top end of the market, it shouldn't be too difficult to find accommodation and operators who can cater for your particular needs. The important thing is to check beforehand with tour companies, hotels and airlines that they can accommodate you specifically.

Contacts for travellers with disabilities

On the Web

Access-Able ☻www.access-able.com. Online resource for travellers with disabilities, including detailed information on cruise lines that cater for disabled travellers.
Jim Lubin's Disability Resource ☻www.makoa .org/index.html. Extensive database of links for disabled travel around the world.

In the US and Canada

Directions Unlimited 123 Green Ln, Bedford Hills, NY 10507 ☏1-800/533-5343 or 914/241-1700. Travel agency specializing in bookings for people with disabilities.
Mobility International USA 45 W Broadway, Eugene, OR 97401 ☏541/343-1284, ☻www .miusa.org. Information and referral services, access guides, tours and exchange programmes. Annual

membership $35 (includes quarterly newsletter).
Society for the Advancement of Travelers with Handicaps (SATH) 347 Fifth Ave, New York, NY 10016 ☏212/447-7284, ☻www.sath.org. Nonprofit educational organization that has actively represented travellers with disabilities since 1976.
Wheels Up! ☏1-888/38-WHEELS, ☻www. wheelsup.com. Provides discounted air fare, tour and cruise prices for disabled travellers, and publishes a free monthly newsletter. Comprehensive website.

In the UK and Ireland

Irish Wheelchair Association Blackheath Drive, Clontarf, Dublin 3 ☏01/818 6400, ☻www.iwa.ie. Useful information provided about travelling abroad with a wheelchair.
RADAR (Royal Association for Disability and Rehabilitation) 12 City Forum, 250 City Rd, London EC1V 8AF ☏020/7250 3222, minicom ☏020/7250 4119, ☻www.radar.org.uk. A good general source of advice on holidays and travel for people with disabilities.
Tripscope The Vassall Centre, Gill Ave, Bristol BS16 2QQ ☏0845/758 5641 ☻www.tripscope. org.uk. This registered charity provides a national telephone information service offering free advice on UK and international transport for those with a mobility problem.

In Australia and New Zealand

ACROD (Australian Council for Rehabilitation of the Disabled) PO Box 60, Curtin ACT 2605; suite 103, 1st floor, 1–5 Commercial Rd, Kings Grove 2208 ☏02/6282 4333, TTY ☏02/6282 4333, ☻www.acrod.org.au. Provides lists of travel agencies and tour operators for people with disabilities.
Disabled Persons Assembly 4/173–175 Victoria St, Wellington, New Zealand ☏04/801 9100 (also TTY), ☻www.dpa.org.nz. Resource centre with lists of travel agencies and tour operators for people with disabilities.

Directory

Children While many people see the Caribbean as an adult-oriented honeymoon and cruise ship destination, it's also a great place for children – the calm, shallow waters are ideal for new swimmers, and there are no worries about inoculations. With a pretty universally beneficent attitude to children, the Caribbean is an easy place for families to travel independently, and an increasing number of all-inclusive resorts also cater for children, offering kids' meals, activities and watersports. Be sure to check with your accommodation about bringing children as some hotels prefer couples only. When children are catered for, however, facilities can range widely from the odd banana boat ride, evening disco, afternoon tennis match or tortoise race to comprehensive activity programmes involving nature walks, arts and crafts, pool games and even field trips.

Cigarettes Smoking is legal and very much on display in the Caribbean, although you are unlikely to see many locals enjoying the infamous hand-rolled Cuban and Dominican cigars. Many of the larger resorts will have nonsmoking areas, but visitors should ensure they request a nonsmoking room when they book – the alternative can often smell like a freshly filled ashtray. Smokers wanting to take advantage of duty-free prices are advised to do so in their home airport, as airports in smaller Caribbean islands can offer minimal – if any – choice.

Electricity Most islands in the Caribbean use 110V (US) sockets, some have 220/240V (UK) only and some have both. Larger hotels will usually be able to provide you with an adaptor, but you should bring your own just in case. (See box.)

Getting married The Caribbean is one of the most popular wedding destinations in the world, as well as one favoured by many honeymooning couples. You can't, however, simply turn up and expect to be married straight away – islands have different requirements about the length of stay prior to the ceremony. Some require a notarized letter

Electricity

Anguilla	110v
Antigua and Barbuda	110/220v
Aruba	110v
Bahamas	120v
Barbados	110v/220v adaptors
Bonaire	120v
British Virgin Islands	110v
Cayman Islands	110v
Cuba	110v, some 220v
Curaçao	110/220v
Dominica	220v
Dominican Republic	110v
Grenada	220/240v
Guadeloupe	110/220v
Jamaica	110/220v
Martinique	220v
Puerto Rico	110v
Saba	110v
St Barts	220v
St Eustatius	110/220v
St Kitts and Nevis	230v
St Lucia	220v
St Martin/St Maarten	110/220v
St Vincent and the Grenadines	220/240v
Trinidad and Tobago	115/220v
Turks and Caicos	110v
US Virgin Islands	120v

declaring the single status of the bride and groom or an affidavit for couples under the age of 18. Residency requirements can be anything from newly arrived to fifteen days. Island tourist offices will give information on marriage requirements on their island, although many of the classier establishments will arrange everything for you. If in doubt, contact the tourist office of your chosen destination – or check their website for details.

Hurricanes The hurricane season begins around June or July, lasts six months or so and is most threatening between August and October. If a hurricane watch is posted, it means hurricane conditions are possible within the next 36 hours; if a warning is posted, conditions are expected usually within 24 hours. Advice about dealing with watches and warnings is usually posted in hotels and guesthouses, but should you be away from your accommodation, get indoors and stay away from windows. Be aware, too, that a tornado will often follow a hurricane.

Time All islands in the Caribbean are on Atlantic Time, one hour ahead of Eastern Standard Time and four hours behind Greenwich Mean Time. Be aware that not all islands adjust for Daylight Savings Time.

Tipping Tipping rates, which can vary in the islands, are covered more specifically in the individual chapters. Hotels normally include a service charge in their bills but if your accommodation doesn't include the charge, or if you want to make sure that the staff get tipped (and not the management), aim to give around US$1 a night per guest to housekeeping staff directly and per bag to porters. (Note that staff at all-inclusives are not meant to be tipped at all.) Restaurants often add ten to fifteen percent automatically to their bills, as do most taxi drivers, but the percentages vary from island to island – and in Puerto Rico a tip of up to 20 percent can be expected.

Women travellers Though violent attacks against women travellers are rare, many women find that the constant barrage of hisses, hoots and comments in parts of the Caribbean (Puerto Rico, Cuba, Jamaica, the Dominican Republic and the French-influenced islands, for instance) comes close to spoiling their holiday; unless, of course, you're visiting the region with romance in mind, as many women are. If you're not interested, don't be afraid to seem rude; even the mildest polite response will be considered an indication of serious interest. Be aware too that a woman on her own in a restaurant or bar will be seen as fair game; usually a firm "no" works in deterring unwanted attention. In any event, never be afraid to ask for help if you feel lost or threatened.

Guide

Guide

Bahamas

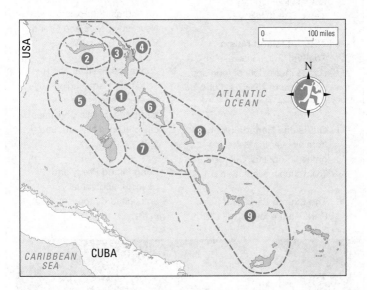

Bahamas highlights

✳ **Sea kayaking in the Exumas**
Glide through turquoise
waters, stopping for a picnic
along the way. See p.126

✳ **The beaches of Eleuthera**
A different deserted strand
of soft white or pink sand
to explore each day of the
week. See p.118

✳ **The Cat Island Music
Festival** Traditional rake 'n'
scrape music, lots of food and
an excuse to socialize Out
Island style. See p.130

✳ **Out Island Regatta** Sloops
from all over the Bahamas
gather in April for George
Town's main event. See p.124

✳ **The Exuma Land and Sea
Park** Nature lovers will thrill
to the fertile coral reefs,
untouched beaches and
native wildlife here. See
p.128

✳ **Diving and snorkelling** The
Bahamas offer some of the
very best diving and snorkelling in the world, especially
off Andros, the Exumas,
New Providence and Grand
Bahama. See p.79

✳ **Junkanoo Festival** Thousands of masquerading
revellers take to the streets
for this hedonistic Christmas
celebration in Nassau. See
p.85

✳ **Long Island** Pretty and
peaceful and virtually
untouched by tourism. See
p.132

△ Out Island Regatta

Introduction and basics

Graced with beautiful beaches of soft pink and white sand, evocative wind-swept panoramas, abundant sunshine and countless opportunities for diving, snorkelling and fishing, the islands of **the Bahamas** are well established as one of the world's top draws for both intrepid explorers and casual holiday makers. An island chain beginning a mere 55 miles east of Miami, Florida, the Bahamas offer an array of tourist hotels, all-inclusive resorts, rustic lodges and cottage rentals. More than three million travellers each year choose the islands as their holiday destination for watersports, sun worship, casino gambling and, on some of the slightly more remote spots, eco-tourism.

The Bahamas encompass around seven hundred mostly uninhabited islands, cays (pronounced "keys") and rock outcroppings, strewn in a wide arc extending from just off the Atlantic coast of Florida to the waters surrounding Cuba, where Great Inagua sits only sixty miles from shore. Although deep oceanic troughs surround some of the islands, most are encircled by shallow, crystalline water that is turquoise and jade-hued during the day and glows with purple luminescence at night. This combination of shallow and deep water makes diving and snorkelling both challenging and intriguing, with numerous reefs, blue holes and underwater canyons waiting to be explored just beyond the surf.

Where to go

The islands' most popular destinations are **New Providence** where the capital **Nassau** and the resort areas of **Cable Beach** and **Paradise Island** are found, and **Grand Bahama** with its vacation towns of **Freeport** and **Lucaya**. Both New Providence and Grand Bahama offer glamorous accommodations in high-rise hotels and boutique inns as well as budget motels, nightclubs, fine restaurants, shopping and plenty of beaches. Some travellers, however, may prefer the quiet, remote charms of one of the so-called **Out Islands** such as **Abaco**, **Andros**, **Eleuthera**, **Harbour Island** or **the Exumas**, or even further off the beaten track on **Cat Island** or **Long Island**, where the accommodations can be equally luxurious but rustic and the beaches and reefs virtually deserted. While they share their spectacular

setting in a warm blue-green sea, each island of the Bahamas has its own distinctive character and pace, which makes **island-hopping** a pleasure as well as an adventure.

When to go

The southern Atlantic high-pressure system and constant trade winds make Bahamian weather consistent throughout the year, with temperatures averaging 24ºC (75ºF) during the **dry winter season** from December to May, and 5–8 degrees warmer in the **summer rainy season**. Just as a steady cooling breeze moderates the hottest hours of the day, nights in the Bahamas are temperate and, in the northern islands, even cool. Late summer and autumn comprise **hurricane season**, delivering the occasional menacing tempest as well as less destructive tropical storms. While the northern Bahamas got hit with a double whammy from Hurricanes Jeanne and Frances in the autumn of 2004, historically, the Bahamas are rarely in the direct paths of hurricanes, which usually bypass the islands to the south before hitting mainland North America directly.

Predictably, **winter travel** is a major draw, with December-to-May prices as much as 25 percent higher than during the rest of the year. **Late spring** and **early summer travel** are popular with bargain hunters, divers, and anglers and sailors drawn by the summer round of fishing tournaments, regattas and clear, still water. Travelling during the **Christmas holiday season** can be hectic and wearisome, with tourists thick on the ground and many locals taking trips to the North American mainland. Likewise, college

Websites

ⓦ**www.bahamas.com** The Bahamas Ministry of Tourism site, covering everything from travel info, watersports and accommodation to local cuisine.

ⓦ**www.bahamasdiving.com** Includes lists of diving operators and live-aboard operators, information on diving training and links to dive-specific features.

ⓦ**www.bahamasflyfishingguide.com** has tips for where to fish in the Bahamas, what flies you should use, and listings for fishing guides and fishing lodges in the islands.

ⓦ**www.bahamasnet.com** Comprehensive website with details on accommodation, activities and restaurants, and a calendar of events.

ⓦ**www.thenassauguardian.com** Website of one of the two leading dailies, with the usual departments plus links to other local papers.

students often crowd the major resorts during **Spring Break** in February and March, while other travellers escape to the Bahamas during late summer and autumn to enjoy a respite in that relatively tranquil period, the odd hurricane notwithstanding.

Arrival

The major international **airports** of the Bahamas are located in **Nassau** and **Freeport**, and are usually reached via connecting flights from North American cities. Although a few carriers offer flights from Miami or Fort Lauderdale to Out Island airports, and some hotels offer charter connections to the island's resorts, most Out Island travellers fly through Nassau, or take ferries and boats to the more remote destinations.

Cruise lines such as Disney and Carnival call at Freeport and Nassau, where visitors can do some shopping and exploring for a day or two.

Information, websites and maps

The best source of **information** on the Bahamas is the Bahamas Ministry of Tourism; you can contact the branch nearest you before you leave home. Once in the Bahamas, you can visit the local tourist offices at Nassau and Grand Bahama airports and in the main towns.

Information on the Out Islands is available from the Bahamas Out Island Promotion Board (☎305/931-6612 or 1-800/688-4752, ⓦ www.bahama-out-islands.com), which distributes small **maps** of each Out Island as well. All major bookstores carry maps of the Bahamas. The best tourist maps of Grand Bahama and New Providence are the Trail Blazer series produced by Dupuch Publications, available through ⓦwww.bahamasnet. com or free throughout Nassau and Freeport/Lucaya. Detailed maps of each of the Out Islands have been locally produced and are available on several of the Out Islands, as noted in the relevant sections below.

Money and costs

The local **currency** is the Bahamian dollar (B$), divided into 100 cents. Coins come in denominations of 5, 10, 15, 20 and 50 cents, as well as $1 and $2. Notes are issued in denominations of $1, $3, $5, $10, $20, $50 and $100. The Bahamian dollar is on a par with the US dollar, and both currencies are accepted throughout the country; as such, there is little need to formally change US dollars before travelling here. Big islands like New Providence, Grand Bahama and Abaco have major **banks** and financial institutions near the tourist centres, and have numerous **ATMs** as well.

Many **Out Islands** have few, if any, banks and most have no ATMs, so it's best to visit these more remote islands with credit cards, travellers' cheques and some cash. Note that **credit cards** are widely accepted at resorts and are almost always required to reserve and rent cars. You can use credit cards pretty much everywhere in Nassau and Freeport, Harbour Island and the Abacos, but you will need cash to pay for anything other than your hotel on the more isolated Out Islands.

Costs on the major islands are comparable to US prices. Hotels, save for motel-style lodges in downtown areas of major cities, average at least US$95–125 per night for a double room, while luxury resorts charge up to 25 percent more. Note that all hotel rooms in the Bahamas are subject to a 10–15 percent **resort tax**, and some slap on an energy surtax and a mandatory service fee on top of that. Most places do not include these fees in their advertised prices. Some Out Island lodges are less expensive, though the costs of food and transportation in the Out Islands are greater because goods and services are imported. Many resorts and hotels offer **all-inclusive packages** or **three-day/ seven-day rates**, which can reduce costs considerably, and at least a few hotels at every destination offer **self-catering** options, which may also lower costs, especially for longer-term stays.

Getting around

In general, **island-hopping** through the Bahamas is easy, though it can be costly. The Out Islands are well linked to Nassau by daily inter-island flights and ferries several times a week, although travelling from

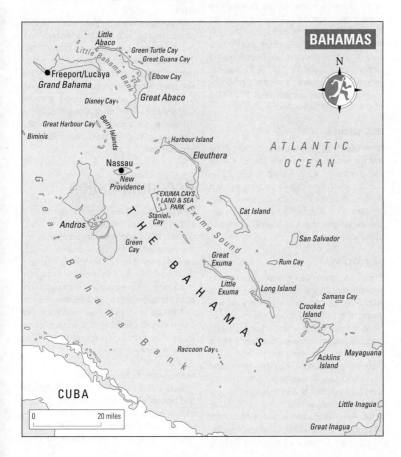

one Out Island to another generally requires returning to Nassau first. This means on average a $70–$110 **air fare** for each leg of the journey; for example, from Long Island to Nassau, and then on to George Town. Due to flight schedules, island-hopping will sometimes require an overnight stop in Nassau, adding another $100 or so to transit costs.

Ferry tickets are generally about half the price of flying, but most do not make daily runs, meaning you will almost certainly need to stop over in Nassau a night or two, or use a combination of flight and ferry to get around.

Nassau and Freeport both have excellent and inexpensive public **bus services**, and $1 will get you anywhere within each city. However, neither service the airport, which is the preserve of **taxi** drivers. Average taxi rates for each island are noted in the relevant sections of the chapter, but are on the high side. For example, a taxi from the Potter's Cay ferry dock in downtown Nassau to the airport costs about $28. On all the islands, **rental cars** are readily available. An economy-sized car costs approximately $60–$80 a day or $350–$450 a week.

By plane

Inter-island transportation is usually done **by air**, especially on the national carrier Bahamasair (☎242/377-5505 or 1-800/222-4262), which flies regular routes between Nassau and the Out Islands. Meanwhile, smaller, Nassau-based carriers offer **charter services** to the Out Islands and other destinations.

By boat

If you have more time at your disposal (and maybe less cash), an interesting way of exploring the Bahamas is by **ferry** or **mail boat**. The Bahamas government operates nineteen mail boats, which also carry cargo and passengers between Nassau and all the Out Islands – trips that can vary from a few hours to several days. Call the dockmaster on Potter's Cay, Nassau (☎242/393-1064) for up-to-date details and schedules. The very efficient Bahamas Fast Ferry (☎242/323-2166; ⊛www.bahamasferries.com) runs from Nassau to Harbour Island, Eleuthera, Georgetown in the Exumas, Abaco, and Andros.

Individual **boat rental** is also a good option for inter-island transit, with many marinas featuring choice spots for anchorage.

By car, bicycle and motor scooter

Almost all the major **car rental agencies** are found on New Providence and Grand Bahama, including Alamo, Avis, Budget, Dollar and Hertz. The international rental agencies don't operate in the Out Islands, but there are generally several private operators with at least a few vehicles available for rent, as listed in each section below. Cars drive on the left side of the road in the Bahamas, although many vehicles are right-hand drive, which makes things interesting, especially after dark when the headlights from on-coming cars can be blinding.

Bicycling can be a pleasant way to explore some islands, with **motor scooters** and **motorcycles** a possibility for longer trips. These are generally available from resorts or rental agencies in tourist centres. Large resorts also often rent guests golf carts to drive around the grounds, and on Harbour Island, Treasure Cay and Hope Town on Abaco, golf carts are the vehicle of choice. However, it is generally easy enough to get to most places you want to go **on foot**.

Accommodation

Although there are relatively few inexpensive places to stay in the Bahamas, the islands do offer many **accommodation** choices for travellers. Honeymooners and large families will find plenty of options among the large and small hotels, resorts, bed-and-breakfasts, inns and lodges. Popular among snowbirds and spring-breakers are the **all-inclusive resorts** that line the beaches in New Providence and Grand Bahama, while families and groups of friends may care to vacation at rental villas, vacation homes and long-term condos, most of which offer self-catering, some privacy and reduced rates for longer stays.

Every island has a fair number of **hotels** and **resorts** which can vary in quality, though almost all feature swimming pools, beach access, water sports, island tours and in-house restaurants. On larger islands like New

Providence, Grand Bahama and Harbour Island, some of these hotels rival any in the world for luxury and nightlife.

Scattered throughout the islands are traditional **Bahamian guesthouses**, anything from converted two-storey homes to small efficiency units surrounding a pool. Some guesthouses can be pretty basic, especially in the more southerly islands, while others are luxurious and spacious. There are lodges catering exclusively to **divers** and **anglers**, many of which are located at Out Island destinations. **Yachters** on the other hand may simply remain on board ship at one of the many marinas around the islands. The only place where unguided **camping** is permitted in the Bahamas is in the Exuma Land and Sea Park (see p.128).

Food and drink

Traditional **Bahamian meals** may include seafood like grouper, conch and snapper (usually grilled or baked in a tomato sauce), along with tropical fruits like guava and papaya. As former members of a British colony, Bahamians have adopted many traditional English dishes, or adapted them to suit local tastes. These include macaroni cheese, peas and rice, boiled potatoes and other vegetable dishes. A Bahamian **breakfast** may consist of anything from fried eggs, bacon, toast, tomato and coffee to more Caribbean-influenced dishes like johnny cakes, a heavy cornmeal bread jazzed up with coconut. **Lunch** tends towards seafood stews and soups or large conch salads.

Hunting the Green Flash

A favourite pastime among rum-soaked beach bums and sailors in the Bahamas is scanning the horizon at sundown for a glimpse of the elusive **green flash** – a brilliant burst of emerald-green light that sometimes punctuates a Bahamian sunset. Just as the sun sinks into the sea, the upper part of the orb – often just a sliver along its very top – suddenly changes colour from yellow, orange or red to bright green for a second or two before the sun slips below the horizon.

This natural wonder is caused by the refraction or bending of light waves from the sun as they enter the Earth's atmosphere. The full scientific explanation involves several laws of physics and some algebra (see ⓦwww.mintaka.sdsu.edu.eu or ⓦwww.usatoday.com/weather/askjack). The less right-brained might be more interested in Jules Verne's 1882 novel *Le Rayon Vert* ("The Green Ray"), inspired by an ancient legend (perhaps of Verne's own invention) according to which the green flash is imbued with mystical power and that "he who has been fortunate enough once to behold it is enabled to see closely into his own heart and to read the thoughts of others",

The green flash can be seen from many locations around the globe – sightings have been reported from the top of the Empire State Building in New York and in the Arctic – but the Bahamas provides ideal viewing conditions: an expansive, unimpeded seascape and what scientists call "a well-layered atmosphere", meaning, according to Dr. Andrew Young of the University of California at San Diego, "where the index of refraction increases without interruption towards the surface of the Earth". Dr Young offers some tips for flash-hunting:

The horizon must be lower than your eye – so sit in a beach lounger or on an elevated deck rather than lying prone on the beach.

Clear air provides optimal viewing. If the air is full of dust, smog or haze, the green light rays will be scattered by atmospheric debris before they reach your eye.

The flash is often small, so looking through binoculars or a telephoto lens will increase the odds of seeing one.

However, it is unhealthy to look directly at the sun until it is very close to the horizon. Also, due to the construction of the human eye, your sensitivity to red light is temporarily weakened if you have been staring at a red or orange sunset. Thus, yellow light may appear green to you. To avoid these self-induced green flashes, don't look at the sun until it is nearly down. Alas, if you want to see this wonder of nature, you will have to choose between it or just another spectacular Bahamian sunset, at least for one night.

With the rise in tourism in the Bahamas, many different types of **imported culinary styles** have flourished here as well. On New Providence, Grand Bahama and Harbour Island, you can find restaurants serving Continental, Mediterranean and Greek cuisine, and even Mexican and pan-Asian dishes, in elegant surroundings with excellent service and fine wines. Many of these restaurants are located at major hotels and resorts and require reservations and jackets for gentlemen while other eateries cater to a more eclectic crowd of locals and visitors. There are also a clutch of lovely restaurants serving gourmet fare tucked away in various corners of the Out Islands; at least one on each land mass.

Every town or settlement in the Bahamas has its share of **take-away restaurants**, featuring traditional offerings like fried chicken, french fries and deep-fried seafood. Most Out Island restaurants serve fairly simple and uniform fare, usually fish, conch or fried chicken, with fresh Bahamian lobster a rare treat. Island desserts are often delightful, especially the coconut concoctions, rice pudding, gingerbread and fruit cocktail.

The generally devout Bahamians are not much for **drinking** wine or liquor, although the national beer, Kalik, is a fine elixir enjoyed throughout the islands. Most bars can serve you up a colourful tropical cocktail with a little umbrella in it, like a sweet and delicious Goombay Smash (coconut rum, pineapple and orange juices, with a squeeze of fresh lime juice) or a rosy Bahama Mama (rum, bitters, crème de cassis, grenadine, nutmeg and citrus juice), Fruit juice and soft drinks are popular, and major brands like Coke and Pepsi are predictably ubiquitous. Fast-food chains have also invaded the Bahamas, although the Out Islands are still a Big Mac-free zone. Here fast food means a conch burger, pig's feet or sheep's tongue souse.

Phones, post and email

Batelco is the national telephone company of the Bahamas, and it maintains an excellent phone service for all but the most isolated islands. **Public phones** are available in all tourist areas, though some Out Islands phones may be out of service for long periods of time. **Long-distance calls** may be made from public phones by using phone cards purchased from Batelco or through the local long-distance operator. Beware the non-Batelco operated public phones that take credit cards. The costs for making a long-distance call can be breathtakingly high – \$35 for five minutes to Canada, for example.

Postal service to and from the Bahamas is fairly reliable. Postcards from the islands to North America, Europe and South America require a 50-cent stamp, while airmail letters cost 65 cents per half-ounce.

Modem connections and **email** are a still-developing feature of most Bahamian telephone networks, but are gradually becoming available on most islands and in most hotels. If getting online is a necessity for you, it's advisable to check in advance with your hotel or resort.

The **country code** for the Bahamas is ☎242.

Opening hours, festivals and holidays

Shops are typically **open** Monday to Saturday 9am–5pm. **Banks** generally operate Monday to Thursday 9am–3pm and Friday 9am–5pm, although Out Island banks may have very limited opening hours or open only one or two days per week. On the whole, things shut up pretty tight on **Sundays**.

Visiting the islands during one of the many **festivals** held throughout the year is a good way to experience Bahamian culture. Thousands of costumed revellers, drummers and dancers fill Bay Street in Nassau for the all-night Junkanoo rush-outs on December 26 and New Year's Eve. Junkanoo parades and parties are also held in villages on Eleuthera, Green Turtle Cay in the Abacos and on Grand Bahama.

Many Out Island settlements hold **Homecomings** during July or August, when Out Islanders who have left to seek their fortunes in Nassau or elsewhere come home for a week of community parties, music, games and often a sailing regatta. During spring and summer countless **fishing tournaments** and **regattas** take place, including the famous Bahamas Family Island Regatta at George Town in the Exumas during the last week of April. Long Island and Abaco also host popular regattas. Other fun times include the Eleuthera Pineapple Festival in early June in Gregory Town and the Cat Island Music Festival, also in June.

Bahamians, especially those in Fox Hill in Nassau, celebrate **Emancipation Day** on the first Monday in August, marking the abolition of slavery with parades and food, as well as cultural events. Fireworks and parades highlight **Independence Week**, which culminates on July 10. Bahamian tourist centres provide lists of the many festivals, holidays and craft shows that occur year-round.

Outdoor activities

Sunny weather, sandy beaches, exquisite reefs, shallow water, steady winds and proximity to the Gulf Stream make the Bahamas an ideal choice for all manner of **sports** and **outdoor activities**. Islands like Bimini are

rightfully regarded as great spots for **fishing** (especially for wahoo, tuna, barracuda, shark, grouper and snapper), while many Out Islands like Andros, Long Island, Cat and Abaco are famous for their **bonefishing** – so named after the silvery catch. Likewise, the islands' shallow, calm waters have made **sailing** a popular activity, especially around the Exumas, Abaco and Eleuthera.

Nearly every resort, hotel and lodge offers a range of **aquatic sports**, including diving, snorkelling, boating, windsurfing, parasailing and swimming. **Golf** and **tennis** are provided at resorts and hotels on the major islands, with golf courses located in Lucaya on Grand Bahama, at Cable Beach in Nassau, on Paradise Island and on Great Exuma. **Biking**, **hiking** and **sea kayaking** are growing in popularity as well, and a number of operators specialize in trips to isolated spots throughout the islands. **Birdwatching** is a major draw, especially for seabird species like the rare Bahamian parrot on Abaco, and the flamingos on Inagua. There's also **horse riding** at stables on New Providence and Grand Bahama.

History

The name Bahamas probably comes from the Spanish "Baja Mar", meaning "shallow seas", an apt description of the area attributed to Columbus. After the European discovery of the islands in 1492, and the subsequent rapid annihilation of the aboriginal Lucayans, the islands remained a backwater until a few English settlers from Bermuda arrived on Eleuthera in 1647. Soon after, farmers colonized New Providence and established Charles Town, the name of which was changed in 1690 to Nassau in honour of England's new ruler, William, Prince of Orange and Nassau.

With the islands ruled by a series of incompetent royal governors, Nassau gradually slipped into chaos and piracy, becoming home to such notorious figures as the pirate **Blackbeard** and his ilk, who preyed on Spanish and French ships as they passed through the islands loaded with gold and other riches from the Spanish Main and the Caribbean en route to Europe. Not until the arrival of Royal Governor

Woodes-Rogers in 1717 was piracy finally curtailed.

During the American Revolution, several thousand **Loyalists** came to the Bahamas from the North American colonies, settling in Abaco, Eleuthera, the Exumas and Long Island and creating an economy and society based on plantations run by slave labour. However, their cotton, tobacco and fruit crops failed due to crop diseases and soil exhaustion.

After the **abolition of slavery** here in 1834, island residents turned to salvaging from shipwrecks, sponging, fishing and subsistence farming to make a living.

During the American Civil War, Nassau and West End on Grand Bahama became boom towns built on **blockade running**, later turning to rum-running during America's Prohibition of the 1920s and early 1930s. **Tourism**, popular since the mid-nineteenth century, gained a firmer foothold after World War II with the advent of modern air travel, seven-storey cruise ships and air conditioning. On July 10, 1973, after 325 years of British rule, the Bahamas became an **independent**, democratic state supported by tourism, banking and fishing.

In the 1970s, a less welcome form of economic growth emerged as **drug smuggling** boomed throughout the Bahamas. George Town was the scene of what was, at the time, the largest seizure ever of pure cocaine: 247 pounds worth over two billion dollars. The Bahamian government subsequently launched an intensive campaign to rid the islands of drug runners. Things have calmed down considerably since then, and the islands have resumed their sleepy, god-fearing way of life.

The last decade has seen a dramatic expansion in the **tourism** industry, with the opening of the massive *Atlantis Resort* on Paradise Island, which is the largest employer in the Bahamas. Similarly, the economy of Grand Bahama got a boost with the construction of the *Our Lucaya* five-star resort in 2000, although that island suffered millions of dollars of **hurricane** damage in the autumn of 2004, from which it is still recovering.

1.1

New Providence

NEW PROVIDENCE is the thumping heart of the Bahamian archipelago. Despite its tiny size – 21 miles long and 7 miles wide – New Providence holds more than two-thirds of the country's population and is the site of the capital **Nassau**, a thriving city of around 100,000 residents. Initially settled because of its sheltered harbour and strategic location on the shipping route used to transport the riches of the New World to Europe, the island has during its nearly 230-year history been a refuge for pirates and privateers, site of illicit smuggling, haven for fishermen, and a buzzing centre of tourism, with nearly two million visitors now arriving annually.

On the northeastern side of the island, the high-rises of downtown Nassau spread over a gentle slope climbing up from the harbour. Tourist action is focused around **Prince George Wharf** and along **Bay Street**, one block inland from the water, where duty-free shopping hits a fever pitch when the cruise ships are in port. Two long toll bridges east of downtown Nassau connect the city centre to **Paradise Island**, a glitzy tourist enclave centred on the mega-resort *Atlantis*, with many other hotels, shops, restaurants, multimillion-dollar vacation homes and a couple of peaceful, secluded get-aways. Paradise Island's main natural attractions are **Cabbage Beach** and **Paradise Beach**, covering most of the north coast and offering soothing vistas of deep blue water and trade winds that cool even the hottest of afternoons.

Much of eastern New Providence has been covered by urban sprawl, and if you take your holiday here, be warned that you won't be communing with nature. Lovely **Cable Beach**, with its powdery white sand, is completely surrounded by high-rise hotels, exclusive resorts, private estates, condominiums and time-shares. Continuing westward past Cable Beach, you will come across more secluded strands of beach, including **Orange Hill Beach** and **Love Beach** near Gambier Village, where the *Compass Point Resort* is situated.

Beyond the western tip of the island is exclusive **Lyford Cay**, where celebrities like Sean Connery live in hermetically sealed luxury. New Providence's **south shore** has few notable beaches and a few hotels. Diving and snorkelling draw many enthusiasts to the south shore's outer reef and reef walls.

Although the **central interior** of New Providence is mainly marshy scrub, local **eco-tourism** operators offer canoeing on **Lake Killarney** as well as combination biking-kayaking tours.

Arrival and information

Nassau International Airport (☎242/377-7281), the hub of Bahamian air transport, is located on the west-central part of New Providence, a fifteen-minute taxi ride from downtown Nassau and only ten minutes from Cable Beach. While there are no buses from the airport, there are plenty of **taxis**, with the fare for two people to Cable Beach $15, downtown Nassau $22 and Paradise Island $27. Current taxi rates are posted on a billboard at the taxi stand at the airport.

The Ministry of Tourism operates an **information booth** at the airport, while in downtown Nassau there are two information booths that provide useful maps and brochures. The smaller one can be found near the Straw Market on Bay St (Mon–Fri

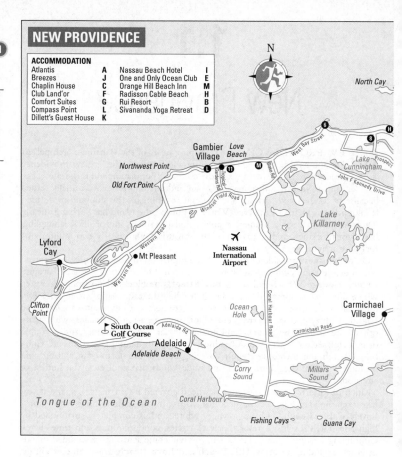

NEW PROVIDENCE

ACCOMMODATION

Atlantis	A	Nassau Beach Hotel	I
Breezes	J	One and Only Ocean Club	E
Chaplin House	C	Orange Hill Beach Inn	M
Club Land'or	F	Radisson Cable Beach	H
Comfort Suites	G	Rui Resort	B
Compass Point	L	Sivananda Yoga Retreat	D
Dillett's Guest House	K		

9am–5pm; ☎242/356-7591), while the larger office is located in Rawson Square, about two blocks east of the market (Mon–Fri 8.30am–5pm, Sat 8.30am–4pm, Sun 8.30am–2pm; ☎242/326-9781).

Getting around

Getting around New Providence and Paradise Island is easy, as both islands are fairly compact and few destinations are ever more than fifteen or twenty minutes apart. **Taxis** are ubiquitous, with almost all hotels and resorts having taxi stands (otherwise, dispatchers can be reached at ☎242/322-5111 and 323-4555). If you're travelling early in the morning, make a **taxi reservation** the night before.

Nassau's **buses**, known as **jitneys**, are frequent and convenient, serving all parts of Nassau, Cable Beach and surrounding areas for US$1. The #10 jitney runs along West Bay Street to Cable Beach, Sandy Point, Orange Hill and Gambier Village. You can pick it up at bus stops along this route. In downtown Nassau, this jitney leaves from the main stop at Frederick and Bay streets, or from a stop outside the *McDonald's* across from the *British Colonial Hilton Hotel*. Eastbound lines go from downtown to the Paradise Island Bridge and can be accessed on Bay Street east of the Straw Market. However, the easiest way to reach Paradise Island is by **ferry**, which runs

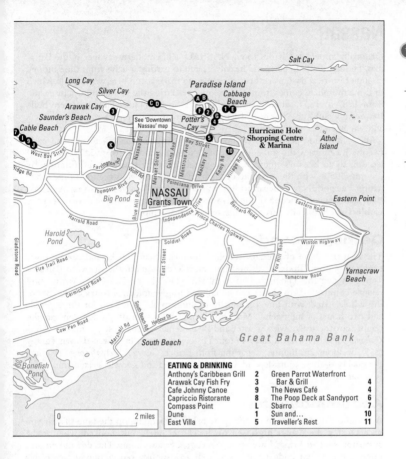

EATING & DRINKING

Anthony's Caribbean Grill	2	Green Parrot Waterfront	
Arawak Cay Fish Fry	3	Bar & Grill	4
Cafe Johnny Canoe	9	The News Café	4
Capriccio Ristorante	8	The Poop Deck at Sandyport	6
Compass Point	L	Sbarro	7
Dune	1	Sun and…	10
East Villa	5	Traveller's Rest	11

every few minutes from Prince George Wharf to Paradise Island across the harbour (daily 9am–6pm; $3 one-way).

To explore the rest of the island, you will probably want to **rent a car**. Avis has four locations on New Providence: downtown Nassau on Cumberland Street, across from the *British Colonial Hilton* (☎242/326-6380); on Paradise Island at the Paradise Shopping Centre (☎242/363-2061); in Cable Beach (☎242/322-2889) and at the airport (☎242/377-7121). Other rental agencies include Budget (downtown ☎242/363-3095, airport ☎242/377-7405), Hertz (airport ☎242/377-8684), Dollar (downtown ☎242/325-3716, airport ☎242/377-7301) and Orange Creek Car Rentals (☎242/323-4967), on West Bay Street in Cable Beach. Rates range from $49–$119 for 24 hours. If you are travelling in high season (Dec 15–April), it is advisable to book a car in advance. You can rent **motor scooters** and **bicycles** at local outlets as well.

Another option for **touring** New Providence is through Majestic Tours (☎242/322-2626), which acts as agent for a variety of operators offering bus tours as well as historical, snorkelling and boating expeditions. It has booths in many of the major hotels in Nassau, as well as Cable Beach and Paradise Island. Other tours are advertised in the tourist magazine *What's On*, available almost everywhere in Nassau.

Nassau

Originally known as Charles Town, **NASSAU** is the modern-day face of the Bahamas. Though dingy in parts and heavily geared to parting tourists from their money, enough historical flavour has been preserved to make a stop here worthwhile. Much of this atmosphere comes from its development during the so-called Loyalist period from 1787 to 1834, when many of the city's finest colonial buildings were built. Before this build-up, Nassau had largely been a rustic haven for pirates, privateers and wreckers.

After alternating periods of decline and prosperity in the nineteenth and early twentieth centuries, the spike in trade and construction that followed World War II led directly to Nassau's emergence as a global centre for **tourism** and **finance**. By the mid-1950s, with the dredging of the harbour and the construction of the international airport, Nassau began to host more than a million visitors a year. A decade later, after the construction of the **Paradise Island Bridge** and the development of **Cable Beach**, the city was receiving twice as many more.

Getting around

The historic centre of Nassau occupies about six square blocks, and can be easily explored on foot. **Taxis** are also readily available throughout the city, with Bahamas Transport and the Taxi Cab Union (☎242/323-5111 or 323-4555) as the most reliable companies. Any driver can be enlisted to give informal **tours** of the city or the whole island, with the cost usually running to about US$60 for three people and two hours of sightseeing. Most hotels offer **bike rentals**, though you can also rent a **scooter** at Knowles Scooter and Bike Rental, located just outside the *British Colonial Hilton Hotel*. You can also tour Historical Nassau by **horse-drawn surrey** ($15 for about 25 minutes, departing from Prince George's Wharf area), although the quality of these tours depends on how interested and knowledgeable your guide is (it varies).

Accommodation

Accommodation in Nassau can be quite pricey, depending on the time of year you visit. During the winter **high season** hotels are often fully booked, whereas the **summer season** brings lower prices and greater availability. The downtown area offers some decent budget options as well as a swanky old colonial hotel. Cable Beach boasts several chain hotels and a couple of exclusive resorts, while a few miles further west are a range of more secluded options.

Nassau

British Colonial Hilton Nassau 1 Bay St ☎242/322-3311 or 1-800/742-4276, ☜www .nassau.hilton.com. Built in 1922 and once the epitome of elegance in colonial Nassau, the *Hilton* still offers plush, upscale accommodation after a $70 million refurbishment in 2004, but sits sandwiched between the harbour and the busy main street in downtown Nassau, flanked by banks and shops, with the landscaping leaning more towards brick and cement than greenery. The 305 rooms have opulent gold and claret decor, Internet access, CD players and TVs with pay-per-view movies, but no balconies. The oceanside rooms have a spectacular view but no balconies. There is a formal dining room and a small swath of beach and a pool bar with a view of the cruise ship dock and Paradise Island. ❻

Dillet's Guest House at the corner of Dunmore Ave and Strachan St, West Nassau ☎242/325-1133, ☜www.islandeaze.com. A couple of miles west of downtown Nassau and within walking distance of the beach and bus routes, a rambling 60-year-old Bahamian house in a residential neighbourhood, set in an acre of gardens and hammocks, with large, comfortable rooms done up in modern decor. Includes breakfast and tea at 4pm. ❺

El Greco Hotel West Bay and August streets ☎242/325-1121. Centrally located across from the beach and near downtown on the main road, with 26 basic rooms positioned around a pool and courtyard. ❺

Graycliff West Hill St ☎242/322-2796, ☜www. graycliff.com. Perched on a hill above Nassau, a glamorous British Colonial pile with secluded rooms opening onto a garden and private cottages where Churchill and the Beatles once slept, decorated in rich woods and luxurious fabrics and set in lush grounds. The hotel has one of the city's top restaurants. ❽

Holiday Inn Nassau West Bay St ☎242/356-0000 or 1-800/HOLIDAY, ⊛www.holiday_inn.com/nasjunkanoo. Offering standard hotel rooms with a spotty reputation for cleanliness, located right on the main thoroughfare, with no grounds or greenery, three blocks from downtown Nassau. There is a public beach across the road, a heated pool in a cement courtyard with a view of the street, and several restaurants nearby. ❼

Mignon Guest House 12 Market St ☎242/322-4771. Clean, bright six-room budget choice with simple, homy rooms, air conditioning, shared baths and a fridge and microwave for guest use. ❷

Parthenon Hotel West St ☎242/322-2643, ⊕322-2644. A quiet, no-frills option downtown, the *Parthenon*'s eighteen rooms are in a two-storey L-shaped building that overlooks a garden. Continental breakfast is available for US$3. ❸

Cable Beach and around

Breezes West Bay St, Cable Beach ☎242/327-5356, ⊛www.superclubs.com. A huge all-inclusive package hotel (part of the *Superclubs* chain) with standard hotel rooms, serving up countless activities, including a full range of aquatic sports, to busloads of holiday-makers. ❾

Compass Point West Bay St, Gambier Village ☎242 327 4500, ⊛www.islandoutpost.com. A few miles west of Cable Beach on the #10 bus route, an upscale but unpretentious collection of eighteen rainbow-coloured, delightfully and luxuriously furnished cottages and guest rooms, some with kitchens. Built on a small patch of land between the road and the ocean, but artfully designed to create an atmosphere of privacy and relaxation.

The open-air bar is a great spot for lunch and a drink and there is an elegant restaurant for dinner. ❾

Nassau Beach Hotel West Bay St, Cable Beach ☎242/327-7711 or 1-888/627-7278, ⊛www.nassaubeachhotel.com. A venerable Nassau institution, with many appealing features, but looking a bit ratty around the edges. There is a nice beach, an attractive sculptured pool set amidst tall palms and flowers, a state-of-the-art fitness centre, pleasant staff and one of the best casual restaurants in Nassau – *Cafe Johnny Canoe*, with live music a few nights a week. The low-rise hotel has an intimate feel, built in a U-shape that encloses the pool and faces the ocean, and the 403 balconied, carpeted rooms are nicely if unimaginatively furnished. However, some of the bathrooms are a decade overdue for renovation and maintenance is spotty in areas. Ask for a room high up facing the pool or the open ocean. ❺

Orange Hill Beach Inn West Bay St, at Blake, Love Beach ☎242/327-7157, ⊛www.orangehill.com. Four miles west of Cable Beach, away from the hustle and glitz, a laid-back, small motel popular with divers, with large, bright and comfortable rooms built around a small swimming pool. There's a relaxed bar and restaurant and a beach just two minutes' walk down over the hill. Downtown Nassau is a short bus ride away, and the airport a five-minute, $9 cab ride. ❻

Radisson Cable Beach Casino and Golf Resort West Bay St ☎242/327-6000 or 1-800/333-3333, ⊛www.radisson-cablebeach.com. Bringing a touch of Las Vegas to the Bahamas, this 700-room high-rise hotel draws many guests with gambling and golf, but also boasts eighteen tennis courts, a health club, three pools and abundant watersports. Plush, nicely decorated common areas, lushly landscaped grounds and comfortable guest rooms with the standard amenities round out the offerings. ❻

Historic Nassau

The heart of **historic Nassau** is **Rawson Square** on Bay Street, just up from Prince George Wharf, where the major cruise lines dock. The square is the authentic crossroads of old Nassau, where tourists, government workers, hawkers and musicians congregate – especially during Christmas **Junkanoo festivities**, when up to 30,000 onlookers jam the square and surrounding streets and balconies to watch the all-night parade.

Just west and north of the square, the **Hairbraider's Centre** features Bahamian women braiding hair for about US$1 a strand. Across Bay Street, south of Rawson Square, **Parliament Square** is the centre of Bahamian government, with the grand colonial edifices of the British Empire, constructed in the early 1800s. These include the Opposition Building, House of Assembly and Senate, where a statue of **Queen Victoria** looks down sternly from the steps. Behind the Senate is the **Supreme**

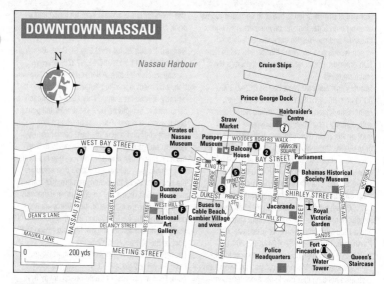

DOWNTOWN NASSAU

ACCOMMODATION				EATING & DRINKING					
British Colonial		Holiday Inn		Athena Café	2	Conch Fritters		Island Pasta	
Hilton	C	Junkanoo Beach	A	Bahamian Kitchen	5	Bar & Grill	4	Market	B
El Greco Hotel	B	Mignon Guest House	E	Café Matisse	6	Gaylord's	7	Segafredo	
Graycliff	F	Parthenon Hotel	D	Chez Willie	3	Graycliff	F	Espresso	1

Court building, and its lovely **Garden of Remembrance** honouring Bahamian casualties of two world wars.

Back on Bay Street, a few blocks west of Prince George Wharf, is Nassau's famous **Straw Market**. Filling much of a square block, the covered market squeezes in 150 vendors peddling everything from beads, tote bags and T-shirts to shark-tooth necklaces and expensive hand-carved wooden turtles. Just behind the market, the waterfront area is bounded by **Woodes–Rogers Walk**, named after the British colonial governor credited with ridding Nassau of pirates. It's worth a quick stroll for the view of the teeming harbour, usually chock-a-block with multistorey cruise ships.

Just west of the Straw Market, the **Pompey Museum**, on the corner of Bay and George streets (Mon–Fri 10am–4pm; $1; ☎242/236-2566), is located in Vendue House, on the site of the eighteenth-century slave auction, subsequently renamed to honour the slave who led a rebellion on Exuma in the 1830s. One of the city's oldest buildings, though gutted by a fire in 2001, it houses a collection of artefacts and documents tracing the history of Bahamian slavery.

A couple of blocks away, on the corner of George and King streets, kids especially will have great fun going through the small but well-done **Pirates of Nassau Museum**, complete with a replica of Nassau's seedy eighteenth-century waterfront, with creepy sounds and interactive displays (Mon– Sat 9am-6pm, ☎242/356-3759). Nearby, the fully restored eighteenth-century **Balcony House**, at 52 Market St near Bay, is believed to be the oldest wooden house in Nassau (Mon–Wed & Fri 10am-4.30pm, Thurs & Sat 10am–1pm; donations welcome; ☎242/302-2621).

Hillside area and west

South of Rawson Square, roughly bounded by Elizabeth Avenue to the east and Cumberland Street on the west, the **Hillside area** has a historical flavour enlivened by small **cafés** and some architecturally interesting pastel-coloured colonial buildings.

A block south of Parliament Square on Shirley Street is the **Nassau Public Library and Museum**, an octagonal building that was the first site of the Bahamian Parliament and later the city jail (Mon–Fri 10am–9pm, Sat 10am–4pm; free). The cluttered rooms house a remarkable collection of maps, photographs and engravings. Across from the library on the south side of Shirley Street is the restful **Royal Victoria Garden**, where you're free to wander among three hundred species of tropical plants on the former grounds of its namesake hotel, now a crumbling ruin. Following East Road, which runs along the eastern edge of the grounds, the road forks at East Hill Road. A right turn here will take you along a stretch containing much of Nassau's historic **architecture**, most prominently **Jacaranda House**, a two-storey private residence with peaked roofs and carved mansards.

Moving west, East Hill Road turns into West Hill Road, where you'll find both the **Dunmore House**, built in the 1790s by governor Lord Dunmore and now a private home, and **Graycliff**, an imposing Georgian residence from the 1720s and now an exclusive hotel (see "Accommodation", p.84). The Bahamas **National Art Gallery** is located on the corner of West Hill Road and West Street (Tues–Sat 11am–4pm, ☎242/328-5800 or 5801), showcasing a collection of Bahamian painting, sculpture, textiles and photographs. Alternatively, stay on East Road past the Royal Victoria Gardens and take a left turn on Sand Road, which will link up with Elizabeth Avenue, where the road slopes up toward the highest points in Nassau: the 1793 **Fort Fincastle** and the **Water Tower** (daily 9am–5pm; free), providing fabulous views of the harbour. Just east of the Water Tower, the unique **Queen's Staircase** is a deep limestone gorge into which stairs were carved for the convenience of Nassau's elite.

The areas west of downtown are best visited by hopping on the #10 jitney from in front of the *British Colonial Hilton Hotel*. A mile or so from downtown is **Fort Charlotte**, on a magnificent overlook between Nassau Street and Chippingham Road (daily 9am–4.30pm; free). Begun in 1787 by Lord Dunmore, the fort offers daily tours by guides occasionally sporting period costumes. Opposite Fort Charlotte is **Arawak Cay**, a man-made island and popular local hangout featuring food shacks and patio restaurants where Bahamian cooks serve up conch salad, cracked and fried conch and other local delicacies. Weekends are a good time to visit, when there is occasionally live music.

Cable Beach

Five miles west of downtown Nassau, and named after the first underwater phone cable that reached here in 1892, **CABLE BEACH** is home to numerous hotels, restaurants and sports facilities, along with a major golf course and tennis courts. Along the beach, whispering **casuarina trees** line the sands, and offshore lie **North Cay** and **Long Cay**, which make nice day-trips for snorkellers and picnickers. At the end of Cable Beach is **Delaporte Point Beach**, a chic assortment of Venice-style apartment condos, fancy shops and restaurants.

Eating and drinking

Thanks in part to its international influx of tourists, Nassau's **restaurants** feature a wide variety of cuisines, highlighted by Bahamian seafood prepared by local chefs using fresh ingredients. Every large hotel also has its own restaurants, some of them world-class. The free and widely available *Dining and Entertainment Guide* contains a complete listing of restaurants, diners and take-aways.

Nassau

Athena Café Bay St, at Charlotte ☏242/326-1296. Attracts large numbers of hungry cruise ship day-trippers with tasty (though overpriced) Greek food, served on a pleasant second-storey verandah.

Bahamian Kitchen Trinity Plaza, at Market St ☏242/325-0702. Authentic Bahamian home-cooking – wonderful grouper, snapper and conch dishes for US$10 – served in spartan surroundings.

Café Matisse on Bank Lane behind Parliament Square ☏242/356-7012. One of the nicest places to dine in Nassau, a sophisticated but relaxed bistro with great service and a menu including seafood and fresh pasta, highlighted by duck-filled ravioli and seafood pizza. Occasional Thursday or Sunday night jazz. Proper dress required and reservations recommended.

Chez Willie West Bay St ☏242/322-5364 or 5366. Just west of the *British Colonial Hilton*, this expensive though cordial French restaurant serves delicious mussels and steak tenderloin.

Conch Fritters Bar and Grill Bay St, across from the *British Colonial Hilton* ☏242/323-8778 or 8801. Convenient, pleasant location and tasty, inex-

Nassau tours and activities

Tours

Horse-drawn surrey rides $15 for about 25 minutes, leaving from Prince George's Wharf and taking you past the Bahamian Parliament and other major sights of old Nassau.

Majestic Tours ☏242/322-2606 or 326-5818, ⒲www.majesticholidays.com. Has agents in most hotels and handles bookings for an extensive menu of Nassau–Paradise Island tour operators, including bus tours of Nassau, boat excursions to the Out Islands and nearby cays, snorkelling expeditions, canoe trips, booze cruises, cycling day-trips, tours of the rum distillery and a variety of other activities.

Nassau Walking Tours ☏242/325-8687 or 328-8687. Offers a 90min walking tour of historic Nassau, departing daily (except Sunday) at 10am & 2pm from the bust of Sir Milo in Rawson Square. $10.

Boat excursions

Bahamas Fast Ferries ☏242/323-2166, ⒲www.bahamasferries.com. Puts on day-trips to historic Dunmore Town on Harbour Island, off Eleuthera, including a walking tour, lunch and cabana facilities on lovely Pink Sand Beach. $159 adult, $99 child.

Barefoot Sailing Adventures ☏242/393-0820 or 393-5817. A real sailing excursion (ie, no engine noise) with a small group, to Rose Island and nearby cays, for snorkelling and a barbecue on the beach. Half-day outings $55, full day with picnic $89, sunset champagne cruise $49.

Flying Cloud Catamaran Cruises ☏242/363-4430, ⒲www.bahamasnet.com/flyingcloud. Half-day sailing and snorkelling excursions to Rose Island on a catamaran (daily 9.30am & 2pm except Mon morning & Sun; $45), as well as evening cruises (Mon, Wed & Fri 6pm; $50) and a five-hour Sunday outing to Rose Island with snorkelling and a barbecue lunch on the beach (10am; $60). Children pay half price. All trips leave from the Paradise Island Ferry Terminal, but transportation to and from your hotel is included.

Powerboat Adventures ☏242/393-7116 or 393-3223, ⒲www.powerboatadventures.com. Runs an exhilarating day-trip to the Exuma Cays by high-speed powerboat, followed by snorkelling, a visit to the resident giant iguanas, an elaborate picnic lunch on the beach, a nature walk and time for relaxation. Recommended. $100.

Sea Island Adventures ☏242/325-3910 or 328 2581, ⒲www.seaislandadventures.com. Full-day excursions to Rose Island, off New Providence, including snorkelling, use of kayaks, beach volleyball and other games, and picnic lunch. $60.

Diving and snorkelling

Long, deep reefs and drop-off walls line the south shore of New Providence, and shallow reefs fringe the western side. The main diving centre is **Coral Harbour** along the south shore, where several dive operators maintain shops and boats, although all operators provide complimentary transportation to and from your hotel. Most opera-

pensive food, namely burgers, conch done several ways, buffalo wings and jerk chicken.

East Villa East Bay St, 3/4 mile past the Paradise Island Bridge ☎242/393-3385 or 3387. Chinese and Continental cuisine in an elegant formal dining room; considered the best restaurant on the island by some residents. Reservations recommended.

Gaylord's Dowdeswell St, near Victoria Ave ☎242/356-3004. In a charmingly ornate 1870s mansion, an upscale Indian restaurant with delicious samosas and tandoori. Special vegetarian dishes are also available.

Graycliff West Hill St ☎242/322-2796. Located in the eponymous hotel, with four elegant candlelit dining rooms in a restored colonial mansion and a 300,000-bottle wine cellar. The lengthy menu features French cuisine and Bahamian seafood dishes, as well as charcoal-grilled Ecuadorian white jumbo shrimp, Canadian sea scallops and meat dishes garnished with peppercorns brought in from Madagascar. The Humidor Churrascaria dining room specializes in Brazilian barbecued steak.

Island Pasta Market in the *El Greco Hotel*, West Bay St ☎242/323 8155 or 322 1188. Moderately

tions also offer snorkelling and swimming trips and combination snorkel-picnic packages, as do most hotels and resorts. All have similar rates, with a day of snorkelling for $45, two-tank dives for around $85 and $250 for open-water PADI certification. Among the most popular and well-established operations are:

Bahama Divers ☎242/393-1466 or 1-800/398-DIVE in the US and Canada, ⊛www .bahamadivers.com. Local office is located at the Paradise Island Bridge on Paradise Island.

Nassau Scuba Centre ☎242/362-1964, ⊛www.divenassau.com.

Stuart's Cove Dive Bahamas ☎242/362-4171 or 1-800/879-9832 in the US, ⊛www .stuartcove.com. This large operation, with a well-stocked dive shop, is based at South Ocean Beach on the south side of the island. In addition to an extensive menu of snorkelling and diving excursions and certification courses, they offer underwater "field trips" in one-person submarines that look like a cross between a motor scooter and a space suit ($99).

Fishing

The waters around New Providence are renowned for their deep-sea **sport fishing**, especially for grouper, snapper, deepwater amberjack, blackfin tuna, bonito and blue marlin. One reliable operator is the Charter Boat Association (☎242/363- 2325), with a fleet of ten vessels. Other charter services include Born Free Charters (☎242/393-4144, ⊛www.born-free.com), Chubasco Fishing Charters (☎242/324-3474, ⊛www. chubascocharters.com), Hunter's Charters (☎242/394-5037 or 557-3229) and Captain Jesse Pinder, who can also arrange fly-fishing trips (☎242/393-3739 or 394-1376).

Other outdoor activities

Bahamas Outdoors ☎242/362-1574, ⊛www.bahamasoutdoors.com. Runs cycling, birdwatching and canoe day-trips in New Providence's little visited interior, with groups limited to six people. Half-day outings $59 per person, full-day excursions $99.

Dolphin Encounters ☎242/363-1003, ⊛www.dolphinswims.com. Trips to visit and swim with the dolphins at Blue Lagoon Island, leaving four times a day from the Paradise Island ferry terminal. Observation/close encounter (petting)/swim with dolphins $20/$85/$165 respectively.

Sailing is a Nassau pastime, and sailing boats are available for rent at most marinas and yacht harbours. Rates vary widely depending on the size and type of vessel and whether or not it's crewed; you'll need to reserve in advance and provide proof of experience if you are renting a boat without a crew. Marinas to try include Brown's Boat Basin (☎242/393-3331), East Bay Yacht Basin (☎242/394-1816), Lyford Cay (☎242/362-4131), Nassau Harbour Club (☎242/393-0771), Nassau Yacht Haven (☎242/393-8173) and Atlantis (☎242/363-3000).

priced North American-style pasta dishes and salads served in a colourful, family-friendly atmosphere. Dinner only and reservations recommended.

Segafredo Espresso Charlotte St, between Bay and Woodes Rogers Walk. A small stainless-steel and black-leather coffee bar, serving Italian coffee, tasty deli sandwiches and pastries.

Sun and... Lakeview Rd, off Shirley St ☎242/393-1205, 393-2644 or 327-7976. Considered one of Nassau's culinary highlights. Elegant, formal dining with a menu of imaginative, beautifully presented French cuisine. Jackets required for men and reservations recommended. Dinner only.

Cable Beach and around

Cafe Johnny Canoe at the *Nassau Beach Hotel*, West Bay St, Cable Beach ☎242/327-3373. Colourful, popular spot for good food and people-watching; recommended dishes include the Bahamian fried chicken, meat loaf and macaroni cheese, and luscious desserts. Dining inside at comfy casual booths or outside on a covered terrace.

Capriccio Ristorante West Bay St, across from *Sandals*, Cable Beach ☎242/327-8547. Nice little Italian eatery, with four tables inside and a few more on a covered terrace.

Compass Point West Bay St, Gambier Village ☎242/327-4500. Casual though expensive open-air dining by the ocean, with a typically seafood-focused menu.

The Poop Deck West West Bay St, on Sandy Point Beach ☎242 393 8175. Moderately priced waterfront eatery popular with residents and guests for seafood and sundowners. Closed Mon.

Sbarro next to the *Nassau Beach Hotel*. Good for a quick bite or take-away – fast-food pizzas, pasta and fried chicken.

Swiss Pastry Shop West Bay St, across from *Sandals*. An excellent quick stop in Cable Beach for coffee, sweets and pastries.

Traveller's Rest West Bay St, near Gambier Village. Great casual lunch-time escape from the city, with shaded patio seating overlooking the beach at Orange Hill, offering great banana daquiris. Service can be almost comically slow, so be prepared to relax with a drink.

Nightlife and performing arts

Generally, **nightlife** in Nassau and on Cable Beach is to be found in the major resort hotels at a variety of bars and clubs. The biggest "floor show" in town is at the rather tired-looking *Kings and Knights Night Club* at the *Nassau Beach Hotel*, where King Eric and his Knights perform steel drum music with **limbo** and **fire dancing**, while the *Drumbeat Club* on West Bay features **Junkanoo music** and limbo as well.

On Mackey Street, the **Dundas Centre for the Performing Arts** (☎242/393-3728) provides a year-round schedule of music, theatre and dance, featuring both local and foreign artists. The monthly free tabloid *What's On*, available at all hotels and at many shops and restaurants around town, contains a section on the latest nightlife offerings.

Paradise Island

Across the short span of the Paradise Island Bridge from Nassau's harbour, **PARADISE ISLAND** consists of 686 acres of hard-pack coral and wind-blown limestone oolite sand. Until the mid-1960s this was Nassau's boat-building centre and supported a population of wild hogs and domesticated pigs. This former "**Hog Island**" also acted as a get-away for rich tourists, home to places like the posh *Ocean Club*, a 59-room Georgian charmer with a central courtyard garden and tennis courts.

In 1967, when the Paradise Island Bridge linked the island with Nassau, a small airport was built at the island's eastern end, and *Resorts International* created a huge hotel complex catering to package tourists. With a recent second bridge now assisting the increased traffic flow, Paradise Island has become a hugely popular destination, almost chock-a-block now with hotels, casinos, shops and holiday-makers. Whether or not you will enjoy your visit depends on your definition of "getting away from it all". If your tropical daydreams are full of lounging by the pool people-watching, gambling the night away in the casino, enjoying some fine dining and escapist activities like waterslides and paragliding, you will have a good time here. If, however, your idea of getting away from it all means getting away from your fellow human beings, you'll find the Paradise Island carnival overwhelming. Still, the island has some quiet backwaters, namely a marvellous **north coast** where pink sands meet the soft turquoise of the Atlantic Ocean.

The island

Most visitors to Paradise Island arrive through **Nassau International Airport** and, as there is no public bus service from the airport, travel by taxi to their Paradise Island hotel ($27). From downtown Nassau, the island is easily accessible by **water taxi** or **ferry**, which leave frequently from Prince George's Wharf and from the Paradise Island Ferry Dock on the other side (9am–6pm; $3 each way).

Only four miles long and half a mile wide, Paradise Island tapers to a point on its western end where there is a small **lighthouse**. The best **beaches** are on the north side facing the Atlantic Ocean, while the south side is dotted with marinas, docks and wharves. At the foot of the Paradise Island Bridge, drivers encounter a huge roundabout, the northern axis of which leads to the **Atlantis** hotel and its casino. North of the hotel is **Cabbage Beach**, two miles of fabulous blush-coloured sand, and further east, separated by a small anvil-shaped headland, is **Snorkeler's Cove Beach**, a striking and often deserted stretch where one can snorkel in peace.

Two main east–west roads cross the island: the first, **Paradise Island Drive**, heads east from the roundabout, passing the *One and Only Ocean Club* and other resorts and restaurants, and leading to the island's eastern end, home to private residences, a few exclusive hotels, the airport and a golf course. The only sights in the vicinity are the **Versailles Gardens** and **The Cloister**, built to resemble medieval ruins by the developers of the *One and Only Ocean Club*. The other street, **Paradise Beach Drive**, running west from the roundabout, heads out to the now-defunct *Club Med* and provides access to **Pirate's Cove Beach**, a secluded, windswept stretch, and **Paradise Beach**, two miles of sand that live up to the name.

Getting around Paradise Island is quite easy and many people simply walk to their destinations. The **Casino Express**, a shuttle bus making the rounds of the major hotels for a US$1 fare, is based at the *Atlantis* hotel. For longer trips or when it is hot out, **taxis** circulate on the main roads and carry passengers across the Paradise Island Bridge for shopping in Nassau.

Accommodation

Paradise Island is dominated by the sprawling, pricey *Atlantis* resort, which continues to gobble up real estate on the island, having recently acquired the former *Club Med* property. Still, there are plenty of other **accommodations** available on the island, ranging from secluded, exclusive luxury resorts to relatively inexpensive, charming guesthouses and comfortable, standard hotel rooms near the beach.

Atlantis Casino Drive ☎242/363-3000 or 1-800/321-3000, ⌨www.atlantis.com. A huge, package-tourist hotel with 2239 rooms, 230 suites, 17 eateries, 18 bars, 11 swimming pools and 3 spectacular aquariums housing 250 species of marine life and 50,000 fish (tours available for outside guests; $29), with every kind of recreation on offer – a casino, watersports on a strip of white sand beach and in the artfully designed swimming pools and man-made lagoon, a putting course and a golf course, fitness centre, tennis courts, library, children's day camp, concerts by big-name performers, a comedy club, a shopping arcade stocked with designer gear and trinkets, and a movie theatre. The whole complex has been developed on the theme of the mythical civilization of Atlantis, and there is little here to suggest that you are in the Bahamas. If you just want to relax by the pool with a cool drink and are in the mood for glitz, decadence and lots of company, you will love it. If not, you might go mad here. ❾

Chaplin House ☎242/363-2918. Located on the peaceful, secluded western tip of Paradise Island (call from the Paradise Island ferry dock for pick-up by water taxi), it is hard to imagine a greater contrast with *Atlantis*. Three homy, casually elegant, sun-bleached white clapboard cottages are set in a green, tree-shaded garden, each with a deep wooden verandah appointed with white wicker chairs for relaxation. Some rooms are directly on the beach, the others within steps of it, and all have a view of the water. On one side is Nassau Harbour, on the other, a gorgeous, private stretch of Paradise Beach. There's no TV or telephones in the rooms (though phone and Internet are available on request in the main house), but many contented returning guests. There are four studio units with kitchenettes ($95–105), a one-bedroom cottage that sleeps four with full kitchen ($120–140) and one oceanfront double room with full galley kitchen ($175). ④–⑦

Club Land'or Paradise Beach Drive ⓦwww. clublandor.com, ☎1-800/552-2839. Overlooking the marina, 72 attractive one-bedroom suites with kitchens and balconies in a three-storey building surrounding a quiet, green courtyard where breakfast and lunch are served by the pool. Guests have access to the beach a 5min walk away at *Atlantis*, there is a formal dining room, laundry onsite and a shuttle bus to the grocery store every Friday and Saturday. ⑨

Comfort Suites Casino Drive ☎242/363-2234 or 1-800/451-6078, ⓦwww.comfortinn.com. A three-storey pink hotel with 320 junior suites, nicely furnished rooms with a king-size bed, sofa, cable TV and bathroom. There is a pool and spa and Cabbage Beach is nearby. ⑦

One and Only Ocean Club Paradise Island Drive ☎242/363-3000 or 1-800/321-3000, ⓦwww. oceanclub.com. Once a private estate, now a chic hotel with a casual sophistication, set alongside a gorgeous beach and exquisite gardens, with a great restaurant and jaw-dropping prices. ⑨

Riu Resort Casino Drive ☎242/363-3500, ⓦwww. riu.com. Ornate, very grand beachfront hotel with a European feel. Hundreds of nicely furnished pink and floral rooms, all with balconies (the best views are on the ocean side on the seventh storey and higher), five restaurants, including the blue and white-tiled breakfast room, a Japanese glass pagoda on the beach and white linen and silver service in a formal dining room. All-inclusive. ⑨

Sivananda Yoga Retreat West Island ☎242/363-2902, ⓦwww.sivananda.com. Lovely, peaceful retreat for yoga practice and training, with accommodation in basic, comfortable cabins or camping. Located on the secluded western tip of the island on four acres of private beach, shaded by palms and accessible only by water taxi. Daily yoga classes and vegetarian meals included. ②

Eating, drinking and nightlife

Only a handful of **restaurants** on Paradise Island are unconnected to hotels or resorts, and dining can be a rather expensive endeavour. *Atlantis* seems to have places to eat around every corner: the elegant *Villa d'Este* has freshly made pasta, *Atlas Bar and Grill* hamburgers and ribs, the *Bahamian Club* steaks and grilled seafood, and the *Clock Tower* pizza and salad. *Fathoms Seafood Restaurant* at *Atlantis* has glass walls affording diners a blue-lit view of the exotic creatures in the aquarium. All are uniformly expensive (think $15 for a hamburger). With the exception of the *Riu* all-inclusive resort, all hotel restaurants are open to guests staying elsewhere, but most require reservations for dinner.

Drinking and **nightlife** hereabouts is largely confined to hotel bars and lounges. Most of these are found at *Atlantis*, which features Las Vegas–style entertainment with a dozen watering holes, notably *Club Pastiche* and *Dragons Lounge and Dance Club*, as well as a **comedy club**. Other hotels also have spots featuring drinking, music and dancing, such as the *Oasis Lounge* in the *Club Land'or*.

Anthony's Caribbean Grill in the Paradise Shopping Plaza. A colourful, family-friendly eatery serving good pizza, lobster, chicken and burgers for around $10.

Dune at the *One and Only Ocean Club* ☎242 363 2501. The *place du jour* for expensive gourmet cuisine in a spare, glass-walled dining room with wraparound views of the ocean. The menu is a melange of French and Asian cooking infused with Bahamian fresh seafood. For example, local grouper served in a tomato sauce accompanied by smooth coconut soup and shitake mushroom cakes.

Green Parrot Waterfront Bar and Grill at the Hurricane Hole Marina. A pleasant open-air retreat from the hustle and bustle of Paradise Island holiday-makers, serving drinks and light food, including a tasty chicken caesar wrap.

The News Café at the Hurricane Hole Shopping Plaza. Serves inexpensive breakfasts, sandwiches and salads on an outside patio with a view of the road.

Outdoor activities

Paradise Island **beaches** are famous for their swimming and sunbathing. At the far western edge of the island, **Paradise Beach** is nicely secluded, though lined with resort properties that charge swimmers a small fee. More spectacular is three-mile-long **Cabbage Beach**, one of the longest in the Bahamas, a sunny pink stretch that links the inlet at the *Atlantis* to Snorkeler's Cove. Because of the trade winds along the beach, **parasailing** has become very popular here, often resulting in a brilliant display of sails outlining the glowing horizon. There are all kinds of day-trips and activities on offer, and all operators offer free transportation from your hotel, whether you are staying on Paradise Island or elsewhere. See the boxed list of activities and outfitters on p.88–89. A visit to the magical **aquarium** at *Atlantis* is not to be missed, although breathtakingly expensive (tours several times daily; $29 adults, $25 child) and the price of admission does not entitle you to access the resort's beachside eateries afterwards.

1.2

Grand Bahama

Fifty-five miles east of Miami, **GRAND BAHAMA** exists largely as a big playground for North Americans, built from the ground up on a hundred-mile-long flat slab of bleached limestone bristling with tall, thin pine trees and edged by a ribbon of powdery white sand and multihued bands of blue-green water.

Most of the approximately half-million annual visitors to Grand Bahama do not stray far beyond the urban conglomeration of **Freeport** – three miles inland from the south coast – and its seaside suburb of **Lucaya**, which are together home to most of the island's 47,000 residents. Long regarded as a cut-rate package holiday destination passed over by more discerning travellers in favour of Nassau and Paradise Island, Grand Bahama has come into its own in recent years with the opening of several nice resorts in Lucaya and points outside the city. With miles of undeveloped coastline and largely free from traffic and urban sprawl, the charms of Grand Bahama are more than a match for anything on offer on New Providence. It will be a hard slog, though, for travellers looking to experience Bahamian history and culture. Lots of Bahamians live and work on Grand Bahama, but it was settled only in the 1950s, and sprang up almost overnight as a "destination" for tourists rather than as an organic Bahamian community. Grand Bahama's biggest attraction for visitors is probably its **accessibility**, with a daily **ferry service** from Florida and **direct flights** from several North American cities.

Among Freeport/Lucaya's attractions are four championship golf courses, two casinos, a good range of restaurants and several nice beaches within easy reach, especially

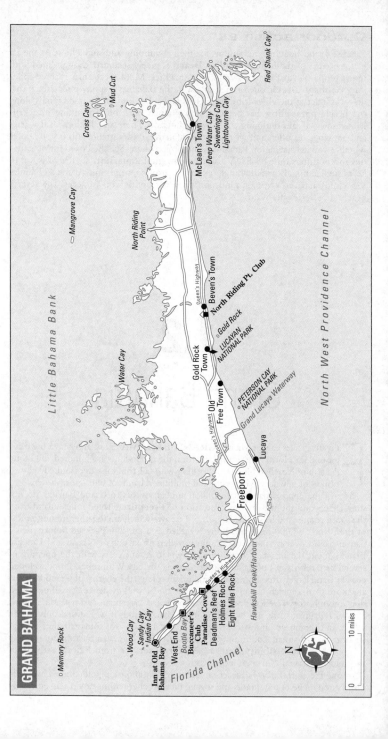

GRAND BAHAMA

Memory Rock

Little Bahama Bank

Wood Cay
Sandy Cay
Indian Cay
Inn at Old Bahama Bay
West End
Bootle Bay
Buccaneer's Club
Paradise Cove
Deadman's Reef
Holmes Rock
Eight Mile Rock

Cross Cays
Mud Cut

Mangrove Cay

Water Cay

North Riding Point

McLean's Town
Deep Water Cay
Sweetings Cay
Lightbourne Cay

Red Shank Cay

Queen's Highway
Beven's Town
North Riding Pt. Club

Gold Rock
LUCAYAN NATIONAL PARK

Gold Rock Town

Queen's Highway
Old Free Town

PETERSON CAY NATIONAL PARK

Grand Lucaya Waterway

Freeport

Lucaya

Queen's Highway

Hawksbill Creek/Harbour

Florida Channel

North West Providence Channel

N

0   10 miles

the mile-long **Lucayan** strand and the less built-up **Taino**, **Churchill**, and **Fortune beaches**. During daylight hours, there is an almost endless variety of well-organized day-trips and outdoor activities, including excellent diving and snorkelling, boat excursions, nature tours, kayaking, horse riding and duty-free shopping. Night-time entertainment – manufactured solely for the pleasure of vacationers – ranges from live music, dance clubs and sunset booze cruises to bonfires on the beach.

If the idea of miniature golf or the sight of other tourists is not to your taste, it's easy enough to escape the crowds. To the east of Freeport/Lucaya are the unspoilt and empty expanses of **Barbary**, **High Rock** and **Gold Rock** beaches, as well as the **Lucayan National Park**, which encompasses walking trails, limestone caves and mangrove creeks that can be explored by kayak. Also, an hour east of Freeport are two quiet fishing villages at **McLean's Town** and **Sweeting's Cay**, offering a glimpse of life in the Bahamas before the invention of Club Med. There are two worthwhile destinations west of Freeport: **Paradise Cove at Deadman's Reef** is the site of Lucayan archeological excavations as well as great snorkelling from the beach. Further west, scruffy **West End** has a wildly romantic history of pirates, sunken treasure and rum-running, although it isn't much to look at these days. The recently reopened, luxurious and secluded *Inn at Old Bahama Bay* on the western tip of the island may stimulate a change in the settlement's economic fortunes.

Some history

After the eradication of the native Lucayans at the hands of **Spanish conquistadors**, Grand Bahama remained virtually uninhabited for several hundred years. Bands of **pirates** and **privateers** often lurked at the west end to ambush ships sailing through the Florida Channel and heading to Europe loaded with gold and other treasures, and many Spanish galleons and British men-of-war wrecked on the reefs encircling the island. During the American Civil War, the island experienced a sudden spurt of growth when the village of West End briefly became a staging ground for Confederate **blockade-runners** smuggling guns and supplies into the southern states, just as it later became a base for **rum-runners** during Prohibition in the 1920s.

When American businessman **Wallace Groves** acquired the rights to harvest timber on Grand Bahama in 1946, the island was still largely empty and undeveloped, but the tycoon set about creating a **winter playground** for the rich and famous, almost overnight. However, by the 1970s and 1980s, the novelty and glamour of the once-burgeoning casinos and hotels began to fade, and Freeport and Lucaya were left mainly to continuous waves of college students on spring break and to cruise-ship day-trippers. After some years of decline, Grand Bahama has enjoyed a dramatic **economic rejuvenation** in the last five years, fuelled by a number of giant, five-star resort complexes, helping the island shake off its image as Nassau's poorer, more unsophisticated cousin. Whether this latest tourism boom can translate into long-term stability and prosperity, however, remains to be seen.

Arrival and information

Coming in by plane, you'll land at **Grand Bahama International Airport** (℡242/352-6020), located on the northern outskirts of Freeport. Although many hotel packages include **free transfers** to and from the airport, you may have to take a **taxi** or **rent a car**. Taxi ranks and car-rental agencies are found at the front entrance to the terminal (see "Getting around", overleaf, for more), and the usual taxi fare to Freeport hotels is around $12, and to Lucaya $17.

If you arrive by cruise ship, ferry from Florida or on the mail boat from Nassau, you will come ashore at **Freeport Harbour**, five miles west of Freeport proper. Several **cruise ships** call here every week, including the *MSV Discovery Sun*, a quadruple-decker passenger ferry/cruise ship taking a daily five-hour route between Fort Lauderdale and Freeport, with casino, swimming pool, buffet meals, games and floor-show ($179 round-trip; ☎1-800/937-4477 in Florida, 1-800/866-8687 in the rest of the US and Canada and 305/597-0336 elsewhere, ⊛www.discoverycruiseline.com). The ticketing office in Freeport is located at the Tanja Maritime Centre (☎242/352-2328), on Queen's Highway near the Port Facility.

There are five full-service **marinas** in Freeport/Lucaya, three of which are official ports of entry to the Bahamas. Dockage rates range from 75 cents to US$1.50 per foot/per day. All have electricity and freshwater hookups, as well as showers, bathrooms and laundry facilities.

The Grand Bahama Island Tourism Board (PO Box F 40251, Freeport, Grand Bahama Island, Bahamas; ⊛www.grand-bahama.com) has **information booths** at the airport, the cruise-ship dock and in the Port Lucaya Marketplace, as well as a main office in Freeport's International Bazaar. Copious maps, brochures and activity guides are available in most hotel lobbies, shops and restaurants around town, with free **maps** of Grand Bahama, Freeport and Lucaya available almost everywhere. Finally, the *Grand Bahama Island Snorkelling Map* is on sale at the UNEXSO shop in Lucaya, located next to the *Pelican Bay Hotel* on the harbourfront.

Getting around

Most visitors rarely venture beyond the resorts of Freeport/Lucaya, where the major attractions can easily be reached by foot, bicycle, motor scooter, public bus or organized bus tours. Complimentary **shuttle buses** to beaches, restaurants and the town centres of Freeport and Lucaya are offered by most hotels, and dinner shuttles are also available from some of the restaurants on the outskirts of town.

For those who want to roam further, a variety of transport options are available. **Car rentals** start from around $80 a day plus fuel, and include companies like Avis at the airport (☎242/352-7666) and Port Lucaya (☎242/373-1102), Brad's (☎242/352 7930), Dollar (☎242/352-9325), Hertz (☎1-800/654-3131 from North America, otherwise ☎242/352-3297) and Thrifty (☎242/352- 9308).

Bahama Buggies (☎242/352-8750, ⊛buggies@batelnet.bs) rents bright-pink **dune buggies** for $50 a day plus optional $15 insurance, while **motor scooters** can be rented for $50 per day in the car park across from *Reef Village* in Port Lucaya, at *Running Mon Resort and Marina* and at the *Island Palm Resort*; rentals can also be arranged through your hotel. Well-maintained single-gear **bicycles** can be rented by the hour, day or week in Lucaya at *Reef Village*. If you are planning to put in some heavy mileage, though, bring your own bike, as these single-gear bikes are heavy and built for short excursions rather than bike touring.

Taxi companies include Freeport Taxi (☎242/352-6666) and the Grand Bahama Taxi Union (☎242/352-7101); any hotel can also call one for you. A **passenger ferry** makes a ten-minute trip on the inland waterway between Port Lucaya and the *Flamingo Bay Hotel* at the *Ritz Bay Resort* on Taino Beach (hourly 8am–11pm; $3 one-way, $5 round-trip), leaving from the dock behind the *Flamingo Bay Hotel* at Taino Beach and the dock at Port Lucaya next to the *Ferry House Restaurant*. The ferry is not licensed to carry luggage, so only day-packs and handbags are permitted.

Freeport/Lucaya and other nearby communities are connected by a fleet of privately owned minivan **buses**. To travel between Freeport and Lucaya, catch the bus in front of Freeport's International Bazaar or on the corner of Seahorse Road and Royal Palm Way in Lucaya. Bus stops throughout the city are marked by pink and white shelters. On busy routes, the buses leave when they are full and a ride costs a mere dollar anywhere within the city limits. Buses to settlements east and west of Freeport/Lucaya leave regularly from the **main bus stand** in the car park of Winn Dixie Plaza in downtown Freeport.

Freeport and Lucaya

A utilitarian town with no organic centre or street life – everyone lives in the sub-urbs – **FREEPORT** is not an especially pleasant place for strolling or sightseeing, though it's easy enough to navigate on foot for visiting shops and restaurants. Free-port's main commercial district is centred on **The Mall**, located between **Ranfurly Circus** – named after the British royal governor who supported the city's develop-ment in the 1950s – and **Churchill Square**, about ten blocks north. Surrounding the city centre, The Mall is bound on one side by West Mall Drive, and on the other by **East Mall Drive**, where most of the hotels and restaurants are located. Tourist activity is focused on the south end of **East Mall Drive**, around Ranfurly Circus and the **International Bazaar**, a faded warren of tacky shops and cafés marked by red Japanese-style Torii gates. In addition to several serviceable but uninspired res-taurants, a straw market and assorted souvenir stands, there are duty-free shops selling jewellery, perfume, Cuban cigars, rum, resort wear and crystal.

East from Ranfurly Circus on Sunrise Highway, and south on Seahorse Road, **Port Lucaya** and the beachfront hotels of **LUCAYA** comprise a resort area with a more cheerful atmosphere than Freeport's, with carefully tended lawns and shrub-bery, and tidy, candy-coloured shops and houses. A seaside suburb first developed in the 1960s, Lucaya is dominated by the massive *Our Lucaya Beach and Golf Resort*, fronting **Lucayan Beach**, with two golf courses. Across the street from *Our Lucaya* is **Port Lucaya Marketplace**, a busy, colourful tourist market overlooking the boats at **Port Lucaya Marina**, with shops selling the standard duty-free assortment of goods, open-air stalls displaying straw work and other souvenirs, and several lively restaurants and bars packed with vacationers.

Accommodation

Grand Bahama was hammered by the hurricanes of autumn 2004, but with a few exceptions, the tourist infrastructure been refurbished and reopened for business. When choosing **accommodation**, keep in mind that Freeport lies several miles inland, and although there are a number of nice hotels in town, it is not an especially attractive place. If you do stay here, you can take one of the complimentary **shuttle buses** to the beach at Xanadu or Lucaya (five and ten minutes away by car, respec-tively). The main advantage of staying in Freeport is generally lower room rates than those found in Lucaya. Note also that Freeport and Lucaya are besieged with college spring-breakers in February and March, and if you don't want to party with them, either choose another time to travel or stay away from the resort strip.

Freeport

Best Western Castaways Resort East Mall Drive ☎242/352-6682 or 1-800/WESTERN, ⊕www.castaways-resort.com. Recently renovated with 139 attractive rooms and suites overlooking the pool or street, an excellent budget option for Freeport and within a few minutes' walk of several restaurants and the town's main sights, such as they are. Has a pool, bar and restaurant, with complimentary beach shuttle service. ❺

Island Palm Resort East Mall Drive ☎242/352-8485, ⊕ispalm@batelnet.bs. A decent budget choice, with bright and cheerful rooms surrounding a courtyard and a small pool. Offers an outdoor bar, a restaurant that becomes a disco at night, motor scooter rentals and complimentary shuttle bus to the beach at Lucaya's *Island Seas Resort*. ❺

Royal Islander Hotel East Mall Drive ☎242/351-6000, ⊕royalisland@hotmail.com. A small gem with a palm-shaded courtyard, restaurant, Jacuzzi, pool and poolside bar serving light meals. Rooms are nicely appointed, and free transportation to Xanadu Beach is provided. ❺

Royal Oasis Golf Resort and Casino Ranfurly Circus, next to the International Bazaar ☎242/350-7000 or 1-800/545-1300 in the US and Canada, ⊕www.theroyaloasis.com. Currently closed due to hurricane damage but expected to reopen in late 2005, this is the gaudy doyen of Freeport hotels, built in the 1960s and featuring a casino that has long been a mainstay of the local economy. Boasts twelve tennis courts, a fitness centre, two golf courses, seven restaurants and 965 guest rooms that garner mixed reviews from visitors. ❼

98

FREEPORT/LUCAYA

N

Grand Bahamas International Airport

Regency Theatre

▲ Deadman's Reef & West End

Xanadu Beach

QUEENS HIGHWAY

QUEENS COVE ROAD

THE MALL DRIVE

EAST MALL DRIVE

FREEPORT

THE MALL SOUTH

WEST SUNRISE HIGHWAY

EAST SUNRISE HIGHWAY

Ranfurly Circus

Pinetree Stables

CORAL ROAD

CORAL ROAD

SERGEANT MAJOR DRIVE

BALAO ROAD

SEA HORSE ROAD

LUCAYA

▲ The Lucaya Golf Course

▲ The Reef Golf Course

Lucayan Beach

Silver Point Beach

Fortune Hills Golf Course ▲

EAST BEACH ROAD

WEST BEACH ROAD

WEST BEACH ROAD

MIDSHIPMAN ROAD

Taino Beach

CHURCHILL DRIVE

Churchill Beach

FORTUNE BAY DRIVE

Fortune Beach

See Inset for detail

0   1 mile

ACCOMMODATION

Best Western Castaways Resort	B
Flamingo Bay Yacht Club & Marina Hotel	L
Island Palm Resort	A
Island Seas Resort	G
King's Court Resort	I
Our Lucaya Beach & Golf Resort	N
Pelican Bay at Lucaya	K
Port Lucaya Resort & Yacht Club	J
Ritz Beach Resort	M
Royal Islander Hotel	C
Royal Oasis Golf Resort & Casino	D
Running Mon Marina & Resort	F
Wyndham Club Fortuna	H
Xanadu Beach Resort & Marina	E

EATING & DRINKING

Banana Bay Beach Bar & Restaurant	8
Cally's	9
Churchill's Chophouse	6
Club Caribe	10
Coconuts Grog and Grub	1
The Ferry House	7
Geneva's Place	9
Irie's	2
Margaritaville Sand Bar	3
The Prop Club	4
The Pub at Port Lucaya	9
The Ruby Swiss	5
Silvano's Italian Restaurant	4
The Stoned Crab	5
Sugar Mill Bar and Grill	2
Tranquility Shores	3
Willy Broadleaf	N
Zorba's	9

Inset detail

N

The Lucayan Golf Course ▲

MIDSHIPMAN ROAD

Lucayan Marina Village

Port Lucaya

Bell Channel

Reef Tours

Pat & Diane/ Fantasia Tours

Police

UNEXSO

Superior Watersports

Port Lucaya Market Place

Lucayan Beach

▲ The Reef Golf Course

Xanadu Beach Resort and Marina Sunken Treasure Drive ☎ 242/352-6782, ⓦ www .xanadubeachhotel.com. Overpriced, disorganized monument to 1980s kitsch on a litter-strewn patch of beach. Only worth visiting as a last resort (or if you're a Howard Hughes fan; this was his final residence before moving to Las Vegas, where he died shortly thereafter). ❺

Lucaya and around

Flamingo Bay Yacht Club and Marina Hotel Taino Beach ☎ 242/373-4677, 373-4682 or 1-800/824 6623, ⓔ taino@batelnet.bs. Part of the grandly named but rather tacky and disorganized *Ritz Beach Resort*, which also includes the *Ritz Beach* and *Taino Beach* time-share condominium complexes and the Pirates of the Bahamas Theme Park. The three-storey, 68-unit *Flamingo Bay Hotel* sits on the edge of the waterway which connects Taino Beach to Port Lucaya, and is three minutes' walk across the parking lot and grounds to a fine white-sand beach. The pastel and white rooms are pleasant enough but a bit worse for wear. There are tennis courts, watersports, minigolf and ping pong to amuse, and the small, palm-shaded pool with its waterfall and underwater grotto bar is a delightful flight of fancy; however, the whole place suffers from poor management and badly trained staff. You could wait hours to be served in the bare-bones dining room or the otherwise inviting beachside patio café. ❺

Island Seas Resort Silver Point Drive ☎ 242/373-1271, ⓕ 373-1275. Small, isolated beachfront hotel with a pleasant, relaxed atmosphere, featuring one- and two-bedroom suites with kitchens and living quarters, a large swimming pool with rock garden and waterfall, swim-up bar and open-air restaurant. Offers watersports, bicycle rentals and free shuttle bus to the International Bazaar. ❻

King's Court Resort 4 Kings Rd ☎ 242/373-7133, ⓦ www.kingscourtbahamas.com. Modest but comfortable efficiency units in this family-owned, homy and clean place with a loyal clientele. Kitchenettes, TV, laundry facilities and a small dipping pool. ❹, with seven nights for the price of six.

Our Lucaya Beach and Golf Resort Seahorse Rd ☎ 242/373-1333, or in North America 1-877/OUR-LUCAYA, ⓦ www.ourlucaya.com. Five-star resort to be compared favourably with anything on offer in Nassau or Paradise Island. Lucaya has 1350 beautifully appointed rooms in three seafront complexes. The secluded *Lighthouse Pointe* is currently closed for renovations following hurricane damage, but is set to reopen in November of 2005. The *Westin* soars ten stories in the middle of the resort, offering floor-to-ceiling views of the ocean – ask for an

oceanview room. The low-slung *Sheraton* complex caters primarily to families, though the atmosphere can get frantic and very noisy during college spring break (Feb–Mar). The resort's beautifully landscaped grounds include two golf courses, seven acres of white sandy beach, nine swimming pools, four tennis courts, fourteen restaurants and bars, a fitness centre, spa and casino. ❺

Pelican Bay at Lucaya Seahorse Rd ☎ 242/373-9550 or 1-800/852-3702, ⓦ www.pelicanbayhotel. com. Small, lovely hotel built around a quiet courtyard with a swimming pool, Jacuzzi and open-air bar serving light meals. Elegant rooms have tile floors, refrigerators and balconies furnished with adirondack chairs, while the 96 luxury suites have kitchens as well. All guests have access to the beach at *Our Lucaya* resort across the street. ❼–❾

Port Lucaya Resort and Yacht Club Seahorse Rd ☎ 242/373-6618 or 1-800/582-2921, ⓦ www .portlucayaresort.com. Situated across from Lucayan Beach, this place features boat slips outside each of the hotel's 160 rooms, plus balconies overlooking the swimming pool or marina. Also with Jacuzzi and on-site restaurant. Very good value for the money, but occasionally noisy. ❹

Ritz Beach Resort Taino Beach ☎ 242/373-4677, 373-4682 or 1-800/824 6623, ⓔ taino@batelnet. bs. Located on a lovely stretch of beach, some of the opulent gilt-and-marble condo suites in this time-share are rented by the night or week. They are Las Vegas-grade glitzy, with sunken baths in the bedroom, lots of mirrors and glass, a kitchenette, dining and sitting area, and a waterfall-fed Jacuzzi on the private balconies overlooking the ocean. Guests share the swimming pool, tennis courts, watersports and other amenities with the *Flamingo Bay Hotel* and *Taino Beach Club* condos, but also their unprofessional service (see *Flamingo Bay* listing above).

Wyndham Club Fortuna Fortune Beach ☎ 242/373-4000, ⓦ www.wyndham.com and www.vivaresorts.com. Done up in bright yellows and greens, with a constantly jammed lobby and music blaring out of every door, this all-inclusive summer camp for adults and families receives mixed reviews from guests. Some complain of erratic plumbing and tatty rooms, others report having the time of their lives – though the staff get high marks all around for friendly service. Found a couple of miles east of Lucaya on a stretch of powdery white sand at Fortune Beach, the resort has 276 rooms, two restaurants, two discos, tennis courts, a gym, sauna and children's day camp in a complex of twenty-odd buildings spread over

26 acres of nicely landscaped grounds, with a large swimming pool next to the beach. Organized activities include diving, snorkelling and other watersports, day-trips around the island, dance

classes, theme parties and live entertainment nightly. You've got to like company to enjoy it here. **6–7**

Eating and drinking

In general, hotel **restaurants** have most of the area's best food options, with *Our Lucaya* resort especially good for its thirteen eateries with eclectic cuisine and dramatic decor. There are a dozen or more moderately priced places to eat in **Port Lucaya Marketplace**, most with pleasant outdoor seating and a view of the marina, people passing by and the occasional outdoor entertainment in Count Basie Square in the centre of the Marketplace. There are a few popular local **cafés**, but most residents prefer take-away – traditional dishes or fast food – to dining out. Also worth noting are the **beach bars** and restaurants along Taino Beach and Churchill Beach. Dining in Freeport/Lucaya is predictably expensive, though there are a few cheap eateries around.

Also, on the beaches just east of Freeport/Lucaya are some cheerful and relaxed beach bars and restaurants that make a good change of pace. Note that the restaurants on **Taino Beach** listed below are not within walking distance of the ferry dock – you will need to drive to reach all of them; some establishments offer complimentary transportation.

Freeport/Lucaya resorts

Cally's Port Lucaya Marketplace. Serving tasty and affordable Greek and Bahamian dishes, including Greek salad and savoury grilled vegetable wraps. Cheerful and relaxed atmosphere with indoor and outdoor seating on the wooden verandah.

Churchill's Chophouse in the *Manor House, Our Lucaya* resort. An elegant glass-and-mahogany dining room open for dinner only, serving steak, lobster and other seafood dishes with a fine selection of vintage wines.

The Ferry House on the waterfront at Port Lucaya ☏242/373-1595. Featuring an imaginative menu with dishes like grouper braised in Nassau Royale sauce and shrimp with a ginger glaze, as well as staples like chicken and pasta. Elegant dining room is sunny and inviting at breakfast, and candlelit with harbour views at dinner.

Geneva's Place East Mall Drive, at Kipling. Popular and lively local eatery serving Bahamian and American food at reasonable prices.

Irie's behind the *Westin, Our Lucaya* resort. A cosy replica of a colonial-Caribbean house featuring Cuban, Jamaican, Puerto Rican and Haitian cuisine, with traditional (though pricey) stews and seafood dishes like snapper steamed in banana leaf and served with plantains and voodoo fritters.

The Prop Club on the beach at the *Westin, Our Lucaya* resort. A casual restaurant and sports bar decked out like an aircraft hanger. Inexpensive menu features pizza margherita, chicken, ribs and tropical drinks. With a pool table and nightly music and dancing.

The Pub at Port Lucaya outside at Count Basie Square. A busy, outdoor patio restaurant serving a moderately priced international menu.

Silvano's Italian Restaurant in the *Pub on the Mall* on East Mall Drive. Inexpensive Mediterranean-based menu and decor, with a rough stone floor and sunny yellow walls, plus three additional tables on an terrazzo outside, though traffic somewhat spoils the ambience. Be sure to save some room for ice cream from **Silvano's Ice Cream Parlour** next door, which also serves breakfast, pastries and sandwiches.

Willy Broadleaf on the ground floor of the *Westin, Our Lucaya* resort. A series of themed dining rooms offering breakfast, lunch and dinner buffets ($20–$40), with eclectic Middle Eastern and Indian dishes, Mexican favourites, fresh pasta, crepes and sweets like baclava and Bahamian guava duff, a traditional island dessert.

Zorba's Port Lucaya ☏242/373-6137. Tasty and inexpensive Greek favourites like souvlaki, pita wraps and salads, with a no-frills seating area.

Taino, Churchill and Fortune beaches

Banana Bay Beach Bar and Restaurant on Fortune Beach. A delightful, moderately priced spot for breakfast or lunch, in the whimsically painted turquoise, pink and blue café with its palm tree cut-outs, tropical fish tank and wall murals – or even better, on the broad wooden deck overlooking a lovely stretch of beach. Imaginatively presented lunch plates include conch burgers, cheese quesadillas, crab cakes, sandwiches and mouthwatering desserts. Caters primarily to day-trippers off cruise ships, but worth the short drive out from Freeport.

Club Caribe on Churchill Beach at Mather Town, east of Lucaya off Midshipman Rd ☎ 242/373-6866. Serving hearty, inexpensive burgers and fries, seafood, and frozen cocktails, with pleasant outdoor seating at umbrella-shaded picnic tables on a breezy wooden deck with a view of the turquoise sea. Call for transportation from Freeport or Lucaya. Closed Mon.

Tranquility Shores (formerly *Kaptain Kenny's*) on Taino Beach. A huge, two-storey, buoy-strung timber restaurant and beach bar, great for a day or night out. Also has hammocks, beach loungers and a full range of watersports.

Margaritaville Sand Bar on Churchill Beach, off Midshipman Rd next to *Club Caribe* ☎ 242/373 4525. The interior of this small, candy-striped bar is cool and dark, with a sand floor and coloured lights. You can have burgers, sandwiches, conch fritters and occasionally wild boar at picnic tables under a thatch roof overlooking the beach, and play some volleyball. The bar hosts a bonfire on the beach every Tuesday night, with a steak or fish dinner, dancing contests and a DJ. Transportation from Freeport/Lucaya available daily for diners.

The Stoned Crab on Taino Beach next to *Tranquility Shores* ☎ 242/373 1442. An upscale seafood restaurant with a relaxed, tastefully designed dining room overlooking the beach; you'll know you've found it by its distinctive double pyramid roof. Serving seafood platters, steak, chicken and pasta dishes. Dinner only.

Nightlife and entertainment

There is no shortage of things to do **after dark** in Freeport/Lucaya. One popular way to spend the evening is on one of the numerous **sunset dinner** or "**booze cruises**" leaving nightly from Port Lucaya. Otherwise, you can usually find a beachside **bonfire** and **fish fry** almost any night of the week at one of the major hotels or restaurants. Inside *Our Lucaya Resort* (bars daily 6pm–2am; ☎ 242/373-1333), the *Manor House's* swank *Churchill Bar* features live jazz Thursday to Sunday nights.

There are several lively **bars** in the Port Lucaya Marketplace, patronized mainly by beach bums and yacht cruisers. In Freeport, locals and visitors mix on the dance floor at *Club 2000* (Thurs–Sun 10pm–3am; ☎ 242/352-8866) and at *Amnesia* (☎ 242/351-2582), both on East Mall Drive near the International Bazaar. For visual refreshment, there are two **cinemas** on East Mall Drive with several daily showings: Columbus Theatres (☎ 242/352-7478 or 7577) and RND Cinemas (☎ 242/351-3456). Finally, two local **amateur drama** societies put on plays throughout the year, the Freeport Player's Guild and the Regency Theatre (both at ☎ 242/352-5533), located in the same theatre on Regency Boulevard, just west of the Ruby Golf Course.

The rest of the island

The two main attractions outside Freeport – Lucayan National Park and Paradise Cove – lie on opposites sides of the town. Straddling the Queen's Highway 25 miles to the east, **Lucayan National Park** (daily 9am–4pm; $3; ☎ 242/352-5438) encompasses forty acres of mixed forest, limestone caverns and sinkholes, mangrove creeks, a spectacular beach and several nature trails all less than a mile long. A trail from the car park on the north side of the highway leads to a six-mile-long **underwater cave system**, one of the world's longest. One of them, Ben's Cave, is named after Grand Bahamian Ben Rose, the first diver to explore the entire cave system. Others have died trying to repeat this feat, but certified divers may explore the underwater stalactites and stalagmites of the tunnels with a permit obtainable from the Bahamas National Trust (☎ 242/359-1821, ✉ exumapark@aol.com); UNEXSO also offers guided expeditions (see box overleaf). The opening of Ben's Cave, accessible by a steep staircase, is home to a large colony of bats and is closed to visitors in the summer months when they nurse their young. Nearby, in Burial Mound Cave, another limestone sinkhole, divers discovered the skeletons of four indigenous Lucayans.

Heading west from Freeport along Queen's Highway, a sign on the left marks

Grand Bahama tours and outdoor activities

Boat excursions

Pat and Diane/Fantasia Tours booth at *Port Lucaya* resort ☏242/373-8681. Organizes an array of daily boat cruises, including a four-hour trip to Peterson Cay National Park for swimming, snorkelling and picnicking. US$59, kids $35.

Reef Tours at Port Lucaya Marketplace ☏242/373-5880. Offers several daily tours aboard a glass-bottomed boat, lasting about an hour and costing US$25, kids $15. As a second option, the catamaran *Fantasea* departs each morning on a two-hour trip, at a cost of $30 per person.

Smiling Pat's Adventures ☏242/373-4837, ⊛www.smilingpat.com. Provides different outings every day, from all-day boat excursions to Abaco and Peterson Cay National Park to beach-hopping trips and spear-fishing expeditions. Full-day excursion $35–$70.

Diving and snorkelling

East End Adventures ☏242/373-6662, ⊛www.bahamasecotours.com. A quality outfitter offering a seven-hour "Blue Hole Snorkelling Safari", which explores the marine life of blue holes off the eastern end of Grand Bahama, followed by a barbecue lunch on a deserted cay. Group size is limited to eight. Adults US$85, kids $35.

Paradise Cove at Deadman's Reef ☏242/349-2677, ⊛www.deadmansreef.com. Twenty minutes' drive west of Freeport on a secluded beach, a place to snorkel over lush reefs, float in a glass-bottomed kayak or relax on the sand. A snack bar and grill serves tasty beach food as well. Includes transport to and from your hotel, lunch and equipment usage. US$30, kids $23.

Superior Watersports Pork Lucaya Marketplace ☏242/373-7863. Uses a large motorized catamaran for hour-long snorkelling trips along Treasure Reef, departing four times daily. Another catamaran departs daily at 11am for a five-hour "Robinson Crusoe Beach Party", including 90 minutes of snorkelling followed by a full buffet lunch and volleyball on a deserted beach. US$59, kids $39.

the turn-off to **Paradise Cove** at **Deadman's Reef** (☏242/349-2677, ⊛www.deadmansreef.com), and a beautiful stretch of white sandy beach backed by tall grass and bush, with great snorkelling around the teeming reef just offshore. Deadman's Reef is the site of an important archeological find – the remains of a Lucayan settlement from the twelfth or thirteenth century that was discovered in 1996.

Practicalities

East of Freeport, the *North Riding Point Club* (☏242/353-4250, ⊛bonefish @grandbahama.net) is a relaxed yet elegant hideaway catering exclusively to serious **fishermen**, with accommodation in nicely appointed wooden cottages, each sporting a screened-in porch (one week of fishing all-inclusive $3225 per person based on double occupancy). Kayak Nature Tours (☏242/373-2485, ⊛www.bahamasvg. com/kayak) offers a unique view of Lucayan National Park on its easy paddling **kayak expeditions** through a mangrove creek, followed by a guided nature walk and picnic lunch on the beach ($69). Public buses pass by here three times a day.

Underwater Explorer's Society (UNEXSO) based at Port Lucaya ☎242/373-1244 or 1-800/992-3483 and 954/351-9899 in the US, ⊛www.unexso.com. Well-established operation with equipment rental, courses and day or night snorkelling and diving trips, including swimming with dolphins and sharks, as well as visits to wrecks, reefs and blue holes. One/two-tank dives $35/$70; night dive $49; dive with sharks $89; dive with dolphins $159.

Other outdoor activities

The Dolphin Experience ticket booth at UNEXSO ☎242/373-1250 or 1-888/365-3483, ⊛www.dolphinexperience.com. Departing from the UNEXSO dock, a twenty-minute boat ride leads to Sanctuary Bay, where the dolphins live in a quiet cove. Three experiences are offered: petting dolphins, swimming with them and spending the day assisting their keepers. One of the most popular tourist activities on Grand Bahama. Swim with dolphins $169; dolphin encounter (pet a dolphin) $75 adult, $37.50 for children.

East End Adventures ☎242/373-6662, ⊛www.bahamasecotours.com. Offers excellent all-day excursions to the unspoiled eastern tip of the island, visiting fishing villages, bumping along bush trails and sampling wild fruit before arriving at Sweeting's Cay for a conch-cracking demonstration. Final destination is the pristine beaches of Lightbourne Cay for picnic lunch, sunbathing and snorkelling. Group size limited to eight people. US$110, kids $55.

Kayak Nature Tours ☎242/373-2485 or 1-800/440-4542, ⊛www.grandbahamanaturetours.com. Runs enjoyable paddling excursions, including day-trips in Lucayan National Park, kayaking/snorkelling tours to Peterson Cay National Park (US$69), strenuous all-day paddling trips to the tiny remote settlement of Water Cay ($110) and guided, cycling nature tours as well ($69). Tour group sizes are limited and tours include transport and picnic lunches.

Pinetree Stables ☎242/373-3600, ✉pinetree@batelnet.bs. Offers a pleasant, two-hour guided trail ride through a pine forest and along the beach. Twice daily rides, no experience necessary. US$65, reservations required, closed Mon.

West of Freeport at Paradise Cove, the Smith family operate two well-maintained, two-bedroom beachfront **cottages**, a one-bedroom apartment and a two-bedroom villa for rent within steps of the water (☎242/3420-2677, ⊛www.deadmansreef.com; ❺–❼). The family also runs a friendly and relaxed snack bar and rents snorkelling gear and glass-bottomed kayaks, and does day excursions from Freeport/Lucaya. The nearby *Buccaneer's Club* (☎242/349-3794) is an atmospheric seaside **restaurant** with a touch of the Bavarian beer garden about it, with indoor or outdoor dining on the terrace and serving seafood and German cuisine. Courtesy pick-up from Freeport/Lucaya is available. Further west, the *Inn at Old Bahama Bay* (☎1-800/444-9469 or 242/350-6500, ⊛www.oldbahamabay.com) is a secluded luxury **resort** offering privacy, beautifully appointed rooms, three restaurants, walking and snorkelling trails, tennis, a swimming pool and a sheltered curve of white sandy beach for $510 a night.

1.3

The Abacos

The northernmost of the Bahamian islands, **THE ABACOS** are the most accessible of all the Out Islands and, consequently, the most developed, visited and affluent. In fact, a significant proportion of the 10,000 residents are reset-tled Americans and Canadians. In high season, the North American visitors temporarily inhabiting the dozens of clapboard cottages, palatial beach houses and small waterfront hotels seem to outnumber the Bahamian residents, lending the larger communities an atmosphere more akin to the less trammelled of Florida's coastal towns than to the rest of the Bahamas.

Beginning two hundred miles east of Miami and 75 miles north of Nassau, the Abacos are stretched in a band some two hundred miles long, though the islands themselves are rarely more than four miles wide at any point. The two main islands, **Little Abaco** and **Great Abaco**, are joined by a causeway, forming a boomerang jutting into the Atlantic. Running parallel to this landmass is a chain of approximately 25 cays that constitute a 200-mile-long barrier and reef system off the Abacos' Atlantic coast, enticing boaters, divers and other holiday-makers to their many hidden coves and beaches.

The hub of activity and services in the archipelago is **Marsh Harbour** (popula-tion 4000), located halfway down the Atlantic coast of Great Abaco, with easy access from here to the **Loyalist Cays**, which fan out in an arc a twenty-minute ferry ride offshore. The Loyalist Cays were originally settled by small bands of American royalist sympathizers following the American Revolution. **Hope Town** on Elbow Cay and **New Plymouth** on Green Turtle Cay are lovingly preserved historic set-tlements with tidy, freshly painted eighteenth- and nineteenth-century wooden cot-tages lining their narrow lanes, most of which are now vacation rentals. The smaller fishing villages and long stretches of beach on **Man O' War Cay** and **Guana Cay** also make enjoyable destinations. South of Marsh Harbour on Great Abaco, the spectacular unbroken sandy coastline from **Cherokee Sound** to **Casaurina Point** offers pleasing vistas, solitude and a couple of spots for beachfront refreshment. At the southern tip of Abaco, **Sandy Point** is the jump-off point for serious bonefish-ers. North of Marsh Harbour, the isolated but bustling resort community at **Treas-ure Cay** boasts a long stretch of white sandy beach.

The pine-covered Abacos have a temperate-to-subtropical **climate**, with cool winters and mild, windy summers, and an average yearly rainfall of 50-60 inches. In addition to threading their way through the cays, sailors may find ideal **yachting** in the shallows of the western coast, a fascinating landscape of mangrove islands, rocks and cays known collectively as **The Marls**. On the east side, **fringing reefs** and several **deep canyons** offer excellent **diving and snorkelling**. The Abacos are also fabled **sport-fishing grounds**, and a large percentage of the Bahamian residents make their living from the sea.

Some history

The Spanish slave trade obliterated the original Lucayan population of the Abacos. After a few hundred years of solitude, the archipelago was first settled in 1783 when a few hundred **Loyalist emigrants** from New York, the Carolinas and Florida fled the fallout of the American Revolution. Some of these original settlers were black Americans who arrived near present-day Treasure Cay, founding the village of

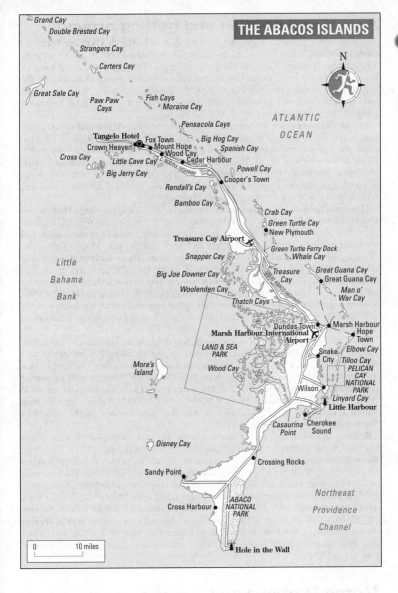

THE ABACOS ISLANDS

Grand Cay
Double Brested Cay
Strangers Cay
Carters Cay
Great Sale Cay
Paw Paw Cays
Fish Cays
Moraine Cay
Pensacola Cays
ATLANTIC OCEAN
Tangelo Hotel Fox Town Big Hog Cay
Crown Heaven Mount Hope Spanish Cay
Cross Cay Wood Cay
Little Cave Cay Cedar Harbour
Big Jerry Cay Powell Cay
Cooper's Town
Rendall's Cay
Bamboo Cay
Crab Cay
Green Turtle Cay
New Plymouth
Treasure Cay Airport
Green Turtle Ferry Dock
Whale Cay
Snapper Cay
Little Bahama Bank
Big Joe Downer Cay
Treasure Cay
Great Guana Cay
Great Guana Cay
Man o' War Cay
Woolenden Cay
Thatch Cays
Dundas Town Marsh Harbour
Marsh Harbour International Airport
Hope Town
Elbow Cay
More's Island
LAND & SEA PARK
Snake City
Tilloo Cay
Wood Cay
PELICAN CAY NATIONAL PARK
Wilson
Linyard Cay
Little Harbour
Casaurina Point Cherokee Sound
Disney Cay
Crossing Rocks
Sandy Point
Northeast Providence Channel
Cross Harbour
ABACO NATIONAL PARK
Hole in the Wall

0   10 miles

Carleton, named after the Governor of British North America, Guy Carleton. The Loyalists eventually colonized the areas around Marsh Harbour and the cays offshore, bringing with them their New England **architecture** of clapboard houses, steeply pitched roofs and tiny gardens surrounded by picket fences. This **Abaco style** survives today in the island's bright plantings of oleander, hibiscus and bougainvillea, its narrow streets and a grand old tradition of boat-building carried on by the descendents of the original Loyalist settlers.

Arrival, information and getting around

The main entry point for most visitors to the Abacos is **Marsh Harbour International Airport**, located at the midpoint of Great Abaco. There is also an **airport** located near **Treasure Cay** that primarily serves guests staying at the resort there or those heading to Green Turtle Cay. Several airlines service Marsh Harbour, and the tiny terminal is often overflowing with people coming and going. It is a short **cab ride** from the airport into town (US$10) or on to the ferry dock ($12) to catch a ferry to Hopetown, Guana Cay or Man O'War Cay.

Two **mail boats** make the journey from Nassau to Great Abaco and Green Turtle Cay every week, while Bahamas Fast Ferries (☎242/323-2166, ⊛bahamasferries. com) also has a **ferry service** on Friday and Sunday between Nassau and Sandy Point, at the southern tip of Abaco ($50 one-way for a passenger without a vehicle). Note that Sandy Point is 50 miles and a $135 taxi ride from Marsh Harbour, although the Islander Express **bus** (☎242/366-4444 or 457-9958) has occasional service between Sandy Point and Marsh Harbour.

There is a **tourist information office** (☎242/367-3067) in Marsh Harbour on Queen Elizabeth Drive, in a small shopping centre in the heart of town. The glossy periodical *Abaco Life* (⊛www.abacolife.com) is widely available in the islands and publishes regular features on island history, events and the like. **Maps** of the Abacos are also widely available from tourism operators. The weekly newspaper *The Abaconian* (⊛www.abaconian.com) is a good source for local news and up-to-date listings for restaurants, hotels, emergency services and ferry schedules. For yachting information, see the *Cruising Guide to the Abacos* by Steve Dodge (☎386/423-7880, ⊛www.wspress.com). Abaco Cruisers Net (⊛barometerbob.com) has local weather and yachting news, while ⊛www.oii.com is a good source of tourism information and local news.

There are several **car rental agencies** in Marsh Harbour, but demand frequently exceeds supply and reservations should be made well in advance. Centrally located Rental Wheels (☎242/367-4643, ⊛www.rentalwheels.com) offers excellent service and well-maintained cars and vans from $65/$300 a day/week as well as **motor scooters** and **bicycles** for $45 and $10 a day, respectively. Alternatively, try A&P Auto Rentals (Don McKay Blvd; ☎242/367-2655), H&L Rentals (at the Shell station downtown; ☎242/367-2840) or Sea Star Car Rentals (☎242/367-4887, ⊛www.go-abacos.com/seastar).

Renting a motor boat is a great way to explore the cays and the coastline. In Marsh Harbour, **boat rentals** are available from Blue Wave Boat Rentals (☎242/367-3910, ⊛troy@bluewaverentals.com), Rich's Rentals (☎242/367-2742), Rainbow Rentals (☎242/367-4602, ⊛rainbowrentals@abacoinet.com) and Sea Horse Boat Rentals at Boat Harbour Marina in Marsh Harbour and Hope Town Harbour (☎242/367-2513, ⊛www.seahorseboatrentals.com). Prices range from $100 to $150 a day for a 21-foot powerboat, with discounts for rentals by the week. Albury's Ferry Service (☎242/367-3147 or 365-6010, ⊛www.oii.net/alburysferry) operates regular **ferries** several times a day from Marsh Harbour to Elbow Cay, Man O'War Cay and Guana Cay ($20 return). Green Turtle Cay Ferry services New Plymouth from Treasure Cay (see p.112).

Marsh Harbour and around

Founded in 1784 by Loyalists, **MARSH HARBOUR** started life as a **logging**, **sponging** and "**wrecking**" town, with boat-building as a secondary industry. These days, **tourism** is the town's major source of income, and its marinas are filled with yachts and surrounded by swanky holiday villas. Tidy and functional rather than picturesque, the town has a pleasant holiday atmosphere and offers most of the services you might require, including a post office, bookshop, grocery stores, gift and clothing shops, several marinas and tour operators for diving, fishing and kayaking. There are also several pleasant waterfront **bars** and **restaurants** offering live music a few nights a week. With the exception of the swath of beach in front of the *Abaco Beach Resort*, there is **no local beach**, but the town makes an ideal base from which to explore the surrounding cays and the rest of Abaco, where white sand and turquoise water are in abundant supply.

Accommodation

Marsh Harbour was hit hard by the hurricanes in the autumn of 2004, but reconstruction and renovations have been intensive, and local businesses are for the most part back in operation.

Abaco Beach Resort and Boat Harbour ☎1-800/468-4799 or 242/367-2158, @www.abacobeachresort.com. On a strip of beach a short walk from the town centre, a sprawling peach stucco complex with eighty comfortably appointed (though overpriced) oceanfront rooms, six two-bedroom cottages and a large marina, along with pool, swim-up bar, a casual restaurant, tennis courts, beach volleyball, kayaks and snorkelling and diving trips arranged. ⑧

Conch Inn Marina and Hotel ☎1-800/688-4752 or 242/367-4000. Located on Bay St in the centre of town facing the harbour, nine rooms renovated and newly furnished following a thorough washdown from Hurricanes Jeanne and Frances in 2004. Each with bar fridge, coffeemaker, TV, a/c and use of the swimming pool. There is a small, plain restaurant and a pleasant outdoor bar serving light food and heavy drinks. Hotel marina has 75 slips and an excellent dive shop. ⑤

Lofty Fig Villas ☎242/367-2681, ☎242/367-3372. Centrally located on Bay St, across from the *Conch Inn*, six charming, tastefully decorated, quiet, private and very well-kept one-bedroom efficiency units grouped around a small kidney-shaped swimming pool. Set in grounds dotted with trees and flowers, each villa has its own screened-in porch, kitchen and television, with a barbecue out by the pool. ⑤

Pelican Beach Villas Pelican Shores Rd ☎1-800/642-7268. On a secluded peninsula a couple of miles from the centre of town, six cute cotton candy-coloured two-bedroom cottages fronting a small scallop of beach facing the open sea. Each has a kitchen, TV and rattan furniture, with docking for boats, a small swimming pool, showers and laundry facilities. Can be windy, but serene. ⑤

Eating and drinking

Marsh Harbour **eateries** are for the most part casual and pleasant, but a bit pricey, catering primarily to tourists with menus heavy on seafood and tropical cocktails. Bahamian home-style cooking is served up at several reasonably priced restaurants that draw a local crowd. Most places are situated within easy walking distance of one another along Bay Street, the main road which runs along the waterfront. For **picnic provisions** and self-catering, head to *Da Best Bakery*, locally renowned for their oatmeal raisin cookies. Solomon's, in the big blue building in the centre of town, is a well-stocked **grocery store**, and Bahamas Family Markets, near the traffic light, offers fresh produce, baked goods, Internet access and local news.

The Conch Inn Bay St ☎242/367-4000 or 1-800/688-4752. Popular for its fabulous breakfasts of jumbo French toast and great dinners of calypso grouper and stuffed jalapenos, plus fine gumbos and stews. Reservations recommended for dinner.

Hummingbird Restaurant and Bar in Memorial Plaza on Queen Elizabeth Drive. A dark and cool refuge from the heat, recommended for delicious, inexpensive Bahamian home-cooking and a grouper burger marinated in jalepeno pepper sauce and olive oil. Open only for breakfast and lunch during the week, with supper served on weekends.

Jaime's Bay St. This popular, inexpensive local restaurant has home-cooked Bahamian favourites and good ice cream. The fried chicken is highly recommended.

Java Coffee Along the main road heading towards the ferry dock, this is a great place to start your day, with fresh coffee and pastries, comfy sofas and a patio where you can watch everyone else heading to work.

The Jib Room at the Marsh Harbour Marina. Come here for reasonably priced seafood, burgers, "drunken chicken" (chicken marinated in sherry) and salads at picnic tables indoors and outside facing the marina. Open Wed–Sat 11.30am–2.30pm and Wed & Sat evening for a BBQ supper, with music and dancing on Sat night.

Mangos on the waterfront in downtown Marsh Harbour ☎242/367-2366. This white-linen service restaurant has a menu featuring pork tenderloin with mango sauce, grilled chicken with garlic and ginger, veal piccata, cracked conch and ribs, as well as home-made desserts such as coconut tart and pineapple sorbet. Patio seating was torn off by the recent hurricanes, but should reopen sometime in 2005. Dinner only.

Sapodilly's Lookout and Bar on Bay St. A local hotspot, with tables on a rainbow-painted wooden deck, comfy wicker chairs and an open-air bar. The moderately priced menu features sandwiches and burgers served with Bahamian sides like rice and peas, coleslaw and plantains, as well as salads and seafood dishes. Live music Friday nights.

Wally's Bay St ☎242/367-2074. In a two-storey pink colonial house facing the water, elegant dining on a pleasant covered patio furnished with white wicker furniture and chintz tablecloths, with extra seating inside. The menu features burgers and conch salad for lunch, dinners with grilled lamb chops and cracked conch, and tropical libations. Open for lunch only Mon–Thurs, lunch and dinner Fri & Sat.

Outdoor activities

Abaco Outback (☎242/367-5358, ⊛www.abacooutback.com) offers full and half-day **kayaking** excursions in the little-explored Marls on the eastern shore of Great Abaco, as well as **birding expeditions**, **hikes** and **off-road cycling trips** in undeveloped southern Abaco. Dive Abaco, whose office is at the *Conch Inn* (☎242/367-2787 or in the US 1-800/247-5338, ⊛www.diveabaco.com) offers a full slate of **snorkelling** and **diving** trips at two dozen sites around Abaco. Abaco Island Tours, located in *Sapodilly's* restaurant (☎242/367-2936 or 375-8718, ⊛www. abacoislandtours.com), arranges all kinds of day-trips in concert with local outfitters, including **historical** and **nature tours** of the cays and south Abaco, picnics on the beach, birdwatching, kayaking, snorkelling and diving. Guided **fishing** can be arranged through Jay Sawyer (☎242/367-2089 or 367-3941), Captain Justin Sands (☎242/367-3526) or J.R. Albury (on Abaco ☎242/366-3058 or in the US 1-800/827-6199, ⊛www.bonefishabaco.com).

South of Marsh Harbour

The highway heading south from Marsh Harbour is a straight shot barrelling through a stretch of pine forest and scrub until you reach the turn-off to **Cherokee Sound** and **Little Harbour**, 13.5 miles south of Marsh Harbour. Follow the signs to *Pete's Pub* in Little Harbour, about eight miles in from the highway, or to the *Sand Bar* (erratic opening hours; call ☎242/366-2210 before you go) in Cherokee Sound a few miles further on along the same road; both are fun and popular destinations for lunch or a sundowner on the beach.

Back on the highway heading south, 17.5 miles south of Marsh Harbour is the turn-off to the settlement of **Casaurina Point**, where a few bungalows front an absolutely spectacular curve of white-sand beach and turquoise water that runs uninterrupted all the way back to Cherokee Sound. There are no accommodations or other services here, but it is a nice destination for a swim and a picnic.

Continuing south on the highway, you pass **Abaco National Park**, a nature preserve crisscrossed by overgrown logging roads. Note that taking a rental car on these rough tracks is prohibited. Abaco Outback runs birdwatching and cycling tours in this area out of Marsh Harbour (see "Outdoor activites", above).

Fifty miles south of Marsh Harbour the highway ends at the island and ends at **Sandy Point**, a quiet fishing settlement overlooking Disney Island, formerly Gorda Cay, where cruise ship passengers are let out to play. There is a marine mammal research centre here as well as some good bonefishing. *Nancy's Seaside Inn* near the wharf is a good spot for a cool drink.

△ Sand patterns, the Bahamas

North of Marsh Harbour

The highway running north from Marsh Harbour passes a few small roadside settlements before reaching **Treasure Cay**, 24 miles north of Marsh Harbour. Not really a cay, but rather a slender peninsula, Treasure Cay is an isolated and self-contained resort community, with its own shops, post office, bank, health clinic, restaurants and marina, plus a miles-long stretch of beach.

The centre of activity is the *Treasure Cay Beach Hotel Resort and Marina* (☎242/365-8801 or 1-800/327-1584, ⊛www.treasurecay.com; ❻), offering several hundred comfortable if uninspired and slightly shabby rooms, suites, condos and small, self-catering villas, with golf, tennis and dive packages. This place is usually thronged with fun-seekers and spring-breakers and it is where the action is in these parts – but if you are looking for privacy, it is probably not for you. A more low-key local option is the *Banyan Beach Club* (☎242/365-8111, ⊛www.banyanbeach.com; villa US$1900/week), which has condos with two or three bedrooms and ocean views.

Continuing northwards, the S.C. Bootle Highway cuts through **Little Abaco,** passing a number of quiet beaches while the coastline gradually grows rockier and the forest denser. By the time you pass **Cedar Harbour**, the shores are overtaken by rock-shallows and finally heavy mangroves. *Nettie's Snack Bar* at Cedar Harbour is a good spot for conch and fried fish.

The end of the line is tiny **Crown Haven**, a quiet tumbledown village with a wooden wharf and a struggling lobster business. A **ferry** to Grand Bahama leaves from here daily at 7am and 2.30pm (Abaco ☎242/365-2356; fare $40 one-way, children $20) with a bus connection into Freeport, where you can rent a car.

1.4

The Loyalist Cays

J ust off the eastern side of Great Abaco, the **Loyalist Cays** are scattered in a sweeping arc fanning out from Marsh Harbour. Elbow Cay, Man O' War Cay and Great Guana Cay are accessible by a twenty-minute ferry ride from Marsh Harbour. Further north, Green Turtle Cay is accessible by a ten-minute ferry from Cooper's Town, 23 miles north of Marsh Harbour.

The cays were first settled by small bands of **United Empire Loyalists** who found themselves on the wrong side at the end of the American Revolution. They re-created their tidy little New England villages here, and scraped a modest living from fishing, sail-making and boat-building. Their clapboard cottages are now painted gay tropical colours and rented out to vacationers.

Each of the cays has a slightly different atmosphere. **Green Turtle** and **Elbow Cay** have been largely turned over to holiday-makers, and the primary activities here are relaxing and catering to those on holiday. **Guana Cay** is less developed but becoming more so due to a long, lovely stretch of largely empty beach. **Man O' War Cay** is still a working fishing community, with a few vacation homes dotting its shores. The cays are crowded in comparison to other Out Islands of the Bahamas, but make good destinations for a day-trip or a short holiday for those content to stroll around the village or along the beach, do some snorkelling or diving, sit at a waterfront bar with a cool drink or read a good book.

Elbow Cay and Hope Town

Five-mile long **Elbow Cay** is home to six hundred residents, many of whom are descendants of Loyalist settlers. **HOPE TOWN**, the only village, is located at the cay's northern end, traversed by two narrow lanes known as **Back Street** and **Bay Street** – which locals call "Up Along" and "Down Along". The village is a compact and picturesque collection of a hundred tightly packed and brightly painted clapboard houses, many surrounded by white picket fences and flower gardens; most of these have been converted into holiday rentals.

Local attractions include the **Elbow Cay Lighthouse**, a candy-striped pole visible for miles (but unapproachable by foot from the centre of the village – you have to get the ferry to drop you here), and the **Wyannie Malone Museum** (Mon–Sat 10am–3pm; $3 per person or $5 per family), which houses an eclectic collection of island memorabilia. Hope Town also serves as a good base for visits to the natural sanctuaries of the **Pelican Cay Land and Sea Park** and **Sandy Cay National Sea Park** nearby. Island Marine Boat Rentals rents Boston Whaler power boats (☎242/366-0282, ⓦwww.islandmarine.com) for those wishing to explore the surrounding waters. Froggies Out Island Adventures (☎242/366-0431, ⓔfroggies@batelnet.bs) offers **scuba**, **snorkelling**, picnicking and **boating excursions**.

Practicalities

Many visitors **arrive** on Elbow Cay on their own sailboats. For others, there is regular **ferry** service from Marsh Harbour to Hope Town (Albury's Ferry ☎242/367-0290; $20 round-trip). As there are few cars on the island, visitors and residents must walk or take **golf carts**; Island Cart Rentals (☎242/366-0448, ⓦwww.islandcartrentals.com) rents them for $40/$240 a day/week.

There are several nice options for **accommodation** on Elbow Cay. Straddling both shores on a secluded spot south of Hope Town, the *Abaco Inn*, on Bay St (☎242/366-0282, ⓦwww.abacoinn.com; ⑥), has fourteen rooms and eight one-bedroom villas with kitchenettes, as well as a pool, watersports and an elegant dining room. In the middle of the village, overlooking the harbour and the town, *Hope Town Harbour Lodge and Marina* (☎242/366-0095 or 1-800/316-7844, (ⓦwww.hopetownlodge.com; ⑥) offers twenty tightly set but cosy rooms, watersports, a pool with a popular outdoor bar and a nice restaurant. On the southern tip of the island, *Sea Spray Resort and Marina* (☎242/366-0065, ⓦwww.seasprayresort.com; ⑥) has brightly painted one-bedroom villas perched on a bluff overlooking the sea, each with kitchen, a/c, satellite television and broad wooden verandahs complete with hammocks, as well as a good dockside restaurant, a seafront pool, the *Garbonzo Reef Bar* and access to watersports. Closer to the village but still private and away from the crowds, *Turtle Hill Cottages* (☎1-800/339-2124 or in the US ☎508/540-2519 or 242/366-0557, ⓦwww.turtlehill.com; ⑥) has a clutch of two- and three-bedroom light wood-panelled villas near the Atlantic beach. *Hopetown Hideaways* (☎242/366-0224, ⓦwww.hopetown.com; ⑥) offers dozens of lovely **cottage** and **beach house rentals** all over the island starting at $1000 a week for a one-bedroom cottage.

All the resorts have decent **restaurants** and **pool bars**, but one of the most popular local eateries is *Cap'n Jack's* on the water near the harbour. Serving three meals a day and open late for drinks, the restaurant is locally famous for its conch burger and macaroni cheese, with live music on Wednesday and Friday nights. *Vernon's Grocery*, up the hill from *Cap'n Jack's*, sells sandwiches and flavourful key lime pie, while *The Harbour's Edge*, recently renovated following a visit from hurricanes Frances and Jeanne, is a popular spot for a drink and a bite.

Green Turtle Cay

Eight miles north of Treasure Cay, **Green Turtle Cay** is the most popular and well-visited of the Loyalist Cays, with a striking array of bays, inlets and sounds, with one very well-preserved New England-style fishing village, **NEW PLYMOUTH**. While simply wandering the town's streets is enjoyable, you can also check out the **Albert Lowe Museum**, housed in a 200-year-old colonial house displaying a fine collection of photographs, model ships and paintings. In the museum's basement, more art is viewable at the **Schooner's Gallery**, while on the outskirts of town, at the head of Black Sound, the **Alton Lowe Studio** is the best gallery in the area. The cay is dotted with white-sand beaches rimmed by close-in reefs ideal for **snorkelling** and **diving**. Several operators offer **boat rentals** and **sport fishing** (one is Captain Rick Sawyer, ☎242/365-4261, ⊛www.abacoflyfish.com), as well as **diving packages**, including Brendals Dive Centre on White Sound (☎242/365-4411, ⊛www.brendal.com).

Practicalities

To get here, take the **Green Turtle Ferry** ($7 one-way; ☎242/365-4166 or 4128), which departs from the Airport Ferry Dock near Treasure Cay on Abaco (with connections from Treasure Cay Airport) eight times a day from 8.30am to 5pm. It also departs from New Plymouth seven times daily from 8am to 4.30pm. There is also a **marina** at *Green Turtle Club and Marina* (☎242/365-4271 or 1-800/OUTISLA, ⊛www.greenturtleclub.com).

The most popular forms of transit on the cay are **golf carts**, **motor scooters** and **bicycles**, which can be rented at *Cay Cart Rentals* (☎242/365-4406), *C&D Rentals* (☎242/365-4161) or almost any resort. There are two **taxi** services on the cay, Omri and McIntosh Taxis (☎242/365-4406 for both), although it is very easy to **walk** everywhere you might want to go.

The major **resorts** on Green Turtle Cay are located either around White Sound or in a cluster between New Plymouth and Gilliam Bay. Some isolated **cottages** are available in the far north of the island, or on the Atlantic shore closer to New Plymouth. Rental agencies include *Coco Bay Cottages* (☎242/365-4464) and *Linton's Beach and Harbour Cottages* (☎242/365-4003). *Bluff House Beach Hotel* (☎1-800/745-4911 or 242/365-4247, ⊛www.bluffhouse.com; ⑤) has a commanding view on a hilltop and offers hotel rooms, townhouse suites and large villas, as well as two miles of beach, tennis courts, boat rental and a marina. *Green Turtle Club and Marina* (☎242/365-4271 or 1-800/OUTISLA, ⊛www.greenturtleclub.com; ⑦), has 32 poolside rooms and eight villas, along with a full-service marina and a waterside restaurant and pub.

Guana Cay

Accessible by a short ferry ride from Marsh Harbour, **GUANA CAY** – sitting just north of Elbow Cay – is a popular destination for day-trippers. Inhabitants of the small **fishing settlement** here have seen their community change dramatically with the influx of tourists in recent years, and plans for a new resort development on the cay have met with local resistance. The island is seven miles end to end, and the big draw is a five-mile stretch of powdery white sandy beach, dotted with a couple of beach bars and small hotels, with great **snorkelling** and **diving** along the Great Abaco Barrier Reef, which sits fifty feet offshore.

Practicalities

From central Marsh Harbour, Albury's Ferry (☎242/367-0290; $20 return) picks up passengers at the Union Jack Dock and the *Conch Inn* several times daily for the twenty-minute ferry run to Guana Cay. There are also several daily return trips to Marsh Harbour.

For **accommodation**, the delightful *Dolphin Beach Resort* (☎242/365-5137 or 1-800/222-2646, ⊛www.dolphinbeachresort,com; ❼) has seven simple one-, two- and three-bedroom cottages plus four double rooms, each with kitchenette, screened-in porch, TV, video and CD player. There are hammocks strung in the trees, a small pool and a five-mile stretch of beach steps away. There is a bar, and the casual *Blue Water Grill* is open for lunch and dinner by reservation (closed Tues; ☎242/365-5230). *Guana Seaside Village* (☎1-877/681-3091 or 242/365-5106, ⊛www.guanaseaside.com; ❺) is a casual beachside inn offering simple, comfortable and airy rooms done up in white and pastels. Cute two-bedroom cottages with kitchenettes are also available for $1450–2200 a week. *Ocean Frontier Hideaway* (☎1-888/541-1616 or 519/389-4846, ⊛www.oceanfrontier.com; ❼) has a handful of log cabins closely grouped around a small pool, each equipped with a microwave, coffeemaker and a mini-fridge.

Most visitors to Guana Cay end up at *Nipper's* (☎242/365-5143), a colourful beach **bar** and **grill** on a broad wooden deck overlooking the ocean, offering tropical cocktails, cold beer and beach food as well as a regular Sunday Pig Roast and live music. *Dive Guana* (☎242/365-5178, ⊛www.diveguana.com) offers full and half-day **diving** and **snorkelling** excursions as well as open-water certification.

Man O' War Cay

Man O' War Cay has been a centre for **boatbuilding** for generations. The small harbour bristles with sailboat masts, and beyond it a sleepy, pleasantly calm settlement straddles a low hill. The small grid of tidy streets are lined by picket fences and cottages sporting window boxes full of flowers. The Atlantic shore has a long stretch of undeveloped beach to stroll. The island is easily explored on foot, and what little traffic you see is of the golf cart variety. A few dozen snowbirds have built vacation homes along the shore, and there are a few cottages for rent to those who want a quiet, sunny place to unwind.

Practicalities

There is regular **ferry** service from Albury's Ferry Dock in north Marsh Harbour to Man O' War Cay (☎242/367-0290; $20 return). The trip takes about 20 minutes. On Man O' War Cay, the *Hibiscus Café* (☎242/365-6380) serves simple, tasty **meals** such as coconut-fried fish burgers, conch cooked up several ways, lobster, salads and sandwiches. It is up the slope from the dock, to the left. Another option is the *Man O' War Cay Marina* (just to the left of the dock, facing the land), which offers deep-fried fare at its open-air, waterside snack bar. There are a couple of **shops** in the village where you can buy provisions and souvenirs. Jody Albury (☎242/367-5119, mobile ☎242/375-8068, call 5–10pm) will take you bonefishing, and if you want to explore the neighbouring cays, David Albury (☎242/365-6502) has motor boats for rent for $118 a day/$675 a week. There is **no hotel** on Man O' War. For condo and cottage rentals, try at the Island Treasure Gift Shop (☎242/365-6072). They are also the contact for Golf Carts R Us rentals.

1.5

Andros and North Bimini

Bahamians call **ANDROS** their "Big Back Yard", an appropriate description considering the thick bush that dominates the island, which in the north consists mainly of tropical and deciduous trees like **Andros pine** and **lignum vitae** – the latter virtually the national tree of the Bahamas – and in the south, a mix of mangroves, mud flats and tidal swamps. Not surprisingly, amid this rugged natural terrain, there are seemingly as many **birdwatchers** as there are birds, making the island an essential stop for avian enthusiasts.

However, what really makes Andros unique is its magnificent **barrier reef**, the third longest in the world after those in Australia and Central America. Running parallel to the island's east coast for 167 miles, the Androsian reef is a massive inner bar of **elkhorn coral** that lies 10 to 200ft underwater and helps protect the island from tropical storms and hurricanes. It's also a truly spectacular place to explore, whether you **dive**, **snorkel** or **fish**, with an outer wall that plunges down spectacularly through a myriad of canyons, caves, blue holes and sand chutes. In the shallower waters inshore, the sights are just as stunning, featuring a bright assortment of reef fish, starfish, sea cucumbers and southern manta rays, among countless other species.

The island is divided into three zones: **North Andros**, home to most of the population; Central Andros, better known as **Mangrove Cay**; and **South Andros**, the most lightly populated and remote section. Aside from the north end, many parts of the rest of the island received electricity only in the last twenty years, and still have a rather poor, antiquated road system. This gives the region a rather charming and isolated character, a rustic appeal for those with the patience to deal with it.

Only fifty miles due east of Miami, the **Biminis** are the closest Bahamian islands to the US mainland – on a clear night it's possible to see the shimmering glow of Florida's biggest city. Composed of seventeen small, flat islands, the chain occupies a leeward position on the edge of the Great Bahama Bank, which helps explain why the entire eastern (or windward) shore of the two largest islands, North and South Bimini, are one long white-sand beach. The local economy depends on fishing and most visitors are drawn here for some of the best sport-fishing around. **Alice Town** on the very southern tip of **North Bimini** is the largest settlement in the Biminis, with a population of 600; it's also the hub of tourist services.

Arrival, information and getting around

Located 25 miles west of New Providence, Andros is easily reached **by air** from Nassau or mainland Florida. Bahamasair (☏242/339-4415, or in the US ☏1-800/222-4262) is the main carrier between Nassau's International Airport and any of the four airports on Andros. The airline also has daily flights from Nassau to Bimini. Note that the airport for the Biminis is situated on South Bimini; if you are headed for North Bimini, a shuttle bus will transport you from the airport to the ferry dock where you can catch a water taxi to Alice Town ($12 total).

Ferries and **mail boats** are a cheap and easy way to reach Andros and the Biminis from Nassau. Ferries can make the journey in just under three hours, although, depending on your destination and route, they may sometimes take up to seven hours. Fares are US$30 one-way.

Tourist information offices are located throughout the island, though the best site is at Fresh Creek (☎242/368-2286), located opposite the city park on the south side of the creek. There are only a few good options for **getting around** the island, mainly because there are so few roads, and major settlements are widely separated. Renting a car can be a frustrating endeavour, and is typically best forsaken in lieu of **walking** and **bicycling**.

Taxis meet all incoming flights at the airport, though cab companies on Andros are mainly individual operators who can vary dramatically in service and price. With no official tour operators on the island, most taxi drivers also double as **tour guides**, and offer informal sightseeing jaunts, particularly on North Andros, for around US$300 per day for two people. Some hotels and resorts may also include a complimentary taxi service for guests.

North Andros

The most common pastime on **NORTH ANDROS**, and the major draw for many of the island's visitors, is the sport of **bonefishing**. Although many of the creeks, flats, bights and rivers here sport countless numbers of hungry bonefish, the **North Bight** is the focus of the fishing scene, about thirty miles from Andros Town airport.

You can always find a great assortment of fishing boats parked at the wharf at nearby **Nicholl's Town**, a small burg of six hundred residents living in breeze-block and tin-roofed homes and scattered wooden shacks, lying near the island's north tip along a beach fringed by tall palm trees. To the east lies the pleasant fishing village of **Lowe Sound**, which has a guesthouse for visitors, several small bars and restaurants, and a few recommended bonefishing guides like Arthur Russell (☎242/329-7372).

Less appealing, the town of **San Andros**, further south along the east coast, consists of a few concrete houses surrounded by pine forest, with a nearby harbour at **Mastic Point**. Both settlements are tiny and virtually without services. On the island's rugged west coast, the tiny fishing village of **Red Bays** is the only real settlement, reachable by a bumpy, unpaved fifteen-mile road from San Andros.

South of San Andros airport, the delightful *Small Hope Bay Lodge* is the island's premier diving and fishing destination, while two miles south of Small Hope Bay is **Fresh Creek**, which actually encompasses two distinct settlements connected by a lovely single-lane bridge. The first, **Coakley Town**, is home to a few shops, restaurants and bars, as well as a large lighthouse on a cape. The town also has the only full-service marina around, the Andros Lighthouse Yacht Club and Marina, though the *Chickcharnie Hotel* has slips as well. Across the bridge, **Andros Town** has a tourist office, a pleasant park with a few disused tennis courts, and the **Androsia Batik Factory** (Mon–Sat 8am–5pm; ☎242/352-2255), one of the few commercial enterprises on Andros. Operated by the Birch family, which also owns *Small Hope Bay Lodge*, the factory produces batik fabrics, using wax to create patterns on brightly coloured cloth. You can buy it by the bolt or done up in dresses, blouses, trousers, T-shirts, scarves and household linens that make popular keepsakes for visitors and are a decorating staple in hotel rooms throughout the Bahamas.

The rough road south from Fresh Creek to Cargill Creek runs through bush and pine scrub, and is devoid of settlements. Still, the towns of **Cargill Creek** and nearby **Behring Point** are in the midst of prime bonefishing country, and worth making the effort to visit if you don't mind the drive.

Practicalities

Most of the activities and tours of North Andros are based around bonefishing, and are often organized by the island's **lodges** and **resorts**. The *Andros Lighthouse Yacht Club and Marina* in Fresh Creek (☎242/368-2305 or 1-800/688-4752, ⊛www.androslighthouse.com; ⑥), is built around a central patio, with large, comfortable rooms with a/c, TV and fridges overlooking an eighteen-slip marina, and offering bonefishing and island tours. Further north, on an island off Staniard Creek, *Kamalame Cay* (☎242/368-6281, ⓦwww.kamalame.com; ❾) is a secluded luxury resort with gorgeous guest villas tucked into private corners of its 96 acres. At Cargill Creek, the best lodge is *Andros Island Bonefishing Club* (☎242/368-5167, ⓦwww.androsbonefishing.com; $2797 per person for a week of fishing, all-inclusive) with simple and neat guest rooms and a cheerful clubhouse.

The island's premier diving and snorkelling lodge is *Small Hope Bay Lodge* in Calabash Bay (☎242/368-2014 or 1-800/223-6961, ⓦwww.smallhope.com; ❽ including meals), a lovely limestone and pine resort with guest cottages on the beach, a converted old boat for a bar and batik decor in the rooms. Diving and snorkelling trips are available, along with a beachside hot tub, kayaks, bonefishing, saltwater flyfishing and reef fishing. **Dining** is excellent here, as it is at most of the lodges. Other good choices for meals include *The Conch Sound Resort* and *Green Windows Inn* in Nicholl's Town, and in Fresh Creek, *Hank's Place*, known for its great fried chicken.

Mangrove Cay and South Andros

Most of the hotels and resorts in central and southern Andros are located directly on the beach, typically a rather narrow strip of soft, white sand. Offshore, the barrier reef is close enough for **snorkelling** and features stunning, close-up views of Caribbean spiny lobster, natural sponges, southern manta rays, parrotfish and iridescent displays of coral.

In central Andros, around **MANGROVE CAY**, the main settlement of **Little Harbour** is most interesting at its northern end, known as **Moxey Town**. With a tiny dock for harvesting fishing catches and bringing in ferries, Moxey Town has a few restaurants and bars, and good access to the offshore reef as well. The main diving centre on Mangrove Cay is the *Seascape Inn* (see below), with special snorkelling and diving packages, kayak dives and weekly night trips for advanced divers.

A few miles beyond Mangrove Cay, **SOUTH ANDROS** features thirty miles of coastal road edging white sands and coconut palms, and premier birdwatching and nature-hiking opportunities on its inland terrain. From **Drigg's Hill** to the north (where the ferry from Mangrove Cay disembarks), it's a slow and bumpy 25-mile trip to the road's southern end at Mars Bay. **Congo Town** is the site of the airport, offering a few places to eat, an ocean walk through coconut palms and, in the town centre, a **cemetery** where many of the island's founding families are buried. Everything west of here is mangrove and dense bush.

There are many attractive vistas on the road south and several worthwhile stops, namely **Long Bay**, departure point for long hikes into bromeliad- and orchid-covered hinterlands; **High Rock**, site of a magnificent blue hole perfect for diving and swimming; and little **Duncombe's Court**, a hole-in-the-wall village with a few restaurants. **Mars Bay**, at the road's southern terminus, is a pleasant little village with a quaint town square and a busy fishing dock, where loads of grouper and conch are stacked for cleaning and shipment.

Practicalities

As with North Andros, most of the **activities** and **accommodation** to the south are centred around hotels and resorts. Nestled in a palm grove on a white-sand beach, the refurbished *Seascape Inn* in Moxey Town (☎242/369-0342, ⓦwww.seascapeinn.com; ❻ including breakfast) has five simple but comfortable cabanas on the beach, excellent breakfasts and dinners, and a popular bar. In Kemp's Bay, the *Royal Palm Beach Lodge* (☎242/369-1608, ⒺZrahmings@batelnet.bs; ❸), has ten rooms, a courtyard, palm tree decor and a small bar and restaurant. At New Bight, near Drigg's Hill and Congo Town, is the recently opened *Tiamo Resort* (☎242/357-2489, ⓦwww.tiamoresorts.com; ❾), a lovely small resort with eleven beachside timber cottages with a spare, sophisticated decor, housing a maximum of 22 guests. Located between Drigg's Hill and Congo Town, *Emerald Palms Resort* (☎242/369-

2713 or 1-800/824-6623, ⓦwww.emerald-palms.com; ❼) gets rave reviews from contented guests. The resort resembles a relaxed seaside village with 22 pleasantly appointed cottages with kitchenettes, TV, a/c (but no phones), and more guest rooms in the main lodge. Bonefishing, hiking, blue-hole swimming and kayak **tours** are all available, along with **diving** equipment rental. The resort also offers a fine restaurant serving an eclectic blend of European and Bahamian cuisines, though the area has a few other good **dining** options as well. Congo Town's *Square Deal* and *Flamingo Club* are solid choices, and in Drigg's Hill, the *Blue Bird Club* (☏242/369-4546) offers decent food and nightly dancing. In Kemp's Bay, *Big J's on the Bay* (☏242/369-1954) is the most popular place to eat, while *Cabana Beach Bar* and *Lewis' Bar* are good watering holes.

North Bimini

The lightly settled Biminis are a fabled destination for fishers. South Bimini, where the international airport is located, has only a few residents and a smattering of retirement homes. Just 150 metres across a narrow channel is **Alice Town** on **NORTH BIMINI**, capital of the tiny Bimini island chain. Popularized by Ernest Hemingway, who described it as a hard-drinking fishing refuge, the town's numerous hotels and marinas continue to provide plenty of activity for anglers, divers and snorkellers, as well as a freewheeling, somewhat ribald atmosphere reminiscent of the town's glory days.

With more than two hundred hotel rooms in a six-block-square area, Alice Town has a number of notable **fishing clubs** and **resorts**. Best known is the *Compleat Angler Hotel*, King's Highway (☏242/347-3122; ❹), where Hemingway drank, fought and wrote the novel *To Have and Have Not*. It houses a collection of Hemingway memorabilia including rare photographs of the author. Almost as famous, the original *Bimini Big Game Fishing Club and Hotel*, also on King's Highway (☏242/347-3391 or 1-800/737-1007, ⓦwww.biminibiggame.com; ❼), has hotel rooms, two penthouse suites and twelve cottages around an attractive swimming pool and patio, and offers marina services along with excellent food and drink. Both the *Bimini Bay Guest House* (☏242/347-2171; ❹), an Art Deco treasure, and the *Bimini Blue Water Resort* (☏242/347-3166; ❹), where Hemingway wrote in a cottage called the Anchorage, offer comfortable surroundings and fine food.

King's Highway, the only paved road on the island, is lined with several **restaurants**, swinging **pubs** and garish souvenir stands. All of the hotels listed above have pleasant dining rooms and decent food. *Captain Bob's*, a popular spot for breakfast and lunch, is locally famous for its filling omelettes and French toast made with sweet Bimini bread. For a splash-out evening meal, try the *Gulfstream Restaurant* (☏242/347-3391; reservations recommended) at the *Bimini Big Game Fishing Club*, where the speciality is fresh kingfish. The *New Red Lion Pub* (☏242/347-3259; Tues–Sun dinner only) is the place to head for tasty barbecue ribs or seafood in a fun, relaxed atmosphere, while the *Compleat Angler* is the local evening hotspot, with live music several nights a week.

1.6

Eleuthera

The long, thin island of **ELEUTHERA** is the most populous of the Out Islands, with 10,000 residents scattered in a dozen fishing villages spread up and down its long coastline. Less than two miles wide for most of its length, the landscape here is rolling and green, farmed for citrus fruit, tomatoes and vegetables or clothed in tall grass punctuated by the occasional grove of pine or coconut trees. Running mainly along the water's edge, the north–south Queen's Highway offers long views of the turquoise sea and occasionally of both coasts at once. The other three islands, tiny Harbour Island, Spanish Wells and its bedroom community of Russell Island, surround the northern tip of Eleuthera.

Eleuthera is lightly touristed and boasts miles and miles of pristine pink, white and golden-brown sandy **beaches** with a crashing surf backed by dunes on the Atlantic coast. Along the Bight side, limpid sapphire shallows are fringed by soft sand and tall palms, shell-strewn strands or rocky cliffs. In the middle of the island, the genteel community of **Governor's Harbour** is the capital of Eleuthera and was one of the earliest (c 1648) settlements in the Bahamas. To the north is Gregory Town, built on a steep hillside surrounding a deep horseshoe-shaped harbour, and the self-proclaimed pineapple capital of the Bahamas. Further south, Tarpum Bay and Rock Sound are picturesque working fishing villages. Outside of a few comfortable small resorts, there is little in the way of organized activities for tourists.

By comparison only, pretty **Harbour Island** – or 'Briland, as it's also known – bustles with activity. The historic village of Dunmore Town boasts several upscale luxury resorts, fine restaurants and bars, and a couple of dive outfitters, as well as the three-mile-long **Pink Sand Beach**.

Arrival, information and getting around

Eleuthera has **airports** at Rock Sound at the southern end of Eleuthera, Governor's Harbour at the island's midpoint, and North Eleuthera at the north end of the island, with daily service from Nassau and Florida on Bahamasair, Continental and US Airways. Note that if your destination is Harbour Island or Spanish Wells, you should land at North Eleuthera Airport. For all other destinations on Eleuthera, you should land at Governor's Harbour or Rock Sound Airport.

Bahamas Fast Ferries (US$55 one-way, $100 round-trip; ☎242/323-2166, ⊛www.bahamasfastferries.com) operates daily **ferry** services between Nassau, Harbour Island and Spanish Wells, and twice-weekly services to Governor's Harbour. Government **mail boats** call once a week at several points on the island.

There are Ministry of Tourism **information offices** in Governor's Harbour (☎242/332-2142) and Dunmore Town on Harbour Island (☎242/333-2621), theoretically open during regular business hours, but in practice more sporadically. Tarbox Publications offers an excellent, well-detailed four-sheet **map** of Eleuthera, Harbour Island and Spanish Wells, including their respective beaches and other local attractions (US$10), available at the *Rainbow Inn* and other local shops.

There are no public buses on Eleuthera, and no organized tours. **Taxis** are readily available at the airports and ferry docks. If you are staying on Eleuthera and planning to do some exploring, you will need to **rent a car**. This is highly recommended, as one of the great pleasures of a stay on Eleuthera is meandering through its villages and seeking out its many lovely beaches. Wilfred Major (☎242/334-2158) offers excellent service and rents well-maintained vehicles from $70/$350 a day/week.

Accommodation

Eleuthera is dotted with lovely rental **cottages**. Island Dreams (☎242/334-2356, ⓦwww.bahamas-island-dreams.com) has several appealing cottage rentals in and around Tarpum Bay and Rock Sound, from $500 a week.

Cartwright's Oceanfront Cottages Tarpum Bay ☎242/334-4215. Offers three cosy two- and three-bedroom cottages on the waterfront at the western edge of town, with a homy and eclectic decor and a great view of the sea. ❺

Cigatoo Resort Governor's Harbour ☎242/332-3060, or in North America ☎1-800/467-7595, ⓦwww.cigatooresort.com. Has 24 clean, bright and modern rooms set in nicely landscaped grounds around a swimming pool, with tennis courts and a bar and restaurant. ❻

Cocodimama two miles south of Governor's Harbour airport on the Queen's Highway ☎242/332-3150, ⓦwww.cocodimama.com. A small beach resort with three two-storey cottages on the beach. Twelve spacious, pleasingly decorated rooms feature Balinese furniture, clay-tile floors and private balconies with hammocks, and a swath of white sandy beach and calm water. Windsurfing, kayaking and snorkelling gear available for guest use. Closed Sept–Nov. ❼

The Cove Eleuthera two miles north of Gregory Town ☎242/335-5142 or 1-800/552-5960, ⓦwww.thecoveeleuthera.com. A small, casual resort with a lovely sheltered cove for swimming and snorkelling, bicycle rentals, snorkelling gear, a swimming pool and patio with a spectacular view. There's a laid-back restaurant inside, and tennis courts and a dramatic coastline to explore by kayak. Features 24 comfortable rooms with ceramic-tiled floors, some with kitchenettes. ❻

The Duck Inn on the Queen's Highway in Governor's Harbour ☎242/332- 2608, ⓦwww.theduckinn. com. Located on the waterfront, with three charming wooden cottages built in the early 1800s and carefully restored with lots of creature comforts and delightful touches. There's a lush enclosed garden, outdoor barbecue, kayaks for guest use and an orchid nursery. Cottages sleep two to eight. ❺

Morgan's Bonefish Harbour Gregory Town ☎242/335-5077, ⓦmorgansbonefishharbour.com. Two cute rustic cottages for rent on a secluded bluff within walking distance of town, with kayaks and hammocks for guest use and guided fishing trips arranged. Studio sleeping two and a one-bedroom sleeping three. ❹

Nor'Side Resort Rock Sound ☎242/334-2573. Perched on a high bluff overlooking the Atlantic, a cluster of four hexagonal cottages with eight studio apartments, sand-floored bar and a restaurant serving the best home-cooked Bahamian meals on the island. ❺

Rainbow Inn ten miles north of Governor's Harbour airport on the Queen's Highway ☎242/335-0294, or in North America ☎1-800/688-0047, ⓦwww.rainbowinn.com. A relaxed resort with hexagonal wooden cottages (some with kitchens) built around a swimming pool overlooking the sea. Facilities include tennis courts, free bicycle use, kayaks, hobie cats, snorkelling gear and trips, hammocks and the best gourmet restaurant on the island. Closed Sept to mid-Nov. ❻

Governor's Harbour

Governor's Harbour is a gracious seaside town and fishing community of a few hundred residents with a distinctly colonial feel and a tangible expatriate presence. Located at the midpoint of Eleuthera, with plentiful and charming accommodations and restaurants and several beautiful beaches close at hand, it makes a good spot to base yourself to explore the island. Daintily painted wooden cottages with gingerbread trim line the steep lanes which climb the hillside, surrounded by stone walls overflowing with hibiscus and oleander blooms. The harbour, dotted with fishing boats and pleasure craft, is enclosed by a curve of white sand joined to **Cupid's Cay** by a narrow causeway. Cupid's Cay, a small hunk of flat rock, was the site of the first settlement on Eleuthera, by the Company of Eleutheran Adventurers, exiles from Bermuda in 1648 (although a big sign proudly declares it to have been 1646). A church, a few cottages and the ruins of nineteenth-century wooden houses remain. The **mailboat** and passenger **ferries** dock at the north end of the cay.

On the south side of the harbour in front of the candy-pink **library** is **Arthur's Beach**, where there is a community fish fry every Friday and Saturday night. Over the hill on the Atlantic side is **Club Med Beach** – possibly the finest on the island – a broad swath of powdery pink sand, often deserted since the closure of the *Club Med* resort, now just a cluster of overgrown buildings set back from the beach. To reach the beach from the centre of Governor's Harbour, take Haynes Avenue up the hill from the Queen's Highway, past the *Cigatoo Resort* and down the other side, where you come to a T-junction. From here, take the wooded path just to the right of the junction, which arrives after 200 yards or so at the beach.

The rest of the island

North of Governor's Harbour the Queen's Highway passes through several small fishing villages as well as the larger hillside settlement of **Gregory Town**. Along the way, through rolling farmland and long stretches of dense bush, side roads off the highway lead to beautiful empty **beaches** on both the Caribbean and Atlantic coasts. After you pass through the **Glass Window** – a rocky, wave-doused moon-scape where Eleuthera is barely a car-width wide – there's little to detain visitors (though you must come this way to catch a **ferry** to Harbour Island or Spanish Wells).

South of Governor's Harbour are two picturesque fishing villages worth a visit: sleepy **Tarpum Bay** and prettily painted **Rock Sound**, both of which offer refreshments and accommodations. The remaining highlights of southern Eleuthera are several stunning beaches, including **Ten Bay**, **North Side** and **Lighthouse**. There is not a lot to do down this way besides stroll along the shore and listen to the sound of the waves from the verandah of any number of beachfront rental cottages, but that is basically the point for many visitors.

Eating and drinking

Eating and **drinking** is a casual affair on Eleuthera. You can find some hearty Bahamian cooking and a local drinking hole in most settlements, and there are a few very nice restaurants for a memorable meal. Island **nightlife** is pretty subdued. The *Rainbow Inn* offers live music with dinner a few nights a week, and you can play a game of pool and listen to the jukebox at *Mate and Jenny's*.

Cocodimama two miles south of Governor's Harbour airport on the Queen's Highway ☎242/332-3150. Part of a small resort, with romantic seating on a wide terrace on the sands with a great sunset view. Nice choice for a special night out, serving Italian and Bahamian cuisine and featuring dishes such as gorgonzola cheese salad, grouper in a white wine sauce and crepes with Cointreau and ice cream. Breakfast, lunch and dinner service.

Dolcevita Restaurant and Lounge at the *Rainbow Inn*, ten miles north of Governor's Harbour airport on the Queen's Highway ☎242/335 0623, ⓦwww.dolcevitabahamas.com. Atmospheric hexagonal restaurant with excellent Italian cuisine, an extensive wine cellar, sublime home-made key lime pie, and live music with Dr Seabreeze on Wed and Fri. Closed Mon.

Mate and Jenny's just off the highway in South Palmetto ☎242/332-1504. Moderately priced casual restaurant with a dark and cosy interior, the rafters strung with yachting pennants and a pool table. Offers delicious conch pizza, seafood, steak, sandwiches and potent tropical cocktails. Closed Tues.

Nor'Side Resort Rock Sound ☎242/334-2573. Great Bahamian home-cooking and cool drinks in a lovely setting on a bluff overlooking the Atlantic.

Pammy's Queen's Highway, Governor's Harbour. A popular local spot with fine, home-style Bahamian food like fried chicken, conch fritters, burgers and sandwiches, with traditional side dishes like cole-slaw, fried plantains, peas 'n' rice and macaroni cheese.

Rosie's Café and Bakery on the Queen's Highway in James Cistern. Serving fine break-fasts and lunches at reasonable prices. Also sells delicious home-made bread and banana-and-pineapple loaf.

Harbour Island

Sitting two miles off the northeast side of Eleuthera, **Harbour Island** is a different world altogether. Tourism is the name of the game on this tidy green island – just three miles end to end and less than half a mile across – focused on the spectacular **Pink Sand Beach**, which runs the length of the Atlantic side. There is not a high-rise or tour bus in sight, however. The island's only settlement is the picture-perfect village of **Dunmore Town**, which climbs a low hill overlooking the harbour. With neat narrow streets lined with freshly painted clapboard cottages, flower boxes and white picket fences, it evokes a New England seaside town. It was, in fact, built mainly by Loyalist exiles and their slaves from the American colonies at the end of the eighteenth century. These days, a clutch of intimate and exclusive beach **resorts** and heritage inns cater to a wealthy clientele.

Water taxis ($4 each way) depart regularly from the wharf on Eleuthera to make the ten-minute trip to the dock in the centre of Dunmore Town, within walking distance of all hotels and restaurants and the famous Pink Sand Beach. If you're coming from **Nassau**, Bahamas Fast Ferries (☏242/323-2166, ⊛www.bahamasferries. com) has daily service to Harbour Island, and the government **mail boat** calls here weekly. Although the island is easy enough to navigate **on foot**, most locals buzz around on **golf carts**, which can be rented on the dock when you arrive or arranged through your hotel.

Accommodation

Island Real Estate (☏242/333-2278 or 2377, ⊜islandrealest@batelnet.bs) handles bookings for more than eighty properties on Harbour Island, ranging from self-catering studio **apartments** to beachfront **villas** staffed with a cook and house-keeper.

Bahama House Inn ☏242/333-2201, ⊛www. bahamahouseinn.com. Charming bed and breakfast with seven guest rooms in a rambling late eighteenth-century mansion with a private garden and a view of the harbour from the wraparound verandah. The guest rooms (one with a kitchen) evoke the colonial era with painted wood floors, high antique beds, polished mahogany wardrobes and colourful scatter rugs. Breakfast is served on the ground floor in a warm, inviting open space with an old-fashioned kitchen and solid wooden tables. There are deep comfy sofas for chatting or watching television and a cosy library nook. No kids under twelve. ❻ including breakfast.
Coral Sands Hotel ☏242/333-2350, ⊛www. coralsands.com. The largest, most modern hotel on the island, situated on the beach and offering some choice rooms with expansive ocean views and mahogany four-poster beds in the Lucaya block as well as less luxurious but still pleasant and comfortable rooms done up in wicker in the Caribe block, all with patios or balconies. Also tennis courts, swimming pool, bar and restaurant. ❽
The Landing ☏242/333-2707, ⊛www. harborislandlanding.com. An elegant historic inn overlooking the harbour. The guestrooms are spare and airy, exquisitely restored to evoke the colonial period with four-poster beds with gauzy canopies and crisp white linens, polished dark wood floors,

antique furnishings and dramatic original artwork. Some rooms have private balconies. The inn has one of the finest restaurants on the island, a cosy and popular bar, and a quiet upstairs sitting room for guests which opens onto the verandah. ❾
Ramora Bay Club ☏242/333-2325, or in North America ☏1-800/688-0425, ⊛www.romorabay. com. This small hotel has an unpretentious and cosmopolitan sophistication. Cottages housing thirty guest rooms and suites are staggered down a gentle green slope facing the harbour with a view of Eleuthera across the water. The decor is an eclectic and imaginative mix of Indian textiles, modern art and bold colour. Each room has a private patio and is furnished with fresh tropical flowers, CD player, TV, VCR and phone, with a selection of music, movies and books in the main house. Breakfast and lunch are served at wrought-iron café tables in a sunny alcove adjoining the terrace, and dinner is served by candlelight in an intimate dining area. There are tennis courts, a swimming pool with lounge chairs facing the harbour, an open-air bar and watersports arranged through Ocean Fox Dive shop. ❽
Tingum Village Hotel ☏242/333-2161. Several rustic, self-catering cottages and apartment units set in a quiet grove of coconut palms, with close beach access and the famous *Ma Ruby's* restaurant. ❺

Eating

In addition to the **restaurants** listed below, along the waterfront on Bay Street are several **kiosks** selling fresh conch salad, hamburgers and chips, with wooden benches situated with a view of the harbour.

Angela's Starfish Restaurant ☎ 242/333-2253. A simple, inexpensive local restaurant perched on top of Barracks Hill that receives rave reviews for its seafood dinners. Its unfortunate proximity to the dump (out of sight over the hill) can occasionally be a problem when the wind blows the wrong way and you want to sit outside, but the dining room is scrupulously clean. Note: "No bare backs and no profanity."

Arthur's Bakery Crown St, at Dunmore. Scrumptious cinnamon buns, rich chocolate brownies, fresh baked pies, pastries and breads fill the display cases. The aroma and soft jazz music wafts through the sunny café serving tasty breakfasts and lunches.

Browser Café Murray St ☎ 242/333-3069. A charming, moderately priced courtyard café attached to the *Briland Brush Strokes Art Gallery*, dishing up delicious coconut French toast, omelettes and fresh-squeezed orange juice as well as Bahamian platters of tuna and grits, boiled fish and souse for breakfast, with home-made soups and chowder, salads and sandwiches for lunch, and daily specials like grouper served with fried plantains.

Commander's Beach Bar at the *Coral Sands Hotel*. The patio bar has a sweeping view of the beach and a tasty lunch menu featuring a rock lobster salad sandwich, salads, burgers including a vegetarian burger, seafood nibbles and yummy frozen drinks.

Gusty's perched atop Barracks Hill on the west side of town. Serves seafood with live music a couple of nights a week and has a mystique imbued by occasional visitations from the patron saint of laid-back island living: Jimmy Buffett. Open for dinner from 6pm.

Hammerheads Bar and Grill at the Harbour Island Marina ☎ 242/333-3240. An attractive lunch and dinner spot serving snacks, salads, sandwiches, jerk chicken, strip steak, veggie quesadillas and drinks on a deck overlooking the marina.

Harbour Lounge on Bay St facing the government dock. With tables on a wide verandah, this popular people-watching spot has specialities including spicy tequila shrimp, a grouper sandwich and pumpkin soup. Closed Mon, dinner only Sun.

The Landing south of the government dock ☎ 242/333-2707. An elegant and romantic candlelit dining room with warm yellow walls, dark hardwood floors, white linen and silver. The menu features fresh pasta, lobster, steak and squid with aioli. Closed Wed.

Sports and outdoor activities

There are no organized activities on Eleuthera, although several of the resorts offer bicycles, kayaks and snorkelling equipment for guest use, as noted above. On Harbour Island, Ocean Fox Dive Shop, at the Harbour Island Marina (☎ 242/333-2323), offers **snorkelling** and **diving** excursions, **boat rentals** and **fishing** charters, as does Valentine's Dive Center (☎ 242/333-2080, ✺ www.valentinesdive.com). Robert Davis presents ninety-minute **historical tours** of Dunmore Town (US$100; ☎ 242/333-2337) for up to three people, along with **horseriding** on the beach (US$20 for a half-hour, $30 for a full hour).

1.7

The Exumas

With a name like a contented sigh, **THE EXUMAS** bear a fitting label. Over three hundred and sixty-five islands, cays and rock outcroppings of various shapes and sizes make up the Exuma chain, lying in a narrow band stretched over one hundred miles along the eastern edge of the Great Bahama Bank. The islands are mainly low-lying chunks of honeycombed limestone rimmed by powdery white sand and covered in dense vegetation. Viewed from the air, the shallow flats, reefs and sand bars surrounding the islands create whimsical swirls of turquoise and white, like a finger painting by a gifted child. At ground level the landscape holds beautiful vistas of sand and brush, pristine expanses of soft white beach fringed in places with towering coconut palms and dunes covered with emerald green vines and exotic blooms. Most of the island chain's population of 3000 live at the southern end of the archipelago, in the small, bustling capital of **George Town** and environs on **Great Exuma**, in neighbouring settlements on **Little Exuma**, or on **Staniel Cay**, **Little Farmer's Cay** and **Blackpoint** in the southern **Exuma Cays**. Those Exumians not engaged in fishing or farming cater to a small but growing tourist trade.

The Exumas are one of the best places in the Bahamas for those looking for an active outdoor vacation. Boasting crystal clear warm waters and an abundance of marine life, they are a choice destination for divers, snorkellers and sailors. The islands are flanked by prime bonefishing and deep-sea fishing grounds and several fishing guides operate throughout the islands. Shallow protected waters and dozens of deserted sandy coves make the chain ideal for sea kayaking, and several outfitters run expeditions through the cays. The remote **Exuma Land and Sea Park** in the northern part of the chain is an area of extraordinary beauty, splendid in its isolation and desolation. If all that sounds like too much work, there is no shortage of beautiful, empty beaches to lounge on and gaze out at the blue-green sea.

Arrival, information and getting around

Most visitors will arrive in the Exumas at George Town. **George Town International Airport** is located eight miles north of town on Great Exuma, and receives two Bahamasair **flights** daily from Nassau. American Eagle and Lynx Air fly to and from George Town daily from Miami and Ft Lauderdale, respectively.

Ferries and **mail boats** from Nassau arrive at the government dock in the centre of George Town, within walking distance of most hotels, restaurants and services. Bahamas Fast Ferries (☎242/323-2166, ⓦwww.bahamasferries.com) departs Nassau for the overnight trip to George Town on Mondays and Wednesdays, returning on Tuesdays and Thursdays. The well-maintained *Grand Master* mail boat ($40 one-way; ☎242/393-1064) departs Nassau on Tuesdays at 2pm, arriving in George Town early Wednesday morning, and depending on tides and cargo, returns Wednesday night or Thursday morning, arriving in Nassau twelve hours later.

Note that if your primary interest is visiting the **Exuma Land and Sea Park**, you would be better off landing at **Staniel Cay**, just outside the parks' southern boundary. The *Captain C* **mailboat** calls at Staniel Cay, Blackpoint, Farmer's Cay and the Ragged Islands, departing Nassau on Tuesdays for the twelve-hour trip ($70 one-way; ☎242/393-1064). Alternatively, Flamingo Air (☎242/377-0354; $70 one-way) flies from Nassau to Staniel Cay daily except Saturdays. If your plan is to explore all of the Exumas and you don't own your own sailboat, it is difficult – though not impossible – to get to Staniel Cay from George Town. There are no commercial flights connecting the two, and it requires a combination of cars and boats or an airplane charter.

Located in the centre of George Town above Thompson's Car Rental, the **Bahamas Ministry of Tourism** provides information (Mon–Fri 9am–5pm; ☎242/336-2440, ☎242/336-2431) and a selection of **maps** and brochures.

There are no public buses on the Exumas and no shuttle services from the airport, but **taxis** meet every flight and any hotel will call one for you. The eight-mile trip to George Town costs around US$25 for two passengers. For reliable and courteous service, call Leslie Dames (☎242/357-0015). **Hitchhiking** is easy on the Exumas, and many residents rely on it for travelling and commuting to work. Great and Little Exuma are easily explored by **rental car**. Three companies with reasonable vehicles are Airport Rent-a-Car (☎242/345-0090 or 358-8049), Thompson's Rentals, in the centre of George Town (☎242/336-2442), and Uptown Rent-A-Car across the street (☎242/336-2822). All charge around $70 a day, plus a $200 deposit.

Birdsong and picturesque rest stops make travelling by **motor scooter** or **bicycle** a fun way to get around, especially heading south from George Town. You can rent well-maintained 21-speed bikes at Starfish Exuma Adventure Center (☎242/336 3033) for $15 half-day and $100 per week. The Exuma Dive Centre (☎242/336-2390) and Prestige Cycle Rentals (☎242/345-4250), both opposite Regatta Park in the centre of town, rent motor scooters for $35 a day or $175 per week. You can also rent a **motor boat**, **sailboat** or **kayak** to explore the coastline and the numerous cays offshore. Exuma Dive Centre (☎242/336-2390) has 17ft boats for $80 a day or $400 per week, while Minns Water Sports (☎242/336-2604) offers similar package deals, with discounts for rentals of three days or more.

Great Exuma and Little Exuma

Sitting head to toe at the southern end of the Exuma chain and joined by a narrow bridge, **GREAT EXUMA** and **LITTLE EXUMA** are the largest and most settled islands in the archipelago. The capital **George Town** is a bustling, slightly ramshackle little hub in the middle of 35-mile long Great Exuma. Here you will find a compact collection of pastel-coloured cement block buildings, plenty of small hotels, restaurants and nightly entertainment drawing the yachting and diving crowd. The town's most appealing sights lie offshore, however, in the azure and emerald depths of **Elizabeth Harbour** and the offshore cays. These include **Stocking Island**, with its long windswept beach (reached by ferry from the *Peace and Plenty Hotel*), and **Crab Cay**, site of the ruins of a Loyalist plantation. In late April, usually sleepy George Town springs into party mode for the **Out Island Regatta**, which draws crews from across the Bahamas to race their sloops and spectators from around the world. North and south of George Town are several modest settlements, including **Rolle Town** and **Williams Town** at the tip of six-mile-long Little Exuma, which make a pleasant day-trip by car or bicycle.

Accommodation

Accommodations on Great and Little Exuma range from a five-star resort to rustic cottage rentals. If you're planning to visit during the Out Island Regatta in late April, you must book months in advance. Most accommodation is found in George Town and environs, with a few other nice choices north and south of town.

George Town

Bahamas Houseboats office near the mailboat dock ☎242/336-BOAT, ☎www .bahamashouseboats.com. Economical, 35ft floating apartments with large windows, a/c, fully equipped galleys, CD players, outdoor barbecues and water slides on the top deck. Each comes with a motorized dinghy to get to shore. Daily rates from US$300 (three-day minimum) or US$1750 per week. ⑨

Club Peace and Plenty in the centre of the village ⓣ242/336-2551 or in the US ⓣ1-800/525-2210, ⓦwww.peaceandplenty.com. Comfortable rooms with wicker furniture, satellite TVs and balconies overlooking the pool or Elizabeth Harbour. ⑥

Minns Cottages half a mile from the centre, on the Queen's Highway ⓣ242/336-2033, ⓕ242/336-2645. Quiet cottages in a shady grove with screened-in porches, nice ocean views, tiled floors, fully equipped kitchens and satellite TV. One- and two-bedroom cottages ⑤

George Town outskirts

Coconut Cove Inn Queen's Highway ⓣ242/336-2659, ⓕ242/336-2658. A mile and a half north of town, a small beachfront hotel with twelve modern rooms featuring private balconies, most with ocean views. Also restaurant, palm-shaded terrace, beach bar and shuttle buses to and from George Town. ⑥

Coral Gardens Bed and Breakfast Hooper's Bay five miles north of George Town ⓣ242/336-2880, ⓦwww.bahamasbliss.com. A pleasant B&B run by a friendly and knowledgeable English couple, perched on a breezy hilltop with views of both coasts. Three rooms with refrigerators and shared baths in the main house, a five-minute walk to a secluded beach, and two beachfront apartments sleeping two and four. A rental car is available for US$40 per day. ③

Hotel Higgins Landing Stocking Island ⓣ242/336-2460, ⓦwww.higginslanding.com. Exquisite secluded resort with five timber guest cottages furnished with antiques, each with a private ocean view. ⑦

Peace and Plenty Beach Inn Queen's Highway ⓣ242/336-2250 or in the US ⓣ1-800/525-2210, ⓦwww.peaceandplenty.com. Quiet retreat a mile and half north of town, featuring sixteen well-appointed rooms with private balconies and ocean views, as well as beach access, pool, restaurant, outdoor bar and shuttle to and from George Town. ⑥

South of George Town

Club Peace and Plenty Bonefish Lodge Queen's Highway at Hartswell ⓣ242/345-5555 or in the US ⓣ1-800/525-2210, ⓦwww.ppbonefishlodge.com. Handsome timber and stone lodge with wraparound verandah overlooking Little Exuma, catering to serious fishers. Featuring eight rooms with tile floors, ceiling fans, deep balconies and ocean views, as well as a restaurant and bar. Fishing packages include lodging, meals, bonefishing guides and use of kayaks, bicycles and snorkelling equipment. Three nights and two days US$998 per person, seven nights and six days $2562. ⑨

La Shanté Beach Club Forbes Hill, Little Exuma ⓣ242/345-4136. Spectacular beachside setting in a secluded cove, with three double rooms and one one-bedroom apartment, offering basic accommodation without ocean views. Restaurant serves lunch and dinner on a terrace overlooking the beach. Doubles ④, one-bedroom apartment ⑥

Master Harbour Villas ⓣ242/345-5076 or 242/357-0636, ⓦwww.exumabahamas.com/masterharbour. Three miles south of George Town in a private grove of coconut palms, three white clapboard cottages set on a rocky shore overlooking Crab and Redshank cays, with high ceilings, overhead fans and motorboat rental for guests. One-bedroom villa ⑥, two-bedroom ⑧ and four-bedroom ⑨.

North of George Town

Four Seasons Resort at Emerald Bay ⓣ242/336-6800 or 1-800/819-5053, ⓦwww.fourseasons.com/greatexuma. A huge new upscale resort on a secluded beach fifteen miles north of George Town, with an eighteen-hole golf course designed by Greg Norman, two restaurants offering formal and informal dining, and featuring local seafood and Italian cuisine, a full service spa, gym and three swimming pools set on lushly landscaped grounds. ⑨

Eating and drinking

George Town offers several pleasant **restaurants** to choose from, ranging from open-air pool **bars** to smart casual gourmet fare. South of George Town, *La Shanté Beach Club*, on the beach in Forbes Hill, makes a good spot for lunch, while in Williams Town, *Mom's Bakery*, *The Arawak Club* and *Santana's Grill* all serve tasty snacks and simple seafood meals. North of George Town, *Big D's Conch Spot*, on the beach at Steventon, is a local favourite, and the basic but friendly *Kermit's Hilltop Tavern* in Rolle Town and *The Fisherman's Inn* in Barreterre can fix you up if you are up that way.

The Bistro at February Point ⓣ242/336-2661. A mile south of George Town, on a terrace at the edge of a white sandy beach, an alfresco restaurant with delicious seafood and meat dishes for lunch and dinner, as well as Wednesday night pizza. Free transfers to and from George Town for supper. The menu ranges from moderate to expensive.

The Chat and Chill An open-air beach bar at Volleyball Beach on Stocking Island. A cheap and breezy place for burgers, seafood, cool drinks and a swim. Open daily 11am–7pm. Note that you can't reach here by the ferry; you must take a water taxi or your own boat.

Cheater's Restaurant and Bar ☏242/336-2535. Inexpensive no-frills roadhouse two miles south of George Town on the Queen's Highway, serving tasty home-style Bahamian food. Open for lunch and supper Mon–Fri 10am–11pm and Sat 8am–11pm for breakfast as well. Tuesday night fish fry with rake 'n' scrape music.

Club Peace and Plenty Restaurant ☏242/336-2551. Located off the hotel lobby and set in a glassed-in alcove with a nice view of Stocking Island, the upscale menu features fish, lobster and steak. Open for breakfast, lunch and dinner.

Coconut Cove Inn ☏242/336-2659. One of the best restaurants in the Exumas, with an extensive moderately priced menu, cosy atmosphere and attentive service. Offers delicious pizza, pasta and steak and seafood platters. The chef will prepare your day's catch, and the beachside *Sand Bar* serves sandwiches and snacks Fri 3–9pm. Breakfast daily 7.30–9.30am, dinner Tues–Sun 6–9pm; reservations recommended by 4pm.

Eddie's Edgewater Club ☏242/336-2050. Popular, inexpensive local spot overlooking Victoria Pond and offering native dishes, pool tables and live music on Mon & Sat.

Hamburger Beach Snack Bar at *Peace and Plenty* beach shack on Stocking Island. An array of inexpensive hotdogs, burgers, soft drinks, beer and ice cream. Daily 11am–3pm.

Sam's Place ☏242/336-2579. Upstairs in a grey timber building overlooking the marina, the best place in George Town for breakfast, specializing in Bahamian boiled breakfasts and American-style bacon and eggs and pancakes. Also good lunchtime seafood, sandwiches and burgers, great oceanside views and quick and friendly service.

Two Turtles Inn ☏242/336-2545. An outdoor patio bar overlooking the wharf, and a great place for lunchtime sandwiches, salads, burgers and conch dishes. Friday nights, there is a barbecue with live entertainment.

Outdoor activities

Several outfitters based in George Town offer an array of **outdoor activities**. Starfish Exuma Adventure Center (☏242/336-3033 or in North America ☏1-877/398-6222, ⊛www.kayakbahamas.com) offers excellent guided **history** and **eco-tours** of Elizabeth Harbour, Crab Cay and Stocking Island by boat, along with **cycling trips** on quiet island byways and paddling excursions through the cays off George Town. Day-trips include beach picnics and snorkelling, and full-moon, sunset and sunrise **paddling excursions** are also available, as well as two- to six-day kayaking and camping trips ($1395 for a week) and week-long **sailing excursions** through the Exuma Land and Sea Park ($1795). Full-day kayaking or nature tours with some hiking and a boat excursion cost $95; a half-day outing or three-hour full-moon paddle is $60–$70. Kayaks can be rented from Starfish for $30/$45/$225 for an hour/day/week; bicycles for $15/$30/$125 including a helmet and a map of the islands.

Sea kayaking in the Exumas

One of the best ways of exploring the Exumas is by **sea kayak**, and several outfitters offering guided expeditions through the cays. Starfish The Exuma Activity Center (see above) rents kayaking equipment and offers excellent paddling **day-trips**. North Carolina Outward Bound, (☏ 828/299-3366, ⊛www.ncobs.org), offers nine- and twelve-day **sea kayaking courses** in the southern cays (several times through the year, between November and June, $2495 and $3295). Ecosummer Expeditions (☏1-800/465-8884 in Canada and the U.S. or ☏ 250/674-0102, ⊛www.ecosummer.com) offers a nine-day **guided expedition** through the Exuma Land and Sea Park in March, ($1795, excluding air fare to Nassau or George Town, respectively.) Further north in the Exumas, Ibis Tours ☏914/738-5334 or 1-800/525-9411 in the US, ⓔinfo@ibistours.com) runs eight-day guided trips through the Exuma Land and Sea Park putting in at Staniel Cay, from March to May ($1795 excluding air fare).

The Exumas are one of the best places in the world to **snorkel** and **dive**. Exuma Scuba Adventures (☎242/336-2893 or 357-2259, ⓦwww.exumascuba.com) operates out of *Club Peace and Plenty*, while the Exuma Dive Center (☎242/336-2390, ⓔexumadive@bahamasvg.com) offers snorkelling and diving excursions and rents watersports equipment.

The islands also offer superb **deep-sea fishing** and **bonefishing** waters, and a number of good fishing guides are based in George Town and the surrounding area: Cely's Fly Fishing (☎242/345-2341), Cooper's Charter Service (☎242/336-2711), Fish Rowe Charters (☎242/345-0074) and Abby MacKenzie (☎242/345-2312).

The Exuma Cays

Off the northern tip of Great Exuma, the **Exuma Cays** is a forty-mile-long chain of a couple of hundred mainly uninhabited islands stretched along a northwest trajectory ending forty miles east of Nassau. These cays, of various shapes and sizes, share a similar topography of white sand, honeycombed black coral rock and hardy vegetation, surrounded by a rich marine environment.

The Southern Cays

The only permanent settlements in the cays are at the southern end of the chain, on sleepy **Little Farmer's Cay**; on Great Guana Cay in the scruffy village of **Blackpoint**; and on tidy, green and nicely painted **Staniel Cay**. Staniel Cay has a noticeably prosperous air, owing largely to its popularity with yacht cruisers and expatriate residents. Staniel Cay is also the gateway to the **Exuma Land and Sea Park**, with an airstrip, two marinas, volunteer-run clinic, and several restaurants and shops.

Arrival and getting around

Fishing expeditions and **day-trips** from Great Exuma to the southern cays can be arranged through Captain Martin (☎242/358-4057) or Reverend A.A. MacKenzie (☎242/355-5024) in Barreterre on Great Exuma. A good destination is **Leaf Cay**, home to a colony of giant iguanas. The *Captain C* **mailboat** ($120 round-trip) serves the communities of the southern Exuma Cays – including Staniel Cay – from Nassau. It does not call at George Town and the schedule varies somewhat from week to week, so call ahead to the dockmaster at Potter's Cay (☎242/393 1064). Flamingo Air (☎242/377-0354) flies to Staniel Cay every day except Saturday from Nassau.

Accommodation

Happy People Marina ☎242/355-2008, ⓕ242/355-2025. Adequate motel-style rooms on the Staniel Cay waterfront and a nice two-bedroom apartment. ❹ and ❽ respectively.
Sampson Cay Club and Marina ☎242/355-2034, ⓦwww.sampsoncayclub.com. Just north of Staniel Cay on a small cay bordering the Exuma Land and Sea Park, a newly renovated operation with five cottages, a grocery store, restaurant and bar. Rent a 13ft Boston Whaler powerboat to explore the park for US$80 per day. Call for cottage rental rates.
Staniel Cay Yacht Club and Marina ☎242/355-2024, ⓦwww.stanielcay.com. Five cute wooden cottages with coffeemakers, small refrigerators and verandahs overlooking the water, with cottages sleeping four to seven people also available. ❺

Eating

Club Thunderball on the north side of Staniel Cay overlooking Thunderball Grotto. An eatery serving native dishes for lunch and dinner and offering a pool table and weekend dancing. Closed Mon.
Happy People Restaurant and Bar ☎242/355-2008. Next to the hotel and marina, a local hangout open for breakfast, lunch and dinner, serving Bahamian dishes, sandwiches and burgers. Call in advance.

Staniel Cay Yacht Club Restaurant and Bar
℡242/355-2024. Near the dock, a colourful and relaxed eatery with a nautical theme, offering

American and Bahamian food and home-made desserts. Reserve by 5pm for dinner that night.

The Exuma Land and Sea Park

Beginning five miles north of Staniel Cay in the middle of the chain, the **Exuma Land and Sea Park** encompasses fifteen sizeable cays and many smaller outcroppings over 176 square miles – 22 miles long and eight miles wide. Bound on the east by the deep waters of Exuma Sound, and on the west by the shallow reefs and sandbars of Great Bahama Bank, the park was established in 1958 as a marine conservation area by the **Bahamian National Trust**, a nonprofit agency devoted to the preservation of the country's natural environment.

There are no commercial developments, resorts or restaurants within the park boundaries, and the major events are spectacular sunrises and sunsets. The **park headquarters** is at the north end of **Warderick Wells Cay**, twenty miles north of Staniel Cay in the middle of the park (Mon–Sat 9am–noon & 3–5pm, Sun 9am–1pm; ℡242/359-1821, ℅exumapark@aol.com). Seven miles of well-marked **hiking** trails crisscross Warderick Wells Cay, leading through groves of thatch palm and silver button-wood, past limestone sink holes and along a broad tidal creek-bed to lookout points and Loyalist plantation ruins. A dozen white **beaches** dot the secluded palm-fringed coves on the leeward side of the island. The other cays in the park offer similar delights.

Practicalities

Most visitors to the Exuma Land and Sea Park arrive on their own **sailboats** or with organized **kayaking** or **diving** expeditions. There are 22 moorings at the north anchorage of Warderick Wells by the park headquarters, and four more at the south anchorage. The mooring fee is $15 a night. The park asks that you call them the morning before you intend to arrive so they can assign you a mooring. There are no hotels or resorts within the park boundaries, but there are dozens of soft sandy beaches on which you can pitch your tent. **Camping** fees are $5 a night. The Bahamas National Trust functions entirely on private donations and relies on camp-ers to drop their payment at the park headquarters or mail it in after they leave.

The park is most easily reached from Staniel Cay, where you will have to **rent** or **charter** a boat to take you into the park. The *Staniel Cay Yacht Club* (see "Accommodation", opposite) rents thirteen- and seventeen-foot Whalers for $85 and $235 per day respectively including fuel. You might also ask on the dock for a local fisherman who could take you into the park. Alternatively, Captain Bill Hirsch (℡305/944-3033, ℅www.myknottymind.com) will run you up to Warderick Wells (a forty-minute boat ride) for $100 if he's in the area; he also offers **guided tours** of the park aboard his yacht *M/Y Knotty Mind* for $450 per day for up to four people, all-inclusive. From Nassau, Captain Paul Harding of Diving Safaris Ltd (℡242/393-2522 or 242/393-1179) can fly you directly to Warderick Wells or any other place in the park in his **floatplane**. The **sailboat** *Cat Ppalu* (toll-free in the US ℡1-800/327-9600 or 305/888-1226, ℅www.blackbeard-cruises/c-adven.html) makes **guided diving trips** through the park several times a year from Nassau, with plenty of time made for exploring the cays topside ($1395 per person with room for twelve).

The Northern Exumas

Although the northern boundary of the Land and Sea Park lies at the Wax Cay Cut, the Exuma chain continues northwards for another ten miles. The **Northern Exumas**, however, are most easily reached from Nassau, forty miles to the west. Three companies offer **day-trips** to the cays, departing from the dock on Paradise Island. Island World Adventures (℡242/394-8960) makes a daily excursion to Saddleback

Cay in a 45ft speedboat, Out Island Voyages (☎242/394-0951 or 1-800/241-4591) offers sailboat journeys out to the cays and Powerboat Adventures (☎242/327-5385, ⊛www.powerboatadventures.com) leads a full-day outing to the Sail Rocks and Allan's Cay, including snorkelling, a barbecue lunch on the beach and a visit with the islands' resident giant iguanas.

1.8

Cat Island and San Salvador

A world away from the cruise ship crowds, casinos and duty-free shops of Nassau and Freeport, **CAT ISLAND** and **SAN SALVADOR** offer peace and a taste of Bahamian life before the advent of mass tourism. With economies traditionally based on farming and fishing, the islands have experienced economic difficulties in recent years and many of their young people leave for service jobs in New Providence and Grand Bahama. Nevertheless, both islands have considerable quiet charms to attract visitors, including long splendid stretches of powdery white and blush-coloured beaches, top-notch snorkelling and diving, and a few exquisite beach lodges far from the bustle of the outside world.

Cat Island

Lying 130 miles southeast of Nassau, small, boot-shaped **CAT ISLAND** is a relaxed and unspoiled place with sparkling beaches, small settlements and a few sizeable hills. The **southern end** of the island presents great opportunities for diving, with steep cliffs and offshore reefs, while the entire **east coast**, accessible only by dirt roads, offers a continuous strand of idyllic seaside, with hidden coves and rugged shores. The **west coast**, with its mud creeks and estuaries, is great for bonefishing. The major settlements are **Arthur's Town** in the north, the pre-Hollywood home of Sidney Poitier, and **New Bight** in the south, a sprawling town that runs for two miles along the road. Cat Island is served by a single good paved road, the **Queen's Highway**, which runs the length of the 48-mile island.

There are several choice beaches on the island. **Fernandez Bay**, just north of New Bight, is an exquisite curve of white sand and turquoise sea in a sheltered cove. The Atlantic beaches are wilder, harder to reach and home to big waves and high winds – a tempting challenge for windsurfers and swimmers. At the southern end of the island, **Greenwood Beach** is eight miles of blush-coloured sand and crashing surf. Towering over the island terrain near New Bight, **Mount Alvernia** stands 206ft above sea level – the highest point in the Bahamas – and offers a sweeping view of the island's rolling terrain and coastline.

Hiking and **birdwatching** are both excellent at the southern end of the island, where ponds and lakes abound. The island's major celebrations include the annual

Cat Island Regatta in early August, attracting hundreds of yachters, and the Cat Island Music Festival in early June.

Arrival and information

Bahamasair ($82 one-way; ☎242/377-5505, ⊛www.bahamasair.com) flies to Cat Island from Nassau several times a week, while Cat Island Air ($75 one-way; ☎242/377-3318) has daily flights between Nassau and New Bight. Continental ($333 round-trip; ☎1-800/231-0856), Air Sunshine (☎954/434-8900) and Lynx Air ($350 round-trip; ☎954/772-9808, ⊛www.lynxair.com) all fly to New Bight from Fort Lauderdale. At the south end of the island, *Hawk's Nest Resort* (☎242/342-7050 or 1-800/688-4752) has a private airstrip and a **marina**.

There are no formal **information** services on either Cat Island or San Salvador, but material is available through Nassau's Ministry of Tourism (☎1-800/224-2627, ⊛www.bahamas.com), or the Out Island Tourist Board (☎305/931-6612 or 1-800/688-4752, ⊛www.bahama-out-islands.com).

Accommodation

Accommodation on Cat Island is in a clutch of small and secluded resorts, each with their own individual charms. There are a few bare-bones budget options, including the *Bridge Inn* (☎242/342-3013; ❷), a decent motel-style place, though it's devoid of charm.

Fernandez Bay Village New Bight ☎242/342-3043 or 1-800/940-1905, ⊛www.fernandezbayvillage .com. On an exquisite secluded curve of white sand backed by casaurinas and palm trees, this casually elegant beach lodge is one of the gems of the Bahamas. Eight pleasingly and thoughtfully appointed stone and timber guestrooms and cottages are tucked in along the shore, each with a private terrace, air conditioning, ceiling fans and outdoor shower rooms so you can bathe by starlight and fall asleep to the sound of the waves. Wonderful buffet meals are served in the open, airy main lodge and on the terrace with a sunset view, fresh flowers and candlelight. There are sea kayaks and snorkel gear for guest use, as well as a collection of board games, well-stocked bookshelves, a nice gift shop, a thatch-roofed honour bar, hammocks and lounge chairs shaded by umbrellas. A local musician entertains guests a few nights a week, and there is a nightly bonfire on the beach. ❽

Greenwood Beach Resort 3.5 miles north of Port Howe, then 2 miles east on a coral road ☎242/342-3053 or 1-800/688-4752, ⊛www. greenwoodbeachresort.com. In an isolated spot on the Atlantic coast, this relaxed family-run resort is popular with divers, offering twenty cheerful, simple rooms a few steps from a gorgeous eight-mile strand of blush-coloured sand with crashing surf. There is a small swimming pool and hot tub, a colourful, airy restaurant and bar in the main lodge where guests eat together at a long table, a dive shop offering dives and certification courses ($50 for a one-tank dive, $350 for PADI open-water certification) and a meal plan available for $48 a day for three meals. ❹

Hawk's Nest Resort and Marina Devil's Point ☎242/342-7050 or 1-800/688-4752, ⊛www. hawks-nest.com. Set on four hundred acres of beachfront at the isolated southeast tip of the island, this laid-back small hotel caters to fishers, boaters and private pilots, with ten nicely decorated oceanview rooms done up in wicker and ceramic tile, situated about 100 yards from the water. There is also a large house for rent with two bedrooms. Meals are served in a small, simple dining room with a view of the pool, a few hundred yards from the beach (make reservations for dinner by 2pm). There is a 28-slip marina, an airstrip and three dive instructors on staff. ❼

Sammy T's Resort Bennett's Harbour ☎242/354-6009 or 242/427-5897, ⊛www. sammytbahamas.com. This small seaside resort earns rave reviews from visitors, with a handful of tastefully appointed natural wood and stone cabins just steps from a long, lovely strand of white-sand beach. Each cabin is equipped with a kitchen, a/c, DVD player and movies, and a bedroom and sitting room. There is a game room, fitness centre, bar and restaurant in the main house, serving imaginatively prepared local seafood and other dishes. ❼

Eating and drinking

Most resorts offer **dining** in casually elegant surroundings (outside guests call ahead for reservations). Dinner on the terrace overlooking the beach at *Fernandez Bay Village* resort (℡242/342-3043, reservations required) is a memorable experience, with fine food, candlelight and bonfire on the beach. Most of the major settlements also have a few road-side **eateries** and a **bar** where you can sample local fare. In New Bight, the *Blue Bird Restaurant and Bar* is recommended for tasty fried chicken, seafood and Bahamian delicacies like pig's feet and sheep's tongue souse, and occasional rake 'n' scrape music and dancing, while in the far north at Smith's Bay, *Hazel's Seaside Bar* is a relaxed spot for a quiet drink at sunset.

San Salvador

Two hundred miles east of Nassau, small **SAN SALVADOR** is the easternmost island in the Bahamas. Only twelve miles long and five wide, this low-lying island features saline lakes and brine ponds surrounded by palmetto brush, a beautiful shore of uninterrupted white sands and a **western reef** that offers some of the best diving and snorkelling in the country. Despite this, its renown for aquatic sports is a relatively recent phenomenon. Although it was the original place where Columbus first encountered the New World, San Salvador remained a backwater until diver Bill McGehee promoted the beauty and diversity of its western reef in the 1970s. Later, *Club Med* added its own endorsement, building a resort north of **Cockburn Town** (pronounced "Coburn") in 1992. Though it's the main settlement on the island there's little to keep you in Cockburn, other than a few accommodation options.

Typical **island tours** take in the lovely **East Beach**, **Dixon Hill Lighthouse**, and the **Bahamian Field Station** (for prime birdwatching and hiking), each taking about four hours and available through the two major resorts (see below). Likewise, either resort can arrange **sport fishing** and **underwater photography** – which is quickly becoming something of a cottage industry in San Salvador.

Practicalities

Bahamasair offers twice-weekly **flights** from Miami and Nassau to Cockburn Town, while Florida-based Air Sunshine flies to Cockburn Town out of Fort Lauderdale. *Riding Rock Inn* provides charter air service for its guests.

There are only a few choices for **accommodation** on San Salvador, most clustered around Cockburn Town. *Riding Rock Inn*, southwest of the airport (℡242/331-2641 or 1-800/272-1492; ❹), offers diving packages, as well as cottages and furnished rooms with patios. Cockburn Town has a number of grocery stores, **restaurants** and **bars**, though most visitors predictably dine at their hotel.

1.9

Long Island and the Southern Bahamas

South of Cat Island, **Long Island** is pretty, peaceful and virtually untouched by tourism. Its roughly 3200 residents live in a dozen or so small fishing settlements dotted along its seventy-mile-long coastline. For visitors, Long Island has the double virtue of unspoiled natural beauty and a handful of lovely small resorts offering appealing accommodation, fine dining and a full range of activities, including excellent **diving** and **snorkelling**. Long Island also boasts superb **fishing** year round, and there are numerous beautiful beaches to explore.

Lastly, the most remote islands of the Bahamian archipelago, the Southern Bahamas lie about 250 miles southeast of Nassau. Consisting of Long Island, Crooked and Acklins islands, Great Inagua and Mayaguana, the south islands are comparatively free of tourist development and offer a taste of the slowly vanishing traditional Out Island life.

Long Island

Most locals on **LONG ISLAND** earn their living from the sea, as they have for generations. The island has a long tradition of boat-building, and the **Long Island Sailing Regatta**, held at **Salt Pond** in mid-May for the past 35 years, is one of the premier social events in the Out Islands. The rest of the year, life in the tidy little villages is pretty quiet, with many of the young people off seeking their fortunes in Nassau or elsewhere. Long Islanders are a devout lot and on Sunday mornings, the numerous **picturesque whitewashed churches** up and down the island fling open their doors and the air is filled with hymns and birdsong.

For sunseekers, at the north end of the island there's a pristine expanse of powdery white sand and turquoise water that stretches for three miles along **Cape Santa Maria**. There's also a soft golden curve of sand facing **Guana Cay** in the middle of the island, where there is good snorkelling from shore, and secluded **Lowes Beach**, stretching for several miles along the Atlantic side to the south. Long Island's rolling and varied landscape of steep rocky cliffs, sheltered white-sand coves, green velvety pastures specked with grazing goats and quaint seaside villages such as **Seymours**, **Simms**, **Millers** and **Clarence Town**, with its photogenic historic churches, make for pleasant sightseeing by car or bicycle.

At **Hamilton's Cave** near the village of **Cartwrights** are several underground chambers filled with colourful stalactites, stalagmites and pictographs; the site of a rich find of Lucayan artifacts in recent years. Another worthwhile expedition by car or bicycle is to the **Columbus Monument**, which tops a rocky bluff at the northern tip of the island, with a fantastic panoramic view of sapphire and jade bonefish flats and the white-sand-rimmed clots of land that Columbus surveyed on his two-week tour through the Bahamas in 1492.

Arrival and getting around

There are two **airports** on Long Island, one at Deadman's Cay in the centre of the island and the other at Stella Maris at its northern end. Bahamasair (☎242/352-8341) operates one flight a day from Nassau to Long Island, stopping first at Stella Maris and then Deadman's Cay before heading back to Nassau. If you are staying at the *Stella Maris Resort* (☎242/338-2050), their plane flies several times a week to George Town on Great Exuma and to Nassau ($102 one-way, five-seat charter $690).

Two government **mailboats** serve Long Island. The *Mia Dean* departs Potter's Cay in Nassau on Tuesday at noon, reaching Clarence Town at the southern end of Long Island twelve hours later ($45 one-way). The *Sharice M* departs Nassau Mondays at 5pm, calling at Deadman's Cay, Salt Pond, Simms and Seymours in north Long Island after a fifteen-hour crossing (also $45 one-way). Call the dockmaster's office on Potter's Cay for information (☎242/393 1064).

There are two full-service **marinas** on the island. The Stella Maris Marina (☎242/338 2055), with fifteen boat slips, is located near the *Stella Maris Resort* at the north end of the island, while the Flying Fish Marina, in Clarence Town (☎242/337-3430, ✉flyfishmarina@batelnet.bs), also has fifteen slips and one nicely appointed double guest room (❹).

There is **no public bus service** on Long Island. Both airports are a couple of miles from the nearest hotel or guesthouse, but **taxis** meet every flight. If you plan to do some exploring on your own, you will need to **rent a car** or **motor scooter**, which can be arranged through your hotel. At the northern end of Long Island, Alfred Knowles (☎242/338-5009) and Joe Williams (☎242/338-5002) in Glinton's both rent cars for $65 a day.

With varied scenery and little traffic, Long Island is a wonderful destination for **cyclists**. The two biggest resorts on the island – *Cape Santa Maria Beach Resort* and *Stella Maris Resort* – have serviceable touring bikes for guest use, but if you are planning to put in a lot of miles, bring your own bike. It is reasonably safe to **hitch-hike**, but not many people do it.

Accommodation

Cape Santa Maria Beach Resort in North America ☎1-800/663-7090 or at resort ☎242/338-5273, ☻www.capesantamaria.com. A small cottage resort situated on a pristine strand of powdery white beach on a flat, sandy peninsula at the northern tip of Long Island. Twenty double rooms in ten beachfront cottages are decked out with colourful tropical fabrics, clay tile floors and rattan furniture, each with a screened-in porch. There is an attractive dining room and bar and a fitness centre, and the resort offers a full range of water sports as well as fishing trips. Meal plans and all-inclusive packages available. Closed Sept & Oct. ❾

Chez Pierre no phone, ✉anne@chezpierrebahamas.com, ☻www.chezpierrebahamas.com. Located on a serene stretch of beach at Miller's Bay (halfway between Deadman's Cay and Stella Maris), *Chez Pierre* has earned rave reviews from guests for the beautiful simplicity of its six elevated timber cottages and for the gourmet cuisine served in the casually elegant lodge. There are kayaks and snorkel gear for guest use, and fishing, car rental and other activities can be arranged. ❻ including breakfast and dinner.

Greenwich Creek Lodge Cartwright's ☎242/337-6278, ☻www.greenwichcreek.com. Situated on the mangrove-edged shore and catering to serious bonefishers, this well-maintained two-storey timber lodge with wraparound verandahs houses eight nicely furnished doubles (containing two beds) and four king rooms, some with TV. There is a small dipping pool and a common room where meals are served. Based on double occupancy, a week of bonefishing including accommodation, meals and a guide costs $2100. They also offer deep-sea and reef fishing charters. ❼ including breakfast.

Lochobar Beach Lodge ☎242/327-8323 or 337-3123 or c/o Mrs. Judy Knowles at *Earlie's Tavern* (☎242/337-1628) in Mangrove Bush, ☻www.the-bahamian.com/lochobarbeach/. A secluded idyll for those who really want to get away from it all, on an exquisite curve of white-sand beach at Lochobar Bay south of Clarence Town. The two-storey timber and stucco lodge houses two beautifully rustic studio apartments and a one-bedroom apartment sleeping up to five, with French doors that open onto a balcony or patio steps from the beach. ❻ **Stella Maris Resort** in North America ☎1-800/426-0466 or at resort ☎242/338-2050, ⊛www.stellamarisresort.com. Sitting atop a green hill with views of both coasts, this is a friendly, unpretentious resort with two dozen bright, comfortable guestrooms housed in a couple of one- and two-storey buildings tucked into a gentle slope, each with a private verandah. There are also several cottages scattered along the rocky oceanfront, three swimming pools, a Jacuzzi, tennis courts and a tennis pro on staff. The main lodge is a cosy place to gather in the evening, with a pleasant bar, a lounge with satellite TV, books and games and an airy appealing dining room. A scenic oceanfront drive leads to several secluded beaches within walking distance, and there is free transportation to other nearby beaches. Snorkelling, diving and fishing trips are offered daily. Meal plans and all-inclusive packages available. ❻

Eating and drinking

Cape Santa Maria Resort North Long Island ☎242/338 5273. Has a beautifully atmospheric dining room in a glass-walled two-storey timber beach-house facing the white sand at Cape Santa Maria. The menu features gourmet seafood dishes and imaginative American cuisine. Reservations required.

Harbour Restaurant Clarence Town ☎242/337-3247. A clean and pleasant lunch room with windows overlooking the harbour, near the government dock. The menu is tasty versions of your basic seafood, deep-fried food and sandwiches.

Kooter's Mangrove Bush ☎242/337-0340. A pleasant place for a pit stop, with shaded picnic tables on a wraparound wooden verandah directly on the water. Serving burgers, sandwiches, conch, salads, ice cream and soft drinks. On Sun, open for ice cream only.

Max Conch Bar and Grill Deadman's Cay ☎242/337-0056. A colourful local favourite serving conch cracked, frittered and marinated, as well as fried chicken, burgers and fries at an outdoor kiosk with bar stools and tables.

Oasis Bakery and Restaurant one mile north of Clarence Town on the Queen's Highway ☎242/337-3003. A lovely spot for breakfast or lunch with tables set on a deep wooden verandah overlooking a small pond. Fresh-baked bread, pastries and cookies to eat in or take home, plus inexpensive sandwiches, pizza, burgers and conch done several ways for lunch. Closed Sun.

Stella Maris Resort ☎242/338-2050. A pleasant bar and a bright airy hilltop dining room with a sunny, sophisticated decor of potted greenery, honey-coloured rattan, linen tablecloths and huge windows on three sides with pleasing views of flowering trees and the ocean beyond. The delicious breakfast buffet is especially recommended. Reservations advisable.

The Southern Bahamas

The **southernmost islands** of the Bahamas have few inhabitants and receive few visitors. Those who do venture down this way are drawn primarily by the abundant wildlife – the rich fishing grounds that surround the islands and the flamingos, sea turtles and rare birds which inhabit the densely overgrown interior.

While there were around fifty Loyalist cotton plantations on **Crooked** and **Acklins islands** two hundred years ago, today just four hundred people live on each in a smattering of small coastal villages, most without electricity or running water. While the islands may lack appeal as sightseeing destinations, they make up for it with some of the finest tarpon and bonefishing around. For non-fishers, there are several nice stretches of beach to explore. The nicest place to stay on Crooked Island is *Pittstown Point Landings* (☎1–800/752-2322 or 242/334-2507, ⊛www.pittstownpointlandings.com; ❼) on a white-sand beach at Landrail Point. On Acklins, the tidy, nicely appointed cottages at *Acklins Lodge* (⊛www.acklinsislandlodge.com, see site for list of booking agents) are recommended by fishermen.

Great Inagua lies 321 miles southeast of Nassau at the southern tip of the Bahamian archipelago. The shallow waters of Lake Windsor cover one quarter of Inagua's interior, and much of the remaining area is low, flat bush and swamp. The island sits squarely in the path of the relentless trade winds, which combined with a strong, hot sun provide ideal conditions for solar salt production. There is only one settlement on Inagua – **Matthew Town**, at the southwest corner of the island – with a population of about 1200, most of whom are employed at the **Morton Salt Works**, which you can tour by arrangement (☎242/339-1847) The nineteenth-century **Great Inagua Light House**, still operational on a point of land a mile south of Matthew Town, makes a great destination for a short hike.

The bulk of the island – 127 square miles – has been set aside as **Inagua National Park**, a protected conservation area for a large colony of West Indian **flamingos** who nest on the shores of Lake Windsor. Within the National Park is the **Union Creek Turtle Reserve**, a protected habitat and research station devoted to giant sea turtles. The park entrance is twenty miles east of Matthew Town, and to visit you must first make arrangements with the park warden, Henry Nixon, who also takes bookings for the rustic bunkhouse in the park ($25 per person; ☎242/339-1616, ℻242/339-1850).

In Matthew Town, you have a choice of simple but clean **guestrooms** with private bath, a/c and TV at the *Morton Salt Company Main House* (☎242/339-1267, ℻242/339-1265; ❸) or *Walkine's Guest House* (☎242/339-1612; ❸), half a mile south of Matthew Town across the road from the beach.

Mayaguana is about as far off the beaten track as you can get in the Bahamas. It receives few visitors apart from the occasional passing yacht cruisers, sport fishermen and scientists who come to study the unique bird and lizard life on the island. Electricity and telephone service arrived only in 1997. The island has about 320 residents in three small settlements tucked in along the shore on the western side of the island. *Baycaneer's Resort* in Pirate's Well (☎ & ℻242/339-3605, ⊛www.bahamasnet.com/baycaneerbeach; ❹) has sixteen **rooms** and a restaurant on an empty white-sand beach which runs for several miles in both directions. Local **fishing guide** Leroy Joseph (☎242/339-3065) can take you out for a day of fishing, snorkelling or sightseeing by boat.

Bahamasair (⊛www.bahamasair.com) has **air service** to each of the southern islands two or three times a week. The government **mailboats** call at each island once a week; ring the dockmaster at Potter's Cay, Nassau (☎242/393-1064) for departure times, which can vary from week to week. There is a government-operated **ferry** ($5) from Cove Point, Crooked Island and Lovely Bay on Acklins.

Turks and Caicos

Turks and Caicos highlights

✱ **Grace Bay beach** Still uncrowded and fabulous for walking or swimming, this truly is one of the great beaches of the world. **See p.143**

✱ **Little Water Cay** Mingle with some prehistoric rock iguanas before snorkelling in this cay's crystal waters. **See p.146**

✱ **Salt Cay** Choose between a festive guesthouse and a fantastic old plantation, whatever your budget allows. **See p.158**

✱ **Grand Turk** The quaint colonial streets of this languid island are lined with fine examples of local architecture. **See p.156**

△ Iguana on Little Waters Cay

Introduction and basics

The tiny but gorgeous islands of the Turks and Caicos, recently fashionable with the cognoscenti, are scattered over a long swath of sea to the south of the Bahamas. Classy development on the main island of Providenciales, together with truly fantastic beaches and great diving on all of the islands, undeniably places the country in the upper rank of top-end West Indian resorts.

The country comprises two groups of islands – eight inhabited and around forty uninhabited – separated by the Columbus Passage, a deep-water channel 22 miles wide and up to 6000 feet deep. To the east, the **Turks Islands** include Grand Turk and Salt Cay, the former the long-time home to government, the latter a tiny island named after the salt industry that once dominated the country. To the west, the chain of **Caicos** Islands includes South, Middle and North Caicos – each with its own charms – and the island of Providenciales, known as Provo and home to the great majority of the nation's tourist development.

The major attractions on all of the islands are concentrated along their coasts: truly sensational white-sand beaches that stretch for miles, and world-class diving, snorkelling and deep-sea fishing and bonefishing. Inland, there's not much to see other than low-lying scrubby vegetation and, particularly in the Turks Islands, large expanses of featureless *salinas*, from which Bermudian settlers and traders harvested salt during the islands' early development.

Where to go

Most visitors head to **Provo**, which receives nearly all of the country's international flights and has the major hotels and restaurants. Even if you plan to stay there, however, you should consider excursions to one or more other islands, either as day-trips or to spend a night or two. Particularly recommended are **Grand Turk**, a terminally calm, easy-going place just a thirty-minute flight away, notable for its great colonial architecture, the National Museum and more fantastic diving and beaches – or a boat trip around the spectacular **Caicos Cays** to **Middle** or **North Caicos**, where you can check out

some dramatic caves or the remains of an old plantation house.

When to go

The Islands are a year-round destination, with the most popular periods being from mid-December to mid-April and during the school holidays in July and August. Rainfall is low year-round but, particularly from September to November, the weather can get a bit sticky as the trade winds die down. The hurricane season here is the same as elsewhere in the Caribbean; the islands took a blow in October 2004, though the damage was fortunately limited.

Arrival

All international **flights** arrive on the island of Providenciales. American Airlines flies there daily from Miami, and three times a week from New York. British Airways flies on Sundays from London, stopping in Nassau en route. Air Canada flies in from Toronto on Saturdays. Bahamasair leaves Nassau on Tuesdays, Thursdays and Saturdays. Finally, Air Jamaica flies in from Montego Bay from Friday to Monday.

Information and websites

Before you leave home, brochures and **information** can be had from the Turks and Caicos Tourist Board, with a helpful Web presence at ⊛ www.turksandcaicostourism. com. For information while on the islands, you can visit either of the Tourist Board's offices, on Front Street on Grand Turk, and

Websites

ⓦ **www.tcimaill.tc** "Gateway to the island", with useful island contact details and events listings.

ⓦ **www.tcmuseum.org** Website of the superb national museum on Grand Turk, with lots of interesting features on the islands' history.

ⓦ **www.turksandcaicos.tc** A good general website for the island, with excellent links to accommodation, transport and similar sites.

ⓦ **www.turksandcaicos.tc/freepress** The island's principal newspaper, published fortnightly.

ⓦ **www.turksandcaicostourism.com** The offical website of the Turks and Caicos Tourist Board.

in Stubbs Diamond Plaza on Provo. See the box above for several worthwhile Turks and Caicos **websites**.

Money and costs

The official currency of the Turks and Caicos Islands is the **US dollar**. Costs are fairly high as most food, drink and other items are imported. There is a government room tax of 7–9 percent, and most hotels and restaurants automatically add a 10–15 percent **service charge**, so check your bill to ensure you're not paying twice. Unless a service charge is added, **tipping** is customary, with 15 percent being average. Most places take credit cards.

Providenciales and Grand Turk each have several banks with ATMs.

There is a $35 **departure tax**.

Getting around

Travelling between the main islands of the Turks and Caicos is relatively easy, with three local **airlines** offering frequent connections: Air Turks and Caicos (ⓣ 649/946-4181, ⓦ www.interislandairways), TCA (ⓣ649/946-

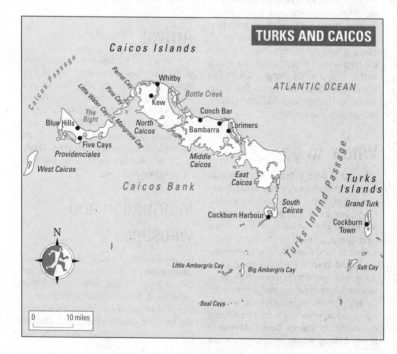

4255) and Skyking (℡ 649/946-4594 or 941-5464, 🌐 www.skyking.tc). Skyking has twelve daily scheduled half-hour flights each way between Provo and Grand Turk, three stopping in South Caicos to pick up and drop off in both directions. Round-trip fares cost $120. Air Turks and Caicos has daily flights, too, between Provo and North and Middle Caicos and Salt Cay (between $60 and $150 round-trip) and between Grand Turk and Salt Cay ($30).

Each of the islands has a taxi service, and there will invariably be a **taxi** waiting for passengers at the airports. For **car and jeep rental**, typically around $60 a day, it's best to try in Providenciales or Grand Turk. Elsewhere you may struggle to get a rental; it's worth asking at your hotel.

Accommodation

There are plenty of **places to stay** in the Turks and Caicos, though most options lean towards the upper end of the price scale. Providenciales, or Provo, has by far the most choices for visitors, though there are fine places to stay on the other islands in the Caicos chain as well. Pickings are somewhat more slim on the Turks Islands, with fewer luxury resorts, but you should still be able to find a suitable spot.

Food and drink

Visitors are spoilt for culinary choice on Providenciales, with a fantastic range of restaurants catering to most budgets, though – with most of the **food** imported – there are few bargains. On the other islands, however,

> The **country code** for the Turks and Caicos Islands is ℡ 649.

the options are strictly limited, which is not surprising, given the relatively low number of visitors. The main island speciality is the delicious conch – served raw in salads and cooked in fritters, chowder, or "cracked" (in batter) – and you'll find plenty of excellent fresh fish, particularly snapper and grouper. Make sure you try traditional "native" food at least once, probably best at *Dora's* on Provo.

As for drinking, there is a wide variety of imported **beers** on offer, as well as the local Turks & Caicos brew, and a surprisingly good selection of **wines** (at least on Providenciales).

Public holidays

Aside from the Caribbean-wide **holidays** listed on p.60, Turks and Caicos also celebrate the holidays listed below.

January 1	New Year's Day
March 14	Commonwealth Day
March/April	Good Friday
March/April	Easter Monday
May 30	National Heroes Day
June 12	Queen's Birthday
August 1	Emancipation Day
September 30	National Youth Day
October 10	Columbus Day
October 24	International Human Rights Day
December 25	Christmas Day
December 26	Boxing Day

History

The first inhabitants of the Turks and Caicos Islands were **Amerindians**, whose sites and relics have been found dotted across the islands; the more important recent finds include the one at the Conch Bar Caves in Middle Caicos. The Amerindian period is well documented at the National Museum in Grand Turk.

As elsewhere in the Caribbean, there is a major debate here about the first European visitor to the islands. While the island of San Salvador in the Bahamas has probably the strongest claim to be where **Christopher Columbus** first set foot in the Americas in 1492, there are many exponents of the theory that in fact his ships actually first pulled up to shore at Grand Turk.

With Spanish slaving ships raiding the islands for Amerindian labour for the gold mines of South America, by 1513 the population had been reduced to zero. As for the colonial powers, ownership of the islands passed between Spain, France and Britain, but none was interested in setting up base. Between 1690 and 1720 Providenciales and the Caicos Cays were used as hiding places by **pirates**, and stories of buried gold and jewels still bring treasure hunters to the islands.

By the late seventeenth century, though, it was a new "treasure" that drew occasional visitors here: **salt-rakers** from Bermuda, who had discovered the ease with which salt could be produced from shallow salt-water ponds (or *salinas*) which were constructed across the islands. This was particularly true in Salt Cay, Grand Turk and South Caicos, where large numbers of trees were chopped down to discourage rainfall (resulting in the largely bare landscape that endures today). "White gold", as the stuff came to be known, was a highly lucrative crop, much of it sent off to Newfoundland for salting cod, and some of the remaining grand houses on Salt Cay are testament to that profitable era. By 1781 the rakers had established a permanent settlement in Grand Turk.

Meanwhile, the Caicos Islands stayed uninhabited until after the American War of Independence, when thousands of defeated **Loyalists** fled from the southern states such as Georgia and the Carolinas. Some were granted large tracts of land by the British government, from Providenciales to Middle Caicos, in recompense for what they had lost in North America. Around forty Loyalists arrived during the 1780s, bringing with them more than one thousand slaves, and began farming cotton.

Though immediately successful – **Caicos cotton** was said to be among the finest in the world – the cotton industry went into decline after only a generation, with hurricanes and pests taking a heavy toll. Though a few planters moved to the Turks Islands and went into salt production, almost all of the planters had left the country by the mid-1820s, leaving their slaves behind to a subsistence existence of farming and fishing, much like the original population of Amerindians.

For the next century, the economy was sustained by the remnants of the salt industry, but there was little population growth and the pace of life was extremely slow. Things began to change with the arrival of a group of American investors in the 1960s, who laid the foundations for **tourist development**, building a small airstrip on Provo and erecting the first hotel – *Third Turtle* – in Turtle Cove. A trickle of foreign visitors began to arrive, turning into a steady stream once Club Med insisted on a proper airport to service their Grace Bay resort in the mid-1980s, and then a small flood with the arrival of further resorts through the 1990s – including the ultra-trendy and prohibitively expensive *Parrot Cay* hotel and spa, home away from home to models, movie stars and fashion designers. The new millennium brings the prospect of Provo's rapid development spreading out to islands like North Caicos and uninhabited West Caicos, where ground was broken in 2003 for an ambitious new five-star resort.

2.1

The Caicos Islands

The **CAICOS ISLANDS** form a rough semicircle, running from the lovely and uninhabited island of West Caicos up through the major tourist centre of Providenciales and a chain of tiny islands – the Caicos Cays – to North Caicos, then down through the largest island of Middle Caicos and uninhabited East Caicos, to the once busy but now largely ignored island of South Caicos.

North and Middle have their individual charms and can be easily accessed from Providenciales by plane or via a fabulous boat trip from Leeward Marina that takes you round the Caicos Cays – a highlight of any stay in the islands.

Providenciales

PROVIDENCIALES, usually referred to as Provo, is the mainstay of the country's tourist industry. With little in the way of cultural life or historical interest, for decades only a handful of visitors made their way here, attracted particularly by the superb opportunities for diving and fishing in the offshore waters. Tourism began to heat up in the 1980s with the arrival of Club Med, and rocketed through the 1990s as investors spotted the great potential for resorts. The opening of *Beaches* (part of the enormously successful Sandals resort chain) in the late 1990s put Provo on the map as far as large-scale tourism was concerned, but it remains an easy-going getaway nonetheless.

There's no town to speak of on the island. **Downtown**, as the business centre is known, is a rather ugly group of shops and offices that you'll pass through on your way from the airport. The three original settlements (which can loosely be described as villages) are little visited by tourists: **Blue Hills**, a pretty residential area that runs alongside the sea north of the airport; **Five Cays**, a drab collection of homes and shops on the south of the island; and a similar cluster around the *Beaches* resort known as **The Bight**.

For many visitors, particularly those staying at the all-inclusives on the north coast, the only sightseeing worth venturing out for is a wander along the six miles of magnificent beach on **Grace Bay**, running from Leeward in the far east of the island along to the native settlement known as the Bight. It's a spectacular stroll beside a turquoise sea, with occasional shade beneath the casuarina trees, and however large the crowd outside the hotels, you'll invariably find a deserted spot to pitch camp.

More adventurous visitors will want to take advantage of the **boat trips** that run to the Caicos Cays from Leeward Marina, where you can spot rock iguanas, hunt for sand dollars and make a picnic on a deserted island.

Arrival and getting around

Nearly all visitors arrive at **Luddington Airport**, roughly in the centre of the island, where there's always a string of taxis waiting outside; a ride to the hotels along Grace Bay costs $12–20. There are also a couple of car rental desks here as well.

A **bus service** operates along the island's main artery, Leeward Highway, but it does not run to the airport or by any timetable. There is also a shuttle service

PROVIDENCIALES

EATING & DRINKING	
Banana Boat	I
Bay Bistro	F
Coyaba	G
Danny Buoy's	2
Grace's Cottage	1
Sharkbite	3

ACCOMMODATION	
Airport Inn	K
Allegro	D
Beaches	H
Caribbean Paradise Inn	B
Club Med	G
Coral Gardens	J
Erebus Inn Turtle Cove	A
Ocean Club	C
Royal West Indies Resort	F
Sibonne	I
Turtle Cove Inn	I

0   2 miles

between the main hotels and restaurants on Grace Bay. If you want to explore the island for a day or two it's worth **renting a car** (or a jeep if you want to make a trip to Malcolm Roads); try Rent-a-Buggy (℡649/946-4158) or Avis (℡649/946-4705). Expect to pay $55–60/day including insurance. **Scooters** can be rented from Scooter Bob's (℡649/946-4684) for $30/day.

For **taxis**, try Nell's (℡649/231-0051 or 941-3228) or Provo Taxi (℡649/946-5481).

Accommodation

Due to the resort boom of the past decade there are plenty of **hotels** on Provo, though most are at the top end in terms of price and quality. By far the most popular are the **all-inclusives** – like *Beaches* and *Allegro* – but there are several other excellent options, such as *Sibonne*, dotted along the north coast.

If you're thinking of renting a **villa**, Lynnette Simpson at Elliot Holdings (℡649/946-5355, ⊛www.elliotholdings.com) has a superb range of places starting from around $1800/week.

Airport

Airport Inn Airport Rd ℡649/941-3514, ⊛www.tcnational.tc/hotel.htm. Far from the beach (though they'll provide a free ride to get there), this is the cheapest option on Provo, with nineteen clean and tidy rooms with a/c. Some rooms have kitchenettes, all have cable TV, and there's a local restaurant and bar on site. Fifteen percent discount on car rental. ❸

Turtle Cove

Turtle Cove Inn Resort Turtle Cove ℡649/946-4203, ⊛www.turtlecoveinn.com. A ten-minute walk from the nearest decent beach, but a relaxed and reasonably priced little place near the marina and a couple of good restaurants. The friendly *Tiki* bar is popular with locals, and there's a small, shaded pool. ❹

Grace Bay

Allegro Grace Bay ℡649/946-5555, ⊛www.allegroresorts.com. Not the best-looking hotel on Provo, but this 186-room all-inclusive compensates guests by being on a magnificent stretch of Grace Bay. It also features the nation's main casino, aimed at casual blackjack and roulette players. There are three restaurants, a piano bar and a nightclub with regular live music, as well as a large pool, tennis courts, fitness centre and good watersports facilities. Rooms have rattan furniture, colourful throws, a/c and fans. ❻

Beaches Grace Bay ℡649/946-8000, ⊛www.beaches.com. This superb all-inclusive resort – part of the impressive Sandals chain – is aimed at families, with top-class facilities for entertaining children, including a Pirate's Island, a Sega arcade centre and their own restaurant and disco. Rooms are spacious, colourful and evenly distributed across a wide area, all within a short walk of the glorious beach and a number of pools. Watersports facilities are top-notch, while the nine restaurants are all excellent, ranging from Italian and French to Caribbean and Japanese, some catering to adults only. ❽–❾

Caribbean Paradise Inn Grace Bay ℡649/946-5020, ⊛www.paradise.tc. One of the cheapest options in the Grace Bay area and not a bad spot, the hotel is a five-minute walk from the beach and right by the Ports of Call shopping area and restaurants. There are one hundred rooms, all with either a king or two double beds, plus cable TV, a fridge, telephone and a/c. ❹

Coral Gardens Grace Bay ℡649/941-3713, ⊛www.coralgardens.com. This small block of smart and good-value one-, two- and three-bedroom condominiums is popular with repeat visitors to the island. All condos are good-sized, with private balconies, sea views, fully equipped kitchens and daily maid service. Close to a good snorkelling site. ❺–❻

Royal West Indies Resort Grace Bay ℡649/946-5004, ⊛www.royalwestindies.com. Attractive, comfortable and very popular condo-resort on a great stretch of beach, with well-kept gardens and a huge pool. The staff are particularly friendly and helpful. ❽–❾

Sibonne Grace Bay ℡649/946-5547, ⊛www.sibonne.com. One of the best and best-value options on the island, this small boutique hotel sits beside a magnificent stretch of white sand and houses the *Bay Bistro*, one of Provo's finest restaurants. The attractively landscaped two-storey hotel has 27 medium-sized rooms, all with a/c, and a tiny pool. ❻–❼

Leeward Marina and boat tours

At the eastern end of the island, neat little **Leeward Marina**, overlooking the first of the Caicos Cays (see box below) that stretch around to North Caicos, is home to most of the boat tour groups. You can just about make out the mangrove swamps of Mangrove Cay directly across the channel and, looking to your left, the sandy beaches of Little Water Cay where rock iguanas strut their stuff. If it's a calm day, it's worth renting a kayak from the Big Blue ($20 per hour for a double; ☏649/946-5034) for an hour or two of cruising across to the cay and stopping on a deserted sandbank or beach to look for shells.

If you're feeling less energetic, there are a number of professional operators based at the marina who run excellent **sailing boat or speedboat trips** to Little Water Cay to see the iguanas and to other nearby cays for shelling and picnics, normally stopping for some excellent snorkelling en route. Even more adventurous, and definitely worth trying, are the speedboat trips that go around all of the cays to Middle Caicos, where you can visit the Conch Bar Caves. The journey takes about

The Caicos Cays

Strung out in a chain between Providenciales and North Caicos are the **Caicos Cays**, a dozen tiny islands, of which all but two are uninhabited. Though there are airstrips for the private planes of the millionaire residents of Pine Cay and Parrot Cay, the most likely way to set foot on any of the cays is by taking a boat trip from Leeward Marina (see above) – one of the undoubted highlights of any visit to the country. All beaches are open to the public and you're pretty much free to wander around at your leisure on all the uninhabited islands.

Five minutes by boat from Provo, the nature reserve of **Little Water Cay** is home to several thousand rock iguanas. These reptiles – unique to the region – were once found throughout the islands, but development has led to their virtual extinction elsewhere. Here, wooden boardwalks have been put up across the cay to allow you access to the heart of their protected habitat. You'll see dozens of iguanas – up to two feet long – sunning themselves on the beach or foraging around in the scrub.

Northeast of the cay, **Water Cay** is fringed by small, sandy cliffs and fantastic white sand, while the adjoining **Pine Cay** has a small hotel and about 35 private homes dotted around its beaches and interior providing winter retreats for their wealthy and mostly US-based owners. The twelve-room *Meridian Club* hotel (☏203/602-0300, in the US ☏1-800/331-9154, ⊛www.meridianclub.com; ❾) is one of the finest of its kind in the world, priding itself on being simple but classy ("barefoot elegance" is the apposite slogan), with nature trails crossing the cay, and kayaks, snorkelling, fishing and diving all available for guests. No children under 12 are allowed.

Beyond Pine Cay as you head east, **Fort George Cay** once housed a fort erected in the eighteenth century by the British to deter pirates from concealing themselves and plunder pinched from Spanish galleons sailing further south. The fort is long gone, though two of its iron cannons can be seen by snorkellers in shallow water just off the northwest shore.

Last in the chain and closest to North Caicos, **Parrot Cay** (formerly known as Pirate Cay, and thought to have been a refuge for pirates such as Calico Jack, Anne Bonney and Mary Read) saw an ultramodern multimillion-dollar hotel (☏649/946-7788, ⊛www.parrot-cay.com) open its doors in the late 1990s. With just fifty rooms and six villas, some with private swimming pools, and a fabulous spa, the place is altogether grander (and, most would say, rather snootier) than the *Meridian Club* on Pine Cay. Prices starting at $500 a room ($2000 for a villa) mean that it's for the rich only, and in true copy-cat style a bunch of celebrities have beaten a steady trail to this island since the likes of Paul McCartney stayed. Bruce Willis and Donna Karan are building holiday homes on the cay.

ninety minutes each way, and you'll stop off en route to see the iguanas and to do some snorkelling.

The main **speedboat operators** are Silver Deep (☎649/946-5612) and J&B Tours (☎649/946-5047). Both run similar trips for similar prices; expect to pay around $35 per person for the visit to Little Water Cay and $150 to Middle Caicos. Big Blue (☎649/946-5034) runs slightly pricier tours, with more emphasis on "eco-adventures", like visiting the mangrove swamps or nature trails on Middle Caicos.

Sailing trips are run by Sail Provo (☎649/946-4783) and Beluga (☎649/946-4396) on comfortable catamarans or trimarans; as well as trips to the cays and snorkelling and shelling trips, both offer sunset cruises for around $50 per person.

The Caicos Conch Farm

Tucked away in the wilds of Leeward, east of the marina, the **Caicos Conch Farm**, on Leeward Highway (Mon–Sat 9am–4pm; $6, $3 for children), is the only one of its kind in the world. Started in 1984, the farm is responsible for rearing queen conch – a giant sea snail, famous for its gorgeous pink shells and pearls – for export and for sale in the islands. Conch – pronounced *konk* – are subject to numerous predators in the sea, including sharks, stingrays, porcupine fish and octopus. At the farm they are protected, first in large hatcheries and then, as they grow towards adulthood at three to five years, in pens at sea.

Twenty-minute **tours** of the farm are given frequently – if you arrive mid-tour you can still join in; the guide will fill you in afterwards on the parts you missed.

Long Bay and the Hole

Just a short drive along the road that runs west of the Conch Farm, **Long Bay Hills** is a residential area on the south side of the island with an impressive stretch of sand. Unfortunately, millions of conch shells washed up on the shore by the prevailing winds make access to decent swimming awkward, though you'll notice that some local house owners have tried to clear a path out to the ocean. Even then, however, the water is shallow for some way out and the sand more silty than you'll find on the north shore.

Follow signs to the hidden and rather dramatic **Hole** (always open; free), an eighty-foot drop down to a wide green pond. Brave souls have been known to scramble down for a swim in the icy water – but there are no ropes or other protection, so be careful and make sure to keep small children well away.

Blue Hills and Malcolm Roads

West of Long Bay, Leeward Highway cuts straight across Provo to its tiny commercial centre, downtown. Just before you reach downtown, turn off to the right for what is perhaps the prettiest drive on the island. After about half a mile, take the right fork leading onto a coastal road that passes **Blue Hills**, the most attractive of Provo's original settlements. As well as an astounding variety of churches, and a graveyard where all the graves face out to sea, there are some great bars on the beach serving fish and conch snacks and lunches.

If you've got a jeep, past Blue Hills you can turn left to join a more substantial road a few hundred yards inland (the continuation of the road you avoided earlier by forking right). Continue west towards Malcolm Roads beach and Northwest Point. Where the road divides, take the left turn (ignoring signs for the Crystal Bay condominium project) down a diabolical track about four miles long to Malcolm Roads. As you crawl down this rocky road, look out for osprey nests, large bundles of twigs and sticks, assorted palms and cacti that characterize the island's original vegetation, and great views over the bays as well as the virtually inaccessible inland ponds known for their spectacular birdlife.

The beach at **Malcolm Roads** (also known as "Sam's Beach") is one of the most beautiful spots in the country, and well worth the tortuous route to get there. The surf often crashes in on the magnificent beach here, and you can expect to have it to yourself, though you may see dive boats moored offshore at some great dive sites. Bring water as there's no shelter and no facilities; you can also clamber around some rocky outcrops to find tiny coves for swimming. Steer clear of the small group of thatched, wooden tiki-huts that were put up here for a French game show in the early 1990s; untended since then, and blown about by occasional hurricanes, they have fallen into disrepair, with rotten floorboards and rusty nails a peril to the unwary.

Five Cays, Chalk Sound and the south

There's little in the way of tourist development on the south side of the island, where you'll find one of Provo's original settlements at Five Cays (named after the small group of rocks just offshore) and the gorgeous Chalk Sound national park and semicircular Taylor Bay.

To get there from downtown, turn down the main road virtually opposite the airport road. A left turn at the gas station leads to **Five Cays** – an uninspiring and unkempt jumble of houses, schools and small businesses. However, make sure you stop at the excellent *Liz's Bakery* (daily 6am–6pm) on the main road for some freshly baked breads, cakes and pastries.

Continuing south on the main road towards the island's main dock at South Dock, a turn to the right just before you reach the sea leads to the gloriously milky blue **Chalk Sound**, a stunning lagoon in a national park; bear in mind, though, that it's not a great place to swim because of the silty bottom. The Sound is protected from the sea on its southern side by a narrow peninsula, which is indented with a series of bays, overlooked by grand and very expensive private homes. **Sapodilla Bay** is the first and largest of the bays, with a handful of yachts normally moored just offshore. At the eastern end of the bay, reached by a rocky path just west of the run-down *Mariner's Hotel*, are a number of inscriptions in the rock that were carved by shipwrecked sailors in the early nineteenth century.

Beyond Sapodilla Bay, **Taylor Bay** has a perfect crescent of sand. Like Chalk Sound and Sapodilla Bay, however, it's not a great place to swim.

Eating and drinking

There is a good range of places to **eat** in Provo, from fine French and Italian restaurants to local hostelries dishing up traditional island food. As you'd expect, seafood has pride of place on most menus, but there's plenty to keep you happy if you're a meat-eater. Vegetarians will struggle to find much in the way of variety. There are no places specifically catering to drinkers.

Grace Bay

Bay Bistro *Sibonne*, Grace Bay ☎ 649/946-5396. Sip a cocktail at the bar and watch a fabulous sunset before sidling into this easy-going bistro. The fish and lobster are superb, whether marinated in ginger and soy or simply pan-fried on the grill, and there's a smaller selection of fine cuts of beef or lamb. Finish with the lemon *crème brûlée* – it's huge, but you'll manage it. Starters cost $5–10, mains $16–35. Lunch and dinner, closed Tues.

Coyaba *Coral Gardens Hotel* ☎ 649/946-5186. Fabulous food in a garden setting near the beach, with seafood specialities like tuna ceviche, fish chowder, fresh snapper with orange or spiny

lobster with vanilla among the highlights. Expect to pay $22–40 for a main course. Dinner only.

Danny Buoy's Grace Bay main road ☎ 649/946-5921. The ubiquitous Irish-themed pub has now reached Provo, serving pints of Guinness as well as local Turks Island beer. Food is inexpensive and filling, with wraps, burgers and the like for around $10, and there are daily happy hours from 4–7pm, sports tournaments and quizzes. Lunch and dinner daily.

Grace's Cottage *Point Grace Hotel*, Grace Bay ☎ 649/946-5096. Gorgeous little cottage with outdoor seating on a terrace, serving wonderful food with an emphasis on the freshest catch.

Expect to find dishes like pumpkin and coconut soup or jerked wahoo, and to pay around $50–60 for two courses.

Downtown

Dora's Leeward Highway ☏ 649/946-4558. Dora has run this place – best of the native restaurants – for nearly two decades and still dishes out excellent and relatively inexpensive fare from curried chicken, lobster and goat to beef stew and creole snapper or grouper. Open all day.

Hey Jose! Central Square, Leeward Highway ☏ 649/946-4812. Longstanding island favourite for Mexican dishes (enchiladas, burritos and fajitas) and pizzas at $10–20 per head. Lunch and dinner Mon–Sat.

Tasty Temptation Butterfield Square, Downtown ☏ 649/946-4049. This established bakery sells a great selection of plain or filled croissants, rolls and sandwiches from around $5 as well as giant muffins and good coffee. Mon–Fri 6am–3pm.

Turtle Cove

Banana Boat Turtle Cove ☏ 649/941-5706. Pleasant family-friendly place at Turtle Cove marina, with a moderately priced range of fish and seafood platters, including excellent cracked conch and snapper or grouper in a spicy creole sauce. Avoid karaoke night on Saturdays.

Sharkbite Turtle Cove ☏ 649/941-5090. This great spot overlooking the marina offers tasty meals from almond-crusted grouper in curry sauce ($19) to cracked conch ($13) and burgers ($10). Alongside the restaurant there's a long and busy bar, and a handful of games to keep the kids occupied.

Nightlife and entertainment

Nightlife on Provo is fairly quiet. Local soca and reggae bands play irregularly at a variety of venues around the island, and it's great to have a dance under the stars; ask at your hotel for what's on. If you want to chance your hand, head to the casino at the *Allegro* to play blackjack and roulette, and finish off with a bop in the hotel's nightclub.

The biggest party of the year is held around "Provo Day", which takes place in late July and early August. There is a beauty pageant, a regatta and a parade of floats and a big weekend party with live music and stalls (normally around the easy-to-find ballpark in downtown) selling beer and local food like souse and conch fritters.

Watersports and other activities

The **diving** around Provo is as good as you'll find anywhere in the Caribbean. Although the best wall diving is a lot further from shore than you'll find in Grand Turk, there is a great variety of excellent sites here, including those at Northwest Point and at West Caicos, between sixty and ninety minutes by boat from Turtle Cove marina. There are also good shark and other dives to be found closer by off the island's north shore.

Reputable **operators** include the longstanding Provo Turtle Divers (☏ 649/946-4232, ⊛ www.provoturtledivers.com), which also offers snorkelling tours and glass-bottomed boat rides, Dive Provo (☏ 649/946-5029, ⊛ www.diveprovo.com), and Big Blue Unlimited (☏ 649/946-5034, ⊛ www.bigblue.tc), which also run whale-watching trips in February and March – when humpback whales pass by the island – and kayaking tours of the cays near Provo. Expect to pay around $45/75/100 for a one-tank/two-tank/three-tank dive, $60 for a night dive or $160 for a resort course which includes a two-tank dive. A four- or five-day open-water certification course, involving four or five two-tank dives, costs $400–450.

The best places to **snorkel** on Provo are near the *Coral Gardens* hotel and at Smith's Reef, just east of the entrance to the Turtle Cove marina on the north coast. At both places you'll find good reefs just offshore. Alternatively, ask the dive operators when they have a snorkelling trip going out (normally $30 per person) or take one of the island/snorkelling trips offered by the outfits at Leeward Marina.

Other **watersports** are also well catered for, and the larger hotels all have good facilities for their guests. At Grace Bay, Windsurfing Provo (☏ 649/241-1687) offer rental and instruction on windsurfers, kitesurfers and small sailing boats.

Fishing charters offer superb deep-sea fishing for marlin, wahoo, tuna and shark, difficult but exhilarating bonefishing in the shallow flats around the islands and bottom-fishing for grouper, snapper and parrotfish. For deep-sea fishing, try Sakitumi (☎649/946-4065) expect to pay $590/490 for a full/half-day's fishing for up to six people or $150 if they'll take you on your own. For bonefishing or bottom-fishing, try Catch the Wave (☎649/941-3047) or Silver Deep (☎649/946-5612), both at Leeward Marina. In July there's a huge billfish tournament, with boats coming from around the world to hunt for the biggest blue marlin in the sea.

There is a magnificent **golf** course at Provo Golf and Country Club (☎649/946-5991, ☻www.provogolfclub.com), rated by many as one of the finest in the region, where you'll pay $130 each for 18 holes and a cart or $70 for nine holes. Many of the hotels have private **tennis** courts.

Listings

Banks Scotiabank and First Caribbean have branches in Downtown. Hours are Mon–Thurs 8.30am–2.30pm, Fri 8.30am–4.30pm.
Emergencies ☎911.
Internet access There are no Internet cafés, but most hotels will let you log on for a modest charge.
Laundry Pioneer Cleaners, Butterfield Square, Downtown ☎649/941-4402.

Medical services Associated Medical Practices, Leeward Highway (☎649/946-4242, ☻www .doctor.tc); Grace Bay Medical Centre, Grace Bay (☎649/941-5252).
Police ☎649/946-4259.
Post office Airport Rd (Mon–Fri 8am–noon & 2–4pm).

North Caicos

NORTH CAICOS is the most lush and in many ways the most beautiful of the nation's islands. Receiving more rainfall than anywhere else, the vegetation is denser and taller here than on the other islands, and many islanders keep vegetable patches and grow fruit trees, including tamarind, papaya and sapodilla. As you'd expect, the beaches are great, too. Property speculators have pushed land prices to dramatic heights in the hope that North Caicos will become the "next big thing". Their optimism seems to be paying off, as tourist development is slowly beginning to increase, but for now the island remains delightfully quiet, like Provo a decade ago.

Arrival, information and getting around

There are no international flights to North Caicos, and most people arrive by **plane** from Providenciales with Air Turks and Caicos. **Boat**s do make trips from Leeward Marina as part of day excursions from Providenciales.

There is no tourist office on the island. Cars can be rented from Gardiners (☎649/946-7141), and there are **taxis** at the airport to meet incoming flights. If you want to tour around by taxi, M&M (☎649/946-7338) charges $25 per hour.

Accommodation

Most of the **hotels** on North Caicos are scattered along the lovely sandy beaches of Whitby; the *Bottle Creek Lodge* is a delightful place on the other side of the island.

Bottle Creek Lodge Bottle Creek ☎649/946-7080, ☻www.bottlecreeklodge.com. Comfortable eco-friendly accommodation in two cottages and an apartment, overlooking the turquoise creek that divides North from Middle Caicos. Not ideal for the beach, but a very relaxed place offering free

sailboats and kayaks for exploring Middle Caicos and nearby cays. The owners will also arrange expeditions around the island. ❼
Pelican Beach Hotel Whitby ☎649/946-7112, ☻www.pelicanbeach.tc. Laid-back and longstanding small hotel with excellent

ocean views from the a/c upstairs rooms and unpretentious but comfortable furnishings and decoration. There's a cosy bar, and you can expect to find good local food at the roomy restaurant. **6**
Prospect of Whitby Whitby ☎649/946-7119, ⓦwww.prospectofwhitby.com. Probably the nicest

place to stay on the island, this is an Italian-run all-inclusive hotel on a fabulous beach. With just 23 good-sized and a/c rooms, it has an intimate feel, while the restaurant is excellent and scuba diving, windsurfing and tennis are included with the package. **9**

The island

At the west end of the island, **Sandy Point** is a small fishing community and your likely arrival point if you're coming by boat from Provo. Just offshore lie three prominent rocks known as **Three Mary Cays**; one of them has a huge osprey nest, whose occupant is often seen gazing imperiously over passing vessels. Back on land, and a short drive from Sandy Point, birdwatchers can douse themselves in bug spray and make for **Cottage Pond**, a small nature reserve with a deep sinkhole that's inhabited by ducks, grebes and other birds, or (a little further east) for **Flamingo Pond**, a large expanse of brackish water where you can normally spy a flock of flamingos (though it's hard to get close to them, and you'll need binoculars for a decent view).

On the north side of Flamingo Pond, **Whitby** is home to North Caicos's main hotels and guesthouses and fringes onto a number of excellent white-sand beaches with good snorkelling just offshore. On the western edge of Whitby, the powdery sands of Pumpkin Bluff Beach are especially magnificent while, on the eastern side of the village, Pelican Point is a good place to snorkel.

South of Whitby, the road leads inland to the farming settlement at **Kew** – the only one of the country's original settlements not based on the coast – named after the botanical gardens in London and home to many of the island's most productive fruit and vegetable growers. There are also a post office, church and general store.

A mile to the west of Kew are the extensive though unspectacular ruins of **Wades Green Plantation**, currently under ongoing restoration, where you're free to wander around the remains of the massive kitchen, overseer's house, stables and walled garden plots. Built in 1789 by Wade Stubbs, the plantation developed high-quality cotton and was a rare success story for the area; upon his death in 1822, Stubbs owned over 8000 acres on North and Middle Caicos and Providenciales as well as 384 slaves, many of whom took his surname. Consequently, today Stubbs is one of the most common names in the islands.

On the eastern side of the island is **Bottle Creek**, North Caicos's largest settlement, whose houses spread out along the ridge that overlooks the creek between North and Middle Caicos. The peace and quiet and the colours of the creek make this a gorgeous spot, especially if you're passing through by boat, though there's little specific sightseeing. A vehicle ferry crosses the creek at weekends; otherwise ask around in Bottle Creek for a ride to Crossing Place in Middle Caicos (five minutes by boat). Bear in mind that you'll want to arrange a taxi for the other end (see overleaf).

Eating and drinking

Away from the hotels, there's not much in the way of **restaurants** or bars, and **nightlife** tends to be quiet.

Club Titters Bottle Creek ☎649/946-7316. This local place dishes up tasty and inexpensive fare all day, including grouper with peas and rice and cracked conch, and there's occasional live entertainment at weekends.
Papa Grunt's Seafood Restaurant Whitby ☎649/946-7301. Expect to find lots of local fish and conch (served in a variety of ways) on offer here, along with fried chicken and burgers. Most dishes cost $6–10.

Pelican Beach Hotel Whitby ☎649/946-7112. Good mixture of local and international food at this hotel's eatery, with plenty of fine grilled snapper and grouper, served up with peas and rice, as well as ribeye steaks and lobster salad for $15–20. The place can lack atmosphere when it's quiet, but there's a very easy-going vibe.

Middle Caicos

Home to just three hundred people, **MIDDLE CAICOS** is the country's larg-est island and one of its quietest. Despite the abundance of great beaches, espe-cially at **Mudjin Harbour** near Conch Bar and further east at **Bambarra**, tourist development has been very slow and there are few facilities for visitors; you'll find just a handful of guesthouses and a couple of taxi drivers. If you're after peace and quiet, you couldn't find many better refuges in the country, but don't expect the watersports or food choices of other islands.

Middle Caicos was settled by **Lucayan Indians** between the eighth century and around 1540, by which time Spanish slave traders had killed or shipped off the local population for servitude in South American mines. The island remained uninhabited until Loyalists and their slaves arrived from North America after the Revolution. As elsewhere in the islands, the settlers' attempts at growing cotton made little progress and, within a generation, they had departed, leaving their former slaves to run the three north coast settlements that survive today.

Arrival, information and getting around

TCA and Air Turks and Caicos operate daily **flights** to Middle Caicos from Providenciales, some of them stopping at North Caicos en route. There is also a ferry from Bottle Creek in North Caicos on Saturdays from 8am ($2 per person, $20 for a car), landing at Crossing Place in the west of the island.

You won't find a tourist office on the island or a car rental outlet, but there are a couple of local **taxi** drivers who prowl around the airport and will be delighted to take you on a tour of the island – reckon on around $25 per hour. Try Earnest Forbes (☏649/946-6132) or Cardinal Arthur (☏649/946-6107). They'll also be happy to organize fishing trips for you on the shallow waters south of the island.

Accommodation

There are just a couple of **places to stay** for visitors to Middle Caicos.

Blue Horizon Resort Mudjin Harbour ☏649/946-6141, ☻www.bhresort.com. A handful of large and comfortable cottages perched on the hilltops above the harbour, with fine views over the coastline. It's a fabulously relaxed place, a short walk from a superb beach – sometimes pounded by waves, at other times blissfully calm – though don't come expecting much in the way of entertainment or nightlife. The staff will organize snorkelling or hiking expeditions on request. Meals available by reservation. ⑥–⑦

Taylor's Guesthouse Conch Bar ☏649/946-6161. A good place for those on a tight budget, five minutes' walk from the beach. The inexpensive rooms are clean and well kept in a large, attractive wooden house, all with fans and TV. There's also a small restaurant on site. ③

Around the island

One of the main draws in Middle Caicos is a series of limestone **caves** at Conch Bar. Formed over millennia by water slowly carving into the soft rock, the extensive network was once home for the Lucayan Indians, almost certainly here at the time of Columbus, and various of their artefacts – including tools and pottery – have been removed to the National Museum in Grand Turk. Tours of the caves need to be arranged in advance, either through a tour company in Provo or by booking a tour with one of the Middle Caicos taxi drivers (see above).

If you are here on a tour, you'll probably spend some time at **Mudjin Harbour**, a short drive east of the caves. It's a dramatic setting with tall cliffs dropping down to the sea, a rocky promontory just offshore and waves often crashing onto a yellow-sand beach. As you go down to the beach there's a short trail off to the left that leads to the top of the cliff where you'll have fantastic views down the coast and across the scrubby, undeveloped interior of the island.

East of here the road leads to the small settlement of **Bambarra**, where there is a large and very quiet white-sand beach framed by casuarina trees; at low tide you can wade out along a sandbank for half a mile to the delightful beach at Pelican Cay. Continuing further east, **Lorimers** – named after a local plantation owner – is one of the most remote settlements in the country, though there's little here for visitors besides the Crossing Place Trail (see below).

The high point in the island's calendar is **Middle Caicos Expo**, a great weekend party in August during which former residents return and others flood in to hear live bands and hang out at the beer tents set up on Bambarra beach.

Eating and drinking

Given the tiny population of the island (and the fact that most of it consists of either elderly people or children), there's nowhere much to head to for **a night out**, other than a small bar in Conch Bar where local guys gather in the evening to drink beer and play dominoes. Plan quiet nights in your hotel, guesthouse or villa and lay in beer from the **grocery store** in Conch Bar.

Hiking and biking

The **Crossing Place Trail** makes Middle Caicos one of the best places in the country for hiking and biking. It's an ancient path that leads from Lorimers in the east around the north coast of Middle Caicos to Crossing Place (literally that) in the west, from where it's possible to cross to North Caicos at low tide. After years of being overgrown, the path was recently cleared by the National Trust, and you can now follow the track for some four and a half miles. Part of the path is on the beach and passes through Mudjin Harbour, with trail markers along the way. It's a great way of seeing the island, mostly along the flat and not particularly strenuous parts, though you may want to arrange for a taxi to pick you up at the end of the route.

There is also a seven-mile **biking trail** on pretty easy terrain from Conch Bar to Bambarra beach, with good snorkelling spots along the way. Bikes can be rented from Sport Shack in Conch Bar for around $15 a day.

△ Arts and crafts, Grace Bay

2.2

The Turks Islands

The small group of **TURKS ISLANDS** has just two inhabited islands: **Grand Turk**, the home of government, and tiny **Salt Cay**, with its population of under a hundred. Both places are quiet and quaint, showcasing attractive remnants of the colonial era, with great beaches and diving to keep you entertained during the day but little in the way of nightlife.

Grand Turk

Despite the government's best efforts, major development continues to elude the small but delightful island of **GRAND TURK**. Frustrating as this is to the powers that be – who see their young people emigrating to Providenciales or abroad for jobs – those who make the effort to get here will find a charming and unspoiled island.

A series of expansive, muddy-coloured **salinas** dominate the centre of the island, testament to the salt trade that first brought development to Grand Turk. West of here in the island's capital, Cockburn Town, and running beside the sea, Front Street has much of the country's finest colonial-era **architecture** as well as the tiny but superb **National Museum**. The **diving** and **fishing** on Grand Turk are world-class and the **beaches** magnificent. Consider renting a car or scooter for a day to tour the island, which will only take you a few hours to explore, or ask a taxi driver for a guided tour.

Arrival and getting around

There are no international flights into Grand Turk and you'll need to come in via Providenciales, from where there are more than a dozen **flights** a day costing $120 return.

Car rental can be arranged from Tony's (☎649/946-1879) for around $55 a day; scooters from Val's (☎649/946-1022) for $30 a day. Taxis are found at the airport or can be reached by phone – try K's (☎649/946-2239).

Accommodation

Though Grand Turk has none of the five-star hotels that you'll find on Provo, there's a good range of **places to stay**.

Arches of Grand Turk Lighthouse Road ☎649/946-2941, ⓦwww.grandturkarches.com. Four very comfortable a/c townhouse units, a short walk from the beach, and great for families. ⑦
Osprey Beach Hotel Front St ☎649/946-1453, ⓦwww.ospreybeachhotel.com. Comfortable and tranquil little place right on the beach, with sixteen tidy rooms, each with a patio or a balcony overlooking the sea. There's a small restaurant a short walk from the main hotel, and a tiny pool around

which the owners hold occasional barbecues. ⑤
Turks Head Hotel Front St ☎649/946-2466, ⓦwww.grand-turk.com. One of Front Street's many charming colonial buildings from the 1840s, the *Turks Head* pulls in business travellers and tourists with its attractively furnished rooms and period charm, all just a short walk from the beach. At quiet times it can feel rather soulless, but the bar is normally busy with locals in the evening and there's a good restaurant on site. ⑤

Cockburn Town

Although **Cockburn Town** is the country's capital, don't expect to find a bustling city. The government has spent a great deal to smarten the place up, but it hasn't brought in the masses, with most tourists still coming here for diving more than sightseeing. Comprising just a couple of streets of nineteenth-century homes and warehouses, it's rare to find much activity and the streets are often empty. Stroll down the main drags of **Duke Street** and **Front Street**, which run alongside the gorgeous blue ocean, and you might encounter a gaggle of smartly dressed children making their way to school or a languid cow munching from some overhanging foliage.

The island's **architectural highlights** are centred on these two streets. At the southern end of Front Street, the *Salt Raker Inn* and *Turks Head Hotel*, two of Grand Turk's oldest hotels, are fine examples of the wooden houses built in the 1840s by Bermudian shipwrights who came here to collect salt. Other colourful buildings like the General Post Office line this area of Front Street, many of them constructed with ballast and timbers taken from the trading ships of the time, and covered with purple and orange bougainvillea, as well as the occasional Turk's-head cactus, recognizable by its red fez-shaped flower.

The Turks and Caicos National Museum

Continuing up Front Street from the hotels, you'll come to the **Turks and Caicos National Museum** (Mon–Fri 9am–4pm, Sat 9am–1pm; $5; ⊛www.tcmuseum .org), chief among the island's highlights. Here you can examine the remains of the Molasses Reef wreck, the oldest recovered shipwreck in the Caribbean, dating from around 1515. After the wreck was discovered in the 1970s, some morons mistook it for a treasure ship and blew sections of it apart with dynamite looking for treasure. Key remains on display include the enormous main anchor, cannon and other weapons, hand- and foot-cuffs of prisoners and some tools.

The exhibits upstairs span the islands' history from pre-Columbian times to the present, and include a room given over to artefacts – notably pottery – from the Lucayan Indians and another explaining the islands' reefs and aquatic life. Also on display are items recording key visits to the island, from astronauts John Glenn and Scott Carpenter – who splashed down near here in 1962 and were brought to Grand Turk for debriefing – to present-day British monarch Queen Elizabeth II and members of her family who have visited periodically over the past forty years.

Governor's Beach and around

Of the good **beaches** that line the west and east coasts, the pick of them is **Governor's Beach**, where the powdery sands shelve into a turquoise sea. To get there, head south on the road from Cockburn Town, ignoring the turn-off to the airport, and continuing towards the Governor's residence, known as **Waterloo**. Just before you reach the imposing white walls, turn off to the right along a track that runs past the small nine-hole **golf course** in the grounds of the house (call ☏649/946-2308 to book a round for $25). At the end of the track, take the path through the bush to a superb stretch of white sand, backed by casuarina trees and fronting onto a magnificent turquoise bay. Be sure to bring water, as there are no facilities on the beach and you're likely to have it all to yourself.

Eating, drinking and nightlife

There's not much sophistication to **dining** out in Grand Turk, but there are plenty of decent options and prices are reasonable. Nightlife is quiet, though there's usually some late-night music and dancing at *Nookie Hill* on Friday and Saturday and occasional bands at the *Turks Head* or *Water's Edge*.

Calico Jacks *Turks Head Hotel*, Front St ☎649/946-2466. Tasty food from an experimental and eclectic menu, covering everything from grilled lobster ($25) and fish and chips ($9) to spicy grouper ($15) and stone-crab claws ($22). Sit outdoors under the trees at lunchtime but remember the bug spray. Daily breakfast, lunch and dinner.

Regal Beagle Hospital Rd ☎649/946-2274. Shack-like restaurant dishing up tasty and inexpensive native lunches and dinners for $4–10, such as conch fritters, stewed beef, goat curry and fried chicken. Daily for lunch and dinner.

Water's Edge Front St ☎649/946-1680. The best food on the island, served on a pier poking out into the gorgeous waters off the west coast, and usually busy at lunch and dinner. The well-tended bar is often lively, and the cracked conch, conch salad and grilled fish are a treat. Expect to pay $20–25 for a three-course meal.

Watersports and diving

Superb **diving** opportunities, many of them very close to shore, include fantastic deep and shallow dives at twenty sites along the five-mile wall that starts just off the west coast. You'll find magnificent coral formations, abundant reef life and plenty of shipwrecks.

The three **operators** are Blue Water Divers (☎649/946-2432, ⓦwww .grandturkscuba.com), Oasis Divers (☎649/946-1128, ⓦwww.oasisdivers.com) and Sea Eye Diving (☎649/946-1407, ⓦwww.seaeyediving.com). All offer one and two-tank dives (from $40 and $60, respectively) and PADI certification courses, and are happy to take snorkellers along if they're going to train at a shallow site. **Snorkellers** should also make for the old pier at South Dock, not the most attractive place to dive but teeming with fish, and try to get on a boat ride to deserted Gibbs Cay where the snorkelling is fantastic and where you'll bump into some friendly southern stingrays.

Listings

Banks Scotiabank has a branch on Front Street. Hours are Mon–Thurs 8.30am–2.30pm, Fri 8.30am–4.30pm.
Emergencies ☎911.

Medical services Grand Turk Hospital ☎646/946-2333.
Police ☎649/946-2299.
Post office Front Street (Mon–Fri 8am–noon & 2–4pm).

Salt Cay

Tiny **SALT CAY** is one of the most appealing islands in the country, both for its natural beauty and its historical interest. Although measuring barely six and a half square miles and home to just eighty people, the island was once an important source for the Bermudian salt-rakers, whose relics still litter the place and provide much of the charm: fabulous old white-washed houses as well as the salt pans from which the "white gold" was laboriously scraped. Add to that some sugary white beaches (particularly along the north coast), great diving and snorkelling, and a small but fine range of accommodation, and you've got another great place to chill out.

Arrival, information and getting around

Flights with TCA and Air Turks and Caicos leave from Provo for Salt Cay daily and cost $150 return. There are also daily flights between Grand Turk and Salt Cay, though these are less frequent and cost $25 each way. The government **ferry** runs between Grand Turk and Salt Cay, leaving Grand Turk on Mondays and Fridays at 3pm and costing $12 per person return.

There's no tourist office on the island and just a couple of taxis.

Accommodation

Salt Cay has a range of **accommodation** options to suit most budgets; magnificent as *Windmills* is, there's plenty of choice for those without money to burn.

Mount Pleasant Guest House ☏ 649/946-6927, ⊕ www.mtpleasant.tc. Superb value, this timber-beamed nineteenth-century salt trader's home on the great north coast beach has been catering mainly to divers for over a decade. There's a comfortable lounge/library for guests, and rooms are colourful and quiet. The restaurant and gazebo bar are the most popular on the island. Single ⑥, double ④

Pirate's Hideaway ☏ 649/946-6909, ⊕ www.pirateshideaway.com. Four comfortable suites and a friendly owner make this a good option just across from the beach. There's a small bistro and bar. ⑥

Windmills Plantation ☏ 649/946-6962, ⊕ www.windmillsplantation.com. Fabulous and fabulously expensive, *Windmills* is built like a traditional West Indian plantation house. Wooden walkways connect the main house, with its wooden verandahs and gingerbread fretwork, to the other guest rooms, all furnished with superb antiques and custom-designed furniture that includes four-poster beds. The restaurant is top-notch and the capable proprietors will arrange whatever activity you need. ⑨

Around the island

Like Grand Turk, the centre of Salt Cay is dominated by the flat, shallow **salinas** that supplied the island's once-thriving salt industry. Recognizing the salinas' commercial potential, the salt traders built stone walls and sluice gates to create smaller ponds so that the water would evaporate more quickly under the baking sun. Windmills were built to speed up the process, but it was fiercely hard manual work scraping the salt into piles. Trading ships from Bermuda carrying limestone rocks as ballast (later used to build the traders' smart houses) then transported the rough salt to trade along the eastern seaboard of the fledgling United States.

For centuries, salt was the source of the island's wealth, but the industry was subject to stiff international competition and went into decline for decades before it finally ground to a halt in the 1960s. Nothing much has happened here since, and Salt Cay's population has slowly melted away, the remaining people mostly elderly or children, their numbers supplemented by a trickle of tourists.

On the west side of the island, **Balfour Town** is the principal settlement, home to government buildings, the local school and a couple of stores. It's also where you'll find the **White House** dominating the shoreline. The most spectacular of Salt Cay's two-storey jalousie-windowed limestone houses, it was built by local salt magnate Joshua Harriot after the great hurricane of 1812 had flattened his wooden home with a 15ft tidal wave. Elsewhere you'll see more recent and pastel-coloured wooden houses, with little courtyards and low stone walls to keep stray cattle at bay.

The island's best **beach** runs along the entire north coast, a magnificent swathe of sand, with massive elkhorn coralheads in a couple of places just offshore harbouring schools of fish and perfect for snorkelling. The rocky east coast is dominated by sharp-edged ironshore limestone, with a series of small bays dotted along it. It also has the island's highest point at Taylor's Hill, 60ft above sea level.

For **divers** there are a handful of good sites five minutes by boat off the west coast of the island, where you'll find spotted eagle rays and a wealth of brightly coloured fish as well as deep-water gorgonians and black coral trees. Ten miles further south, the encrusted wreck of HMS *Endymion*, an eighteenth-century British warship complete with cannon, lies in thirty feet of water.

The island's principal **dive operator**, Salt Cay Divers, based at the *Mount Pleasant Guest House*, (☏ 649/946-6906, ⊕ www.saltcaydivers.tc), also rents bikes and organizes horseriding tours of the island. From January to March, humpback whales make their way to the nearby Mouchoir Banks to breed, and while a fortunate few will spot them blowing from the shore, you might be better off joining one of the whale-watching tours organized by Salt Cay Divers (and their Grand Turk equivalents).

Eating and drinking

You'll do almost all of your **eating** and **drinking** at hotels and guesthouses, where prices are reasonable. The food at the *Mount Pleasant* (see opposite) restaurant is particularly good, and you should also make tracks to the *One Down, One To Go* bar (☎646/946-6901) in Balfour Town for a drink and a game of pool, and some local colour.

3

Cuba

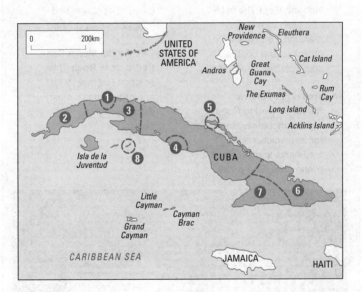

Cuba highlights

❋ **Cuban music in Havana** Check out at least one of the excellent salsa, jazz or *son* groups that regularly make the rounds of the best-known clubs. See p.192

❋ **Habana Vieja** The old city, filled with elegant mansions, centuries-old churches and cobblestone plazas. See p.183

❋ **Trekking in Sierra Maestra** Head to Cuba's highest mountain range for its revolutionary landmarks and excellent hiking trails. See p.230

❋ **Viñales valley** Bizarre limestone hillocks lend this valley a dreamlike air. See p.197

❋ **Baracoa** Isolated by verdant mountains, quirky Baracoa has retained much of its charm and hospitality. See p.220

❋ **Castillo del Morro San Pedro de la Roca** This colossal fort makes for one of Santiago's most dramatic sights. See p.229

△ Habana Vieja

Introduction and basics

Evocative and beguiling, the last decade has seen Cuba slough off its outdated image of a country isolated from the Western world to become the jewel of the Caribbean. Communist credentials notwithstanding, Cuba well understands the commercial power of rebranding and has reinvented itself as the home of sun, salsa and rum with chutzpah and an apparent insouciance which are intrinsic to the country.

Shaped by one of the twentieth century's longest-surviving **revolutions**, until recently Cuba's image had been inextricably bound up with its politics, rather than its long satiny beaches, offshore cays and jungle-covered peaks. Now, the country is changing and Cuba today is characterized as much as anything by a frenetic sense of transition as it shifts from socialist stronghold to one of the Caribbean's major **tourist destinations**, running on capitalist dollars.

Yet at the same time, it can seem to visitors that nothing has changed here for decades, even centuries: the classic American cars, moustachioed cigar-smoking farmers, horse-drawn carriages and colonial Spanish architecture have apparently all been unaffected by the breakneck pace of **modernization**. Newly erected department stores and shopping malls, state-of-the-art hotels and resorts are the hallmarks of this new, emerging Cuba. This improbable combination of transformation and stasis is symbolic of a country riddled with contradictions and ironies. In a place where taxi drivers earn more than doctors, and where capitalist reforms are seen as the answer to preserving socialist ideals, understanding Cuba is a compelling but never-ending task.

Despite favouritism toward tourists and the crippling US trade embargo, there is surprisingly **little resentment** directed at foreign visitors. In most of the country it's easy to come into contact with the locals: the common practice of renting out rooms and opening restaurants in homes allows visitors strong impressions of Cuba and its people even in a short visit. It's a good thing, too, since Cubans are renowned for their love of a good time. Their energy and spirit are best expressed through **music** and **dance**, both vital facets of the island's culture. As originators of the most influential Latin music styles, such as *bolero*, *rumba* and *son*, which spawned the most famous of them all – **salsa** – people in Cuba seem always ready to party.

There are occasional reminders that Cuba is a highly **bureaucratic** one-party state. Going to the police, finding your hotel room double-booked or simply needing to make an urgent phone call can prove to be frustratingly complicated. As such, having a certain determination and a laid-back attitude are essential requirements for a pleasant trip to Cuba, particularly when exploring less visited parts of the country. Things are becoming easier all the time, though, with the introduction of a wider variety of more efficient services; unfortunately these improvements also mark an irreversible move away from what makes Cuba unique.

Where to go

No trip to Cuba would be complete without a visit to the capital city, **Havana**, whose time-warped colonial core, **Habana Vieja**, is crammed with architectural splendours dating back to the sixteenth century. West of the capital, **Pinar del Río** is the best area for getting close to nature. The resorts best suited for hiking are **Las Terrazas** and **Soroa**, but it's the peculiar *mogote* hills, which look more like gargantuan boulders than hills, of prehistoric **Viñales valley** that attract the most attention.

The country's premier holiday destination and beach resort is **Varadero**, two hours' drive east of Havana, while on the opposite side of the province, the **Península de Zapata** boasts a potent mix of beaches, wildlife excursions and other attractions. Further east, **Trinidad**, a small colonial city, lures coach parties and backpackers in

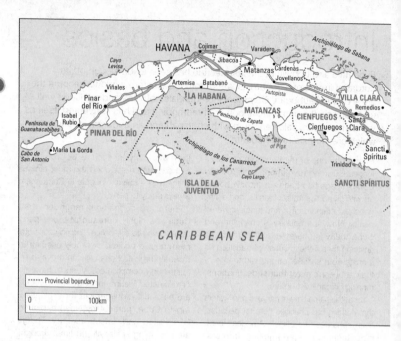

equal numbers. However, the most popular destinations in this central part of the country are the luxurious resorts of **Cayo Coco** and **Cayo Guillermo**. Beach-goers also won't want to miss **Guardalavaca**, on the northern coast of Holguín province, where there are ample opportunities for watersports.

While **Guantánamo** province, forming the far eastern tip of the island, is best known for its infamous US naval base, it is the jaunty seaside town of **Baracoa** that is the region's most enchanting spot. The country's most vibrant and energetic city after Havana is **Santiago de Cuba**, on the island's south-east coast, which, like the capital, has a lively historic centre. Trekkers and revolution enthusiasts will want to follow the Sierra Maestra as it snakes west of here into **Granma** province, offering various revolutionary landmarks and nature trails. Finally, lying off the southwest coast of Havana province, luxurious and anodyne **Cayo Largo** is the only sizeable beach resort off the southern coastline of Cuba.

When to go

Cuba generally has a **hot** and **sunny** tropical climate. While the average annual temperature is 24°C (75°F), temperatures can drop to 15° (59°F) or lower in January and February (considered winter), especially at night and in the mountains. These months fall in the **dry season**, which runs roughly from November to April. May to October is considered the **wet season**, when you can expect it to rain at least a couple of days during a two-week holiday. Downpours don't usually last long, however, and are quickly followed by sunshine. September and October are the most threatening months of the annual **hurricane season** that runs from June to November.

The peak **tourist season** runs from about December to March and July to August (high summer). Prices and crowds are most rampant in summer when the holiday season for Cubans gets under way. As much of the atmosphere of the smaller resorts is generated by tourists, they can seem somewhat dull out of season – although you'll benefit from lower prices. The cities, particularly Havana

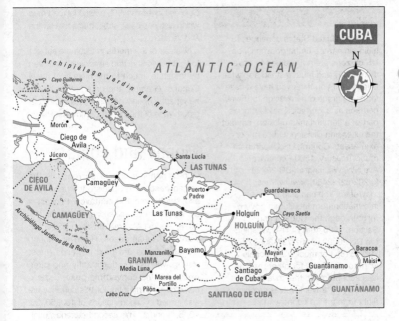

and Santiago, are always buzzing and offer good value for money all year round.

Arrival

The majority of international flights arrive at Havana's **Jose Martí Airport**, although the international airports at Varadero, Holguín, Ciego de Avila, Santiago de Cuba, Cayo Coco, Cayo Largo, Santa Clara and Camagüey also receive (mainly charter) flights. Though there are no scheduled ferry services from neighbouring countries a limited amount of European cruise ships dock at the **marinas** in Havana and Santiago de Cuba. It is, however, quite possible to sail by **private yacht** or cruiser to a number of spots on the island. Normal visa requirements apply and you should make sure you have these before you embark on your trip. Whilst it is not currently a legal requirement to notify the Cuban authorities of your arrival it is common maritime courtesy to do so. You should **radio ahead** when possible.

Entry requirements

Citizens of most Western countries must have a ten-year **passport**, valid for at least six months, a **tourist card** (*tarjeta de turista*) and an **onward ticket**. Tourist cards are valid for thirty days and although you can buy one from Cuban consulates you will get more efficient service if you buy it from your tour operator or travel agent. The charge in the UK is £15–20, in Australia Aus$35, in New Zealand NZ$44 and in Canada Can$24. **American citizens** (see box overleaf) can travel to Cuba on tourist cards purchased in Canada, Mexico or other countries, and the Cuban authorities will on request stamp the card instead of your passport when you enter and leave Cuba.

Note that you will pass through **customs** much more smoothly if you have entered the name of a state hotel on your tourist form as your destination. If you don't have an address you may have to pay on the spot for three nights' accommodation in a hotel of the state's choosing.

Since the United States continues to maintain a trade embargo with Cuba, **US citizens** are not allowed to travel there freely and must instead apply for a licence. If you think you have a case for being granted permission to travel, perhaps as a journalist, student or as part of a humanitarian mission, contact the Licensing Division, Office of Foreign Assets Control, US Department of the Treasury, 1500 Pennsylvania Ave NW, Washington DC 20220 (☎202/622-2480, ⊛www.treas .gov/ofac). You can also get information from the Cuban government through the Cuban Interests Section, 2630 16th St NW, Washington DC 20009 (☎202/797-8609 or 797-8518). For most US nationals who want to visit Cuba for other reasons less acceptable to the government, like tourism, travel involves catching a flight from a third country.

Information, websites and maps

There is a shortage of printed travel literature in Cuba and getting hold of any kind of tourist **information**, particularly outside the major resorts, can be difficult. Before you leave home, therefore, it's worth contacting the nearest branch of the Cuban Tourist Board (⊛www. cubatravel.cu/oficinas.asp), which has information for visitors. In Cuba itself the only tourist information network is **Infotur** (⊛www.infotur. cu), which still only has a handful of branches (three in Havana and one in Matanzas), but also has desks in many hotels and at the José Martí International Airport. Concentrating on booking organized excursions, hotel room reservations and car rental, Infotur has very little information on public transport other than the Víazul bus service (see "Getting around", p.168). Also, the staff, though generally helpful, do try to steer visitors towards the state-run tourist apparatus.

Finding a trustworthy **map** once in Cuba is also difficult. The exception is the invaluable

Guía de Carreteras ($6), a national road map which also has basic street maps for Havana and Varadero.

All areas of the **media** in Cuba are subject to tight censorship and are closely controlled by the state, much to the dismay of many Cubans. *Granma*, the only national daily newspaper, openly declares itself the official mouthpiece of the Cuban Communist Party.

Money and costs

Cuba's national unit of **currency** is the Cuban **peso** or, in Spanish, the *peso cubano*, divided into 100 **centavos**. Banknotes are issued in denominations of 100, 50, 20, 10, 5, 3 and 1. At time of writing US$1 was worth 26 Cuban pesos. However, though Cuban salaries are paid in pesos, most visitors will use predominantly and often exclusively the **convertible peso**, or *peso convertible*. Banknotes for this currency are also issued in denominations of 100, 50, 20, 10, 5, 3 and 1. This second currency, originally introduced in 1995, has now completely replaced the US dollar, which was legal tender on the island until November 2004. Since then all products and services which were previously priced in dollars are now charged in convertible pesos, at an exchange rate of one for one, making it the king currency in Cuba. Although the convertible peso can be thought of as a US dollar equivalent, there are some important distinctions to be aware of. Firstly, convertible pesos are useless outside Cuba so make sure you exchange any leftover notes before you leave the country. Secondly, although the international exchange rates for US dollars are the same rates applied to the convertible peso, actually exchanging US dollars for convertible pesos is costly, as this is subject to a **service charge** of ten percent. It therefore makes sense to arrive in Cuba with British pounds, Canadian dollars, euros or other internationally recognized currencies, ready to change them into convertible pesos.

You'll need to keep in mind that on the island pesos and convertible pesos are both represented by the **dollar sign** ($). The most commonly used qualifier for pesos is *moneda nacional*; thus one peso is often written $1MN.

Websites

While the majority of **websites** on Cuba are US-based – many of them politically oriented and quite interesting – there is also an increasing number of Cuban state-run sites.

ⓦ**www.afrocubaweb.com** Fantastically detailed site covering absolutely anything even remotely connected to Afro-Cuban issues, from history and politics to music and dance.

ⓦ**www.cuba.com** This US-based site claims to be "The official web site to Cuba" and is designed for US citizens who want in-depth and impartial information in English about the island from a visitor's point of view.

ⓦ**www.cubatravel.cu** The Cuban Ministry of Tourism site with practical information and advice on a wide range of issues from customs regulations to accommodation and transport.

ⓦ**www.cubaupdate.org** An excellent source of information that details tours organized by the Center for Cuban Studies.

ⓦ**www.cubaweb.cu** The Cuban government's official site includes news reports from the Cuban press, plus information on travel, investment and many other subjects.

Unless otherwise stated, any reference made simply to pesos in this book will be to Cuban pesos, not convertible pesos, while we use the $ symbol by itself to signify convertible pesos only.

All official tourist-oriented facilities, including all state-run hotels, most state-run restaurants and pretty much all goods sold in shops, are **charged** in convertible pesos. You'll also be expected to pay in convertible pesos for rooms in people's homes, meals in *paladares* (small, privately run restaurants) and most private taxis, though there is some flexibility in these cases. Entrance to cinemas and sports arenas, local buses, snacks bought on the street and food from *agromercados* are all paid for with plain old Cuban pesos.

Hard currency is king in Cuba, so it's a good idea to **exchange** your money into convertible pesos as soon as you arrive. You can do this at the *bureaux de change* in Havana and Varadero airports, at most of the four- and five-star hotels and at selected banks around the country. Although **travellers' cheques** are easily exchangeable in many banks, a significant number of shops and restaurants still refuse to accept them. Travellers' cheques issued by a US bank are unusable in Cuba, though American Express cheques issued outside of the US are accepted. **Credit cards** – Visa and MasterCard in particular – are more widely accepted, but in most small-to medium-sized towns plastic is useless as a method of payment. Moreover, no card issued by a US bank (including American Express, regardless of country of issue) can be used in Cuba. Credit cards are more useful for obtaining cash advances, most efficiently through branches of the Banco Financiero Internacional. There are very few **ATMs** in Cuba and though their number is slowly increasing you shouldn't count on being able to find one outside of the major resorts. **Bank opening hours** are usually Monday to Friday 8am to 3pm; at weekends, when most banks are closed, it is virtually impossible to obtain money.

Accommodation aside – for which you should expect to pay a minimum of $15–25 a night – your daily **budget** can vary quite considerably. Eating street-vendor type meals, you can get away with a daily food budget of just $5, or about 125 pesos. At restaurants and *paladares* allow $5–15 for food; add at least another $5 if you want to attend a live performance or go to a club. If you travel by tourist bus expect to pay upwards of $15 per journey. Private taxis can sometimes work out cheaper than buses if you share them with three or four other convertible peso-paying travellers – this way, a 100km trip can cost as little as $5–10 each. A rental car will add another $50–70 a day.

Getting around

Mastering Cuban **transport** can be a fascinating, if sometimes frustrating, experience; understanding its nuances can take years. However, with a public bus service aimed at tourists, a proliferation of car rental agencies and an abundance of reasonably priced state-run taxis, it's actually much easier for most foreign travellers to get around the country than it is for many Cubans, whose incomes keep them confined to the inferior peso-priced transport services.

Hitching a lift in Cuba, or *coger botella* as it is known locally (meaning literally "catching a bottle"), is as common as catching a bus. Crowds of people wait by bridges and junctions along the major roads waiting for vehicles to stop. Drivers often ask for a few pesos, and tourists, though they are likely to attract a few puzzled stares, are welcome to join in. The usual hitchhiking precautions apply.

By bus

Bus travel, the most common method of transport, is divided into two separate and very different services for inter-provincial routes, one operated by **Astro**, the other by **Víazul**. Though technically available to anyone willing and able to pay the fares, Víazul (☎ 7/881-14-13) is effectively a bus service for tourists. Although limited to the larger towns, cities and resorts, it is by far the quickest and most reliable way to get around independently.

That said, most bus routes are still the exclusive domain of Astro (☎ 7/870-33-97), which is characterized, for Cubans at least, by long queues, overcrowding and a complicated system of timetables and tickets. Foreign passport holders are afforded the privilege of jumping queues should they choose to pay in convertible pesos rather than pesos though there are usually only two to four seats for this purpose on most Astro buses; to guarantee a seat you should arrive at the bus station at least an hour before departure. Before you do that, however, ring to check whether the bus is actually leaving, particularly if you are in a non-touristy area. Most town or city bus stations have a separate office where convertible peso tickets are sold. Even if you choose a destination covered by Víazul you may decide that the Astro fare (usually between half and two-thirds of the price of a Víazul ticket) justifies the less comfortable conditions.

By train

Cuba is the only country in the Caribbean with a functioning **rail system** and, though slow, trains are a good way of getting a feel for the landscape. You'll need your passport to buy a ticket, which you must do directly from the train station at least an hour before departure. The main line, which links Havana with Santiago, also serves Matanzas, Santa Clara, Ciego de Ávila, Camagüey and Las Tunas. *Servicio Regular* trains, which are perfectly comfortable but lack air conditioning, leave once daily, stopping at all the main-line stations. **Fares** work out at around $4 per 100km, with Havana to Santiago, for example, costing $30. *Servicio Especial* trains run every three days and are more expensive ($43 from Havana to Santiago), though they do have air conditioning and are significantly faster.

By car

Given that so much of Cuba is not properly served by public transport, the most convenient (though substantially more expensive) way to get around the island is undoubtedly in your own **rental car**. Also, traffic jams are almost unheard of and, away from the cities, at least, many roads are almost empty.

There is a confusing array of car **rental agencies**, despite the fact that they are all state-run firms. Apart from **prices**, which are rarely less than $35 a day and more often between $50 and $70, the essential difference between the agencies is the type and make of car they offer. Havanautos (Calle 1ra esq. 0, Miramar, Havana ☎7/203-98-15 or 203-96-57, reservations ☎204-06-47 or 204-06-48, ⊛www.havanautos.cu) and Transautos (Calle 40-a esq. 3ra, Miramar, Havana ☎7/204-76-44, reservations 204-55-32, ⊛www.transtur.cu) have the most branches throughout the island as well as the widest range of vehicles. For any chance of getting a car that isn't the most expensive model, it's essential to book at least a day in advance. All agencies require you to have held a driving licence from your home country or an international licence for at least a year, and that you be at least 21.

Driving in Cuba is on the right-hand side of the road. There is only one motorway in the whole country – el autopista – and from Havana it cuts through the country down to the eastern edge of Sancti Spíritus province and in the other direction to the provincial capital of Pinar del Río; it fluctuates between six and eight lanes. Road markings are almost nonexistent and the 100km/hr speed limit would undoubtedly lead to accidents were there more traffic. The main alternative route for most long-distance journeys is the two-lane Carretera Central, a more scenic though far more congested road with an 80km/hr speed limit. The quality of minor roads varies enormously and potholes are commonplace. Driving anywhere outside the cities is dangerous at night, but to mountain resorts like Viñales or Topes de Collantes, where the winding hillside roads are both narrow and without crash barriers, it's positively suicidal. The high proportion of cyclists on the road (the vast majority without lights) and the amount of horse-drawn transport are also cause for caution.

By taxi

Taxis have become one of the most popular expressions of private enterprise. The official metered state taxis are the easiest to spot and getting hold of one by telephone isn't usually a problem. **Cost** depends primarily on the size of the car. For the smallest hatchback taxi in a provincial town you will be charged around 30 (convertible peso) centavos per kilometre, whilst in Havana a saloon car can cost as much as 90 (convertible peso) centavos per kilometre, with luxury taxis even pricier.

As ubiquitous are individually owned cars, predominantly 1950s American classics or Russian Ladas, which are run as taxis by their owners. The local name for these is máquinas or taxis particulares, but those that carry tourists are referred to throughout this guide as **private taxis**. Officially, drivers can charge in either convertible pesos or pesos, depending on their licence, but most will try to charge tourists in convertible pesos. Intra-

city journeys typically cost between $2 and $5, but negotiation is part and parcel of the unofficial system. For longer trips, there is usually a specific area of a town, invariably next door to a bus station, where taxis wait for long-distance passengers. As a rough indicator, a driver will be looking for between $20 and $30 per 100km.

Peso taxis are known as colectivos, into which drivers fit as many passengers as possible. More akin to a privately run bus service, they are used almost exclusively by Cubans and can be flagged down from the roadside, though they are likely to ignore tourists, probably on the assumption that foreigners are unlikely either to understand the system or to be carrying pesos. It is generally accepted in Havana that a trip within the city in a colectivo will cost ten pesos. The rest of the country is similar.

Accommodation

Broadly speaking, accommodation in Cuba falls into two types: **state** and **private**. You'll find at least one state hotel in every large town, for which you should budget at least $30 per room per night. Private accommodation, in casas particulares, works out cheaper at between $20 and $30. Only in major tourist areas like Havana will you need to pay more. At the higher-end state hotels, expect to pay $100 or more a night. During low season, some hotels lower their rates by about ten percent.

State-owned **tourist hotels** are the most convenient type of accommodation in Cuba – you can usually get a room by turning up on spec, although reservations are recommended. Upon arrival, specify how many days you intend to stay to avoid having your room booked out from under you by someone else.

For many visitors, staying in casas particulares – "private houses" – is an ideal way to gain insight into the country and its people. Like a guesthouse, proprietors rent out rooms in their home. Most offer breakfast and an evening meal for an average of $5. Touts (called jineteros or intermediarios) wait to meet potential customers at buses; note that if you're brought to a casa particular by one you can expect to be charged an extra $5 per night. Many *casas particulares* operate illegally without paying taxes. They are usually no cheaper than their registered counterparts and, although you are not breaking the law by staying in one, if you encounter a problem you will get little sympathy from the authorities.

Campismos, sort of quasi-campsites, are an excellent countryside option, and all provinces have at least one. Not campsites in the conventional sense, they instead offer basic accommodation in rudimentary concrete cabins. At around $5 a night per cabin they are extremely reasonable. For more details contact Cubamar, Calle 15 no. 752 esq. Paseo Vedado, Havana (☎ 7/66-25-23 or 30-55-36, ✉ cubamar@mit.cma.net), which runs the best sites.

Food and drink

While you'll usually be able to **eat** decently in Cuba, mealtimes are not the gastronomic delight enjoyed on many other Caribbean islands. Restaurants are divided into two categories: state restaurants and small, privately run *paladares*. Covering both convertible peso establishments and peso eateries, **state restaurants** differ greatly in quality – the best offer up tasty meals in congenial settings while the worst are atrocious. Peso restaurants, which you'll find away from the tourist areas, cater essentially to Cubans. The quality tends to be poor, though you can occasionally get a passable meal very cheaply. As a visitor you're more likely to eat in the convertible peso establishments which, particularly in the large cities and tourist areas, have better-quality, more varied food, often including some international dishes, like Chinese and Italian. By way of contrast, state-run roadside cafés are unhygienic and poorly managed and should be avoided.

Paladares are a godsend. Usually run out of a spare room in someone's home, they offer visitors a chance to sample good Cuban home-cooking in an informal atmosphere. They are plentiful in Havana, and while most large towns have at least one, some smaller towns may not have any at all. Prices are uniform, with a meal costing $5–10. They

can seat no more than twelve people and are subject to tight restrictions on what they can serve: beef and seafood are prohibited (though you may be offered them anyway) and lamb and mutton are banned in some provinces. **Chicken** and **pork** are always on the menu and although there will be few, if any, set **vegetarian** options, *paladares* are more accommodating than state restaurants in terms of off-menu ordering, making them a good choice for non-meat-eaters.

Also privately run, from front gardens and driveways, the peso **street stalls** dotted around cities and towns are invariably the cheapest places to eat and an excellent choice for home-made snacks and impromptu lunches.

One of the worst problems you will encounter when eating out is **overcharging**, which is so widespread that it's unlikely you will make it through your trip without being overcharged at all – and some unfortunates report overcharging at virtually every meal. The most likely reason for this is that Cubans see tourists as a font of wealth and, as such, fair game for extortion. Failsafe trouble-shooting methods include asking for the menu when you're ready to pay and tallying your own bill accordingly. Point out any discrepancy calmly – you'll gain nothing by having a fit – and it will usually be amended without comment (or apology).

Breakfast in Cuba is commonly a bread roll eaten with eggs. **Lunch** also tends to be light, and following the locals' lead and snacking on maize fritters or *pan con pasta* – bread with a garlic mayonnaise filling – from the peso street stalls is the best bet for a midday meal. The basis for a typical **dinner** is fried chicken or a pork chop or cutlet. Although there is not as much fish and seafood on offer as you might expect, what you can get is excellent, particularly the grilled lobster, prawns and tuna. Note that apart from garlic and onion, spices are not really used in Cuban cooking. Accompanying your meal will almost always be **rice and beans**, known as *congrí*, *moros y cristianos* or *arroz con frijoles* depending on preparation. Other traditional **vegetable side dishes** are fried plantain, cassava and salad. The best places to buy **fruit** are the *agromercados*, where you can load up cheaply with whatever is in season. Particularly good are the mangoes, juicy oranges and sweet pineapples.

For drinking **water**, it's best to stick with bottled, readily available from all convertible peso shops and hotels; otherwise tap water should be boiled. Canned **soft drinks** are widely available, and peso food stalls serve non-carbonated soft drinks made from powdered packet mix – these cost just a couple of pesos, though you should be cautious about the water they're made with. With the same caveat, try the *granizado* (slush) served from portable street wagons; *guarapo*, a super-sweet frothy drink made from pressed sugar cane; and, a speciality in the east of the island, *Prú*, a refreshing drink fermented from sweet spices and tasting a little like spiced ginger beer. **Coffee** is the beverage of choice for many Cubans, and is served most often as pre-sweetened espresso. **Tea** is less common but is available in the more expensive hotels and better restaurants.

As for **alcohol**, if you like *ron* (rum) you'll have plenty of options. Havana Club reigns supreme, but also look out for Caribbean Club and Siboney. Cuba is also famous for its cocktails, including the ubiquitous **Cuba Libre**. Made from white rum, Coca Cola and a twist of lime, it's second only in popularity to the **Mojito** – white rum, sugar, sparkling water and mint. Lager-type **beer** (*cerveza*) is plentiful and there are some excellent national brands, particularly Cristal, Hatuey and Bucanero. On average, cocktails cost $3–4 while a beer will run you $1–3, though ritzier places will of course charge more.

Phones, post and Internet

Although a more efficient digital **telephone** system has replaced much of the antiquated analogue system, using the phone in Cuba is still fairly complicated and frustratingly unreliable. **Payphones** are of three distinct types. The most common are coloured blue and are often found in glass-walled phone cabins (a kind of large, walk-in phone booth), in hotels and an increasing number of public places. These phones don't accept coins, only what are called Chip prepaid **phone cards** (as opposed to the Propia phone cards used by most Cubans), sold in convertible pesos in denominations of $5, $10 and $20. National **rates** are reasonable, starting at 5c per minute for calls within the same province. These are the only payphones which allow international calls: currently, a payphone call to the US or Canada costs $2 per minute, or $4.40 per minute to Britain or Australia. However, calling the US from Cuba is now subject to a US-based **tax**, an extra cost of US 24.5¢/min not included in the officially listed call rates. The older, least reliable payphones, which only accept 5¢ peso coins, are still the only kind of public phone in the majority of Cuban towns and villages. There are, however, newer **peso payphones** appearing around the country and these are just as reliable as their blue, convertible peso counterparts. They are grey with a digital display, and most are coin-operated, accepting 5 centavo, 20 centavo and 1 peso coins; some also accept peso phone cards (though these cards are available only to Cubans).

To **make a call** within the same province if calling from a prepaid card phone, simply dial ☎0 followed by the area code and number. If dialling from a phone in a *casa particular* or from one of the old peso phones you will not need to dial the area code of the place you are calling but instead you will need to dial the exit code for the place from where you are making the call. The exit code, available either through the operator (☎00 or ☎110) or from the telephone directory, can itself depend upon where you are calling to.

For **interprovincial calls** you will need to dial first the appropriate prefix (usually ☎0 but there are a number of variations depending on where you are in the country) to get onto the national grid, then the area code, followed finally by the number. Some interprovincial calls are only possible through the operator. If you are consistently failing to get through on a direct line dial ☎00.

For **international calls** without the assistance of an operator, possible from the newer payphones but only on a relatively small proportion of private phones, dial the international call prefix, which is ☎119, then the country code, the area code and the number.

The **country code** for Cuba is ☎53.

Cuba's **postal service** has seen a slight improvement in recent times; it now takes weeks instead of months for airmail to leave the island. If you send anything other than a letter, either inland or overseas, there's a significant chance that it won't arrive at all, as pilfering is widespread within the postal system. You should also be aware that letters and packages coming into Cuba are sometimes opened as a matter of policy. Stamps are sold in both *convertibles pesos* and plain old pesos at post offices, from white and blue kiosks marked *Correos de Cuba* and in many hotels. All large towns and cities have a post office, normally open Monday to Saturday from 8am to 6pm. The full range of postal services, including DHL and EMS, is offered in some of the larger hotels, usually at the desk marked *Telecorreos*.

Getting online in Cuba is easier than ever, with all major cities now counting at least one cybercafé and many hotels renting out email and Internet facilities, though their rates are sometimes exorbitant; in Havana they commonly charge between $7 and $10 an hour. The best places to get online are the new Telepunto centres, currently found only in some provincial capitals, which contain anywhere from three to ten Internet terminals and offer a number of other services including fax, prepaid phone cards and telephone cabins. Some of their services are offered in pesos but foreign visitors are likely to be charged in *pesos convertibles* and will be required to show your passport for Internet access. Currently, Telepunto charges are 10¢/min with a minimum charge of $6, giving you an hour online.

Having always been keen to control the flow of information to the Cuban public, the government has, unsurprisingly, **restricted** its citizens' access to the Internet. However, though private home Internet connections are illegal, access to Cuban-based email accounts are not and there are an increasing number of Cuban homes using email, mostly in Havana.

Opening hours, holidays and festivals

Cuban offices are normally **open** for business between 9am and 5pm Monday to Friday, with many of them closing for a one-hour break anywhere between noon and 2pm. Shops are generally open 9am to 6pm Monday to Saturday, normally closing for lunch, while the shopping malls and department stores in Havana stay open as late as 8pm. Sunday trading is increasingly common, with most places open until noon or 1pm, longer in the major resorts. **Banks** generally operate Monday to Friday 8am to 3pm, but this varies.

Cultural **festivals**, like the International Theatre Festival and the International Festival of New Latin American Film have won Havana global acclaim. Lesser-known festivals celebrating dance, literature and other arts, as well as a whole host of smaller events in other provinces, are also worthwhile. If you're around in July, Cuba's main

---

Cuban music

Music forms the pulsing backdrop to virtually all entertainment in Cuba, and if you're looking to hear traditional Cuban music, like that popularized by the Buena Vista Social Club, you won't come away disappointed. Along with Santiago and Varadero, Havana offers the best variety of places to soak up home-grown salsa, from lavish salsa palaces and open-air venues to hotel salons. Better still, you can also hear all the soulful *son* (which is the foundation, really, of most Cuban music), *boleros* (slow and romantic ballads) and *guajiras* (country music influenced by *son*), as well as *salsa* (itself an offspring of *son*), in any of the **Casas de la Trova** – atmospheric music halls specializing in traditional Cuban tunes that often have live groups – located throughout the country. For something a bit more riotous, Cuban street parties, held on holidays and at **carnival,** feature live bands, which expertly tease seductive moves from heaving crowds.

Public holidays and festivals

Public holidays

January 1 Liberation Day. Anniversary of the triumph of the revolution.
May 1 International Workers' Day.
July 25–27 Celebration of the day of national rebellion.
October 10 Anniversary of the start of the Wars of Independence.
December 25 Christmas.

Festivals

January

Cubadanza Gran Teatro, Habana Vieja ☎7/31-13-57, ⊕paradis@turcult. get.cma.net. Cuban contemporary dance festival featuring performers from around the country.
Havana Jazz Festival Teatro Nacional, Havana ☎7/79-60-11. See the best of Cuban jazz, including the legendary Irakere with Chucho Valdés, play around the town at different venues. International guest stars also feature.
Festival de Música Electroacústica "Primavera en La Habana" Habana Vieja ⊛www.mundoclasico.com. Festival of electro-acoustic music held every even-numbered year in the bars, museums and cafés around Habana Vieja.

July

Fiesta of Fire Festival Santiago de Cuba ☎226/2-35-69, ⊕upec@mail. infocom.etecsa.cu. Santiago's week-long celebration of Caribbean music and dance culture takes place at the beginning of July.

Santiago Carnival ☎226/2-33-02, ⊕burostgo@binanet.lib.cult.cu. Cuba's most exuberant carnival holds Santiago in its thrall during the first two weeks of July with costumed parades, congas, salsa bands and late-night parties.
Havana Carnival ☎7/62-38-83, ⊕rosalla@cimex.com.cu. Carnival festivities in Havana take place in late July/early August, with parades and street parties around the city centre for about three weeks.

August

Cubadanza Gran Teatro Habana Vieja ☎7/31-13-57, ⊕paradis@turcult.get. cma.net. The summer season of the Cuban contemporary dance festival which draws performers from all over the country to Havana.

September

Havana International Theatre Festival ☎7/31-13-57, ⊕paradis@turcult.get. cma.net. Excellent ten-day theatre festival showcasing classics and contemporary Cuban works at various theatres around the city.

December

International Festival of New Latin American Film Havana ☎7/55-28-54, ⊕rosalla@cimex.com.cu. One of Cuba's top events, this ten-day film festival combines the newest Cuban films with the finest classics, as well as providing a networking opportunity for leading independent film directors.

carnival, which takes place in Santiago, is unmissable; also well worth checking out are the carnival celebrations held in Havana.

Sports and outdoor activities

On the whole, participatory **sports** and **outdoor activities** in Cuba are still in the development stage. Watersports are the main exception, with dive sites all around the island. Featuring some of the richest and most unspoilt waters in the world, Cuba has great **scuba diving** and **snorkelling**. As well as reefs there are numerous underwater caves, tunnels and even shipwrecks to explore. Most of the major beach resorts, including Varadero, Santa Lucía and Guardalavaca, have well-equipped diving centres. Varadero, with its three marinas and two diving clubs, is one of the best places for novice divers.

Hiking is another good option and all three mountain ranges in Cuba have hiker-friendly resorts. Designated hikes tend to be quite short, rarely more than 5km, and trails are often unmarked and difficult to follow without a local guide. Furthermore, orienteering maps are all but nonexistent. This may be all part of the appeal for the more adventurous but it is generally recommended that you hire a guide, especially in adverse weather conditions.

The most popular spectator sport in Cuba is **baseball**, a national obsession. Games in the national league, the Serie Nacional de Béisbol, take place between sixteen teams over a regular season which usually begins in October or November and runs through the playoffs in March or April, finishing with the finals a month later. Every provincial capital has a baseball stadium and, during the season, teams play five times a week, so there's a good chance of catching a game if you're in the country during the winter months.

The national **basketball** league, the Liga Superior de Baloncesto, also has a relatively high profile in Cuba and is the most worthwhile alternative to baseball for sports fans. In fact, the smaller arenas and the faster pace of the sport itself often give the atmosphere at a basketball game an edge over the national sport. There are only four teams in the league and games take place predominantly in Havana, Pinar del Río, Santa Clara and Santiago. The basketball season usually lasts from August to December.

Entrance to sports stadiums and arenas in Cuba costs only a peso or two and tickets are always sold at the gate rather than in advance.

Crime and safety

Despite increasing worries about crime, Cuba is still one of the **safest destinations** in the Caribbean and the majority of visitors will experience a trouble-free stay. The worst you're likely to experience is incessant and annoying attention from touts and hustlers, known as *jineteros*. **Women travellers**, however, particularly those travelling solo, should brace themselves for nonstop male attention. While violent sexual attacks are virtually unheard of, unaccompanied women are generally assumed to be on holiday because

they're looking for sex. Fortunately, the persistent come-ons will be more irritating than threatening.

The most common assault upon tourists is **bag-snatching** or **pickpocketing**, so take the usual precautions and only carry the minimum amount of cash you require. Also avoid leaving personal possessions on view in a rental car. Some hotels are not entirely secure, so put any valuables in the hotel security box, if there is one, or at least stash them out of sight. Registered *casas particulares* are, as a rule, safe. You should always carry your passport (or a photocopy) as the police sometimes ask to inspect them.

The **police** are generally indifferent to crimes against tourists – and they may even try to blame you for not being more vigilant. If you're the victim of theft, you may find it more useful to contact **Asistur** (☎ 7/33-85-27 or 33-89-20), a 24-hour assistance agency based in Havana and Santiago; they'll be able to arrange replacement travel documents, help with financial difficulties and recover lost luggage.

Drugs, specifically marijuana and cocaine, are increasingly common in Cuba. The authorities take a very dim view of drug abuse and prison sentences are frequently meted out, even for possession of small amounts.

The **emergency number** for the Cuban police differs from place to place. In Havana dial ☎ 82-01-16 or 60-01-06; in Varadero, Trinidad and Santiago dial ☎ 116.

Health

Providing you take common-sense precautions, visiting Cuba poses **no particular health risks**. It is essential, however, to bring your own medical kit, including painkillers and any other supplies you think you might need, as they are hard to come by on the island and the choice is extremely limited.

Cuba's famous free health service does not extend to foreign visitors; in fact the government uses its impressive medical advances to earn extra revenue for the regime. There are specific **hospitals** for foreign visitors, most of them run by Cubanacan (🌐 www.cubanacan.cu/espanol/turismo/salud) and its subsidiary Servimed, an institution set up in 1994 to deal exclusively with health tourism. If you do wind up in hospital in Cuba, one of the first things you should do is contact Asistur (see opposite), who usually deal with insurance claims. For minor complaints you shouldn't have to go further than the hotel doctor. If you're staying in a *casa particular*, your best bet if feeling ill is to inform your host, who should be able to arrange a house-call with the family doctor.

As with much else on the island there are two types of **pharmacies** in Cuba: tourist pharmacies operating in *pesos convertibles* and peso pharmacies for the population at large. The majority are run by Servimed and you should ask for the nearest *clínica internacional* within which they are normally located.

History

Cuba was inhabited for thousands of years before Columbus by **Amerindians** who had worked their way up through the Antilles from the South American mainland. The last group, the Taíno, who arrived sometime around 1100 AD, were a mostly peaceful people, largely unprepared for the conflict they were to face with the arrival of the Spanish.

On October 27, 1492, **Columbus** landed on the northeastern coast of Cuba. On his second voyage in 1494, he erroneously concluded that Cuba was part of the mainland of Cathay, or China. Not convinced that Columbus had discovered a western route to Asia, Spain's King Ferdinand sent an another expedition to the island, and in 1509 Diego Velázquez landed near Guantánamo Bay with three hundred men. Those Indians who were not killed died later from European diseases or the harsh living and working conditions forced upon them.

As **Spain** consolidated its American empire, Cuba gained importance thanks to its location on the main route to Europe. The population grew slowly, with African **slaves** being imported as early as the 1520s to replace the dwindling indigenous population; by the end of the sixteenth century there was almost no trace of the **Taíno** natives.

The Cuban **economy** came to be based heavily on agriculture. Cassava, fruits, coffee, tobacco and sugar were amongst the chief exports and the island slowly became a source of potentially significant wealth. The first half of the eighteenth century saw Cuban society become more sophisticated, as a clear Cuban identity emerged, distinct from that of Spain. By the end of the century the colony had established its first newspaper, theatre and university.

However, economic progress was **restricted** as the colony was forced to trade exclusively with Spain. This was to change with the British seizure of Havana. Engaged in the Seven Years' War against Spain and France, the British sought to weaken the Spanish position by attacking Spain's possessions overseas. On August 12, 1762, the British took control of Havana and opened up new markets in North America and Europe. Within a year, Cuba was back in Spanish hands, but the impact of the British occupation was enormous, as previously unobtainable products flowed into Cuba. In 1776 the newly independent US started trading directly with Cuban merchants.

In 1791 revolution in Haiti, then known as Saint-Domingue, destroyed the sugar industry there and Cuba became the largest producer of **sugar** in the region. Rising demand and rising prices, combined with scientific advances in the sugar industry and improved transportation on the island during the first half of the nineteenth century, transformed the face of Cuban society.

Meanwhile, as the size of the slave population increased, the conditions of slavery worsened, and **slave rebellions** became more common. The rebellions were symptomatic of an increasingly divided societal structure, one which pitted *criollos* against *peninsulares*, black against white, and the less developed eastern half of the country against the more economically and politically powerful west. A reformist movement emerged and grew more and more radical; in the early 1840s, the colonial government reacted with a brutal campaign of repression known as La Escalera. The authorities killed hundreds, soldiers were sent over from Spain and the governor's power was increased to allow repression of even the slightest sign of rebellion.

In 1865 the **Reformist Party** was founded by a group of *criollo* planters, providing the most coherent expression yet of the desire for change. A revolution plotted by a group of landowners, headed by Carlos Manuel de Céspedes, got no further than the planning stage when the colonial authorities sent troops to arrest the conspirators. Pre-empting his own arrest on October 10, 1868, Céspedes freed the slaves working at his sugar mill, effectively instigating the **Ten Years War**, the first Cuban war of independence. The Pact of Zanjón (1878), signed by the Spanish, ended most of the hostilities but failed to address the fundamental causes of conflict, including political representation for the *criollos* and the end of slavery. It was not until 1886 that slavery was **abolished**, whilst in 1890, when universal suffrage was declared in Spain, Cuba was excluded.

No one did more to stimulate interest in Cuban independence than **José Martí**. From his base in New York he worked tirelessly, trying to gain momentum for the idea of an independent Cuba. In 1892 he founded the **Cuban Revolutionary Party** (**PRC**), which began to coordinate with groups inside Cuba as preparations were laid for a Second War of Independence. Martí was killed in his first battle, but the revolutionaries fought their way across the country until on January 1, 1896, they reached Havana province.

Riots in Havana gave the US the excuse they had been waiting for to send in the warship *Maine*, ostensibly to protect US citizens. On February 15, 1898, the *Maine* blew up in Havana harbour, killing 258 people; the US accused the Spanish of sabotage and so began the **Spanish-American War**. To this day the Cuban government remains adamant that the US blew up its own ship in order to justify its intervention in the war, but evidence is inconclusive.

On December 10, 1898, the Spanish signed the **Treaty of Paris**, handing control of Cuba, as well as Puerto Rico and the Philippines, to the US. In 1901 Cuba adopted a new constitution, devised in Washington without any Cuban consultation, which included the **Platt Amendment**, declaring that the US had the right to intervene in Cuban affairs should the independence of the country come under threat. The intention to keep Cuba on a short leash was made even clearer when at the same time a US **naval base** was established at Guantánamo Bay. On May 20, 1902, under these terms, Cuba was declared a republic and Tomás Estrada Palma, the first elected Cuban president, headed a long line of US puppets.

With the **economy** in ruins following the war, US investors moved in. Havana and Varadero became flooded with casinos, strip-clubs, hotels and sports clubs, and the island gained a reputation as an anything-goes destination, a reputation enhanced during the years of Prohibition in the US. However, the global economic crisis, which followed the Wall Street Crash of 1929, caused widespread discontent, and opposition to the government became increasingly radical – but was ruthlessly repressed. Amidst the chaos emerged a man who was to shape profoundly the destiny of Cuba.

A young sergeant, **Fulgencio Batista**, staged a coup within the army and replaced most of the officers with men loyal to him. He installed Ramón Grau San Martín as president, and then continued to prop up a series of Cuban presidents until in 1940 he was himself elected.

Batista was not, at least during the early years, the hated man that communist Cuba would have people believe. Some of his policies had widespread support and, despite the backing he received from the US, he was no puppet. By the time he lost power in 1944 Cuba was a more independent and socially just country than it had been at any other time during the pseudo-republic. Carlos Prío Socarrás led the country until 1952 when Batista, who had left Cuba after his defeat in 1944, returned to fight another election. On March 10, 1952, two days before the election, Batista, fearing failure, staged a **military coup** and seized control of the country. He abolished the constitution and went on to establish a dictatorship bearing little if any resemblance to his previous term as Cuban leader.

Amongst the candidates for congress in the 1952 election was **Fidel Castro**, a young lawyer who saw his political ambitions dashed when Batista seized power. Effectively frozen out of constitutional politics by Batista's intolerance of opposition, on July 26, 1953, Castro and around 125 others attacked an army barracks at Moncada in Santiago de Cuba. Castro regarded the attack "as a gesture which will set an example for the people of Cuba". The attack failed and those who weren't shot fled into the mountains where they were soon caught. Castro would certainly have been shot had his captors taken him back to the barracks, but a sympathetic police sergeant kept him in the relative safety of the police jail. A trial followed in which Castro gave what has become one of his most famous speeches, uttering the immortal words, "Condemn me if you will. History will absolve me." He was sentenced to fifteen

years' imprisonment but had served less than three when, under popular pressure, he was released and sent into exile.

Now based in Mexico, Castro set about organizing a **revolutionary force** to take back to Cuba; among his recruits was an Argentinian doctor named **Ernesto "Che" Guevara**. They called themselves the Movimiento 26 de Julio, the 26th of July Movement. Waging a war based on guerrilla tactics, the rebels gained the upper hand against Batista's forces. Eventually, the army surrendered to the rebels and Fidel Castro began a victory march across the country, arriving in Havana on January 8, 1959.

Though the revolutionary war had ended, this date marks only the beginning of what in Cuba is referred to as the **Revolution**. The Agrarian Reform Law of May 1959 set the tone, by which the land, much of it foreign-owned, was either nationalized or redistributed amongst the rural population. Education became the focus for the reshaping of the country, while public health saw great gains in the early years of the revolution and is an area that continues to elicit praise. As the decade wore on, the regime became more intolerant of dissenting voices, declaring all those who challenged government policy to be counter-revolutionaries.

During the first few years of the revolution, as **Cuba–US relations** soured and the revolution seemed to be swinging further to the left, the Cuban upper-middle and upper classes sought refuge overseas, predominantly in the US. Between 1960 and 1962 around 200,000 emigrants left Cuba, forming large exile communities, especially in Florida.

As huge sectors of Cuban industry were nationalized and foreign businesses, most of them US-owned, found themselves dispossessed, the US government retaliated by freezing purchases of Cuban sugar, restricting exports and then, in 1961, breaking off diplomatic relations. The US backed counter-revolutionary forces within Cuba as well as terrorist campaigns aimed at sabotaging the state apparatus. Finally, President Kennedy opted for all-out invasion and on April 17, 1961, a military force of Cuban exiles, trained and equipped in the US, landed at the **Bay of Pigs** in southern Matanzas. However, the revolutionaries were ready for them and the whole operation ended within 72 hours.

In December of that year, in the face of economic and political isolation from the US, the Cuban leader declared himself a Marxist-Leninist. The benefits for Cuba were immediate as the **Soviet Union** agreed to buy Cuban sugar at artificially high prices whilst selling them petroleum at well below its market value. Then, in 1962, at Castro's request, the Soviets installed over forty **missiles** on the island. Kennedy declared an embargo on any military weapons entering Cuba. Krushchev ignored it, and Soviet ships loaded with more weapons made their way across the Atlantic. Neither side would back down and nuclear weapons were prepared for launch in the US. A six-day stalemate followed, after which a deal was finally struck and the world breathed a collective sigh of relief – the **Cuban Missile Crisis** had passed.

The 1960s saw new economic policies aimed at reducing Cuba's dependence on sugar production. However, the mass exodus of professionals during the early years of the decade, coupled with the crippling impact of the US embargo, made this all but impossible. In the end, Cuba became even more dependent on sugar than it had been prior to the revolution.

In 1975 the government adopted its first **Five Year Plan**, setting relatively realistic targets for growth and production. With rises in the price of sugar on the world market and increased Soviet assistance, there were tangible improvements. The policy changes were carried on into the next decade as the economy continued to make modest improvements, though the mass exodus of 125,000 Cubans in the **Mariel boatlift** of 1980 demonstrated that, for many, times were still hard. As

more private enterprise was permitted, however, Castro became alarmed at the number of people giving up their state jobs and in 1986 issued his Rectification of Errors. The economy returned to centralization and, with increasing sums being ploughed into defence, Cuba survived only with heavy Soviet support.

In 1989 the bubble burst. The **implosion of the Soviet Union** led to a loss of over eighty percent of Cuba's trade. In 1990, the government declared the beginning of the **Special Period**, a euphemism that essentially meant compromise and sacrifice for all Cubans. Public transport deteriorated dramatically as the country lost almost all of its fuel imports, strict rationing of food was introduced and power cuts became frequent.

In 1992, the US government took advantage of Cuba's crisis to tighten the trade embargo further as thousands of Cubans risked their lives trying to escape the country across the Florida Straits. Forced to make huge ideological readjustments, the government embarked on one of its most ideologically risky journeys yet, when, in August 1993, the US dollar was declared legal tender. With this came other reforms as the Cubans sought to rebuild the economy by appealing to the worldwide tourist trade.

Former President Jimmy Carter's visit to Cuba in May of 2002 was the first visit to Cuba by a former or sitting US leader since 1959. While Carter promoted reconciliation with the US, and expressed his support for easing the embargo, President George W. Bush vowed to keep the **embargo** in place until Castro implements democratic reforms. Compounding the situation around the same time was the Bush administration's inclusion of Cuba in the "Axis of Evil".

The **economic hardships** following the collapse of the Soviet bloc and the measures taken by the government to deal with them have made Cuba's lack of social and political freedoms more apparent than at any time since the

1960s. However, whether Cuba is the country decried in right-wing circles as suffering at the hands of a dictator or, as more moderate pundits suggest, a country whose people would elect a similar government were they not denied the privilege, many Cubans support the ideologies of the revolution, even though they feel frustrated by their political impotence. So convinced are they that the present situation will last forever that it is not uncommon to hear people surmise that *if* Fidel dies, rather than *when*, things may change.

3.1

Havana and around

Havana is in a class of its own on the island, with five times as many inhabitants as the next largest Cuban city, Santiago de Cuba. Nowhere else are the contradictions which have come to characterize the country as pronounced as they are here in the capital. The restoration projects which have returned some of the finest colonial architecture in the Caribbean to its original splendour continue, but there is still a long way to go before they reach many of the city's overcrowded, neglected neighbourhoods. There is a sense in some parts of the capital that Havana is on the move, with visitors pouring in, new nightspots appearing regularly and an increasing variety of products in shops which, not long ago, either didn't exist or stood empty. Yet, on the other hand, time stands still, or even goes backwards, in a city where 1950s Chevrolets, Buicks and Oldsmobiles cruise the roads and significant numbers of people seem to spend most of the day in the street or on their crumbling, nineteenth-century doorsteps. Although the tourist industry and foreign cash are infiltrating every level of life in the capital, the city is far from a slave to tourism. Cuban **culture** is at its most exuberant here, with an abundance of theatres, cinemas, concert venues and art galleries. Along with Santiago, Havana is host to the country's most diverse **music scene**, where world-famous *salsa* and *bolero* orchestras and bands ply their trade while, bubbling under the surface, the newer rock and hip-hop subcultures are gaining momentum.

East of the city are the region's best **beaches**, including the top-notch Playas del Este. South of the city is the Museo Ernest Hemingway, the writer's long-time Cuban residence, while slightly further west, the impressive Jardín Botánico Nacional offers some picturesque scenery.

Havana

Founded on the western banks of a fabulous natural harbour, what was once the entire city of **HAVANA** now forms the most captivating part of **Habana Vieja**, the old city and the capital's tourist centre. This UNESCO-declared World Heritage Site is one of crumbling magnificence and restored beauty. Any sightseeing you do will fan out from here, taking in the fine museums, colonial buildings, elegant plazas, sweeping boulevards and narrow, atmospheric streets bristling with life.

Most visitors to Havana restrict themselves to Habana Vieja and **Vedado**, a leafy district of the city occupying the western half of the seafront promenade, the Malecón, where many of the post-colonial mansions have been converted into public works and ministry offices or museums. The best way to appreciate Vedado's compact, quiet suburban streets is on foot. From here, you could walk the couple of kilometres to the famous **Plaza de la Revolución**, where giant monuments to the two most famous icons of the Cuban struggle for independence, Che Guevara and José Martí, present unmissable photo opportunities. Beyond Vedado to the west, on the other side of the Río Almendares, **Miramar** – modelled on mid-twentieth-century Miami – ushers in yet another change in the urban landscape. A commercial district is emerging on its western fringes, accompanied by a number of luxury hotels, whilst some of Havana's most sophisticated restaurants are scattered around Miramar's leafy streets.

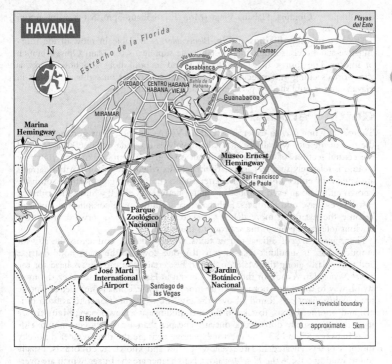

Arrival and information

All international flights land at **José Martí International Airport** (℡7/33-56-66 or 33-57-77), about 15km south of the city centre. The vast majority deposit passengers at Terminal Three where most of the airport services are concentrated, including a few shops, a restaurant and a bureau de change, though there are car rental desks in each of the three terminals. From the airport, it's most likely you'll take a taxi; the half-hour journey into Havana shouldn't cost much more than $15.

Arriving by bus, you'll be dropped off at either the **Víazul terminal** (℡881-14-13 or 7/881-56-52), on Avenida 26 over the road from the city zoo, or the Astro-operated **Estación de Omnibus** (℡879-24-56), near the Plaza de la Revolución. Both bus stations are a $3–5 taxi ride from most centrally located hotels, and there's a car rental desk at the Víazul terminal. Trains pull in at Habana Vieja's **Estación Central de Ferrocarriles** (℡7/861-76-51 or 862-19-20), where you'll probably have to find yourself a private taxi or one of Havana's army of *bicitaxis* – three-wheeled, two-seater bicycle cabs. If you arrive on one of the two or three cruise ships that dock in Havana every week, you will disembark at the splendid **Terminal Sierra Maestra** (℡7/866-65-24 or 862-19-25), which faces the Plaza de San Francisco in Habana Vieja.

The state-run Infotur operates several **information centres**, with the best-stocked found at Obispo no. 521 e/ Bernaza y Villegas in Habana Vieja (daily 9am–7pm; ℡7/33-33-33 or 862-45-86, ✉obispodir@cubacel.net) and in Playa, in the western suburbs, at 5ta. Ave. y 112 (daily 9am–6pm; ℡7/204-70-36, ✉miramardir@cubacel.net). You can book rooms and excursions through these centres, though for a better choice of **maps and guides**, head for El Navegante at Mercaderes no. 115

e/ Obispo y Obrapía, Habana Vieja (Mon–Fri 8.30am–5pm, Sat 8.30am–noon; ☎57-10-38).

The free monthly **listings guide**, *Bienvenidos*, is available in most of the four- and five-star hotels, though the most reliable supplier is the main Obispo branch of Infotur. The tourist magazine *Prisma*, found in bookshops and hotel stores, is also worth seeking out, especially as it often carries articles on sights and events in Havana and is published in parallel Spanish/English text.

Getting around

There's only one way to experience Habana Vieja – on foot – but **getting around** the rest of the city will almost inevitably involve a taxi ride of some kind. Most of the central sections of Havana are laid out on a grid system and finding your way around is relatively simple, particularly in Vedado, where the vast majority of streets are known by either a number or a letter: streets running roughly north to south are known either by an even number or a letter between A and P, whilst those running east to west have odd numbers. Habana Vieja is a little more complicated, not least because the narrower, more densely packed streets allow less forward vision; the obvious reference point is the seafront to the north.

There are plenty of official tourist **taxis**, which will take you across the city for around US$5. It shouldn't take long to flag one down in the main hotel districts and particularly along the Malecón, but to be certain you can always head for the *Hotel Nacional* in Vedado or the Parque Central in Habana Vieja. However, the most stylish way to travel, and not necessarily more expensive, is in any number of vintage pre-revolutionary cars found all over the city, most of which operate as both official and unofficial taxis. To take in the surroundings at a slower pace, **bicitaxis** are ideal though usually don't work out any cheaper than a car; a fifteen-minute ride costs between $2 and $3. The most inexpensive taxis are the three-wheeled novelty motor scooters encased in large yellow spheres and known as **cocotaxis**, usually found waiting outside the *Hotel Inglaterra*. Far cheaper are the **buses**, which are over-crowded and infrequent and there is no route information at bus stops, though if you decide to brave it, your journey will cost no more than 40 centavos (less than 3¢).

Accommodation

Accommodation in the capital is abundant and in most of the main areas you'll find rooms starting from $25 – as well as those at upwards of $200 a night. You'd do well to make a **reservation**, particularly in high season (November to April) when the town is packed. Many visitors choose to stay in the state hotels in **Habana Vieja**, handy for many of the key sights and well served by restaurants and bars. Quieter **Vedado** features some of the city's more spectacular *casas particulares*, but you'll need transport to make the trip to Habana Vieja.

Habana Vieja

Casa de Eugenio Barral García San Ignacio no. 656 e/ Jesús María y Merced ☎862-98-77. Deep in southern Habana Vieja, this exceptional large-apartment *casa particular* with very hospitable landlords is spotlessly clean and beautifully furnished with antiques. The three double bedrooms all have a/c and one has a TV. Price includes full breakfast. ❷

Casa del Científico Paseo del Prado no. 212 esq. Trocadero ☎7/862-45-11 or 863-35-91, ℱ 33-01-67. The least expensive hotel this close to the Parque Central and, unlike most of Havana's remodelled colonial buildings, this aristocratic

residence has barely been touched, leaving much of the original opulent decoration and a more rough-hewn finish. Rooms are comfortable but a little basic, some share bathrooms and there's a spacious rooftop terrace. ❷

Chez Nous Brasil no. 115 e/ Cuba y San Ignacio ☎7/862-62-87, ℮cheznous@ceniai.inf.cu. This majestic *casa particular* has three balconied first-floor rooms for rent, all with a/c, TV and minibar. From the airy, leafy central patio a spiral staircase leads up to the spacious roof terrace where there's another room with en-suite bathroom. The savvy owners speak English and French. Bookings essential. ❷

Florida Obispo no. 252 esq. Cuba ☎ 7/862-41-27 or 861-56-21, ✉ reservas@habaguanexhflorid a.co.cu. A perfect blend of modern luxury and colonial elegance with marble floors, iron chandeliers, birds singing in the airy stone-columned central patio and potted plants throughout, this hotel is one of the outstanding success stories of the Habana Vieja restoration project. ❻

Hostal Conde de Villanueva (aka *Hostal del Habano*) Mercaderes esq. Lamparilla ☎ 862-92-93, ⓦ www.hostalcondevillanueva.cu. Despite its relatively small size this place boasts a fantastic cellar-style restaurant, a wonderful courtyard and a relaxing smokers' lounge and bar. ❻

Hostal Valencia Oficios no. 53 esq. Obrapía ☎ 867-10-37 and 7/861-64-23, ✉ hostales@hvhc. ohch.cu. Plain but pleasant rooms in a beautiful building that feels more like a large house than a small hotel. Highlights include a cobbled-floor courtyard with hanging vines. ❸

Inglaterra Paseo del Prado no. 416 esq. San Rafael, Parque Central ☎ 860-85-93 to 97, ✉ reserva@gcingla.gca.tur.cu. Superbly located on the Parque Central, this classic nineteenth-century hotel could do with sprucing up in places and is less luxurious though just as expensive as some of its neighbours. However, the atmospheric interior is full of genuine colonial hallmarks and the rooms are of a high standard. ❻

Vedado

Bruzón Calle Bruzón no. 217 e/ Pozos Dulces y Boyeros ☎ 7/877-56-84. More like a youth hostel than a hotel, though the small, dark rooms and paucity of frills or hot water are all redeemed by the reasonable price. Near the Plaza de la Revolución. ❸

Casa de Angela Arenal Calle 6 no. 620 e/ 25 y 27 ☎ 7/37-20-9. Airy and cool throughout its white interior this stately colonial house with two a/c rooms is one of the best choices in the area. Both have televisions and share an interconnecting bathroom, with the largest room en suite. Other attractions include a covered patio laden with overhanging hibiscus, an alfresco eating area and parking for two cars. ❸

Casa de Mélida Jordán Calle 25 no. 1102 e/ 6 y 8 ☎ 7/83-352-19, ✉ melida@girazul.com. A big stylish house set back from the road and surrounded by a marble verandah overlooking an expansive garden. Two of the three rooms have their own bathrooms and all are beautifully furnished. The largest room has twin beds and the other two doubles, although extra beds can be added. English is spoken by the helpful and friendly owners and there are various extra services available. A superb choice. ❸

Habana Libre Calle 23 esq. L ☎ 7/33-40-11, ⒻⒻ 33-31-41. Large, slick city hotel with lots of shops, a terrace pool, three restaurants, numerous bars and a cabaret, making it a solid, if somewhat anonymous, choice. ❼

Hotel Nacional Calle O esq. 21 ☎ 7/33-35-64, ✉ reserva@gnacio.gma.cma.net. The choice of visiting celebrities for decades, this handsome hotel looks like an Arabian palace and is deservedly recognized as one of Havana's best hotels. Beautiful rooms, smooth service and excellent facilities. ❽

Habana Vieja

By far the most visited part of the city, bursting with centuries-old buildings and buzzing with a strong sense of the past, **Habana Vieja** – or Old Havana – is the richest sightseeing area in the city. Its narrow streets, refined colonial mansions, countless churches, cobblestone plazas and sixteenth-century fortresses make it one of the most complete colonial urban centres in the Americas. Yet there is much more to Habana Vieja than its physical make-up. Unlike many of the world's major cities, the tourist centre of Havana is also home to a large proportion of the city's residents, with some of its poorest families crammed into apartment buildings right next door to the museums and hotels to which tourists flock in ever-increasing numbers.

The **Plaza de la Catedral** and the nearby **Plaza de Armas** are both good starting points for your visit, while for the other unmissable sights head up **Obispo**, Habana Vieja's busiest street, to the **Parque Central**. If you intend to do all your sightseeing in one fell swoop you might want to restrict yourself to a maximum of three or four museums, as the half-hearted displays and incoherent collections which occupy many of them can become disheartening. That said, several of the city's museums are excellent, most notably the **Museo de la Revolución** and the **Museo Nacional de Bellas Artes**.

A word of warning: Habana Vieja is the **bag-snatching** centre of the city, with an increasing number of petty thieves working the streets, so use extra precaution. Even at night, however, there is very rarely any violent crime.

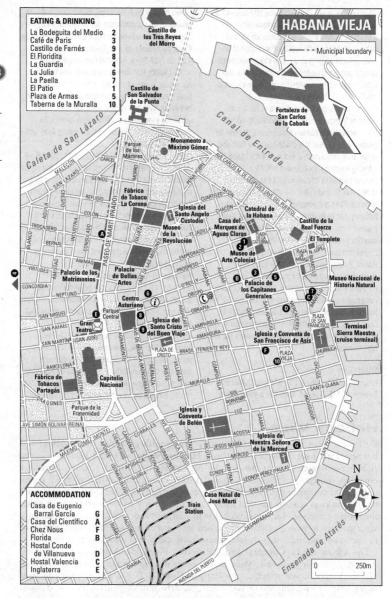

EATING & DRINKING

La Bodeguita del Medio	2
Café de Paris	3
Castillo de Farnés	9
El Floridita	8
La Guardia	4
La Julia	6
La Paella	7
El Patio	1
Plaza de Armas	5
Taberna de la Muralla	10

HABANA VIEJA

- - - Municipal boundary

ACCOMMODATION

Casa de Eugenio Barral García	G
Casa del Científico	A
Chez Nous	F
Florida	B
Hostal Conde de Villanueva	D
Hostal Valencia	C
Inglaterra	E

Plaza de la Catedral

The **Plaza de la Catedral**, in northeastern Habana Vieja, is one of the most architecturally coherent squares in the old city, enclosed on three sides by a set of symmetrical, eighteenth-century aristocratic residences. The striking **Catedral de la Habana** (Mon–Sat 10.30am–4pm, Sun 9.30am–noon; Mass at 10.30am; free), hailed as the consummate example of the Cuban Baroque style, dominates the plaza with its swirling detail, curved edges and cluster of columns. While the less spectacular interior bears an endearing resemblance to an archetypal local church, it features lavishly framed portraits by French painter Jean Baptiste Vermay and other artwork.

Opposite the cathedral, the Casa de los Condes de Casa Bayona, built in 1720, houses the **Museo de Arte Colonial** (daily 9am–7pm; $2, guided tour $1 extra, $2 to take photos). Its comprehensive collection of well-preserved, mostly nineteenth-century furniture and ornaments offers a clear insight into aristocratic living conditions during the later years of Spanish rule in Cuba. The predominantly European-made artefacts have been collected from colonial residences around the city and include mahogany dressers, gold and porcelain vases and a fantastic antique piano. The most sophisticated of the colonial mansions on the plaza is the **Casa del Marques de Aguas Claras**. Its serene fountain-centred courtyard encompassed by pillar-propped arches and simple coloured-glass portals is actually part of the delightful *El Patio* restaurant, so you'll need to eat there to see it.

Plaza de Armas and the Castillo de la Real Fuerza

A couple of blocks southeast of the Plaza de la Catedral, on San Ignacio and then on O'Reilly, the area around the **Plaza de Armas**, the oldest and most animated of Habana Vieja's squares, was where Havana established itself as a city in the second half of the sixteenth century. Based around an attractive, leafy, landscaped core, the plaza at its busiest seethes with tourists as live music wafts from the *La Mina* restaurant in the corner and browsers crowd around the stalls of the outdoor book market.

The refined **Palacio de los Capitanes Generales**, on the western side of the plaza, was the seat of the Spanish government from the time of its inauguration in 1791 to the end of the Spanish-American War in 1898. It's now home to one of Havana's best museums, the **Museo de la Ciudad** (daily 9am–6pm; $3, $2 extra for guided tour), a fine representation of the city's colonial heritage. A number of the upstairs rooms have been precisely restored, including the sumptuous Salón del Trono (Throne Room) with its dark-red, satin-lined walls intended for royal visits (though in fact no Spanish king or queen ever did visit colonial Cuba). Most striking is the Salón Dorado (Gold Room), where the governor of the city used to receive his guests amidst golden furniture and precious porcelain.

There's more to see around the rest of the square, particularly in the **Museo Nacional de Historia Natural**, on the corner of Obispo and Oficios (Tues–Sat 9.30am–5pm, Sun 10am–3.30pm; $3, $4 with guide). Though unimpressive compared to many of its counterparts elsewhere in the world, this is nevertheless one of the city's more substantial collections, most likely to go down well with kids. The essentials are covered on the ground floor, where simple models and rather primitive interactive video displays attempt to tell the history of life on earth, while one floor up, Cuban wildlife is the dominant theme.

In the square's northeastern corner, the incongruous classical Greek architecture of **El Templete** church (daily 9.30am–6pm; $1) marks the exact spot of the foundation of Havana and the city's first Mass in 1519. In the same corner, just beyond the northeastern border of the plaza, is the **Castillo de la Real Fuerza**, a solid sixteenth-century fortress surrounded by a moat. It is placed well back from the mouth of the bay, a location which allowed the English, in 1762, to take control of Havana without ever coming into the firing range of the fortress's cannon. Today the ground floor houses an excellent collection of ceramic art in the **Museo de la Cerámica** (daily 8.30am–6.30pm; $1), where pre-Columbian-style vases sit alongside quirky modern pieces, such as a pottery typewriter.

Parque Central

From the Plaza de Armas a walk up busy Obispo leads to the **Parque Central**, straddling the border between Habana Vieja and Centro Habana and within shouting distance of the Capitolio Nacional. Although the speeding traffic detracts somewhat from the whole, the grandeur of the surrounding buildings, characteristic of the celebratory early twentieth-century architecture in this section of town, lends the square a stateliness that's quite distinct from the residential feel which pervades the rest of Habana Vieja. The attention-grabber is undoubtedly the **Gran Teatro**, between San Martín and San Rafael (☎7/861-30-96), an explosion of balustraded balconies, colonnaded cornices and sculpted stone figures striking Classical poses. For a proper look inside, you'll have to attend one of the ballets which make up the majority of performances here; these usually take place at weekends, and tickets can be bought from the box office just inside the main entrance and usually cost around $10.

Capitolio Nacional

Just beyond the southwestern corner of the Parque Central looms the familiar-looking dome of the **Capitolio Nacional** (Mon–Sat 9am–7pm, Sun 9am–3pm; $3). Opened in 1929 (and bearing a striking resemblance to the Capitol Building in Washington DC, though little is made of this in Cuban publications), it was the seat of the House of Representatives and the Senate prior to the Revolution. The two ornate main chambers are now the centrepiece of visitor tours, and the walk round, with or without a free tour guide, shouldn't take you longer than twenty minutes as only one floor is open to the public, much of it behind ropes. Nevertheless, the sheer size of the magnificent polished entrance hall known as the Salón de los Pasos Perdidos (The Room of Lost Steps) and the breathtaking gold and bronze Rococo-style decoration of the Hemiciclio Camilo Cienfuegos, a theatrical, echoing conference chamber, are enough to leave a lasting impression.

Fábrica de Tobacos Partagás

Behind the Capitolio stands one of the country's oldest cigar factories, the **Fábrica de Tobacos Partagás** (tours every 30min Mon–Fri 9.30–11am & 12.30–2pm; occasionally Sat same hours; $10), which was founded in 1849 and is still churning out such famous makes as Cohiba, Bolívar and Partagás. Although steeply priced compared to most museum entrance fees, the 45-minute tour is easily among the most fascinating things to do in the city, with English-speaking guides taking you through the various stages of production – drying, sorting, rolling and boxing – all performed in separate rooms under one roof. There's even an area used as a kind of cigar school, from where, after a nine-month course, those who graduate will move upstairs and join the hundred or so workers making some of the finest cigars in the world. Here, a sea of expert workers – expected to produce between 80 and 250 cigars during their eight-hour shifts – are read to while they work, from a newspaper in the mornings and from a book in the afternoons. It's entirely uncontrived and there's a very genuine sense of observing an everyday operation, with most of the workers almost oblivious to the flashing of cameras. There is also an excellent **cigar shop** just inside the entrance.

Museo Nacional de Bellas Artes

The **Museo Nacional de Bellas Artes** (Tues–Sat 10am–6pm, Sun 10am–2pm; $5 for one building, $8 for both) is the most spectacular of Havana's museums, containing by far the largest collection of art in the country. This has been divided between two buildings: the Art Deco Palacio de Bellas Artes, opposite the Museo de la Revolución on Trocadero, is the showcase for exclusively Cuban art, while the rest of the world is represented in the Centro Asturiano, across Agramonte from the Parque Central.

The best way to tackle the **Cuban collection** in the **Palacio de Bellas Artes** is to take the lifts in the entrance lobby up to the top floor and walk round clockwise, as the exhibits are laid out in chronological order. The most historic pieces are on the gantry that runs most of the length of the first two rooms, including a great lithograph of nineteenth-century Havana by Eduardo Laplante. The rest of the top floor leaps straight into the twentieth century, beginning with paintings by Victor

Manuel García (1897–1969), including his portrait of a gypsy girl, *Gitana tropical*, considered a national treasure and one of the most widely reproduced paintings in Cuba. Here also is the morbid work of Fidelo Ponce de León (1895–1949), whose penchant for depictions of illness and death are evident in the works on display, such as *Tuberculosis*, a group portrait of gaunt-faced subjects. Amongst the more modern stuff, the jumbled-looking *Esta es la Historia* ("This is history") by Gilberto de la Nuez (1913–1993) is a large picture made up of numerous tiny scenes, all set against the same background but in fact each portraying a separate and significant moment in Cuban history.

The grandiose **Centro Asturiano** is divided up by country of origin, with collections from Britain, Italy, Spain and France, as well as Dutch, Flemish, Latin and North American rooms and a smaller Asian section. No single collection particularly stands out, as many of the artists are lesser-known painters and there are no classic or renowned works on display. However, there are several paintings by notable artists, including *Malvern Hall* by John Constable and *Kermesse* by Jan Brueghel (the younger), interesting as much for the fact that they somehow ended up in Cuba as for their artistic merit. Most of the fourth floor is dedicated to the ancient art of Rome, Egypt and Greece, with highlights of the Egyptian section including a 3000-year-old tomb.

Museo de la Revolución

From the Parque Central it's a two-minute walk along Agramonte to Havana's most famous museum, the **Museo de la Revolución** (daily 10am–5pm; $4, $2 extra for guided tour), defiantly housed in the sumptuous presidential palace of the 1950s dictator General Fulgencio Batista. The events leading up to the triumph of the revolution in 1959 are covered in unparalleled detail, but your attention span is unlikely to last the full three storeys. Visitors work their way down from the top floor, which is the most engaging part of the museum and where you should concentrate your efforts. The events of the revolutionary war and the urban insurgency movements during the 1950s were surprisingly well documented, and there are some fantastically dramatic pictures, like one of the police assault on the Socialist Party headquarters. Some of the classic images of the campaign waged in the Sierra Maestra by Castro and his band of followers will look familiar, but even serious students of Cuban history will struggle to keep track of the chronology as they overdose on battle plans and miscellaneous firearms. Located outside, to the rear of the museum, is the **Granma Memorial**, where the boat which took Castro and his men from Mexico to Cuba to begin the revolution is preserved within a giant glass-walled hall.

Centro Habana

For many visitors, the crumbling buildings and bustling streets of **Centro Habana**, crammed between the hotel districts of Habana Vieja and Vedado, are glimpsed only through a taxi window en route to the city's more tourist-friendly areas. Yet this no-frills quarter has a character all of its own, as illuminating and fascinating as anywhere in the capital. Overwhelmingly residential, its late eighteenth- and nineteenth-century neighbourhoods throb with life, particularly **El Barrio Chino**, Havana's Chinatown, and there's no better place to really savour the essence of the city, particularly because here it's not on display but up to you to discover.

That said, this part of town is for the most part not that attractive on the surface. Full of broken sewage systems, potholed roads and piles of rubbish, Centro Habana has not yet enjoyed the degree of investment and rejuvenation that Habana Vieja has, save for the **Malecón**, where there are at last visible signs of part of the famous seafront promenade being returned to its former glory, with a growing number of cafeterias appearing along the stretch and a few buildings having been renovated in recent years.

El Barrio Chino

About a block inside Centro Habana from Habana Vieja's western border, the grand entrance to **El Barrio Chino**, Havana's Chinatown, is likely to confuse most visitors, as it's placed three blocks from any noticeable change in the neighbourhood's appearance. The entrance, a rectangular concrete arch with a pagoda-inspired roof, is south of the Capitolio Nacional, on the intersection of Amistad and Dragones, and marks the beginning of the ten or so square blocks which, at the start of the twentieth century, were home to some ten thousand Chinese immigrants. Most of the Chinese that came to Cuba arrived as indentured labourers during the mid-nineteenth century, and were used by the Spanish and other colonial powers as an alternative to African slaves following the outlawing of the slave trade. Today only a tiny proportion of El Barrio Chino, principally the small triangle of busy streets comprising Cuchillo, Zanja and San Nicolás – collectively known as the **Cuchillo de Zanja** – three blocks west of the arched entrance, is discernibly any more Chinese than the rest of Havana. Indeed, the first thing you are likely to notice about El Barrio Chino is a distinct absence of Chinese people, the once significant immigrant population having long since dissolved into the racial melting pot. The Cuchillo de Zanja itself does feature, however, a tightly packed little back-street **food market** composed mostly of simple fruit and vegetable stalls and lined with eccentric-looking restaurants where the curious and unique mixture of tastes and styles is as much Cuban as Asian. For some of the best Chinatown restaurants you'll need to look elsewhere in the neighbourhood, particularly on Dragones.

The Malecón

The most picturesque way to reach Vedado from Centro Habana is to stroll down the **Malecón**, Havana's famous seawall, which snakes west along the coastline west from La Punta for about 4km. Crowded with schoolchildren hurling themselves into the churning Atlantic, sun-worshippers and wrinkled anglers, it's the city's defining image, and ambling along its length, drinking in the panoramic views, is an essential part of the Havana experience. But don't expect to stroll in solitude: the Malecón is Havana's front room and you won't be on it for long before someone strikes up a conversation. People head here for free entertainment, particularly at night-time when it fills up with guitar-strumming musicians, vendors offering cones of fresh-roasted warm nuts, and star-gazing couples, young and old alike. In recent years it's grown in popularity for the city's expanding clique of gays and transvestites who put its sinuous length to good effect as a nightly catwalk and meeting place, especially the area close to the *Hotel Nacional*. Shutterbugs should visit in the early evening when a good sunset bathes the wall (and the locals) in a photogenic glow.

Pot-holed, sea-beaten and lined with battered old buildings, the Malecón looks much older than its hundred years, but construction only began in 1901 after nearly a century of planning. As with many public works projects in colonial Cuba, it was beset with funding problems and it wasn't until after independence that building got slowly under way, the seawall advancing the length of Havana in slow sections. Each decade saw another chunk of wall erected, until in 1950 it finally reached the Río Almendares. Today, after decades of neglect, it's slowly being spruced up again, with a number of its buildings freshly painted and soulless roadside cafeterias installed every few blocks. Reports from the US reveal that the fast-food giants, anticipating the end of the trade embargo, have already staked their claim on various buildings. Until they move in, this is the most Havanan part of Havana, so enjoy it while you can.

Vedado

The cultural heart of the city, graceful **Vedado** draws the crowds with its palatial hotels – the backbone of so much of Havana's social scene – contemporary art galleries, concerts, restaurants, bars and nightspots. Threadbare but character-filled cinemas lie dotted throughout the area, with the names of the latest North American (and occasionally Cuban) films picked out in wonky and incomplete peg letters on billboards above the entrance. Loosely defined as the area running west of Calzada de Infanta up to the Río Almendares, Vedado is less ramshackle than other parts of the city and more intimate. Plenty of crowds lend a veneer of activity but look closely and you'll see that many people are actually part of a bus queue, waiting their turn to enter Havana's massive ice-cream parlour, *Coppelia*, or are *jineteros* keeping watch for the next buck. Vedado divides into three distinct, easy-to-negotiate parts intersected by four main thoroughfares: the broad boulevards of Avenida de los Presidentes (also known as Calle G) and Paseo, running north to south, and the more prosaic Linea and Calle 23, running east to west.

The most obvious part is modern **La Rampa** (Calle 23), and the streets immediately to the north and south, racing with battered Chevrolets and Buicks and landscaped in high-rise 1950s hotels and utilitarian buildings. It's a relatively small space, but it dominates your immediate impression of Vedado, firstly because the peeling, 50-year-old, skyscrapers are such a rarity in Cuba and, secondly, because as a visitor you end up spending a fair amount of time here – confirming or booking flights, changing money in the hotels, souvenir-shopping in the street markets and dollar shops or eating at the restaurants. Although it's an area for doing rather than seeing, you will find some worthy museums, including the **Museo Napoleónico** on San Miguel (Mon–Sat 10am–5pm; $3, guided tour $3 extra), a treasure trove of artefacts relating to the erstwhile French emperor. Nearby, the **Universidad de La Habana** comprises a series of beautiful buildings in verdant grounds, attended by well-behaved students who personify the virtues of post-revolutionary education.

Beyond here, to the south, the **Plaza de la Revolución** sports immense monuments to the twin heroes, José Martí and Ernesto "Che" Guevara, as well as the exhaustive **Museo José Martí** (Tues–Sat 10am–6pm; $3, $5 including lookout point), which charts Martí's luminary career. The uncompromising concrete sweep of the plaza itself forms a complete contrast to the area's other key attraction, the atmospheric **Necrópolis de Cólon** (daily 8am–5pm; $1), one of the largest cemeteries in the Americas, with some of the most grandiose and stunning tombs in the country.

Vedado shows its third face further west and north. This quieter area is less distinct but broadly encompasses the area north of Calle 23 up to the Malecón, bordered to the west by the Río Almendares and stretching east roughly as far as Avenida de los Presidentes. Here, the back streets narrow and avenues are overhung with leaves from the pine, rubber and weeping fig trees planted in the mid-nineteenth century to create a cool retreat from the blistering tropical sun. Many of the magnificent late- and post-colonial buildings that line these streets – built in a mad medley of Rococo, Baroque and classical styles – have now been converted into state offices and museums, though others retain their role as lavish albeit stricken homes. Particularly noteworthy is the **Museo de los Artes Decorativos**, 502 Calle 17 (Tues–Sat 11am–7pm; $2, $1 extra with guide, $3 extra to take a camera), a dizzying collection of fine furniture and *objets d'art*. Further afield, dotted around Linea, Paseo and Avenida de los Presidentes, are several excellent galleries and cultural centres, notably the **Casa de las Américas** (Sala Contemporánea Mon–Fri 10am–5pm; free; Galería Latino-Americana Mon–Thurs 10am–5pm, Fri 10am–noon; US$2), set up to celebrate Pan-Americanism and displaying quality artworks from all over Latin America as well as hosting regular musical events.

Miramar and the western suburbs

Miramar and the western suburbs are Havana's alter ego: larger than life, with ice-white Miami-style residences, flash business developments, spanking new hotels and curvy Japanese cars streaking along wide avenues. The area is divided into four main suburbs: oceanfront **Miramar**, reached from the Malecón through the tunnel under the Río Almendares; **La Sierra** to its immediate south; **Kohly** tucked further south; and **Almendares** to the west; but you'll often hear the whole area referred to as **Playa** and sometimes addresses are listed as such. Although the houses and embassies are good for a gawp, most visitors venture over the river do so for the **entertainment**, particularly the famous *Tropicana* cabaret in Marianao, and the international **restaurants**, which provide a welcome respite from pork, rice and beans. The **Marina Hemingway** on the outskirts of Miramar also pulls in scores of yachties.

Habana del Este

Many people omit the sights in **Habana del Este**, across the bay from Habana Vieja, from their itinerary, erroneously believing them to be inconveniently located, but those who do make it this far can trace a series of links in the city's history. Broadly speaking, Habana del Este comprises the area on the immediate east side of the bay, visible from the western side and flanked by the Via Monumental.

A visit to the castles and fortifications that collectively make up the **Parque Morro-Cabaña**, on the east side of the harbour, is really worthwhile. Part of the Havana skyline, they dominate the view across the harbour and, along with the fortifications in Habana Vieja, comprise the city's oldest defence system. The **Castillo de los Tres Reyes Magos del Morro** (daily 8am–8.30pm; $3, $2 extra for lighthouse) was built between 1589 and 1630 to complement the **Castillo de San Salvador de la Punta** on the opposite side of the bay, but the dual fortifications failed spectacularly when the British invaded overland in 1762 and occupied the city for six months. From the high parade grounds, studded with rusted cannons and Moorish turrets, you could easily spend an hour or so surveying the bay. A highlight of the visit is watching the sun set over the sea from the summit of the **lighthouse** that was built on the cliff edge in 1844.

Roughly 250m further east, the **Fortaleza San Carlos de la Cabaña** (daily 8am–11pm; $3) needs more time to do it justice. Built as the most complex and expensive defence system in the Americas, work on the fortress was begun in 1763 as soon as the Spanish traded the city back from the British. However, its defensive worth was never proven, as takeover attempts by other European powers had largely died down by the time it was finished. It took eleven years to complete, and you can see why with one look at the extensive grounds, whose cobbled streets lined with houses (where soldiers and officers were originally billeted) now shelter a miscellany of workshops, artisans' boutiques and restaurants.

The easiest way to get to Habana del Este is to take a metered ($4) or private taxi ($2–3), or a bus (40¢) from the bus stop near the Monumento Máximo Gómez on the Malecón in Habana Vieja – get off at the first stop after the tunnel. From the fortifications it's a brisk half-hour walk to the seventeen-metre-high **Cristo de La Habana**, the gigantic hilltop Christ figure, or a pleasant ride on the foot-and-bicycle ferry (1 peso) that leaves every thirty minutes from Avenida del Puerto e/ Sol y Luz, ten minutes' walk south from Plaza San Francisco and the main Sierra Maestra Terminal.

Eating

Havana offers the most varied culinary scene in Cuba, even if the setting of many establishments is more notable than the food. The best restaurants tend to be in Miramar and the western suburbs, while numerous *paladares* dish up good-value portions of local fare. There are several **ethnic** restaurants in Havana; the most common are Chinese, Italian and Spanish. **Vegetarians** will find decent though predictable choices (pizza and omelettes featuring heavily) at most places, although the city is now benefiting from several well-equipped vegetarian restaurants. Vegans, however, should resign themselves to a diet of salad and fries. Stick to the hotels for **breakfast** as elsewhere the choice is a bit patchy; the *Habana Libre* does a particularly fine buffet for about $12. The best option for **lunch** is to grab a snack from one of the **street stalls** dotted around Centro Habana and Vedado, which sell tasty fritters and pizzas for just a few pesos each.

Habana Vieja and Centro Habana

La Bodeguita del Medio Empedrado e/ San Ignacio y Cuba, Habana Vieja ☎ 7/867-13-74 to 75. A Havana classic which relies more on its secret-hideout ambience and Hemingway associations than its standard, though fairly priced, Cuban cuisine. Papa's usual tipple, a *mojito*, has become the house speciality.

Castillo de Farnés Ave. de Bélgica esq. Obrapía, Habana Vieja. With a refreshingly original menu (by local standards, at least), the Spanish cuisine here includes the tasty *arroz indiana*, a mixed meat and rice dish, and well-prepared seafood.

El Floridita Monserrate esq. Obispo, Habana Vieja ☎ 7/867-13-00 or 867-13-01. Expensive seafood dishes in one of the most exclusive restaurants in the old city. It's another Hemingway heritage site and a velvet-curtain doorway leads through from the equally famous bar to an elegant circular dining area.

La Guarida Concordia no. 418 e/ Gervasio y Escobar, Centro Habana ☎ 7/862-49-40. The meat and fish menu at this unbeatable *paladar* breaks with all the Cuban norms, the food bursting with flavour and the whole place run with unusual professionalism. Set in the aged apartment building where the acclaimed *Fresa y Chocolate* was filmed, the décor is eye-catchingly eclectic. Reservations are essential and a meal here unmissable.

La Julia O'Reilly no. 506a e/ Bernaza y Villegas, Habana Vieja. Top-quality cooking and flavourful *comida criolla* are the main attractions of this homy little *paladar*, which has pork dishes down to a science.

La Paella in the *Hostal Valencia*, Oficios no. 53 esq. Obrapía, Habana Vieja. Authentically prepared, moderately priced Spanish food including six different kinds of paella and an ample selection of light meals and aperitifs.

El Patio Plaza de la Catedral, Habana Vieja. The serenity of this leafy, eighteenth-century mansion courtyard goes a long way to justifying the above-average prices, as does the excellent choice of main dishes, with an emphasis on seafood, set vegetarian meals and plenty of optional extras.

Vedado

Carmelo Calzada e/ D y E. You can choose among a range of well-prepared dishes at this excellent vegetarian restaurant. Dishes like steamed okra and fried aubergine made a welcome change from run-of-the-mill tomato and cucumber salad. Staff sometimes run an informal all-you-can-eat service for visitors ($3) so check beforehand.

Coppelia Calle 23 esq. L. Havana's massive ice-cream emporium contains several peso cafés and a peso convertible open-air area, serving rich sundaes with exotic flavours like coconut and guava. Closed Mon.

Decameron Linea, no. 753 e/ Paseo y Calle 2. Decor and ambience are inspired and low-key, while a mix of Italian, Cuban and European food contributes to the cosmopolitan air. The giant pizzas are possibly the largest in town, the pasta is nicely *al dente* and there's a decent attempt at salade nicoise. Strong and sweet *mojitos*, plus attentive service, gild the lily.

Doña Clara Calle 21 no. 107 e/ L y N. The best stall for lunch snacks at rock-bottom prices. Ice-cold soft drinks, *papas rellenas* and guava pies.

Nacional Calle O esq. 21. The $18 all-you-can-eat buffet restaurant in this hotel's basement provides one of Havana's best feeds, with an extensive range of fish and meat and a welcome array of green vegetables.

Nerei Calle 19 esq. L. Elegant mid-range *paladar* where you can dine alfresco on escalope of pork, pork cooked in garlic or fried chicken, all served with yucca, fried banana and salad. The house speciality – rubbery squid – is best avoided.

La Roca Calle 21 esq. M ☎ 33-45-01. Although somewhat pricey, this tranquil seafood restaurant is great for a blow-out meal of lobster or grilled red snapper. A reservation is usually unnecessary.

La Torre Calle 17 no. 55 Edificio Focsa piso 36. Mesmerizing views from the city's second tallest building are matched by the excellent French menu. Definitely worth splashing out $40 or so to dine on foie gras, fillet of beef with rosemary, shrimps caramelized in honey, and profiteroles.

Miramar and the western suburbs

Club Almendares Calle 49c y 28a, Reparto Kohly. A country club-style venue with two restaurants. The popular outdoor pizza house serves excellent Italian-style thin-crust pizzas and pasta dishes for less than $5, whilst the fancier *Restaurant Almendares* offers decent lobster, paella, fried rice and Cuban cuisine for upwards of $7 per dish.

Villa Diana Calle 49 e/ 28a-47, Reparto Kohly. A classy establishment offering a $12 set meal of grilled and roast meats, accompanied by some good live music.

Drinking, nightlife and entertainment

A typical night out in Havana is a giddy whirl of thumping *salsa* or soulful *boleros*, well oiled with rum, and often a hefty bill attached for you and all your newly acquired Cuban friends. What Cuba does best is **live music**, so you should definitely try to catch at least one of the excellent *salsa*, jazz or *son* groups that regularly do the rounds of the best-known clubs.

A more spontaneous night out is a bit difficult, as there's no single area with a buzz. **Bar crawls** involve a lot of walking, although the Plaza de la Catedral district is usually quite lively at night, with most of the attention focused on *El Patio* bar and restaurant. However, for sheer *joie de vivre* you can't beat Havana's best option – taking some beers or a bottle of rum down to the Malecón and mingling with the crowds beneath the stars. Another option is the **cinema**, a popular form of entertainment with Cubans, with plenty of atmospheric fleapits dotted around Vedado. As a visitor, you may be charged in convertible pesos ($2–3).

Bars and cafés

La Bodeguita del Medio Empedrado e/ San Ignacio y Mercaderes, Habana Vieja. Made famous by Hemingway, this usually overcrowded but always atmospheric bar no longer attracts Havana's bohemian set, but retains some of the spirit of the 1930s and 1940s, despite the queues of tourists.

Café de Paris San Ignacio esq. Obispo, Habana Vieja. Popular with an even mix of tourists and locals, this simple little bar enjoys a party atmosphere stirred up by a live band on a nightly basis.

Plaza de Armas in the *Hotel Ambos Mundos*, Obispo no. 153 esq. Mercaderes. Not on the Plaza de Armas itself but featuring good views of it, this fabulous rooftop patio-bar is also a restaurant. Lolling on the tasteful garden furniture amongst the potted plants is as relaxing an option as you could wish for in Habana Vieja.

Taberna de la Muralla San Ignacio esq. Muralla, Plaza Vieja. The smoothest, best beer in Havana, Cerveza Plaza Vieja, is not only, and uniquely, on tap here but is brewed on the premises by the Austrian company that set the place up. Benches and tables fill two large halls and a corner of the plaza outside, where the buzz created by this place looks unlikely to die down soon.

Cabarets, discos and live music

Cabaret Nacional San Rafael esq. Paseo del Prado, Habana Vieja. Below the Gran Teatro, this seedy basement cabaret and disco is more than just a pick-up joint, though it is certainly that, too. The show starts around 11pm and the disco usually gets going at about 1am. Entrance is between $5 and $10 depending on the night.

Casa de la Cultura Aguiar no. 509 e/ Amargura y Brasil, Habana Vieja ☎63-48-60. In the converted Convento de San Francisco, this centre for local talent runs a full programme of evening performances, ranging from folk music to rap. Entrance is usually between 2 and 5 pesos.

Casa de la Música Ave. de Italia (Galiano), Centro Habana ☎7/862-41-65. This is the biggest, snazziest and one of the newest and hippest club and live music venues on this side of the city. All the hottest names in Cuban *salsa* play here, where you can enjoy the music from a table or on the sizeable dance floor. Afternoon performances start at 4pm and at night the club is open 10pm–4.30am. Entrance $10–25, depending on who's playing.

Listings

Banks and exchange The *cambio* in the *Nacional* hotel has the longest opening hours (daily 8am–noon & 1–7pm), while Banco Internacional de Comercio (Mon–Fri 8.30am–3pm) at Empedrado esq. Aguiar is the best bank in the old city for foreign currency transactions.

Car rental There's a concentration of rental agencies on or within a few blocks of the Malecón, between the *Hotel Nacional* and the Cupet-Cimex Tángana petrol station in Vedado. Micar is the cheapest and has offices at the Galerías de Paseo shopping mall at Paseo esq. 1era in Vedado and

two of the most central at Calle 21 esq. M, Vedado (☎7/55-17-44), and Calle 1era esq. Paseo, Vedado (☎7/55-35-35; open 24hr).

Embassies Embassies in Havana include the Canadian Embassy, Calle 30 no. 518, Miramar, Playa (☎ 7/204-12-22, ℉ 204-20-44); the British Embassy, Calle 34 no. 702–704, Miramar, Playa (☎7/204-17-71, ℉204-81-04); and the US Special Interests Section, Calle Calzada y L, Vedado, Havana (☎7/33-35-31, ℉33-37-00). There are no consulates or embassies for Australia or New Zealand; citizens are advised to go to either the Canadian or UK embassies.

Immigration and legal Asistur, Paseo del Prado no. 212 esq. Trocadero (℡ 33-89-20 or 33-83-39 or 7/867-13-15, ℻ 33-80-87), deals with insurance claims and financial emergencies and is open 24hr. There's also an office a few doors down at no. 254 (℡ 33-85-27 or 7/867-13-14). Otherwise, try the Consultoria Juridica Internacional in Miramar at Calle 16 no. 314 e/ 3ra y 5ta (Mon–Fri 8.30am–noon & 1.30–5.30pm; ℡ 204-24-90 or 7/204-26-97).

Medical Call ℡ 40-50-93 to 94 or 57-70-41 to 43 for a state ambulance, or contact Asistur on ℡ 7/867-13-15 for a tourist ambulance. The Clínica Internacional Cira García in Miramar at Calle 20 no. 4101 esq. Ave. 41 (℡ 204-0330 to 31 or 204-2673) is run predominantly for foreigners, while two floors are reserved for foreign patients at the Hospital Hermanos Ameijeras, San Lázaro no. 701 e/Padre Varela y Marqués González, Centro Habana

(switchboard ℡ 7/57-60-77).

Pharmacies Farmacia Internacional at Ave. 41 no. 1814, esq. 20, Miramar (℡ 24-50-51), is one of the best-stocked in Havana.

Police Habana Vieja's police headquarters are in the mock-colonial fort at Tacón e/ San Ignacio y Cuba. The main station in Centro Habana is at Dragones e/ Lealtad y Escobar ℡ 7/862-44-12. In an emergency ring ℡ 7/882-01-16 or 860-01-06.

Post offices The branch at Ave. Salvador Allende esq. Padre Varela, Centro Habana (Mon–Sat 8am–6pm), offers peso services only. The branch in the Gran Teatro building, at Paseo del Prado esq. San Martín, offers fax and telegram services as well as poste restante facilities (daily 8am–6pm).

Taxis Havanautos (℡ 7/24-24-24) offer a 24hr pick-up service. Try also Turistaxi (℡ 7/33-66-66), Habanataxi (℡ 7/41-96-00), or Panataxi (℡ 7/55-55-55).

Around Havana

East of the city, **Guanabacoa** is a quiet provincial town with numerous attractive churches and a fascinating religious history. However, for most people, the big attractions are the boisterous **Playas del Este**, the nearest beaches to the city, where clean sands and a lively scene draw the crowds. South of Havana, the **Museo Ernest Hemingway**, a perfect preservation of the great writer's home, is the most neatly packaged day-trip destination. Not far away, the sprawling **Jardín Botánico** is the best bet for a relaxing escape from the city grime. Outside the city proper, public transport is scarce and unreliable, and you'll really need a car to see many of these sights, though there are **local buses** to the Playas del Este (4 daily; 1hr) from the Parque de la Fraternidad in Habana Vieja.

Guanabacoa

Two kilometres inland along the Vía Monumental from the tunnel under the bay is the turn-off to **GUANABACOA**, a little town officially within the city limits but with a distinctly provincial feel. The site of a pre-Columbian community, and then one of the island's first Spanish settlements, it's the strong tradition here of Afro-Cuban religion which holds the most appeal for visitors. This tradition centres on a visit to the town's **Museo Histórico de Guanabacoa** (Mon–Sat 9.30am–4.30pm, closed Tues; ℡ 7/97-95-10; $2), at Martí no. 108 e/ Quintin Bandera y E.V. Valenzuela, two blocks from the understated main square, Parque Martí. The collection of cultish objects relating to the practices of Santería, Palo Monte and the Abakuá Secret Society, all forms of Afro-Cuban religious worship, give the museum its edge. One room is set up to reflect the mystic environment in which the *babalao*, the Santería equivalent of a priest, would perform divination rituals, surrounded by altars and African deities in the form of Catholic saints. There are also some interesting bits and pieces, including furniture and ceramics, relating to the town's history.

The most accessible and intact of the town's five **churches** is the run-down **Iglesia Parroquial Mayor** on Parque Martí, with its magnificent, though age-worn, altar. Otherwise, once you've checked out the Afro-Cuban-style knick-knacks in the **Bazar de Reproducciones Artísticas**, two blocks down from the museum at Martí no. 175, and eaten at *El Palenque*, the basic outdoor **restaurant** next door, you've done the town justice.

Playas del Este

Fifteen kilometres east of Cojímar, on the outskirts of the city, the Vía Blanca reaches Havana's nearest beaches – Playa Santa María del Mar, Playa Boca Ciega and Playa Guanabo – collectively known as the **Playas del Este**. Hugging the Atlantic coast, these three fine-sand beaches form a long, twisting, ochre ribbon, which vanishes in summer beneath the crush of weekending Habaneros and tourists. There's not a whole lot to choose between the beaches, although as a general rule the sand is better towards the western end.

There is an abundance of really good self-catering and hotel **accommodation** around the beaches, and if you're based in Havana for most of your holiday this could provide an excellent mini-break. Those craving creature comforts should head for the big hotels in Santa María, though budget travellers will find the best value in the inexpensive hotels and *casas particulares* in Guanabo. Other than the rather anonymous, all-inclusive *Club Arsenal* (☎7/97-12-72; ❼) there's nowhere to stay in Playa Boca Ciega. Although a number of **restaurants** serve cheap meals, these all tend to be rather alike, and your best bet is to eat at the *paladar* in Guanabo; otherwise, see if a *casa particular* can recommend somewhere.

Museo Ernest Hemingway

Eleven kilometres southeast of Habana Vieja, in the suburb of San Francisco de Paula, is **La Vigía**, an attractive little estate centred on the whitewashed nineteenth-century villa where Ernest Hemingway lived for twenty years until 1960 and wrote a number of his most famous novels. Now known as the **Museo Ernest Hemingway** (Mon–Sat 9am–4pm, Sun 9am–noon; ☎7/91-08-09; $3), it makes a simple but enjoyable excursion from the city. To get there by car, take the Vía Blanca through the southern part of the city and turn off at the Carretera Central, which cuts through San Francisco de Paula. Alternatively you can brave the M-7 *camello* bus, one of the converted juggernauts used for longer bus journeys in and around the city; catch it at the Parque de la Fraternidad and walk from the bus stop to the museum. A taxi to the museum from Habana Vieja or Vedado should cost about $10.

On top of a hill with splendid views over Havana, the single-storey colonial residence has been preserved almost exactly as Hemingway left it – with drinks and magazines strewn about the place and the dining-room table set for guests. Frustratingly, entrance into the rooms is forbidden, but by walking around the encircling verandah you can get good views of most rooms through the windows. In the well-kept gardens, Hemingway's fishing boat is suspended inside a wooden pavilion and you can also visit the graves of four of his dogs, next to the swimming pool.

The museum closes when it rains to protect the interior from the damp and to preserve the well-groomed grounds, so time your visit to coincide with sunshine.

Jardín Botánico Nacional

About a 25-minute drive south of the city via the airport road (Avenida Rancho Boyeros) and then branching right onto Avenida San Francisco is the entrance to the **Jardín Botánico Nacional** (Wed–Sun 8.30am–4.30pm; ☎7/54-41-08 or 54-72-78; 60 centavos, $3 for guided tour). The grounds are split into sections according to continent, with the different zones blending seamlessly into one another. Highlights include the collection of 162 species of palm from around the world, and the picture-perfect **Japanese Garden**, built around a beautiful little lake and donated by the Japanese government in 1989 on the thirtieth anniversary of the revolution. The Japanese Garden is also the best place to stop for **lunch**, in *El Bambú* (open 1–3.30pm), where $10 lets you eat your fill from a tasty vegetarian buffet. Near the main entrance are the indoor **Pabellones de Exposiciones**, two large greenhouse-style buildings with raised viewing platforms and twisting pathways, one housing a fantastic collection of cacti, the other a jungle of tropical plants and flowers.

Although you can explore the botanical gardens yourself, a lack of posted information means you'll learn far more by taking the one- to two-hour **guided tour**, whether in the tractor-bus or having a guide in your own car (at no extra cost). There's usually at least one English-speaking guide available. Tours leave every hour or so from just inside the main entrance, near the useful **information office**. There's also a small **shop** selling ornamental plants. At weekends, for those people that want to head straight for the main attraction, a park bus takes passengers from the entrance directly to the Japanese Garden (every 30min; $1).

3.2

Pinar del Río

Despite its relative proximity to Havana, life in **Pinar del Río** is a far cry from the noise, pollution and hustle of the capital. The butt of a string of national jokes, native Pinareños are caricatured as the island's most backward country folk, a reputation that fits in with the slower, more relaxed feel to the province. Most of the highlights are well away from the population centres, the majority situated in and around the green slopes of the **Cordillera de Guaniguanico**, the mountain range that runs down the length of this narrow province, invitingly visible from the *autopista* running alongside. Hidden within the relatively compact **Sierra del Rosario**, the eastern section of the *cordillera*, the peaceful mountain retreats of **Las Terrazas** and **Soroa** provide perfect opportunities to explore the tree-clad hillsides and valleys. Both are set up as centres for eco-tourism, though of the two Las Terrazas offers best the chance to get a little bit closer to the local community. Most visitors head straight for what is justifiably the most heralded location in Pinar del Río, the **Viñales valley**, whose unusual flat-topped mountains, or *mogotes*, are unique in Cuba and worth the trip alone.

Las Terrazas

Eight kilometres beyond the signposted turn-off at Km 51 of the *autopista* is **LAS TERRAZAS**, a harmonious tourist resort and small working community that forms the province's premier eco-tourism site. The motorway suddenly seems a long way behind as the road takes you into a thickly wooded landscape and up to a junction where, after a left turn, you'll reach a tollbooth ($3 per person; resort guests free), which marks the beginning of the main through road for Las Terrazas. It's here, just a few metres past the checkpoint, where you'll turn for the **Cafetal Buenavista**, a hilltop colonial coffee plantation accessible by car or as a hike destination (see "Hiking trails at Las Terrazas" box overleaf), where you can also enjoy great views and a restaurant. About 2km further beyond the tollbooth, a left-hand turn leads several hundred metres down to a complex of red-roofed bungalows and apartment buildings, beautifully set into the grassy slopes of a valley, at the foot of which is a lake. The cabins belong to the resident population, which numbers around a thousand and has lived here since 1971 as part of a government-funded conservation and reforestation project, covering some fifty square kilometres of the Sierra del Rosario. A large proportion of the locals work in tourism, either directly or indirectly, many as employees at **Moka** (☎82/77-86-00 to 03, ✉commoka@teleda.get.tur.cu; ❹, lakeside cabin ❺), a resort hotel that blends perfectly with its surroundings.

There are several official **hiking trails** around Las Terrazas, none more than 6km; the three best are covered in the box below. There is no better way to experience the diversity of the Sierra del Rosario than along these routes, which collectively offer the most comprehensive insight available into the region's topography, history, flora and fauna. Whilst you are free to follow the trails independently, it's generally better to hire a guide from the complex's visitor centre, **Rancho Curujey** (☎82/77-29-21 or 78-55-5), as you'll learn a lot more and you won't get lost. The visitor centre is also where you can get hold of a map. Though the centre has no formal opening hours, it's generally a good idea to arrive at around 8.30am before staff disappear on hikes and excursions. To get to the **restaurant** and the one or two other buildings that make up Rancho Curujey, take the signposted right-hand turn off the main through road just before the left turn that leads down to the village and hotel. **Guides** cost between $15 and $35 per person on a pre-booked excursion, depending on the size of the group and your specific requirements. It works out considerably cheaper if you're in a group of six or more; you may be able to join another visiting group if you call a day or so in advance, or if you arrive at or before 9am.

Soroa

The tiny village of **SOROA** nestles in a long, narrow valley sixteen kilometres southwest of Las Terrazas, the two resorts linked by a single mountain road which allows you to travel between them without returning to the motorway. To get here, follow the main road through Las Terrazas until you reach a tollbooth, marking the western end of the resort, where you should turn left. If you do arrive direct from the *autopista* look for the turning marked by the first petrol station en route to Pinar del Río from Havana. Soroa's location is cosy and inviting, but as access into the hills is limited and the list of attractions brief, this place is best for a short stint rather than a protracted visit.

All of the official attractions are based around the **Villa Soroa** (☎85/75-21-22 or 75-20-41, ✉85/27-84-65; ❸), a well-kept hotel complex encircling a swimming pool. Most of what you'll want to see is within ten minutes' walk of the reception building, but if you've driven up from the *autopista* the first place you'll reach, 100m

---

Hiking trails at Las Terrazas

Ruta del Cafetal Buenavista (2.5km each way). One of the more back-breaking hikes, the route here follows a trail barely distinguishable amid dense foliage. There are occasional views of the complex below on the way up to the Cafetal Buenavista (daily noon–4pm), an excellent reconstruction of a nineteenth-century coffee plantation.

Sendero La Serafina (5km each way). This trail, through rich and varied forest, is the best route for birdwatching and is much enhanced by going with a guide who'll be able to point out the red, white and blue *tocororo*, the endemic *catacuba* and the enchanting Cuban nightingale amongst the 73 species which inhabit the *sierra*. This is the most physically demanding of the hikes on offer.

Sendero Las Delicias (3km each way). Starting on the same course as the Cafetal Buenavista trail, this path bypasses the turn for the coffee plantation and continues up to a *mirador* at the summit of the Loma Las Delicias, for some magnificent views.

or so from the hotel, is the car park for **El Salto** (open during daylight hours; $2), a twenty-metre **waterfall** and one of Soroa's best-known attractions.

Back at the car park, follow the sign pointing in the direction of the small bridge to **El Mirador**, the most easily accessible local viewpoint. A thirty-minute hike scales an increasingly steep dirt track, though it's mercifully shady and a set of steps has been installed for the final stretch. There are a number of possible wrong turns on the way up; follow the track with the horse dung. At the summit you'll find vultures circling the rocky, uneven platform. **El Castillo de las Nubes** is the more developed of Soroa's two hilltop viewpoints and the only one you can drive to. The road up to the summit, which you'll have to follow even if walking as there are no obvious trails through the woods, is between the car park for El Salto and the hotel. It shouldn't take you more than twenty minutes on foot to reach the hilltop **restaurant**, housed in a building resembling a toy fortress with a single turret (the *castillo* – or castle – in question). It's worth stopping for a meal (daily 11.30am–4pm), as the views are fantastic.

Viñales

The jewel in Pinar del Río's crown, the **Viñales valley** is by far the most visited location in the province. Though only 25km from the provincial capital, Pinar del Río, the valley feels far more remote than that, with an almost dreamlike quality that's inextricably linked to the *mogotes*, the 160-million-year-old boulder-like hills, which look like they've been dropped from the sky onto the valley floor.

Despite the influx of visitors, the region has remained largely unspoilt, with the tourist centres and hotels kept in isolated pockets of the valley, often hidden away behind the *mogotes*. Most of the locals live in the small **village of Viñales**, reached in a five-hour bus ride from Havana. If time is limited, concentrate your visit on the **San Vicente** region, a valley within the valley, much smaller and narrower than Viñales and home to the **Cueva del Indio** cave system. On the other side of the village, the **Mural de la Prehistoria** is by far the most contrived of the valley's attractions.

Accommodation

There's an even spread of good **places to stay** in Viñales, with average costs relatively low. Both *Los Jazmines* and *La Ermita* offer comprehensive programmes of **activities** and **excursions**, including horseriding, trekking and birdwatching.

Campismo Dos Hermanas on the road to the Mural de la Prehistoria ⑦82/79-32-23. This *campismo*, hidden away within the *mogotes*, is better equipped than most, despite having no a/c or fans in its well-kept cabins. The cheapest of the official options, this is the place to come to share your stay with Cuban holidaymakers, but be prepared for the blaring music around the swimming pool in peak season. ❶
Casa de Doña Hilda casa no. 4, Km 25 Carretera a Pinar del Río ⑦8/79-60-53. Two rooms for rent – the biggest (with bath, fridge and colour TV) is in its own small bungalow, next door to the main house where the other smaller room is located. A large dirt courtyard joins it all together, and parking is available. ❶
La Ermita Carretera de Ermita Km 2 ⑦8/79-60-71 to 72, ⓔlaermita@laermita.co.cu. Gorgeous, open-plan hotel in immaculate grounds high above the valley floor. With some of the best views in

Viñales, this tidy complex features three apartment buildings, a central pool, tennis court and a wonderful balcony restaurant. Rooms are attractive and reasonably well equipped. ❸
Hostel Inesita Salvador Cisnero no. 40 ⑦8/79-60-12. Run by an elderly couple, the two rooms (one with a/c) in this *casa particular* in the heart of the village are in a separate apartment taking up the entire top floor of the house. With a wide balcony running around it, this is one of the best places to stay. ❶
Los Jazmines Carretera de Viñales Km 25 ⑦8/79-63-39, ⓔgerencia@jazmines.esipr.cu. The first hotel along the road into Viñales has an unbeatable hillside location; almost all the tasteful rooms in the colonial-style main building have panoramic views. Most rooms are in a separate, modern building, with a few housed in tile-roofed cabins. There's a pool, a well-stocked shop, two bars, a small disco and taxi and car rental. ❸

Mogote Dos Hermanas and the Mural de la Prehistoria

Less than a kilometre west of the village, the flat surface of the valley floor is interrupted by the hulking mass of the **Mogote Dos Hermanas**, a pair of archetypal *mogotes* and the face of Viñales as seen on the front of most tourist brochures. It plays host to the misleadingly named **Mural de la Prehistoria** (daily 8am–7pm; $2), hidden away from the main road down a dust track. Rather than the prehistoric cave paintings you might expect, the huge painted mural, measuring 120m by 180m, desecrating the face of one side of the *mogote*, is in fact a modern depiction of evolution on the island, from mollusc to man, impressive for its scale though its size also makes it an eyesore. The bar, restaurant and souvenir shop just off to the side of the mural do nothing to alleviate the contrived nature of the place, although it's not an unpleasant spot to have a drink and a bite to eat. The **restaurant**'s speciality is "Viñales-style" pork, roasted and charcoal-smoked, the highlight of an otherwise limited menu.

The Cueva del Indio

By taking the left-hand fork at the petrol station at the northeastern end of the village, you can head out of Viñales through heavily cultivated landscape to the narrower **San Vicente** valley, around 2km away. Past the lacklustre Cueva de San Miguel, it's a two-minute drive or a twenty-minute walk north to San Vicente's most captivating attraction, the **Cueva del Indio**, 6km north of the village (daily 9am–5pm; $5). Rediscovered in 1920, this entire network of caves is believed to have been used by the Guanahatabey Amerindians, both as a refuge from the Spanish colonists and, judging by the human remains found here, as a burial site. The walls are marked with natural wave patterns, testimony to the flooding which took place during the caves' formation millions of years ago. Only the first 300m of the tunnel's damp interior can be explored on foot, before a slippery set of steps leads down to a subterranean river, where a tour guide in a boat steers you for ten minutes through the remaining 400m of accessible cave. The boat drops you off out in the open, next to some souvenir stalls and a car park, around the corner from where you started.

3.3

Varadero and Matanzas

Varadero is Cuban tourism at its most developed: a world apart from most of Cuba, but for its thousands of foreign visitors, the familiar face of the Caribbean. The Península de Hicacos, on which Varadero makes its home, reaches out from the northern coastline of the western **province of Matanzas** into the warm currents of the Atlantic as the ocean merges with the Gulf of Mexico. Its 25-kilometre stretch of fine white-sand beaches and turquoise waters are enough to fulfil even the most jaded sun-worshipper's expectations. On the opposite side of the province, the **Península de Zapata**'s sweeping tracts of unspoilt coastal marshland and wooded interior are easy to explore, thanks to an efficiently run tourist infrastructure. It's perfectly suited to a multitude of activities, including walking through the forests, birdwatching on the rivers, scuba diving in crystal waters and, to a lesser extent, sunbathing on admittedly less-than-perfect beaches. The peninsula also boasts a recent history featuring an event as renowned as any other in the entire revolution: the invasion at the **Bay of Pigs**.

Varadero

Cuba's answer to the Costa del Sol in Spain or Cancún in Mexico, **VARADERO** is dominated by tourism and almost nowhere on this slender peninsula are you out of sight of a hotel. However, anyone hoping for a polished, Disney-style resort will be disappointed. With hotels, shops and nightclubs spread out across the peninsula, there are areas where activity is more concentrated, but nowhere is there the buzz you might expect from the major holiday resort on the largest Caribbean island. None of this detracts from what most people come here for, namely the **beach**: a seemingly endless runway of blinding white sand. This is also the best place in Cuba for a wide variety of **watersports** in one place, including scuba diving, fishing and boat trips, with three marinas and two diving clubs offering a broad range of activities.

Varadero is divided into three distinct sections, though all are united by the same stretch of beach. The bridge from the mainland takes you into the **main town** area, where all the Cubans live and where nightlife, eating and entertainment are most densely concentrated. The streets here are in blocks, with *calles* numbering 1 to 65 running the width of the peninsula; dissecting them is **Avenida Primera**, the only street running the five-kilometre length of the whole town. The two-kilometre section of the peninsula west of the town, separated from the mainland by the Laguna de Paso Malo, is the **Reparto Kawama**, largely the exclusive domain of hotel guests. The majority of the all-inclusive luxury hotels lie **east of the town** on a part of the peninsula wholly dedicated to tourism.

Arrival, information and getting around

All international and most national flights arrive at the **Juan Gualberto Gómez Airport**, 25km west of Varadero (☎45/61-30-16). There's an information centre and several car rental agencies here, and although there's no public bus service many hotels pick up guests with reservations. It's worth talking to the driver or tour guide to see if there are any spare seats, or there are plenty of taxis which will take you to the centre of Varadero for $25. Inter-provincial **buses**, whether Víazul (☎45/61-48-86) or Astro (☎45/61-26-26), arrive at the small **Terminal de Omnibus** on Calle 36 and Autopista Sur. The daily services from Havana take two and three-quarter hours, or nearly six hours from Trinidad. There are many hotels within easy walking distance of the terminal, some less than five minutes away, and there are often two or three **taxis** waiting out front. If not, call Taxi OK on ☎45/66-73-41. At least half of central Varadero's hotels are within a $5 ride of the bus terminal.

The three most prominent national tourist travel and **information** agencies are represented in the lobby of most hotels, whilst they each also have their own offices. All offer very similar services, including excursions and hotel bookings. The Rumbos **Centro de Información Turística** at Ave. 1era esq. Calle 23 (daily 8am–8pm; ☎45/66-76-30) is the best place to pick up written information. **Cubatur**, at Calle 33 esq. 1era (daily 8.30am–8.30pm; ☎45/66-74-01 or 66-72-17), is also helpful, while the travel agent for **Havanatur**, Tour y Travel, has the largest number of outlets on the peninsula, with the most central office at Calle 31 e/ 1era y Ave. Playa (daily 9am–6pm; ☎45/66-71-54 or 66-31-74).

Most people get around in **taxis**; there's a constant stream of them along Avenida Primera, and a taxi rank between calles 54 and 55, next to the Cubana office.

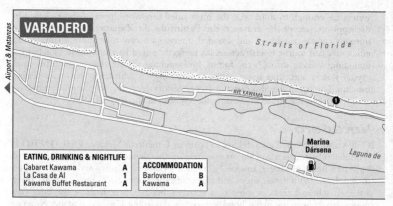

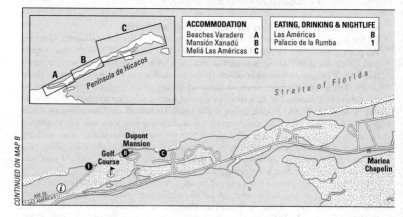

Accommodation

Varadero has no shortage of **accommodation**, but there isn't the variety you might expect, except at the more expensive end of the market. An overwhelming proportion of the hotels east of the town are all-inclusives, and the further east you stay the more restricted you are to your hotel grounds, as places become increasingly isolated.

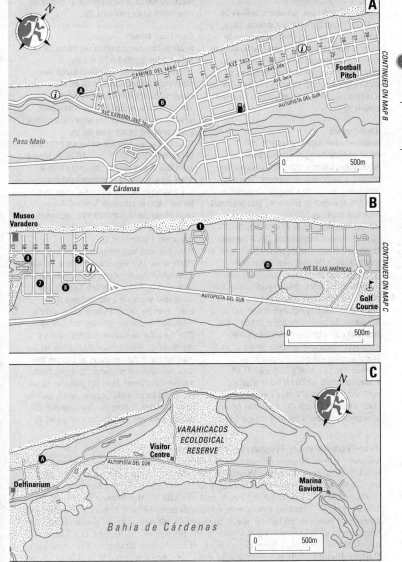

However, wherever you stay, the distance from hotel to beach is never more than a ten-minute walk. Locals continue to rent rooms in their houses in Varadero, despite the government ban on **casas particulares**, with prices at around $20–30 per room. Touts offering to take you to one are never far away, though the bus station is as good a place as anywhere to find them.

Reparto Kawama

Kawama Calle 0 y Ave. Kawama Ⓣ5/61-44-16 to 19, Ⓔreserva@kawama.gca.cma.net. Large, landscaped, all-inclusive complex, bordered by 300m of beach, centred on a neo-colonial terraced main building founded in 1930 as a gentlemen's club. Choose from private or shared houses or modern apartments, all tastefully furnished. There's a fantastically chic restaurant and cosy basement cabaret. 8

The town

Barlovento Ave. 1era e/ 10 y 12 Ⓣ5/66-71-40, Ⓔreserva@ibero.gca.cma.net. Stylish and sophisticated complex with over 200 rooms, yet retaining a harmonious atmosphere. There's an atmospheric lobby with a fountain, a captivating pool area enveloped by palm trees, plus tennis and basketball courts. 7

Los Delfines Ave. 1era e/ 38 y 39 Ⓣ45/66-77-20 to 21, Ⓦwww.horizontes.cu. This is the most tasteful and attractive of the smaller landscaped-garden hotels in the town area, its low-rise accommodation blocks linked together by outdoor corridors cutting across grassy lawns leading right down to the beach from the main street. 4

Dos Mares Calle 53 y Ave. 1era Ⓣ5/66-75-10, Ⓦwww.horizontes.cu. Untypical of Varadero, this agreeable little hotel is of the kind more often found in provincial colonial towns. Makes up for its lack of facilities with bags of character. 3

Pullman Ave. 1era e/ 49 y 50 Ⓣ5/66-71-61, Ⓦwww.horizontes.cu. One of the smallest and most adorable hotels in Varadero, whose main building features a castle-like turret. Very relaxing atmosphere and ideal if you want to avoid the hullabaloo laid on as entertainment at most of the other hotels on the peninsula. 3

East of town

Beaches Varadero Carretera Las Morlas, off Autopista Sur Ⓣ5/66-84-70, Ⓦwww.beachesvaradero.com. A pastel-coloured, five-storey main building stands at the top of the spacious grounds of this tastefully designed hotel. The emphasis is on sophisticated comfort, with soft-cushion seats around the lobby bar, a relaxing lounge area and an airy piano bar. 7

Mansión Xanadú Autopista del Sur km 7 Ⓣ45/66-84-82, 66-77-50 or 66-73-88, Ⓕ66-84-81. Housed in the flush Dupont Mansion, this unique hotel is one of the smallest and most original places to stay in Varadero. All six of the refined rooms face the sea, each one individually furnished, two with colonial American originals. The hotel also features a delightful wine cellar and one of the peninsula's best restaurants, *Las Américas*. 7

Meliá Las Américas Autopista Sur Km 7 Ⓣ5/66-76-00, Ⓦwww.solmeliacuba.com. This is the most stunningly designed complex on the peninsula, with paths weaving their way through the intricately landscaped grounds to a secluded part of the beach. Even the pool drops down a level while it twists itself around the pathways and pond. 7

Villa Cuba Ave. de las Américas, Km 3 e/ C y D Ⓣ5/66-82-80, Ⓔreserva@vcuba.gca.cma.net. The main building of this impressive all-inclusive features staircases and gangways zigzagging through a network of different floors and platforms. Spread out around the open-plan complex, which stretches down to the beach, there are various smaller residences, some with their own swimming pool. 8

The Town and Reparto Kawama

Varadero is low on sites of cultural or historic interest, and those that do exist are quickly exhausted. **Central Varadero**, specifically the area between calles 56 and 64, has the highest proportion of things to see, as well as the greatest concentration of shops and restaurants. At the beach end of Calle 57, the **Museo Varadero** (daily 10am–7pm; $1) contains exhibits of varying degrees of local historical, cultural and zoological interest, including some memorable photographs of pre-revolutionary Varadero in its aristocratic heyday, such as the portrait of the straight-faced local sailing club. Over the road from the grounds of the Museo Varadero is the entrance to **Parque Josone** (daily noon–midnight; free), sometimes referred to as Retiro Josone, the most tranquil and picturesque spot in central Varadero. The design is simple, with no intricately designed gardens, just sweeping well-kept lawns dotted with trees, and a small lake with its own palm-tree-studded island. There are four restaurants and an often-closed cafeteria to help prolong what would otherwise be a short visit.

Reparto Kawama, the slender strip of land at the western end of the peninsula, no more than thirty metres wide in places, is occupied almost exclusively by five upmarket hotels. The best reason to visit, if you're not staying at one of the hotels, is the **Casa de Al**, a restaurant housed in the only building likely to catch your eye in this neighbourhood, the former holiday home of Al Capone. The spacious

△ One of Cuba's vintage autos

grey stone villa-residence with its arch doorways and terracotta-tile roof is one of the few remaining hallmarks of the pre-1959 exclusivity of Varadero and certainly stands out for style and opulence amongst the neighbouring hotel villas and apartment blocks.

Eastern Varadero

To the east of town, about 2km from central Varadero and next door to the *Meliá Las Américas* hotel, is the **Dupont Mansion** (daily noon–midnight). Built in 1926 by the American millionaire Irenée Dupont at a cost of over US$700,000, it has hardly changed since Dupont and his family fled the island in 1959, and stands testament to the wealth and decadence of the pre-revolutionary years in Varadero. It was once open to the public as a museum, but these days to appreciate the splendidly furnished rooms you have to eat at the restaurant or sip a cocktail in the dignified bar, from where there are fine views of the coastline.

At the eastern extreme of the peninsula, three square kilometres of land have avoided development and been declared the **Varahicacos Ecological Reserve**. Billed by its founders as "the other Varadero", it's only part of the peninsula where you can experience relatively unspoilt landscapes, with a chance of viewing the flora and fauna up close, focusing predominantly on the local birdlife and including an impressively large 500-year-old cactus. The reserve's **visitor centre** (daily 8am–5pm) is by the side of the road, about a kilometre past the Marina Chapelin. For individuals, the charge for being guided around any of the three set routes is $2.50–3.50, but you can also arrange tailor-made excursions.

The beach

Of course, it's the **beach** which attracts most attention, a golden carpet of fine sand stretching from one end of Varadero to the other and bathed by placid, emerald-green waters. From the Dupont Mansion to the western tip of Varadero the beach is accessible to anyone, whether a hotel guest or not. There is actually very little to differentiate any one section of this ten-kilometre highway of sand from another, though there tends to be a livelier atmosphere on the stretch between calles 57 and 61, where the *Albacora* restaurant looks over the beach. This stretch is also the noisiest part of the beach, and in general if you want peace and quiet stay away from the beachfront hotels and restaurants, most of which are rarely reticent about blasting music out across the sand. Though in the summer months the place unsurprisingly becomes very crowded, the beach is so long that you will always find room to sunbathe in relative tranquillity.

Eating

For an international holiday resort the quality and variety of food in Varadero's **restaurants** is remarkably mediocre, though the choice is wider than anywhere else outside Havana. It's well worth trying some of the restaurants in the deluxe hotels,

---

Watersports and activities

Most **watersports and activites** in Varadero are organized through one of the three following marinas: **Marina Dársena**, Vía Blanca, 1km from the Varadero bridge (☏45/66-80-63, ℻66-74-56), which does good-value fishing trips around northern Varadero, lasting four, six or eight hours (daily; $200–300); **Marina Chapelin**, Autopista Sur Km 12 (☏45/66-75-50 or 66-78-00, ℻66-70-93), which does a two-hour "Jungle Tour" on two-person ski-bikes (hourly 9am–4pm; $39); and **Marina Gaviota**, at the end of Autopista Sur, Punta Hicacos (☏45/66-77-55 or 56), which runs fishing trips with an open bar on board a motorized yacht (9am–3pm; $250 for up to four people, plus $25 per extra person).

where the quality of food is often higher, thanks to their more direct access to foreign markets, while even the all-inclusives usually open their doors to non-guests. Like *casas particulares*, *paladares* are forbidden by law in Varadero.

Reparto Kawama

La Casa de Al in the grounds of *Villa Punta Blanca*, Ave. Kawama. Better-than-average Spanish food at slightly above-average prices in one of the most impressive restaurant buildings in Varadero.

Kawama Buffet Restaurant in the *Hotel Kawama*, Calle 0 y Ave. Kawama ☎45/66-71-56. Dine on a terrace overlooking the beach from a regularly changing menu which can include anything from pizza to rump steak. A meal here will usually cost upwards of $20 per person.

The town

Antiguedades Ave. 1era e/ 58 y 59. A small selection of exquisite seafood dishes at around $15 each, served with decent-quality side orders so often lacking elsewhere. From pictures of jazz greats and bygone Hollywood stars to a wall of old clocks and even a rocking chair hanging from the ceiling, somehow nothing in this atmospheric Aladdin's cave of a restaurant looks out of place.

El Bodegón Criollo Ave. Playa esq. 40. Varadero's version of Havana's famous *Bodeguita del Medio* has a similarly bohemian look and vibe, its walls covered in handwriting and signatures; it's also one of the best-known purveyors of Cuban cooking in the area and most main dishes are priced around $10 or less.

La Vega Ave. Playa y 31. Hearty portions of paella for less than $10 and other rice dishes at similarly reasonable prices are the highlights on the menu at this restaurant themed on a tobacco plantation ranch.

East of town

Las Américas Dupont Mansion, Autopista Sur Km 7 ☎45/66-77-50. One of the classiest and most expensive restaurants on the peninsula, with seating in the library, out on the terrace and down in the wine cellar. The international menu won't win any awards but is a cut above the average; more outstanding is the selection of cocktails and wines. Expect to pay at least $30 per person for a full meal.

Drinking, nightlife and entertainment

Nightlife is almost entirely restricted to the hotels, most of which offer something more akin to a school disco, with music to match, than a fully equipped nightclub. The majority are open to non-guests, although some of the all-inclusives may restrict entrance to their own clientele. The most popular alternative to a night on the dance floor is an evening at the **cabaret**, almost all of which are, again, run by the hotels. There are considerable differences in ambience, but wherever you go the shows themselves are basically the same displays of kitsch glamour, overly sentimental crooners and semi-naked dancers. There are surprisingly few places to go for **live music** in Varadero, the hotels again being your best bet.

Bars and cafés

Casa del Habano Ave. 1era e/ 63 y 64. Upstairs at this excellent cigar shop is a dinky, stylish, balconied bar which makes a good place for a quiet drink. Closes by 10pm.

El Galeón in the *Hotel Dos Mares*, Calle 53 y Ave. 1era. One of the most characterful bars in town, set just below street level and with a slight Mediterranean feel. A good place to come if you're fed up with hotel bars – this is just a straight-up, laid-back place to get a drink.

Piano Bar Centro Cultural Artex, Calle 60 e/ Ave. 2da y Ave. 3era. A sleek little bar, suited to something more refined than the karaoke that it hosts most nights of the week. Avoid the singing by leaving before 11pm.

Clubs and discos

Havana Club Calle 62 y Ave. 2da. The biggest nightclub in town and a popular pick-up joint. Often the last place to close at night. Cover $10. Daily 10.30pm–3am.

Palacio de la Rumba at the end of Ave. de las Américas just beyond the *Bella Costa*. Often referred to simply as *La Rumba* and as lively a night as anywhere in Varadero. Having paid the $10 to get in, there's an open bar and therefore a guaranteed night of lost inhibitions. Daily 10pm–5am.

La Red Ave. 3era e/ 29 y 30. There's a good mix of Cubans and foreigners at this popular and friendly club, which gets packed out at weekends. Cover $3. Daily 10pm–4am.

Cabarets and live shows

Cabaret Kawama in the *Hotel Kawama*, Calle 0 y Ave. Kawama. One of the more stylish cabarets, set in a cosy underground jazz-style nightclub. Cover $5 for non-guests. Mon–Sat 11pm–late.

Continental in the *Hotel Internacional*, Ave. de las Américas ☎45/66-70-38. You'll have to pay $25 to see Varadero's best and most famous cabaret. Exceeded in reputation only by the *Tropicana* in Havana, the exaggerated costumes and heartfelt renditions of cheesy love songs make this a classic show. There's a disco afterwards. Tues–Sun 9pm–3.30am.

Tropicana 50m off the Vía Blanca (the road to Matanzas) at the Río Canímar bridge, 30km from Varadero ☎45/26-53-80, reservations ☎26-55-55 or 66-86-66. The Matanzas version

of Havana's world-famous cabaret nightclub is set in a huge outdoor auditorium and is no less spectacular than the original, with a full cast of over one hundred singers and dancers and lasers shot into the night sky during showtime, attracting party-goers from Varadero. Ticket prices start at $35 and can go as high as $70 if you opt for all the extras which include a meal, transfers to and from your hotel and a table close to the stage. Show nights are Thurs–Sat 8.30pm–2.30am, showtime from 10pm. After the show there is a disco.

Península de Zapata

Forming the whole of the southern section of the province is the **Península de Zapata**, a large nature reserve covered by vast tracts of wild and unspoilt swampland and dense forests. It's equally appealing as a more orthodox holiday destination, situated on the Caribbean side of the island, with over 30km of accessible coastline and crystal-clear waters. As one of the most popular day-trips from Havana and Varadero, the peninsula has built up a set of relatively slick and conveniently packaged diversions. **Boca de Guamá** draws the largest number of bus parties with its **crocodile farm**; it's also the point of departure for the boat trip to **Guamá**, a convincingly reconstructed lakeside Taíno Indian village. The beaches at the **Playa Girón** and **Playa Larga** resorts, where the famous **Bay of Pigs** invasion took place in 1961, are less spectacular than those of Varadero, but there are enough palm trees and white sand to keep most people happy. There's a greater emphasis on scuba diving than sun-bathing here, most of which takes place relatively close to the shore.

The travel agent and tour operator **Rumbos** runs most of the attractions and organizes all excursions on the peninsula; the best place to go for **information** is the Rumbos-run **La Finquita** (☎459/32-24), a snack bar-cum-information centre by the side of the *autopista* at the junction with the main road into Zapata. Rumbos also runs *buros de turismo* in the lobbies of the *Hotel Playa Larga* (☎459/72-94) and the *Hotel Playa Girón* (☎459/41-10). **Public transport** in this area is virtually non-existent and unless you're content to stick around one of the beach resorts you're best off **renting a car** or scooter. Both Havanautos (☎459/41-23) and Transautos (☎459/41-26) rent out cars from Playa Girón, while scooters are available from either of the two beachfront hotels. That said, the hotels all run various excursions of their own and, if you take advantage, then having your own transport becomes less of an issue.

Boca de Guamá and Guamá

Eighteen kilometres from the *autopista*, down the Carretera de la Ciénaga, **Boca de Guamá** is a heavily visited roadside stop. Boca, as it's referred to locally, is famous for the **Criadero de Cocodrilos** (daily 9am–4.30pm; $5), a crocodile-breeding farm, where a short path leads from the car park to the small swamp where the beasts are fenced in. The stars of the show are left more or less to themselves and you may have trouble spotting even one on the short circuit around the swamp. For a more dramatic encounter, it's best to visit at one of the twice-weekly feeding times, though unfortunately there is no regular timetable.

Boca also serves as the departure point for boats travelling to **Guamá**, the second part of the package usually offered to day-trippers. Located on the far side of the open expanse of the Laguna de Tesoro, Guamá is intended to re-create the living conditions of the Taíno, the last of the Amerindian groups to arrive in Cuba, around a thousand years ago. A perfectly straight canal lined by fir trees leads to the **Laguna de Tesoro**, the largest natural lake in Cuba. The first of the neatly spaced islets, where you'll be dropped off, is occupied by life-sized, posed Taíno statues, each representing an aspect of their culture. Cross the footbridge to reach the diminutive **museum** detailing Taíno life and featuring a few genuine artefacts.

Passenger **boats** seating 35 people leave Boca for the village at 10am and noon every day; alternatively you can cross in a five- or six-seat **motorboat** any time between 9am and 6.30pm. In either case, an English-speaking guide is available and the round-trip costs $10 per person.

Playa Girón

Following the road down to and then along the coast, it's a drive of around 35km from Boca de Guamá to **Playa Girón**, where the course of Cuba's destiny was played out over 72 hours in April 1961. Aside from the hotel and beach, the main reason for stopping here is the **Museo Girón** (daily 9am–noon & 1–5pm; $2), a two-room museum documenting the events prior to and during the US-backed invasion. Outside the building is one of the fighter planes used in the defence of the island; inside, there are depictions of life before the 1959 revolution, along with dramatic photographs of US sabotage and terrorism in Cuba immediately prior to the **Bay of Pigs**. The museum goes on to document the invasion itself, with some incredible photography taken in the heat of battle and, most poignantly, photographs of each of the Cuban casualties. To bring it all to life it's worth asking the staff if you can watch the museum's ten-minute documentary, filmed at the time of combat.

The **Hotel Playa Girón** (☎459/41-10 or 41-18, ⊛www.horizontes.cu; ⑤), a stone's throw from the museum, is the largest of all the tourist complexes on the peninsula, with most of its family-sized, fully furnished bungalows facing out to sea. There's a diving centre, pool, tennis court, car rental and all the usual services. The beach is more exposed than that at Playa Larga, to the northwest, and though it's blessed with the same transparent green waters, there is an unsightly three-hundred-metre-long concrete wave-breaker which creates a huge pool of calm seawater but ruins the view out to sea.

3.4

Trinidad and around

W hile **Trinidad** attracts more tourists than many of Cuba's larger cities, its status as a UNESCO-declared **World Heritage Site** has ensured that, as in Habana Vieja, its marvellous architecture has remained unspoiled. Plenty of other Cuban towns evoke a similar sense of the past, but there is a harmony about central Trinidad's cobbled traffic-free streets, its jumble of colonial mansions and its red-tiled rooftops, that sets it apart. Wandering the streets of the colonial district in particular, there is something of a village feel about the place

– albeit a large and prosperous village – where horses are as common a sight as cars. From Trinidad, most of the province's highlights are within easy reach. In fact, the city's proximity to the **Península de Ancón** and its Caribbean beaches, and the lush mountain slopes around the **Topes de Collantes** hiking resort, make it one of the best bases on the island for discovering the diversity of Cuba's landscape.

Trinidad

The historic centre of the city is the main attraction of **TRINIDAD**, and it's there that you'll spend most of your time. In general, if you're walking on cobbled stones you're in the UNESCO-protected part of the city, often referred to as the "old town". Beyond these streets there are a number of less feted but equally historic buildings, especially in the northern limits of Trinidad, where the absence of motor vehicles and the buzz of human activity lend the muddy streets a strong sense of the past.

Arrival and information

Inter-provincial buses use the **bus terminal** (☎419/24-48) at Piro Guinart e/ Maceo e Izquierdo, just inside the colonial centre and within easy walking distance of a number of *casas particulares*. Arriving on the coastal road by **car** from the west will bring you into town on Piro Guinart, which leads directly up to the two main roads cutting through the centre of the city, José Martí and Antonio Maceo. From Sancti Spíritus and the east, the Circuito Sur takes cars closer to *Las Cuevas* hotel, but a left turn at Lino Pérez will take you into *casa particular* territory. Incidentally, the Cuban phenomenon of towns and cities with **old and new street names** is particularly prevalent and confusing in Trinidad. All street signs show the new names, as used in the addresses listed here.

For **information**, try **Cubatur** at Maceo no.129 esq. Francisco Javier Serquera (daily 9am–7pm; ☎419/63-14, ✉cubaturtdad@ip.etecsa.cu), which has a desk for taxis and car rental, as well as being an agent for Inter-Cuba flights (☎419/62-12). **Rumbos** at Maceo esq. Simón Bolívar (daily 9am–7pm; ☎419/64-95) has fewer facilities, but both can arrange excursions and help with other activities such as diving or horseriding. Neither agency sells **maps** but you can buy those at the **post office** on Maceo e/ Colón y Francisco Javier Zerquera.

Accommodation

Trinidad has one of the best selections of **casas particulares** in the country and they're spread throughout the city, with a concentration on and around Maceo and José Martí.

Casa Bastida Maceo no. 587 e/ Simón Bolívar y Piro Guinart ☎419/31-86. A very spacious triple with a streetside balcony and roof access, overlooking a pleasant outdoor terrace. This was once also a *paladar*, and the meals are still of excellent quality. ❶

Casa María del Carmen Suárez Guerra Juan M. Márquez no.70 e/Piro Guinart y Ciro Redondo ☎419/41-97, ✉yoel.suarez@caramail.com. Two beautifully appointed rooms in a *casa particular par excellence*, dotted with colonial *objets d'art*. There is a lovely central patio, a rooftop terrace with views over the nearby church and the friendly owners can arrange tours to local sites. ❶

Casa Muñoz José Martí no. 401 e/ Fidel Claro y Santiago Escobar ☎419/36-73, ✉trinidadmunoz@yahoo.com. One of the finest colonial residences in Trinidad, this house is crammed with original nineteenth-century furniture, and features two bathrooms, three large bedrooms, a fantastic rooftop terrace, parking and English-speaking owners. Expect to pay about $5 more than average prices and book in advance. ❷

Las Cuevas Finca Santa Ana ☎419/61-33 or 64-34, ☎61-61. A twenty- to thirty-minute walk east from the Plaza Mayor, this large cabin complex is superbly located on a hillside overlooking the town and coast. There's access to the cave network

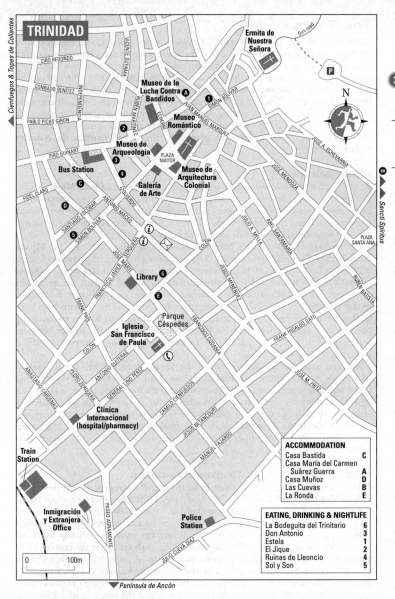

TRINIDAD

Cienfuegos & Topes de Collantes

CIRO REDONDO

CONRADO BENÍTEZ

PABLO PICHS GIRON

VICENTE SUYAMA

RUBÉN MARTÍNEZ

ECHERRI

JUAN MANUEL MARQUEZ

Ermita de
Nuestra
Señora

Dirt road

P

Museo de la
Lucha Contra
Bandidos **A**

1 SIMÓN BOLÍVAR

JOSÉ A. ECHEVARRIA

Museo
Romántico

2

Museo de
Arqueología **3**

PLAZA
MAYOR

PIRO GUINART

Bus Station **C**

4

Museo de
Arquitectura
Colonial

JOSÉ MENDOZA

FIDEL CLARO

D

SANTIAGO ESCOBAR

ANTONIO MACEO

O'GORLLO

Galería
de Arte

COLÓN

JULIO A. MELLA

ABEL SANTAMARIA

PLAZA
SANTA ANA

SIMÓN BOLÍVAR

5

JOSÉ MARTÍ

FRANCISCO JAVIER ZERQUERA

i

i

FRANK PAÍS

Library **6**

E

COLÓN

Iglesia
San Francisco
de Paula

Parque
Céspedes

JESÚS MENÉNDEZ

FRANCISCO CODAHIA

FRANK HIDALGO GATO

RUBÉN BATISTA

AMASTASIO CÁRDENAS

PEDRO ZERQUERA

ANTONIO SUITERAS

GENERAL LINO PÉREZ

JOSÉ M. FRITZ

Clínica
Internacional
(hospital/pharmacy)

CAMILO CIENFUEGOS

JESÚS BETANCOURT

Train
Station

MANUEL FAJARDO

PASEO AGRAMONTE

Inmigración
y Extranjera
Office

Police
Station

JULIO CUEVA DIAZ

0   100m

Península de Ancón

N

3

3.4 | CUBA | Trinidad and around

B ▲▲ Sancti Spíritus

ACCOMMODATION

Casa Bastida	C
Casa María del Carmen	
Suárez Guerra	A
Casa Muñoz	D
Las Cuevas	B
La Ronda	E

EATING, DRINKING & NIGHTLIFE

La Bodeguita del Trinitario	6
Don Antonio	3
Estela	1
El Jique	2
Ruinas de Lleoncio	4
Sol y Son	5

over which the site was built, a music-based show every night, a tennis court and the only pool in town. **4**

La Ronda José Martí e/ Colón y Lino Pérez ☏419/22-48 or 40-11. The only hotel in central Trinidad, this is an easy-going place near Parque Céspedes, with pleasing little rooms, a patio, rooftop bar and agreeable restaurant. More character than comfort, but no worse off for it. **2**

The Town

Trinidad boasts the highest number of museums per capita in the country, three on the central **Plaza Mayor**, including the memorable **Museo Romántico**, with another two no more than a few minutes' walk away. However, simply wandering around the narrow streets in the shadows of the colonial houses, whose shuttered porticoes form a patchwork of blues, greens, reds and yellows, is one of the highlights of any tour of Trinidad and it's worth conserving enough time and energy to do just that, even if it means missing out some of the museums. If you're prepared to walk a little further, north of the Plaza Mayor there are wide-reaching views from the hillside that overlooks Trinidad, marked by the ruined **Ermita de Nuestra Señora** church.

Plaza Mayor

At the heart of the colonial section of Trinidad is the beautiful **Plaza Mayor**. Comprising four simple fenced-in gardens, each with a palm tree or two shooting out from one of the corners, and dotted with various statuettes and other ornamental touches, this is the focal point of the old town, surrounded by colourfully painted colonial mansions adorned with arches, balconies and terraces.

Overlooking the plaza on the corner of Echerrí and Simón Bolívar is the **Museo Romántico** (Tues–Sun 9am–5pm; $2), containing one of the country's most valuable collections of antique furniture, packed into its fourteen rooms. Dating from 1808, the house itself is a magnificent example of elegant, yet restrained, nineteenth-century domestic Cuban architecture, built for the Brunet family, one of the wealthiest in Trinidad during the sugar-boom years. The contents have been gathered together from various buildings all over town, with highlights including the exquisite dining room, with its Italian marble floor, and the master bedroom featuring a four-poster bed and French wardrobe, miraculously constructed without nails or screws.

Working your way clockwise around the square from Echerrí, you'll find the **Museo de Arquitectura Colonial** (daily 9am–5pm, closed Fri; $1), a sky-blue and white building with a plant-bedecked courtyard, whose central theme is the development of domestic architecture in Trinidad during the eighteenth and nineteenth centuries. Its maps, pictures and exhibits needn't delay you for long before nipping into the **Galería de Arte** (daily 8am–5pm; free), at the bottom end of the square, from where – through the open shutters upstairs – there is a perfectly framed view of the plaza.

Museo de la Lucha Contra Bandidos

A block north of Plaza Mayor, where Echerrí meets Piro Guinart, the **Museo de la Lucha Contra Bandidos** (Tues–Sun 9am–5pm; $1) can be easily picked out by the dome-topped, yellow- and white-trimmed bell tower that's become the trademark image of Trinidad. Displays here concentrate on the counter-revolutionary groups – the *bandidos*, or bandits – that formed during the years immediately following Castro's seizure of power in 1959. The most striking exhibits are in the central courtyard, where a military truck and a motorboat mounted with machine guns stand as examples of the hardware employed by and against the *bandidos* in their struggle to overthrow the revolutionary government. But even if the museum's contents don't appeal, it's well worth paying the entrance fee to climb the tower for the panoramic view over the city and across to the hills and coastline.

Ermita de Nuestra Señora

As it heads up and away from Plaza Mayor, Simón Bolívar leads out of Trinidad's historic centre and through a less pristine part of town; soon the road becomes a dirt track leading steeply up to the **Ermita de Nuestra Señora**, a dilapidated church marking the last line of buildings before the town dissolves into the countryside.

There's nothing to see of the church but its ruins, though it's worth making the easy fifteen-minute walk up the hill for the views alone. Just beyond the ruined church you can easily cut across to the *Las Cuevas* complex, on the adjoining hillside, where non-guests can use the hillside **swimming pool** for $1.

Eating, drinking and nightlife

With so many of the colonial mansions converted into **restaurants**, eating out is one of the easiest ways to soak up Trinidad's gracefully ageing home interiors. Although the choice of food is almost exclusively restricted to *comida criolla*, the quality is, as a rule, far higher than in most of Cuba's larger cities. **Breakfast** isn't easy to come by in Trinidad, but *Hotel La Ronda* is usually willing to serve up eggs, bread, fruit and coffee for around $4.

For **drinking**, you're best off in the restaurants listed below, many of which have separate bars. *Don Antonio* is as pleasant as anywhere and, on the same street, *Ruinas de Lleoncio* is open later and has an upstairs balcony bar. For a little more contemporary local authenticity try *La Bodeguita del Trinitario* at Colón no. 91 e/ José Martí y Maceo.

Nightlife in Trinidad is decidedly subdued. By far the liveliest place is **Parque Céspedes**, where an open-air disco is held every weekend, the modern *salsa* and pop music geared very much to the large crowd of young locals. Aimed more towards tourists is the *Casa de la Trova* at Fernando Echerrí no. 29, Trinidad's best-known **live music** spot. There is a constantly changing cast of musicians playing *salsa*, *bolero* or *son* every night (cover $1).

Restaurants

Don Antonio Izquierdo e/ Simón Bolívar y Piro Guinart. Open for lunch only, there's a fair selection here, from meat dishes to salmon or lighter meals such as tuna salad or vegetable omelette. The canopied courtyard and comfortable interior are equally appealing.

Estela Simón Bolívar no. 557 e/ Juan Manuel Marquez y José Mendoza. Although there are only three (meat-based) main courses on offer at this peaceful, backyard *paladar*, a feast of extras is laid on and the two-tier patio within high walls and under tree-tops makes this one of the most relaxing spots in town.

El Jigue Rubén Martínez Villena esq. Piro Guinart. Friendly place in a colonial residence, specializing in chicken dishes. Portions are on the small side, but are reasonably priced and of a high quality.

Sol y Son Simón Bolívar no. 283 e/ Frank País y José Martí. Choose from a number of spaghetti dishes, an array of fish, or plenty of chicken and pork plates. Everything is carefully prepared and full of flavour, served in a romantically lit courtyard. The best place to eat in the city.

Around Trinidad

From Trinidad some of the province's foremost attractions lie within easy reach. Probably the least energetic option is the twenty-minute drive to the **Península de Ancón**, one of the biggest beach resorts on the south coast, though still tiny by international standards. Another alternative is to head west out of the city for about 3km, then take a right turn onto the mountain road into the **Sierra del Escambray**, whose borders creep down to the outskirts of Trinidad. Here, 15km from the turn-off, is **Topes de Collantes**, a rather run-down resort that nevertheless offers some excellent hikes in the surrounding national park.

There are organized **excursions** to the mountains, which you can book at either the Rumbos or Cubatur information centres in Trinidad. Alternatively, there are plenty of **private taxis** near the bus station on Piro Guinart in the city. A day-trip to the mountains can be negotiated for $20–30, depending on the car and the driver you pick, whilst a trip to the beach should only cost half as much.

Península de Ancón

The **Península de Ancón** – a five-kilometre finger of land curling out into the placid waters of the Caribbean, backed by rugged green mountains – enjoys a truly marvellous setting. Covered predominantly in scrub, the peninsula itself is not terribly impressive but does boast at least 1.5km of sandy **beach** and an idyllic stretch of largely undisturbed coastline. Shrubs and trees creep down to the shore and there is more than enough fine-grained sand, the best of it around the hotels, to keep a small army of holiday-makers happy. On the beach, the **International Diving Centre** (daily 9am–5pm) rents out pedal boats, kayaks, surfboards and the like. Opposite the *Hotel Ancón* (see below), on the other side of the peninsula, **Marina Cubánacan Trinidad** (☎419/62-05, ✉marinastdad@ip.etecsa.cu) offers a selection of boat trips, including diving and fishing trips, from around $50 per person.

To **get here** from Trinidad, follow Paseo Agramonte out of town and head due south for 4km to the village of Casilda. Continue for another 4km west along the northern edge of the Ensenada de Casilda, the bay clasped between the mainland and the peninsula, and you will hit the only road leading into Ancón. The taxi fare is around US$6 one-way. Of the **places to stay**, *Hotel Trinidad del Mar* (☎419/65-00 to 07, ✉reservas@brisastdad.co.cu; **❼**) is the newest, flashiest hotel on the peninsula and by far the most comfortable and luxurious place to stay around here. *Hotel Ancón* (☎419/61-20 to 26, ✉miguel@ancon.co.cu; **❹**), right on the best bit of beach, is an older, family-oriented all-inclusive where most activity on the peninsula is focused; facilities include a number of bars and places to eat, plus a pool, two tennis courts, a basketball hoop, a volleyball net and pool tables.

Topes de Collantes

Rising to the northwest of Trinidad are the steep, pine-covered slopes of the Guamuhaya mountain range, more popularly known as the **Sierra del Escambray**. These make for some of the most spectacularly scenic – and dangerous – drives in Cuba, whether you're cutting through between Trinidad and Santa Clara, or over to Cienfuegos where most of the range, including its highest peak (Pico San Juan, 1140m), lies. Three kilometres from central Trinidad along the Trinidad–Cienfuegos coast road, a right turn takes you the 15km or so into the mountains to the scattered houses of Vegas Grandes village; immediately beyond is the resort of **Topes de Collantes**. Don't expect too much in the way of eating, entertainment or nightlife, but as a base for **hiking** this is the obvious starting-point for visiting the much larger area encompassed by the 175-square-kilometre Topes de Collantes national park.

The best way to take advantage of what's on offer is to follow one of the designated **trails**, the most popular of which heads to the **Salto del Caburní**, a 62-metre-high waterfall surrounded by pines and eucalyptus trees; at the base of the cascade is a small natural pool perfect for swimming. This 2.5-kilometre trek – which takes around three hours there and back – begins at the northernmost point of the resort complex (see below) and takes you on one of the more clearly marked trails, down steep inclines through the dense forest to the rocky falls.

Unless you book a tour in Trinidad (which you can do through Rumbos or Cubatur), the place to get advice and maps – both absolutely essential as some of the trails are almost completely unmarked – is the park's information centre, the **Carpeta Central** (daily 8am–5pm; ☎42/54-02-19, ✉topescom@ip.etecsa.cu), a few minutes' walk from most of the hotels. English-speaking guides can also arrange **excursions** from a basic choice of four trails priced at $16–25 per person; this will usually include a lunch and there is normally a minimum of eight people required.

Practicalities

Although the rather worn-out resort is unlikely to lure you into staying the night, it might prove necessary if you want to stick about long enough to enjoy more than one of the trails. There are four **hotels** within the resort, two of which are permitted to rent rooms to non-Cubans. Best is *Villa Caburní* (☎42/54-03-30; ❸), at the start of the trail to the eponymous waterfall, which has 29 tiny, ice cream-coloured bungalows – each with its own little lawn and parking space – spread around a grassy area like a model 1950s American village. Most have two double rooms, bathroom and kitchenette, and all feature wonderful views of the mountains. The only place to **eat** outside of the hotels, where the food is only average, is the *Restaurante Mi Retiro*, 3km along the road back to Trinidad, where meat-based dishes are served on a verandah on top of a small hill in a scenic valley enclosed by two big hills shaped like camels' humps.

3.5

Cayo Coco and Cayo Guillermo

Spanning the trunk of the island, 450km east of Havana, the provinces of Ciego de Ávila and Camagüey form the farming heart of Cuba, their handsome lowland plains given over to sugar cane, fruit trees and cattle pasture. Though the eponymous capitals of both provinces are well worth visiting, the main draws hereabouts are the paradisiacal **Cayo Coco** and **Cayo Guillermo**. These cays lie to the north of Ciego de Ávila and offer the twin pleasures of superb beaches and virgin countryside. And with one of the longest offshore reefs in the world, the cays offer excellent **diving**, while they are also home to a variety of wildlife, prompting the government to designate them an ecologically protected zone.

There's a ban on locals visiting the resorts, so getting to the cays without the umbrella of a tour guide, state taxi or rental car can be a bit of a mission. Don't try to go in a private taxi, as your driver will have monumental hassle with the authorities before being routed back home, leaving you dumped at the barrier. All **road traffic** enters the cays along the causeway – where passports are checked and rental cars looked over to make sure they're not harbouring nationals – and then takes the fork for either Coco or Guillermo. **Flights** from Havana arrive daily at the airstrip on the west of Cayo Coco, from where hotel representatives whisk passengers off to their accommodation. **Tour buses** drop you off at the hotels.

Once on the cays, the best way to **get around** is by moped. Transautos rents mopeds, jeeps and sand buggies from its office at the *Sol Club Cayo Coco*. **Maps** of the cays are available from all the hotels and give a good impression of the islands but are distinctly lacking in specifics. There's no tourist office, but each hotel has a public relations officer who can provide general **information**.

Cayo Coco

With 22km of creamy white sands and cerulean waters, **Cayo Coco** easily fulfils its hyperbolic tourist-brochure claims. The islet is 32km wide from east to west, with a high round hill rising from the middle. The best beaches are clustered on the north coast, dominated by the all-inclusive hotels, whose tendrils are gradually spreading along the rest of the northern coastline.

The big three **beaches** take up most of the narrow easternmost peninsula, which juts out of the cay's north coast. Spanning the tip, and home to the *Sol Club Cayo Coco*, **Playa Las Coloradas** is exceptionally picturesque, with fine sand and calm, shallow waters. It's a good place for watersports and is busy with cruising **catamarans and pedalos** – a $50 all-inclusive day-pass, which includes all meals and drinks, lets you join in. The fee is waived for guests at the all-inclusive hotels. Three kilometres west, **Playa Larga** and **Playa Las Conchas**, divided by name only, form a continuous strip of silvery sand. They are arguably the best beaches on the island, although very crowded during the organized activities laid on by the *Hotel and Club Tryp Cayo Coco*. Non-guests are welcome to use the beaches during the day – access is through the hotel – but are required to pay $40 for an all-inclusive day-pass; access is restricted at night.

For solitude, head west along the main dirt road to **Playa Los Flamencos**, demarcated by a stout stucco flamingo, which boasts 3km of golden sands and clear waters where tangerine-coloured starfish float through the shallows – this is a good place for **snorkelling**. The beach gets busy in the daytime but wandering away from the lively, expensive bar should guarantee some privacy.

Away from the beach strip, dirt roads – perfect for rented mopeds – allow easy access into the lush wooded **interior**, where hidden delights include sightings of hummingbirds and pelicans, some gorgeous lagoons and **Sitio La Güira**, a re-creation of an old Cuban peasant village. Although it's something of a novelty theme park, a number of interesting exhibits rescue it from tackiness; entrance is free, there is an on-site restaurant (see below), and riding and walking tours are offered ($5 an hour for the horse; rates for a guide are negotiable). At the western tip of the island is **El Bagá Nature Reserve** (Mon–Sat 8.30am–5pm; free), well situated in radiant countryside. The park is speckled with lakes and crisscrossed by several trails, enlivened by various well-tended animal enclosures where iguanas, crocodiles and *jutías* (indigenous rodents similar to large guinea pigs) are all on display. The easiest – albeit most pedestrian – way to see the park is on one of the **guided walks** leaving from the Visitors' Centre at the reserve's entrance on the hour from 9am to noon and then at half past the hour from 1.30pm to 3.30pm.

Accommodation

With no towns or villages to offer *casas particulares*, **accommodation** on Cayo Coco is almost totally limited to a few plush **all-inclusives**, grouped together on the main beach strips. The only alternative is right at the other end of the scale, bedding down at the **beach hut** on Playa Los Flamencos (ask at the *Flamenco* bar).

All-inclusive hotels

Blau Colonial Playa Larga ☎ 33/30-13-11. This luxury hotel is built in the style of a colonial village and, though somewhat twee, its red-tiled roofs, wooden balconies and cobbled pathways are quite attractive and help create a friendly and warm atmosphere. The pool is expansive while the six restaurants on site provide endless choice. ❻

Hotel and Club Tryp Cayo Coco Playa Larga ☎ 33/30-13-00 and 30-13-11, ⓔ ventas2. tcc@solmeliacuba.com. The strip's oldest hotel is actually two hotels combined: the *El Club* part has modern, ochre-coloured buildings shaded by healthy palms while the more characterful colonial village-style *El Colonial* is painted in muted blues, greens and pinks. Guests can eat at the range of restaurants in either section and are ferried between the two by a toy-train bus. Although reminiscent of a theme park, and equipped with all the usual mod cons including nursery, fitness centre and beach activities, it actually feels more Cuban than the other all-inclusives on the strip because the buildings have a passing resemblance to authentic Cuban architecture. ❼

Hotel Playa Coco Carretera a Cayo Guillermo ⓣ33/30-25-50, Ⓦwww.gaviota-grupo.com. A good-looking hotel with a couple features to set it apart from the herd, including pastel-coloured blocks of rooms in tangerine, lemon and cobalt blue evenly spaced over a well-tended lawn, a soft, blonde-sand beach well peppered with parasols and a shallow stretch of sea. As well as a long adults' pool there is also a separate kids' pool. A Japanese restaurant adds an unusually cosmopolitan touch. ⑦

Meliá Cayo Coco Playa Las Coloradas ⓣ33/30-11-80, Ⓔjefe.reservas.mcc@solmeliacuba.com. This opulent hotel is aimed squarely at the romance market, with deluxe chalet-style accommodation set around a natural lagoon, a large pool and a full range of activities, including sauna, gym and watersports. The lack of a disco makes it peaceful and quiet, there are special deals for honeymooners and you can even get married here if you want to. ⑨

El Senador Playa Las Coloradas ⓣ33/30-14-70, Ⓦwww.el-senador.com. A fairly anonymous, modern hotel with accommodation in rather featureless mustard-yellow blocks that benefit from big windows but lack balconies, along with some pricier but far more attractive rustically luxurious wooden villas spread around a lagoon and connected by a boardwalk. The facilities are excellent with international and Chinese buffets, a variety of à la carte restaurants, four swimming pools and a state-of-the-art gym. ⑦

Sol Club Cayo Coco Playa Las Coloradas ⓣ33/30-12-80, Ⓔjefe.reservas.scc@solmeliacuba.com. Painted in bright tropical colours, this popular family-oriented hotel has a mini-club for kids, free non-motorized watersports, a buffet, snack bar and beach grill and a lively atmosphere with excited children running around causing mayhem. ⑧

Eating, drinking and nightlife

With all **food** and **drinks** included in your hotel bill (if you're staying on the cays, that is) you probably won't need to look elsewhere for meals, although there are a few places that cater for day-trippers. If you've paid for a day-pass at one of the hotels, you can dine there and go on to the hotel disco afterwards. *Sol Club Cayo Coco* has a disco with **live salsa** and tacky floorshows, but the one at *Hotel and Club Cayo Coco* is better, with a raucous palm-wood bar overlooking the sea at the end of a pier, and a house DJ alternating *salsa* with Europop.

Cueva del Jabalí This natural cave 5km inland from the hotel strip takes its name from the one-time resident wild boar evicted to make way for the restaurant, which serves moderately priced roast pork and grilled meats. It's best during the day, when you can admire the peaceful countryside, but is more animated in the evening with a glittery cabaret. Closed Sun & Mon.

Playa Flamenco Bar A friendly, though pricey, beach bar with trestle tables under a palm wattle roof, serving Cuban cuisine (and occasionally lobster) to the strains of a mariachi band.

Playa Prohibida Bar A tiny beach bar serving tasty barbecued chicken and fish.

Sitio La Güira A ranch restaurant in the midst of Cayo Coco's re-created village, specializing in *escabeche* – meats and fish prepared in a pickle made from oil, vinegar, peppercorn and herbs – and holding a *Guateque*, "a farm party with animation activities and lessons on typical dances". Closes at 10pm.

Cayo Guillermo

Bordered by pearl-white sand melting into opal waters, **Cayo Guillermo** is a quieter, more serene retreat than its neighbour. It is here that the cays' colony of twelve thousand **flamingos** (celebrated in all Cuban tourist literature) gathers and, although they are wary of the noise of passing traffic, while crossing the causeway you can glimpse them swaying in the shallows and feeding on the sandbanks. As the presence of the birds testifies, there is a wealth of fish, notably marlin, in the waters and the cay's marina offers a range of deep-sea fishing expeditions. At only thirteen square kilometres the cay is tiny, but its 4km of stunning beaches seem expansive. It's quite a trek from the mainland if you are not staying overnight, but arriving early and spending a day lounging on the sands and exploring the offshore **coral reef** definitely merits the effort.

All the hotels and beaches are strung along the north coast, apart from gorgeous **Playa Pilar** on the western tip of the cay. This was Ernest Hemingway's favourite hideaway in Cuba and is named after his yacht, *The Pilar*. With its limpid waters and squeaky-clean beaches, Playa Pilar is the top beach choice on Guillermo, if not the entire cays, though there are no facilities other than a small beach bar. The two other beaches on Guillermo are **Playa El Medio** and **Playa El Paso** on the north coast, serving the *Sol Club Cayo Guillermo* and *Villa Cojímar* respectively. Popular with package-tour holiday-makers, both have shallow swimming areas and lengthy beaches, though El Medio also has towering sand dunes, celebrated as the highest in the Caribbean.

Practicalities

Accommodation on Cayo Guillermo is restricted to several slick all-inclusives largely patronized by Italians. *Club Villa Cojímar* on Playa El Paso (☎33/2-23-52; ❼) provides four-star services, with snazzy rooms, a large pool, two restaurants and ample sports facilities. On Playa El Medio, *Sol Club Cayo Guillermo* (☎33/30-17-60, ℉30-17-48, ✉reserve@cguille.solmelia.cma.net; ❼) has similar facilities with pleasant, spacious rooms – some with a sea view. On Playa El Paso, *Meliá Cayo Guillermo* (☎33/30-16-80, ✉jefe.rrpp.mcg@solmeliacuba.com; ❾) is a swish luxury hotel that's stylishly and imaginatively decorated in cool aquamarines, and is popular with divers on account of its in-house diving centre. *Iberostar Daquiri*, Playa el Paso (☎33/30-16-50, ℉30-16-41, ✉info@iberostarcaribe.com; ❼) offers colonial-style bungalows and a private beach, along with the usual amenities. **Day-passes** for all the hotels (inclusive of meals and drinks) will set you back $40, but you can use *Sol Club Cayo Guillermo*'s stretch of beach for free. Outside the hotel **restaurants** you are limited to a floating bar and a beach restaurant on Playa Pilar, a simple wooden lean-to where you can eat excellent but pricey barbecued fish and lobster as skinny cats rub around your ankles. Opening times fluctuate, but service around lunchtime is usually guaranteed.

The **Marina Cayo Guillermo**, at the entrance to the cay near the *Club Villa Cojímar*, runs deep-sea fishing excursions for $200/400 for a half/full day; dive trips to the best sites around Cayo Media Luna, the tiny crescent cay off Playa Pilar (each dive costs $35); and yacht "seafaris" (around $25 per person) with time set aside for off-shore swimming and snorkelling.

3.6
Northern Oriente

Traditionally, the whole of the country east of Camagüey is known simply as the "Oriente". Running the length of the north coast, the three provinces that make up the **northern Oriente** – Las Tunas, Holguín and Guantánamo – form a mountainous landscape fringed by flatlands, with some of the country's most breathtaking peaks and stunning white-sand beaches.

Possibly the quietest and least dynamic province in Cuba, Las Tunas is justifiably overlooked by visitors pushed for time. By contrast, larger Holguín province has a variety of attractions, not least the **Guardalavaca** resort, whose beaches and lively atmosphere draw scores of holidaymakers. Of the three provinces it is undoubtedly Guantánamo, with the notorious US naval base at **Caimanera**, that is best known. Many Cubans living in this region are of Haitian and Jamaican origin – the result of late nineteenth- and early twentieth-century immigration – while an indigenous heritage is still visible in the far east. In fact, this is the only place in Cuba where vestiges of pre-Columbian peoples still exist.

The provincial capital of Guantánamo, small and quiet **Guantánamo town**, is a very ordinary place, though it forms a useful jumping-off point for the seaside settlement of **Baracoa**, one of Cuba's most enjoyable destinations. Sealed off from the rest of the island by a truly awe-inspiring range of rainforested mountains, fantastic for trekking, Baracoa's small-town charm is immensely welcoming and a visit here is the highlight of many trips.

Guardalavaca and around

Despite being the province's main tourist resort, **GUARDALAVACA**, on the north coast 112km from Holguín, retains a charmingly homespun air. Surrounded by hilly countryside and shining fields of sugar cane, it combines small-scale intimacy with a vibrancy lent by its youthful visitors. Four hotels are centred on the lively **Playa Guardalavaca** and there's a more exclusive satellite resort at **Playa Esmeralda**, about 5km away. **Guardalavaca town**, which backs onto the resort, is little more than a clutch of houses, though the surrounding area has enough sights to keep you busy for a couple of days should you tire of sunning yourself on the beaches.

The beaches and local excursions

A 1500-metre-long stretch of sugar-white sand dappled with light streaming through abundant foliage, **Playa Guardalavaca** is a delight. One of its most refreshing aspects is that, unlike many resort beaches, it's open to Cubans as well as tourists, which gives it a certain vitality. A shady boulevard of palms, tamarind and sea grape trees runs along the centre of the beach, the branches strung with hammocks and T-shirts for sale. Groups of friends hang out chatting or resting in the shade, while children play in the water. Those seeking solitude should head to the eastern end, where the beach breaks out of its leafy cover and is usually fairly deserted. Midway along, a restaurant serves simple snacks and drinks, and there are stands renting out **snorkelling equipment** so you can explore the coral reef offshore.

A five-kilometre trip west from Guardalavaca, along the Holguín road, **Playa Esmeralda** – also known as Estero Ciego – boasts clear blue water, a smooth swath of powdery sand speckled with thatched sunshades and two luxury hotels hidden from view by thoughtfully planted bushes and shrubs. If you want unashamed, hassle-free luxury, where the intrusion of local culture is kept to a bare minimum, this is the place for you. The beach is owned by the hotels but is open to non-guests, although you'll have to pay for a day-pass (around $40) for facilities, meals and drinks. Also in the resort is a **horseriding centre**, opposite the hotels, with negotiable rates for treks into the countryside, and *Hotel Sol Club Río de Luna*'s **dive centre**, Easy Sport (⊕24/3-01-02), offering dives for $50 and courses for between $50 and $500.

All the hotels arrange excursions to the fascinating **Taíno burial ground**, uncovered about 3km away in the Maniabon hills, which incorporates a re-creation of a Taíno village that really brings the lost culture to life. Close to Playa Esmeralda, at the Bahía de Naranjo, an offshore **aquarium** offers an entertaining day out. Visits can be arranged with the hotels. Alternatively, one of the most rewarding pastimes is to rent a bicycle or moped and head off into the countryside to enjoy stunning views over the hills and sea.

Accommodation

As a prime resort, Guardalavaca's **accommodation** consists of all-inclusive hotels at the top end of the price range, and while most deliver the standards you would expect for the price tag, a couple fall slightly short. As the region has grown up with the tourist industry, there are no peso hotels nor any registered *casas particulares*, although you might be able to find unregistered accommodation in the houses near the beach.

The three hotels around **Playa Guardalavaca** are interconnected, with guests at each entitled to vouchers that allow them to eat in the restaurants of the others; *Delta Las Brisas Club Resort* is based at Playa Las Brisas, 1.5km to the east. All four of these offer free **watersports**, including kayaks, catamarans and diving classes in the hotel pools (open-water dives cost extra), although you have to pay for the jet-skis and rides on the inflatable yellow banana. The two hotels at **Playa Esmeralda** are decidedly fabulous, facing the low peaks of the Cerro de Maita mountains and with a full complement of facilities.

Playa Guardalavaca

Las Brisas ☎24/3-02-18, ⓦwww
.brisasguardalavaca.com. The plusher of the two hotels based at Playa Guardalavaca, *Las Brisas* boasts four restaurants, two snack bars, a beauty salon, massage parlour, kids' camp and watersports, as well as mercifully restrained variety show-style entertainment. There's a choice between rooms and suites within the hotel block or more privacy in newer bungalow-style rooms, although all are equally luxurious (suites have hot tubs). Non-guests can wallow in luxury by buying a $25 day-pass which covers meals and use of facilities. ⑧

Club Amigo Atlántico Guardalavaca ☎24/3-01-80, ⓔbooking@clubamigo.gvc.cyt.cu. The *Atlántico* is a friendly and unpretentious resort that feels more Cuban than the others and attracts a varied clientele. It's a free-form complex (compiled from three previously independent hotels) with blocks of guestrooms, pools, bars and restaurants dotted around in a seemingly random layout and connected by meandering pathways. There's a variety of accommodation options catering for a range of needs and budgets but also varying in quality: the "Villa" section is easily the most appealing with cool, airy houses painted in soothing pastels with balconies and simple but attractive furnishings; the "Tropical" and "Standard" areas offer plain but decent rooms – some with a sea view – strung along shadowy corridors, while the best-avoided "Bungalow" section seems stuck in a 1970s time warp. ⑥–⑦

Playa Esmeralda

Paradisus Río de Oro ☎24/3-00-90, ⓔparadisus.ro@solmeliacuba.com. Undoubtedly one of the best in Cuba, this hotel is aimed at those seeking Caribbean-style five-star luxury. The accommodation blocks, attractive two-storey villas in muted yellow, orange and rose, are set amongst gorgeous gardens brimming with fragrant tropical plant life, home to clouds of butterflies. The hotel boasts four excellent à la carte restaurants including, unusually, a Japanese one serving a range of sushi delights, as well as an airy buffet restaurant where tiny, fearless birds will share your meal if you are not careful. ⑨

Sol Club Río de Luna y Mares ☎24/3-00-30 or 60. This complex comprises two hotels that have been joined together to operate as one. The "Luna" section is more attractive and offers spacious, light-filled accommodation in three-storey blocks arranged around a central pool while the "Mares" section features well-appointed rooms grouped in a single block. Altogether there are two buffet restaurants, four à la carte restaurants and eight bars. Facilities include tennis, sauna and gym, and excursions into the surrounding countryside are also offered. ⑨

Guantánamo town and around

GUANTÁNAMO town is only on the tourist map because of the proximity of the **US Guantánamo naval station**, 22km southeast, but the base plays a very small part in the everyday life of the town itself. For the most part, this is a slow-paced provincial capital, marked by a few ornate buildings, attractive but largely featureless streets and an easy-going populace. Many visitors come to see the US base and although you can get to the two lookout points, **Mirador Malones** and **Caimanera**, with a little planning, there really isn't a lot to see and you cannot enter the base itself.

Buses from Santiago, Baracoa, Havana and Holguín arrive at the **Astro Terminal de Omnibus**, Carretera Santiago, 2.5km out of town. Daily trains from Santiago, Havana and Las Tunas pull in at the central **train station**, housed in a squat Art Deco folly on Pedro A. Pérez. The main **hotel**, *Guantánamo*, 5 km from the centre at Ahogados esq. 13 Norte, Reparto Caribe (☎21/38-10-15; ❷), is a typical, hulking, old-style Cuban hotel. Much nicer is the intimate *Casa de los Sueños*, 500m further along the street, at Ahogados esq. 15 Norte (☎21/38-16-01; ❷), with three double rooms. *Casa de Elsye Castillo Osoria*, Calixto García no. 766 e/ Prado y Jesús del Sol (❷), is a friendly *casa particular* with a sunny courtyard.

There are several **restaurants** in the centre, though few are well stocked with food. *El Colonial* and *La Cubanita*, neighbouring *paladares* on Martí esq. Crombet, both serve adequate portions of pork or chicken with rice and beans for around $5, while the *Guantánamo* hotel restaurant, *Guaso*, boasts a more interesting menu than most, with a house speciality of chicken "Gordon Blue" – stuffed with ham. The tastiest food, including fritters, milkshakes and hot rolls, comes from the **street stands** clustered at the south end of Pedro A. Pérez, while *Coppelia*, at Pedro A. Pérez esq. Varona, does bargain bowls of ice cream for a couple of pesos.

Mirador Malones

The more easily accessible of the two naval base lookouts, **Mirador Malones** is 32km from town, on the east of the bay, near Boquerón. At the top of a steep hill of dusty cacti and grey scrubs, a purpose-built platform is equipped with a restaurant and high-powered binoculars. From a distance of 6km, and at 320m above sea level, the view of the base is rather indistinct, but you can make out a few buildings and see the odd car whizzing past. The real wonder is the view of the whole bay area: dramatically barren countryside, luminous sea and unforgiving desert frequented by hovering vultures. You can arrange a trip with a guide through the *Guantánamo* hotel in town (see above; $6 per person plus around $15 for an unmetered taxi).

Caimanera

Bordered by salt flats that score the ground with deep cracks, **CAIMANERA**, 23km south of Guantánamo, takes its name from the giant caiman lizards that used to roam here, although today it's far more notable as the last point in Cuba before you reach the US naval base. The village is a restricted area, with the ground between here and the base one of the most heavily mined areas in the world, although this hasn't stopped many disaffected Cubans from braving it in the hope of escaping to America. Until 1995, many who chanced it, along with those who were brought to the base after being rescued from makeshift rafts in the Florida Straits, were allowed into the US on humanitarian grounds, but illegal Cuban immigrants are now returned to Cuban territory. The village is entered via a **checkpoint** at which guards scrutinize your passport before waving you through. The lookout is within the grounds of the prosaic but functional **Hotel Caimanera** (☎9/94-14-16; ❷), which has a view over the bay and mountains to the base – though even with binoculars ($1), you only

---

Guantanamera: the song

Synonymous with the beleaguered history of the US naval base, Guantánamo is an enduring legacy of the struggle between the US and Cuba. In name at least, it's one of the best-known places in Cuba, thanks to the immortal song **Guantanamera** – written by Joseito Fernández in the 1940s as a tribute to the women of Guantánamo. Made internationally famous by North American folk singer Pete Seeger during the 1970s, it has become something of a Cuban anthem and a firm – if somewhat hackneyed – favourite of tourist bar troubadours the world over, a sad fate for the song which includes words from José Martí's most famous work, *Versos Sencillos*.

see a sliver of it. You can use the lookout without being a guest of the hotel but you must phone ahead to let them know you are coming: staff then alert the checkpoint of your imminent arrival. A taxi from town costs $15–20, and you will need a guide, which you can arrange through the *Guantánamo* hotel.

③ Baracoa

In the eyes of many who visit, **BARACOA** is quite simply the most beautiful place in Cuba. Set on the island's southeastern tip and protected by a deep curve of mountains, its isolation has so far managed to protect it from some of the more pernicious effects of tourism creeping into other areas of the island. Surrounded by awe-inspiring countryside – whose abundance of cacao trees makes it the nation's **chocolate** manufacturer – Baracoa is fast becoming an absolute must on the travellers' circuit.

On a spot christened Porto Santo by Christopher Columbus, who arrived here in 1492 and, as legend has it, planted a cross in the soil, Baracoa was the first town to be established in Cuba, founded by Diego de Velázquez in 1511. The early conquistadors never quite succeeded in exterminating the indigenous population and direct descendants of the **Taíno** population are alive today, with Baracoa the only place in Cuba where they survive. Their legacy is also present in several myths and legends that are habitually told to visitors, including the notion that anyone who takes a dip in the Río de Miel, to the west of town, will return to Baracoa a second time.

Half the fun of a visit to Baracoa is **getting there**. Before the revolution, the town was only accessible by sea, but the opening of **La Farola**, a road through the mountains that provides a direct link with Guantánamo, 120km away, changed all that, and a flood of cars poured into town. Considered to be one of the triumphs of the revolution, the road was actually started during Batista's regime but was temporarily abandoned when he refused to pay a fair wage to the workers, and work was only resumed in the 1960s. Today, it makes for an amazing trip through the knife-sharp peaks of the Cuchillas de Baracoa mountains.

Arrival, information and getting around

The airport, **Aeropuerto Gustavo Rizo** (☎4/2-52-80), is near the *Porto Santo* hotel, on the west side of the bay, 4km from the centre; taxis wait to take you into town for $2–3. Buses pull up at the **Astro bus terminal**, west on the Malecón, with services to and from Santiago (10–11 weekly; 6hr), Guantánamo (10–11 weekly; 4hr) and Havana (1 every other day; 20hr); it's a short walk down Maceo to the centre, or you can take a *bicitaxi* for ten pesos. The private peso trucks that arrive from over the mountains via La Farola drop off on Maceo.

There's no official **information** bureau in town, but the staff at the *El Castillo* hotel are extremely helpful. The best way to **get around** is on foot, as most of the places you'll want to see are within easy reach of the centre. To travel further afield, catch a *bicitaxi* or unmetered **taxi** from outside the tobacco factory at Calle Martí no. 214. There's little point relying on public transport – buses are scarce and always jam-packed. **Excursions** to the surrounding countryside can be arranged through the *El Castillo* hotel (see below). For a less official trek, pay a visit to "Castro" at the Fuerte Matachín museum (☎4/21-22), a knowledgeable town character who will be happy to negotiate a tailor-made trip for you.

Accommodation

In *El Castillo*, Baracoa has one of the most characterful **hotels** in Cuba, though the sheer volume of visitors means that this and the two other hotels in town are often full. However, the taxes on private accommodation are low and you'll find a number of superb **casas particulares**, all within a few streets of one another.

Casa de Isabel Artola Rosell Rubert López no. 39 e/ Ciro Frías y Céspedes ☎4/52-36, ⓔartolar2002@yahoo.es. A very hospitable, pretty little house with two rooms near the town centre.

One bedroom has twin beds making it a good choice for friends sharing. The owners also provide meals and a laundry service. ❷

Casa de Sr Dulce Maria Máximo Gómez no. 140 e/ Pelayo Cuervo y Ciro Frias ☎ 4/22-14. A charming little room with one double bed and one single, as well as a private bathroom and a kitchen with fridge. Good for a longer stay. ❷

Casa de Ykira Mahiquez Maceo 168A e/ Céspedes y Ciro Frías; ☎ 4/24-66. Casual accommodation on a friendly street one block from the main square. The owner knows almost everyone in town with a room to let, so if her place is full she'll be able to point you elsewhere. ❷

El Castillo Calixto García ☎ 4/51-65. Perched high on a hill overlooking the town, this former military post, one of a trio of forts built to protect Baracoa, was built between 1739 and 1742 and is now an intimate, comfortable and very welcoming hotel. Glossy tiles and wood finishes give the rooms a unique appeal, while the handsome pool patio ($2 for non-guests) is the best place in town to sip *mojitos*. Very popular and often fully booked, making reservations essential. ❹

The Town

Although many will be happy simply to wander through the town, enjoying its easy charm, there are several tangible attractions. Baracoa's most notable exhibit is **La Cruz de la Parra**, the celebrated cross which is reputed to have been erected by Christopher Columbus himself. It is housed in the picturesque **Catedral de Nuestra Señora de la Asunción**, on the edge of leafy **Parque Independencia**, a local gathering point. On the east side of town you'll find the **Fuerte Matachín**, one of a trio of forts built to protect colonial Baracoa, and now the site of the town museum (daily 8am–noon & 2pm–6pm; $1). Further east is the main beach, **Playa Boca de Miel**, shingled in jade, grey and crimson stones, and a lively summertime hangout. Converted from the second of the town's fortifications, which overlook the town from the northern hills, the **El Castillo** hotel is a peaceful retreat, while on the western side of town, the third fort, **Fuerte La Punta**, is now a restaurant and overlooks the **Playa La Punta** – the best bet for solitude seekers.

Baracoa has a strong tradition of local art, with reasonably priced originals sold at **La Casa Yara**, Maceo no. 120 (Mon–Fri 8am–noon & 1–6pm, Sat & Sun 8am–noon), along with coconut-wood jewellery, handmade boxes and other trinkets. Art is also available from the **Casa de la Cultura**, at Maceo no. 124 – look out for paintings by Luís Eliades Rodríguez.

Eating

After the monotonous cuisine found in much of the rest of Cuba, **food** in Baracoa is ambrosial, drawing on a rich local heritage and the region's plentiful supply of coconuts. Tuna, red snapper and swordfish fried in coconut oil are favourite dishes and there is an abundance of clandestine lobster, as well as a few vegetarian specials. Look out for *cucurucho*, a deceptively filling concoction of coconut, orange, guava and lots of sugar, sold in a palm-leaf wrap. Other treats for the sweet-toothed include the locally produced Peter's chocolate and the soft drink *Prú*, widely available from *ofreta* stands, a fermented blend of sugar and secret spices that's something of an acquired taste.

Casa Tropical Martí no. 175 e/ Céspedes y Ciro Frias. A central *casa particular* with a cool interior and a friendly atmosphere that offers food to non-guests. Excellent swordfish and generous helpings of shellfish, when available, are served in a courtyard beside an ailing papaya tree.

El Castillo Calixto García ☎ 4/21-25. The Saturday night buffet at this hotel restaurant offers possibly the best meal you will have in town: a feast of Baracoan dishes featuring coconut, maize, local vegetables and herbs, all for $10.

La Colonial Martí no. 123 e/ Maraví y Frank País ☎ 4/31-61. A homey place offering standard, though well-prepared, Cuban dishes for $6–8 per person. It gets very busy, so reservations are recommended, as is early arrival.

La Punta Ave. de los Martires, at the west end of the Malecón. An elegant 24hr restaurant in the grounds of La Punta fort, serving traditional Cuban and Baracoan food, some spaghetti dishes and the house speciality, *bacan*, a delicious baked dish with meat, green bananas and coconut milk. There's a cabaret show on from 9pm to midnight, so arrive early if you want a peaceful meal.

Nightlife and entertainment

Baracoa has quite an active **nightlife**, perhaps surprisingly so for such a small town, though it's essentially centred on two small but boisterous venues near Parque Independencia. The most sophisticated option is twilight cocktails at the *El Castillo* rooftop bar. Baracoa's small **cinema**, Cine-Teatro Encanto, Maceo no. 148, screens Cuban and North American films every evening.

485 Aniversario de la Fundación de la Ciudad Maceo 141, in front of Parque Independencia. Known by all as "el cuatro ocho cinco", this is *the* place to hang out in town. In a room reminiscent of a village hall, *salsa* bands play for a mixed crowd of Cubans and visitors, while across the courtyard, a fire escape leads to a precarious roof-top disco where you've every chance of taking a dive over the edge. Downstairs 9pm–3.30am; upstairs 9pm until they decide to close.

Casa de la Cultura Maceo e/ Frank País y Maraví. A haven of jaded charm, with live music and dancing on the patio nightly. Tends to get going around

9 or 10pm.

Casa de la Trova Victorino Rodríguez no. 149B e/ Ciro Frias y Pelillo Cuevo. Concerts take place in a tiny room opposite Parque Independencia, after which the chairs are pushed back to the wall and exuberant dancers spill onto the pavement. Mon–Fri 9pm–midnight, Sat 9pm–1am.

La Terraza Calle Maceo 120. A lively open-air terrace bar whose varied repertoire includes magic shows and comedians, as well as dancing to western disco music with a smattering of *salsa*. Popular with Cuban couples and visitors. Cover $1. Open daily 8pm–3am.

3.7

Santiago de Cuba and Granma

T he southern part of Oriente – the island's easternmost third – is defined by the **Sierra Maestra**, Cuba's largest mountain range, which binds together the provinces of Santiago de Cuba and Granma. Rising directly from the shores of the Caribbean, the mountains make much of the region largely inaccessible, a quality appreciated by the rebels who spent years waging war here.

At the eastern end of the *sierra*, the romantic provincial capital **city of Santiago de Cuba** draws visitors mainly for its music, at its best in July when **carnival** drenches the town in *rumba* beats, fabulous costumes, excitement and song. This talent for making merry has placed Cuba's second city firmly on the tourist map, but there's much more to the place than carnival. Briefly the island's first capital, Santiago has a rich colonial heritage and played an equally distinguished role in

△ Church of Our Lady of Charity, El Cobre

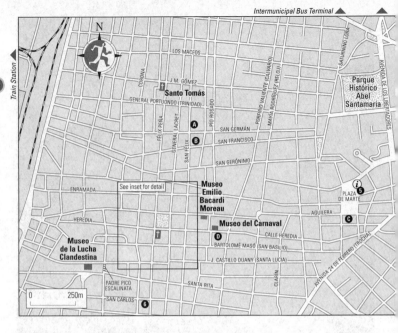

more recent history, as the place where Fidel Castro and his small band of rebels fired the opening shots of the revolution. Further west, bordering Granma province, the heights of the Sierra Maestra vanish into awe-inspiring cloud forests, and although access to the **Parque Nacional Turquino** – around Pico Turquino, Cuba's highest peak – is often restricted, you can still admire it from afar. Unlike Santiago de Cuba, which is centred around its main city, the province of Granma has no definite focus. The small black-sand beach resort at **Marea del Portillo** gives Granma some sort of tourist centre, but the highlight of the province, missed by many, is the **Parque Nacional Desembarco del Granma**, lying in wooded countryside at the foot of the Sierra Maestra and easily explored from the beach of **Las Coloradas**.

Santiago de Cuba city

Nowhere outside Havana is there a Cuban city with such definite character or such determination to have a good time as **SANTIAGO DE CUBA**. Set on a deep-water bay and cradled by mountains, the city is credited with being the most Caribbean part of Cuba, a claim borne out by the laid-back lifestyle and rich mix of inhabitants. It was here that the first slaves arrived from West Africa, and today Santiago boasts a larger percentage of black people than anywhere else in Cuba. **Afro-Cuban culture**, with its music, myths and rituals, formed its roots here, with later layers added by French coffee-planters fleeing revolution in Haiti in the eighteenth century. Santiago's proximity to Jamaica has encouraged a natural crossover of ideas and it is one of the few places in Cuba to have a strong Rastafari following, albeit a hybrid one – devout Jamaican Rastas are teetotal vegetarians who don't wolf down huge plates of fried pork with lashings of beer.

The leisurely pace of life doesn't make for a quiet city, however, and the higgledy-

SANTIAGO DE CUBA

Moncado Barracks
& Museo Histórico
■ 26 de Julio

Ayuntamiento   Casa de
                Cultura

Museo de
Ambiente Cubano   Parque   Casa
                   Céspedes Granda Hotel

Catedral de
Nuestra Señora
de la Asunción

0   100m

ACCOMMODATION

Casa Colonial Maruchi	A
Casa de Arlex Rojas Cruz	B
Casa de Leonard y Rosa	C
Casa de Raimundo Ocaña y Bertha Peña	D
Casa Granda	F
Gran Hotel	E

EATING, DRINKING & NIGHTLIFE

Bar Claqueta	9
Casa de la Cultura	7
Casa de la Trova	8
Casa Granda	F
Coppelia	4
La Corona	6
Los Dos Abuelos	5
La Maison	3
Pico Real	1
Pista Bailable	2

piggledy arrangement of narrow streets around the colonial quarter rings night and day with the beat of drums and the toot of horns. **Music** is a vital element of *Santiaguero* life, oozing from the most famous Casa de la Trova in the country, not to mention numerous impromptu gatherings. Although music and the July carnival are good enough reasons to visit, the city offers a host of other attractions too. Diego Velázquez's sixteenth-century merchant house and the elegant governor's residence, both around **Parque Céspedes**, and the commanding **El Morro** castle at the entrance to the bay, reflect the city's prominent role in Cuban history. Added to this, the part played by townspeople in the **revolutionary struggle**, detailed in several fascinating museums, makes Santiago an important stopoff on the revolution trail.

Arrival, information and getting around

Flights arrive at the **Aeropuerto Internacional Antonio Maceo**, near the southern coast 8km from the city (☎22/69-10-52). Metered and unmetered **taxis** wait outside and charge around $10–15 to take you to the centre, while there is sometimes a bus that meets flights from Havana, charging around 5 pesos for the same journey. You can arrange car rental at the Havanautos desk (☎22/68-61-61) at the airport or at agencies in town, including Cubacar on Avenida de los Defiles (☎226/5-45-68).

Inter-provincial buses pull in at the **Astro bus terminal** on Avenida de los Libertadores, 2km from the town centre (☎22/62-30-50). Next door, tourist buses arrive at the **Víazul bus depot** (☎22/62-84-84); there are daily services to and from Havana (15hr 30min). A taxi to the centre from either terminal costs $3–4. Provincial buses use the **Terminal de Omnibus Intermunicipal**, on Paseo de Martí, north of Parque Céspedes (☎22/62-43-25).

Arriving by **train** (10 weekly services from Havana; 14hr) you'll alight at the station near the port, on Paseo de Martí esq. Jesús Menéndez (☎22/62-28-36), from where horse-drawn buggies and *bicitaxis* can take you to the centre for around $3, while a taxi will cost around $5.

Information

Santiago does not have an official tourist **information** bureau but the staff at the two Rumbos offices – one on Parque Céspedes at Heredia 701 esq. San Pedro, the other, shared with a couple of other tour companies, at the *Hotel Santiago de Cuba* – can help with general enquiries. You can buy **maps** in the Librería Internacional on Parque Céspedes under the cathedral and at the shop in the *Hotel Casa Granda*'s basement. Santiago's weekly newspaper, the *Sierra Maestra* (20¢), is available from street vendors and occasionally from the bigger hotels, and has a brief **listings** section detailing cinema, theatre and other cultural activities.

Getting around

Although a large city, Santiago is easy to negotiate, as much of what you'll want to see is contained within the historic core around Parque Céspedes. Even the furthest sights are no more than around 4km from Parque Céspedes, making it an excellent city for **exploring on foot**. However, taxis are the best way to reach outlying sights, as the buses are overcrowded and irregular.

Metered taxis wait on the cathedral side of Parque Céspedes or around Plaza de Marte and charge between forty and eighty centavos per kilometre, with a $1.50 surcharge, while the **unmetered taxis** parked on San Pedro negotiate a rate for the whole journey; expect to pay about $3–4 to cross town. A cheaper option for the brave – or foolhardy – are the **motorbike taxis** that hare round town as fast as their two-cylinder engines can carry them. These congregate at the corner of San Pedro and Aguilera, by the Casa de Cultura, and all rides within the city cost 10 pesos.

In the *Hotel Casa Granda* you'll find Havanatur (Mon–Sat 8am–5pm; ☎226/86-1-52), one of the two agencies in Santiago offering **city tours**. Opposite the hotel, its rival, Agencia de Viajes Rumbos (daily 8am–5pm; ☎226/2-22-22), is friendlier and can also make bookings at state hotels elsewhere in the country. Both agencies offer similarly priced **excursions** throughout the province.

Accommodation

Accommodation in Santiago is plentiful and varied. Except during carnival in July, when rooms are snapped up well in advance, you can usually turn up on spec, though making a reservation will save you the possibility of having to trudge around the city looking for a place, especially as accommodation is spread over a wide area.

Hotels

Casa Granda Heredia no. 201 e/ San Pedro y San Félix ☎22/68-66-00, ✉reserva@casagran.gca.tur.cu. A tourist attraction in itself on account of its beauty, the regal *Casa Granda* is a sensitively restored 1920s hotel overlooking Parque Céspedes. From the elegant, airy lobby to its two atmospheric bars, it has a stately, colonial air matched in its tasteful rooms. ❻

Gran Hotel Enramada esq. San Félix ☎22/65-30-20, ✉ana@ehtsc.co.cu. A very central, friendly hotel operating in convertible pesos for visitors and regular pesos for Cubans. While it no longer merits the "grand" of its title, the vaguely colonial exterior and faded charm of the rooms are very appealing if you don't mind roughing it a

bit – the somewhat grubby bathrooms don't look their best in the harsh fluorescent lights. Singles, doubles and triples all come with a/c and many with a tiny balcony overlooking the busy shopping street. ❸

Casas particulares

Casa de Arlex Rojas Cruz San Francisco no. 303 e/ San Félix y San Bartolome ☎22/62-25-17. Although there isn't much natural light in either of the two a/c rooms, this colonial house is still a good option. It boasts a tranquil patio furnished with rocking chairs, is home to two docile dogs and is run by entertaining owners. ❷

Casa Colonial Maruchi San Félix no. 357 e/ San Germán y Trinidad ☎22/62-07-67, ⓦwww

.casasantiagodecubacolonial.sitio.net. Two rooms are available in this magnificent colonial house. Vintage brass beds, exposed brickwork and wooden beams add romance. Breakfast is included in the price. An excellent place to stay. ❷

Casa de Leonard y Rosa Clarín no. 9 e/ Aguilera y Heredia ☎ 22/62-35-74. One smallish, rather dark a/c room with a hot-water bathroom in a wonderful eighteenth-century house featuring period ironwork, wooden walls, high ceilings and red and blue stained-glass windows. Out back is a serene courtyard filled with leafy palm trees and vibrant flowers. ❷

Casa de Raimundo Ocaña y Bertha Peña Heredia no. 308 e/ Carnicería y Calvario ☎ 22/62-40-97, ✉ co8kz@yahoo.es. A charming, very central household with an attractive, sunny patio, unfortunately bedevilled by noisy passing traffic. Two rooms, both with a/c, and private bathrooms with hot water. ❷

The historic centre and around

While many of the sights are gathered in the **colonial quarter** to the west side of town – and you will need at least a day to do this area justice – you'll also want to take some time to explore the newer suburbs out to the east and north. The other sights of interest are dotted randomly on the outskirts and can be squeezed into the tail end of a visit to other areas.

The colonial district's must-sees are clustered around the picturesque **Parque Céspedes**, the spiritual centre of Santiago. Originally the Plaza de Armas, the first square laid out in the town by the conquistadors, it is more of a plaza than a park, and is usually bustling with activity. A known pick-up spot, it also draws everyone from brass bands to old folks to tourists, and is great for people-watching. On its south side stands the handsome **Catedral de Nuestra Señora de la Asunción** (daily except Tues 8am–noon; Mass daily at 6.30pm, plus Sun 9.30am). The first cathedral in Cuba was built on this site in 1522, but repeated run-ins with earthquakes and pirates made their mark, and *Santiagueros* had to rebuild several times. The present cathedral was completed in 1818. A Baroque-style edifice, its twin towers gleam in the sunshine and its doorway is topped by an imposing herald angel, statues and four Neoclassical columns. Cherubs and angels are something of a theme in the interior, strewn across the ceiling and up the walls. The prize piece of the cathedral, though almost hidden on the left-hand side, is the tremendous **organ**, now disused but still replete with tall gilded pipes. Lining the wall is a noteworthy frieze detailing the history of St James, patron saint of Santiago. A tiny **museum** (Mon–Sat 9am–5pm; $1), in a small upstairs room round the cathedral's east side, has a small collection of calligraphic correspondence between various cardinals and bishops, portraits of all the past bishops of the cathedral and not much else. It's the only museum of its kind in Cuba and worth checking out if you're into that sort of thing.

On the north side of the square is the brilliant-white **Ayuntamiento**, or town hall, dating from the sixteenth century. During colonial times, the building on this site was the Casa del Gobierno, the governor's house, though the first two structures were reduced to rubble by earthquakes and the present building, erected in the 1940s, is a copy of a copy. It's not open to the public, but you can still admire the front cloister covered in shiny red tiles and fronted by crisply precise arches, with snowflake-shaped peepholes cut into the gleaming walls and shell-shaped ornamentation below the windows. The balcony overlooking the park was the site of Fidel Castro's triumphant speech on New Year's Day 1959.

The magnificent stone structure on the west side of the park, built in 1515 for Diego Velázquez, one of the first conquistadors of Cuba, is the oldest residential building in Cuba. It now houses the **Museo de Ambiente Cubano**, Parque Céspedes esq. Félix Pena (Mon–Sat 9am–5pm, Sun 9am–1pm; $2, $1 extra for each photo taken), a wonderful collection of early and late colonial furniture, curios, weapons and fripperies which offers one of the country's best insights into colonial lifestyles, and is so large that it spills over into the house next door. Much of what's on display is imported from Europe and shows off the good life enjoyed by the bourgeoisie, but the most interesting items are native to Cuba, like the *pajilla* chair with latticework back and seat, invented in Cuba to combat the heat, and the reclining *pajilla* smoking chair with an ornate ashtray attached to the arm, made for the proper enjoyment of a fine cigar.

A couple of blocks southwest of Parque Céspedes, in the **El Tivolí** district, the **Museo de la Lucha Clandestina**, perched on the Loma del Intendente (Mon–Sat 9am–5pm; $2; English, Italian and Spanish guides available; no photographs), is a tribute to the pre-revolutionary struggle. Spread over two floors of a reproduction of a historically important eighteenth-century house, the museum comprises a photographic and journalistic history of the final years of the Batista regime and is a must for anyone who desires to understand the intricacies of the events leading up to the revolution. The best exhibits are those that give an idea of the turbulent climate of fear, unrest and excitement that existed in the 1950s in the lead-up to the revolution. Adjoining the museum is the celebrated **Padre Pico escalinata**, a towering staircase of over five hundred steps, built to accommodate the almost sheer hill that rises from the lower end of Calle Padre Pico.

Heading east from Parque Céspedes lands you on the liveliest section of **Calle Heredia** with its craft stalls, music venues and museums, amongst them the quirky **Museo de Carnaval** at no. 301 Heredia (Tues–Sat 9am–5pm, Sun 9am–noon; $2, plus $1 per photo taken or $5 for camcorder). Be sure to stop here if you can't make it for the real thing in July. Thoughtfully laid out on the ground floor of a dimly lit colonial house, the museum is a bright and colourful collection of psychedelic costumes, atmospheric photographs and carnival memorabilia. When the museum closes, the flamboyant carnival atmosphere continues with a free, hour-long **dance recital**, the Tardes de Folklórico (folklore afternoon; Tues–Sat 5–6pm, Sun 11am–noon), which is given outside on a patio to the back of the museum.

In the street parallel to Heredia, on the corner of Aguilera and Pío Rosado, the suberb **Museo Emilio Bacardí Moreau** (Tues–Sat 10am–8pm, Sun 10am–6pm; $2, $1 extra for each photograph) is the one Santiago museum you should definitely visit if your time is limited. Styled along the lines of a traditional European city museum, it was founded in 1899 by Emilio Bacardí Moreau, then mayor of Santiago and patriarch of the Bacardi rum dynasty. Its colonial antiquities, excellent collection of Cuban fine art and archeological curios – including an Egyptian mummy – make it one of the most comprehensive hoards in the country.

East of the historic centre, Avenida de los Libertadores, the town's main artery, holds the **Moncada barracks** where Santiago's much-touted **Museo Histórico 26 de Julio** (Mon–Sat 9am–5pm, Sun 9am–1pm; $1, $1 extra for each photograph) fills you in on Fidel Castro's celebrated – though futile – attack on July 26, 1953. With a commanding view over the mountains, the building, peppered with bullet holes, is a must-see, if only for the place it has in Cuban history. While the exhibits are not without flashes of brilliance when it comes to telling the story, they are otherwise rather dry.

Out of the city

Presiding over the bay eight kilometres outside the city is Santiago's most magnificent sight, the **Castillo del Morro San Pedro de la Roca**, or "El Morro" (Mon–Fri 9am–5pm, Sat & Sun 8am–4pm; $4, $1 extra for a camera or $5 for a camcorder), a statuesque fortress built by the Spanish between 1633 and 1639 to ward off pirates. However, despite appearing to be indomitable – with a heavy drawbridge spanning a deep moat, thick stone walls and, inside, expansive parade grounds stippled with cannons trained out to sea – it was nothing of the sort, and in 1662 the English pirate Christopher Myngs, finding to his surprise that the fort had been left unguarded, made a successful rearguard attack. Ramps and steps cut precise angles through the heart of the fortress, which is spread over three levels, and it's only as you wander deeper into the labyrinth of rooms that you get a sense of how awesomely huge it is.

Eating, drinking and nightlife

As in most of the country, the majority of Santiago's **restaurants** fall back on the old favourites of pork or chicken accompanied by rice and beans, although many state restaurants, especially the ones at the top end, usually have a tasty seafood dish or two as well. However, you won't be at a loss for places to try, with plenty of restaurants and cafés around the centre all serving decent meals at affordable prices. Away from the state arena, choice is very limited as high taxes and tight controls on what food can be served have pushed most of the **paladares** in town out of business, but some *casas particulares* make meals for their guests.

As for **bars**, since much of the action in Santiago revolves around live music there are few places that cater specifically for drinkers, although the *Hotel Casa Granda* has two excellent bars. **Musical** entertainment in Santiago is hard to beat, with several excellent live *trova* (traditional Cuban music) venues – all a giddy whirl of rum and high spirits with soulful *boleros* and *son*. Keep an eye out for the superb Estudiantina Invasora *trova* group, who often play at the *Casa de la Trova* (see overleaf). You don't have to exert too much effort to find the best music; it often spills onto the streets at weekends. The best nights are often the cheapest and it's rare to find a venue charging more than $5. Around **carnival** time in July, bands – including some of the biggest names in Cuban salsa – set up just about everywhere, with temporary stages in many of the open spaces, notably at the Guillermón Moncada Baseball Stadium on the Avenida de las Américas and parks around the centre.

Discos tend to draw a young, sometimes edgy and high-spirited crowd, including many of the *jinetero* and *jinetera* types who hang out in Parque Céspedes trying to win your attention. It's a situation that attracts a lot of police interest and trouble spots are often closed without warning in a bid to stem the flesh trade. At those discos that are open, you can expect to pay between $1 and $5 entrance.

Cafés and restaurants

Casa Granda Heredia 201 e/ San Pedro y San Félix. This hotel restaurant is the best place in town for breakfast, with an extensive hot and cold Continental, English and Caribbean buffet. Also scores highly for lunch and dinner, with lemon roast chicken, steak and lobster as well as some drinkable wines. Prices for mains start from $6.

Coppelia Ave. de los Libertadores esq. Garzón. Freshly made ice cream at unbeatable peso prices in an outdoor café that looks like a crazy golf course. Very popular locally, so arrive early before the best flavours sell out. Closed Mon.

La Corona Félix Pena no. 807 esq. San Carlos. Excellent bakery with an indoor café, serving up a wide variety of breads, sweets and pastries filled with custard or smothered in super-sticky meringue.

La Maison Ave. Manduley esq. 1 no. 52, Reparto Vista Alegre ☎ 22/64-11-17. A swanky restaurant in the La Maison fashion-house complex, serving good steaks, red snapper and seafood specialities including paella and "surf 'n' turf" grill. Entrée prices start at $8.

Bars and clubs

Bar Claqueta Santo Tomás e/ San Basilio y Heredia. A small, welcoming open-air club with excellent, energetic live music from the two resident bands, Los Amantes del Son and Sonora Huracán.

Casa de la Cultura San Pedro, on Parque Céspedes. Formerly a high-society club, this gracefully decaying venue is perfect for classic sounds. There's often a band playing on Saturdays, a fairly regular *rumba* night, occasional classical music performances and, on the first and third Sunday of every month, a daytime show featuring a *trova* group.

Casa de la Trova Heredia no. 208 e/ San Pedro y San Félix. A visit to the famous, pocket-sized *Casa de la Trova* is the highlight of a trip to Santiago, with musicians playing day and night to an audience packed into the single tiny room or hanging in through the window. Although this venue attracts much tourist attention, it is still the top choice in town for hearing excellent music. Entrance costs $2–5 depending on who's playing.

Los Dos Abuelos Pérez Carbo 5, Plaza Marte. A variety of local groups play *son* and *guaracha* on this bar's pretty patio, shaded by fruit trees, at 10pm every night. There's an extensive range of rums and snacks available.

Pico Real in the *Hotel Santiago de Cuba*, Ave. de las Américas y Calle M. Rooftop bar and a good setting for a panoramic soak, though expect a livelier scene in the evening, with a nightly fashion show (around $25), followed by a small-scale *salsa* disco.

Pista Bailable Teatro Heredia, Ave. de las Américas s/n ☎ 22/64-31-90. Pumped-up *salsa*, *son*, *bolero* and *merengue* tunes all get the crowd dancing at this unpretentious local club, with live music some nights.

Granma and the Sierra Maestra

Protruding west from the main body of Cuba, cupping the Bahía de Guacanayabo, **Granma** is a tranquil, slow-paced province, bypassed with impunity by those pressed for time. That said, a visit to the small, simple rural town of **Pilón** gives a worthy insight into life beyond the tourist trail. On the southwestern tip of Granma's coastline, **Las Coloradas**, where Fidel Castro and his revolutionaries came ashore on the *Granma*, is the highlight of any revolution pilgrimage, while nearby the **Parque Nacional Desembarco del Granma** has several excellent guided nature trails.

The **Sierra Maestra**, Cuba's highest and most extensive mountain range, stretches along the southern coast of the island, running the length of both Santiago and Granma provinces. The unruly beauty of the landscape – a vision of undulating green-gold mountains and remote sugar fields – will take your breath away. That said, once you've admired the countryside there's not an awful lot else you can do: national park status notwithstanding, much of the Sierra Maestra is periodically declared out of bounds by the authorities, who sometimes give the reason of an epidemic in the coffee crops but more often give no reason at all; the area is possibly still used for military operations. Should you get the opportunity to go trekking here, seize it as there are some excellent trails, most notably through the stunning cloud forest of the **Parque Nacional Turquino** to the island's highest point, **Pico Turquino** (1974m).

Pilón

The tiny sugar town of **PILÓN**, 175km west from Santiago de Cuba, is a step back in time, with open-backed carts laden with sugar cane zigzagging across the roads and the smell of boiling molasses enveloping the town. There's little to do, but the two beaches, **Playa Media Luna**, with beautiful views over the Sierra Maestra and a rocky coastline good for snorkelling, and the narrow white-sand **Playa Punta**, are refreshingly different from those at the smart resorts. The small but engaging **Casa Museo Ceila Sánchez Manduley** (Mon–Sat 9am–5pm, Sun 9am–1pm; $1), erstwhile home of revolutionary Ceila Sánchez, offers a ragtag assortment of exhibits, from Taíno ceramics to shrapnel from the wars of independence.

There's nowhere to stay or eat in Pilón, though the local service station on the Marea de Portillo road sells sweets, snacks and cold drinks. Bus service from Santiago is erratic; if you don't have your own transport, the most dependable way to reach the town is to catch one of the *colectivo* trucks that leave from the Astro bus terminal on Avenida de los Libertadores.

Parque Nacional Desembarco del Granma

West of Pilón, the province's southwestern tip is commanded by the **Parque Nacional Desembarco del Granma**, which starts at the tranquil holiday haven of **Las Coloradas**, 47km from Pilón, and stretches some 20km west to the tiny fishing village of Cabo Cruz. The forested interior of the park is littered with trails, but the most famous feature is the **Playa Las Coloradas**, on the western coastline, where the *Granma* yacht deposited Fidel Castro and his 81 comrades on December 2, 1956, on their clandestine return from exile in Mexico.

Named after the red colour that the mangrove jungle gives to the water, the beach is completely hidden and you can't see or even hear the ocean from the start of the path that leads down to the **Monumento Portada de la Libertad** (Mon–Fri 8am–5pm, Sat & Sun 8am–2pm; $1, including guide), which marks the spot of the landing. Flanked on either side by mangrove forest hedged with jagged saw grass, the kilometre-long path presents a pleasant walk even for those indifferent to the revolution, and even the most jaded cynics will find the enthusiasm the guide has for his subject hard to resist. His compelling narrative (in Spanish) brings to life the rebels' journey through murky undergrowth and razor-sharp thicket.

The tour also takes in a life-size replica of the **yacht**, which the guide can sometimes be persuaded to let you clamber aboard, and a rather spartan **museum** with photographs, maps and an emotive quotation from Castro on the eve of the crossing that neatly sums up his determination to succeed: "*Si salimos, llegamos. Si llegamos, entramos, y si entramos triumfamos*" ("If we leave, we'll get there. If we get there we'll get in, and if we get in we will win.")

The only **accommodation** in the area is the *Villa Las Coloradas*, on Playa Las Coloradas (⓪), which has simple, clean chalets with air conditioning and hot water, along with a restaurant and bar. Bookings should be made via Cubamar (☏7/83-12-891) and are essential at weekends, when this is a favourite target for Cubans. Las Coloradas is somewhat out of the way; if you are not driving, your best bet is to hitch from Pilón or arrange private transport in Santiago.

3.8

Cayo Largo

South of the mainland, the little-visited Isla de la Juventud (Island of Youth) is the largest of over three hundred scattered emerald islets that make up the **Archipiélago de los Canarreos**. Most visitors to the archipelago, however, are destined for its comparatively tiny neighbour **CAYO LARGO**, arguably Cuba's most exclusive holiday resort.

Some 140km east of the Isla de la Juventud, the cay is a narrow, low-lying spit of land fringed with powdery beaches, and is totally geared to those on package holidays. The tiny islet, measuring just 20km from tip to beachy tip, caters to the quickening flow of European and Canadian tourists who swarm here to enjoy the excellent watersports, diving and Club Med-style hotels. In November of 2001, **Hurricane Michelle** wrought havoc on the cay; large-scale evacuations took place and some of the hotels were heavily damaged. Now, though, all the damage has been repaired and plans are under way for even more hotels.

Arrival, information and getting around

The only way to reach **Cayo Largo** is by **plane**, and its airport sees numerous international arrivals, as well as domestic flights on a rickety Russian twenty-seater from Havana (2 daily; 40min); you'll be required to book accommodation along with your flight. The tiny Vilo Acuña airport is 1km from the main belt of hotels and courtesy hotel buses meet every flight.

Though there is no main **tourist office** on the cay, the representatives of various tour companies who share a desk at the *Sol Club Cayo Largo* offer general information and organize excursions. You can buy **maps** at all the hotel shops or from the post office in front of the *Isla del Sur* hotel and there's a **bank** on the corner of the village plaza. The cay is also relatively well represented on the Web, with informative sites at ⊛www.cayolargodelsur.cu and ⊛www.cayolargo.net.

The island is small enough to negotiate easily and courtesy **buses** regularly do the circuit of the hotels, running from early morning to midnight. A free **ferry** leaves from the marina to Playa Sirena and Playa Paraíso twice daily at 9.30am and 11am, returning at 3pm and 5pm. There's also a speedboat service running intermittently, charging $2. The best way to take in the east of the island is to rent a moped, dune buggy or jeep from the office at the *Sol Club Cayo Largo*.

Accommodation

Hotel standards are high and rooms are not overly cheap as they tend to be block-booked by overseas package-tour operators at a specially discounted rate. All the hotels are all-inclusive, and some group together to offer a range of shared facilities. A selection are reviewed below – the price codes represent what you'll pay if you book through a Cuban tour operator. Note that the *Villa Coral*, *Isla del Sur* and *Villa Lindarmar* hotels (see opposite) form something of a cooperative; they all share a phone and fax number (☎45/24-81-11 to 18, ℻24-81-60) and guests from each hotel are welcome to eat and use the facilities at any of the others.

Isla del Sur Though its reception is sunny and pleasant, this is a slightly dowdy hotel, patronized by an almost exclusively Italian clientele, with old-style shadowy, lurid green corridors. The rooms are simple but comfortable, almost all with sea views, and there's a buffet restaurant, snack bar and lively 24hr lobby bar. ❼

Sol Cayo Largo ☎45/24-82-60, ✉jefe.reservas.scl@solmeliacuba.com. An appealing, buzzy, Caribbean-themed hotel with airy rooms painted in tropical colours in smart blocks set around palm trees and rather parched lawns. With an all-inclusive buffet, beach grill and à la carte restaurants, two swimming pools, free non-motorized watersports, a health centre, tennis courts and a football field, this is the biggest and plushest place on the cay, with a clientele of twenty-something couples, families and retirees all mingling happily. ❾

Villa Coral This family-oriented hotel offers rather gaudy pink and green blocks with red-tiled roofs, divided by neat beds of sea shrubs and palms to ensure a sense of privacy. Rooms have spacious balconies and smart sun terraces, with shaded seating surrounding a sparkling circular pool. ❼

Villa Lindamar A stylish complex that backs onto an ample stretch of beach lined with sun shades and loungers. These thatched cabins, each with its own porch and hammock, are perched on stilts, over-looking a garden of sea grass and hibiscus bushes, and feel self-contained and private – a definite plus. ❽

Exploring Cayo Largo

Life on the cay began in 1977 when the state, capitalizing on the extensive white sands and offshore coral reefs, built the first of eight hotels that now line the western and southern shores. There is still ample room for development, however, and while plans are under way for more hotels, the cay has a long way to go before it is spoilt; indeed so sparse is the infrastructure away from the hotels that at times hanging out in the resort can seem rather monotonous. The artificiality which works well in the hotels fails somewhat in the **Isla del Sol village** on the west of the island, which has a distinctly spurious air: it's just a sparse collection of a shop, restaurants, a small museum, a bank and, behind the tourist facade, blocks of workers' accommodation.

There's rather more activity around the beaches to the south and along the hotel strip, where warm shallow waters lap the narrow ribbon of pale downy sand. Protected from harsh winds and rough waves by the offshore coral reef, and with over 2km of white sands, **Playa Sirena** enjoys a deserved reputation as the most beautiful of all the beaches and is consequently the busiest. There's a road to the beach from the *Sol Pelícano* but, as it's frequently covered by rifts of sand, you're better off catching one of the ferries or speedboats from the marina (see below). There's a **café** on the beach serving drinks, sandwiches and snacks. Further south along the same strand, **Playa Paraíso** is almost as attractive and popular as Sirena, with the added advantage that the shallow waters are ideal for children. Heading east, **Playa Lindamar** is a serviceable 5km curve of sand in front of the *Lindamar, Sol Pelícano* and *Villa Coral* hotels and is the only one where you can play volleyball and windsurf.

With over thirty dive sites in the clear and shallow waters around the cay, Cayo Largo is also known as one of Cuba's best **diving areas**. Particularly outstanding are the coral gardens to be found in the shallow waters around the islet, while other highlights of the region include underwater encounters with hawksbill and sea green turtles, as well as trips to the tiny **Cayo Iguana** where the eponymous reptiles are tame enough to be fed by hand. The cay boasts two dive centres, one at the Marina Puerto Sol and the other on Playa Sirena, although both are managed by the marina and offer identical packages (☎5/4-82-13, ⓦwww.puertosol.net). One dive costs $35, including all equipment and transfer to the dive site, and prices per dive decrease with subsequent dives. The marina also runs **catamaran excursions** that include snorkelling at the coral gardens, a visit to Cayo Iguana, lunch, an open bar and paddling in the Fifth Canal – an area where the deliciously warm waters of the Caribbean sea never exceed a depth of one metre ($65).

Eating, drinking and entertainment

Although some hotels have two-way cooperative systems whereby their guests can eat at either hotel, most all-inclusive packages confine visitors to the buffet **restaurants** of the hotel they are booked into, where the food is a fairly standard range of international dishes. Of these, the *Sol Club Cayo Largo* has the largest selection and the cheeriest atmosphere. It also has an à la carte restaurant serving more sophisticated fare at which non-guests can pay to eat. *Villa Coral* has a pleasant and airy snack bar in a pink-tiled pool area, serving small pizzas, sandwiches and ice cream.

Down in the quiet of the village, the thatched *Taberna del Pirata* **bar**, on the plaza overlooking the picturesque harbour, is a great spot to enjoy the cooling sea breezes as you watch the sun go down. Next door, the *El Criolla* restaurant has a distinctive Wild West flavour with a wooden ceiling, cow-hide-covered chairs and some ornamental saddles. It serves classic Cuban chicken and pork dishes as well as lobster and shrimp cooked in a variety of ways. Other than the *Taberna del Pirata* bar, there is no **nightlife** on the island outside of the hotels. The bar in the reception of the *Isla del Sur* is open 24 hours a day and has a buzzy atmosphere. The *Sol Club Cayo Largo* is probably the liveliest spot at night, with a friendly lobby bar and a larger one by the pool that's mercifully set back from the stage where an entertainment team puts on nightly cabaret shows with enforced hilarity. Should you feel like providing the entertainment yourself, there's also a karaoke bar. For a cover charge of $15, guests from other hotels can join in the festivities and drink at the open bars.

The Cayman Islands

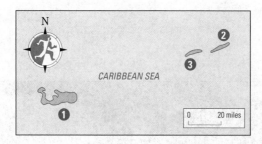

N

CARIBBEAN SEA

1
2
3

0   20 miles

The Cayman Islands highlights

✳ **Bloody Bay Wall** Swim amongst luminescent corals and colourful fish at Little Cayman's premier wall dive. See p.257

✳ **Seven Mile Beach** Miles of soft white sand and sparklingly blue, gentle surf draw visitors to this popular and easily accessible stretch. See p.248

✳ **Stingray City** Superb spot where you can get friendly with the local stingray population. See p.246

✳ **Botanic Park Colour Garden** Meander through a living rainbow: 2.5 acres of colour-coordinated flora. See p.249

△ Sandcastle-building on Seven Mile Beach

Introduction and basics

Just northwest of Jamaica, the **Cayman Islands** have truly grown up during the past forty years, driven by tourism and banking. Today they boast one of the highest per capita incomes in the world and rank as the world's fifth largest offshore financial centre. On the tourism side of development, they attract more than two million visitors a year (most by cruise ship) and have been a scuba-diving paradise since the 1960s.

Although one of the countries hit hardest by **Hurricane Ivan** in September 2004, the Cayman Islands have quickly bounced back. Despite the storm, the financial sector hardly had a pause in business and has continued to grow. And tourists are returning to find newly refurbished accommodations and restaurants along with the same alluring beaches and azure waters.

Of the 44,000 people who live in Cayman (rather than "The Caymans", "Cayman" is the accepted abbreviated name), 40 percent were born elsewhere. While expatriates move here from all over the world, Jamaicans, Americans and Canadians predominate, and the majority of visitors come from the US. The islands are just a 90-minute flight from Miami, Florida, and being a British overseas territory, English is the official language – making for a quick, convenient and easy getaway for North Americans. Since the fast-food chains along with many hotels and products also hail from the US, it's sometimes easy to forget you're in the Caribbean and think you're somewhere in, say, Florida instead.

That being said, Cayman does have its unique draws, the chief one being superb **scuba diving**. Like many islands, the Cayman Islands are essentially tops of underwater mountains, and the submerged terrain here is especially dramatic: spectacular underwater walls, caverns and healthy coral reefs have made this one of the world's best spots for diving and snorkelling. With its crystal clear water and sandy **beaches** (Grand Cayman's Seven Mile Beach is among the finest in the Caribbean), Cayman is also an ideal destination for those who enjoy other watersports or just soaking up the sun. A variety of tropical birds flock here as well, making **birdwatching** a popular activity. Life in Cayman is laid-back; if rousing casinos and wild nightlife are what you seek, these are not the islands to visit – there's no gambling of any kind, but there are plenty of places to sip a cocktail while watching the sunset. Families will be pleased to find that many larger resorts have daily kids' camps, restaurants often have a children's menu, and most attractions have discounted rates for young ones.

Grand Cayman is the most developed of the three islands and where you will find the largest choice of accommodation, restaurants and attractions. The Sister Islands **Cayman Brac** (pronounced "brack") and **Little Cayman** have far fewer options in lodging and dining and most travellers to these islands choose all-inclusive packages. Compared to Grand Cayman, the pace is far mellower here. They've yet to put up stop lights on either island, and on Little Cayman bikes are the transportation of choice.

None of the islands is densely populated; much of each is uninhabited swampland or rough ironshore, and other than in the busier west end of Grand Cayman, homes are rather sparsely dotted along the coastlines. All three islands are low-lying and arid, though Cayman Brac does have a ridge that rises to 140 feet above sea level, the country's highest point. The **vegetation** throughout is predominately scrub brush and mangrove. There are also colourful flowering **plants** and **trees** such as the brilliant flamboyant tree that grows as high as 40 feet and develops a blossoming orange canopy that spreads across the roadways. Bougainvillea flowers almost year-round, gracing island homes with vibrant swatches of fuchsia, white and lemon-yellow.

Where to go

To soak up the sun on a gorgeous stretch of sand within reach of assorted restaurants and bars, head to **Seven Mile Beach**, just north of George Town on Grand Cayman. For a total escape, spend some reflective time **hiking** or **birdwatching** on quiet Cayman Brac, or quieter Little Cayman.

The main reason to come to Cayman, though, is the premier diving attractions on all three islands: frolic with the friendly rays at **Stingray City** off Grand Cayman, shore-dive just a few yards off Cayman Brac, or head to **Bloody Bay Wall** just off Little Cayman for superb underwater adventure; snorkellers can explore the wall in about 20 feet of water while a short distance away divers can slip into a 6000-foot abyss.

When to go

The **average temperature** hovers around 24°C (75°F) in winter and 29°C (85°F) in the summer. If travelling during the holiday season (late Nov to early Jan), be sure to reserve hotels and vehicles a few months in advance. Off-season (April to mid-Nov) lodging rates can drop twenty percent or more and the islands are less crowded.

There are **two seasons**: "rainy", lasting from mid-May to October, followed by the "dry" season, November to April. Don't let the term "rainy season" deter you from visiting; in general you'll encounter brief afternoon showers followed by sun and higher humidity than in the drier months. **Hurricane** season, though, is from June 1 to November 30 (at its worst in September), and while chances of your holiday coinciding with a major storm are slim, Cayman is by no means immune: Grand Cayman will likely take years to fully recover from the devastation of Hurricane Ivan in 2004. Note that most resorts on Little Cayman close for the month of September.

Arrival

Virtually all flights touch down first at **Owen Roberts International Airport** (☎ 345/949-7811) on Grand Cayman, with connecting flights to Cayman Brac and Little Cayman usually departing the same day (there's also one direct flight weekly from Miami to Cayman Brac).

Year-round, **cruise lines** such as Carnival, Disney and Celebrity dock daily at the **Port of George Town**.

Information, websites and maps

Once you arrive on Grand Cayman, you'll find an array of brochures and maps at the **information booth** at Owen Roberts International Airport. At the time of writing, there was also a small temporary booth (set up post-Ivan) at the North Terminal cruise ship dock in George Town Harbour, but plans for a new facility there were in the works. Similarly, the Department of Tourism (☎ 345/949-0623, ⊛ www.caymanislands.ky) had its temporary headquarters in the Leeward Two building of the Regatta Business Park on West Bay Rd, but was scheduled to move in 2006 to the Cayman Corporate Centre in downtown George Town. There are also some brochures and maps at the airport on Cayman Brac, and the Brac Department of Tourism (☎ 345/948-1849) has its office in the West End Community Park.

Websites

⊛ **www.caymanislands.ky** The official website of the Cayman Islands Department of Tourism, where you can read up on Cayman and plan your vacation.

⊛ **www.caymannetnews.com** Online version of a local tabloid newspaper which has stories filled with insight as well as innuendo. A great place to get an insider's look at the islands.

⊛ **www.cimoney.com.ky** Curious about offshore banking? All the information you might want is right here.

⊛ **www.divecayman.ky** Details on dive sites, resorts and dive operators. An interactive dive map with pop-up windows that take you directly to a dive site with a full listing on what you will see there.

Hurricane Ivan

On September 11, 2004, the Caribbean's most powerful storm in a decade reached Grand Cayman and battered the island for as many as 36 hours, killing two people and causing nearly US$3.5 billion in damage. **Hurricane Ivan** brought with it wind gusts of up to 220mph and an 8-foot rise in sea level, hurling entire homes from their bases and depositing them on the roads alongside mountains of sand, mangled cars and felled trees. According to official reports, 83 percent of homes were damaged, more than 5000 cars were destroyed and the island had no power for five days (and in parts, none for many months). More than 10,000 people left the island in the month of September, many of whom flew home to their native countries and may not return.

But major storms are nothing new to Cayman; in recent memory are Michelle which hit in 2001 and Gilbert in 1988 – and there are still memorials on Cayman Brac for the worst storm of the twentieth century which hit there hardest in 1932. Despite the devastation these storms bring, Cayman is fortunate to have a high level of **insurance coverage**, especially as compared with other countries in the Caribbean, and a greater capacity to rebuild. With tourism contributing at least half of the GDP, the islands were quick to reopen to visitors after Ivan in November of 2004. At the time of writing, the Department of Tourism was confident that, while it may take some years before the vegetation returns and all the rebuilding is complete, Cayman will effectively be **back to normal** for tourists by the 2005/2006 high season.

Money and costs

The official currency is the **Cayman Islands dollar (CI$)**, which comes in $1, $5, $10, $25, $50 and $100 notes; the coins are 1, 5, 10 and 25 cents. The Cayman dollar is based on 100 Cayman cents. The exchange rate is fixed at 80 Cayman cents to one US dollar. Both Cayman and US dollars can be used everywhere on the islands, although change will generally be given in CI$. All other currencies will need to be exchanged at either a bank or your hotel, but travellers' cheques and all major credit cards are widely accepted.

Although Grand Cayman has more than 300 licensed **banks**, only a handful provide customer banking service as most visitors know it. These include Scotiabank, Bank of Butterfield, Royal Bank of Canada, Cayman National Bank and First Caribbean International Bank. **ATMs** accepting Visa and MasterCard linked to the Cirrus and Plus systems are located along West Bay Road as well as at Owen Roberts International Airport on Grand Cayman. **Bank hours** are generally Mon–Fri 9am–4pm. There is one bank on each of the Sister Islands, both of which keep limited hours, but no ATM on Little Cayman.

Though there are special deals and packages, the Cayman Islands are far from a bargain hunters' paradise; **prices are fixed** and haggling is not the norm here. High-season prices kick in from late November and begin to drop in April.

Getting around

Island Air (℡345/949-5252), based in Grand Cayman, and *Cayman Airways Express* (℡345/949-2311 or 1-800/GCAYMAN) offer four trips daily between all three islands. The flight between Grand Cayman and either of the Sister Islands takes about 40 minutes and costs just over US$100 return. Although the Sister Islands are only about five miles apart, no ferries run between them.

Car Rentals are available on all three islands, although they are not the norm on Little Cayman where the transportation of choice is a bicycle. To drive a car on any of the islands, a visitor's licence is required and available for US$7.50 at rental agencies and at the central police station in George Town on Grand Cayman. Roads are in excellent condition on Grand Cayman and Cayman Brac, but a bit rough on Little Cayman. Petrol costs about US$4 per gallon. Remember to drive on the left and wear a seatbelt.

The **bus** system on Grand Cayman is efficient, but there are no buses on either of the Sister Islands. **Taxis** are available on Grand Cayman and Cayman Brac, but not on Little Cayman.

Accommodation

Cayman is **expensive** by any standards; expect to pay at least US$100 per night for even the most modest accommodation. **Packages** (diving, fishing, golfing) can be a way to save and are offered throughout the year; other specials are sometimes advertised on the Department of Tourism website (ⓦwww.caymanislands.ky). If you're serious about diving, you might consider staying on a live-aboard dive boat; check ⓦwww.divecayman.ky for listings.

Renting a **villa** on any of the three islands is another popular option; there are more than a hundred available and you may even find yourself with a private stretch of beach (many have a pool and maid service). You can try Cayman Villas (☎345/945-4144 or 1-800/235-5888, ⓦwww.caymanvillas.com) or the Department of Tourism website which lists all available properties.

A 10 percent **government tax** is added to all bills, and most properties also tack on a **service charge** of 10–15 percent. When making reservations, be sure to ask if the quoted rate includes these additional charges.

Food and drink

Thanks to Cayman's historical connection to Jamaica, it's no surprise to find **jerked meats** – heavily spiced meats smoked over hardwoods in enclosed barbecue grills – as one of the island specialities. **Turtle**, though not as popular as it once was, is part of traditional Cayman cuisine and usually prepared in stews. Also prevalent is **conch**, popularly served as fritters but traditionally prepared in stews or as steak, or occasionally as ceviche – sliced thin and marinated in lemon or lime with bits of tomato and onion.

Cayman-style **fish** can really be any fish pulled fresh from the sea and sautéed with pepper, onions and green peppers. Typical sides are plantains, yams and rice and peas cooked in coconut milk. **Heavy cake** is a real treat and can be found in small grocers and at some petrol stations. Made with grated cassava root, white yam or papaya, it is sweetened with sugar and has the consistency of a thick bread pudding.

You can find **locally grown produce** such as mango, grapefruit, ackee, coconut and breadfruit along with home-made goodies at most supermarkets on the islands. Though restaurants tend to specialize in Continental or international fare, traditional Cayman cuisine occasionally appears on menus. You'll find a truer taste of island food in the outer districts of Grand Cayman and on Cayman Brac.

The local brew in Cayman is **Stingray Beer**, a fairly nondescript lager that tourists tend to enjoy more than locals. **Rum Punch**, made with orange and pineapple juices, rum, and grenadine, is as popular here as elsewhere in the Caribbean. More unique to Cayman is the **Cayman Lemonade** made with sweet and sour mix, peach schnapps, cranberry juice, vodka and rum. There's no distillery in Cayman, but **Tortuga Rum Company** makes its own Cayman blend of Jamaican and Barbados rums.

In restaurants and hotels on all three islands, the **tap water** is desalinated sea water and fine for drinking.

Phones, post and email

When making a **phone call**, watch out for hotel surcharges: they can be double the already expensive per-minute rate. A less expensive option is to purchase a phone card, available in most stores, and make your call on a public phone, readily available throughout the islands and in most hotel lobbies.

The main **post office** branch is in downtown George Town at Edward St and Cardinal Ave (Mon–Fri 8.15am–5pm; ☎345/949-2474), and has a philatelic bureau; there are also branch locations throughout the island. The main post office on Cayman Brac is in West End, and there is one post office on Little Cayman.

Grand Cayman has all the latest high-tech communications infrastructure and devices. There are an ever-increasing number of **Internet** cafés, including *The Thai Restaurant* in downtown Georgetown (CI\$6/hour) and *Café del Sol* in the Marquee Shopping Centre off West Bay Rd (CI\$4/hour). Several hotels on Cayman Brac and Little Cayman offer access as well, some of them with available wireless connections. There is no public access on Little Cayman, but the West End post office on Cayman Brac has one computer available (CI\$6/hour).

The **country code** for the Cayman Islands is ☏345.

There are no embassies in Cayman as it is a British Territory; the closest location is in Jamaica. For assistance, call the Department of Tourism main office at ☏345/949-0623 or the Government Administration Building at ☏345/949-7900.

Public holidays and festivals

The main event on Grand Cayman is the annual **Pirates' Week** (☏ 345/949-5078, ✉ www.piratesweekfestival.com), a ten-day celebration held in late October. George Town is centre stage for the major activities at the weekends, but special events take place all over the island and include street dances into the wee hours, sports contests, a mock pirate invasion, glittering parades and treasure hunts. It's a popular event with islanders and tourists, so book hotel accommodations well in advance.

Spring brings **Batabano** (☏ 345/949-7121, ✉ www.caymancarnival.com), Cayman's annual **Carnival** which takes place at various venues around the island over four days in early May, featuring parades and live soca and calypso bands, along with street stalls offering tasty Cayman and Caribbean delicacies. April, meanwhile, sees the Cayman Islands International **Fishing Tournament** (☏345/945-3131, ✉www.fishcayman.com), where international anglers compete to catch blue marlin, yellowfin tuna, wahoo and the like for hefty cash prizes.

Little Cayman also has its share of events, the most popular being the **Annual Mardi Gras Festival** (☏ 345/948-1010). This is small-town parade atmosphere at its best; many people visit during this time just to take part and there are always more participants than spectators.

Sports and outdoor activities

Given the clear, warm sea it's no surprise that **watersports** predominate, the greatest variety being available on Grand Cayman. **Scuba diving** and **snorkelling** are by far the most popular; visibility can exceed 100 feet (see box overleaf). For those who prefer to stay dry, a glass-bottom boat or an air-conditioned submarine will shuttle sightseers down to this amazing world underwater.

There is as much to do on top of the water: deep-sea fishing, bonefishing on the flats around Little Cayman, windsurfing (especially good on the breezy East End of Grand Cayman), jet skiing, parasailing, sailing and simply swimming or floating around on the salty sea.

Grand Cayman has well-maintained and challenging **golf** courses, although at the time of writing they were still recovering from Ivan. At the *Hyatt Regency*'s Britannia Golf Club, the Jack Nicklaus signature course (greens fees US\$85–110) is actually

Public holidays

January 1 New Year's Day
Fourth Monday in January National Heroes' Day
February Ash Wednesday
March/April Good Friday, Easter Monday
Third Monday in May Discovery Day
First Monday after second Saturday in June Queen's Birthday
First Monday in July Constitution Day
First Monday after November 11 Remembrance Day
December 25 Christmas Day
December 26 Boxing Day

Scuba diving

Excellent conditions and unique terrain have made the seas around the Cayman Islands the domain of **scuba divers**. The underwater landscape is dominated by a massive trench (Cayman Trench), which plunges down some 25,000 feet to the deepest point in the Caribbean Sea. The drop-off is dramatic, with 6000ft cliffs in some places no more than a few hundred yards offshore. To scuba divers, diving these walls is akin to exploring the Grand Canyon; they explode with life – sea fans, barrel sponges and sea whips abound as does a plethora of marine creatures that crawl, hover and dart around the reefs. Given the popularity of the sport, dive operators and packages are abundant, but despite the traffic, Cayman's strict marine park regulations (with maximum fines of CI$500,000) keep damage in check.

Hurricane Ivan did mar some dive sites, mainly on Grand Cayman – depositing debris on the reefs and removing soft corals and sponges; however, if you're a first-time diver in these waters, chances are you won't even notice the damage. In the short-term, though, returning divers may prefer to go to the Sister Islands as they were less impacted by the storm and conditions there have traditionally been more pristine.

Every hotel on Little Cayman has an affiliated dive operation, as do both resorts on Cayman Brac. On Grand Cayman, there's a wide variety of **dive shops**; the following are just a few of the best.

Grand Cayman dive shops
Bob Soto's Reef Divers George Town ☎345/949-2871 or 1-800/BOB-SOTO. Most likely reopening in Jan 2006.
Don Foster's George Town and Seven Mile Beach ☎345/949-5679 or 1-800/83-DIVER.
Eden Rock South Church St ☎345/949-7243.
Red Sail Sports Seven Mile Beach and Rum Point ☎345/945-5965 or 1-877/RED-SAIL.

---

two courses in one: a par 58 executive-style, or short, course, and a par 70 championship course. The Links at Safehaven (greens fees US$80–120) is an eighteen-hole, par 71 championship course.

The Sister Islands offer some distinct nature-based sports. Cayman Brac sets itself apart from the other islands with the various **hiking trails** that criss-cross the island. Be sure to wear sturdy shoes as some of the trails are over sharp ironshore coral, and bring water as it's easy to get dehydrated in the heat. On the less strenuous side, there's excellent **birdwatching** on Little Cayman, where the centre of the island is dominated by a mangrove swamp – the red-footed booby, black frigate and snowy egret are commonly seen here.

History

Christopher Columbus is the first European credited with discovering the islands in 1503, though frankly he stumbled upon them. While en route between Panama and Hispaniola he got blown west off course and recorded seeing two small islands (Little Cayman and Cayman Brac) "full of tortoise". Thus he dubbed them "Las Tortugas", Spanish for turtle, though the name didn't last. A few decades later in 1586, British explorer Sir Francis Drake passed through, recording that the islands were flush with "great serpents… like large lizards". These were caimans – marine reptiles related to crocodiles, after which the islands were renamed.

Except for the animals and marine creatures, it's generally assumed the islands were uninhabited until seafarers began using them as **replenishment centres** in the sixteenth century. English, Dutch, French and Spanish explorers all made use of the abundant supplies of fresh water and food available here, including sea turtles and wildfowl. Historians dispute whether any of these explorers were pirates, but legend has it that in the eighteenth century **Blackbeard** stashed his treasures in Cayman caves.

The **Spanish** and **British** were the two main colonial powers battling for control of the islands in this region. The Cayman Islands became part of the British Empire in 1670 under the Treaty of Madrid, which also bestowed nearby Jamaica and other islands onto the British. Most of the original settlers to Cayman were English, Welsh and Scottish who came from Jamaica, some of whom brought their **African slaves** with them to work on cotton plantations, cut mahogany and farm the rocky land for produce. Many Caymanians also turned to the sea to earn a living as merchant marines or turtle fishermen. Under this arrangement, for the next two hundred years or so the Cayman Islands were governed as a dependency of Jamaica.

By the 1950s, with a population of just a few thousand, life in Cayman was still quiet and uncomplicated, with boat building, thatch rope making and turtle fishing the mainstays of the economy. But a post-World War II economic boom opened possibilities for the island.

Propelled by a reputation of **political stability** and a relatively crime-free atmosphere, Cayman began taking strides to follow the example of Bermuda and the Bahamas in creating an **offshore finance** industry and developing a high-end **tourism** sector. Crucial factors encouraging visitors were the opening of Owen Roberts International Airport in 1954 and the work of the Mosquito Control and Research Unit to eradicate the pesky and widely spread mosquito in the 1960s (which didn't altogether succeed). Financial investors were drawn by **bank secrecy laws** (now relaxed since their strictest form in 1976), an efficient telecommunications system and no direct taxation. In 1962 when Jamaica gained independence, the Cayman Islands preferred to remain under the British Crown, in part with the aim of securing continued foreign investment.

The industries grew rapidly, and by 1998, more than 40,000 companies were registered in Cayman, banking assets exceeded US$500 billion and yearly tourist arrivals surpassed one million (mainly by cruise ship). Today, finance and tourism are the mainstays of the Cayman economy.

In recent years, Cayman's prosperity suffered a setback when Hurricane Ivan slammed into the island in September 2004. But the country has made a quick recovery, and barring any additional storms of Ivan's magnitude in the near term, Cayman's financial future continues to look bright.

4.1

Grand Cayman

With a total landmass of 78 square miles, **GRAND CAYMAN** is the largest, most populated and most developed of the three Cayman Islands. As such it receives the greatest number of visitors and certainly feels the most like a traditional Caribbean vacation spot, with a small colonial capital, a beautiful stretch of beach and lots of typical resorts that will set up your whole holiday for you.

The island is carved into five districts, of which only two see much traffic – George Town and West Bay, which comprise the entire western portion. The capital city of George Town is on the western coast in the district which bears its name. Each week nearly 40,000 cruise ship passengers shoulder their way along the narrow sidewalks of the harbour town's main streets, where duty free shops hawk everything from Cuban cigars to fine emeralds. The crowds are never overwhelming but do lend an air of activity to an otherwise fairly quiet place. Once you've covered downtown, you'll likely head to **Seven Mile Beach**, just a ten-minute drive away and arguably one of the finest stretches of sand in the entire Caribbean, its fine powder and calm waters making an alluring destination.

It's easy to explore the rest of the island in a day or two, and while each of the eastern districts certainly has its charm and a far mellower pace than George Town, there are few stops of much interest. **East End** does have some prime places for diving, and the beach at **Rum Point** makes a nice escape from the bustle of the west. No place on the island is much more than an hour from any other, so you can base yourself anywhere and come and go as you please.

Getting around

The main roads around Grand Cayman are paved frequently as needed (most recently just after Ivan) and are in good condition. You might find it easiest to **rent a car** to get around on them, though the public bus service is efficient, and taxis are relatively comfortable, with fixed rates that aren't too astronomical.

Rentals are available across the street from the airport and at some hotels. Many agencies provide complimentary pick-up/drop-off. The major US rental companies operate here – Avis, Budget and Dollar – along with some island-based ones like Coconut Car Rentals (☎345/949-7703), which offers various discount specials. Economy-size car rentals start at US$50 per day in high season.

The **bus terminal** is adjacent to the public library on Edward Street in downtown George Town and serves as the dispatch point for all buses. The fleet of minibuses is distinguished by blue licence plates with white numbering, and each bus displays its route on large round colour-coded stickers. All districts are served by bus, though you may have to transfer, and fares range from CI$1.50 to $3.50. Daily bus service is reliable, beginning at 6am and running until 11pm for the West End, 9pm for the East End (with extended service on Fridays and Saturdays).

Taxis are available from the airport, all resorts and from the taxi stand at the cruise ship dock in George Town. While you won't often see them cruising for fares, you can also call for one – numerous operators are in the phone book. Rates are fixed and posted at the downtown dock and at the dispatch stand at the airport; cabbies rarely try to rip off visitors. Rates from the airport to the Seven Mile Beach resorts run about US$20 one-way.

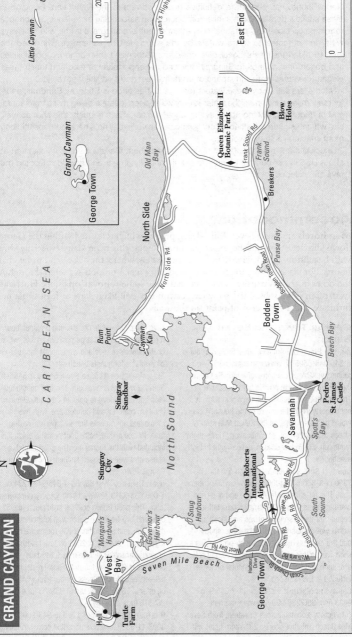

GRAND CAYMAN

CARIBBEAN SEA

N

West Bay

Morgan's Harbour

Hell

Turtle Farm

Seven Mile Beach

Governor's Harbour

Snug Harbour

North Sound

Stingray City

Stingray Sandbar

Rum Point

Cayman Kai

North Side

Old Man Bay

North Side Rd

Queen's Highway

Gun Bay

The Wreck of the Ten Sails

East End

Queen Elizabeth II Botanic Park

Frank Sound Rd

Frank Sound

Blow Holes

Breakers

Pease Bay

Bodden Town

Bodden Town Road

Beach Bay

Savannah

Spott's Bay

Pedro St James Castle

Owen Roberts International Airport

South Sound

George Town

West Bay Rd

Harbour Drive

South Church St

Walker's Rd

Smith Rd

Crewe Rd

Red Bay Rd

South Sound Rd

GRAND CAYMAN

Little Cayman

Cayman Brac

Grand Cayman

George Town

0   20 miles

0   2 miles

Stingray City and Stingray Sandbar

Heralded as the "world's best twelve-foot dive", **Stingray City**, in Grand Cayman's North Sound, has become a definitive goal for divers in the Caribbean. Plunging in these shallow depths about a mile from shore is an astounding experience, the chance to mingle up close and personal with Atlantic southern stingrays in the wild. The rays were first attracted to these waters by the scraps left by fishermen, who used the area to clean their fish. Local dive operators recognized the economic possibilities and began offering trips to Stingray City, and the opportunity to feed and touch these elegant creatures, with wingspans of up to five feet and skin like wet velvet.

Snorkellers will enjoy these waters too, but just as good is **Stingray Sandbar**, a further few miles east where the water is only waist-deep (despite being miles from shore) and perfect for splashing about even without a mask. Rays frequent this spot as well, and weren't scared off either by locals who set up volleyball nets here, perhaps thinking more snacks would be involved.

Check out any number of boat operators throughout the island – excursions start at about US$35 per person; be sure to ask if snorkelling gear and squid for feeding the rays are included.

Accommodation

Most **hotels** are along Seven Mile Beach proper, which is located within the George Town district. As would be expected, hotels along this main drag, especially those with beachfront, are pricier than those located elsewhere; they also tend to be chain resorts. For places with a touch more personality, seek out spots scattered throughout the other districts. Virtually every hotel has done some **renovations** since Hurricane Ivan, often quite substantial, so wherever you stay will likely have at least some new furniture and a fresh coat of paint on the walls.

George Town and Seven Mile Beach

Annie's Place 282 Andrew Drive, Snug Harbour ☎345/945-5505, ✆www.anniesplace.ky. Two rooms available in the home of a friendly Caymanian couple, each with private bath and cable TV. The included full breakfast is served in a lovely open courtyard in the centre of the house. A car would be handy here, as the Seven Mile strip is fifteen to twenty minutes' walk away. Three-night minimum stay in low season, seven-night in high season. ⑤

Comfort Suites Seven Mile Beach ☎345/945-7300 or 1-800/517-4000, ✆www.caymancomfort.com. This all-suites hotel (studios and one- and two-bedrooms) has rather small rooms but is popular for its reasonable prices and location within walking distance of restaurants, shops and the cinema. The beach (not on-property) is a short walk away, and there's a pool, beauty salon, dive shop and bar on site. Continental breakfast included in the rates. ⑧

Courtyard Marriott West Bay Rd ☎345/946-4433 or 1-800/228-9290, ✆www.marriott.com/gcmcy. Located across the street from Seven Mile Beach, this five-storey, 231-room hotel will save you plenty while not shirking on amenities. A restaurant, bar and large pool are on site, while chairs, towels, a café and watersports facilities are all available for guests beachside. ⑧

Eldemire's Guesthouse South Sound ☎345/949-5387, ✆www.eldemire.com. The first guesthouse (and one of the few) to open in Cayman, *Eldemire's* is clean, colourful and comfortable, with twelve rooms and apartments that all have a/c, ceiling fans, TV and private bath. Continental breakfast is included with the rooms (not the apartments), as is use of a well-equipped kitchen. One mile from George Town. ⑤

Hyatt Regency West Bay Rd ☎345/949-1234 or 1-800/633-7313, ✆www.hyattregencygrandcayman.com. This posh British colonial-style resort has 53 one- and two-bedroom suites with kitchenettes on the beach, and an additional 236 rooms are due to reopen in February of 2006 on lush landscaped grounds. Amenities include a Jack Nicklaus-designed golf course, top-notch sushi restaurant, full-service spa and fitness centre; tennis will be on offer in 2006. Rates start at US$285 for a room, US$575 for a suite. ⑨

Ritz-Carlton West Bay Rd ☎345-943-9000 or 1-800/241-3333, ✆www.ritzcarlton.com. Stretching

144 acres from Seven Mile Beach to North Sound, the newly opened Ritz-Carlton is the ultimate in luxury, with twice-daily maid service, large marble bathrooms, private balconies and goose down pillows in every room. Sensational restaurants and a tennis centre, private nine-hole golf-course and La Prairie Spa ensure guests feel fully pampered. Rates start at $450. ⑨

Sunset House South Church St ☎345/949-7111 or 1-800/854-4767, ⓦwww.sunsethouse.com. This popular full-service dive resort – the only Caymanian-owned hotel in Grand Cayman – includes an underwater photo centre (courses available), oceanside pool and plenty of offshore diving along the ironshore (no beach here, so dive gear stays sand-free). Hungry divers can refuel at the onsite restaurant, and George Town is a fifteen-minute walk away. ⑥

Westin Casuarina Seven Mile Beach ☎345/945-3800 or 1-800/WESTIN-1, ⓦwww.westin.com /casuarina. Marble baths and a gorgeous 700ft stretch of beachfront (lined by the largest freshwater pool on the island) are the main attractions at this upscale resort. The luxurious spa is a perfect place to soothe sun-kissed skin, and the highly rated Cuban-Caribbean restaurant has a fine selection of cuisine, wine and cigars; there's also a famous Sunday brunch at the more casual *Ferdinand's*. Rates start at US$349. ⑨

Wyndham Sunshine Suites West Bay Rd, Safehaven ☎345/949-3000, 1-877/786-1110, ⓦwww. sunshinesuites.com. Don't let the location behind a strip mall put you off from this pretty yellow all-suites hotel. Each suite is effectively one room, sectioned into sleeping and eating areas including a well-equipped kitchen. There's a pool and open-air bar and grill on site, and a dive centre, restau-

rants and shopping are all within walking distance. Rates include Continental breakfast. ⑦

Outer Districts

Cobalt Coast Sea Fan Drive, West Bay ☎345/946-5656 or 1-888/946-5656, ⓦwww.cobaltcoast. com. Just a few miles north of bustling Seven Mile Beach is this jewel of a place, an intimate dive resort with eighteen well-appointed and colourful rooms and apartments. There's no beach here, but you can easily slip into the water from the long pier that extends from the ironshore; there's also an oceanside pool. One of the island's best wall dive sites is a mere few hundred yards away: the unspoilt North Wall, a 6000ft drop. ⑧

Retreat at Rum Point North Side ☎345/947-9135, ⓦwww.retreatrumpoint.com. One-, two-, and three-bedroom beachfront condos with central a/c, well-equipped kitchens and screened-in porches. The sandy peninsula is lovely for swimming and short strolls, and the beach at Rum Point is just around the corner. Tennis and racquetball also on offer. Ideal location for those who want a nice beach away from the hustle of Seven Mile. Reopening Nov 2005. ⑨

Turtle Nest Inn Bodden Town ☎345/947-8665, ⓦwww.turtlenestinn.com. Built in the style of a Spanish villa with a red-tile roof, whitewashed walls and graceful arches, this inn on the beach has seven bright and cheery one-bedrooms with kitchens, along with one small village-view room (no kitchen). The pool faces the sea and there's superb snorkelling just offshore. Weekly dinners on the terrace add a touch of camaraderie to a longer stay. Book ahead, as the *Inn* is full almost year-round. Single room ⑥, one-bedroom ⑦

George Town

GEORGE TOWN is generally dense with tourists from visiting cruise ships, with as many as seven ships docking daily year-round. The numerous cigar and gem shops – which though duty- and tax- free are still no bargain – keep shoppers busy, but otherwise George Town is a fairly quiet little place with businesspeople running around in suits plying the financial trade. Driving the congested streets can be tricky, but you can park at the Picadilly Car Park on Elgin Avenue just south of Shedden Road; the town is best explored on foot.

The **Cayman Islands National Museum**, on the bay at Harbour Drive and Shedden Rd (Mon–Fri 9am–5pm, Sat 10am–2pm, closed first Mon of every month; US$5; ☎345/949-8368), is a good spot to start a walking tour and to get oriented on Cayman history. The 170-year-old building has served variously as a courthouse, a church and a jail and was refurbished as a museum in 1990, with the former jail converted into a gift shop. Of the historical displays inside the museum, most interesting is a three-dimensional model revealing the Cayman Islands as small peaks of massive underwater mountains.

From the museum, walk a few blocks north along the water on Harbour Drive to the small **Elmslie United Memorial Church**, built in 1920 by architect-shipbuilder Captain Rayal Bodden and bearing his signature design: a ceiling that mimics the upturned hull of a schooner. North to Fort Street, and then right heading east, you'll come upon **Heroes Square**, reconstructed in 2003 to commemorate the islands' quincentennial, with a palm-tree framed fountain, historical milestones depicted in murals on a Wall of History, and a Wall of Honour recognizing 500 Caymanians who have significantly contributed to Cayman's development. On the south side of the square is the **Law Courts** building and on the north side the **Legislative Assembly Building**, both modern constructions reminiscent of trapezoids, one upside-down and the other right-side-up. If the assembly is in session, you're welcome to observe from seats in the upper gallery.

Next door to the Assembly is another Bodden building, **Peace Memorial Town Hall**. Though once the hub of community activity, Ivan forced it to close and currently no reopening date is scheduled. Cross over to the east side of the square to Bodden's third civic project, the **public library**, which like the church has an upturned hull ceiling, although it's currently closed and not due to reopen until 2006; the temporary location is on the ground floor of the Commerce Building on Dr Roy's Drive.

Continue south along Edward Street to the columned **post office**, built in 1939. There is no home delivery of mail on the islands, hence the nearly three thousand post boxes at this location.

To get back to the bay, head back west along Cardinal Avenue, flanked by sparkling duty-free shops. On South Church Street, there's a small beach at **Eden Rock** where you can rent snorkel/scuba gear and swim out to one of the finest **snorkelling** reefs on the island. If you prefer not to get wet, Atlantis submarines will shuttle you down 100 feet in air-conditioned comfort. You can't miss the store, which has a yellow model submarine right on South Church Street. Tours last a little over an hour (daily 8.30am–3.30pm, depending on cruise ships; US$84 per person, US$24 for a second dive; ☎345/949-7700) and advance booking is recommended.

Seven Mile Beach and West Bay

Actually only five and a half miles long, **Seven Mile Beach** is a wide, powder-soft stretch of white sand that curls around the west side of the island. The waters are generally calm, warm and crystal-clear, owing to a lack of winds coming from the northwest. The slope heading out to sea is an easy and gradual one, ideal for swimming or just wading in. It's by far the most popular beach around; even so, it never gets towel-to-towel. If you do want to slip away from the crowds, walk north to where there are fewer hotels.

The community of **WEST BAY** begins at the northern edge of Seven Mile Beach and is the second most populated district on the island. Though most of the area is residential, the **Turtle Farm** on West Bay Rd (daily 8.30am–5pm; ☎345/949-3893) draws tourists on a regular basis to see its thousands of green sea turtles flopping about in large open-air tanks. At the time of writing, the farm was still rebuilding after 2001's Hurricane Michelle (Ivan did little damage) and the temporary setting is rather gloomy, although children especially enjoy the chance to watch hatchlings and hold baby turtles. Tours are self-guided and take less than a half-hour to complete. A small percentage of turtles here are raised to meet the local demand for turtle meat, but most are bred for research, and conservation-minded visitors can sponsor their release into the wild.

Also in West Bay is the town of **Hell**, named for a jagged patch of uninhabitable ironshore and, although scarcely worth the visit, popular for the opportunity to send postcards stamped by the local post office.

The rest of the island

Travelling on from the west end of the island, you'll encounter the districts of Bodden Town, East End and North Side which each offer the odd sight that reveals a fuller picture of life on Grand Cayman.

The first stop of note, eight miles on from George Town in the town of Savannah, is **Pedro St James Castle** (daily 9am–5pm; US$8; ☎345/947-3329), not so much a castle but rather a traditional plantation house. The island's oldest stone building (built in 1780), Pedro St James is known as the birthplace of democracy in the Cayman Islands: it was while meeting here in 1831 that Cayman residents decided to hold their first election. In the 1990s the site was painstakingly restored to traditional splendour, including the sprawling grounds, which are full of tropical fruits and native flora. The **visitor centre** was built with a state-of-the-art multimedia theatre, where the story of the castle unfolds in a twenty-minute video. Hurricane Ivan forced the closure of the entire complex, though at the time of writing it was expected to reopen by the fall of 2005.

East of the castle is **Bodden Town**, Grand Cayman's original capital (which moved to George Town in the late nineteenth century for its more protected harbour). The town's landscape has changed dramatically since Ivan, which hit here particularly hard; there's a newly widened beach lining the coast, but rebuilding the largely residential area may take some years. The main attraction here is the kitschy **Pirates Cave** (daily 9am–5pm; adults US$8, kids US$5; ☎345/947-3122) in which the property's owners have placed fake treasure and pirate-bedecked mannequins – although plans are in the works to properly explore the cave system, largely plugged since the hurricane of 1932. Adding to the effect is, across the road, the oldest **cemetery** on the island, where pirates are rumoured to be buried.

Next along the south shore road is the tiny community of **Breakers**, where a white lighthouse has been transformed into a restaurant, making a lovely stop for a hearty meal (Caribbean and Italian fare) on the seaside. Just after the lighthouse, the road becomes Frank Sound Road, off which you can watch plenty of spray from crashing waves and blowholes worn into the ironshore. As the road turns towards **East End** it becomes **Queen's Highway**; looking out to sea here at the island's easternmost point you can see remnants of the **Wreck of the Ten Sails**, where ten ships successively crashed into the reef one fateful day in 1794.

The highway loops around East End until heading back west along the northern coast of the island through **North Side**. It dead-ends at **Rum Point**, a favourite stretch of white-sand beach second only to Seven Mile, where you are welcome to use the facilities and snorkel about in the shallow waters. Along with chairs and hammocks, there's a reasonably priced beach bar here good for burgers and salads, and Red Sail Sports has watersports equipment for rent. A ferry usually runs between Rum Point and the *Hyatt* Marina in the channel off the *Hyatt* hotel property on West Bay Road, though service has been suspended since Ivan and no reopen date has been set.

The return trip to George Town from Rum Point requires backtracking through North Side again, but a bypass at Old Man Bay halfway towards East End shortcuts the journey. Along the way is a turn-off for the 65-acre **Queen Elizabeth II Botanic Park** (daily April–Sept 9am–6.30pm, Oct–March 9am–5.30pm; last admission 4.30pm; US$7.50; ☎345/947-9462). Much of the park is a woodland nature preserve where more than half of Cayman's native plants grow naturally, including orchids, palms, mahogany and cacti. Near the entrance to a mile-long walking trail through the preserve, you'll pass an enclosure where you can catch a glimpse of the endangered native **blue iguana**, raised at a breeding facility in the grounds. Also in the park is 3-acre lake, a good place to spot rare aquatic birds like the West Indian whistling duck, and nearby is a 2.5 acre **colour garden**, a clever series of similarly hued plant and flower collections designed to bloom year-long. There's also a traditional Cayman sand garden of medicinal plants and fruit trees on display.

Eating and drinking

Of the three Cayman Islands, Grand Cayman has by far the most dining choices with respect to cuisine. There are **gourmet options** galore and **international**

tastes like Thai, Chinese and Italian are easily found. Most restaurants are on West Bay Road along the Seven Mile Beach corridor. **Local food**, such as rice and peas, jerked meats and fried plantain, is most common on menus in the outer districts.

There are many well-stocked and conveniently located **supermarkets**, including Foster Food Fair, which carries gourmet and vegetarian products. The self-serve lunch buffet at the **Fort Street Market**, a grocery store in downtown George Town on the corner of Fort and Panton streets (weekdays 7am–3pm), has a fine selection of island dishes prepared in-house; you can have a meal here for under US\$10.

Bed West Bay Rd. The servers here may wear pajamas and the booths might resemble four-poster beds, but the cuisine is anything but casual (note that Miami and New York have followed suit with their own take on this boudoir theme, going a step further and replacing tables and chairs with actual beds). Entrees here vary from curries to lasagne to an array of vegetarian options, but locally caught yellow-fin tuna is the signature dish and an island favourite. A small adjacent lounge has tapas and live music. Dinner daily.

Café Mediterraneo Galleria Plaza on West Bay Rd ☎345/949-8669. Portions are large and the wine selection ample at this Italian restaurant, known around town as *Café Med*. The best seats are inside in the plush semi-private booths; the roadside setting means dinner by candlelight on the patio isn't especially romantic. Thursdays are *salsa* nights, and the dance floor is packed for a free course at 9pm, with would-be dancers practising until closing time at 1am.

Champion House Two 43 Eastern Ave, George Town ☎345/949-7882. Of the two restaurants at this address, be sure to go to *Champion House Two* at the back (*Champion House One* is a little seedy). *Two* serves fabulous island fare in a comfortable, air-conditioned setting. The inexpensive menu features items like turtle stew, curried goat, and codfish and ackee (a fruit resembling scrambled egg when prepared).

Coconut Joe's West Bay Rd ☎345/943-5637. An eclectic menu with everything from Tortuga Rum BBQ ribs to sizzling fajitas and Japanese rice bowls. Breakfast is tasty, too, and Starbucks coffee addicts can get their fix here. Come evening, *Coconut Joe's* is hopping, with an outdoor projection-screen TV showing sports nightly, a festive deck and drink specials like the massive Beergarita (a Corona tipped into a 48oz margarita). Weekdays breakfast and lunch only, weekends breakfast, lunch and dinner.

Grand Old House South Church St ☎345/949-9333. Outdoor oceanside gazebos provide an elegant backdrop for romantic dinners. The gourmet cuisine is international with a local flair; the

speciality is seafood, with dishes like medallions of lobster tail sautéed with shallots, mushrooms and tomatoes in a Chardonnay cream sauce. Meals are complemented by a fantastic wine selection, with dinners accompanied by a pianist playing into the sunset. Reservations are essential. Mon–Fri 11.45am–2pm, daily 6–10pm.

Heritage Kitchen Boggy Sands Rd, West Bay. Well worth the twenty-minute drive from downtown George Town for great local food and a relaxed outdoor setting. Indulge in fish tea (basically a fish stew touted as an aphrodisiac) or one of the freshly fried fish options (CI\$10). If you're brave, try one of the home-made hot sauces, made from some of the world's hottest peppers – the habanero and the scotch bonnet. Open Wed, Fri & Sat 5pm–late.

Kaibo Restaurant and Bar 585 Water Cay Rd, Cayman Kai ☎345/947-9975. Known as the *Kaibo Yacht Club*, there's a full-service marina here but don't be put off – no membership is needed at this relaxing beach bar and grill serving burgers, salads and sandwiches at reasonable prices. Don't miss the signature battered fries, the best on the island. An uncrowded stretch of sand is perfect for lounging the day away (free use of beach chairs).

The Reef Grill at Royal Palms Seven Mile Beach ☎345/945-6358. At weekends especially, the beach bar here is a popular spot; free lounge chairs are snapped up and there's often a pick-up game of beach volleyball. For a more formal affair, head to the adjacent restaurant, where the best tables are outside in a garden setting. Seafood reigns supreme – their calling-card dish is coconut-crusted grouper with pineapple salsa and boniato. Reservations recommended.

The Wharf Restaurant and Bar West Bay Rd ☎345/949-2231. Reservations are a must to sit waterside, where you can watch tarpons and the occasional stingray or turtle swimming just below you. Grilled Caribbean spiny lobster in a lemon butter sauce along with basil and pistachio-crusted Chilean sea bass are the favourites here. A harpist serenades tables three nights a week. Mon–Fri 11.30am–2.30pm, daily 6–10pm.

△ Scuba diving on Bloody Bay Wall, Little Cayman

Nightlife

It may seem like things are quiet in the evenings on Grand Cayman, but that's mainly because venues are spread out, so there's no main strip for nightlife. There are a number of fun **outdoor bars** and **dance clubs**, most of them in the Seven Mile Beach area, if you know where to look. Fridays are the biggest nights out – on Saturdays, everywhere closes by midnight by law. On Sundays before bank holidays, many bars will apply for extended Monday hours and open Sunday night (effectively Monday) from one minute past midnight until 3am.

Calico Jack's Public Beach, West Bay Rd ⊕ 345/945-7850. The perfect island beach bar, just steps away from the water on a gorgeous stretch of sand with hardly a condo in sight. Live music Friday and Saturday nights with dancing on a wooden deck or, even better, on the sand. Come for the sunsets and happy hour from 5–7pm. No cover. Mon–Sat 9am–midnight, Sun 11am–6pm if the cruise ships are in.

The Next Level West Bay Rd ⊕ 345/946-6398. The Next Level draws locals, ex-pats and tourists alike with nightly DJs playing reggae, calypso, hip-hop and house. A Friday and Saturday night dress code means no hats or beach attire. Cover charge from CI$5–20 most nights, sometimes all-you-can-drink. Mon–Fri 10pm–3am, Sat 9pm–midnight.

OBar Queen's Court, West Bay Rd ⊕ 345/943-6227. A hot spot for a predominately twenty-something ex-pat and tourist crowd, with a plush red interior and a generally packed dance floor – DJs spin music from hip-hop to Top 40 remixes and house. No cover. Mon–Fri 10pm–3am.

The Office 99 Shedden Rd, George Town ⊕ 345/945-5212. At this office, ties are left at the bar and games are on TV. Working folk come here to unwind and enjoy some of the cheapest drinks on the island. The restaurant next door caters free appetizers on Friday evenings, usually gone by about 6.30pm. Karaoke Wed and Saturday nights. Mon–Fri 10am–1am, Sat 10am–midnight, Sun noon–midnight.

4.2

Cayman Brac

About ninety miles northeast of Grand Cayman, and accessible by a half-hour plane hop, lies tiny **CAYMAN BRAC**, only fourteen square miles and home to around 1800 people. With none of the fast-food outlets or tourist bustle of the larger island, the Brac (as it's colloquially known) offers the chance for an isolated Caribbean vacation; this is where residents of Grand Cayman come to get away from it all.

There's no main town here, nor any major developments, but all modern amenities are available, including decently-stocked grocery stores, post offices, a bank and a handful of restaurants. Those looking to keep busy come for the supreme **diving**, although growing numbers are also being drawn by land activities like **caving** and **hiking**, enough to keep you occupied for a day or two, and popular here because of the Brac's unique landscape among the three islands. The island is named after the striking limestone bluff ("brac" means "bluff" in Gaelic) which runs along its spine, culminating with great ocean views at its peak of 140 feet on the eastern coast – a perfect place to catch the sunrise. Much of the bluff surface is covered by woodland and is a **birdwatching** haven.

Around the island

The best way to explore the Brac is to get on one of its numerous **trails**, accessible off the main road and marked by large white and blue Heritage Site signs that designate the name of the trail (see box overleaf). Don't miss the one along Bight Road, which cuts across the bluff from east to west within the **Brac Parrot Reserve**, threading its way through a tropical woodland brimming with native trees, including candlewood and wild fig, plus varieties of cacti and orchids. There are a few entrance points, one of which leads along a 600ft stretch of wooden boardwalk, a perfect place to watch for the rare, emerald-green Cayman Brac **parrot** which has its nesting colonies here.

Cayman Brac is not known for miles-long strips of sand: the coastline is chiefly ironshore, and the few small beaches, most located on hotel property, have a fair amount of seagrass in their waters. The **public beach** is the best stretch around these parts, and has picnic tables and showers on offer – it's on the same south side as most hotels and just a ten-minute bicycle ride away.

The ironshore does, however, make for great snorkelling and shore-diving. Along with natural formations like Handcuff Reef on the north shore and Radar Reed in Stake Bay, perhaps the most popular site is the wreck of the *Captain Keith Tibbetts*, a Russian destroyer sunk on purpose in 1996 just yards off the northwest coast. The Department of Tourism (☎345/948-1649) can suggest additional places to go and give specific directions. The Brac's **diving** in general is superb, with few sites much more than a ten-minute boat ride away. The marine life is abundant, among which you'll find eels, lobster, turtles and the occasional octopus, along with walls encrusted with purple sea fans and massive barrel sponges. Note that Bloody Bay Wall off Little Cayman can also be visited from Cayman Brac.

The **Cayman Brac Museum** in Stake Bay (Mon–Fri 9am–noon & 1–4pm; donation suggested; ☎345/948-2222) was the first museum to open in the Cayman

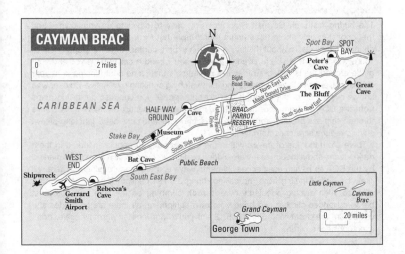

Islands, in December 1983. Upstairs is an exhibit on the 1932 hurricane that killed more than 100 people on Cayman Brac, with pictures of the event and write-ups by Caymanians who experienced the storm. Also of note here is a display on the Caymanian catboat, developed in 1904 on Cayman Brac and used for turtling through the mid-twentieth century.

Practicalities

Flights arrive at **Gerrard Smith International Airport** (☏345/948-1222) on the western tip of the island. You'll probably want to have a **car** or **scooter** to get around, both for exploring the island and for accessing various shore dive and snorkelling spots; the handful of agencies can arrange for complimentary drop-off and pick-up at your hotel or the airport. Rentals start at US$35 a day for a mid-size car or US$30 for a scooter. At US$10, **bicycle** rentals are a cheaper but less equipment-friendly alternative.

Because there aren't many restaurants on the Brac, the two **resorts** here offer a meal plan; other accommodation options have use of a kitchen (other than private villas, all are listed here). At both resorts, **dive packages** are the norm (and diving is "valet-style": drop off your gear when you arrive, and it will be cleaned and carried for you throughout your stay), but be sure to ask exactly what's included.

Brac Caribbean & Carib Sands South Side ☏345/948-1121, or 1-866/843-2722, ⊛www.866thebrac.com. Two condo complexes on the beach, offering spacious one- to four-bedroom units, a small shared fitness room, a pool on each property and one of the island's few restaurants, *Captain's Table*. Diving is arranged with nearby Reef Divers at *Brac Reef Beach Resort*. ⑦
Brac Reef Beach Resort South Side ☏345/948-1323, ⊛www.bracreef.com. Despite the just standard rooms, divers love this property for its reasonable rates and knowledgeable dive staff. The poolside bar is popular with locals, and the illumi-

nated dock off the beach attracts sea creatures at night, like tarpon, stingrays and the occasional octopus. A tennis court and the island's only spa (with room for one) are also onsite. The three-night-minimum dive package includes five dives, all meals, government tax and service charge at US$411 per night.
Divi Tiara Beach Resort South Side ☏345/948-1553 or 1-800/367-3484, ⊛www.divitiara.com. Cheery pastel exteriors at this beachside resort help counteract rather drab interiors. The PADI Gold Palm dive outfit (the main draw) has a shop, photo centre and instruction room; there's also a pool,

Hiking the Brac

The **hiking trails** on Cayman Brac are fairly easy to navigate on your own – and the longest is only about three hours round-trip – but for a unique experience and a chance to really learn about the island from an expert, contact the Brac Department of Tourism (☏345/948-1849) to arrange a guide. You'll **need a car** to drive you and your guide around the island, but otherwise remarkably there's no cost (tipping is at your discretion), and you'll get taken caving, birdwatching or hiking by a native-Bracker who knows every inch of the island. If that doesn't appeal, you can also get hiking maps from the DOT, or from your hotel. Sturdy shoes are essential as many trails weave through sections of sharp ironshore; carry some water and consider a light long-sleeve shirt to reduce scratches from twigs.

There are hundreds of **caves** within the bluff (about 200 people sheltered in them during Ivan), and although many are hidden or difficult to reach, five have been marked by the DOT as having easy accessible entryways and are worth exploring. There will likely be bats dangling from the ceiling; bring a small penlight if you want a better glimpse. Also gaining popularity here is **rock climbing** on the bluff, but you must be an advanced climber and bring your own equipment, as there are no guides and climbs are rated between 5.8 and 5.12 – if you're not familiar with this scale, don't even consider a climb.

tennis court and beach bar to keep you occupied. The three-night-minimum dive package includes daily two-tank dives, all meals and government tax at US$319 per night.

La Esperanza Stake Bay ☎345/948-0591, ⓦwww.laesperanza.net. Located on the island's north side, this property has a handful of small and rustic but clean two- and three- bedroom apartments. There's a grocery, restaurant and bar across the road, but you'll need a car to reach the beach and dive shops. ❸

Walton's Mango Manor Stake Bay ☎345/948-0518, ⓦwww.waltonsmangomanor.com. A well-run B&B on three acres of landscaped gardens stretching from the bluff to the ocean, where there's a private swimming beach. Nestled among the fruit trees is an intimate synagogue (one of only a handful in the Caribbean), open to all as a place to reflect. All five rooms come with private bath; also available is a pretty two-storey beach villa perched right along the sea. Rooms ❹, Villa ❻

4.3

Little Cayman

On string-bean-shaped **LITTLE CAYMAN**, road signs read "iguanas have the right of way" – fitting for an undeveloped island on which the two thousand or so of these primordial-looking creatures greatly outnumber the people. Although just a few square miles smaller than the Brac, this least developed of the Cayman Islands has merely around 100 full-time residents, of whom just one was actually born and raised here, and only a handful are Caymanian. Even more so than Cayman Brac, Little Cayman attracts visitors looking for untrammelled seclusion (Brackers come here on vacation); there's only one small very-general store and one restaurant, and homes are few and far between.

Those who come tend either to love it or hate it. This is not a lush tropical paradise: the landscape is flat and the vegetation mostly low-lying shrubs, mangroves and sea-grape trees. In the winter, the pond beds of the **marshy interior** dry up and, depending on the prevailing winds, as the water level changes a sulphurous odour sometimes wafts over parts of the island. Most visitors are scuba or wildlife enthusiasts eager to take advantage of a top dive site and an inland nature sanctuary, and since prices are highest here of the three islands, others may prefer Cayman Brac for a secluded escape. It's less than a ten-minute hop between the two, so if you're intrigued you can easily spend just a day here; **flights** cost about US$50 return. From Grand Cayman, it's a pricier journey at around US$100, but still just forty minutes away. If you'd like a guide, MAM's Island Tours (☎345/948-0026, ⓦwww.mamstour.ky) will pick you up at the airport and take you on a day's tour of the island for around US$50 per person. If you see a handful of people anywhere you go, consider it crowded.

Around the island

The mangrove-filled wetlands in the centre of the island are home to as many as 200 species of birds, including West Indian whistling-ducks, egrets, frigates and herons. Just a few steps east of the airport is a 1.2 mile-long nature reserve known as **Booby Pond**, home to a nesting colony of 20,000 red-footed boobies, the largest in the Western Hemisphere and a Ramsar site (designating it a wetland of international importance). The **National Trust Visitors Centre** (☎345/948-1010) at its western tip has a balcony offering panoramic views of the marshy reserve, along with telescopes for close-ups of the birds, which are fairly easy to spot. Volunteers are on-hand Monday to Friday from 3 to 5pm to answer questions, but you're welcome to enjoy the view in your own time.

To get up close and personal with animals that won't readily fly off, head to Candle Road on the southwestern end of the island, a favoured hangout for **West Indian iguanas**, which can grow to be as long as four feet. They tend to roam about in the afternoons and are used to being fed (preferably fruit), but take care as they are wild and can be aggressive; attempts at handfeeding are very unwise.

Most resorts in Little Cayman are along the southern shore, which is also where the best **beaches** are found (although they're somewhat narrower and rockier since Hurricane Ivan; the southside took the brunt of the storm). In most spots, even by the resorts, the water isn't especially inviting – it's shallow and the bottom is covered with turtle grass. For the best swimming and snorkelling, visit **Point O' Sands** on the southeastern tip; just stay to the west of the point, as the current is strong at the reef mouth on the eastern side. Or, kayak out to what's likely to be your own private island: **Owen Island** off South Hole Sound, a great picnic spot.

Diving and fishing

For divers, Little Cayman is a true gem. Aside from having obvious assets like phenomenal water clarity and abundant marine life, it doesn't get the numbers other destinations do (in part because of stringent marine park restrictions), making dives here all the more special. The famed **Bloody Bay Wall**, a mere ten- to fifteen-minute boat ride from most hotel docks, is hailed as one of the **world's best dive sites**. Like North Wall on Grand Cayman, Bloody Bay features a sheer drop-off plunging 6000ft down into the depths; here, though, conditions are at their most pristine, especially post-Ivan. These reefs are lush with coral and sponge life, and friendly groupers as well as seahorses, sharks, eagle rays and elegant arrow crabs are common sights.

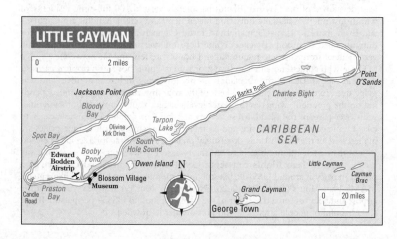

Anglers can partake in deep-sea **fishing**, bonefishing on the flats and tarpon fishing at the fifteen-acre **Tarpon Lake** on the south shore. Hotels can arrange for gear and guides through the *Southern Cross Club* (℡345/948-1099) and *McCoy's Diving and Fishing Lodge* (℡345/948-0026).

Practicalities

On the southwest end of the island, **Edward Bodden Airstrip** (only partially paved) handles incoming flights. Once here, although there's no public transport, there's little need for a **vehicle**, though you might like one for a day. A short walk from the airport, McLaughlin Rentals (℡345/948-1000) rents Ford Explorers and the like starting at US$75 per day. You can easily drive around the island in an hour. **Bicycles**, available at most properties, are the best way to get around.

Every **hotel** on Little Cayman has a **meal plan**, but cottages with kitchens are available as well (other than private villas, all options are listed here). Non-diver options are always available, but since dive packages are the norm, rates listed here – all based on double occupancy – include dives as specified; multi-night packages are usually cheaper. Unlike most all-inclusives, many places here have fewer than twenty rooms, and can feel quite cosy.

Little Cayman Beach Resort Blossom Village ℡345/948-1033 or 1-800/327-3835, ⓦwww. littlecayman.com. The island's largest hotel, with forty rooms, spa, dive and photo shop, tennis court and fitness room. Nearby sister properties *Conch Club Condos* and *The Club* have rather luxurious one-, two- and three-bedroom condos available, most right on the beach. The three-night-minimum dive package includes five dives, all meals, government tax and service charge at US$475 per night; condos start at US$235.

Paradise Villas Blossom Village ℡345/948-0001 or 1-877/322-9626, ⓦwww.paradisevillas.com. Perhaps the best buy on the island for non-divers: twelve simple ocean-front one-bedroom villas, each with patio, kitchenette, a/c and cable TV. There's a pool on site, along with the island's only restaurant should you prefer not to cook. Dive packages available with the property's Paradise Divers operation. ❼

Pirates Point Resort Preston Bay ℡345/948-1010, ⓦwww.piratespointresort.com. The island's finest chef keeps the repeat guest rate high at this well-run and informal resort, with homey (and a bit kitschy) touches like guests' inventive artwork, made from materials found on the beach during their stay. Ten bungalow rooms are clustered around the property; those seaside are the most appealing. Rates, including two-tank computer dives daily, all meals and alcoholic beverages, start at US$520.

Southern Cross Club Blossom Village ℡345/948-1099 or 1-800/899-2582, ⓦwww.southerncrossclub .com. A small but full-service diving and fishing resort comprising a handful of pretty pastel cinder-block cottages dotted along a beautiful 800ft stretch of beach; there's also a small pool, alfresco bar and intimate dining room. Five-night minimum stay at US$732 per night includes three-tank dives daily, service charge, government tax and all meals.

Jamaica

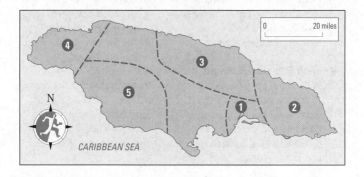

N

CARIBBEAN SEA

Jamaica highlights

✳ **Jamaican nightlife** Whether it's reggae icons singing out under the stars or dancehall queens winding and grinding to ragga, Jamaican nightlife is unmissable. See p.271

✳ **Climbing Blue Mountain Peak** The superb panoramic views from the top stretch from Jamaica's south coast to the north. See p.290

✳ **West End sunset, Negril** With a string of excellent bars to choose from, Jamaica's extreme western tip is the best place to watch the sun go down with a cocktail in hand. See p.324

✳ **Hellshire beach on Sundays** Best visited on Sundays, when the beach comes alive with booming sound systems, dancing and sizzling grills. See p.285

✳ **Frenchman's Cove and Blue Lagoon, Portland** Take in the cove's soft white sand, warm waters and fabulous reef or dip into the nearby lagoon. See p.296

✳ **Treasure Beach** Supremely laid-back yet stylish south coast bay, from where you can take a boat ride to the sublime *Floyd's Pelican Bar*. See p.327

△ West Indies team on Sabina Park

Introduction and basics

Rightly famous for its beaches and music, beautiful, brash Jamaica is much more besides. There's certainly plenty of white sand, turquoise sea and swaying palm trees, but there are also spectacular mountains and rivers, tumbling waterfalls and cactus-strewn savannah plains. Far more than just a resort, the island also boasts vibrant towns and cities such as sprawling Kingston, which inspired the music of Bob Marley and countless other home-grown reggae superstars.

Jamaica is a country with a swagger in its step – proud of its history, sporting success and musical genius – but also with a weight upon its shoulders. The island faces the familiar problems of a developing country, including dramatic inequality of wealth and social tensions that occasionally spill over into localized violence and worldwide headlines. As a result Jamaicans are as renowned for being as sharp, sassy and straight-talking as they are laid-back and hip. People don't beat around the bush here, and this can sometimes make them appear rude or uncompromising. Particularly around the big resorts, this directness sometimes is taken to extremes at times, with approaches from vendors and hustlers extremely frequent.

But there's absolutely no reason to be put off. As a foreign visitor, the chances of encountering any trouble are minuscule, and the Jamaican authorities have spent millions making sure the island treats its tourists right. As the birthplace of the "all-inclusive" hotel, Jamaica is well suited to those travellers who want to head straight from plane to beach, never leaving their hotel compound. But to get any sense of the country at all, you'll need to do some exploring. It's undoubtedly worth it, as this is an island packed with first-class attractions, oozing with character and rich with a musical and cultural heritage; if you're a reggae fan, you're in heaven.

Where to go

Most of Jamaica's tourist business is concentrated in the resorts of **Montego Bay**, **Ocho Rios** and **Negril**, which together attract hundreds of thousands of visitors every year. Montego Bay is a busy, commercial city with hotels lined up along its lively main strip, a stone's throw from a couple of Jamaica's most famous beaches. There's a great entertainment scene, especially during the annual August **Reggae Sumfest** festival. To the west is Negril, its low-rise hotels slung along seven miles of fantastic white sand and two miles of dramatic cliffs. It's younger, more laid-back and with a longstanding reputation for hedonism that still carries a hint of the truth. East of MoBay, and the least individualistic of the big three, Ocho Rios embodies high-impact tourism – purpose-built in the 1960s to provide the ultimate package of sun, sand and sea. It's not an overly attractive place, and the beaches don't compare favourably with Negril and MoBay, but its tourist infrastructure is undeniably strong – the place is packed with shops, restaurants, bars and watersports – and you're right by some of Jamaica's leading attractions, including the famous **Dunn's River waterfall**.

Jamaica's quieter east and south coasts offer a far less packaged – perhaps more rewarding – experience, and there are plenty of real gems worth hunting out. In the island's east, lush, sleepy **Port Antonio** and its increasingly popular neighbour, **Long Bay**, provide gateways to some of Jamaica's greatest natural attractions, like the cascading waterfall at Reach. The south coast offers different pleasures, from gentle beach action at easy-going **Treasure Beach** – the perfect base from which to explore area delights such as the YS waterfalls – to boat safaris in search of local wildlife on the Black River.

Last, but in no way least, **Kingston** is the true heart of Jamaica, a thrilling place, pulsating with energy and spirit, that is home to more

than a third of the island's 2.5 million people. This is not just the nation's political capital but the focus of its art, theatre and music scenes, with top-class hotels, restaurants and shopping, a clubbing scene that is second to none and legendary fried fish on offer at the fabulous **Hellshire beach**. A stunning backdrop to the city, the cool, coffee-smothered **Blue Mountains** offer plenty of hiking possibilities, while the nearby fishing village of **Port Royal**, once a pirate refuge, provides historic diversion.

When to go

Jamaica's tropical climate is at its most appealing during the peak **mid-December to mid-April** tourist season, when rainfall is lowest and the heat is tempered by cooling trade winds; it can also get quite cool at night at this time, so it's worth packing a sweater or

light jacket, particularly if you plan to attend all-night concerts. Things get noticeably hotter during the **summer**, and particularly in September and October the humidity can become oppressive. September is also the most threatening month of the annual **hurricane season**, which runs officially from June 1 to October 31; however, on average, the big blows only hit about once a decade.

Prices, and **crowds** at the attractions and beaches, peak during high season. Outside this period it's quieter everywhere, and though the main resorts throb with life pretty much year-round, quieter areas like Port Antonio and Treasure Beach can feel a little lifeless. The good news is that in the off-season hotel prices fall by up to 25 percent, there are more bargains to be had in every field of activity and a number of festivals – including the massive annual Reggae Sumfest in Montego Bay – inject some zip.

Arrival

Most airlines fly into Donald Sangster Airport in **Montego Bay**, but many also land at Norman Manley in **Kingston** as well – more convenient if you're heading for Port Antonio, Ocho Rios or the Blue Mountains. For information on transportation to and from each airport, see p.310 and p.273, respectively.

Information, websites and maps

Before you leave home, it's worth contacting the **Jamaica Tourist Board** (JTB), which will send out lots of glossy brochures on the island. Also take a look at their website (see box overleaf), which has information on the main tourist attractions, schedules of events and accommodation listings. Once in Jamaica, you can get the same information from JTB desks at the Kingston and Montego Bay airports, as well as JTB offices in those cities. Jamaica has no entertainment listings magazine, so to find out what's going on, you have to rely on the radio (particularly Irie FM on 105.5 and 107.7 FM), newspapers, flyers and banners posted up around the towns. The best road **map** is *Discover Jamaica*, distributed free by JTB offices abroad and on the island.

Money and costs

Jamaica's unit of currency is the **Jamaican dollar** (J$), divided into 100 cents. It comes in bills of J$1000, J$500, J$100, J$50 and J$20, and coins of J$20, J$10 and J$5. It's

Websites

⊛ **www.jahworks.org** Great reggae site concentrating on the more conscious aspects of Jamaican music.

⊛ **www.jamaicagleaner.com** Searchable website of the island's most widely read daily paper, with all the news and lots of features.

⊛ **www.jamaicans.com** All things Yard, from language, culture and music to cookery and tourist info, plus busy message boards.

⊛ **www.jamaicatravel.com** The Jamaica Tourist Board site, with lots of pretty pictures, resort rundowns and good links.

⊛ **www.top5jamaica.com** Links to the most popular Jamaican websites, divided by category.

worth keeping a sharp eye on J$100 and J$1000 bills, which look alarmingly similar. At the time of writing the **rate of exchange** is roughly J$68 to US$1 and J$110 to £1. This is prone to fluctuation, and as a result, the US dollar has emerged as an unofficial parallel currency, with prices for tourist-oriented goods and services usually quoted in US$.

Accommodation is likely to be your major expense, although extremely basic rooms can be found for as little as US$30. Expect to pay US$70–100 for a room with air-conditioning and cable TV. Accommodation aside, if you travel around by bus or shared taxi and get your food from markets and the cheaper cafés and roadside stalls, you can just about survive on a daily budget of around US$40 per day. Upgrading to one decent meal out, the occasional taxi and a bit of evening entertainment, expect to spend a more realistic US$50–70; after that, the sky's the limit.

Banking hours are generally Monday to Thursday 9am to 2pm and Friday 9am to 3 or 4pm. Cambios, which are widespread throughout the country, are often more convenient, opening later and offering better exchange rates. FX Trader, with branches islandwide, is one to look out for; call ☎1-888/398-7233 to find the nearest outlet. Exchange bureaux at the main airports offer

rates slightly lower than the banks, and at hotels the rate is invariably significantly lower.

Lastly, don't hesitate to **negotiate** on prices, particularly in taxis and at markets and roadside stalls. Even hotels and guesthouses are generally fair game for a bit of bargaining when things are slow.

Getting around

Buses and minibuses are inexpensive if not comfortable. Renting a car offers maximum independence but will eat heavily into your budget; if you just want to make the odd excursion or short trip, it can be cheaper to take a taxi, or even hire a private driver. For longer trips, internal flights are reasonably priced.

By bus

Jamaica's **buses** (privately owned minibuses and, in Kingston and Montego Bay, government-owned full-sized single-decker buses) can be a little disquieting: timetables are nonexistent outside Kingston, drivers can show little interest in the rules of the road and passengers are often squeezed in with scant regard for comfort.

On the other hand, public transport is a great way to meet people, and it's also absurdly **cheap** – about J$100 per 50 miles for a bus and J$150–200 per 50 miles for minibuses. Each town has a bus terminal of sorts, often near the market. The destination is usually written on the front of the vehicle, along with its name ("Nuff Vibes", "Tings Coulda Worse" and the like). The conductor shouts out the destination before departure, scouting the area for potential passengers and cramming in as many as possible. Buses and minibuses stop anywhere en route to pick up or drop off passengers (except in major towns, where they are restricted to bus stops and terminals). If you want to get off somewhere before the terminus, just tell the conductor; to get on a bus, stand by the side of the road and flag it down.

By car

If you can afford it, **renting a car** is the best way of seeing Jamaica. However, rental prices are high, starting at around US$70 per day in high season, including government tax (rates can go as low as US$40 a day at slow times). Third-party insurance is normally included in the price; if you don't have a credit card that offers free collision damage waiver, you'll have to pay another US$12–15 per day to cover potential damage to the car.

There are **rental companies** all over the island, with the best selection in Kingston, Montego Bay and Ocho Rios, and we've listed them throughout the chapter. Though local companies often offer the best rates, going with a known name will normally ensure guaranteed roadside assistance and a better vehicle; larger companies will also allow you to pick up and drop off in different major towns for no extra fee. Major international rental companies with offices in Jamaica are Budget (☎868/952-3838), Hertz (☎868/979-0438) and Thrifty (☎868/952-5825). The best local operator, with excellent support services across Jamaica and rates that often beat the international companies, is Island (☎868/926-8861).

Driving in Jamaica is on the left and (unless otherwise specified, as on the new highway along the south coast from Kingston) speed limits are set at 30mph/50kph in towns and minor roads and 50mph/80kph on highways. Roadside speeding checks by way of radar gun are increasingly frequent, and speeding tickets start at J$5000; the safest bet is to always stick to 30mph/50kph unless you seen a sign indicating otherwise. Wearing front seatbelts is mandatory, and police frequently levy fines on those who don't wear them.

If you don't drive – or don't want to – it might be worth **hiring a local driver**, which will cost around US$100 a day.

By taxi

Taxis in Jamaica are either the gleaming white vans and imported cars of the Jamaican Union of Travellers Association (JUTA; ☎868/927-4534, 926-1537 or 952-0623), the official – and expensive – tourist carriers, to beaten-up old Ladas. Licensed taxis carry red number-plates with "PP" or "PPV" on them, but there are also a number of rogue taxis. The authorities advise against using these.

On the whole, **fares** are hefty – around US$20 for ten miles, and you'll always pay a little more if you take a taxi licensed to a hotel. Meters are nonexistent, so always establish a price before you get in (or over the phone if you're calling for one). The first quoted price may well be just an opener, particularly if you hail a vehicle on the street; don't be afraid to negotiate. Once a price is agreed, a tip is unnecessary.

Shared taxis or "route taxis" are usually crammed with as many passengers as the driver/owner can fit in, and operate on short, busy set routes around the main towns, picking up and dropping off people anywhere along the way in the same manner as the buses and minibuses. Prices are much closer to bus fares than to taxi rates.

By motorbike

Renting a **motorbike** or **scooter** can be an exhilarating way of touring the island. Outlets abound in the main resorts, and at US$35–50 per day, prices are very reasonable. Though in theory you'll need to show a driving licence, these are rarely asked for. Under Jamaican law, all motorcycle riders must wear helmets.

By plane

If you're heading across country, it's well worth considering one of the **internal flights** provided by Air Jamaica Express (☎868/923-6664, ✪www.airjamaica.com). They're quick and efficient, though not exactly a budget option; the one-way fare from Montego Bay to Kingston, for example, is US$75. Flights shuttle among the domestic airports at Tinson Pen in Kingston (☎868/924-8850), Montego Bay (☎868/952-4300), Port Antonio (☎868/913-3692), Negril (☎868/957-4251 or 4972) and Ocho Rios (☎868/726-1344).

Accommodation

Although Jamaica has many more **accommodation** options than most other islands, it's rare to find anywhere to stay for less than US$20 per night in the large resort areas, and you usually need to pay more than twice that for a place with reasonable security and comfort. Jamaica also has some of the world's finest luxury hotels, and there are plenty of options in the middle.

It is always worth **haggling** over the price of a room. Even in high season, a lot of hotels have surplus capacity, and in low season you have even more bargaining power. Prices in the resort areas tend to be more seasonal than elsewhere; in this chapter rates are for the low season (mid-April to mid-Dec) or most of the year.

Jamaica has no youth hostels and the cheapest places to stay are usually small, family-run **guesthouses** with pretty basic facilities. The low-cost rooms (US$20–35) that we recommend are normally clean and have some measure of security, though you can expect them to be cramped and box-like, with spartan furniture, shared bathrooms and a fan. Moving up in price, and into hotel territory, US$40–60 will normally secure a more tolerable place with a comfortable bed, hot water and, usually, a bar and maybe a place to eat. Once you're paying US$75, you can expect your hotel to have a swimming pool, a restaurant and air-conditioning; over US$100 you'll get a considerable degree of luxury.

Jamaica was the birthplace of the **all-inclusive** hotel, where a single price covers your room and all meals, and often all drinks, watersports and tips too. As it's pretty much unheard-of not to pre-book via a travel agent (usually as part of a flight-inclusive package) at these places, we've not listed any in the chapter, but if you do want to go all-inclusive, visit the websites of the two main operators in Jamaica, *Sandals* (ⓦ www.sandals.com) and *Superclubs* (ⓦ www.superclubs.com); these companies have a range of properties in all the main resorts.

Throughout Jamaica, there are hundreds of **villas** available for rent, normally by the week. Ranging from small beachside chalets to grand mansions, these are typically self-catering places, often with maid service, and can make a reasonably priced alternative to hotels for families and groups. JAVA, the Jamaica Association of Villas and Apartments (ⓣ 868/974-2508, ⓦ www.villasinjamaica.com), represents scores of villas islandwide; you can book via their website.

Food and drink

From fiery jerk meat to inventive seafood dishes and ubiquitous rice and peas, the Jamaican diet is surprisingly varied, and the Rasta preference for natural cooking means you can get good vegetarian food fairly easily. Snacking is good, too, with beef, vegetable or chicken patties the staple fare, and there is a vast selection of fresh fruit and vegetables.

The classic – and addictive – Jamaican **breakfast** is ackee and saltfish. The soft yellow flesh of the otherwise bland ackee fruit is fried with onions, sweet and hot peppers, fresh tomatoes and boiled, flaked salted cod. It's usually served with the delicious spinach-like callaloo, boiled green bananas and fried or boiled dumplings.

At most of Jamaica's cheaper restaurants and hotels, chicken and fish are the mainstays of **lunch** and **dinner**. Chicken is typically fried in a seasoned batter, jerked or curried, while fish can be grilled, steamed with okra and pimento pods, brown-stewed in a tasty sauce or "escovitched" – served in a spicy sauce of onions, hot peppers and vinegar. "**Jerking**" is the island's most distinctive cooking style. Meat – usually chicken or pork, but occasionally fish and lobster – is seasoned in a mixture of island-grown spices, including pimento, hot peppers, cinnamon and nutmeg, and then grilled slowly, often for hours, over a fire of pimento wood and under a cover of wooden slats or corrugated zinc sheets in a customized oil drum.

Rice and peas (rice cooked with coconut, spices and red kidney beans) is the accompaniment to most meals, though you'll sometimes get bammy (a substantial bread made from cassava flour), festival (a light, sweet, fried dumpling), sweet or regular potatoes (the latter known as Irish potatoes), yam, dasheen (like a yam, but chewier), Johnny cakes or fried or boiled dumplings.

Jamaica's **water** is safe to drink, and locally bottled spring water is widely available. For a tastier nonalcoholic drink, look no further than the roadside piles of coconuts in every town and village, often advertised with a sign saying "ice-cold jelly". Other **soft drinks** include Jamaica's own Ting (a refreshing sparkling grapefruit drink), Malta (a fortifying malt drink), throat-tingling ginger beers and fresh limeade. Fresh natural **juices** – tamarind, June plum, guava, soursop, strawberry and cucumber – are always delicious, if occasionally over-sweet. Jamaican Blue Mountain **coffee** is among the best and most expensive in the world, though the other local brews, such as High Mountain, Low Mountain or Mountain Blend, are also good.

The national **beer** is the excellent Red Stripe. Heineken is widely available, as is locally brewed Guinness, which competes with the sweeter Dragon as the island's stout of choice. Wray and Nephew make the classic white overproof **rum**: cheap, potent, available everywhere and best knocked back with a mixer of Ting. If you're after taste rather than effect, try gold rums such as Appleton Special or Myers, and the older, aged varieties such as Appleton Estate twelve-year-old.

Post and phones

Though fairly efficient, Jamaica's **telephone system** is expensive for overseas calls; local calls are far cheaper, but watch out for the shocking surcharges imposed by most hotels. You can bypass the high charges, though, by using a locally available international calling card. The **mail** service is less dependable. **Internet** access is available in all of the major resorts for anything from J$150 to US$6 for half an hour.

Phones

Most hotel rooms have a **phone**, and phone booths litter the island; the latter accept phonecards only, available from hotels, post offices and gift shops. One of the cheapest and easiest ways to make international and local calls is to buy a Worldtalk calling card; they can be used from public, private and hotel phones for both international and local calls. Most European **mobile phones** will work in Jamaica, and several British companies have roaming agreements with local provider Digicel (though you'll pay a premium, of course). Unless they're tri-band, US phones won't work in Jamaica. Owners of European or tri-band phones might want

to consider purchasing a SIM card from any Digicel dealer (you'll find one in every town) and inserting it into the phone; these cost around J$1500, and you add credit by way of the pay-as-you-go "Flex" system. Calls to local and international numbers are surprisingly cheap.

All Jamaican **telephone numbers** (except some freephone ones) have seven digits. To dial locally (within the same parish), simply key in the number. To get a number in another parish, prefix the number with "1"; you also use the "1" prefix when dialling mobile (cellular) numbers.

The **country code** for Jamaica is ☎876. For domestic and international **directory assistance** phone ☎114.

Mail

It's amazing how long it takes for **mail** to get across the island. Don't expect a letter from Kingston to the north coast (or vice versa) to arrive in less than a week. International mail is also slow – reckon on around ten days to a fortnight for airmail to reach Europe or North America. Most towns and villages have a **post office**, normally open Monday to Friday from 9am to 5pm; smaller postal agencies in rural areas keep shorter hours.

Opening hours, festivals and holidays

Jamaican **business hours** are normally 8.30am to 4.30/5pm Monday to Saturday, although some shops and offices close at noon on Saturdays. Museums normally close for one day a week, either Sunday or Monday, while most other places you'll want to visit are generally open daily.

Most of Jamaica's special events are timed to coincide with the winter tourist season. The main exceptions are Montego Bay's **Reggae Sumfest** in August and spring break, when young Americans take over the big resorts for a fortnight of raucous, beer-fuelled cavorting. April is **Carnival** time and, though not on the same scale as Trinidad's, it is a growing event. **Emancipation Day** and **Independence Day** celebrations – concerts, dance and theatre performances

January 1 New Year's Day
February Ash Wednesday
March/April Good Friday,
Easter Monday
May 23 Labour Day
August 1 Emancipation Day
First Monday in August
Independence Day
Third Monday in October National
Heroes Day
December 25 Christmas Day
December 26 Boxing Day

and parades – are held in late July to early August; contact the Jamaica Tourist Board for details. The JTB's annual **calendar of events** is available from offices on the island and abroad, and is posted on the JTB website, ⊛www.jamaicatravel.com.

Sports and outdoor activities

Sport is a Jamaican obsession – hardly surprising in a country that has produced so many world-class athletes. The island is also a great place to indulge your own sporting passion, with excellent watersports and top-class golfing in particular.

Cricket is the national game, and bringing it up in conversation is a sure-fire icebreaker. The atmosphere at matches is very Jamaican – thumping reggae between overs and vendors hawking jerk chicken and Red Stripe. There are cricket pitches throughout the island; visit ⊛www.windiescricket.com for schedules.

Scuba diving and **snorkelling** are concentrated on the north coast between Negril and Ocho Rios. The state of the reefs is variable, but there are still some gorgeous sites very close to the shore. The resort areas are packed with operators offering dive and snorkelling excursions; the most reputable are listed in the Guide.

Jamaica boasts no fewer than twelve **golf** courses, from the magnificent championship Tryall course near Montego Bay (☎868/956-5681) – home to the annual Johnnie Walker International – to less testing nine-hole links in Mandeville and Port Antonio (☎868/993-7645). All are open to the public, except during tournaments (Tryall sometimes closes to nonmembers in winter). Greens fees vary from US$10 to US$100 in winter, less in summer.

Crime and safety

While Jamaica's murder rate is undeniably high – the average is about a thousand per year – the JTB is keen to stress that you are more likely to be mugged in New York than Montego Bay. Nonetheless, robberies, assaults and other **crimes** against tourists do occasionally occur, and it's wise to apply the precautions you'd take in any foreign city.

Hustling can be a major annoyance in Jamaica. Especially in Montego Bay and Negril, young hopefuls aggressively (or humorously) accost foreigners in the street with offers of transport, ganja, aloe massages, hair-braiding and crafts. While an inevitable few street touts see tourists as easy prey for exploitation, most are just trying to make a living in an economically deprived country. Best advice is to keep things in perspective and employ a dash of humour.

Though tourism officials are loath to acknowledge it, many people do come to Jamaica in search of what aficionados agree is some of the finest **marijuana** in the world. If you're fairly young, expect to be offered ganja in the tourist areas; if you're not interested, calmly and firmly refuse. Bear in mind, too, that the possession, use, export or attempted smuggling of any quantity of ganja is against the law in Jamaica and carries stiff penalties.

The **emergency number** for the Jamaican police is ☎119.

History

Jamaica's first inhabitants were Taíno (also called Arawak) Indians, who arrived from South America around 900 AD and led a simple life of farming and fishing until the arrival in 1494 of Columbus, who claimed the island for Spain. Spanish settlement began in 1510, first at Sevilla Nueva on the north coast and then at the site of today's Spanish Town, just northwest of Kingston.

Spanish Town was completely sacked by the **British** in 1596, and again in 1643. In 1655, fifteen British ships, having failed in their assault on the island of Hispaniola, turned their sights on neighbouring Jamaica. They quickly captured Spanish Town, but the Spanish weren't defeated until five years later, when the last of them fled to Cuba. In the process, the Spanish freed and armed their slaves, most of whom fled to the mountainous interior. The **Maroons**, as they were called, later waged successful guerrilla war against the British.

Under British rule, new settlers were enticed to Jamaica with gifts of land. The colonists established vast **sugar cane** plantations. In the eighteenth century, the island became the world's biggest producer of sugar. The planters amassed extraordinary fortunes, but their wealth was predicated upon the appalling inhumanity of **slavery**.

Despite heavy opposition from a West Indian lobby desperate to protect its riches in the colonies, pressure from the Church finally brought about the **abolition of slavery** in 1834. Across the country, missionaries set up "free villages", buying land, subdividing it and either selling or donating it to former slaves. Meanwhile, planters found another source of cheap labour by importing 35,000 indentured labourers from India in the 1830s.

Jamaica's sugar industry took another major blow in 1846, when a free-trade-minded British government passed the **Sugar Duties Act**, forcing Jamaica's producers to compete on equal terms with sugar producers worldwide. At the same time, the development of beetsugar in Europe reduced demand for the West Indian product.

The **economic downturn** that followed abolition and the introduction of free trade in sugar took its toll on the freed slaves. Wages were kept pitifully low, taxes were imposed and unemployment rose as plantations were downsized or abandoned altogether. There were numerous **riots**, the most significant of which took place in 1865, when a major rebellion broke out in Morant Bay in St Thomas. Fearing islandwide insurrection, the governor ordered a show of strength from the armed forces. Little mercy was shown as 437 people were killed, while thousands more were flogged and terrorized. The brutal suppression caused horror througout Jamaica and Britain and the governor was dismissed for his part in the atrocities. His assembly abolished itself, and in 1866, Jamaica became a **Crown Colony**.

The early twentieth century saw considerable economic prosperity. Inevitably, though, most of the new wealth bypassed the black masses, and serious poverty remained throughout the island. By the 1930s, as the **Great Depression** took hold worldwide, unemployment spiralled and riots became commonplace. Strikes erupted too, with a major clash in 1938 between police and workers at the West Indies Sugar Company factory in Frome leaving several people dead. Partly as a result of the Frome incident, strike leader **Alexander Bustamante** founded the first trade union in the Caribbean in 1938 – the Bustamante Industrial Trade Union (BITU). An associated political party was born too, with the foundation of the **People's National Party** (PNP) by the lawyer Norman Manley. Both events gave a boost to Jamaican nationalism, already stirred by the campaigning of black-consciousness leader **Marcus Garvey** during the 1920s and early 1930s.

After serving as a major Allied base during World War II, Jamaica experienced new- found prosperity in the late 1940s, thanks to early **tourism** and the first **bauxite** exports. In 1944, a new constitution introduced universal adult suffrage, and first elections for a government that would work in conjunction with the British-appointed governor were held. Bustamante's newly formed **Jamaica Labour Party** (JLP) won, and gradually the island's two political parties drifted in different ideological directions, with the JLP adopting a basic liberal capitalist philosophy, and the PNP leaning towards democratic socialism.

The JLP stayed in power until 1955, when the PNP were elected on a manifesto that placed independence firmly on the agenda. Following the collapse of the short-lived West Indies Federation, Jamaica became an **independent state** within the British Commonwealth on August 6, 1962, with Bustamante as its first prime minister.

The early years of independence were marked by rising **prosperity**, as foreign investment increased, particularly in the bauxite industry. The JLP continued in power until the key elections of 1972, when the PNP – now led by Norman Manley's charismatic son Michael – swept to power. Manley set out to improve the conditions of the black majority, and his reforms included a minimum wage, the distribution of land to small farmers and increased funding for the island's education and healthcare sectors, all of which were financed by taxation, in particular of the internationally owned bauxite industry.

The bauxite companies promptly scaled down their Jamaican operations, and the ensuing economic decline was compounded by the 1973–1974 **oil crisis**. Manley sought to promote a greater degree of self-sufficiency, rejecting closer ties with the US in favour of an alignment with communist Cuba. US reaction was furious; economic sanctions were applied and it became increasingly difficult for Jamaica to attract foreign investment.

Politics became ever-more polarized during the Manley years. The opposition JLP, led now by Edward Seaga, launched blistering attacks on the "communist" administration. The 1976 election – won by the PNP again – saw a disturbing increase in **political violence**, particularly in the ghettos of Kingston. Despite criticism from human rights groups, Manley's response to the violence was to impose a state of emergency and severe anti-crime legislation was put in place. Jamaica entered the economic doldrums, and was forced to turn to the IMF for assistance.

Violence flared again during the 1980 election campaign, with hundreds of people killed in shoot-outs and open gang warfare. Amid the carnage, Jamaican voters turned to the JLP. In turn, the JLP turned to the US, but were still obliged to continue the cutback of government services begun under the PNP. The JLP's honeymoon with the Jamaican people proved short-lived; in 1989, Michael Manley and the PNP were returned to office. Ill health forced Manley's resignation in 1992; his successor, **P.J. Patterson**, the first black man to become Jamaica's prime minister, won the election of 1993 on a far less radical platform (he was re-elected in the 1997 and 2003 polls). The demands of the World Bank and the IMF continued to be met and a generally liberal economic policy followed.

Tourism, bauxite and agriculture remain the mainstays of the Jamaican economy, but the island carries a huge burden of **debt** to foreign banks, and much of the foreign currency earned is required to repay interest and capital on that debt. Consequently, education, roads and public transport have suffered, and the lot of the average Jamaican remains hard. **Crime**, though, is the key concern for most people. Kingston's "garrison communities" are these days delineated by the whims of drug dons rather than by political allegiances, and gun battles have resulted in far too many riots and curfews in the capital.

Despite these problems, there remains much to be **positive** about in Jamaica. Tourism remains strong and Jamaican culture remains vibrant. Whatever the challenges, it is hard to quench the island's spirit, and while many islanders predict that "things will get worse before they get better", Jamaica's future, on balance, seems bright.

Music

Close your eyes practically anywhere in Jamaica and you'll hear **music.** Radios blare on the street, buses pump out nonstop dancehall and every Saturday night the bass of countless sound-system parties wafts through the air. Music is a serious business here, generating an average of a hundred record releases per week and influencing every aspect of Jamaican culture from dress to speech to attitude. Reggae and DJ-based dancehall dominate, but Jamaicans are catholic in their musical tastes: soul, hip-hop, jazz, rock 'n' roll, gospel and the ubiquitous country and western are popular.

Jamaica's music scene first came to international attention with **ska**, the staccato, guitar-and-trumpet-led sound heard in Millie Small's smash hit *My Boy Lollipop* and Desmond Dekker and the Aces' *007 (Shanty Town)*. By the mid-1960s, ska had given way to the slowed-down and more melodic **rocksteady** sound. Rocksteady didn't carry the swing for very long, though, and by the late 1960s it had been superseded by the tighter guitars, heavier bass and sinuous rhythm of **reggae**. Bob Marley's lyrics, drawn from the tenets of Rastafari, emphasized repatriation, black history, black pride and self-determination. Reggae became full-fledged protest music – anathema to the establishment, which banned it wherever possible.

The 1970s stand out as the classic period of **roots reggae**. But while Burning Spear was singing *Marcus Garvey* and *Slavery Days*, the era also offered a sweeter side: the angelic crooning of more mainstream artists like Dennis Brown or Gregory Isaacs found an eager audience, their style becoming known as **lovers' rock**. As the 1970s wore on, studio technology became more sophisticated and producers began manipulating their equipment to produce **dub** – some of the most arresting and penetrating music ever to emerge from Jamaica. With a remarkable level of inventiveness and often limited means, dub pioneers King Tubby, Prince Jammy and Scientist brought reggae back to basics, stripping down songs so that only bass, drums and inflections of tone remained. Snippets of the original vocals were then mixed in alongside sound effects (dog barks, gunshots). Before long, scores of DJs clamoured to produce dub voice-overs. The craft was mastered by U-Roy, who released talk-based singles to great success throughout the 1970s.

As the violent elections of 1976 and 1980 saw the pressure in Kingston building up, the sound systems multiplied and the DJs "chatted" on the mike about the times, analysing the position of the ghetto youth in Jamaica. But reggae struggled to find direction and purpose after the death in 1981 of **Bob Marley**; his legacy of cultural consciousness began to seem less relevant to the ghetto world of cocaine-running and political warfare.

Meanwhile the lewd approach and overtly sexual lyrics – or "slackness" – of DJs such as Yellowman became hugely popular, leading to the rise of **dancehall**, a two-chord barrage of raw drum and bass and shouted patois lyrics. Dancehall is now the most popular musical form in contemporary Jamaica; names to look for include Beenie Man, Bounty Killer, Lady Saw, Elephant Man and Sean Paul.

Dancehall, though, isn't to everyone's taste, and the battle between cultural and slackness artists continues. The culturally conscious lyrics and staunch Rastafarian stance of the late Garnet Silk, who burst on the scene in the mid-1990s, led the way for artists such as Capleton, Sizzla and Luciano, while singers such as Beres Hammond and Ritchie Spice continue to release wonderful reggae tunes.

5.1

Kingston and around

Fast, furious and fascinating, **KINGSTON** is unlike anywhere else in the Caribbean. Given its troubled reputation, it's hardly surprising that few tourists visit, and though the scare stories are absurdly exaggerated, Jamaica's capital is not a place for the faint-hearted. With a population fast approaching one million, the city seethes with life, noise and activity; it's a side of Jamaica that couldn't be more different from the resorts. The live-for-today vitality of the place is tempered by a cool elegance and a strong sense of national history. In addition to being the seat of government and the island's administrative centre, Kingston is Jamaica's **cultural heart**, the city that spawned Bob Marley, Buju Banton, Beenie Man and countless other reggae stars, and it's *the* place to experience the best of local art, theatre and dance.

Though undeniable, practically all of the **crime** and violence in Kingston is confined to the ghettos, and as these are not places for casual sightseeing, you're actually no more at risk here than in any other big city. Take the usual precautions – don't walk the downtown streets alone, take cabs after dark, keep jewellery and valuables out of sight – and you're unlikely to run into any problems. If you do decide to visit, you'll find that not only is it easy to steer clear of the troubled areas, but that there's little of the persistent **harassment** that bedevils parts of the north coast.

A handful of interesting museums, galleries and the botanical gardens can easily fill a couple of days of sightseeing; the island's best clubs, theatres and some great restaurants will take care of the evenings. In addition to the lovely Blue Mountains, plenty of other attractions surround the city. The area is littered with historic sites, such as the forts of the English buccaneers in atmospheric **Port Royal**, while white-sand **Hellshire** and **Lime Cay beaches** are the perfect places for a dip in the ocean.

Some history

There was little development in Kingston until 1692, when thousands of Jamaicans fled a violent **earthquake** that devastated Port Royal. Kingston's population was further expanded in 1703, when more Port Royalists fled to the other side of the harbour after a devastating **fire**. In 1872, when Kingston replaced Spanish Town as Jamaica's capital, many wealthy families were already moving beyond the original town boundaries to the more genteel areas that today comprise **uptown** Kingston. Meanwhile the less affluent, including a growing tide of former slaves, huddled downtown and in the **shanty towns** that began to spring up on the outskirts of old Kingston, particularly west of the city.

Jamaica's turn-of-the-twentieth-century boom, engineered by tourism and agriculture, largely bypassed Kingston's poor. The **downtown** area continued to deteriorate, neglected by government and hit by a catastrophic earthquake in 1907. Those who could afford to continued to move out, leaving behind an increasingly destitute population that proved fertile recruitment ground for the **Rastafari** movement during the 1920s and 1930s. Since then the faith, with its message of love, peace and rebellion against the "Babylon system" of the establishment, has attracted a significant following in Jamaica and the wider Caribbean, and its tenets have formed the basis of many a classic reggae tune.

In the 1960s, efforts were made to give the old downtown area a face-lift. Redevelopment of the waterfront resulted in a much-needed expansion of the city's **port facility** and a smartening up of the harbour area. A mini **tourist boom** was sparked by the new-look Kingston (and by the growing popularity of reggae music abroad). But the redevelopment of downtown was only cosmetic. Crime soon proliferated, and tourists headed for the new beach resorts on the island's north coast as the city sank into a quagmire of unemployment, poverty and crime. Today there are hints that the capital's fortunes may be turning, with some serious attempts to tackle crime and improve economic fortunes; still, Kingston remains a divided city.

Arrival and information

All international and some domestic flights land at **Norman Manley International Airport** (℡876/924-8546 or 8452) on the Palisadoes – the strip of land that frames Kingston Harbour southeast of the city. A number of **car rental** firms have desks in the arrivals area; others will meet you there on request. The best option is Jamaica's biggest outfit, Island Car Rentals, 17 Antigua Ave (℡876/926-8012) and at the airport.

City **bus** #98 runs from just outside the arrivals area to downtown roughly every half-hour (around J$50). However, as buses drop you downtown (not a good idea for a new arrival toting suitcases), you're far better off opting for a **cab** – the fare for the thirty-minute journey to New Kingston is JS$1500, and there are plenty of JUTA drivers around. You can **change money** in the arrivals lounge.

The domestic airport of **Tinson Pen** (℡876/978-8068; 923-6664 for Air Jamaica Express flights), where some (but not all) domestic flights land, is just to the west of downtown on the fringe of some of the city's less desirable communities. A cab into central Kingston from here should cost around J$600. Taxis usually meet the flights; otherwise, call one of the operators listed in the "Getting around" section below.

The main office of the **Jamaica Tourist Board** is slap in the middle of New Kingston at 64 Knutsford Blvd (Mon–Fri 9am–4.30pm; ℡876/929-9200); staff can answer basic queries and dole out JTB pamphlets, but it's not really geared up to assist visitors. There's a smaller, more tourist-oriented booth at Norman Manley airport (℡876/924-8024).

Getting around

Finding your way around Kingston is pretty straightforward. Downtown uses a grid system, while uptown is defined by a handful of major roads; the mountains to the northeast serve as a good compass. The heat and the distances between places mean you're not going to want to do a lot of **walking**, though the downtown sights are easily navigable on foot. It's not advisable to walk the streets at night in any part of the city; Kingstonians don't.

Taxis are the best way of getting around the city and reasonably cheap; a ride from New Kingston to downtown costs around J$300. Although it is standard practice to call for a taxi, particularly at night, they can almost always be flagged down on the main streets (look out for red "PP" or "PPV" plates). There are bustling ranks downtown at Parade, and along Knutsford Boulevard. Reputable taxi firms include Blue Diamond (℡876/937-1604) and Eagle Force (℡876/923-4236).

Unfortunately, **public transport** in Kingston is not really a viable option for visitors. Fares are absurdly cheap – no more than J$50 for any journey around the city – but overcrowding and the fact that all services radiate from terminals at less-than-salubrious Half Way Tree and at Parade mean it's not worth the hassle. If you want to take a **tour** of the city, see p.283 for details of reliable firms.

Accommodation

Most of Kingston's **hotels** are scattered around the uptown district of **New Kingston**, a convenient base for sightseeing and close to many restaurants, theatres, cinemas and clubs. Prices are not as seasonal as in the resort areas, and there are few discounts available during the summer. Although it is wise to reserve in advance, finding a room is rarely a problem.

Alhambra Inn 1 Tucker Ave ☎876/978-9072
or 9073, ✉alhambra@cwjamaica.com. Pretty
complex set back from the road near the National
Stadium, with a pool, outdoor restaurant and
lots of greenery. The rooms offer king-size beds,
telephone, a/c and cable TV, and are superb value;
rates include breakfast. ❹
Altamont Court 1 Altamont Terrace ☎876/929-
4497, ⓦwww.cariboutpost.com/altamont. The best
mid-range option in New Kingston, in the heart of
the action but tucked away from the noisy main
drag, with a swimming pool, Jacuzzi, restaurant
and bar. The comfortable rooms have a/c, cable TV,
phone, hairdryers and wireless Internet access, and
there are some lovely split-level suites too. Rates
include breakfast. ❹, suites ❻
Christar Villas 99 Hope Rd ☎876/978 3933,
ⓦwww.christarvillashotel.com. Appealing studios
and suites with kitchen, a/c, phone and cable TV;
the more luxurious units have private Jacuzzi, gym
equipment and wireless Internet access. Business
centre, gym, pool, Jacuzzi, sun deck, a/c restaurant
and popular bar on site, a great location near the
Bob Marley Museum and free airport transfers
(Mon–Sat 8am–5pm). ❹
Courtleigh 85 Knutsford Blvd ☎876/929-9000,
ⓦwww.courtleigh.com. Easily the most appealing
of the New Kingston high-rise hotels, with a tasteful lobby decked out in Chinese style, a business
centre, good restaurant, popular bar/nightclub, a
pool, gym and luxurious rooms with a balcony and
lots of welcome extras, from hairdryer to Internet
jack. ❻
The Gardens 23 Liguanea Ave ☎876/927-5957,
ⓦwww.forrespark.com. With a central location
and a relaxing ambience, this delightful complex is
one of Kingston's best choices. Set in landscaped
grounds with a pool, the expansive two-bedroom
townhouses have full kitchen and living room;
you can rent just a room as well as a whole unit.
Rooms ❸, townhouses ❻
Hilton Kingston 77 Knutsford Blvd ☎876/926-
5430, ⓦwww.hilton.com. Lively, glitzy complex

dominating New Kingston, with a huge pool, nightclubs, restaurant and bar. Rooms afford good views
and have a/c, satellite TV, phone and hairdryer. ❻
Holborn Manor 3 Holborn Rd, Kingston 10
☎876/926-0296, ⓕ876/906-5281. Very basic
but friendly family property in New Kingston. The
somewhat dingy en-suite rooms (cold water only)
have fan, phone and cable TV, and there's a dining
room on site. Breakfast is included in rates. ❸
Indies 5 Holborn Rd ☎876/926-2952, ⓦwww.
indieshotel.com. Compact, clean and appealing
little hotel next to Holborn Manor, set on two levels
around a garden courtyard and small restaurant.
Rooms have a/c and phone – you pay a little more
for a TV. ❸
Knutsford Court 16 Chelsea Ave ☎876/929-
1000, ⓦwww.knutsfordcourt.com. Formerly Sutton
Place hotel, and newly refurbished, with lots of
greenery outside and redecorated rooms with all
mod cons. Business centre, coin-op laundry, pool
and restaurant on site; rates include Continental
breakfast. ❻
Mikuzi 5 Upper Montrose Rd ☎876/978 4859
or 813 0098, ⓦwww.mikuzi.com. Wonderful and
unique guesthouse set in and around a lovely
colonial-era house in residential New Kingston. The
eclectic en-suite rooms have stylish, funky decor,
fans and kitchenettes; some have a/c and cable TV;
there are also a couple of budget cottages in the
pretty flower-filled gardens. Very friendly. ❷–❸
Sandhurst 70 Sandhurst Crescent ☎876/927-
8244, ⓕ876/927-7239. Excellent value in a
peaceful spot near King's House and behind the
Bob Marley Museum, with a nice pool and a terrace
restaurant overlooking the mountains. Rooms range
from simple fan-only to units with a/c, cable TV and
verandah. ❸–❹
Sunset Inn 1A Altamont Crescent ☎876/929-
7283, ✉sunsetinn@mindspring.com. Rather
cramped but functional, in a great New Kingston
location, with a range of clean, pleasant en-suite
rooms with fridge, a/c and cable TV; some have a
kitchenette. ❸–❹

The City

Kingston's main sights are divided between the area known as "downtown", which
stretches north from the waterfront to the busy traffic junction of Cross Roads, and
"uptown", spreading up into the ritzy suburbs at the base of the mountains. **Downtown** is the industrial centre, its factories and all-important port providing most
of Kingston's blue-collar employment. You may be surprised at how attractive and
easy-going **Uptown** feels. Most of Kingston's hotels, restaurants, clubs and shopping
centres are here, and it's where you'll spend most of your time. Some of the residential districts are simply beautiful, while the central high-rises suggest a modern city
anywhere in North America.

Cross Roads & Uptown

N

ROUSSEAU ROAD

RETIREMENT ROAD

OLD HOPE RD

CALEDONIA

TOM REDCAM AVE

LYNDHURST

CALEDONIA CRES

ROAD

SLIPE ROAD

MARESCAUX ROAD

Mico College

CAMP ROAD

TRENCH TOWN

JONES TOWN

DEVON AVE

PRICE LA

TORRINGTON RD

TORRINGTON AVE

EVE LA

ROSEDALE AVE

ORANGE LA

HEROES CIRCLE

CIRCLE

National Heroes Park

National Heroes Memorial ⊙

HEROES CIRCLE

CONNOLLEY AVE

PRINCE OF WALES ST

REGENT ST

PRINCE ALBERT ST

HTICHIN ST

WILD ST

JOHN ST

SARAH ST

STEPHEN ST

HANNAH ST

ARNOLD ROAD

WATER ST

GOODWIN PARK RD

SLIPE PEN ROAD

ORANGE STREET

UPPER KING ST

NEW NORTH STREET

NORTH STREET

Sabina Park Cricket Ground

MELBOURNE RD

Holy Trinity Cathedral ✝

NORTH STREET

SOUTH CAMP ROAD

SPANISH TOWN ROAD

Jubilee & Coronation Market

TIVOLI GDNS

Bus Terminal

HEYWOOD ST

CHARLES ST

BEESTON ST

Ward Theatre ■

N PARADE

W PARADE

St William Grant Park

S PARADE

Kingston Parish Church

WEST ST

PECHON ST

MATHEWS LA

PRINCESS ST

DUKE ST

LUKE L

BARRY ST

★ Taxi Rank

Jewish Synagogue ■

✝ Coke Chapel

SUTTON ST

EAST ST

MARK LA

JOHNS LA

HANOVER ST

GEORGE'S LA

ROSEMARY LA

MAIDEN LA

EAST QUEEN ST

LAWS ST

BARRY ST

WILDMAN LA

SMITH LA

JAMES ST

TEXT LANE

CLOVELLY RD

WIDCOMB LA

BLAKE ROAD

VICTORIA AVE

St Andrews Scots Kirk ✝

Institute of Jamaica ■

GOLD ST

FOSTER LA

LADD LA

HIGH HOLBORN ST

FLEET ST

BECKFORD ST

W QUEEN ST

KING ST

CHURCH ST

TEMPLE LA

TOWER ST

WATER LANE

Moby Dick ▣

WATER LA

HARBOUR ST

PORT ROYAL ST

Craft Market

National Gallery ■

OCEAN BLVD

Negro Aroused Statue ●

Bank of Jamaica ⌒

NETHERSOLE PL

Jamaica Conference Centre ■

Airport, Rae Town, Port Royal & Morant Bay

Tuff Gong Studios, Causeway & Portmore

Trench Town Culture Yard & Tinson Pen Airport

Kingston Harbour

0   500 yds

DOWNTOWN KINGSTON

Downtown

Flattened by an earthquake in 1907, **downtown Kingston** has lost most of its grand eighteenth-century architecture, though a handful of historic buildings can still be found along Rum Lane, Water Lane and King Street. Much of Kingston's economic strength still derives from its impressively huge natural **harbour**, one of the world's best, but grimly polluted these days. Once buzzing with trading ships, the wind-whipped waterfront is a good spot to start exploring; it's also the departure point for the ferry to Port Royal. The chief beneficiary of the city council's 1960s' effort to beautify downtown, the waterfront saw its historic buildings swept away and replaced by spanking new high-rises. Today these modern monuments define the eastern end of the waterfront's main strip, Ocean Boulevard. Housed in an unprepossessing iron building at the western end of Ocean Boulevard, the **Craft Market** (closed Sun) is the least expensive place on the island to buy souvenirs, and shopping here is usually a hassle-free experience.

The National Gallery

Just up from the waterfront, the air-conditioned **National Gallery**, at 12 Ocean Blvd on the corner of Orange St (Tues–Thurs 10am–4.30pm, Fri 10am–4pm, Sat 10am–3pm; J$100, guided tours on request at J$800, call ☏876/922-1561 to arrange), is one of the highlights of a visit to Kingston. The permanent collection here is superb, ranging from delicate woodcarvings to flamboyant religious paintings, while the Annual National Exhibition (normally Dec–Feb) showcases the best of contemporary Jamaican art.

Ten galleries on the first floor cover the **Jamaican School**, 1922 to the present. The school is generally deemed to have begun with Edna Manley's 1922 *Beadseller*, a dainty little statue that married Cubism to a typical local image (the Kingston "higgler", or female street vendor) to create something distinctly Jamaican. Manley's sculpture and the dark, brooding local scenes of John Dunkley (1891–1947) dominate the first galleries. Dunkley and Manley paved the way for other Jamaican artists to paint what they saw around them.

The paintings of Carl Abrahams in the later galleries show a move towards abstraction that is capped by the Jamaican surrealism of Colin Garland and the ghostly images of David Boxer. Realism returns with the powerful re-creation of a Trench Town ghetto in Dawn Scott's *A Cultural Object*. An entire room houses the **Larry Wirth Collection** of African-style sculpture and paintings by Shepherd Mallica "Kapo" Reynolds. Downstairs, the **A.D. Scott Collection** displays a selection of Edna Manley's sculptures alongside some of the finest works of the island's most important artists, including Gloria Escoffery and Barrington Watson.

Uptown

The phrase "Uptown Kingston" is used as a catch-all for areas of the city north of Cross Roads, including the business and commercial centres of **Half Way Tree** and **New Kingston** as well as residential areas such as **Hope Pastures**, **Mona** and **Beverly Hills**. The heart of **Uptown** is the high-rise financial district of **New Kingston**, found in an eccentric triangle bounded by Trafalgar Road, Old Hope Road and Half Way Tree Road.

Though there are only a couple of low-key attractions in New Kingston itself, there are plenty of facilities ranged along the central Knutsford Boulevard, and chances are that you will stay and do much of your eating and drinking in or around this area. Some of the interesting sights are within walking distance; the rest are a short taxi ride away.

Knutsford Boulevard

With its back-to-back restaurants, bars, offices and banks, the "Strip", as New Kingston's main street is often known, is a permanently busy strip of tarmac, all honking taxi horns and scurrying office workers. Past its first straight stretch south of Trafalgar

UPTOWN KINGSTON

①, Stony Hill & North Coast   **Jack's Hill**   **②&③**

King's House

Sovereign Centre

Bob Marley Museum **⑥**

Jamaica House

⑦   **C**

Devon House

⑨ ⑧

Vale Royal

D

St Andrews Parish Church

HALF WAY TREE

TRAFALGAR

NEW KINGSTON

E   **⑩**

⑫   **⑪**   **⑬**

G

New Kingston Shopping Centre

⑰   **⑭ ⑮**

Jamaica Tourist Board   **⑯**

Putt-n-Play

I

J

⑱

K

⑲

Emancipation Park

OXFORD RD

National Arena

National Stadium

N

Little & Little Little Theatres

Parish Library

Carib Theatre   CALEDONIA AVE

ROUSSEAU RD   LYNDHURST RD

0   500 yds

Downtown ▼   ▼ Downtown

Gardens & Blue Mountains   **④ ⑤**   Hope Botanical

Beverly Hills

ACCOMMODATION			
Alhambra Inn	**H**	Holborn Manor	**E**
Altamont Court	**J**	Indies	**F**
Christar Villas	**C**	Knutsford Court	**G**
Courtleigh	**L**	Mikuzi	**D**
The Gardens	**A**	Sandhurst	**B**
Hilton Kingston	**I**	Sunset Inn	**K**

EATING, DRINKING & NIGHTLIFE			
Akbar and Thai Gardens	12	JamRock	15
Ashanti	4	Livity	5
Carlos Café	19	Norma's on the Terrace	8
Casson's	11	Our Place	7
Chasers Café	2	Red Bones Blues Café	10
Cuddy'z	17	Starapple	6
The Deck	13	Up on the Roof	16
Escape 24-7	14	Village Café	3
The Grog Shoppe	9	Weekendz	1
Hot Pot	18		

Road, the street bends and widens, flanked now by high-rise hotels. Past the tennis courts and colonial architecture of the Liguanea Club, a private members' enclave where James Bond took cocktails on the terrace in *Dr No*, a turn-off to the right leads to the only real attractions in the area. **Putt and Play** (Mon–Thurs 5–11pm, Fri 5pm–midnight, Sat & Sun 11am–midnight) is a prettily landscaped eighteen-hole mini-golf course which attracts a healthy clique of Kingston teenagers after dark, and families at the weekends; as well as golf, there's go-karts, trampolines and bouncy castles. There's usually a lively crowd at the bar and restaurant after dark. Across the road is **Emancipation Park** (no set hours; free), opened in 2002 as a memorial to the 1838 cessation of slavery. It's a manicured and well-maintained space, with more concrete than grass, piped jazz from speakers ensconced in fake boulders, a jogging track and a concert stage where regular free concerts are staged. At the south end of the park stands Laura Facey's controversial sculpture *Redemption Song*, a stunning and majestic study of a Jamaican couple whose prominent breasts and genitals led to calls for its immediate removal after it was first installed. Though the park is a nice spot to take a breezy breather in the daytime, it comes into its own at night, when couples canoodle and families turn out to promenade and gaze at the central "sky cascade" fountain, the jets of water lit by coloured lights to delightful effect.

Devon House

Trafalgar Road forms a T-junction with Knutsford Boulevard, and then swings east towards Hope Road. Opposite the junction of Trafalgar and Hope Road are the green lawns and shady trees of the **Devon House** complex, a cool oasis in the midst of the city that's centred around the palatial Devon House itself (Mon–Sat 9.30am–5pm, tours run throughout the day, last tour at 4.30pm; J$250 including guided tour). The house was built in 1881 by Jamaica's first black millionaire, building contractor George Stiebel. Born in Kingston in 1820, Stiebel made his fortune gold-mining in Venezuela, returning home in 1873 to snap up properties throughout Jamaica. Among these was Devon Pen, where he built the house that was his Kingston home until he died in 1896. Bought by the Jamaican government in 1967, it has gradually been furnished with West Indian and European antiques as well as more modern Jamaican reproductions. It makes for a diverting hour's exploration, in spite of the enforced tour, which can be rushed and monosyllabic – don't be afraid to take your time.

The landscaped grounds make a fine place for a leisurely stroll, but most people head straight for the former stables in the middle of the lawns, where the central courtyard, with its benches, trellises and flowerbeds, is surrounded by a number of **shops** and **cafés**. You can pick up good-quality (if expensive) souvenirs from the gift shops, a heavenly home-made Devon House "I Scream" (try the soursop or Guinness flavours), a smoothie or blended juice from the *Jamaica Juice* bar, or an excellent cooked lunch, patty or gooey cake from the *Brick Oven* bakery. *Café What's On*, with tables outside and in the a/c interior, has good sandwiches, bagels, rotis, cappuccinos and Internet access. There are also a couple of great restaurants here, detailed in "Eating" (see overleaf); note that there's also an NCB ATM in the stables area.

The Bob Marley Museum

For reggae fans, the **Bob Marley Museum**, at 56 Hope Rd (Mon–Sat 9.30am–5pm, tours every 20min, last tour at 4pm; J$500; ☎876/927-9152, ⊛www.bobmarley-foundation.com), is the whole point of a visit to the capital, and even if you're not a serious devotee, a visit is an obligatory part of any Kingston itinerary. Marley's Kingston home from 1975 until his death from cancer in 1981 is still much as it was when he lived here, a gentle and surprisingly low-key monument to Jamaica's greatest musical legend. During the hour-long guided tour you'll see legions of silver, gold and platinum discs and scores of awards as well as concert memorabilia and a rather bizarre hologram of Marley in action. Upstairs there is a re-creation of Wail 'n' Soul – Marley's tiny, shack-like Trench Town record shop. You'll also see Marley's kitchen, bedroom, stage outfits, and the room where he was almost assassinated during the 1976 election campaign – the bullet holes still much in evidence. The tour ends behind the house in the theatre that once housed Marley's Tuff Gong recording studio. There's moving footage of the "One Love" concert of 1980, at which Marley brought together rival political party leaders Michael Manley and Edward Seaga, and a film of interviews with Marley. There's an excellent photo gallery, too.

To the right of the museum entrance are a juice bar/restaurant and a series of high-quality, Rasta-oriented craft shops and a CD outlet. A small shop at the back of the complex sells stylish clothes and shoes from the Cooyah and Zion Roots Wear lines.

Hope Botanical Gardens

A quarter of a mile east of the Marley museum on Old Hope Road, the **Hope Botanical Gardens** (daily 6am–7pm; free) were established in 1881 by government on 200 acres of land that were formerly part of the Hope Estate sugar cane plantation. Despite taking a battering from hurricanes Gilbert and Ivan, in 1988 and 2004 respectively, the gardens remain a lovely escape from the clamour of the city and a popular venue for weekend strolls, picnics and get-togethers, with sweeping lawns, bouganvillea walks, a disintegrating maze and a dizzying variety of unusual trees, including a great collection of palms. After exploring, you can grab a bite at the wonderful *Ashanti* vegetarian restaurant (see below) in the middle of the gardens; come on a Sunday afternoon and you'll get live music as you eat. Adjacent to the gardens is a small, sadly underfunded and eminently missable **zoo** (Mon–Fri 10am–5pm, Sat & Sun 10am–6pm; J$20).

Eating

After the sun goes down, the Kingston area is hard to beat for open-air dining. Uptown – which is where you'll want to be in the evenings – you'll find a wider choice of **restaurants** than anywhere else in Jamaica and an excellent standard of food. Most places offer variations on traditional Jamaican fare, but you'll also find good Chinese, Indian and Italian cuisine. If you want a meal with a view, head to Port Royal for the waterside restaurant at *Morgan's Harbour* hotel, or any of the fish places dotted around the village. For informal lunches, visit the **food courts** at Sovereign Centre in Hope Road, Island Life Plaza on St Lucia Avenue, the huge Marketplace complex in the Constant Spring Arcade or the two Manor Plazas on Constant Spring Road. For **patties**, *Tastee's* has a convenient branch on Knutsford Boulevard, while the *Juicy Beef* outlet on Hope Road, just up from Sovereign Centre, also does great breakfast; try the porridge. If you're after truly authentic **jerk chicken**, try any of the smoking oil-drum barbecues set up on street corners; one of the best is outside the open-air Dragon Plaza shopping mall, just up from the Sovereign Centre on Hope Road in Liguanea.

Akbar and Thai Gardens 11 Holborn Rd ☏876/922-3247. The best Indian food in town, with all the regular dishes (including plenty of vegetarian options) served up in a tastefully decorated a/c indoor dining room. In the shady backyard of *Akbar* restaurant, *Thai Gardens* offers decent Thai food, with the full range of starters – fish cakes, spring rolls – as well as red and green curries and noodle dishes.

Ashanti Hope Gardens. Relaxing, inexpensive open-air restaurant in the centre of the gardens, offering a daily-changing lunch/early dinner vegetarian menu that always includes a delicious thick soup (split peas, red peas, pumpkin) and main dishes such as soya and veg balls served with rice, salad and ratatouille. Veg burgers with chutney, natural juices and soya ice cream also available.

Casson's 1d Braemar Ave. English pub with typical Brit meals including sausages and mash and Sunday lunch with all the trimmings, served up in a pleasant air-conditioned dining room adjacent to the bar.

Carlos Café 22 Belmont Rd. Friendly place off Oxford Road with appealing decor and excellent service. Decent and fairly inexpensive, food ranges from salads and sandwiches to steaks, seafood and pasta.

Cuddy'z 25 Dominica Drive ☏876/920 8019. New venture operated by ex-Windies cricket superstar Courtney Walsh, this slick, modern a/c restaurant offers a wide-ranging, mid-priced international-style menu of build-your-own salads, steaks, ribs, pasta and local favourites.

The Grog Shoppe Devon House ☏876/926-3512. A shady spot on the Devon House grounds serving standard Jamaican meals at lunchtime and more European fare (and prices) in the evening. There are regular theme nights, such as all-you-can-eat crab night; call ahead to check. Closed Sun.

Hot Pot 2 Altamont Terrace. Popular spot for typical Jamaican meals in the heart of New Kingston, with excellent breakfasts, including cornmeal and banana porridge and saltfish combinations, and lunches of fish and bammy, curry goat, stewed beef and the usual Jamaican staples.

JamRock 69 Knutsford Blvd. A perfect and popular combination of bar, hangout, restaurant and patisserie; favourite among Jamaican dishes is the sumptuous "Jerk Nyamwich", and you can also get salads, soups, burgers, sandwiches, excellent patties, pastries and espresso or cappuccino.

Livity 166 Old Hope Rd. Tables ranged around an open-air courtyard, and a delicious vegetarian menu: soups (pumpkin, split peas, etc), brown lentil, tofu and soya stews, salads, patties, channa or hummus wraps, veggie burgers, natural juices/ smoothies and cakes or soya ice cream.

Norma's on the Terrace Devon House ☎876/968-5488. Upscale eatery, situated on the terrace of the old Devon House stables and serving gourmet Jamaican food with an international twist. Menus might include peppered beef salad, smoked marlin and seafood chowder; afternoon teas feature delectable pastries. It's also good for a late-night espresso accompanied by one of the superb desserts.

Our Place 102 Hope Rd. Laid-back place offers excellent Jamaican cooking and attracts a regular crew of lunchers. All the staples, from conch soup to curry goat, and evening specials such as janga (freshwater shrimp) night on Fridays. The bar is nice for a quiet drink.

Red Bones Blues Café 21 Braemar Ave ☎876/978-8262, ⊛www.redbonesbluescafe.com.
Stylish, upmarket restaurant-cum-music venue with a distinguished but laid-back atmosphere, serving imaginative Jamaican-style food at table on the outdoor covered terrace or the indoor dining room. Good wine list.

Starapple 94 Hope Road ☎876/927 9019. Set in a lovely old house, all creaky polished floors and gingerbread tracery, and offering a solid, mid-priced Jamaican menu, from yam and saltfish, oxtail and beans, steamed fish and all the usual variations. Interesting veggie options include callaloo quiche, vegetable rundown and aloo and channa curry.

Up on the Roof 73 Knutsford Blvd ☎876/929 8033. Fabulous setting, with a decked terrace over-looking the hustle below and an a/c dining room. The upscale Caribbean creole menu is inventive and delicious: "Junction" shrimp with lime garlic jerk mayo and crabcake salad make great starters, while mains include all the classic dishes from around the region, from Bajan flying fish and coocoo to Cuban pork loin or Trini curry and roti. Good veggie options too.

Drinking and nightlife

Kingston has legions of great places to get a **drink**, and many of them also double up as restaurants; *Casson's*, *Red Bones*, *Our Place*, *Up on the Roof* and the *Grog Shoppe* (see above) are all good bets. Many of the bars also have poetry, open-mic and film nights, which are great for tapping into the current Kingston scene – expect a cover charge of around J$300. There are also scores of **clubs** around town, ranging from state-of-the-art places featuring big-name DJs to more sedate in-hotel affairs and dancehall dives. Anticipate a cover of around J$500. It's also worth keeping a lookout for posters and press advertisements for one-off nights at places such as Mas Camp Village, or all-inclusive parties staged at outdoor venues in and around the city; these are usually well attended by a friendly uptown crowd, and invariably lots of fun. For more on what's on, visit ⊛www.whaddat.com.

Live music in the capital is less predictable; some of the best shows are the annual round of Heineken Startime concerts, featuring the best of Jamaica's vintage artists. Big shows are promoted in the press, on the radio and by way of posters and ban-ners slapped up around town. Annual celebrations include **Carnival**, with numerous events held around the time of Lent. It's similar to the Trinidadian festival, but on a far smaller scale and with more organized parties than street parades. For more on Carnival, visit ⊛www.jamaicacarnival.com or ⊛www.bacchanaljamaica.com.

Bars

Carlos Café 22 Belmont Rd ☎876/926-4186. Outdoor bar with an uptownish feel, which stages various themed nights, from Martini Mondays to Latin on Thursdays.

Chasers Café 29 Barbican Rd. Popular hangout with a decent beer selection. Monday offers karaoke, Tuesday is oldies night, there's disco each Friday night and sports on TV throughout the week.

Cuddy'z 25 Dominica Drive ☎876/920 8019. Operated by cricketing legend Courtney Walsh,
who often passes through to the delight of patrons, this newly opened sports bar is a lively place for a drink or to catch a baseball, cricket or football game shown on numerous TVs, the big screen at the back of the mini basketball court or one of the monitors in the "Superbooths", which also have Internet access and instant messaging that enables you to send messages to other patrons or pics to your mates back home.

The Deck 14 Trafalgar Rd. Easy-going and central outdoor bar under a mango tree, popular with a friendly, older set. Different snacks on offer each night, and low-key music from a DJ; women get half-price drinks each Thursday between 5pm and 8pm.

Escape 24-7 24 Knutsford Blvd. Semi-outdoor bar in a great central location, popular with a youngish crowd and offering good – if sometimes ear-shattering – music, inexpensive drinks (a rarity in the vicinity) and basic light meals such as fish and chips.

Weekendz 80 Constant Spring Rd. Outdoor club-bar, set back from the road in gardens and attracting a mixed-age, friendly crowd. Weekends are busiest, with a music policy ranging from dancehall and reggae to R&B, hip-hop and house, and there are imaginative themed nights; current special is "Public Stonings", an open-mic night where patrons register displeasure with performers by pelting them with stale bread.

Peppers 31 Upper Waterloo Rd. Late-opening and permanently popular outdoor bar that pulls in post-work drinkers and then younger clubbers, who come for a snack or to dance to sound-system DJs.

Village Café Orchid Village Plaza, Barbican Rd. Open-air, split-level venue at the top of this small plaza that stages a range of popular and ever-changing events such as Thursday's Fashion Night and open mic on Tuesdays.

Clubs

Asylum 69 Knutsford Blvd ☎876/929-4386. Kingston's clubland stalwart, pumping out the reggae and dancehall for a lively, loyal crowd. There's a different music policy each night, but Wednesday nights, when more conscious reggae is played, are typically the best introduction; Thursday's dancehall night is more hardcore, with Stone Love on the decks.

Epiphany Too 73 Knutsford Blvd ☎876/754-9184. Indoor club next door to *Asylum*, attracting a mixed crowd; dancehall night on Friday is usually busy. Open Wed–Sat.

Jonkanoo Lounge in the *Hilton Kingston*, 77 Knutsford Blvd ☎876/926-5430. Relatively sedate, as you'd expect from a hotel-based venue, but a good and very upmarket (if rarely crowded) disco with occasional live bands.

Priscilla's 109 Constant Spring Rd. Pleasant and easy-going roof bar with views over the city; Sixties and Seventies Jamaican music on Friday and Saturday nights attracts the older media and professional set.

Quad 20–22 Trinidad Terrace, off Knutsford Blvd ☎754 7823. Kingston's newest club, this upmarket indoor venue has *Christopher's Jazz Café* on the ground floor, a comfortable a/c lounge with a weekday happy hour (5–8pm). Above, *Oxygen 2* is a flashy North American-style nightclub, playing commercial dance music for a youngish crowd. The top-floor *Voodoo Lounge* is aimed at the slightly more mature, with music from the 1960s to 1990s and a small outdoor deck. Cover charges vary from J$200 to J$600.

Waterfalls 9 Mona Plaza, Liguanea ☎876/977-0652. Indoor club that's best on a Friday, when Winston "Merritone" Black spins an excellent oldies selection.

Theatre and cinema

Kingston's **theatre** scene is limited but buoyant, with a small core of first-rate writers, directors and actors producing work of a generally high standard. Most of the plays are sprinkled with Jamaican patois, but you'll still get the gist. **Comedies** (particularly sexual romps and political satire) are popular, and the normally excellent annual **pantomime** – a musical with a message, totally different from the English variety – is a major event, running from December to April at the **Ward Theatre** (☎876/922-0453) and, later, the **Little Theatre** (☎876/925-6129).

Kingston's **cinemas** invariably screen recent mainstream offerings from the States. Tickets are around J$300, and there's usually a snack interval in the middle of the show. Most of the cinemas are uptown and include the **Palace Cineplex** (☎876/978-3522) at the Sovereign Centre, the **Island Cinemax** (☎876/920-7964) at the Island Life Centre on St Lucia Avenue and the plush **Carib Cinema** at Cross Roads (☎876/926-6106).

Shopping and galleries

A multitude of American-style malls means that **shopping** in Kingston is nothing if not convenient. The major players are the New Kingston Shopping Centre on Dominica Drive, the Sovereign Centre on Hope Road and the multitude of malls on Constant Spring Road.

Tours from Kingston

All of the places around Kingston can be explored on an **organized tour** from the city. Although you shouldn't need a tour to see Port Royal, which is easy to reach on the ferry and small, safe and relaxed enough to wander around alone, it's not a bad option for Spanish Town, which is a bit awkward to get to and – as a major industrial city – can feel rather unwelcoming. However, you'll get a fuller perspective on all the sights by engaging the services of a tour company, many of which offer individualized, small-scale jaunts. **Our Story Tours** (℡876/1-377 5693 or 876/1-699 4513, ⓔcrompton@hotmail. com) is brilliant for historical perspectives, offering custom-designed tours of Kingston, Spanish Town, Port Royal and horse racing at Caymanas Park as well as farther afield – Colbeck Castle, Mountain River Cave, Sligoville, St Thomas; costs start at US$75 per person including any entry fees; trips to Caymanas Park for racing start at $50 per person. Moving up a step, **My Tropic Escape** (℡876/925-6918, ⓦwww.mytropics-cape.com) offer brilliant specialized, personalized and very luxurious tours that really allow you to get a flavour of Jamaica. In the capital, the "Natural Mystic – Source of Jamaican Culture" trip takes in the National Gallery and Bob Marley's former home, the Trench Town Culture Yard in downtown Kingston; the "Roots Rock Reggae" tour includes a trip to a top studio where you get to record your own CD. The "Grounation" tour features a trip to a Rastafarian camp in the hills and a bathe in a waterfall; other excursions range from a Blue Mountain coffee experience to a day-trip between the waterfalls and black-sand beaches of St Mary by boat, as well as jaunts to Cockpit Country and to go whitewater rafting. Prices vary according to group size; get in touch for details. **Sun Venture** (℡876/960 6685 or 469-4444, ⓦwww.sunventuretours.com) is your best choice if heading into the Blue Mountains; trips include High Blue, with some light hiking, a waterfall swim and a trip to Cinchona botanical gardens, as well as the trek to Blue Mountain Peak. Again, prices vary according to group size.

For **books**, the bookshop at the University of the West Indies in Mona is far and away the superior choice for both novels and books on Jamaica; there are branches of the reliable Sangster's on Knutsford Boulevard and in the Sovereign Centre. Reggae fans are in shopping heaven in Kingston. There are **record shops** in most of the shopping malls, and downtown's Orange Street has several places stocking everything from dancehall to rocksteady and reggae classics.

For **souvenirs**, try the Crafts Market downtown, or the malls on Constant Spring Road, which hold excellent, reasonably priced craft shops such as Craft Cottage, in the Village Plaza mall, 24 Constant Spring Rd.

Listings

Airlines Air Canada, Norman Manley Airport (℡1-800/813-9237 or 876/924-8211); Air Jamaica, 72 Harbour St (℡876/922-4661), Norman Manley Airport (℡876/924-8331); American Airlines, 26 Trafalgar Rd (℡876/920-8887), Norman Manley Airport (℡1-800/433-7300 or 876/924-8248); British Airways, 25 Dominica Drive (℡876/929-9020), Norman Manley Airport (℡1-800/AIRWAYS or 876/924-8187); BWIA, 19 Dominica Drive (℡876/929-4231), Norman Manley Airport (℡876/924-8364 or 8377); Cayman Airways, 23 Dominica Drive (℡876/926-1762), Norman Manley Airport (℡1-800/G-CAYMAN or 876/924-8092); Cubana, 22 Trafalgar Rd (℡876/978-3406), Norman

Manley Airport (℡876/978-3410 or 3411).
Ambulances For a public ambulance, call ℡110 or St John's Ambulance on ℡926-7656; for a private one call ℡978-2327.
Banks and exchange The main banks have branches city-wide including: Bank of Nova Scotia at 2 Knutsford Blvd, 6 Oxford Rd and 125–127 Old Hope Rd; Citizen's Bank at the Sovereign Centre, 17 Dominica Drive and 15A Old Hope Rd; National Commercial Bank at 32 Trafalgar Rd, 133 Old Hope Rd and 37 Duke St. Most of those uptown have ATMs. However, you'll get better rates at FX Trader (Mon–Sat 9am–5pm), just off the north end of Knuts-ford Boulevard next to the John R Wong supermarket.

Embassies Almost all of the embassies and consulates are based in New Kingston. They include the British High Commission, 28 Trafalgar Rd ☎510 0700; the American Embassy, 2 Oxford Rd ☎929 4850; and the Canadian High Commission, 3 West Kings House Rd ☎926 1500.

Hospitals Kingston's public hospitals are the University Hospital at Mona (☎876/927-1620) and the Kingston Public Hospital downtown on North St (☎876/922-0210). There are a number of private hospitals in New Kingston, including Medical Associates, 18 Tangerine Place (☎876/926-1400) and Andrews Memorial, 27 Hope Rd (☎876/926-7401).

Internet Innovative Superstore in the Sovereign Centre on Hope Rd in Liguanea offers Internet access in air-conditioned surroundings for J$150 per half-hour; on the opposite side of Hope Rd, the Liguanea Post Office in the Post Office Mall offers free half-hour sessions.

Police The main station is at 79 Duke St (☎876/922-9321).

Post offices The most convenient post office is within the Post Office Mall, opposite the Sovereign Centre on Hope Rd in Liguanea (Mon–Fri 7am–7pm, Sat 9am–1pm).

Spectator sports International and major domestic soccer and cricket matches are played, respectively, at the National Stadium (☎929-4970) and Sabina Park (☎967-0322). Horse-racing can be seen at Caymanas Park (☎922-3338).

East of Kingston

The main route east out of Kingston, Windward Road, follows the coastline. It scythes through an industrial zone of oil tanks and a cement works that towers over the ruined defensive bastion of Fort Rock, now the **Rockfort Mineral Baths** (Tues–Sun 7am–5.30pm; US$100), where you can take a therapeutic soak in the mineral-rich waters; a two-seater Jacuzzi bath costs J$700, and a dip in the public pool J$150. Massages are also available, using all-natural essential oils. A mile or so further on, turning right at the roundabout takes you on to the **Palisadoes**, a narrow ten-mile spit of land that leads out past the international airport to the ancient city of **Port Royal**, from where it's a short hop to the tiny island of **Lime Cay**.

Port Royal

PORT ROYAL captures the early colonial spirit better than any other place in Jamaica. Originally a tiny island, this little fishing village is now joined to the mainland by the **Palisadoes**, a series of small cays that silted together over hundreds of years and, with a bit of human assistance, now form a roadway and a natural breakwater for Kingston's harbour which affords fantastic views of the city.

After wresting Jamaica from Spain in 1655, the British turned the island into a **battle station**, with five separate forts and a palisade at the north to defend against attackers coming over the cays. As added protection, they encouraged the buccaneers who had for decades been pillaging the area to sign up as **privateers** in the service of the king. Merchants took advantage of the city's great location to buy and sell slaves, export sugar and logwood, and import bricks and supplies for the growing population. The privateers wreaked havoc on the ships of Spain, and the fabulous profits of trade and plunder brought others to service the town's needs; brothels, taverns and gambling houses proliferated, and by the late seventeenth century, the population had swollen to six thousand.

The huge **earthquake** that struck the city on June 7, 1692, dumped sixty percent of Port Royal into the sea, killing two thousand people in seconds; within a week, a thousand more had died. Most of the remaining population fled for Kingston; almost all who remained later died or deserted when a massive fire swept the island in 1703.

Despite the destruction, Port Royal continued to serve as the country's **naval headquarters** until the advent of steamships saw the Royal Navy close its dockyard in 1905. Though Port Royal still retains its naval traditions as home to the JDF naval wing and the Jamaican coastguard, it's a far less exotic place today, a small and tidy fishing village, proud of its very low crime rate and happy to serve up some of the tastiest fresh **fish** you'll find anywhere in Jamaica.

Getting there

Since the ferry from downtown Kingston was scrapped in 2004, the only way to get to Port Royal is to **drive** (follow signs southeast from Kingston to the airport, and keep going past the turn-off) or take a **taxi** (around US$25). Local **buses** do run several times a day to Port Royal Square, but you'll have to board and disembark downtown, at the often dodgy Parade bus stand.

The Town

Look back to sea from anywhere in Port Royal and you'll get not only a great view of the harbour, but a clear idea of the area's strategic military importance and a glimpse of its former limits.

What remains of Port Royal is easily navigable on foot. Five minutes' walk from the ferry terminal, behind the old garrison wall, are the decaying red bricks of the **Old Naval Hospital**, the oldest prefabricated structure in the New World. The ramshackle structure now holds the offices of the National Heritage Trust.

Ten minutes' walk away and on the main Church Street, **St Peter's Church** (irregular opening hours) was built in 1726 and, apart from the roof, has survived largely intact. It's unremarkable apart from an intricately carved mahogany and cedar organ. More interesting are the ancient tombs in the small and rambling graveyard. A left turn out of the church leads down the main road to fascinating **Fort Charles** (daily 9am–5pm; J$100). Originally known as Fort Cromwell, Charles was the first of the five forts to be built here, though it never saw any action. In the courtyard, a **museum** provides a lucid history of Port Royal and its maritime history, and displays items – bottles, coins, cannonballs, shipwrights' tools, a rather nasty-looking urethral syringe and a set of ankle shackles used to restrain slaves – dredged up from the underwater city.

The raised platform on the other side of the small parade ground is known as **Nelson's Quarterdeck**; the great commander (still under 21 when he was stationed here) used to pace up and down here spoiling for a fight with the French. From the quarterdeck you can see how the land has built up around the fort as the sea has continued to deposit silt – over a foot per year – against the former island. The two structures that now stand between the fort and the water both date from the 1880s. The squat, rectangular **Giddy House** was an ammunition store, while the circular bunker beside it was the **Victoria and Albert Battery** – an emplacement for a nineteenth-century supergun that was fired only once, at a British soldier attempting to desert.

There are a couple of **beaches** around Port Royal, but both sea and sand are pretty dirty; if you want to **swim**, you're better off taking a boat out to Lime Cay (see below). The waters offshore of Port Royal offer excellent **scuba diving**, with plenty of wrecks to explore. The dive shop at *Morgan's Harbour Hotel* (see below) was temporarily closed at the time of writing, but if you're interested in diving, call to see if they've reopened. The hotel can also arrange deep-sea **fishing** and evening drop-line fishing.

Lime Cay

Just fifteen minutes by boat from Port Royal, **Lime Cay** is a tiny undeveloped island with fine white sand, clear and clean turquoise waters and easy snorkelling, perfect for a day on the beach. It was here that Ivanhoe ("Rhygin") Martin – the cop-killing gangster and folk-hero immortalized in the classic Jamaican movie *The Harder They Come* – met his demise in 1948, but this gorgeous swath of sand is better known today as the beach of choice for well-to-do Kingstonians. At the weekend, there's a sound system and food and drinks on sale; at other times, take your own picnic. Boats to Lime Key run regularly from Port Royal for around J$400 per person return (J$500 at weekends and public holidays); try *Y-Knot*, or *Morgan's Harbour Hotel* (see overleaf).

The grandest place to **stay** in Port Royal (and a five-minute drive from the airport) is the elegant and atmospheric *Morgan's Harbour Hotel* (☎876/967-8030 or 8040, ✉mharbour@kasnet.com; ❻), all dark wood and seafaring charm with a pool and an open-air bar; rooms have all mod cons, and there's a nice pool by the sea's edge. The only other option is the charming *Admiral's Inn* (☎876/353-4202 or 856-5636, ☎876/750-0391; ❷), in the housing development behind Church Street; ask anyone for Aunt Jean if you have difficulty finding it. The spick-and-span en-suite rooms have king, twin or double beds, a/c, fridge and microwave, and there's a pretty garden out back for chilling out. The owners offer Lime Key trips and airport pick-ups and drop-offs with advance notice.

Morgan's Harbour Hotel has a good and reasonably priced restaurant, *Sir Henry's*, which affords marvellous views of the city and cooks up excellent seafood and "international" dishes. Several cheaper **eateries** near the ferry pier serve Port Royal's best fish; the most popular is *Gloria's Rendezvous* at 5 Queen St, where you can enjoy a tasty plate of fish and bammy and watch the pelicans and frigate birds fishing just offshore. *Buccaneer's Roost* around the corner offers pretty much the same thing, but has a pleasant outdoor dining area upstairs. The best time to eat in Port Royal is Friday evening, when a sound system sets up in the main square and locals have stalls selling fried fish and bammy and other seafood delicacies; the curried crab and conch soup sold at the *Martin's Sweetness* cart is particularly delicious, and usually runs out around 7pm. For a drink, a meal or a dance on the deck at the weekend and during the week, head to *Y-Knot*, a lovely bar right by the sea's edge adjacent to *Morgan's Harbour*; you can also get a good seafood meal here.

Hellshire and around

Southwest of Kingston, a **causeway** (closed to outgoing traffic from Monday to Friday 6.30–9am, and to incoming traffic Monday to Friday 4.30–7pm) connects the city to the bland but booming dormitory town of **Portmore** in the neighbouring parish of St Catherine. Portmore lies at the eastern fringe of the **Hellshire Hills**, an arid and scrubby expanse of "makko" thorn bushes and towering cacti that shelters the closest beaches to the capital. Virtually the only inhabitants are the migrant birds, a few conies and a handful of Jamaican **iguanas**, once thought to be extinct. From the small fishing community of Port Henderson, the signposted road to the Hellshire beaches runs under the flanks of the hills. Follow the road to **Hellshire beach** (no set hours; free), separated from the less enjoyable Fort Clarence beach (Mon–Fri 10am–5pm, Sat & Sun 8am–6pm; J$100) by a barrier reef that makes the Hellshire water a lot calmer. Hellshire buzzes at the weekends, with booming sound systems and a party atmosphere. Most Jamaicans come here for the **fish restaurants** as much as the sea and sand, and Hellshire fried fish or lobster, best eaten with vinegary home-made pepper sauce and festival sweetbread, beats anything you'll find in town. Cookshops are lined along the top of the beach, and you'll be approached by operators as you drive in. By far the best option is *Prendy's on the Beach*, directly opposite you as you drive in; as well as fried fish, they do a fabulous steamed fish in pumpkin broth. Other operators worth a try are *Flo's* and *Seline's*, the latter with some wonderful wall art. At weekends, **watersports operators** offer jet-ski rental and snorkelling equipment, and there are horse rides for children, while you can get an excellent therapeutic massage or a spot of reflexology from the highly professional Tommy (aka Nathan Griffiths; ☎876/872 1839), who's usually to be found around *Prendy's*.

5.2

The Blue Mountains and Portland

Towering behind Kingston, the **Blue Mountains**, named after the mists that colour them from a distance, are an unbroken, undulating spine across Jamaica's easternmost parishes. At 28 miles, the mountains form one of the longest continuous ranges in the Caribbean, and their cool, fragrant woodlands, dotted with coffee plantations, offer some of the best **hiking** on the island. The most popular hike is to **Blue Mountain Peak** – at 7402ft, the highest point in Jamaica – but there are dozens of other trekking possibilities, such as the marked trails within the gorgeous Holywell Recreational Park. Otherwise, **coffee** is the chief interest is here, and you can visit several of the estates producing some of the most expensive – and delicious – beans on earth.

On the other side of the Blue Mountains (here officially known as the **John Crow** range), the northeastern parish of **Portland** is justifiably touted as one of the most beautiful parts of Jamaica, with jungle-smothered hillsides cascading down to a postcard-perfect Caribbean shoreline. If you stay in the parish capital of **Port Antonio**, you'll be close to the lovely **Reach** waterfalls and fabulous swimming at the magical **Blue Lagoon**. Inland, you can hike in pristine tropical **rainforest** or take a gentle rafting trip on the **Rio Grande**.

Getting around the mountains

You'll need a **car** to get the most out of the mountains. The principal access road, the B1, cuts straight through the slopes, connecting Kingston with Buff Bay on the north coast; a right fork at the small village of **The Cooperage** leads to Mavis Bank, the main access point for Blue Mountain Peak. Landslides are inevitable in the wet season and you can expect bumpy roads throughout the year. You'll need to be extra-attentive when behind the wheel here. Though the roads appear wide enough only for a single vehicle, delivery trucks loaded with precariously balanced crates frequently barrel up the slopes, sounding their presence with blasts on the horn. It's wise to turn off the radio here and listen for oncoming traffic, and also toot your horn at every corner.

Public transport will only take you as far as the main settlements – from Papine in northeast Kingston, **buses** (roughly J$80) go to Newcastle via Irish Town (with the occasional minibus managing to get up as far as Holywell) and to Mavis Bank via Gordon Town. Ask around in Papine Square the day before you plan to travel, and avoid starting out on a Sunday when services are greatly reduced. **Cycling** is an attractive option if you've got your own mountain bike (finding one to rent can be difficult). Several hotels run day-long biking expeditions, among them the *Mount Edge Guesthouse* (☎876/944-8151, ⊛www.jamaicaeu.com; US$40; see p.290). Blue Mountain Tours (☎876/974-7075 or 1-800/982-8238; US$89 including transfer, brunch, lunch and refreshments) will pick you up from Ocho Rios and Runaway Bay, drive you up into the mountains and let you freewheel sixteen miles or so down to Fishdone waterfall near Buff Bay.

THE BLUE MOUNTAINS

ACCOMMODATION

Forres Park	I
Gap Café	A
Holywell Cabins	C
Jah B's	H
Mount Edge Guesthouse	D
Starlight Chalet and Health Spa	B
Strawberry Hill Hotel	E
Whitfield Hall	F
Wildflower Lodge	G

Papine to Section

At Papine in northeast Kingston, the city slams to an abrupt halt as it meets the southern edge of the Mona Valley. From here, Gordon Town Road (B1) winds slowly upwards into the riverine hills. The road forks at the tiny village of **The Cooperage**; turning right brings you towards Mavis Bank and ultimately Blue Mountain Peak, while the left fork leads up a winding road for three miles to the friendly settlement of **IRISH TOWN**. Just over 3000 feet above sea level, it's a small farming community dominated by one magnificent **hotel**, *Strawberry Hill* (℡876/944-8400, ⓦ www.islandoutpost.com; ⓿). This is among the most attractive places to stay in all of Jamaica, with beautifully landscaped gardens, a glorious decked pool providing panoramic city vistas, a sauna and an Aveda spa. It's fashionable amongst a well-heeled Kingston set, and is a favourite venue for society weddings and photo shoots. Bob Marley was also brought here to convalesce after being shot in 1976. Perched on the hillsides, the twelve individually designed luxury cottages – from studios to two-bedroom villas with full kitchens – offer fabulous views.

Even if you don't stay here, **eating** at *Strawberry Hill* is a must. The setting on the Great House balcony overlooking Kingston is exceptional, and the menu offers an eminently successful combination of fresh local ingredients and sophisticated international-style cooking. The Sunday brunch (11.30am–4pm; book ahead) is an immensely popular local institution and very reasonably priced at US$40. If you're after a less formal meal in Irish Town, the *Crystal Cove*, at the roadside just south of the village, offers excellent Jamaican cooking (including jerk chicken at the weekends) and lots of good-natured chat.

From Craighton, the road continues through the tiny village of **Redlight**, named after the former brothels that kept the Irish coopers entertained. There are a few basic bars and a couple of hole-in-the-wall stores where you can buy provisions. Four thousand feet up and multiple switchback turns from here is **NEWCASTLE**, an old British military base still used by the JDF as a training facility. The main road

Hiking in the Blue Mountains

There's no charge to enter most parts of the Blue Mountains; however, visitors pay J$200 to enter the managed Holywell Recreational Park area and walk its trails. Park information is available from each of the Blue and John Crow national parks' three **ranger stations**, located at **Holywell**, **Portland Gap** and **Millbank**. Theoretically always open (though Holywell is the liveliest and by far the most accessible), these stations can provide advice on weather conditions and trail access, and ordnance survey maps are on display. None of the ranger stations has a phone, but you can make prior contact through the Jamaica Conservation and Development Trust in Kingston (℡876/920 8278–9, ⓦ www.jcdt.org).

No matter where you're walking in the Blue Mountains, it's almost always advisable to use a **guide**; given the changeable weather conditions and poor hiking maps (in a terrain with few obvious landmarks), it's very easy to get lost. Security can also be a problem for unaccompanied hikers, particularly on the Kingston side of the mountains. A guide will ensure your safety, clear overgrown paths and provide an informed commentary. You can arrange a guide through any of the accommodation options listed in this section, but if you just want a day tour or guided hike, contact Sun Venture, 30 Balmoral Ave, Kingston 10 (℡876/960-6685, ⓦ www.sunventuretours.com), which offers trips to the gorgeous Cinchona gardens, as well as various day-long mountain walks (US$60–80), and a hike up the peak trail, with a night at *Wildflower Lodge* in Penlyne Castle (US$130). Prices are based on groups of two to four people and transport is included. You can also arrange guided hikes through the Mount Edge and Forres Park guesthouses (see overleaf & p.291); the latter can take you up to the Peak, to a coffee plantation on the Peak's foothills, and on birding tours.

cuts across the **parade ground**, emblazoned with insignia of the various regiments stationed here during the past century or so. The views across the mountains and down to Kingston are dazzling, while behind you, immediately above Newcastle, **Catherine's Peak** (5060ft) marks the highest point in the parish of St Andrew.

For **accommodation**, just below Newcastle and clinging to the side of the valley, *Mount Edge* (☎876/944-8151, Ⓦwww.jamaicaeu.com; ❶–❸) is a laid-back counterculture-ish guesthouse-cum-restaurant. The simple rooms inside the main house and separate but small units just outside are perfect for backpackers, while the bar is a great place to chill out. Meals (cooked to order; call ahead for dinner) are also available, ranging from crab in coconut milk to crayfish. Otherwise, you can press on to the *Gap Café* (Mon–Thurs 10am–5pm, Fri–Sun 10am–6pm; ☎876/997-3032) at **Hardwar Gap**, 4200ft above sea level and some two miles up past Newcastle. Constructed in the 1930s, it's a pretty, flower-wreathed place offering yet more fabulous views. It serves American and Continental breakfasts, and excellent lunches and dinners (J$500–900). There's also a small room for rent (❺ including breakfast); it's nicely decorated and offers TV and a compact kitchen; breakfast is included in the rates.

Just beyond the café is the entrance to the 300-acre **Holywell Recreational Park**, affording a spectacular unbroken view over Kingston, Port Royal and Portmore when not bathed in mist. Easily accessible from the city, this "park within a park" is the busiest part of the mountains, latticed with enjoyable, well-maintained hiking trails. Just past the entrance is the ranger station, where you pay your entry fee (U$10); you can also pay an additional US$20 for guided walks along Holywell's well-maintained trails, best of which is the signposted Oatley Mountain jaunt (2 miles; 40min), an easy, varied circular hike through the tunnel-like jungle. If you want to **stay**, there are three cabins (1-bed and studio ❷, 2-bed ❸), which you'll need to book well in advance through the Jamaica Conservation and Development Trust, 95 Dumbarton Ave, Kingston 10 (☎876/920-8278 or 8282, Ⓦwwww.jcdt.org). These sleep four to six people, and the very basic facilities – foam-mattressed beds without bedding, indoor cooking range, fridge and cold shower – take second place to the marvellous setting, a Kingston view from your balcony and complete seclusion. You can also camp for J$100 per person. You may be able to buy local produce from vendors at the weekends, but it's safer to bring everything you'll need with you, or plan on taking all your meals at the *Gap Café*.

Section

Past Holywell, the scenery becomes more beguiling as you wind your way higher, with fantastic clear views over mountain gaps planted with neat rows of coffee. The next break in the trees comes at **SECTION**, a friendly little settlement that's home to several small-scale coffee farmers – it's a great place to both enquire about a local hiking guide and buy some coffee (a pound of beans should cost about J$500). The small shop can supply you with beers and snacks, and if you want cheap and very basic **accommodation** (around US$30), ask at the Dennis family's cavernous concrete house opposite. The road forks at Section; the left turn winds seventeen scenic miles down to the north coast at Buff Bay. Around nine miles from Buff Bay, (turn left just before the Silver Hill Bridge at a sign for the Avocat Primary School) is Fishdone waterfall, port of call for Blue Mountain Bike Ride tours and a great place for a swim, with a wide, clear pool and a fat gush of a cascade.

Back at Section, taking the right fork in the road brings you eastwards via several switchback turns towards **Silver Hill Gap**, a stunning spot some 5000ft above sea level and offering awesome views across coffee-planted peaks. The *Starlight Chalet and Health Spa* (☎876/969-3116 or 985-9380, Ⓦwww.starlightchalet.com; ❸), is an isolated and extremely appealing **hotel** on a gorgeous flower-filled bluff. The rooms are modern and comfortable, with balconies and private bathrooms, and there's a sauna and steam room (US$75 including full body massage). Try the good, inexpensive Jamaican meals served up in the **restaurant**, which, like the attached bar, is open to non-guests; call ahead if you plan to eat. There are a couple of bicycles available for guests to use, and several short trails surround the property, one leading down the valley to a swimmable river; guides are available. Staff also offer guided **hikes** to nearby destinations such as Cinchona botanical gardens (US$20), and a picnic at Clydesdale (US$10).

Mavis Bank and Blue Mountain Peak

Back down the hill at The Cooperage, the right-hand fork of the Gordon Town Road passes through the comparatively lively village of Gordon Town. Turn right at the bridge over the Gordon Town River, and a bumpy half-hour drive takes you to neatly arranged **MAVIS BANK**. Nestled in the Yallahs River valley, it's the last full-scale settlement on the route to Blue Mountain Peak. There's little to the tiny village itself; the main attraction is the government-owned **JABLUM coffee factory** (Mon–Fri 10am–2pm; US$8; tours by appointment on ℡876/977-8015) on the west side. The factory is Jamaica's main Blue Mountain coffee-processing plant, and an engaging tour takes you through the whole process.

The main reason to visit Mavis Bank, however, is hiking up to **Blue Mountain Peak**. As only the sturdiest of Land Rovers can take the abominable road up to Penlyne Castle, where the peak trail starts, it's best to make arrangements in advance; contact SunVenture (see box p.289), which will take care of everything, or call one of the lodges at the base of the trail (see below) and arrange for a pick-up, which costs J$1500 one-way per vehicle. You can **stay** at *Forres Park* (℡876/927-8275 or 5957, ⓦwww.forrespark.com; ❹), a delightful collection of self-contained wood cabins set around a large house that holds appealing, comfortable rooms with private bathrooms. **Meals** are available on request (non-guests are also welcome), as are guides for the peak trail, hikes in the Mavis Bank area and birding trips.

From Mavis Bank, it's a fabulous drive up to Abbey Green, just over five miles northeast. On the way up, you'll turn left through **HAGLEY GAP** – a one-street village where you can buy provisions and get a hot meal – after which you'll traverse one of the least road-like roads in Jamaica, with huge gullies carved through the clay by coursing water and a constant scree of small boulders in your path. At some 4500 feet above sea level, **ABBEY GREEN** is a completely different world, where wind whistles through eucalyptus trees and mists billow over the mountainside only to evaporate in the sun. You're unlikely to meet anyone save the odd coffee-grower or scallion farmer. The only buildings of note are the two hiking hostels; of these, *Whitfield Hall* (℡876/926-6612 or 927-0986; bunks ❶, cabin ❸) is the most atmospheric, set in an old stone planters' house, with a grand piano, a log fire, low ceilings and a prewar kitchen. You sleep in bunks or in a self-contained cottage. A few hundred yards down the road is the more comfortable *Wildflower Lodge* (℡876/929-5395; bunk ❶, private rooms ❷, cottage ❸), a modern two-storey house set in gorgeous flowered gardens. Bedding choices include private double rooms with bathrooms as well as bunk beds and a self-contained cottage; there's also a gift shop, cavernous kitchen and dining room. Another option, on the hillside just below *Wildflower*, is the simple, friendly guesthouse run by local Rasta Jah B (℡876/977-8161; ❶); meals are available. Whichever lodge you choose, it's a good idea to arrange to have a **hot meal** ready for your return. Any of the lodges will be able to provide a peak guide for around US$30.

The highest point on the island, **Blue Mountain Peak** (7402ft) seems daunting, but isn't the fearful climb you might imagine – though it's hardly a casual stroll, either. It's magnificent by day, thrilling by night. From Penlyne Castle, the climb to the peak is around eight miles and can take anything from three to six hours depending on your fitness level. Most people start at around 1am and catch sunrise at the peak (at around 5.15 to 6.15am, depending on the time of year). If you synchronize your walk with a full moon, you'll get beautiful natural floodlighting – but take a flashlight anyway. Regular signposts make the route easy to follow without the aid of a guide, but in this remote area it's sensible to go with someone who knows their way. Don't stray onto any of the tempting "short cuts" – it's illegal, you'll damage the sensitive environment and you'll almost certainly get lost.

The Portland Gap ranger station, around a third of the way up, offers the opportunity to refill your water bottles. From here it's another three and a half miles to the peak. At around 7000ft, the plateau at **Lazy Man's Peak** is where many hikers call it a day, but it's worth struggling on for another twenty minutes, as a far more spectacular panorama awaits you at the peak. As the sun burns off the mist, you can make out Cinchona and, on a good day, Buff Bay and Port Antonio's Navy Island to the north, and Kingston, Portmore and coastal St Thomas to the south.

Portland

North of the Blue Mountains, **PORTLAND** is rightfully touted as the most beautiful of Jamaica's parishes – a rain-drenched land of luscious foliage, sparkling rivers and pounding waterfalls. Small-scale **Port Antonio** is the largest settlement, a relaxed country town with some inexpensive accommodation options. To the east lie a string of fabulous **beaches** and swimming spots, including the lovely Blue Lagoon, while if you head into the interior, you can be poled down the **Rio Grande** on a bamboo raft or hike through the rainforest along the centuries-old trails of the Windward Maroons. An increasing number of visitors are venturing further east along the coast for the even more laid-back pleasures of **Long Bay** – with a growing young travellers' scene and the best surf in Jamaica – while the roadside vendors in **Boston Bay** offer some of Jamaica's best jerk pork and chicken in a lovely oceanside setting.

Some history

Portland's early economy was dependent on sugar, with large estates scattered around the parish. However, as the industry declined in the nineteenth century, the parish's fertile soil proved ideally suited for **bananas**. As the country's major banana port, Port Antonio boomed, ushering in an era of prosperity for the town and the region. Cabin space on the banana boats was sold to curious tourists, and the place became a favourite of glitterati such as William Randolph Hearst, J.P. Morgan, Bette Davis and Errol Flynn.

Celebrities still sequester themselves in Portland, and there's a burgeoning backpacker scene at Long Bay, but despite the revitalizing of areas such as Port Antonio's harbourfront, with its spanking new marina and waterside promenade, the area can't yet compete for the mainstream vacationer, losing out to the more accessible and better-marketed resorts of Montego Bay, Negril and Ocho Rios. Agriculture is still important, though, and the movie business periodically injects much-needed cash into the economy – films shot here include *Cocktail*, *The Mighty Quinn*, *Club Paradise* and *Lord of the Flies*. That said, the area is still a long way from the prosperity of its heyday – something which many find its greatest charm.

Port Antonio

A magnet for foreign visitors during the 1950s and 1960s, the quiet town of **PORT ANTONIO** feels more like an isolated backwater these days. But that may change following the recent redevelopment of the harbour; across the bay, the hotel and beaches at Navy Island (currently closed, but call the tourist board on ☎876/929-9200 for an update) are slated to receive some much-needed attention, too. Though Port Antonio has no dedicated attractions save the new waterside promenade, it's a friendly and beguiling place with a bustling central market and a couple of lively clubs.

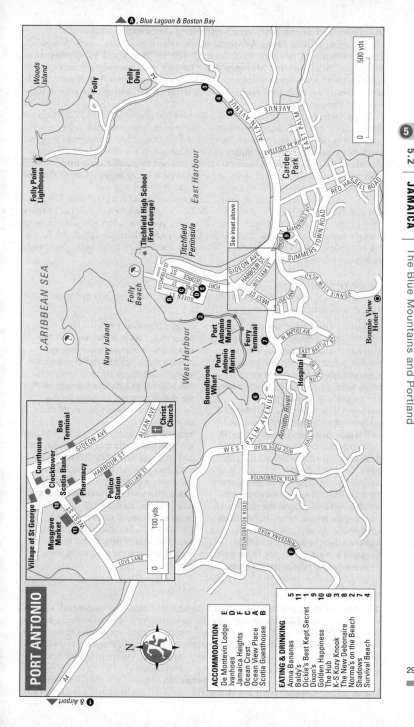

PORT ANTONIO

N

ACCOMMODATION
De Montevin Lodge   E
Ivanhoes   D
Jamaica Heights   F
Ocean Crest   C
Ocean View Place   A
Scotia Guesthouse   B

EATING & DRINKING
Anna Bananas   5
Baldy's   11
Dickie's Best Kept Secret   1
Dixon's   9
Golden Happiness   10
The Hub   3
K-S Kozy Knook   6
The New Debonaire   8
Norma's on the Beach   2
Shadows   7
Survival Beach   4

▲ Ⓐ, Blue Lagoon & Boston Bay

Woods Island

Folly Point Lighthouse

Folly

Folly Oval

CARIBBEAN SEA

Navy Island

West Harbour

East Harbour

Folly Beach

Titchfield Peninsula

Titchfield High School (Fort George)

Boundbrook Wharf

Port Antonio Marina

Ferry Terminal

See inset above

Carder Park

Bonnie View Hotel

Hospital

Annotto River

GIDEON AVE

ALLAN AVENUE

EVELEIGH PK RD

EAST PALM

RED HASSELL ROAD

SUMMERS TOWN ROAD

MANNINGS AVE

BONNIE VIEW ROAD

WEST ST

LOVE LANE

W. BAPTIST AVE

EAST BAPTIST AVE

NUTTALL RD

WEST PALM AVENUE

RICE PIECE ROAD

HALL'S AVE

BOUNDBROOK ROAD

SWINGBANK ROAD

Ⓕ

TITCHFIELD ST
KING ST
QUEEN ST
GEORGE ST
FORT ST
HARBOUR ST
WILLIAM ST

Village of St George

Courthouse

Bus Terminal

Clocktower

Scotia Bank

Pharmacy

Police Station

Christ Church

Musgrave Market

GIDEON AVE
ALLAN AVE
HARBOUR ST
WILLIAM ST
WEST ST
LOVE LANE

0   100 yds

0   500 yds

Ⓘ & Airport

Arrival, information and getting around

Flights arrive at **Ken Jones Aerodrome**, six miles west of town in St Margaret's Bay, from where a taxi into town costs US$10–15. **Buses** and **minibuses** from Kingston (3hr 30min) and Montego Bay (5hr) pull in at the main terminus by the seafront on Gideon Avenue, or by the town's central square on West Street (which also serves as the main **taxi rank**). If you're **driving**, the A4 highway runs straight into and through the town.

To get your bearings, head up to the *Bonnie View Hotel* (signposted off Harbour Street at Port Antonio's eastern outskirts), overlooking the entire town and providing great views of the twin harbours, Navy Island and the shimmering reefs. You can **walk** between the handful of sights in Port Antonio, while most places of interest outside town (and all of the beaches) can be reached by **public transport**. Shared taxis run along the main road as far as Long Bay; you'll pay around J$40 to Dragon Bay/Frenchman's Cove, J$60 to Boston Bay and J$80 to Long Bay.

Since you'll want to get out of town a lot, **renting a car** is a good idea. Try Eastern Car Rentals, 16 West St (☎876/993-3624), or Derron's, east of town at Drapers (☎876/993-7111); both companies will deliver to your hotel. If you're just planning a single day-trip it can work out cheaper to use a taxi. Alternatively, call the cheerful Mr Palmer (☎876/993-3468 or 707-4276), the Port Antonio taxi cooperative (☎876/993-2684) or JUTA (☎876/993-2684).

Accommodation

Port Antonio has plenty of good **accommodation**, and prices here are some of the lowest in all Jamaica.

De Montevin Lodge 21 Fort George St, Titchfield ☎876/993-2604, ⓔdemontevin@cwjamaica.com. Good value in a lovely old gingerbread house, a relic from colonial days. Clean, cool and simple rooms with cable TV, balconies and shared or private bathrooms, and great food from the restaurant downstairs. ❷, en-suite ❸

Ivanhoes 9 Queen St, Titchfield ☎876/993-3043, ☎876/993-4931. Scrupulously clean and tidy no-frills guesthouse opposite the ruins of the old *Titchfield Hotel*. Each of the appealing, reasonably priced rooms has a private bathroom and a fan; meals are available. ❶–❷

Jamaica Heights Spring Bank Rd (off Boundbrook Rd) ☎876/993-3305 or 2156, ⓦwww.jasresort.com. This mellow, very friendly little place is easily the best option in town. The lofty location affords grand views of the twin harbours, and the spacious rooms have clean, simple decor, wood floors, four-poster beds and big balconies. There's a pool, a trail to a river and waterfall, and lovely meals

available. Brilliant value. ❹

Ocean Crest 7 Queen St, Titchfield ☎876/993-4024, ⓔlydiaj@cwjamaica.com. Friendly place offering a slightly higher standard of accommodation than its neighbours. The clean, homey units have TV, ceiling fan and private bathroom; the three newest ones afford good views over the town. There's a shared kitchen and lounge, and meals are available. ❷

Ocean View Place Chilly Lane ☎876/715-3473 or 457-1342. A five-minute drive from the main road (take the second right past the Folly turn-off) and offering nice views over the sea, this Jamaican-owned place is great value. With locally made wooden fittings, all rooms have double beds, fans, cable TV and use of a kitchen. ❷

Scotia Guesthouse 15 Queen St, Titchfield ☎876/993-2681. Very basic accommodations in an atmospheric wooden house. Most of the fan-cooled rooms share bathrooms; en-suite units cost a bit more. ❶

The Town

The obvious starting-point for a stroll around Port Antonio is its **central square**, with a landmark **clocktower** opposite the red-brick, two-storey Georgian **courthouse**, built in 1895 and fronted by an elegant fretworked verandah. On the other side of the road is the **Village of St George** shopping mall, a striking if somewhat bizarre melange of European architectural styles that houses a rather desultory parade of stores (including Don J's Internet café at shop 10).

Due north from here, the **Titchfield peninsula** juts out into the Caribbean Sea, bisecting Port Antonio's **twin harbours**. The tip of the peninsula once held the British **Fort George**, whose ancient cannons and crumbling walls today form part of Titchfield High School. The short wander up from town takes you past the **De Montevin Lodge** hotel – high-Victorian gingerbread architecture at its best, but there's little else to see now that the peninsula's pretty beach has been fenced-off as part of the new **Port Antonio Marina** (open daily, but no set hours; free; ☎876/715-6044, ⓦwww.themarinaportantonio.com). Opened in 2002 to great fanfare, the development features a wide waterside promenade, state-of-the art marina facilities, landscaped gardens, a pool, a restaurant and shops (including a gift shop, an ice-cream parlour and a well-stocked chandlery). Although a few small cruise ships have called and there are usually a few yacht-owners milling around, there's a rather deserted air to the place due to the fact that its huge gates completely cut it off from the rest of the town. The complex also includes the town's only strip of sand, **Folly Beach**, which has been tidied up, planted with palms and remains a lovely place to swim, with clear waters and great views of Navy Island across the narrow channel of water. On the other side of the marina, next to the spanking new boatyard, **Boundbrook Wharf** is still the loading point for bananas being shipped to Europe and the United States. This is the place that inspired the banana boat song *Day O*, and the hulking freighter, which arrives on Friday afternoons and leaves the following day, is an impressive sight. The marina is also the departure point for Lady G'Diver, the only scuba operator in the area (☎876/715-5957 or 995-0246, ⓔladygdiver@cwjamaica.com); they offer dives, certification, and rent scuba equipment.

Back in the centre of town on West Street, which shoots off from the clocktower, there's a welcome dose of local bustle in the form of **Musgrave Market**, crammed with stalls selling fresh produce, fish, meat, clothes and a handful of crafts and souvenirs.

Eating

Port Antonio isn't a gourmand's paradise, but you can get good, inexpensive Jamaican **meals** at a handful of places around town. Patties are available from several outlets along West Street, and there's a branch of *Juicy Beef*, which sells lobster and chicken patties, on William Street (parallel to Harbour Street at the eastern end of town). You can get great baked goods at *CC's Bakery*, 25 West St.

Anna Bananas Allan Ave. A seaside restaurant overlooking the bay, thus one of the better choices in the area. Popular with tourists and locals alike, the food is reliable Jamaican, from curry lobster to brown-stew chicken; breakfast, lunch and dinner are served daily.

Dickie's Best Kept Secret On the A4 just west of town ☎876/1-809-6276 (mobile). On a knoll as you round the far bend of Port Antonio's west harbour, this simple wooden house scaled down the cliffside is easily missed, but is one of the best choices around. The moderately priced four-course dinners are fabulous (order the morning before you want to eat); choices include ackee on toast, garlic lobster and steamed fish. You can also drop by for breakfast, lunch or afternoon tea.

Dixon's Bridge St. Take-away lunch joint offering delicious vegetarian food (salads, curried tofu stew, stir-fried veg, etc) at rock-bottom prices. There's an airy upstairs room if you want to eat in.

Golden Happiness Harbour St, at West. Cavernous diner serving reliable Chinese food with a Jamaican twist; good for a quick and inexpensive lunch.

The Hub 2 West Palm Ave. Just west of the main drag near the old train station, this is a popular place for affordable Jamaican food: rundown, liver or callaloo for breakfast, and stew beef, stew peas, cow foot, or baked chicken for lunch and dinner.

The New Debonair 22 West St. Hole-in-the wall eatery serving inexpensive local fare daily from 7am to midnight. Jamaican breakfasts, and lunches and dinners such as roast pork and beef, curry goat and chicken, and escovitched, steamed or sweet-and-sour fish.

Norma's on the Beach Port Antonio Marina. The latest venture from one of Jamaica's most celebrated chefs, offering casual dining (lunch and dinner) at tables by the waterside. The mid-priced menu includes starters such as crab-backs or tomato mozzarella salad, while the sophisticated main courses range from teriyaki ribeye steak to grilled chicken glazed with june plum preserve.

Shadows 40 West St. Excellent omelettes for breakfast and good Jamaican and Chinese meals, served at the pleasant outdoor gazebo or in the smarter, less atmospheric a/c restaurant.

Survival Beach Allan Ave. Inexpensive vegetarian lunches and dinners and fresh seafood in a friendly, easy-going setting with outdoor tables on a little strip of sand by the water.

Rafting and hiking in the Rio Grande valley

Portland's interior – the **Rio Grande valley** – is a fantastically lush and partially impenetrable hinterland of tropical rainforest, rivers and waterfalls. The **Rio Grande** – one of Jamaica's major rivers – pours down from the John Crow Mountains through the deep and beautiful valley of real virgin forest, with none of the soil erosion and deforestation found on the south side of the Blue Mountains. The paucity of good roads means it's not a heavily visited area, but it does offer some marvellous **hiking**, as well as the chance to slide down the waters of the Rio Grande aboard a bamboo raft. Once just an easy way to transport bananas to the loading wharf in Port Antonio, **rafting** has been Portland's most popular attraction ever since Errol Flynn began organizing rafting races here for his friends in the 1950s. From the put-in point at **Berridale**, six miles southwest of Port Antonio, rafts meander down the river on a three-hour journey through some outstanding scenery before terminating at the Rafters' Rest complex at St Margaret's Bay. The raft captain stands at the front and poles the craft downstream, stopping periodically to let you swim or buy snacks from vendors positioned along the route. **Tickets** are sold at the put-in spot by Rio Grande Attractions Ltd (℡876/995-778; US$48 per raft), or by hotels and tour groups in Port Antonio. Because it's a one-way trip, **transport** can be a problem. If you're driving, you can leave your car at Berridale and have an insured driver take it down to Rafters' Rest for around US$10. A taxi to Berridale and back to Port Antonio from Rafters' Rest costs around US$10–15 each way.

If you fancy seeing the valley on foot, call into the **Valley Hikes** office, upstairs at 26 Harbour St (℡876/993-3881, ⓔvalleyhikes@cwjamaica.com). An eco-friendly, non-profit group employing valley citizens as guides, Valley offer a comprehensive package of walks and excursions, from a gentle two-hour stroll to McKenzie Falls to a strenuous climb up to the White River. Excursions in the lower Rio Grande valley cost US$10 per hour per person plus transportation, but there are plenty of more adventurous (and costlier) options such as an overnight trip to Nanny Town (US$150), as well as horse-riding and rafting.

Drinking and nightlife

The few places to head for a **drink** in town are often very quiet. The best and busiest option is *Baldy's*, a breezy rooftop bar above the Town Talk Plaza, opposite the courthouse, which usually has music pouring from the speakers and plenty of friendly chat – it's an excellent spot for watching the shenanigans at the market below. Just east of town, there are a couple of low-key rum bars right by the sea on Allan Avenue – try the friendly *K-S Kozy Knook*, with a large circular bar and plenty of dominoes action; a similar scene is found in town at *The Hub* at 2 West Palm Ave, or at *Shadows,* 40 West St.

The fluorescent-streamer-bedecked UV palace of the *Roof Club* at 11 West St (nightly; J$150) is a Portland **clubbing** institution and one of the best, most laid-back, friendly places in Jamaica for a night on the tiles. It's busiest for Ladies' Night on Thursdays, when women get in free; DJs play the latest dancehall, R&B and hip-hop alongside a dollop of more conscious tunes. On Friday nights, you might also want to check out Crazy Friday's, a popular dancehall session held in the garage building at the corner of East Palm Avenue and Summerstown Road.

East of Port Antonio

The coastline east of Port Antonio is a tropical fairytale landscape of jungle-smothered hills rolling down to fantastic beaches, from upmarket **Frenchman's Cove** and **Dragon Bay** to laid-back **Winnifred** and **Long Bay**. It also boasts

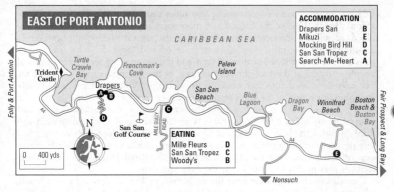

the sublime **Blue Lagoon**, made famous by the eponymous 1980 movie starring Brooke Shields and Christopher Atkins. Further east, the smoking, sizzling jerk stands at Boston Bay are an essential stopoff en route to **Reach Falls**, a lavish natural cataract in the hills pounding down into a deep pool. A series of smart hotels vie for business with a handful of less expensive guesthouses, the latter mostly slung along the palm-fringed, wind-whipped beach at funky, laid-back Long Bay.

East to Winnifred

Just past Port Antonio's eastern outskirts, Allan Avenue swings past the **Folly Peninsula**, site of the sorry ruin of what was, briefly, one of the grandest houses in Jamaica. Built by an American banker in 1902, it stood for less than thirty years – a victim of shoddy construction. The remaining Grecian-style pillars retain an evocative look, and the ruins have appeared in many music videos and films. Around a few more bends is the fantasy **Trident Castle**. Built by European baroness Zigi Fami, owner of the *Jamaica Palace* hotel, the turreted white edifice is now the property of the *Trident Hotel* and is occasionally rented out for private functions.

Three miles east of Port Antonio is **Frenchman's Cove**. The formerly sumptuous hotel villas here have deteriorated, but the grounds are still beautifully maintained, and the **beach** (daily 9am–5pm; J$200), though small, is one of the most splendid in Jamaica. The curve of fine sand is enclosed by verdant hills, and a freshwater river, its bottom lined by white beach sand, runs straight into the sea. Food and drink are usually available from a tent set up on the sand (Tues–Sun), and you can rent loungers or take a boat tour to nearby beaches or the Blue Lagoon (US$10 per person). Just opposite the gates to the beach, local man Delroy keeps a couple of lovely horses and offers rides (US$25 per hour) along local beaches and into the interior. To find him, ask at the gates or call ☎876/383 1588. The signposted entrance to Frenchman's Cove is opposite the turn-off to the eighteen-hole San San Golf Course (☎876/993-7645).

The next option for a swim is privately owned San San beach, open to tourists for around US$5 and somewhat neglected; you're far better off pressing on to the **Blue Lagoon**. Enclosed by greenery-smothered cliffs, the remarkably turquoise lagoon is a result of several underwater streams running down from the mountains. The whole effect is incredibly picturesque, and it's a peaceful place to swim, made more unusual by the sensation of chilly spring water at the surface mixing with warm seawater below. You can swim for free from a pebbly "beach" or from the fenced-off restaurant complex, which usually charges a fee but was closed at the time of writing.

There's more marvellous swimming four miles east at supremely laid-back **Winnifred Beach**. One of the biggest and most appealing beaches on this side of the island, its wide, golden crescent of sand is justly popular with locals; however at the time of writing plans were afoot to fence off and "upgrade" what was one of Jamaica's last undeveloped swathes of sand, and impose an entry fee. Protests by local people outraged at the thought of losing one of the few places they can swim for free have been vociferous, but whatever the outcome, Winnifred remains a marvellous place for a day by the sea. The small reef is perfect for snorkelling (bring your own gear) and protects the bay from the waves, and at the eastern end a small mineral spring offers a freshwater rinse. Winnifred has good, unobtrusive food and drink facilities; the best is *Painter and Cynthia's*, tucked into the western corner and serving up delicious platefuls of ackee and saltfish, chicken and fresh fish; however new official restaurants were planned as part of the slated redevelopment, so these facilities may not be in existence by the time you visit.

The coast road swings away from the sea parallel to Winnifred; to get to the beach, take the road opposite the *Jamaica Crest Resort* and follow it for half a mile or so. You can park and walk down to the sand where the tarmac ends; if it hasn't been raining recently, you should be able to drive right down onto the beach.

Practicalities

There are several upmarket **accommodation** options on the coast east of Port Antonio. Green-conscious *Mocking Bird Hill* (℡876/993-7267, ⓦwww.hotelmockingbirdhill.com; ⑤) boasts a lovely airy setting on a peaceful bluff above San San, with great Blue Mountain views, too. The comfortable rooms have balconies, and there's a pool and a good restaurant. Italian-style *San San Tropez* (℡876/993-7213, ⓦwww.sansantropez.com; ④) is another possibility. Its large rooms have a/c and cable TV, and there's a pool and renowned restaurant on site. A less expensive option is *Drapers San*, right on the road at Drapers (℡876/993-7118, ⓦwww.go-jam.com; ③), a funky, friendly, Italian-run guesthouse with an eclectic collection of rooms, some with kitchen, some with shared bathroom; all have fans and mosquito nets. Breakfast is included, and the owner is a great source of local information. Next door, *Search-Me-Heart* (℡876/353-9217, ⓦwww.searchmeheart.com; ③ including breakfast) is a pretty Italian-Jamaican guesthouse offering three airy en-suite bedrooms with fan; guests can use the kitchen and laundry room, and there's a large verandah and well-kept garden. Within walking distance of the beach (also accessible from the main road just past the Winnifred turn-off – keep an eye out for the sign on the left), *Mikuzi* (℡876/978-4859 or 329-8589, ⓦwww.mikuzi.com; rooms ②, cottage ③), set in pretty gardens and painted in fetching shades of orange and purple, consists of a couple of compact, nicely decorated rooms with fan and kitchenette, and a self-contained cottage (sleeping up to four) with screened windows, kitchen, living room and a verandah.

There are a few **places to eat** this side of Port Antonio. For a formal meal, head to *Mille Fleurs* at *Mocking Bird Hill Hotel*, where the terrace restaurant offers imaginative and expensive dishes based on Jamaican staples. The Italian chefs at *San San Tropez* serve up bruschetta, smoked marlin salad, fresh pasta, fantastic thin-crust pizzas and fish and meat dishes, as well as lovely home-made ice-cream. As you'd expect, there's a good wine list. A less expensive option is *Woody's*, a friendly family-run café on the coast road at Drapers offering great burgers (including veggie burgers); the lovely Jamaican staples such as fish with pumpkin rice, pepperpot soup, jerk pork or chicken and curries have to be ordered a day in advance.

Boston to Long Bay

Though blessed with a perfectly good public beach, **BOSTON BAY**, further east along the A4, is better known for its collection of **jerk stands**. Jerking of meat originated in this part of the country, and the pork and chicken sold here is still reckoned to be the best in Jamaica. You'll pay around J$380 for a pound of chicken, and J$300 for a pound of pork; both are best eaten with a dollop of ketchup and jerk sauce and accompanied by roast yam, breadfruit or a hunk of fresh hardough bread and, of course, an ice-cold Red Stripe.

Still owned by the widow of Errol Flynn, the rolling pasturelands past Boston Bay give way to **LONG BAY**, home to a relaxed tourist scene. With its wide swath of surf-pounded honey sand, Long Bay attracts a smattering of European backpacker types, some of whom have settled here and opened guesthouses. Two simple, friendly beach bars, *Cool Runnings* and *Chill Out,* cater to the demand for entertainment. It's a far cry from the developed resorts on the north coast: tourists are outnumbered on the beach by local people, and there's a lot of ganja-wreathed hanging out. There isn't much to the village, which has grown up piecemeal on either side of the main road. The north end of the beach is best for **surfing**; the locals should be able to help you find a board, and they'll also know who can take you out **fishing**. **Swimming** is excellent here, too, but watch out for a dangerous undertow and rip tides; never swim out further than you can stand.

When you're able to drag yourself away from the beach, head a few miles further east to a signposted turn-off that swings inland from the coast road to spectacular **Reach Falls**, where the Drivers River cascades thirty feet into a wide, green pool. You can stand right underneath the falls for an invigorating water massage. From the base of the falls, there's a lovely walk upriver through the rainforest. At the time of writing, Reach Falls were officially closed pending redevelopment (though visitors were still able to swim here – the charge is negotiable, but it's well worth doing).

Practicalities

There's a wealth of budget **accommodation** in Long Bay. Of the many inexpensive options on the inland side of the road, try *Likkle Paradise* (☎876/913-7702; ❷), which has spotless rooms with fans and private bathrooms; guests can use the kitchen. *Fishermen's Park* (☎876/913-7482; ❶–❷) is a rambling family home offering atmospheric local-style rooms with cold-water bathrooms, fans and mosquito nets. Over on the beach, *Yahimba* is two African-style huts (☎876/913-7067, ✉coolrunnings@irieweb.net; ❸) adjacent to the *Cool Runnings* bar, with mosquito nets, verandahs overlooking the water and private bathrooms with hot water. More upmarket options include *Seascape* (☎876/913-7762, ✆www.jamaica-beachvillas.com; ❸), with two comfortable three-bed villas; rooms can be rented separately, and rates include breakfast. Twenty minutes' drive east of town, past the small fishing community of Manchioneal, there's another lovely and unique accommodation option. Run by knowledgeable and chilled-out Dutch emigrée Free-I, *Zion Country Beach Cabins* (☎876/993-0435, ✆www.zioncountry.com; ❷ including breakfast) are ranged up a landscaped hillside and offer simple accommodation with gorgeous views over the bay. There's a private beach, and Free-I offers great tours in Portland and the rest of the island.

For **food** and **drink**, the appealing *Cool Runnings* offers tasty meals (fish in coconut, chicken in satay sauce, calamari fritters, pizza). There's usually good **music**, and occasionally parties (including a monthly full-moon beach party with a bonfire and conscious reggae) or sound-system jams. Just east with a slightly roomier thatch-roofed patio, *Chill Out* offers good meals (burgers, pizzas and salads as well as good Jamaican food, including curry goat at weekends); the excellent Jolly Boys mento band play on Sundays (4–7pm) and there are sound-system dances once a month. Either of these is a great place for a drink, and there are also several friendly **rum bars** on the main road.

5.3

Ocho Rios and around

With its high-rise blocks, buzzing jet skis and duty-free stores, the classic resort town of **Ocho Rios** typifies the commercial feel of Jamaica's north coast. Home to a wealth of slick attractions – from the famous **Dunn's River Falls** to **Dolphin Cove**, as well as a couple of lovely **botanical gardens** – the town is geared to the needs of cruise shippers and beach vacationers. East of town, the quiet coastal villages of **Oracabessa** and **Port Maria** boast a funky beach club and Noel Coward's former home, while west of town hotels line the shore at the resort-oriented coastal sprawls of **Runaway Bay** and **Discovery Bay**. The lush St Ann hills hold one of Jamaica's major draws, the **Bob Marley Mausoleum** at the singer's birthplace, Nine Mile.

Ocho Rios

The first town in Jamaica to be developed specifically as a resort, **OCHO RIOS** (usually just called "Ochi") abounds with neon-fronted duty-free stores, fast-food chains, bars, clubs and visitor-oriented restaurants. Local culture takes a back seat to the tourist trappings here, so this isn't the place to get an authentic flavour of Jamaica. It's not the best choice amongst the island's "big three" resorts for the classic Caribbean beach holiday, either – the town's strip of hotel-lined sand just can't compete with the beaches of Negril and Montego Bay, and the club and bar scenes are less vibrant. Nonetheless, the nightlife is improving, and Ochi compensates for its deficiencies with a certain neon energy.

Organized tours and activities

In terms of quality and choice, the Ocho Rios roster of **organized tours** is second only to Montego Bay – you'll see fliers advertising them at practically every tourist-oriented spot in town. The tours market here has been pretty much sewn up by the highly professional Chukka Cove Adventure Tours (℡876/972-2506, ⊛www.chukkacove.com); choices include **tubing** along the White River from Spanish Bridge; **jeep safaris** (5hr; US$70), which include lunch and a stop at Dunn's River Falls; **mountain-bike rides** (3hr 30 min; US$50), which are 95 percent downhill and include a spot of snorkelling; **quad-bike safaris** (2hr; US$60); and **horseriding** trips (3hr; US$60). The newest innovation from Chukka is the brilliant **canopy tour** (2hr 30 min; US$65) at Cranbrook Flower Forest, where nine horizontal traverses, ranging from 105 to 660ft long, have been strung up between platforms in the treetops. Once harnessed up, you soar along via a system of pulleys and carabiners. Costs for all trips cover return transportation from Ochi and refreshments. Hooves (℡876/972-0905) offers **horseback trail rides** around the Seville Great House at St Ann's Bay that include swimming your horse (2hr 30min; US$60); they also offer inland hacks (2hr "Bush Doctor" ride, US$55), and will do private rides on request; add US$5 if you want transport to and from Ocho Rios. Ochi isn't far from the **Blue Mountains**, and Blue Mountain Tours (℡876/974-7075 or toll-free on 1-800/982-8238) will transport you up into the mountains for a spectacular sixteen-mile downhill bike ride to a waterfall near Buff Bay on the north coast (US$89 including transfer, brunch, lunch and refreshments).

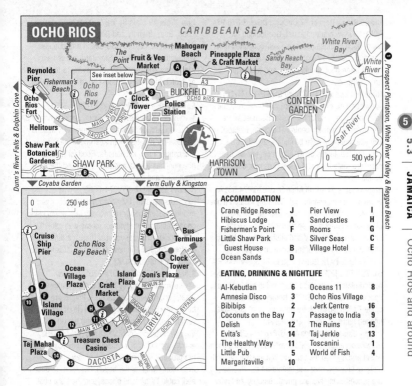

OCHO RIOS

CARIBBEAN SEA

White River Bay

The Point
Fruit & Veg Market
Mahogany Beach
Pineapple Plaza & Craft Market
Sandy Reach Bay
White River

Reynolds Pier
Fisherman's Beach
Ocho Rios Bay
See inset below
A3
BUCKFIELD
OCHO RIOS BYPASS
CONTENT GARDEN

Ocho Rios Fort

Helitours

Clock Tower
Police Station

Salt River

Shaw Park Botanical Gardens
SHAW PARK
HARRISON TOWN

N

0   500 yds

Dunn's River Falls & Dolphin Cove ◄
◄ Coyaba Garden   ▼ Fern Gully & Kingston

0   250 yds

Cruise Ship Pier
Ocho Rios Bay Beach
Bus Terminus
EVELYN STREET
JAMES AVENUE
Clock Tower
Ocean Village Plaza
Craft Market
Island Plaza
Soni's Plaza
NEWIN ST
Island Village
Taj Mahal Plaza
Treasure Chest Casino
MAIN STREET
GRAHAM STREET
RENNIE RD
MILFORD STREET
OCHO RIOS BYPASS
DACOSTA
MILFORD ROAD
DRIVE

Prospect Plantation, White River Valley & Reggae Beach ►

ACCOMMODATION

Crane Ridge Resort	J	Pier View	I
Hibiscus Lodge	A	Sandcastles	H
Fishermen's Point	F	Rooms	G
Little Shaw Park		Silver Seas	C
Guest House	B	Village Hotel	E
Ocean Sands	D		

EATING, DRINKING & NIGHTLIFE

Al-Kebutlan	6	Oceans 11	8
Amnesia Disco	3	Ocho Rios Village	
Bibibips	2	Jerk Centre	16
Coconuts on the Bay	7	Passage to India	9
Delish	12	The Ruins	15
Evita's	14	Taj Jerkie	13
The Healthy Way	11	Toscanini	1
Little Pub	5	World of Fish	4
Margaritaville	10		

Arrival and information

All **buses** pull in at the terminus behind Main Street. It's within walking distance of most hotels, but taxi drivers usually hang around plying for fares. If you're **driving** in from Montego Bay, the coast road forks as you enter town; left takes you onto the one-way section of Main Street, where the majority of hotels are located, while right takes you along DaCosta Drive, which connects with the bypass (the route to hotels east of town) and with Milford Road, which leads to Fern Gully and, eventually, Kingston. If you drive in from the east, you'll enter town via the bypass; there are numerous signposted exits onto Main Street. Domestic flights touch down at **Boscobel Aerodrome**, a thirty-minute drive east of town; a cab to town should cost about US$30. **Cruise ships** dock at the pier on the west end of the town's main bay; taxi drivers line up to meet ships in the hope of getting some business from the few passengers who haven't already arranged day tours. A ride into town should cost around US$10.

Accommodation

There are numerous **lodging places** in Ochi, including many all-inclusive resorts. There are also a huge amount of villas to rent in and around town, which can work out to be surprisingly inexpensive if you're travelling in a group, and allow you the freedom to cook for yourself. One of the most appealing is *Goldenfoot* (℡650/941-1760, ⊛www.agoldenfootvilla.com; ❻), a gorgeous two-bedroom place overlooking the sea twenty minutes' drive east of Ochi. With stylish decor, a pool, lovely gardens and all mod cons (including a great outdoor shower area), it makes a great escape from the hustle and bustle. For details of other villas, contact the Jamaica Association of Villas and Apartments (℡868/974-2508, ⊛www.villasinjamaica.com).

Crane Ridge Resort 17 DaCosta Drive ☎876/974 8051, ⑩www.craneridge.net. Overlooking the town, each of these agreeable self-contained units has a/c, satellite TV, phone, balcony and kitchenette. A large pool, tennis courts and restaurant/bar are on site. ❹

Hibiscus Lodge 83-87 Main St ☎876/974-2676, ⑥mdoswald@cwjamaica.com. Set back from the road in beautiful gardens, this is the most attractive hotel in the town centre. The clean, pleasant cliffside rooms all have balconies, and there's a pool, hot tub, tennis court, sun deck, sea access, excellent restaurant and a bar. Rates include breakfast. ❺

Fishermen's Point off Main St ☎876/974 5317, ⑩www.fishermanspoint.net. Centrally located highrise on the road to the cruise ship pier, offering clean and comfortable apartments with private balconies. a/c, cable TV and kitchenettes. Friendly staff, Jamaican restaurant and a small pool. ❹

Little Shaw Park Guest House 21 Shaw Park Rd ☎876/974-2177, ⑤974-8997. Easy-going, familyowned place overlooking town, set in gardens with space for camping (US$25). Homey rooms with cable TV, fan; some share bathrooms, others have kitchen facilities. Meals are available. ❸

Ocean Sands 14 James Ave ☎876/974-2605, ⑩www.oceansandsresorts.com. Hidden behind Main Street and right on the sea, this is a lovely base, with a slip of beach, a pool and restaurant/bar. Rooms are spotless, with a/c and private balcony, and rates include breakfast. Excellent value. ❸

Pier View 19 Main St ☎876/974-2607, ⑤974-1384. Busy, friendly and laid-back apartment development, next to UDC beach and popular with younger travellers. Standard rooms have fan, fridge and cable TV; you pay more for a/c and kitchen. All have access to the pool and sun deck. ❸–❺

Sandcastles 120 Main St ☎876/974-5626, ⑩www.sandcastlesochorios.com. Backing onto the beach (guests get free access), these airy studios and one- or two-bedroom apartments each have a/c, cable TV and kitchenette. Good for families (the pool has a slide and kids' area) and there's a restaurant and bar. ❹

Rooms Main St ☎876/974-6632, ⑩www.roomsresorts.com. Overlooking the beach, this middle-market, newly renovated place offers clean, comfortable resort-style a/c rooms with cable TV and wireless Internet access. There's a fitness centre, pool, bar and restaurant, and rates include Continental breakfast. ❹

Silver Seas Main St ☎974 2755, ⑩www.silverseas.com. Slightly faded but atmospheric old hotel, popular with backpackers. Rooms are simple but comfortable, and all have sea views and private verandahs. Large garden, pool and bar on site. ❸

Village Hotel 54-56 Main St ☎876/974-3193, ⑩www.geocities.com/villagehotel. Friendly, familyrun property slap in the centre of town and a five-minute walk to the beach. Rooms have queen bed, cable TV, a/c and phone, and there's a pool, restaurant and bar. ❹

△ Dolphins at Ocho Rios

The Town

Home to most of the town's hotels, bars, banks, shopping plazas and restaurants, as well as the bustling craft market, Ochi's permanently busy **Main Street** holds little interest for sightseeing. You're likely to spend your days lazing on the **beach** – variously known as UDC, Mallards, Turtle and Ocho Rios Bay (daily 8.30am–6pm, last entry at 4.30pm; J$50). Tucked under the tower blocks and accessible from the western end of Main Street near the *Pier View* and *Sandcastles* hotels, and from Island Village via the back of the cruise ship pier, the white-sand beach is wide, fairly attractive and well maintained, with showers, changing rooms, bars and plenty of activity. Patches of sea grass and occasional pollution mean that this isn't one of the north coast's most appealing places to swim, however, particularly when it's overshadowed by the massive bulk of docked cruise ships across the bay.

These days, the main centre of activity in Ochi is the **Island Village** complex at the far west end of Main Street (no set hours; free; ⊛ www.islandvillageja.com). An unashamed and not unattractive attempt to capture cruise-shippers' dollars, this is a shopping complex-cum-theme park of wooden, fretworked buildings painted in faded ice-cream colours housing shops, restaurants and attractions, all arranged around a grassy central plaza with fountains, a Bob Marley statue and a stage where free entertainment – dance, poetry, drumming and the like – are put on at various points throughout the day. The entrance hall contains the **Cove Theatre** (☎ 876/875-8353; J$350), a digital cinema screening the latest US releases, and **Reggae Explosion** (daily 9am–5pm; US$7), an expertly executed exhibition dedicated to Jamaican music and culture. It's an illuminating collection of photographs, music and video clips of all of the island's musical heroes, from Prince Buster to Bounty Killer, as well as African reggae stars such as Alpha Blondy. Presented chronologically, the displays cover mento, ska, roots reggae, dub and dancehall – the latter section has a dancefloor on which you can follow footprints of various popular dance styles. Understandably, the section devoted to Bob Marley is the largest, with plenty of rare photos and a re-creation of Lee Perry's infamous Black Ark studios. There's also a rotating display of paintings by Jamaica's pre-eminent artists, on loan from the National Gallery in Kingston. Island Village's other main attraction is its pretty stretch of **beach**, a heavily manicured curve of white sand where you can indulge in all manner of watersports or get a massage, hair braid or fancy nail job as well as take a swim.

The only other stretch of sand in Ochi that's not the private domain of an all-inclusive hotel is **Mahogany Beach**, set at the eastern stretch of Main Street as it climbs uphill (turn off just past the *Hibiscus Lodge* hotel). This compact wedge of

Watersports

Although there isn't that much to see underwater at Ocho Rios's main beach – you'll find much richer pickings east of the harbour or at the reef at the bottom of Dunn's River (see below), the sand is lined with **watersports concessions**. Prices are set and displayed on boards at the main entrance, and offerings range from jet-skiing to banana boat rides, water-skiing and parasailing. You can also take a glass-bottom boat ride; many go along the coast towards Dunn's River Falls. For **scuba diving**, try Resort Divers at 2 Island Plaza (☎ 876/974-5338), which also offers deep-sea fishing from US$300 per half-day.

Many private boats offer **pleasure cruises**. Day-trips go to Dunn's River for snorkelling and climbing the falls, with an open bar and lunch or snacks; sunset cruises include drinks only. Most operators offer dinner cruises, too. Visitors usually book via the agents who stake out the beaches. One of the better operators is Red Stripe (☎ 876/974-2446), which runs a day-cruise to Dunn's River (Tues, Wed & Sat 12.30–3.30pm; US$59, including an open bar and entry into the falls) and a sunset party cruise (Thurs–Sat 5–7.30pm; US$39) with drinks and jerked snacks.

beach with calm, clean waters and good snorkelling is a low-key place for a swim. Management of the bar changes frequently; entry was free at the time of writing, but a small charge is sometimes levied.

Dolphin Cove and Dunn's River Falls

Heading west of town along Main Street, a boardwalk allows easy pedestrian access to Ochi's two biggest, and best, organized attractions. The first, some ten minutes' walk from the centre, is **Dolphin Cove** (daily 8.30am–5.30pm; ☎876/974-5335, Ⓦwww.dolphincovejamaica.com). The main draw at the landscaped, theme-park-style complex is the chance to interact with the trained bottlenose dolphins kept in a fenced-off section of the bay. There are three choices of "interactive programme": the "Touch Encounter" (US$39), in which you stand in knee-high water and get to stroke a dolphin and have your photo taken (US$14); the "Encounter Swim" (US$89), which gets you into the water to kiss and play with the animals; and the "Swim with Dolphins" (US$155), in which you spend a bit more time in the water, and get a dorsal pull and a foot push. While it's all very organized, nothing much can take away from the delight of being so close to the dolphins. Elsewhere in the complex, there's a pool containing sharks and rays; a nature trail with stops for petting macaws, touching starfish and snakes; a small beach (you can hire snorkel equipment and canoes); a restaurant; and a great gift shop. The entrance fee of US$15 allows you to stay and explore all day; lunch costs US$12. Dolphin programmes start daily at 9.30am, 11.30am, 1.30pm and 3.30pm; it's advisable to book ahead, and you must arrive half an hour before the programme starts. There are changing facilities and lockers on site, but most people arrive in their bathing suits.

A couple of minutes' walk further west, **Dunn's River Falls** (daily 8am–5pm, last ticket 4pm; US$10, plus a tip for the guide) is Jamaica's best-loved waterfall and a staple of tour brochures. Masked from the road by restaurants, craft shops and car parks, the wide and magnificent 600ft waterfall cascades over rocks down to a pretty tree-fringed, white-sand beach that's far cleaner than the one in town. There's a lively reef within swimming distance, and snorkel gear is available to rent. With water running so fast you can hear it from the road below, the falls more than live up to their reputation, despite the concrete and commerciality. The main activity is climbing up the cascade, a wet but exhilarating and easily navigable hour-long clamber (last climb starts at 4pm). The step-like rocks are regularly scraped to remove slippery algae, and visitors form a hand-holding chain led by one of the very experienced guides. Wear a **bathing suit** – you're showered with cool, clear water all the way up. Most people also rent "sticky feet" shoes to help grip on the stones. There's a restaurant and bar, craft and hair-braiding shacks and full changing facilities at the beach and at the top of the falls.

Shaw Park and Coyaba

From the main roundabout at Ochi's western outskirts, a twenty-minute walk starting along Milford Road takes you to two of Ochi's better-known pastoral attractions, both on the ill-maintained Shaw Park Road (turn right from Milford Road 100ft from the junction at the Shaw Park signpost). Some 550ft above sea level, **Shaw Park Botanical Gardens** (daily 8am–5pm; US$10) afford stunning aerial views of town and do a cracking trade with cruise ship passengers. The former grounds of a long-gone hotel, the 25-acre gardens are resplendent with unusual flowers, plants and trees – including a huge banyan – set amidst grassy lawns; there's even a near-perpendicular (but non-swimmable) waterfall. You can walk unaccompanied, but the knowledgeable gardeners-cum-guides will initiate you into the wonders of tropical horticulture. There's an on-site bar, and crafts and jewellery on sale at the gift shop.

About five minutes further up Shaw Park Road, **Coyaba River Garden and Museum** (daily 8am–5pm; US$5) is another favourite tour bus stop-off, a meditative and restful miniature hothouse of lush, well-watered flowerbeds. Wooden

△ Rafting on the Martha Brae River

walkways allow easy viewing of the tropical foliage, and the flowerbeds are bisected by streams teeming with fish and turtles, with glass panels providing views of the underwater goings-on. Housed in an elegant cut-stone building, the museum has a limited but thoughtful collection of exhibits spanning Jamaican history; special weight is given to St Ann's own Marcus Garvey and Bob Marley. The new attraction here is a gorgeous **waterfall** (US$5 extra) which you can splash about in and climb à la Dunn's River. Surrounded by foliage, its steep, fast cascade has been made accessible via wooden steps and platforms. "Sticky feet" shoes are available for rent.

Prospect Plantation, Reggae Beach and White River Valley

A ten-minute drive east of town, **Prospect Plantation** (1hr 25min guided tours Mon–Sat 10.30am, 2pm & 3pm, Sun 11am, 1.30pm & 3pm; US$32; ☎876/974-2058) is a slick managed attraction designed to introduce the more sedentary visitor to the delights of tropical farming. You sit atop an open trailer and trundle through sugar cane patches and groves of coconut palm, pimento, lime, ackee, breadfruit, mahoe and soursop trees, stopping to sample fruits, admire the bay views and potter around a stone church. A far better way to tour the plantation is on **horseback** (2hr; US$58). You'll need to book all rides one day in advance, and the horses rest on Sundays.

A few minutes' drive east of Prospect along the A3 is **Reggae Beach** (Mon–Fri 9am–5pm, Sat & Sun 9am–6pm; US$5). A pretty curve of coarse yellow sand, it's cleaner than the strip in town, though there's also some sea grass. Pluses include brightly painted showers and changing rooms, rope swings from the trees, plenty of shade and a good snack shop – and, as it's a little way out of town, it's usually very quiet.

The only other thing to do hereabouts is to head inland along the road that cuts into the hills from the main highway just past Prospect Plantation, and makes its very potholed way to the well-signposted **White River Valley** (daily 8am–6pm; ☎876/917-3373 or 972-2506, ⊛www.whiterivervalleyja.com). Some 400 acres of verdant flatlands and fruit orchards ranged around the White River itself, and a regular haunt of cruise ship tour buses, it's a beautiful spot, with a rather swanky "village" of brightly painted wooden buildings housing a restaurant, bar and gift shop. A boardwalk leads from here to a swimming spot on the White River, where you can take a swim in the cool, clear waters (US$8) or picnic on the banks. You can also choose to partake of a number of activities such as hiking (US$28), horseriding (US$50) and kayaking (US$40), but by far the best choice is **tubing** down the river (US$40), passing the gorgeous Spanish Bridge en route.

Eating

As many of Ochi's **restaurants** aim to please the foreign palate, Italian, Indian, Chinese and American fare is available in addition to the Jamaican staples, and there are a couple of excellent vegetarian options. There are several patty shops around town, including a branch of *Juicy Beef* by the clocktower and *Tastees* a little further up Main Street, as well as numerous **fast-food** joints. For Jamaican food on the hop, head to one of the smoking jerk stands that set up around the clocktower in the evenings.

Al-Kebutlan 1 James Ave. Rasta-oriented indoor diner offering good Ital-style breakfasts (including plantain, cornmeal and oat porridges) and various vegetarian delights for lunch and dinner, as well as the full array of natural juices.

Bibibips 93 Main St. Set back from the road, with tables overlooking the sea, this place serves excellent fish dishes as well as coconut curry chicken, seafood crepes, vegetable stir-fry, Rasta pasta and all the usual Jamaican favourites. Service is excel-

lent and prices are fair.

Coconuts on the Bay Off Main St. On the road to the cruise ship pier, this open-air restaurant offers an appealing, mid-priced and wide-ranging menu from spring rolls and stuffed jalapeño peppers to salads, wraps, fajitas and Jamaican staples. Good service.

Delish 16 Main St. Funky café with a good on-site bakery, serving natural juices and tasty and good-value Chinese and Jamaican lunches.

Evita's Eden Bower Rd ☎876/974-2333. The best-advertised pasta on the north coast, served on a gingerbread verandah overlooking the bay. Huge choice of starters, salads and soups; main courses include pasta – even "Lasagne Rastafari" with ackee, callaloo and tomatoes – and seafood. Expensive, but worth the splurge.

The Healthy Way Ocean Village Plaza. Energetic and efficient vegetarian take-away, with a couple of tables, offering veggie/tofu burgers and patties, soups, Ital juices, fruit salad, cakes and a different main dish each day.

Little Pub 59 Main St ☎876/974-2324. American and Jamaican breakfast and lunch in a roadside café with a juice bar on site. Dinner – from filet mignon or surf 'n' turf to lobster thermidor – is dished up in the "entertainment area". Prices range from moderate to expensive.

Ocho Rios Village Jerk Centre just before the roundabout on DaCosta Drive. Renowned for the consistently good and sensibly priced jerk pork, chicken, fish and barbecued spare ribs as well as the piped dancehall, which draws in an evening crowd of drinkers.

Passage to India Soni's Plaza, 50 Main St ☎876/795-3182. Rooftop restaurant serving excellent Indian cuisine. The menu is pretty comprehensive; breads are particularly good, as are the lassi yogurt drinks and desserts.

The Ruins 17 DaCosta Drive. The main restaurant, built around a waterfall, is a pretty and upmarket spot for a Chinese meal in the evenings; next door, an annexe serves inexpensive lunches.

Taj Jerkie Taj Mahal Plaza, Main St. Prettily decorated tourist-oriented diner offering a sanitized but professional jerk experience.

Toscanini Harmony Hall ☎876/975-4785. A ten-minute drive east of the centre under the eaves of pretty Harmony Hall, and easily Ochi's best restaurant. Service is great, and the relatively expensive menu features all the Italian classics. Vegetarians are well served, and the puddings are sublime. Closed Mon.

World of Fish 3 James Ave. Popular place for a late supper; fish is served any which way, with bammy, festival or rice and peas. The outdoor seats are perfectly placed for soaking up the James Avenue shenanigans.

Nightlife and entertainment

Given Ocho Rios's dedication to the cruise ship trade, its nightlife can seem a bit limited, mostly revolving around whatever's going on at *Margaritaville* in Island Village – though the *Treasure Chest* **casino** on Main Street is usually lively and is good for an inexpensive drink even if you don't want to hit the slot machines; it's open 24 hours a day. If you want to get away from the all-pervasive Americana, the pretty outdoor bar at *Toscanini* restaurant (see "Eating," above) offers a more sophisticated ambience, with some great wines available and a Friday happy hour (6.30–8.30pm). At completely the other end of the scale, there are rum bars and a couple of decidedly locals' clubs along James Avenue – it's best to go with a Jamaican companion, as the area can be a bit risky after dark. Finally, the stellar **Ocho Rios Jazz Festival** brings Ochi to life every June, with concerts at venues around town – for more information call the tourist board or the Jazz Hotline (☎876/927-3544) or visit ✪www.ochoriosjazz.com.

Amnesia Disco above the Mutual Security building, 70 Main St. The nightclub of choice for most locals, with an indoor, air-conditioned dance floor and an outdoor bar area. Wednesday is a fairly quiet "Warm-Up" Night; Thursday is the busy Ladies' Night, when women get in free; Friday sees an after-work jam with drinks promotions; on Saturdays there's a party night, with dancehall, R&B, hip-hop and dance; and there's an old hits party on Sundays. Entrance is J$200.

Bibibips 93 Main St. Laid-back but upscale clifftop bar popular with tourists and locals alike. One of the best places in town for a few drinks; occasional live music.

Coconuts on the Bay off Main St. On the road to the cruise ship pier, the gazebo bar of this friendly restaurant is a great, hassle-free spot for a drink, with great cocktails and welcome sea breezes.

Margaritaville Island Village, Main St ✪www.margaritaville.com. This neon-bedecked US-style place is Ochi's busiest nightspot, right on the beach and offering plenty of wet-and-wild action on the waterslide and in the pool, as well as good cocktails and dancing. The roster of theme nights, some all-inclusive, changes regularly (pick up flyers around town), and big-name DJs usually play at weekends.

Oceans 11 off Main St. Overlooking the Island Village beach on the road to the cruise ship pier, this professional and slick spot is a nice place for a drink, with karaoke on Tuesdays and Latin night on Thursdays.

Ocho Rios Village Jerk Centre DaCosta Drive. Popular with an older Jamaican crowd, and good for a few rums or a game of dominoes in the open air.

Shopping

Shopping is big business in Ocho Rios. The town's three **craft markets** (daily 7am–7pm) have enticed many a hapless soul to leave Jamaica laden with "Yeh mon it irie" T-shirts and the like. Among the dross you'll find really nice T-shirts and sculptures. The main market is to the right of Ocean Village Plaza, while the smaller Pineapple Place and Coconut Grove markets are further east towards *Hibiscus Lodge* and the all-inclusive hotels. **Island Village** has the usual roster of T-shirt and craft emporia as well as the self-explanatory Hemp Heaven, a well-stocked branch of Book Land and an outlet selling the wonderfully aromatic Starfish aromatherapy products. Don't miss the gorgeous **art gallery** and shop at Harmony Hall (Tues–Sun 10am–6pm), ten minutes' drive out of Ochi on the way to Tower Isle. Set in a beautifully restored great house, it features works by renowned contemporary Jamaican artists and a variety of crafts and books.

East of Ocho Rios

As the clamour of Ocho Rios recedes, the A3 coast road switchbacks through the countryside towards the slow, close-knit communities of **Oracabessa** and **Port Maria**, where tourism is only just starting to take hold. Though ostensibly quiet, the area has long been a favourite haunt of the rich and famous. Noel Coward and Ian Fleming (creator of James Bond) both lived here in the Fifties and Sixties, and their old homes, **Firefly** and **Goldeneye**, are still standing, with Firefly now a prime tourist site and Goldeneye the centrepiece of a luxury villa complex.

Oracabessa

Lit in the afternoons by an apricot light that must have inspired its Spanish name *Oracabeza*, or "Golden Head", **ORACABESSA**, some sixteen miles east of Ocho Rios, is a friendly one-street town with a covered produce market (main days Thurs & Fri) and a few shops and bars. A centre for the export of **bananas** until the early 1900s, Oracabessa became something of a ghost town when the wharves around the small natural harbour closed in 1969, taking with them the rum bars, gambling houses and most of the workers. The town snoozed quietly until the mid-1990s, when the **Island Outpost** corporation (owned by Chris Blackwell, the former boss of Island Records and the producer of Bob Marley's most well-known albums) bought seventy acres of prime coastal land and opened up the village's main draw, the **James Bond Beach Club** (Tues–Sun 9am–6pm; US$5), signposted just off Main Street along Old Wharf Road. Jamaica's most stylish beach, the pretty but tiny strip of white sand offers brightly painted changing rooms, a watersports centre and a bar and restaurant. The expansive lawns are a regular venue for large-scale **concerts**.

East of the turn-off for James Bond Beach, Oracabessa merges into the residential community of **Race Course**. This is the site of **Goldeneye**, the unassuming white-walled bungalow in which Ian Fleming wrote almost all of the James Bond novels. Now an exclusive hotel, it's off-limits to all but the very well-heeled.

Port Maria and Firefly

The diminutive capital of St Mary, **PORT MARIA**, nestled around a crescent bay some five miles east of Oracabessa, is one of Jamaica's most picturesque towns – but once you've taken in the bay view and strolled the few shopping streets, there's little to keep you here. Most people turn off the main road before getting into town and travel the precipitous route up the hill to **Firefly** (daily 8.30am–5.30pm; US$10), the Jamaican home of Noel Coward and his partner Graham Payn from 1956 to Coward's death in 1973. The house remains much as Coward left it, with the table laid as it was on the day the Queen Mother came to lunch in 1965. Coward died here and is buried on the property. It's worth going to Firefly for the view alone. The panorama takes in Port Maria bay and Cabarita Island to the east, with the peaks of the Blue Mountains poking through the clouds, while to the west lies **Galina**

Point, where a **lighthouse** overlooks the northernmost tip of Jamaica – you may even see Cuba on a clear day.

West of Ocho Rios

The coast road west of Ocho Rios swings past a couple of engaging attractions. Some eight miles west of town is the former site of **Seville**, Jamaica's first Spanish settlement, now an overgrown wasteland dotted with the crumbling remains of once-impressive buildings. The best way to see it is on horseback; see box p.300 for details of the rides offered here by Hooves. Across the road is **Seville Great House and Heritage Park** (daily 9am–5pm; J$150; ☎876/650-1500), one of the few sites on the island focusing on the lives, customs and culture of Taínos and Africans (as well as the Spanish and British), with a great collection of artefacts arranged in chronological order, and intelligent interpretive information; call ahead for a free tour (1hr). There's more equine action at **Chukka Cove**, the most prestigious equestrian facility and polo ground in Jamaica – matches are open to observers most weekends; call or check the website for schedules (☎876/972-2506, ⓦwww.chukkacove.com). The immaculate stables also offer fabulous three-hour beach rides as part of their roster of excursions (see box p.300). A mile or so past Chukka Cove, a tiny paved road cuts inland towards the signposted **Cranbrook Flower Forest** (daily 9am–5pm; US$10; ☎876/770-8071), an exquisitely landscaped, 130-acre nature park with several grassy lawns, a fishing pond where you can catch your lunch and have it cooked for you, and a swift-running river with plenty of swimming spots; it's also the home of the pulleys and ropes of Chukka Adventures' fabulous new Canopy Tour (see p.300). It's the perfect place for a **picnic**: bring your own or buy it on site.

Runaway Bay and Discovery Bay

Halfway between Ocho Rios and Falmouth, the neighbouring mini-resorts of **RUNAWAY BAY** and **DISCOVERY BAY** bask in isolated indolence. Dominated by lavish all-inclusives, neither demands much of your time unless you've checked into one of the hotels. Runaway is the more developed of the two, though beyond the hotel fences and Italianate marble lobbies, life jogs along at a slow pace. There's little obvious activity in town; for swimming, sugary-sanded **Cardiff Hall public beach**, opposite the Texaco petrol station, is popular with locals. Midway between the two bays are the **Green Grotto Caves** (daily 9am–5pm; US$20), a system of expansive limestone caves that's been made accessible to the public. The guides inject plenty of humour into their tours, but nothing really justifies the entrance fee.

Even more pacific than its neighbour, with fewer hotels, Discovery Bay is more a coastal clutch of shops, snack bars and houses than a town. But it does have the fantastic **Puerto Seco beach** (daily 8am–5pm; J$200 Mon–Fri, J$250 Sat & Sun), which, despite gleaming sand and crystal-clear water, is relatively deserted on weekdays.

Marley's mausoleum and the St Ann interior

Both the B3 from Runaway Bay and the inland road from Discovery Bay lead towards **ALEXANDRIA**, a tiny hamlet where you turn left for the only tourist attraction in the St Ann interior, Bob Marley's Mausoleum, at his former home of **NINE MILE**. Though the red-earthed pastures and sweeping hills and gullies of the Dry Harbour mountains are stunning, there are few specific points of interest. You'll need to have your own transport or charter a taxi to get here; a round-trip in a taxi from Runaway or Discovery bays should cost US$80–90, and from Ochi around US$100. From Alexandria, the narrow road off the B3 to the **Bob Marley Centre and Mausoleum** (daily 9am–6.30pm; US$12 ☎876/995-1763, ⓦwww. bobmarleyfoundation.com) winds through the hills past **Alva** and **Ballintoy**. You

Bob Marley – king of reggae

Born February 6, 1945, **Robert Nesta Marley** was the progeny of an affair between seventeen-year-old Cedella Malcolm and 51-year-old Anglo-Jamaican soldier Captain Norval Marley, who was stationed in the Dry Harbour mountains. Marley's early years in the country surrounded by a doting extended family and by the rituals and traditions of rural life had a profound effect on his development. He clung to the African side of his heritage and revelled in the rich cultural life of downtown Kingston, where he spent most of his later life.

Fusing African drumming traditions with Jamaican rhythms and American rock guitar, Marley's music became a symbol of unity and social change worldwide. Between 1961 and 1981, his output was prolific. Following their first recording *Judge Not* on Leslie Kong's Beverley's label, his band, The Wailers (Marley, Bunny Livingstone and Peter Tosh), went on to record for some of the best producers in the business. In 1963, the huge hit *Simmer Down* meshed perfectly with the post-independence frustration felt by young Jamaicans, and the momentum of success began in earnest. International recognition came when the Wailers signed to the Island label – owned by Anglo-Jamaican entrepreneur Chris Blackwell. The first Island release was *Catch a Fire* in early 1973, and the eleven albums that followed all became instant classics. After the departure from the group of Peter and Bunny in 1974, Marley continued to tour the world with a new band – Bob Marley and the Wailers.

After being injured in a 1976 **assassination** attempt, Marley left Jamaica to recover and record in Britain and the States. Two years later, he returned to perform at the historic **One Love Peace Concert**. Marley ended his performance by enticing political arch-enemies Michael Manley and Edward Seaga on stage to join hands in a show of unity. But Marley's call for unity and freedom was not restricted to Jamaica; one of his greatest triumphs was performing the protest anthem *Zimbabwe* at the independence celebrations of the former Rhodesia.

In the midst of a rigorous 1980 tour, Marley was diagnosed as suffering from cancer; he died a year later in Miami, honoured by his country with the Order of Merit. The Bob Marley Foundation, administered by his wife, Rita, continues to sponsor the development of new Jamaican artists, and many of the Marley children have forged their own musical careers – look out for the marvellous **Junior Gong**. In the hearts of Jamaicans, though, the master's voice can never be equalled.

know you're in Nine Mile when you see red-gold-and-green flags flying high above a bamboo-fenced compound to the side of the main road. If driving, you'll be directed into the compound car park. There's also a vegetarian restaurant and a small gift shop selling CDs and high-quality Marley memorabilia. Led by a Rasta guide, the tour includes the wooden shack that Marley lived in between the ages of six and thirteen, an outdoor barbecue where Marley cooked up Ital feasts, and the Rasta-coloured "meditation stone", immortalized in the song *Talkin' Blues*. The **mausoleum**, a concrete building painted with Rasta colours and depictions of black angels, encases the marble slab that holds Marley's remains. If you don't fancy making your way to Nine Mile independently, you can join one of the jeep **tours** run by Chukka Cove (see box p.300; US$55).

If you want to linger in Nine Mile, you can stay in the relatively basic **hotel** opposite the complex, run by extended members of the Marley family; rooms cost around US$50 a night and you can have meals cooked for you or use the kitchen yourself. The place comes alive every **February 6**, when Marley's birthday is celebrated with a sound-system jam and live show.

5.4

Western Jamaica

Home to two of the island's busiest resorts, western Jamaica is firmly on the tourist track. **Montego Bay**, once Jamaica's tourist capital, is losing out a bit to the hedonistic pleasures of **Negril** at the extreme western tip. In many ways, though, MoBay, as it's usually called, still delivers. Sitting pretty in a sweeping natural harbour and hemmed in by a dazzling labyrinth of protected offshore reefs, it remains the *grand dame* of Jamaican resorts and is particularly lively during its world-renowned summer **reggae festival**. Sybaritic Negril, boasting the longest continuous stretch of white sand in Jamaica and a front-row sunset seat, has a geographical remoteness that lends it a uniquely insouciant ambience. "Discovered" by wealthy hippies in the 1970s, it is still immensely popular with those who favour fast living and corporeal indulgence, and is easily the best place outside Kingston for **live reggae** and **nightclubs**. There are plenty of natural attractions around Negril, too, including the pleasant river walk at **Mayfield Falls** and the blue hole at **Roaring River**.

Montego Bay

Jamaica's second largest city, **MONTEGO BAY** nestles between the gently sloping Bogue, Kempshot and Salem hills, and extends some ten miles from the haunts of the suburban rich in Reading at its western edge to the plush villa developments and resort hotels of Ironshore and Rose Hall to the east. It's made up of two distinct parts: the main tourist strip **Gloucester Avenue** (rechristened by the marketing men as the "Hip Strip"), and the city proper, universally referred to as "**downtown**" – a split so sharp that most tourists never venture further than the dividing roundabout.

The "Hip Strip" wouldn't exist were it not for Montego Bay's prize asset: a dazzling bay with miles of **coral reef** (now designated a marine park) and some beautiful **beaches**. Much of the coastline has been snapped up by the hotels, but there are three main public beaches along the length of Gloucester Avenue, all with showers, changing rooms, snack outlets and watersports concessions and a minimal entrance fee.

Arrival, information and getting around

More than eighty percent of visitors to Jamaica arrive at **Donald Sangster International Airport** (®www.sangster-airport.com.jm), three miles east of the town centre and a mile from Gloucester Avenue. It has a 24-hour **cambio** and a branch of the NCB bank, a tourist-board desk (daily 9am–10pm) and numerous hotel, ground-transport and car rental booths. **Luggage trolleys** aren't permitted past immigration, but the official red-capped porters will carry your bags for a small charge (J$50 per bag). Larger hotels provide free airport transfers, but you can charter a **taxi** from any of the omnipresent JUTA drivers – the trip to Gloucester Avenue, Queens Drive or downtown should cost no more than US$10. If travelling *very* light you can take one of the local **shared taxis** that leave from the petrol station past

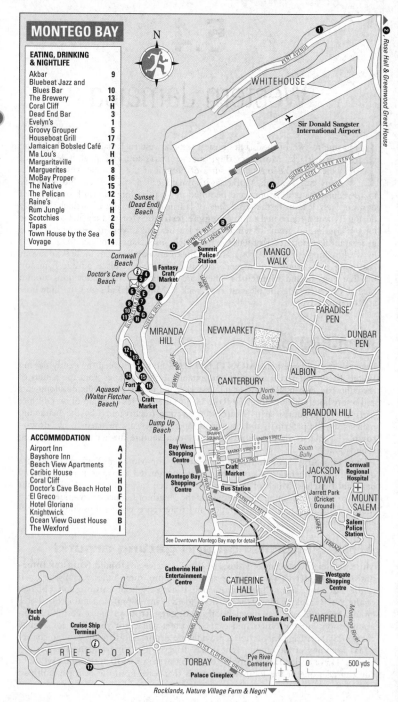

MONTEGO BAY

EATING, DRINKING & NIGHTLIFE

Akbar	9
Bluebeat Jazz and Blues Bar	10
The Brewery	13
Coral Cliff	H
Dead End Bar	3
Evelyn's	1
Groovy Grouper	5
Houseboat Grill	17
Jamaican Bobsled Café	7
Ma Lou's	H
Margaritaville	11
Marguerites	8
MoBay Proper	16
The Native	15
The Pelican	12
Raine's	4
Rum Jungle	H
Scotchies	2
Tapas	G
Town House by the Sea	6
Voyage	14

ACCOMMODATION

Airport Inn	A
Bayshore Inn	J
Beach View Apartments	K
Caribic House	E
Coral Cliff	H
Doctor's Cave Beach Hotel	D
El Greco	F
Hotel Gloriana	C
Knightwick	G
Ocean View Guest House	B
The Wexford	I

Rocklands, Nature Village Farm & Negril ▼

Organized tours

Hundreds of **tour companies** operate out of Montego Bay; most have booths at the airport as well as offices along Gloucester Avenue and offer similarly priced trips to independent plantations and great houses. The **best operators** are slightly more adventurous: Barrett Adventures, Rose Hall (℡876/995-2796, ⓦwww.barrettadventures.com), puts together customized packages to off-the-beaten-track waterfalls, farms and beaches from US$100 per person per day. Alternatively, hire a **local driver** and do some independent sightseeing. Reliable and friendly Dale Porter, aka "Shaka" (℡876/316-2184), offers all-day tours for around US$100; he can usually be found outside *Caribic House Hotel*.

Chukka Blue Adventure Tours (℡876/979-6599, ⓦwww.chukkaadventuretours.com) offer a number of very slick tour options in the area. These include **quad-bike (ATV) safaris** (1hr 45min; US$60) around the Rose Hall estate; **ride and swim horseback tours** (2hr 30 min; US$60) west of town at Moskito Cove, which includes a ride through a former sugar plantation and a ride in the sea; **tubing along the Great River** (2hr 30min; US$55); **jeep safaris** (5hr; US$70 including lunch), including a walk up a waterfall and a swim in a mineral pool and lots of four-wheel-drive action; and an exhilarating **canopy tour** (2hr 30min–3hr; US$65), similar to the Ocho Rios operation but including a traverse over the Great River and one 1000ft traverse. All costs include refreshments and return transportation from local hotels.

If you want to go **horse riding**, by far the best option is the immaculate Half Moon Equestrian Centre (daily 9am–5pm; ℡953-2286, ⓦwww.horsebackridingjamaica.com) at the *Half Moon* hotel. There's a Jungle Jaunt (45min; US$50), good for beginners and with a short lesson included; more experienced riders can opt for the longer Tryall Trail (1hr 45min; US$60) into the countryside. By far the best option is the Sand Shuttle (1hr 45min; US$60), through the hotel gardens and onto the beach. Unlike other Jamaican beach rides, where the horses simply trot through deep water, this allows you to actually swim your horse back to shore; far less strain on the legs and immeasurably more fun.

River rafting (ⓦwww.jamaicarafting.com) is a more sedate pleasure, best done along the Martha Brae River, 45 minutes' drive east of MoBay near Falmouth. You can either turn up at the Rafter's Village departure point (signposted from Falmouth's main square) and pay US$42 for a 1hr 15min trip on a two-person raft, or opt to be transported there and back, which costs US$45 per person; to book the latter, call ℡876/952-0889.

Tour sites

Listed below are the best tour sites and most popular organized excursions. Each can be seen independently as well as on a package.

Croydon in the Mountains Catadupa, St James ℡876/979-8267, ⓦwww.montego -bay-jamaica.com/ajal/croydon. Half-day; US$60; Wed & Fri. Croydon Estate is a 132-acre working coffee and pineapple plantation in the foothills of the Catadupa mountains in the St James interior. A half-day tour includes barbecue lunch and fruit tasting.

Hilton High Day Tour St Leonards, St James ℡876/952-3343, ⓦwww.jamaicahiltontour. com. 7hr; US$64; Tues, Wed, Fri & Sun. Gentle and enjoyable trip up into the hills through Montpelier and Cambridge to the diminutive Hilton plantation house, whose small grounds contain a piggery and stables. Breakfast and lunch are included, as are a stroll around the village and local school, a bus ride to the German settlement of Seaford Town and its museum, and a drive back through the western outskirts of Cockpit Country.

John's Hall Adventure Tour c/o *Relax Resort* ℡876/971-6958, ⓦwww. johnshalladventuretour.com; US$50; Mon, Wed, Fri & Sat. A bit more than the usual plantation tour, with an informative stop at St James Parish Church, the Town Hall museum and a primary school visit along the way to this small farm on the outskirts of MoBay, where you look at local trees and plants, as well as goats, pigs and mongoose, and have an excellent Jamaican lunch.

the airport's car park, which charge around J$30 for the same journey. There is no public bus service from the airport.

Cruise ships dock at the complex on the Freeport Peninsula, and taxi drivers are on hand to ferry passengers into town (US$10–15) or further afield.

The main **Jamaica Tourist Board** office (Mon–Fri 8.30am–4pm, Sat 9am–1pm; ☎876/952-4425) is at the end of the access road to Cornwall Beach, just off Gloucester Avenue. For online information on Montego Bay check out ⓦwww.montego-bay-jamaica.com.

Unfortunately there is no public transport serving downtown Montego Bay or the strip, and consequently any tourist walking the streets will be assailed with offers by passing **taxis**. Be prepared to haggle and always settle the price before you get in. However, if you're spending most of your time on the strip, you can easily get around on foot.

Accommodation

The range of **accommodation** in Montego Bay is huge. This is prime **all-inclusive** territory, with the swankiest enclaves out at suburban Ironshore just east of town. Most people, however, stay along the Gloucester Avenue **strip** – busy, buzzing and swarming with hustlers – and the best of the bunch there are listed below. Many hotels include free airport transfers, and more distant properties throw in a free beach shuttle. Unless otherwise stated, rooms have air conditioning, cable or satellite TV and phone.

Airport Inn Queen's Drive ☎876/952-0260 or 330-7180, ℉929-5391. Two minutes from the airport, and clean and reliable. All rooms have kitchen facilities, and there's a pool and bar/restaurant. ❷

Bayshore Inn 27 Gloucester Ave ☎876/952-1046, ℉979-5087. Cheerful, brightly decorated en-suite rooms at the less frantic end of the strip. Reduced-rate weekly rentals available. ❸

Beach View Apartments Gloucester Ave ☎876/971 3859, ⓦwww.marzouca.com. Appealing and inexpensive self-contained apartments in a great location. All have tiled floors, big bathrooms and a separate living area with kitchenette; one can sleep six, the others four. Rates include airport pickup and a daily pass to Aquasol beach. ❸

Caribic House 69 Gloucester Ave ☎876/979-9387, ⓦwww.caribicvacations.com. Small hotel popular with European backpackers, in a great location opposite Doctor's Cave Beach. Adequate rooms with fridges; some have ocean views. ❸

Coral Cliff Gloucester Ave ☎876/952-4130, ⓦwww.coralcliffjamaica.com. Tucked behind the Disney-esque gaming lounge and restaurant, the rooms here are functional and comfortable; there's a pool on site. ❺

Doctor's Cave Beach Hotel Gloucester Ave ☎876/952-4355 or 4359, ⓦwww.doctorscave.com. One of the better strip hotels, across from Doctor's Cave Beach, with stylish decor, gorgeous tropical garden, pool, hot tub, restaurant, bar and small gym. Rooms are pretty uniform, but the friendly atmosphere wins a lot of points. Rates include breakfast. ❺

El Greco Queen's Drive ☎876/940-6116, ⓦwww.elgrecojamaica.com. Sprawling complex of self-contained apartments perched high above the strip (access is via the lift of the adjacent *Montego Bay Club* resort). The modern suites have kitchens and balconies; tennis courts, pool and restaurant/bar are on site. Rates include breakfast and a pass to Doctor's Cave Beach. ❺

Hotel Gloriana 1-2 Sunset Blvd ☎876/979-0669, ⓦwww.hotelgloriana.com. Cheap and cheerful place, popular with Jamaicans as well as tourists. Rooms are basic but nice, with fridges and balconies; units with kitchens are available. There's a pool, whirlpool, restaurant and bar. ❷–❸

Knightwick Corniche Rd ☎876/952 2988, ℮tapas45@hotmail.com. Large, comfortable rooms in an elegant hacienda-style building above *Coral Cliff*. Run by a friendly live-in couple, with breakfast on the verandah included, this is one of the most appealing and best-value options on the Strip. ❸

Ocean View Guest House 26 Sunset Blvd ☎876/952-2662. Modest guesthouse between the strip and the airport offers basic rooms and a friendly atmosphere. Meals are available. ❷

The Wexford Gloucester Ave ☎876/952-2854, ⓦwww.montego-bay-jamaica.com/wexford. Overlooking the only green space on the Strip, this reliable MoBay old-timer has clean, bright rooms with tiled floors, tropical-style decor and king beds; some have sweeping ocean views. There's a pool, bar and restaurant on site. ❺

The Strip: Gloucester Avenue and the beaches

Occupying the whole of **Gloucester Avenue** and stretching north into **Kent Avenue**, Montego Bay's glittering oceanfront tourist strip builds to a bottleneck around Doctor's Cave Beach during the daytime, with taxi drivers shadowing your every move and gift shops competing for business. At night the action switches to MoBay's most happening joint, *Margaritaville*, and street vendors stake out jerk chicken stands and carts selling snacks. Gloucester Avenue is home to most of MoBay's tourist hotels and restaurants as well as the best beaches, bars and clubs, so even if you don't check into a strip hotel, you'll spend a lot of time here.

Starting at the roundabout that filters Howard Cooke Boulevard, Queens Drive and Fort Street traffic, the first stretch of Gloucester Avenue is a kind of no-man's-land, bordered by the only sizeable undeveloped beach in town. On the inland side, arranged around steep steps that make a useful shortcut to Sewell Avenue and Queen's Drive, **Fort Street Craft Market** is a relatively relaxed spot for a bit of bartering; stalls sell the usual array of carvings and T-shirts. Opposite the market, and still popularly referred to by its old name of Walter Fletcher Beach, **Aquasol Theme Park** (daily 10am–10pm; US$5; ⊛www.aquasoljamaica.com) has the most comprehensive **sports facilities** of MoBay's three main beaches. It offers watersports (jet-skis US$75, glass-bottom boat rides US$20, snorkelling US$24; all per half-hour), tennis and basketball courts, and a go-kart track (five laps cost US$4 in a one-person kart, US$5 in a two-person kart). The wide expanse of sand, childrens' playground, a decent seafood restaurant, a fish-fry kiosk and an attractive decked bar have made the beach popular with young tourists and the attendant hangers-on as well as Jamaican families. The water is usually lovely, but beware after a bout of wet weather, when the town's gullies discharge into the sea across the bay.

Though Gloucester Avenue runs parallel to the water, the sea is mainly obscured by the buildings. The only place to fully appreciate the sweep of the bay is from the strip's only **green space**, opposite the restaurants and bars at Miranda Ridge; there are a couple of benches from which you can watch the sunset. The bucolic illusion is rudely shattered just past the park at **Margaritaville** (daily 10am–3am; ⊛www.margaritaville.com), a mini-lido-cum-restaurant-cum-bar that proudly displays the second-tackiest facade along the strip, including a smoking volcano with vomit-like lava tumbling down the walls. *Margaritaville*'s bar and outdoor eating deck are built right over the sea; below there's a watersports area with boat berths and swimming platforms. On the roof there's a hot tub, sun deck, and – best of all – a 110ft water slide which sluices down into the sea and draws hordes of tourists and locals alike. Directly opposite, topped by a thatched African-style roof and with its faux waterfall and tableaux of life-size jungle animals spilling over onto the pavement, is the **Coral Cliff** complex, where the numerous arcade games, slot machines and ice-cold a/c might tempt you to take a break from the heat.

The strip builds in intensity as it approaches the magnificent Doctor's Cave Beach, becoming a seamless parade of bars, cafés and identikit duty-free shops. **Doctor's Cave Beach** itself (daily 8.30am–sunset; J$300; ⊛www.doctorscavebathingclub.com) is Montego Bay's premium portion of gleaming white sand and translucent water. The rapidly deepening waters really are the best in town, and following extensive refurbishment, facilities are excellent, including spotless showers and changing cubicles, a restaurant and bar and a snack counter. On the downside, there's little shade (umbrella rentals are available but extortionate) and it can get very crowded.

Past Doctor's Cave is the diminutive **Fantasy Craft Market**, tucked behind a row of duty-free stores and offering some bargains. Opposite the market, and with its own driveway off Gloucester Avenue, **Cornwall Beach** is a lovely strip of sand, but was closed at the time of writing for an upgrade. An entrance fee usually applies; ask at the tourist board to see if it's opened up to visitors again.

Watersports

Montego Bay is justifiably famed for its deep turquoise waters and abundant reef systems, some close enough to swim to from the main beaches. Discarded rum bottles and tyres can be disconcerting, but the deeper reefs are alive with fish, rays, urchins and the occasional turtle and nurse shark. There are hosts of similarly priced **watersports operators** on each beach and within the larger hotels; we list the most reputable below. Information is available from the Montego Bay Marine Park office at *Pier 1* (℡876/971-8082, ⓦwww.mbmp.org); the park's rangers also offer excellent and informative snorkelling trips around the bay for a small fee.

Diving and snorkelling

The following offer guided dives (around US$50), certification courses (from US$350) and equipment rental (from US$15). Like every other watersports operator in Montego Bay, they also rent **snorkel gear** for around US$15 a day; some also offer guided snorkelling tours of the best reefs.

Captain's Watersports and Dive Centre at the *Round Hill Hotel*, Hopewell ℡876/956-7050 ext 378.

Fun Divers Wyndham, Rose Hall ℡876/953-3268.

Jamaica Scuba Divers at the *Half Moon Hotel*, Ironshore ℡876/953-9266.

Resort Divers at *Jack Tar Village* and *Holiday Inn* ℡876/940-1183 or 953-9699.

Boat trips

With an open bar and sometimes lunch, **boat trips** are always popular and usually fun, if bawdy humour is your bag. Most depart from the *Pier One* complex downtown and sail around the bay to the airport reefs, with a stop for snorkelling. Calico sailing cruises runs "Pirate Cruises" aboard *Calico*, the only wooden sailing ship in town (℡876/952-5860, ⓦwww.calicosailingcruises.com); 3hr daytime cruise US$40; 2hr evening cruise US$25); dinner cruises are also available (US$60), with food from the *Town House* restaurant. The well-maintained catamarans *Tropical Dreamer* and *Day Dreamer* (℡876/979-0102; 3hr cruises; US$48) offer cruises along the coast to *Margaritaville*, where you get out and have a go on the water slide. There's also a snorkelling stop on the way.

Glass-bottom boats operate from all the main beaches and sail out to the airport reefs for around US$25 for half an hour. MoBay Undersea Tours (℡876/940-4465, ⓦwww.mobayunderseatours.com; 2hr; US$40) has a **semi-submersible** that takes you ten feet underwater to view the reef; a diver goes overboard to feed the fish, and it's a nice way to get close to the coral without getting wet. Tours leave at 11.30am and 1.30pm from *Pier One*. One step up from the semi-sub is the **Sea-Trek** tour (25min; US$60) operated by Chukka Blue (℡876/979-6599, ⓦwww.chukkaadventuretours.com), in which you don a spaceman-type helmet fed with a continuous supply of air and walk along the seabed to the reef. It's a pretty unusual experience, and not to be missed, particularly if you've never tried scuba diving. Tours leave daily at 9.30am, 11.30am, 1.30pm and 3.30pm from Doctor's Cave Beach; round-trip transportation from hotels is included, as are refreshments and the Doctor's Cave entry fee.

A fully equipped **sport fishing boat** costs around US$350 per half-day; try the *Irie Lady* (℡876/953-3268) or *No Problem* (℡876/381-3229).

The hotels peter out as Gloucester becomes **Kent Avenue** (known locally as Dead End Road) at the junction with Sunset Boulevard and continues to hug the coast before ending abruptly at the wall marking the distant section of the airport runway. The adjacent **Sunset/Dead End Beach** (or **Buccaneer Beach**) is a thin but attractive strip of public sand; it's popular with Jamaicans, despite the racket of aircraft landings and take-offs. The water is shallow and there are no facilities, but snorkelling is good and the view over the bay is fabulous, providing the best free sunset seat in town.

The last of the strip proper, **Sunset Boulevard** is home to a small complex of shops and bars. At the airport roundabout, the boulevard becomes part of **Queen's Drive**, a fast traffic route that runs parallel to Gloucester Avenue. Pavements are sporadic up here and walking can be risky, though the views over the bay are fantastic.

Downtown: Sam Sharpe Square and the craft market

Downtown MoBay announces itself with its very own stretch of undeveloped shoreline opposite the dividing roundabout. **Dump-Up Beach** looks pretty enough, particularly from a distance, but this is one of the dirtiest parts of the bay. Shooting off from the roundabout, the main route into the centre of town is **Fort Street**, a clamorous thoroughfare with dancehall flooding out from storefronts and all manner of pushcarts and vehicles jostling for space with the thick human traffic. Past here, over the bridge across North Gully, you enter town proper. The lively covered fruit and vegetable market to the left is popularly known as the **Gully** (the correct name, William Street Market, is seldom used).

St James Street comes to an abrupt end at **Sam Sharpe Square**, the heart of downtown, with a central fountain and a seemingly permanent stream of traffic. The square is bordered by a jumble of old and new architecture, including **The Cage**, built in 1806 as a lock-up for disorderly seamen and runaway slaves. Just outside is a **bronze statue** of national hero Sam Sharpe by Jamaican sculptor Kay Sullivan.

Market Street weaves towards the sea from Sam Sharpe Square, passing the brand-new Georgian-style **Town Hall**, home to a small but illuminating **museum** of local history (Tues–Fri 9am–5pm, Sat 10.30am–3.30pm; J$150); occasional art exhibitions are held here, too. Past the Town Hall, pedestrianized Market Street leads to MoBay's

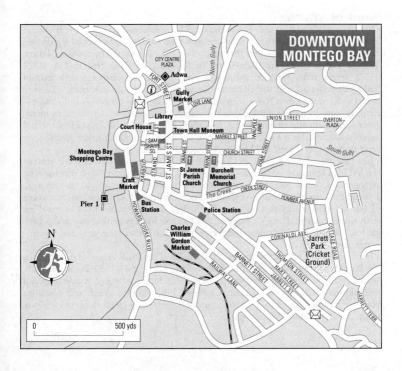

main **craft market**. With 200-odd brightly painted stalls selling a colossal variety of craft items, it's a great place to pick up some souvenirs and is surprisingly hassle-free. Otherwise, there's little to see downtown, and given the prevalence of pickpockets, it's not a great area for a wander.

Day-trips from MoBay

Tourist town that it is, Montego Bay is within easy distance of a glut of managed attractions. Most are on the roster of tour companies, but all can also be seen independently. Most popular is **ROSE HALL**, six miles east from MoBay and site of the infamous **Rose Hall Great House** (daily 9.15am–5.15pm; US$15). Built between 1770 and 1780 by planter and parish custos (mayor) John Palmer, the dazzling white-stone structure is set back from the A1 and surrounded by gardens, woods and a swan-filled pond. The rather mechanical 45-minute tours that run every fifteen minutes make much of the vastly embellished legend of Annie Palmer, the "White Witch of Rose Hall", a planter's wife who supposedly dabbled in the occult and who's said to have dispatched numerous husbands by shady means. As the house was unoccupied and widely looted during the nineteenth century, almost all of its current contents have been transported from other great houses or from overseas.

Five miles east from Rose Hall, the A1 opens up to a magnificent sea view at diminutive **GREENWOOD**. Perched on a hill overlooking the sea, the off-white stone of **Greenwood Great House** (daily 9am–6pm; US$12) dominates the few houses and bars below. Surrounded by luscious flowering gardens, the house has managed to retain most of its original contents. Built in 1790, Greenwood contains its owners original library and a wonderfully eclectic collection of objects. The tour, which ends in a bar set up in the original kitchen area, is much more enjoyable than the breakneck run round Rose Hall.

West of MoBay

On the west side of Montego Bay at the small community of Reading, the B8 winds inland off from the smooth tarmac of the new highway to a brace of well-signposted natural attractions. Look out for the signpost on the right for the turn-off to **Nature Village Farm** (Mon–Fri 10am–6pm, Sat & Sun 11am–7pm; free; mobile ℡912 0172), several miles along an appallingly potholed road. A sweeping collection of basketball, volleyball and netball courts, soccer pitches and a go-kart track, it's a very scenic spot on the Great River with manicured lawns, bamboo groves and an open-air restaurant on a deck overlooking the water. The cook-to-order Jamaican menu, from curried shrimp to sandwiches and salads, omelettes and fries, is excellent and inexpensive, and this is a marvellous spot to get away from it all. You can swim in the river from several places, and kick back afterwards with a game of pool.

Just two miles beyond Lethe at Copse, the road curves; look out for a dirt road to the left by a lamppost – this takes you down to **Animal Farm** (Mon–Fri tours by arrangement, Sat & Sun 10am–5pm; $200; ℡876/815-4104, ✍fly.to/animalfarm), a delightful, environmentally conscious and well-tended smallholding run completely on solar energy that makes a worthwhile stop, especially if you're travelling with small children. There's a huge array of exotic birds, a petting zoo and a herb garden, all with good labelling and, below the main part of the property, a swimmable river.

Back on the B8, turn off to the left from the B8 at the small village of Anchovy for the **Rocklands Feeding Station** (daily 2–5pm; US$8; ℡876/952-2009), regularly visited by more than a hundred species of birds, including orange quits, vervains and the long-tailed doctor bird, Jamaica's national bird. Hummingbirds will perch on your outstretched finger to drink sugar water here; feeding peaks at around 4.30pm, when the air thrums with tiny wings.

Eating

Montego Bay has its fair share of swanky **restaurants** alongside the more usual Jamaican eateries. Pricier tourist restaurants almost always offer special deals; look out for flyers around town. There's a *KFC* and a *Pizza Hut* just beyond the downtown end of Gloucester Avenue, and a *Burger King* opposite Margaritaville; *McDonald's* is east of town at the Blue Diamond Mall in Ironshore.

Adwa City Centre Mall, Fort St. Great air-conditioned vegetarian diner on the mall's top floor, offering breakfast (ackee, porridge), wholewheat ackee, veg or soya patties, salads and lunches/dinners of ackee and tofu stew, curried tofu, veggie "chicken" and "lamb" dishes and all manner of pulse and vegetable combinations. Smoothies, natural juices and power drinks also available.

Akbar Gloucester Ave ☎876/979-0113. The sister of the renowned Kingston purveyor of fine Indian and Thai cooking serves excellent curries and noodle dishes in an air-conditioned dining room with tasteful Asian decor. Prices are moderate to expensive.

The Brewery Miranda Ridge, Gloucester Ave. Late-opening bar and restaurant above the strip. Extremely varied menu with daily specials, a big burger selection, lots of salads and excellent fajitas. Good value and pretty views over the bay.

Evelyn's Kent Ave, Whitehouse. Basic locals' seafood joint right on the water, serving all things piscatorial with rice, bammy or roti; try the curry conch. Great cooking, inexpensive prices and a casual, laid-back vibe.

Groovy Grouper Doctor's Cave Beach ⊛www.groovygrouper.com. On a raised deck overlooking the sand, this mid-priced seafood restaurant comes into its own at night, when lights twinkle in the greenery and the bay views are fabulous, but it's good for a local-style meal anytime – pepper shrimp, crab cakes, jerk calamari as well as fish, lobster and chicken. Best value is the all-you-can-eat Friday night seafood buffet for US$20.

Houseboat Grill Freeport Rd ☎876/979-8845. Fantastic, unique setting in a beautifully converted houseboat moored on Bogue Lagoon; you board by way of a rope-pulled launch, and a window in the floor allows perusal of the marine life gliding underneath. The menu is superlative and sophisticated, mixing Jamaican cooking with international dishes; the pepper shrimp with scotch bonnet beurre blanc is unmissable, and the desserts are pure indulgence. One of the best in town.

Jamaican Bobsled Café Gloucester Ave ☎876/940-7009. Gorgeous New York-style pizzas, with dough made in-house daily and a variety of succulent toppings. Local deliveries available.

Ma Lou's at the *Coral Cliff* 165 Gloucester Ave ☎876/952-4130, ⊛www.coralcliffjamaica.com.

Upscale, indoor air-conditioned restaurant serving Caribbean-wide specialities; stick to the Jamaica specials and you can't go far wrong.

Margaritaville Gloucester Ave. The loudest place on the strip, offering an international menu with a Mexican flavour, and American-style service with the emphasis on fun.

Marguerites Gloucester Ave ☎876/952-4777. Right on the seafront next to *Margaritaville*, this is perfect for a romantic meal, with elegant decor, faultless formal service, upscale atmosphere and a delicious Continental menu specializing in seafood; the crème brûlée is wonderful.

MoBay Proper Fort St. Brilliant, inexpensive little place on the approach to the strip that's popular with locals and offers a welcome remedy to the all-encompassing Americana. Reliable Jamaican lunches and dinners, from red peas soup and stewed chicken to steamed or brown-stewed fish – the specially seasoned "Stretchcovitched" pork is not to be missed, and there's a fish fry on Friday nights.

The Native 29 Gloucester Ave ☎876/979-2769. The best place on the strip for a sit-down Jamaican meal – take advantage of reduced-rate buffets and lunch specials. Try the "Boonoonoo's Platter" of ackee, curry goat, jerk chicken and escovitched fish, rice and peas and plantain.

The Pelican Gloucester Ave ☎876/952-3171. Long-established restaurant popular with locals and tourists. Highlights include American/Jamaican breakfast, the daily lunch specials, and the rum pudding and coconut or banana cream pie for dessert.

Raine's St James Place, Gloucester Ave. Popular kiosk café between Doctor's Cave and Cornwall beaches with all-day breakfasts, burgers and home-made cakes.

Scotchies near the *Holiday Inn*, Ironshore. A bit of a trek out of town, but worth the effort if you're after some excellent jerk cooking: pork, chicken and seafood are served with festival, breadfruit, yam or sweet potato and you eat at palm thatch-shaded tables set back from the road.

Tapas Corniche Rd ☎876/952-2988. Innovative and delicious Mediterranean food in a place that's upscale but affordable, and blessedly detached from the strip; take the small road to the left of *Coral Cliff* hotel. Try such delights as salmon fillet with shrimps and a lime beurre blanc or pork with scallions, apricots and pimento liqueur.

Town House by the Sea Gloucester Ave ☎876/952-2660. A new location for this MoBay stalwart, right by the sea next to Doctor's Cave

Beach. The sophisticated menu includes starters such as lobster and shrimp cakes, and mains from filet mignon to chicken kebabs and a few pasta dishes. Also good for lunch, with a daily special (J$200) alongside sandwiches and salads. Free pickups for dinner from local hotels.

Drinking, nightlife and entertainment

Aside from the shenanigans at the permanently packed *Margaritaville* and *Coral Cliff*, Montego Bay is not particularly lively at **night**. Nonetheless, there are several places to sink a few beers or pickle yourself in rum punch (the *Groovy Grouper* on Doctor's Cave Beach and *Voyage* at Aquasol beach are good for a drink by the sea), and there are regular concerts and sound-system dances in and around town.

There are two **cinemas** in town showing the latest US releases: the Palace Multiplex off Alice Eldemire Drive (☎876/979-8359) is the more luxurious, while over in Ironshore there's the Diamond Cinema at the Blue Diamond Shopping Centre (☎876/953-9540).

Bars and clubs

Voyage Aquasol beach, Gloucester Ave. The beach bar here offers lovely views across the bay, excellent margaritas, sea breezes and a pool table; a gaming lounge is planned for the upstairs level. Jamaican food available, too.

Bluebeat Jazz and Blues Bar Gloucester Ave. Upmarket, icily air-conditioned little bar with high-tech jazz-themed decor, offering expensive cocktails and great live jazz or blues nightly.

The Brewery Miranda Ridge, Gloucester Ave ☎876/940-2433. Friendly place for a drink and/or a dance, with a cosy indoor bar and great bay views from the verandah. Usually packed with young Jamaicans and large groups of American tourists. Tuesday and Friday are karaoke nights, and there's a daily happy hour (4–6pm). Look out for Saturday night promotions featuring well-known Jamaican DJs.

Coral Cliff 165 Gloucester Ave ☎876/952-4130, ⒲www.coralcliffjamaica.com. No expense has been spared on this temple to American-style entertainment and decor, centred around the 170 ringing, buzzing slot machines of the gaming lounge (drinks are free when you're playing). Open 24 hours, the *Rum Jungle* bar attracts a mixed crowd of tourists, well-to-do locals and flashily dressed gigolos, and offers a huge range of cocktails as well as nightly live entertainment – free except for the Viva Xaymaca performance on Tuesdays (9.30pm; US$35), a professional cabaret-style music and dance production that takes you through five centuries of Jamaican culture. Downstairs, the more family-oriented *Chillin* area (Mon–Thurs 4pm–2am, Fri–Sun 10am–2am; free) has high-tech arcade games in a winter-wonderland setting; here, too, you'll find the *Ice Bar*, where everything from the bar itself to the shot glasses is crafted from ice.

Dead End Bar Kent Ave. Laid-back spot perfect for sunset- and plane-watching. Thursday night is given over to a beach party, with a comprehensive mix of reggae, soca and hip-hop. Sunday features classic reggae and rocksteady.

Houseboat Grill Freeport Rd. This restaurant-on-a-boat has a cosy indoor bar downstairs and a breezy upper deck good for a romantic cocktail under the stars. Excellent martinis, great bar snacks and friendly staff. Happy hour daily 5–6pm.

Jamaican Bobsled Café Gloucester Ave. Right in the heart of the strip and bedecked with memorabilia from the infamous Jamaican bobsled team – you can even have your picture taken in one of their sleds. Reasonably priced drinks and a friendly atmosphere; ten percent of profits are ploughed back into the team.

Margaritaville Gloucester Ave ☎876/953-4777, ⒲www.margaritaville.com. Hugely popular bar, club and restaurant that usually draws the biggest evening crowd – if you're looking for guaranteed action and don't mind gigolos galore, this is the place. Lively themes each evening: Wednesday is an all-inclusive pyjama party (J$600) and there are party nights (J$500) from Thursday to Saturday, with DJs (sometimes big names from Kingston) playing dancehall, R&B, hip-hop and the odd commercial dance tune. Dancefloor opens at 10pm; the "Boogie Bus" offers free pick-ups (9, 10 & 11pm) and drop-offs (midnight–3am on the hour) from local hotels; call ahead to arrange.

MoBay Proper Fort St. The best place on the strip to get a flavour of downtime Jamaican style, with karaoke on Thursdays, old hits night on Fridays and jazz on Sundays; Wednesdays see the "Fort Street Jam", which spills out onto the street with crafts stalls, local snacks such as roast yam and saltfish or pan chicken, and live reggae. At other times, borrow one of the board games from behind the bar or test your skills at the pool table.

Pier 1 Howard Cook Blvd ☎876/952 2452, ⊚www.pieronejamaica.com. A lovely setting for a dance, extending along a pier into the harbour, with a regularly changing roster of club nights. Best at the weekends. Cover around J$300.

Shopping

The best **craft market** is the huge Harbour Street complex (daily 7am–7pm), packed with straw and wickerwork, belts, clothes, jewellery, T-shirts and woodcarvings. The Fort and Fantasy craft markets along the strip (daily 8am–7pm) are worth a look but tend to be a little more expensive with less variety. The **Gallery of West Indian Art**, 11 Fairfield Rd, Catherine Hall (⊚www.galleryofwestindianart .com) has a huge range of works and is renowned for its hand-carved and painted wooden animals, while the **Bob Marley Experience** at Half Moon Shopping Village claims to have the largest collection of Marley T-shirts in the world. Downtown, **record stores** offer custom-made reggae tapes (around US$3) as well as CDs and vinyl; one of the better ones is El Paso, at 3 South Lane, overlooking Sam Sharpe Square.

Negril

Jamaica's shrine to permissive indulgence, **NEGRIL** metamorphosed from deserted fishing beach to full-blown resort town in little over two decades. American hippies first started visiting what was then a virgin paradise in the 1970s, setting the tone for today's free-spirited attitude, but these days, the presence of deliberately risqué resorts like the infamous **Hedonism II** has ensured that Negril is widely perceived as a place where inhibitions are lost and pleasures of the flesh rule. The traditional menu of ganja and reggae draws a young crowd, but the north-coast resort ethic has muscled in too. All-inclusives of every ilk pepper the coast and hotels line every inch of the beach, while hustling has increased to an irritating degree.

But Negril shrugs off such minor issues and remains supremely chilled-out. Pristine miles of sand, comprehensive watersports facilities, open-air dancing to first-rate live music, a wide range of eating and drinking joints, gregarious company and the best sunsets on the island are all on offer here. Many foreigners have stayed on permanently, blurring the distinctions between tourists and locals and making for a relaxed, natural interaction that's a refreshing change from other resorts.

Arrival, information and getting around

Buses from MoBay and the north coast drop off passengers on the A1 (Norman Manley Boulevard) just before Negril's central roundabout; if you're staying on the boulevard (ie the beach rather than the cliffs), ask the driver to drop you off outside your hotel. Buses from Savanna-la-Mar and the south coast terminate at the top end of Sheffield Road, where you can charter a **taxi** to the West End or beach for about US$5. Domestic flights land at **Negril Aerodrome** at Bloody Bay. Taxis wait there, but fares can be ridiculous – a reasonable price is US$7–10.

For **information**, visit ⊚www.negril.com. The *Yacht Club*, on West End Rd (☎876/957-9224, ⊚www.yachtclub.com), offers accommodation, watersports, bike rental and taxi services as well as informal advice.

You don't need a **car** if you're going to stay in town. **Shared taxis** run the length of the beach and West End Road all day every day; you can flag them down anywhere en route. A trip from the roundabout to the lighthouse or Bloody Bay costs about J$50. **Chartering a taxi** can be expensive, but competition is high, so haggle – US$5 from the roundabout to Bloody Bay is reasonable. There is no local bus service to the roundabout from the beach or cliffs. Other than **walking**, the most

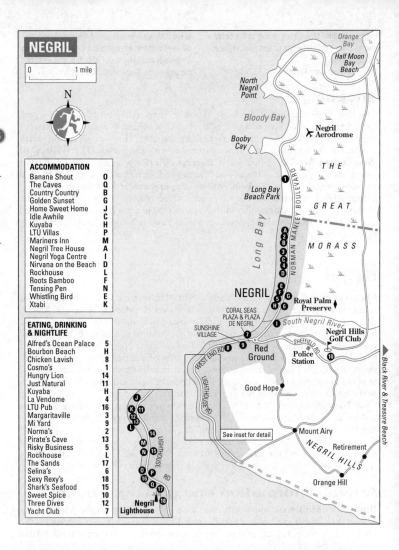

NEGRIL

0 — 1 mile

N

ACCOMMODATION

Banana Shout	O
The Caves	Q
Country Country	B
Golden Sunset	G
Home Sweet Home	J
Idle Awhile	C
Kuyaba	H
LTU Villas	P
Mariners Inn	M
Negril Tree House	A
Negril Yoga Centre	I
Nirvana on the Beach	D
Rockhouse	L
Roots Bamboo	F
Tensing Pen	N
Whistling Bird	E
Xtabi	K

EATING, DRINKING & NIGHTLIFE

Alfred's Ocean Palace	5
Bourbon Beach	H
Chicken Lavish	8
Cosmo's	1
Hungry Lion	14
Just Natural	11
Kuyaba	H
La Vendome	4
LTU Pub	16
Margaritaville	3
Mi Yard	9
Norma's	2
Pirate's Cave	13
Risky Business	5
Rockhouse	L
The Sands	17
Selina's	6
Sexy Rexy's	18
Shark's Seafood	15
Sweet Spice	10
Three Dives	12
Yacht Club	7

Orange Bay

Half Moon Bay Beach

North Negril Point

Bloody Bay

✈ **Negril Aerodrome**

Booby Cay

THE

Long Bay Beach Park

GREAT

Long Bay

MORASS

NEGRIL

CORAL SEAS PLAZA & PLAZA DE NEGRIL

SUNSHINE VILLAGE

South Negril River

Royal Palm Preserve

Negril Hills Golf Club

SHEFFIELD RD

Police Station

Red Ground

WEST END RD

LIGHTHOUSE RD

Good Hope

See inset for detail

Mount Airy

NEGRIL HILLS

Retirement

Orange Hill

▶ *Black River & Treasure Beach*

LIGHTHOUSE RD

Negril Lighthouse

---

popular modes of transportation are moped, motorbike and bicycle. Motorbikes rent for around US$45 per day, mopeds from US$35 and bicycles around US$15; there are numerous outlets along Norman Manley Boulevard and the West End.

Accommodation

Negril has over two thousand **beds**, split between the cliffs and beach. Easily the more popular location, the **beach** reeks of commercial vitality. The quieter **West End** offers more privacy, but steep open-access cliffs make it a bad choice for those travelling with children. There are more budget options here and rates are often open to negotiation, especially if you're planning a long stay; check out ⓦwww.negril.com.

"Rent-a-dread"

Jamaica is a carnal kind of country, and while there's no sex tourism industry as such, monetary-based holiday liaisons are a well-established convention. Middle-aged women strolling hand in hand with handsome young studs has become so normal that pejorative epithets – "**Rent-a-dread**" or "**Rastitute**" – for the young men who make a career out of these cynical liaisons have entered the lexicon.

Negril is a centre for this kind of trade-off, and many women regularly return specifically to partake of an injection of "Jamaican steel". As a result, single women are almost unanimously assumed to be out for one thing only – prepare yourself for a barrage of propositions.

Male tourists are less involved in the holiday romance scenario, but **female prostitutes** are common and men should expect to be frequently propositioned. If you do choose to indulge, make sure that you practise safer sex; one in five prostitutes are HIV-positive, and STDs – including syphilis – are rife.

As Negril ostensibly prohibits buildings taller than a palm tree, a lot of accommodation is in traditional circular palm-thatched **cottages**; also popular is the **pillar cabin**, a round cottage set on top of a stone column, with a shower below. There are also a few places where you can **camp**, though only Roots Bamboo has 24-hour security for its campsite; if you're willing to rough it and risk it, there are plenty of cabins and campsites with few facilities and negligible security on the morass side of Norman Manley Boulevard.

The beach

Country Country ☎876/957-4273, ⓦwww.countryjamaica.com. Brightly painted fretworked cottages set on a lovely stretch of beach. The rooms are spacious and have a fridge, cable TV, a/c and ceiling fans, and there's a beachside restaurant and bar. Rates include breakfast. ❻

Golden Sunset ☎876/957-4241, ⓦwww.thegoldensunset.com. Long-established and reliable, though across the road from the beach, offering clean rooms or cabins with fans (a/c costs more), bathrooms, kitchenettes and patios. ❷–❸

Idle Awhile ☎876/957-9566, ⓦwww.idleawhile.com. Sophisticated and intimate little hotel with beautifully designed and furnished rooms; all have a/c, cable TV, wireless Internet access, fridge and phones. There's a restaurant on site, and guests get a pass to the excellent sports facilities of the *Swept Away* resort. ❻

Kuyaba ☎876/957-4318, ⓦwww.kuyaba.com. "Rustic cottages" set along a pretty landscaped track leading to the beach, with porches, a/c and fans; some have kitchenettes. There are more luxurious (and expensive) options in the main block. Good restaurant on site, and rates are sensible. Cottages ❸, rooms ❹

Negril Tree House ☎876/957-4287, ⓦwww.negril-treehouse.com. An appealing complex of clean, comfortable rooms and villas with a/c, phone and cable TV. Two bars, a restaurant, a pool and watersports are on site. ❺

Negril Yoga Centre ☎876/957-4397, ⓦwww.negrilyoga.com. Yoga centre and guesthouse overlooking the Great Morass. Attractive cottages of varying degrees of luxury surrounded by greenery; all beds have great Sealy mattresses. Wholefood cooking and yoga classes available, and there's a communal kitchen. ❷–❸

Nirvana on the Beach ☎876/957-4314, in the US ☎716/789-5955, ⓦwww.nirvananegril.com. Attractive, fully screened a/c wooden cottages with kitchens, two bedrooms and kooky decorative touches, set in an unusually beautiful sand garden shaded by tall trees and dotted with sculptures and hammocks. Friendly atmosphere. ❻

Roots Bamboo ☎876/957-4479, ⓦrootsbamboo.com. Friendly, efficient place that's one of Negril's most popular budget options. Cottages are small but cosy; some have private bathrooms, and there's also a communal row. There's also a campground ($20 per tent) with 24hr security. ❷

Whistling Bird ☎876/957-4403, ⓦwww.negriljamaica.com/whistlingbird. Pretty wooden beach cottages (one to three bedrooms), with wireless Internet access, a/c, cable TV, fridge and phone, set in a lovely garden with cook-to-order restaurant. Very private and alluring. Extremely genial staff. ❺

West End

All properties are on West End Road or its continuation, Lighthouse Road.

Banana Shout ⊤876/957-0384, in the US ⊤941/927-6996, ⓦwww.bananashout.com. Simple but attractive cottages right on the cliffs. Each has kitchenette, ceiling fan and hammocks on the verandah. There's a diving platform, sun deck, private cave and exceptional sunset views. ❹

The Caves ⊤876/957-0269, ⓦwww. islandoutpost.com. Utterly gorgeous, very secluded and supremely romantic place that offers the very best of Negril, from candlelit dinners in a cave to a private hot tub with a sunset view. Aveda spa treatments, sauna, watersports equipment and a saltwater pool are on site, and the stylish, individually decorated rooms are faultless, with batik bathrobes and CD players. Rates include wonderful meals and drinks. ❾

Home Sweet Home ⊤876/957-4478, ⓦwww. homesweethomeresort.net. Small, cheerful resort with swimming pool, Jacuzzi, restaurant and cliffside sun deck. All rooms have ocean views. Popular with young Canadians. ❺

LTU Villas ⊤876/957-0382, ⓦwww.negril.com/ ltu. A great-value option offering spacious rooms in quiet gardens opposite one of Negril's best bars, the LTU Pub. Each room has a lounge, fridge and balcony; some have TV, and those with a/c cost a little more. ❷–❸

Mariners Inn ⊤876/957-4220, ⓦwww. marinersnegril.com. Medium-size retreat with attractive rooms and apartments. Facilities include a dive centre, swimming pool and games room patronized by local pool wizards. Great sea swimming and a boat-shaped bar. ❹

Rockhouse ⊤876/957-4373, ⓦwww. rockhousehotel.com. Enviable location, Mediterranean styling, magnificent thatched bar/restaurant, yoga room and saltwater pool are highlights. The thatched studios and villas (some of which sleep four at no extra charge) have glass-doored patios overlooking the ocean, outdoor showers, fans and four-poster beds, and there's an innovative and expensive restaurant. ❺–❻

Tensing Pen ⊤876/957-0387, ⓦwww.tensingpen. com. Stylish and exclusive retreat in pretty clifftop gardens with imaginatively decorated bamboo and wood cottages, a yoga room and a lovely restaurant and bar. Some of the cliffs are linked by a tiny suspension bridge. Breakfast included in the rates. Bungalows ❺, cottages from ❽

Xtabi ⊤876/957-0121, ⓦwww.xtabi-negril. com. Lovely West End veteran with flowering gardens and a network of caves. Accommodations in wooden cabins with private sun decks and sea access or two-storey concrete cottages with kitchens. Also pool, open-air restaurant and bar, and countless swimming platforms. Rooms ❸, seafront cottages ❼

The Town

Negril doesn't really have a centre – just a roundabout feeding its three main roads – and most people leave the beach or cliffs only to change money, buy petrol or find a ride out of the area. However, **Sheffield Road** is the least tourist-oriented part of town and the closest approximation of a real heart, with the police station, market stalls, petrol station, restaurants and constant crowds dodging beeping mopeds. To the right of the roundabout are two **shopping plazas** – Coral Seas Plaza and Plaza de Negril; the car park in front is known as **Negril Square**, a base for taxi drivers, black-market currency touts and would-be guides. Nestled behind is **Red Ground**, a residential area that houses most of Negril's permanent population.

The beach

Negril beach is a near-perfect Caribbean seashore. The seven-mile stretch of whiter-than-white sand is lined by palms and sea grapes, the water is warm, translucent and still, and the busy reefs are ornately encrusted. It's also packed with tourists, locals and holidaying Jamaicans. While it's great for lively socializing, the high concentration of human traffic inevitably draws plenty of vendors and hustlers. Approaches are constant and high-octane, and along with the usual crafts, hair braiding and aloe massage, you'll probably be offered sex and drugs with alarming frequency.

Though hotels guard "their" portion of beach with security men and strings of floating buoys, by law the sand is public up to the shoreline. The beach is roughly divided by the bank of all-inclusives at the outcrop splitting Long Bay and Bloody Bay. Beginning at the roundabout, **Long Bay** is the most heavily developed, by day a rash of bronzing bodies and flashing jet skis, by night a chain of disco-bars dedicated to reggae, rum punch and skinny-dipping. At the far end, the hotels give way to the grassy stretch of **Long Bay Beach Park**, with picnic tables, changing rooms, a snack bar and considerably fewer people.

The West End

The **West End** begins at the roundabout in the centre of town and meanders along the cliffs for some three miles, becoming Lighthouse Road at Negril Lighthouse and winding inland to Orange Hill and ultimately Sheffield Road. The first stretch is the liveliest, with jerk shacks, bars, juice stalls and craft shops lining the inland side and restaurants hanging over the sea's edge. There are a couple of ramshackle **beaches** where fishermen moor their canoes but the murky water makes swimming inadvisable. The road opens up a little once you get to the fancy Kings Plaza and Sunshine Village shopping malls, but the true West End begins over the next blind bend; the road narrows, the water clears and the hotels that carve up the rest of the cliffs begin in earnest.

As this is Jamaica's extreme westerly point, the **sunset view** from the West End is the best you'll see. Sunset-watching is an institution here; most bars and restaurants offer sunset happy hours and the half-hour or so before dusk is the closest the West End gets to hectic. Coach parties descend in droves upon undeservedly popular **Rick's Café**, where you pay for your drinks with plastic tokens, cameras click and local lads dive off the cliffs; see below for some less commercialized spots to watch sunset.

After *Rick's* the road becomes a country lane and the hotels are interspersed with near-wild coastline. A main point of interest is **Negril Point Lighthouse**, standing 100 feet above sea level at Jamaica's westernmost tip. Built in 1894, the 66-foot tower now flashes a solar-powered beam ten miles out to sea. Workers who live on site are usually willing to take you up all 103 leg-quivering steps to the top.

Around Negril

As most visitors to Negril are after a beach holiday rather than sightseeing, there aren't many managed attractions in the area. But if you fancy getting out of town, there are a few good options nearby. For some peaceful beachlife, head east out of town along Norman Manley Boulevard. Just outside Green Island, the nearest village to Negril, the unspoilt **Half Moon Bay Beach** (daily 8am–10pm; J$60 entrance, redeemable at the bar when you buy a drink) is full of the paradisiacal charm that originally brought tourists to Negril. The wide curve of white sand has no braiding booths, jet skis or hassle, just a little sea grass and some small islets; nude bathing is perfectly acceptable and snorkel equipment cheap. The **restaurant** serves excellent chicken, fish and sandwiches. On the way to Half Moon is **Rhodes Hall Plantation** (☎876/957-6333, ⊕www.rhodesresort.com.com), a 550-acre coconut, banana, plantain and pear farm with two private beaches – one a shallow, sea-grassy reef beach with a freshwater mineral spring bubbling under the brine, the other a more conventional sugar-sanded curve. Volleyball and football/basketball pitches and a restaurant/bar are adjacent, but the main draw is **horseriding**. The well-kept mounts trot into the hills and along the beach (US$50–60, depending on length of ride).

Mayfield Falls

One of the most popular excursions from Negril heads into the low-lying **Dolphin Head Mountains** to the 22 mini-cascades and numerous swimming spots at **Mayfield Falls** (daily 9am–5pm). The falls are very hard to find independently, and most people visit as part of an organized tour run by one of two operators, Original Mayfield Falls (☎876/957-4729) and Riverwalk at Mayfield Falls (☎876/974-8000). Both offer tranquil guided walks through bamboo-shaded cool water with swimming holes every twenty yards. Tours (US$65 per person, plus tip) include transport from Montego Bay or Negril and lunch; you pay US$10 if you get there under your own steam. Wear

Many **hotels** will let you swim from their piece of cliff for the price of a drink, and though they all look pretty similar, some stand out. *Drumville Cove* has a friendly attitude towards non-guests and a spectacular portion of cliff, while *Rockhouse* boasts a stylish saltwater swimming pool, a bar, excellent sea access and complete seclusion. The limestone cliffs are riddled with **caverns**, with a popular network below *Xtabi* hotel. The rather chic *Pirate's Cave* watering hole is in prime position for the exploration of **Joseph's Cave**, one of the largest along the West End, made famous in the movies *Dr No*, *Papillon* and *20,000 Leagues Under the Sea*; there's a staircase from the bar which leads down into the cave. The cliffs are at their highest around *Rick's Café*, the venue of daily **cliff-diving** demonstrations; a less prominent place to have a go yourself is the *LTU Pub* next door, while the most stylish spot from which to take the plunge is *The Sands*. Past the lighthouse, the cliffs peter out, coastal winds whip the sea into a frenzy and swimming becomes a little risky, but there is a sheltered spot just past the point where Lighthouse Road turns inland – turn straight onto the piece of undeveloped land and climb down the rocks.

a swimming costume and bring water shoes, as the stones are tough on bare, water-softened feet. Mosquitoes can also be a problem, so bring repellent as well.

Roaring River Park

An easy escape about five miles north of Savanna-la-Mar is gorgeous **Roaring River Park** (daily except Sat 9am–5pm) near the small community of **Petersfield**, approached on a rutted road that you'll probably need directions to find, though there are plenty of signposts from town. Set in a former plantation and still surrounded by cane fields, the first point of interest is an extensive system of **caves** (US$10) that have been developed with tourists in mind. A guide takes you through the caverns, where steps, concrete walkways and lighting let you appreciate their full magnitude. Bats flit about, and there are two mineral pools for a disquieting swim in pitch-blackness. The guide then takes you through the surrounding gardens (US$4), where a dazzling swimmable **mineral pool** is overhung by trees and flowers.

Eating

Negril caters to a cosmopolitan crowd and some of the classiest, albeit somewhat pricey, dining is found in **hotel restaurants**; the best of these are included in the listings below. Thanks to Negril's hippy associations, there are plenty of **vegetarian** options, and you'll also find a lot of **pasta**, as the area attracts a huge number of young Italians. Vendors based at the first stretch of West End Road sell roast or fried fish, jerk chicken and soup.

Sheffield Road

Sweet Spice The best place on Sheffield Road for cheap, delicious Jamaican food to take away or eat in.

The beach

Cosmo's ☎876/957-4330. One of the best, busiest spots on the beach, equally popular with Jamaicans and tourists. Excellent, moderately priced seafood – conch soup is a speciality – and the usual selection of chicken variations.

Kuyaba ☎876/957-4318. Upscale thatch-roofed, open-sided restaurant with good food and regular crowds. The menu includes lobster and shrimp, crab and pumpkin cakes, vegetarian dishes and pasta. Good cocktails, too.

Norma's at the *Sea Splash* hotel ☎876/957-4041. Upscale spot on the sand for dinner, from imaginative takes on seafood staples to peppered steak, pastas and lamb chops, as well as great breakfasts (try the Caribbean benedict, with smoked marlin and calalloo) and burgers, salads and sandwiches for lunch.

Selina's Excellent breakfast joint with friendly service, moderate prices and an extensive menu: eggs, filled bagels, banana pancakes and the like, as well as Blue Mountain coffee.

La Vendome at the *Charela Inn* hotel ☎876/957-4648. Celebrated, sophisticated and expensive French-Jamaican cuisine, from duck à l'orange to snapper in coconut. Great home-made breads, and live entertainment on Thursdays and Saturdays.

West End

Chicken Lavish Choice spot for domino players, serving chicken and fish, Jamaican and Chinese style; steaks and pork chops, too.

Hungry Lion ☎876/957-4486. The best vegetarian food in town, with seafood as well and gorgeous local art on the walls. A walled courtyard affords privacy, and the fairly priced food is always good – try the dill fishcakes or veggie kebabs.

Just Natural Fresh and cheap Jamaican food, calalloo omelettes, pasta, burritos and vegetarian options are served in a beautiful shady garden.

LTU Pub Laid-back venue with cliffside dining. Eclectic menu offers seafood, stuffed jalapeños, chicken filled with callaloo and cheese, and some German dishes.

Pirate's Cave Popular and efficient bar and grill, with stylish decor, moderate prices and excellent grilled chicken and ribs.

Rockhouse ☎876/957-4373. Romantically set on a boardwalk right over the sea, with excellent service and an expensive menu that includes vegetable tempura, seafood linguine with garlic, and conch fritters.

Shark's Seafood A few tables in the open air on the covered verandah, with great, inexpensive Jamaican seafood (try the octopus), this is a good place to soak up some old-style West End atmosphere. Breakfasts and natural juices also available.

Three Dives Expansive jerk restaurant on the cliffs, with a nightly bonfire and tasty chicken, pork, lobster and fish.

Drinking and entertainment

Most **bars** want you to spend the **sunset** with them, and provide drinks promotions or happy hours as an incentive. As the cliffs give the best view, bars along the West End tend to be livelier at dusk, with the action moving to the beach after dark. The larger places are distinctly tourist-oriented; if you want some local flavour, try the **rum bars** and **beer shacks** along Sheffield Road or West End Road near the roundabout.

Jungles (see below) is the only proper **club** in town, but there's also weeknight dancing at the **beach bars**, which use their portions of sand as dancefloors. DJs play dancehall or Euro-disco, and the **live music** usually consists of a no-name reggae band singing Bob Marley covers. Ask around to see what's on each night.

Large **stage shows** featuring well-known reggae artists are advertised on roadside billboards and through a car-with-megaphone system. Main **venues** for large shows are *Bourbon Beach* (formerly *DeBuss*), *Alfred's* or *Risky Business* on the beach and *Samsara* or *Kaiser's* on the West End. Stage shows rarely begin before 11pm and often go on until 3 or 4am; cover charge is usually about US$10.

Norman Manley Boulevard

Alfred's Ocean Palace Busiest bar on the beach with thrice-weekly live reggae and crowds of happy holiday-makers dancing on the sand. Great fun, but watch out for the hustlers, particularly on gig nights.

Bourbon Beach Piped or live music every night in a covered area and a section of the beach. The jerk chicken is famously good.

Jungles ☎876/957-4005. Negril's only true club is a fairly lavish place with a smoky, packed indoor dancefloor downstairs and a breezy upper deck with pool, table tennis and a restaurant. Each night has a different theme and music. Cover charge US$10. Closed Mon and Tues.

Margaritaville All of Jamaica's major resorts now have a *Margaritaville*, and the Negril branch is as popular as the others, with a nightly bonfire, beach volleyball, two-for-one drink offers and big TV screens for sports fans. Hugely popular with

American students, with various themed nights (some all-inclusive) throughout the week.

Risky Business Popular American-style beach bar complete with big-screen sports via satellite and regular drinks promotions.

West End Road

LTU Pub Very cool bar, vastly superior to next-door *Rick's*, offers cliffside drinking, diving, snorkelling and food to boot. Ask the barman to make you a Bob Marley – and then try and drink it.

Mi Yard High-rise bar that's tourist-friendly but positively Jamaican. Open 24 hours a day for music, dominoes, drinking and jerk; always packed after 2am.

Pirate's Cave Popular sunset spot, with a long cocktail list and a friendly, convivial atmosphere.

Rick's Café Overpriced tourist trap puts on the West End's main sunset event. An appallingly tuneless band play reggae while local boys dive from the high cliffs.

The Sands Part of the stylish *Caves* hotel, and displaying the same funky and chic decor, this is a wonderful sunset spot, with beach chairs to take in the show, a diving platform, a covered lounge with sofas and good barbecue. The sand came courtesy of Hurricane Ivan, and was retrieved from the West End Road during the cleanup efforts.

Sexy Rexy's This small shack makes a surprising amount of noise around sunset, with reggae blaring from the speakers and plenty of smiles from the entertaining owner.

Yacht Club Large thatched bar overlooking the sea. Cheap Red Stripe all day until 7pm, live music at weekends and wonderfully shady clientele. Come for a heavy drinking session with the hippies who "discovered" Negril and other local characters; the staff are helpful and friendly. It's surprisingly safe and often great fun.

5.5

The south coast

I f you want to catch a glimpse of Jamaica as it was before the tourist boom, head **south**. Mass tourism has yet to reach the southern parishes – none of the all-conquering all-inclusives have opened here yet, and the beaches aren't packed with sun-ripened bodies – but there are some fantastic places to stay, and great off-the-beaten-track places to visit. It takes a bit of extra effort to get here, but it's definitely worth it. The parishes that make up south-central Jamaica are immensely varied; the landscape includes mountains, cactus-strewn desert, lush jungle and rolling fields. To the west, in the beautiful parish of St Elizabeth, **Treasure Beach** – an extremely laid-back place with decent beaches and some lovely accommodation options – is the area's main draw. If you want to do some sightseeing, you can visit the **rum factory** at Appleton or the fabulous **YS waterfall**, or drive around the tiny villages of the attractive **Santa Cruz Mountains**. **Black River** is the main town – an important nineteenth-century port that today offers popular **river safaris** and a handful of attractive colonial-era buildings. New roads have opened up large parts of the south coast in the last few years and it's now possible to drive along large stretches of it without losing sight of the sea. The scenery is often wild and unspoilt down here, though you'll **need a car** to see most of it; buses and minibuses tend to stick to the main, inland roads, making side-trips down to coastal villages as required.

Treasure Beach

The easy-going, snoozy little community of **TREASURE BEACH** has become the main tourist centre on the south coast, particularly popular with a laid-back bohemian crowd. It has a good range of **accommodation** options, including a delightfully eclectic collection of villas and beach cottages to rent. There are also some great places to **eat** and a couple of diverting attractions, while the bays here boast some pretty **beaches**. The **Santa Cruz Mountains** rise up from the sea just east of Treasure Beach and run northwest, providing a scenic backdrop for the village and protecting

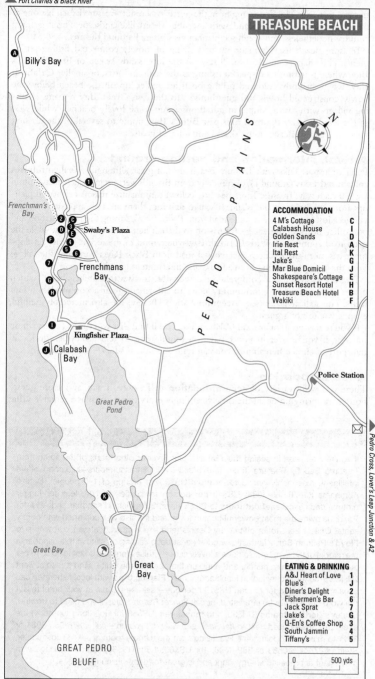

TREASURE BEACH

Billy's Bay Ⓐ

Frenchman's Bay

Ⓑ ①

Swaby's Plaza Ⓒ
②③④
Ⓕ ⑤ ⑥
⑦
Ⓖ
Ⓗ

Frenchmans Bay

P E D R O   P L A I N S

ACCOMMODATION	
4 M's Cottage	C
Calabash House	I
Golden Sands	D
Irie Rest	A
Ital Rest	K
Jake's	G
Mar Blue Domicil	J
Shakespeare's Cottage	E
Sunset Resort Hotel	H
Treasure Beach Hotel	B
Wakiki	F

Ⓘ

Kingfisher Plaza

Ⓙ **Calabash Bay**

Police Station

Great Pedro Pond

Ⓚ

Great Bay

Great Bay

EATING & DRINKING	
A&J Heart of Love	1
Blue's	J
Diner's Delight	2
Fishermen's Bar	6
Jack Sprat	7
Jake's	G
Q-En's Coffee Shop	3
South Jammin	4
Tiffany's	5

GREAT PEDRO BLUFF

0   500 yds

▶ Pedro Cross, Lover's Leap Junction & A2

5.5 | **JAMAICA** | The south coast

the area from rain clouds coming from the north. As a result, Treasure Beach has one of the **driest** climates on the island, with a scrubby, desert-like landscape. This is farming country nonetheless, and you'll see plantations scattered around the area.

Treasure Beach itself is made up of a string of loosely connected fishing settlements. The chances are that you'll stay on the long sandy sweep of **Frenchman's Bay**, where tourism has displaced fishing as the main industry, or smaller **Calabash Bay**, where brightly coloured fishing boats are pulled up on the beach below the newly constructed hotels and guesthouses. To the east, **Great Bay** remains a fishing village with just a couple of guesthouses and some lovely beaches, while west of Frenchman's Bay the road runs past **Billy's Bay**, home to several of the classiest villas in Treasure Beach, some shacks and a lot of goats.

Arrival, information and getting around

Public transport links with Treasure Beach are not great, although several **minibuses** and **shared taxis** (around J$70) run daily from Black River; a regular taxi costs around US$30 each way; Treasure Tours (see box below) can organize reasonably priced pickups from anywhere in the island. If you're **driving**, there are two approaches to the village. Most traffic arrives via the road from Pedro Cross, passing the police station and post office north of the village. A turn-off to the left here leads to Great Bay, while the main road continues towards Calabash Bay, where most of the recent tourist development has taken place. The newer, coastal road from Black River runs into the village from the west past a string of small bays and intermittent guesthouses.

Treasure Beach has a comprehensive **website**, ⓦwww.treasurebeach.net, which covers everything from community news to information on accommodation and tours. The staff at *Jake's* (see "Accommodation," below) are also incredibly helpful, even if you're not a guest.

If you're staying in or around Calabash Bay, you'll find that you can get everywhere on foot; if you're over in Great Bay, you might want to rent a bicycle, the locals' transport of choice hereabouts; you can rent one from *Q-En's* – see p.332.

Accommodation

There is a wide variety of **accommodation** in Treasure Beach, and more guesthouses are springing up all the time. Seemingly every other house is a rentable **villa**;

Organized tours and activities

If you're interested in seeing the YS Falls, Gut River or other parts of the south from Treasure Beach, Treasure Tours (ⓣ876/965-0126, ⓔtreasuretours@info.com) offers intelligent, reasonably priced **tours** (from US$90 for groups of 1–3 people). Dennis Abrahams (ⓣ876/965-3084; US$40 per person for parties of two, less for bigger groups) does excellent **boat tours** to Black River, Sunny Island sandbar and Alligator Pond; he owns the most powerful boat in town, and it's also well equipped with comfy seats. One of best tours offered by Dennis (and every other boatman in town) is to **Floyd's Pelican Bar**, a fantastic wooden construction sitting on stilts atop a sandbar in the middle of the sea; he also does a lovely sunset cruise along the coast for US$18 per person, including rum punch, and a trip up the coast to the white-sand beach at Font Hill (US$130 for two including lunch and drinks). **Fishing trips** with local fishermen can usually be arranged for around US$100 per day – ask the people at your hotel to put the word out that you're interested, or call *Sunset Resort Hotel*. If you need to unwind, Shirley's **herbal steams** (US$30) and **massages** (US$60 for hour-long full-body) are excellent. She's based next to *Ital Rest*, and will pick you up – call ⓣ876/965-3231 or 3111 to make an appointment. Practising from the therapy room at *Jake's*, Joshua Lee Stein (ⓣ876/965-0583 or 389-3698; 1hr US$60, 1.5hr US$80) blends massage with movement and healing energy work and is great for deep-tissue massages.

these vary from simple beach cottages to luxurious homes; call Treasure Tours on ☏876/965-0126 for details of places to suit all budgets. Most of the places below are listed on, and bookable via, ⊛www.treasurebeach.net.

4 M's Cottage Frenchman's Bay ☏876/965-0131, ℮fourmscottage@hotmail.com. Six small, simply furnished and appealing en-suite rooms presided over by the dynamic Miss Effie. Beds are swathed with mosquito nets and windows screened. There's a kitchen that guests can use (though meals are available) and a bar in the front garden. ❸

Calabash House Calabash Bay ☏965-0126. Right on the sea, this is a cute, clean three-bedroom cottage with a kitchen, a/c rooms, a nice verandah and excellent rates. You can have the whole place for US$140 per night, or rent a room only. Meals are available. ❷

Golden Sands Frenchman's Bay ☏876/965-0167, ℮goldensandguesthouse@yahoo.com. Long-standing and deservedly popular place in a prime position on Frenchman's beach. The simple tile-floor rooms have fan, screened windows and a bathroom, and share a communal kitchen. One self-contained a/c cottage is also available (❹), and there's a bar and restaurant. ❷

Irie Rest Billy's Bay ☏876/965-0034, ⊛www.geocities.com/irierestguesthouse. Extremely friendly place set back from, but within walking distance of, the beach. Rooms are simple and inviting, with a/c, screened windows and en-suite bathrooms; some have huge screened verandahs. There's a bar-cum-restaurant and a cool communal area with a stereo and satellite TV. Brilliant value. ❷

Ital Rest Great Bay ☏876/965-3231. Two cottages only at this gentle and beautifully landscaped place near the beach, each with separate rooms upstairs and down (ask for upstairs for the views and the breeze), and with kitchen and verandahs facing the sea. Small bar, restaurant and herbal steam room on site (US$50 for a steam and massage). Turn right just before the *Seacrab* restaurant and then take the first right. Rooms ❷, cottage ❸

Jake's Calabash Bay ☏876/965-0635, ⊛www.jakesjamaica.com. With an easy-going but cultured atmosphere, this delightful venue on its own tiny beach is the nicest, and liveliest, place to stay hereabouts. The gorgeous and unique rooms and cottages are decorated in funky colours and have CD players and coffee-makers. There's a pool and restaurant, and the bar draws a genial local crowd. ❹–❾

Mar Blue Domicil Old Wharf, Calabash Bay ☏876/965-3408, ⊛www.marblue.com. German-run place right on the beach, with fabulous attention to detail. Spotless and fresh, rooms have a/c, balconies overlooking the sea, CD and DVD players, bathrobes, hairdryers and irons with boards. There's a bar and an excellent restaurant, two pools and breakfast is included in the rates. ❻

Shakespeare's Cottage Frenchman's Bay ☏876/965-0120. Excellent budget option, with four basic but clean rooms with fans and shared bathrooms, and a kitchen for guests' use. ❶

Sunset Resort Hotel Calabash Bay ☏876/965-0143, ⊛www.sunsetresort.com. Extremely friendly, efficient resort in a lovely seaside setting, with a fabulously kitsch astroturfed central area. Huge, comfortable rooms have a/c, fans, cable TV and coffee-maker; self-catering cottages are also available, and there's a pool and restaurant/bar. ❺–❼

Treasure Beach Hotel Frenchman's Bay ☏876/965-0110, ⊛www.treasurebeachjamaica.com. Big, attractive resort on one of the best stretches of beach, with two pools, a restaurant and bar. Modern suites with oceanfront views all have a/c, ceiling fan and cable TV. ❺

Wakiki Calabash Bay ☏876/965-3660. Rangy place set back from the road and overlooking the beach, with basic, clean rooms with fans and private bathrooms, and a communal kitchen. Brilliant if you're on a budget. ❶

The beach

If you're in the mood for sightseeing, there are a couple of places worth checking out just outside Treasure Beach (see p.333). Otherwise, it's just you and the **beach**. The swimming is excellent, though the undertow can get strong at times – ask at your hotel about present conditions. Although rocky headlands create occasional obstacles, you can stroll for miles on certain parts of the beach, particularly west of the *Treasure Beach Hotel*. If you want to explore by **bicycle**, you can rent a mountain bike from *Q-En's* (see overleaf) for US$10 per day

Eating and nightlife

Evenings are pretty low-key in Treasure Beach, but there are a few good options for **food** and a couple of **bars** that keep late hours and get very full at the weekends.

BREDS

A nonprofit association established in 1988 to promote local awareness of local cultural heritage and the environment, and to provide educational opportunities and healthcare for the residents of Treasure Beach, **BREDS** (☎876/965-3000, ⊛breds.org), short for "bredrin", Jamaican slang for friend, has had a tangible positive impact on quality of life in Treasure Beach. The brainchild of, among others, Jason Henzell of *Jake's* fame, BREDS embodies the strength of this close-knit community, very much a place where people look out for one another. By way of grants and endowments, as well as the profits from annual events such as a triathlon and fishing tournament and sale of T-shirts and postcards, BREDS has constructed some thirty homes for less well-off locals, provided computers and office equipment for the local school, added a marine light to Frenchman's Beach to ensure safe navigation through the reef and conducted regular beach and town cleanups. Following the extensive damage wreaked on the area by Hurricane Ivan in September 2004, BREDS also helped to raise much needed funds: in collaboration with ⊛treasurebeach.net, the US-based Treasure Beach Foundation and the Treasure Beach Women's Group, a massive US$44,000 was collected, which was later matched by the United Way of Jamaica, bringing the total to US$88,000, all of which has been used to regenerate Treasure Beach and widen St Eliazbeth. BREDS has also established the Treasure Beach Response Unit, training 27 local volunteers in various basic medical techniques to become "first responders" in the event of emergencies. There are now at least four volunteers on call 24 hours a day to respond to emergencies – an essential service in a town with no hospital (the nearest is in Black River) and where the majority of residents (and visitors) don't have access to a car. The organization is always on the lookout for visitors who can contribute to the cause, whether materially or in terms of skills sharing, and BREDS merchandise is on sale at *Jake's*. For more on upcoming projects, visit the website above.

A&J Heart of Love Frenchman's Bay. Formerly the renowned *Trans-Love Café*, and maintaining the excellent reputation of its predecessor, this laid-back thatched patio is the essential stop for breakfast or brunch, with fresh bread, cakes and fruit salads, muesli, French toast, homemade fruit jam, marvellous Spanish omelettes, baguette pizzas, sandwiches and salads. Open till 5pm.

Blue's in the *Mar Blue* hotel, Old Wharf, Calabash Bay ☎965 3408. Stylish hotel restaurant right by the sea, serving sophisticated, imaginatively presented, moderate to expensively priced dishes concocted by the German owner/chef. The menu changes daily, but staples include soups (crab or tomato with gin), cheese plates, curry chicken and shrimp and lobster with aioli.

Diner's Delight Frenchman's Bay, opposite Swaby's Plaza. Simple local place serving Jamaican food at excellent prices: callaloo with saltfish, liver, steamed fish with okra, etc.

Fishermen's Bar Frenchman's Bay. Easy-going local hangout up a lane off the main road with a small disco and a pool table out back. Very popular at the weekends with both locals and tourists, particularly Sunday nights. It stays open after every place else has closed.

Jack Sprat Calabash Bay. Part of the *Jake's* empire, this fabulous café demonstrates what eating out in Jamaica should be like. With tables under the sea-grape trees, a sandy path down to the beach and a stylish verandah dining area, this is the perfect place for a relaxed, inexpensive meal. Baguette sandwiches and seafood – fish cooked any style and served with bammy, as well as shrimp, curry conch and conch soup – are available alongside excellent pizzas. Pastries, cakes and Devon House ice cream satisfy the sweet tooth. There's a beach bonfire on Saturday nights.

Jake's Calabash Bay ☎876/965-0365. Open-air restaurant within the hotel, this is usually one of the busiest places in town, serving moderately priced Jamaican fare with a sophisticated twist. The breakfast, lunch and dinner blackboard menus change daily; highlights include breakfast banana porridge, pumpkin soup, curried shrimp and lobster cooked in various ingenious ways. Tables are under shade trees, and there's a good wine list.

Q-En's Coffee Shop Swaby's Plaza. Open from 7.30am daily for great ackee or omelette breakfasts (served till noon), and good Jamaican lunches and dinners. Pastries and coffee are available all day.

South Jammin Frenchman's Bay. Unpretentious and popular bar serves up burgers, pizza and seafood. There's a pool table and a cute pocket-sized garden.

Tiffany's Frenchman's Bay. Rather incongruously smart place, with candlelit tables inside or on the terrace, good service and a range of moderately priced lobster, octopus and fish dishes.

Black River

Although it's St Elizabeth's largest town, **BLACK RIVER**, 18 miles west of Treasure Beach along the main A2 coast road, is a relatively quiet spot, with just one central shopping street, and most travellers only nip in briefly to take a boat trip on the river. It wasn't always this way: in the mid-nineteenth century the town derived substantial wealth from exporting **logwood**, used to produce black and dark-blue dyes for the textiles industry. For a brief period the town was one of the most influential in Jamaica. But the introduction of synthetic dyes meant the end for the logwood trade, and today the only signs of those illustrious days are some wonderful but decrepit old gingerbread houses. **Buses** and **minibuses** stop behind the market, just off the High Street.

The nicest thing to do in Black River is to stroll along the **waterfront** and check out the old wooden buildings, many with gorgeous colonnaded verandahs and gingerbread trim and most in a perilous state of collapse. The **Waterloo Guesthouse**, built in 1819, is reputed to have been the first place in Jamaica to get electricity – installed to provide air-conditioning for racehorses kept in the old stables – and to have boasted the island's first telephone. Nearby, the gleaming white **Invercauld Hotel**, built in 1889, reflects the confidence of the town during its heyday.

The main reason most people come to the town, however, is to take a **boat safari** on the **Black River**, which, at 44 miles, is Jamaica's longest. So named because the peat moss lining the river bottom makes the crystal-clear water appear inky black, the Black River is the main source for the **Great Morass** – a 125-square-mile area of wetland that spreads north and west of the river and provides a swampy home for most of Jamaica's surviving crocodiles as well as some diverse and spectacular birdlife. The boat tour is a very pretty trip into the Great Morass, although the term "safari" promises rather more excitement than it delivers. You are almost sure to see crocodiles (albeit fairly tame ones), and there are some marvellous **mangrove swamps** where you can normally spot flocks of roosting egrets as well as whistling ducks, herons and jacanas. To go on the ninety-minute tour (five daily; US$15 per person), turn up at the dock by the bridge or contact St Elizabeth River Safari (☎876/965-2374) or Black River Safari Boat Tours (☎876/965-2513).

If you're in the mood for some **lunch** or **dinner** whilst here, head over the bridge just west of town to *Cloggy's on the Beach*, in a lovely setting by the sea, with tables inside by the bar or under thatched gazebos on the sand. Great conch soup, curry conch or lobster, or a plate of fish (steamed with okra and pimento is delicious), served with rice, bammy and festival.

Middle Quarters and YS Falls

As you drive northeast from Black River, you'll reach an intersection directing you north for Montego Bay or east towards Santa Cruz and Mandeville. Head east and you'll soon pass **Middle Quarters**, a small crossroads where groups of women sell spicy, salty and delicious **pepper shrimp** from the Black River – perfect to add to your picnic if you're heading to the YS waterfall. Feel free to sample from the proffered bags before you buy, and reckon on around J$150 for a small bag (you're likely to get fresher fare from the roadside *Auntie's One-Stop* bar just beyond the crossroads). Shortly after Middle Quarters, a left turn takes you two and a half miles north to **YS**, an area dominated by the **YS farm**, home of the magnificent YS Falls. The name is thought to derive from the farm's original owners in 1684, John Yates and Richard Scott, whose initials were stamped on their cattle and the hogsheads of sugar that they exported. Today the 2300-acre farm raises pedigree red poll cattle – a Jamaican breed that you'll see all over the country – and grows papaya for export.

The **YS Falls**, a series of ten greater and lesser waterfalls, are great fun (Tues–Sun 9.50am–3.30pm; US$12). A jitney transports you across the farm's land and alongside the YS river to a grassy area at the base of the falls, where there's a changing room. You can climb up the lower falls or take the wooden stairway that leads to a platform beside the uppermost and most spectacular waterfall. There are ropes for aspiring Tarzans and pools for bathing at the foot of each fall. If water levels are low, you can also swim under the main falls and climb up into a cave behind them. Early morning is a good time to go, before the afternoon clouds set in and the tour buses arrive. Take a picnic and a book and you can comfortably spend a few hours loafing around on the grass and in the water. Cold beers and soft drinks are available nearby.

A **car** is extremely handy if you're heading for the falls, as they're a little off the beaten track. If you're relying on public transport, **buses** run along the main A2 highway south of YS between Black River and Santa Cruz. Ask the driver to drop you at the junction, and you can usually find **taxis** waiting to run passengers up to the YS farm – make sure you negotiate a price before you get in (around J$150 is standard).

The Appleton Rum Estate

Some six miles east of YS Falls, the **Wray and Nephew Rum Estate** at **APPLETON** (Mon–Sat 9am–3.30pm; US$12; ☎876/963-9215, ⍟www.appletonrum.com) has a great setting in the Black River valley among thousands of acres of sugar cane fields. At 250 years old, this is the oldest rum producer in the English-speaking Caribbean and the best-known of Jamaica's several brands.

You'll need a car to get here, or you can take a taxi from the nearby village of Maggotty. It's a good idea to call ahead to arrange a visit, if only to avoid arriving at the same time as a big tour party. The thirty-minute **tour** starts with a complimentary drink, followed by a whirlwind trip through the factory and warehouses and then outside to an old press, where donkeys used to walk in circles to turn a grinder that crushed juice out of the sugar cane. The tour concludes in a "saloon", where you can sample all seventeen kinds of rum and various rum-based liquors. The prices in the adjacent shop are far lower than supermarket prices.

6

Dominican Republic

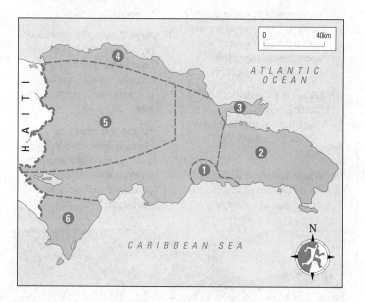

DOMINICAN REPUBLIC

Dominican Republic highlights

✻ Colonial Santo Domingo Chock-full of 500-year-old architecture – including the hemisphere's first cathedral, university, hospital and more. See p.348

✻ Watersports in Cabarete A bustling international enclave with the best windsurfing and kiteboarding in the hemisphere. See p.371

✻ Hiking the Cordillera Central Pristine alpine wilderness in the Caribbean's highest mountains. See p.379

✻ Whale-watching in Samaná An unforgettable spectacle of humpback whale migration; catch it from December to February. See p.363

✻ Old-style Cuban son at the Mauna Loa Catch a Buena Vista-style Cuban *son* show in a plush Santo Domingo ballroom. See p.353

✻ Playa Cosón The best beach on the island bar none, with no crowds, gentle turquoise currents, swaying palms and soft white sand stretching for miles. See p.367

✻ Parque Nacional Los Haitises Boat rides through a surreal snarl of mangrove swamps and prehistoric caves in the island's remote southeast. See p.360

△ Catedral Santa María de la Encarnación, Santo Domingo

Introduction and basics

Occupying the eastern half of the island of Hispaniola, the **Dominican Republic** (or the DR, as it's often known) is a hugely popular destination, thanks to the portion of the country that most resembles the image of a Caribbean playland: the crystal-clear waters and sandy beaches lined with palm trees, of which the DR has plenty. This vision of leisurely days spent by the sea and romantic nights filled with *merengue* and dark rum is supported by what turns out to be the largest all-inclusive resort industry in the world.

Set on the most **geographically diverse** Caribbean island, the DR also boasts virgin alpine wilderness, tropical rainforests and mangrove swamps, cultivated savannas, vast desert expanses and everything in between within its relatively small confines – slightly smaller than the US states of New Hampshire and Vermont combined, providing staggering opportunities for eco-tourism and adventure travelling.

The DR also lays claim to some of the more intriguing culture and history in the area, dating back to its early cave-dwelling groups, the **Taínos**, who recorded much of their activities in the form of rock art – it's quite likely you'll find yourself clambering down a dark cave to view some of these preserved paintings during your stay. In addition, as Dominicans are often quick to point out, their land was the setting for Christopher Columbus's first colony, La Isabela, and Spain's first New World city, Santo Domingo, at the end of the fifteenth century. Though the island quickly lost this foothold, the events that took place during its brief heyday did much to define the Americas as we know them.

Where to go

The southeastern part of the country probably has the loveliest all-inclusive resort zones, **Bávaro** and **Punta Cana**, both with pristine coastline stretching for kilometres on end. These are slightly overshadowed, if not in attractiveness then in sheer magnitude, by the complex at **Playa Dorada** along the north coast. Fortunately, this is close by **Puerto Plata**, an historic city worth examining for its wealth of Victorian architecture and proximity to developed stations like windsurf-

ing capital **Cabarete**, to the east. More great beaches are scattered about the **Samaná Peninsula**, poking out at the country's extreme northeast, from where you can also check out migrating humpback whales. In the mountainous interior, a few **national parks** make for good hiking terrain; while midway along the southern coast, **Santo Domingo** is an obvious draw, for its history and big urban feel.

When to go

The northern hemisphere's winter is **high tourist season** in the Dominican Republic; this is when the Dominican climate is at its optimum, having cooled down just a bit. You'll therefore save a bit of money – and have an easier time booking a hotel room on the spot – if you arrive during the **spring** or the **autumn**, which is just fine, as the temperature doesn't really vary all that much from season to season. Keep in mind, though, that the Dominican Republic is right in the centre of the Caribbean hurricane belt, and gets hit with a major one every decade or so; August and September are prime **hurricane season**, though smaller ones can occur in the months preceding and following.

Getting there

The cheapest and most frequent **flights** depart from gateway cities such as **Miami** and **New York**. Flights from the latter average about US$450–550, though if you fly late-night on JetBlue you can get there for as little as US$100 one-way. As there are no nonstop scheduled flights to the Dominican

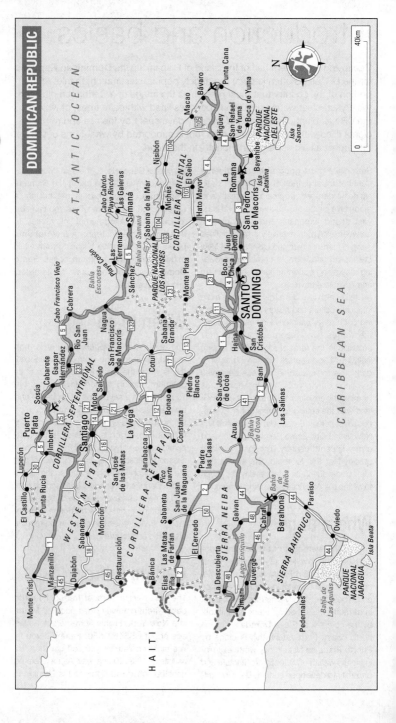

Republic from the UK, many **British** and **Irish** visitors to the Dominican Republic arrive on a charter flight as part of a package holiday, though you can also fly via the States or various stops in Europe; try Iberia Airlines for the least expensive deals. Visitors from **Australia** and **New Zealand** will need to travel first to the US or Europe and pick up onward connections from there. Most flights fly into Santo Domingo, though some land at Puerto Plata. Options for arriving in the Dominican Republic by **ship** are mostly limited to hitting the country as one of the ports of call on a longer Caribbean cruise. Otherwise, it is possible to arrive via **ferry** from Mayaguez, Puerto Rico, on *Ferias del Caribe* (℡ 809/688-4400, Puerto Rico ℡ 787/832-4800), but it's a long, uncomfortable overnight trip. Ferries depart Mayaguez three times a week; the cost is US$109–247 one-way (price depends on the ticket class), plus the US$10 entry tax.

Information, websites and maps

The glossy promotional material handed out by Dominican Consuls and tourist agencies are pretty to look at but seriously lacking in hard facts. With the emphasis on the package vacations that have earned the country so much money, they hold little value for independent travellers. Their **maps** are likewise relatively useless, though there are several excellent ones of the country available, including the 1:600,000 Dominican Republic map published by Berndtson & Berndtson. Better places to go for answers to specific questions are the websites listed below.

Money and costs

The official Dominican currency is the **peso** (RD$), which comes in notes of 5, 10, 20, 50, 100, 500, 1000 and 5000; there are also 10, 25, 50 centavo (100 centavos = 1 peso) and 1 peso coins, though only the last sees much use. The **exchange rate** typically hovers at around 30–35 pesos to the US dollar. It's impossible to find Dominican pesos outside the country, and visitors are well advised to come armed with a substantial amount of US dollars, as these are the most readily accepted (and exchangeable) foreign currency in the land. The best places to change money are the banks, which offer good exchange rates; **keep your receipts**, as this allows you to exchange the pesos back into hard currency (dollars or euros) on departure; otherwise you're stuck with the pesos. At a pinch, smaller *casas de cambio* are fine, though you should avoid the street moneychangers.

Websites

The Dominican Republic maintains a large presence on the **Web**, though, as ever, ferreting out a specific piece of information can take some time. The following are a few tried-and-true sites.

ⓦ **www.activecabarete.com** Terrific website devoted to Cabarete, with a detailed interactive map and a complete listing of hotels, restaurants, bars, current wind conditions, a calendar of events and other local services.

ⓦ **www.debbiesdominicantravel.com** A dizzying array of links to hundreds of Dominican-related sites and a deep archive of travellers' personal accounts of all-inclusive vacations.

ⓦ **www.dr1.com** The most heavily trafficked Dominican message board, and the best place to get DR info on the Web. Also has a good daily news bulletin that you can sign up to receive.

ⓦ **www.popreport.com** An exhaustive news bulletin and comprehensive roundup of tourist attractions and businesses in the Puerto Plata area.

ⓦ **www.superpagesdr.com** Home page of the Dominican Republic's premier phone company, with a comprehensive yellow pages covering the entire country.

The Dominican Republic is one of the last true **budget destinations** in the Caribbean. Package deals are relatively low-priced, and in many parts of the country shoestring travellers can spend as little as US$50/£27 per day. The savings are spread unevenly, though, and some things are pricier here than elsewhere: riding from town to town via public transport can cost as little as US$0.35/£0.20, but car rental will set you back at least US$45/£28 a day.

Getting around

The Dominican Republic's **bus** companies provide an excellent, inexpensive service over much of the country. Lines at the stations move quickly, there's plenty of room for luggage on the vehicles and trips are relatively pleasant. Even more extensive, and cheaper, is the informal network of **guaguas** – ranging from fairly decent minibuses to battered, overcrowded vans – that cover every inch of the DR; in most cases, you should be prepared for some discomfort, and you'll have a hard time fitting in much luggage. **Taxis** are another option for getting around the cities, and by foreign standards are relatively cheap; reputable operators are listed throughout the chapter.

Car rental is common as well, but the cost is generally high. **Domestic airlines**, on the other hand, are reasonably economical, and can make sense if you're not exploring much beyond the main centres. Finally, a number of tour operators in Santo Domingo, Puerto Plata and the all-inclusive resorts organize individual itineraries and packages with transport included.

By bus

Caribe Tours (in Santo Domingo ☎809/221-4422) boasts by far the most extensive bus network, while **Metro** (in Santo Domingo ☎809/566-7126) can get you from the capital to the Cibao, Puerto Plata and the Samaná Peninsula. Both have comprehensive brochures available in their stations, listing destinations and departure times. In addition, you'll find several regional bus companies, though vehicles and drivers tend to vary more in quality. Unless it's a public holiday, you

won't need advance reservations, but you should arrive at least an hour before the bus leaves to be sure of getting a seat. As the bus companies strive to stay in competition with *guaguas*, rates are extremely cheap. Even a cross-country trip from Santo Domingo to Samaná or Monte Cristi will set you back no more than RD$250, while shorter trips range around RD$140.

By guaguas, públicos and motoconchos

The informal system of **guaguas**, an unregulated network of private operators, is a distinctive Dominican experience that you should try at least once. Aside from the local colour, they're worth using because they're incredibly cheap and cover far more of the country than the bus companies. To catch a *guagua*, either ask for the location of the local station or simply stand by the side of the road and wave your arms at the first one that passes; they're typically battered minivans with a man drumming up business by hanging out of the side door and shouting at the top of his lungs. For longer trips, you'll often have to transfer *guaguas* at major towns, but even the longest leg of the trip will cost no more than RD$60; more often, you'll pay only RD$20.

Santo Domingo to the southeast and the Barahona region are often served by far more comfortable, air-conditioned **minibuses**; along the Silver Coast, the vans are augmented by private cars called **públicos**, which charge RD$5 and only go to the next nearest town and wait to fill up before heading off. *Públicos* also make up part of the city transport system in Santo Domingo, and dominate it in Santiago. City routes rarely cost more than RD$2. In Puerto Plata and other smaller towns, city transit is instead in the form of **motoconchos**, inexpensive, small-engined motorbikes that ferry you from place to place; they're faster than the *públicos* but can be dangerous.

By car

Car rental is expensive in the DR, though you can cut your costs a bit – and avoid a lot of hassle – by booking in advance with an international operator. Rates start around US$45–50 per day, with unlimited mileage but no discount for longer rental periods; you should also get full collision insurance, an extra US$10–12 per day. Even with collision, though, you're contractually responsible for any damage up to RD$25,000, but it's still worth taking out in case of catastrophic damage to the car. You should therefore take special care to note *all* dents, scratches and missing parts before signing off. Dominicans drive on the right-hand side of the road, often at a breakneck pace. You'll have to keep a careful eye out along the highways, as large commercial buses and cargo trucks constantly veer into the opposite lane to pass slower vehicles.

Accommodation

The Dominican Republic has become the most popular destination in the Caribbean thanks to its preponderance of **all-inclusive hotels**, which make package vacations here far cheaper than elsewhere in the region, with prices varying widely depending on the package that you book; look to spend around US$40-80 per person per night. The all-inclusives do, though, have their downside: the food is usually not that great, and you'll be stuck in a walled-off complex for the whole of your trip, which can get a bit claustrophobic. There are, however, plenty of other options for travellers wanting to get out and see the country: luxury high-rise resorts along the capital's Malecón, independently operated beach hotels, rooms for rent in Dominican family homes and an assortment of bearable budget hotels, many with private bath, hot water and a/c. Away from the main tourist spots expect to pay around US$30-50 for the night; in resort towns prices rise to US$75-140. Reservations are essential for the all-inclusives, where you'll get up to 75 percent off the price by booking with a travel agent before you arrive as part of a package.

There are no youth hostels in the DR, but a good way to cut expenses is the traditional *pensiones* still found in many towns, though over the past two decades they've begun to die out. There are also no campgrounds, and few travellers choose to camp here because of the lack of regulation.

Food and drink

If you take all your **meals** at an all-inclusive hotel, you'll get little sense of how Dominicans eat and drink; the "international" buffet fare on offer at these resorts can't compete with the delicious, no-nonsense cooking at the many mom-and-pop restaurants just outside their walls. Dominicans call their cuisine "comida criolla", and it's a delicious – if often a bit greasy – blend of Spanish, African and Taíno elements, with interesting regional variants across the island. Dishes usually include rice and beans – referred to locally as *la bandera dominicana* (the Dominican flag) – using either *habichuelas* (red beans) or the tiny black peas known as *morros*. Most often the rice is supplemented with chicken, either fried, grilled or served *asopao* (in a rich, soupy sauce). Invariably main courses come with *plátanos* (deep-fried green plantains, which locals often inundate with ketchup), and a small coleslaw salad. Outside of the major cities, **vegetarians** will often have to stick to rice and beans.

Local **breakfasts** are traditionally starchy and huge, and typically include *huevos revueltos* (scrambled eggs), sometimes *con jamón* (with bits of ham mixed in); *mangú*, mashed plantains mixed with oil and bits of fried onion; and *queso frito*, a deep-fried cheese. Dominican **lunches** are the day's main meal. Aside from the omnipresent chicken, popular main courses include *mondongo*, a tripe stew strictly for the strong of stomach; *mofongo*, a tasty blend of plantains, pork rinds and garlic; and **bistec encebollado**, grilled steak topped with onions and peppers. Special occasions, particularly in rural areas, call for either *chivo* (roast goat) with *cassava*, a crispy, flat bread inherited from the Taínos; or *sancocho*, a hearty stew with five different kinds of meat. For the very best in Dominican eating, go for the **seafood**, which is traditionally prepared one of five ways: *criolla*, in a flavourful, slightly spicy tomato sauce; *al ajillo*, doused in a rich garlic sauce; *al horno*, roasted with lemon; *al orégano*, in a tangy sauce with fresh oregano and heavy cream; and *con coco*, in a tomato, garlic and coconut milk blend especially prevalent on the Samaná Peninsula. The best local fish are the *mero* (sea bass), *chillo* (red snapper) and *carite* (kingfish). Other popular seafoods include *langosta* (clawless lobster), *lambí* (conch), *camarones* (shrimp), *pulpo* (octopus) and *cangrejo* (crab).

As far as **drinks** go, Dominican **coffee** is among the best in the world. Most Dominicans take it *solo*, with a great deal of sugar added, which is the way it's sold for RD$1 by morning street vendors, and handed out for free in the petrol stations. Dominican *café con leche* is made with steamed milk and is extremely good. *Jugo de naranja*, fresh orange juice squeezed as you order it, is another omnipresent Dominican morning drink; be sure to ask for it *sin azúcar* (without sugar). Later in the day you should sample the fresh coconut milk sold by street vendors, and the many Dominican *batidas*, popular fruit shakes made with ice, milk and either papaya, mango, pineapple or banana.

There are several Dominican **beer** brands, but by far the best and most popular is Presidente, served in both normal-sized and surreally large bottles, and comparing favourably with beers from across the world. Also popular are the very good, inexpensive local **rums**, Brugal, Barceló and Bermúdez.

Phones, post and email

It's not hard to keep in touch with home by phone or fax while you're in the DR because storefront **phone centres** are scattered about the country, though the price can be a bit steep. These phone centres are run by DR's many private telephone companies. The oldest, most venerated and by far the most omnipresent company is Verizon, which charges RD$5 per minute to North America; RD$18 per minute to Europe; and RD$26 per minute to Australia and New Zealand. The rates are a couple of pesos cheaper if you use a Verizon calling card, sold at Verizon phone centres in denominations of RD$25, 45, 95, 145, 245 and 500. You also have the option of going to one of Verizon's competitors that have sprung up over the past decade, the most popular

of which is Tricom; they charge RD$5 per minute to North America; RD$15 to Europe and RD$24 to Australia and New Zealand. Local calls cost RD$1 per minute, but it's important to note that a telephone call between towns in the DR is considered long-distance, and charged at the same rate as North American calls; all areas of the DR, however, are under one **area code**, ☎809. If at all possible avoid calling collect with any of these companies, as the prices are exorbitant.

Dominican *correos*, or **post offices**, are notoriously slow; even if you use special delivery (highly recommended) you'll still have to allow at least three weeks for your postcard or letter to reach North America, and at least a month for it to reach Europe or Australasia. Postage costs RD$3 to North America, RD$4 elsewhere.

Email is steadily growing in importance, with many phone centres in the larger cities offering Internet and email access, and a few private cybercafés cropping up in the resort areas.

Opening hours, festivals and holidays

Business hours in the Dominican Republic are normally 8.30am–6pm Monday to Friday, and 8.30am–12.30pm on Saturday. About half of the stores still close for the midday siesta. Banks are generally open Monday to Friday 8.30am–noon and 2–5pm, with a few open on Saturday. Pretty much everything is shut on Sundays, with the exception of some restaurants and most bars.

The Dominican Republic has a bewildering barrage of **festivals**. On every day of the year, there seems to be some kind of celebration somewhere, the majority of which are regional *fiestas patronales*, held in honour of the city's or town's patron saint. These traditional fiestas are one of the great pleasures of a trip to the DR; the box opposite covers only a few of the top events.

Major holidays and festivals

January
Virgen de Altagracia, January 21, honours the country's patron saint and is there-fore the most important religious day in the Dominican calendar, including a several-day pilgrimage to Higuey.
Duarte Day Holiday in honour of the Father of the Country, with public fiestas in all major towns on January 26.

February
Carnival The pre-eminent celebration of the year, held on every Sunday in Febru-ary and culminating on February 27. The biggest festival is in La Vega, with Santo Domingo a close second.
Independence Day Celebration of independence from Haiti and the culmination of the Dominican Carnival (Feb 27). The place to be is Santo Domingo.

April
Semana Santa The Christian Holy Week (variable, usually early to mid-April) is also the most important week of Haitian and Dominican *vodú*. Festivals take place in the Haitian *bateyes* (sugar plantations) and in Haina.

May
Espiritu Santo Huge celebrations in the capital's barrio Villa Mella, pueblo Santa María near San Cristóbal and the El Pomier caves, and San Juan de la Maguana; held seven weeks after Semana Santa.

June
San Pedro Apostol A colourful mummer festival in San Pedro de Macorís on June 29, with roving bands of masked singers and dancers performing dance dramas on the street.

August
Festival of the Bulls Higuey's *fiesta patronal* (Aug 14), with processions coming into the city from all sides – some from as far as 30km – with cowboys on horseback and large herds of cattle.

December
Christmas *Guloya* festivals in San Pedro de Macorís, Haitian voodoo celebrations in the Haitian *bateyes* and rural groups of Caribbean-style Navidad carollers in the campos (Dec 25).
Festival of the Bulls Traditional cattle festival in Bayaguana (Dec 28).

Outdoor activities

Opportunities for **watersports** are natu-rally tremendous, ranging from swimming, snorkelling and scuba diving, surfing and windsurfing, to deep-sea fishing and whale-watching. Though many beaches are protected from powerful ocean currents by natural barriers, others have dangerous rip-tides along them, and should be avoided by all but the strongest of swimmers.

The vast majority of Dominican **reefs** have been damaged beyond repair by careless local fishing practices, notably the daily dropping of anchors by thousands of small vessels. The only place you'll still find a large system of intact reefs is the stretch west of Puerto Plata, between La Isabela and Monte Cristi. By no coincidence, this is also by far the most remote coastal region in the country, and devilishly difficult to access for scuba diving and snorkelling. A number of tour operators and most all-inclusive hotels in the resort towns can take you to the more modest reefs around the island.

The north coast resort of Cabarete is known internationally as the **windsurfing** and kiteboarding capital of the Americas. Learning here is a challenge due to the strength of the waves and wind, though a dozen different clubs offer equipment rental and tutoring. Surfing is less organized and done mostly by locals. Popular venues include Playa Encuentra near Cabarete, Playas Grande and Preciosa just east of Río San Juan and Playa Boba north of Nagua.

The country's five separate mountain ranges provide several options for **mountain sports**; most popular are mountain biking, horseriding and several-day mountain treks. Cabarete's Iguana Mama is the one major mountain-bike tour outfit in the country, offering challenging day-trips into the Cordillera Septentrional and week-long mountain-bike and camping excursions from one side of the country to the other. The best hiking can be found along the trails leading from disparate parts of the Cordillera Central to Pico Duarte, the highest peak in the Caribbean. Horseriding excursions are also quite popular. In addition to the plethora of outfits that offer day-rides along the country's many beaches, you'll find quality mountain-riding operators in Cabarete, Punta Cana, Las Terrenas and Jarabacoa. Also in the mountains, Jarabacoa is the centre for white-water rafting and kayaking.

Finally, though there are several small, nondescript **golf courses** spread across the island, three of them stand head and shoulders above the pack: the Pete Dye-designed Teeth of the Dog course at *Casa de Campo* in La Romana, and the excellent Robert Trent Jones courses at Playa Dorada and Playa Grande on the Silver Coast. All three have the majority of their holes set on spectacular open oceanfront and are occasionally used as tournament venues.

History

Before Columbus, the island of Hispaniola was inhabited by the **Taínos**, an Arawak group that had migrated up from the Amazon basin and maintained an advanced culture on the island for centuries. This all came to an end in 1492, when **Christopher Columbus** "discovered" the New World. After stopping off at the Bahamian island of San Salvador, Columbus landed in what is today the Dominican Republic, where he encountered the Taínos. Attempting to circle around the island, his ship the *Santa Maria* grounded against a coral reef on December 25, 1492, forcing him to set up a small fort there — which he named La Navidad, leaving 25 men there before heading back with his remaining ships.

Upon returning in late 1493, Columbus found his fort burned and the settlers killed. He established his first small colony further east – La Isabela, today the village of **El Castillo** – where he set up a trading settlement to trade cheap European goods in return for large quantities of gold. La Isabela soon fell apart. Settlers died in the hundreds from malaria and yellow fever, and one disgruntled colonist hijacked a ship and headed back to Spain to complain. Columbus followed him back in 1496, and during his absence the colony was abandoned, with most Spaniards resettling at **Santo Domingo** along the mouth of the Ozama River. When Columbus returned in 1498, the colonists refused to obey his orders, and in 1500 he was sent back to Spain in chains.

Spain's King Ferdinand replaced Columbus with **Nicolás de Ovando**, with instructions to impose order on the unruly outpost. Ovando instigated the monumental construction in today's Zona Colonial and engaged in the systematic destruction of Taíno society, apportioning all Taínos to Spanish settlers as slaves and forcing their conversion to Christianity. Lacking resistance to Old World diseases and subjected to countless acts of random violence, the Taínos were quickly exterminated through overwork, suicide and disease.

To make up for the steep decline of forced labour, the Spaniards began embarking on **slaving expeditions** throughout the Caribbean and Central America in 1505, laying the foundation for future Spanish colonies. By 1515 the Spaniards had wiped out enough Native Americans that they began looking to slave labour from Africa, setting in motion the African slave trade. Santo Domingo's power slowly eroded as Spain branched out across the Americas, and by the end of the sixteenth century was little more than a colonial backwater. The French began encroaching in 1629, settling the island of Tortuga and branching out from there onto the western side of Hispaniola. When the French colony's slaves revolted in the early nineteenth century, they had little trouble invading and occupying Spanish Hispaniola, ruling it for 21 years. Only in 1843 were the Spanish colonists able to boot the invaders out, and for the first time establish the Dominican Republic as an independent country.

But this independence did not last long. A series of warlords known as *caudillos* tore the country apart in their quest for money and power, and in 1861 strongman Pedro Santana sold the island back to Spain. The Spaniards didn't last long, though; almost immediately a new revolutionary movement was formed, and the occupiers were forced to withdraw in 1865. A renewed period of extended **civil warfare** between *caudillos* ensued until the United States intervened in 1914. The Americans stayed for over eight years, successfully reorganizing the nation's financing but instituting a repressive national police. When the US left, this new police force took control, and its leader **Rafael Leonidas Trujillo** maintained absolute totalitarian control over the Dominican Republic for three decades. In the late 1950s, though, Cuba's **Fidel Castro** took an interest in overthrowing the dictator, and concerns about a possible communist takeover prompted the CIA to train a group of Dominican dissidents, who assassinated Trujillo in a dramatic car chase on May 30, 1961.

Upon Trujillo's death, Vice President **Joaquín Balaguer** rose to power, and continued his totalitarian practices. Balaguer was deposed in a popular 1965 uprising, but the US military again intervened and soon placed him back in control. Only in 1978 was he forced to hold free and fair elections – and was promptly thrown out of office, only to win it back in 1986 after an extended economic crisis. Balaguer managed to edge out his rivals again in 1990, but left the presidential race in 1994 when it was obvious that he would not beat **Leonel Fernández**, who ran a slick, centrist American-style campaign and edged the competition out by a few thousand votes. 1998 saw the first back-to-back free and fair elections in the Dominican Republic's history, as Fernández gave way to political opponent **Hipolito Mejia**. Hipolito made a mess of the Dominican economy, though, and is now known locally as "Huracán Hipolito" for his disastrous fiscal policies. As a result, Leonel returned to power in late 2004 and he's already making headway on the host of economic problems inherited from his predecessor.

6.1

Santo Domingo and around

Santo Domingo isn't the tropical paradise most travellers come to the Caribbean in search of, but at the core of the rather bewildering sprawl the old Spanish colonial capital – the very first European city of the New World – lies magically intact along the western bank of the Río Ozama. This was the domain of **Christopher Columbus**: founded by his brother Bartolomé, ruled by him for a time and claimed a decade later by his son Diego. After five centuries, the Columbus palace can still be found alongside the cobblestone streets and monumental architecture of the walled, limestone city the family built.

Far more than just history makes Santo Domingo an integral part of any trip to the Dominican Republic; it is, after all, the modern face of the country, and as such has a nonstop liveliness not seen in many other places. The vitality extends, though in a slightly more disappointing manner, to the very reachable beaches east of the city, at **Boca Chica** and **Juan Dolio**, both fairly built-up resorts.

Santo Domingo

Most visitors to **SANTO DOMINGO** understandably make a beeline for the **Zona Colonial**, Santo Domingo's large, substantially intact colonial district, home to dozens of wonderful old buildings and a dramatic setting right on the river. Many never bother to venture outside of this expansive, historic neighbourhood, but while

it rates the most attention you should also make the effort to check out at least a few other diversions – especially around the barrios of the **Gazcue** and **Malecón** – throughout the city.

Arrival and getting around

The majority of visitors arrive at **Aeropuerto Internacional Las Américas** (☎809/412-5888), the country's largest, located 13km east of the city proper. The airport is far enough away from the city centre to make a **taxi** the most efficient way into town if you're not renting a car; you shouldn't pay more than RD$500.

If arriving by **bus**, you'll have no trouble finding a taxi or public transport from your terminal, including Caribe Tours at Av 27 de Febrero and Navarro (☎809/221-4422); Metro at Máximo Gómez 61 and Av 27 de Febrero (☎809/566-7126); and Terrabus at Guarocuya 4 (☎809/531-0383).

There is no official **public transit** system in Santo Domingo, but the informal network of *públicos* and *guaguas* manage to cover every inch of the city and can get you pretty much anywhere for under RD$10. Just stand on the corner of a major street and wave your arms at the first car with a taxi sign. More comfortable are private **taxis**; the most reputable operator is Apolo (☎809/537-0000).

Accommodation

There's a wide variety of **accommodation** in the city, but budget rooms in decent neighbourhoods are hard to come by. Most expensive are the high-rises along the **Malecón**, which have great rooms and service. If you've got this kind of money, though, consider one of the smaller *pensións* tucked away in the **Zona Colonial**, which are more intimate and welcoming than the large waterfront hotels. For peace and quiet at a more reasonable rate, head to one of the small hotels in residential **Gazcue**.

Zona Colonial

Aida El Conde 474 and Espaillat ☎809/685-7692. The only hotel with balcony rooms on El Conde and a good bargain for clean, simple accommodation. ②

Conde de Penalba El Conde 111 and Meriño ☎809/688-7121, ⊛www.condepenalba.com. A fair compromise between comfort and colonial character, this small hotel, on the second floor of a century-old building on Parque Duarte, boasts good service, comfortable rooms (a/c, cable TV, phone) and excellent showers. You pay for the location, though. ⑤

Nicolás Nader Luperón 151 and Duarte, ☎809/687-6674, ⊛www.naderenterprises. com/hostal. A well-regarded, small luxury hotel with spacious, tastefully decorated rooms in a colonial-era mansion. ③

Palacio Duarte 106 and Ureña ☎809/682-4730, ⊛www.hotel-palacio.com. Perhaps the best place in the old city for the money, featuring large rooms, attentive service and all the amenities in a 1628 mansion. ③

Malecón and around

Maison Gatreaux Llúberes 8 ☎809/687-4856.

Large, great-value rooms with a/c, comfortable beds and especially strong, hot showers. US$2 extra for cable TV. ②

Renaissance Jaragua Malecón 367 ☎809/221-2222, ⊛h.jaragua@verizon.net.do. Massive luxury resort with big rooms, great service, swimming pool, hot tub, four restaurants, bar, disco, casino and a tropical garden. ⑥

Gazcue

Felicidad Aristides Cabrar 58 ☎809/221-6615. Clean rooms in a small *pensión* with hot water. Not particularly attractive but the neighbourhood is quiet and pretty. ①

La Grand Mansión Danae 26 ☎809/689-8758. Unpretentious and functional on a quiet residential street, with private hot-water bath and nice rooms. ①

Quisqueya Cayetano Rodriguez 201 ☎687-6037. Unremarkable, mid-range private rooms and a dormitory with RD$140 beds – one of the best deals in town for budget travellers and in a safe location – though it's a good long walk to the colonial district from here. Very big with Peace Corps volunteers, so it's a good place to meet people who know a bit about the country. ①–③

The Zona Colonial

Though the **Zona Colonial** – straddling the western mouth of the Río Ozama – is crammed with monumental architecture, it's very much a living neighbourhood thanks to the many cafés and clapboard row-houses where thousands of people live and work. The most important monuments can be seen in a single day; thorough exploration requires two or three.

The town gates east to Parque Colón

A good place to begin exploring is the massive **Puerta de la Misericordia** (Gate of Mercy) on Hincado and the Malecón, a sixteenth-century fortified city entrance. On February 27, 1844, Ramón Mella fired off the first shot of the revolution against Haiti here. Follow Mella's torchlit route up Hincado to Calle El Conde and the **Puerta El Conde**, an imposing stone structure where Mella first raised the new national flag. The gate leads into beautiful **Parque Independencia**, a popular meeting-place encircled by a traffic-choked ring road.

Stretching east from Parque Independencia is **Calle El Conde**, once Santo Domingo's main thoroughfare but closed off to motorized traffic in the 1970s and now a broad promenade lined with cafés, restaurants and stores. Follow it eight blocks to **Parque Colón**, a pleasant open space surrounded by beautiful colonial and Victorian buildings. At the west end of the park is the nineteenth-century town hall, while to the north you'll find a series of cigar and souvenir shops.

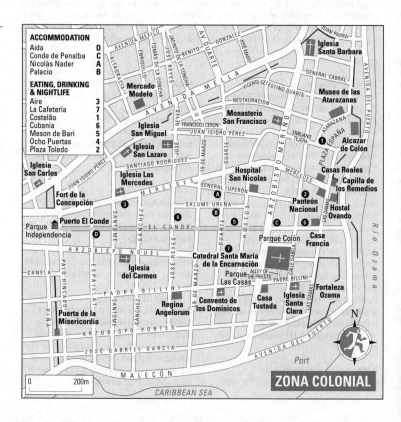

The cathedral and around

Most imposing of the buildings along Parque Colón is the **Catedral Santa María de la Encarnación** (daily 8am–6pm), originally intended to be the religious centre of the West Indies. Built between 1521 and 1540, the cathedral's **western facade** is a prime example of Plateresque architecture, a style that features an over-abundance of fanciful ornamentation. The gold Habsburg seal and statuary that once surrounded the main portals were stolen by Sir Francis Drake – the current ones are modest reproductions. Inside, under a Gothic-styled ribbed vault, and just to the right of the pulpit, **Santa Ana Chapel** bears the tomb of colonial administrator Rodrigo de Bastidas and the only surviving original stained-glass window, depicting an angel hovering over Virgin and Child. Beside it, the **Chapel of Life and Death** has a Rincón Mora window – reminiscent of Chagall – showing a decidedly deranged John the Baptist baptizing a clean-shaven Christ.

Pass through the cathedral's southern door and you'll enter the enclosed **Plaza of the Priests**, once the city cemetery. Across the plaza, the **Alley of the Priests**, an attractive walkway lined with bougainvillea, leads past the old priests' quarters. Exiting onto the street from here, it's a block north to **Iglesia Santa Clara**, the New World's first nunnery. Built in 1552, it was severely damaged by Drake and renovated by a blustery local businessman named Rodrigo Pimentel.

From the entrance to the Alley of the Priests you can also walk a half-block west to **Plaza Padre Billini**, at Billini and Meriño, a small public plaza backed by a row of expensive antique, jewellery and clothing shops. If you're in no mood to shop, cross to **Casa Tostado**, on the plaza's southeast corner, built in 1503. Inside you'll find the **Museum of the Nineteenth-Century Dominican Family** (Mon–Sat 9am–4pm; RD$5), featuring a number of antique furnishings.

Calle de las Damas

Calle de las Damas (Street of the Ladies), the first road laid out by Nicólas de Ovando when he moved the town to the river's west side, received its name in 1509, thanks to the retinue of women who would accompany Diego Columbus' wife María de Toledo down the street to church. On the street's southern end **Fortaleza Ozama** (daily 9am–7pm; RD$10) was long Santo Domingo's most strategic site. Built in 1502 and enlarged over the centuries, it's set on a steep bank over the mouth of the Ozama and was the departure point for the Spanish conquests across the Americas. The largest structure is the medieval **Tower of Homage**, the most impenetrable part of the fortress and long used as a prison. Also on the grounds are the old arsenal and the excavated remains of the provisional fort from 1502.

Across the street you'll pass two more restored colonial buildings before arriving at **Casa Francia**, originally the home of conquistador Hernán Cortes. It was here that he plotted his conquest of Mexico; you'll find his family's coat of arms in the second gallery. Across the street, **Hostal Nicólas de Ovando** incorporates the homes of the Ovando and Davila families, both prominent in the early colony. Attached to the hotel's north wall is **Capilla de los Remedios**, the Davilas' private chapel, with an especially pretty triple-arched belfry.

Casa Davila looks directly across at **Plaza María Toledo**, a broad walkway with a sixteenth-century fountain, and the **Panteón Nacional** (Mon–Sat 9am–7pm; free), built from 1714 to 1745 as a Jesuit convent. In 1955 Trujillo renovated it and reinterred most of the major military and political figures from Dominican history. The building's Neoclassical, martial facade seems particularly suited for its sober task, topped with a prominent cupola flanked by statues of Loyola and Jesus. The interior has been completely redone, with Italian marble floors and an enormous central chandelier. Beside the Panteón is **Casa de las Gárgolas**, named after the prominent row of five grimacing gargoyles above the door.

Plaza España

Calle de las Damas ends at **Plaza España**, an attractive, tiled open space surrounded on all sides by monuments and with terrific views across the river – hence the outdoor cafés that proliferate. An intact section of the old town wall still skirts the eastern plaza, extending to **Puerta San Diego**, the colonial-era entrance from the port.

At the southern end of the plaza, **Museo de las Casas Reales** (Tues–Sun 9am–6pm; RD$50; ☎809/682-4202), built between 1503 and 1520, was the administrative centre of the West Indies, housing the Royal Court, Treasury and Office of the Governor. Inside, the museum's rather hodgepodge collection includes a few Taíno artefacts, Spanish navigational instruments, and an armoury donated by Trujillo with examples of weaponry used here since Columbus. Opposite the Casas Reales is the **Alcazar de Colón** (daily 9am–5pm; RD$50), the fortified palace of the Columbus family, built by Diego from 1511 to 1515. This building is the finest local example of the late Gothic style called **Isabelline**, characterized by plain, linear surfaces adorned only with Islamic portals and delicate vine ornaments. The museum itself holds an array of sixteenth-century ornaments, including religious tapestries, a display case of period silverware and a sixteenth-century harp and clavichord.

Bordering the Alcazar to the north is a winding row of colonial storefronts known as **Las Atarazanas**. Follow it to the end where the Reales Atarazanas, once the colonial port authority, contains the **Museo de las Atarazanas**, Colón 4 (daily 9am–6pm; RD$15; ☎809/682-4834). Inside you'll find the recovered booty from the wreck of the sixteenth-century Spanish galleon *Concepción*, sunk during a hurricane in the Bahía de Samaná.

El Convento de los Dominicos and around

Back to the south of El Conde, towards the Malecón, stand three ancient churches worth a detour. The oldest, the 1510 **Convento de los Dominicos**, Billini and Hostos (Mon–Fri 7–9am & 5.30–7pm, Sun 7.30am–noon & 7–8pm), held the New World's first university, San Tomé de Aquino. Its striking stone facade is framed by decorative two-dimensional pillars; blue *Mudéjar* tiling runs along the top of the portal, and a profusion of red Isabelline vine ornamentation surrounds the circular window in the centre. A block east on Billini/José Reyes is nunnery **Regina Angelorum** (Queen of the Angels), with huge external buttressing, decaying gargoyles and a sombre stone facade. Knock on the caretaker's door in the back to have a peek inside, where you'll find an eighteenth-century Baroque altar with a stunning silver retable. Smaller but prettier is **Iglesia del Carmen**, erected at Arz Nouel and San Tomé in 1590. Its facade boasts a decorative Isabelline red-brick portal topped by a fanciful Islamic peak.

The Malecón

The **Malecón**, the capital's oceanfront boardwalk, commences within the Zona Colonial. An intact section of the old city wall follows for 100m to **Fort San José**, built on a strategic oceanfront promontory after an attempted invasion by the British in 1655. The cannons that remain appear to point across the street at a fifty-metre high statue of **Fray Montesino**, a sixteenth-century priest who preached against the Taíno genocide. Further on you'll find **La Obelisca**, placed by Trujillo in 1941 to honour repayment of long-outstanding debt to the US. A kilometre west is another obelisk, **El Obelisco**, built in 1936 to commemorate Santo Domingo's temporary re-christening as Ciudad Trujillo. Informal **party zones** abound along the capital's boardwalk, with especially lively scenes occuring nightly at the municipal port at Calle del Puerto, La Parillada along the San Jose fort and at the intersection with Av Máximo Gómez.

Gazcue

West of the Zona Colonial and north of the Malecón is rambling, tree-shaded **Gazcue**, a middle-class neighbourhood highlighted by the **Plaza de la Cultura**, Máximo Gómez and Ureña, a complex of museums alongside the National Theatre.

The first stop should be the magnificent **Museo de Arte Moderno** (Tues–Sun 10am–6pm; RD$10; ☎809/685-2154), four storeys dedicated to twentieth-century Dominican art, with a superb permanent collection on the second and third floors. Look out in particular for the paintings of **Candido Bidó**, whose stylized idealizations of *campesino* life have won international acclaim. The museum owns six Bidós, all of them on the second floor, including his most famous, *El Paseo a las 10am*, a stylized painting of a Dominican woman in a sunhat with a handful of flowers.

The plaza's other main attraction is the **Museo del Hombre Dominicano** (Tues–Sun 10am–5pm; RD$20; ☎809/687-3623), which holds an extraordinary collection of Taíno artefacts and has a good anthropological exhibit on Dominican *fiestas patronales*. Less enticing is the **Museo de Historia y Geografía** (Tues–Sun 9.30am–5pm; free; ☎809/686-6668), which takes you through an uneven collection of historical memorabilia from the past two centuries.

East of the Ozama

Though most attractions lie west of the Río Ozama, there are a few scattered points of interest along the eastern bank and beyond. The best-known of these is the **Columbus Lighthouse** (daily 9.30am–5.30pm; RD$30; ☎809/592-1492), known locally as **El Faro** ("the lighthouse"), a monument completed in 1992, the 500th anniversary of Columbus' "discovery". Within this mammoth, cross-shaped concrete edifice stands the baroque **mausoleum of Christopher Columbus**, which supposedly holds the body of Columbus (a church in Seville makes a similar claim) with dozens of flowery angels hovering above the marble casket alongside a 24-hour honour guard.

El Faro towers over the western end of **Parque Mirador del Este**, a pleasant stretch of manicured woodlands spanning the length of the barrios east of the Ozama. At the park's far eastern tip are a series of large caves dotted with freshwater lagoons. Known as **Los Tres Ojos**, "The Three Eyes" (daily 9am–5pm; RD$10), the Taínos used them for religious ceremonies; more recently they've been the setting for some half-dozen Tarzan movies. The setting is quite peaceful and gives off a true jungle atmosphere, despite being located inside Santo Domingo city limits.

Eating

Dining options range from the omnipresent *comedores* and *pica pollos* to gourmet restaurants with speciality cuisines from around the world. At the more expensive restaurants, expect to spend RD$300–400 per person for a meal with a drink.

Zona Colonial

La Cafetería El Conde 253. Best of the cafés along El Conde and a hangout for local artists. Delicious breakfasts with fresh orange juice and *café con leche*.

Costelão Atarazana 23 ☎809/688-2773. This new traditional Brazilian *churrascaria* easily takes over the mantle of best place to eat on Plaza España, with all-you-can-eat 900-peso meals that include chicken wings, grilled pork, steak, chicken, veal, pork ribs, quail, rabbit, sausage and red snapper.

Plaza Toledo Isabela la Católica and Luperón. Beautiful outdoor courtyard featuring linguini with shrimp or criolla sauce and delicious dessert crepes.

Malecón

Fogarate Malecón 517. Some of the best Dominican food in the city, doled out in a fun atmosphere full of multicoloured thatched roofs. Try the traditional *asopao* rice with chicken dish served in

Dominican syncretism

The syncretic religion **vodú dominicana** – the mixing of European and African religions in South America and the Caribbean – is very much a part of Dominican culture, though Eurocentrism and official disfavour make it an object of shame. Cousin to Haitian voodoo, it came about during the colonial era, when European Christianity was imposed on African slaves from the Congo and West Africa. The Africans mixed Catholicism with their own belief system, and over time various Christian saints came to be linked to deities imported from Africa.

Vodú involves ceremonies using altars covered with depictions of saints, offertory candles, plastic cups of rum and crosses honouring the **Guedes**, bawdy cemetery spirits known to spout lascivious songs when they possess humans. **Possession** is an integral part of *vodú* ceremonies, both by saints and the spirits of dead Taíno warriors. You'll see *vodú* paraphernalia, including love potions, spray cans that impart good luck in the lottery and Catholic icons at the many *botánicas* in towns throughout the country.

a beat-up tin bowl.

Vesuvio Malecón 521. Most renowned restaurant in the city, deservedly so for its vast array of delicious, if expensive, pastas. Next door they have a more downscale dining room for pizza, sandwiches and crepes.

Gazcue

Don Pepe Pasteur 41 and Santiago ☎809/686-8481. This is the place to go if you've budgeted for one big splurge, with by far the freshest and most well-prepared seafood in the city. The menu is a display of fresh seafood on ice, including lobster and an assortment of fish.

La Mezquita Independencia 407. Outstanding little seafood restaurant with a cosy dining room and a loyal local following. Specialities include grouper (called *mero*, served criolla or *al orégano*), octopus,

and sea snail.

El Provocón 4to Santiago and José Pérez, with other locations throughout the city. Outdoor patio offering heaping portions of grilled chicken, rice and beans and salad. Open 24 hours.

Outer districts

Lumi's Park Av Lincoln 809 just north of 27 de Febrero. Fun outdoor tropical garden atmosphere in which you can enjoy home-style Dominican *mofongo* (fried salt pork and mashed plantains) and grilled steaks.

Tacos del Sol Av Lincoln 609 and Locutores. Popular outdoor Mexican joint with tacos, burritos and fajitas, though the frozen daiquiris and pleasant outdoor plaza are what attract the crowds.

Drinking, nightlife and entertainment

The Malecón is the traditional focus of **nightlife**; along with some of the city's finest dance halls, the boardwalk is crowded with outdoor restaurants that start getting packed around 10pm and stay open into the early morning. There are also clubs across the city that specialize in **Cuban son**. Weekends see plenty of activity, but the busiest night for local clubs is Monday, when most are booked with big-name acts.

The Zona Colonial is a great place to go **bar-hopping**. At night the ruins are especially atmospheric, and dotted around them are a variety of neighbourhood joints, jazz bars and slick New York-style clubs. The other major centre is the Plaza Central, where most wealthy young Dominicans hang out. The Malecón also has a number of informal setups with a liquor shack surrounded by tables and chairs; most popular of these is *Plaza D'Frank*, two blocks west of the *Centenario Hotel*.

Bars

Cubania El Conde 53 between Isabela and Las Damas, Zona Colonial, ☎809/333-7001. Features nightly live *son* with top Cuban musicians who are brought in for the week, and excellent Cuban food such as *ropa vieja*, *bistec encebollado* and

black bean shrimp and rice. For drinks go with the *mojito criollo* which – unlike *mojitos* outside the Caribbean – is made with local yerba buena instead of mint.

Meson de Bari Hostos and Ureña, Zona Colonial. Atmospheric after-work gathering place notable for

Baseball in Santo Domingo

Baseball is the most exciting spectator sport in Santo Domingo due to the high level of play and the passions of the fanatical crowds; two separate professional teams, **Licey** and **Escogido**, play in the winter professional league from mid-November to early February; games are at Estadio Quisqueya, Máximo Gómez and Kennedy (tickets RD$50–150; ☎809/565-5565, ⊛www.beisboldominicano.com).

its soundtrack of traditional *bachatas*, *merengue perico ripao* and old-style Cuban *son*.

Ocho Puertas José Reyes 107, Zona Colonial. Trendy techno bar set in a gorgeously restored colonial warehouse, with lounge rooms and a young, wealthy scene.

Discos and live music

Fusion Rose El Conde and Las Damas, Zona Colonial. Best club in Santo Domingo for hip-hop, house and dancehall music, and the most popular place in the Zone for young locals. The crowds here are friendly and drink prices are reasonable. RD$100 cover for men, women get in free.

Jet Set Independencia 2253, Malecón ☎809/535-4145. Very nice seventh-floor disco with great views of the city. RD$50 cover.

Jubilee Malecón 367, in the *Renaissance Jaragua Hotel*, Malecón ☎809/688-8026. Luxurious hotel disco featuring great sound and light systems, though serving expensive drinks. RD$100 cover.

La Guácara Taina Av Mirador del Sur, Gazcue, ☎809/530-2666. Probably the most famous club in the city, set in a huge, multi-level natural cave, that now focuses almost exclusively on electronica and is a popular spot for ravers, who call it simply "The Cave".

Mauna Loa Calle Héroes de Luperón at Malecón, Centro de los Héroes ☎809/533-2151. Super-suave nightclub and casino with tables looking out onto a big-band stage reminiscent of the Roaring Twenties. If you love *Buena Vista Social Club*, this place is a must. RD$25 cover.

Monumento del Son Av Charles de Gaulle and Los Restauradores, barrio Sabana Perdida. Famous outdoor *son* hall 5km north of the Las Américas highway.

Vieja Havana Av Máximo Gómez, barrio Villa Mella. Great outdoor *son* hall best on Thursday and Sunday nights, when they hold old-style dance contests.

Listings

Airlines Air Canada, Ricart 54 (☎809/567-2236); American, El Conde 401 (☎809/542-5151); JetBlue, Aeropuerto Las Américas (☎809/365-2350).

Banks Banco Popular (24hr ATMs), Calle Isabela la Católica and Tajeras; Calle Duarte and Mella. Scotiabank (24hr ATMs), Av Duarte and Mella; Calle Isabela la Católica and Mercedes.

Embassies Canada, Marchena 39 (☎809/685-1136); UK, 27 de Febrero 233 (☎809/472-7111); US, Calle Nicolás Pensión (☎809/731-4294).

Hospitals Centro Médico Semma, Perdomo and Joaquín Peres (☎809/686-1705); Clínica Abreu, Beller 42 (☎809/688-4411).

Internet InetB2.com, El Conde and José Reyes (☎809/682-6138).

Pharmacies Carol, Ricart 24 (☎809/562-6767); San Judas Tadeo, Independencia 33 (☎809/685-8165).

Police Dial ☎911 from any phone.

Post office Av Héroes de Luperón just off the Malecón (☎809/534-5838).

Telephone Verizon, El Conde 137; Tricom, Hermanas Mirabal 127.

Wiring money Western Union, Av Lincoln 306 (Mon–Sat 9.30am–noon & 2–5pm).

Around Santo Domingo

Those looking for a bit of Caribbean beach should head to **Boca Chica**, a festive, though overrun resort town 10km east of the airport; further along is **Juan Dolio**, a strip of resort-heavy beachfront.

Boca Chica

Once one of the island's prime swimming spots, **BOCA CHICA** curves along a small protected bay, with transparent Caribbean water paralleling a long line of beach shacks. Sadly, the town has become so overwhelmed with tourism – and an accompanying plethora of shysters and informal "guides" – that it's no longer the best spot along the coast to spend some time, and a major draw these days is prostitution. Sitting on the **beach** is the main daytime activity, and the waters are low and calm enough for a good swim. Expect a big crowd at weekends.

Accommodation

There are plenty of **hotels** in Boca Chica, including three **all-inclusives** (only two are on the beach) and a sprinkling of small **hostels** all across town.

Dominican Bay Vicini and 20 de Diciembre ☏809/412-2001, ℱ523-6310. Best local all-inclusive resort, with beautiful grounds, modern rooms and good food. ❸
Europa Calle Dominguez and Duarte ☏809/523-5721, ℮htleuropa@verizon.net.do. Highly recommended little French-run hotel with 33 ocean-view rooms and outstanding service. ❷
Tropic Lost Paradise Vicini and Del Sur ☏809/523-4424. Check here first if you're on a rock-bottom budget. Pretty basic rooms but they're clean and safe. ❶

Eating and drinking

Boca Chica has several quality **restaurants**, but the very best places to eat are the beachside food shacks serving fresh seafood. The **bars** are all along the main strip, Calle Duarte.

Boca Marina Prolongación Duarte 12 ☏809/523-6702. Fantastic seafood that's relatively pricey but well worth it. Try the red snapper or dorado filet, heaping plates of grilled shrimp, ceviches and fried calamari. The waterfront setting is ideal; if you bring your bathing suit, you can jump off the edge of the restaurant and swim between courses.
D'Lucien Duarte 1. Pricey patio restaurant with views of the promenade and fresh seafood displayed on ice.
Terraza Quebec Vicini 45. Good French-Canadian restaurant with *filet de poisson*, a good house lasagne and fresh seafood.

Juan Dolio

Just east of Boca Chica begins a 25-kilometre-long line of rocky coast dotted with all-inclusive resorts, collectively known as **JUAN DOLIO**. This resort area has never quite matched Boca Chica, its northern rival, but a couple of its new resorts are the equal of any all-inclusives in the country – if it weren't for the beach. Though the sand is perfectly acceptable, dead coral under the water makes swimming and walking in the water uncomfortable, and the beaches are no match for what you'll find at Punta Cana. Nonetheless, you can have a good time here, primarily because of a couple of great independent hotels and the plethora of local nightlife.

Accommodation

Barceló Talanquera Carretera Las Américas Km 13 ☏809/526-1476, ℱ526-2408. The tops of the Juan Dolio resorts, with palatial grounds, great rooms and suites, plus shopping gallery, three swimming pools and sports facilities. ❻
Fior di Loto Calle Central 517 ☏809/526-1146, ℱ526-3332, ℮hfdiloto@verizon.net.do. Highly recommended independent hotel decorated in the style of a Rajasthan palace in India, with twenty well-appointed rooms of varying sizes. The restaurant here is outstanding as well, and it's a great place to meet other travellers. ❷

Eating, drinking and nightlife

For **dining**, stick to the two excellent Italian restaurants along Juan Dolio's main strip. The best place for **nightlife** depends on which night of the week it is; this is based on local tradition rather than any particular events that take place. The entire Juan Dolio crowd heads to the pleasant indoor bar *Café Giulia* (Vila del Mar 288) on Mondays, the outdoor *Chocolate Bar* (Calle Central 127) on Fridays and the full-out dance hall *El Batey* (Calle Central 84) on Saturdays.

Fior di Loto Calle Central 517. Tremendous pastas, traditional Dominican seafood dishes and some really excellent Indian curries set amid a pleasantly off-beat dining room with Far Eastern artefacts and private couches shielded by billowing curtains.

Restaurante El Sueño Calle Central 330. Formal Italian fare in a relatively swank outdoor patio and with outstanding service. In addition to the pastas, which are excellent, try the chicken scallopini in white wine sauce or bass fillet in mushroom sauce.

6.2

The southeast

The Santo Domingo valley stretches east along the coast from the capital, encompassing vast tracts of sugar cane. North of these fields roll the verdant hills of the Cordillera Oriental, which terminate at the bowl-shaped swamp basin of Parque Nacional Los Haitises. This is the Dominican Republic's **Southeast**, known primarily for its popular resort zones **Bávaro** and **Punta Cana**, bookends of a thirty-kilometre strip of uninterrupted sand lined with all-inclusives.

Past these attractions, the Southeast is fairly poor, rural and bereft of must-see sights – with the exception of two national parks. **Parque Nacional del Este**, poking into the Caribbean at the southeastern tip of the Dominican Republic, continues the theme of great beachfront, especially along **Isla Saona**, while the mangrove swamps of **Parque Nacional Los Haitises** hide several Taíno caves you can visit by boat.

San Pedro de Macorís

Crowded **SAN PEDRO DE MACORÍS**, seventy kilometres east of Santo Domingo, owes its uneven development to the boom-and-bust fortunes of the sugar industry. Victorian civic monuments built during the crop's glory years stand along the eastern bank of the Higuamo River, a far cry from the squalor of the surrounding neighbourhoods. Many of the 125,000 people of San Pedro are descendants of *Cocolos* – "The English", as many of them prefer to be called – imported during the early twentieth century as seasonal field labour. Their presence is most obvious during the **Cocolo festivals** held at Christmas and the Feast of San Pedro (June 24–30), when competing troupes of masked dancers known as **mummers** wander door to door along the major thoroughfares in elaborate costumes and perform dance dramas depicting folktales and biblical stories.

Continuous urban migration has made the bulk of San Pedro a pretty miserable place, and the first view of its smokestacks and sprawling slums is a bit off-putting. What redeems it is its **Malecón**, a bustling seaside boardwalk with public beaches at either end. Head north from the Malecón onto Avenida Charro at the *Hotel Macorix* to get a quick glimpse of the Victorian architecture built during the city's heyday. Foremost is the 1911 **Iglesia San Pedro Apostol**, Av Charro and Independencia, a three-aisled whitewash church with a prominent bell tower. Time has been less kind to the old **town hall** a block south of the church, partially in ruins and occupied by a metalwork factory.

Far more than for architecture, though, San Pedro is famous for its baseball players, including Pedro Guerrero, George Bell and Sammy Sosa – and a pilgrimage to **Estadio Tetelo Vargas**, Av Circunvalación and Carretera Mella, a spacious, tattered concrete temple to the sport, is compelling for serious fans. Look in Santo Domingo newspapers for schedules; tickets are available during the winter baseball season on the night of the game for RD$200–300.

5km east of San Pedro on the highway to La Romana, you'll find prominent national park signs marking the entrance to the newly renovated **Cueva de las Maravillas** (Tues–Sun 10am–6pm; adults RD$100, children under 12 RD$50; ⓦwww.cuevadelasmaravillas.com). This is a truly first-rate attraction, with scores of Taíno petroglyphs, beautifully odd geologic formations and easy walkways with motion-sensor lighting that make the caverns easy to explore during the one-hour guided tours. Only a few of the guides speak English, but those that do are well versed in the cave's history and the significance of the various petroglyphs.

Practicalities

Though San Pedro is fairly large, there's not much in the way of **accommodation**; the top hotel in town is the amenity-laden *Howard Johnson Hotel Macorix*, Malecón/ Deligne (☎809/529-2100, ✉hj.macorix@verizon.net.do; ❷), which has impeccable service and a patio/swimming pool area that thrums with live *merengue* at weekends. For **food** head straight to *Robi Mar*, on Av Charro across from Iglesia San Pedro, a romantic little riverside restaurant hidden behind the clapboard stalls where local fishermen sell the day's catch; specialities include garlic shrimp and melt-in-your-mouth grilled dorado. San Pedro's **nightlife** is clustered along the ocean boardwalk; the current hot spot is the high-tech disco *Lexus*, and there are outdoor beer halls with ocean views and dancing all along the Malecón.

La Romana and Casa de Campo

LA ROMANA, 37km east of San Pedro, has been a one-company town since the South Porto Rico Sugar Company built the mammoth Central Romana mill in 1917; it was the only sugar operation not taken over by Trujillo during his reign. The mill was sold to Gulf & Western in 1967, who used the profits to diversify their holdings in the area, constructing the lavish *Casa de Campo* resort. The town itself is not especially interesting, though **nightlife** is good and a walk along the rambling barrio that borders the river's western bank makes for a pleasant hour. Also worth a visit in winter is **Michelin baseball stadium**, on Abreu and Luperón at the city's west end, home of the La Romana Azucareros (check Santo Domingo newspapers for schedules; RD$100–250 for tickets) – perhaps not as exciting as the games in San Pedro, but good play nevertheless.

Just east of La Romana, the **Casa de Campo** resort, accessible via a marked Highway 4 turn-off, is a massive complex. It costs a bit more than the all-inclusives along Bávaro Beach, but you'll be spared the security paranoia and compulsory plastic wristbands of most deluxe Dominican accommodations. The complex encompasses seven thousand manicured acres set along the sea and boasts two golf courses, a 24-hour tennis centre, fourteen swimming pools, equestrian stables, a sporting clay course and so forth. In addition to the spacious, comfortable rooms, there are 150 luxury private villas with butler, private chef and maid. The crowning pleasure is **Playa Minitas**, a gorgeous strand of beach protected by a shallow coral reef – nice enough that some spend their whole vacation on it.

Flanking the resort to the east is another Gulf & Western brainchild, **Altos de Chavón**, a high-concept shopping mall perched atop a cliff looking out over the Chavón River. Constructed to the specifications of a sixteenth-century Italian village with artificially aged limestone, it exudes dreary kitsch like few places in the country, its cobblestone streets littered with double-parked tour buses and its "Tuscan" villas crammed to the gills with dime-store souvenirs.

Practicalities

Accommodation at *Casa de Campo* (☎809/523-3333, ⊕www.casadcampo.com; ❼–❽) won't disappoint, as rooms are large, well appointed and include all the amenities one would expect for the price. Decor is more in line with top-flight corporate hotels, as opposed to the dreary motel rooms you'll find in most Dominican all-inclusives. Within town, the solid but somewhat drab *Olimpo*, Abreu and Llúberes (☎809/550-7646, ⊕550-7647; ❷), qualifies as the best overnight option, with good service, a/c, telephone and cable TV.

Casa de Campo used to have far better **food** than the other Dominican all-inclusives, but quality has deteriorated sharply over the past few years; the best option is their beachfront seafood restaurant, which does good lobster and blackened grouper fillets. Nevertheless, they do offer meal plans costing US$12 for breakfast, US$50 for breakfast and dinner and US$65 for all three meals. The best restaurants in La Romana are around the town's *parque central*, including *Shish Kebab*, on Calle Reales a block south of the park, a decent little Lebanese joint, and the more formal *La Casita*, Richiez 57 and Doucuday (☎809/349-6155), whose Italian menu includes seafood pastas and lobster in cognac. La Romana's **nightlife** nets few tourists but can be a lot of fun. Head first to *Fava* disco on Gonzalvo just off the park.

Bayahibe and Parque Nacional del Este

The former fishing village of **BAYAHIBE** was once the most beautiful and remote spot along the entire coast, but due to over-building by the big all-inclusive hoteliers, the place has been ruined and retains little intrinsic beauty or interest. The only reason to stop here is to use it as base camp from which to visit **Parque Nacional del Este**, a park just east of Bayahibe on a peninsula jutting south into the Caribbean. The national park maintains a maze of forests, trails, caves and cliffs, home to an impressive array of birdlife and signs of early Taíno activity. Not much of the park, however, is conveniently accessible; no roads lead directly into its interior, and the best method of approach is to hire boats from Bayahibe to hit specific points along the rim.

The most popular part of the park – and rightfully so – is **Isla Saona**, an island off the southern coast lined with alternating stretches of idyllic, coconut tree-backed beachfront and mangrove swamp, unpopulated except for two tiny fishing villages. The larger ships stop off at **Mano Juan**, a strip of pastel shacks with a hiking trail that leads inland, an expensive restaurant and a couple of modest beachfront eateries, or **Piscina Natural**, a sand bar with a clear lagoon behind it good for swimming.

Another good option is to **hike** into the interior of the park to the Cuevas José María, a set of stunningly beautiful caves 10km from Bayahibe. Inside them is a treasure-trove of Taíno rock art, including 1200 pictographs depicting the major events of Taíno mythology (for example, when the first cave spirits were transformed into human beings by the light of the sun) and some historical events, including a 1501 peace treaty that the Taínos established with the Spaniards.

6

6.2

DOMINICAN REPUBLIC | The southeast

△ One of the Dominican Republic's many waterfalls

Practicalities

The road that leads into town ends at a car park crowded with tour buses that shuttle package-resort patrons to the larger catamarans docked a few metres further on. If you're on your own, you can sign on for a trip to Saona at **Scubafun** (℡809/833-0003; US$75), a local tour operator located right in the village centre.

Budget **accommodation** in Bayahibe is plentiful but somewhat dreary; they tend to be downscale *cabañas* run by local families and with cold water bath and few amenities. The most pleasant of these are *Trip Town*, Malecón (**❶**), and *Nina*, Calle Segunda (**❶**, with breakfast **❷**), both on the waterfront. Of the **all-inclusives**, *Club Dominicus*, which is located southeast of town on the border of Parque Nacional del Este, is best (℡809/686-5658, ℻221-6806; **❻**), a lavish compound frequented mostly by Italian tourists that offers good food, a great beach, numerous watersports, tennis, aerobics and a dive centre. You can choose between a standard a/c hotel room and a more primitive but private bungalow.

For **lunch** go to the small unmarked *comedor* across from the police station, which has good fresh fish dishes daily. At night you can try *Kettly Berard* on Calle Segundo, a small Haitian-run establishment with good Creole cuisine – though you'll be subjected to a bit of harassment from the family salesman trying to sell you cheap souvenirs.

Boca de Yuma

On the northeastern tip of Parque Nacional del Este sits *pueblo* **BOCA DE YUMA**, for the most part passed over by tourism because of its lack of appealing beaches, though its setting along squat, ocean-pounded bluffs is undeniably impressive. Though there are no hotels in town, it's a nice enough spot to spend a day, with a decent little beach across the river which you can reach via a RD$10 ferry.

The other major nearby attraction is the fortified **Casa Ponce de León**, located northwest of town in *pueblo* San Rafael de Yuma (Mon–Sat 9am–5pm; RD$10). The home of conquistador Ponce de León, who settled here after land was cleared and the locals slaughtered in the Higuey war of 1502–1504, established an extremely profitable farm that provided Santo Domingo and the gold mines of San Cristóbal with cassava bread and salt pork. It's now maintained by the parks department, who have renovated the two-storey house into a museum meant to evoke de León's life and times. San Rafael is about 9km north of Boca de Yuma, so if you don't have a car use one of the hourly *guaguas* that ply the route between the two towns.

Punta Cana and Bávaro

From Higuey, an unpleasant, completely concrete town 50km or so north of Boca de Yuma known throughout the country as a holy city because it holds a basilica that honours the nation's patron saint, the Virgin of Altagracia, a paved road winds 35km east to the tropical playgrounds of **PUNTA CANA** and **BÁVARO**, two resort areas on either end of a long curve of coconut tree-lined beach. Go elsewhere if you want to explore the country, as these resorts tend to be cities unto themselves: most encompass vast swathes of beachside territory, expansive tropical gardens and several separate hotels. Fortunately, the beach is big enough that it doesn't get overly crowded despite the 700,000 visitors each year; with enough fortitude you could walk some thirty kilometres without seeing the sand interrupted once.

Practicalities

If you're not flying to the resorts via charter at **Aeropuerto Punta Cana** (℡809/688-4749), from where you'll be ferried to your hotel by bus, you'll have to get here by private car or *guagua* from Higuey. **Taxis** are usually waiting at the airport and the entrance to the resorts; otherwise, call ℡809/552-0617 for pickup.

Most people staying in the **all-inclusives** are on package tours, so it's rare to actually call up such a hotel and request a room for the night. You'll get much better deals in any case if you book at home through a travel agent. In the unlikely event you'll be **eating** outside of the resorts, go to *Capitan Cook* in the town of Cortecito, with a beachfront patio where you can feast on grilled seafood, served up from a mammoth barbecue pit that's set up right on the sand.

Resorts and inns

Bávaro Beach Resort ☎809/686-5797, ℗686-5859. Lovely grounds and spacious rooms, though the buffet food is lacklustre. Book a room in the Beach or Garden complexes, closer to the water, or the Palace, which is not all-inclusive and slightly more expensive, allowing you to eat outside the resort. ⑥

Cortecito Inn Calle Playa Cortecito ☎809/552-0639, ℗552-0641. This is the place if you don't want to go all-inclusive. It's right by the beach, some rooms have private balconies, and there's a swimming pool and restaurant too. Breakfast included. ⑤

Melía Caribe Tropical ☎809/686-7499, ℗686-7699. The very best of the resorts, slightly more expensive but well worth it, with opulent contem-porary architecture, sculpted tropical gardens and a choice of suites or bungalows. Luxurious amenities include bathrobes, a daily newspaper of your choice and a glass of champagne. ⑤–⑦

La Posada de Piedra Calle Playa Cortecito ☎809/221-0754. One of the few budget options, with a half-dozen water view rooms located in the large beachfront home of a local family; accommodations are not exactly luxurious, but they are meticulously clean and fairly quiet. ②

Ríu Resort ☎809/221-7171, ℗682-1645. Classy Julio Iglesias brainchild with swimming pools punctuated by artificial palm islands, not to mention great food and service. Some rooms come with a private hot tub. Casino, tennis courts, dive school, windsurfing and deep-sea fishing. ⑦–⑧

The beaches and inland

If you're not staying at one of the resorts, head to the public-access beach at **Cortecito**, a kilometre north of the first Bávaro turn-off from the highway. The only village left along the entire stretch, it's an agreeably laid-back hangout populated by backpackers, independent European vacationers and a slew of Dominican vendors with souvenir stalls set up along the sand.

Hato Mayor and Sabana de la Mar

Despite its lush surroundings in the pretty rolling hills and orange groves of the Cordillera Oriental, overcrowded **Hato Mayor**, 40km north of San Pedro de Macorís on Highway 4, is one of the poorest towns in the region and has little of interest for visitors. Most get only a passing glance anyway while driving Highway 103, the only paved road to Sabana de la Mar and Parque Nacional Los Haitises. You're unlikely to want to **spend the night** in Hato Mayor, but at a pinch you can head to *Centenario*, Mercedes/Hincado (☎809/553-4649; ①), the only formal hotel in town, with clean rooms and private bath but no hot water.

Sabana de la Mar is a dusty little port unremarkable but for its use as a setting-off point for the highly recommended boat tours of Parque Nacional los Haitises (see below). It also happens to be fairly convenient to the Samaná Peninsula; ferries depart twice a day from the wharf at the northern end of town (daily 11am & 5pm; RD$50). You won't really want to use Sabana de la Mar as a base for anything – the hotels are pretty substandard – but just east of the town (and close to the entrance of Los Haitises) is *Paraiso de Caña Hondo* (☎809/556-7483; ②), which has a small restaurant and a very nice set of rooms, plus a natural pool with cascades.

Parque Nacional Los Haitises

Parque Nacional Los Haitises, a massive expanse of mangrove swamp that protects several Taíno caves, 92 plant species, 112 bird species and a wide variety of marine life, spreads west of Sabana de la Mar around the coastal curve of Bahía de

Samaná. Though twelve hundred square kilometres in total, only a small portion of that is open to the public, accessible by organized tours.

The **Ruta Litoral** – the standard 2.5-hour boat tour – hits three main areas of interest within the park. First up is **Cueva Arena**, a large grotto that has numerous Taíno drawings of families, men hunting, supernatural beings, whales and sharks. You can stop for a half-hour at the beach cove here if you'd like, from which you get a good look at **Cayo Willy Simons** – once a hideout for the infamous pirate – recognizable by the dozens of birds circling around: pelicans, herons, terns, frigates, even an occasional falcon. The next stop is to grottoes **San Gabriel** and **Remington**, both with Taíno faces carved into their walls. From here you'll pass the ruins of a 100-year-old banana wharf, with pelicans perching on the remaining wooden supports, to reach **Cueva de la Linea**, which was once intended to hold a railroad station for the sugar cane that was grown in the area.

Practicalities

You'll need to hire a **guide** from Sabana de la Mar for the trip, which runs to around RD$700 for up to four people. They can be picked up at the national park office at the town pier. The port of entry to the park is a tiny pier called **Caña Hondo**, entered via a signposted turn-off on the road to Hato Mayor at the village's southern end. From there you'll travel 12km along a bumpy dirt road to the pier before you set off along a mangrove-lined canal and into the bay.

6.3

The Samaná Peninsula

t's not hard to appreciate the beauty of the **Samaná Peninsula**, a thin strip of land poking from the Dominican Republic's northeast. Perhaps the most appealing part of the whole country, the region boasts a coast lined with beaches that conform strictly to the Caribbean archetype of powdery white sand and transparent green-blue sea.

Besides bumming on the beach, visitors come to see the thousands of **humpback whales** that migrate to the Bahía de Samaná during the winter. Whale-watching has become a thriving local industry, peaking between mid-January and mid-March. Most whaleboats depart from **Santa Bárbara de Samaná** (generally shortened to Samaná), the largest town on the peninsula and a welcome break from the more typical beach-oriented tourist resorts. If the hustle and bustle of more typical Dominican towns becomes too much for you, head east to **Las Galeras**, a pristine horseshoe of sand that, despite considerable development in recent years, still maintains an air of tranquillity. Along the peninsula's north coast you'll find the beautiful beaches of the remote expat colony of **Las Terrenas**, a burgeoning hangout for independent travellers.

The **Carretera 5 (C-5)** that skirts the Dominican north coast leads all the way from Puerto Plata to Santa Bárbara de Samaná. At Sánchez, which nestles in the

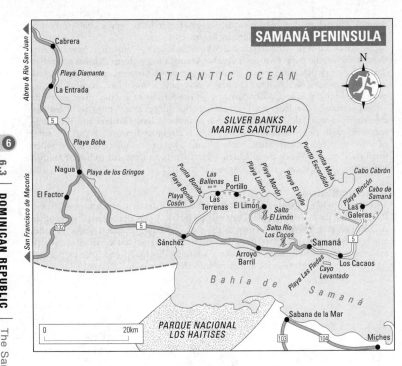

northwestern corner of the rectangular bay, another good road with spectacular views crosses the mountains to Las Terrenas. Travellers heading this way can catch the half-hourly pick-up trucks from the Texaco station on the C5. Recently paved roads now link Samaná with Las Galeras and Las Terrenas although the road to the latter gets a little rougher after El Limón.

Samaná

Protected on its southern side by an elongated strip of land that breaks apart into a series of small islands, **SANTA BÁRBARA DE SAMANÁ** is a very pretty harbour town that's given over to independent tourism, with nary an all-inclusive resort within the city limits. The town is also the main embarkation point for **whale-watching** and other boat trips.

Arrival, orientation and accommodation

Driving into town, the C-5 that stretches along the country's north coast leads directly onto the Malecón, a pretty concrete boardwalk that divides the shops and restaurants from the ocean. Together, the C-5 (known locally as Avenida Rosario Sánchez) and the Malecón are the only major thoroughfares in the city. Incoming **buses** stop in the centre of the Malecón, easy walking distance from most hotels, while *guaguas* stop and set off from the large city market (El Mercado), right on the C-5 and close to a few budget accommodations but a half-kilometre north of the seafront. Samaná has an array of **accommodations**, from luxury resorts to dirt-cheap options, but the latter are not quite as comfortable as those you'll find in Las Terrenas to the north.

Bahia View Av Circunvalación ☎ 809/538-2186. Exceptionally clean budget hotel with a friendly proprietor and better than average rooms with private showers. ❷

Casa de Huespedes Mildania Calle Fco. Del Rosario Sánchez 41 ☎ 809/538-2151. Clean and tidy rooms with private showers in an immaculate Dominican house. ❷–❸

Hotel Docia Duarte 1 ☎ 809/538-2041. Wildly popular small hotel off the Malecón, though it's hard to see why. Clean, basic and well placed, but nothing special. ❶

Gran Bahía Carretera 5 6km east of town ☎ 809/538-3111, ✆ www.occidental-hoteles.com. One of the great gems of Caribbean resorts, with a majestic oceanfront setting east of town, immaculate grounds and well-maintained rooms. ❹

Tropical Lodge Malecón ☎ 809/538-2480, ✆ www.tropical-lodge.com. One of the best hotels on the peninsula, with modern rooms, hot showers, bay views, an outdoor hot tub looking out over the harbour and attentive service. ❸

The Town

Samaná is undeniably charming, with pretty, spacious neighbourhoods, winding streets that amble up the hills and a warm sense of community. The centre of activity is the city's **Malecón**, a broad, concrete boardwalk across the street from numerous outdoor cafés, storefront shops and patches of park. At night the Malecón's restaurants and bars buzz with activity and music, a fairly mixed scene of Dominicans, expats and foreign visitors.

A few blocks back from the waterfront, the old First African Wesleyan Methodist Church of Samaná, popularly known as **La Churcha**, on Santa Bárbara and Duarte (daily 9am–6pm), tangibly maintains what African-American culture is left in Samaná. The prefabricated, tin-roofed structure was originally shipped over by the English Methodist Church in 1823, in support of a recently emigrated African-American community that still remains here. These days it's known as the Dominican Evangelical Church.

Whale-watching

Humpback whales have used the Dominican Republic's Samaná Bay and Silver Bank coral reef sanctuary as a **nursery and breeding ground** for untold millennia. They return each winter after spending nine months fanning out across the North Atlantic and by mid-January more than twelve thousand of them move around the waters of the country's northeast coast. They're at their liveliest in Samaná's tepid depths, as males track females, compete for attention and engage in courting displays, while mothers teach their calves basic survival skills.

Adult humpbacks grow to 15m long, weigh up to forty metric tons, and are black with distinctive white patches. Among the behaviours that you may see while whale-watching are **breaching** – hurtling the entire body above the surface before landing back down in a spectacular crash – and the **trumpet blow**, a tremendous, low blast that can be heard from several kilometres away. Humpbacks also engage in **whale songs**, an eerie combination of moans and chirps formed into short phrases that are shuffled and put together in a basic form of communication. All of this is done to advance the serious business of **mating and birthing**. The female gestation period is a full year, so calves that are conceived in the bay one year are given birth here the next; there's a good chance you'll see at least one of the babies, which can weigh a ton and are light grey.

Whale-watching as a local tourist industry was begun in the 1980s by Kim Beddall, then an itinerant scuba instructor with no formal training as a marine biologist – although she's since been instrumental in the implementation of a code of conduct for whale-watch boats. Beddall still runs excellent **whale boat tours** through her Whale Samaná/Victoria Marine operation, Malecón (☎ & ✆ 809/538-2494; US$45) that allow you to get an up-close look at the humpbacks; sitings are guaranteed in season.

Eating and drinking

Samaná's best **restaurants** are concentrated on the four blocks of the Malecón around the port, with waterside expat joints serving great French and Italian and several good spots for Dominican food. The expats also have a number of **bars** along the waterfront, while locals have set up a festive clutch of beach shacks serving beer, rum and fried chicken on the Malecón just west of the port.

Café de Paris Malecón 6. French-run expat hangout serving up delicious pizzas and crepes. **Le France** Malecón. Reasonably priced gourmet Dominican dishes with some French fare as well, in a relaxed open-air patio. The *gambas* (small bay shrimp) are wonderful and the chocolate cake's to die for. Also the best people-watching spot on the waterfront.

L'Hacienda E De León 6. Below *Naomi* disco, affordable French food and the best steaks in town.

Nightlife

Samaná has a great **nightlife** scene during the busier times of the year, with most of the action centred around the outdoor food and liquor shacks on the western end of the Malecón. The prime spot on the Malecón, however, is *Naomi* (cover RD$40), a slick, dark, bustling meat market with great light shows and sound system, playing a mix of *merengue* and European techno.

Around Samaná

Samaná's best attribute is its convenience as an inexpensive base from which to explore some of the peninsula's more compelling sights. Ferries leave three times daily to nearby **Cayo Levantado**, the original Bacardi Island photographed in the 1970s rum campaign. Although it's undisputedly beautiful, the huge tourist infrastructure that's been set up around it somewhat destroys its desert island charm; and unless you're visiting as part of a whale-watching tour, there are better places on the peninsula to spend a day on the beach. Along the eastern tip of the peninsula, and easily reachable by *guagua*, a series of attractive beaches lead toward **Las Galeras**, as pretty a spot as any along the coast, and the even better beach at **Playa Rincón**.

Las Galeras

A horseshoe-shaped beach cove sheltering a modest village at the far eastern end of the peninsula, **LAS GALERAS** has seen considerable changes over the last few years. Despite the construction of *Casa Marina Bay*, a large all-inclusive, and numerous other hotels near the main beach entrance, it still maintains a peaceful, timeless ambience. The solitude that Las Galeras was once famous for has now gone but it's been replaced with some tasteful amenities that should make most visitors' stays more comfortable. The beaches, however, are still as stunning as always.

Accommodation

Most of Las Galeras's **hotels** are found along the main road or spread out to the north and south behind the beach.

Casa Por Que Non Calle Las Galeras ☎809/538-0011. Two light and airy rooms attached to a private house with a lovely garden. Excellent breakfasts every day and home-cooked dinners by arrangement. Open during winter only. ❷
Club Bonito Beach Road South ☎809/538-0203, ⊛www.club-bonito.com. A beautifully designed and fabulously decorated establishment littered with odd maritime artefacts. Has large rooms, a colourful garden and a nice pool. The restaurant is well worth a try too, for its outstanding pastas and Italian-style seafood preparations. ❹

Paradiso Bungalows Calle Las Galeras ☎809/967-7295. The best of the several private bungalows on offer, right off the beach with a cosy, tropical communal garden. ❷
Todo Blanco Beach Road South ☎809/538-0201, ✉todoblanco@hotmail.com. Tasteful to the extreme and a genuine haven of tranquillity, with huge rooms, a pretty garden and a superb authentic Italian restaurant. ❹
Villa Serena Beach Road North ☎809/538-0000, ⊛www.villaserena.com. Housed in a beautiful faux-Victorian mansion with a large, manicured

tropical garden on the beach, facing a small desert island. Perfect for honeymooners as both the setting and the rooms are exceedingly romantic.

Their restaurant is one of the best in town, with traditional French cooking fused with tropical fruits and spices. ⑥

Eating

There are plenty of **eating** options scattered along the main road on the way into town and also a good selection of restaurants in the main hotels.

Chez Denise Calle Las Galeras. Traditional French food and creperie on a terrace near the beach.
Dominican Kitchen Calle Las Galeras at the beach entrance. Not so much a restaurant as a collection of shacks serving excellent seafood dishes. Prices can vary for tourists so check before ordering.

Patiserrie Francais Calle Las Galeras. A great breakfast spot with a good selection of pastries and croissants, real orange juice and strong coffee, served in a cramped but pretty courtyard, just off the main street.

Playa Rincón

Hidden from the rest of the peninsula by the upper prong at its easternmost end, **Playa Rincón** boasts the top Samaná beach bar none. From the Samaná–Las Galeras road follow the signposted paved road north for approximately 8km and then turn right onto a rocky dirt road that leads to the beach (❹; recommended). Alternatively take a boat from Las Galeras, departing at 9am from Dive Samaná, *Casa Marina Bay Resort* (US\$10). Of all the warm, clear waters on the island, Rincón has the very finest – moderately deep with manageable waves and a bright turquoise transparency that can't be matched – combined with a three-kilometre stretch of whiter-than-white sand and a sprawling coconut forest behind it. For now the only buildings are a couple of Dominican fish shacks serving fresh seafood at both ends of the beach; check prices before eating but expect to pay around RD\$100 per person. This is an eminently more enjoyable day out than Cayo Levantado.

Las Terrenas and around

Set midway along the peninsula's remote northern coast, the former fishing village of **LAS TERRENAS** has grown over the past twenty years from a backwater to an expat-dominated resort town renowned for its buoyant nightlife. Though development has led to a new paved road from Sánchez and a town centre which, along with the beach, is lined with restaurants, bars and shops, the inland Dominican barrio remains much the same as it was two decades ago.

Las Terrenas makes for a pleasant base camp from which to explore the northern part of the Samaná Peninsula; on either side are less developed beaches such as **Playa Bonita**, and a day-trip to the **El Limón waterfall** is also highly recommended.

Arrival and getting around

The best way to get to Las Terrenas if you don't have your own car is a RD\$40 *guagua* leaving every hour from the Samaná Malecón. Once you arrive, you probably won't have too much trouble just **walking** where you want to go – the town's layout is exceedingly straightforward, with just one main thoroughfare, the Carretera Las Terrenas – but if you need a lift anywhere, **motoconcho** rides within town are RD\$50 during the day, double that at night. If you do have your own car, you're best off skipping the pothole-scarred road between Las Terrenas and Sanchez and instead driving a few extra kilometres from Samaná north to the town of El Limón and then due west to Las Terrenas via a newly paved road.

Accommodation

Development in Las Terrenas has meant the loss of most of its rock-bottom **accommodation** options. What remains are pricier inns and *cabañas*, though none that should be too much of a strain on anyone's budget. Note that nearby Playa Bonita (see overleaf) also has a collection of more secluded hotels.

Casas del Mar Calle El Portillo ☎809/360-2748. Clean *cabañas* with welcoming proprietors, access to the beach and a scenic location slightly away from the main part of town. ❸

Las Cayenas Calle Playa Cacao ☎809/240-6080, ☏240-6070. A popular American hangout, *Las Cayenas* is a little inn in an old beachfront manor with a palm-shaded patio area. ❹

Kanesh Village ☎809/240-6333, ⊛www.kanesh. com. Small three-building complex with six full-service apartments for rent. Clean with adequate beds, modern bathrooms and some have kitchens. Very good Indian food is available in the restaurant as well. Located 200 metres behind Playa Las Ballenas on a small dirt road west of town. ❹

Tropic Banana Calle Playa Cacao ☎809/240-6110, ⓔhoteltropic@verizon.net.do. The oldest hotel in Las Terrenas, and still one of the very best. The well-kept rooms are large, with private balconies, and the extensive palm-covered grounds include a swimming pool and tennis court. ❷

Villas Eva Luna Calle Playa Las Ballenas ☎809/978-5611, ⊛www.villa-evaluna.com. Highly recommended small hotel with five great villas that sleep up to four, with private terraces, kitchen and king-size bed, on quiet grounds set 200 metres off the western beach. The two larger villas have a/c. The best part here is the food, prepared by a gourmet French chef in the *table d'hôte* mode: each guest tells the chef what they want 24 hours in advance and your group eats from a common table at dinner time. ❻

The Town

Aside from spectacular day-trips to the surrounding countryside, the **beach**, which stretches uninterrupted 2km in either direction from town, is the focus of daytime entertainment. Just west of the Carretera is a less lively beach area, which stretches a full 2km to **Playa Las Ballenas** – a section of the beach named after three oblong islands in the waters just beyond it that resemble breaching humpback whales – before ending in a patch of swamp. The beach east of the intersection has just recently been built up, and has a slightly funkier feel, dominated by low-end *cabañas* and bars until the construction peters out entirely.

Eating and drinking

In keeping with its expat-dominated culture, Las Terrenas's **restaurants** have a fully international flavour with Italian, Spanish, French, Mexican and even Indian options available. Most of the hotels along the beach have their own restaurants and **bars** and these tend to cater as much for passing trade as they do for residents. The social scene, too, tends to be based around the beachfront joints, with most of the action close to the main road.

Barrio Latino Calle Playa Cacao. Bustling café with a huge menu including good breakfasts and pizzas. Good for people-watching too.

Casa Boga Calle Playa Cacao. A beachside shack that serves the best fish in town, along with ice-cold Presidente beer.

Casa Coco Calle El Portillo. Reasonably priced pizzeria with a candlelit outdoor seating area.

Chez Nadine Calle Principal, in the tiny plaza just north of Scotiabank. This place absolutely must not be missed. This new French bakery and *salon de thé* is a godsend to Las Terrenas as it is run by a former Parisian master baker and has pastries and croissants that are simply unbelievable. Try the lemon tart, chocolate mousse with passion fruit and the caramel and walnut pastries.

Comedor Jahaira The only place to go for *comida criolla* in Las Terrenas, and incredibly inexpensive. From the town centre, head up the Carretera Las Terrenas and take the second dirt track on the right after the Centro Commercial.

Kanesh Village Calle Playa Las Ballenas, 200m back from the beach, ☎809/240-6333. It's worth going out of your way one night for some of the excellent and authentic-tasting Indian food available here, which needs to be ordered at least one day in advance. Located a little bit west of town.

Nuevo Mundo Carretera Las Terrenas. This is the place to party in Las Terrenas, an insanely popular disco a few metres south of the main crossroads.

West of Las Terrenas: Playa Bonita and Playa Cosón

Playa Bonita, 13km of uninterrupted beach that begins just west of Playa Las Ballenas, boasts the kind of powdery white sand you might expect to see only in tourist brochures. There's been a fair bit of development in recent years but this has been done carefully and the **hotels** do little to detract from the beauty and serenity of the heavenly beaches. Indeed, if you're looking for natural beauty, peace and quiet, you're far better off staying here than in Las Terrenas. The best of the bunch is *Atlantis Hotel & Restaurant* (☎809/240-6111, ✆hotelatlantis@verizon.net.do; ❷), whose rooms are palatial and pretty; try to book either the Jamaica or the Grenada room, both with panoramic views of the beach. Also nice is the *Acaya* (☎809/240-6161, ✇acaya.free. fr; ❷), a modern hotel with a/c and all the amenities, including swimming pool, free snorkelling gear and a thatch-roofed beachside restaurant. The cheapest rooms on the beach and excellent value are *Casa Grande* (☎809/240-6349, ✇www.casa-grande.de; ❷), five good-sized rooms in a large house.

From Playa Bonita's entrance, a sand road provides access for four-wheel-drives and motorbikes, past a beachfront populated at most by a few small groups of people taking advantage of the isolation to swim or sunbathe naked, until, after 6km, you reach **Playa Cosón**, a small fishing village holding two gourmet beach shacks with tables and chairs on the sand, serving grilled, fresh-caught fish for a few pesos.

East of Las Terrenas: El Limón

Eleven kilometres east of town, and little more than a crossroads with a few shacks attached, dusty **El Limón** seems unpromising at first, but does make an ideal base for excursions to the magnificent El Limón waterfall to the south. Upon arrival you'll be beset by several local *buscones* trying to steer you to one of the excursion outfits; the best is Casa Santi, just south of the crossroads on the road to Samaná. The **waterfall** is accessible by horse from the town and takes 2.5 hours round-trip, well worth it to see the 50m of torrential white water dropping from a cliff in the middle of the wilderness. Expect to pay around RD$500 for the round-trip with a good lunch included.

From Las Terrenas, a **motoconcho** here costs RD$100, and during the day *guaguas* ply the El Limón route once an hour during the day for RD$25. Getting back is more of a problem if you're depending on public transport – it's standard practice to hitchhike from here. Every hour or so, a *guagua* will pass by.

6.4

The Silver Coast

The Dominican Republic's **Silver Coast**, 300km of prime waterfront property on the country's northern edge, is the most popular tourist destination in the Caribbean. With a seemingly unending supply of great beaches around the booming towns of **Puerto Plata** and **Cabarete**, such a designation is no surprise. The Carretera 5 skirts the coast all the way east from Samaná to just past Puerto Plata, making **getting around** this part of the region a breeze. The country's two major bus companies ply the highway, along with *guaguas* and plentiful *público* taxis. Heading west of Puerto Plata is more of a challenge (but not impossible) if you don't have a four-wheel-drive vehicle.

Puerto Plata and Playa Dorada

PUERTO PLATA and **Playa Dorada** comprise the mass tourism capital of the Caribbean. The city of Puerto Plata is a vibrant Dominican town of 200,000 that's well worth exploring for its historic architecture and nightlife. Its core, the **Old City**, borders the port to the east, a narrow grid of streets that was once the swankiest neighbourhood in the country. Around the original town sprawls a patchwork maze of industrial zones and concrete barrios known as the **New City**, formed over the past century with the growth of the town's industry. Most visitors, though, are here for package tours to the Playa Dorada complex – located a kilometre east of the city limits – a walled-off vacation factory that pulls in over a half-million tourists each year.

Arrival and getting around

Six kilometres east of town, **Aeropuerto Internacional Luperón** (☎809/586-1992), usually referred to as Puerto Plata Airport, is the main northern entry point into the country. There is a Banco de Reservas **currency exchange** (Mon–Fri 8.30am–6.30pm) within the strip of shops lining the front of the airport, alongside a number of **car rental** offices. While most of the more expensive hotels have shuttle buses, any of the *motoconchos* can take you into town for RD$20, and there are plenty of taxis to take you to points further out. Arriving by **bus** is another option; the city is a major junction point for Caribe Tours (☎809/586-4544) and Metro (☎809/586-6062), whose vehicles arrive here from the south (via Santo Domingo and Santiago) and the east (via Samaná).

Central Puerto Plata is compact enough to make **walking** your best option for getting around. If you want to go to Playa Dorada or Costambar, you may want to take one of the ubiquitous *motoconchos*, which should cost RD$20 (RD$10 within town). Cheaper but far slower are the **public buses** shuttling between Playa Dorada and the Parque Central. The price is RD$3 but it can take up to 45 minutes to get from one side of town to the other. **Taxis** are relatively expensive (RD$150 to Playa Dorada), but are the fastest mode of transport and far safer than *motoconchos*.

Accommodation

The best luxury **hotels** are east of town within Playa Dorada, but as they are **all-inclusives** your freedom is limited some. If you want to explore the city itself there are plenty of moderately priced options in and around the old town and the Malecón.

Puerto Plata

Porto Fino Ave Hermanas Mirabal ☎809/586-2858, ☎586-5050. Clean and comfortable air-conditioned rooms, way nicer and quieter than the *Victoriano* (see below) for only a few bucks more. A long way from town and the action though. ❶

Puerto Plata Beach Malecón just west of Av Hermanas Mirabal ☎809/586-4243. Formerly an all-inclusive beach resort, this place has extremely comfortable rooms and full-service apartments for a rock-bottom price. The only problem is that they don't have a generator for the rooms, which means you may be stuck in darkness for several hours each day. ❸

Sofy's Bed and Breakfast Las Rosas 3 and Ginebra ☎809/586-6411, ✉gillin.n@verizon.net.do. A cosy private home with a hibiscus-filled courtyard patio and two large rooms rented to travellers. Price includes free laundry service and a terrific cooked breakfast. ❷

Victoriano San Felipe 33 ☎809/586-9752. A true budget option with clean but depressingly plain rooms and warm water. Can be very noisy at night. ❶

Playa Dorada

Gran Ventana ☎809/320-2111, ⊛www.victoriahoteles.com.do. The newest and best of the resorts in Playa Dorada. Great, comfortable rooms, extensive sports and beach facilities and excellent service. ❻

Jack Tar Village ☎809/320-3800, ☎320-4161. The oldest of the Playa Dorada resorts and long highly regarded – but don't expect the same kind of four-star service you'd get back home. Two large swimming pools and a popular, user-friendly casino. Adults only. ❻

Paradise Resort ☎809/320-3663, ⊛www.amshamarina.com. Known for its excellent restaurants, sports facilities and children's programme. Rooms and grounds well maintained, and ethnic "theme nights" keep the buffet food varied. Popular with the British. ❻

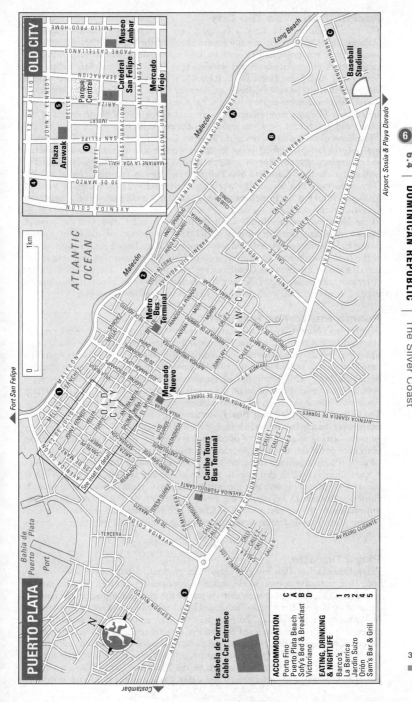

PUERTO PLATA

OLD CITY

ACCOMMODATION
Porto Fino	C
Puerto Plata Beach	A
Sofy's Bed & Breakfast	B
Victoriano	D

EATING, DRINKING & NIGHTLIFE
Barco's	1
La Barrica	3
Jardin Suizo	2
Orión	4
Sam's Bar & Grill	5

Isabela de Torres
Cable Car Entrance

ATLANTIC OCEAN

NEW CITY

OLD CITY

Bahia de Puerto Plata

Port

Baseball Stadium

Metro Bus Terminal

Mercado Nuevo

Caribe Tours Bus Terminal

Plaza Arawak

Parque Central

Catedral San Felipe

Mercado Viejo

Museo Ámbar

Long Beach

Malecón

▲ Fort San Felipe

▲ Costambar

Airport, Sosúa & Playa Dorado ▶

Puerto Plata: The Old City

The once-exclusive **Old City**, a compact area bounded by Avenida Colón, the Malecón and Calle López, visually retains much of the Victorian splendour of its past, when it was populated by wealthy landowners, dock workers and European merchants. A good place to begin wandering is the colonial-era **San Felipe** fort (9am–noon & 2–5pm; closed Wed; RD$30), a limestone edifice perched atop a rocky point at the seaside Malecón off Avenida Colón. The Spaniards constructed it in 1540 as a defence against corsairs and a prison for smugglers. Once past the unnecessary freelance tour guides that surround it, you can climb up several of the towers and gun turrets, or down into the old prison cells.

The heart of the Victorian city is the **Parque Central**, at the corner of Separación and Beller, a fast-paced focal point for transportation and tourism. Shaded benches and the central **gazebo** supply a much needed dose of tranquillity. South of the park looms the large **Catedral San Felipe**, which blends Spanish Colonial and Art Deco influences. The remaining three sides of the park are surrounded by some of the best **Victorian architecture** in the city, notably a colossal white gingerbread mansion on the northwest corner.

One block east of the Parque Central on Duarte and Castellanos, the popular **Museo Ámbar** (Mon–Sat 9am–6pm; RD$50) comprises two floors of amber-related exhibits in a renovated mansion called Villa Berz, built a century ago by one of the town's wealthiest German tobacco families. The museum's collection, culled from the amber mines in the Cordillera Septentrional south of Puerto Plata, consists of Jurassic and Triassic leaves, flowers, spiders, termites, wasps, ants and other insects trapped in amber, along with one small lizard several million years old.

Puerto Plata: The New City

Puerto Plata's **New City** spreads outwards in three directions from the Old, roughly bounded by the port, Circunvalación Sur and Avenida Hermanas Mirabal, though additional, less developed barrios exist beyond this convenient circumscription. The centre of the city's social life is the two-kilometre-long **Malecón**, a sunny, spacious boardwalk lined with hotels and all manner of commerce. During the day it's a popular place to hang out or lie on the beach, while at night a strip of bars open up along with numerous restaurants and outdoor shacks selling Dominican fast food. The Malecón begins at **Long Beach**, on the town's far eastern end – not the most picturesque beach by any stretch, but with a convivial mood, peopled largely by *merengue*-blaring teens. A row of **outdoor bars** extends for several hundred metres from here down the adjoining Avenida Hermanas Mirabal.

Puerto Plata's crowning attraction is the suspended **cable car ride** (Thurs–Tues 8.30am–5pm; RD$200) that goes to the top of **Mount Isabela**. The entrance is at the far western end of town past the port, just off the Circunvalación Sur on Avenida Teleférico. It's not to be missed; the views of the city on this 25-minute trip are stupendous. At the summit a statue of **Christ the Redeemer**, a slightly downsized version of the Rio de Janeiro landmark with its arms spread out over the city, crowns a manicured lawn.

Playa Dorada

Playa Dorada, just 1km east of Puerto Plata on the C-5 but truly a world away, is walled off from the outside world; inside its confines are fourteen separate massive resorts, and meandering between them is one of the best golf courses in the country, designed by Robert Trent Jones. Frequented by a half-million package tourists per year (the majority from Canada and Europe), the main draw is obviously the **beach**, 2km of impeccably white sand dominated by a variety of hotel-run activities, including beach volleyball, *merengue* lessons and parasailing, along with numerous local souvenir vendors and hair braiders. Even if you're not a guest, getting through the front gate is not a problem. Either sneak onto the beach via entries beside the *Dorado Naco* complex or just east of the *Playa Dorada Hotel*, or buy a **day pass,** available from each resort and costing from US$35 to $50, and entitling you to five hours on the grounds, including meals and drinks.

Eating

Most of Puerto Plata's **restaurants** are scattered within the Old City and along the Malecón, the latter also lined with cheap food shacks.

Barco's Malecón 6. A great people-watching spot on the Malecón with a sidewalk patio and a second-floor terrace. They serve good pizzas, lamb and goat dishes.

Cafe Cito on the Sosúa Highway, across from the *Costa Dorada* resort complex ☎809/586-7923. The best restaurant in town has recently moved and is now situated 500m west of Playa Dorada. Great food – try the filet mignon – and jazz music make for a memorable night out.

Jardin Suizo Malecón 13-A. Top-end international fare in a smart but relaxed building close to the water's edge. Seafood specials including excellent tuna steaks.

Sam's Bar & Grill Ariza 34. Established meeting place for fellow travellers, with good-value daily specials. The American breakfasts and Philly cheese steak are highly recommended.

Drinking and nightlife

Fed by a metropolis full of dance-crazy Dominicans and vacationing foreign hordes, Puerto Plata's **nightlife** establishments are crammed with dancers until dawn. While Playa Dorada resorts and their restaurants are off limits to non-guests (except for day passes), the discos are open to all.

La Barrica Circunvalación Sur and Av Colón, Puerto Plata. Hip, strictly Dominican music disco catering mostly to city-dwellers cutting vicious moves. There are no lights in the entire club – the waiters use flashlights. No cover.

Hemingway's Cafe in *Playa Dorada Plaza*, Playa Dorada. Haven for crazed drunken tourists intent on having a good time. Friday's ear-splitting karaoke night is the most popular; Thursdays and Saturdays feature good rock 'n' roll. No cover.

Orión 30 de Marzo and 12 de Julio, Puerto Plata. Rough-and-tumble local nightclub, but the most popular dance spot in town, featuring strictly *merengue* and *bachata*. RD$40 cover.

East of Puerto Plata

The resort development that began around Puerto Plata has over the past two decades gobbled up most of the prime beachfront east of the city. As such, you'll have to keep going all the way east, for approximately 70km, to the small, friendly fishing village of Río San Juan to find anything approaching unspoiled coastline. Even closer, though, and easier for those with limited time, is the bustling resort town of **Cabarete**, a windsurfing enclave that's quickly being swallowed by tourism construction.

Cabarete

Stretched along the C-5 between the beach and lagoon that bear its name, **CABARETE** is a crowded international enclave that owes its existence almost entirely to **windsurfing**. The main beach, Playa Cabarete, has ideal conditions for the sport, and the multicultural cross-section of its aficionados attracts a growing community from across the globe.

Arrival and accommodation

Virtually all of Cabarete is on the **Carretera 5**. Buses, *guaguas* and *motoconchos* will drop you off along the main strip, a crowded patchwork of restaurants and bars, tour operators and souvenir shops.

Agualina Carretera 5 ☎809/571-0805, ⊛www.agualina.com. Unbelievably nice full-service apartments right on Kite Beach, with an in-house kiteboarding school called Dare2Fly. Unlike most similar places, these rooms are not only spacious and comfortable, they're also stylishly done.

Highly recommended if you're going to spend most of your time on Kite Beach. 6–7

Casa Blanca Carretera 5 ⓣ809/571-0934, ⓦwww.casablancacabarete.com. Solid mid-range budget option with spare but reasonably spacious rooms, some of them right on the beach and with terrace, and a common kitchen area. Free gear storage and a modest but pleasant pool area. 3–4

El Magnifico Carretera 5 ⓣ809/571-0868, ⓦwww.hotelmagnifico.com. Three different buildings with eye-catching architecture and wild ethnic-style interiors set around a tranquil pool area. This place is a real haven yet it's just a 5min stroll from the town centre. 4

Residencia Dominicana Calle Las Orquideas ⓣ809/571-0890, ⓔresdom@hipaniola.com. Small hotel with good, clean rooms and a peaceful garden and pool. Located on the Orquideas road, south of the C-5, at the eastern end of town. The place usually fills up, so it's a good idea to reserve in advance. 2

Villa Taina Carretera 5 ⓣ809/571-0722, ⓦwww.villataina.com. Classy hotel with top-notch service and a selection of stunning, individually designed rooms, some with sea views. 4

Exploring Cabarete

What there is of a town consists of the hectic strip of restaurants and hotels along the C-5, just behind the water. The real action here is centred nearly completely on the **beach**. During the day it's full of windsurfers; calm water and light breezes during the morning make it a perfect place for beginners, but as the day wears on, and the trade winds kick in with full force, the experts take over. Further out from the centre, both east and west, you can have the beach to yourself. At night, the bars and restaurants spill out onto the sand, helping create a hedonistic atmosphere.

Two kilometres further west, on a white-sand beach hidden behind Punta Goleta, Cabarete is playing its part in the birth and infancy of a new sport – **kiteboarding**. In many ways similar to windsurfing, kiteboarding needs less wind to really get moving and the best riders perform huge jumps and tricks that would be impossible with a sail. See the info on Dare2Fly in the box below for details about how you can try out this new sport.

Eating and drinking

Cabarete has an array of good **dining** options, most of them opened by European expats, and hence serving some unusual cuisines for this part of the country. The entire town is packed with **bars**, but a select few garner the majority of the business.

Cabarete adventure sports outfitters

Carib BIC Center ⓣ809/571-0640. Slick windsurfing/kiteboarding outfit with a great equipment shop and a well-trained, friendly staff always willing to give you pointers. The best part is their new Board Test Center, which allows you to test boards from different manufacturers, including F2, Mistral, BIC, Tabou, Naish, Real Winds and Roberto Ricci. US$170 for ten hours of use on the water; US$200 for using the test centre; US$150 for 6hr classes; US$35 equipment insurance.

Iguana Mama ⓣ809/571-0908, ⓦwww.iguanamama.com. Offers US$30 mountain-bike day-trips and week-long bike tours of the island, as well as hikes up Mount Isabela (see p.370) and several-day treks through the Cordillera Central to Pico Duarte (see p.379). They also do whale-watching in Samaná Bay for US$125/day, horseriding for US$25/half-day and a whole stack of cultural tours.

Vela/Spinout/Dare2Fly ⓣ809/571-0805, ⓦwww.velacabarete.com. The best-stocked of Cabarete's windsurf centres with free daily clinics and a lively social scene. The small bar is a great place to relax and does great lunches. US$180 for ten hours actually out on the water; US$120 for 3hr classes; US$25 equipment insurance. Their Dare2Fly station on Kite Beach offers equipment rental and kiteboarding lessons daily. US$330 for a three-day introductory course with equipment; US$250 for a week's kite equipment hire only.

Casa del Pescador Carretera 5. The best seafood in town, served in an idyllic candlelit atmosphere right on the beach.

DND (Do Not Disturb) Carretera 5. This is the latest hot spot, a super-cool tapas bar with a super-comfortable couch lounge and ambient electronica à la *Buddha Bar*. The tapas are excellent and they also have reasonably priced Thai food like coconut curry shrimp and pad Thai.

Friends Carretera 5. Next door to *Panadería Dick* (see next column), this is a nice breakfast and lunch spot serving hearty sandwiches, salads and fruit shakes. Great fresh muffins, cookies and banana pancakes.

Lax Carretera 5. Popular bar with an amiable lounge atmosphere that's more relaxed than most of the beachside spots, with live music on Sundays. Best place in town to chill out with friends.

Miro's Carretera 5. The best of Cabarete's beach restaurants, with fantastic fish dishes and a good selection of wine. The Moroccan tuna is out of this world.

Onno's Carretera 5. Lively bar/restaurant which really gets going in the small hours – plays mainly European and American hits.

Panadería Repositera Dick Carretera 5. Various gourmet breads for a few pesos, great Danishes and croissants. Excellent breakfasts with fresh-squeezed orange juice and cappuccino.

West of Puerto Plata

The contrast between east and **west of Puerto Plata** couldn't be more striking. In place of the paved highways and resort complexes you'll find vast stretches of untrammelled wilderness along rough dirt tracks, though some are slowly being converted into freeways. One thing that doesn't change, however, is the proliferation of lovely **beaches**.

El Castillo and La Isabela

From Puerto Plata, the Carretera de las Américas branches off from the C-5 and heads 50km west to **EL CASTILLO**, a seaside village located on the site of Columbus's first permanent settlement. It's easy to see why he picked it, since the town is set on a splendid bay of tranquil, blue water with a solid wall of imposing, Olympian peaks.

Just off the main highway, before you make town, is the entrance to **Parque Nacional La Isabela** (9am–5.30pm, closed Sun; RD$30), which preserves the ruins of La Isabela, the first European town in the New World. Centred on the private home of Columbus himself, which is perched atop a prominent ocean bluff, the park also encompasses the excavated stone foundations of the town and a small museum with Columbus-era relics, including a few Spanish skeletons that apparently died of malaria and yellow fever.

A few kilometres further on, you enter the village, draped over a steep hillside above Playa Isabela, which attracts few beach-goers and is instead marked mainly by small wooden boats. A kilometre offshore is an intact **coral reef** where there's a healthy, multicoloured reef bed that's home to thousands of tropical fish and sea creatures. The *Rancho del Sol* hotel (see below) can arrange **diving** (US$50) and **snorkelling** (US$35) day-trips.

If you're looking to **spend the night**, check out *Rancho del Sol* (☎809/543-8172; ❷), located off the Carretera de las Américas at the town entrance, which rents simple but well-maintained duplexes with kitchen and bath. Meanwhile, *Miamar*, Calle Vista Mar (☎809/471-9157, ℱ471-8052; ❷, breakfast included), is a modern hotel with a swimming pool and enormous rooms with lovely ocean views. For good Dominican cuisine try *Milagro*, near the entrance to *Rancho del Sol*, a small and friendly *comedor* with a good selection of local dishes.

Playa Ensanata and Punta Rucia

From El Castillo a dirt road extends west and heads to a series of beaches that relatively few foreign visitors make it to. There are two rivers to be crossed en route, and a 4x4 is recommended. After 14km, a turn-off heads north to **Playa Ensanata**, where many Dominican families come to take advantage of the shallow waters. The beach is lined with shacks where you can eat grilled, freshly caught fish extremely cheaply. Just around the point from Playa Ensanata, **Punta Rucia** is yet another beautiful beach, featuring bone-white sand and more great mountain views. It attracts fewer people than Ensanata and is dotted with fishing boats, but has several good places to stop for lunch or a beer. There are a few down-home Dominican seafood **restaurants** on Punta Rucia as well, but no hotels.

Monte Cristi

West from Punta Rucia, the roads deteriorate even further and the only sensible way to make for the Haitian border is to turn south back onto the C-1 at **Villa Elisa**. The further west you go, the more the landscape transforms itself – gone are the swaying palms and grassy pastures, replaced by scrubby cactus plants and dusty dry soil inhabited mainly by goats. The *carretera* terminates at the westernmost outpost of the Silver Coast, **MONTE CRISTI**, founded in 1501 and at one point one of the country's most important ports. These days it resembles a dusty frontier town bearing only the occasional tarnished remnant of its opulent past along wide, American-style boulevards. Most visitors are here to use the town as a base from which to explore the local **beaches** and the **Parque Nacional Monte Cristi**, an expanse that protects a towering mesa named El Morro and an enormous river delta.

To reach the park, take the beach road north of the city towards **Playa Juan de Bolaños**, the area's most popular beach but quite disappointing in comparison to others on this coast. Once past the restaurants that clutter the beach's entrance, the road arrives at the entrance to the eastern half of the park, which is divided in two by Monte Cristi's beaches. Its eastern section is often referred to as **Parque El Morro**, after the flat-topped mesa that takes up a good chunk of it. Climbing the mesa is a lot easier these days as the park office has built a set of steps up from the road's highest point (RD$50 entrance fee). At the foot of El Morro's eastern slope is a lovely and unpopulated **beach** accessible by parking at the end of the road and continuing down on foot. The western half of the national park encompasses a dense mangrove coast dotted with small lagoons; informal tours are led from the *Los Jardines* hotel (from RD$300 per person; see below), on which you'll see several river deltas thick with mangroves and perhaps even a couple of crocodiles.

Practicalities

The best **accommodation** option in Monte Cristi is *Cayo Arena*, Playa Juan de Bolaños, 250m west of the beach entrance (℡809/579-3145, ℻579-2096; ❸), a set of large, full-service apartments right on the beach with ocean-view balconies, a/c, kitchenettes, swimming pool, bar and 24-hour security. Also on the beach, a little more basic but definitely better value is *Los Jardines,* Playa Juan de Bolaños (℡809/579-2091, ⓦwww.elbistrot.com; ❷), which has simple rooms with cold-water showers. Note that these hotels get busy over the weekend and the rates go up accordingly. The best **restaurant** in town is *El Bistrot*, Calle Bolaños (℡809/579-2091), which serves great seafood dishes in an atmospheric courtyard.

6.5

The Cibao

Cibao (rocky land) is the word Taínos used to describe the **Cordillera Central** mountain range that takes up much of the Dominican Republic's central interior. These mountains are the highest peaks in the Caribbean, including Pico Duarte, the Caribbean's tallest at 3087m. The heart of the range is protected as **Parques Nacionales Bermúdez** and **Ramírez**.

Today, though, Dominicans use the term Cibao more to describe the fertile Cibao Valley, a triangle of alluvial plain that contains some of the deepest topsoil in the world. In the valley sits vibrant **Santiago**, the country's second largest city after Santo Domingo, well positioned for short excursions into the neighbouring farmland.

The region is penetrated by the **C-1**, also known as the Autopista Duarte, that links the northwest with the southeast, via Santiago and Santo Domingo. But, with most of interest gathered in the northern reaches, many vistors also take advantage of the good roads that hurdle the Cordillera Septentrional from the north. Once in the mountains, the best progress is made by following the biggest and best roads between towns, even when the distance travelled is far greater, which is often the case. Buses link most of the towns and *guaguas* make up for any shortfall.

Santiago

Founded in 1504 as a mining town and demolished by an earthquake in 1562, **SANTIAGO** has been associated with tobacco since it was introduced for export to the French in 1697, and is also the home of *merengue périco ripao* – the classic Dominican music using accordion, *tambora* and *güira*. Today the Domincan Republic's second city is a growing metropolis that seems less and less provincial, though its economy is still based on its status as an agricultural depot and centre for the cigar industry. There's a good club scene based mostly around the indigenous music, so you won't lack for fun at nights. During the day, **downtown Santiago** supplies enough cultural diversions to merit a full day or two of ambling about.

Arrival and getting around

All three highway entrances to town – the Autopista Duarte, the Carretera Duarte and the Carretera Turística – lead directly to the city centre. If you're arriving by **bus**, your station will likely be on the north or east side of town, from where you can get a RD$100 taxi closer to the heart of downtown. If you arrive by *guagua*, you'll end up at one of the city's **guagua stations**, one on the corner of 30 de Marzo and Cucurullo (from Mao, Monciòn and Santo Domingo) and on Calle Valerio a block west of Parque Valerio (from San José de las Matas and Puerto Plata). Another arrival point is the **Cibao International Airport** (☎809/582-7179), a twenty-minute drive (or a RD$200 taxi ride) from the centre.

A complex system of battered public taxis – referred to locally as **motoconchos** – should cover most **city transport** needs; a one-way ride costs RD$20. **Private taxis** wait at the city parks, though you can call directly for pick-up: reliable operators include Camino (☎809/971-7788). As always, you're best off sticking with an established international firm for **car rental**. Options include Budget, 27 de Febrero

(☎809/724-7868); Honda, Estrella Sadhalá and 27 de Febrero (☎809/575-6077); and Nelly, Av Salvador E. Sadhalá 204 (☎809/583-6695).

Accommodation

Santiago is pretty well set up for **accommodation**, from budget options up to the *Gran Almirante*, the one five-star hotel in town.

Centro Plaza Mella 54 ☎809/581-7000, ℱ582-4566. Large western-style hotel with large comfortable rooms, a gym and a worthwhile restaurant. ❺

Colonial Cucurullo and 30 de Marzo ☎809/247-3122, ℱ582-0811. Great little budget hotel with excellent service, clean rooms, a/c and TV. ❷

Dorado Cucurullo 88 ☎809/582-7563. Good-value cheapie with fan and hot water. Not quite as nice as *Colonial*, but comfortable enough. ❶

Gran Almirante Estrella Sadhalá and Calle 10 ☎809/580-1992, ✆www.hodelpa.com. Luxury hotel in a wealthy northeastern suburb with all the amenities. ❸

The City

Most places of interest are **downtown** and within walking distance of one another. In fact, many visitors spend their whole stay in the area bounded by the main city park and the **Monumento a los Héroes de la Restauración** (Mon–Sat 9am–noon & 2–5pm; free), Santiago's distinctive symbol and most impressive sight. Built by Trujillo in honour of himself, it was quickly rededicated upon his death to the War of Independence with Spain. It's possible to climb the stairs up the monument – a statue of Victory personified as a woman tops its seventy-metre pillar – to take in the breathtaking panorama of Santiago and the surrounding valley and mountains.

Calle del Sol, which borders the monument to the west, is the city's major shopping district and the heart of downtown activity, lined with department stores, banks and sidewalk stalls selling clothing, household wares and fast food. Follow Del Sol north to 30 de Marzo and the **Parque Duarte**, a bit overcrowded but covered by a tree canopy and lined with horse-and-carriage drivers. At the park's southern end stands the **Catedral Santiago** (1895), a concrete building with intricate carvings on its mahogany portals. Just across the street the excellent **Museo del Tabaco**, on 16 de Agosto and 30 de Marzo (Tues–Fri 9am–noon & 2–5pm, Sat 9am–noon; free), housed in a old Victorian tobacco warehouse, presents a history of the crop's use dating back to Taíno times. Three blocks south of the park, **La Habanera Tabaclera**, 16 de Agosto and San Luis (Mon–Fri 8.30am–4.30pm; free), is the oldest working Dominican cigar factory and one of the few in the city that offers tours, though free samples are not included.

In the opposite direction, a few blocks northwest of the park, sits the fascinating **Museo Folklórico de Tomas Morel**, Restauración 174 (Mon–Fri 8.30am–1.30pm & 3.30–5.30pm; free). Inside is a remarkable collection of papier-mâché Carnival masks, alongside various Taíno artefacts and early Spanish household items. The masks, though, are the main focus, with an array of spectacularly baroque and evil-looking demons.

Eating

You'll have no problem finding plenty to **eat** in Santiago, whether it's at fine dining establishments, low-key *comedores* (small Dominican kitchens) or American fast-food chains.

Camp David Carretera Turística Km 12 ☎809/223-0666. Former Trujillo mountain home, now converted into a gourmet restaurant and hostelry that offers a long list of choice seafood dishes and steaks. Look for the turn-off on the Carretera Turística, then drive up a winding road for 2km.

Daiqui Loco JP Duarte and Oueste. Festive outdoor bar with the best grilled sandwiches and burritos in town. Frozen daiquiris are also a speciality.

Olé JP Duarte and Independencia. Creole restaurant with Dominican standards and American-

style pizzas in a thatch-sheltered terrace.
Rancho Luna Carretera Turística km 7 ☏ 809/736-7176. Top-quality steakhouse and piano bar with excellent service, a huge wine list and great views over the city.

Drinking and nightlife

Santiago **nightlife** is rowdy, diverse and seemingly nonstop; most clubs are completely empty until midnight and don't close until dawn.

Alcazar in the *Gran Almirante*, Estrella Sadhalá and Calle 10. The best disco in town: it doesn't get hopping until 1am, but stays full until 7am. Dress sharply. RD$50 cover.

Bar Code Cuba 25. Popular courtyard bar with live Caribbean music. Definitely one of *the* places to hang out.

Francifol Del Sol at Parque Duarte. Classy pub with the coldest beer in town. A good place for drinks and conversation.

Kukaramacara Av Francia in front of the monument. The hottest spot in the monument area, an open-air building that's perpetually packed with locals and features late-night drum jam sessions, great Dominican and Mexican food, plus the obligatory cold Presidentes and frozen tropical drinks.

San José de las Matas

The easiest excursion into the mountains from Santiago is **SAN JOSÉ DE LAS MATAS**, a sleepy hill station looking out over the northern Cordillera Central. There's little to do within town but take a leisurely walk and admire the views; for one such lookout, take the dirt path behind the post office, on 30 de Marzo, to a **cliff-top park** with a good vantage over the neighbouring mountains. Most points of interest lie a bit outside San José, such as the **Balneario Vidal Pichardo Trail**, 10km north at the confluence of the rivers Anima and Bao, which is ideal for a day's hike.

If you're arriving from Santiago, it will likely either be by *guagua* (hourly; RD$35), or by car – simply head west on Calle 30 de Marzo, cross the Hermanos Patiño bridge and continue west for 28km. Most visitors choose to make a day-trip of the town, but those looking to **stay the night** will find a couple of good hotels, including *Hotel Restaurant San José*, 30 de Marzo 37 (☏ 809/578-8566; ❶), with basic rooms, ceiling fans and hot water. *Los Samenes* is as good a place to eat as any, serving typical Dominican platters.

The Cordillera Central

The **Cordillera Central** contains the Caribbean's tallest, most beautiful mountains. For the most part, the roads are horrific, and so getting from place to place often requires a convoluted route, leaving the mountains via one paved road and then re-entering them via another. To head deeper into the range you'll need a donkey; blazed trails lead to **Pico Duarte** from several points.

La Vega

LA VEGA, just 30km south of Santiago, started out as one of Columbus's gold-mining towns. Aside from the ruins of this old settlement, **La Vega Vieja**, there's little in today's noisy, concrete city to hold your attention. However, La Vega's **Carnival** celebrations in February are generally acknowledged to be among the most boisterous and authentic in the nation. A twenty-block promenade is set up between the two main parks, along which parade platoons of demons in impressively horrific masks, the making of which is somewhat of a local speciality craft.

There are no good in-town **hotels**; most lack even the most basic amenities like toilet seat, mosquito net or hot water. *San Pedro*, Cáceres 87 (☏ 809/573-2844; ❶), is the least seedy and cleanest, but is still not especially comfortable. You'll fare slightly better with local **restaurants**, notably the second-floor *Salón Dorado* above Engini Car Wash, Cáceres and Restauración, which has a hip decor, fun crowd and pool tables. The **bus** stations, Caribe Tours (☏ 809/573-3488), Metro (☏ 809/573-7099) and Vegano Express (☎809/573-7079), are all on the Carretera La Vega, just off the Autopista Duarte. **Guaguas** to Jarabacoa set off from the corner of 27 de Febrero and Restauración.

Jarabacoa

JARABACOA, a sleepy mountain resort peppered with coffee plantations, is popular with wealthy Dominicans for its cool summers, and with foreign travellers for the nearby natural splendour and adventure sports opportunities. While there's little to do in the town itself, the pine-dominated mountains immediately surrounding the town hold three large waterfalls, several rugged trails fit for day-hikes, three rivers used for white-water rafting and the busiest starting-point for treks up Pico Duarte; see the box below for local outfitters.

Arrival and accommodation

Located some 30km southwest of La Vega, Jarabacoa is well served by **public transport**. *Guaguas* do the road from La Vega at hourly intervals and Caribe Tours, with a station at the main crossroads across from the Esso station, runs four buses daily from La Vega, Bonao and Santo Domingo. *Guaguas* pick up and drop off at Esso in the centre and by the Shell station on the Constanza road.

With the recent increase in visitor numbers, Jarabacoa's **accommodation** options have improved radically. In addition to the possibilities listed below, you can **camp** around Manabao or at Balneario la Confluencia; if you want to get further away from civilization, most farmers will let you camp on their land, provided you ask first.

Brisas del Yaque Luperón ☎809/574 4490. Clean, modern hotel just off the town centre. Nothing special but perfectly comfortable. The rooms come with a/c, TV, hot water and a fridge. ❷

Gran Jimenoa Av La Confluencia, Los Corralitos ☎809/574-6304, ⊛www.granjimenoa.com. Best hotel in town with large a/c rooms in a new building overlooking a pleasant pool area. By far the most comfortable of the Jarabacoa hotels, though there's basically zero service. ❷

Hogar Mella 34 ☎809/574-2739. The best budget hotel in town, with very basic rooms (beds are a bit uncomfortable), but also boasting private showers, clean rooms and a pleasant courtyard. ❶

Pinar Dorado on the road to Constanza, km 1 ☎809/574-2820, ⓔpinardorado@verizon.net.do. Pleasant Swiss chalet-style architecture and amiable staff. The hotel has nice rooms (if a bit worn around the edges) with TV, a/c, hot water, private balconies, restaurant and bar. ❷

The Town

Most of the action in town is centred on the major crossroads, a few blocks north of the small **parque central.** The point at which the Río Yaque del Norte and Río Jimenoa meet is a popular spot for swimming, a half-kilometre north of the main crossroads.

The most popular local attractions are the three **waterfalls** (*saltos*), which are all enough of a trek that you'll want either your own transport or a ride on a *motoconcho*

Jarabacoa tour operators

Franz's Aventuras del Caribe Hato Viejo 21 ☎809/242-0395, ⊛www.hispaniola.com/whitewater. Budget white-water rafting trips, plus basic kayaking and canyoning. They also arrange early morning pick-ups from the hotels along the north coast.

Rancho Baiguate on the road to Constanza, km 5 ☎809/574-6890, ⊛www.ranchobaiguate.com.do. One of the island's biggest tour operators, with most of their clients coming on excursions from the all-inclusives on the north coast. As well as culture tours they also run adventure trips including white-water rafting, canyoning, paragliding, mountain trekking, mountain-biking, jeep safaris and horseriding. Longer trips include a guided hike to Pico Duarte.

Pico Duarte and the Cordillera Central's national parks

Two national parks, **Bermúdez** and **Ramírez**, protect much of the mountains, cloud forests and pines present in the Cordillera Central, each encompassing over seven hundred square kilometres. By far the best way to explore the region is on an organized trek up **Pico Duarte**, at 3087m the tallest mountain in the Caribbean, which is actually located between the two parks but generally approached via Bermúdez.

A number of strenuous treks lead up the peak, which towers over the centre of the range alongside its sister mountain La Pelona. The most popular one starts from the tiny *pueblo* of La Ciénega, 25km southwest of Jarabacoa, where you'll need to register for the 46km round-trip at the park's entrance office on the far side of the village. You'll have to pay the RD$100 **park entrance** and hire at least one **guide** for every five people (RD$200/day plus meals). It's also a good idea to rent at least one **mule** (RD$250/day) – chances are the guide will insist upon it – to carry water and food as well as to get you down safely if things go wrong.

The best bet is to arrive in the afternoon, sort out the formalities and then camp down in the village with a view to starting out early the next morning. The first leg is a comfortable 4km riverside stroll to a bridge across the river at **Los Tablones**. Once over the river, however, the climbing starts for real and you'll gain over 2000m in the next 14km, mostly on a badly eroded track that wends its way through some wonderfully wild woodland. Regular stops at official picnic sights allow you to get your breath back and to peep out through the canopy for a glimpse of the totally pristine wilderness that surrounds you. You'll spend the night in a ramshackle cabin at **La Comparticíon** and then scramble up the last 5km at around 4.30am to be on the bare rocky summit for sunrise. It's quite a stirring sight to watch the sun creep over the horizon, casting a bright-red hue on the banks of cloud beneath your feet.

Treks can be made any time of the year, but should never be attempted without a waterproof coat, winter clothing, a sleeping bag and hiking boots. You'll also need to bring enough food for yourself and the guide (this is best bought in Jarabacoa). It's definitely worth considering the two **tour operators** who operate trips up this trail: Iguana Mama, in Cabarete (see p.372); or Rancho Baiguate, in Jarabacoa (see box opposite), as they'll take care of all the logistics for you.

(RD$50–100 one-way). Most popular is the crashing **Lower Salto Jimenoa**, 3km east of town off the Carretera Jarabacoa (daily 8.30am–7pm; RD$5), which boasts a deep pool good for swimming. **Salto Baiguate**, 1km south of town on the road to Constanza (daily 8.30am–7pm; free), is a bit taller, plus it has a large cave and a swimming hole at its base. The steepest Jarabacoa waterfall is the **Higher Salto Jimenoa**, or Salto Jimenoa Uno, as it's often called. This isn't so easy to find but if you head out on the road to Constanza for 7km, you'll pass through a small *pueblo* before coming to a few shacks on the right. Almost directly opposite these is a jeep-size driveway that quickly deteriorates into a narrow and steep footpath. Continue down to the bottom and scramble over some huge slabs to the pool at the waterfall's base. It's a pretty awesome sight: the water drops 75m from a hidden lake above, and thunders into a huge pool at its base. The spray at the bottom creates its own rainbows and it's easy to see why this was chosen as a setting for a scene in *Jurassic Park*.

Eating

Jarabacoa has a couple of quality restaurants catering to the Dominican families that weekend here. *Don Luis*, at the corner of Colón and Duarte, is a good mid-range restaurant facing the *parque central*, serving steak, seafood and the usual Dominican staples. At the main crossroads at the town entrance, *El Rancho* is an excellent high-end restaurant serving good pizza plus specialities like baked chicken stuffed with banana.

6.6

Barahona

Occupying the coast west of Santo Domingo and taking its name from the major city at its centre, the **Barahona Region** was once the focus of Trujillo's personal sugar empire; vast tracts of cane still take up much of the land north of **Barahona** city, but today this is one of the country's poorest regions. As a result, the stunning Barahona **coastline** is almost completely undeveloped, making it perfect for independent travellers willing to rough it a bit in exchange for unblemished natural beauty.

Barahona and around

BARAHONA city isn't an especially pleasant place. Founded in 1802 and once the informal capital of Trujillo's multimillion-dollar sugar industry, the city has fallen on hard times due to the closing of the local sugar mill. That said, the locals are friendly and it does have a couple of good hotels, making it a useful base to explore the undeveloped coastline that stretches west of the city. If sticking around, head either to the Malecón, which is quite beautiful, or the *parque central*, a major hangout at night.

Most visitors arrive **via guagua or car**; coastal Highway 44 connects the city with Azua, Baní and Santo Domingo to the east before continuing west all the way to the border. If spending the night, most **accommodations** are within a couple of blocks of the seaside Malecón. The best of the lot is a bit pricey, the Costa Larimar, Malecón 18 (T809/524-3442; ❺–❻), which has just about every amenity you can think of and a prime beachfront location to boot. The best of the rest is the *Gran Barahona*, Mota 5 (T809/524-3442; ❷), with comfortable rooms that have a/c, TV and hot water. There's a decent array of **places to eat**: *Melo's Café*, Anacaona 12 (T809/524-5437), is the best of the lot, an unpretentious diner with delicious American breakfasts and nightly dinner specials. Also well worth checking out is *Brisas del Caribe*, a seafood restaurant on the far eastern end of the Malecón; the creole shrimp and broiled kingfish are house specialities.

West of Barahona

The gorgeous coastline **west of Barahona** is the region's premier attraction, yet it remains virtually undiscovered by outsiders. The first major beach spot is Baoruco, 15km west of Barahona along Highway 44, a tiny fishing village with the best hotel in the Barahona region, *Casa Bonita* (T809/696-0215, F223-0548; ❺), with great views, a patio with a swimming pool and an elegant restaurant.

Five kilometres beyond Baoruco, *pueblo* **San Rafael** holds an enticing beach, if one with a strong, crashing surf. Fortunately, a **waterfall** thrums down the nearby mountains and forms a natural swimming pool at the entrance. **Paraiso**, another 5km to the west, is the biggest town along this stretch, but still doesn't boast much in the way of facilities. It does have a long strand of superb sandy beach, along which stands *Hotel Paraiso* (T809/243-1080; ❶), a decent place to stay for the night.

A better beach lies yet 5km further west, in **Los Patos**, where the ocean is joined again by a river descending from the mountains to form a freshwater swimming pool. The beach, surrounded with dense mangroves, stays pretty active throughout the week, and beach vendors are set up to take care of most visitors' needs.

East of Barahona

Heading **east of Barahona** towards San Cristóbal and the capital stand a string of colonial-era towns that appear congested and unappealing at first sight, but hide beaches that make stopovers worthwhile. First up is **Azua**, 60km east of Barahona on Highway-2. Though there's nothing left of the original city, Azua is one of the oldest European cities in the New World, founded by future conqueror of Cuba Diego Velázquez in 1504. What is still here, though, is the five-kilometre-long **Playa Monte Río**, a short drive south of town, which offers beautiful views of the rolling El Número mountains. There's very little development around the beach; rather, the calm waters are lined with fishing boats and a few locally run outdoor restaurants.

Tucked away in the mountains along the Río Ocóa between the town of Azua and Baní is **San José de Ocóa**, 27km north of the Carretera Sánchez along Highway 41, attracting weekenders from across the country, most of whom are eager to beat the valley heat, visit the local river *balneario* (swimming hole) and take advantage of the lovely, sometimes rugged, mountain landscape. The town itself is an easy-going and fairly modest hamlet, unremarkable but for its majestic setting. Just south of town, though, is **El Manantiel**, another swimming spot a kilometre down a dirt road off the highway, where you'll find several good places to bathe among the boulders and ice-cold cascades. **Accommodation** options in town are plentiful but decidedly no-frills, intended as they are to serve families who don't mind shacking up several to a room. The best of the lot is the spartan *Sagrato de Jesús*, Cañada/San José (☎809/558-2432; ❶), not especially luxurious but acceptable with private cold-water bath. *Baco*, a half-block west of the *parque central*, serves quality **meals** like *chivo guisado* (goat stew) or chicken with rice, beans and plantains.

Another 40km east on the Carretera Sánchez, less than 20km east of the San José turn-off, coastal **Baní** has in recent years turned relatively prosperous, an upswing that has spurred much population growth, if not exactly prettified the place. There are few diversions within the town, but the nearby beaches are the main draw. Best of the bunch is **Las Salinas**, a small town consisting of little more than a few dozen houses scattered about a white-sand beach, 16km southwest at the end of the Carretera Las Calderas. Sand dunes, saltpans and rolling hills surround the village, which makes for a fine place to do some **windsurfing**; taking advantage of these conditions is the *Salinas High Wind Center*, Puerto Hermosa 7 (☎809/310-8141; ❹), a small but extremely nice resort catering mostly to wealthy Dominicans.

Puerto Rico

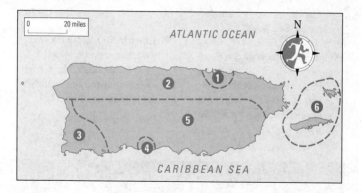

Puerto Rico highlights

* **Old San Juan** Wander among some of the oldest and best-preserved colonial architecture in the Americas in this district, perched on a dramatic headland. See p.399

* **El Yunque** Hike, birdwatch or orchid hunt amid the 43 square miles of tropical rainforest that smother the island's eastern mountain range. See p.408

* **La Ruta Panorámica** Stunning views of the jungle-like Puerto Rican interior greet you at every turn along this winding mountain road. See p.421

* **Desecheo** There are many magnificent diving sites in the remarkably clear waters around this lone 360-acre rock just offshore from Rincón. See p.411

* **Mosquito Bay** Wonder at the trillions of sparkling organisms in one of the world's brightest bioluminescent bays on Vieques. See p.426

* **Culebra** This laid-back and beautiful island off Puerto Rico's east coast has superb snorkelling and the country's best beaches. See p.427

△ Iguana crossing road, Culebra

Introduction and basics

Puerto Rico – or Borinquén, as the island's pre-Columbian inhabitants called it – commands a pivotal spot in the Caribbean, the last substantial island before the sprawling arm of the Antilles swoops south towards Venezuela, fragmenting into the tiny Leeward and Windward Islands. Puerto Rico's unique status as a commonwealth of the US, however, keeps it a world apart from its island neighbours, over a distance that can be measured not just in kilometres, but in dollars. It's a place that combines island life with a level of infrastructure seldom seen in the region: excellent interstate highways allow travellers to zip from coral reef to five-star restaurant, and hikers can traipse through the spectacular El Yunque rainforest on well-paved trails maintained by the US National Forest Service. American influence is strongest in San Juan, where even the ramparts of El Morro – which staved off European aggressors for 500 years – haven't managed to prevent the influx of American fast-food and retail chains. But the capital's core retains a distinctly Latin character, with Old San Juan host to a treasure-trove of pastel Spanish colonial architecture on exquisitely restored cobblestoned streets.

Despite the threat of overdevelopment, most of the 35-by-100-mile island has managed to elude despoilment. Even in the crowded capital, it's hard to find a sullied beach, and nature is largely untouched outside the major cities – especially in the jungly, mountainous interior; on the relatively hidden beaches along the south coast; and on the offshore islands. Puerto Rico's diversity makes it just as appealing to the eco-tourist as to the sun-worshipper. Quite apart from the plentiful picture-postcard beaches, there are excellent opportunities for **diving, snorkelling, sailing, fishing, surfing, caving, birding** and **hiking**.

Where to go

No matter where you are in Puerto Rico, you're never more than a couple of hours by car from **San Juan**, whose colonial architecture in its old town is a must-see. More historic vestiges can be found in the southern cities of **Ponce** and **San Germán**.

Numerous pretty and isolated beaches are within easy reach, some fringed with otherwordly, pristine coral reefs. For diving and snorkelling, choose from **Desecheo** off the west coast, the beautiful offshore islets of **Vieques** and **Culebra** in the east, or the **Wall** running just off the southwest

coast. With advance planning you can also reach the uninhabited island of **Mona**, the so-called "Galápagos of the Caribbean", a wildlife reserve halfway to the Dominican Republic.

Hikers won't want to miss **El Yunque**, the only tropical rainforest in the US park system, with exotic and rare flora and fauna. There are also good walks in the **Cordillera Central**, especially through the San Cristóbal Canyon outside Barranquitas. The subtropical dry forest of **Guánica** in the southwest is not only a World Biosphere Reserve, but also has the added attraction of excellent birdwatching opportunities.

And the spelunking is superb: the vast labyrinth of caves in the **northwestern karst country** is among the largest in the world, set amid abruptly eroded limestone landscape around the **Río Camuy** which features giant sinkholes and peculiar haystack hills.

When to go

Puerto Rico's pleasant **tropical climate** is virtually seasonless, with an average temperature of 82°F (28°C) from November to May, slightly higher the rest of the year; note it can be considerably cooler in the mountains. Rainfall varies around the island – heaviest in El Yunque, which receives up

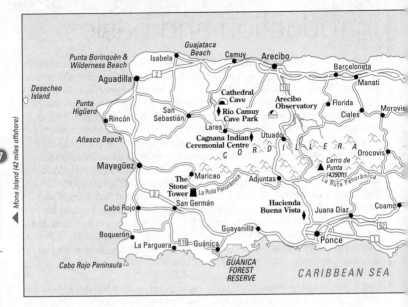

to 200 inches a year, while Guánica's dry forest in the southwest gets as little as 30 inches. But make sure to bring an umbrella, whenever you go.

Hurricanes are so common in Puerto Rico that they got their name here; the English word for these storms with winds of over 75mph comes from the name of the Taíno god of malevolence, Jurakán (pronounced hu-ra-kan). Hurricane season runs from June to November, when the weather is hottest and wettest. The highest risk is in September, when in 1998 winds of 120mph were recorded during Hurricane George. Call the National Weather Service on ☎787/253-4586 for current information.

Arrival

San Juan is one of the world's top **cruise ship** destinations, with most of the pleasure boats docking at the **port** by the old town. But you are most likely to arrive at the **Luis Muñoz Marín International Airport**, 14km east of San Juan in the suburb of Carolina.

Information, websites and maps

The **Puerto Rican Tourism Company**, or PRTC (⊛ www.gotopuertorico.com), has offices in San Juan at the Luis Muñoz Marín International Airport (☎787/791-1014) and Old San Juan (☎787/722-1709), in Ponce (☎787/843-0465), Vieques (☎787/741-0800), Aguadilla (☎787/890-3315) and Cabo Rojo (☎787/851-7015). Like concierges all over the island, the helpful and multilingual staff are more than eager to suggest and book hotels and restaurants, arrange activities and even intervene in case of theft or illness. Be sure to grab a copy of their annual 70-page *Travel Planner* (⊛ www.travelandsports.com), which has lists of accommodation and phone numbers for many transportation and recreation services. It is also broken down and expanded into five handy booklets covering separate regions.

The PRTC's flagship publication is *Que Pasa?* (⊛ www.qpsm.com), a bimonthly glossy with a calendar of events, feature-length stories on various attractions and regions, and helpful listings. Another

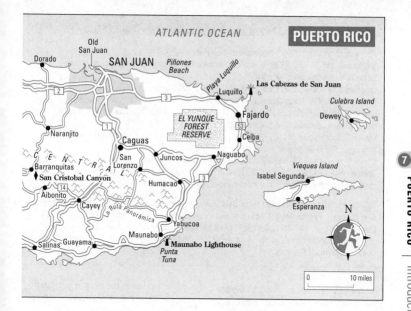

useful publication, *Places to Go* (🌐 www. enjoypuertorico.com), is free at hotels and tourist offices.

Basic **maps** of the island are available at PRTC offices (or at 🌐 www.travelmaps.com), and can be found in all the publications mentioned. Street and road maps are also sold in bookstores, but even the Official Transportation Map is by no means comprehensive.

Money and costs

Puerto Rico uses **US currency**, which generally comes in bills of US$1, $5, $10, $20, $50 and $100; the dollar (sometimes referred to as a peso) is made up of 100 cents in coins of 1¢ (penny), 5¢ (nickel), 10¢ (dime) and 25¢ (quarter). Major credit cards are widely accepted at hotels and restaurants.

Although Puerto Rico's GNP is lower than that of any of the fifty states, **prices** are not drastically cheaper than on the mainland, although it is cheaper than other parts of the Caribbean. On a strict budget (which would mean forgoing a car) you can get away with spending less than $100 a day, while you can travel in style on over $200 a day. In San Juan, the least you can expect to pay for accommodation with a/c and your own bath is US$65 for a single/double room (all hotels in listings have a/c and bath unless mentioned); an average lunch at a modest establishment runs US$7 to $12, with comparable dinners from US$12 to $22. The standard tip is 15 percent.

ATMs – called ATHs ("a todas horas", or "at all hours") – are abundant in cities; you'll find them in banks, supermarkets, casinos and most of the larger hotels. In smaller towns and rural areas, you'll have to look a little harder. If you're at a loss, ask for directions to the local Banco Popular. Official banking hours are 8.30am to 2.30pm from Monday to Friday, though many stay open until 4pm.

Expect to pay 11 percent **tax** on rooms with casinos, otherwise 9 percent on rooms without. There is no tax on food and merchandise.

Getting around

If you **rent a car**, you'll make the most efficient use of your time. While you may get a cheaper deal from a local rental company,

The following services all originate in San Juan:

Blue Line ☎787/765-7733, Plaza de Recreo, Río Piedras (destinations include Isabela, Aguadilla and Rincón)

Chóferes Unidos de Ponce ☎787/764-0540, Braumbaugh y Saldana, Río Piedras; ☎787/722-3275, Plaza Degetau, Parada 18, Santurce (to Ponce and around)

Línea Borícua de San Sebastián ☎787/765-1908, Avda Gonzalez 1012 (inland destinations towards San Sebastián)

Línea Caborrojeña ☎787/723-9155, Avda Las Palmas, Santurce (to the southwest, including Cabo Rojo and San Germán)

Línea Sultana ☎787/765-9377 (to Mayagüez and Rincón)

Terminal del Este ☎787/250-0717, Calle Arzuaga y Capuchinos (by the Correo), Río Piedras (to Fajardo and other destinations east of San Juan)

Daily domestic flights depart from San Juan's international airport for Ponce, Vieques and Culebra. Flights for the offshore islands also depart from the Fernando L. Rivas Dominici Airport (☎787/729-8790) in Isla Grande, near the San Juan neighbourhood of Miramar, and from Fajardo. Vieques and Culebra can also be reached by regular daily ferries from Fajardo.

national chains such as Avis (☎800/874-3556), Hertz (☎800/654-3131) and Budget (☎787/791-0600) are likely to be more reliable, and offer 24-hour emergency service. Weekly rates for an economy car in San Juan start at around US$280. AAA (☎787/791-2609) also operates emergency roadside assistance for members. Driver's licences from the UK, US, Canada, Australia and New Zealand are valid for up to three months.

Highways are relatively fast (although driving habits can be profoundly erratic) and fairly well maintained (watch for potholes). As in the US, motorists drive on the right side and speed limits are posted in miles per hour. Unlike the US, distances are posted in kilometres and road signs are in Spanish. On the whole signposting is poor and often quite bewildering. Off the main highways signs usually show road numbers rather than town names; note that "INT" (for *intersección*) above a road number denotes a forthcoming turning *onto* that road. The lack of any decent maps available compounds the problem, so a compass can come in handy.

As most Puerto Ricans have their own cars, there is no official public transportation network outside the San Juan metropolitan area, although there is a rather confusing and fragmented system of **públicos** – part-bus, part-taxi. They are an inexpensive, if not exactly efficient, way to traverse the island,

transporting up to ten people over somewhat flexible routes and distances Monday to Saturday. A trip from San Juan to Ponce costs about US$10 one-way, US$20 round-trip. Each town has its own terminal; most don't have phone numbers, however, so you have to go there in person to ask about schedules.

In San Juan, many terminals are in Río Piedras, although some lines going west are based in Santurce (see box above). You can also ask to be picked up at your hotel, but expect to pay an additional US$3–5. Don't be surprised if you have to wait at least an hour, at either the terminal or your hotel. While *públicos* are inexpensive, they make frequent stops, so travel over great distances can be extremely slow.

Accommodation

Puerto Rico has a wide range of **accommodation** options, from rustic mountain cottages to fancy beachfront high-rises. For a room endorsed by the PRTC, with air conditioning and TV, you'll spend anywhere from US$65 to over US$1000 – if you're willing to pay for it. For lower prices, you'll have to settle for a fan and share a shower in typically basic and dingy surroundings; ask the PRTC for any suggestions. The very finest hotels cost a minimum of US$200 a night. During high season, mid-December to mid-April (when you should definitely book ahead, especially weekends), prices are generally US$20–30 higher at small inns and hotels, and as much as US$50–100 higher at luxury establishments. The rest of the year prices drop, as do the number of tourists.

Puerto Rico has established a system of over 20 state-sanctioned **paradores** (☎ 888/642-6923). These so-called country inns are intended to be convenient for accessing the island's beaches, mountains and towns, and most are located in picturesque settings west of San Juan. The PRTC can provide a complete list (or visit ⓦwww. gotoparadores.com), but don't always assume these places will be first-rate.

The Compañía de Parques Nacionales (☎787/622-5200, ⓦwww.parquesnacionalespr. com) runs a number of vacation centres with very economical accommodation around the island's national parks. There are also almost 20 legal **campgrounds** – mostly on beaches or in national parks and forests – but camping is not straightforward as you have to book at least two weeks in advance. Contact the Department of Natural Resources (☎787/724-3724) who will provide a **permit**; cost varies according to site.

Food and drink

In recent years, Puerto Rico – and San Juan in particular – has commanded a growing reputation as the culinary hot spot of the Caribbean. World-renowned chefs at vanguard restaurants prepare dynamic **Nuevo Latino** cuisine – a twist on traditional *criollo* cooking, with an emphasis on fish, fruits, tubers and dark rum sauces or marinades with tropical ingredients. You'll also find every manner of ethnic food in the capital, including Indian, Thai, French and even Romanian.

Criollo fare, however, is still the staple of the Puerto Rican diet. Meats are mostly served with rice and red beans (*habichuelas*) or *tostones* – fried green plantains. *Sofrito* – a sauce made from cilantro, onions, garlic and peppers – is used to season many dishes, as is *adobo*, a mixture of garlic, oregano, paprika, vinegar and oil. The food is typically tasty but much of it is starchy and fried in animal fat, and pork is far more popular than fish outside of the major cities.

The system of over 30 state-sanctioned **restaurants**, called *mesones gastronómicos*, presumably ensures a standard of decency among participating restaurants (most of which serve traditional criollo food), but the quality can vary widely. See the PRTC's website for a complete list; they are also listed in *Travel and Sports or Que Pasa?* under their respective destinations.

Budget travellers can fill up at cheap rice-and-beans joints all over the island or seek out savory criollo staples like *asopao de pollo* (stewed chicken) and *plátanos* (plantains) or *lechón asado* (roast pork) and *mofongo* (a ball of crushed, fried plantains and seasonings), sold from trailers or the backs of pickup trucks. You can also snack on *empanadillas* (pasties with all manner of savory fillings) very cheaply. *Reposterías* are a good bet too: found in San Juan and in strip malls islandwide, they have some of the island's best coffee, along with breakfast *postres* – slightly sweet pastries filled with jam or cheese; they also sell soups, tortillas, seafood salads and fresh bread. Note that in all but the best restaurants, fresh vegetables are hard to come by, but supermarkets like *Pueblo* usually carry a good supply.

Coffee in Puerto Rico is strong, served black or with heated milk *(café con leche)*, and very sweet. Look out for signs for refreshing *coco frío* – chilled coconuts punctured with drinking straws. While not as common, **fresh-fruit drinks** made from mangos, papayas and oranges (known as *jugo de china*) are also available. The *batidos* (milkshakes) are also worth a try. Not surprisingly, **rum** (*ron*) is the national drink – *piña colada* being a favourite – as Puerto Rico is the world's largest producer of this sugarcane-based liquor; more than twenty brands are distilled here. The locally brewed **beer** is Medalla; Presidente, from the Dominican Republic, is also popular.

Tap water is generally safe to drink. However, it's wise to stick to bottled water (widely available) after storms. If in doubt, ask the locals.

> The **country code** for Puerto Rico is ☎787. The emergency number is ☎911.

Mail and communications

Post offices, located in most major and small towns, are open from 8am to 5pm weekdays, though some have Saturday morning hours.

Outside Puerto Rico, dial ☎787/555-1212 for **directory information**. Attendants usually answer in Spanish but will switch to English at your request; within Puerto Rico, dial ☎411. All telephone numbers are seven digits long and preceded by ☎787 (or, increasingly, ☎939 for some mobile telephones), which must be used for both local and long-distance calls; for long-distance, dial a "1" first. US cell phones work in Puerto Rico, but coin-operated pay phones are also easy enough to find in populated areas. Decent **Internet** service is available but not abundant; you will find it at larger hotels and the occasional cybercafé.

Opening hours, holidays and festivals

In general, **business hours** in Puerto Rico are Monday to Friday 8.30am–5.30pm, with many businesses closing for lunch (noon–1pm).

On **public holidays** (see box), government offices, banks and schools are closed, and museum hours and transportation schedules may change.

The following **festivals** are the most popular organized events in Puerto Rico. In addition to these, each town celebrates its patron saint's day (*fiesta patronal*) and the ten days leading up to it. Check PRTC's website (Ⓦwww.gotopuertorico.com) for details.

Festivals

January

San Sebastián Street Festival Old San Juan. Take to the streets of old town as it becomes unusually and enjoyably animated.

February/March

Carnaval Ponce. Celebration during the six days preceding Lent, featuring parades of traditional *vejigantes*, or masked revellers.

May/June

Casals Music Festival San Juan. Two weeks of orchestral music with world-renowned musicians. **Heineken Jazzfest** San Juan. Four days of Latin jazz, performed by Puerto Rican and international musicians, at the Sixto Escobar Park in Condado. **San Juan Bautista Day/Noche de San Juan** (around June 23) San Juan's *fiesta patronal*. Parties and festivities in Old San Juan culminate with crowds walking backwards into the sea three times, in honour of St John the Baptist.

Public holidays

January 1 New Year's Day
January 6 Three Kings' Day
Second Monday in January Eugenio María de Hostos's Birthday
Third Monday in January Martin Luther King, Jr., Day
Third Monday in February Presidents' Day
March 22 Abolition Day
March/April Palm Sunday, Good Friday, Easter Sunday
Third Monday in April José de Diego Day
Last Monday in May Memorial Day
July 4 Independence Day
Third Monday in July Luís Muñoz Rivera's Birthday
July 25 Constitution Day
July 27 José Celso Barbosa's Birthday
First Monday in September Labour Day
October 12 Columbus Day
November 11 Veterans' Day
November 19 Discovery of Puerto Rico Day
Fourth Thursday in November Thanksgiving Day
December 25 Christmas Day

Santiago Apostol Festival Loíza. Good place to experience the customs of Santería. Very African in flavour, with costumed parades and *bomba* drumming. Not to be missed.

November

National Bomba y Plena Festival Ponce. African-based drumming and singing, by performers from all over the island.

December

Festival of Inocentes Hatillo. On the 28th, watch children chased through the streets by costumed revellers commemorating King Herod's infamous massacre.

History

Some two thousand years ago, the **Arcáicos** were the first indigenous tribe to arrive in Puerto Rico. Later came the **Igneris**, and finally the **Taíno** from 600 AD, who dubbed the island "Borinquén", or "Borikén" – "the land of the valiant and noble lord". This last group had a long-lasting effect on Puerto Rican culture and bloodlines; many Puerto Rican words come from the Arawak language they spoke, and it is estimated that sixty percent of Puerto Ricans today have some Taíno ancestry.

Nevertheless, pure Taíno had virtually ceased to exist by the end of the sixteenth century. Those the Spanish hadn't killed they had bred with, while the remainder had either fled or been wiped out by disease. But taking the Spanish for gods, the peaceful Taíno people welcomed the arrival of **Christopher Columbus** in 1493, on his second voyage to the Americas. It was not until 1508 that colonization started on the island, which Columbus had named San Juan Bautista. That year, the first settlement was founded by the island's first governor, Ponce de León, on the south side of what is now San Juan Bay. Originally named Caparra, it was soon renamed Puerto Rico (or rich port) – it was not until later that the name of the city and the island were switched through a cartographic error.

Having converted the Taíno to **Christianity**, the Spanish wasted no time in setting them to work mining the little gold there was on the island, which had all but run out within a few decades.

Somewhat disillusioned with these so-called gods, the Taíno decided to test their immortality by drowning a Spanish soldier; they realized their mistake when he failed to come back to life. An uprising ensued in 1510, resulting in a bloody massacre. The remainder of the Taíno either fled the island, took refuge in the mountainous interior or ended up as slaves. The church then sanctioned intermarriage in 1514, rendering permissible the practice of keeping Taíno mistresses. Their offspring, called *mestizos*, sustained Taíno heritage, together with the *jíbaros* hiding in the hills. The rapid disappearance of the Taíno meant that West African slaves were already being imported by 1513 to tend to plantations of sugar cane, plantains, bananas, citrus fruits and ginger; by 1530 they constituted almost two thirds of the island's population.

In 1521 **San Juan** was officially founded in its final position, having moved across the bay from Caparra because the new site offered far superior fortification against invaders and protected the entrance to the bay. By 1539, *sanjuaneros* had recognized both the strategic value and vulnerability of their port – as had Spain's European rivals – and began constructing the formidable stone fortification called Fuerte San Felipe del Morro, which still stands at the headland of Old San Juan. After Francis Drake failed to take the city in 1595, the British managed to seize and burn San Juan in 1598, but were soon defeated by dysentery. The Dutch also attacked successfully in 1625, again burning the city, but were likewise eventually overcome by disease.

By now little more than a strategic stronghold, Puerto Rico was largely overlooked by Spain and began to languish. Impoverished islanders resented that they saw so little return on their labour for the Spanish. They were not allowed to participate in government, trade with other nations, or move around the island. In rebellion, they began trading sugar and rum illegally, so the island soon became a hotbed of pirates and contraband.

The Spanish empire, in one of its last gasps, sent **General Alejandro O'Reilly** to establish order in the latter half of the eighteenth century. He built roads and schools and encouraged literate, conservative Spaniards to immigrate to the island, while dropping trade restrictions and lowering taxes. By the turn of the century, Puerto Rico was thriving. In the wake of the French Revolution, slaves began revolting in the French Caribbean colonies, driving white plantation owners to Puerto Rico, and boosting sugar and rum production on the island, where slavery wouldn't be abolished until 1873. Puerto Rico began a lucrative exchange with the US, exporting sugar, rum and coffee.

Starting in 1810, a movement spearheaded by **Simón Bolívar**, the "Liberator", resulted in the independence of almost all Spain's colonies by the mid-1820s, except for Puerto Rico, Cuba and the Philippines. To keep the islanders happy and nurture their loyalty,

the Spanish further lowered taxes and opened up more ports for trade. And to *guarantee* their loyalty, they established a military government that lasted 42 years.

This failed to prevent an independence movement from brewing, although the first serious uprising in Puerto Rico did not to come until 1868 with the "Cry of Lares", which proclaimed the Republic of Puerto Rico. By 1897 Puerto Rico finally got what it wanted: **independence from Spain** as an autonomous state. But only a year later, American forces landed in Guánica Bay and took Puerto Rico for themselves – the islanders offered no resistance, putting a swift and easy end to the **Spanish–American War**. The Americans wanted the island primarily as a naval base, as well as for trade, so it wasn't until 1917 that its inhabitants became US citizens.

Puerto Rico's economy suffered terribly from the **Great Depression** in the 1930s, and revolutionary movements continued to simmer. This led to several bloody altercations between radicals and police, notably the 1937 Ponce Massacre in which nineteen protesters died. In 1948, Luis Muñoz Marín, head of the Popular Democratic Party, was elected the island's first governor under US jurisdiction (which he remained until 1968), and its first constitution was drafted. Under "Operation Bootstrap", tax breaks encouraged US manufacturing companies to set up on the island, thus kick-starting industrialization and making the island less dependent on agriculture – by now mostly sugar, coffee and tobacco.

After World War II, huge numbers of Puerto Ricans in search of the American Dream emigrated to the US mainland, mostly New York. Here a new hybrid culture evolved whose people became known as **Nuyoricans** – famously depicted in Leonard Bernstein's 1957 musical *West Side Story*. Today, there are reckoned to be some eight million Puerto Ricans living outside the island, about half of them on the American mainland.

A botched assassination attempt on US President Truman in 1950 by Puerto Rican nationalists notwithstanding, the US granted the island **commonwealth** status in 1952. Puerto Rico became the "Estado Libre Asociado" (free associated state) it remains today, which allows self-government in internal affairs as well as fiscal independence, although islanders cannot vote in presidential elections. Furthermore, the US Congress retained full authority to determine the status of the territory and apply federal law as appropriate.

In the first referendums addressing the issue of **sovereignty** in 1967, Puerto Ricans overwhelmingly voted to remain a commonwealth, rather than become a full US state or independent nation. Two much narrower referendums followed in 1993 and 1998, and although both were voted down in favour of the status quo, a much larger proportion favoured statehood.

The move for **independence** wo. most recent victory with the eventua termination of the US Navy's bombing practices on Vieques in 2003, after years of bitter protest. But support for outright independence is very small, considered something of a pipe dream. Puerto Ricans recognize the need for – and inevitability of – change, with supporters of an adjusted version of the status quo only slightly outweighing those in favour of becoming the 51st state. The problem lies in the fact that Puerto Rico has developed strong ties with the US, while it also jealously protects its Hispanic heritage – most notably the language. While it will certainly be hard to wean the island off the hefty subsidies it receives each year from the US government, few Puerto Ricans are willing to forsake the conspicuous bonus of having a US passport.

7.1

San Juan

ounded in 1521 by Ponce de León, the capital of Puerto Rico, **SAN JUAN**, is the oldest city on US territory. The metropolitan area of San Juan is home to half of the island's almost four million citizens; it is also the heart of Puerto Rican tourism. The city is best known for its beautifully restored historic district, **Old San Juan**, situated on a rocky peninsula girded by twenty-feet thick walls jutting into the crashing Atlantic surf. Unlike other such gems of Spanish colonial architecture, San Juan also offers miles of smooth, clean beaches, a wide range of accommodation, fabulous restaurants and a lively nightlife.

Along with Old San Juan, resort-filled **Condado** is the most popular neighbourhood for visitors thanks to its excellent beachfront and fine boutiques, and these two sections of the capital share the highest concentration of restaurants and lodging options. There's plenty more to explore: further east is up-and-coming **Santurce** with its numerous art galleries and trendy nightclubs; and the beachfront neighbourhoods of **Ocean Park** and **Isla Verde**, beyond which are the deserted palm-fringed beaches of **Piñones**. To the south lies the financial district of **Hato Rey**, and then **Río Piedras** with its easygoing college-town vibe.

Excellent day-trips can be made to some of the island's top attractions: east to **El Yunque** rainforest and famous **Luquillo Beach**; or west to the **Río Camuy Cave Park** and the striking **Arecibo Observatory** in the karst country.

Arrival and information

San Juan is fifteen to thirty minutes' drive west from the airport along Rte 26 (Avenida Baldorioty de Castro). Major **car rental** agencies operate airport offices. By **taxi**, it costs US$8 to Isla Verde, US$12 to Condado and US$16 to Old San Juan. The **public bus** is air-conditioned and cheap (just 25¢ a throw), but the trip can take a full hour. The #C45 from the airport only goes as far as Isla Verde, where you have to change to the #A5 to get to the bus terminal in Old San Juan, located on the bay side, near the **cruise ship** port. If you're going on to Condado, you'll have to change again to the #B21 at the terminal – it is also possible, however, to intercept the #B21 route earlier by getting off the #A5 at Avenida José de Diego. If you're getting off at the bus terminal, the main **taxi** rank in Old San Juan is a block away at the southwest corner of Plaza Colón.

The **Puerto Rican Tourism Company** (PRTC) has two offices in the airport; the main one is in terminal C on both levels. Their invariably friendly staff will help you arrange transportation and lodging, even going so far as to call around for the best deals. Terminal C also has a handy luggage deposit service. The **PRTC**'s other main office for walk-in advice is in Old San Juan on Calle Comercio, near the docks in a pink building known as **La Casita** (Mon–Wed 8.30am–8pm, Thurs & Fri to 5.30pm, Sat & Sun 9am–8pm; ☎787/722-1709). Its headquarters are in another colonial structure, **La Princesa**, on Paseo de la Princesa (Mon–Fri 9am–4pm; ☎787/721-2400).

Getting around

If you're staying in Old San Juan or Condado for just a few days, you may prefer to remain **on foot**; both neighbourhoods are compact enough for strolling. For getting around outside these areas, bus travel is cheap but it can be tedious and unpredictable – the Metrobus service does work more efficiently, however, while the city's size makes the use of taxis prohibitively expensive. **Renting a car** is definitely the most convenient way to get around if you can spare the cash.

By car

If you rent a **car**, it's probably worth spending a little extra on insurance, particularly if you intend to drive in the capital: Puerto Rican drivers can be very unpredictable. You'll need to **drive defensively** and stay alert at all times. Don't be caught off guard, for instance, if a car suddenly passes you on the sidewalk or shoulder. Rubbernecking is great sport – mostly on the part of men checking out the pretty girls, a phenomenon that's almost comically exaggerated in San Juan – and doesn't exactly lend itself to careful driving. It's also not uncommon to encounter cars turning without signalling, barrelling down the centre of the road, or not using headlights at night.

Prepare yourself for many narrow **one-way streets**, which are indicated (or not, in some cases) by *tránsito* signs with arrows pointing in the direction of traffic. When in doubt, drive slowly and note the direction of parked cars.

Parking can be a nightmare. Although parking on the street is often free, many businesses don't have car parks, so vehicles line up on the sidewalk, and many drivers think nothing of straddling two spaces. Certainly avoid driving into the old town – there are several parking lots in the port area.

By taxi

Plenty of **taxis turísticos** cruise the streets during the day in Condado and Old San Juan; in other neighbourhoods, you may have to call first. Taxis are supposed to charge US$1 to start and 10¢ for each 1/13th of a mile, but in practice drivers never turn on their meters, so agree on a price before you get in. If you call for a cab, ask the dispatcher the cost and confirm it with the driver when you're picked up. Two companies to call are Major Taxi (☎787/723-2460) and Metro Taxi (☎787/725-2870).

If you're travelling at night, don't expect to hail a cab from just anywhere on the street; taxis run much less frequently after 10pm. Be sure to call in advance from a safe location as you may end up waiting as long as an hour for a cab to show up.

By bus

Buses (known as *guaguas*, pronounced *wah-wahs*) can be slow, and also infrequent at weekends and after 9pm, but their routes cover most of the city and you can't beat the price – 25¢ on Metropolitan Bus Authority vehicles and 50¢ on the more frequent Metrobus. Schedules, which are often hard to come by, are sometimes available at the bus terminal, or at PRTC offices at the airport. *Sanjuaneros* orient themselves according to the numbered stops, or *paradas*. If you ask for directions, you may be told that somewhere "está cerca de parada 23" (is near stop 23).

Some bus routes (see box above) pass through rough neighbourhoods en route to more popular tourist areas. Always watch your valuables, and take care to get off at the right stop – you can always ask the driver.

By train

A light rail **train** system, or *tren urbano*, that's been under construction for many years, is scheduled to be up and running at some point during 2005. At the time of this book's writing, there was only one operational line, from the western suburb of Bayamón, across the bay from the old town, via Río Piedras to the edge of Santurce, where it connects with Metrobus routes into the centre of San Juan.

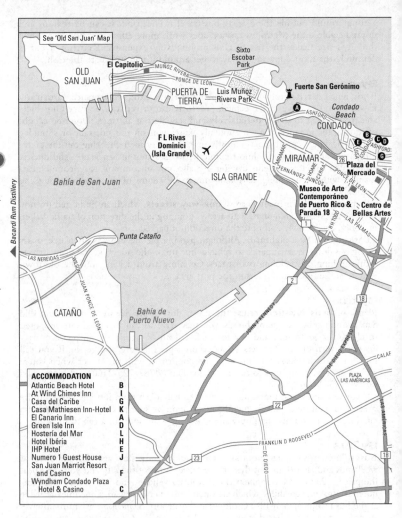

ACCOMMODATION

Atlantic Beach Hotel	B
At Wind Chimes Inn	I
Casa del Caribe	G
Casa Mathiesen Inn-Hotel	K
El Canario Inn	A
Green Isle Inn	D
Hostería del Mar	L
Hotel Ibéria	H
IHP Hotel	E
Numero 1 Guest House	J
San Juan Marriot Resort and Casino	F
Wyndham Condado Plaza Hotel & Casino	C

Accommodation

Most of San Juan's **accommodation** is concentrated in Old San Juan, Condado, Ocean Park and Isla Verde. Old San Juan boasts the city's two most remarkable places to stay – *La Galería* and *Hotel El Convento* – as well as a few flophouses, but not much in between. More popular Condado has a wider range of price options (including some excellent bargains), in addition to being a central location on a prime stretch of beach with some of the city's finest restaurants. Ocean Park is also nice, but much quieter, and has a selection of affordable, unique guesthouses. Isla Verde contrasts some fancy all-inclusive beachfront **resorts**, which are worlds unto themselves, with some much cheaper places along the freeway, still just a few blocks from the beach.

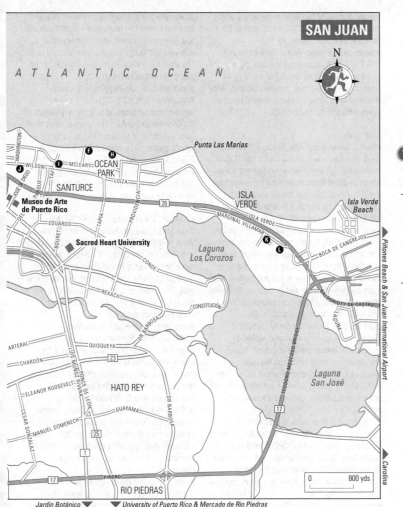

SAN JUAN

ATLANTIC OCEAN

N

Punta Las Marías

WASHINGTON
WILSON
MCLEARY
JOSE DE DIEGO
TAFT
PARQUE
OCEAN
PARK
LOIZA
SANTURCE
Museo de Arte de Puerto Rico
EDUARDO
JOBURT
TAPIA
PROVIDENCIA
DEL PARQUE

Sacred Heart University

CONDE
REXACH

ISLA VERDE
MARGINAL VILLAMAR
ISLA VERDE

Isla Verde Beach

26

Laguna Los Corozos

CONSTITUCIÓN
DR BARBOSA

BOCA DE CANGREJOS

K L

ARTERAL
QUISQUEYA
CHARDÓN
23
LUIS MUÑOZ RIVERA
PONCE DE LEON
ELEANOR ROOSEVELT
CESAR GONZALEZ
MANUEL DOMENECH
25
HATO REY
GUAYAMA
DR BARBOSA

Laguna San José

17

TEODORO MOSCOSO BRIDGE
BALDORIOTY DE CASTRO
LAGUNA

1
PINERO
17
RIO PIEDRAS

0   800 yds

Jardín Botánico ▼   ▼ University of Puerto Rico & Mercado de Río Piedras

▶ Piñones Beach & San Juan International Airport

▶ Carolina

Old San Juan

Hotel El Convento Calle Cristo 100 ☎787/723-9020, ⊛www.elconvento.com. Seventeenth-century nunnery restored to become one of San Juan's smartest hotels. A five-storey quadrangle with long breezy arcades, vaulted ceilings and balconies overlooks a patio with several restaurants. There's a small pool, Jacuzzi and gym, a casino and designer shops. Rooms with mahogany beams and rich colour schemes have cable TV, VCR, stereo systems, refrigerators, phones and bathrobes. ❾

Hotel Milano Calle Fortaleza 307 ☎787/729-9050, ⊛home.coqui.net/hmilano. This nineteenth-century building with rooftop bar and restaurant overlooking San Juan Bay has modern rooms featuring cable TV, phone and mini-fridges; some rooms have harbour views, some are also very small, check first. ❹

La Galería Calle Norzagaray 204–206 at San Justo ☎787/722-1808, ⊛www.thegalleryinn.com. Enchanting, rambling, lovingly restored eighteenth-century house with hidden courtyards, fountains, luxuriant plants and friendly tropical birds. Some of the 24 luxury rooms, all unique, have balconies overlooking the Atlantic. The rooftop garden is the highest spot in Old San Juan. Antiques and art by the owner are for sale. Continental breakfast is served in an indoor garden. **7**

Vicente Castro Guest House Calle Tanca 205 ☎787/722-5436. Something of a dive, but if you're on a shoestring budget, this is the one to go for – very run-down, but in an excellent location, safe and jovial staff. Shared showers, more expensive rooms have a/c, the rest fans. **1**

Condado

Atlantic Beach Hotel Calle Vendig 1 ☎787/721-6900. This Condado hotel has been a gay landmark for decades. The boisterous indoor/outdoor bar on a wide swath of beach showcases live drag shows and DJs almost daily, and there's also a rooftop deck and Jacuzzi. Simple but clean rooms have a/c, TV and a room safe. **5**

At Wind Chimes Inn Calle McLeary 1750 on Taft ☎787/727-4153, ⊛www.atwindchimesinn.com. This intimate restored Spanish villa a few blocks from the beach is enclosed by a stucco wall with arched entryways, interior patios and gardens, and has a pool with fountain and an outdoor bar. Rooms have private bath, a/c, ceiling fan, cable TV and phone with jack for Internet access. **5**

Casa del Caribe Calle Caribe 57 ☎787/722-7139, ⊛www.casadelcaribe.com. Walled-in escape with interior garden and patio located one block from restaurants and the beach; same owners as *At Wind Chimes*. Thirteen rooms have safe, cable TV, phone with jack for Internet access and offstreet parking. Continental breakfast is included. **4**

El Canario Inn Avda Ashford 1317 ☎787/722-3861, ⊛www.canariohotels.com. The *El Canario* has the best location of Condado's middle-market hotels. Small, basic, clean rooms have safes, cable TV and phones; Continental breakfast included. Patio and garden area is home to resident *coquís*, a type of small tree frog. **5**

Hotel Ibéria Avda Wilson 1464 ☎787/722-5380. Small, Spanish-style hotel in a residential part of Condado, with a restaurant, solarium and terrace. There are some 30 simple rooms with cable TV and phone. **4**

IHP Hotel El Consulado Avda Ashford 1110 ☎787/289-9191, ⊛www.ihphoteles.com. Distinguished-looking former Spanish consulate with tile floors, balconies and terracotta roofs. Clean, spacious rooms have cable TV, Internet access and safes; some with balconies. **5**

San Juan Marriot Resort and Casino 1309 Ashford Ave ☎787/722-7000, ⊛www.marriottpr.com. Looming 21 storeys over Condado, this major resort is popular with business travellers and

convention-goers. It hosts two restaurants, a 24hr business centre, two tennis courts, health club and spa, game room, casino, two oceanside pools, a whirlpool and lounge with live Latin jazz and *salsa*. The spacious, generic rooms have TV/VCR, phone, safety box and hairdryer. **9**

Wyndham Condado Plaza Hotel & Casino Avda Ashford 999 ☎787/721-1000, ⊛www.wyndhamcondadoplaza.com. At the very end of the Condado peninsula, this enormous, fancy hotel (with something of an airport feel about it) has a private beach, seven restaurants, several pools, Puerto Rico's largest casino and live *salsa*. Richly coloured, elegant rooms are bright and spacious with private terraces – mostly overlooking the ocean or lagoon – and 24hr room service. **7**

Ocean Park and Isla Verde

Casa Mathiesen Inn-Hotel Calle Uno 14, Isla Verde ☎787/726-8662, ⊛www.casamathiesen.com. Safe, no-frills option off a busy freeway, with same owners as the similar *Green Isle* next door. A couple of blocks from the beach, with swimming pool. Clean, unexciting rooms have cable TV, phone and safe box; some with kitchenette. Ask for a room away from the street. **3**

Green Isle Inn Calle Uno 36, Isla Verde ☎787/726-4330, ⊛www.greenisleinn.com. Great bargain in a safe but charmless area, near the beach, with a pool on the premises. Spacious rooms with cooking facilities, cable TV and phone. Meagre Continental breakfast included. **3**

Hostería del Mar Calle Tapia 1, Ocean Park ☎787/727-3302. Simple but appealing, directly on the beach. Rooms with phone and cable TV; some have ocean views and kitchenette. On-site restaurant in gazebo overlooking the ocean serves vegetarian and macrobiotic fare, steaks and seafood. **4**

Numero 1 Guest House Calle Santa Ana 1, Ocean Park ☎787/726-5010, ⊛www.numero1guesthouse.com. Lives up to its name, attracting many repeat customers, many of whom are gay. Features an interior garden, swimming pool, terrace with ocean views and an excellent bar and restaurant (*Pamela's*). Twelve elegant rooms with phone. Continental breakfast included. **6**

Wyndham El San Juan Hotel & Casino Avda Isla Verde 6063, Isla Verde ☎787/791-1000, ⊛www.wyndham.com/hotels/SJUES/main.wnt. Probably San Juan's most luxurious hotel, with pretensions to Old World style. Has spacious rooms, its own beach, fourteen landscaped acres and pretty much everything else you might want, including one of the city's trendiest nightclubs. **9**

Old San Juan

As recently as the 1970s, **OLD SAN JUAN** (Viejo San Juan) was a reminder of better times, a run-down collection of Spanish colonial relics, in little better shape than the collapsed empire that constructed them. Now, however, after extensive and careful restoration, this seven-blocks-square area is considered one of the best-kept troves of Spanish colonial architecture and has become a World Heritage Site. Steep, narrow streets are distinctively cobbled with smooth, iridescent bricks known as *adoquines*, originally used as ballast in ships, and feature buildings – some of the oldest in the Western hemisphere – with bright pastel facades and wrought-iron balconies abloom with plants and flowers.

The old town occupies the headland of a 4km long island (connected by bridge to the mainland) that shelters the San Juan Bay, for centuries a key port in the New World. It was originally known as Puerto Rico, or "rich port", because its position made for such a fine stop for shipping, though in 1521 its name was switched with that of the island, which Columbus had called San Juan in honour of St John the Baptist. For a while, the entire city was enclosed by thick, imposing walls to ward off British, Dutch and French intruders jealous of this strategic location. Now, only a portion of the wall, known as **La Muralla**, as well as the ramparts of **El Morro** and **San Cristóbal**, remains.

The bay used to be a central hub for exports of New World riches, a regular stop-off for boats transporting gold, silver, sugar, coffee, slaves, tobacco and rum. Today the port is busy with **cruise ships**, as the old town plays host to hordes of holiday-makers who help to make tourism one of Puerto Rico's biggest industries.

If you only have a day here, you're best off losing yourself among the streets to soak in some of the history, or joining an organized walking tour of the most important buildings (ask the PRTC). If the heat and steep, crowded streets get to be a bit much, you can always ride the **free trolley** that leaves from the bus terminal on Calle La Marina (Mon–Fri 6am–8pm, Sat & Sun 8am–8pm, departs every 15min). You can get on or off anywhere along the route.

La Muralla

Begin your wanderings in the old town along the **Paseo de la Princesa**, a busy cobblestoned promenade, and head west along the southern city wall. The prim, grey and white Neoclassical building you'll see before you come to Calle Presidio is known as **La Princesa**. Built as a prison in 1837, it now houses the main PRTC offices, as well as a gallery showcasing the work of contemporary Puerto Rican artists.

Known as **La Muralla**, the city wall is an impressive sight, up to twenty feet thick in some places. Until the late nineteenth century, it encircled all of Old San Juan with 3900 metres

---

Useful San Juan bus routes

All of the following buses, with the exception of #C45, start or finish at the Old San Juan bus terminal.

Bus	Route
Metrobus 1	Río Piedras, Hato Rey, Santurce, Old San Juan
Metrobus Express	Río Piedras, Hato Rey, Old San Juan
#A5	Old San Juan, Parada 18 (Stop 18), Isla Verde, Los Angeles, Iturreguí
#C10	*Acuaexpreso* ferry, Hato Rey, Borinquen Ave, Eduardo Conde, Loiza St, Condado, Isla Grande, Parada 18
#B21	Old San Juan, Condado, Parada 18, Fernández Juncos, Plaza Las Américas
#C45	Iturreguí, Airport, Isla Verde, Piñones, Loíza

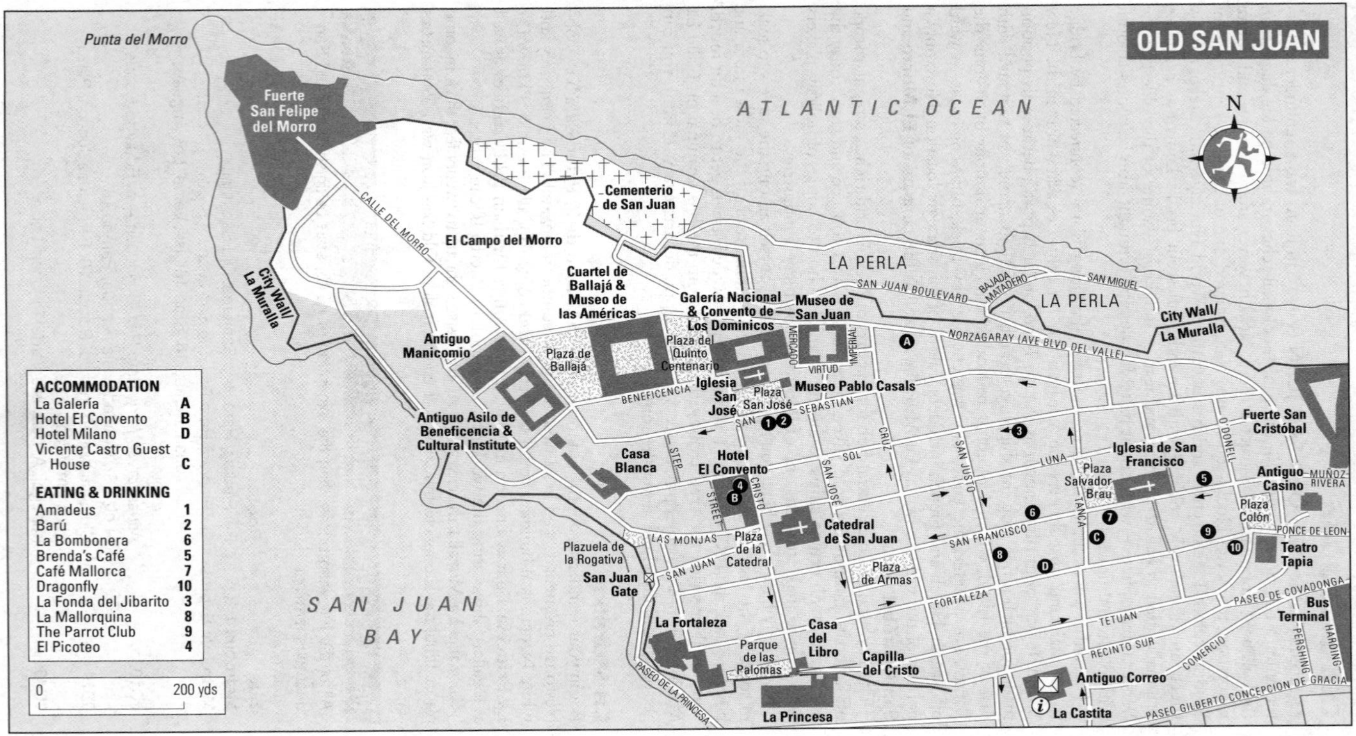
OLD SAN JUAN
N
ATLANTIC OCEAN
Punta del Morro
Fuerte San Felipe del Morro
City Wall/ La Muralla
CALLE DEL MORRO
El Campo del Morro
Cementerio de San Juan
LA PERLA
SAN JUAN BOULEVARD
BAJADA MATADERO
SAN MIGUEL
City Wall/ La Muralla
Cuartel de Ballajá & Museo de las Américas
Galería Nacional & Convento de Los Dominicos
Museo de San Juan
MERCADO
IMPERIAL
VIRTUD
NORZAGARAY (AVE BLVD DEL VALLE)
Antiguo Manicomio
Plaza de Ballajá
Plaza del Quinto Centenario
Iglesia San José
Plaza San José
Museo Pablo Casals
BENEFICENCIA
SEBASTIAN
SAN
Antiguo Asilo de Beneficencia & Cultural Institute
Casa Blanca
STEP
Hotel El Convento
CRISTO
STREET
SOL
CRUZ
SAN JOSÉ
SAN JUSTO
LUNA
Fuerte San Cristóbal
O'DONELL
Iglesia de San Francisco
Plaza Salvador Brau
TANCA
Antiguo Casino
MUÑOZ RIVERA
Plaza Colón
PONCE DE LEON
Teatro Tapia
Catedral de San Juan
SAN FRANCISCO
LAS MONJAS
Plaza de la Catedral
Plazuela de la Rogativa
SAN JUAN
San Juan Gate
Plaza de Armas
FORTALEZA
TETUAN
RECINTO SUR
COMERCIO
PASEO DE COVADONGA
Bus Terminal
PERSHING
HARDING
PASEO GILBERTO CONCEPCION DE GRACIA
SAN JUAN BAY
La Fortaleza
Parque de las Palomas
Casa del Libro
Capilla del Cristo
La Princesa
PASEO DE LA PRINCESA
Antiguo Correo
La Castita
ACCOMMODATION
La Galería A
Hotel El Convento B
Hotel Milano D
Vicente Castro Guest House C
EATING & DRINKING
Amadeus 1
Barú 2
La Bombonera 6
Brenda's Café 5
Café Mallorca 7
Dragonfly 10
La Fonda del Jibarito 3
La Mallorquina 8
The Parrot Club 9
El Picoteo 4
0 200 yds

of sandstone, culminating in the fortress of El Morro at the headland. Construction began in 1539 but was only finished by 1783. Until 1897, when part of the wall was destroyed to facilitate urban development, the city was accessible only through six huge, heavily guarded wooden doors that closed at nightfall. Today only three remain, one of which, **La Puerta de San Juan**, stands at the far end of Paseo de la Princesa. Completed in 1635, this sturdy red door was the first of the entrances to be built and was the check-in point for Spaniards delivering colonists and goods.

After going through the gate, turn left and you'll come to a tall sculpture known as **La Rogativa**. This striking, Giacometti-like bronze, set dramatically against the bay, commemorates the city's 1797 salvation from the British, who were scared off when they mistook a night-time procession of praying, candle-bearing women for the arrival of enemy reinforcements. A little further is the **Casa Blanca**, entrance at San Sebastián 1 (Tues–Sat 9am–noon & 1–4.20pm; ☎787/725-1454), which is now a period museum but was home for 250 years to the family of Juan Ponce de León, whose own untimely death denied him the chance of ever living there, and finding peace in its charming gardens.

Fuerte San Felipe and around

Following Recinto Oeste to the headland's northwest tip, eventually you reach the unmistakeable **Fuerte San Felipe del Morro** (daily 9am–5pm, tours in English depart at 11am & 3pm; US$3; ☎787/729-6754), known simply as **El Morro**. A bulwark if ever there was one, this hulking fortress dominates the headland of San Juan Bay, rising 140ft above the Atlantic. Built between 1539 and 1783, the thick walls are so old and weathered they have begun to look like outcroppings of bedrock, as though its six levels of towers, barracks, secret passageways, dungeons and ramps were carved from a natural cliff. The views of the ocean, back over the city and towards the mountains beyond are splendid.

Heading back towards town across the windswept Campo del Morro – a famously good spot for flying kites – to Calle Norzagaray, you'll reach the imposing Cuartel de Ballajá. Built in 1864, it served as a barracks for the Spanish army until their abrupt exit in 1898, when a gaping hole was blown in its wall by the American invaders. Today it houses the **Museo de las Américas** on the first floor (Tues–Fri 10am–4pm, Sat & Sun 11am–5pm; free; ☎787/724-5052, ⊕www.prtc. net/~musame), which showcases North and South American folk art – don't miss the collection of *santos* (saints carved in wood).

Further along Calle Norzagaray in the old market place built in 1855, once the commercial centre of the city and now one of its best museums, is the **Museo de San Juan** (Tues–Sun 10am–4pm; free; ☎787/724-1875). It provides an excellently presented and digestible overview of the city's history, culture and geography.

Between the two museums is the new **Plaza del Quinto Centenario**, dominated by a curious column studded with shards of nearby-excavated pottery, which was built to commemorate the five-hundredth anniversary of the island's discovery by Columbus in 1493. On the plaza's east side is the **Convento de los Dominicos**, which housed the Dominican monks who also built the adjacent **Iglesia San José** (weekdays except Thurs 7am–3pm, Sat 8am–1pm, Sun Mass at noon). Both recently restored buildings were begun in 1523, making the church the second oldest in the New World: its vaulted ceilings are a fine example of the Gothic style in Spanish colonial architecture. The church faces south onto **Plaza San José**, on the east side of which is the **Museo Pablo Casals**, Calle Sebastián 101 (Tues–Sat 9.30am–5.30pm; US$1; ☎787/723-9185), which displays manuscripts, photographs and instruments of the much-loved virtuoso Spanish cellist who lived in Puerto Rico from 1956 until his death in 1973.

Along Calle del Cristo

Down Calle del Cristo from Plaza San José, heading back towards Paseo de la Princesa, you'll pass plenty of restaurants and cafés, several of which are in *El Convento*, once a Carmelite nunnery, now restored into a smart hotel but still worth nosing around. At the corner of Caleta de San Juan, you'll reach the **Catedral de San Juan** (daily 8am–5pm; Mass Mon–Fri 12.15pm, Sat 7pm, Sun 9am & 11am), the construction of which was begun in 1535, but most of what you see today – after centuries of hurricanes, earthquakes and invaders – was rebuilt in the early nineteenth century, with some rare examples of the original Gothic balustrades, archways, ceiling and stairwell remaining. You'll also find Juan Ponce de León's tomb as well as the relics of the early Christian martyr San Pío, transferred from Rome to satisfy the whims of a former bishop.

A block further, turn right down Calle Fortaleza, at the end of which is **La Fortaleza**, or the Palacio de Santa Catalina (Mon–Fri 9am–3.30pm; free; ☎787/721-7000 ext 2211). Finished in 1540, it is touted as the oldest executive residence of its kind in the western hemisphere. The island's original fortress, it proved to be inadequately sited, and instead this palatial mansion has served as the Puerto Rican governor's home since the seventeenth century. While there is no access to the government offices, visitors may take a free, guided tour through the dungeon and lush Moorish gardens; dress appropriately.

At the south end of the Calle del Cristo is the **Capilla del Cristo** (Mon, Wed & Fri 10.30am–3.30pm), a dainty stone chapel erected in 1753 at the edge of a precipice overlooking San Juan Bay. Some say it was built to celebrate the miraculous survival of a young man who lost control of his horse and plummeted over the cliff; others maintain that he died, and the chapel was intended to ward off future mishaps.

To one side of the chapel is the **Casa del Libro**, at Calle del Cristo 255 (Tues–Sat 11am–4.30pm; ☎787/723-0354), dedicated to the art of bookmaking, with a collection of 7000 books – including 200 that predate the sixteenth century. Opposite is the **Parque de las Palomas**, which not only has an open view over the bay but is also believed to be inhabited by magical pigeons. Superstitious locals encourage the normally bothersome creatures to land on them, as this is considered to be a good omen.

Fuerte San Cristóbal and the north end

At the northeastern corner of Old San Juan, entered at the east end of Calle Norzagaray, is the sprawling **Fuerte San Cristóbal** (daily 9am–5pm; tours in English at 10am & 2pm; US$3; ☎787/729-6777), San Juan's second stronghold. Whereas El Morro defended against attacks by sea, San Cristóbal was intended to prevent land-based assaults. Built from 1634 to 1785 over 27 acres, it was the largest Spanish military base in the Americas. Today, the maze-like fortress is maintained by the National Park Service, and visitors can explore its secret tunnels, moats, dungeons and 150-foot high walls.

La Perla, the slum clinging outside the northern city wall between El Morro and San Cristóbal, is a deceptively quaint-looking neighbourhood that is best avoided. Desperately impoverished, it gained notoriety with Oscar Lewis's 1966 grim novel, *La Vida*, and has been an enclave of crime for centuries. Many of San Juan's early colonizers are buried nearby, in the **Cementerio de San Juan**, which can also be dangerous and, like La Perla, is best observed from a safe distance above the wall.

Condado

Balancing on a peninsula straddling the Atlantic and the Laguna Condado, highrise **CONDADO** was built in the 1950s as the island's first resort area, and after a decline in the 1980s it has again boomed in popularity. Today its wide, tiled sidewalks lined with palms, fancy boutiques, trendy restaurants and resort hotels and casinos make it San Juan's slickest neighbourhood. Next to Old San Juan, it's the best area to explore on foot, particularly the main drag, **Avenida Ashford**.

Just a block from Avenida Ashford is 3km **Condado Beach**, the best stretch of sand in town, though far from the best on the island. It's certainly the most accessible beach for the great number of tourists who stay in the luxury hotels here, and its smooth sand and good swimming make it pleasant enough. There are lots of watersports available, and plenty of outdoor bars and restaurants are to be found on the beach itself, or within walking distance.

Condado also has a lively **nightlife**, and some of the hotels book fantastic live *salsa* bands. **Gay travellers** will also find this area to be very gay-friendly.

Ocean Park, Isla Verde and Piñones

East along the coast from Condado, other beachfront neighbourhoods attract their fair share of visitors. When Avenida Ashford becomes Calle McLeary, you'll find yourself in **OCEAN PARK**, an affluent residential district on a wide swath of palm-lined sand. Thanks to a city code barring the construction of buildings over three storeys, it feels more intimate than Condado, and while there isn't much of interest here for the sightseer, there are several lovely inns and guesthouses and a handful of good restaurants.

The next major beachfront area, further east and just before the airport, is **ISLA VERDE**. Some charmless budget accommodation is contrasted by a few luxury, all-inclusive hotels that give you no need to leave the premises. Like all the waterfronts in San Juan, the beach is good for sunbathing and swimming, though its location – two blocks from the freeway (Rte 26) and its service roads – is hardly ideal.

The #C45 bus east from Isla Verde follows Rte 187 along 8km of completely wild beaches on the edge of **PIÑONES STATE FOREST**. Only minutes from the frenetic city centre, the waterfront here has a far more Afro-Caribbean feel, and the place can get very lively at weekends. Roadside kiosks sell raw oysters (avoid), seasoned pork and *coco frío*, while there is also an excellent **bike path** along the shore and good **surfing**. The forest itself is thick with almond and palm groves and shelters the island's largest mangrove lagoon, making it an important **wildlife refuge** and home to more than 45 bird species, including pelicans and herons. Be aware that thefts are not uncommon, so watch out for yourself and your vehicle.

Santurce

Slightly inland and south of Ocean Park, **SANTURCE** is a neighbourhood in transition with a growing art scene that's outstripping its dodgy reputation. By the 1950s San Juan had grown enough to engulf the settlement of Santurce, and many important government departments were established there. It became a fashionable business and residential neighbourhood, but more recently has had its share of social problems. It has a lively main drag, which is pretty safe during busier daylight hours, but even now it is not recommendable to wander alone through Santurce's outer reaches (beyond around Parada 25). The city's main art museums, as well as some of its best restaurants and nightclubs, are located on or near Avenida Ponce de León – although you may not want to go there by yourself at night.

The **Museo de Arte de Puerto Rico** is just off Avenida Ponce de León at Avda José de Diego 299 (Tues–Sat 10am–5pm, Sun 11am–6pm; US$6, US$3 students; ☎787/977-6277, ⊛www.mapr.org). Its permanent collection, in the Neoclassical west wing, traces the evolution of Puerto Rican art from the sixteenth century to the present. The modernist east wing is decorated with a five-storey stained-glass window by local artist Eric Tabales, which overlooks an attractive five-acre sculpture garden and lily pond. The museum also houses chef Wilo Benet's masterpiece of a restaurant, *Pikayo*.

For the performing arts, just opposite is the **Centro de Bellas Artes Luis A. Ferré** (☎787/724-4747), which puts on a varied programme of events including theatre, concerts, dance and opera. For late-night entertainment, it also has one of Santurce's several fashionable nightclubs.

San Juan's other important art museum is more central, where Ponce de León intersects Avda Roberto H. Todd. The **Museo del Arte Contemporáneo de Puerto Rico** (Mon–Fri 8am–5pm, Sat 9am–5pm; free; ☎787/977-4030, ⊛www.museocontemporaneopr.org) has the island's best paintings, sculpture, photography and new-media works by young internationally known Puerto Rican artists, like Nelson Sambolín, Lope Max Diaz and Rafael Ferrer.

Tucked away off Calle Canals, with an entrance marked by large, metallic avocados, is one of San Juan's most genuine attractions. The airy **Plaza del Mercado** is packed with stalls selling fresh produce, sandwiches, flowers, meats, cheese and the like, and is always crowded with locals doing their daily shopping. It also heats up during weekends, when the surrounding bars put on live music and a wide variety of people hang out here to all hours of the night.

Hato Rey

A 3km ride from central Santurce south on Metrobus #1 along Avenida Ponce de León (or you can take the Metrobus Express direct from the Old San Juan bus terminal) will take you to the heart of a very different part of town: **Hato Rey**, San Juan's financial district. There, Ponce de León is lined for a mile with high-rise office buildings, as well as hotels and restaurants catering to the business trade. Amidst the pricey shops, there are a few good contemporary art galleries. The best of the lot, **Galería Botello** at Avenida F.D. Roosevelt 314 (Mon–Sat 10am–6pm; ☎787/754-7430) – which also has an outlet in Old San Juan on Calle del Cristo – sells the work of some of the island's most acclaimed younger artists, like Mari Mater O'Neill, whose reputations extend as far as New York and Europe. The work is reasonably priced, by London or LA standards, and is worth a look.

For those who just can't stay away from this kind of thing, **Plaza Las Américas** – the Caribbean's largest mall with some 300 stores – (Mon–Sat 9am–9pm, Sun 11am–5pm; ☎787/767-5202) is on Avenida F.D. Roosevelt, off Rte 18.

Río Piedras

Continue south from Hato Rey down Avenida Ponce de León for another 2km, and you will reach **RÍO PIEDRAS**, San Juan's equivalent of a college town, only with palms and terracotta rather than ivy and bricks. The main campus of the **University of Puerto Rico** (☎787/763-4408 or 764-0000) is located to the east of the last stretch of Ponce de León. The university hosts cultural events throughout the year, and the campus itself is a nice place for a stroll, with a youthful vibe and cheap bars and restaurants nearby, as well as the island's best bookshops all in a row – particularly La Tertulia at Ponce de León 1002 (☎787/765-1148).

A five-minute walk east is the not-to-be-missed **Mercado de Río Piedras** (Mon–Sat daylight hours), four blocks of indoor and outdoor shopping along the Paseo de Diego, with everything from rare fruits to high heels on display. It's "bien puertorriqueño" (very Puerto Rican), and full of bargains, especially if you know how to haggle.

One kilometre south of the campus, at the junction of Rte 1 and 847, is the university's 75-acre **Jardín Botánico** (daily 6am–6pm; free; ☎787/767-1710). It's a pretty spot to escape the stresses of the city, and you can stroll through clove, cinnamon and nutmeg trees, and find shade under 50 different types of palms. The Herbarium has 36,000 specimens (call ahead to arrange a viewing), and is particularly strong on heliconias and orchids.

Eating

San Juan is garnering a reputation as the **culinary capital of the Caribbean** – a smorgasbord of both international cuisines and endless variations on Puerto Rican staples. The highest concentration of good restaurants are in Old San Juan (particularly on Calle Fortaleza near Plaza Colón) and Condado (along Avenida Ashford), but fine food can be found pretty much anywhere that draws visitors; even Miramar, the residential district south of Condado, has its fair share of classy eateries.

Old San Juan

Amadeus Calle San Sebastián 106 ☎787/722-8635. Excellent nouvelle Caribbean cuisine served until 2am to a hip crowd in a handsome, eighteenth-century brick and stone building; try the dumplings with guava sauce and arrowroot fritters or the smoked salmon and caviar pizza; entrees run US$10–26.

Barú Calle San Sebastián 150 ☎787/977-7107. Fine Mediterranean-cum-Caribbean dishes (from US$10 to $24) are on offer in this elegantly designed locale, where you can dine either in the smarter indoor space or the more casual and airy patio.

Brenda's Café Calle San Francisco 353 ☎787/725-0027. With a relaxed atmosphere, this eccentrically decorated, bohemian restaurant serves excellent vegetarian food at very reasonable prices.

Café Mallorca Calle San Francisco 300 ☎787/724-4607. People line up at this eatery for its famous pastries and hot chocolate; also on offer is good *café con leche*, fruit salads, pancakes and eggs for breakfast, and *criollo* staples for lunch and dinner. You can eat well for US$5–10. Closes at 7pm.

Dragonfly Calle Fortaleza 364 ☎787/977-3886. Chic spinoff of the *Parrot Club* (same owner), offering Nuevo Latino dishes with an Asian twist (US $15 to $20). Wonderful halibut ceviche with ginger, coconut milk and scallions, and Moo-shoo Mongolian beef wraps. Live music Tues, Thurs & Sat until midnight. Entrees US$15–28.

El Picoteo *Hotel El Convento*, Calle del Cristo 100 ☎787/723-9202. The cheap way to experience *El Convento*. Choose from over a hundred different tapas or more substantial, moderately priced Spanish dishes, and enjoy the cool breeze on the open terrace overlooking *El Convento*'s central courtyard.

La Bombonera Calle San Francisco 259 ☎787/722-0658. Century-old inexpensive institution for morning pastries, excellent coffee, sandwiches and *criollo* classics like rice with squid or marinated roast pork and fried plantains for $7-8. Daily 7.30am–8pm.

La Fonda del Jibarito Calle Sol 280 ☎787/725-8375. This unpretentious and inexpensive bistro-style restaurant is as popular with locals as with tourists. The lamb stew and goat fricassee are excellent.

La Mallorquina Calle San Justo 207 ☎787/722-3261. Expensive for *criollo* fare, but the Old World atmosphere fits the bill. Established in 1848 and

run by the Rojas family for about a hundred years, it is reputedly San Juan's oldest restaurant. Try the garlic soup and lobster *asopao*.

The Parrot Club Calle Fortaleza 363 ☎787/725-7370. This requisite Old San Juan experience is pure Nuevo Latino, and the inspiration for many other restaurants. A mixed crowd dines on impeccable dishes, while listening to mellow live Latin jazz on Tues, Thurs and Sat. The house special: rare tuna broiled with dark rum and orange essence with yucca and cassava mash. Entrees US$18–29.

Condado

Ajili-Mojili Avda Ashford 1006 ☎787/725-9195. So successful that it has had to move to a bigger location with great views over the Condado lagoon. The superb classic *criollo* cuisine prepared by chef Mariano Ortiz – such as savoury pork loin sautéed with onions, and plantain-encrusted shrimp in white-wine herb sauce – attracts a loyal following of upscale *sanjuaneros*. Entrees US$18–30.

La Patisserie Francés Avda Ashford 1504 ☎787/728-5508. This cheery place with Spanish tiles and wrought-iron furniture is a nice spot for a breakfast of stuffed croissants, or lunching on fresh fish or vegetable salad topped off by gorgeous pastries.

Marisquería Miró Avda Condado 74 ☎787/723-9593. Award-winning Catalán chef José La Villa prepares intensely memorable fish dishes like baked halibut in *cabrales* cheese sauce and seafood with black rice. Entrees US$19–23.

Zabó Calle Candina 14 ☎787/725-9494. Elegant setting with a distinct gay vibe in an early twentieth-century mansion featuring dining on the verandah. Chef Paul Carroll's masterpieces include guava-glazed spare ribs with fried yucca and papaya salad, and fresh fish over black bean mash in a mango-rosemary curry. Entrees US$18–36.

Ocean Park and Isla Verde

Che's Calle Caoba 35, Ocean Park/Isla Verde, near Punta las Marías ☎787/726-7202. Argentine-style grill with reputedly the most tender, flavoursome *parrillada* (grilled, marinated meat) in Puerto Rico and good Chilean and Argentine wines. Entrees US$13–28.

Dunbars Calle McLeary 1954, Ocean Park ☎787/728-2920. A sprawling, collegiate dive with upscale bar food that's boisterous even during midweek. Live music at weekends. Entrees US$12–23.

Panadería España Avda Baldorioty de Castro, Calle Marginal, Isla Verde ☎787/727-3860. Good place to stock up for a picnic, a block from the beach. Excellent sandwiches, *café con leche*, tortillas and thick chicken soup with vegetables, all for US$5 to $10.

Repostería Kasalta Calle McLeary 1966, Ocean Park ☎787/727-7340. This stainless-steel emporium of cured meats and cheeses, breads, wines and fine imported goods is a requisite stop. The *café con leche* is superb.

Miramar and Santurce

Augusto's Cuisine *Hotel Excelsior*, Avda Ponce de León 801, Miramar ☎787/725-7700. Somewhat stuffy hotel restaurant offering serious French and Continental cuisine. Chef Augusto Schreiner delivers the likes of veal brains *au beurre noir* with capers and a hot chocolate soufflé to die for. Entrees US$25–36.

Chayote *Hotel Olimpo Court*, Avda Miramar 603, Miramar ☎787/722-9385. International cuisine by chef/owner Mario Pagan features unlikely blends of fresh tropical ingredients. Menu items include ceviche in rosewater essence with sweet yam croquettes or halibut with yam gnocchi in fresh corn cream sauce. Entrees US$25–31.

La Casona Calle San Jorge 609, Santurce ☎787/727-2717. Open since 1972, this elegantly restored Spanish mansion surrounded by an attractive cocktail garden may require a taxi ride to get to, but it's worth the effort. Top-quality Spanish fare; paella marinara is the house speciality. Dress smartly.

Pikayo Museo de Arte de Puerto Rico, Avda José de Diego 299, Santurce ☎787/721-6194, ⊛www.pikayo.com. The constantly changing menus by celebrated chef Wilo Benet and views over a sculpture garden have earned this ultra-chic spot inside the new museum a deservedly revered status. The lamb chops with ripe plantain *salpicón* and conch spring rolls with orange *sofrito* sauce are extraordinary. Entrees US$28–52, with a $65 six-course tasting menu.

Drinking and nightlife

There's plenty going on at night in San Juan. The old town has the highest concentration of good **bars** and **clubs**, quite apart from its lively restaurants like the *Parrot Club*, *Dragonfly* and *Amadeus* (see p.405). Puerto Rico being the birthplace of **salsa** (see box opposite), there's lots of it around – in particular, Condado's smart hotels put on some classy shows. Calle San Sebastián in Old San Juan and the Plaza del Mercado in Santurce both have a good choice of inviting small bars that come alive at weekends, some with live music, while on or near Avda Ponce de León in Santurce are some of the city's most progressive dance clubs. For hip-hop and its popular local variant, reggaeton, try *Club Lazer* or *The Noise* at Calle Tanca 203.

Old San Juan

Bar Rumba Calle San Sebastián 152, Old San Juan ☎787/725-4407. With its young crowd, it's one of the liveliest bars on San Sebastián. Live music, from *salsa* to heavy metal, Thursday to Sunday.

Carl Café Plazoleta Rafael Carrión, Edificio Banco Popular, Old San Juan ☎787/725-4927. Excellent regular jazz trio plays to a discrete, older crowd in this classy, upmarket venue.

Club Lazer Calle Cruz 251, Old San Juan ☎787/721-4479. A favourite with locals and one of the old town's serious hip-hop clubs. On several floors and an outdoor rooftop area.

El Batey across from *El Convento*, Old San Juan. This dark, grungy fixture, open until 6am, is usually mobbed. Has a very "local bar" feel, despite the number of outsiders.

Nuyorican Café Callejón de la Capilla, Old San Juan ☎787/977-1276. Also a theatre and cinema, this alternative venue has live *salsa* at weekends, when the narrow pedestrian alley outside gets packed with locals drinking at the kiosk opposite.

Oleo Lounge Recinto Sur 305, Old San Juan ☎787/977-1080. Above an art gallery near the docks, which sometimes throws exhibition parties. Slick spot, also a restaurant.

Señor Frogs behind the *Wyndham Hotel*, Old San Juan ☎787/977-4142. This spacious club in the port area is surprisingly popular with both tourists and locals, but is hardly at the cutting edge of San Juan's nightlife. Also serves food.

Condado

Sol de Luna Avda Ashford at Plaza Ventana al Mar ☎787/806-8153. A swish new open-air bar by the sea where San Juan's smarter youths can gather in very large numbers, spilling out into the square when the weather is fine.

Fiesta Lounge Wyndham Condado Plaza Hotel & Casino, Avda Ashford 999 ☎787/721-1000. Popular with the older generations and with a seafront terrace, some of the best *salsa* and *merengue* bands play in the hotel lounge, where plenty of locals come to dance – free entry, dress smart casual.

Music in Puerto Rico

Puerto Rico is probably most famous as the cradle of **salsa**, in which a very diverse stew of musical influences have produced a distinctly Latin result. *Salsa* is a fusion of Caribbean folk music (mostly from Puerto Rico and Cuba) and North American jazz, set to complex African rhythms. First developed by migrant Puerto Ricans in New York nightclubs during the 1940s, and most famously poularized by the late Tito Puente, *salsa* is experiencing a resurgence of popularity on the island, thanks to the likes of Puerto Rico's very own superstar, Ricky Martin. Though it's hard to find *salsa* played live anywhere but in the best nightclubs these days, every town seems to have a spot where locals of all ages gather to listen and dance to the likes of Celia Cruz and Afro-Cuban All-Stars.

The musical dance tradition called **bomba** still has a presence in Puerto Rico. Much like Cuban *rumba*, it's based on intricate West African percussion. The drummer – traditionally using an old barrel with leather stretched over one end – provokes a response from a dancer, inciting a sort of rhythmic duel where honour can be at stake, as each attempts to outdo the other. The island's other important folk music is **plena**, said to have originated in Ponce in the early twentieth century, with its counterparts in the Spanish *romance*, the Dominican *merengue*, the Trinidadian *calypso* and the Mexican *corrido*. The sometimes moralistic lyrics of a lead singer are repeated by a choir, set to the music of a ten-string guitar, called a *cuatro*, and a hollowed gourd, like a maraca, called a *guiro*. Interestingly, *plena* was once a means of reporting news as singers effectively recited the day's events.

Santurce

Café de la Plaza Calle Dos Hermanos 176, Santurce. One of the most popular bars around Santurce's fun Plaza del Mercado; live music on Thursdays.

Cups Calle San Mateo 1708, Santurce ☎787/268-3570. This lesbian bar has a low-key atmosphere and a good mix of types and nationalities.

El Teatro Avda Ponce de León 1420, Santurce ☎787/722-1130. San Juan's most progressive club pumps underground dance music to a hip crowd. Open to 4am Thursday to Saturday.

Eros Avda Ponce de León 1257, Santurce ☎787/722-1131. Basically a gay club, but all persuasions come here on Saturdays. *Salsa* and New York-style house with dance, drag and strip acts. Open to 4am at weekends.

Luxor Avda Roberto H. Todd 1, Santurce ☎787/562-4051. Never mind the curious Egyptian statuary, this is a very trendy techno club that pulls in internationally renowned DJs.

Isla Verde

Borinquén Grill & Brewing Co Avda Isla Verde 4800, Isla Verde ☎787/268-1900. The atmosphere and location – along a service road – are unremarkable, but the beer is home-made here in San Juan's only microbrewery. Happy hour 4pm–7pm.

Club Bablyon Wyndham El San Juan Hotel & Casino, Avda Isla Verde 6063 ☎787/791-1000. Hard techno bangs out till late slightly incongruously from within this rather grand hotel. Lots of people-spotters, fancy dressers and pretty girls.

7.2

Around San Juan

Given how easily accessible most of the island is from the capital, there is a wealth of excellent day-trips that you can do without checking out of your hotel (which can arrange transport). Make sure to save at least one day to visit the lush **El Yunque** national rainforest, 40km southeast of the capital. Another tempting target that's very close by is **Playa Luquillo**, a palm-lined *balneario* (public beach) on the northeast shore.

In the other direction from San Juan is the peculiarly abrupt landscape that characterizes the the northwest of the island – the so-called **karst country**, which was formed as rivers originating from the rainforest of the Cordillera Central carved their way to the ocean through porous limestone, creating vast networks of sinkholes and tunnels. The area conceals several popular attractions: world-class spelunking in its extensive underground network of caves, most easily accessed through the **Río Camuy Cave Park**; the world's largest radio telescope, lodged in a sinkhole, at the **Arecibo Observatory**; and Taíno petroglyphs and ceremonial grounds at the **Caguana Indian Ceremonial Centre**.

El Yunque

The Caribbean National Forest, commonly known as **EL YUNQUE** (daily 7.30am–6pm; free; ☎787/888/1880, ⊛www.fs.fed.us/r8/caribbean), looms over eastern Puerto Rico, shrouded in mist. The 28,000-acre forest sits on the Sierra de Luquillo (supposedly the abode of the powerful but benevolent Taíno spirit Yuquiyú), which rises 3500ft above sea level, making it easily visible from San Juan rooftops, 40km away. The only rainforest in the US Forest System, El Yunque is deluged with more than 100 billion gallons of rainfall a year, and is home to more than 225 native tree species and a panoply of rare flora and fauna, most notably the endangered *cotorro*, or Puerto Rican parrot, of which there are only thirty still remaining, all of them here.

Below 2000ft, the forest is relatively dry, containing **tabonuco**, **palm** and **ausubo** trees, and more than 50 types of **orchid**. Some of the trees in the **palo colorado**, the section of forest that grows above 2000ft, have stood for more than a thousand years – in fact, this is where you'll find the only remaining virgin forest on the once tree-covered island. The region above 2500ft is dominated by mountain palms, ferns and mosses. The highest level of growth is **cloud forest**, also known as dwarf forest, where trees, stunted by strong trade winds, rarely grow higher than twelve feet tall.

While the mountain is more often than not under cloud, on good days there are excellent views, particularly on trails starting from the **Palo Colorado Information Centre** (daily 9.30am–5pm) at Km 11.8, almost a kilometre from the top. Overall, there are 27km of well-marked pathways (many paved) to explore. The most popular, **El Yunque Trail** (2–2.5hrs), ascends through cloud forest to El Yunque peak; for **waterfalls**, take the **Coca** or **La Mina** trail. Keen hikers take on the almost 6.5km **Tradewinds Trail** which climbs **El Toro**, the **highest peak** in the forest, at 3522ft. Wear good walking shoes and light, loose clothing; also bring a poncho or umbrella in case of rain.

Practicalities

While El Yunque is not served by public transportation, organized tour buses do pick-ups at San Juan hotels most days. You can also hire a private guide through the forest's **Rent-a-Ranger** programme (☎787/888-1880). By car from San Juan, head east on 26, which becomes 3 in Carolina towards Fajardo. Turn right onto 955 at Río Grande and make a quick left onto 191, which after 5km brings you to the forest. On your right you'll see the entrance to **El Portal Tropical Forest Centre** (daily 9.30am–4.45pm; US$3), which has an elevated canopy walkway and where you can learn about rainforests. Visitor information, maps and brochures are also available.

Camping is legal with a permit (obtainable near the entrance on 191 at the Catalina Work Centre) in certain parts of the forest, including El Toro. You can also stay in the beautifully situated *Casa Cubuy Ecolodge* (☎787/874-6221, ✪www.casacubuy. com; ④), a haven on the south side of the forest that is overlooked by the vast majority of the million people who come here each year. The hotel, which also organizes walks, is reached by continuing on 3 past Fajardo and Naguabo, after which you turn right onto 31 and right again onto 191, which you follow to the end. There is a series of waterfalls nearby: just a couple of minutes away is an idyllic bathing pool below a dramatic cascade, surely one of the prettiest spots in Puerto Rico. Further downstream is **El Salto de Río Blanco**, where the river gashes through a 20–30-foot-high corridor of rock, providing excellent rock jumping opportunities for athletic locals.

Northeastern coast

Many day-trippers from San Juan round out a morning trip to El Yunque with an afternoon at **PLAYA LUQUILLO**, more formally known as *Balneario la Montserrate* (daily 8.30am–5pm; parking US$2; ☎787/889-5871). Being just 45 minutes from the capital on Rte 3, and with calm waters perfect for swimming, the crowds – especially at weekends – are no surprise. Kiosks sell everything from *piña coladas* and beers to grilled meats and *empanadillas*. For starry nights rather than city lights, you can also camp here (30 campsites with bathhouse; US$13 a night or US$16 with hook-up).

To dodge the crowds, head to the east end of the beach and round the corner to **Playa Azul**, also pretty and much quieter. Farther east still, the waves get considerably rougher at **La Pared**, the local surfer beach, beyond which stretches another long, utterly deserted beach backed only by vegetation.

Some 10km on, at the northeastern tip of the island are **Las Cabezas de San Juan** (three two-hour tours a day, Wed–Sun, admission by reservation only; adults US$7; ☎787/722-5882), a clutch of promontories poking into the Atlantic. Crowned by Puerto Rico's second oldest lighthouse – from where there are great views back inland to El Yunque – it is now Puerto Rico's most complete nature reserve, with trails and boardwalks through dry forest, mangroves, lagoons and beaches, and an excellent eco-tourism destination.

Karst country

With an unusual name as well as peculiar features, the "**karst country**" covers the area northeast of Mayagüez and south of Arecibo between the northwest coast and the Cordillera Central. Just a couple hours' drive west of San Juan there is a good choice of places to visit, a couple of which would make for a full day's sightseeing – although you don't necessarily need to start from San Juan (Rincón, for example, is closer).

An hour west of San Juan near Arecibo, turn off Rte 22 onto Rte 129, continuing until Km 18.9, where you'll come to the **Río Camuy Cave Park** (Wed–Sun 8am–3.45pm, closed if it rains; US$10; ☎787/898-3100). It's the third largest underground river cave system in the world, with eighteen entrances into its 268 acres of tunnels, sinkholes, stalagmites, stalactites and underground rivers. A two-hour tour takes you first by trolley through palm and banana trees down to Clear Cave Junction, a 200-foot-deep sinkhole. You then descend underground on foot past enormous boulder-like stalagmites, rocks that fold like drapery or drip like candles, and underground bats that flit overhead in caverns up to 170 feet high. In places, the raging River Camuy is visible far below. The tour also takes you to the Tres Pueblos sinkhole, a vast chasm that measures 650 feet wide and 400 feet deep – large enough to fit El Morro.

Adventurous visitors can rappel down a rock wall to view **Cathedral Cave**, featuring 42 Taíno petroglyphs, or descend hundreds of feet into sinkholes and body-raft through an underground river; contact Aventuras Tierra Adentro in San Juan for details (☎787/766-0470). At US$85 to US$100 per person, the trips aren't cheap, but the experts who lead them have the highest regard for safety.

You don't just need to have an interest in the night sky to want to visit the nearby **Arecibo Observatory** (Wed–Fri noon–4pm & Sat–Sun 9am–4pm; $4 adults; ☎787/878-2612, ⓦwww.naic.edu), the largest radio telescope in the world. Coming from San Juan along Rte 22, follow Rte 129 south for 8km, then turn left onto 134, and after 2km left again onto 635. After another 3km, turn right onto 625, which ends at the observatory. Its massive 1000-foot-wide dish – covering a gaping sinkhole – is such an impressive spot that it's a popular film location (including *Contact* and the James Bond film *Goldeneye*) as well as tourist attraction. At the visitor centre, you can learn about astronomy and find out how the observatory, used to discover planets outside the solar system, studies radio emissions from galaxies, quasars and pulsars. There are some who darkly whisper that the distinctly otherworldly-looking telescope is where the US government looks out for alien life forms.

The **Caguana Indian Ceremonial Centre** (daily 8.30am–4.30pm; $2; ☎787/894-7325) is equally worthy of a visit, considered the most important pre-Columbian archeological site in the West Indies; to get here turn off Rte 22 from San Juan onto 10, then right after Utuado onto 11 to Km12.3. This pretty spot, thought to have been inhabited from around 1200 AD, is the largest Taíno ceremonial centre in the Antilles, containing petroglyphs and a dozen *bateyes* – used for ceremonial ball games of religious importance, many of them are lined with stone monoliths engraved with mythological figures. The park is also effectively a botanical garden showcasing the indigenous flora, while a museum displays Indian artefacts.

7.3

Porta del Sol
and the southwest

Western Puerto Rico holds some of the island's greatest natural treasures, not least the pretty, sun-bathed **beaches** which have earned the region its name as the **PORTA DEL SOL** (⊛ www.gotoportadelsol.com), or gateway to the sun. Beach-lovers apart, many are also drawn here for the world-class **diving** opportunities available from the uninhabited offshore islets of **Mona** and **Desecheo**, as well as along **the Wall** near La Parguera. There's also the world's largest **subtropical dry forest** outside **Guánica**, designated a World Biosphere Reserve by the UN, while the architecture in **San Germán** rivals the capital's, and far predates Ponce's.

If that's not enough, the natural beauty of the southwest in particular is almost enough to warrant a visit alone, caught between the looming Cordillera Central and the alluring Caribbean Sea. Positioned midway between Ponce and San Germán, **Guánica**, and nearby La Parguera, make the best hubs for exploring this area, offering the more appealing accommodation options.

In the northwest, you will want to base yourself in **Rincón**, the **surfing** capital of Puerto Rico, and it is from here that you can make the short trip to Desecheo. It also makes a convenient departure point for **Mona**, which lies stranded halfway between Puerto Rico and the Dominican Republic. It takes advance planning, but this "Galápagos of the Caribbean" will reward your efforts (see box overleaf).

Rincón and around

Surfers have been coming to **RINCÓN** in droves since the 60s, some of them staying on and forming a substantial ex-pat community. You can see why: the beaches around the small town of Rincón are among the island's finest, and good enough reason to come here, even if you don't surf (the season is October to April).

Rincón is also known for its romantic sunsets, best seen at the island's most westerly point at the restored **Punta Higüero lighthouse**, to the north of town. The pretty surrounding park overlooking the sea is also a good spot for **whale watching** in the winter – February is the best month. Next door is the innocuous-looking dome of Latin America's first nuclear power station, no longer operational. On either side of the cliffs below the lighthouse is a series of excellent **beaches** where the surfers congregate, although in calm weather there's also good snorkelling around Tres Palmas beach, where elkhorn coral proliferates.

For some more serious **snorkelling** or **diving**, you shouldn't leave Rincón without exploring the otherwordly, incredibly clear waters around the 360-acre protrusion of rock that is **Desecheo**, just 23km offshore. There are underwater ravines, pinnacles and grottos, where flying gurnards, peacock flounders, snappers, triggerfish, octopus and nurse sharks are to be spotted. Your best bet is Taíno Divers, Rte 413, Black Eagle Marina (☏ 787/823-7243, ⊛ www.tainodivers.com), whose professional staff run daily boat trips taking 45 minutes; $55 for snorkelling or $120 for two dives, includes kit.

Other beaches in the northwest

If you get bored of the beaches at Rincón itself, there are plenty more within easy reach. Half an hour's drive north is the aptly named **Wilderness Beach**, as well as Gas Chambers Beach a short walk south, both well-kept secrets by the surfing community. While the water here can be a bit rough for swimming, it's a wild, picturesque setting, just south of the cliffs of Punta Borinquen and adorned with a romantic ruined lighthouse, victim of an earthquake in 1918. It's not easy to find, reached by turning left off Rte 107 through Punta Borinquen golf course, just before you get to Aguadilla airport.

Rounding the northwestern tip of the island beyond Isabela is the isolated and beautiful **Guajataca Beach**, backed by steeply rising grassy slopes. It is accessed through a disused railway tunnel just off Rte 2, and it's worth the walk to the far end of its expansive shore, where waves collide vigorously with outcrops of rock.

About 10km South of Rincón on Rte 115 and then onto 401 are the much calmer waters of serene Añasco bay, where coastal hills rise up to the north. The main reason to come here is the *balneario* of **Tres Hermanos**, a vast stretch of sand, lined with palm trees, and with facilities for camping, including bathrooms and showers (☏787/826-0996).

Practicalities

Rincón has one of Puerto Rico's widest and best selections of **accommodation**, ranging from budget dormitories to charming rustic guesthouses to seriously exclusive hotels. The classiest hotel in Rincón, and perhaps all Puerto Rico, is *The Horned Dorset Primavera*, Rte 429, Km 0.3 (☏787/823-4030, ⊛www.horneddorset.com; ❾). It has eight immaculate luxury suites with mahogany four-poster beds in a Spanish colonial mansion on a private beach, and the best restaurant in town. At the other end of the scale is Rincón Inn, Rte 115, Km 11.6 (☏787/823-7070, ⊛www.rinconinn.com; ❷), with good basic accommodation as well as a youth hostel-style dormitory, and *Cowabungas*, an Internet café and ice cream parlour downstairs. To the north of town, beyond the lighthouse, is a collection of good, relaxed **guesthouses**, including *Beside the Pointe on the Beach*, Rte 413, Km 4.4 (☏787/823-8550, ⊛www.besidethepointe. com; ❹), right on the beach with eight rooms, some with sea views and kitchens. It has a decent restaurant, *Tamboo Seaside Grill*, serving grilled food on a wooden deck overlooking the sea, and also *Tamboo Tavern*, one of the most happening bars in town, especially on Monday nights. *The Lazy Parrot Inn & Restaurant*, Rte 413, Km 4.1

Mona

You will have to brave the 68km crossing and plan in advance to enjoy spectacular **Mona**. The diving around this uninhabited 13,000-acre island is unparalleled, with visibility averaging 150–200ft and 270 kinds of fish lurking in its waters. Depending on the time of year, you may see sailfish, dorado, tuna and marlin, while sharks, rays, turtles, pods of dolphins and even pilot whales. In the winter months, migrating humpback whales often come close to shore. With 200-foot high cliffs rimming the mostly flat, dry island, Mona has 8km of empty beaches, hiking trails and caves to explore, as well as diverse wildlife that includes giant iguanas (among them the endangered Mona Iguana), red-footed boobies and countless other sea birds.

The Mona Passage is notoriously rough and the journey can take from three to six hours. Oceans Unlimited (☏787/823-2340, ⊛www.oceans-unlimited.com) has a seaworthy boat, and will only take qualified divers on day-trips ($175 for a three-tank dive), but it's worth camping out for at least a night anyway. You will probably have to organize your trip before arriving in Puerto Rico, as boats go infrequently and it's a protected nature reserve which requires advance permission from the Department of Natural Resources to visit (☏787/724-3724).

(☎787/823-5654, ⊛www.lazyparrot.com; ❹) sits on top of a hill with beautiful views and a charmingly meandering outdoor area, including pool. It also has an excellent restaurant.

Rincon's large youthful population, thanks to the hordes of surfers it attracts, means the **nightlife** can get quite animated, and there are plenty of cool beach bars where you can hang out. *Pools Beach Bar*, above Pools Beach (☎ 787-823-8135), is another favoured night spot, as is *The Spot*, by the Black Eagle Marina (☎787/823-3510). Both serve decent food and can get very busy. A more exclusive destination is the fashionable beachside bar at *Villa Cofresí Hotel*, Rte 115, Km 12.0 (☎787/823-2450, ⊛www.villacofresi.com); try their *piratas*, a potent rum-based concoction served in a coconut.

San Germán

An hour's drive southeast of Rincon, **SAN GERMÁN** is arguably the oldest settlement in Puerto Rico, and makes an excellent day-trip, although it is just as close from Ponce on the south coast. It has the island's oldest architecture outside the capital – some 36 acres of it on the National Register of Historic Places – and its faded colonial charm is wonderfully evocative of bygone days.

San Germán was originally founded as early as 1506, and it was the island's second city long before Ponce usurped its position. In 1514, Spain divided Puerto Rico into two "partidos", under the control of San Juan and San Germán. Known as the Wandering City because its early inhabitants were forced into an almost nomadic existence by constant attacks from Caribe Indians and French corsairs, San Germán's current location was not settled until 1573.

The simple **Iglesia de Porta Coeli** on the Plazuela de Santo Domingo (Wed–Sun 8.30am–4.30pm; ☎787/892-5845) is the island's oldest church outside San Juan, now operating as a museum of religious artefacts. Maps with information of nearby historic buildings are available here, and there are fine views of the surrounding countryside from the top of its steep front steps. It was originally built in 1607 as the chapel for a Dominican monastery; an adjacent convent was destroyed in 1874, except the remaining front wall. The church's original bell was removed in the eighteenth century and buried when it was realized that, while it might have helped to warn against imminent danger, the bell's resounding ringing also guided approaching pirates to their loot. Attacks subsequently ceased but (rather more mysteriously) to this day the bell has not been recovered, despite concerted efforts to find it.

The more elaborate Spanish Baroque **Catedral de San Germán de Auxerre** dominates the Plaza Francisco Mariano Quiñones, a block west of Plazuela de Santo Domingo. Although a chapel has stood there since 1573, what remains today was built in 1688 and restored after an earthquake in 1737. It is notable for the *trompe l'oeil* fresco on the nave's ceiling, lit by a brilliant crystal chandelier. Doors open half an hour before Mass at 7am and 7.30pm, or you can call ☎787/892-1027 to see if the priest will let you in. At the opposite end of the square is the Antigua Casa Alcaldía, from where tours of the town by **trolley** depart from Thursday to Sunday (normal business hours; free).

There are no decent places to stay in San Germán, but if you're hungry the seafood and *criollo* dishes at *The Oasis*, a government-sanctioned *mesón gastronómico* in a musty old hotel at Calle Luna 72 (☎787/892-1175; ❸), should do.

La Parguera

Some 10km directly south of San Germán on the coast is the fishing village of **LA PARGUERA**, surrounded by a maze of mangrove swamps, channels, canals, coral reefs and cays. The diving here is superb, and the village makes a pleasant hub from which to explore the surrounding region, with decent restaurants, a lively bar culture, and a good selection of agreeable hotels. In general, the atmosphere is unusually young and lively for a place of its size, despite efforts by the local authorities to quieten things down by imposing curfews.

Divers are drawn to La Parguera's innumerable coral reefs offshore, many of them still unexplored. About 8km from the coast, **the Wall** runs for 35km from Guánica to Cabo Rojo at the island's southwest tip and drops to 2000ft, with visibility up to 120ft. Snorkelling, too, is excellent: barracudas, morays, manatees, nurse sharks and sea turtles abound. For equipment and details on expeditions, contact Parguera Divers at *Posada Porlamar* (☎787/899-4171) or Paradise Scuba (Rte 304 in town, ☎787/899-7611), who rent kayaks for $10 an hour as well.

In a nearby mangrove swamp, La Parguera has its own bioluminescent bay, known as **La Bahía Fosforescente**. This remarkable phenomenon is not literally "phosphorescent" – the bay contains millions of minute organisms called dinoflagellates, which glitter when disturbed. Sadly, pollution from powerboats and sewage means the bay is now only one-tenth as bright as it once was, and nothing compared to dazzling Mosquito Bay on Vieques. Nevertheless, for $5 you can catch a glass-bottomed boat that leaves from the pier every night after dark, while for $25 Paradise Scuba will take you there to swim.

Practicalities

There are a number of interesting **places to stay** in La Parguera. *Posada Porlamar*, Rte 304, Km 3.3 (☎787/899-4015, ⊛www.parguerapuertorico.com; ❹), offers 24 comfortable and well-equipped units styled like the area's "floating houses" on stilts in the water. Surrounded by mangroves and hillsides, they're very private. A stone's throw away, state-approved *Parador Villa Parguera* (☎787/899-7777, ⊛www .villaparguera.com; ❹) has luxurious units with private balconies and lovely views, as well as a pool, good restaurant and cabaret acts on Saturday. There is also a selection of cheap guesthouses, a particularly reasonable one being *Flamboyán Guest House*, Calle Principal 239 (☎787/899-3534; ❷).

The cheapest **food** in the village is by the pier, where vendors grill a variety of fresh fish for less than US$4, when they're there. On the main drag just above, in addition to the *parador* (see above) there is plenty of good, inexpensive grub. On Friday and Saturday nights live music accompanies good pub food at *Parguera Blues Café*, Centro Comercial El Muelle, Avda Los Pescadores (☎787/899-4742). For some tasty Mexican fare in relaxed, open-air surroundings, try out *Restaurante Gaucataco* (☎787/808-0303) on the main road approaching the pier.

Guánica and around

Home to **Bosque Estatal de Guánica**, the world's best example of subtropical dry forest, the diverse and wild landscape around **GUÁNICA** is dotted with blanched trees curling like arthritic old bones and suggestively-shaped cacti called *dildos*, while at the water's edge are some splendid beaches and mangrove swamps whose groping roots ensnare everything in their way. There's not much to the dusty town of Guánica itself, but nearby hotels are ideal for exploring the southwest, with lots to do within a thirty-minute drive.

Bosque Estatal de Guánica

Scientists surmise that a mere one percent of the world's subtropical dry forest remains; almost 10,000 acres of it survive in the **Bosque Estatal de Guánica**, or Guánica State Forest, a United Nations World Biosphere Reserve just to the east of town (daily 8.30am–5.30pm; free, guide to trails US$1; ☎787/821-5706) that accommodates some 700 plant species and over 100 types of bird. It has the best **bird-watching** in Puerto Rico and boasts several rare species, including the Puerto Rican emerald-breasted hummingbird, the yellow-shouldered blackbird and (rarest of all) the endangered **Puerto Rican nightjar**. The forest also contains bullfinches, the Puerto Rican woodpecker, the lizard cuckoo, and crested toads and leatherback turtles.

The park has a half-dozen beaches on the mainland and a number of offshore cays, including the popular snorkelling spot, **Gilligan's Island** ($5 return boat trips leave from outside *San Jacinto Restaurant*, see below). There is also a selection of unchallenging **hiking** trails – some very short, although they can be hot and buggy, so bring plenty of sunscreen and insect repellent. It's worth wearing light clothing that will also protect you from the spiny vegetation. The hikes mostly depart from the **ranger station** at the end of Rte 334, where you can get very basic maps of the trails and information on the flora and fauna. In a couple of hours you can walk down to the beautiful and isolated Ballena and Tamarindo beaches and back, most directly via the Ballena trail which passes a thousand-year-old lignum vitae tree. You can also drive to those beaches on Rte 333, and from the roadhead follow the coast around into the driest part of the forest, studded with cacti.

Practicalities

Conveniently located approximately midway between Ponce and San Germán, the town of Guánica has a better selection of **accommodation** than either of its neighbours. In fact, *Mary Lee's by the Sea*, Rte 333, at Km 6.7 (☏787/821-3600, ⓦwww.maryleesbythesea.com; ⑥) is one of Puerto Rico's most charming places to stay. Situated by a mangrove swamp, with kayaks and motorboats to take guests to beaches on cays across the water, it has eight cheerful, sprawling apartments with a very tropical feel, some with sea views. Nearby, the swish, all-inclusive *Copamarina Beach Resort*, Rte 333, Km 6.5 (☏787/821-0505, ⓦwww.copamarina.com; ⑦), has a private beach, two pools, Jacuzzi, boat launch, beachside bar, boat rentals, gym, Internet access and two excellent restaurants (see below) – they also run diving trips to the Wall. For **campsites**, you'll have to travel into the Bosque Estatal de Susúa, above Guánica on Rte 368, Km 2.1, where Almacigo I and II (☏787/833-3700) have space for 175 people, campfire areas, running water and bathrooms. Permits required from the Department of Natural Resources (☏787/724-3724).

Guánica has a (limited) number of good **restaurants**. *San Jacinto Restaurant*, Rte 333, Km 66 (☏787/821-4941), is a lively locals' favourite by the Gilligan's Island ferry dock, serving *criollo* staples, many with fresh fish and seafood, for around US$12–20. For something a bit more upscale, *Restaurant Alexandra* at the *Copamarina Beach Resort* is expensive but well worth the price for its grilled fish and meat dishes with inventive tropical marinades and sauces. *Copamarina's* more casual option is the reasonably priced *Las Palmas Café*, open until 6pm. *Criollo* staples, burgers and sandwiches will cost you less than US$12.

7.4

Ponce

After San Juan, Puerto Rico's second city is **PONCE**, best known for its art museum and handsome centre, an excellent example of nineteenth-century *criollo* architecture. The city is liveliest during **Carnaval**, when the streets fill with parades of musicians, floats, dancers and *vejigantes* – revellers in devilish-looking painted masks. Things also heat up in November during the **Fiesta Nacional de Bomba y Plena**, when drummers and dancers gather to compete. In between festivals, there are a number of interesting sights on the outskirts of town, including **Tibes Indian Ceremonial Centre** and **Hacienda Buena Vista**.

Historically fiercely independent from the capital, Ponce's heyday was in the late nineteenth century, underpinned by riches generated from its surrounding sugar and coffee plantations. But Ponce's growth was not sustained and nowadays if arriving from San Juan you will need to shift down a gear or two to adjust to its sleepier pace of life. Note that on Mondays and Tuesdays many of Ponce's cultural and historical institutions are closed.

Some history

Known as La Perla del Sur ("the pearl of the south"), the settlement of Ponce was recognized by the Spanish in 1692, and named after **Loíza Ponce de León**, the great grandson of Juan Ponce de León. It developed into an important cultural and commercial centre – essentially a southern capital of the island, largely due to its proximity to the sea. By 1831, it was designated a harbour, but trade was permitted only with Spanish ships. However, with the northern capital a good distance away over the Cordillera Central, it was hard for the governor to keep tabs on the southern city.

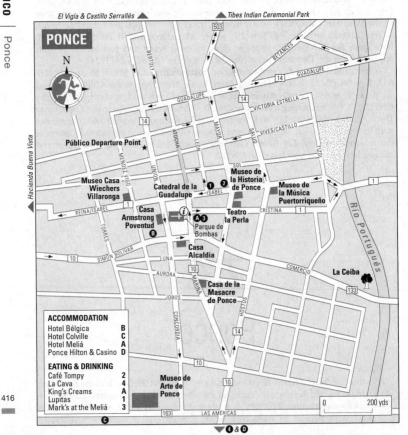

Contraband flourished for the better part of the nineteenth century, as did the **arts** under the auspices of the Serrallés family, the makers of Don Q and Captain Morgan's rum. The family commissioned European architects to construct mansions downtown, and imported European paintings, music and books. The city became known as a haven for liberal ideas, safe from San Juan's allegiance to Spain, and eventually became a breeding ground for the **nationalist movement**. As a means of throwing off Spanish sovereignty, the city was glad to surrender to American troops when they entered Puerto Rico near Ponce in 1898, bringing the Spanish-American War to an end and ceding Puerto Rico to the US. What the city's inhabitants didn't realize, however, was that the Americans would put a stop to illegal trade and herald a precipitous **downturn** in Ponce's good fortune. Power was centralized in the capital and growth in the sugar industry in nearby towns like Salinas and Guánica as well as the loss of trade with Spain and Cuba pushed Ponce into a phase of economic decline. But the city flourished in the arts and has provided three of the island's six Puerto Rican **governors** since 1946. Fifty years later, in 1995, US$500 million was invested in the restoration of the historic centre in a successful bid to jump-start **tourism**, leaving Ponce today fresh-faced and a pleasure to wander around.

Arrival, information and getting around

Ponce is a 90-minute drive from San Juan via Rte 52. Alternatively, Cape Air makes daily half-hour flights from San Juan into **Mercedita Airport** (☎787/842-6292), located about 7km east of Ponce on Rte 5506, off Rte 1. A taxi ride into the city centre costs about US$10 from the airport. **Públicos** leave from and arrive at Calle Unión, north of the Plaza de las Delicias in the historic part of town. See the list of *público* lines on p.389.

The **PRTC's** Ponce office (☎787/843-0465) is in the Paseo del Sur shopping centre on Rte 1. Information is more conveniently available at the **Ponce Municipal Tourist Office** (☎787/284-3338), located in the Parque de Bombas building on the Plaza de las Delicias.

Ponce has several **taxi** companies, the most reliable of which is the Asociación de Taxis de Ponce (☎787/842-3370). A free sightseeing **trolley** tour leaves from outside Casa Armstrong-Poventud and runs through the historic district to Castillo Serrallés. Otherwise, you can fairly easily walk around the parts of Ponce you'll want to see.

Accommodation

The old **hotels** in downtown Ponce have more character than the chains outside the historic district, though they are still a little run-down. As a base for exploring the southwest, you may want to consider staying in Guánica or La Parguera, both within half an hour's drive of Ponce.

Hotel Bélgica Calle Villa 122 ☎787/844-3255, ⓦwww.hotelbelgica.com. Although it's more charming than the *Meliá*, with a super-affable innkeeper, this hotel in the heart of the historic district is showing its age. Ask for a high-ceilinged room. ❸

Hotel Colville Avda Muñoz Rivera 1295 ☎787/843-1935 or 473-0463. Poor service, but still a reasonable option for the budget traveller, with TV and a/c, near the art museum. ❷

Hotel Meliá Calle Cristina 75 ☎787/842-0260, ⓦhttp://home.coqui.net/melia. Faded grand hotel with an excellent restaurant, *Mark's*. Excellent for seeing the historic district. Spacious rooms, some with fabulous views right over the Plaza de las Delicias and around. ❺

Ponce Hilton and Casino Avda Caribe 1150 ☎787/259-7676, ⓦwww.hiltoncaribbean.com/ponce. Expensive, glittery compound outside of town, facing a small, rocky Caribbean beach, with two restaurants, three bars, a pool, tennis courts, golf course, fitness area, spa and full business centre. ❼

△ La Fortaleza, Old San Juan

The historic district

Ponce is a much younger city than San Juan. It did not blossom until the late nineteenth century, when the oldest remaining buildings in the city centre were constructed – although much was rebuilt after a particularly damaging earthquake in 1918. Nevertheless, Ponce has some fine architecture – mostly in the Neoclassical style – concentrated around the quite delightful **Plaza de las Delicias**, which is punctuated with refreshing fountains (the illuminated Fountain of Lions came from the 1939 New York World's Fair) and 100-year-old Indian laurel topiary. The space actually comprises two squares, Plaza Federico Degetau and Plaza Luis Muñoz Rivera, divided by **Our Lady of Guadalupe Cathedral** (Mon–Fri 6am–3.30pm, Sat & Sun 6am–noon). Although there has been a chapel on the site since 1670, it was completely destroyed in 1835 and rebuilt in phases; most of the existing structure dates from its final restoration after the 1918 earthquake, when both its towers were toppled.

Behind the cathedral is Ponce's signature red-and-black striped Moorish-inspired **Parque de Bombas**, or firehouse – now a museum (daily except Tues 9.30am–6pm; free; ☎787/284-3338). It was built for the 1883 World's Fair hosted by Ponce, and then donated to its very active fire company – a token of appreciation for having saved so many other buildings from the string of natural disasters that has struck the city. It became a social gathering place and music hall for the firemen's band, directed by Juan Morel Campos, a key figure in the development of Puerto Rican music who is commemorated by a statue in the plaza. **Casa Armstrong-Poventud** faces the cathedral's west end, with an ornately embellished facade and caryatids flanking the heavily carved wooden doorway. Built by a Scottish banker as a private home in 1900, it now houses the Instituto de Cultura Puertorriqueña Sur, which was founded to promote Puerto Rico's cultural heritage.

The museums

Make sure to spare some time for Ponce's excellent museums, themselves in noteworthy buildings. Beside the hulking Neoclassical **Teatro La Perla** is the **Ponce History Museum**, Calle Isabel 53 (daily except Tues 10am–5pm; free, including

---

The Ponce Massacre

The early twentieth century was a rough time for Ponce. Profits stalled, hurricanes destroyed coffee production, the price of sugar bottomed out and the US favoured San Juan for development over its uppity nationalist rival to the south. By the time the Great Depression took hold, Ponce had had it. Revolution fomented more fervently than ever, leading to one of the US's most egregious injustices towards the territory of Puerto Rico: the **Ponce Massacre**.

Along with the influx of European art and culture in Ponce had come a substantial number of students and intellectuals. On March 21, 1937, a group of Puerto Rican nationalists gathered outside what is now the museum commemorating this event, to stage a march celebrating the abolition of slavery and protest against the imprisonment of their leader. They had permission, but their North American governor, General Blanton Winship, revoked it at the last minute. Nevertheless, about 100 unarmed men and women turned up, to find themselves face to face with many more police officers armed with machine guns, rifles and pistols. When the marchers began to sing the national anthem, La Borinqueña, a shot rang out, culminating in a blaze of gunfire. Twenty-one men, women and children died, including two policemen shot by their own companions; around 200 more were wounded. The police blamed the protesters, so they were tried – and found innocent. A subsequent investigation by eminent Puerto Ricans on behalf of the American Civil Liberties Union corroborated this finding and determined that a massacre had taken place.

guided tours; ☎787/844-7071), which provides a useful introduction to the city's 300-year history, appropriately emphasizing its non-conformist stance on Puerto Rican politics – being housed in what was the seat of the Ponce Nationalist Association. For a US$20 deposit, you can borrow a guidebook (in Spanish and English) to 45 historically and architecturally significant structures in town. A block further down Calle Isabel is the **Museum of Music** (Wed–Sun 8.30am–4.30pm; free; ☎787/848-7016), in the rum-making Serallés family's elegant city centre house. It gives an interesting overview of Puerto Rican music and has a thorough display of the instruments used; *ponceños* are rightly proud of their musical tradition, and claim that *plena* (see box p.407) was invented there. The **Museum of the Ponce Massacre**, at the corner of Calles Marina and Aurora (Wed–Sun 8.30am–4.30pm; free ☎787/844-9722), commemorates this infamous episode (see box p.419), which took place right outside the museum, and also examines the history of the Puerto Rican independence movement in general.

Outside the historic district

If you have the time, a few sights outside Ponce's historic district warrant a visit – in particular, the **Museo de Arte de Ponce**, just south of the centre at 2325 Avda Las Américas (daily 10am–5pm; US$4, children US$2, students US$1; ☎787/848-0505, ⓦwww.museoarteponce.org), considered the best art museum in the Caribbean. With over 3000 works, the collection is strongest on the British Pre-Raphaelites, with important paintings by Lord Leighton (don't miss *Flaming June*) and Burne Jones. It is also good on Italian Baroque, French Academy and the Spanish Golden Age; look out for works by Van Eyck, El Greco, Velázquez, Rubens, Goya and Delacroix, as well as Puerto Rico's two most esteemed masters, José Campeche and Francisco Oller.

Just northwest of town, sharing a hill with the 100-foot-tall, 70-foot-wide cross of **El Vigía** – from which the Spanish kept watch over the waters around the port of Ponce – is the **Museo Castillo Serallés** (daily except Mon 9.30am–5pm; US$3; ☎787/259-1774). Ironically, this lavish 14,000-square-foot, Spanish Revival mansion was built during the Great Depression. Home to the Serallés family, whose riches stemmed from their Don Q and Captain Morgan's rum, it has a commanding view over Ponce and is now worth about US$25 million. It was passed from one family member to another until the mid-1980s when it became too impractical to keep up. Today, many of the family's eccentric period possessions lie around the house, including cutting-edge technology of the early twentieth century, bizarre grooming equipment and eerie-looking dolls. There is also a permanent exhibition on Ponce's rum-making industry.

About 3km north of Ponce, at Km 2.2 on Rte 503, **Tibes Indian Ceremonial Centre** (daily except Mon 9am–4pm; US$2; ☎787/840-2255) was discovered in 1975 after Hurricane Eloise struck. It exposed 187 graves, some dating from 300 AD, making it the oldest burial ground in the Caribbean. There are also pre-Taíno *bateyes* (courts used for ceremonial ball games), tools, pottery and a star-shaped stone formation with points facing the direction of sunrise and sunset during the solstice and equinox.

At the accurately restored **Hacienda Buena Vista** (Wed–Sun by reservation only; US$7; ☎787/722-5882), about 16km north of town, at Km 16.8 on Rte 123, you can get a glimpse of what life was like on a nineteenth-century coffee plantation. Slaves were used to grow coffee, cacao, plantains, pineapple, yams and corn, although the hacienda was one of the first on the island to use industrial machinery, such as the corn mill, cotton gin and coffee depulper.

Eating and drinking

For a metropolis of its size, the quality of the **food** in Ponce is wanting, especially if you've been spoiled by San Juan's impressive range of options. A few places will tide you over, however, and *Mark's at the Meliá* is excellent. As for **drinking**, there's a surprising shortage of enticing places; in the centre, *Mark's* and *Lupita's* are as good an option as any of the few run-of-the-mill bars you might happen across.

Café Tompy Calle Isabel ☎ 787/840-1965. Good café con leche, hearty criollo cooking and sandwiches are available at this neighbourhood hangout for around $5.

King's Creams Plaza de las Delicias, underneath Hotel Meliá. Delicious ice creams with unusual tropical flavours; perfect for a stroll around the plaza.

La Cava Ponce Hilton and Casino, Avda Caribe 1150 ☎ 787/259-7676. Continental menu that changes regularly; past offerings include duck foie gras with toasted brioche and an excellent black

and white soufflé. There's also a champagne and cigar bar. Entrees US$25–28.

Lupita's Calle Isabel ☎ 787/848-8808. Filling, reasonably priced Mexican food in a courtyard setting; sometimes has live music.

Mark's at the Meliá Hotel Meliá, Calle Cristina 75 ☎ 787/842-0260. Renowned chef Mark French prepares inventive variations on criollo staples, like mofongo with barbecue tamarind duck or corn-crusted red snapper with yucca purée. Entrees US$18–28.

7.5

La Ruta Panorámica

The often wild and sparsely populated interior of Puerto Rico – dominated by the Cordillera Central, which runs like a mountainous rudder, east to west, along the length of the island – is best explored along **LA RUTA PANORÁMICA**. A 266km assemblage of about forty roads, the Panoramic Route can be heartstopping – not just for its dazzling natural beauty, but also for its unpredictable twists through mist-shrouded peaks, sheer canyons and impenetrable forests. Often there are no dividers and precipitous drops away from the narrow road.

In the mountains, the temperature is much cooler, the air heavy and wet, and the vegetation lush and jungle-like. You'll hear sounds of roosters and coquís; see houses built on stilts and towns wrapped in fog; and pass through coffee plantations clinging to abrupt hillsides, shaded with banana trees. At various points along the route, you'll catch glimpses of both the Atlantic and the Caribbean, with impressively open views of large chunks of the island's coastline.

It matters little whether you start in the east at **Maunabo**, or in the west at Mayagüez. But to do the entire length – without stopping – would take a full and very exhausting day, so plan on at least two days and take your time on the sometimes hair-raising roads. Unless otherwise indicated, all the stops described below lie directly on the route, so follow La Ruta Panorámica signs carefully, and be aware that they are not always used. The route numbers change constantly and it can get confusing: a compass can provide reassurance that you are going in roughly the right direction, as adequate maps are not available.

Maunabo to Bosque Estatal de Carite

Going from east to west, the best starting point is the beach town of Maunabo on the island's southeast corner, where you can charge up your batteries at the peaceful, pretty **beaches** of Playa Larga and Playa Los Bohíos on either side of the picturesque nineteenth-century **lighthouse** at Punta Tuna. From Maunabo take Rte 3 inland to Yabucoa crossing over the lush Cuchilla de Panduras, the easternmost stretch of the Cordillera Central.

Once into the Cordillera proper, the first major stop is the town of **Guavate**, legendary for its *lechón*, juicy roast suckling pig cooked on an outdoor spit. You will find a proliferation of restaurants specializing in *lechón* if you follow Rte 184 north off La Ruta Panorámica to Km 27. Customers are charged by the weight of their plate (about US$6 a pound) – the best is *El Monte*. Locals come in droves at the weekend, when loud live music fills the outdoor seating area.

Many *sanjuaneros* come to the Guavate region for the 6600-acre **Bosque Estatal de Carite**, less than an hour south of San Juan, where you can hike, camp, fish, bird-watch, swim and escape the heat; there is a ranger station by the *lechonerías* (Mon, Thurs & Fri 8–10am ☎787/747-4545, as well as a campsite ☎787/864-8903). Three **rivers** originate here – the Río Grande de Loíza, the Río Grande de Patillas and the Río de la Plata; the reserve, which stretches over the Sierra de Cayey, protects this important watershed from erosion caused by development. There are two campsites and 25 **hiking trails** (ask for maps at the ranger station) the most popular of which starts from **Charco Azul**, a bluish freshwater **swimming hole** within walking distance of Rte 184.

San Cristóbal Canyon and Barranquitas

Turn back on Rte 184 and continue west some 40km to **San Cristóbal Canyon**, a stunning, 500-foot-deep volcanic gorge that stretches for 8km and is home to Puerto Rico's highest **waterfall**, on the Río Usabón. The ravine offers some of the island's best **hiking** opportunities, although the path to it is not easy to find without being able to ask locally for directions, while the slopes are extremely steep and can be dangerous in wet weather.

For those confident enough to go it alone, turn off 162 onto 725, and after just under a kilometre, turn left. After a further half-kilometre going steeply downhill, park your car when the road turns sharply right and levels out to head back onto the 725 by a school. The path begins from that corner, descending abruptly for some 15 minutes until you are confronted with the strikingly beautiful **Neblina waterfall**, whose pool makes for wonderful bathing as you gaze up at the narrow streams of water spraying off the crags above. You can **hike** some way downstream; you will have to clamber down the left-hand side of a second smaller waterfall to reach the third, which is not passable. Allow about three hours there and back. Less experienced walkers can take an organized tour: they leave from *La Piedra* restaurant (☎787/735-1034) on Rte 7718, Km 0.8, next to the Parque Mirador, at 8.30am on Saturdays; call ahead to make a reservation or to arrange a private hike. Bring water and sturdy hiking shoes.

Nearby on Rte 162 is the charming little hill town of **Barranquitas**, best known as the 1859 birthplace of **Luis Muñoz Rivera**, champion of Puerto Rican independence before Spain ceded rule to the US. Rivera is remembered at the **Casa Natal Luis Muñoz Rivera**, Calle Luis Muñoz Rivera 10 (Tues–Sat; 8.30–4.30pm; free; ☎787/857-0230), a museum in the very simple *criollo* home where Rivera was born. Meanwhile, the **Mausoleo Familia Muñoz Rivera**, Calle Padre Berrios 7 (same hours as Casa Natal; free), contains the remains of Rivera and his son, Luis Muñoz Marín, another extremely important political shaper of modern Puerto Rico and founder of the Popular Democratic Party. Barranquitas makes a convenient place to break the journey for the night, especially if you're planning to see the San Cristóbal Canyon. Try *Hacienda Margarita* to the north of town on Rte 152, at Km 1.7 (☎787/857-0414; ❸), in a commanding spot overlooking the Barranquitas valley.

Bosque Estatal de Toro Negro to Maricao

From Barranquitas, head south on Rte 162 and west onto Rte 143, an uphill drive which will take you into the 7000-acre **Bosque Estatal de Toro Negro**.

Continuing for some 16km above 3000ft, this is the most remote and highest stretch of La Ruta Panorámica. You'll find a **ranger station** at Km 32.4 on Rte 143 at the Area Recreativa Doña Juana. You can **camp** nearby at Los Viveros (⊕787/844-4660), but apply for a permit fifteen days in advance at the Department of Natural Resources in San Juan (⊕787/724-3724). You can also get sketchy maps indicating the 18km of **treks** available. The most impressive takes you on a two-hour circuit up to an observation tower with commanding views over the island. Further west on 143, turn right off La Ruta Panorámica onto 149, which will bring you to the Salto de Doña Juana, a pretty **waterfall** thundering down right beside the road.

Back onto Rte 143, you will pass just beneath the highest peak in Puerto Rico, **Cerro de Punta** (4389ft), crowned with a clutch of radio and television towers. To reach the very top, turn right 5km after the turning for 577 at a wide passing point once the 143 has begun to descend, and then follow an almost impossibly steep metalled road back up until you reach the mirador beside the giddying pylons. The views from up here are stunning, with both coasts visible on a clear day.

From where La Ruta Panorámica crosses over the fast Rte 10, it is just a twenty-minute drive south to central Ponce, an easy option for spending the night. Continuing west will bring you across some of the most poorly maintained, narrow and windy stretches of the route, although also some of the most beautiful. Some of the best views along the whole route are to be had from **La Torre de Piedra** (Stone Tower) on Rte 120, south of Maricao. From the tower, you can survey almost the whole western half of the island, with particularly extraordinary views towards the southwest from beyond Ponce to the very tip of the Cabo Rojo peninsula.

Maricao, near the western end of the La Ruta Panorámica, hosts a **coffee harvest festival** in mid-February, but its natural setting alone makes it worth a visit any time of year. The town is snug in the mountains, with some steeply inclined streets, and gorges and streams just on the outskirts. A wonderfully sequestered spot is Salto Pepe Curet, a small **waterfall** reached by taking Rte 105 out of town; turn right after the bridge onto 425, which you follow to the end, from where it is five minutes further on foot.

7.6

Vieques and Culebra

E ven if you're staying in Puerto Rico for just a week, it's worthwhile to catch a ferry or hop onto a puddle-jumper to **VIEQUES** or **CULEBRA**, the two little-developed islets lying off the eastern coast that are known as the Spanish Virgin Islands – and geologically are part of the Virgin Islands. Snorkelling, diving, fishing and swimming here are about as good as it gets, while idyllic, often isolated, beaches abound on both islands. You may need to adjust to "island time", as a laid-back atmosphere prevails, particularly since the US finally ceased its controversial bombing practices on Vieques in 2003.

Travelling to the offshore islands

The Spanish Virgin Islands are easily reached by **plane** from San Juan or the port town of **Fajardo** on the eastern coast, via Vieques Air Link (☎888/901-9247, ⑭www.vieques-island.com/val/) or Isla Nena (☎787/741-1577). Flights from San Juan leave for Vieques from the international airport (US$79 one-way) and to both islands from Isla Grande airport, which is somewhat cheaper (US$45 one-way to Vieques; US$50 to Culebra). Flights are much cheaper from Fajardo, an hour's drive from San Juan (US$20 one-way to Vieques; US$25 one-way to Culebra). Either flight takes just around a half-hour.

The **Puerto Rican Port Authority** (☎800/981-2005 or 787/863-0705 in Fajardo; ☎787/741-4761 in Vieques; ☎787/742-3161 in Culebra) also runs regular **ferries** three times a day to and from both Vieques and Culebra. The trip takes about an hour and is dirt-cheap: US$2 to Vieques and US$2.25 to Culebra. There is also a less frequent service running direct between Vieques and Culebra. Bringing a car is considerably more complicated (and expensive), and involves reserving a space at least two weeks in advance. Call for schedules and to make reservations.

Vieques

Just 11km off the eastern shore of Puerto Rico, 34km-long **VIEQUES** feels a world away. Despite the controversial construction in 2000 of a five-star resort at Martineau Bay, near the airport, its countryside remains untrammelled. Many locals still get around on horseback and chickens still stop cars in the roads, which are devoid of traffic or traffic lights.

Ironically, the lack of widespread development on the island is largely thanks to the occupation of its western and eastern thirds in 1941 by the US Navy, which used these portions for **bombing practice** for decades afterwards. For years, this was undoubtedly the most substantive complaint about life under the US flag, provoking widespread protest on the Puerto Rican mainland and even from celebrities and politicians stateside. But it took the killing of a local civilian by a stray bomb in 1999 to make anything happen, providing the impetus for President Bill Clinton to start phasing out military training on Vieques. This was successfully achieved in 2003, and you can now (safely) explore networks of empty bunkers dotted around the western end of the island. But while you may now be able to enjoy the place without being disturbed by rumbling noises in the distance, unfortunately much of this beautiful island is still off limits due to the danger of accidentally treading on unexploded bombs, although several nature reserves have also been set up.

Arrival, information and getting around

You'll land on Vieques, whether by air or by sea, in **Isabela Segunda**, the rather plain town on the north side (referred to around the rest of the island as "the far side"). It has the island's only **post office** and **ATM**, but that's no reason to stay; indeed, best to press right on to the south side of the island.

For **information**, contact the tourism office (☎787/741-0800), or rely on any of the hotels listed below.

Only Sombé beach (see overleaf) is easily accessible by foot from Esperanza; for the remaining beaches you will need **transport**. *Públicos* generally run from 8am to 6pm, though Ana Luz Robles operates 24 hours (☎787/313-0599). Otherwise, bring or rent a car (try *Acevedo's*, Rte 201, Km 1.5; ☎787/741-4380); scooters (*Extreme Scooter Rental*, near ferry dock; ☎787/435-9345) are a cheaper and more manoeuvrable alternative. Call *La Dulce Vida* (☎787/435-3557) for mountain bike rental and tours.

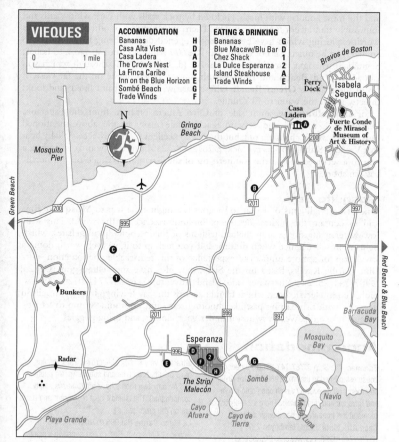

VIEQUES

0 ⎯⎯⎯⎯ 1 mile

ACCOMMODATION	
Bananas	H
Casa Alta Vista	D
Casa Ladera	A
The Crow's Nest	B
La Finca Caribe	C
Inn on the Blue Horizon	E
Sombé Beach	G
Trade Winds	F

EATING & DRINKING	
Bananas	G
Blue Macaw/Blu Bar	D
Chez Shack	1
La Dulce Esperanza	2
Island Steakhouse	A
Trade Winds	E

Around the island

Just a fifteen-minute drive south from Isabela Segunda takes you to **Esperanza**, the main town on Vieques's Caribbean coast. Without question, the beaches on this side of the island are superior (the Atlantic beaches tend to be rocky) and the landscape more attractive.

The main drag in Esperanza – known by its large ex-pat population as the **Strip**, otherwise Calle Flamboyán – has a lovely white seaside promenade, or *malecón*, and a picturesque collection of indoor/outdoor restaurants and guesthouses. Heading east from town are Vieques's three most popular beaches. A ten-minute walk around the headland at the eastern end of the Esperanza beachfront – where pelicans as well as locals are to be found fishing – will take you to the *balneario* **Sombé** (Sun Bay), a 3km crescent of bone-coloured sand lined with trees and coconut palms where wild horses graze. The beach can be busy at weekends, but on weekdays or in the off season, it's easy to feel as though you have it entirely to yourself.

East along the dirt road from Sombé is **Media Luna**, a tidy, half-moon cove with baby-bath water. The beach is backed by sea grapes and almond trees, and the water is incomparably calm and warm. Further on, **Navío** is another attractive stretch, and the most popular with locals, enclosed by rock walls with stark white sands and impossibly translucent turquoise waters. There are a number of other lovely beaches worth exploring which have been recently opened up, and being harder to get to are likely to be quieter, if not empty. On Rte 977 halfway from Esperanza to Isabela Segunda, turn right into the nature reserve (daily 6am–6pm), through which you can access **Red Beach** and **Blue Beach**, among others; while on the far western tip of the island is **Green Beach**, whose narrow stretch of palm-lined sand looks directly across the water to El Yunque.

For **snorkelling**, the south side of Cayo Afuera offshore from the Esperanza beachfront is magical and easy to reach, while many of the above-mentioned beaches are worth checking out; but there are excellent spots only accessible by boat that Vieques Sailing (by ferry dock; ☏787/508-7245) can take you to, including a trip to a secluded reef at the southern tip of the Bermuda Triangle on the north-eastern shore.

Mosquito Bay

One of the highlights of a visit to Vieques is a night-time trip to **Mosquito Bay**, said to contain the highest degree of bioluminescence in the world. This shallow-water mangrove swamp shelters trillions of microscopic dinoflagellates, which light up in self-defence when disturbed. If you feel up to it, it's well worth doing a kayak trip for a more immediate experience of this remarkable phenomenon – use Blue Caribe Kayaks, based on the Strip; they also have snorkelling gear (US$25; ☏787/741-2522). Otherwise, ride Island Adventure's (☏787/741-0720, ⊛www. biobay.com) electric boat, which trundles across the bay leaving glittery contrails in its wake, with fish darting past like shooting stars, and stops mid-swamp to let passengers take a dip. Wear a swimsuit under your clothes, and bring goggles.

Accommodation

Bananas The Strip ☏787/741-8700. Pioneer guesthouse established in the mid-1980s. Twelve rustic, airy rooms off breezeway which open onto jungle and have a/c and refrigerators. There's a lively bar, so rooms at the front are noisier, though safer. ❸

Casa Alta Vista Calle Flamboyán 297 ☏787/741-3296, ⊛www.casaaltavista.net. Homely and well-run, with ground-floor shop and scooters available for hire. Clean rooms with a/c have access to a roof terrace. ❸

Casa Ladera Playa Monte Santo, Rte 200 ☏917/570-7558, ⊛www.casa-ladera.com Pretty villa by beach on north coast with ocean views, private terraces and pool. Three units with two spacious bedrooms each, and modern kitchens. Includes DVD player with movie library. Great deal for four or more. ❻

The Crow's Nest Rte 201, Km 1.5 ☏787/741-0033, ⊛www.crowsnestvieques.com. Located ten minutes from the beach by car on a forested hill overlooking the Atlantic. Spacious rooms with private bath and kitchenette. There's a pool and excellent restaurant. ❹

Inn on the Blue Horizon Rte 996, Km 4.2 ☏787/741-3318, ⊛www.innonthebluehorizon. com. Vieques's most beautiful place to stay, in an elegant seafront, Mediterranean-style structure,

attracts a very fashionable crowd. Three cabins have private balconies and sea views. No phones or TVs; only two rooms have a/c (breezes amply compensate). The island's best restaurant and bar are on the premises. ❼

La Finca Caribe Rte 995 ☏787/741-0495, ⊛www.lafinca.com. Rustic, eco-sensitive lodging in a pretty hillside setting offering run-down but charming and spacious cottages with hammocks everywhere, open-air showers, and tropical vegetation. The main house, also for rent, sleeps 6–20. ❹

Sombé Beach ☏787/741-8198. Legal camping on *balneario* with outdoor showers, toilets and changing rooms. ❶

Trade Winds The Strip ☏787/741-8666, ⊛www. enchanted-isle.com/tradewinds. Vieques's first guesthouse has spacious, tidy a/c rooms, four with terraces facing the Caribbean. Friendly innkeeper and good seaside open-air restaurant. ❹

Wyndham Martineau Bay Resort and Spa Rte 200, Km 3.2 ☏787/741-4100, ⊛www. wyndham.com/hotels/VQSMB/main.wnt. The luxury option. On the north side of the island, the large rooms all have fine Caribbean views. Three beaches on the property, which also includes two tennis courts, a respectable restaurant, various bars and a spa. ❾

Eating, drinking and nightlife

Bananas The Strip ☎787/741-8700. Tasty half-ounce burgers, chicken wings and other bar grub are on offer at this lively, sometimes raucous, inexpensive open-air bar.

Blue Macaw/Blu Bar *Inn on the Blue Horizon*, Rte 996, Km 4.2 ☎787/741-3318, ⊛www. innonthebluehorizon.com. Locals mingle with New York and LA fashion types in the *Blue Macaw*, an elegant, open-air setting with sea views, offering Continental cuisine with the occasional tropical twist. The *Blu Bar* is well known among the jet-set and travel writers. Entrees US$19–24.

Chez Shack Rte 995 ☎787/741-2175. Located 10km northwest of Esperanza in forest surroundings, the *Shack* offers excellent reasonably priced grilled fish, including lobster, plus a live steel band on Mon nights.

Island Steakhouse *The Crow's Nest* Rte 201, Km 1.5 ☎787/741-0011. Alfresco dining combined with the island's best steaks, even available together with lobster, for moderate to expensive prices. The second-floor deck has a great view of El Yunque. Open Fri–Tues; happy hour Tues 5–7pm.

La Dulce Esperanza Calle Almendro ☎787/741-0085. This sweet, tiny place tucked away behind the Strip serves as a bakery from 7am–11am, where you can snack on healthy versions of standard Puerto Rican pastries. Reopens at 5pm to turn into a pizza joint by night.

Trade Winds The Strip. Rustic porch with ceiling fans overlooking the Caribbean. The menu features moderately priced savoury fresh grilled fish and steaks in tropical marinades and sauces.

Culebra

14km north of Vieques, and 27km east of Fajardo, tiny **CULEBRA** is surrounded by two dozen islets and cays that afford **snorkelling** and **dive** sites touted as some of the Caribbean's best. Just as spectacular are the island's miles and miles of stunning **beaches**, many of them wild and deserted. A rusty tank can be found on the famous Flamenco beach as a reminder of when the US Navy used Culebra for bombing practice, until protests caused them to move to Vieques in 1975. Since 1909, the entire coastline and large portions of the 7000-acre interior have been designated a **wildlife refuge** to protect the rare sea birds and turtles that nest here.

You'll likely have no other choice but to concern yourself with that natural environment while you're here; home to about 2000 inhabitants, the island has no nightclubs or resorts, and only one sleepy town, called **Dewey**, a ragtag assemblage of two-storey wooden lean-tos, bars and restaurants whose streets are full of washed-up drifters just hanging about.

Arrival, information and getting around

The minuscule **airport** is just north of Dewey, right by the main roads that run across the island. The **ferry** arrives at one end of Calle Pedro Márquez, Dewey's main strip, if you can call it that. It is home to Banco Popular, which has an ATM machine, a branch of the US Post Office, and the Town Hall (☎787/742-3288), which also houses a rather limited **tourist information office**. Far more useful is the Culebra Tourist Guide, ask around for a copy or order from ⊛www.culebraguides.com.

Públicos will run you to beaches and pick you up at a specified time – try Willy's (☎787/742-3537). If need be, you can rent four-wheel-drive vehicles, but book ahead and be aware that many of the roads are in bad condition. Jerry's Jeeps (☎787/742-0587) is right by the airport. Otherwise, **bikes** may well be the way to go, available for US$10 a day from Culebra Bike Shop (☎787/742-2209). To get to the outer cays, rent a **kayak** from your guesthouse; get dropped off and collected later with Ocean View Water Taxi (☎787/360-9807 or 787/742-2601) or fun Tanamá Glass Bottom Boat (☎787/501-0011) for around $40; or even hire your own boat with Culebra Boat Rental (☎787/742-3559).

Around the island

In 1909, President Theodore Roosevelt learned of the migratory bird colonies here and curtailed human exposure by establishing the **Culebra National Wildlife Refuge**, which encompasses one-third of the island's 7000 acres. Overseen by the US Fish and Wildlife Service (☎787/742-0115, ⊛www.fws.gov/southeast/culebra), these protected lands are the domain of endangered sea turtles, including the seven-foot-long leatherback turtle (which can weigh up to 1400 pounds); and some 50,000 sea birds, of thirteen species, including terns, boobies, white-tailed and red-billed tropic birds, and laughing gulls. Between March and April, extra hands are needed to help out with **leatherback turtle breeding**, an extraordinary experience to behold. For more information or to sign up as a volunteer, call ☎877-772-6725.

On the north coast, about 3km north of Dewey, you'll come to a perfectly shaped bay that shelters the deservedly world-famous **Flamenco Beach**, a *balneario* with showers and legal campsites. The arcing white sand is as fine as baking flour, and the wide, smooth beach allows a gentle entrance into the water. As with most other island beaches, it's deserted and paradisiacal during the week, much busier at weekends.

Playa Zoni, way over on the island's eastern side, and **Playa Brava**, to the north, are both fine beaches, though trickier to reach. To get to Zoni, take Rte 250 from Dewey and continue on right to the end of this hilly road. For Brava, turn left off Rte 250 at Km4 by the Culebra Museum, go to the end of this road until it turns into a battered track and follow that on foot for a good twenty minutes to the beach. Be warned that Brava, a favourite with surfers, can be extremely rough, so don't swim there alone. Undertows and rip tides are common on the north side of the island.

Some of the Caribbean's best **diving** and **snorkelling** is on Culebra, whose reefs are protected by the US Fish and Wildlife Service. The whole of its sheltered western shore, angled towards the south, is fringed with a pristine coral reef where calm and clear waters provide excellent visibility for the barracuda, stingray, blue tang, brain corals, lavender sea fans, trumpet fish, parrot fish and hawksbill turtles that lurk around the island. A twenty-minute scenic hike over the hill from the entrance to Playa Flamenco (or a water taxi from Dewey) will take you to lovely **Playa Tamarindo** and **Playa Carlos Rosario**, which provide easy access to the reef, perfect for snorkelling. Of the offshore cays, **Culebrita** is a favourite for observing underwater wildlife, as well as for its splendid beaches and ruined lighthouse, built in 1882. Culebra Dive Shop (☎787/742-0566) can take you **diving** at Culebrita, and also has information on **kayak rental**, **fly fishing** for bonefish, **snorkelling**, and **underwater photography**. Also try Culebra Divers (☎787/742-0803).

Accommodation

Club Seabourne Carreterra Fulladoza, Km 1.5 ☎787/742-3169, ⊛www.clubseaborne.com. Excellent, clean cottages, villas and rooms, some with furnished balconies overlooking the water. Pool and excellent restaurant and bar on premises. Rather upscale for Culebra. ⑧
Culebra Beach Villas Flamenco Beach ☎787/767-7575, ⊛www.culebrabeachrental.com. Attractive beachfront villas and apartments with full kitchens; it's understandably very popular, so book early. ⑤
Flamenco Beach ☎787/742-0700, ⊛www. gobpr.net/culebra. This legal campground on the *balneario* is a mob scene at weekends and in summer. ①

Mamacita's Calle Castelar, Dewey ☎787/742-0090, ⊛www.mamacitaspr.com. Handful of modest apartments and rooms above one of Dewey's most popular restaurants. ④
Posada La Hamaca Calle Castelar, Dewey ☎787/742-3516, ⊛www.posada.com. Clean, inexpensive, basic rooms in the heart of "town" near the canal. Terrace overlooking water. ④
Villa Boheme Carreterra Fulladoza ☎787/742-3508, ⊛www.villaboheme.com. Very pleasant rooms, some with sea views, balconies or sun decks. Those that don't have a room with kitchenettes can use the communal kitchen and barbecue. Beach gear rentals are available. ④

Eating, drinking and nightlife

Club Seabourne Carreterra Fulladoza, Km 1.5
☎787/742-3169, ⊛www.clubseaborne.com. Fish
and chips, seafood stroganoff, lobster, and steaks;
all a bit upscale for Culebra.

Dinghy Dock across the drawbridge on Carreterra
Fulladoza ☎787/742-0233. Overlooking the bay,
gourmet breakfasts – smoked salmon, eggs
benedict, etc – and grilled foods for dinner, costing
US$14–20. Lively bar.

El Batey Calle Escudero towards airport from
Dewey ☎787/742-3828. Great, cheap grilled
burgers and *criollo* food, kitchen closes after lunch.

Worth visiting Saturday night for hot, hot *salsa* and
serious local Boricúa vibe.

Mamacita's Calle Castelar, Dewey ☎787/742-
0090, ⊛www.mamacitaspr.com. Waterside dining
under a tin-roof gazebo, where you can enjoy
criollo food, burgers and burritos, accompanied
by calypso and reggae music. The bar is popular
with locals.

Oasis Calle Pedro Márquez, Dewey ☎787/742-
3175. Superb, inexpensive pizzas with gourmet
toppings, tasty salads and the "coldest beer on
Culebra" attract a hip but unpretentious crowd.

The Virgin Islands

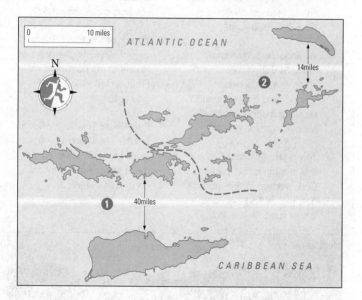

The Virgin Islands highlights

✳ **Charlotte Amalie, St Thomas** Take advantage of the duty-free savings on everything from discount rum to diamonds. See p.442

✳ **Magens Bay Beach, St Thomas** This half-mile-long stretch of powder on St Thomas is consistently voted one of the best beaches in the world. See p.446

✳ **Virgin Islands National Park, St John** Over 12,000 acres divided between pristine land for hiking and stunning marine areas for snorkelling. See p.456

✳ **Jump-Up, St Croix** Catch this monthly street party in Christiansted for live music, dancing, stilt walkers and lots of food. See p.467

✳ **Bomba's Full-Moon Party, Tortola** Decadent bash presided over by the self-proclaimed King of Tortola. See p.480

✳ **The Baths, Virgin Gorda** Scramble through the grottoes, caves and pools created by these outsize volcanic rocks. See p.487

✳ **Wreck of the RMS *Rhone*** View the haunting remains of *Rhone* at the bottom of Sir Francis Drake Channel. See p.484

✳ **Painkillers** The *Soggy Dollar* in White Bay, Jost Van Dyke is said to have invented these intense rum concoctions. See p.494

△ The Baths beach on Virgin Gorda

Introduction and basics

World-famous beaches or secret stretches of glowing sand, lush green mountain peaks or colonial port towns, a castaway's complete seclusion or the revelry of an all night party – whatever your fancy, the **Virgin Islands** have a bit of something to satisfy it. Made up of over one hundred islands, cays, islets, reefs and rocks, the islands attract in excess of two million visitors a year for the **fishing**, **sailing**, and spectacular **snorkelling** and **diving**. No two islands are the same and their proximity to one another makes it easy – and advisable – to island hop. The colonial legacy, which has seen many flags flying over the islands in the past three hundred years (Dutch, French, Danish, British and Spanish to name a few), has left some charming historic architecture, particularly in the towns of the United States Virgin Islands, together with atmospheric ruins of sugar plantations and a culture that is something of a melting pot.

A territory of the USA, the **United States Virgin Islands (USVI)** can, with their international cuisine, mini-shopping malls and American-style amenities, initially seem rather too much like its big brother with the added advantage of duty-free shopping. But further exploration reveals the strong roots of West Indian culture, no more so than at Carnival time when the streets of St Thomas are overtaken with colourful costume parades, bands and food stalls selling delicious creole food. The **British Virgin Islands (BVI)** are less touched by tourism and the majority of visitors are yachters – the calm waters, gentle breezes, sheltered bays and short distances between anchorages have long made the BVI a **sailing** paradise.

The mainstay of the **economy** in the Virgin Islands is tourism, though the USVI have a lucrative sideline in the Hess Oil Refinery and a reasonable manufacturing industry, while the BVI receive significant income from licence fees paid by foreign companies taking advantage of the BVI's tax exemptions.

Where to go

Most visitors to the Virgin Islands head straight for St Thomas, though it can feel overcrowded and familiar; more serene surroundings await on St Croix and St John, especially the latter, which offers excellent **hiking.**

In the BVI, the main draws are the wondrous **reefs** and sandy **beaches**, along with myriad watersports and boating activities; **Brewer's Bay Beach** in particular has excellent snorkelling, while the well-preserved wreck of the **RMS Rhone** off Salt Island is the highlight of any visit. To the east, peaceful Virgin Gorda is home to the unusual natural attraction known as **The Baths**, colossal boulders surrounded by pools teeming with marine life.

When to go

The Virgin Islands' **climate** is subtropical, with temperatures ranging from 26°C to 31°C (79–89°F) in summer to 22°C to 28°C (72–82°F) in winter. Easterly trade winds keep the humidity low, with May and June the stickiest months. Heavy rain is rare except during **hurricane season** (June–Nov) when most of the annual rainfall of 100mm arrives, though most of it is in the form of brief showers. The last major hurricanes to hit the Virgins, Hurricane Luis and Hurricane Marilyn, occurred within two weeks of each other in September 1995 and caused several billion dollars of damage. Unsurprisingly, there are good deals to be had in hurricane season – November is the best because off-season prices are still in effect, yet the weather is often just as good as in December. Some hotels and restaurants will close for the months of August and/or September.

Arrival

The main gateways to the Virgin Islands are the **Cyril E. King International Airport** on St Thomas and **Henry E. Rohlsen Airport** on St Croix. There are no direct flights to the BVI; you have to go via St Thomas or San Juan, Puerto Rico – American Eagle, LIAT and Air Sunshine all operate daily flights from San Juan to Tortola and Air St Thomas flies from San Juan to Virgin Gorda.

Cruise ships arrive in **Charlotte Amalie, St Thomas**; **Frederiksted, St Croix**; and **Road Town, Tortola**. If you are arriving on your own boat you must clear customs. See the end of the Getting Around section for a list of customs points.

Information

All main towns in the Virgin Islands have **tourist offices**. The official agencies are the **US Virgin Islands Department of Tourism** (ⓦ www.usvitourism.vi) and the **BVI Tourist Board** (ⓦ www.bvitourism.com). Your lodgings may also be an excellent source of local information – resorts and large hotels in particular will often help guests (and sometimes non-guests) set up trips, car rental and activities, especially on the smaller islands without official tourist offices.

Money and costs

The **currency** for the US and British Virgin Islands is the **US dollar**. Branches of major **banks**, most with **ATMs**, are located in most towns. Major **credit cards** are accepted widely on the islands at hotels, restaurants and car rental agencies. However, there's always a risk that some small out-of-the-way place won't take them or their system is down, so it pays to travel with some cash if you plan to go off the beaten track. **Travellers' cheques** are also widely accepted and most hotels allow guests to cash personal cheques. Be warned that there's a government **room tax** (8 percent in the USVI; 7 percent in the BVI) on all accommodation and an 8–15 percent service charge on everything else in hotels, so check bills before **tipping**. The standard tip for good service is 15 percent in restaurants and bars; around 10 percent for taxis.

Getting around

Hopping **from island to island** is easy either by air or, more popularly, using the network of inter-island ferries. Just remember to bring proof of citizenship when passing back and forth between the BVI and USVI. **On the islands** themselves you can do much of your exploring on foot using taxis, rental cars, bikes or boats for longer distances.

By air

Getting between the islands **by air** is relatively easy. Between **St Thomas and St Croix** there are a couple of options: American Eagle and Cape Air fly this route (about US$100–135 round-trip) or there's Seaborne Airlines' seaplanes (several daily; 15min; ☎340/773-6442, ⓦwww.seaborneairlines.com) – cheaper and more of a thrill. There's no airport on **St John** so you need to take a ferry either from Charlotte Amalie (nearest to the airport; US$7 one-way; 40min), or Red Hook (US$3 one-way; 20min). The car ferry (same ports) costs US$35 round-trip.

To get **from the USVI to BVI** there are scheduled flights from St Thomas to: Tortola (daily with LIAT, CaribAir, Air Sunshine; Mon, Wed & Fri with Clair Aero (☎284/495-2271); Virgin Gorda (Mon–Sat with Air St Thomas); and Anegada (Mon, Wed & Fri with Clair Aero). From St Croix there are daily flights to Tortola with Air Sunshine. Charter flights to Tortola, Virgin Gorda and Anegada are always available with Fly BVI. Within the BVI, there are regular flights by Fly BVI and Clair Aero.

By bus and car

On the main islands of the USVI there's a government-operated **bus** service, **VITRAN** (☎340/774-5678), which makes designated stops (look for rainbow-coloured buses on signposts). While buses are cheap (generally US$1 per trip and 25¢ per transfer), they are not very reliable and stops aren't always conveniently located and trips, especially in and around Charlotte Amalie, can be a slow process. Apart from the irregular shared taxi vans on Tortola there is no public transport on the BVI. In most cases you'll find it easier on both the USVI and BVI to get a taxi or, better still, rent a **car**, which is easily done on most of the major islands. Book your car in advance if you're coming during peak season and expect to pay upwards of US$45–55 per day (weekly rates are lower). Note that in the USVI and BVI cars **drive on the left** side of the road. On the BVI you'll need a **BVI driving licence** (US$10) that can be issued by the car rental company. **Taxis** in the Virgin Islands charge by the destination so it pays to pack in as many people as you can. Rates are set by the government and taxi drivers are required to carry a rate card; ask to see it if you're unsure of the fare and always agree on your price before you set off.

By sea

There is an excellent network of **inter-island ferries**, though it's advisable to call ahead for times as they often change. As a rough guide to prices, a return fare between Tortola and St. John is US$40; between Tortola and Virgin Gorda US$20. Between St Thomas and St Croix there is a high-speed catamaran (75min; Dec–May only; US$64 round-trip).

Alternatively you may prefer to **charter a yacht**, either with a crew or by yourself (bareboat). Either way you're looking at upwards of US$2000 per week for a boat in high season, and if you're going **bareboat** you'll have to demonstrate that you have sufficient sailing experience. You'll also need accurate maps and charts to navigate the many reefs surrounding the islands. You must clear **customs** on entry to the USVI (unless you are coming from a US port) at Charlotte Amalie, Cruz Bay, Christiansted or Frederiksted. In the BVI, customs points are at Great Harbour, Jost Van Dyke, Spanish Town on Virgin Gorda, and Road Town and Soper's Hole on Tortola.

Ferries between the BVI

Jost Van Dyke Ferry Service and M/V When ⓣ284/494-2997. Between West End, Tortola and Jost Van Dyke.
Marina Cay Ferry ⓣ284/494-2174. Free ferry connecting Beef Island to Marina Cay.
North Sound Express ⓣ284/495-2138. Between Beef Island and Virgin Gorda.
Paradise Express – New Horizon Ferry Service ⓣ284/496-8200. Between West End, Tortola and Jost Van Dyke.
Peter Island Ferry ⓣ284/495-2000. Between Tortola and Peter Island.
Saba Rock Ferry ⓣ284/495-9966. Between the North Sound and Saba Rock.
Smith's Ferry Services ⓣ284/494-4454. Between Tortola, Virgin Gorda, and Anegada.

Ferries between the USVI and BVI

Inter-Island ⓣ340/776-6597 or 284/495-4166. Between Red Hook, St John, Tortola, Virgin Gorda and Jost Van Dyke.
Native Son ⓣ340/774-8685 or 284/495-4617, ⓦwww.nativesonbvi.com. Between Tortola (Road Town and West End) and St Thomas (Charlotte Amalie & Red Hook).
Nubian Princess ⓣ284/495-4999. Between West End Tortola and St John and Red Hook, St Thomas.
Smith's Ferry Services ⓣ284/494-4454. Between Tortola (Road Town and West End), Virgin Gorda and St Thomas.
Speedy's ⓣ284/495-5240. Between Tortola, Virgin Gorda and St Thomas.
Tortola Fast Ferry ⓣ284/494-2323 or 340/777-2800, ⓦwww.tortolafastferry.com. Between Charlotte Amalie, St Thomas and Road Town, Tortola

Ferries between the USVI

Inter-Island ⓣ340/776-6597. Between Red Hook and St John.
Transportation Services ⓣ340/776-6282. Between Charlotte Amalie, Red Hook and St John (Cruz Bay).
Virgin Islands Fast Ferry ⓣ340/719-0099, ⓦwww.virginislandsfastferry.com. Between Charlotte Amalie and St Croix (Gallows Bay), high season only.

Accommodation

Accommodation in the Virgin Islands covers the entire scale from campsites with bare sites to super-luxury resorts on private islands. There aren't any youth hostels in the Virgin Islands but you'll still be able to find some budget accommodation in most places. **Campsites** range US$12–35 for a bare site. The next rung up, **guesthouses**, vary widely in quality, price and size from basic rooms above a bar to cosy beachside inns, but you can expect to pay around US$50–120 for a double room per night.

Hotels range from small places (mainly in towns and villages) with a pool and bar (for around US$75–180) to resorts with beachfront accommodation and all facilities (upwards of US$150). Bear in mind the room tax (see above). If you're planning on a lengthy stay it might be worth checking out renting a private villa or home.

Depending on the season, rates can vary widely. Depending on the room you choose, it's generally 20–40 percent cheaper during low season (May 1 to Dec 14). If you are visiting in high season you should book a few months in advance to be sure of getting the place you want.

Food and drink

Because the Virgin Islands have flown several flags during their history there is a rich culinary heritage combining Dutch, English, French, African, West Indian and other influences. And while there's plenty of fine international cuisine to be had (albeit to a lesser extent on the smaller BVI such as Jost Van Dyke and Anegada), you should definitely try out the many wonderful West Indian dishes showcasing the best of creole cuisine. Generally speaking, you'll pay around US$6–15 for a meal at a café or standard restaurant; US$18–30 for an entrée at more upmarket places. The USVI has the full range of international cuisine; eating on the BVI you're more likely to have to stick to West Indian food, with international dishes confined mainly to upmarket places or snack-style places serving sandwiches, burgers and pizzas.

Restaurants often close for several hours between meals, generally 3–5pm and many places close before 10.30pm. As always you should reserve in popular places and call ahead for those in out-of-the-way spots to make sure they're open. When it comes to dress, the BVI are a little more formal than most other islands. For some of the smarter restaurants men are advised to wear long trousers and a collared shirt.

In the Virgin Islands, West Indian fare is the food of choice for locals. An average dish consists of spiced meats, lots of starches and very few vegetables. Conch, a shellfish that has a similar texture and taste to squid, and goat, which is very similar to pork, are served almost any way you can imagine. A popular dish that often sells out quickly is conch in butter sauce. Common side dishes include fried plantains, fry bread called johnny cakes, and fungi, which is a sort of stuffing made from corn meal and okra. Many fish and chicken dishes are served with fruit salsa, or a coconut milk sauce. Spicy foods, such as foods rubbed with Caribbean curries or Jamaican jerk spices, are also popular. For a quick and inexpensive meal, locals grab a roti – meat, potatoes, carrots and onions simmered in a creamy curry sauce and folded between warm flatbread, occasionally with some chutney on the side. Be careful when you eat a chicken roti, because locals eat them with the bones. Similar is a pate, a deep-fried pasty with fillings such as beef, goat, chicken, conch or saltfish. Kallaloo (or callaloo) is a seasoned stew of assorted greens, meats, and seafood.

Rum – in particular Cruzan rum made on St Croix – is definitely the spirit of choice and rum punch is the most popular rum drink. Locals drink a mixture of two shots of dark rum, a teaspoon of sugar and a splash of water. Virgin Island beers include Caribe (very similar to Corona), Foxey's Lager and Blackbeard Ale, but you can also get foreign beers like Red Stripe, Heineken and Guinness.

Phones, post and the Internet

Local calls on public payphones typically cost 35 cents for five minutes. To call the islands from overseas dial the international dialling code + 1 + area code + number. For international calls you are best off using one of a number of prepaid phone cards which are available in US$10 increments from shops, post offices and most hotels. If you carry a mobile phone, try dialing ☎6611 to enquire about use on the island, though it's best to enquire with your carrier well in advance of making your trip.

Post offices (open generally Mon–Fri 7.30am–4.30pm & Sat 7.30am–noon) can be found in most main towns. However,

> The **country code** for the BVI is ☎284; for the USVI it's ☎340.

many hotels will sell you stamps and mail letters for you.

Some hotels offer free **internet access** to guests; otherwise you'll have to log on at one of the cybercafés – they're not widespread but most major towns will have one. The main USVI **newspapers** are *The V.I. Daily News* and *The Independent* – both on St Thomas, and *The St Croix Avis*. There's also a free weekly called *Island Delights* which is a good source of **entertainment** listings. In the BVI it's the *BVI Beacon* (Thurs) and *The Island Sun* (Sat), plus the free weekly, *Limin' Times*, which carries **listings** of upcoming events.

Opening hours, holidays and festivals

For the most part in the USVI and BVI **businesses** are open Monday to Saturday 8am–5pm, and **shops,** museums and historic sights Monday to Saturday 9am–5pm. On the USVI **bank opening hours** are Mon–Fri 9am–3pm, and some open Saturday morning; BVI banks close slightly earlier at around 2.30pm. Government buildings are open 9am–5pm weekdays. Always **call ahead** to make sure your destination is open, especially in the off-season. Both the USVI and the BVI celebrate local **public holidays** as well as many of the holidays celebrated in their mother countries. The government and banks close for major holidays, but stores, restaurants and tourist attractions generally

stay open. The main cultural event to look out for in the Virgin Islands is **Carnival** – a couple of weeks of costumed street parades including mocko jumbies (stilt walkers), calypso and steelpan bands, street stalls and all-night partying and dancing. St Thomas Carnival – the second largest in the Caribbean after Trinidad – takes place the last two weeks in April (see p.448). Some other Virgin Islands have mini-carnivals – Virgin Gorda's is in mid-February and St John's the first few days of July – and if you happen to be in

Public holidays

USVI
January 1 New Year's Day
January 6 Three Kings' Day
January Martin Luther King Jr's Birthday (third Mon)
Third Monday in February Presidents' Day
March 31 Transfer Day
March/April Maundy Thursday, Good Friday, Easter Monday
Last Monday in May Memorial Day
July 3 Emancipation Day
July 4 Independence Day
July Supplication Day (date varies)
First Monday in September Labour Day
Second Monday in October Columbus Day
November 1 Liberty Day
November 11 Veteran's Day
Fourth Thursday in November Thanksgiving Day
December 25 Christmas Day
December 26 Boxing Day

BVI
January 1 New Year's Day
March 11 Commonwealth Day
March/April Good Friday, Easter Monday
May/June Whit Monday
June 11 Queen's Birthday
July 1 Territory Day
August BVI August Festival Days
October 22 St Ursula's Day
November 12 Birthday of Heir to the Throne
December 25 Christmas Day
December 26 Boxing Day

Emergency phone numbers

For **emergencies**, you can dial T911 in the USVI on any telephone for fire, police or medical assistance. In the BVI the number is T911 or 999. For **marine emergencies**, call Virgin Islands Search and Rescue (VISAR) by dialling the emergency numbers or via VHF Ch.16.

the BVI the last two weeks of July you'll be swept along in the nightly entertainment and music of the **BVI Summer Festival**.

Watersports and outdoor activities

The Virgin Islands are a paradise for almost any **watersports** you can imagine – diving, snorkelling, windsurfing, parasailing – as well as fishing, sailing and hiking. See the individ-ual island accounts for details of companies offering anything from snorkelling day-trips to weeklong sailing courses. **Fishing** is a popular pastime on the islands – wahoo are hot from August to February, marlin September to January, mahi mahi from February to May and tuna November to January. However, note that the removal of any marine organism from BVI waters is illegal for non-British Virgin Islanders without a recreational **fishing permit**. Call the Fisheries Division at ℡284/494-3429 for information.

History

Although there is some evidence that the Virgin Islands were populated by Amerindian tribes as far back as 1500 BC, the earliest tribe known to have settled here was the Igneri, the first wave of **Arawaks**, who arrived from South America in huge canoes, landing on St Croix sometime between 50 and 650 AD. The next wave of Arawaks – the Taíno – arrived around 1300; skilled in agriculture they set about farming the islands of St Croix, St John and St Thomas only to be displaced in the early part of the fifteenth century by the aggressive warrior tribe known as the **Caribs**. By the time Columbus set foot on the islands in 1493 during his second voyage, the Caribs were well established and the indigenous Arawak tribes had dwindled to a fraction of their original number. Columbus named the islands **Las Virgenes**, "the virgins" – their sheer number and pristine condition reminding him of the legend of St Ursula, a feisty fourth-century European princess, and her "army" of 11,000 virgins, who were raped and killed by a Hun prince and his henchmen. After the Spaniards pretty much wiped out the entire population of native peoples, the islands were safe for colonization and ripe for mass planting of sugar cane.

The first half of the seventeenth century witnessed a period of intense **colonial squabbling** with the British, Dutch, Spanish and French establishing proto-colonies on various islands until the **Danes** interceded in 1666 and began their period of domination over the islands west of St John, while the **English** gained control of the eastern section of islands. The Danes are credited with developing their islands into some of the busiest ports in the West Indies; the **slave trade** boomed, **pirates** were a common (and often welcome) sight, but more importantly, **sugarcane** flowered into a major cash crop. However, owing to many factors, including natural disasters and the **emancipation of the islands' slaves** (1834 in the British West Indies, 1848 in the Danish West Indies), the economy of the islands soured in the early to mid-1800s.

The **US** didn't get their hands on the Danish West Indies until the twentieth century. Worried that the Germans would use the islands as submarine bases in **World War I**, the US government purchased them from the Danes in 1917 for US$25 million – to the approval of much of the population who anticipated American investment in education and health. Meanwhile in the BVI, a "crown colony" since the 1870s, rumblings of dissatisfaction were beginning over their negligent and distant ruling power. The effect was catching and by the **Thirties** most citizens of the USVI were feeling similarly let down by the US: their expected improvements in living conditions hadn't materialized and the islands had become little more than a US naval base with the attendant problem of unruly sailors. A visit by President Roosevelt in 1934 revitalized the US attitude to the USVI and before long huge improvements to the islands' infrastructure were in full swing. But by the end of the **Forties** both territories were actively seeking more **independence** and the right to elect their own government – the BVI got theirs in 1967 when they were permitted a ministerial system of government headed by an elected Chief Minister. The following year, the USVI gained the right to elect their own governor. No news is good news – since that time the highlights of island history have been the tragic devastation of **hurricanes**. The most potent were Hugo in 1989 which hit St Croix not once but twice on a sudden change of direction and Marilyn which left St Thomas eighty percent devastated in 1995.

Today, the USVI are considered a territory of the United States and have one seat in Congress. Islanders are US citizens and pay taxes, but they cannot vote for the President of the United States. The BVI are a dependent territory of Britain and are overseen by a governor appointed by the British monarch, though they are more or less self-governing. The governor presides over the five-member Executive Council, while the Legislative Council consists of a twelve-member elected body with a ministerial system.

8.1

The United States Virgin Islands

Known as America's Paradise, the **UNITED STATES VIRGIN ISLANDS,** with its sea-swept landscapes, historic towns, duty-free shopping and luxurious resorts, bask in a combination of familiar yet exotic that makes them one of the most popular cruise-ship destinations in the Caribbean. America aside, it's the Danes who have had the most influence on the look of the islands. Successful sugar cane exporters and slave dealers, they built most of the major towns, and there are plentiful reminders of their presence in the **colonial architecture** of the historic cities of Charlotte Amalie and Christiansted and in the ruins of sugar plantations scattered across the green mountainous slopes. But it's the slaves and their descendents that have defined the culture, creating their own forms of music and developing a rich cuisine.

Of the sixty islands, islets and cays (most of which are uninhabited) that make up the USVI, the biggest and busiest are St Thomas, St Croix and St John. Each has a distinctive mood and culture, and you haven't really seen the USVI until you've checked out all three. **St Thomas**, with its picturesque capital, Charlotte Amalie, is the most American of the islands – hip and stylish (at least compared to the rest of the Caribbean) with upmarket shops and restaurants and a history born of trade

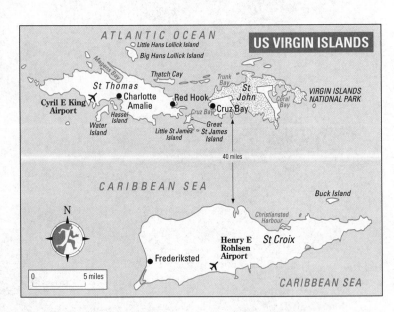

rather than sugar. **St John,** the greenest of the three, is also the smallest, and its National Park, part on land, part underwater, is the major attraction for its miles of hiking trails and quiet beaches. **St Croix**, the largest of the islands, is the most distant so sees little of the hordes that flock to St Thomas and St John, though its rich culture and the ports of Christiansted and Frederiksted still attract visitors with a mix of historic sights, shopping and good restaurants.

St Thomas

The most accessible and Americanized of the Virgins, **ST THOMAS** is high on the list of Caribbean destinations for cruise ships and honeymoons. Its mercantile roots – the port at **Charlotte Amalie** has been an important merchant centre since the 1700s – still prevail and Charlotte Amalie's renovated old warehouses now house a wealth of galleries, restaurants and shops. It can all seem a bit too sanitized, but if you look deeper – a trip to the western side of the island or *Ashley's Mobile Restaurant* is a good start – you'll find Caribbean culture alive and kicking. The small town of **Red Hook** offers all the amenities of Charlotte Amalie on a smaller scale. It doesn't have much in the way of historical buildings, but the harbour hops with yachters and those seeking ferries for St John and beyond. The north and east of the island have the nicest **beaches**, including **Magens Bay**, consistently voted one of the world's best. Be aware that beaches, shops and the roads themselves can get congested depending on the number of cruise ships in port.

Arrival, information and getting around

St Thomas's **Cyril E. King Airport** is three miles west of Charlotte Amalie. VIT-RAN **buses** run from the airport to Charlotte Amalie; the first leaves at 6am and the last at 9.30pm. **Taxis** (for 2 persons) to Charlotte Amalie cost around US$5; for resorts on the eastern end of the island it's US$10–20. Most major **car rental** companies have offices at the airport and in Havensight Mall (see also below).

Information booths at the airport offer free brochures and maps, including helpful publications such as *St Thomas This Week* and the *West Indies Visitor's Guide*. In downtown Charlotte Amalie, there is a USVI Division of Tourism office across from Nisky Center mall (☎340/774-8784). There's also a National Park Service visitor centre across the street from the ferry dock in Red Hook. **Post offices** are located in Emancipation Garden, Charlotte Amalie (☎340/774-3750); on Veteran's Drive, Charlotte Amalie (☎340/774-6980); and at the Havensight Mall (☎340/776-9897). Charlotte Amalie has a few **Internet cafés** including Beans, Bytes & Websites in the Royal Dane Mall (☎340/777-7089); Little Switzerland Internet Café, Main Street (☎340/776-2010); and Soapy's Internet Café across from Havensight Mall.

Getting around the island, VITRAN **buses** (☎340/774-5678) operate services to Red Hook (hourly 5.30am–8.30pm) and to the west as well. **Taxis** come in all shapes and sizes – vans, cars and trucks; reputable operators include Allie's Taxi Stand (☎340/777-8007); East End Taxi Service, Ferry Dock (☎340/775-6974); and Islander Taxi & Tour Services (☎340/774-4077). From town to the east of the island, including Red Hook, the fare for two people is US$10–15. General two-hour sightseeing tours go for about US$40.

Although you don't need a **car** on St Thomas, it will give you a much better feel for the island and you can even take the car ferry (US$35 round-trip) over to St John for the day. Options include Avis (☎340/774-1468); Budget (☎340/776-5774); Discount Car Rental (☎340/776-4858); and Tri Island Car Rental (☎340/776-2879). You might opt for a **scooter** from Biz Rentals (☎340/774-5840) in Havensight or Zip Rentals (☎340/715-1501) in Red Hook.

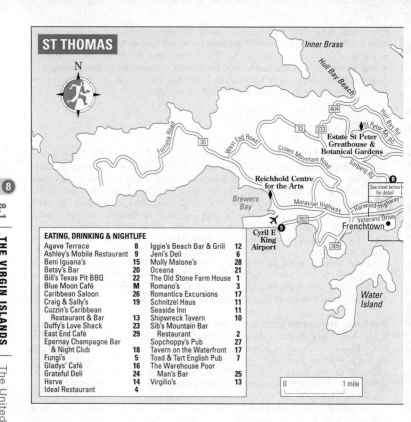

ST THOMAS

N

Inner Brass

Hull Bay Beach

404

33 333

St Peter Mt Rd

Hull Bay Rd

Estate St Peter
Greathouse &
Botanical Gardens

Foruna Road

30

West End Road

Crown Mountain Road

Solberg Rd

Reichhold Centre
for the Arts

Brewers
Bay

Moravian Highway

Harwood Highway

Veterans Drive

302

Frenchtown

Cyril E
King
Airport

305

See inset below
for detail

Water
Island

EATING, DRINKING & NIGHTLIFE

Agave Terrace	8	Iggie's Beach Bar & Grill	12
Ashley's Mobile Restaurant	9	Jeni's Deli	6
Beni Iguana's	15	Molly Malone's	28
Betsy's Bar	20	Oceana	21
Bill's Texas Pit BBQ	22	The Old Stone Farm House	1
Blue Moon Café	M	Romano's	3
Caribbean Saloon	26	Romantica Excursions	17
Craig & Sally's	19	Schnitzel Haus	11
Cuzzin's Caribbean		Seaside Inn	11
Restaurant & Bar	13	Shipwreck Tavern	10
Duffy's Love Shack	23	Sib's Mountain Bar	
East End Café	29	Restaurant	2
Epernay Champagne Bar		Sopchoppy's Pub	27
& Night Club	18	Tavern on the Waterfront	17
Fungi's	5	Toad & Tart English Pub	7
Gladys' Café	16	The Warehouse Poor	
Grateful Deli	24	Man's Bar	25
Herve	14	Virgilio's	13
Ideal Restaurant	4		

0   1 mile

Charlotte Amalie and around

CHARLOTTE AMALIE sweeps around St Thomas Harbour in a striking combination of red-roofed whitewashed buildings backed by lush green villa-dotted hills. Up to eleven cruise ships can occupy the harbour on any given day and hundreds of ferries and yachts pass through each week, so that at times the population of 12,500 seems to double and the streets jam with bargain-hunting tourists. Many of them head straight for the famous **shopping district** whose renovated merchant warehouses contain shops selling everything from cut-rate diamonds, perfume and fine textiles to monstrous Cuban cigars. But there's much more to Charlotte Amalie than shopping – the town is full of historic sites like the **99 Steps**, **Fort Christian** and the **St Thomas Synagogue**. Named Charlotte Amalie in honour of the wife of Danish King Christian V, the Danish influence here is strong – much of the historic **colonial architecture** is still standing and streets are commonly referred to by the Danish word *gades*. On the peninsula due west of Charlotte Amalie, the smaller, quieter neighbourhood of **FRENCHTOWN** has been home to most of St Thomas's French descendants for centuries. You will find some fantastic restaurants and bars here and the quaint yellow one-room cottage that houses the **French Heritage Museum** (☎340/714-2583, Mon–Sat 9am–6pm, free).

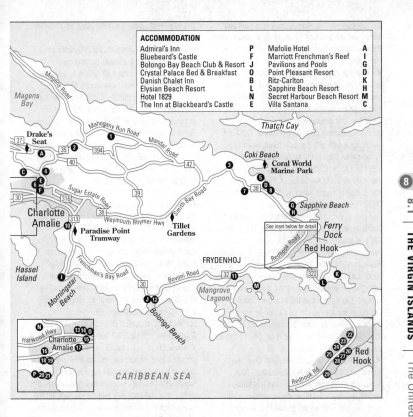

ACCOMMODATION

Admiral's Inn	**P**	Mafolie Hotel	**A**
Bluebeard's Castle	**F**	Marriott Frenchman's Reef	**I**
Bolongo Bay Beach Club & Resort	**J**	Pavilions and Pools	**G**
Crystal Palace Bed & Breakfast	**O**	Point Pleasant Resort	**D**
Danish Chalet Inn	**B**	Ritz-Carlton	**K**
Elysian Beach Resort	**L**	Sapphire Beach Resort	**H**
Hotel 1829	**N**	Secret Harbour Beach Resort	**M**
The Inn at Blackbeard's Castle	**E**	Villa Santana	**C**

Accommodation

Charlotte Amalie and Frenchtown contain the majority of the island's small **hotels**, **historic inns** and **cosy B&Bs**. While they generally have pools, easy beach access is not an option and this is reflected in the price. There are only a few resorts nearby. For groups, the many **villas and private homes** tucked in the hills are a better option; try *Calypso Realty* (☎340/774-1620 or 1-800/747-4858, ⊛www.calypsorealty .com); *McLaughlin Anderson Luxury Villas* (☎340/776-0635 or 1-800/537-6246, ⊛www.mclaughlinanderson.com); *Paradise Properties* (☎340/779-1540 or 1-800/524-2038, ⊛www.st-thomas.com/paradiseproperties); or *VIP Villa Rentals* (☎407/464-9181 or 1-800/788-4847, ⊛www.viprentals.com). Unlike St John and St Croix, there is no camping on St Thomas.

Hotels and inns

Admiral's Inn Villa Olga, Frenchtown ☎340/774-1376 or 1-800/544-0493 ℱ340/774-8010. The only lodging of note in Frenchtown, half a mile away from the hustle and bustle of town. Of the twelve rooms, the four with the ocean views (and balconies) are more expensive. There is no restaurant on premises, but just downstairs is *The Pointe*. ⑤

Crystal Palace Bed and Breakfast Charlotte Amalie ☎340/777-2277. This classy mansion with

wrought-iron gates, is located in the heart of the historic district. Ask for a room overlooking the harbour. There are five rooms, some with private bath. ④

Danish Chalet Inn Solberg Road, Charlotte Amalie ☎340/774-5764 or 1-877/407-2567, ⊛www. danishchaletinn.com. Located in the hills above downtown, this West Indian-inspired B&B was recently renovated and at US$98 a night it's a good deal. The fifteen rooms have private baths and a/c. Check-in and amenities such as a pool and restaurant are provided by its 32-room sister hotel *Palms Court Harborview Hotel* (⑤) right across the street. ❹

Hotel 1829 Government Hill, Charlotte Amalie ☎340/776-1829 or 1-800/524-2002, ⓦwww.hotel1829.com. This bright orange building with huge mahogany shutters and a cool brick, fieldstone and natural wood interior is the most atmospheric small hotel on the island. The front porch, complete with bamboo furniture and cooled by overhead fans, is the perfect place to read a novel by Graham Greene, for whom, it is rumoured, the hotel was a favourite haunt. Rooms vary in size but all are good value, with prices starting at US$105 for a single. ❻

The Inn at Blackbeard's Castle Government Hill, Charlotte Amalie ☎340/776-1234 or 1-800/344-5771, ⓦwww.blackbeardscastle.com. At the centre of this hilltop hotel is the tower of so-called Blackbeard's Castle. The rest of the grounds are decorated with wonderful bronze statues of pirates including a mammoth one of the hotel namesake himself. The figures and the way the rooms and pools are spread out up and down various stairways gives the place the fascinating air of a ship. Garden rooms are cheaper at US$115 but the suites are worth the extra cash. ❼

Mafolie Hotel 7091 Estate Mafolie, Charlotte Amalie ☎340/774-2790 or 1-800/225-7035, ⓦwww.mafolie.com. The rooms in this hillside retreat are clean, the view of the harbour is stunning and free shuttles are provided to Magen's Beach and one-way to downtown in the morning.

The hotel restaurant is a great place for a sunset meal or cocktail. ❺

Villa Santana 2D Denmark Hill, Charlotte Amalie ☎340/776-1311, ⓦwww.st-thomas.com/villasantana. Built in the mid-1850s by exiled Mexican general Santa Anna (remember the Alamo?) from stolen money, this six-unit inn is located at the crown of Denmark Hill within easy walking distance to downtown. Units have been created out of the general's library, wine cellar, kitchen and so on, and are a steal at around US$125–135 per night. There is also the three-bedroom El Establo with full kitchen and two and a half baths which rents by the week at $2400. ❺

Resorts and condos

Bluebeard's Castle Bluebeard's Hill, Charlotte Amalie ☎340/774-1600 or 1-800/524-6599, ⓕ340/774-5134. Originally a fort built in 1735, this 170-room hotel overlooks the harbour and has a pool, fitness centre and tennis courts. A taxi is necessary to go just about anywhere and there are a lot of steps to climb. Standard rooms, starting at US$195, have most amenities, and all suites, US$395, have kitchenettes. ❽

Marriot Frenchman's Reef 5 Estate Bakkeroe, South Shore ☎340/776-8500 or 1-800/524-2000, ⓦwww.marriott.com. Though not without its imperfections – some rooms look a bit worn – the lavishly landscaped grounds are spacious and offer two private beaches, oceanfront tennis courts, five restaurants and bars everywhere you turn. All the rooms look to sea, and you can watch the cruises slip past. ❾

The Town

Most of Charlotte Amalie's sights are within the same square mile and can easily be explored on foot – the bustling **downtown** shopping area occupies the numerous narrow streets linking Waterfront Drive and Main Street (Dronningens Gade) while historic sights cluster on the slopes just east on **Government Hill**. Further east of downtown **Havensight Mall** offers yet more shopping and a couple of touristy diversions, or you can hop on a ferry to the calm beaches of **Hassel and Water Islands** in St Thomas Harbour.

Downtown

The town comes alive daily at around 5.30am at the outdoor **market** (fish and produce early on, clothing and crafts later) at Vendor's Plaza, in front of **Emancipation Park**, a shady respite from the hustle and bustle, which commemorates the 1848 emancipation of the island's slaves. Just below the park, on Waterfront Highway, is the red-brick **Fort Christian** (Mon–Fri 8am–4.30pm & Sat 10am–3pm), the oldest standing building on the island. Danish troops resisted attacks from the Spanish, British, French and pirates here and during its 300-year life the fort has also been a jail, church, courthouse, and home for the governor. Inside, the **Virgin Islands Museum** (Mon–Fri 8.30am–4.30pm; free) evocatively charts the islands' history from pre-colonial times to the present day. Due south, on Veteran's Drive, the lime-

The legend of Blackbeard

Blackbeard, made infamous in Robert Louis Stevenson's novel *Treasure Island*, is said to have walked the streets of Charlotte Amalie when the island was a legal refuge for pirates, who sold their contraband freely – wild days when anything and everything was legal and the town was affectionately known as Beer Hall. Born Edward Teach in Bristol, England, Blackbeard was the meanest man the seas have ever seen – a heavy drinker (rum mixed with gunpowder) and a notorious lady-killer (it is said he murdered all fourteen of his wives). Before boarding a target vessel he would light slow-burning fuse matches and tie them into his long hair and beard giving him a hellish appearance. When he was finally beheaded from behind while fighting the captain of a crippled vessel, his body was dumped into the sea where, legend has it, it swam three times round the ship before sinking.

green **Legislature Building** (daily 8am–5pm) is the place where the Danes transferred ownership of the islands to the US in 1917; today it's the seat of the USVI governing body. Head north on a steady climb up Government Hill, taking a break first at Norre Gade, where the Georgian-style **Frederick Lutheran Church** stands on the site of the first Danish church in the Virgin Islands, which was destroyed by fire. The current structure, built by black parishioner Jean Reeneaus, dates to the early nineteenth century. Northeast of the church, on Kongens Gade, the imposing white mansion of **Government House** (Mon–Fri 8am–5pm; free), built in 1867, was originally a meeting place for the Danish Colonial Council. Now the administrative headquarters of the US Virgin Islands it also houses a museum showcasing work by famous local artists like Camille Pissarro and Pepino Mangravatti. Just to the west is the start of the palm-lined **99 Steps** (there are actually 103), which lead north towards the top of Government Hill affording exquisite views of the harbour and beyond. Laid in the mid-1700s by Danes living in the hills, they were the original access to the waterfront and to **Blackbeard's Castle**, otherwise known as Fort Skytsborg, said to have been the tower the legendary pirate Blackbeard (see box above) used for an unobstructed view of the ocean.

On the way back to the main shopping area, stop off at Crystal Gade to see the charming **St Thomas Synagogue** (Mon–Fri 9am–4pm) with its white pillars, stone walls, mahogany pews and sand floor (symbolizing the Exodus from Egypt). The building dates to 1833 and is the western hemisphere's second oldest synagogue, not to mention the longest continually in service in America. Next door, the **Weibel Museum** (same hours; free) is an interesting exhibition of the three hundred years of Jewish history in the islands. Just before you hit the shops check out the **Camille Pissarro Gallery**, 14 Main St, where the artist was born in 1830. One of the founders of the French Impressionist school, Pissarro grew up on this street, working for his father; his experiences here would become the subjects of some of his later paintings.

Havensight

At the eastern end of the bay, Havensight has a few malls, the cruise ship dock and a couple of interesting but expensive attractions. For US$84, **Atlantis Submarines**, Havensight Cruise Ship Dock (☎340/776-5650), has a two-hour tour that will take you out to Buck Island to board a sub that descends 90ft below the water's surface. You can peer through portholes at stingrays, sharks and whatever else happens to swim by. Going to the other extreme, **St Thomas Skyride**, 9617 Estate St, across the street from the Havensight Mall (☎340/774-9809; US$16), operates gondolas that whisk you 700ft above sea level up the side of Slag Hill for stunning views of downtown, the harbour and Water and Hassel islands. Overpriced food and drinks await you at the top.

Water and Hassel islands

Hop on a ferry from Crown Bay Marina just west of Charlotte Amalie's harbour (US$5 one-way) for a relaxing day-trip across the harbour to Hassel Island and Water Island. **Hassel Island**, part of the Virgin Islands National Park system, is a relaxing place for fun exploration but there's not much to see here, apart from the relics of an old British military garrison from their occupation during the 1800s and the shell of a failed hotel (the hotel from Herman Wouk's novel *Don't Stop the Carnival*). **Water Island** (ferry from Crown Bay Marina; US$3 one-way) has a small population but is now considered the fourth USVI; bring a picnic and spend the day lazing on its glorious sandy beaches or cycling round the island. **Water Island Adventures** (☎340/714-2186) does bike tours, mostly on paved roads (US$60) and will pick up groups (eight minimum) from the cruise dock in Charlotte Amalie for a narrated tour of the harbour as you make your way to the island.

Around Charlotte Amalie

With a car or by taxi it's worth seeking out some of the attractions just outside Charlotte Amalie. On Route 40 north of town, **Drake's Seat**, sometimes crowded with tour buses, is a popular lookout point where it is said Sir Francis Drake himself sat to look out for his fleet and watch for enemy ships. On the same road, roughly two miles west, the mountainside perch of **Estate St Peter Greathouse and Botanical Gardens** (daily 8am–4pm; ☎340/774-4999; US$10) is worth a trip for the breathtaking views alone. Once you've got your breath back, grab a complimentary rum punch, shop for local art and take a tour of the luscious gardens which boast over two hundred species of plants and trees.

Two and a half miles east of town on Route 38 at Tutu, **Tillet Gardens** (☎340/775-1929, ⊛www.tillettgardens.com) was once a Danish farm; it's now St Thomas's answer to an artists' colony, where you'll find all sorts of artisans at work and a shop to buy their wares. Call ahead to time your visit with one of the occasional jazz and classical concerts.

Beaches

On the **north side** of the island, the mile-long sandy stretch of **Magens Bay Beach** (US$3) three miles north of Charlotte Amalie on Route 35 is the island's longest beach and is almost always included in lists of the world's best beaches. Protected by two dramatic peninsulas (the one to the east is the upmarket area of Peterborg where the elite keep their villas – Bill Clinton once stayed here at *Sand Dollar Villas*), it's the perfect beach for swimming and sunbathing, though the snorkelling isn't much to speak of. There's a grill serving sandwiches, pizza and burgers, and waitresses in bikinis walk the beach taking drink orders. On your way out, hit *Udder Delights* for one of their famous milkshakes. Round the peninsula to the west, **Hull Bay Beach**, also on Route 37, is a favourite with the locals, especially surfers who ride the choppy waves rolling in from the Atlantic. In the distance you can see Inner and Outer Brass, two cays that are part of the US Virgin Islands. *Larry's Hideaway* on the road in provides hot grub, drinks and the occasional live band.

Beaches on the **south side** of the island aren't as good but are easy to get to. **Brewers Bay Beach**, on Route 30, three miles west of town, is fairly unpopulated, except for students from the nearby university, and it has a few snack trucks, while **Morningstar Beach** at *Marriott Frenchman's Reef*, on Route 315 one mile south of Havensight, is the closest and easiest to access from Charlotte Amalie. On the waterfront at Charlotte Amalie, look for the small ferry called *The Reefer*, which provides access throughout the day (make sure to ask time of last return trip) for US$5 each way (free for *Marriott* guests). Back on Route 30 and two miles east, **Bolongo Beach**, surrounded by the *Bolongo Bay Beach Club and Resort*, offers grill grub, frozen drinks and pick-up volleyball games. The beach at **Secret Harbour** on the southeast of the island is great for sunsets. Snorkelling along the point to the right is good and a popular hangout for sea turtles. The east side **Sapphire Bay Beach**, just north of Red Hook, is popular with both locals and tourists and is another fine place to don your mask and snorkel.

Eating and drinking

St Thomas's **restaurants** offer a complete range of menus, venues and prices. Throw a stone in **Frenchtown** and you'll hit any number of intimate places popular with locals and out-of-towners. While the finest spots abound with entrees approaching Manhattan prices, there are options for all budgets, from roadside stands to burger joints to ethnic cuisine. For an unusual dining setting put on some finer clothes and make a reservation with *Romantica Excursions* (☏340/775-0027, @www.romanticaexcursions. com), St Thomas's finest dinner cruise. There is a bar, a piano player and a set menu with several choices for US$89 per person plus gratuity. The *Romantica* sails Tues–Sun from its berth at the promenade on Veteran's Drive. They sometimes do Sunday brunches and on Mondays the boat becomes a classy nightclub.

Charlotte Amalie

Ashley's Mobile Restaurant Cyril E. King Airport ☏340/774-1533. Known for their quick and authentic West Indian dishes, *Ashley's* serves what many hold to be the best stewed chicken with rice on the island. An excellent final meal before catching your flight out. Daily 7am–9pm.

Beni Iguana's *Grand Hotel* Court ☏340/777-8744. This sushi bar with outdoor courtyard is located in the historic district, part of the Grand Galleria, a collection of shops just north of Emancipation Park. The peanut-based iguana sauce is quite good and their "Famous Mussels" are a mouth-watering speciality. Sushi plates cost US$4–15. Lunch Mon–Sat 11am–3pm, dinner Mon–Sat 5–9pm.

Bill's Texas Pit BBQ Veteran's Drive ☏340/776-9579. This mobile outdoor pit serves slow-smoked barbecue with a thick, tangy sauce. Portions are large and the most expensive item on the menu is a rib plate with a side and a roll for US$9. The chicken is a bit cheaper at US$7. There are four locations, two of them in the Sub Base and Red Hook areas.

Cuzzin's Caribbean Restaurant and Bar 7 Back St ☏340/777-4711. Located in an eighteenth-century stone building in the heart of the downtown shopping district, *Cuzzin's* serves up everything from stewed goat to burgers. But it's the West Indian dishes like conch in butter sauce, sides like *fungi* and drinks like *maubi* (a root) that top the bill. Lunch Mon–Sat 11am–5pm, dinner Tues–Sat 5–9.30pm.

Gladys' Café Waterfront at Royal Dane Mall ☏340/774-6604. Bacon, eggs, French toast or fresh tropical fruit for breakfast, or well-priced West Indian fare for lunch, including the hard-to-find local favourite saltfish and dumplings. Gladys also makes three mean hot sauces and sells them by the bottle.

Herve Government Hill ☏340/777-9703. An eclectic fusion of contemporary American, French and Caribbean fare (lunch around US$10; dinner US$28–35) on a hilltop location with amazing views just minutes from Main Street. A great bouillabaise and the black sesame-crusted tuna with ginger-raspberry sauce is a dream.

Ideal Restaurant 2329 Comandante Gade ☏340/777-5321. This is the best roti in town with prices ranging from US$6 for the veggie version up to US$11 for conch or shrimp.

Jeni's Deli Emancipation Park A good place to pick up a sandwich or salad and the prices are decent (US$6–10).

Shipwreck Tavern Al Cohen Plaza across from Havensight Mall ☏340/777-1293. If you just want a burger and a beer, this watering hole will set you up with three-quarters of a pound of beautiful beef. Other than that it is more of a late-night munchies place.

Tavern on the Waterfront 30 Dronningens Gade ☏340/776-4328. Live jazz and the beautiful mahogany ceiling create an inviting atmosphere, but the menu with a choice of well over a dozen delicious appetizers and a nice variety of seafood and steak entrees is more than reason enough to stop by. Also this is probably the only place in the Caribbean to get Polish pierogis and cabbage rolls. Entrees cost US$18–32.

Virgilio's 18 Dronningens Gade ☏340/776-4920. Beyond the fountain and huge mahogany front doors is a cosy, elegant Italian restaurant, but don't be intimidated – the dress is casual. Pasta is the popular choice (US$20–26) but the veal is the signature dish.

Frenchtown

Betsy's Bar 59 Honduras ☏340/774-9347. Betsy just might be the coolest bartender on the island, and her bar is a local favourite. There's decent bar food (burgers and munchies) and live music at weekends.

Craig and Sally's 22 Honduras ☎340/777-9949. Hands down the most intimate restaurant with the most delicious food on St Thomas. The menu is creative and ever-changing (though the eggplant cheesecake is a regular item and recommended) and there's a wine list with over 450 vintages. Lunch Wed–Fri and dinner Wed–Sun. Reservations are highly recommended though some drop-in patrons elect to have an appetizer at the bar while they wait.

Epernay Champagne Bar and Night Club 24A Honduras ☎340/774-5348. A small, hip, intimate bistro with an extensive menu serving everything from pizza to sushi to shrimp bok choy (US$18) plus twenty wines by the glass. The bar is a great place for early evening cocktails, and there's a nightclub upstairs.

Oceana Villa Olga ☎340/774-4262. Set on the terrace of an old stone house which once served as the Russian embassy, this upscale restaurant serves innovative international cuisine with views off the point of the Frenchtown peninsula. There are twenty wines by the glass. Try the oven-roasted sea bass with couscous and roasted red pepper sauce. Entrees are US$23–45. Mon–Sat 5.30–10pm, open Sundays during high season.

Nightlife and entertainment

Nightlife in Charlotte Amalie revolves around **bars**, particularly on Main Street, with live music and the occasional DJ. There's also more cultured entertainment – art shows, community theatre and eclectic music ensembles; pick up a copy of *St Thomas This Week* for what's on when. The most anticipated (and drunken) event of the year is **Carnival** (☎340/776-3112, ⓦwww.vicarnival.com) – St Thomas's is one of the oldest and largest celebrations in the Caribbean and really kicks into gear the last two weeks of April. The revels take place all around downtown Charlotte Amalie with elaborate costumed street parades, a dancing till dawn frenzy called J'ouvert, music competitions like the famous Panorama and a final blowout when fireworks light up the harbour. For a little primer, read Herman Wouk's novel *Don't Stop the Carnival*.

Bars and clubs

Betsy's Bar (see p.447). Live entertainment, ranging from rock 'n' roll to reggae on Friday and Saturday nights (no cover charge).

Epernay Upstairs (see above). This loungey, late-night dance club is popular with the island's professional set. DJs spin disco, house, hip-hop, jazz and much more until 2am.

The Green House Bar and Restaurant ☎340/774-7998. After the dinner crowd has left, the music starts pumping with DJs or live reggae bands.

Shipwreck Tavern (see p.447). Two-dollar Coronas, big screen TVs and heavy-duty burgers make this place a favourite among sports fans.

Tavern on the Waterfront (see p.447). The island's best spot for live jazz; check the schedule for a variety of great local performers.

Entertainment venues

Pistarkle Theatre ☎340/775-7877, ⓦwww.pistarkletheater.vi. Located at Tillet Gardens, this 200-seat air-conditioned venue is one of the island's main outlets for theatre and dance.

Reichhold Center for the Arts Rte 30, west of the airport ☎340/693-1559. Located at the University of the Virgin Islands, St Thomas's largest performance space showcases local and international music, theatre, dance and ballet.

Red Hook and around

Most of St Thomas's resorts are found on the east side of the island, whose main settlement, **RED HOOK,** consists mostly of a couple strips of shops, restaurants and bars nestled around the bay of the same name. It caters mostly to the hundreds of folks who get on and off ferries leading to and from St John, Tortola and other Caribbean islands, and to the high-end resorts nearby, and is a fun little place to shop, eat and grab a drink or three. The late-night bars have more of a natural party atmosphere, and travellers linger longer than cruise ship patrons do in Charlotte Amalie. The main tourist attractions on this side of the island are the **beaches** and the **Coral World Marine Park**, on Route 38 at Coki Point (daily 9am–5pm; US$18, US$9 children; ☎340/775-1555). This 4.5-acre park boasts an imaginative array of marine and non-marine attractions including the Undersea Observatory, Sea Trekkin' (the fee of US$68/adults, US$59/children, includes admission) – an air helmet that enables you to walk along an underwater trail just off shore, Caribbean

Reef Encounter (an 80,000-gallon tank teeming with reef life), Turtle Pool, Touch Pool and shark and stingray tanks. **Coki Beach** on Smith Bay right next to Coral World Marine Park is probably the best beach for **snorkelling** on the island, though it can get really crowded. Come early to avoid the throngs of cruise-ship snorkellers. There's a great natural reef, plus all the amenities you could want: snack trucks, drinks, rental equipment and much more. You can get on the **Internet** at Grateful Deli (see overleaf).

Accommodation

Staying on the east side of the island you'll be limited to upmarket resort **accommodation**, all of which has easy access to a beach.

Bolongo Bay Beach Club and Resort 50 Estate Bolongo, South Shore ☏ 340/775-1800 or 1-800/524-4746, ⊛www.bolongobay.com. Though all rooms have a sea view, the draw of *Bolongo* is its social activities rather than the quality of the accommodations, which don't quite live up to the price. That said, the staff are personable, there are three pools, a hopping nightlife thanks to the hotel bar (see *Iggie's Beach Bar and Grill*) and beach volleyball. The all-inclusive plan is a good deal and there are also condos available for US$470 per night. ❽

Elysian Beach Resort 6800 Estate Nazareth, Eastside ☏ 340/775-1000 or 1-800/426-5445, ⓕ 340/776-0910. Set on 8.5 acres of waterfront, the 180-room resort has tennis courts, health club, pool, a palm-lined beach and several restaurants (most notably *Palm Court*). Grounds are well manicured and the rooms are clean and spacious if a little dull. ❽

Pavilions and Pools 6400 Estate Smith Bay, Eastside ☏ 340/775-6110 or 1-800/524-2001, ⊛www.pavilionsandpools.com. Each of the 25 villas has a bedroom (some have two), kitchen (maids do the dishes), living room and large bathroom, and the rooms are spacious and well decorated. Spaced well apart to ensure privacy, all villas come complete with their own four-foot pool and patio, and though not on the waterfront, the complex is a short walk to Sapphire Bay Beach, one of the finest. There's a café on site that serves breakfast and dinner. ❽–❾

Point Pleasant Resort 6600 Estate Smith Bay, Eastside ☏ 340/775-7200 or 1-800/524-2300, ⊛www.pointpleasantstthomas.com. Some of the best deals on the island can be found at this mountainside resort. The suites are pleasant, the pool is right on the ocean and there are two great restaurants (*Agave Terrace* and *Fungi's*) on the premises. The Junior Suite goes for about US$255 per night in high season and there are also three

2-bedroom villas. There's beach access and equipment for snorkelling, windsurfing and kayaking. ❾

Ritz-Carlton 6900 Great Bay Estate, Eastside ☏ 340/775-3333 or 1-800/241-3333, ⊛www.ritzcarlton.com. If you've got the money and can put up with the attitudes of regular *Ritz* guests, then you can't get much better than this. Set on fifteen acres of beautifully landscaped beachfront land, the resort blends European architecture with Caribbean charm. For the price the rooms are small but here you are paying top dollar for the friendly staff who cater to your every need. Resort staples like multiple restaurants, a spa, beach, watersports options, tennis courts and fitness centre are also on site. The resort has its own catamaran for sunset cruises. ❾

Sapphire Beach Resort 6270 Great Bay Estate, Eastside ☏ 340/775-6100 or 1-800/524-2090, ⊛www.sapphirebeachresort.com. Families will be pleased with nicely decorated, spacious rooms and villas that can accommodate up to six people. The views of the BVI are precious, and the beach is one of the finest on the island for its pure white sand and excellent snorkelling. Smaller rooms have kitchenettes. Snorkelling and basic windsurfing lessons are included, and there is a dive shop on site. There's a beach party every Sunday from 2.30–5.30pm. ❾

Secret Harbour Beach Resort Ridge Rd, Red Hook ☏ 340/775-6550 or 1-800/524-2250, ⊛www.secretharbourvi.com. Set in a peaceful relaxing corner of the island not far from town, *Secret Harbour* enjoys an envious location on a very calm little cove. All rooms have sea views and are comfortable and clean but a little plain. There are also eight rooms with excellent handicap access as well as beach wheelchairs. The dive shop downstairs, Aqua Action, is the only one in the VI that specializes in scuba for people with disabilities. The on-site restaurant, *Blue Moon Café* (see overleaf), is quite good. ❾

Eating, drinking and nightlife

There's great waterfront **food** and a hopping **nightlife** to be had in Red Hook or, for a more local experience, head off to one of the several restaurants in the hills on the north side of the island. At the more upmarket restaurants you'll need to dress smart casual. If you want to make up a beach picnic or stock up your kitchenette head for Marina Market across from Ferry Dock.

Restaurants and cafés

Agave Terrace 4 Estate Smith Bay, *Point Pleasant Resort* ☎340/775-4142. One of the better resort restaurants and one of the better fine-dining choices on this side of the island. There's a great view of St John and the BVI and often some live steel pan music. The Alaskan king crab legs are wonderful (the menu is mostly Caribbean), and the lobster bisque is recommended. An extensive wine list. Try the Agave Snowball for dessert – vanilla ice cream coated with hot fudge and roasted coconut.

Bill's Texas Pit BBQ Across from Ferry Dock, Red Hook ☎340/776-9579. Best barbecue on the island, be it chicken, ribs or brisket.

Blue Moon Café *Secret Harbour Beach Resort* ☎340/779-2262, ⓦwww.bluemooncafevi.com. Great food with a seaside sunset view while you sip a glass from an award-winning wine list. Try some seared tuna with mango soy sauce and wasabi mashed potatoes. There's live steel pan music on Tuesdays and Fridays and the bar is open until 11pm. Dinner entrees start at US$18.

East End Café American Yacht Harbor, Red Hook ☎340/715-1442. Reasonably priced Italian fare has made the *East End Café* popular with both locals and tourists. Serves lunch and dinner.

Grateful Deli Red Hook Plaza, Red Hook ☎340/775-5160. A fantastic assortment of salads but also does great sandwiches on fresh home-made speciality breads. Many locals start the day off here with a cup of great coffee. Very reasonable prices (most everything under US$7) make this a good place to pack your picnic for the beach. Friendly, reliable service. Open 7am–6pm Mon-Sat, 7am–3pm Sun.

Molly Malone's American Yacht Harbor, Red Hook ☎340/775-1270. This open-air, garden-setting Irish pub serves great shepherd's pie and corned beef and cabbage, plus has a great breakfast menu. Perfect for just having drinks too, or watching sporting events on TV.

The Old Stone Farm House Northside ☎340/777-6277. With a setting in a 200-year-old farmhouse and creative cuisine like three-day Asian duck, this fantastic experience every time.

Romano's 97 Smith Bay, Smith Bay ☎340/775-0045. A swanky Italian restaurant off the beaten path, Romano's is worth tracking down for the delicious food and excellent service. While there

are pastas on the menu, this is northern Italian, so meatier, fare. If you're adventurous, go for the veal tongue or the classic osso bucco. Always crowded, but it's worth waiting at the bar.

Schnitzel Haus Frydenhoj, Red Hook ☎340/776-7198. Authentic German restaurant specializing in veal – the wiener schnitzel is recommended. Only open Mon–Fri 6–9pm.

Seaside Inn Frydenhoj, Red Hook ☎340/775-7313. Don't let the plain look of the place deter you. Popular with locals for real Creole-style seafood, it is open for dinner Mon-Sat after 7.30pm. You pick your prey from the daily catch and pay by weight. Try the Old Wife (trigger fish). Plates are US$15–20 and include sides and a particularly good *fungi*.

Sib's Mountain Bar Restaurant 33-5 Estate Elizabeth, Northside ☎340/774-8967. Mostly locals come to the bar to catch up on gossip, play pool or watch football over beer and burgers; the other half is an excellent restaurant. You can sit in the garden next to an artificial creek and see where the owner grows peppers for Sib's Mt Lava hot sauce. Does a popular brunch too.

Sopchoppy's Pub American Yacht Harbor, Red Hook ☎340/774-2929. Basic salads, subs, Mexican munchies and quite decent pizzas. Good for take-away or when drinking is more important than eating (bar overlooks the harbour).

Toad & Tart English Pub Rte 38 a few minutes west of Red Hook ☎340/775-1153. Sociable spot for fish and chips and Yorkshire pudding washed down with your favourite UK draught beers.

Bars and clubs

Caribbean Saloon American Yacht Harbor, Red Hook ☎340/775-7060. There's a DJ most nights but the real draw is the kitchen which can satisfy late-night munchies until 4am. It's on the second floor overlooking the harbour.

Duffy's Love Shack Red Hook Plaza, Red Hook ☎340/779-2080. During high season, the music is deafening and the crowds spread out into the parking lot. Shots and special potent cocktails are the favourites here. Look for drink specials such as the Hour of Power starting at midnight on Fri & Sat when drinks are two for one.

Fungi's 4 Estate Smith Bay, *Point Pleasant Resort* ☎340/775-4142. Located on the beach below the resort (park above and walk down). An informal place to eat and drink, *Fungi's* is a great spot to listen to a little reggae. Steel pan on Fridays and usually Karaoke on Wednesdays and Sundays. Has some excellent home-made BBQ sauce and local sides with the plates. US$9–15.

Iggie's Beach Bar and Grill 50 Bolongo Bay, Bolongo Bay Beach Resort ☎ 340/775-1800. There's frequent live music in an open-air beach bar setting as well as theme nights such as Carnival night when the firewalkers and conga lines come out.

The Warehouse Poor Man's Bar 18A Smith Bay, Red Hook ☎ 340/775-1507. Located across from the ferry dock, this upstairs dive bar is a pour-your-own affair – meaning you make your drink as strong as you please.

Watersports and outdoor activities

The majority of the **dive sites** are around many of the small cays and the most popular, such as Buck Island, Cow and Calf Rocks, are to the southeast. The *W.I.T Shoal*, a 400-ft freighter in 90ft of water is the best of the wrecks. Most wrecks are visited from St Thomas rather than St John, the notable exception being *Major General Rogers*, a 120-ft Coast Guard vessel intentionally sunk off St Thomas in 1972 which rests at 40–60ft. Other diveable wrecks are to the west through Savana Passage and near Sail Rock and so dive shops might be limited to Charlotte Amalie. Pillsbury Sound between St Thomas and St John is often protected from the weather and features shallow sites visited by operators from both islands. Divers should be aware that certain sites are visited by cruise ship passengers and a boat of 20 day-trippers is not uncommon. If that sort of thing bothers you, you might want to see where your operator is heading and how many cruise ships are in port.

Whether you are going **sport fishing** for the big boy-blue marlin or just looking to catch some tuna to throw on the grill, there are plenty of boats out of St Thomas. The following will be able to hook you up: American Yacht Harbor at Red Hook (☎ 340/775-6454); Charter Boat Center, Red Hook (☎ 340/775-7990); or Sapphire Beach Marina, Eastside (☎ 340/775-6100). For **golf** lovers the Mahogany Run Golf Course, Route 42 near Magens Bay (☎ 340/777-6006, ☜ www.mahoganyrungolf.com), is St Thomas's only golf course – an eighteen-holer that skirts the coastline. You can rent clubs and shoes – greens fees for nine holes plus cart are around US$100. Most resorts have **tennis** courts open to non-guests for a nominal fee – try *Bluebeard's Castle Hotel* (☎ 340/774-1600); *Marriott Frenchman's Reef* (☎ 340/776-8500); or *Wyndham Sugar Bay* (☎ 340/777-7100). There are also two public courts at Sub Base and Lindberg Bay. If you are prepared to tackle some hills or just pedal around the port, GNC-Endurance Sports (☎ 340/774-2311) at Port of Sail Mall rents **bikes**.

Watersports

Admiralty Dive Center *Windward Holiday Inn* ☎ 340/777-9802 or 1-888/900-3483, ☜ www.admiraltydive.com. Offers the standard training courses through divemaster. Two-tank boat dives for US$90. Offers some unexceptional dive packages; however, the half- and full-day of near-shore trolling fishing charters are nicely priced at US$300/$550.

Aqua Action *Secret Harbour Beach Resort* ☎ 340/775-6285 or 1-888/775-6285, ☜ www.aadivers.com. The dive shop offers certification and Discover Scuba courses and keeps dive groups small, two to ten people.. Owner Carl Moore is specially certified as a divemaster for people with disabilities, and courses/dives are available for a broad spectrum of special needs clients including quadriplegics.

Caribbean Parasail Adventures Frydenhoj ☎ 340/775-9360. Strap yourself in and be pulled high up in the air for US$60 for a ride of about ten minutes. This outfit will pick you up and drop you off at your resort.

Chartering the World ☎ 340/775-6972 or 1877/775-9834. Just give them a call, tell them what kind of sailing, sport fishing or powerboat adventure you're looking for and they'll do the rest.

Chris Sawyer Diving American Yacht Harbor, Red Hook ☎ 340/777-7804. This PADI five-star underwater centre can help you with all your diving needs. Their dive speciality is the wreck of the *Rhone* in the BVI (see p.484). Certification also available.

Limnos Charters American Yacht Harbor, Red Hook ☎ 340/775-3203. Limnos offers all kinds of package sails to the US and British Virgin Islands with crews knowledgeable on the history and folklore of the islands and surrounding seas.

Nauti Nymph Powerboat Rental American Yacht Harbor, Red Hook ☎340/775-5066. Choose the way you want your boat outfitted (snorkelling, water-skiing) and set out on your own adventure under your own control. Boats (25–29-footers) are pricey (up to US$300 per day), but it's the best way to go.

VI Snuba Excursions Coki Beach ☎340/693-8063, ⊛www.visnuba.com. If you aren't scuba certified and haven't the time for a course, then snuba – part snorkelling and part scuba – is for you. After twenty minutes of instructions you dive a maximum depth of 20 feet at the end of a regulator attached to a scuba tank floating above you on a small raft.

Virgin Islands Eco-Tours 2 Estate Nadir, Red Hook ☎340/779-2155. Learn about Mangrove Lagoon while touring the Virgin Islands Marine Sanctuary by kayak and seeing quite a different snorkelling scene. Recommended.

West Indies Windsurfing Vessup Beach ☎340/775-6530. If your resort doesn't offer wind-surfing lessons, give these guys a call and they'll have you flying across the seas in no time.

Shopping

St Thomas, and Charlotte Amalie in particular, is the shopping capital of the USVI. As Charlotte Amalie is a **duty-free** port with low taxes on luxury goods, there are big savings to be made there on jewellery, clothes, perfumes, cosmetics, alcohol and electronics. The heart of the **shopping district** is the six-block grid between Tol-bod Gade to the east and Trom Peter Gade to the west. The Vendor's Plaza, a daily outdoor **market** (9am–5pm), just south of Emancipation Garden, offers better deals than the shops along Main Street. The following are a taster of some of the best places to bargain hunt around the island. All, with the exception of Elizabeth Jane's, are in Charlotte Amalie.

Club Cigar Main Street ☎340/774-8100. The best selection of cigars on the island for less than you would pay in the US.

The Crystal Shoppe 14 Dronningens Gade ☎340/777-9835. A large selection of fine crystal from Waterford, Hernd, Bellek and Lladro among others.

Diamond's International Main Street ☎340/774-1516. If you're in the market for a pristine diamond, these guys have the largest selection of loose rocks in the Caribbean, though better deals can be found. There are two other locations: along the waterfront and at Havensight Mall.

Elegant Illusions Copy Jewels Port of Sale ☎340/777-4670. If shopping for jewellery downtown has your wallet screaming, then do your buying here.

Elizabeth Jane's American Yacht Harbor, Red Hook ☎340/779-1595. A wide selection of sterling silver jewellery at the best prices.

Island Newsstand Tolbod Gade and Norre Gade ☎340/774-0043. If you can't do without your daily newspaper from back home, there's a good chance this stand will have it.

K-Mart Nelson Mandela Square ☎340/714-4902 Don't laugh, the popular US department store has a great selection of duty-free liquor at the cheapest prices in town. Stock up on your Cruzan rum here.

Local Color Hibiscus Alley ☎340/774-2280. Local artists like Sloop Jones display their utilitarian art: painted clothes ranging from dresses to shirts to hats.

Native Arts and Crafts Cooperative Tolbod Gade ☎340/777-1153. Every kind of art you could imagine made by local artists at rock-bottom prices.

Parrot Fish Music 2 Store Tvaer Gade ☎340/776-4514. This CD shop offers the island's greatest selection of Caribbean music, from reggae to calypso to pan bands. Staff will play samples for those unfamiliar with the various genres.

Royal Caribbean Havensight Mall ☎340/776-8890. One of three locations of the largest camera store in St Thomas. Often carries underwater housings for digital cameras.

Tropical Memories Royal Dane Mall ☎340/776-7536. Paintings, textiles, pottery, blown glass and carved masks – all by USVI artists.

Tropicana Perfume Shop 2 Main Street ☎340/774-0010. Has the largest selection of perfumes in the Virgin Islands at prices lower than US prices.

St John

Located just three miles east of St Thomas and only accessible by boat, **ST JOHN**, the smallest and most pristine of the USVI, is the perfect hideaway and a paradise for nature lovers. Twenty square miles of lush mountains rise from perfect white-sand beaches, and with two-thirds of the island designated a **National Park** – one of the largest areas of wilderness in the whole of the Caribbean – there's an abundance of flora and fauna, including wild cats and burros (be careful, they bite), hummingbirds and iguanas to look out for. You really need to come for longer than a day-trip to get the most out of the scenery, miles of hiking trails, numerous secluded beaches, and many reefs to snorkel. A hike into the mountains will also take you past man-made sights – ruins dating from the eighteenth century when the island had over one hundred successful sugar plantations and a population of two hundred whites and one thousand slaves. The main town on St John is **Cruz Bay**, home to half of the island's five thousand inhabitants and the best of the island's shopping, eating and nightlife.

Arrival and information

You'll find maps and brochures on the **ferry dock** in Cruz Bay (next to the ticket booth); grab a free copy of the *St John Guidebook*, which has a great map of Cruz Bay. The **tourist office** is located in town next to the post office. There is also a **National Park Visitor Centre** (daily 8am–4.30pm; ☎ 340/776-6201), at the creek in Cruz Bay, on the other side of the car ferry dock, north of the town centre. The exhibits will give you a taste of what you can expect to encounter on your hike and the centre will provide maps of the park for self-guided walks, help you plan your trip or book you onto guided hikes with park rangers. There is a post office in Cruz Bay (Mon–Fri 7.30am–4.30pm and Sat 7.30am–noon; ☎ 340/779-4227).

Connections (☎ 340/776-6922, ✆ www.connectionsstjohn.com), located in the heart of Cruz Bay, is known as "information central" for the island and beyond and does a little bit of everything for those living and vacationing here. They can help book accommodation, recommend restaurants and schedule watersports activities. For boaters, they monitor VHF channel 72. You can check your email, as well as receive snail mail, get a document notarized and receive cash via Western Union; they even issue money orders. You can also access the **Internet** in Cruz Bay at *Quiet Mon Pub & Cyber Celtic Café* (☎ 340/779-4799) for US$10/hour.

Getting around

VITRAN **buses** park at the head of the ferry dock and leave about every half-hour, making stops in the Park, Coral Bay and the East End of the island. Otherwise, tell the driver where you need to go and he or she will be happy to help you out. **Taxis** – usually brightly painted pick-up trucks with open-air canopies – are plentiful in Cruz Bay and are also available for island tours (about US$16 per person for a one-and-half-to two-hour tour). Don't be surprised if drivers try to pack in other people going your way. If you need to call a taxi ahead of time, try the Taxi Commission (☎ 340/693-8036); St John Taxi Services (☎ 340/693-7530); and C&C Taxi Tours (☎ 340/693-8164). **Bike and car rental** outfits are available; in fact, you'll probably be hounded by agents of the latter as soon as you step off the dock but a quick walk around Cruz Bay will present you with many options, most around US$55 per day. You can also call Avis (☎ 340/776-6374); Best Car Rental (☎ 340/693-8177); Conrad Sutton Car Rentals (☎ 340/776-6479); Hertz (☎ 340/693-7580); Hospitality Car & Jeep Rentals (☎ 340/693-9160); and St John Car Rental (☎ 340/776-6103).

Accommodation

The island holds all kinds of **accommodation options**, from beach camping, eco-cabins, and private boarding rooms to beachfront resorts and mountain villas, but given the small size of St John the number of rooms is more limited and prices are

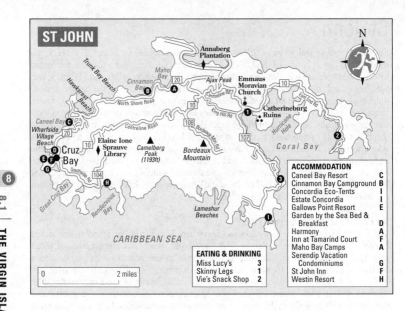

generally higher. The smaller inns in **Cruz Bay** and the campgrounds outside of town, which also have eco-accommodations complete with a/c and kitchenettes, are best for travellers on a budget. For groups a villa may be the best option. A few great places to start your search include Caribbean Villas and Resorts (☎340/776-6152 or 1-800/338-0987, ⊛www.caribbeanvilla.com); Destination St John (☎340/779-4647 or 1-800/562-1901, ⊛www.destinationstjohn.com); Private Homes for Private Vacations (☎340/776-6876, ⊛www.privatehomesvi.com); and Windspree (☎340/693-5423, ⊛www.windspree.com).

Hotels and inns

Estate Concordia 20–27 Estate Concordia, east of Cruz Bay/Coral Bay ☎340/693-5855 or 1-800/392-9004, ⊛www.maho.org/Concordia. These nine units, located on the southeastern end of the island overlooking Salt Pond, are really out of the way – rental car and a serious need for peace and quiet are required. All rooms are spacious and modern with terracotta floors and comfortable furniture and have balconies. Prices are US$135–210 depending on size and whether you have a partial or full view of the water. ⑥–⑦

Garden by the Sea Bed and Breakfast Enighed, Cruz Bay ☎340/779-4731, ⊛www. gardenbythesea.com. Just walking distance from town and located between Frank and Turner bays in a tropical jungle surrounded by banana trees and coconut palms, this tranquil B&B offers colourful West Indian charm with a private snorkelling beach. Rooms have exposed-beam ceilings, four-poster beds, and there are lovely garden showers. Recommended. ⑧

Harmony Maho Bay, northeast of Cruz Bay ☎340/776-6240 or 1-800/392-9004, ⊛www. maho.org/harmony. Located just above the *Maho Bay Camps*, these studios are a step above tent accommodation, offering creature comforts while adhering to Maho's eco-friendly environment. The electricity comes from the sun, rain is collected for the running water in your kitchenette and private bath, and wind scoops help pull breezes through lofted rooms that have laptops monitoring your energy consumption. Recommended. ⑦

Inn at Tamarind Court Cruz Bay ☎340/776-6378 or 1-800/221-1637, ⊛www.tamarindcourt.com. This pink, twenty-room, B&B-style inn offers all the amenities and solitude you'll need while keeping you close to all the action in Cruz Bay. Accommodation ranges from single rooms with shared baths (US$75) to more spacious apartments with full kitchens and private baths for US$240. All have cable TV and a/c. The courtyard bar and restaurant are open for breakfast and dinner, though they might be noisy for some guests. ④/⑥

Serendip Vacation Condominiums Enighed, Cruz Bay ☎340/776-6646 or 1-888/800-6445; ⊛www. serendipstjohn.com. These one bedroom ($196) and studio ($131) units offer great sunsets and views of St Thomas, but some may find them a bit plain for the price. ⑥–⑦

St John Inn Off Rte 104, Cruz Bay ☎340/693-8688 or 1-800/666-7688, ⊛www.stjohninn.com. On the outskirts of Cruz Bay, this little hideaway offers thirteen rooms, all of which are individually named and decorated. All rooms have a fridge, microwave and private bathroom, some have wooden armoires, wrought-iron beds or four-poster mahogany beds, kitchenettes and ocean views. Prices range from US$140 to 195 depending on the room. ⑥–⑦

Resorts

Caneel Bay Resort Rte 20, north of Cruz Bay ☎340/776-6111 or 1-888/767-3966, ⊛www. caneelbay.com. Opened in 1955 and set on a 170-acre peninsula bordered by the Atlantic and the Caribbean, this early eco-resort was the brainchild of Laurence Rockefeller. While there are no phones (they offer wake-up knocks rather than calls) or TVs or radios, who needs them with so much to do (or rather not to do) on this lush estate? Rooms are beautifully decorated with dark woods and rose-coloured tiles and most offer views of one of the seven beaches and the sea beyond. There are three restaurants and a wine bar/cigar room and a beach for each day of the week if you don't want to repeat one. Best deals are the garden rooms, which have the largest showers. Recommended. ⑨

Gallows Point Resort Gallows Point, just south of Cruz Bay ☎340/776-6434 or 1-800/323-7229, ⊛www.gallowspointresort.com. The only resort within walking distance of Cruz Bay, set on a four-acre peninsula overlooking the Caribbean. The suites accommodate up to four people and all have fully equipped kitchens, spacious living rooms and water views. While the property doesn't really have a beach, there is a walkway down to the water where the snorkelling is good. A harbour-view room is only US$205 per night during the low season. *ZoZo's Restaurant* (see p.459) is on site. ⑨

Westin Resort Rte 104, southeast of Cruz Bay ☎340/693-8000 or 1-800/937-8461, ⊛www. westinresortstjohn.com. Sitting on a 47-acre

compound overlooking Rendezvous Bay, this small self-serving community means that you never have to leave the premises, though Cruz Bay is just a US$6 taxi ride away. Convenient golf cart shuttles carry guests back and forth between the beach, restaurants, bars, shopping centre, deli, spa, tennis courts and gym. There are 282 guest rooms and suites, as well as 67 villas. The concierge desk helps book all sorts of off-premises activities. ⑨

Campgrounds

Cinnamon Bay Campground Rte 20, northeast of Cruz Bay ☎340/776-6330 or 1-800/539-9998, ⊛www.cinnamonbay.com. Forty smallish cottages (⑤) with patios, cooking equipment and utensils, charcoal grill, propane stoves and communal bathrooms. Or you can go for one of the sixty canvas tents (US$58–80) with solid floors (10ft by 14ft). The tents don't have electricity but lanterns are provided. For those really wanting to rough it, there are 26 bare campsites (US$27) with a picnic table and charcoal grill. There is a restaurant and weekly activities, some for a nominal fee.

Concordia Eco-Tents Coral Bay ☎340/776-6240 or 1-800/392-9004, ⊛www.maho.org. One of *Maho*'s sister eco-complexes on the eastern side of the island, these digs offer a few more modern amenities. The tents ($125) offer wind and solar power, kitchenettes with running water, private toilets and solar-heated showers. A work exchange programme is also available. Four of the seven newest units offer wheelchair access.

Maho Bay Camps Maho Bay, northeast of Cruz Bay ☎340/776-6240 or 1-800/392-9004, ⊛www.maho.org. Stanley Selengut started these camps in 1976 before the term eco-tourism even existed. Now Maho has 114 units tucked in the hills above Maho Bay connected by above-ground wooden walkways that leave the earth below relatively unscathed. The tent cottages have cots, linens, towels, cooking and eating utensils and propane stoves are included. There are cold-water communal showers, the water from which is recycled to irrigate the vegetation. There are flush toilets and a restaurant that offers healthy fare and veggie options and the store sells most foodstuffs and sundries you'll need. They also offer a four-hours-per-day work programme in exchange for lodging. Recommended. ⑤

Cruz Bay and around

CRUZ BAY didn't become a port until the mid-1800s, when Danish soldiers from St Thomas used it as an outpost. Unlike towns on the other main USVI there's not much in the way of architecture, but it's a great place to spend a leisurely day shopping, eating and drinking. As you get off the ferry, in front of you, beyond the collection of taxis, there's a municipal park and pavilion – ideal for sitting with a smoothie or a beer and take a load off. Keeping the water on your left, if you walk down Northshore Road, you'll see on your right **Mongoose Junction**, an upmarket outdoor mall, which is worth a look. **Wharfside Village Beach**, to your right as you exit the ferry dock, is the only beach in Cruz Bay, and while technically you can swim it's not recommended as this is a busy harbour. You're better off using the beach for powerboat rentals, sea-kayak tours and booking dive trips. Surrounding the beach is the outdoor mall, Wharfside Village. Apart from Cruz Bay the only other commercial area on the island is **Coral Bay**, the site of St John's first Danish colony, which now hosts a growing number of restaurants and shops catering mostly to the locals. It's also home to the **Emmaus Moravian Church**, the oldest church on St John. Dating to 1733, this was the original place of worship for the Danes who settled a colony here.

The Virgin Islands National Park

This spectacular and varied **National Park** encompasses about 7200 acres above ground and 5600 acres of marine sanctuary. The land was donated – with the stipulation it would be used for a National Park – to the federal government in 1956 by the then owner Laurence Rockefeller. Before you head off into the wilderness get some information from the **National Park Visitor Centre** at Cruz Bay (see p.453), which has an exhibition and free literature, and get hold of a copy of the Park Service's monthly schedule of ranger-led activities, such as adventure hikes, snorkelling trips, history programmes and nature walks. For some easy self-guided **beach hikes** that leave from Cruz Bay, ask the park ranger about trailhead locations for Lind Point, Salomon and Honeymoon (the unofficial nude beach). You'll need to drive or get a taxi to the start of the self-guided trails to the Annaberg Sugar Mill Ruins (see below), Cinnamon Bay Loop and the Francis Bay Trail. All of these trails are a half-mile over easy terrain. For the more adventurous, there's the **Reef Bay Trail**, on Centerline Road, accessible by bus. This three-mile hike takes you downhill through rainforest (look for the kapok trees, with their cloaked roots), cactus woodland, past petroglyphs and sugar mill ruins before bringing you out at a beach. You can either hike back up or arrange, for a small fee, for a boat to take you back to Cruz Bay (individuals arrange through the Park Service; groups call Sadie Sea ☏ 340/776-6421).

The rest of the island and the beaches

Besides the obvious natural beauty, there are a few low-key attractions around the island. A five-minute drive out of the town centre, the **Elaine Ione Sprauve Library**, Enighed Estate, Rte 104 (Mon–Fri 9am–5pm; free; ☏ 340/776-6359), is an eighteenth-century house containing an extensive collection of Caribbean reference materials unavailable anywhere else in the world and a display of photographs and artefacts. Four miles northeast of town, above Leinster Bay, a walk around the ruins of the well-preserved 1733 **Annaberg Plantation** (US$4 included in Trunk Bay beach fee) will give you your best impression of what a sugar plantation was like, plus some amazing views of the British Virgin Islands. If this whets your appetite for more ruins, visit the **Catherineberg Sugar Mill Ruins** (Rte 10), once a sugar plantation and rum factory, which, after the revolt of the 1730s served as the headquarters for the slave uprising. On the east side of the island the hills rise to a peak at **Bordeaux Mountain** (1277ft), the highest spot on St John. Stop for a scoop of ice cream or have some lunch or dinner on patios overlooking Lameshur Bay.

Beaches

St John has its fair share of white-sand **beaches** and stunning azure bays where you can sunbathe, nap in a hammock, float in tranquil waters and snorkel the reefs. Most offer dressing facilities and restrooms and some have amenities such as beach bars, snack huts, T-shirt shops and watersports rentals. Only Trunk Bay Beach charges admission, and by law all beaches (up to 15ft) are public, even those that skirt private resort property. For smaller, more out-of-the-way beaches, such as those on the eastern part of the island like Lameshur and Salt Pond, get a map from the National Park's Contact Station in Cruz Bay. Northeast of Cruz Bay there's a fine selection of beaches, including **Trunk Bay** (US$4 fee), St John's best and most popular beach. The **snorkel trail** here (marked by red, white and blue buoys) has underwater plaques to help you identify the coral and fish you see, but it won't knock your socks (or flippers) off. Better snorkelling is towards the west end of the beach. There are also food and facilities, and snorkel equipment for rent. VI Snuba Excursions (☎340/693-8063) offers **snuba** here, but you'll need a reservation.

Further east, at **Cinnamon Bay,** part of the National Park's campground, you can rent kayaks, snorkel equipment, bicycles and even get a windsurfing lesson. This is also really the best place for **surfers** to catch a northern swell in winter. For a break from the beach, head out on the Cinnamon Bay Nature Trail, which loops through ruins and returns you to the beach. **Hawksnest Beach**, on the other side of the peninsula from the *Caneel Bay Resort* (see p.455), is a favourite with locals because it's not tourist-heavy. There's snorkelling, changing facilities and picnic tables here. Advanced snorkellers might consider kayaking out of **Maho Bay** to Whistling Cay, Mary Point or Johnson's Reef. **Salt Pond Bay** near Coral Bay has a rocky beach better for exploring than lounging on. Tide pools and some good snorkelling await.

Eating and drinking

There are great **dining** options on St John for people on all budgets. If you're self-catering, the island has several grocery stores, though don't be surprised by the prices and the limited supply of perishables. Although most **restaurants** and **bars** are located in Cruz Bay (or very close), some are now starting to spring up in Coral Bay.

Asolare Rte 20, Caneel Hill ☎340/779-4747. One of St John's oldest estates and a romantic spot for dinner – come early for drinks and the sunset over Cruz Bay before tucking into the Asian-inspired dishes.

Banana Deck Cruz Bay ☎340/693-5055. The ribeyes are a speciality (US$20–30) at this open terrace which is the home to all things banana, from splits and banana caramel cheesecake to banana rum. Entrees run US$17–30, and the place is often packed so make a reservation.

Chilly Billy's Cruz Bay ☎340/693-8708. The various lunch sandwiches are quite good (US$7–11) but the main event here is breakfast: eggs Benedict (US$10.50), Belgian waffles, and a Bailey's-battered apple raisin bread French toast.

The Fish Trap Cruz Bay ☎340/693-9994, ⍟www.thefishtrap.com. With at least six types of fresh fish on the menu daily – such as tuna, salmon, swordfish and shark – this is an excellent choice for the seafood lover. Plates, including pasta, lobster, steaks and shellfish, range from US$17–32; for dessert, there's coconut cake with rum caramel sauce. Closed Mondays. Early bird specials 4.30–6.30pm.

J.J.'s Texas Coast On the municipal park, Cruz Bay ☎340/776-6908. Always a cheap, reliable option, *J.J.'s* serves tasty breakfast burritos (US$4.95) as well as lunch or dinner outside or at

tables around the indoor bar.

The Lime Inn Cruz Bay ☎340/776-6425. A mainstay since 1984, this open-air restaurant with full bar serves good seafood, steaks and an all-you-can-eat shrimp feast ($19.95) on Wednesday night. Owner Rich Meyer's hook hand adds to the seafaring ambience. Tuesday is lobster night and reservations are required. Entrees US$17–26.

Morgan's Mango Wharfside Village ☎340/693-8141. Open only for dinner, this Caribbean-inspired eatery offers a cornucopia of flavours to tempt your taste buds. The flash-fried flying fish is tasty, the ceviche is refreshing and the citrus chicken is divine. Veggie dishes also available.

Paradiso Cruz Bay ☎340/693-8899. A St John's standout, this comfortable Mongoose Junction restaurant should be one of your first stops for dinner. Ask for a table on the wraparound, second-floor terrace and watch the world pass below. Entrees go between US$25–36.

Ronnie's Pizza & Mo' Cruz Bay ☎340/693-7700. The best pizza on the island is served here by the slice or by the pie Mon–Sat 11.30am–9pm; they also deliver.

The Stone Terrace Cruz Bay ☎340/693-9370. At this fine-dining restaurant up a stone staircase and overlooking the bay you can feast on interesting light dishes such as king crab in garlic butter with arugula and mango salad (US$14), garlic and chive wontons (US$9) and a seared tuna spinach salad with ginger potato cakes and cellophane noodles (US$14), or opt for bigger deals such as pan-seared scallops with truffled wild mushroom tomato broth ($32).

Tage Cruz Bay ☎340/715-4270, ⓦwww. tagestjohn.com. St John's newest culinary wonder, *Tage* serves "Neo-Northern Californian" fare. Ted Robinson, the former chef at *Paradiso*, conjures up some amazing creations such as pan-roasted day boat scallops with a potato pillow and wild mushrooms, leeks and gruyere, aged balsamic vinegar and white truffle oil, or a white chocolate tarragon souffle. There is a comprehensive California wine list. Entrees are US$27–35. Open 6–9.30pm Mon–Sat.

Uncle Joe's BBQ Cruz Bay ☎340/693-8806. Ask locals and their eyes will light up at the mere mention of this outside grill and picnic tables not far from the ferry landing. Hands down, this is the best barbecue on the island, so go early before the food runs out – because it does.

Vie's Snack Shop Hansen Bay ☎340/693-5033. More like a snack shack, there's not much here for your eyes to feast on. But the conch fritters, some swear, are the best in the Caribbean. Other snacks include meat pies and johnny cakes. For dessert, grab a home-made coconut tart.

ZoZo's Cruz Bay ☎340/693-9200. A favourite among locals who want to splurge on some killer Italian food like a handmade lobster ravioli that is out of this world.

Nightlife and entertainment

While there are no discos, clubs or theatres on the island, there are lots of great **bars** and festivals that give you a chance to tilt a few back and party. For those with more refined tastes, the bar at *Caneel Bay* offers nightly calypso, pan bands and fine wines from 8.30pm to 11pm.

The Beach Bar Wharfside Village ☎340/777-4220. This is the perfect spot for a burger and a beer after a tough day on the water. For appetizers, try the flying shrimp. A grilled tuna sandwich is another solid bet (US$10). Always hopping around happy hour from 3–7pm. Live music three or four times a week and a jazz jam on Sundays from 4–7.30pm.

Duffy's Love Shack Behind the municipal park, Cruz Bay ☎340/776-6065. The better half of the Duffy's party empire that started in St Thomas, this Tiki bar is the closest thing to a disco that the island has. The food's good enough but the real attraction is the drink menu featuring Bikini-tinis, Shark Tanks or Tiki God Rum Punches, all of which come in their own signature glasses. Get a Volcano, a flaming drink for 2–4 people which comes complete with light show and Jimmy Buffet song. Wednesday is ladies' night and they drink for free 9pm–midnight. Cash only.

Fred's Restaurant, Bar and Cut-Rate Store Cruz Bay ☎340/776-6363. The food is miss-able but the dancing and live reggae music on Wednesday night (local reggae greats InnerVisions) and live calypso on Friday night really hit the spot. Hailed as the biggest Friday night party around. Often a US$5 cover charge though some avoid it by listening from the street or a table at *The Lime Inn Restaurant*.

The Frontyard Cruz Bay ☎340/693-9275. This pavilion-style bar seems more of a backyard. Live bands (mostly rock and blues) at the weekends and a four-hour happy hour (2–6pm) with great specials for those drinking on the cheap. There are pool tables and games as well. Open until 4am.

The Inn at Tamarind Court 34E Enighed ☎340/776-6378. A soothing open-air terrace bar and restaurant with country rock on Wednesday night and reggae on Saturday night.

Larry's Landing Wharfside Village ☎340/693-8802. A pour-your-own bar facing the beach that offers pool and gambling games. There are also TVs here for you to watch the big game.

Miss Lucy's Restaurant and Bar Estate Friis past Coral Bay ☎340/693-5244. This beachside establishment serves West Indian fare for lunch and dinner. There's a Sunday jazz brunch and full-moon parties.

Skinny Legs Coral Bay ☎340/779-4982. You'll know you've made it when you see a parking lot full of rusted-out beaters and ratty dogs scratching their fleas. This local shack bar, adorned with old flip-flop and broken-sandal mobiles and smashed windsurfing boards, is a fun drinking spot popular among the boating crowd and locals. There's occasional live music. Sandwiches and great burgers only for US$5–7.

Woody's Seafood Saloon Cruz Bay ☎340/779-4625. The sight of people spilling onto the street means you've arrived at *Woody's* – a small joint serving fried seafood and a party of booze and beautiful waitresses. Open until 2am most nights. The crowd here is perenially happy, and you can down shots with names like Surfer on Acid.

Watersports and outdoor activities

Arawak Expeditions (℡340/693-8312) runs half- and full-day **mountain-bike tours** for US$50–90 per person. If you want to try some **fishing**, Bite Me Charters (℡340/693-5823, ⊛www.bitemechartersvi.com) does full, three-quarter and half-day trips aboard *See Bee*, a 30ft Sea-Vee, for US$400–800 for four people, US$50 extra per person up to six. Dorado Sport Fishing (℡340/693-5664) has a 32ft catamaran, which leaves from Coral Bay for trips to catch wahoo, tuna, dolphin, marlin and sailfish off the South Drop of St John. Fishing, drinks, bait and tackle are all included at a price of US$100 per hour or US$675 for 8 hours. For the ultimate fishing experience arrange a trip on *The Marlin Prince* (℡340/693-5929, ⊛www.marlinprince.com), a custom 45ft Viking with an air-conditioned gallery, shower, and even a washer/dryer. They provide all types of fishing, even flyfishing for marlin, but their speciality is tournament fishing. Expect to pay US$1100 for a boat for six for a full day of marlin mania. You can go **horseriding** with Carolina Corral, Coral Bay (℡340/693-5778) on an hour-long ride that climbs the Johnny Horn Trail to the top of Hurricane Hole (US$35). Half-day and night-time rides are also available. Richard Wiltshire at Villa Vakoola (℡340/693-5737) also puts together personalized rides, prices depending on length of the excursion. There are public **tennis** courts on the outskirts of Cruz Bay (open till 10pm; free) or courts at *The Westin* (℡340/693-8000; non-guests US$15 an hour).

Watersports

St John offers a little of everything for **watersports** enthusiasts. All kinds of chartered **sailing** excursions are available – most leave Cruz Bay at about 10am, returning at 4pm and include lunch. You can go through one of the services mentioned below, enquire inside Connections (see p.453) or just look at advertisements tacked on telephone posts. Snorkellers should stop in at the National Park Visitor Centre at Cruz Creek and pick up a pamphlet that gives good descriptions of the best sites. It's best to buy your own mask before you come or at a dive shop in Cruz Bay – rentals are often shabby and if they don't fit right, water will seep into your mask and ruin the experience. **Divers** will not find much on their own, but there's PADI training and excursions for certified divers can be booked to shipwrecks, larger reefs and underwater caves. Popular sites include Carvel Rock, Cow and Calf Rocks and wreck dives to the *Major General Rogers* (see p.451) and the *RMS Rhone*, just off the BVI's Salt Island (see p.484)

Adventures in Paradise Cruz Bay ℡340/779-4527 or 1-888/448-5499, ⊛www.bookstjohn.com. Offers nearly everything – sport fishing, sailing and powerboat charters, kayak rentals, scuba and snorkel trips and parasailing.

Arawak Expeditions ℡340/693-8312 or 1-800/238-8687, ⊛www.arawakexp.com. This adventure outfitter leads kayak expeditions (US$50 for half-day, US$90 for full-day) around St John and surrounding islands. Longer trips include camping on deserted beaches and inn-to-inn multi-island packages.

Cinnamon Bay Watersports Center ℡340/776-6330 or 1-800/539-9398. You can rent snorkel equipment, kayaks and small sailboats at this campground facility. They also offer windsurfing lessons and can help book other watersports activities.

Cruz Bay Watersports Palm Plaza, Cruz Bay ℡340/776-6234, ⊛www.divestjohn.com. This ultimate dive shop offers PADI and NAUI training

and daily two-tank dives that leave at 8.30am and return by 12.30pm (US$85). Packages are available. Ask about the popular Jost Van Dyke trip, which is equal parts snorkelling and drinking, or The Baths of Virgin Gorda.

Low Key Watersports Wharfside Village, Cruz Bay ℡340/693-8999 or 1-800/835-7718, ⊛www.divelowkey.com. There's a high-spirited crew at this PADI five-star training facility that offers great night dives and wreck dives to the *Major General Rogers* and the *RMS Rhone*. General two-tank dives go for US$80.

Maho Bay Water Sports Center *Maho Bay Camp* Offers a wide variety of snorkel, sailboat, and windsurfing rentals, as well as a comprehensive scuba diving programme.

Noah's Little Arks Wharfside Village, Cruz Bay ℡340/693-9030. A small fleet of 11ft inflatable dinghies rests in the sand at Wharfside beach. The rafts give you the freedom to motor yourself around the island for exploring and snorkelling, and each comes with a map of the reefs and a fish ID chart. Use that reef map – if you break the motor you pay for it.

Ocean Runner ☏ 340/693-8809, ⊛ www. oceanrunner.vi. Offers 22 to 28ft powerboat rentals for half- or full day. You must have experience with boats, but basic lessons and day captains are available. Prices vary by season and size of boat, but be ready to pay at least US$225 for a full day.

Proper Yachts Mongoose Junction ☏ 340/776-6256. This outfit, which has been catering to watersports enthusiasts since 1970, charters bareboats and captained yachts for snorkel and scuba trips or sightseeing sails.

Sea Gypsy Charters ☏ 340/693-8020, ⊛ www. cathypacko.com. Let Captain Catherine Packo,

licensed Coast Guard captain, divemaster and marine naturalist, take you out on *Lucky Dog*, her powerboat. These eco-tours include snorkelling around St John for a couple of hours ($60) or in the British Virgin Islands for the day ($145) including the caves of Norman Island and a stop for lunch on the *Willie T*.

VI Snuba Excursions Trunk Bay ☏ 340/693-8063, ⊛ www.visnuba.com. If you are interested in diving but find it a daunting prospect, try this snorkelling/diving hybrid called snuba. Basic instructions will you started and then you will swim along the bottom attached to an air tank that floats at the surface. The cost is US$65. Maximum depths are about 15ft and the activity is suitable for anyone at least eight years old.

St Croix

ST CROIX, the largest of the USVI, measuring twenty-eight miles by seven miles, is also the most remote, lying forty miles south of St Thomas. For many years this peaceful gem has been accessible only by air or cruise ship but now that a high-season fast ferry connects the island to St Thomas, it's a must-see for all visitors to the USVI. The landscape, more gentle than its neighbours, is a mixture of rocky sierras, fertile coastal plain and rainforest and, of course, St Croix has its fair share of picturesque beaches. Architecturally the island is a few steps ahead of the other Virgins – the towns contain plentiful and beautiful examples of Danish colonial architecture and the landscape is dotted with the ruins of plantations and stone windmills from the island's days as king of the Caribbean sugarcane industry. Culturally, St Croix is a fusion of cuisines, ideas and customs, its employment opportunities (the Hess Oil refinery and tourism) and proximity to the US (and potential for US citizenship) attracting people from all over the Caribbean.

The island holds two major towns: historic **Christiansted**, on the northeast coast, and **Frederiksted**, on the west coast. The latter only really comes to life when cruise ships dock but Christiansted is almost always lively. Don't leave without a visit to the tiny but spectacular **Buck Island**, off the northeast coast. The island has been administered by the National Park Service since 1948 and is a paradise of beaches, reefs and hiking and snorkelling trails.

Arrival and information

The **Henry E. Rohlsen Airport** is located on the southern side of the island. VITRAN **buses** (☏ 340/773-1290 ex2291) are supposed to run between the airport and Christiansted every hour (ask at the airport for a route map and schedule) but are not very reliable; a **taxi** from the airport will cost about US$15 to Christiansted and US$10 to Frederiksted. **Tourist offices** – at the airport, in Frederiksted (at the pier; ☏ 340/772-0357) and in downtown Christiansted (☏ 340/773-0495) – will load you up with maps, brochures and advice. There are **post offices** in Christiansted, Gallows Bay, Richmond, Sunny Isle, Kings Hill, Frederiksted and Mars Hill. You can access the **Internet** for about US$10/hr in Christiansted at A Better Copy, 52 Company St (☏ 340/692-5303) or Strand Street Station Internet Cafe, Pan Am Pavillion (☏ 340/719-6245), and in Frederiksted at Rotsen Express, 1 Market St (☏ 340/277-6950).

The music of the Virgin Islands

The official music of the Virgin Islands, **quelbe** (kwail-bay) or **"scratch"** music, originated in the VI as a fusion of the rhythms and chants of the slaves with the melodies performed by old European fife and drum bands. The first native musical ensembles used home-made flutes, bass drums and European snare drums, but over time guitars and tambourines and a dried gourd which was "scratched" with a wire prong were added. The dance steps of European quadrilles and jigs were adapted and quelbe was born. The lyrics often spoke of the rough life or some off-color scuttlebutt. The subject matter hasn't changed much but modern bands have incorporated electric bass, saxophone and congas.

The best place to catch quelbe these days is at Mount Victory Camp on St Croix, where Jamesie Brewster, the 76-year old "King of Scratch", and his band of All-Stars can often be heard at Sunday pig roasts.

8

Opening hours on St Croix tend to coincide with the arrival of cruise ships. In Frederiksted, for example, while most of the restaurants remain open daily, shops remain closed until a cruise pulls into port (about twice a week during the high season and once every two weeks in low season). Outside of Christiansted, you should always call ahead to make sure your destination is open, especially in the off-season.

Accommodation

There are all kinds of **accommodation** on St Croix – camping, eco-cabins, bed and breakfasts, hotels and beachfront resorts – and because the island is less visited than the other USVI, prices are usually cheaper. For those on a **budget**, the cheapest hotels can be found in Frederiksted and Christiansted. Those seeking luxury should bear in mind that resorts on St Croix are less swanky than their St Thomas or St John counterparts and none has five stars.

If you're looking for a more natural experience and a way to save a little dough, **eco-tourism** is a great option. The **Nature Conservancy**, which offers hikes, and the **St Croix Environmental Association** (see p.470), which has scheduled two-hour hikes for US$25, are great places to start. **Mount Victory Camp** (℡340/772-1651 or 1-866/772-1651, ⊛www.mtvictory.camp.com) is the only **eco-camping** option on the island. Located north of Frederiksted on Mahogany Road, the grounds were built entirely by owner Bruce Wilson. Constructed with free-form pieces of fallen mahogany, teak and other hardwoods, five canopied tent platforms feature beds, linens, coolers, propane stoves, cookware, utensils and running water. There is a clean communal bathroom with flush toilets and solar-heated showers. Bare sites are also available. While you have to provide and cook your own food, Wilson offers information and help in booking every sort of outdoor adventure you can imagine, including scuba diving and recommended eco-hikes led by local herbalist **Ras Lumumba Corriette** (see p.470).

Getting around

There aren't many bus stops on St Croix and they're not very conveniently located. **VITRAN** runs between Christiansted and Frederiksted (Mon–Sat every 30min; Sun every hour) but **shared taxi vans** running along Queen Mary Highway are just as good an option. They stop on demand, which can be time-consuming, but they're cheap and are widely used by commuting locals (US$2 before 6pm, but be warned they are very few and far between after 6pm though the price is only US$0.50 more). If you need to call ahead for one, try St Croix Taxi Association (at the airport, ℡340/778-1088); Antilles Taxi Service, Christiansted (℡340/773-5020); Caribbean Taxi Service Tours (℡340/773-9799); or Frederiksted Taxi Tours (℡340/772-4775).

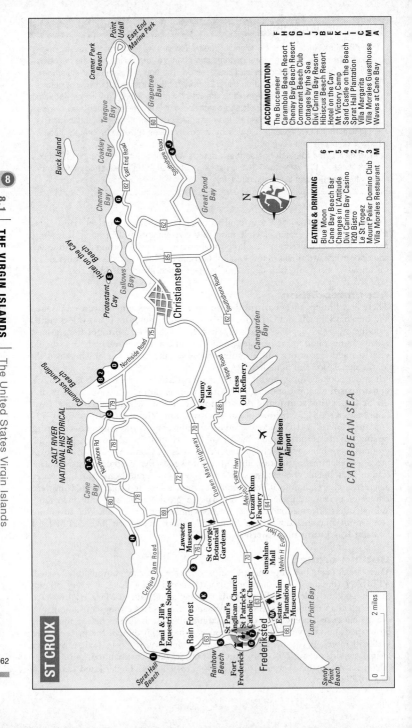

ST CROIX

ACCOMMODATION

The Buccaneer	F
Carambola Beach Resort	H
Chenay Bay Beach Resort	G
Cormorant Beach Club	D
Cottages by the Sea	L
Divi Carina Bay Resort	J
Hibiscus Beach Resort	B
Hotel on the Cay	E
Mt Victory Camp	K
Sand Castle on the Beach	I
Sprat Hall Plantation	C
Villa Margarita	M
Villa Morales Guesthouse	I
Waves at Cane Bay	A

EATING & DRINKING

Blue Moon	6
Cane Bay Beach Bar	1
Changes in L'Attitude	5
Divi Carina Bay Casino	4
H2O Bistro	2
Le St Tropez	7
Mount Pelier Domino Club	3
Villa Morales Restaurant	M

CARIBBEAN SEA

N

0   2 miles

The St Croix Heritage Trail

One way to see the best of the island is to take the **St Croix Heritage Trail**, a 72-mile driving route that offers close-up glimpses and detailed information about over 200 sites and attractions around St Croix. The route marked by road signs displaying an old sugar mill weaves through the hills between Frederiksted and Christiansted, mostly on Centerline Road. Pick up a map at their website (ⓦwww.stcroixheritagetrail.com), or at any tourism office, and many hotels also have information and maps. If you don't have your own car, ask taxis for their special Heritage Trail Tour rates.

Alternatively, most hotels and resorts have cut-rate shuttles that will take you back and forth from Christiansted and Frederiksted at prearranged times (ask ahead). From the East End, **taxis** – generally station wagons, trucks or minivans – to Christiansted will cost between US$20 and US$30 for a round-trip, almost double that for Frederiksted. St Croix is a great island for driving around, especially along the **St Croix Heritage Trail** (see above).

Should you find the need for a car, several **car rental** firms have offices in and around Christiansted and at the airport: Avis (ⓣ340/778-9395); Budget (ⓣ340/776-5774); Olympic Rent-a-Car (ⓣ340/773-8000); Centerline Car Rentals (ⓣ340/778-0450); Hertz (ⓣ340/778-1402); and Thrifty (ⓣ340/773-7200).

Christiansted and around

CHRISTIANSTED was established in 1735 by the Danes, who named the town after Christian VI of Denmark. Located on the north central coastline, it is the capital of St Croix and its most historic and developed city. Because of a building code installed by the forward-thinking Danes, much of Christiansted's original architecture still exists. In some cases, you can still see original street signs written in Danish. The streets are laid out so simply that it's almost impossible to get lost, and because of this it's a great walking city. It has a pleasant, aged feel, its handful of historic sights mingling with small courtyard restaurants and a laid-back bar scene down on the Wharf, on the city centre's northern edge. And once you've tired of the town's low-key attractions, you can indulge in plentiful watersports and beach activities not far off, or go on nature excursions to nearby **Buck Island**.

Accommodation

Christiansted

Carringtons Inn Estate Herman Hill ⓣ340/713-0508 or 1-877/658-0508, ⓦwww.carringtonsinn.com. A five-room bed-and-breakfast on a hill overlooking Christiansted. The owners are delightful and pay great attention to details for the guests, including fresh flower arrangements and excellent breakfasts. Recommended. ⑤

The Danish Manor Hotel 2 Company St ⓣ340/773-1377 or 1-800/524-2069, ⓕ340/7731913. The rooms are basic, very few have a nice view and the pool looks a bit stagnant. But at US$80 for a double it is as cheap as you'll get in high season. ④

Hotel Caravelle 44A King Cross St ⓣ340/773-0687 or 1-800/524-0410, ⓦwww.hotelcaravelle.com. A 43-room, European-style hotel located just off the Wharf downtown, this is a favourite among those who want nice digs but would rather spend their money enjoying the island than on their accommodation. ⑤

Hotel on the Cay Protestant Cay ⓣ340/773-2035 or 1-800/524-2035, ⓦwww.hotelonthecay.com. This seven-acre island, located in Christiansted's harbour, is just a ninety-second ferry ride from the wharf. Rooms have kitchenettes and balconies, and though the place is showing wear and tear, the price is not bad and many watersports are available. ⑤

King Christian Hotel King's Wharf ⓣ340/773-6330 or 1-800/524-2012, ⓦwww.kingchristian.com. Clean bright rooms located right on the boardwalk, and the Superior rooms have views of the sea and fort. Offers good low-season weekend packages with diving and a rental car. ⑤

Pink Fancy 27 Prince St ☎ 340/773-8460 or 1-800/524-2045, ✆ www.pinkfancy.com. An extremely cute and well-kept, gay-friendly historic inn (the oldest part of the four-building complex is a Danish townhouse from 1780) that in the 1950s was a favourite hangout of stage stars like Noel Coward. Rooms have four-poster beds, kitchenettes and names like "Sweet Bottom" and "Upper Love." There are also two-bedroom cottages for US$275 for four people. No steel drums here; this courtyard listens to opera and classical. Best value in town. **⑤**

Around Christiansted

The Buccaneer 25200 Gallows Bay ☎ 340/773-2100 or 1-800/255-3881, ✆ www.thebuccaneer.com. Situated on 340 pristine acres, with three beaches offering good snorkelling, an eighteen-hole golf course, eight tennis courts and huge rooms with four-poster beds, this is the island's finest resort. **⑨**

Carambola Beach Resort Estate Davis Bay ☎ 340/778-3800 or 1-888/503-8760, ✆ www.carambolabeach.com. Designed in the Tahitian Rockefeller style of Caneel Bay, with rattan chairs, mahogany beds and terracotta floors, but showing some signs of wear and tear. Two restaurants, tennis courts, spa and a lovely stretch of beach. Good hiking in the hills along the coast and the golf course here is the best on the island. **⑧**

Chenay Bay Beach Resort Rte 82 ☎ 340/773-2918 or 1-800/548-4457, ✆ www.chenaybay.com. Located on sedate Chenay Bay, east of Christiansted, this three-star resort offers fifty, tightly situated West Indian-style cottages, all with kitchenettes, located on a former sugar plantation. The restaurant is good, especially for more traditional Caribbean items and Saturday features a pig

roast and carnival-style entertainers. Enquire about package deals. **⑨**

Cormorant Beach Club 4126 La Grande Princesse ☎ 340/778-8920 or 1-800/548-4460, ✆ www.cormorantbeachclub.com. Just west of Christiansted, this gay-friendly resort, now under new management is on its way up after a period of deterioration. It is a peaceful delight situated on a white-sand peninsula surrounded by the ocean. **⑧**

Divi Carina Bay Resort 25 Estate Turner Hole ☎ 340/773-9700 or 1-800/823-9352, ✆ www.divicarina.com. Though remote (a rental car is a must) this is not your peace and quiet type of resort. There is always activity seaside or at the casino across the street. All 130 rooms overlook the sea and have kitchenettes. There are also wheelchair-accessible guestrooms. **⑧**

Hibiscus Beach Resort 4131 La Grande Pincesse ☎ 340/773-4042 or 1-800/442-0121, ✆ www.hibiscusbeachresort.com. A 38-room resort right up on the beach with views to Buck Island, and offering a variety of packages including diving deals. Bathrooms have showers only. The on-site restaurant *H2O* is quite good. **⑦**

Villa Margarita 9024 Salt River ☎ 340/713-1930 or 1-866/274-8811, ✆ www.villamargarita.com. Walking distance from Salt River Marina, the grounds are seaside but nothing special. Rooms, however, are nice, all with kitchenettes and balconies with a great view of the sea, and the suites go for US$110. **⑤**

Waves at Cane Bay Rte 80 ☎ 340/778-1805 or 1-800/545-0603, ✆ www.canebaystcroix.com. Situated west of Christiansted on Cane Bay, this is the place to stay if you want to literally roll out of bed, don your scuba gear and hit the water. Shore dives to the wall are possible and guests are provided with snorkelling gear, maps and instructions. **⑥**

The Town

Christiansted is the best-preserved colonial city in all the Virgin Islands and has a number of historic public buildings and churches. The best place to start a tour of the town's sights is the **Scale House** at the top of King Street by the Wharf (daily 8am–4.45pm; ☎ 340/773-1460), which was built in 1856 as the weigh house for all the goods that passed through the harbour and nowadays houses the Christiansted visitor's centre. Close by, the **Customs House** currently serves as the headquarters for the National Park Service (Mon–Fri 9am–5pm). **Fort Christianvaern**, off Hospital Street (daily 8am–5pm; US$3), constructed in 1749, is St Croix's finest example of Danish military architecture: its cannons still point out to sea, and inside you can take a guided or self-guided tour through the dungeon's torture chambers, visit the officers' kitchen and the barrack rooms, and take in the building's history by way of text and well-displayed weapons, documents and other artefacts. The same ticket grants admission to the **Steeple Building** across the road (daily 8am–4.45pm), the island's first Danish Lutheran church, built in 1753 and now housing the national park museum, which offers exhibits on the history of the church, St

Croix's indigenous tribes, sugar plantations, rum factories and slavery. The **West Indies Guinea Warehouse**, closed to the public for renovations, is on the same street and used to house the trading company that basically built the town of Christiansted. A short walk north, **Government House**, on King Street, was originally the mansion of a Danish merchant, built in 1747, but today this long, bright-yellow building (one of the prettiest in town) houses the local government. If it's open, slip into the courtyard, where you'll be met by a flowing fountain and lush greenery. Afterwards, take in the **Lutheran Church of Lord God of Sabaoth**, further down King Street, built by the original Danish settlers in 1734, but later renamed the Dutch Reformed Church. It houses the original altar from the Steeple Building. Nearby, Company Street is the home of a regular Wednesday and Saturday **market** at which local farmers, fishermen and local craftsmen sell their goods on the site of the original 1735 slave market.

Around town

There are one or two sights beyond the town's limits that are worth seeking out. Around three miles west of Christiansted, the **Salt River National Historical Park and Ecological Preserve** is nowadays a freshwater channel by which lavish yachts enter the marina. But it was also the place where Columbus first sent sailors ashore here in 1493. This is also the site of many successful excavations, which have rendered artefacts from some of the indigenous peoples, and guided hikes are available. In the opposite direction from Christiansted, east, **Point Udall** is worth the trip – the easternmost point of the United States, and one of the most peaceful spots on the island. It's a windblown spot, but ideal for escaping the crowds, and hiking down one of many trails to the beaches at the **East End Marine Park** where the protected waters of **Jack's** and **Isaac's Bay** butt up against lush, rolling hills protected by the Nature Conservancy. The snorkelling here is excellent. A mile out to sea to the north, **Buck Island Reef National Monument** is St Croix's crown jewel, with picture-perfect deserted beaches, great hiking and an underwater trail for snorkellers. It was proclaimed a National Monument in 1962 by President John F. Kennedy, and consists of 700 acres of Caribbean reef and sea and 180 acres of land. Most hotels can set up an excursion for you, which will leave from the Christiansted wharf or Green Cay Marina. These guided tours can also drop you off on your own secluded beach with a picnic lunch and a bottle of wine. Best check with the National Park Service (☎340/773-1460) regarding rules for visiting on your own boat.

Beaches

The beach at the *Hotel on the Cay*, across the harbour from Christiansted, is the closest **beach** to town. It's accessible only by the regular US$3 ferry, and offers watersports rentals, a restaurant and bar. Further away, the beach at **Cane Bay**, six miles or so west of Christiansted off Route 80, has great snorkelling, plus a dive shop that offers trips, a beach bar and restaurant. Closer to town, **Columbus Landing Beach** is the beach off the Salt River where Columbus's men first came ashore.

Eating and drinking

Despite being the least touristed of the USVI, St Croix has a wide selection of cuisine at all price levels. There are several little roadside attractions scattered around the island such as *South Shore Cafe* (☎340/773-9311) with its pepper ice cream and a little sugar-cane juice stand along Centerline Road closer to Frederiksted. But the island also has some of the best high-end dining spots in the Caribbean. While there are a few great **places to eat** in Frederiksted (see p.469), Christiansted is the culinary capital of St Croix, and it's a mostly casual experience with no need to dress up.

Bacchus 52 Queen Cross St ☎340/692-9922. Expensive, but without a doubt one of the best dining experiences you'll have in the Virgin Islands. Request a table overlooking the street and choose something special from the largest wine list on the island. Open Tues–Sun 6–10pm. Recommended.

Cane Bay Beach Bar Rte 80 ☎340/778-5669. Burgers and beer on the beach at Cane Bay, west of town. Cash only.

Fort Christian Brew Pub 55 King's Alley ☎340/713-9820. Hot sandwiches, pastas, jambalayas and other Cajun favourites. While the food is always a safe bet, the local-brewed beer is a must-try. Located on the boardwalk overlooking the water.

H2O Bistro *Hibiscus Beach Resort* (see p.464). You can eat breakfast, lunch or dinner right on the beach. The menu is quite good, the quality excellent. Entrees ($18-32) include some creole and cajun choices, as well as crab cakes, coconut shrimp and filet mignon. The wraps are quite good and sizeable. For breakfast try the rum-soaked French toast.

Harvey's Restaurant and Bar 11B Company St ☎340/773-3433. Reasonably priced fare ($5-12), specializing in creole dishes and barbecue. Lunch Mon–Sat from 11.30 to when the food runs out. You don't want to be late for the seafood kallaloo on Fridays. Also a good place to sample local drinks like sorrel, soursop and maubi (a root).

Kim's 45 King St ☎340/773-3377. Dine among locals at this dirt-cheap West Indian eatery. The conch in butter sauce melts in your mouth. Mon–Sat 11am–9pm.

Luncheria 6 Company St ☎340/773-4247. Cheap and savoury Tex-Mex food with killer margaritas for just a buck. Open Mon–Sat 11am–9pm.

Morning Glory Coffee and Tea Off East End Road ☎340/773-6620. Owner and third-generation coffee roaster Margo Loe ensures you get a top-notch cup of joe at this Gallows Bay café. She also has a full breakfast menu and wraps and salads for lunch. Mon–Sat 7am–3pm.

Rum Runners Christiansted boardwalk ☎340/773-6585. The steaks are particularly popular and with the lobster are the only things over US$20 on the dinner menu. Eggs Benedict is a must-try for breakfast ($9). Or just stop by for great happy-hour drink prices to wash down a half-pound of peel and eat shrimp with a tequila lime cocktail sauce for just under US$10.

Savant's Hospital Street ☎340/713-8666. Upscale restaurant that serves a fusion of Thai, Mexican and Caribbean cuisine in a stylish atmosphere on the eastern edge of town. Mon–Sat 5.30–10pm. This place is small, the service is great, and reservations are a must.

Shenanigan's 1102 Strand St/Pan Am Pavilion ☎340/713-8110. Fast and friendly Southern cooking for travellers on a budget. You can get breakfast for around US$5.

Singh's Fast Food 23B King Street ☎340/773-7357. Serving up local food for over 30 years, this deli-style outfit has great roti and a variety of stews including curried goat. At US$1.50 a "Double" (spicy chick pea and potato sandwich) is a great snack option.

Turtles Deli 55/56 Company St ☎340/772-3936. Good-sized gourmet sandwiches (US$8–9) on a variety of fresh-made breads.

Tutto Bene 2006 Eastern Suburb ☎340/773-5229. A small favourite since 1991 in a new location, serving northern Italian fare with a Caribbean twist. A "taste of Tutto Bene" is a nice assortment of antipasti. Reservations suggested. Daily 6–10pm.

Zeny's Bar and Restaurant 39–40 King Cross St ☎340/773-4393. Cheap and authentic Puerto Rican fare located next to Market Square. Go for simple fried pork chops and curried stews or try local favourites such as saltfish and dumplings or sautéed pig feet. Daily 8am–11pm.

Nightlife and entertainment

While nowhere on St Croix is known for its crazy **nightlife**, Christiansted is your best bet. During high season, take a moonlit stroll along the waterfront and you're bound to find a party of clinking beer mugs and live music. Cover charges almost don't exist on the island, so you can poke into any place and have a drink while you check out the scene. Most restaurants have bars, which offer live music (mostly on weekend nights), ranging from jazz to rock to reggae to calypso to acoustic. If you want to get a great taste of Caribbean **steel panning**, find out where local Bill Bass (⊛www.billbasssteelpans.com) is playing. **Hermit crab races** are held at around 5pm on Monday, Wednesday and Friday at *Fort Christian Brew Pub*, *Divi Resort* and *Stixx* (on the waterfront), respectively. Sponsor a crab for a couple dollars and if he emerges first from a giant circle, you win a prize. Look for **full-moon parties** at Cane Bay. Some of the resorts, such as Chenay Bay Beach Resort have theme nights during high season. The social scene changes often, especially with high and low season; local newspapers are a good place to look for your options.

Watch for the **Jump-Up** (@www.gotostcroix.com/jumpup), a Carnival-like street party that takes place in downtown Christiansted regularly during tourist season between 6pm and 10pm. Expect live music, dancing, mocko jumbies (stilt walkers), crafts and lots of food. The **Whim Plantation** (☎340/772-0598) hosts a Candlelight Concert series throughout the year and the 1100-seat **Island Center for the Performing Arts** (☎340/778-5272) is the place to look for plays and concerts.

Bars, clubs and nightlife

Cane Bay Beach Bar (see opposite). Often has live reggae or steel pan bands and music during Sunday brunch 10.30am–2pm. Watch for pig roasts and full-moon parties when the crowds spill into the road and onto the beach.

Cheeseburgers in Paradise East End Road ☎340/773-1119. This small, informal eatery offers live music ranging from acoustic guitar and calypso to rocking blues bands Thursday to Sunday nights, generally beginning at about 7pm.

Club 54 54B Company St ☎340/773-8002. Check out this indoor/outdoor space, with multilevel decks and a tropical setting, for regular DJs and live performers. Open Wed–Mon until 3am.

The Deep End Bar Green Cay Marina. Live jazz every Friday at 7pm.

Divi Carina Bay Casino 54 Estate Turner Hole ☎340/773-7529. Located on the southeast end of the island, this is currently the island's only casino, a modest collection of slots and table games open Mon–Thur 12pm–4am; Fri 12pm–Mon 4am. Often has live music at the weekends.

Moonraker 43A Queen Cross St ☎340/713-8025. A DJ plays club music and Top 40 at this upstairs dance bar.

Off the Wall Bar and Grill Cane Bay ☎340/778-4771. Anything from jazz to steel pan to Jimmy Buffet covers nightly 6–9pm during high season. No shirt, no shoes, no problem. US$5–15 for various burgers, sandwiches and pizzas.

The Terrace Lounge *Buccaneer Hotel*. Live music nightly 8.30–11pm. There's often a piano player at happy hour.

Shopping

With few exceptions, Christiansted is where you'll find the best assortment of shops, the speciality being jewellery of all kinds (especially the "Crucian" bracelet), and the usual array of local arts and crafts – on which, of course, no tax is payable. The Caribbean Bracelet Company, King's Alley Walk, is good for jewellery; the Iona Skye Gallery, 2220 Queen Cross St, is the outlet of a husband-and-wife team of jewellery-makers; Many Hands, in the Pan Am Pavillion, has a great range of local arts and crafts, pottery, jewellery and music; while Mark Austin, 3AB Queen Cross St, hand-paints beach pails, garden watering pails, calabash bowls, frames, and more. Finally, the Mitchell–Larsen Studio, 58 Company St, sells all types of hand-blown glassware made by its resident artisans.

Frederiksted and around

FREDERIKSTED, seventeen miles away on the west coast of the island, is smaller than Christiansted, though it is closer to the airport and its harbour attracts weekly cruise ships. Frederiksted doesn't have much in the line of old buildings – at the local post office, a mural of **The Fireburn** captures well the spirit and anger of the rioters that burnt much of the town in 1878 in protest at harsh economic conditions. Many of its clapboard buildings date from the turn of the twentieth-century but sit on original stone foundations that date back to the mid-1700s. The main strip of Strand Street, which skirts the newly renovated palm-lined waterfront, offers shopping, restaurants and the **Caribbean Museum Center for the Arts**, but overall Frederiksted is a fairly sleepy place until the cruise ships pull into port. In town, be sure to visit **Fort Frederik**, a large red-coloured building and ramparts next to the pier that was built in 1760: it was the site of the slave emancipation of 1848. Inside, there's an art gallery and museum (Mon–Fri 8.30am–4pm). Other architectural highlights include **St Paul's Anglican Church**, built in 1812, and **St Patrick's Catholic Church**, built in the 1840s, both on Prince Street. Frederiksted is a bit dodgier at night and anywhere off the main strip should be regarded with caution during the evening, though the more adventursome might find the various local bars pumping out *reggae*, *bachata*, *salsa* and *merengue* intriguing.

Around town

Outside Frederiksted, there are a few places to take in on a leisurely day-trip. The **St George Village Botanical Garden** is perhaps the highlight, a few miles inland at 127 Estate St in Kingshill (daily 9am–5pm; US$6; ☎340/692-2874), with beautiful botanical gardens flourishing amid the ruined buildings of an old estate. Just south, across the Queen Mary Highway, the **Cruzan Rum Factory** offers tours and liberal samples (Mon–Fri 9–11.30am & 1–4.15pm; US$4; ☎340/692-2280), and the **Estate Whim Plantation Museum**, back towards Frederiksted on Route 76 (Mon–Sat 10am–4pm; US$8; ☎340/772-0598), has been restored as it was during Danish times, with a period museum of agricultural tools and other exhibits. If you like this, try also the **Karl and Marie Lawaetz Museum** on Route 76, which also devotes itself to mid-eighteenth century life on the farm; don't miss the nearby **St Croix Leap** (☎340/772-0421) on Mahogany Road, a woodworking studio that sells jewellery, furniture and other crafts by local craftspeople.

For a unique experience, you must make a happy-hour trip to the **Mount Pellier Domino Club**, east of town on Route 76 (☎340/772-9914). Go for the beer-drinking pigs – yes, you throw them a can of non-alcoholic beer, they crush it between their jaws, drink it dry and then spit out the can – and stay for the ambience (dirt floor and thatched roof) or a mean game of dominoes. Other pigs are not so lucky and you can find them most Sundays at **Mount Victory Camp's pig roasts** which are truly a community event. This is the place to hear **Quelbe** music (see box p.461) and dance under the great mango tree. Or if jazz is more your thing, watch for **Sunset Jazz** when a large local crowd brings beach blankets, lawn chairs and picnics to the beach near Fort Frederiksted the third Friday of every month.

Beaches and activities

There are several **beaches** around Frederiksted that offer great amenities. **Rainbow Beach**, half a mile north on Route 63, has good snorkelling and several beach bars and restaurants, such as *Changes in L'Attitude* (☎340/772-3090), which offers so-so Tex-Mex and general American fare, plus darts, billiards and watersports rentals. At **Sprat Hall Beach**, a mile north on Route 63, there is the *Sunset Grill* (☎340/772-5855), which serves grilled food and drinks for beachcombers. Go **horseriding** next door at Paul and Jill's Equestrian Stables (☎340/772-2880, ⊛www.paulandjills.com), where a two-hour ride into the nearby rainforest costs US$60. The largest beach in the entire Virgin Islands is **Sandy Point**, part of a nature preserve (only open Sat–Sun 10am–4pm) directly south of Frederiksted, which can be reached by following Melvin Evans Highway (Route 66). The final scene of the movie *The Shawshank Redemption* was shot here, but be aware the sand comes and goes with currents and seasonal storms, sometimes leaving large bare rocks at the water's edge. It is best to ask a local about current conditions though it is very beautiful and secluded either way.

Accommodation

Century 21 Island Villas ☎340/773-8821 or 1-800/626-4512, ⊛www.stcroixislandvillas.com. Offers some very fine villas in various locations on the west end and caters to the diving crowd. ❾

Cottages by the Sea 127A Est. Smithfield ☎340/772-0495 or 1-800/323-7252, ⊛www.caribbeancottages.com. Though rather outdated these breezy cottages are being remodelled one by one. Quiet at the edge of Frederiksted though since Hurricane Jeanne whipped up some surge in 2004, the beach will need some time to recover.

Frederiksted Hotel 442 Strand St ☎340/772 0500, ⊛www.frederikstedhotel.com. This is a decent but not fancy modern option if you want to stay in town, with a pool, bar and restaurant, and TVs and phones in most rooms.

Mt Victory Camp (see opposite) Canopied tent platforms are US$85 for two adults and two children, US$10 extra per person. Bare sites for US$35.

Sand Castle on the Beach 127 Est. Smithfield ☏340/772-1205, ✆www.sandcastleonthebeach. com. Located on a beautiful stretch of white sand, this is the nicest hotel on the west end with rooms of various size and price aimed mainly at the gay and lesbian community. The hotel's *Beachside Cafe* serves the best lunch in town.

Sprat Hall Plantation ☏340/772-0305. A guest-house filled with antiques located on twenty acres of an old estate complete with windmill. **⑥**

Villa Morales Guesthouse 82-C Est. Whim ☏340/772-0556. Several basic rooms five minutes from the airport, some with a/c. Nothing special but clean, cheap ($45 for a double, US$10 extra per person up to 4) and the owners are great people. Restaurant on site (see below). **②**

Eating and drinking

Though most of the high-end dining is in or around Christiansted, there are several great places to eat in Frederiksted.

Armstrong's Just east of Frederiksted on Centerline Road this is the place to try all sorts of home-made tropical fruit-flavoured ice cream.

Beachside Cafe *Sand Castle on the Beach* ☏340/772-1266. Choose from a wide variety of fresh seafood as well as duck, chicken, pork, veg-etarian dishes and more. This is the best place for lunch according to many (try a caesar wrap with chicken/shrimp for US$11/14) and reservations are recommended. US$18-26 for dinner entrees.

Blue Moon Victorian House, Strand St ☏340/772-2222. Arguably the best eats in town, this intimate bistro serves Cajun and Caribbean and huge salads. It is also the place to catch some live jazz on Wednesdays and Fridays or for Sunday brunch. Entrees US$16–27.

Coyote Cafe 37 Strand St ☏340/772-2222. Fresh Mexican meets Caribbean fish at this second floor terrace opened by the owners of Blue Moon during the pier renovation. Great for sunset meals. Entrees are around US$15.

Le St Tropez 227 King St ☏340/772-3000. This Mediterranean French restaurant in a charm-ing courtyard serves lunch (Mon–Fri) and dinner (Mon–Sat) with entrees ranging US$17–30.

Lost Dog Pub 14 King St ☏340/772-3526. Something along the lines of a roadhouse bar this is the place for a great pizza (from US$8) although you might wait a long time for your food, especially when it's busy. But you're on island time so belly up to the bar, have a beer and listen to the classic

rock jukebox and the local barflies. Out back is a great courtyard.

Pier 69 69 King St ☏340/772-0069. Good for late night drinks, ooccasional dancing and live music when the cruises come to town. The biggest burger on the island and, talk is, the best steak. Chef Herbie promises you'll never find a hair in the food. (He's bald and quite a character.)

Tropical Java 330 Strand St ☏340/773-5282. The place to go for a cup of joe or some home-made baked sweets. Closed Sat.

Turtles Deli 37 Strand St ☏340/772-3676. Mon–Sat 8.30am–6pm. Good-sized gourmet sand-wiches ($8–9) on a variety of fresh-made breads. Nice seaside patio.

Uca's Kitchen 115 King St ☏340/772-5063 Just straight off the cruise dock, this Rastafarian kitchen may look a little dodgy from the outside – especially on nights when cruises are in port and they open after their posted hours – but don't let that deter you. This is the best vegetarian option on the island as well as one of the more economi-cal choices. The spinach mushroom lasagne is a favourite. Open Mon–Fri 11.30am–5pm (or until the food runs out), Sat 12.30–"until".

Villa Morales Restaurant 82-C Est. Whim ☏340/772-0556. Only open Thurs–Sat but if you want local and Puerto Rican fare, this is the place. The conch in butter sauce is excellent and some former patrons have had the pâté shipped frozen to them thousands of miles away.

Watersports and outdoor activities

There are two types of **fishing** offered on the island – fishing the flats for tarpon, bonefish and permit fish or deep-sea fishing along the edge of the island. Catch-22 (☏340/778-6987) does full and half days on a Bertram 38; Carl Holley (☏340/277-4042, ✆www.fishwithcarl.com) captains *The One-Eyed Wahoo*, a 26-ft Dusky with room for up to four anglers for half- and full-day trips ($350/500); and Fantasy Charters (☏340/773-0917) operates a 30-foot powerboat out of the Gallows Bay St Croix Marina. For **golfers**, Carambola Golf Club, a par-70 course at *Carambola*

Beach Resort (see p.464), is the best on the island and has a four-star rating by *Golf Digest*. A round of eighteen holes with a cart will generally cost you US$50–70, depending on the season. St Croix offers great **hiking**: Ay-Ay, Kingshill (☎340/772-4079), does personalized eco-hiking and tours at any price range by herbalist, naturalist and son of a long line of bush women, Ras Lumumba Corriette. For a special treat, ask him to show you where he lives. **Annaly Bay** is a somewhat serious hike from Carambola Resort with views of the sea-swept northern coast and some gorgeous tide pools to soak in at the end while the waves beat the rocks protecting you. **Nature Conservancy**, 3052 Estate Little Princess, Christiansted (☎340/773-5575) offers tours of its grounds on an old mill plantation and by arrangement gives group tours of the land aspect of the **East End Marine Park** around Jack's Bay and Isaac's Bay. **St Croix Environmental Association**, Arawak Building, Suite 3, Gallows Bay (☎340/773-1989) periodically schedules hikes to places such as Estate Mt Washington, Estate Caledonia, the rainforest and Salt River for around US$25.

Like all Caribbean islands, St Croix is **watersports** crazy. While most activities and trips can be booked along the waterfront in Christiansted, remember that many outfits offer hotel pick-ups and can help booking entire vacations. Also, most hotels and public beaches offer kayak, jet ski and snorkel rentals.

It is possible to dive Buck Island but it is better for snorkelling unless the sea is quite calm and you can get beyond the protection of the reef.

Watersports

Big Beard's Adventure Tours Pan Am Pavillion, Christiansted ☎340/773-4482, ☻www.bigbeards. com. This outfit specializes in snorkelling trips to Buck Island on one of two catamarans. They also do beach barbecues and sunset trips.

Bilinda Charters Green Cay Marina ☎340/773-1641, ☻www.sailbilinda.com. Offers private sails for up to six people aboard Kallaloo, a 37ft sloop. Choose from half-day sails to three destinations, sunset sails and Discover Sailing. Custom trips are also available.

Buck Island Charters ☎340/773-3161. Full- and half-day sails on a trimaran leaving from Green Cay Marina.

Caribbean Adventure Tours ☎340/778-1522 or 1-800/532-3483, ☻www.stcroixkayak.com. Whether you embark on an island sightseeing excursion, a sunset trip or an eco-photo tour, this is the place to call for kayaking.

Llewellyn's Charter, Inc St Croix Yacht Club/ Teague Bay ☎340/773-9027. One of the most respected sailing charters, which has been in service for over twenty years.

Mile Mark Charters ☎340/773-2628. Located on the Christiansted waterfront, these guys offer everything from sailing charters to powerboat rentals to glass-bottom boat tours, and they are the only company authorized to take dive trips to Buck Island and they do so by reservation only (minimum six divers) and when seas allow.

St Croix Water Sports *Hotel on the Cay* ☎340/773-7060. This is the place to go for a parasailing adventure or to rent wave-runners, windsurfers, kayaks and snorkelling gear.

Virgin Kayak Co. Cane Bay ☎340/778-0071. Rents kayaks, including some you can pedal. Runs tours customized to taste and ability, including Salt River Bay tours.

Scuba diving and snorkelling

St Croix has plenty to see beneath the waves and its larger territory, smaller tourist crowds and the fact that there are only seven dive operators all combine to give you some good elbow room. Great snorkelling and shore dives await you in **Cane Bay** where the seven-mile long **drop-off wall** that hugs the northern coastline is just 100 feet out. The island also has nine popular wreck dives (☻www. stcroixshipwrecks.com) and six of them are in **Butler Bay** (another good snorkelling spot) on the west end and can be accessed from shore. Other dive highlights are the **underwater canyon at Salt River** and west end reefs such as **The Swirling Reef of Death**, a photographer's dream. The **Frederiksted Pier** is a great place to see seahorses whether you dive or snorkel. **Buck Island** has an underwater snorkel trail which designated operators will take you to on a tour, but if you are on your own there are some spots on the northwest side that are also quite nice. Be aware of currents lest you look up from the bottom and find yourself halfway to Venezuela. **East End Marine Park's Isaac's Bay** has a nice barrier reef just off shore where at times coral sticks right up out of the water. Many of the beaches on the island are turtle nesting grounds and hawksbill and green turtles are common on dives. The three beaches at **The Buccaneer** resort offer excellent snorkelling but are generally for guests only. Just tell the guard at the entrance you are going to the beachside restaurant. Grassy areas around The Buccaneer resort and Chenay Bay are frequented by spotted eagle rays.

All dive shops give discounts on multiple dives and they often hook up with hotels to offer some excellent packages. And if you can't decide on a shop, check out the **Dive-the-Island Passport** (⊚www.diversevirgin.com). All the operators have collaborated to offer these dive packages, the most basic of which (6 tanks for US$199) includes boat dives with any three operators. This way you are not restricted to the dive sites of a single operator.

Anchor Dive Center Salt River National Park ☎340/778-1522 or 1-800/532-3483, ⊚www. anchordivestcroix.com. This five-star PADI shop is just a five-minute boat ride from the best of the wall dives and surface interval is done on shore which is nice when the seas are a bit rough. Has shops at Carambola and Divi resorts.

Cane Bay Dive Shop Pan Am Pavillion in Christiansted ☎340/773-4663; Strand Street, Frederiksted ☎340/772-0715; and Cane Bay, North Shore ☎340/773-9913, ⊚www.canebayscuba. com. They offer all levels of instruction, rentals and sales and will even customize dive packages. How about a full-moon midnight dive?

Dive Experience 1111 Strand St, Christiansted ☎340/773-3307 or 1-800/235-9047, ⊚www. divexp.com. Friendly and knowledgeable, owner Michelle Pugh has been diving St Croix since the 70s and runs dives to a wide range of sites, not just the wall. Dive the fish feed at the sunken Chez Barge.

N2 the Blue Diving Adventures ☎340/713-1475 or 1-866-712-2583, ⊚www.n2blue.com. This north shore shop rents equipment and does shore dives. It runs a small boat from the pier

in Frederiksted and takes out a maximum of six divers.

St Croix Ultimate Bluewater Adventures ☎340/773-5994, ⊚www.stcroixscuba.com. Located in the Caravelle Arcade in downtown Christiansted, this dive shop offers everything from wreck dives to rental and sales to introductory dives for kids aged 8 and above. You can have your dive recorded on DVD.

Scuba Shack ☎340/772-2483 or 1-888-789-3483, ⊚www.stcroixscubashack.com. This beachfront shop just north of Fort Frederiksted offers NAUI or PADI courses. Sue and Dave Ward will make you feel just like family. Offers nitrox dives and instruction as well as other speciality courses. Kayak rentals available also.

ScubaWest 330 Strand St, Frederiksted ☎340/772-3701 or 1-800/352-0107, ⊚www .divescubawest.com. Specializes in diving from the pier (a shore dive) and runs boats to other west end sites. Has a great package with Frederiksted Hotel that includes 7 nights hotel with breakfast, five 2-tank boat dives and unlimited shore dives for US$602.

8.2

The British Virgin Islands

Forming roughly two chains separated by the Sir Francis Drake Channel, the **BRITISH VIRGIN ISLANDS** are a haven for snorkelling, fishing and diving enthusiasts. The BVI also offers some of the best **sailing** in the world, and the towns and bays bustle with the constant comings and goings of yachts and cruise ships mooring up at the many marinas and anchorages. Less developed than the USVI, the islands maintain their identity – Caribbean influences still dominate in food, music and culture, the British connection is only really evident in the language, and the resorts are modest and in keeping with their surroundings. What the BVI lack in glitz and historical sites they make up for in unspoilt beauty – stunning tree-covered peaks, secluded coves, long palm-fringed sandy **beaches** and spectacular **reefs** whose breathtaking marine life and numerous shipwrecks make for some of the best diving and snorkelling in the Caribbean.

A minority of the islands, all but one of which are covered in steep green hills, contain the majority of the 22,000 population. The largest and most developed, **Tortola**, is the main resort centre and home to the capital, Road Town. Quieter **Virgin Gorda** offers largely upmarket accommodation centred on its own mini-archipelago and watersports playground, the North Sound. Yachters flock to little **Jost Van Dyke** to clear customs and hit its infamous bars, while **Anegada**, the non-hilly Virgin, is a coral atoll teeming with wildlife whose endless beaches, maze

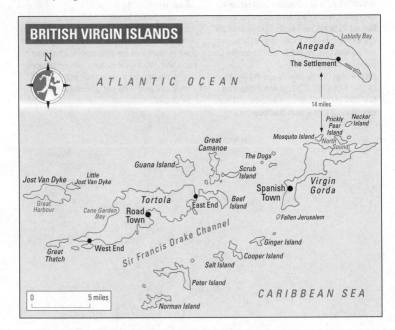

of reefs and bonefishing pull in day-trippers. The **outlying islands**, several of which are privately owned, see transient populations of guests at exclusive resorts or yachters who swim ashore.

Tortola

TORTOLA ("land of turtle doves" in Spanish), with a population of around 15,000, is the commercial and cosmopolitan centre of the BVI. Also the largest of the BVI, Tortola's twenty square miles of stunning mountain scenery rise to a peak of 1780ft, the highest in the BVI, at **Sage Mountain** on the west of the island. **Road Town**, roughly halfway along the more developed southern coast of the island, is home to the governor's residence, and most of Tortola's few historic sights. The **west of the island,** especially the **north coast,** has some of the **best beaches** and resorts and the liveliest nightlife – the **eastern end** is less well established on the tourist track but has some fine, often deserted beaches, including the island's best beach for surfing.

The island is best explored by car; **Ridge Road**, running east–west along the mountains' backbone, offers stunning views across the Francis Drake Channel. It gives access to the Belle View Overlook, **Mount Healthy National Park**, the touristy restaurant/bar *Skyworld*, which offers the island's only 360-degree view, and Sage Mountain National Park (just off Ridge Road).

Arrival, information and getting around

From **Beef Island International Airport** it's a short hop across the Queen Elizabeth II Bridge to East End on Tortola. Taxis cost US$18 for the six miles to Road Town; US$36 for destinations in West End. Hertz has an office at the airport and some other agencies offer a free pick-up and drop-off service (see below). The interisland **ferries** dock at West End, Road Town or Trellis Bay.

Banks, **information** and post offices are all found in Road Town, though you will be able to get hold of maps at the airport and most hotels. Some hotels and resorts offer free Internet access to guests; otherwise, the best deals are at CaribWave Internet Café, Waterfront Drive, Road Town (☎284/494-7549; US$5 for 30min) and Trellis Bay Cyber Café (☎284/495-2447; US$5 for 15min).

Public **transport** is limited to a fleet of shared taxi-vans running to no particular schedule and no particular stops, you just flag them down as they approach – they cost US$2–5 depending on your destination; be sure to enquire first. **Taxis** (often also vans) are easy to come by unless there are several cruise ships in town. There are stands at the ferry docks in Road Town and West End (look out for the brightly coloured stands with men chatting and playing checkers). If you need to arrange for one ahead of time, try BVI Taxi Association, Road Town (☎284/494-2322); West End Taxi Association (☎284/495-4881); and Beef Island Taxi Association (☎284/495-1982). **Car rental companies** on the island include Dede's Car Rental, Fat Hog's Bay (☎284/495-2041); Del's Jeep & Car Rental, Cane Garden Bay (☎284/495-9356); Dollar Rent-a-Car, Long Bay Beach (☎284/494-6093); Hertz, West End (☎284/495-4405); ITGO Car Rental, Wickham's Cay (☎284/494-5150, ⓦwww.itgobvi.com); and Tola Car Rentals, Fish Bay (☎284/494-8652). If you'd rather be out on the water, you can hire a small **dinghy** or even a large **powerboat** to get around – prices range US$50–300 per day (see p.485 for companies).

Road Town

Three-quarters of the island's inhabitants live in **ROAD TOWN**, either downtown, along its outskirts or in the hills above. The **harbour**, which has over the centuries provided shelter for fleets of Dutch, French, Spanish and English ships, fills with cruise ships, yachts and ferries unloading their cargo of tourists into the town's bustling and traffic-packed maze of

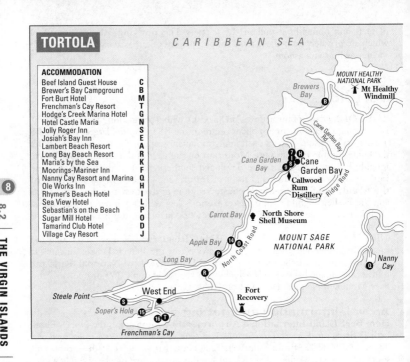

streets. Road Town's sights are all low-key but they're fairly close together and the streets and waterfront have a buzz all of their own with fishing boats unloading their haul and cruise ships docking. Most sights of interest, including the **Folk Museum** and **Botanic Garden**, together with the majority of shops and restaurants can be found on the two principal thoroughfares – historic **Main Street** and the more touristy **Waterfront Drive** – which run parallel to the water.

Maps and brochures are available at the **BVI Tourist Board office** on the second floor of the AKARA Building, Wickhams Cay I (Mon–Fri 8.30am–4.30pm; ☎284/494-3134, ⊛www.bvitourism.com), at the ferry terminal, and in most hotels.

Accommodation

There is no beachfront **accommodation** in Road Town, but the hotels perched on the surrounding hills offer spectacular views of the harbour and the Sir Francis Drake Channel beyond, while those around marinas will have you falling asleep to the tinkling sound of halyards in the wind. If you'd prefer to rent a **villa** or private house try *My Private Paradise* (☎202/554-8880 or 1-800/862-7863, ⊛www.myprivateparadise.com); *Areana Villas* (☎284/494-5864, ⊛www.areanavillas.com); *Island Hideaways* (☎1-800/832-2302, ⊛www.islandhideaways.com); or *Purple Pineapple Villa Rentals* (☎284/495-9567, ⊛www.purplepineapple.com). For accommodation just a few steps from the beach, head for the west of the island – lovely resorts and small hotels skirt Long Bay, Carrot Bay and Cane Garden Bay. **Tropical Nannies** (☎284/495-6493, ⊛www.tropicalnannies.com) can provide babysitting services at your hotel or resort in Tortola or Virgin Gorda if you've brought children and need a break from them.

Fort Burt Hotel Waterfront Drive ☎284/494-2587 or 1-888/873-5226,⊛www.bviguide.com/fortburt.

The commanding harbour views from this hillside retreat, built on the remains of a seventeenth-century

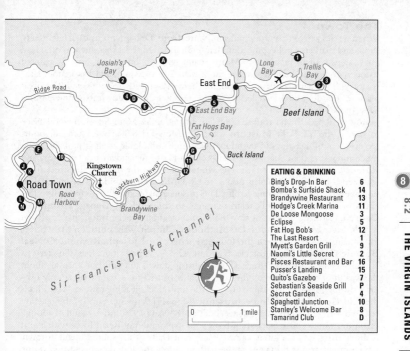

EATING & DRINKING

Bing's Drop-In Bar	6
Bomba's Surfside Shack	14
Brandywine Restaurant	13
Hodge's Creek Marina	11
De Loose Mongoose	3
Eclipse	5
Fat Hog Bob's	12
The Last Resort	1
Myett's Garden Grill	9
Naomi's Little Secret	2
Pisces Restaurant and Bar	16
Pusser's Landing	15
Quito's Gazebo	7
Sebastian's Seaside Grill	P
Secret Garden	4
Spaghetti Junction	10
Stanley's Welcome Bar	8
Tamarind Club	D

fort, make this one of the top options in town. The outdoor patio is perfect for a drink at sunset. Rooms vary in size, but most are large, and several multi-bedroom suites, complete with private pools, are also available. All have balconies, a/c, TV and refrigerators. The restaurant here is one of the best around. ➏

Hotel Castle Maria Waterfront Drive ☎284/494-2553, hotelcastlemaria@surfbvi.com. Sitting on a hill overlooking the harbour just a few minutes from the centre of town, the hotel is fronted by a nice tropical garden. The 33 rooms are plain but have kitchenettes and are very clean. There's a restaurant, bar and pool. Prices for doubles start at US$95. Some rooms have balconies and a view of the harbour. ➍

Maria's by the Sea Waterfront Drive ☎284/494-2595, ✉mariasbythesea@surfbvi.com. Rooms are bright and clean at this moderately priced choice located along the waterfront. The decor is typical Caribbean flavour with floral fabrics and wicker furniture, and each room has a balcony and kitchenette. Special deals are available for stays of seven days or longer. ➎

Moorings-Mariner Inn Waterfront Drive, Wickhams Cay II ☎284/494-2332 or 1-800/535-7289, ☎284/494-2226. Next to the docks for the Caribbean's yacht charter giant, Moorings, the hotel is convenient for the yachting crowd passing through for a night or two, but nothing special for someone in search of a resort. Be aware that the time to be off the boats is noon and check-in not until 2pm. Has all the usual facilities including a swimming pool. ➐

Nanny Cay Resort and Marina Nanny Cay ☎284/494-4895 or 1-866/284-4683, ⊛www.nannycay.com. Almost a little city in itself, this resort overlooking a quaint marina has all you could need – restaurants, two swimming pools, a watersports centre, tennis, volleyball, spa, an Internet café, small supermarket and charter services. For US$100–160 (depending on the season) for a standard studio room for two, it's a steal. ➏

Sea View Hotel Waterfront Drive ☎284/494-2483, ⒻF495-9458. If you shun the resorts, preferring to spend the bulk of your money on food, drinks and adventure, this is the best budget deal around. Basic but clean rooms for about US$50 a night. ➌–➍

Village Cay Resort and Marina Wickhams Cay I ☎284/494-2771, ⊛www.villagecay.com. More a lush, small luxury hideaway than a resort, with 21 large, well-appointed rooms, all of which have views of the harbour below. A great place to embark on watersports adventures. Relax in the waterside restaurant or poolside bar. Standard rooms as low as US$150 for a double in high season. ➐

The Town

When ferries arrive or a cruise pulls in, **Waterfront Drive** with its bars, restaurants, shops and markets can become a sudden traffic jam. Don't let that put you off. Head a few steps west to picturesque **Main Street** which is lined with brightly painted wooden and stone buildings, some more than 200 years old, and has a more laid-back feel. The many shops and restaurants here cater mostly to locals, and it's a great place to look for crafts, jewellery, clothing and spices, or sit down to an inexpensive West Indian meal.

Most of Road Town's tourist sights are strung along Main Street. A good place to start is the **VI Folk Museum** (officially Mon–Fri 8.30am–4.30pm but hours are erratic), though the old traditional West Indian building itself is probably of as much interest as the contents – a small collection of Amerindian, plantation-era and *RMS Rhone* (see p.484) artefacts. The white building at the heart of the street is the eighteenth-century colonial prison – today **HMS Prison** and still operational so not open to the law-abiding public. The prison is flanked by the reforming influences of two of the island's main religions, to the south **St George's Anglican Church**, featuring a copy of the 1834 Emancipation Proclamation that freed the islands' slaves, and to the north the **Methodist Church**. Walk north on Main Street for fifteen minutes to reach the four-acre oasis of the **Joseph Reynold O'Neal Botanic Gardens** (Mon–Sat, closes at dusk; US$3), named after a local dignitary. Its jasmine-scented pathways are a delight to stroll down, and you can learn all about the wealth of tropical flora on display – orchids, banana trees and cactus among others – through self-guided walks. Just past the ferry dock heading towards West End is the **Old Government House Museum** (Mon–Fri 9am–2pm; US$3) the recently restored former governors' residence, built in 1880 and 1926 and now full of antique furniture, murals and artifacts. Finish off your exploration of Road Town with a visit to **Fort Burt**, set on a hillside above Waterfront Drive at the southern end of town, which offers wonderful views of the harbour. Only the foundation and mezzanine remain of this seventeenth-century fort built by the Dutch to guard Road Harbour, so once you've glanced at the ruins, drop in at the *Fort Burt Hotel*, grab a drink and watch the sun set over the bay.

Eating and drinking

Conjuring up delicious dishes with seafood such as conch, mahi mahi and Anegada spiny lobsters, **Tortolan cuisine** is something to be savoured. Meats are often grilled and Tortolans are famed for their barbecue. In Road Town, you'll find superb local cuisine at bargain prices, including a wide selection of well-priced **West Indian and barbecue restaurants**, grilled seafood, simple sandwiches and plenty of vegetarian options. If you're self-catering or just putting together a beach **picnic**, *Riteway Food Market* and the *Ample Hamper*, a gourmet deli, are next to the Village Cay Marina and good places to hit.

C&F Restaurant Purcell Estate ☎ 284/494-4941. Located just east of town, this lively local favourite is difficult to find so call ahead for directions or take a taxi. It's worth it, though; the best barbecue ribs on the island and the barbecued fish and seafood are contenders as well. It's open evenings only and always busy so be prepared to wait. Main courses cost upwards of US$16.

Capriccio di Mare 196 Waterfront Drive ☎ 284/494-5369. An Italian restaurant whose outdoor patio is a great place to sip espresso or enjoy a light meal. The menu includes an array of pizzas, sandwiches and salads, but the tasty bowls of pasta for under US$13 are the main draw.

The mango bellini is also a highlight. Open from breakfast to dinner but most popular for lunch. Closed Sun.

Courtyard Coffee Shop Main Street ☎ 284/499-2194. A good place to take a break from sight-seeing and shopping in the area. Speciality coffees, teas and pastries served from 7.30am.

Crandall's Pastry Plus Fishers Estate south of town ☎ 284/494-5156. This bakery does the best pastries on the island, though the coffee leaves something to be desired. Also sells cakes and West Indian food to go. Open Mon–Fri till 5pm.

The Dove 67 Main St ☎ 284/494-0313, ⊚ www. dovebvi.com. A charming West Indian cottage with a large mango tree standing over the deck is home to one of the newest and finest restaurants in town. The menu changes each evening but the Boston seafood flown in daily is a constant. Try the char-grilled calamari and scallops with browned butter and horseradish vinaigrette for a starter. The steak with chocolate and coffee sauce raises some eyebrows but will make a believer out of you. There is a huge selection of wine including twenty by the glass. Entrees go for US$19–33.

Healthy Choices Wickhams Cay I ☎284/494-4733. A good choice if you're vegetarian or just fancy a break from seafood and grilled chicken. Does low-salt and low-fat soups, salads and veggie meals. The baked patties are highly recommended.

La Dolce Vita 200 Waterfront Drive ☎284/494-8770. Choose from 24 flavours of delicious ice cream served in waffle cones, all of which are home-made.

Le Cabanon Main Street ☎284/494-8660. An airy and relaxed French bistro good for lunch – try the cured ham and goat cheese tartine – or dinner. Black-tie food but T-shirt attire. A light lunch costs around US$8–9; dinners are in the US$18–29 range. When the food stops being served at 10.30 the place becomes an after-hours hangout.

Midtown Restaurant Main Street ☎284/494-2764. Almost always open (7am–11pm daily) and a favourite among locals for cheap, but high-quality local cuisine that includes conch soup, roti and various curried dishes (the curried whelk is excellent). If those don't appeal to you, the baked chicken is a sure bet.

Neato's Chicken Bus near the roundabout in Road Town. Sometimes open until dawn, this late-night snack truck has popular after-bars food and serves up piping hot local soups such as "goat's

water". Two chicken legs and fries go for US$5.

The Pub Waterfront Drive, near Fort Burt ☎284/494-2608. Long-time Road Town favourite doles out everything from burgers to steaks to fresh fish, with nightly specials, such as prime rib on Thursday. Has a great waterfront location to enjoy the happy hour and live music at weekends.

Pusser's Pub in Road Town Waterfront Drive ☎284/494-2467 ex☎117. If you're hankering for some English fare, you can sup a pint and order up a plate of fish and chips at Road Town's nautical take on the English pub, a popular tourist choice. For something a bit more Caribbean, try one of the many rums on offer followed by the jerk chicken or pineapple quesadilla (US$9.95). And where else will you find a jerk pizza?

Rita's Bar and Restaurant Wickhams Cay I/Omar Hodge Bldg ☎284/494-6165. Delicious soups, ribs and seafood, all cooked West Indian-style.

Roti Palace Abbott Hill, just off the southern end of Main Street ☎284/494-4196. Packed with sea-food, meat, curried chicken or veggie options and served with a side of rice and plantains, the rotis served at this eatery are a local speciality not to be missed. Prices are hefty, though, ranging between US$8 and US$16.

Spaghetti Junction Baugher's Bay ☎284/494-4880. An assortment of pasta dishes, some standard, some inventive (try the jambalaya pasta). Tiger shrimp with dill roasted tomatoes is popular. Open Mon-Sat for dinner from 6–10pm, but serving lunch as *The Bat Cave* Mon–Fri. Entrees go for US$9.75–24. They also serve a lot of local food such as boiled fish, stewed conch, and whelk. Prices on these items are US$10–12 and come as complete meals.

Nightlife and entertainment

While Road Town might be the place to find most everything else, its **nightlife** is more mellow than that on the west side of the island. With the exception of *The Bat Cave*, you won't find many clubs or discos with DJs here, but if you're content with some **live music** (check the *Limin' Times* for what's on), **drinking** and **dancing** there's plenty on offer, especially at weekends.

The Bat Cave *Spaghetti Junction Restaurant* ☎284/494-4880. Occupying a new location (fire destroyed the previous digs) with huge pillars, statues and high ceilings, *The Bat Cave* is the closest thing to a disco on the island. When the pasta runs out, things get hopping as DJs rock the house on Fridays and Saturdays. There's an outdoor deck to enjoy the evening air while inside has a/c and is smoke-free (except the fog on the dance floor). Happy hour specials 5–7pm. On Friday nights DJ Commodore, a local favourite, draws crowds in excess of 200 people. Saturday night features live

cabaret-style entertainment. Monday night in the restaurant features live jazz. With four TVs, the bar is also a good spot to catch the big game you're missing.

Le Cabanon (see also above). Perhaps the most international bar on the island when the restaurant shuts down at 10.30 each night. Hours are "flex-ible" and a mostly ex-pat crowd ends the night here.

Moorings-Mariner Inn (see also p.475). ⓦwww.danishchaletinn.com. Located in the hills above downtown, this West Indian-inspired B&B was recently renovated and at US$98 a nice place to hang out but the all-day "happy hour" on Friday sets the weekend off to a good start. During regular daily happy hour, free veggies are served 6–7.30pm. There's live music on Thursdays and Fridays 5–7pm, typically Ruben Chinnery. Bucking the full-moon celebration trend, the bar hosts random "No Moon" parties.

Pusser's Pub (see also p.477). This hopping Road Town institution is popular with locals, tourists and yachters and is the self-proclaimed home of the Painkiller – a potent concoction made with Pusser's own rum.

Village Cay Marina Wickhams' Cay I. Happy hour 4.30–7pm daily with free nachos and wings, and live pan music every Saturday night at 6pm.

West End and around

The west side of the island, with its main area of settlement, **WEST END**, is home to Tortola's resort scene, more relaxed than Road Town and with an abundance of excellent **beaches**, seafront accommodation and nightlife. Popular with yachters and landlubbers alike, the anchorage of **Soper's Hole**, a quaint collection of shops, restaurants and lodgings, is located just across the bay from the West End ferry docks. However, most of the resorts, hotels and small inns are clustered either around **Steele Point**, at the very western tip of the island, or along the stunning beaches and in the hills above **Long Bay**, **Apple Bay**, **Carrot Bay** and especially **Cane Garden Bay**. The western end is also the party side of Tortola; aside from the entertainment laid on by hotels, there are local favourites ranging from *Bomba's* wild full-moon parties to BVI reggae great Quito Rhymer. Tourist sights are few and far between but the **Callwood Rum Distillery** (Mon–Fri 8am–5pm; US$1 for a short tour) at the west end of Cane Garden Bay provides an interesting behind-the-scenes look at one of the BVI's most popular products. Their rum, called Cane Juice, is still made in copper vats the same way islanders did centuries ago and at the end of the tour you can sample a bit and buy some to take home.

Accommodation

Almost all of the **accommodation** – from resorts to cosy inns – on the western end of the island has ocean views. Don't automatically expect air conditioning; many rooms are simply cooled by overhead fans or the sea breezes. This side of the island is also home to Tortola's only **campsite**, at Brewer's Bay, while the hills are clustered with **villas** and **private homes** (see the *BVI Welcome Tourist Guide* for a detailed list). The following companies offer some of the best places: Villas of Fort Recovery (☎284/495-4354 or 1-800/367-8455); Icis Vacation Villas (☎284/494-6979, ⊛www.icisvillas.com); Heritage Villas (☎284/494-5842); Grape Tree Vacation Rentals (☎284/495-4229); and Purple Pineapple Rental Management (☎284/495-4848).

Hotels and resorts

Frenchman's Cay Resort West End ☎284/495-4844 or 1-800/235-4077, ⊛www.frenchmans.com. This small, luxury resort offers self-contained beachside villas with one or two bedrooms. A one-bedroom villa during May is US$160 for one person, plus US$10 per additional person up to four in total. In high season that starts at US$245. The resort has a beach, freshwater pool, balconies, great views, kitchenettes, but no TV or a/c, though a refreshing breeze permeates the place. Closed Sept and Oct. ❼

Jolly Roger Inn West End ☎284/495-4559, ⊛www.jollyrogerbvi.com. At the entrance of Soper's Hole, just down the shore from the West End ferry dock, this five-room inn is definitely for the rough-and-ready traveller. Rooms are basic,

only some have baths, and you can expect to pay about US$22 extra for a/c. ❸–❹

Long Bay Beach Resort Long Bay ☎284/495-4252 or 1-800/729-9599, ⊛www.longbay.com. Located on a 52-acre estate, this is the largest and most well-rounded resort on Tortola, offering rooms, beachfront cabanas and family villas. The deluxe beachfront rooms are the way to go here though they can be pricey (US$355–605), depending on the season. The *Beach Café*, an old stone plantation renovated into a restaurant and bar, adds to the well-prepared meals. Other amenities include watersports, tennis courts, a swim-up poolside bar, small shopping complex and fitness centre. Package deals help cut down the cost. ❾

Myett's Garden Inn Cane Garden Bay ☎284/495-9649, ⊛www.myettent.com. Charming beachfront rooms with nice sunsets, quite close to all the action in the bay which might not be ideal for those seeking solitude. Prices are good in high season (US$165–175) but become magnificent from mid-May to Dec 14 (US$100–110). ❼

Ole Works Inn Cane Garden Bay ☎284/495-4837, ℻495-9618. Built on the remains of a 300-year-old sugar plantation, this eighteen-room inn is owned by renowned reggae performer Quito Rhymer, whose band plays across the street at *Quito's Gazebo* (see overleaf). Rooms are basic but have a/c, and there's a pool and a gym. ❺–❼

Rhymer's Beach Hotel Cane Garden Bay ☎284/495-4639, ℻495-4820. This brightly coloured hotel is right on the beach and offers very simple motel-like rooms, all with a/c, kitchenettes and balconies offering views of the beach. ❸–❹

Sebastian's on the Beach Little Apple Bay ☎284/495-4212 or 1-800/336-4870, ⓦwww.sebastiansbvi.com. The best rooms are the beach-front rooms but they are a little pricey at US$230. The Tropical Yard units drop to US$135 but aren't as nice and don't open onto the beach. The on-site restaurant, *The Seaside Grill*, serves breakfast, lunch and dinner (see overleaf). ❻/❽

Sugar Mill Hotel Little Apple Bay ☎284/495-4355 or 1-800/462-8834, ⓦwww.sugarmillhotel.com. Located in the ruins of a seventeenth-century sugar mill, this elegant, well-managed boutique hotel has 23 guest cottages, all tastefully decorated in colourful West Indian style with wicker furniture. The on-site restaurant is one of the best on the island (see overleaf). It is closed for August and September but otherwise offers good low season discounts. ❾

Camping

Brewer's Bay Campground Brewer's Bay ☎284/494-3463. Something akin to an upscale refugee camp, this campground features US$40 prepared sites that include worn canvas tents, beds, linens, propane lamps and stoves, plus other cooking and eating utensils. These tents are rather crowded together, but as it sits right up on a great beach you can't beat the location. You might prefer a bare site (you provide tents and so on) for US$15 for one or two people. Community bathrooms have showers and flush toilets. There's a beach bar, restaurant and commissary on-site otherwise you'll need a ride to the nearest town. ❶

Beaches

Cane Garden Bay, a mile-long stretch of sand backed by lush green hills, is the most popular and most accessible of Tortola's beaches – a drawback when the cruise ships are in town as the crowds can get unbearable. It's also Tortola's party beach, attracting a mix of locals, tourists and yachters who come in for a day of sun or a night of fun. You can hire all kinds of **watersports** gear here, and there are plenty of restaurants, bars and hotels. The surf may not be nearly as good as at Josiah's Bay Beach (see p.482), but **Apple Bay**, south along the coast from Cane Garden Bay, still pulls the surfers in (especially during January and February when the waves are at their best), as much for the fun atmosphere as the surfing scene. There are restaurants, bars and several hotels on the beach and alongside the road skirting the western side of the island. North along the coast from Cane Garden Bay, palm-fringed **Brewer's Bay Beach** is the most secluded beach on the western side of the island; you won't find any crowds even during the height of the season. The abundant coral also makes it the best beach in the area for **snorkelling**. The island's only **campsite** (see above) is located here, along with a few beach bars and grills.

Eating and drinking

Some of the best **food** can be found on this side of the island. Many of the places listed below have **outdoor decks**, perfect for sipping a cocktail while the sun sets before tucking into a delightful spread of huge Anegada lobster. Always call to check places are open as schedules can vary, especially in the off-season.

Myett's Garden Grill Cane Garden Bay ☎284/495-9649. As well as a Caribbean-fare restaurant, this large open-air bar hops with live music late at night. Start with the tasty conch chowder, and no matter what meal you order – whether it's the Anegada lobster or the veggie pasta – be sure to ask for a side of the locally renowned peas and rice. Entrees are US$17–30.

Pisces Restaurant and Bar Frenchman's Cay ☎284/495-3154. Serves up home-style West Indian breakfasts, lunches and dinners. Open daily 7am–10pm.

Pusser's Landing Soper's Hole ☎284/495-4554. At this dockside bar with both informal outdoor eating and formal indoor dining, the extensive menu ranges from English pub food to seafood cooked in various styles (macadamia encrusted, char-grilled, creole blackened or herb braised). Look for all-you-can-eat shrimp on Tuesdays and at weekends and prime rib specials on Mondays. US$18–27 for entrees.

Quito's Gazebo Cane Garden Bay ☏284/495-4837. The restaurant in the back half of this oceanfront spot offers basic meat, fish and pasta dishes, while the front half has a bar, dance floor and stage where owner and local favourite Quito Rhymer plays his killer reggae. Dinner plates are US$12–30.

Sebastian's Seaside Grill Little Apple Bay ☏284/495-4212. Look right out to sea as you eat breakfast (banana pancakes), lunch (roti) or dinner (fresh fish). No matter what time of day, try one of Sebastian's superb rum coffees or pies.

Stanley's Welcome Bar Cane Garden Bay. Find yourself a hammock on the beach and have a beer to whet your appetite for a decent cheeseburger. A good perch for watching the sunset.

Sugar Mill Restaurant Little Apple Bay ☏284/495-4355. This hotel restaurant, by far one of the best dining experiences on the island, is located in an old stone rum distillery and has a changing menu that's consistently good, including lobster bisque, scallops in puff pastry with a roasted red pepper sauce and almond-crusted lamb loin. The service is excellent. Entrees average around US$28.

Nightlife and entertainment

The centrepiece of the entertainment scene on the western side of the island is the monthly **full-moon party** at *Bomba's Surfside Shack* but there is also a fair share of **live reggae and calypso music** and dancing. If you are looking to keep things mellow, you won't have to look too hard to find relaxing steel pan or acoustic guitar playing.

Bomba's Surfside Shack Cappoon's Bay ☏284/495-4148. Bomba and his driftwood shack decorated with the left clothing of previous partiers are legendary in the BVI for the monthly full-moon parties, when hundreds of people pack the streets in a bacchanalian frenzy of dancing and drinking. Mushroom tea is served while Bomba presides over the party from a huge throne as the self-proclaimed King of Tortola. On a more mundane note, Wednesday and Sunday nights feature live reggae or calypso and the occasional wet T-shirt contest.

Da Wedding Cane Garden Bay ☏284/495-4236. More of a local place, this is down the beach from the rest of the joints and a bit more laid-back. Occasionally features live music.

Elm Beach Bar Cane Garden Bay ☏284/494-2888. Live music on Friday and Sunday nights along with a wonderful barbecue causes this place to really fill up.

Jolly Roger West End ☏284/495-4559. You can find local bands here attracting a mixed crowd every Friday and Saturday night, with dancing on the cramped outdoor patio overlooking Soper's Hole. Near the West End ferry dock.

Myett's Cane Garden Bay ☏284/495-9543. A daily sunset happy hour with free munchies 5–7pm usually followed by live music Friday to Monday nights. Bar closes when the last customer leaves.

Pusser's Landing Soper's Hole ☏284/495-4554. They do a little bit of everything here: happy hour deals (5–7pm), 25¢ chicken wings, live music on weekend evenings and steel drums during Sunday brunch. Call ahead for details on upcoming events. There is an ATM here.

Quito's Gazebo Cane Garden Bay ☏284/495-4837. Reggae performer Quito Rhymer plays at his own restaurant and bar, singing Marley-esque songs with his band, The Edge, on Friday and Saturday nights. One of the few places on the island where everyone from yachters and tourists to locals and the hardcore reggae crowd get together and pack the dancefloor. Arrive early (before 9pm) to bag a spot and avoid the cover charge.

Sebastian's Little Apple Bay ☏284/495-4212. This restaurant's sole live entertainment is Sunday night when local *fungi* bands perform.

East End and around

The development on the **eastern side** of the island has not been excessive but there is definitely a fair share of attractions and activities to offer visitors. You'll find several good bars and restaurants on Beef Island's **Trellis Bay**, which has become a very laid-back beach hangout with a decent beach whose breezes make it an ideal place to learn to windsurf. *Trellis Bay Cybercafe* (☏284/495-2447) is the best source for local information, Internet access, or a fantastic fly-fish sandwich. Don't miss its **full-moon party** when two large metal globes are filled with wood and set ablaze.

△ St John

The restaurants and marina at **Fat Hog's Bay**, to the south of East End, are worth looking into as well. The **beaches** on the east of the island are among its most secluded and peaceful. **Josiah's Bay Beach** is the surfers' favourite but even if you don't hang ten, it's worth a day-trip. Start early with a great beachside breakfast at *Naomi's* (see opposite), before exploring the dramatic beach and body-surfing the killer waves. On your way back, stop at **Josiah's Bay Plantation** to walk through the ruins, check out the artwork in the gallery and enjoy a late lunch on the patio of the *Secret Garden* (see opposite).

Accommodation

The east of the island hasn't got the **accommodation** clout of the west or Road Town, but a few places deserve consideration, especially if you want to avoid the crowds, be near the airport or close to ferries to nearby islands.

Beef Island Guest House Trellis Bay ☏284/495-2303, ℻495-1611. This B&B has a nice location just down the beach from the little community at Trellis Bay and close to the airport and the North Sound Express ferry docks. The four beachfront rooms are simple and fairly well maintained, but only have fans. Each room has its own bathroom, and there's also a common room. ❺

Hodge's Creek Marina Hotel Hodges Creek ☏284/494-5000, ⓦwww.hodgescreek.com. Moderately priced hotel, anchorage and mini-mall overlooking a busy marina and the Sir Francis Drake Channel. There are 29 rooms (five with kitchenettes), all brightly though blandly decorated, and there's also a pool and a great restaurant on site (see below). Make sure you ask for a room with a balcony view of the marina. ❼

Josiah's Bay Inn Josiah's Bay ☏284/495-2818. Heading down towards the beach from Ridge Rd a steep driveway on the left takes you to this simple guesthouse. A single room can be as low as US$65/night in low season, US$80 during high. There is a four-bedroom, two-bath unit with full kitchen and a balcony where the whisper of surf still reaches you from down the hill and this rents for US$1500 for a week. A great deal for a group of surfers or those not interested in glamorous resort decor. ❹

Lambert Beach Resort Lambert Bay ☏284/495-2877, ⓦwww.lambertbeachresort.com. There are 38 rooms and suites in this complex that is about as secluded as you can get on Tortola – you'll need a rental car if you want to go anywhere. The rooms are pleasant, the complex is peaceful, the beach is long and the pool is a stunner. The beachfront and garden rooms have tile flooring, colourful wood furniture and large bathrooms; the hillside rooms are two-bedroom villas with full-size kitchens. Rooms range from mid-level to fairly pricey, and the resort offers a seventh night free except right around Christmas and New Year. ❼

Tamarind Club Hotel Josiah's Bay ☏284/495-2477, ⓦwww.tamarindclub.com. Located on the northeast side of the island and not on the beach, this intimate hotel is off the beaten track. But what it lacks in location it makes up for with charm, good prices, and peace and quiet. Each of the nine rooms is individually decorated and all have basic amenities, including a/c and a mini-fridge. The on-site restaurant is very good and the pool and bar area are idyllic (see opposite). ❺–❻

Eating and drinking

Restaurants on this side of the island are not only varied, but plentiful. On the other hand, **nightlife** is almost nonexistent with the exception of the **Trellis Bay full-moon party** and an occasional live performer in a bar or restaurant.

Bing's Drop-In Bar East End ☏284/495-2627. Primarily a local after-hours dance spot, and a plain old bar the rest of the time. A fun and safe experience for non-locals.

Brandywine Restaurant Brandywine Bay ☏284/495-2301. The gourmet menu at this small estate, which offers fine dining in a peaceful scenic setting, features an array of duck, lamb and seafood dishes in Florentine style. This is some of the finest dining on the island and a good place to go if you want to dress up a bit – because you must. Excellent fresh pasta choices will set you back US$26–34 but you won't be disappointed. Extensive wine list.

Hodges Creek Marina *Calamaya* ☏284/495-2126. This funkily designed terrace restaurant overlooking Hodge's Creek Marina serves West Indian fare. You can't go wrong with the grilled Kaiser sandwich (shrimp, ham, pineapple and cheese), the West Indian roast pork (suckling pig roasted on a spit) or the key lime pie. Entrees go for US$13–30 and there's a US$25 buffet on Thursdays.

De Loose Mongoose Trellis Bay ☎284/495-2303. Located on the water's edge next to the *Beef Island Guest House* (see opposite), this bar and restaurant serves breakfast, lunch and dinner. The menu is light bar fare at good prices. The hamburger and brownie sundae are noteworthy. There's live music every weekend and Sunday night is beach barbecue night. Entrees are US$15–24.

Eclipse Fat Hog's Bay ☎284/495-1646. Dishes at this small, homey spot, overlooking Penn's Landing Marina, range from Spanish paella to Thai green curry to venison; the mahi ceviche is especially worth trying. Serves Mexican and cheese fondue in the lounge. Open daily for dinner only with entrees running US$18–30.

Fat Hog Bob's Fat Hog's Bay ☎284/495-1010. This large, fun-loving place has a spirited ambience that's part Tahitian club room and part American bar and grill. Eat on the patio overlooking the bay or drink at the bar or in the large cocktail lounge. There's a big-screen TV for the major sports events plus live music at the weekends. Open for lunch and dinner. Ribs, steaks and chops start at US$19. Eat a three-pound porterhouse and get a 10% discount for life as a Hog Hero.

The Last Resort Trellis Bay ☎284/495-2520. Located on an islet in the middle of Trellis Bay (call for the free two-minute ferry at the dockside phone). The casual and quirky atmosphere should be enough of a reason to stay, but the food is quite spectacular. The fresh seafood is well prepared, the service is excellent and the dessert list is long.

The warm goat cheese salad and rack of lamb are popular favourites. Al, the singing chef, entertains after dinner. Prices for pasta dishes are around US$18–20, other entrees US$22–28. Closed mid-Aug to mid-Oct.

Naomi's Little Secret Josiah's Bay ☎284/495-2818. This little beachside deck offers great West Indian breakfast, lunch and dinner at dirt-cheap prices. Plates are colourfully presented and portions are hearty – the juicy cheeseburgers and the conch fritters are tops. Perfect for beach-goers and Naomi also loans boogie boards and rents surfboards. Accepts credit cards (when the system is working).

Secret Garden Josiah's Bay ☎284/495-1834. Part of the Josiah's Bay Plantation Art Gallery, this outdoor café set among the ruins of the original plantation buildings is about as peaceful as you can imagine. The menu includes home-made soups, falafel sandwiches and grilled scallops. Main courses start at US$12.

Tamarind Club (see also opposite). If you're staying on the eastern side of the island this cosy hotel restaurant tucked away in the hills above Josiah's Bay is worth a visit. The tables are elegantly set and the decor is a soothing blue, the nearby pool contributing to that feeling. The menu changes often but typically features a couple of fresh fish dishes, lamb, steak and the chef's special chicken recipes. Dinner entrees are US$23–35 and pasta dishes go for a bit less. Open for breakfast, lunch and dinner. Sunday brunch is 11am–4pm.

Watersports and outdoor activities

Tortola has the full range of watersports and boating activities – **snorkelling, diving, windsurfing, powerboating, fishing** and **sailing** (from scenic day charters to full-moon booze cruises). Dolphin Discovery (☎284/494-7675, ⊛www.dolphindiscovery.vg) at Prospect Reef offers various **swim-with-a-dolphin** programmes ranging US$79–129. The only place to play **tennis** is at resorts and hotels with courts. These include *Frenchman's Cay Resort* (see p.478), *Long Bay Beach Resort* (see p.478) and *Moorings-Mariner Inn* (see p.475). All charge about US$7 an hour for non-guests, except *Moorings*, which is free of charge on a first-come first-served basis. **Horse-riding** is a great way to explore the mountains **in the national park**. Shadow's Stables, on Ridge Road (US$60 per hour; ☎284/494-2262), offers rides through Sage Mountain National Park. The owner, Elton "Shadow" Parsons, is descended from a long line of local farmers who tilled the land where the stables now stand; his knowledge of local history and funny stories makes him the perfect guide. If you prefer to use your own legs, there are seven excellent **hiking trails** in Mount Sage National Park; pick up a map at the tourist board. While there are no golf courses on the island, there is Captain Mulligan's Driving Range (☎284/499-1513) where you can whack a bucket of balls ($10) into the sea at Nanny Cay.

Snorkelling, diving, surfing and windsurfing

If you are going **diving**, sinkholes, ledges, caves and canyons await you around the Sir Francis Drake Channel islands. Coral spawning takes place one week after

The wreck of the RMS Rhone

The wreck of the **RMS Rhone** has been voted the Caribbean's number one **wreck dive** by several diving magazines. The 310-foot British mail steamer and passenger ship was torn in two by a devastating hurricane in 1867 and sank to the bottom of Sir Francis Drake Channel, near Salt Island, together with her cargo of cotton and copper and 124 passengers. The bow sits about 80 feet underwater and the stern in about 15 to 50 foot of water. The dive makes for an eerie experience as both parts are very well preserved – the crow's nest is fully intact, not to mention the engine room and the battered propeller. Colourful coral, large schools of fish and other marine creatures live on and around the ship. Most of the dive shops run trips to the wreck – see listings below.

the first full moon in August; check with shops about packages. North Tortola sites are less frequented and best done from Jost Van Dyke. Among offshore locales especially worth seeking out, The Dogs are uninhabited little islands surrounded by excellent reefs and include swim-throughs, a chimney and caves, while Painted Walls is a fine sponge-encrusted scene, as is Alice in Wonderland, so named for the mushroom-shaped coral formations. Of the several wrecks, the *R.M.S. Rhone* (see box, above) is considered the signature dive, though the *Chikuzen*, a 246ft Japanese refrigeration ship resting in 75ft of water is perhaps equally impressive. Though technically a Tortola site, it is best reached from Virgin Gorda on a 45-minute boat ride. Seas are not always suitable to get to this dive site, but it is worth the wait. The **surfing** season runs Nov–March and the swells roll into Apple, Cane Garden and Josiah's bays.

Blue Waters Divers Nanny Cay ☏ 284/494-2847, ⍈ www.bluewaterdiversbvi.com. Offers PADI courses up to divemaster level. Two-tank dives are US$85. They will also rendezvous with your charter boat if you are moored at Norman, Peter, Salt or Cooper Island.

Boardsailing BVI Trellis Bay and Nanny Cay ☏ 284/495-2447, ⍈ www.windsurfing.vi. One of the best options for windsurfing whatever your level. Also does sea-kayaking lessons, tours, rentals and sales, as well as surfng, kiteboarding, and dive gliding (being towed in the water by a boat at 2mph and using a sort of wing which can be tilted to dive the user down to nearly 50 feet on one breath).

Dive Tortola ☏ 284/494-9200 or 1-800/353-3419, ⍈ www.divetortola.com. Sets up rendezvous dives with your charter boat. Two-tank dives are US$90. Packages available and discounts for pre-booking.

High Sea Adventures Fat Hog's Bay ☏ 284/495-1300. Hit the Indians, the Baths, Peter Island or any of the other snorkelling hot spots with Captain Roy. Half-day trips (US$60) include two snorkel sites and full-day trips (US$85) take in four. He also does fishing trips – a one-day outing for four guests costs US$300.

HIHO Road Town ☏ 284/494-7694, ⍈ www.go-hiho.com. Your one-stop option for surfing, windsurfing or kayaking – does sales, rentals, lessons and directions to the best beaches. Their

website has a good surf guide, too.

Naomi's Little Secret Josiah's Bay ☏ 284/495-2818. This little beach restaurant rents surfboards and has free loaner boogie boards.

Sail Caribbean Divers Hodges Creek ☏ 284/495-1675, ⍈ www.sailcaribbeandivers.com. This 5-star PADI facility offers two-tank dives for US$95 as well as afternoon and night dives. You can be picked up from Norman and Cooper Islands as well as Marina Cay. Dive instruction runs the gamut from Discover Scuba to Dive Instructor and other high-level certifications. A second shop runs out of Cooper Island.

UBS Dive Center Fat Hog's Bay ☏ 284/494-0024, ⍈ www.scubabvi.com. Specializes in private, personalized diving. Get your own personal boat and divemaster for the day (9.30am–3.30pm) for US$150 per person for two people; includes all equipment and drinks. The Center also rents a wide variety of watersports equipment and can deliver to your hotel.

Underwater Safaris Moorings Dock, Road Town ☏ 284/494-3235 or 1-800/537-7032. Dives to all the usual spots. Single-tank dives are US$55 and two-tank dives are US$80.

We Be Divin' Road Town/Cane Garden Bay ☏ 284/494-8261, ⍈ www.webedivinbvi.com. Rents gear, does air fills and provides rendezvous diving. Two tanks for US$85. This PADI shop is the only dive shop on the north shore.

Sailing and powerboating

BareCat Charters Frenchman's Cay Marina ☎1-800/296-5287, ⊛www.barecat.com. Offers great charter rates for catamarans. There are several sizes and price ranges for two to ten people.

King Charters Nanny Cay Marina ☎284/494-5820, ⊛www.kingcharters.com. In operation since 1989, it can provide day-trips or powerboat and motor yachts rentals (with or without captain).

M&M Powerboat Rentals Village Cay Marina ☎284/495-9993, ⊛www.powerboatrentalbvi.com. Half- or full-day and weekly rentals of 20, 22 and 25ft boats. The 22ft *Contender* with 150hp motor rents for US$275 per day.

The Moorings, Ltd *Moorings-Mariner Inn*, Road Town ☎284/494-2331, ⊛www.moorings.com. Moorings is the largest charter boat company in the Caribbean. Whether you want to skipper your own boat or sail with a captain and crew they will help you plan your entire vacation.

Offshore Sailing School Road Town ☎1-888/454-8002, ⊛www.offshore-sailing.com. This experienced company offers three- to six-day learn-to-sail courses, including a live-aboard option, and ten-day fast-track to cruising courses. Prices start at US$1195 not including accommodation. Their website has full details of all courses and prices.

Sunsail Charters Hodge's Creek Marina ☎284/495-4740 or 1-888/350-3568, ⊛www.sunsail.com. While not as large as Moorings, Sunsail is a serious rival with its immaculate fleet of boats and friendly service.

White Squall II Village Cay Marina ☎284/494-2564, ⊛www.whitesquall2.com. Take a day-trip to The Baths and Cooper Island or The Caves on Norman Island aboard an eighty-foot classic 1936 Schooner.

Fishing

Blue Ocean Adventures ☎284/499-1134. Half-day, full-day and overnight charters available for fishing tuna, wahoo or Atlantic blue marlin. Price covers everything, including lunch.

Caribbean Fly-Fishing Outfitters ☎284/494-4797. For a unique Caribbean fishing experience, go for tarpon, bonefish and permit on a fly rod.

Fort Burt Marina ☎284/494-4200. A number of

fishing outfits work out of this marina – just give them a call and they'll help you find a charter to suit your needs.

Persistence Charters Ltd ☎284/495-4122. Sail out of Soper's Hole with six friends on a 31-footer (all bait, tackle, drinks and snacks included) for US$400 for a half-day or US$700 for a full-day trip.

Virgin Gorda

VIRGIN GORDA, twelve miles east of Tortola, might just be the perfect Virgin Island – peaceful, blessed with abundant natural assets, and sometimes gloriously deserted. Ten miles long and two miles across at its widest, the island got its name – "fat virgin" – from Columbus in 1493 during his second voyage through the area. The name refers to the landscape – mountainous in the middle and thin at each end. Most visitors to the island stay on the luxury resorts (some accessible only by water) at **North Sound**. Skirted on one side by Virgin Gorda and on the other by several major reefs and a series of small islands – **Mosquito**, **Prickly Pear**, **Saba Rock**, **Eustacia** and **Necker** – the North Sound provides excellent watersports, hiking trails, deserted beaches and some of the best diving and snorkelling in the BVI.

The tourist dollar has yet to make much of an impact on **SPANISH TOWN**, Virgin Gorda's main settlement located at its southern end and home to most of the 2500-plus islanders. Unprepossessing and somewhat poor, it consists mainly of a jumble of run-down, windowless houses with chickens running through the yards. **Virgin Gorda Yacht Harbour** is the island's main marina, where you'll find most of the handful of restaurants and shops, as well as the banks and tourist information centre. The North Sound Road leading from Spanish Town to the small village of **Gun Creek** is the starting point (well signposted or look for the stairs leading into the trees) for two short trails into the **Virgin Gorda Peak National Park**, a 260-acre area that rises to the island's highest point, Gorda Peak, at 1359ft.

VIRGIN GORDA

Cockroach Island

George Dog

West Dog

Great Dog

Seal Dogs

Mountain Point

Mosquito Island

Hay Point Beach

Long Bay

Nail Bay

Little Dix Bay

Mahoe Bay

Savannah Bay

Handsome Bay

Spanish Town

Virgin Gorda Yacht Harbour

Trunk Bay

Spring Bay

The Baths

Copper Mine Point

GORDA PEAK NATIONAL PARK

1359ft

1348ft

North Sound Road

Soldier Bay

Anguilla Point

Prickly Pear Island

Lover's Beach

Vixen Point Beach

North Sound

Gun Creek

Berchers Bay

Deep Bay

Oil Nut Bay

Saba Rock

Eustatia Island

Necker Island

N

0   1 mile

ACCOMMODATION

Biras Creek Resort	D
Bitter End Yacht Club	B
Fischer's Cove Beach Hotel	I
Guavaberry Spring Bay Vacation Homes	J
Leverick Bay Resort	C
Little Dix Bay	G
Mango Bay Resort	F
Oceanview	H
Paradise Beach Resort	E
Saba Rock Resort	A

EATING & DRINKING

The Bath and Turtle	8
Biras Creek	D
Chez Bamboo	7
The Clubhouse	3
The Crab Hole	9
Fat Virgin Café	4
Giorgio's Table	5
The Main Deck/Andy's Chateau	10
Mine Shaft	12
The Restaurant at Leverick Bay	2
The Rock Café	11
Saba Rock Restaurant	A
The Sand Box	1
Thelma's Hideout	6
Top of the Baths	13
The Wheelhouse	8

South of Spanish Town, **The Valley** is an area of even smaller settlements at whose southern tip lies Virgin Gorda's biggest and most photographed tourist attraction – **The Baths**. This bizarre landscape of volcanic **boulders** the size of houses stretches from the wooded slopes behind the beach to the sand and on into the clear aquamarine sea, forming a natural seaside playground of grottoes, caves and pools. The **snorkelling** here is excellent and, not surprisingly, it can get very crowded in high season, so come early or late in the day; there are small coin-op storage lockers and facilitities. There are also lots of restaurants, bars and shops both on the beach and in the hills above, connected via trails.

Arrival, information and getting around

Virgin Gorda's **airport** is just over a mile east of Spanish Town, but most people fly to Tortola's Beef Island Airport and take a ferry. **Taxis** are there to meet flights or you can call Mahogany Rentals and Taxi Service (☎284/495-5469) and Andy's Taxi & Jeep Rental (☎284/495-5511). A taxi from the airport to Gun Creek will cost about US$20, and from the airport to Spanish Town about US$5.

Maps and **brochures** are available from Virgin Gorda's BVI Tourist Board office (☎284/495-5181) at Virgin Gorda Yacht Harbour in Spanish Town. The post office is in Spanish Town, on the road south of the yacht harbour (☎284/495-5224). Get on the **Internet** at The Chandlery (☎284/495-5628) at Yacht Harbor or Java Connection (☎284/495-7421) in Leverick Bay.

You won't really need a car on Virgin Gorda – **boats** are generally the fastest, cheapest and most scenic way to get around. The North Sound Express ferry makes stops between Trellis Bay on Tortola, and Yacht Harbour, *Leverick Bay* and *The Bitter End Yacht Club* on Virgin Gorda. For most other journeys you'll be able to hitch a ride on the **ferries** that most resorts provide for their employees, or catch one of the free ferries that run between *The Bitter End* and Gun Creek and between *Saba Rock* and *The Sand Box* on Prickly Pear Island and anywhere in the North Sound. Call ahead to schedule a pick-up (see list of ferries on p.435). Other options include **private water taxis**, renting your own powerboat, which can be pricey, or simply using the 11ft Boston whalers that most resorts provide free for their guests. When operating your own boat, make sure to enquire about a map of underwater reefs. The two main **taxi firms**, Mahogany and Andy's, both provide special tours, or call Patsy's Taxi Service & Island Tours (☎284/495-5002).

If you find the need for a **car**, rental companies are Island Style Jeep & Car Rental (☎284/495-6300) and L&S Jeep Rental (☎284/495-5297) or call 3P Scooter Rentals (☎284/495-6870) if a **scooter** is more suitable.

Accommodation

The best place to stay is **North Sound** but accommodation here doesn't come cheap. **Spanish Town** has a few inexpensive options but nothing as appealing as the North Sound resorts or rooms in **The Valley**, which are usually fairly simple but have great views and easy access to the beach. For a **private villa or home** try: Virgin Gorda Villa Rentals (☎1-800/848-7081, ⑩www.virgingordabvi.com), Caribbean Villas (☎1-877/248-2862, ⑩www.cvoa.com) or Unusual Villa Rentals (☎1-800/846-7280, ⑩www.unusualvillarentals.com).

North Sound

Biras Creek Resort ☎284/494-3555 or 1-800/223-1108, ⑩www.biras.com. Only accessible by water, this 140-acre resort is the pinnacle of luxury in the North Sound – a mixture of posh pampering and undisturbed freedom, natural beauty and cosmopolitan sophistication. Cottages with locally designed linens and hand-carved wood furniture come with golf carts and mountain bikes for getting around. The outdoor showers, especially those that face the crashing waves, make for the most scenic wash you'll have in the Caribbean. There's a private beach and watersports centre, tennis courts and motorized dinghies available for use, as well as organized helicopter, scuba and sailing trips. But the *pièce de résistance* at Biras is the food (see p.489). ⑨

Bitter End Yacht Club ☎284/494-2746 or

1-800/872-2393, ⓕ 284/494-4756, ⓦ www.beyc. com. *The Bitter End* is a huge, lush waterfront resort (reachable only by water), whose superb amenities include two restaurants, a great English pub, a decked-out commissary, several boutiques and even an outdoor movie theatre. Choose from beachfront villas which are cooled by the breezes or air-conditioned North Sound suites that climb the steep hills like treehouses. There is also a two-bedroom estate house and live-aboard yachts available. There are many activities for the whole family, not to mention good-value packages. ⓽

Leverick Bay Resort ⓣ 284/495-7421 or 1-800/848-7081, ⓦ www.leverickbay.com. This resort offers rooms ($US149) or one- and two-bedroom suites with 7-day minimum stay requirements. All offer great views of the bay. A marina and a collection of shops are also on site. Amenities include a laundry, grocery store, charter services, scuba shop, salon and spa, a restaurant and bar, a pool, tennis court and gasoline. The North Sound Express ferry offers dockside access. Forty-three private villas are also available, some of them at Mahoe Bay. ⓺/⓽

Saba Rock Resort ⓣ 284/495-9966, ⓦ www. sabarock.com. This nine-unit collection of suites and villas, marina, restaurant and bar is perched on a huge rock just barely large enough to support it all in the middle of the North Sound. The one- and two-bedroom villas are the nicest on the property (US$350–500); the beach units are the cheapest (US$150). ⓺

Spanish Town and The Valley

Fischer's Cove Beach Hotel The Valley ⓣ 284/495-5252, ⓦ www.fischerscove.com. Located half a mile south of the Virgin Gorda Yacht Harbour, this small beachside complex offers individual cottages and hotel rooms – some with views of Sir Francis Drake Channel. The Garden View rooms are plain and have patios and are the only rooms with a/c. During high season these rooms go for US$165 a night and there are special deals for stays of seven days or more. ⓺

Guavaberry Spring Bay Vacation Homes Spanish Town ⓣ 284/495-5227, ⓦ www .guavaberryspringbay.com. Just north of The Baths, these one-bedroom (US$195) and two-bedroom

(US$265) houses are a steal. A few minutes from the beach, each unit has a kitchen, living room and a covered deck with great views of the sea and sunsets. There are also 18 privately owned villas of varying sizes and prices. Reserve well in advance as there is a high rate of return clients. No credit cards. ⓻

Little Dix Bay Little Dix Bay ⓣ 284/495-5555 or 1-800/928-3000, ⓦ www.littledixbay.com. A mile north of Spanish Town, this relaxed though very refined resort is set among rolling, flower-filled grounds near a crescent-shaped white-sand beach. The luxurious rooms come with comfortable rattan furniture and terracotta floors, and above all else, the service reigns. This is the sister resort to the highly successful *Caneel Bay* on St John, just a ninety-minute ferry ride away, and a package deal is offered for the pair. There are hiking trails, a fitness centre, floodlit tennis courts and even a tennis pro on hand for lessons. ⓽

Mango Bay Resort Mahoe Bay ⓣ 284/495-5672, ⓦ www.mangobayresort.com. A small beachfront resort heavily influenced by Italian architecture and cuisine, and comprising nine duplex villas and two private homes, located on seven blooming acres. Three of the villas are just thirty feet from the water. There are no tennis courts or gym, but the exquisite beach offers plenty of watersports. Nevertheless, it's rather pricey for what you get. ⓽

Oceanview Spanish Town ⓣ 284/495-5230. There's an ocean view only if you are tall enough standing on the second floor balcony and the rooms are small and have musty carpeting. But at US$70 per room including taxes think of it as camping with a/c and a TV. The owner Jerome O'Neal is a great guy and runs a local bar and eatery with cheap daily plates next door. ⓷

Paradise Beach Resort Mahoe Bay ⓣ 284/495-5871, ⓦ www.paradisebeachresort.com. A small luxury resort tucked between steep hills and a beautiful beach protected by an offshore reef. Studios, one- and two-bedroom villas with ceramic tile roofs are available, all with a balcony and full kitchen and complimentary rowboat and kayak use. You can hire a private chef or a nanny with the resort. Studios with garden views are the best deal here – US$132–187, but between US$275 and US$435 is average. ⓺

Beaches

The Baths are an absolute must-see but may be more like your local swimming pool on the hottest day of the year when the tours show up. Fortunately, Virgin Gorda has plenty of quiet **beaches** offering ample opportunity for long walks on endless white sand, quiet picnics, excellent snorkelling and wonderful sunsets. The best are accessible only by water so you'll need to hire a boat. **Prickly Pear Island** has a collection of secluded beaches including long, sandy Vixen Point, Sand Box Beach and idyllic Lover's Beach – as you'd expect, the smallest and most private of them all. **Hay Point Beach** on the now-deserted island of Mosquito, is another good option.

If you feel like having some facilities nearby, **Deep Bay Beach** is a good bet; it's the official beach for *Biras Creek Resort* but you don't have to be a guest to frolic in the ocean or plant yourself on a beach chair. You can reach Deep Bay by hiking from *The Bitter End* or by hiring your own boat. The best beach for snorkelling, **Long Bay Beach**, just south of Mountain Point, can be reached by road or sea; if you're coming by car take Plum Tree Bay Road, a dirt road that winds due north away from North Sound Road about two miles out of Spanish Town. If you're staying in Spanish Town, **Savannah Bay Beach**, one mile of deserted beautiful white sand, is your closest option. When the beach at The Baths is too crowded, swim (or walk) north around the last outcropping of rocks to **Spring Bay Beach** and **The Crawl** which offer more great boulders, snorkelling and sand without the crowds.

Eating

You can get anything from local food in the villages around Gun Creek to gourmet dining at lavish *Biras Creek Resort*. **Gun Creek** can be reached by ferry (the staff ferries from resorts to Gun Creek are free, but beware: they don't run late) or road. From the ferry dock, it's a short taxi ride or a steep uphill walk to the strip at the top for some cheap and delicious local food. Try *The Twin House* (☎284/495-7469) for large curried and boiled fish meals, *Gunney's* for simple fried chicken or *Angie's* Friday night barbecue. **Spanish Town** has plenty of moderately priced restaurants, most of which also double as bars and dance clubs (see overleaf) later in the evening. If you want to make up a **picnic**, *The Wine Cellar and Bakery* (☎284/495-5250; Virgin Gorda Yacht Harbour) is the best place to get a good bottle of wine, plus fresh baked goods and cheap sandwiches (US$3.50) to go.

North Sound

Biras Creek *Biras Creek Resort* ☎284/494-3555, VHF16. This elegant resort restaurant and bar on a hillside overlooking the North Sound welcomes non-guests for dinner only and by reservation. Though pricey (US$65 per person), the food is delicious; the menu rotates so guests staying a week won't see the same offerings twice. Smart dress is required.

The Clubhouse *Bitter End Yacht Club* ☎284/494-2746. The resort's main restaurant serves steaks, seafood, pasta and a selection of fusion foods in an open-air dining room, just steps from the beach. The buffets for lunch (US$22) and dinner (US$39.50) are popular. Reservations are required.

Fat Virgin Café *Biras Creek Resort* ☎284/495-7052. A small, inexpensive, outdoor restaurant, located at the resort's Marina Village, on the dock just east of the main *Biras* landing, serving everything from baby back ribs to flying fish sandwiches. Some say it is the best burger on the island. If you're staying at another North Sound resort, come by dinghy.

The Restaurant at Leverick Bay Leverick Bay ☎284/495-7154. Have breakfast, lunch or dinner in the shade next to the pool or take a pizza to go. The upstairs terrace is a pleasant setting for dinner off a menu featuring local seafood, steaks and a

rack of lamb. Friday night is a beach barbecue (US$20) with live music, mocko jumbies and a limbo contest. Free moorings, yacht water and ice with the purchase of four dinner entrees.

Saba Rock Restaurant North Sound ☎284/495-7711. A unique dining experience on a small rock between Virgin Gorda and Prickly Pear. The changing nightly buffet (often with prime rib) costs US$25, while the Sunday West Indian buffet includes live pan music in the US$20 price. An à la carte menu offers burgers and sandwiches as well. Open for lunch and dinner. Also offers a free ferry for guests to and from any location in the North Sound.

The Sand Box Prickly Pear ☎284/495-9122. This relaxed beach bar on the island of Prickly Pear is accessible only by water. There are moorings for your boat so you can swim ashore for the day – or arrange for your hotel to drop you off. Grab a sandwich for lunch, laze on the beach and then go back for a fish supper. Main courses go for US$16–23 and Wednesday is Caribbean Lobster night US$19.95.

Spanish Town

The Bath and Turtle Lee Road, Virgin Gorda Yacht Harbour ☎284/495-5239. The menu has a variety of pasta dishes and sandwiches as well as pizzas (around US$14). Some highlights are the tamarind ginger chicken wings (US$7), West Indian chicken sandwiches (US$10.75) or seared tuna with ginger-citrus sauce (US$19.75). Open for breakfast, lunch and dinner. Wednesdays feature live music starting at 9pm.

Chez Bamboo Spanish Town ⊕284/495-5752. Located on the town's main strip, *Chez Bamboo* serves great French-Caribbean food. Curried lobster is not something to be missed and the desserts are excellent. Tucked away behind a sea of trees and vine-covered latticework, the candlelit tables create a perfect setting for a romantic meal. But be prepared to pay for it – main courses run from US$30 to US$45. You can expect live calypso or reggae by local bands on Fridays.

The Crab Hole The Valley ⊕284/495-5307. If you're hankering for some genuine local food, like callaloo soup, salt fish and stewed goat, this inexpensive spot is the place to go.

Giorgio's Table Mahoe Bay ⊕284/495-5684, ⊛www.giorgiobvi.com. Sicilian cooking meets Caribbean seafood at *Giorgio's* where lobster ravioli, swordfish capriccio and sweet potato *gnocconi* are just a few of the spectacular items on the menu. Open for lunch and dinner. Reservations and smart dress required. Entrees US$18–24.

The Main Deck/Andy's Chateau The Valley ⊕284/495-5252. *Andy's* is inside and hosts live music most weekends; its counterpart the *Main Deck* sits on the dock over the water and is a good place for sunset happy hour and grilled local seafood. Pig roasts on Saturdays (US$18). Try a shot of Mamma Wanna, a spiced rum concoction that'll make you giddy. (Allergy warning: They say it contains shellfish in some fashion like the worm in a bottle of tequila.) Appetizers are around US$8, entrees up to US$20.

Mine Shaft Copper Mine Road, The Baths ⊕284/495-5260. Featuring a 360-degree view and the BVI's only mini-golf course, this lively eatery near the old copper mine offers simple grilled items, sandwiches and salads. Tuesday is West Indian barbecue night. Be sure to try their signature drink The Cave-In.

The Rock Café Tower Road ⊕284/495-5472. This Italian restaurant, near The Baths, is a locals' favourite for dining, drinks and dancing. You can eat outside, at tables nestled between boulders similar to The Baths minus the sea, or inside under the a/c. Pasta plates range from US$16–28 but you should consider the café's speciality – the delicious Anegada lobster (US$21 per pound). There is a piano bar here nightly and an occasional live band.

Top of the Baths The Baths ⊕284/495-5497. Located as the name suggests on the hills above The Baths, this eatery serves breakfast, lunch and dinner, and is worth a visit for the views and sunsets or a little pre-meal dip in the pool. A piña colada completes the mood. The food is really good too – and not too expensive (around US$10 for lunch; US$20 for dinner). Try the Fritters of the Day with Top of the Baths sauce followed by the shrimp creole or conch in curry sauce. Live music noon to 3pm during its popular barbecue.

The Wheelhouse Spanish Town ⊕284/495-6739. Good homestyle island cooking for about US$10 a plate at this open-air pavilion right across from the Virgin Gorda Yacht Harbour. It varies day to day, often fried chicken or stewed ribs with coleslaw, pumpkin rice and potato salad. Seafood plates are available for around US$20. Happy hour is 6–7pm and features US$1 beers and quite honestly the best rum punch in the Virgin Islands. Live Caribbean music on the weekend nights.

Drinking and nightlife

Nightlife on Virgin Gorda takes the form of hopping from bar to bar by boat for a mellow drink and live music – many of the **bars** have their own ferries connecting them to anywhere in the North Sound. **Gun Creek** is a good place to start. When you step off the ferry, grab a cold one at *The Last Stop Bar*, then, once up the hill, try the *Butterfly* for beer and dominoes or *Gunney's Cool Corner*, where you can drink cheaply, eat fresh-fried chicken wings (or stewed pig's feet), and play some pool. The party epicentre of the North Sound is *Saba Rock Resort*, with nightly **live music**, drink specials and dancing.

In Spanish Town a few of the restaurants (see above for details) liven up later in the evening. *The Bath and Turtle* has two happy hours daily (10.30–11.30am and 4–6pm) as well as live music, usually pan, calypso or reggae, every Wednesday night. *Chez Bamboo* hops on Friday nights when locals and tourists come to dance and party. The *Mine Shaft* and *The Main Deck* host monthly **full-moon parties**, inspired by *Bomba's Shack* on Tortola (see p.480). *The Wheel House* brings in live bands, often calypso or quelbe. *Thelma's Hideout* (⊕284/495-5646), at the edge of *Little Dix Bay*, might be difficult to find, but it's unmissable: Thelma will drink beer and play darts with you all night long.

Watersports and outdoor activities

Virgin Gorda isn't especially known for its **hiking**, but a few simple nature trails thread the hills connecting *Biras Creek* to *The Bitter End*; both resorts provide free maps to guests and non-guests alike. You can also hike to the top of **Virgin Gorda Peak National Park** (see p.485). Most of the resorts have **tennis** facilities, free to guests but also open to non-guests for around US$6–10 per hour. *Leverick Bay* and *Little Dix Bay* have the most courts.

The North Sound in particular offers excellent **watersports** opportunities – the companies below are recommended. Many outfits operating out of Tortola (see p.484) also provide watersports for travellers on Virgin Gorda, and more specific information on the **diving** can be found in the Tortola section on p.483. Some hotels that don't have their own watersports outfits might also provide recommendations.

Bitter End Yacht Club ☎284/494-2746. The club offers equipment rentals, lessons and charters: kayaks, Lasers, Hobies, Rhodes19s, J24s and Freedom 30s. Also located here is the Bitter End Sailing School.

Charter Virgin Gorda ☎284/495-7421, ⑧www.chartervirgingorda.com. Runs cruises, snorkel trips and fishing excursions out of *Leverick Bay Resort*. A half-day trip is US$800, the full-day US$1200.

Dive BVI ☎284/495-5513 or 1-800/848-7078, ⑧www.divebvi.com. This dive shop at Yacht Harbour (with a branch in Leverick Bay) has been in business since 1975 and offers rentals, sales, dive trips and five-star PADI training. Trips hit all the hot spots – a two-tanker is US$85. Snorkel trips every afternoon including the *Rhone* on Saturday and Anegada on Tuesday and Friday. Very professional and accommodating. Also offers nitrox diving and instruction.

Double "D" Charters ☎284/495-6150, ⑧www.doubledbvi.com. Snorkel, scuba, swim or just kick back on one of these day charters. Choose from a 50ft catamaran or one of two 42ft yachts.

Kilbrides Sunchaser Scuba ☎284/495-9638 or 1-800/932-4286. Located at the *Bitter End*, this is the most established dive outfit in the BVI and Kilbride is a legend in the area. Daily trips include The Dogs, Salt, Ginger and Cooper islands as private charters or groups. Lessons range from beginner to divemaster, and they can also videotape your dive.

Leverick Bay Watersports ☎284/495-7376, ⑧www.watersportsbvi.com. From snorkel gear and sea kayaks to powerboats and dinghies you can rent about anything here. Also good for activities such as water-skiing, parasailing and day-sails and excursions. Accessible by road, a claim the other watersports companies in the North Sound can't make.

North Sound Watersports Prickly Pear Island ☎284/495-7558. For boat charters, day-trips and deep-sea fishing. Jet ski rentals are US$50 for 30 minutes, US$90 for an hour.

SunCoast Charters ☎284/496-6288, ⑧bvikingfisher@hotmail.com. Runs four Bertrams from 28 to 46ft for half- and full-day fishing charters (US$600/900 up to six anglers) or cruises for up to ten people.

Jost Van Dyke

JOST VAN DYKE, named after the seventeenth-century Dutch pirate who made it his hideaway, is a tiny, lightly developed, mountainous island three miles off the northwest coast of Tortola. Though its popularity is increasing, this idyll of wooded hills and secluded bays has changed little since a Quaker colony settled here in the 1700s to farm sugar cane – in fact most of the island's 160 inhabitants (all either Chinnerys or Callwoods) are descended from Quaker slaves. The island has only had electricity for less than fifteen years and there's only one paved road. The growing tourist scene owes much to the yachts that stop here to clear **customs** in Great Harbour. Yet sailors and tourists alike flock here to enjoy the magical combination of friendly locals, unspoilt beauty and party atmosphere: two of its **bars** are famous in the Virgin Islands and have helped earn Jost Van Dyke the title of party capital of BVI.

The three main areas of activity are all on the south side of the island and accessible by car or boat. The focal point is the palm-fringed beach and settlement of **Great Harbour**. The beach isn't the best on the island for swimming but has the advantage of being close to the amenities along sandy laid-back Main Street, where you'll find rooms for rent, a handful of bars, boutiques, a provision store and even an ice cream shop. *Foxy's* (see opposite), tucked in the corner, is the major draw. **White Bay**, half a mile to the west beyond Pull and Be Damm Point, has the island's best beach and is home to its other famous drinking hole, the *Soggy Dollar Bar* (see p.494), as well as a hotel, campground and a few bars and shops. Just over a mile to the east of Great Harbour, **Little Harbour** is a good place to eat – the spiny lobster here may well be the biggest you've seen in your life. On the **eastern side** of the island is a short hike past mangroves and a salt pond to the **Bubbly Pool**, where a gap in the rocky coastline allows the foam of crashing waves to form a sort of natural Jacuzzi. Give a whistle for Grizzly, one of the dogs at nearby *Foxy's Taboo*, who will be more than eager to play guide as his father did before him. To get on the **Internet** your best bet is Christine's Bakery ($3/ten minutes).

Getting around

Taxis in Great Harbour Bay will take you to White Bay for about US$5 and to Little Harbour for US$5 more (or call George's Land Taxi ☎284/495-9253 or White Stone Taxi Service ☎284/495-9487). There's also Paradise Land and **Water Taxi** (☎284/495-9281) which also rents **motorbikes and scooters**. Jost Van Dyke's only paved road is very steep and bumpy in spots and curls around the hills offering views of the bays and harbours along the eastern and southern shore of the island. Abe & Eunicy Rentals (☎284/495-9329) in Little Harbour has **jeeps** for US$50-80 per day. Note that there are **no banks** on Jost Van Dyke. Some establishments accept **credit cards** but the connection to that service is rather unreliable.

Accommodation

It might not last, but major development hasn't yet arrived on Jost Van Dyke. Still, there is representation of all levels of **accommodation** including private villas, a hotel, guesthouses and a **campsite** at White Bay. *White Bay Campground* (☎284/495-9358) offers bare sites for US$15 a night, sites equipped with tents for US$35, plus small and large screen-windowed cabins for US$50-70. Communal bathrooms have showers and flush toilets. Special barbecue, chicken, ribs and fish buffets are offered throughout the week, but there's also a nice shared kitchen for cooking and storing refrigerated foods. Regardless of where you stay, it is a good idea to make reservations as soon as you can. If you choose accommodation with a kitchen, bear in mind that the island has limited groceries; it is best to stock up on Tortola or wherever you are arriving from.

Christine's Guest House ☎284/495-9281. Located upstairs from *Christine's Bakery* and within walking distance of Great Harbour, this small bed and breakfast with two basic rooms for two to three people is popular with sailors in need of a break from cramped and often hot sailboat sleeping. There is a microwave and fridge. ⑥

Perfect Pineapple Inn White Bay ☎284/496-8373. Perched halfway up the hill at the eastern end of the bay, the view from these three structures is of the entire inlet and its beautiful white beach. There is a two-bedroom villa with full kitchen, another structure with three studios with kitchenettes, and a one-bedroom villa. All are spacious with a/c. Just a five-minute walk down

to the beach and the party there. Studios go for US$110–130, the villas for US$200–300 per night. ⑥/⑧

Sandcastle White Bay ☎284/495-9888, ⊛www .sandcastle-bvi.com. The best lodging on the island, although this hotel only updated to electricity in 1996. Six large beachfront cottages (with outdoor showers) are cooled by fans, while the newer, more hotel-like cottages have a/c. There is also a restaurant, bar and beach to enjoy. Day sails, scuba diving and fishing can be scheduled through the bartender. ⑧–⑨

Sandy Ground Estates Little Harbour ☎284/494-3391 or 1-800/284-8300, ⊛www.sandyground. com. Eight secluded villas with a private beach and featuring stunning ocean views from tiled terraces. Most are two-bedroom and are available by the week only. It's out of the way so bring enough food and drink for your stay or ring ahead and ask the staff to stock your villa with provisions. Lots of repeat guests so reserve well in advance. ⑨

Sea Crest Inn Great Harbour ☎ 340/775-6389, ⓦ www.bviwelcome.com. These four beachfront units have private balconies, fully equipped kitchens, cable TV and a/c. Close to the local bar scene;

good for stumbling in late at night, but possibly an occasional annoyance when trying to sleep. ⑤

White Bay Villas White Bay ☎ 284/495-9268 or 1-800-778-8066, ⓦ www.jostvandyke.com. Six lovely villas perched above this idyllic bay and moments from the beach. The villas range in size from a huge plantation with three bedrooms and three bathrooms to a one-bedroom unit. Stays are usually arranged by the week, but the owners try to accommodate shorter stays. ⑧

Eating and drinking

Despite its small size Jost Van Dyke has a surprisingly vibrant **eating and drinking** scene and, with the famous *Foxy* at the helm, it's the party island of the BVI. Most of the fun takes place during the day, particularly at weekends, in a variety of places in Great Harbour Bay, Little Bay and White Bay, some of which are no more than beachside shacks with no running water. Nature's Basket is a simple grocery in Great Harbour that has other odds and ends like sunscreen and film.

Abe's by the Sea Little Harbour ☎ 284/495-9329. A simple dockside joint with good seafood, ribs and chicken (BBQed or curried) for lunch or dinner. Happy hour 5–6pm. Cheap sandwiches available.

Ali Baba's Bar and Restaurant Great Harbour ☎ 284/495-9280. BBQ, ribs, conch, lobster and catch of the day. Every Monday is a pig roast with a live band.

Christine's Bakery Great Harbour ☎ 284/495-9281. This quiet little place is great for breakfast (sandwiches US$3–5) or lunch (US$7–8) – the banana bread is a treat.

Corsairs Great Harbour ☎ 284/495-9294. This beachside restaurant is perhaps a close second to *Foxy's Taboo* as the best food on the island. Serving mostly Italian and seafood dishes as well as some Mexican fare, its menu changes often. Standbys include seafood quesadillas, pasta primavera and jerk chicken wings and main plates go for US$16–22. There's regular live music from local singer/guitarist Ruben Chinnery and the occasional limbo session.

Foxy's Great Harbour ☎ 284/495-9258. This is the bar that put Jost Van Dyke firmly on the yachters' map. When you think about waterfront bars, island music and beach barbecues, *Foxy's* is the standard by which everything else should be compared. Sit at picnic tables under the thatched roof or stretch out on the beach, drinking and eating (lobster, grilled fish, rotis and sandwiches). A legend throughout the BVI, larger-than-life Foxy Callwood himself does impromptu shows – playing calypso and telling stories and jokes (call ahead to see if Foxy feels like playing that day). Barbecue buffet nights are Friday and Saturday. Live music Thurs–Sat.

Foxy's Taboo Diamond Cay ☎ 284/495-0218. Plenty of moorings and dock space at this new

restaurant which is arguably the island's best. Lunch highlights include gourmet pizza, pesto penne pasta, and great burgers. Chicken, fish, steak, lamb and pasta dishes for dinner; the eggplant cheesecake in particular is a culinary event. The bar is open from 10.30am and offers its own microbrewery delights.

Ivan's Stress Free Bar White Bay Campground ☎ 284/495-9358. *Ivan's* has a barbecue (US$20) and live music Thursday nights. The bar operates on an honour system, so be sure to keep your own tab and pay when you leave.

One Love White Bay ☎ 284/495-9829. A thatch-roofed beach bar decorated only with things found in the sea – marine life, buoys, nets, plastic bottles and other cast-offs. Cheap place for a drink and if Seddy is in the mood, he'll show you a few sleight-of-hand tricks that get harder to follow with every rum punch.

Sandcastle Restaurant White Bay ☎ 284/495-9888. Non-guests can make reservations (and should, by 4pm) to eat with guests of the hotel at the large communal table. Jost Van Dyke's only fine-dining option, with a set menu of lamb, duck, crab cakes and the like for around US$35. No dinner on Friday.

Sidney's Peace and Love Little Harbour ☎ 284/495-9271. T-shirts of the guests of parties past dangle from the ceiling at this Jost Van Dyke institution that's been serving up food and fun for over 25 years. Choose from steak, shrimp, ribs, chicken and conch stew, plus hearty helpings of rice and peas, coleslaw, potato salad, steamed vegetables for US$18–25. However, the highlight here is lobster, bigger than anywhere else on the islands. Sidney still catches them himself and cooks them over an open fire the island way. Thursday night has all-you-can-eat lobster and live music for US$39. Self-service at the bar – mix 'em as you like 'em.

Soggy Dollar Bar *Sandcastle Hotel*, White Bay ☎284/495-9888. Named after the wet bills brought by patrons who swim to the bar, *The Soggy Dollar*, located right on the beach, is perhaps best known as the inventor of the Painkiller, a potent mix of dark rum, pineapple and orange juices, coco lopez and fresh nutmeg. Saturday and Sunday are especially fun but can get very crowded. Local musician, Ruben Chinnery, plays a mixture of blues and Jimmy Buffet-esque island tunes every Sunday afternoon. Sandwiches are available at lunch.

Watersports and other activities

Unless you go out with a tour the best **snorkelling** is found on the eastern side around Diamond Cay and Little Jost Van Dyke. White Bay is where most gather for **beach activities**.

Ali Baba's Bar and Restaurant (see p.493). Stop in here to inquire about half-day fishing trips for US$300, all equipment included.

BVI Expeditions Offers US$80 day-trips on a high-speed catamaran to St Thomas.

Jost Van Dyke Watersports ☎284/495-0271,⊛www.jvdwatersports.com. Just down the road from *Foxy's*, this well-run outfit pretty much has the lock on scuba diving (two tanks US$95). They operate by reservation only and will take you to any of 35 unmarked dive sites that only they know about. They also specialize in snorkel eco-tours and offer sportfishing, dinghy and kayak rentals as well as Internet service.

Sea and Land Adventure Sports White Bay ☎284/499-2269,⊛www.bviadventure.com. Rent a variety of toys on the beach ranging from jet boats, kayaks and water trampolines to mountain bikes and ATVs. They also offer snorkel excursions for US$65 per person.

Anegada

The name **ANEGADA** means the "drowned land," and with its highest point a dune topping out at 28 feet it would seem this flat coral and limestone atoll just has its nose above the waves. Lying fourteen miles north of Virgin Gorda, the island is almost completely surrounded by the **Horseshoe Reef**, one of the world's largest and the sinker of many a vessel – the plethora of wrecks only add to the already excellent **snorkelling** that draws day-trippers. Anegada's **lobster** is huge and reputedly the best (restaurants on other islands refer to it by name), its **beaches** are long and undeveloped, and the **bonefishing** is some of the best in the world.

Anegada Harbour, on the southwest coast, is nothing much to speak of – just a long, thin dock with lobster traps tied to its side – but it's a good place to base yourself for exploring the island. The area, which includes Pomato Point and Setting Point, has plenty of lodging, restaurants, bars and gift-shops. The little **Pomato Point Museum** (☎284/495-8038) is worth a visit for its small but evocative display of items recovered from shipwrecks around the island, ranging from cannons to gin bottles. Around four miles east of here (southeast of the airport) is **The Settlement**, where most of the island's 195 inhabitants live. You'll find diners, bakeries, a post office and a police station here. There is also a clinic here with a nurse on duty; but the doctor is on island only once a week.

The best of the beaches, miles of pristine white sand, and snorkelling are on the north coast. At **LOBLOLLY BAY**, a picture-postcard Caribbean paradise with a bar and restaurant, the waters teem with schools of mojarra, needlefish and mantis shrimp as well as the occasional sea turtle or stingray. On the western side of the beach, the dark reef area in the middle of the lagoon contains three small caves and a wreck, among which you'll spot elkhorn and brain coral, angelfish, snapper and huge grouper. **Cow Wreck Beach**, six miles to the west, is another good snorkelling spot and with currents towards the shore it is great for kids; it has a changing room, plus food and drinks. **Jack's Bay** and **Keel Point** are also good places to put your face in the water. Anegada's natural assets aren't limited to its reefs; the centre of the island is a salt pond and the whole island is a **wildlife sanctuary**, home to turtles, birdlife, including osprey and a flock of flamingos, and the endangered rock iguanas, which are bred and protected in its carefully monitored reserves. It is possible to walk to Cow Wreck beach along the shore from the south side at Anegada Harbour. The walk can take just over an hour and a quarter and is best done around sunrise for the beauty of the light and to avoid the heat. No footwear necessary.

Arrival and getting around

Every Thursday and the last Sunday of the month Smith's Ferry Services (☎284/494-4454) runs a fast ferry to Anegada from Road Town, Tortola ($50 return) stopping at Virgin Gorda if you call ahead and make a reservation. This option might be best if you have time and a lot of luggage. Taxis run US$6–8 to most points on the island and some hotels might offer guests a free shuttle from the island's **airport**. Getting around the island is fairly easy – the main road loops round to most of the main places of interest – and, for once, given the flat terrain, **cycling** is a realistic option, for short distances anyway. It gets very hot and dusty on the shadeless roads so always carry plenty of water and a hat. For rentals contact *Lil Bit Cash & Carry* at 284/495-9932. *The Anegada Reef Hotel* (see below), on the front of the harbour dock, can help you schedule everything from bike rental to car rental to a shuttle ride to beaches on the north side of the island (US$8). Scooter rentals are available next to the gift shop ($40). Alternatively, call Anegada Taxi (☎284/495-0228) or rent a vehicle (around US$55 per day) through ABC Car Rentals (☎284/495-9466) or DW Jeep Rentals (☎284/495-9677). Most businesses monitor VHF channel 16 for boaters.

Accommodation

Most of the **accommodation** on Anegada is located on the **south shore** and is fairly basic, though there is something to suit all budgets, including **campsites** on the south side of the island at *Cardie's Ship-Wreck Restaurant* (☎284/499-9870, US$12 for 1 or 2 people). They also can provide tents and bedding for a bit extra. If roughing it is too much for you, try one of the **beachfront cabins**. For **villas** consider *Anegada Seaside Villas* (☎284/495-9466, ✆www.anegadavillas.com), the six-person *Bonefish Villa* (☎284/495-8045) sitting nearly on top of a great place to seek its namesake, or the quite elegant *Lavenda Breeze* (☎888/868-0199, ✆www.lavendabreeze.com).

Anegada Beach Cottages Pomato Point
☎284/495-9234, ✆www.anegadabeachcottages.
com. Three fully furnished seaside cottages with
modern kitchen and bathroom set on a private
beach (no a/c but plenty of cooling sea breezes).
There are two one-bedroom cottages and one
double cottage linked by connecting door. **⑤**
Anegada Reef Hotel Setting Point, Anegada
Harbour ☎284/495-8002, ✆www.anegadareef.
com. This lovely hotel, located at the head of the
harbour, acts as a de facto tour operator arranging
beach shuttles, rental cars and fishing trips. Stay in
one of its sixteen rooms and eat a fantastic lobster
meal in its restaurant. **⑦**
Cow Wreck Villas ☎284/495-9932. There are
two simple beachside villas (1 and 2 bedrooms)
with complete kitchens. The beach offers shallow
snorkelling, great for kids and beginners, and there
are fishing tours available. **⑦**
Lo'Blolly Beach Cottages ☎284/495-8359,
✆www.loblollycottages.com. Four cottages just a

stroll down the beach from *The Big Bamboo* with
a/c, full kitchen, great location, but dim interiors.
Bike, snorkel and kayak rentals available. **⑦**
Neptune's Treasure Anegada Harbour
☎284/495-9439. There are nine comfortable
guesthouses, double and single rooms, all with
private baths, a/c, and fridges. There is also a nice
restaurant and bar. (see overleaf) **④**
Ocean Range Hotel The Settlement ☎284/495-
2019. If you'd rather stay closer to town on the south
side of the island where the waters are better suited
for bonefishing than snorkelling, you're best off here
– six simple units with private outdoor balconies, all
with a/c, TV, private baths and kitchenettes. **③–④**
Sands Hotel Keel Point ☎284/495-8065, ✆www.
anegadasandshotel.com. Located on the north side,
the hotel has rooms with kitchenettes and rests
behind a seaside dune (the highest point on the
island). There is good snorkelling here and the area
is secluded, but the real attraction is the high-season
doubles that start at US$75. **③**

Eating and drinking

Most **restaurants** catch their own **seafood** and will be happy to tell you where and how it was caught. The local speciality, the spindly but huge **Anegada lobster**, is delicious and worth ordering at least once. For dinner at any of the following it's advisable to call ahead and make a reservation and make sure lobster is available if you are interested.

Anegada Reef Hotel (see also p.495). Popular dining spot where hotel guests dine alongside leather-faced boaters for cocktails and a candlelit dinner of grilled fish, chicken, steak and lobster (don't worry, you can still wear your shorts). Main courses start at US$20.

The Big Bamboo The North Side ☎284/495-2019. This pavilion-style restaurant in Loblolly Bay caters to the beach crowd, with a good lunch and dinner menu – crab cakes, fish and shrimp, ribs, and burgers too. The lobster is quite good for such a simple place. All meals come with rice and a side dish, while the drink of choice is the rum-based Bamboo Teaser.

Cow Wreck Beach Bar and Grill ☎284/495-8047. Wash down conch fritters, lobster salad or Belle's famous lobster with the bar's own rum-driven Wreck Punch. Serves lunch and dinner and sells food supplies for boaters. Call them for a shuttle if you plan to eat there.

Dotsy's Bakery The Settlement ☎284/495-9667. Dotsy's delicious home-made tarts, breads and cakes are a great way to start the day; or stop by for lunch or dinner – she also serves up sandwiches, pizza, chicken and burgers. Lunches are in the US$8–9 range but a sandwich can be had for US$2–5.

Neptune's Treasure Anegada Harbour ☎284/495-9439. The owners catch, cook and serve their own grilled fish and lobster – main courses for around US$20. Try a Pink Whoopie, yet another rum and fruit juice concoction, at the bar.

Pomato Point Restaurant Anegada Harbour ☎284/495-8038. Located at Pomato Point, this pleasant airy spot serves dinner only. Chicken, ribs, fish and lobster are available in the US$20–40 range. Check out the Pomato Point Museum (part of the same building) before dinner.

Watersports

Anegada doesn't have much in the way of organized **watersports** but the *Anegada Reef Hotel* (see p.495) can help you book fishing trips and also rents out some snorkelling gear, though the selection is very limited and it is best to bring your own equipment to the island. Alternatively, both Virgin Gorda (see p.491) and Tortola (see pp.483–485) have charter operators that run snorkelling and fishing trips to Anegada. If you want to try your hand at **bonefishing**, give Garfield Faulkner a call at ☎284/495-9569 or ask around The Settlement or at your hotel for a local reference. **Scuba diving** off Anegada is prohibited.

Outlying islands

There are a few islands accessible from Tortola that are worth a visit. **PETER ISLAND**, three miles across the Francis Drake Channel from Tortola, is home to the luxurious *Peter Island Resort and Yacht Harbour* (☎284/495-2000 or 1-800/346-4451, ⓦwww.peterisland.com; ⓞ), which offers sea-view rooms, an all-inclusive range of watersports, tennis, bikes, hiking and sailing activities, and extremely elegant dining at its *Tradewinds Restaurant* and wine room (also open to non-guests). Non-guests can visit the island and use the secluded, palm-fringed beaches – the Peter Island Ferry (call the hotel for a day-pass) connects the island with Road Town on Tortola (US$14 one-way; free if you have a reservation at *Tradewinds*). There's more casual fare – wood-oven pizzas and salads – available at *Deadman's Beach Bar and Grill*. Peaceful, unpretentious and good value, **COOPER ISLAND**, four miles east of Peter Island, has a lone hotel and a few vacation homes. *The Cooper Island Beach Club* (☎284/495-9084 or 1-800/542-4624, ⓦwww.cooper-island.com) offers eleven doubles (ⓞ) without phones or TV set on beautiful **Manchioneel Bay** with its long beach and fantastic snorkelling – the thick, sea grass attracts a dazzling assortment of green turtles, eagle rays and huge queen conch. There are no roads and no cars on the island and the private ferry follows the schedules of arriving guests. Non-guests can call the *Beach Club* to find out when it's running. *Sail Caribbean Divers* (☎284/495-1675, see p.484) has a base on the island and runs a dive boat to Cooper daily from Hodges Creek on Tortola.

Eight-acre **MARINA CAY**, which offers great snorkelling, was made famous by author Robb White and his wife, Rodie, who moved here in 1936, built a home and lived without running water or electricity. His book about the experience, *Two on an Isle*, was made into a movie in the 1950s, starring Sidney Poitier. The only place to stay on the island is *Pusser's Marina Cay Resort* (☎284/494-2174, ⓦwww.pussers .com; ❼), connected to Trellis Bay by a short free ferry ride (eight daily), which has basic rooms (❻–❼) or two-bedroom villas (❾). The hotel can arrange everything from snorkelling and diving to surfing and powerboat rentals. The old White residence is now *The Robb White Bar*, which hosts barbecues and features live music. A more extensive menu is available at the *Pusser's* beachside restaurant, whose bar has a happy hour daily from 4pm to 7pm. Be sure not to miss Michael Bean's happy hour pirate show most days at 5pm at the upstairs bar. The show is reputable enough to draw some loyal fans known as "Beanie babies."

Uninhabited and largely untamed **NORMAN ISLAND**, the westernmost BVI, is only accessible by hired boat and there are no places to stay, yet thousands of people in high season flock here every day to snorkel – and look for gold. Rumours are that there is hidden **treasure** all over the island – three chests of gold have reportedly been discovered since the mid-1700s, and it's stories such as these that have led some to suggest that Norman Island was the model for Robert Louis Stevenson's *Treasure Island*.

The bar/restaurant *The Willy T* (☎284/494-0183, ⓦwww.williamthornton.com) is a converted schooner permanently moored in the Bight, a large bay and a popular anchorage for yachters. It's one of the most raucous and unusual drinking spots in the BVI and the top deck often sees inebriated patrons removing their clothes and diving into the water. *Wet Willie,* (☎284/496-6416) the bar's free ferry, departs at 5pm daily from Todman's across from Nanny Cay Marina and returns at an unpredictable hour around 10pm or later.

GUANA ISLAND is an 850-acre private island resort (☎914/967-6050,ⓦwww .guana.com; ❾) with its own nature preserve and wildlife sanctuary. Formerly a Quaker plantation, the resort offers secluded cottages decorated with simple elegance. With seven beaches and no non-guest access, this may be as secluded as it gets. All meals, transfers and other extras included, as well as a golf cart to get around the island. Honeymoon rates available. You can rent the entire island for a mere US$15,500 per day for up to fourteen guests in high season.

Anguilla

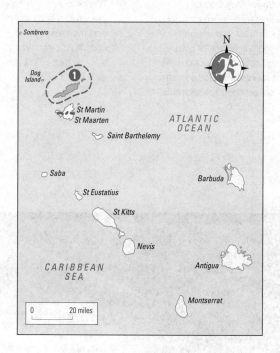

Anguilla highlights

* **Dolphin Discovery** Learn about, interact and swim with dolphins kept in a lagoon at Meads Bay. See p.509

* **Shoal Bay** One of the region's greatest beaches, big enough that you will find your own quiet spot away from the crowds, and dotted with several good restaurants. See p.510

* **Koal Keel** Enjoy a meal at this legendary gourmet restaurant set in the grounds of a former plantation. See p.511

* **Wreck diving** Scuba dive the wrecks both ancient and modern around Anguilla's clear, warm waters. See p.512

△ *Uncle Ernie's BBQ*, Shoal Bay

Introduction and basics

On her 2004 album *Damita Jo*, Janet Jackson describes **Anguilla** as her favourite island for relaxation and escapism – and it is not difficult to see why. With its swaying palm trees and pristine white sandy beaches, Anguilla is the ideal place to curl up with a good book and unwind by the turquoise waters on your own, with a partner or with family. Add to this mix world-class dining and a range of watersports and Anguilla is the quintessential Caribbean holiday destination.

Barely 35 square miles in size, and rising to a highest point of just over two hundred feet, Anguilla has an **interior** that is dry, dusty and covered in scrubby vegetation. However, this fact is largely ignored by an increasing stream of visitors who beat their way here for the glorious turquoise waters and truly stunning beaches. Some of these, particularly **Rendezvous Bay** in the southwest and **Shoal Bay** in the northeast, are among the finest in the Caribbean.

Ignored by the early waves of **tourist development** in the Caribbean, tiny Anguilla has benefited from careful study of the planning mistakes that have blighted its neighbours. Anguilla has eschewed large-scale tourist complexes, successfully aiming for top-quality, high-end development with relatively limited impact on the island's scarce resources, especially important when looking to find that perfect isolated beach spot. This has made it a top destination for stressed-out celebrities and the super-rich who want to get away from it all. And, while more expensive than nearby St Maarten and St Kitts, the best attractions on Anguilla – the **beaches** – are all free.

Where to go

Anguilla's clean white-sand **beaches** are the perfect spot to kick back and relax or pursue more active interests including scuba diving and windsurfing. Many are big enough for you to have your own secluded spot and are sprinkled with a selection of top-quality restaurants. The beaches at **Rendezvous Bay** and **Shoal Bay East** rank among some of the world's finest while at **Mead's Bay** you can swim with dolphins in an enclosed lagoon.

When to go

Like other Caribbean islands, Anguilla is a year-round destination; however, the **best time to visit** is between mid-December and mid-April, when rainfall is low and the heat is tempered by cooling trade winds. At other times of year the weather is often very hot and humid, and storms are not unusual. From June to November is **hurricane season**. And, even if a storm does not hit the island, Anguilla is still prone to flooding, due to its low-lying topography. Note that **prices** for accommodation in particular increase between December and April.

Arrival

Visitors arriving by air will land at the newly expanded **Wallblake Airport** just south of The Valley. Taxis and rental cars are easily procured here. **Private vessels** arriving in Anguilla must go to a port of entry such as Blowing Point or Sandy Ground for immigration and customs clearance and will be required to obtain a permit to anchor in the marine park. The fee is US$15 for private boats and US$23 for charters. For those visitors arriving for a day-trip from nearby St Martin, local taxis can operate as **tour guides**. Alternatively, Malliouhana Travel and Tours (☎264/497-2431, ⊛www.malliouhanatravel.ai) offers sightseeing tours.

Information and maps

At the airport there are a variety of useful publications available, including **maps** and current listings newspapers. In hotels you can also pick up brochures and guides.

ANGUILLA

ACCOMMODATION

Anguilla Great House & Beach Resort	D
Arawak Beach Inn	A
Cap Juluca	F
Cuisinart Resort & Spa	E
Rendezvous Bay Hotel & Villas	C
Shoal Bay Villas	B

0   2 miles

The **Anguilla Tourist Board** office, which has a collection of printed information, is located on Coronation Road in The Valley (8am–5pm Mon–Fri; ☎264/497-2759, ⊛www.anguilla-vacation.com).

Anguilla Life is a quarterly **magazine** available in hotels that contains many articles of interest to visitors. Particularly useful are the restaurant reviews and the diversions section that lists happy hours and events at the island's restaurants and bars. *What We Do in Anguilla* is a monthly listings paper available at the tourist office, the airport and most hotels.

Lastly, the **Anguilla Hotel & Tourism Association** (☎264/497-2944, ⊛www.ahta.ai) has an official publication, *Dream Anguilla*, that can be picked up in member hotels and the tourist board office. It contains a number of glossy photos and useful information.

Money and costs

The island's official unit of currency is the **Eastern Caribbean dollar** (**EC$**), divided into 100 cents. Notes come in denominations of 5, 10, 20, 50 and 100 EC dollars; coins come in 1, 2, 5, 10 and 25 cents. However, because of the large numbers of US visitors prices are usually listed in US$, though both currencies are accepted universally. The **rate of exchange** is fixed to the US dollar at EC$2.70 for each US dollar.

Credit cards are taken in most shops, restaurants and in hotels. **Travellers' cheques** are also accepted – however, to avoid additional currency conversion fees, visitors are advised to take cheques in US$.

Most **banks** in Anguilla have offices in The Valley. Typical opening hours are Mon–Thurs 8am–3pm and Fri 8am–5pm. **ATMs** are located at their branches and also at some supermarkets. National Bank of Anguilla ATMs dispense US dollars while the one at International Caribbean Bank in the Valley issues EC dollars.

There is a **departure tax** at the airport of US$20 (EC$53.00) for adults, US$10 (EC$27) for children (five to eleven years of age); children under 5 years of age are exempt. The tax is payable in cash only.

A **service charge** of between ten and fifteen percent is added to most restaurant bills and ten percent is added to hotel bills – so further tipping is discretionary. A government tax of ten percent is added to hotel bills as well.

Anguilla has little in the way of natural resources for growing crops or rearing animals so most products apart from seafood are imported. This, along with the island's aim of attracting upscale tourists, means that **prices** here tend to be higher than on neighbouring islands or in the US, although favourable exchange rates can make it a bargain for visitors from places with currencies not linked to the US dollar. Prices for restaurant **meals** begin at US$10 and can rise into the stratosphere, while most **rooms** except the most basic cost upwards of US$150 per night at peak times.

Getting around

Anguilla's **roads** are among the best in the Caribbean. A flat wide paved road runs east to west through the middle of the island, and the many other roads branching off it to the hotels and restaurants are in good condition, with only the last few metres running to the coast unpaved. Signposting is also good with entrance roads to most major hotels and restaurants clearly indicated from the main road. There are only a few traffic lights in The Valley and even in the peak season the roads are never congested. The main hazard, in fact, is the stray goats that occasionally bolt without warning onto the road. Petrol stations can be found relatively easily all over the island.

There is **no public transport** system on the the island, so the only way of getting around is by taxi or car rental. Driving is on the left but because most of the cars available from rental firms have the steering wheel on the left, driving can feel a little peculiar. Driving requires a local driving licence which costs US$20 and is valid for three months. Licences can be purchased from all car rental agencies but payment is in cash only. Many hotels have their own fleets of rental cars on offer at competitive rates. **Car rentals** are available from the airport and from a wide number of firms including the big chains and local suppliers: Avis (☎264/497-2642, ℮avisaxa@anguillanet.

com) and Carib (☎264/497-6020, ⊛www.skyviews.com/anguilla/caribrentacar) are two of the best. It is worth shopping around and haggling to get the best **rates** for car rental, though plan to budget between US$30 and $50 per day depending on the type of vehicle.

Rates for **taxi** journeys from Wallblake Airport and from Blowing Point Port to major points on Anguilla, such as hotels, for up to two passengers and two pieces of luggage are fixed (no meters). However for each additional passenger and piece of luggage the fee increases. An extra charge is added for night-time travel between 6pm and 6am. The tourist board website has a full listing of rates. Hotels normally have arrangements with taxi drivers to provide service to guests; alternatively, contact Connor's Taxi Service and Car Rental (☎264/497-6894). Using taxis instead of renting a car can be expensive and is only recommended if you plan to drink alcohol, intend on making only one or two trips during your stay or if you cannot drive.

The flat terrain and quality roads make **cycling** and using a **scooter** relatively easy and enjoyable, too, as there are plenty of roads around the island with spectacular sights along the way. Scooters can be rented from A&S Scooter Rental (☎264/497-8803) for around US$20 per day. Bikes are available at several hotels for modest fees. Mountain bikes and scooters can be rented from On 2 Scooter and Bicycle Rentals (☎264/497-2896) for around US$10 per day.

Accommodation

Most **accommodation** options on Anguilla are at the expensive/luxury end of the scale, many of them on a superb stretch of beach (open to guests and non-guests alike). Everything you need is on the property of the larger ones. There are a few good options in other price ranges, though they may be harder to find at peak times such as Christmas and Easter. Conversely, during the slow season, including most of the summer, prices at the top hotels can fall dramatically. Several hotels offer good **packages** if you pre-book activities such as spa treatments, scuba diving or a wedding and it is a good idea to explore their websites for the best deals rather than through a travel agent. The Anguilla tourist board website listed earlier has a comprehensive accommodation rate guide that allows you to compare prices and amenities of many properties.

Food and drink

There are over seventy **dining** experiences in Anguilla ranging from world-renowned gourmet restaurants to roadside barbecues, beachside bistros and grills. Many of these focus on local **seafood** such as snapper, grouper, conch and lobster. **Island specialities** include pumpkin soup, conch salad and goat stew, though you will rarely find these at more upmarket eateries. What you will not find are the major fast food chains, as these have been prohibited from the island – though one enterprising restaurateur has named their venue *McDonna's*. **Vegetarians** are well catered for with most restaurants offering a variety of choices.

Prices tend to be higher for dinner than for lunch, though dinner menus tend to be more elaborate. The upscale hotels all have terrific dining options and are worth a visit even if you are not a guest in them. Credit cards are accepted in most places except for the smallest transactions. Dinner **reservations** are required for most of the upmarket restaurants, and in peak season, at the most popular venues you may need to book early during your visit or even prior to arrival. Most **bars** serve imported beers, spirits and wines. The **local drinks** to try out include the lethal rum punch concoctions and Anguillian Blue Martinis.

Post, phones and the Internet

Telephone kiosks are scattered around the island and most take phone cards, sold at the many shops, hotels or at the Cable and Wireless office in The Valley (Mon–Fri 8am–5pm, Sat & holidays 9am–1pm; ☎264/497-3100). It is possible to use a credit card from certain public phone kiosks but be aware that these calls can quickly become expensive.

To **place a call** within Anguilla, simply dial the seven-digit number; the 264 prefix is not required. The price of these calls is fixed regardless of length though hotels may add surcharges.

The **post office** can be found on Carter Rey Boulevard in The Valley (Mon–Fri 8am–3.30pm).

Most hotels now offer **Internet** access; some are free while others may charge. The Cable and Wireless office has an Internet access kiosk in their sales area where you can surf the Net for a fee. The Anguilla National Library in The Valley (Mon–Fri 9am–6.30pm, Sat 9am–3pm) also has Internet access on a computer in the main library lobby for EC$5 per half-hour. Customers at *Roy's Place* (see p.509) can take advantage of free wireless Internet access if they bring a Wi-Fi enabled laptop; alternatively, there is a single computer that can be used freely.

Opening hours, holidays and festivals

Shops and businesses are typically **open** Monday to Friday 9am–5pm, with some open at the weekend, too. Restaurant opening times vary and it is worth checking ahead,

Public holidays and festivals

May 3 Labour Day
May 30 Anguilla Day commemorates the beginning of the Anguillian Revolution which took place in 1967. The celebration includes a parade at Webster Park and a six-hour round-the-island boat race.
May 31 Whit Monday
June 14 Celebration of Her Majesty the Queen's Birthday
First week of August Anguilla Summer Festival includes a vibrant celebration of the Anguillian culture through dance, song, beauty pageants, a colourful parade of troupes through The Valley and boat racing.
December 17 Separation Day

particularly for dinner, as many require a reservation in advance. In addition, some places are only open during peak season.

Along with the public holidays of New Year, Easter and Christmas, Anguilla celebrates the **holidays** and **festivals** listed in the box in the previous column. There are a number of additional events taking place throughout each year and the tourist board website lists them.

Sports and outdoor activities

Anguilla offers a variety of **sporting** and **outdoor activities**. Many hotels have excellent facilities and there are some good independent providers as well. **Watersports** such as scuba diving, snorkelling, water-skiing and sailing are well catered for.

Diving

Diving on Anguilla focuses around a number of **wrecks** that have been deliberately sunk and now attract schools of colourful reef fish and interesting coral formations. Uniquely, Anguilla has two **natural reefs** just a few hundred metres apart. The first is along the littoral of Anguilla and is composed of soft corals: sea fan, gorgonians and sponges. The second begins in Island Harbour in the east and continues all the way to Prickly Pear and Dog Island. This outside reef is made up from hard corals such as giant brain, pencil and giant plaque.

Anguilla's clear waters boast seven **marine parks**: Dog Island, Prickley Pear, Seal Island Reef System, Little Bay, Sandy Island, Shoal Bay Harbour Reef System and Stoney Bay Marine Park. All the dive sites are shallow – between 35 and 110ft – which along with the usually high levels of visibility makes it a great place to learn to scuba dive.

The island has two recognized PADI resorts that can be used whichever hotel you choose to stay in: *Shoal Bay Scuba* (☎264/235-1482) and *Anguillian Divers* (☎264/497-4750). Both offer a comprehensive range of dives and instruction, with modern, well-equipped boats.

A **diving permit**, which the above operators can supply, is necessary to scuba dive. Single and multi-tank diving costs can be expensive, however both operators offer dive packages with hotels such as *Rendezvous Bay Hotel*, *Anguilla Great House* and *Shoal Bay Villas*.

Other activities

It is possible to ride **horseback** along the beach and through scenic trails. A popular place to go is the trail out of North Hill Village down to Sandy Ground. Both El Rancho del Blues (☎264/497-6164) and Cliffside Riding Centre (☎264/497-3667) can put you on a horse for around US$35 per hour.

In 2005, a $250 million PGA-standard **golf** course is set to open on Anguilla. Located in the Merrywing Bay area, this will be an 18-hole, 7200-yard championship course that will offer all the facilities you would expect

from such an investment including on-site pros and equipment rental. In the meantime, you can amuse yourself with the aqua golf driving range at Cap Juluca's.

Sailing trips from Sandy Ground to points around the island include those on *Sail Choclat*, a 35ft catamaran that makes lunch and snorkelling trips to the nearby cays and romantic sunset cruises, both with complimentary drinks. To book, contact the operator on ☎ 264/497-3394, or via email at ✉ ruan@anguillanet.com. Prices start at US$50.

There are a variety of game **fish** to pursue around Anguilla, including tuna, wahoo, and marlin. A number of operators offer sport-fishing trips, including Gotcha (☎264/497-2956) and Sandy Island Enterprises (☎ 264/497-0787). Prices vary depending on duration and numbers but start at around US$250 for four passengers.

History

Amerindians are thought to have settled in Anguilla around 1500 BC, living in small settlements dotted around the island. They named the island "Malliouhana", meaning arrowhead or sea serpent. Major remains have been found at more than forty sites including the Fountain, the island's only natural spring, near Shoal Bay.

Though **Columbus** missed the island on his trips to the New World in the 1490s, Spanish explorers who passed by shortly afterwards named the island Anguilla (Spanish for eel) for its long thin shape.

The first Europeans to establish a permanent base here were the **British**, who arrived in 1650 and began growing tobacco and cotton, and raising livestock with a small number of imported slaves. Short on rainfall, and without the size or the quality of soil to enable its plantations to compete with nearby islands, Anguilla never really flourished. Those who could afford to leave made off for more prosperous islands.

For centuries the islanders who

remained managed on little more than subsistence **farming** and **fishing**. Furthermore, they developed a reputation for **boat-building** and **seamanship**, running boats that exported salt and fish and carried local men off for seasonal work in the sugar fields of Santo Domingo (present-day Dominican Republic) and the oil refineries of Aruba and Curaçao.

After **World War II**, with its major Caribbean colonies pressing for independence, Britain showed little interest in continuing to maintain Anguilla. For convenience, it was decided in the 1960s that the island should be administered alongside nearby St Kitts and Nevis, and a union of the islands was put in place. Anguillians, who regarded the politicians on St Kitts as arrogant and bullying, were outraged and demonstrated against the union. They declared **independence**, sending home the policemen installed by St Kitts and calling in a Harvard law professor to draft a national constitution.

Showing a wholly disproportionate reaction, British troops decided to **invade** and crush "The Rebellion". In March 1969 a crack battalion of over three hundred stormed ashore, only to be met by local citizens waving flags and demanding to be put back directly under British rule. Not a shot was fired by the red-faced marines, and the event was dubbed Britain's Bay of Piglets.

Britain resumed **direct responsibility** for Anguilla, which it has maintained to this day, with the island run by an elected government but the British-appointed governor in charge of matters of defence and foreign policy. **Tourism** took off in the 1980s, when day-trippers from nearby Saint Martin/Sint Maarten began to arrive in droves. Today the industry drives the local economy, leaving fewer and fewer of its nearly 10,000 inhabitants dependent on the trade in salt, lobster and fish that sustained previous generations.

9.1

Anguilla

ANGUILLA is centred on its modest capital, **The Valley**, from which roads head both east and west to the island's fine beaches and natural attractions, chief among them shimmering **Shoal Bay East** and **Rendezvous Bay**. There are no towns or villages as such on the island, though you'll find small clusters of houses in **Sandy Ground** and **Island Harbour**.

The island's small size means you are never far from the coast. The Caribbean side is particularly good for watersports such as **scuba diving** and **snorkelling**, while the Atlantic coast is a haven for **windsurfers** and **sailors**. Most of the island's income is derived from **tourism**, though there is a growing financial services industry. **Restaurants** with celebrity chefs and inspired menus along with a plethora of superior **hotels** ensure that Anguilla is firmly targeted by upscale visitors.

Accommodation

Anguilla Great House and Beach Resort
Rendezvous Bay ☎264/497-6061, ⊛www.
anguillagreathouse.com. Attractive and quiet spot, with 27 rooms in a series of cottages spread over a large resort beside Rendezvous Bay, with a good pool and restaurant and watersports equipment. ⑨

Arawak Beach Inn Island Harbour ☎264/497-4888, ⊛www.arawakbeach.com. Several colourful and spacious rooms, all with patios or balconies, furnished with Caribbean art and a stone's throw from the harbour. There's a freshwater pool and the restaurant offers up good food all day. ⑦

Cap Juluca Maunday's Bay ☎264/497-6666, ⊛www.capjuluca.com. Fabulous resort with accommodation strung out along one of the island's best beaches in tasteful and ultra-comfortable Moorish-styled villas. The whole place is designed for maximum relaxation with minimal effort and distraction, right down to the shaded sun loungers discreetly placed at a good distance from your neighbour and periodically called on by staff offering a cooling drink or sorbet. Three acclaimed restaurants and a large selection of spa treatments and other sports activities including tennis, water-skiing and boating are available on site. ⑨

CuisinArt Resort & Spa Rendezvous Bay

☎264/498-2000, ⊛www.cuisinartresort.com. A series of cerulean blue-domed villas, along with a uniquely delightful swimming pool leading down to the beach bar, make this an architecturally unique resort. On the spectacular beach there are a number of activities including windsurfing. Several acclaimed restaurants and boutiques along with spa are also on site. ⑨

Rendezvous Bay Hotel and Villas Rendezvous Bay ☎264/497-6549, ⊛www.rendezvousbay.com. Location, location, location is the first thing to note about this friendly and long-standing hotel, situated on two miles of some of the finest beach in the world and offering some of the best value on the island. Rooms and villas are good-sized and well-furnished, and most have balconies or patios that allow you to step right onto the beach. There's also an excellent cedar tree-lined gourmet restaurant. ⑤

Shoal Bay Villas Shoal Bay East ☎264/497-2051, ⊛www.sbvillas.ai. Choice spot on the white sands at Shoal Bay East with thirteen comfortable and good-sized rooms ranging from studios and one-bedroom apartments to three-bedroom villas. All have their own kitchen and there's a restaurant, a pool and watersports equipment. The villas are conveniently located for the nearby restaurants. ⑨

The interior

Flat, dry and dusty, **the interior** of the island features no waterfalls, rivers, or lush tropical foliage and is covered in sparse scrubby vegetation. Very little of interest can be found inland beyond the island's only town of any size, **The Valley**, and an excellent road that makes getting around straightforward. The Valley is a couple minutes' drive from the airport, though it is not a place where many visitors will spend a great deal of time. It is a functional rather than inspiring place, home to government, banks and the main shops.

The main site of note in The Valley is **Wallblake House**, built in 1787 by a local sugar planter and one of the oldest buildings on Anguilla. The house and its outbuildings of stables and kitchens are not on the scale of plantation houses to be found elsewhere in the Caribbean – a sign that planters here were less successful – but the combination of thick-cut stone and intricately carved timber is of moderate interest. Donated to the Catholic Church in 1959, the house proved too small for holding services and the adjoining St Gerard's church with its peculiar cobbled stone was therefore built in 1966. Entry and a 30-minute tour costs EC$10 (Tues–Fri 10am–noon). On occasion local art galleries will display their work at the house.

In town there are a number of **shops** selling souvenirs, art works and groceries. In addition there is an open-air people's market selling fresh produce. A new modestly sized mall, Eldorados, on the road west of The Valley, offers duty-free shopping. However, better selections and prices are available if you make the short hop by ferry or plane to **Sint Maarten**. A number of other shops are dotted along the main island road, the most notable collection of which is on the corner of Bedneys Road and Rendezvous Road. Most are open Mon–Sat from 9am to 5pm.

In the village of **East End**, situated opposite **East End Pond**, is a small private museum, the **Heritage Collection** (Mon–Sat 10am–5pm; ✆264/235-7440), which showcases the people and history of the island. It houses a modest collection of artefacts, models and pictures.

The coasts

The island's prime attractions are clustered on its **coast**, specifically the magnificent, soft, dazzlingly white-sand **beach** areas. Anguilla has over thirty public beaches that cater to all types, whether you want to do some fun watersports or just relax with a book. The beach areas have not been overdeveloped, either, with two to three hotels per beach being the norm – meaning a quiet spot is never far away. The pleasant ambience extends to waterside **restaurants** and beach **clubs** where you can have a meal or sip cocktails. The absence of pushy hawkers found in other destinations is also welcome. No topless or nude bathing is permitted on any beach, and you are asked not to touch the reef or collect shells that are still in use.

Along the north coast

At over a mile long, **Meads Bay**, situated towards the western end of the island, is one of Anguilla's largest beaches. Quiet and pristine, its calm waters are excellent for swimming and snorkelling, while in the middle of the beach are chairs, parasols, a superb swimming pool and the *Ocean Terrassé* restaurant. At the western end of Meads Bay, **Dolphin Discovery** gives you the chance to swim, snorkel, play with and feed the seven dolphins they keep in the lagoon. Three programmes are on offer daily, each presenting unique opportunities to learn about dolphins and their environment followed by a chance to interact with the friendly creatures directly – the highlight of which is the "footpush". Places are limited, so booking in advance is recommended (prices start at US$119; ☎264/497-7946, ❀www.dolphindiscovery. com). Note that children under the age of eight and pregnant women are not permitted to enter the water. However, the nearby *Corals* restaurant has a perfect vantage point to watch the dolphins and humans being put through their paces. Meads Bay is also a great spot to watch the annual round-island boat races that take place on the first Thursday in August.

A mile west of The Valley, **Sandy Ground** is the island's main low-budget hangout area, with a number of inexpensive places to stay and eat and a friendly, relaxed atmosphere. It's also the key port of entry for privately owned yachts. Here there is an attractive, long, curved beach lined with cliffs, and the tiny village backs onto a large salt pond popular with local birdlife, such as egrets, stilts, herons and other wading birds. Offshore, visible from Sandy Ground, **Sandy Island** is a tiny deserted isle with a handful of palm trees, great for snorkelling and swimming. Boats leave from the pier between 9.30am and 4pm, whenever there is demand, for a small fee and there is a beach bar on the island that sells lunch and drinks.

Surrounded by steep cliffs, **Little Bay** is a small, secluded beach. The snorkelling here is truly exceptional, with steeper drop-offs than other parts of the island; the visibility to the dramatic depths where reef fish gather is extraordinary. To reach Little Bay does, however, represent a challenge. From nearby **Crocus Bay** it is possible to swim or catch Calvin's small boat that departs from a pier next to *Roy's Place*. For US$10, they will leave you there for as long as you require and then collect you (☎264/497-73939). An alternative, more challenging method to reach Little Bay is to climb the rope hanging from the cliff face.

On the island's northeastern coast, **Shoal Bay East** is where you'll find the most popular beach on the island, backed by coconut palms and sea grape. The immaculate white sand shelves gently down to the turquoise waters and though it is often busy, you can always find a patch of your own. Snorkelling gear, lounge chairs and towels can be rented from a number of outlets and you will also find a series of laid-back bars and cafés.

At the west end of Shoal Bay East, a dirt track leads to **The Fountain**, a cave that is the island's most important archeological site, where many Amerindian petroglyphs were found in 1979. The petroglyphs include rare depictions of deities, notably a two thousand year-old carving in a stalagmite of Jocahu, their supreme god; the site may well have been a religious or ceremonial centre and even a place of pilgrimage from other islands. It is said to be the Eastern Caribbean's most intact ceremonial site from this period. Unfortunately, the Fountain is currently closed to the public, though the National Trust has plans to develop the site into a tourist attraction.

Along the south coast

The **south coast** offers Anguilla's more upmarket hotels and, in **Rendezvous Bay**, one of the island's most spectacular and pre-eminent beaches. The two-mile crescent of bright white sand is Anguilla's true natural wonder, where you can collect conch shells of very high quality right off the beach – there's no need to shell out at a souvenir shop here. The views of Saint Martin in the sunset can be enjoyed with a cocktail from a modest number of beachside bars and bistros. Windsurfing, along with a variety of other watersports, is on offer from the hotels that dot the beach, and snorkelling is reasonable at the rocky edges near the hotels, with sea fans and tropical fish rippling under the crystal blue surface.

Further west, there is more shimmering sand at secluded **Maunday's Bay**, smaller than many others mentioned above but still large enough to offer windsurfing, water skiing and sailing. At the far west end of the island is **Shoal Bay West**, yet another beautiful beach. The public access point is hidden behind the West End Salt Pond, but is well worth seeking out. Of particular interest are the spectacular and distinctive modern **villas** here – including a vision of "castles in the sand" – designed by renowned architect Myron Goldfinger. These and others lie just off the sand areas, some of which can cost tens of thousands of dollars to stay in.

Eating, drinking and nightlife

Restaurants are one of Anguilla's key attractions, and dinner in them after a day in the sun is tremendously rewarding if you can get a reservation. There are plenty of choices throughout the island to suit most palettes, and they are also great places to spot Hollywood celebrities, though the etiquette on the island is not to disturb them.

Anguilla has a small number of **nightlife** options and musical diversions, and many resorts and hotels offer their own nightly entertainment. The alternative is a number of local hot spots that offer the opportunity to dance barefoot in the sand to Caribbean tunes. Sandy Ground is usually the liveliest on Fridays and Saturdays, while on Sundays and Wednesdays the place to be is Shoal Bay East. Check one of the **listings** magazines for specifics.

Cedar Grove at the *Rendezvous Bay Hotel* ☏264/497-6549. With a cedar tree-lined dining area, this is one of the best hotel restaurants on the island. Breakfast offers a bewildering array of choices to suit all tastes, while at lunchtime you can go for burgers or delicious but light specialities such as fish salad and marinated shrimps. Evenings see the chef serving up a more formal gourmet dinner menu that includes gumbo soup, fresh lobsters and other delicious seafood creations. The chef creates nightly four-course menus, which can be enjoyed with an impressive selection of wines and exceptional desserts. There's a very popular Caribbean barbecue with live music every Sunday from 7pm.

Gwen's Reggae Bar and Grill Shoal Bay East ☏264/497-2120. Specializing in barbecue and seafood, this is a great place to visit after snorkelling or swimming in the magnificent Shoal Bay; if it all gets too much there are shaded hammocks to lounge around in after your meal. A live band provides entertainment on Sunday afternoons from 1.30pm.

Johnno's Beach Bar and Grill Sandy Ground ☏264/497-2728. Music goes late into the night at this corrugated open-plan wooden-and-tin shack on the beach that dishes up tasty and inexpensive pumpkin soup, grouper, snapper, curried goat and burgers. With live music at the weekends, you are guaranteed a hot and sweaty night dancing away inside or if that gets too much take your Carib beer outside and enjoy the music from the beach with everyone from Hollywood celebrities to youthful locals celebrating the weekend. Closed Mon.

Koal Keel The Valley ☏264/497-2930. Originally constructed as a sugar and cotton plantation, this restaurant is a legend on the island and no visit to Anguilla is complete without dining here. The gourmet menu of Eurasian-Caribbean flavours includes an extensive variety of seafood, salads and a foie gras terrine, plus an awe-inspiring dessert menu. (If you want to get to this part of the menu without earlier courses you can do so by visiting *Le Petit Patissier* downstairs which features unrivalled selections of pastries and desserts baked fresh daily.) Away from the main dining area you will find a wine cellar packed with over 35,000 bottles that can be reserved for private parties. Closed Sun.

Pumphouse Sandy Ground ☏264/497-5154. Historic salt factory turned barefoot bar and American grill boasting over 30 varieties of rum, with soca, calypso and reggae music on offer as well. The menu includes grilled half-chickens, burgers and pizzas. If you want a quiet dinner get there before 9pm when the live music starts.

Roy's Place Crocus Bay ☏264/497-2470. English-style pub on the beach, offering good and reasonably priced sandwiches and fish and chips at lunch, a more formal menu including seafood, sirloin steaks and prime rib in the evening. Friday night happy hour between 5 and 7pm is very popular. Sunday offers a traditional English roast beef lunch along with surf-and-turf specials.

Uncle Ernie's Shoal Bay East ☏264/497-3907. This little stand on the beach is amongst the most famous on the island, serving cold drinks and ice cream, along with a variety of seafood. They have a live band on Sunday afternoons and a happy hour on Tuesdays from 6–8pm that's followed by music.

Scuba diving and snorkelling

In the late 1980s, the Anguillian authorities deliberately sank several ships around their island to develop **artificial reefs**, all of which have since been completely covered in coral. Highlights include the M.V. *Oosterdiep*, which was sunk in an upright position close to an excellent soft coral reef dive in Road Bay. Stingrays, turtles, lobsters, moray eels and yellowtail snappers are commonly sighted. The M.V. *Sarah* lies near Prickly Pear at about 24m and also sits in an upright position. Barracuda, southern stingray, yellowtail snapper, angelfish and trunkfish can be seen here; it's a particularly good spot for underwater photography. Meanwhile, artefacts such as ship's cannon and anchor can be seen in the **Stoney Ground Marine Park**, site of the Spanish galleon *El Buen Consejo*, which sank in 1772. The wreck is shallow enough to be seen by snorkellers at the surface. See p.505 for details on **diving** in Anguilla.

St Martin/St Maarten

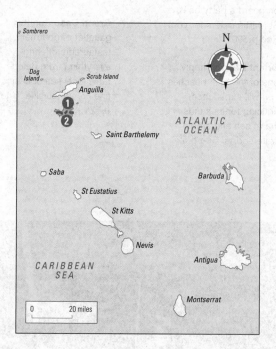

St Martin/St Maarten highlights

✳ **Day on the Water**
Whether you want to
paddle a kayak, sail an
Americas Cup-winning
vessel or spend the day
on board a party boat,
St Martin caters for you.
See p.520

✳ **Orient Beach** Simply
one of the best beaches
you will experience,
enticing for its sands,
warm sea and ample
watersports. See p.524

✳ **Pic Paradis** Escape the
crowds and hike to the
top or just into the rainforest from Loterie Farm.
See p.525

✳ **Grand Case** Run the
gauntlet of gourmet
restaurants offering
everything from delec-
table local seafood to
fine French cuisine. See
p.524

△ Woman diving from yacht, St Martin

Introduction and basics

Shared by the French and the Dutch since the mid-seventeenth century, the tiny island of **Saint Martin/Sint Maarten** is one of the most developed in this part of the Caribbean, with lots of facilities and a huge duty-free shopping area. Opinions about the island are as divided as the island itself. Ask the streams of repeat visitors, cruise ship passengers and time-share owners, and they will tell you that this tiny island is paradise on earth, with fabulous beaches and every type of tourist facility imaginable. Ask others, and you may hear how rapid and barely controlled development has turned a once-beautiful place into "a graceless monument to vulgarian greed", as one disgruntled writer put it.

The truth lies somewhere in between. The island does boast some of the finest beaches in the Eastern Caribbean, particularly at **Orient Beach** on the French side, as well as some stunning scenery, most notably in the interior around **Pic Paradis**, and many excellent restaurants and hotels on both sides of the border. On the other hand, the hunt for the tourist dollar can feel unrelenting and, at times, it is hard to discern the real country under the veneer of concrete development, souvenir shops and the waves of tourists (all particularly acute on the Dutch side in the capital Philipsburg).

If all you want to do is lie on the beach and play in the sea, both Saint Martin and Sint Maarten are not bad options. Travelling between the French and Dutch sides (as many visitors do) is hassle-free, since the **border** is marked at the end of both Bellevue and Belle Plaine by obelisks and there are no border crossing formalities. Ultimately, if the crowds get too much for you, bear in mind that it is a very short flight or ferry ride to some of the quietest, least developed and most rural islands in the entire Caribbean including: Saba, St Barths and Anguilla.

Where to go

There is plenty to see and do while visiting the island. It is suitable for all types of visitor including party-goers looking for lively nights out, families with young children to occupy or upscale visitors mooring their luxury yachts in the marinas while experiencing the fine dining available. **Philipsburg** and

Marigot are the largest towns on the Dutch and French sides respectively, and they both offer plenty of opportunities to shop and eat. There is also a slew of well-maintained **beaches** on both sides of the island, where you can engage in a variety of sporting activities such as sailing or scuba diving.

When to go

The **climate** is usually sunny and warm year-round, with some cooling from trade winds particularly between mid-December and mid-April. Average temperature during this **winter** season is 80ºF (27ºC) and a few degrees warmer but a lot more humid in the **summer**. There are rain **showers** in summer and autumn particularly in late afternoon, while June to November is **hurricane** season. **Prices** for accommodation increase between December and April but good deals can be had at other times.

Arrival

Visitors from Europe and the US pour onto the island at the **cruise ship harbour** or at **Juliana Airport**, both of which are located on the Dutch side. It is not unusual to see traffic jams of cruise liners waiting to moor on the island. On the French side, **L'Espérance Airport**, near Grand Case, handles many regional flights; you may likely land here if coming from Guadeloupe or St Barths. **Taxis** and **rental cars** are easily procured at both airports and are the most effective form of transport to your hotel; not all accommodation is served by (the often overcrowded) buses.

Cruise ship day-trippers can reach Philipsburg from the port on a ferry or by five minutes' walk. Taxi drivers will offer to take tourists to and from the port but this is a very expensive option if you are just going to Philipsburg. If you are heading to one of the other towns the cheapest bet is one of the buses. Taxis are only worthwhile if you have spent so much on duty-free items that you are unable to carry it all back to the ship or if you have difficulty walking.

Information

At Juliana Airport there is a stall near the baggage claim area with a large array of maps,

brochures, magazines and leaflets along with friendly, helpful staff to offer advice. In the town of Philipsburg, where the cruise ships arrive, there is another stand with a similar collection of **information**. There are two **tourist offices** on the island, on the Dutch side in Philipsburg on Buncamper Road (☎599/542-2337, ⚑ www.st-maarten.com) and on the French side in Marigot on Route de Sandy Ground (☎590/87 57 21, ⚑www. st-martin.org). As for local **listings**, your best bets are the *K-Pasa* weekly events guide and the Out 'N About section of Thursday's *Daily Herald*.

Money and costs

On the Dutch side, the currency is the **Netherlands Antilles Guilder** or **Florin (NAf)**,

ST MARTIN/ST MAARTEN

━ ━ ━ Border between French & Dutch sides

▲ Ferry to Anguilla

Ferry to St Barts

ATLANTIC OCEAN

Grand Case Bay
Grand Case ⒶⒷ
Ⓓ French Ⓒ
Cul-de-Sac Ⓔ Ilet Pinel
Ⓖ Bay Orientale
Orient Beach
Caye Verte
Ⓗ
Ⓘ

ST MARTIN

▲ Pic Paradis (424m)
Colombier
Baie de L'Embouchure

Terres Basses
Baie Rouge
Baie de Marigot
Long Bay
Marigot
Simpson Bay Lagoon
Sandy Ground

Ⓙ Cupecoy Beach
Ⓚ Mullet Bay
Ⓛ
Maho Bay
Simpson Bay
Dutch Cul-de-Sac

ST MAARTEN

Oyster Pond ⓂⓃ
Dawn Beach

CARIBBEAN SEA

Cole Bay
Great Salt Pond
Little Bay
Great Bay
ⓄⓅ Philipsburg

N

0   3km

ACCOMMODATION

Alamanda Resort	**I**	Orient Bay Hotel **G**
Alizea	**F**	Oyster Bay Beach Resort **M**
Captain Oliver's	**N**	Pasanggrahan Royal
Grand Case Beach Club	**A**	Guest House **P**
Hevea	**B**	St Tropez Caribe **H**
Holland House Beach Hotel	**O**	Summit Resort **I**
L'Esplanade Caraibes	**C**	Sunrise Hotel **E**
Le Petit Hotel	**D**	Wyndam Sapphire
Maho Beach Resort & Casino	**L**	Beach Club & Resort **K**

though prices are nearly always quoted in US dollars. The rate of exchange is fixed at US$1 to NAf1.78. Notes come in denominations of 500, 250, 100, 50, 25, 10 and 5. Coins are in denominations of 5 and 1, and 50, 25, 10, 5 and 1 cents.

On the French side, the **euro** is the local currency; some, but certainly not all, establishments will quote or accept US dollars in addition to euros. Euro notes are issued in denominations of 5, 10, 20, 50, 100, 200 and 500 euros, and coins in denominations of 1, 2, 5, 10, 20 and 50 cents and 1 and 2 euros.

Exchange of most major currencies can be done at banks and at a multitude of bureaux de change – though be aware that rates vary from place to place. **Banking hours** are Mon–Fri 8.30–11.30am and 1.30–4.30pm. Some banks are also open on Saturday. The best way of getting the right money is to use one of the many **ATMs** found throughout the island. Some ATMs will offer the choice of currency to withdraw: RBTT at the end of Front Street in Philipsburg offers both NAf and US$ while BFC branches on the French side offer euros and US$.

Credit and **debit** cards are accepted almost everywhere. **Travellers' cheques** are accepted too but visitors are advised to bring them in US$ denominations to avoid additional currency conversion fees.

A **departure tax** of US$30 in cash or travellers' cheques is required when leaving via Juliana Airport except for children under 2 years of age and Air France and American Airlines passengers, for whom it is included in the ticket price. If you are heading on to another of the Netherlands Antilles (such as Saba) then the tax is only US$10. Any taxes payable are usually included in the ticket price when departing by plane from L'Espérance Airport. The tax is US$2 by ferry to Anguilla from Marigot's pier.

Hotels add a ten percent tax to bills. The majority of hotels and restaurants add a **service charge** of between ten and fifteen percent; as such, tipping in these establishments is discretionary. Elsewhere **tipping** of ten to fifteen percent is the norm.

The **cost** of staying on the island can vary depending on a number of factors. Tax-free shopping means that bargains on jewellery,

alcohol and tobacco in particular are available. Prices in modest **hotels** during the off-season can start for as little as US$50 per night while in the peak season prices can almost double. There are accommodation options at all points of the price scale and if you choose to go all-inclusive, providing you have all your meals at the hotel, then good value can be had.

Meal costs outside your hotel vary depending on the establishment. A burger, fries and soda from a fast food chain might cost less than US$5 but head up to Grand Case for fine dining and expect to pay upwards of ten times that before you even add wine costs.

Getting around

While paved roads link the major tourist areas, bear in mind that in some areas they can become steep and narrow and sign-posting is limited. The major problem, however, is the sheer volume of **traffic**. Even in off-peak hours traffic can slow to a crawl or even standstill, so if you are holidaying to get away from the daily commute forget it.

The local **bus service** is efficient and cheap. Buses run frequently from 7am to around 10 or 11pm between Philipsburg, Mullet Bay, Simpson Bay, Marigot and usually continue up to Grand Case. The fare is between US$1 and US$2 and drivers will accept dollars or euros (though not always florins if you're on the French side). **Minibuses** run all over the island, charging between US$1.50 and US$3 depending on the distance; the destination is indicated by a placard in the windscreen. Both buses and minibuses can be taken from **bus stops** in Philipsburg and Marigot; elsewhere, you can flag them down as they pass.

If you want to explore the island (and you should certainly do some touring) consider **hiring a car** for a few days. There are nearly one hundred car rental outlets, so competition keeps prices reasonable. In addition to the agencies many hotels also offer rentals, though these tend to be the most expensive option. At the airport just past the arrivals area there are a number of agencies and the rates offered here are pretty competitive (starting from around US$30 per day), especially if you make it clear you are going to shop around. Two good agencies to start with are Avis (St Martin ☎590/87 50 60, St Maarten ☎599/545-2319) and Paradise Car Rental (St Maarten ☎599/545-3737). Driving on the island is on the right-hand side of the road.

Scooters are a good way of getting around and can be rented from many agencies, most of which will deliver to your hotel. Try Defis (☎590/50 41 70, ⊛www.defisagency.com) or GoScoot (☎599/545-4533).

Finally, **taxis** are easy to come by in Philipsburg and Marigot, less so elsewhere. Rates are fixed both from the airport and from the ferry dock in Marigot, while the tourist information booths have available a list of acceptable rates. There are no meters and all charges are set by the government so check the price before you hop in. The rates can quickly mount up elsewhere and can soon make hiring a car more economical. There is a minimum charge and rates do rise after 10pm and then again after midnight. Guided **taxi tours** are available and last two to three hours and are worthwhile if you are a day-tripper. Costs depend on the itinerary you choose and should be agreed upon before you start. In Marigot call ☎590/87 56 54, in Grand Case ☎590/87 75 79 and in Philipsburg ☎599/542-2359.

Accommodation

Most visitors to the **French side** of the island stay either in the Orient Bay area on the northeast coast or in Grand Case on the west coast. On the whole, accommodation in Grand Case is on a smaller scale, while Orient Bay has more of a range, from small boutique places to 400-room resorts. During the low season, **rates** can fall by as much as forty percent (though this is rare at the smaller places).

In contrast to the French side, resorts on the **Dutch side** tend to be large and can feel somewhat impersonal. As you are probably here for the beach, there is no real reason to stay in Philipsburg; you will find a variety of beachfront places scattered along the south coast. Cupecoy in particular is undergoing some regeneration.

Food and drink

The island has always boasted a wide **ethnic mix** within its population – not surprising given its Dutch/French colonial history, slave importation from Africa and immigration from US, Europe, south Asia and the Indian subcontinent – and over the past decade the island has transformed itself into a cosmopolitan melting pot. All of this is reflected in the **dining** choices, with over 350 restaurants providing stimulating local fusion foods, creole creations and exotic Asian dishes, along with more traditional gourmet French and Italian cuisine. **Grand Case** has long been the gastronomic capital of the Eastern Caribbean, with over two dozen gourmet restaurants lining the town's narrow main strip, though **Marigot**'s Marina Port La Royale has rapidly developed casual fine dining restaurants as well.

Seafood is, of course, a speciality, while **vegetarians** are well catered for with most restaurants offering a variety of choices. The local **drinks** to sample include guavaberry liqueur and flavoured home-made rums such as passionfruit, ginger or raspberry. In comparison to other Caribbean islands **prices** often are good value because of the sheer competition any restaurant here faces. Costs escalate quickly at the more upmarket venues but even these are cheap compared to equivalent restaurants in the US or Western Europe. Keep in mind that reservations are required for most upmarket restaurants.

As for **drinks**, most bars and restaurants serve imported beers, spirits and wines, but because of the low duty levied, drinking will not burn a hole in your wallet unless you go for one of the vintage wines on offer.

Phones, post and the Internet

Telephone kiosks can be found all over the island. Most take prepaid phone cards or credit cards, the former of which are much cheaper to use and can be purchased from a variety of outlets, such as post offices and hotels.

To **place a call** within the French or Dutch side of the island (but not from one side to the other), simply dial the subscriber number *sans* area code. Calling one side of the island from the other is treated as an international call (and charged as such) – so when calling from the Dutch side to the French, dial ☏00 599 54 before the number for land lines, or ☏00 599 55 before the number for mobile phones. Reversing the situation, to call the French side from the Dutch, dial ☏00 590 590 before the number for land lines, or ☏00 590 690 before the number for mobile phones.

As for **mobile phones**, on the Dutch side coverage for TDMA handsets is available, while on the French side several GSM network operators exist. Handsets can be rented from BT Electronics in Marigot (☏590/87 81 98) and a number of Cellular One stores dotted around the island including in Philipsburg (☏599/543-0222).

The Main **Post Office** on the Dutch side is in Philipsburg (Mon–Thu 7.30am–5pm, Fri 7.30am–4.30pm; ☏ 599/542-2298), while on the French side the Post Office is in Marigot (Mon–Fri 7.30am–4.45pm, Sat 7.30–11.30am; ☏590/87 53 14).

Internet access is available for a fee at some hotels, and at kiosks across the island. The kiosks can use prepaid cards (acquired at many stores and hotels) or credit cards; costs are high with both, but higher with the latter. There are a number of Internet cafés in each of the major tourist areas. The public library in Philipsburg has a number of personal computers with the cheapest access at US$4 for the first half-hour and US$2 thereafter.

Opening hours, holidays and festivals

Typical **business hours** on the island are Mon–Fri 9am–5pm. Restaurants, bars and retailers are open much longer, however, and throughout the weekend as well. Plenty of nightclubs, meanwhile, open their doors in the early evening and stay busy until dawn.

10

Public holidays and festivals

Both sides of the island have their own **carnivals** each year. On the French side the celebration takes place during Lent, while on the Dutch side seventeen days and nights in April are set aside for the event, with the main parade scheduled to coincide with the birthday of Her Majesty the Queen of the Netherlands, Beatrix, on the 30th of the month. Below is a list of other holidays on the island.

April 30 Queen's Day (Sint Maarten)
May 25 Ascension Day (Saint Martin)
July 14 Bastille Day (Saint Martin)
July 21 Schoelcher Day (Saint Martin)
November 1 All Saints Day (Saint Martin)
November 11 Feast of Saint Martin and Sint Maarten Day
October 21 Antillean Day (Sint Maarten)

Watersports and outdoor activities

The island has an amazing array of **sporting** and **outdoor activities** to indulge in. As you might expect, watersports such as **sailing** and **scuba diving** feature heavily, though there are also plenty of areas to **hike** or to ride a **mountain bike**.

Watersports

Watersports are excellent across the island. Orient Beach in the northeast is the watersports centre of the island, with a host of outlets along the bay renting jet skis, windsurfers and snorkelling gear as well as parasailing and boat trips out to nearby Green Cay and Ilet Pinel. On the Dutch side of the island, Simpson Bay also has plenty of operators hiring out similar equipment.

Diving on the island is good, though not in the top league. The majority of the 55 dive sites are primarily south in the Caribbean although there are a few northern locations in the Atlantic. There are nine PADI-recognized

Dive sites on the island

There are PADI-certified **dive operators** running out of both sides of the island that will collect you from your hotel and take you down to a harbour for a short boat trip to reach most dive spots – particularly useful if your hotel is not near one of the major ports. What follows is a brief list of some of the island's best dive sites.

The top dive spot is the **Proselyte Reef** where British Navy Ship HMS *Proselyte* sank in 60ft of water in 1801. The reef surrounding the frigate rises to with 15ft of the surface, and there are plenty of fish and corals to see and on occasion turtles and rays.

When **Simpson Bay Bridge** was replaced in the late 1980s the remains of the old bridge were submerged and now serve as an artificial reef. Schools of reef fish now congregate and there are a number of other wrecks nearby including an aircraft. The Bridge site is 50ft at its deepest.

Another interesting spot is **Split Rock**, a large boulder that you can swim through. Nearby you'll find **Cable Reef**, where large fish such as pompanos can often be seen. These two sites are both at 55ft.

operators on the island; some of these are tied to cruise ships and are more expensive than the independent ones. A good independent choice is Scuba Fun, which will collect you from your hotel for their full range of dives and courses (☎590/87 36 13, ⊛www .scubafun.com); O2 Limits is another good option (☎ 590/50 04 00, ⊛ www.o2limits. com). For something a bit different, Dive Safaris (☎599/542-9001, ⊛www.divestmaarten. com) runs a **shark awareness dive** a couple times a week where you will see reef and milk sharks having lunch and provide you with a great underwater photo opportunity.

Harking back to the era of Amerindians who used similar vessels to arrive and colonize, **sea kayaking** has become an increasingly popular way to explore the island's waters. Guided trips around the Simpson Bay Lagoon with Trisport (☎599/545-4384, ⊛www.trisportsxm.com) will introduce you to the beaches, historical sites and the mangrove eco-system.

Sailing and excursions

Sailing is particularly popular with visitors and residents with a dozen or so marinas dotted around the island with some of the worlds largest and most beautiful yachts moored in them. Many of these marinas offer the chance to rent and charter vessels. Trips that are feasible from the island vary from voyages to Venezuela to cruising neighbouring islands or just having a day taking in the Simpson Bay Lagoon. You can sail yourself or look to hire a professional skipper to do the work for you. Contact Any Way Marine (☎590/87 91 41, ⊛www.anywaymarine.com) or Aqua World (☎ 599/545-4533, ⊛ www .stmaartenaquaworld.com).

One particularly interesting way of getting yourself onto the water is an **excursion** with the tall ship *Lord Sheffield*, which sails everyday at 11am and anchors at a beach for swimming and snorkelling (☎599/553-4804, ⓔ bookings@lordsheffield.com). The huge catamaran *Golden Eagle* (☎599/530-0068, ⊛www.sailingsxm.com) takes daily trips from Philipsburg to St Barths and various offshore islands, offering hors d'oeuvres and an open bar, and stops for snorkelling and shelling en route. If you'd rather not get your feet wet, Seaworld Explorer (☎599/542-4078, ⊛www. atlantisadventures.com) runs trips on their 34-passenger **semi-submarine** that has an underwater observatory, giving non-divers a chance to see below the waves.

Other activities

Mountain biking tracks are available for all levels of rider. For novices the Cay Bay and Mullet Bay coasts are particularly friendly, while more experienced riders can try out more demanding routes such as the Bellevue Loop, between Port de Plaisance to Marigot or Pic Paradis. Contact Trisport (see above) or Frog's Legs (☎590/87 05 11) to rent a bike.

Apart from the Pic Paradis there are over 25 miles of **hiking** trails through hills, valleys, clifftops and beaches. Hikes are rated from easy to strenuous and vary in length from 90 minutes to four hours; the two-mile Guana Bay hike is especially spectacular. Even though few of the trails take very long and are not particularly isolated you should take plenty of water and protection from the sun. The Sint Maarten National Heritage Foundation (℡599/542-4917) has plenty of information and maps.

Lastly, **horse-** and **pony-riding** on the beach is a splendid experience. There are several stables willing to offer adults and children the opportunity to ride, whether novice or expert, such as Bayside Riding Club (℡590/87 36 64) and Lucky Stables (℡599/544-5255).

History

Amerindian remains dating from as early as 2000 BC have been found near the village of Grand Case on the French side of the island. The vestiges indicate that these people settled in villages, cultivating crops and building boats. Because of the preponderance of salt ponds on the island the Amerindians called it Soualiga, meaning "Land of Salt". While modern knowledge of the island began when **Columbus** sailed past on November 11, 1493, naming the island after Saint Martin of Tours, whose holy day it was, few navigators took much interest for the next century.

During the 1620s **French** and **Dutch colonists** began to settle, with the Dutch building the first fort at Philipsburg in 1631. The **Spanish**, however, were keen on the island for strategic reasons and claimed it, subsequently fighting off a lengthy siege by Dutch troops led by **Peter Stuyvesant**, later to become governor of the Dutch colony of Nieuw Amsterdam (today's New York City) who lost his leg and became known as "Peg-Leg".

By 1648, the Spanish had lost interest in the island, and the French and Dutch governments agreed to divide it in two, populating it with settlers from home. The land was given over to the production of **sugar**, **cotton**, **tobacco** and **salt**, with **slaves** imported from Africa to work on the plantations. However, the soil was poor and the island never prospered, largely sinking into obscurity as the centuries passed.

Despite frequent **disagreements** between the French and the Dutch, including border skirmishes and wholesale invasions and deportations, the boundaries remain pretty much the same today as were agreed on in 1648. The Dutch side, known as Sint Maarten, is part of the **Netherlands Antilles**; the French side is part of France, with representation in the French parliament.

As throughout the region, **tourism** drives the modern economy, bringing floods of visitors and attendant social difficulties, particularly rising crime.

10.1

Saint Martin

French **SAINT MARTIN**, spread over 52 square kilometres, is less commercialized than the Dutch side, despite having some of the finest beaches and restaurants and the most attractive scenery. The pleasant capital, **Marigot**, is worth at least a day of your time, while the delightful long stretch of white sand at **Orient Beach** is the pick of the beaches, with a great choice of watersports to keep you busy. The island's gourmet heart, **Grand Case** boasts a string of excellent restaurants, while **Loterie Farm** offers great hiking away from the crowds into an unspoiled area of rainforest and up to **Pic Paradis**, the island's highest point.

Accommodation

Marigot

Hotel Beach Plaza Baie de Marigot ☎590/87 87 00, ⊛www.hotelbeachplazasxm.com. A pleasant beachfront hotel situated within walking distance of downtown Marigot. The 144 rooms all have private balconies, a/c and TV. Connecting rooms for family stays and handicapped rooms are also available. ❾

Orient Bay and Cul-de-Sac

Alamanda Resort Orient Bay ☎590/52 87 40, ⊛www.alamanda-resort.com. Opened in 2003, this 42-room resort offers views of the beach and ocean, with easy access to some shops and lots of beach activities. The rooms are furnished in a mixture of Caribbean colours and colonial furnishings. ❾

Alizea Cul-de-Sac ☎590/87 33 42, ⊛www. alizeahotel.com. Fabulously landscaped and overlooking gorgeous Orient Bay, this hotel is one of the best options on this side of the island. All rooms have kitchens and are tastefully decorated and furnished, while the restaurant is good and the relative isolation means that it is very peaceful at night. ❼

Orient Bay Hotel Orient Bay ☎590/87 31 10, ⊛www.orientbayhotel.com. A series of cosy pastel-coloured villas arranged around two swimming pools, each with a kitchen, living room and TV. ❽

St Tropez Caribe Orient Bay ☎590/87 42 01. Large but reasonably attractive development, just a short walk from the beach and with all rooms enjoying their own terrace or balcony. ❽

Grand Case

L'Esplanade Caraibes ☎590/87 06 55, ⊛www. lesplanade.com. Welcoming, very relaxed place on the hillside overlooking Grand Case, decorated with curved stone staircases and colourful tiles, and with a quiet pool. All rooms are very comfortable; the standard ones are large and the duplexes are vast. ❾

Grand Case Beach Club ☎590/87 51 87, ⊛www.grandcasebeachclub.com. Seventy-five well-equipped and colourfully decorated condos, all with kitchens and a/c, on the beach in Grand Case. Popular with families, the place also has tennis courts and a restaurant. ❽

Hevea ☎590/87 56 85. Small guesthouse with six cute colonial-style rooms with beamed ceilings, wooden beds and air conditioning. Guests are entitled to discounted food at the hotel's restaurant. ❽

Le Petit Hotel ☎590/29 09 65, ⊛www. lepetithotel.com. Small Mediterranean-style hotel on the beach, with nine studios and a single one-bedroom suite. Each room has a fully equipped kitchen and dining area, tiled floors, rattan furniture, cable TV, plus a/c and ceiling fans. There's no pool, but you can swim at sister hotel L'Esplanade, a short walk away. ❾

Oyster Pond

Captain Oliver's ☎590/87 40 26, ⊛www. captainolivers.com. Attractive resort overlooking the lovely sheltered anchorage of Oyster Pond, half in French and half in Dutch territory. There's a big pool, the fifty large rooms (ask for one with a sea view) are comfortably furnished and air-conditioned, and the restaurant features a miniature zoo so you can watch turtles and nurse sharks swimming under the glass floor while you eat. Delightful Dawn Beach is a short drive away. ❻

Marigot

Sporting a fusion of chic French and tropical Caribbean styles, **MARIGOT** is the main town on Saint Martin, and, although it can be cluttered with traffic, it is pleasant enough, especially if you want to shop, eat or just people-watch. The town has spread along Marigot Bay, with a selection of interesting restaurants and duty-free stores and a sparkling new marina at its western end.

The main focus is the **harbour** at the bottom of Rue de la République, the booking and departure points for ferries to Anguilla and other islands; you'll normally see the ferries lined up alongside a fleet of fishing boats. Just west of here, beyond the taxi rank, lie a group of bars and "lolos", or food shacks, where you can get excellent and inexpensive island fare. Continuing west brings you to the island's largest **public market**, featuring plenty of souvenir stands selling T-shirts, wooden carvings and the like, as well as a host of spice, flowers, fruit and vegetable vendors offering their colourful produce. It's a lively place, and there are a few great bargains for shoppers. The most stalls appear on Wednesday or Saturday but the vendors appear Tues–Sat 6am–3pm.

Moving west from the harbour the waterfront road is not particularly interesting but if you follow the side streets away from the water onto roads such as **Rue du Général Charles de Gaulle** you will stumble across a plethora of stylish, interesting boutiques – such as Hermes, Cartier and Mont Blanc – and plenty of restaurants, along with the grand-looking City Hall. Further west still, the impressive development of the **Marina Port La Royale** houses a number of classy shops selling designer clothes and jewellery, outlets offering boat and fishing trips and loads of bars and restaurants overlooking the water.

Beyond the marina, the main **tourist office** has plenty of information and brochures. You should certainly make a point of stopping at the nearby **archeological museum** (Mon–Sat 9am–1pm & 3–7pm) for its detailed and highly informative exhibits on the Amerindians who lived on the island in the pre-Columbian era as well as more recent history. Evocative black-and-white photographs of quiet streets populated with a handful of children and donkeys and of labourers toiling in the salt industry provide a window into what the island was like before tourism took hold. A welcome antidote to the hustle and bustle elsewhere, the museum affords a glimpse of the untouristed past of Saint Martin.

On the other side of the ferry points you will find **Le West Indies Shopping Mall**, which is the biggest on the island with 22 air-conditioned designer stores, in addition to a spa, beauty salon and a restaurant. Finally, a fifteen-minute climb from the harbour will lead you to **Fort Louis** (always open; free), the remains of a 1789 fort built to protect the town from the raids of British sailors; it offers fine views across the bay.

Sandy Ground and Baie Rouge

Less than a kilometre west of Marigot, the main road curves around to the long spit of land known as **Sandy Ground** that separates the huge Simpson Bay Lagoon from the sea at Nettle Bay. The isthmus is lined with hotels, restaurants (including the very popular *Mario's Bistro*, see p.525) and small shopping malls – though if you're not staying here, the area holds little to detain you. The beaches are not particularly impressive and you are better off heading a couple of kilometres further west to the lovely and normally quiet white sandy stretch at **Baie Rouge**. Here you'll find a handful of traders selling food and drink on the beach and you can rent snorkelling gear from local vendors.

If you are looking for even more privacy on the beach, continue past Baie Rouge and take the right-hand turn-off signposted for **Baie aux Prunes**, which is popular among surfers, or make your way round the headland to **Baie Longue**, where you'll find a vast expanse of white sand, perfect for strolling and shell collecting, though there are a few enclosure walls.

Grand Case

Grand Case has built itself a deserved reputation as one of the finest **dining centres** of the Eastern Caribbean and, as you walk down the main drag that makes up a large part of this tiny town, it's easy to see why. A series of fairly expensive restaurants lines the otherwise unremarkable street, with daily specials chalked up outside and classy wine lists displayed in the windows (see "Eating, drinking and nightlife" p.527 for reviews).

It's far from obvious why the great restaurateurs decided to set up shop in Grand Case since – food aside – there's nothing spectacular about the town. There are a handful of very good places to stay but there's little else specific to bring you here. The sandy **beach** that lines the wide, sweeping bay is nice but modest compared to others on the coast.

Anse Marcel, Cul-de-Sac and Ilet Pinel

Heading east of Grand Case for 1.5km, past the Salinas and the local airport, the road forks, heading south towards fabulous Orient Bay or north for the tiny settlements of Anse Marcel and Cul-de-Sac, from where you can hop on a boat to Ilet Pinel just offshore. **Anse Marcel** is a mini-resort, with a few large hotels, a marina and a pleasant long sandy beach. **Cul-de-Sac** – home to Saint Martin's mayor and characterized by its cute little red-roofed houses – is even smaller, but popular largely as the departure point for trips to the pristine and uninhabited **Ilet Pinel**, where there is excellent snorkelling (rent gear from the shack) and lovely, calm waters for swimming. Boats regularly make the two-minute trip (no set schedule) from the pier in Cul-de-Sac and there are barbecue stalls and drink vendors on the island, and even a small gift shop.

Orient Beach

The area around **Orient Beach**, at the northeastern end of the island, is one of massive commercial development, with hotels, villas and condominiums springing up along a two-kilometre strip. The beach itself, too, is an incredible hive of activity, with restaurants, bars, watersports outlets and most of all hordes of people spread out along its length. Don't be put off by the crowds, though, because this is one of the great beaches in the Eastern Caribbean, a fabulous swathe of white sand bordering an inviting turquoise sea.

Whether you want to rent a jet ski or a windsurfer, take a snorkelling trip or visit an offshore cay, or even if you just want to splash or wander in the shallows, this is a great place to do it. The southern end of the beach, protected from the surf by nearby Green Cay, is the best area for watersports and where the main crowds congregate; beach chairs and umbrellas can be rented here. Note that the very southern end is largely given over to the "clothing optional" crowd.

Butterfly Farm

No prizes for guessing what's on display at the **Butterfly Farm** (US$12; ☎590/87 31 21, ⊛www.thebutterflyfarm.com) just south of Orient Bay, with numerous varieties imported from Indonesia and South America taking it easy on a cabbage leaf or fluttering around under a giant net. It's colourful as well as informative, and a reasonable distraction when you've had enough of the beach. **Tours** led by knowledgeable guides are offered daily from 9am, with the last one beginning at 3pm. Butterflies are most active in the morning and you can witness the new ones emerging from a chrysalis. A pass is given to visitors so that they can return as often as they like during their stay. There is also a small gift shop and café on site.

Oyster Pond

Divided in half by the border, **Oyster Pond** on the coast southeast of Orient Bay is an oyster-shaped and almost completely landlocked anchorage popular with yachters. The marina and most of the hotel/condominium development is on the French side of the border, though the best beach in the area is **Dawn Beach** on the Dutch side – the name says it all for early-risers or those who have not yet got to bed, as this is a great place to watch the sun come up. There is good snorkelling off-shore and, when the waves are rolling in, it's a good place for body surfing (though a little rough for small children). There are great views across to St Barths and, when you need sustenance, there are a couple of good restaurants too.

Loterie Farm and Pic Paradis

While most of the tourist development in Saint Martin is along the coast, **the interior** remains charmingly unspoiled, its peaceful countryside making for an appealing day-trip if you have a car. Just north of Marigot, you can turn right onto a road signposted to **Colombier**, where a scattered settlement of old wooden houses, small farms and picturesque meadows strewn with munching cattle gives a picture of island life that has changed little over the last fifty years.

A little further north still lies **LOTERIE FARM**, a nature-lover's delight and one of the highlights of a visit to Saint Martin. The farm, once a sugar estate, is now a 150-acre working farm where the owners have carved eco-trails that you are free to wander in (US$5; call ahead to book on ☎590/87 86 16). The trails head into the "hidden forest", where you'll find giant silk cotton trees as well as groves of mango and palm fed by quiet streams.

Those with the energy can make their way up to **PIC PARADIS**, at 390 metres the island's highest point and a three-hour trek there and back. Take good footwear, as the trails can be rocky. To get there, follow the main road from Marigot signposted to Pic Paradis. Five hundred metres up a steep hill, a right turn is signposted to the farm, taking you through fields of papayas, melons, bananas and vegetables. If you continue up the hill instead, it's another 2km to the **peak**, past some of the island's most expensive homes, many set back from the road with flamboyant vegetation to guard them from prying eyes. Unless you've got a four-wheel-drive vehicle, you'll need to park at the top and walk for a further ten minutes to get fantastic views out over the island.

Eating, drinking and nightlife

Dining on Saint Martin ranges from fast-food joints to lavish fine dining at some of the Caribbean's best spots. As you might expect there is plenty of French-accented cuisine on offer but there are also lots of other gastronomic styles represented. In addition to the abundance of hotel restaurants and bars there is plenty of choice of venues in the towns and villages surrounding them.

Although **nightlife** on the French side is a little lower-key than the Dutch side there is still plenty on offer. Many hotels lay on their own entertainment during the evenings, while the listings magazines are worth consulting for details of events taking place outside the hotels. In Grand Case, outside of the restaurants, there's little in the way of nightlife except on Tuesday evenings (6–11pm) between January and May when the **Harmony Nights festival** season begins and the main street is given over to pedestrians to enjoy Caribbean bands and dancers.

Marigot and Sandy Ground

Le Bar de la Mer Marigot ☎590/87 81 79. Grilled fish, lobster, sandwiches, pizza and salads make up the main part of the menu in this easy-going and reasonably priced place near the harbour.

La Belle Epoque Marigot ☎590/87 87 70. This pleasant French bistro in Marina Port la Royale could have been lifted from the South of France, offering a wide selection of dishes including exotic crab-based salads and smoked duck breast. There is a wide choice of toppings for the delicious thin-crust pizzas, and a lobster menu too.

Mario's Bistro Sandy Ground ☎590/87 06 36. A favourite with locals and visitors, the waterside location at *Mario's* makes it one of the most romantic places for dinner, and booking is essential. Seafood is the speciality, with delicious starters of scallops and mussels, while well-

△ Cannon, St Martin

prepared main courses include pan-fried snapper, succulent roast duck and a selection of steaks. Dinner only.

La Sucrière Marigot ☎590/40 60 17. Small but elegant French bakery, a pleasant spot to pick up breakfast and enjoy on the premises or while you are on a boat trip from the nearby harbour.

Orient Bay

Kontiki ☎87 43 27. Good if pricey place on the beach, with fresh and tasty grilled fish and chips, wholesome salads, pasta dishes and specials like iced mango and honey soup. The evening starts off with some live music before turning into a dance party complete with a giant bubble machine.

Pedros ☎57 78 25. One of the better cafés on this very popular beach, with friendly waiters dishing up tasty barbecued chicken and fish dishes served with peas and rice. The place is often crowded with those taking a break from the sun with a cold beer.

Grand Case

Lolos A great range of shacks and barbecue pits around an open courtyard, where you can sample cheap local cooking including tasty fish, curried goat, barbecued chicken, spare ribs and the occasional lobster, together with side dishes such as potato salad, peas and rice, macaroni cheese and coleslaw. There's also a location in Marigot.

Spiga ☎590/52 47 83. As consummate a restaurant as you will find on the island, *Spiga*'s Italian roots show through in the black tiger shrimp with spinach gnocchi, the house speciality, while the veal chop and the beef tenderloin with cabernet sauce both have devoted fans. There is an extensive wine list to accompany your meal. Dinner only.

Le Tastevin ☎590/87 55 45. Elegant French-owned place overlooking the water and offering a fine selection of French food, from foie gras and snails to fresh local seafood and steaks, all prepared with skill and imagination. This is one of the best places to eat in town, with prices to match.

10.2

Sint Maarten

Other than the language and some of the names, there is little you could describe as characteristically Dutch about **SINT MAARTEN**. This side of the island, measuring a mere 37 square kilometres, has seen a huge tourist boom since the 1960s, both in overnight and cruise ship visitors, making it one of the most heavily commercialized areas in the region. On the whole, Sint Maarten seems to be geared towards servicing its international visitors and it can be hard to discern much of an individual identity.

The heavily developed town of **Philipsburg** is the main draw for shoppers and cruise ship passengers and has good restaurants, sandwiched in between casinos, T-shirt and duty-free shops and fast-food joints. Situated right on Great Bay, the town has its own large beach.

Relatively few visitors stay in Philipsburg however, and much of the recent development has been along the western end of the island, south of the giant **Simpson Bay Lagoon**, where a series of attractive bays indent the coast. Particularly alluring are **Cupecoy Beach** and **Mullet Beach** in the southwest. Despite the fact that this side of the island can feel crowded, there's plenty of fun to be had on the good-quality beaches and at the multitude of lively bars and restaurants.

Accommodation

Holland House Beach Hotel Philipsburg ☎599/542-2572, ✺www.hhbh.com. Situated in the middle of Philipsburg's shopping area, peace and tranquillity are not likely to be found here; however, the beach is on your doorstep. Most rooms have a kitchenette and refrigerator. ⑥

Maho Beach Resort and Casino Maho Bay ☎599/545-2115, ✺www.mahobeach.com. The *Maho Beach* is a huge resort with six hundred rooms, nine restaurants, its own disco and casino, and excellent facilities. Despite the numbers, the beach is big enough that you can normally find a quiet spot of your own. ❹

Oyster Bay Beach Resort Oyster Pond ☎599/543-6040, ✺www.oysterbaybeachresort. com. Large resort spread over eight acres on the east coast of the island, a short distance from superb Dawn Beach. Rooms are spacious and pleasant and there's a large pool. Rates are high, but you can find good package deals. Service is mixed and restaurant bills cannot be added to your room. ❽

Passangrahan Philipsburg ☎599/542-3588, ✺www.pasanhotel.com. Colonial in feel and once

a guesthouse for royal visitors, *Passangrahan* overlooks the sea on the south side of Front Street and makes a good base for exploring if you want to stay in town. Its former grandeur has faded but it's comfortable enough and there's a welcoming bar and a good restaurant. ⑥

Summit Resort Simpson's Bay Lagoon ☎599/545-2150, ✺www.thesummitresort.com. Popular spot on a bluff overlooking the lagoon, with forty cottages offering appealing accommodation in studios and duplexes. The hotel has a restaurant, bar and tennis courts and offers free shuttle service to Mullet and Cupecoy beaches. ⑥

Wyndham Sapphire Beach Club & Resort Cupecoy ☎599/545-2179, ✺www.sbcwi.com. Situated on the beach at Cupecoy, this luxury resort has terrific views of the ocean. Amenities include several bars and restaurants, a couple of freshwater pools, spa and hair salon, a business centre and a video rental service. All suites have a kitchen with dishwasher, refrigerator, ice machine and cooking utensils. The bathrooms are luxurious with Italian marble tubs. Suites have oceanfront or lagoon terraces/balconies. ❾

Philipsburg and around

Packed with cruise ship visitors during the day, lively **PHILIPSBURG** – the main town of Sint Maarten – makes it an entertaining place to spend a couple of hours, even if shopping is not high on your holiday agenda. Founded in 1733 on a sand bar that separated the sea from a series of inland salt ponds, the small town was named after Scotsman John Philips, one of the island's early pioneers. All four of its main roads run east–west along the thin strip of land that still divides Great Bay from the Great Salt Pond, with busy **Voorstraat** and **Acherstraat** (often called Front Street and Back Street, respectively) facing south onto the blue expanse of the ocean and bursting with duty-free shops.

Although the town is unabashedly in search of the tourist dollar and most of the development is fairly modern, there are a handful of attractive eighteenth- and nineteenth-century buildings dotted along the heaving main drag of **Front Street** and in the grid of quieter streets behind it. There are some good places hereabouts to put your feet up and get a tasty bite to eat. In the evening, when the crowds have gone, the place takes on a different, slightly seedy feel, and can even seem a bit threatening if you move away from the main well-lit areas on Front Street or around Bobby's Marina in the east.

There are a huge variety of **shops** on the recently redeveloped Front Street selling everything from alcohol and cigars, jewellery both look-alike and genuine, cosmetics, perfume, clothes, souvenirs, electronics and food of all varieties. There are also many **bars** and eateries, including a few elegant **restaurants**. The pedestrian area of Front Street is the heart of the main shopping area while Back Street is the focus of cheaper unbranded goods. Away from Front Street there are a number of larger stores selling provisions and alcohol at discount in bulk quantities. Many stores will deliver products back to the cruise ships or your hotel if you cannot carry it all.

Towards the eastern end of Front Street, **Wathey Square** is effectively the town centre and the main focus for visitors, housing the **tourist information kiosk**, a couple of banks and a handful of bars and restaurants. The square is less than a minute's walk from the long, semicircular Great Bay Beach, not one of the most impressive on the island but normally strewn with swimmers and sun-seekers, especially when cruise ships are in town.

On the north side of the square, check out the graceful architecture of the grand old **courthouse**, built in 1793 and serving in its time as a fire station and a jail; today's it's the post office. Just 200m west of the square, the cute little wooden **Methodist church** was built in 1851 and makes for a welcome sanctuary from the hustle and bustle outside.

At the eastern end of Front Street are the more attractive of Philipsburg's historic buildings, a group of elegant **colonial houses** distinctive for their downstairs store or warehouse with steps leading up from the street to a verandah for the living quarters above. Almost at the end of Front Street, the small **Sint Maarten Museum** (Mon–Fri 10am–4pm, Sat 10am–1pm) merits a look for its exhibits on island history from Amerindian times and articles salvaged from local shipwrecks. Just around the corner from here, heading south around the edge of the bay, there's always plenty of boating activity at Great Marina and Bobby's Marina, as well as a couple of good places to eat.

Inland from Front Street you will find a labyrinth of small streets and alleys leading back towards the huge **Great Salt Pond**, where salt-rakers once scraped a living collecting the "white gold". There's nothing particular to head for, with the pond now devoid of activity since the demise of the salt industry after World War II, but amidst the modern concrete buildings are pretty gingerbread cottages and courtyards draped with bougainvillea and hibiscus and, of course, plenty more shopping and dining opportunities.

Sint Maarten Park Zoological and Botanical Gardens

The largest zoo in the Caribbean, **Sint Maarten Park** (US$10, children US$5; daily: winter 9am–5pm, summer 9.30am–6pm; ☎599/543-2030), a few minutes from Philipsburg on Acre Road, features 250 animals and around 80 unique species on display, including several endangered ones, such as golden lion tamarins. It will take less than half a day to fully explore but it is a useful way of amusing children who are unused to the tropical species. The zoo boasts two walk-through aviaries with a large collection of parrots, a petting zoo and a cave where Jamaican fruit bats wheel around as night falls. The grounds include beautifully coloured tropical plants including sea grape, cordia and yellow poui. There is also a large playground, a restaurant and gift shop on the premises.

The southwest coast

The headland at the western end of **Great Bay** divides it from Little Bay and a series of smaller sandy bays that lead around to the great spread of Simpson Bay. The attractive but secluded beach at **Cay Bay**, where Dutchman Peter Stuyvesant was injured in battle against the Spanish, can only be reached by twenty-minute hike or by following an equestrian trail from Cole Bay.

Continuing west towards Juliana International Airport, the road leads for several kilometres along a narrow strip of land that divides the beach at Simpson Bay from the vast **Simpson Bay Lagoon** that dominates this side of the island. There is not much of note here, other than a number of hotels and a host of other, rather unsightly developments, but the lagoon is a popular spot for watersports.

Heading west beyond the airport brings you to further resort development and a series of good white-sand beaches at Maho Bay, Mullet Bay, Cupecoy Beach and Long

Bay (Baie Longue), before you round the headland to Pointe du Plum. **Maho Beach** is often drowned out with noise as planes roar into the airport, particularly at the busiest time between noon and 3pm, when anything left on the beach under the flight path usually ends up being blown into sea by the aircraft engines. Nonetheless the beach is popular and the *Sunset Beach Bar* is invariably packed when the sun goes down.

Mullet Bay tends to be the most crowded of the local beaches, with visitors pouring in for the gentle surf and white sugary sand as well as the ample shade provided by a lovely stretch of palm trees. There is plenty of parking space near the beach but surprisingly few facilities, so bring a towel and some drinks. **Cupecoy** has long been the main beach in the area for nude bathing, a dramatic place with sandstone cliffs and caves, though the once-beautiful beach has been spoiled in recent years by tide erosion. Here you can rent beach chairs and buy food and drinks. Beyond Cupecoy, the turquoise waters of **Long Bay**, actually in Saint Martin, make it a delightful place to swim and take long walks.

Eating, drinking and nightlife

Philipsburg is an excellent place for **eating out**, with a range of places from classy French and Indonesian to simple spots for a snack during a shopping expedition. Consider making a trip in for lunch or breakfast on at least one occasion during your stay. Cupecoy and Simpson Bay offer more upmarket **restaurants** on a par with Grand Case on the French side. The best **nightlife** in terms of bars and nightclubs is also on the Dutch side. For party-goers there is something happening every night, from small Latin-themed bars to happy-hour two-for-one specials and clamorous, booty-shaking music in the nightclubs.

Bliss Maho Beach ☎599/545-3996. A hip restaurant situated on the beachfront; the straightforward menu offers pastas, grills and salads. In the evening the place turns into a lively nightclub, with international DJs making regular appearances. Tuesday is martini night while Thursday is two-for-one drinks. Things pick up around midnight and continue until dawn. Closed Sun.

Busby's Oyster Bay ☎599/543-6088. Choice of meats, pasta and seafood including fresh lobster that you can pick out yourself, all served on a seafront location next to the marina.

Chesterfield's Philipsburg ☎599/542-3484. An informal yacht club-style eatery, with indoor and outdoor seating. There are a variety of seafood dishes on offer, and breakfast is particularly good.

The Greenhouse Philipsburg ☎599/542-2941. During the day, this is a great bar and restaurant to take a break from shopping for lunch. The food is good and happy hour begins at 4.30pm when all the cruise ships have departed and continues until 7pm. It is a favourite of locals and visitors alike particularly on Tuesday when it is two-for-one night. You should not leave the island without trying their rum-based special The Hurricane.

Hot Tomatoes Simpson Bay ☎599/545-2223. Facing the lagoon and marina, the spacious dining room offers a menu of tapas and pizzas and the obligatory selection of seafood prepared in their wood-burning oven. After your meal you can enjoy the live music.

Kangaroo Court Philipsburg ☎599/542-4278.

A good stopping-off point as you tour the town if you can find room, offering an excellent range of coffees as well as tasty muffins, pastries, bagels and sandwiches to raise flagging energy levels. Breakfast and lunch only.

L'Escargot Philipsburg ☎599/542-2483. Colourfully tiled and brightly painted, *L'Escargot* is one of the town's longest-running restaurants. French specialities include frog's legs and caviar as well as a variety of snail options, while the trademark grilled red snapper in pineapple and banana sauce is not to be missed. Friday is cabaret night, which includes dinner and a show.

Sunset Beach Bar Maho Bay ☎599/545-3998. Lively bar on Maho Beach that's a great place to catch the sunset, with cheap beer and a variety of sandwiches, burgers and pizza. There is live music on Wednesday, Friday and Saturday. On your way home it is something of a tradition to check in early and then watch your plane come in to land from this bar.

Temptation Cupecoy ☎599/545-2254. Set in the Atlantis Casino, this cool restaurant casually blends different culinary traditions; you'll see Indian-style grilled chicken served with spinach basmati pilaf and *papadums* served right alongside Italian sausages, for example. The menu also recommends that for couples, "high iodine and phosphorus content in grouper has beneficial effect on sexual potency" – and to help you get in the mood the pianist will happily play your favourite songs.

11

Saba and St Eustatius

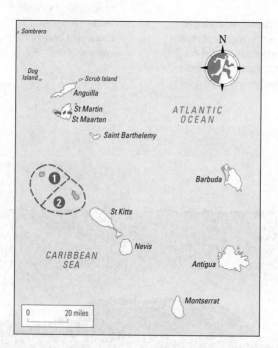

Saba and St Eustatius highlights

* **Mount Scenery, Saba** The hike to the top may be hard work, but the magnificent island views repay the effort. See p.542

* **Saba's island fringes** Pristine reefs and multi-coloured fish abound in the island's superb marine park. See p.542

* **Oranjestad** Take in the Sint Eustatius's colonial past on a gentle wander through town. See p.544

* **The Quill** Explore the spectacular rainforest inside the crater of Sint Eustatius's dormant volcano. See p.547

△ Bird's-eye view of Saba

Introduction and basics

The unspoiled Caribbean endures in an overlooked corner of the region occupied by the tiny Netherlands Antilles isles of **Saba** and **Sint Eustatius**. Sparsely populated and little known even to seasoned travellers to the area, Saba is a true pleasure to visit. Priding itself on showcasing the "Caribbean as it used to be", Saba's superb diving and great hiking more than compensate for the absence of a decent beach. Most refreshing of all – particularly after St Martin, from where nearly all visitors connect – is the lack of tourist development that has kept the island "the unspoiled queen" that the tourist authorities avow.

Similarly, **Sint Eustatius** (or **Statia**, as it is known by locals), 27km to the northwest, moves to the slow pace of island life, with good diving and hiking to be had, the latter especially the case inside the crater of the Quill, the island's dormant **volcano**.

Where to go

Saba and Sint Eustatius are attractive options for the eco-tourist with both offering some of the best **scuba diving** in the Caribbean along with plenty of fascinating **hiking** opportunities. Both have fairly small, low-key **towns** as their capitals.

When to go

The **climate** is usually sunny and warm year-round, with some cooling from trade winds particularly between mid-December and mid-April, aka the peak **tourist season**. Diving visibility at this time of year is particularly good. Between June and November is the **hurricane season** in the Caribbean. Prices however between peak and off-peak season do not vary too much.

Arrival

The closest international airport to Saba and Sint Eustatius is **Juliana Airport** on Sint Maarten, and Winair makes the short connecting flights from there to **Juancho E. Yrausquin Airport** in Saba. After dropping passengers at Saba the flights then continue on to Sint Eustatius to land at

Franklin Delano Roosevelt Airport. Taxis are available at both airports but in Saba it is advisable to arrange transport with your hotel in advance of arrival.

Coming by **ferry** from Sint Maarten (the *Edge*, leaving from Simpson Bay, is a popular high-speed boat), you'll dock at Saba's **Fort Bay**. There are no ferry services operating on Statia, though plans to develop a service are currently under way. **Cruise ships** do not call on Saba as there is no deepwater harbour for them to moor at for extended periods. The roll-on, roll-off pier at **Oranjestad** enables small cruise ships to dock on Statia, though few vessels bother.

Information, maps and websites

On **Saba** in Windwardside, the **tourist office** (Mon–Fri 8am–5pm; ☎599/416-2231, ⓦwww.sabatourism.com) has a large collection of books, brochures and maps, along with extremely helpful staff. A short distance away, at the path leading up to Mt Scenery, you'll find the **Saba Trail Shop**, which also has a collection of maps and books. The Saba National Marine Park (ⓦwww.sabapark.org) and Saba Conservation Foundation produce a series of exceptional visitor information guides and maps which can be picked up in the above locations.

On **Statia**, at the airport there is a small selection of sheets with useful contact information for restaurants and taxis, plus maps. The same information along with a few other brochures can be found at the accommodating **tourism development foundation** in Fort Oranje (Mon–Fri 8am–noon & 1–5pm; ☏ 599/318-2433, ✉ www.statiatourism.com). The Sint Eustatius National Parks Foundation (STENAPA; ☏ 599/318-2884, ✉ www.statiapark.org) is responsible for the maintenance and management of the national and marine park and can offer advice about visiting Statia's attractions.

Money and costs

The official **currency** on Saba and Sint Eustatius is the Netherlands Antilles guilder or florin (NAf), but the US$ is quoted and accepted everywhere. The guilder notes come in denominations of 5, 10, 25, 50, 100, 250 and 500 guilders; coins in 1, 2.5, 5, 10, 25 and 50 cents. The guilder is tied to the US$ at a rate of US$1 to NAf1.78.

Credit cards are accepted in some restaurants, dive operators and in hotels. However some vendors will add a handling fee for credit card transactions, typically around 3 percent. **Travellers' cheques** are accepted too but visitors are advised to take them in US$ denominations to avoid additional currency conversion fees.

Costs are comparatively high on Saba and Sint Eustatius, as the great majority of food, drink and other items are imported. On **Saba** there is a government room tax of 5 percent, and most hotels and restaurants add a 10–15 percent service charge. Tipping of taxi drivers and guides is discretionary. Two US$3 fees are added to hotel bills to defray costs of the marine park and the nature trails. On **Sint Eustatius** a 7 percent tax is added along with a 10 percent service charge for hotels. There are no taxes for restaurant bills but a 15 percent service charge will normally be added to your bill.

On Saba there are a few **banks**, all in the main tourist accommodation area of Windwardside; these are open during the week 8.30am–3.30pm. Note that there are no ATMs on Saba. In Sint Eustatius there are several banks in the capital Oranjestad, as well as the only ATM, issuing both Naf and US$. The banks here are open weekdays from 8.30am to noon and 1.30 to 3.30pm.

Leaving from Saba, a cash-only **departure tax** of US$5 is charged if you're headed to other Netherlands Antilles islands such as Sint Maarten or Sint Eustatius, or US$20 for all other destinations. Leaving from Sint Eustatius, the departure tax is US$5.65 to Netherlands Antilles isles or US$12 for all other destinations.

Getting around

There is **no public transportation** on either Saba or Sint Eustatius; you'll need to either rent a car or hire a taxi to get around, the latter of which is invariably cheaper, as not much driving is needed to cover the islands. **Taxis** will meet you at both islands' airports, though if you're arriving late in the day you might want to ask your hotel to pick you up, as the last taxi might have already left for the day. You can also get a taxi driver to squire you around on a **tour** of either island.

On Saba, if you do decide to **rent a car**, ask your hotel to arrange one for you or call ahead to Caja's (☏ 599/416-2388). On Statia, contact either Arc (☏ 599/318-2595, ✉ www.arcagency.com) or Rainbow (☏ 599/318-2811). There are no scooters or bikes for rent on Saba, though on Statia **scooters** can be rented from Trep Scooter (☏ 599/318-2626). Driving is on the right on both islands.

Hitchhiking is a common means of transport on Saba and locals are usually only to happy to give you a lift. The protocol in Windwardside is to wait by the wall by the Big Rock Market; in the Bottom you should wait by the Department of Public Works; and in Fort Bay, wait by the wall opposite the Saba Deep dive centre.

Accommodation

The **hotels** on Saba and Statia are fairly small and offer only the most basic amenities, and **prices** reflect this. None of the giant or luxurious resorts you find on other Caribbean islands exist here. If you are visiting to **scuba dive** then it is worth investigating the many **packages** the hotels and dive operators have put together; these often offer the best value.

Public holidays and festivals

April 30 Queen's Birthday (both islands).
May 1 Labour Day (both islands).
40th day after Easter (Saba) Ascension Thursday.
Saba Summer Festival late July The week-long carnival includes a queen contest, a calypso king competition, a parade and fireworks display.
Saba Days The first week in December sees sporting events such as international triathlon and basketball, dancing, parades and the Saba "Mr Too Hot To Trot" bathing suit show, along with lots of other activities.
May 29 Ascension Day (Sint Eustatius)
July (Sint Eustatius) Carnival lasting ten days with an early-morning jump-up culminating later in the day with the effigy-burning of King Momo, the spirit of the carnival. Carnival queen and calypso competition are among the other events.
October 21 (Sint Eustatius) Antillean Day celebrated with games and fetes.
November 16 Statia Day, that commemorates the year 1776, when Statia became the first foreign nation to recognize the Union Flag and American Independence by firing its cannons in salute to a US Ship.

Food and drink

There are a few small **restaurants** on both islands, offering mostly international cuisine such as burgers and pizzas, though some have slightly more elaborate menus than others. Most food and drink is **imported** onto both islands and is therefore slightly more expensive than on neighbouring islands. The prices are still reasonable, though.

Phones, post and Internet

On both Saba and Statia there are a handful of **telephone kiosks** that offer international calls via credit card or with prepaid cards that can be purchased at hotels or the airport.

To **place a call** within Saba or Statia, simply dial the final four digits of the phone numbers listed in this chapter. To call Saba or Statia from abroad, dial your country's international access code, then the country code (☎599) and the phone number as listed in this chapter.

As for **post offices**, Saba has one on the main road in Windwardside (open mornings; ☎599/416-3217) and one in The Bottom (☎599/416-2221; open afternoons). Statia's main post office is located on Cottage Road in Oranjestad (Mon–Fri 7.30am–4pm; ☎599/318-2207 or 2678).

Internet access is available on Saba from Island Communication Services in Windwardside at a rate of US$5 for 30 minutes. On Statia, Internet access is available from some hotels for a fee and the public library in Oranjestad for 0.20 NAf per minute.

Opening hours, public holidays and festivals

Although business hours are nominally Mon–Fri 9am–5pm, **opening hours** are in actuality pretty varied on both islands; shops usually open whenever the proprietor sees fit to arrive. It's worth checking with your hotel or locals as to when the establishment in question opens. As for holidays, in addition to the ones listed on p.60, Saba and Sint Eustatius celebrate the **public holidays** and **festivals** listed in the box above.

Outdoor activities

Diving and **hiking** are big draws on both Saba and Statia, with plenty of **reefs** and **trails** to explore. Other activities include **ocean kayaking**, which is available from Dive Statia (☎ 599/318-2435, ⊛ www .divestatia.com).

History

Though **Saba** and **Sint Eustatius** are outposts of the Kingdom of the Netherlands, and shared some early settlement, the islands have had very different histories. **Amerindians** were the first visitors, coming to the islands in long dug-out canoes as they made their way from the river deltas of Venezuela up the chain of eastern Caribbean islands. During their 1493 voyage, Columbus and his crew were the first Europeans to pass the islands; after this, the two changed hands regularly. While Saba became a hideout for **pirates**, Statia went on to become a regional trading superpower before its decline following US independence.

Saba

Geologically, **Saba** is the peak of a volcano that last erupted some five thousand years ago, leaving a steep-sided and now luxuriously vegetated island. The first Amerindian settlers probably arrived around 700 AD and lived in small communities based around fishing and simple farming. A handful of their artefacts are displayed in the museum in Windwardside.

Columbus did not stop in 1493, and the island was largely ignored by European travellers until 1632, when some English were shipwrecked on it, and in 1635 when the French claimed it for themselves. In 1640, the **Dutch** then colonized the island, despatching a team from nearby Sint Eustatius to take up residence near Fort Bay. Unlike many islands in the area, the steep terrain meant that large sugar, tobacco or cotton plantations were not feasible, so **development** remained limited to a handful of small farms. In the late seventeenth century Saba also became a hideout for **pirates** to store their plunder. These pirates were largely British and Irish indentured servants whose work had been taken over by imported African slaves in other Caribbean islands. Many of today's population in Saba revel in their pirate ancestry.

Today, the island remains part of the **Kingdom of the Netherlands**, one of five Dutch islands in the Caribbean with their central administration in Curaçao. Its tiny population is divided fairly equally between the descendants of the black slaves brought in to work the fields and the white farm-owners who ran them, although Sabans are often outnumbered by a combination of students at the **medical school**, expatriates and tourists.

Sint Eustatius

Sint Eustatius, or **Statia**, was settled by **Amerindians** from Venezuela and Guyana, with evidence of their occupation dating to at least 300 AD. They named the island Aloi, meaning "Cashew Island". It is likely that some Amerindians were still here when **Columbus** passed by in 1493, but there were none when the first European settlers arrived, beginning with the French, who stopped here briefly in 1629 and were followed by Dutch settlers from Holland in 1636. Columbus's maps label the island "S Maria de Niebe," which was a name later given to Nevis. The island's next name was **Estasia** after a general in the Roman Army.

Crops including tobacco and sugar were planted and, despite title regularly swapping between European nations (22 times in all), the island flourished. Between 1665 and 1713 the island was occupied eight times by French and English. Between 1781 and 1816, there were five further foreign occupations.

The **eighteenth century** was Statia's heyday, with over eight thousand residents and more than 3500 ships visiting every year during its peak to trade

11

both in local crops and in slaves. Janet Schaw, a Scot visiting the island in the 1770s, described the main town as "a place of vast traffic from every corner of the globe. The ships of various nations which rode before it were very fine… from one end of the town to the other is a continued mart, where goods of the most different uses and qualities are displayed… rich embroideries, painted silks, flowered muslins… exquisite silver plate, the most beautiful I ever saw". The island prospered as a trading hub, particularly with the **colonies** that were later to become the USA, while other Caribbean islands were only allowed to trade with their mother country.

At the time of Ms Schaw's visit, local entrepreneurs were making great profits running arms and supplies to the troops of **George Washington**'s revolutionary army, and the island's most famous moment came in 1776 when Fort Oranje fired its cannons to salute an American ship. Needless to say the British, who largely controlled the eastern Caribbean, were not amused. In 1781 **Admiral Rodney** led an assault on the island in which many ships and property were seized but he did not ruin the city or put the storehouses on fire as suggested by some accounts.

The period after Rodney's invasion saw a gradual **decline** in the island's fortunes, ironically with the US establishing its own trade routes after independence. Along with the **abolition of slavery** in the mid-nineteenth century (which was the death knell of the plantation system and began the relentless exodus of residents), the island returned largely to fishing and subsistence farming. Today Statia is home to around three thousand people largely reliant on **tourism** and **oil storage** for employment.

11.1

Saba

A t the top of the Eastern Caribbean chain, and despite covering just thirteen square kilometres, **SABA** has plenty of small delights. Its quaint villages are neat and attractive places where almost every building by law is painted white with red roof and green shutters, and for the most part tranquil except for the occasional car stereo blaring out. Even more appealing, the island's volcanic origins and limited development mean that spectacular **vegetation** and **scenery** is within easy reach of the main villages, as is an even more spectacular world of **coral** and fish just yards offshore.

Saba's **population** is around 1500, of whom 300 are students at the **Saba University School of Medicine**, which provides students from abroad an opportunity to acquire a medical degree and become a physician. The students spend eighteen months studying in Saba, creating the vibrant feel of a student town on the island.

Unless you are visiting St Martin, in which case you should at the very least make a day-trip here, the main drawback of visiting Saba is the difficulty and cost involved in **getting there**. If that doesn't put you off, and you aren't looking for an island with busy action and nightlife, Saba's a great choice.

Accommodation

Despite its small size, Saba has a good mix of elegant and simple **accommodation** to cater for most budgets. Places to stay are scattered across the island, but most are concentrated in **Windwardside**, which makes the most convenient base for hikers and has the best dining options.

Ecolodge Rendez-Vous Windwardside ☎599/416-3888, ⊛www.ecolodge-saba.com. Designed to attract visitors who want to get close to nature, the *Ecolodge* has a responsible approach towards the environment and energy resources, with twelve individually themed solar-powered cottages, without phones or TV, situated a short way up the Mt Scenery trail. A good place for nature-lovers. ⑥

El Momo Cottages Windwardside ☎599/416-2265, ⊛www.elmomo.com. Five gingerbread cottages, among the cheapest options on Saba, are dotted around the tropical gardens at this basic but easy-going place high on Booby Hill. Bathrooms are shared, there are hammocks to crash out in and the sunset views here are unmatched. ⑥

The Gate House Hell's Gate ☎599/416-2416, ⊛www.sabagatehouse.com. With five bright, spacious rooms and a single villa this small, isolated hotel offers spectacular views of the sea and nearby islands, with a couple of pleasant swimming pools, too. There is a surprisingly large selection of 160+ wines available in the restaurant

and a weekly wine tasting event. ⑥

Juliana's Windwardside ☎599/416-2269, ⊛www.julianas-hotel.com. Bright and cheerful small hotel, with nine decent rooms as well as a separate apartment and two cottages, all with cable TV, private bathrooms and balconies. There is a small pool with sun loungers, and great views up to Mt Scenery and over the ocean. ⑤

Queen's Garden Resort The Bottom ☎599/416-3494, ⊛www.queensaba.com. Attractive and classy resort, set out in an isolated location nearly a kilometre east of town. There's a good-sized pool and Jacuzzis, while the rooms are well equipped with antique furniture, kitchens, TV and fans or a/c. Superb private villas are also available. ⑦

Scout's Place Windwardside ☎599/416-2740, ⊛www.sabadivers.com The largest of Saba's hotels has just fourteen simple but clean rooms, plus pool and restaurant, in a quiet spot just off the centre of the village. This well-equipped place caters largely to divers with good dive packages on offer, but it also makes a good base for walking and hiking. The

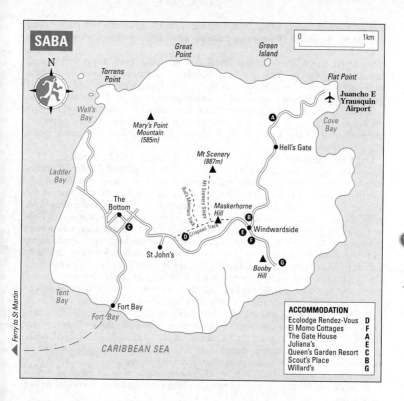

SABA

N

Great Point

Green Island

Torrens Point

Flat Point

Juancho E Yrausquin Airport

Well's Bay

Cove Bay

Mary's Point Mountain (585m)

Mt Scenery (887m)

Ⓐ

Hell's Gate

Ladder Bay

Bud's Mountain Track

Mt Scenery Steps

Maskerhorne Hill

Ⓑ

The Bottom

Ⓒ

Ⓓ

Crispeen Track

Ⓔ

Windwardside

Ⓕ

St John's

Booby Hill

Ⓖ

Tent Bay

Fort Bay

Fort Bay

Ferry to St Martin

CARIBBEAN SEA

0   1km

ACCOMMODATION

Ecolodge Rendez-Vous	D
El Momo Cottages	F
The Gate House	A
Juliana's	E
Queen's Garden Resort	C
Scout's Place	B
Willard's	G

bar is one of the liveliest on the island, popular with tourists, locals and students alike. Ⓐ

Willard's Windwardside ☎ 599/416-2498, ⓦ www. willardsofsaba.com. Saba's most luxurious hotel, with a handful of rooms perched away from it all

on a cliff on Booby Hill overlooking Windwardside and the ocean. There is a large heated pool, a tennis court and a fancy restaurant, and the rooms and shared areas are fitted with attractive furniture. Ⓨ

The island

Saba's tiny airstrip is at the island's northern end. From here, the dramatic road – known simply as "the Road" – rises sharply towards the small village of Hell's Gate. Just outside the airport, a left turn off the Road takes you along Cove Bay Road towards a sign pointing to **Flat Point**, where you can see the remains of an abandoned boiling house, used during the eighteenth century to produce molasses from sugar cane grown on the island. Today Flat Point is a desolate place, with cacti and sea grape scattered around the coastal bluffs and plenty of good tide pools for hunting crabs and sea urchins.

Back on the Road, after a dozen or more switchbacks you reach **Hell's Gate**. Landscape photo-taking apart, there's no great reason to stop here. The main land-mark is the Holy Rosary Church, which was built in the 1960s.

Windwardside

Beyond Hell's Gate, the Road cuts through rainforest-covered cliffs, offering spec-tacular views across the island as it winds towards **WINDWARDSIDE**, the main base for hiking trips and home to the tiny but worthy Saba Museum. It is a charming, relaxed and welcoming village with little traffic, and it makes the best place to stay and eat on the island. Bougainvillea, banana and palm trees line the road, lending colour to village gardens.

At the far end of the village you will find the **Saba Trail Shop**; just beyond here you can start the hike to Mount Scenery. In **Lambee's Place**, once home to Josephus Lambert Hassell, you can find a dive shop, a small café and several art galleries. Hassell, a Saban who took a correspondence course in engineering and – despite official and learned protests that it was impossible – designed and oversaw the construction of "the road that couldn't be built", running from the airport in the north to Fort Bay in the south. A plaque outside the dive shop office recalls Hassell's exploits.

The **Saba Museum** (Mon–Fri 10am–noon & 2–4pm; US$2), housed in a 150-year-old cottage, re-creates with a touch of nostalgia the traditional home of a nineteenth-century Saban sea captain, with a four-poster bed draped with Saban lace (see box below), a piano, maps and sextants in the study, and an old rock oven in the kitchen. Scattered around the house are artefacts from the island's past, among them pre-Columbian Amerindian finds such as a large cooking pot, polishing stones, tools and a cassava griddle. Much of the island's history is told through magazine articles from around the world that recount visits to Saba over the last century (particularly hair-raising are the descriptions of arriving by sea), as well as letters to and from Saban residents written in the eighteenth century. Pride of place goes to a letter from George Bush senior, thanking a Mr and Mrs Stewart for their support (gifts and letters sent to troops) during the first Gulf War. The bust in the pretty grounds is of revolutionary Simón Bolívar, a gift from the government of Venezuela.

Also in Windwardside you will find the **tourist office**, most of the island's restaurants, grocery stores and a number of gift shops including the **Yellow Store**, which is one of the few buildings on the island not decorated in the traditional red, white and green. Among distinctive souvenirs in Saba are Saban lace and spice, both of which can be purchased at the plethora of gift shops in town.

Southeast of Windwardside, **Booby Hill** has a couple of small hotels as well as some of the island's most expensive houses, which command magnificent views out to sea.

The Bottom

Having crossed through Windwardside the Road passes through tiny **St John's** en route to Saba's main village, **THE BOTTOM**, the seat of government and the island's administrative centre. Beyond the town there's a wonderful view of the village, ranks of little white houses with traditional red roofs and green-trimmed shutters, nestled in among the surrounding peaks.

As you drop down the hill to The Bottom, the first buildings on the outskirts comprise the **Saba University School of Medicine**, whose students you will see around the island. Further on is the department of public works in a white-stone old school building and, on your right, the oldest Anglican Church on the island,

---

Saban lace and spice

Once an important export, **Saban lace** is now the traditional souvenir of a trip to the island. The history of local lace-making started in the 1870s, when Mary Gertrude Johnson returned to Saba from Venezuela, where she had learned the art in a Caracas convent. She passed her knowledge on to local women and the skills have been passed down through the generations. It's pretty stuff, if pricey. Saba Artisan Foundation has an outlet selling home-made crafts including lace and linen products.

If you are after something a bit stronger, **Saban spice** is a potent rum-based herby liqueur made locally.

thought to date from the mid-1700s. Beyond here, the tidy streets are lined with old stone walls and white picket fences.

Around the main square, a series of neat buildings house the fire and police stations and the courthouse, while a handful of **munching goats** (that outnumber people by a factor of ten to one) and immaculately dressed schoolchildren are likely to be roaming the nearby streets. At the western edge of the town, the grand **governor's house** (not open to the public) has particularly intricate wooden fretwork and splendid galleries.

Beyond The Bottom

West of The Bottom, a road ploughs through to Saba's only beach of note at **Well's Bay**, where you will find a rather uninspiring patch of sand, though it makes a good spot to snorkel (bring your own gear). It is known to many as the wandering beach, as it is washed away for most of the year and then reappears for four months beginning in the spring.

Heading south the Road winds down through dry, cactus-strewn terrain to the scruffy-looking port at **Fort Bay**, home to the main dive operations and the arrival point for passengers coming to the island by boat. Eight hundred stone steps were carved down to Fort Bay before the road was built to allow supplies including a piano and safe (found in the museum) to be brought in by ship, and remnants of the old trails and the stone walls built to enclose the farms can still be seen around the island.

Eating, drinking and nightlife

For a tiny island, Saba has a surprising variety of places to eat, with **restaurants** in most of the hotels and a good series of other places in Windwardside. As you would expect, the local cuisine is heavily geared towards **seafood**. Vegetarians have good choices too. Most **bars** serve imported beers, spirits and wines. Note that most **close** for lunch by 3pm and for dinner by 9pm unless you make a reservation.

Unless you arrive during one of the festivals, **nightlife** options and musical diversions are limited. Some hotels offer their own evening entertainment but most of the time you will have to entertain yourself.

Brigadoon Windwardside ☎ 599/416-2380. Set in an attractive old Saban house on the edge of the village, this friendly little place offers creole fish dishes featuring grouper and snapper, as well as more typical chicken, steak and lobster options. Thursday is rib dinner and Saturday is sushi hour. Closed Tues. Dinner only.
In Two Deep Fort Bay ☎ 599/416-3438. A good place to catch up on some lunch after a dive trip, *In Two Deep* offers inexpensive sandwiches and burgers, and fine views across the ocean and the tiny harbour.
Rainforest Restaurant Windwardside ☎ 599/416-3888. Serves up a variety of healthy options, with the emphasis on freshness. The menu changes daily depending on what can be gathered from the gardens and caught in the sea. Particularly popular are the Monte Carlo sandwich and the curried shrimp. It is a relaxing place to have lunch after a hike and watch the hummingbirds in the garden.
Saba's Treasure Windwardside ☎ 599/416-2819. Pleasant pub surroundings, with decor describing famous maritime figures that have connections with the island. An impressive selection on the menu notably enormous and very good pizzas and burgers. Closed Sun.
Scout's Place Windwardside ☎ 599/416-2205. One of the busiest places during mealtimes, particularly in the evening when the diving crowd stops in and locals fill the bar. The rotis and burgers are good and cheap, while dinner often includes a fixed-price three-course meal. Daily specials include Saban lobster and spit-roasted chicken.
Swinging Doors Windwardside ☎ 599/416-2506. Daily specials are chalked up outside this lively saloon with an American bar-like feel indoors and garden area outside. Staples like chicken, burgers and ribs are on offer and moderately priced barbecues are held Tuesday and Friday nights. Sunday is steak night.
Tropics Café Windwardside ☎ 599/416-2469. A friendly and inexpensive café with muffins and croissants at breakfast; adequate sandwiches, burgers and omelettes at lunch; and more sophisticated options at dinner, such as sweet pea and basil soup and a seafood "pillow" with a variety of

fish. Friday night is movie night, with the island's only outdoor movie theatre, while Monday is BBQ surf-and-turf night, with steel drum music.
Y11K Windwardside ☎599/416-2539. Eat inside or out on the wooden deck overlooking Mount

Scenery. There are good chicken and shrimp salads to graze on, inexpensive sandwiches and surf-and-turf or pasta dishes. They can also make up a packed lunch for your hike up the nearby mountain trail.

Diving

Superb diving is the reason most tourists make it to Saba. A **marine park** was designated in 1987, and carefully controlled operation of the dive sites scattered throughout the park (which surrounds the entire island) has kept the reefs in pristine condition. The volcanic activity that created Saba also created a spectacular underwater world. Visibility is excellent and, as well as fine coral heads near the surface for snorkelling, there are sheer walls dropping hundreds of feet just offshore. Most of the best dive sites are on the calmer, western side of the island between Tent Bay in the south and Diamond Rock in the north. You will find great pinnacle dives as well as ridges and beautiful healthy coral gardens along with an assortment of sponges and reef fish.

There are nearly 30 different **dive sites** around Saba, most of which require a boat to reach, but the trips are rarely more than ten minutes long. There are several pinnacle sites rising from the ocean floor up to depths of 90ft; these are covered in sponges and corals and provide homes to groupers and turtles – sometimes even black-tip and grey reef sharks. The best of these is the **Eye-of-the-needle**.

Another great spot is the **labyrinth** site, a series of channels around 50ft deep created by old lava flows, on which brain and star corals have formed. You will see lots of fish gathering into this area and brightly coloured tube sponges. **Tent reef wall** is one of the most impressive areas as well, with a steep and extended ledge that plunges into the depths; lots of interesting creatures seek shelter in this wall.

There are three PADI-recognised **dive operators** on Saba, all of which operate boat dives out of Fort Bay: Saba Divers (☎599/416-2740, ⊛www.sabadivers.com), Saba Deep (☎599/416-3347, ⊛www.sabadeep.com) and Sea Saba (☎599/416-2246, ⊛www.seasaba.com). Any of the three will arrange trips to collect you from your hotel in Saba, or wait until the ferry from Sint Maarten arrives before heading out. A marine park **fee** of US$3 is payable at your hotel or to the operator in addition to fees for tanks and other equipment rental. Though the cost of individual dives can be expensive, hotels such as *Scout's Place* and operators like Saba Divers have packages which can bring down the price dramatically if you plan to complete multiple dives.

Hiking

The most popular hike on the island is from Windwardside up **Mount Scenery**, up 1064 concrete steps. The path is easy to follow, starting just west of the trail shop, but it is a tough climb, taking an hour to ninety minutes to reach the top. Do not be put off; it is well worth the effort for the fantastic vistas (sometimes the views from the peak are obscured in cloud so pick your day carefully) and gorgeous tropical and quasi-alpine vegetation. Much of the hike goes through secondary rainforest, with elephant ear ferns and mountain palms among some of the dramatic plants.

At the summit is an undisturbed and beautiful elflike forest of large mountain mahogany trees, their trunks and branches often covered in mosses, bromeliads and ferns. As for **wildlife**, you're sure to see colourful butterflies and birds as you climb, among them hummingbirds, bananaquits and tremblers if you are lucky, and you may spot a harmless racer snake or large iguanas slithering through the undergrowth.

There are several **shelters** en route to the summit, but there is nowhere to get refreshments, so take water with you. As it can get very hot, particularly between noon and 2pm, plan to start your climb early in the morning, preferably on a relatively dry and cloudless day (if it has rained then the trail can be very slippery); take the best-grip footwear you have. Once at the top do not miss the grand lookout over the neighbouring islands; to reach it head left of the communications tower and continue 100m along the pathway. The other scenic views at the top require scrambling through muddy tracks or to haul yourself up a rope (which if it is cloudy can be quite precarious as you cannot see where it leads).

For other **hiking options** on Saba, get hold of a copy of the *Trail Guide* pamphlet and map from the tourist office in Windwardside or the trail shop across the road from the start of the trail. The trail shop also rents walking sticks which are very helpful in the rainforest. They can also assist in finding you a **guide** if you want to explore off the beaten track.

11.2

Sint Eustatius

Despite a fascinating colonial history, **Statia**, as everyone knows the little island of **SINT EUSTATIUS**, is now a tropical but slightly forlorn outpost of the Kingdom of the Netherlands. Once a proud and wealthy "entrepôt", or trading post between America and Europe, the money and people have slipped away, leaving a historical curiosity that makes for an interesting day-trip, but not much more.

As with nearby Saba, the main drawback for those contemplating a trip is the expense and awkwardness of getting here. Those who make the effort will find that they have left the tourists behind for a tranquil and friendly spot, with good **diving** and **hiking** opportunities.

Accommodation

You will almost certainly want to stay in **Oranjestad**, the island's main town, which has a few simple guesthouses and a couple of hotels.

Country Inn Concordia southeast of Zeelandia ☎599/318-2484. Just six rather simple rooms at this longstanding and popular guesthouse ten minutes east of the airport, all with cable TV and a/c. The friendly owners attract repeat visitors and they're happy to cook meals on demand. Nice views of the bay. ❸

Golden Era Hotel Oranjestad ☎599/318-2345, ✉dinaiy@yahoo.com. Twenty clean and tidy rooms in this pleasant if slightly faded little hotel on the shoreline in Lower Town, just below Fort Oranje. All rooms have TV, a/c and private bathrooms. There's a small saltwater pool and a reasonable restaurant by the water. ❻

King's Well Oranjestad ☎599/318-2538, ⊛www. turq.com/kingswell. On the northwest edge of town, *King's Well* has twelve rooms just above Oranje Bay, a short walk from the beach. Rates include a full breakfast. Ask for a room with a view of the ocean. ❹

Old Gin House Oranjestad ☎599/318-2319, ⊛www.oldginhouse.com. The most luxurious of the island's hotels, an old colonial-style building with all mod cons. There's a pleasant pool, shaded with palms and with comfortable sun loungers and hammocks, and the place is handy for town. Choose from fourteen poolside rooms, plus a couple of ocean-view rooms. There is a good restaurant too. ❻

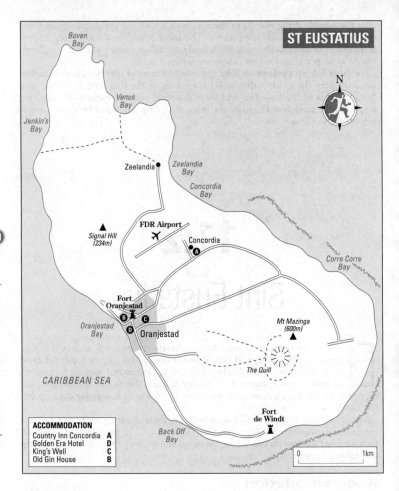

ACCOMMODATION
Country Inn Concordia   **A**
Golden Era Hotel   **D**
King's Well   **C**
Old Gin House   **B**

The island

Virtually all visitors arriving in Statia land at the **Franklin Delano Roosevelt Airport**, which sits in the centre of the roughly pear-shaped island. A short drive to the southwest is **Oranjestad**, the capital and only town, while the **Quill** – a dormant volcano that offers the most dramatic scenery and best hiking on the island – can be seen off to the southeast.

Oranjestad

You will almost certainly be staying in likeable, laid-back **ORANJESTAD** if you stop overnight on Statia. If you are just here on a day-trip, it will take you at least a couple of hours to have a good look around and there are several places where you can get a splendid lunch.

While the town is rather sprawling, you will want to confine your exploring to the main points of interest in the centre. **Upper Town** is where most of the (leisurely) action is, and makes for a pleasant place to wander and visit the island's museum and main colonial buildings. Linked by a footpath to Upper Town, **Lower Town** is the area of the old port, now home to the best local beach and further ruins of the island's once-great past.

Upper Town

Fort Oranje (always open; free) is Oranjestad's dominant building, strategically situated on the cliffside overlooking Lower Town and Oranjestad Bay. The first fortifications were put up by French settlers who came in 1629 but later abandoned the island. The Dutch who followed shortly thereafter enlarged the fort in 1636, leaving it pretty much in its present state. The fort is also the site of the island's **tourist office**.

The fort was restored in 1976, partly to celebrate the American Bicentennial and Statia's role in the USA's independence. With its cannon and old stone and brick walls it makes an evocative place, commanding fine views across the town and out to sea. There is a large bell which is rung with a hammer at 6am, noon and 6pm. Memorials in the cobbled courtyard include a plaque commemorating the momentous salute to the American ship *Andrew Doria* in 1776 and one to Dutch Admiral de Ruyter, who was stationed here in 1665.

Just outside the fort, the expertly restored **Government Guesthouse** is now home to the local governor and the courthouse, while a couple of minutes' walk away to the northeast the little **Sint Eustatius Museum** (Mon–Fri 9am–5pm, Sat 9am–noon; US$2), housed in one of the town's eighteenth-century houses, is one of the finest of its era and well worth stopping by for an hour. Historical finds ranging from Amerindian pottery and tools to colonial glassware and furniture are dotted around the first floor and basement, and there are exhibits that explain the importance of the sea trade to the island during its heyday. As you wander around, you will get a feel of the high quality of life that the island's merchants enjoyed during their brief period of dominance. Admiral Rodney liked the lifestyle so much that he set up his base here after invading the island in 1781.

Among the colonial ruins in the centre of town are the remains of **one of the oldest synagogues** in the Caribbean. Drawn to the island's growing reputation as a trading post, Jewish settlers came here in the early eighteenth century from Europe and Brazil, establishing successful shops and businesses around the port. The synagogue – down an alley across the road from the library – was built in 1739 (to the east, the oldest graves in the Jewish cemetery date back to the same period), though with the gradual Jewish emigration over the twentieth century the yellow-brick building has fallen into sad ruin, its roof gone.

A final relic of Sint Eustatius's golden era, the once-splendid mid-eighteenth century **Dutch Reformed Church** on Kerkweg, half a kilometre south of the Government Guesthouse, is also largely abandoned, though the tower was restored in 1981 and you can climb it free of charge for good views over the town.

Lower Town

Lower Town, the harbour area, carries little sign of its former glory, though you can see the ruins of old warehouses and stores that have collapsed into the sea, largely through hurricane damage and crumbling neglect over the two centuries since. A short stroll along the waterfront and under the cliffs is enough to get a feel for the place's history, after which you will want to make your way to **Oranje Beach** to the north for a snooze on the beige and black sand and a spot of snorkelling along the old seawall. The beach is pleasant enough but you have to watch the traffic jams of enormous tankers around the oil terminal. An artificial reef has been constructed to preserve the beach after years of erosion.

The rest of the island

There is not a great deal to see outside Oranjestad. Heading south the normally deserted main road leads past pretty little Key Bay to the sparse remains of eighteenth-century **Fort de Windt**, from where you will share some great views across the ocean to St Kitts with a handful of roaming goats. It takes about 45 minutes to walk from the centre of town as far as the fort.

North of town the road winds past the airport up to **Zeelandia**, named after the southern province of Holland from where the island's first settlers came. The decent two-mile-long dark-sand beach here makes a good spot for beachcombing and hiking, though not for swimming, as the water is rough and known for dangerous undertows. West of the beach, a dirt track leads north through the scrubland along which you can hike down to another beach at **Venus Bay** or into the **interior**. The nesting areas of four species of turtle can be found on the beach.

Eating, drinking and nightlife

Whether you're here for the day, or spending a couple of nights, there is enough variety of **restaurants** to keep you well fed throughout your stay. Any longer, though, and the menus become a little repetitive. Seafood is the main staple of most menus. Vegetarians have a limited choice of where and what to eat. Goat meat, bull foot soup, peas and rice are the local staples. **Beers**, **wines** and **spirits** are largely imported.

There is virtually nothing in the way of **nightlife** during the week and only marginally more at the weekend. Most places close for lunch by 3pm and for dinner by 9pm, and service is painfully slow at most locations – even by Caribbean standards. Credit cards are not accepted in some spots so check in advance.

Blue Bead Bar and Restaurant Gallows Bay ☎599/318-2873. Attractive little place just above the water in Lower Town that makes a good and inexpensive place for lunch, with tasty salads, sandwiches and fish and chips. Dinner gets pricier, with good local grouper and snapper as well as meat dishes and lobster. Between 2 and 6.30pm the kitchen is closed and only pizzas and French-style sandwiches are offered – good sustenance after returning from a spot of diving. Closed Mon.

Ocean View Terrace Oranjestad ☎599/318-2934. This restaurant, with a good view that overlooks the fort, has one of the largest set of menu choices on the island. Options include burgers, chicken and seafood as well as some locally inspired dishes. It has a good view that overlooks the fort.

Old Gin House Oranjestad ☎599/318-2319. One of the best eating options on the island, serving a variety of French and Caribbean-influenced dishes. Lunch is normally served on the patio and features fresh fish as well as lighter meals; dinner on the elegant terrace normally features lobster, steaks and curried dishes. Due to the fact that this is the best food on the island and there are only six tables, you may have to wait if you show up without a reservation.

Super Burger Oranjestad ☎599/318-2609. A good place to stop for a quick bite as you explore. Locals pop in here for sandwiches, chicken, burgers and ice cream.

Diving

Diving on Statia is excellent. It is one of the few locations in the world that offers **coral reefs**, **walls**, **archeological** and modern **wreck dives** in such close proximity. Over two hundred shipwrecks are thought to litter the water off the west coast of the island, now crusted with coral and teeming with fish, though only a handful of these are accessible to divers. Some of the top dive sites are just minutes from shore, and divers can expect to see turtles, stingrays, puffer fish and perhaps even the rare flying gurnard. Snorkelling is good, too, with many ruined buildings and some of the wrecks lying in shallow turquoise waters just offshore.

The western Caribbean shore is where the majority of Statia's thirty dive sites are located. A **marine park** that prevents any vessel from dropping anchor or any fishing extends all the way along the coastline except in the area where the tankers access the oil terminal. The sites range in depth from 20 to 220ft and visibility is often above 100ft.

Triple wreck, which used to be known as the Supermarket, curiously consists of two coral-encrusted shipwrecks lying just 150ft apart at a depth of 60ft. At the dive site known as the **Grand Canyon** – also sometimes known as Crack in the Wall – pinnacle coral reaches up from the ocean floor and you can see an abundance of life here, including large fish such as black-tip sharks or barracudas. In the southwest, **Anchor Reef** is popular with an extensive variety of sponges, corals and sea fans, while hiding in its many crevices and shelves are lobsters, sea turtles and count-less species of fish. Resting on the seabed nearby at **Anchor Point** is a 14ft-long coral-covered anchor. The body that administers the marine park, STEPNA, has also created **artificial reefs** for future divers by scuttling vessels for coral to attach itself to and for wreck diving courses to be taught. Two of these are **Charlie Brown**, a 330ft-long fibre optic cable-laying ship deliberately sunk in 2003 in 102ft of water, and **Chin Tong**, a Taiwanese fishing vessel submerged in 2004.

There are three PADI-recognized **dive centres** on Statia, all situated within walk-ing distance of each other on the waterfront in Oranjestad: Dive Statia (☎599/318-2435, ⓦwww.divestatia.com), Golden Rock Dive Center (☎599/318-2964, ⓦwww.goldenrockdive.com) and Scubaqua Dive Center (☎599/318-2160, ⓦwww.scubaqua.com). To protect the island's submerged history from souvenir hunters, only divers who are residents of Statia can dive without the accompaniment of a guide from one of the dive operators. If you are not bringing your own dive gear then it is worth asking to inspect the operators' equipment before deciding to rent it, as some of it is a little worse for wear. In addition to guide and gear costs, you must pay US$3 per dive for a **dive pass**, or US$15 for a full year of dives.

Hiking

By far the most popular hiking on Sint Eustatius is up the slopes and into the crater of **the Quill**, a dormant volcano that dominates the landscape of the southern end of the island, rising 2000ft to a crater that is itself nearly 1000ft across. You can follow good and well-signposted trails up and around the slopes of the volcano and into the crater itself, where a spectacular rainforest teems with wild orchids and anthuriums, hummingbirds and lizards.

To reach the Quill, take the road southeast out of Oranjestad and follow the signs leading to the trailhead (a **map** and a **guide** detailing the island's hikes are offered by the tourist office). The footpath begins in low-level scrub, climbing through dry woodland and taller vegetation to the crater, a 45-minute walk away. From the crater rim, you can climb down into the crater itself, though you'll need to take a little care as the path is not always easy to follow. Walking through the thick vegetation to the crater bottom, you may spot coffee, cocoa and cinnamon trees, remnants of the once-cultivated crops, as well as masses of bananas. Look out, too, for the huge silk cotton or kapok trees that can grow up to 150ft tall, as well as members of one of the healthiest populations of **iguanas** in the region.

Alternatively, turn right along the crater rim, following the often slippery **Maz-inga track**, which offers fabulous views into the crater and across to neighbouring islands as you make your way through dense and humid rainforest and woodland forest to the highest point on the island, often shrouded in clouds.

12

St Kitts and Nevis

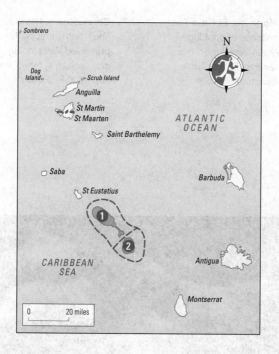

St Kitts and Nevis highlights

* **Brimstone Hill Fortress, St Kitts** Check out the magnificent hilltop views from the most impressive garrison in the Caribbean. See p.560

* **Monkeys, St Kitts** The chances of spotting green vervet monkeys are excellent at Turtle Beach. See p.560

* **Plantation inns, St Kitts and Nevis** Idle the day away with a good book at one of these magnificent inns. See pp.560 & 564

* **Charlestown, Nevis** You'll find impeccably preserved West Indian architecture in Nevis' tiny capital. See p.563

△ Green monkeys on St Kitts

Introduction and basics

The islands of **St Kitts** (short for Saint Christopher's) and **Nevis**, which together comprise the smallest nation in the Western Hemisphere, are unique in the Eastern Caribbean for their remarkable preservation of West Indian culture and attitudes. Nowhere else in the region will you find such pristine examples of colonial architecture, gorgeous plantation inns, ramshackle sugar mills and genuine hospitality.

While there are ample opportunities for diving and snorkelling, hiking and horseriding, just **kicking back** is the order of the day on both islands. And, for sheer atmosphere, St Kitts and Nevis's rambling **plantation inns** offer the islands' most captivating getaways; for the largest concentration of inns, head for St Kitts' northern section or Nevis's Gingerland region.

With the exception of Nevis's Pinney's and Nisbet, the islands' **beaches** are nowhere near as grand as those in other parts of the Caribbean. Still, there are a good number to choose from, especially in St Kitts' **Frigate Bay** area. Nevis's options are fewer, though less crowded, and ideal if privacy ranks high on your list.

Plentiful **marine life** and submerged **shipwrecks** provide interesting **diving** conditions, particularly on the Caribbean Sea side. Exhilarating **hiking** trails head into inland rainforests and up to the summits of Mount Liamuiga and Mount Nevis.

Last but not least, **Basseterre** and **Charlestown**, St Kitts' and Nevis's respective capitals, hold some interesting Caribbean heritage, including charming traditional skirt-and-blouse style houses, as well as British and French influences.

Where to go

The islands of St Kitts and Nevis have a number of attractions of interest to visitors. In particular the restored **plantation inns** make wonderful places to stay and eat. Both islands have a selection of attractive **beaches**, though not in the top league of other Caribbean destinations. There is the usual wide array of **watersports** available on the most popular ones. The respective bustling **capitals** have enough duty-free stores to keep visitors occupied.

When to go

The weather on St Kitts and Nevis is usually sunny and warm all year round, though there is some cooling due to trade winds between mid-December and mid-April. Outside of this period, the temperature is only a few degrees higher, though the humidity increases dramatically, resulting in heavy afternoon downpours. Note that accommodation prices vary widely between peak and off-peak seasons.

Arrival

While modest in size, Nevis's **Newcastle Airport** is one of the newest and sleekest in the Caribbean. By contrast, St Kitts' **Robert Bradshaw Airport** just outside Basseterre is large, chaotic and untidy, with plenty of passengers suffering lost baggage. Both airports have plenty of **taxis** to hire and cars to rent while some hotels and tour operators provide transfer between the airport and your accommodation.

On St Kitts, **cruise ships** dock at **Basseterre**'s deepwater port, capable of mooring ships up to 400ft in length. The port at **Charlestown** on Nevis is also able to receive liners, albeit ones smaller in size.

Three regularly scheduled **ferries** run between the ports in Nevis and St Kitts: the *Carib Breeze/Surf*, the *Sea Hustler* and the *M.V. Geronimo*. Reservations are not required; passengers can simply show up for the 45-minute crossing and purchase tickets at the port. **Information** for all ferries is available on ☏869/466-4636.

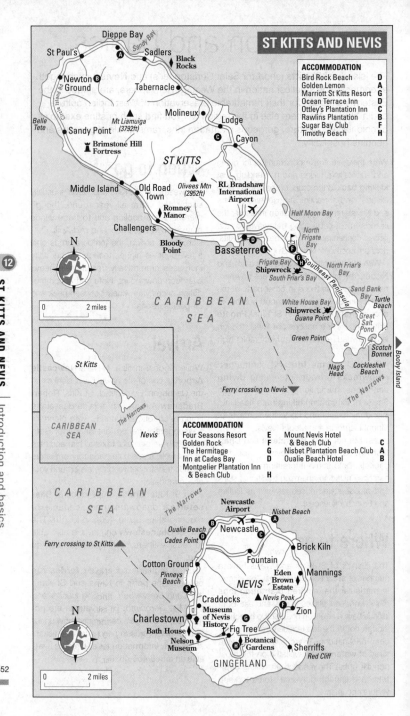

ST KITTS AND NEVIS

ACCOMMODATION

Bird Rock Beach	D
Golden Lemon	A
Marriott St Kitts Resort	G
Ocean Terrace Inn	D
Ottley's Plantation Inn	C
Rawlins Plantation	B
Sugar Bay Club	F
Timothy Beach	H

ACCOMMODATION

Four Seasons Resort	E	Mount Nevis Hotel	
Golden Rock	F	& Beach Club	C
The Hermitage	G	Nisbet Plantation Beach Club	A
Inn at Cades Bay	D	Oualie Beach Hotel	B
Montpelier Plantation Inn			
& Beach Club	H		

Information, maps and websites

Each island has its own **tourism office** and official **website** with links to hotels and services that you can book yourself. Other sources to try are the website of the St Kitts and Nevis Hotel and Tourism Association, ⓦ www.stkittsnevishta.org, which covers accommodation and tour operators, and the government's website, ⓦ www. stkittsnevis.net, which provides general background.

On arrival at either airport there are a number of **information booths** provided by the tourism offices and some of the hotels. The *Four Seasons* hotel has a presence at both airports, while the *Marriott* has a lounge at St Kitts. Lots of useful brochures, **maps** and guides to transport and dining can be picked up from these offices.

For information in **St Kitts** visit the tourism office in Basseterre's Pelican Mall (Mon–Fri 8am–4.30pm; ☏ 869/465-4040, ⓦ www. stkitts-tourism.com). They can assist by supplying maps and brochures, and a knowledgeable receptionist is able to offer advice as well.

For information in **Nevis**, the tourism office is a two-minute walk northeast of Charlestown's pier, on the east side of Main Street (Mon–Fri 8am–5pm, Sat 8am–noon; ☏ 869/469-7550, ⓦ www.nevisisland.com). It is a well-staffed office and they can supply some information and maps.

Money and costs

The islands' unit of currency is the **Eastern Caribbean dollar (EC$)**, which comes in denominations of 5, 10, 20, 50 and 100 EC dollars, and coins in 1, 2, 5, 10 and 25 cents. Prices are usually listed in US$ but both currencies are accepted universally. The **rate of exchange** is fixed to the US dollar at EC$2.70 to US$1, although vendors will sometimes vary conversion rates for cash payments between 2.60 and 2.70. Many will accept US$ and give change in EC$ so try and carry bills in small denominations if you want to avoid this.

Credit cards are taken in most shops, restaurants and in hotels. **Travellers' cheques** are also accepted; however, to avoid additional currency conversion fees visitors are advised to take cheques in US$.

While Nevis is significantly more **expensive** than St Kitts, you can get by on a budget in either place, though you will be relegated to their scarce and hardly spectacular lesser hotels.

Most of the local **banks** have offices in each island's capital. Typical **opening hours** are Mon–Thurs 8am–2pm and Fri 8am–4pm, with some also open on Saturday morning. **ATMs** are located at their branches, at the airports and in some of the larger hotels such as the *Marriott*. Those at the *Marriott* and Royal Bank dispense US$ while the ones at Nevis airport and Scotia banks issue EC$.

A **service charge** of around 10 percent is added to most restaurant and hotel bills. A **government tax** is added on all bills as well, 8 percent on Nevis and 9 percent on St Kitts.

There is cash-only **departure tax** payable at the airports of US$22 or EC$54. When travelling from Nevis to stay on St Kitts for more than 24hrs, a security fee of US$2 or EC$5 is required.

Getting around

The **roads** on both islands are mixed in quality. In order to drive, you'll need to purchase a temporary driver's licence for EC$62, valid for three months and available from car rental agencies. Big chains and local car rental operators exist on both islands and offer plenty of choice and competition. **Rental firms** on St Kitts include Avis (☏ 869/465-6507) and Thrifty/TDC (☏ 869/465-2991), while on Nevis there's also Thrifty/TDC (☏ 869/469-5690) and Noel's (☏ 869/469-5199). Note that if you intend to split your time between Nevis and St Kitts, some agencies arrange dual-island rental packages, which is useful since only the *Carib Breeze* ferry allows you to take a car. Driving is on the left-hand side on both islands. For something more open-air, **scooters** can be rented from M&J on Nevis (☏ 869/469-1369) and Fun Bikes on St Kitts (☏ 869/466-3202).

Public **minibuses** traverse northern St Kitts and all of Nevis from 6am until around 7pm on weekdays and Saturdays. Emblazoned with names like "Reggae Master" and blaring music from open windows, these minivans are easy to spot; you can catch them in the capitals or flag them down on the main roads outside of town; keep in mind that they do not follow any particular schedule. **Fares** are based on distance, with the most expensive trip on both islands EC$4. When you board just call out your destination and the driver and other passengers will make sure you get off in the right place. **Note** that in St Kitts, buses serve the Circle Island Road but not the resort areas south of Basseterre, which is disappointing as the minibuses are by far the most economical way of getting around.

Taxis congregate at both island airports and by the piers downtown in their respective capitals. You will find no shortage of drivers looking to take you on a trip. The tourist offices and airport dispatchers publish lists of **fares** for both point-to-point trips and island tours. There are additional surcharges of 50 percent between 10pm and 6am and for more than two pieces of luggage and more than four passengers. To call for a taxi in St Kitts, dial ☎869/465-8487 or 4253; in Nevis, call ☎ 869/469-9790 (airport taxi stand) or ☎869/469-1483 or 5631 (Charlestown). You can also arrange for a taxi at your hotel.

Lastly, several hotels and tour operators offer private **shuttle buses** between the airport and resorts and the beach. You should check the availability of these when making your reservations.

Accommodation

St Kitts and Nevis have a variety of **accommodation** options. At the top end you have luxurious **plantation inns** and private **villas** that can cost several hundred dollars per night. There are also a number of international chains that offer enormous resort-style lodgings on which competitive offers can be had if you are flexible with dates and avoid peak times like school holidays, Christmas and Easter. Good value can also be had at a number of **all-inclusive** resorts and self-catering **chalets**. Nevis tends to be

more upmarket than St Kitts and therefore is usually a little more expensive than its neighbour.

Food and drink

In addition to the elaborate **dining** on offer in the plantation inns and upmarket hotels (which can cost US$50 for a three-course set-menu meal), there are also a number of inexpensive spots to grab a bite, particularly on the beaches and in the capitals. Fresh **seafood** is the fare of choice at many venues, with the most luxurious offering being the spiny lobster. Other specialities include stewed saltfish, the national dish, and flying fish, served grilled and in sandwiches. The plantation inns tend to favour West Indian **curries** and seasoned vegetables, while Jamaican-inspired dishes such as **jerk chicken** and rotis are quite common at smaller restaurants and some beach grills, usually for less than US$5. **Vegetarians** are reasonably well catered for in most spots.

Most **bars** serve imported beers, spirits and wines though St Kitts does have its own Guinness brewery. One of the most popular **drinks** is a CSR (Cane Spirit Rothschild), a clear sugar-cane liqueur, mixed with Ting, a tangy, grapefruit soda.

Post, phones and Internet

Smart Phone **kiosks** are scattered around the islands and take EC dollar coins and phone cards, sold at the many shops, hotels or at the Cable and Wireless offices on Canyon Street in Basseterre (☎869/465-1000) and Main Street in Charlestown (☎869/469-5000). These offices are open throughout the week and on Saturday morning. To **place a call** within St Kitts or Nevis, just dial the full seven-digit number as listed in this chapter.

The **post office** for Nevis is located on Main Street in Charlestown (Mon–Fri 8am–3.30pm; ☎ 869/469 5521), while the main post office for St Kitts is situated just off the Circus in Basseterre (Mon & Tues 8am–4pm, Wed–Fri 8am–3.30pm; ☎869/465 2521).

Internet access is available for a fee at some hotels and at the Cable and Wireless Offices listed above. Inexpensive access is also available at the public library on Prince William Street in Charlestown (EC$2, free to students, no time limit) and just to the west off the Circus in Basseterre (EC$2 per half-hour).

Opening hours, holidays and festivals

Opening hours for most businesses are typically Mon–Fri 9am–5pm, though many retailers and restaurants are open much longer and at the weekend. As well as the **public holidays** listed on p.60, St Kitts and Nevis celebrate the Queen's Birthday on the second Saturday in June, August Monday on the first Monday in August and Independence Day on September 19.

In addition to closures on holidays, some businesses on St Kitts shut down during **festivals**, the biggest of which is **Carnival**, which runs from just before Christmas until just after New Year, with calypso performances and costumed street dancing. Nevis's main festival, the weeklong **Culturama**, takes place in late July through to early August, with music performances and beauty pageants.

Outdoor activites

As you would expect, St Kitts and Nevis have plenty of **watersports** to take part in, including scuba diving and snorkelling. On land there are spectacular **golfing** facilities and you can go **horseriding** or **hiking**.

Diving

St Kitts has seen pirates carrying out assaults on treasure-laden ships, brutal naval battles, hurricanes, and it was the Caribbean hub for the slave trade, resulting in thousands of **shipwrecks** in the waters around the island, with up to 300 in Basseterre Harbour alone. Despite this potential, St Kitts is not particularly well developed for **diving**, with only a handful of wrecks identified to date and just

fifteen dive sites and three PADI-recognized resorts: St Kitts Scuba (☎ 869/465-8914, ✆ www.stkittsscuba.com), Kenneth's Dive Centre (☎ 869/465-2670) and Pro Divers (☎ 869/466-3483, ✆ www.prodiversstkitts.com).

That said, St Kitts' Caribbean side, where the majority of the sites are found, is well-sheltered and visibility underwater is typically in the 60–100ft range. The dive locations are easily reachable with none more than a short boat trip away, and there are sites of interest for divers of all levels. The 144ft cargo ship **River Taw**, a very good wreck for novices to check out, was deliberately sunk in 1981 to create an artificial reef. Lying close to Basseterre Harbour on a flat sandy bottom at 40ft down, coral, lobsters and plenty of fish can be observed here. On occasion octopus, stingrays and turtles can be found hiding in the nooks and crannies as well. Meanwhile, **Monkey Shoals** is a square-mile coral atoll situated about three miles offshore, directly between St Kitts and Nevis. Around the reef you will find lobster, nurse sharks, stingrays and lizard fish. There are several spots at which to take to the water here but strong currents can often be a problem. You'll need about an hour to navigate the area, which lies at a maximum depth of 50 feet.

Scuba diving options on **Nevis** are even more limited than on St Kitts. There are a very few explored sites and no PADI-recognized resorts on the island although some operators do exist. At Oualie Beach, Under the Sea offers guided **snorkel** trips and lessons (☎ 869/469-1291). They have a half-day experience where you can either go straight onto the water or hear a lecture from a marine biologist followed by demonstrations in the aquarium where you can get hands-on familiarity with a turtle, conch and sea urchin before heading into the water.

Other activities

Unique in the Caribbean (except for Cuba), St Kitts offers visitors the chance to explore the island aboard a train. The **St Kitts Scenic Railway** is a double-decker a/c train that takes you around the island past historic sites, villages and the sugar cane fields. Refreshments and musical entertainment are provided, as is a running commentary. The trip takes around four hours to complete; tickets can be purchased directly from the railway station near the airport (☎869/465-7263, ⊛ www.stkittsscenicrailway.com). Many hotels offer the trip at discounted rates, so shop around before you buy.

There are a couple of **golf** courses on St Kitts. The best of these is the eighteen-hole, 125-acre Royal St Kitts in Frigate Bay (☎869/466-2700, ⊛www.royalstkittsgolfclub.com), while the Golden Rock Golf Club is a smaller, less luxurious facility offering nine holes (☎ 869/465-8103). Meanwhile, on Nevis at the *Four Seasons* there's a championship-standard par 71 golf course.

On the central mountain range in St Kitts the vegetation is rainforest, while higher up it thins out to dense bushy cover that makes for interesting **hiking** opportunities. Greg's Safaris (☎869/465-4121, ⊛www.gregsafaris.com) offers half-day treks in the rainforest area, as well as more strenuous five-hour climbs up **Mt Liamuiga** and into its dormant volcanic crater. Note that the tracks into the interior of St Kitts are not well defined so it is advisable to go with a guide.

On Nevis there's a trail known as the **Upper Round Road** that connects the sugar plantations; this is excellent to **hike**, **mountain bike** or ride along on **horseback**. These wooded areas up in the hills can be rough and rocky in places but the higher the altitude you reach the better the views. As you climb higher the flora and fauna becomes that of the rainforest variety and includes the famous green vervet monkeys. It is also possible to take a challenging hike up **Nevis Peak** itself, a six-hour trip; it's a good idea to go with a guide: Top to Bottom (☎869/469-9080) has numerous trekking options and local herbologist Michael Herbert (☎869/469-3512) also makes the ascent. Mountain Bike Rentals offers tours and equipment at Oualie Beach (☎869/469-9682) while Nevis Equestrian Centre (☎ 869/469-8118) does horse riding around the trails and beaches, plus riding lessons. Many of Nevis's inns also have guides, horses or bikes to rent.

Lastly, Nevis's largest and best **spa** is located at the *Four Seasons* resort (☎ 869/469-1111), with a variety of body treatments and facials available.

History

The first settlements on the St Kitts and Nevis are islands believed to have existed around the coastal areas over 4000 years ago. The early inhabitants were the pre-ceramic **Sibonay** followed by **Arawak** colonists from the area now known as Venezuela; the Caribs arrived later. St Kitts was known as Liamuiga (Fertile Land), while the Carib name for Nevis was Oualie (Land of Beautiful Water).

Christopher Columbus and his crew sighted the islands on their second New World voyage in 1493 and claimed them for Spain, naming them **San Jorge** and **Nuesta Señora de Las Nieves** ("our lady of the snows"), but otherwise left them to the Caribs. Contrary to popular belief, Columbus did not name St Kitts (a shortening of St Christopher's) after himself; rather, the moniker San Cristóbal came later on from inaccuracies in Spanish maps. This in turn was anglicized to "St Christopher's" after

Englishman **Sir Thomas Warner** came ashore in 1623 and established Old Road Town. A small posse sailed for Nevis five years later and set up a camp called Jamestown near Cotton Ground that was destroyed by a tsunami in 1680. Local mythology has it that in certain conditions the submerged town can be seen.

St Kitts did not remain entirely British, as the threat posed by oppressed native **Caribs** prompted Warner to form a union with the French the following year. The combined European legions decimated most of the Caribs in a battle in 1626. The location of the battle, now known as **Bloody Point**, was said to have run red with the Caribs' blood for several days after, and women and children survivors were kept as concubines and slaves.

After that battle the French and British turned on each other with great regularity as the island was split between the two colonial superpowers. The French lorded over the northern and southern coasts and established the modern-day capital, **Basseterre**; the British controlled the leftover areas in between. These areas were occasionally wrested from the British by the French as well, culminating in a one-month siege at **Brimstone Hill** in 1782. The **Treaty of Paris**, signed the following year, officially returned St Kitts to the British and put an end to the squabbles.

Nevis, meanwhile, had no part in the struggle, and instead became the region's most profitable **sugar cane** producer and destination of choice for Britain's rich and famous thanks to its natural spas. In the last quarter of the seventeenth century the plantations made both of the islands amongst the richest in the Caribbean with labour supplied by African slaves and indentured Europeans. They became the depot for the **slave trade** in the Leeward Islands with up to 11,000 passing through annually until **emancipation** in 1838.

The two islands were joined as an **independent federated state** in 1983, following failed geopolitical associations like the Associated States that included neighbouring Anguilla. (There has been a failed attempt since then by Nevis to secede from St Kitts.) Today, the islands have their own distinct style and culture, which not surprisingly is still heavily influenced by Britain and the USA. Though agriculture continues to be a valuable source of income, **tourism** has become increasingly important for both islands – and, while they both have their fare share of monstrous developments, neither has yet become overdeveloped.

12.1

St Kitts

Paddle-shaped **ST KITTS** lies a few miles northwest of Nevis, just across The Narrows. Lush rainforest covers the central mountain range that forms the island's spine, while the surrounding lowlands are largely given over to sugar cane fields. Most visitors tend to head directly to the resort area of **Frigate Bay**, focusing their time in the southern region where all of the island's beaches are found. The best of these fringe the **Southeast Peninsula**, an undulating spit skirted by the island's only white sand.

Nearer to St Kitts' centre, the capital, **Basseterre**, merits a visit for its concentration of traditional skirt-and-blouse-style houses, while traces of the island's imperial past lie closer to its north end, where the star attraction, **Brimstone Hill Fortress**, presides over the Caribbean. The **northern coast** has its own quiet appeal, with fields of overgrown sugar cane sheltering gracious former plantation inns, while the Atlantic side offers dramatic vistas and little else.

Accommodation

The majority of St Kitts' hotel **accommodation** is centred on **Frigate Bay**, and is mostly of the large-resort style. In the north of the island there are a variety of **plantation inns** that offer smaller-scale lodging. Meanwhile, options on the Southeast Peninsula are becoming increasingly popular, particularly with time-shares.

Bird Rock Beach Basseterre ☎869/465-8914, ⓦwww.birdrockbeach.com. With the only real beach around Basseterre, this hotel features 46 standard doubles and a swim-up pool bar, along with botanical gardens and tennis courts. The scuba diving operation Dive St Kitts is situated on the premises. ❹

Golden Lemon Dieppe Bay ☎869/465-7260, ⓦwww.goldenlemon.com. Picturesque and comfortable, this inn has a splendid location on a black-sand beach, eight spacious seventeenth-century main house rooms with gabled roofs and eighteen newer villas with full kitchens and private plunge pools. ❽

Marriott St Kitts Resort Frigate Bay ☎869/466-1200, ⓦwww.stkittsmarriott.com. With 1000 rooms this is easily the largest hotel on the island, if not the Caribbean. There are a multitude of bars and restaurants, as well as a manicured stretch of beach, shopping mall, casino, nightclub and large swimming pool. You also have preferential rates for the nearby spa and golf course. ❽

Ocean Terrace Inn Basseterre ☎869/465-2754, ⓦwww.oceanterraceinn.net. Basseterre's best hotel, set overlooking the bay in tropical gardens, has three freshwater pools, three restaurants and a fitness centre. Choices of accommodation include suites or apartments with kitchenettes. ❺

Ottley's Plantation Inn ☎869/465-7234, ⓦwww.ottleys.com. A few miles south of Black Rocks, this charmingly restored inn has 24 expansive rooms with flounces befitting a princess – Anne, for one, has stayed here – and beautifully manicured grounds. Gourmet dining, spa and tennis are offered along with cottages that have their own private pools. ❾

Rawlins Plantation ☎869/465-6221, ⓦwww.rawlinsplantation.com. Situated inland from the northern coast, *Rawlins* is by far the most authentic inn, with ten distinctive antique-furnished stone cottages, a library sitting room and 25 acres of land infused with the scent of sugar cane. ❾

Sugar Bay Club Frigate Bay ☎869/465-8307, ⓦwww.eliteislandresorts.com. A low-rise resort situated near the Royal St Kitts Golf Club, with 100 rooms, cottages and suites, plus a couple of bars and regular live entertainment. Room-only ❼, all-inclusive ❾

Timothy Beach Frigate Bay ☎869/465-8597, ⓦwww.timothybeach.com. A pleasant and laid-back hotel on the unexceptional South Frigate Bay beach. The sixty rooms, with king-size beds, a/c and wicker furniture, are not fancy, but they are good value. One- and two-bedroom apartments with kitchens are also available. ❺

Basseterre

Settled by the French following the partition of St Kitts in 1628, the island capital, **BASSETERRE**, on the Caribbean coast, is French in name only today. Although boasting some Georgian architecture, it is not a particularly attractive town, though you're likely to spend at least some time here, as it's where ferries and cruise ships arrive, and where you'll find the bus station and taxi rank. There is a selection of reasonable quality **restaurants** and **bars**, along with a tourist office, Internet cafés and the post office. It is also home to a concentration of street disc jockeys with enormous sound systems playing very loud music in competition with each other, giving the town a frantic vibe. You'll not need more than an hour or two to fully explore the town before heading on to more interesting island attractions.

The centre of Basseterre, **The Circus**, reflects the town's British dominion; the roundabout circling the green **Berkeley Memorial Clock** is allegedly modelled after London's Piccadilly, though the only obvious similarity is the traffic. Traces of British rule are also evident in the historical town centre due east, **Independence Square**, where walkways imitating the spokes of a Union Jack are inlaid with red stones. A maiden-topped fountain at its nexus, a gift from Queen Elizabeth to commemorate St Kitts' independence in 1983, marks the spot that once hosted the Lesser Antilles' largest **slave market**; slaves were bathed at the small red fountain on the square's south side prior to mounting the stage. The square looks onto the staid 1927 **Immaculate Conception Cathedral**, its substantial twin-towered facade devoid of the drama associated with Anglican **St George's**, a few blocks northwest of the Circus. The French parish that originally stood here was incinerated in 1706 by the British, who rebuilt their own church several times, complete with menacing spearheads on the ground-floor Gothic windows.

Anglo-French distinctions aside, Basseterre's most remarkable aspect is its preservation of traditional Caribbean **skirt-and-blouse homes** built with stone ground floors topped by wooden levels – the stone prevented flooding, the wood allowed a breeze – and trimmed with dainty gingerbread fretwork. Many demonstrate a certain cultural ingenuity, most obvious along **Fort Street**, where old sentinel walls have been incorporated into their construction. Others are deceptively ancient, having been rebuilt using stones from Brimstone Hill Fortress (see overleaf), following an 1867 fire that ravaged most of the town. (Note that if you want to take pictures of private homes, you should get the owner's permission first.) A decent collection of photographs predating the fire is displayed at the **St Christopher Heritage Society**, at the foot of the Circus (Mon–Fri 9am–5pm, Sat 9am–noon; ⊛www.stkittsheritage.org).

Frigate Bay

St Kitts' only beach resort area, **FRIGATE BAY** lies three miles southeast of the capital, on flatlands sandwiched by the Atlantic and Caribbean. On the Atlantic side is **North Frigate Bay Beach**, a deep golden band fronting un-swimmable waters due to a strong undertow. On the calmer Caribbean side, the narrow South Frigate Bay (also known as **Timothy Beach**) has a watersports shack with snorkelling gear, windsurfers and kayaks; staff also organize three-hour snorkelling trips to nearby reefs and shipwrecks. Between the two beaches are an expansive golf course and a casino.

Frigate Bay is home to the main **hotel district** on the island, with some enormous resorts that include one of the Caribbean's largest, the *Marriott*. Most shopping and entertainment options are within hotel grounds, some of which are open to non-guests, except during peak times such as Christmas. There are a few interesting **shops** dotted around, such as the friendly arts and crafts on offer at A World Apart, next to the *Marriott* (☏869/465-8354).

Southeast Peninsula

The **Southeast Peninsula**, which extends towards Nevis from Frigate Bay, boasts grassy peaks and, more importantly, St Kitts' finest beaches. These only became publicly accessible in 1990, with the opening of the twisting road that cuts through the peninsula's centre. You are likely to spot one of the island's numerous green vervet monkeys as you head south to the peninsula's most happening pocket, **Turtle Beach**, home to a lively beach bar and restaurant. The shores around **Booby Island**, an islet facing the beach, abound with marine life, providing good snorkelling and diving. The one downside is the beach's popularity, particularly with cruise ship day-trippers; if things get too busy, nearby **Cockleshell Beach**, around a hill to the west, is a good alternative. Halfway down the western coast, **White House Bay** fronts a modest stretch of sand with some of the best snorkelling on the island, thanks to a shallow-lying shipwreck just offshore. The two bays at the neck of the peninsula, **North Friar's Bay** and **South Friar's Bay**, get more visitors because of their proximity to Frigate Bay.

Along the Circle Island Road

The northern part of St Kitts, traversed by the **CIRCLE ISLAND ROAD**, is an easy half-day excursion, though if you have the time you should break up the drive with lunch at St Kitts' best West Indian restaurant, *Rawlins Plantation Inn*. Better yet, base yourself at one of St Kitts' charming **plantation inns** that are concentrated in this part of the island. The topography here is typical West Indies, with scores of sugar cane fields, windmills and ramshackle churches.

Bloody Point to Middle Island

Four miles north of Basseterre, the first stop of note on the Circle Island Road is **Bloody Point**, a hillock on the outskirts of **Challengers** village that witnessed a brutal Carib massacre in 1626. A one-hour hike affords glimpses of cartoon-like petroglyphs engraved into the rocky hillside.

After the point, the road heads down to the seaside village of **Old Road Town**, the island's first settlement under Sir Thomas Warner's tenure; the only vestige is a derelict red-brick building that once served as Government House. Better maintained are the **petroglyphs** that predate Warner's arrival, etched on a boulder along the nearby road signposted to Romney Manor; the pregnant-looking character is a fertility idol. At the end of this signposted road you'll find the estate of **Romney Manor**, its smart yellow cottages now home to **Caribelle Batik** (Mon–Fri 8.30am–4pm; ☎869/465-6253, ⊛www.caribellebatikstkitts.com), a popular handicraft boutique. The grounds feature a botanical garden (free) with a 350-year-old saman tree as its centrepiece. The derelict ruins of a sugar plantation lie below, notable for the extensive aqueduct that's used today as the departure point for rainforest hikes.

Back on the main road, another mile north along the Caribbean coast lies **Middle Island** village, where an unkempt cemetery contains Sir Thomas Warner's extravagant marble tomb.

Brimstone Hill Fortress National Park

A few miles north of Middle Island, the conical 800ft **Brimstone Hill** hulks over the flatlands, its name derived from the sulphuric odours exuding from nearby underwater vents. The British must not have minded the smell since they chose the hill's flanks to support a **fortress** so grand it was nicknamed the "Gibraltar of the West Indies". Begun in 1690 and expanded over the course of the following century, the sprawling garrison ultimately proved insufficient defence – it was captured by the French in 1782 after a month-long siege. The Paris Treaty forced its return a year later, but the fortress fell into disuse as relations eased between the warring nations and the dwindling economics of sugar cane production meant island resources no longer needed protection. Abandoned in 1853 and left to deteriorate until 1965, an ambitious restoration project has returned the fortress to its former splendour, and earned it UNESCO World Heritage Site recognition.

The prominent hilltop compound, the **Citadel** (daily 9.30am–5.30pm, ☎869/465-2609, ⍟www.brimstonehillfortress.org) provides spectacular views from its parapets, while the fortifications themselves surround a water catchment system. The enclosing barracks house an eclectic **museum** showcasing military paraphernalia, Carib tools and decorative adornos (small clay figurines) and a rubbing of the petroglyphs at Old Road Town. On the grassy parade, stairs access the lower bastions on a promontory with a tiny **military cemetery** outside the rampart walls. A canteen near the steps serves snacks, or you can picnic and then pick up some souvenirs. Note that the **bus** to Brimstone Hill drops you off on the main island road, after which it is another 2km on foot up a steep hill.

Sandy Point to Black Rocks

Beyond the fortress, the road passes the remains of **Fort Charles**, a 1672 military outpost used as a leper colony from 1890 to 1995, before arriving in **SANDY POINT**, St Kitts' second largest town. The point itself is a rather grubby black-sand beach, while the town occupies the spot on which Thomas Warner and his crew came ashore in 1623. Sandy Point was the centre of the island's tobacco trade in the seventeenth century, and the most fascinating sight in the town is the tobacco warehouses that were constructed during this time.

Lying in the flatlands below the crater-capped **Mount Liamuiga**, the island's highest point at 3792ft, the northern coast is changing dramatically as developers transform it into a resort area. Still, though, the coastal stretch between **Newton Ground** and **Sandy Bay** retains windswept ocean vistas, fields of untamed sugar cane and the ruins of abandoned plantations; what few estates remain now house inns which make for excellent lodging or lunch stops. The main settlement this far north, **Dieppe Bay**, is a former French village that taxi drivers often inform you marks the start of the Atlantic coast. Midway down the Atlantic side is St Kitts' jaw-dropping natural wonder, **BLACK ROCKS**, a jumble of solidified black pyroclastic lava formations that tumble into the sea; there's a viewing area signposted to the left of the main road.

Eating, drinking and nightlife

Most of the best places **to eat** on St Kitts are in the hotels and inns. Even if you do not stay at one of the **plantation inns**, you should make it a point to experience some of their old-world ambience by stopping in for a meal. In addition to extravagant dining, there are plenty of inexpensive spots, particularly in the **capital**, to grab a bite, where roadside shacks grill up great seafood for a fraction of the price you would pay elsewhere. Note that **reservations** are required for the upmarket eateries, particularly in the peak season.

As for **drinking** and **nightlife**, most again centres on the hotels, with some having several bars and nightclubs. Outside of the hotels and resorts, Friday and Saturday nights are the main party nights, as barbecues and makeshift bars are set up across the island.

Ballahoo Basseterre ☎869/465-4197. Perched on an airy verandah overlooking The Circus roundabout, this popular, moderately priced restaurant has a fine seafood menu, including superb lobster *thermidor*. In addition there is a wide selection of Caribbean and international dishes. Closed Sun.
Circus Grill Bar and Restaurant Basseterre ☎869/465-0143. The large choice of items on the menu ranges from lobster to omelettes, with

several vegetarian options. At the fully stocked bar you can try house cocktails or Planters Punch. Closed Sun.
Fisherman's Wharf Basseterre ☎869/465-2754. Moderately priced, tasty seafood served at picnic tables on a breezy pier; head to the buffet to pile on extra fixings like creole rice and mac 'n' cheese.
Marshall's Horizon Villa ☎869/466-8245. The most upscale option in the area, this resort

restaurant has a swanky poolside setting and opulent seafood. The menu includes a combination of many local ingredients tinged with ethnic elements. Dinner only.

Mr X's Shiggidy Shack Bar and Grill Timothy Beach ☎ 869/663-3983 Beachside shack offering grilled fish, lobster and chicken in traditional Kittitian style. The sign outside says topless women get free drinks, giving you an idea of the tone of the place, yet there's live music and a bonfire on Tuesday nights.

Oasis Sports Bar and Grill Frigate Bay ☎ 869/466-9332. American sports bar-style place offering a selection of burgers, steaks, salads, buffalo wings and the like along with a well-stocked bar and lots of TV screens. Happy hour runs from 4 to 6pm daily, while Wednesday night is ladies night, where women get half-price drinks. Open from 4pm Mon–Thurs, from noon on Fri & Sat.

PJ's Pizza Bar and Restaurant Frigate Bay ☎ 869/465-8373. If you tire of your hotel restaurant, this is a good option, serving up Italian cuisine and pizzas in an informal setting. They will even deliver to your hotel room, which can be much cheaper than room service. Closed Mon.

12.2

Nevis

Suffused with sugar cane, gorged with wild bougainvillaea and hibiscus, and sprinkled with overgrown windmills, tiny **NEVIS**'s rural beauty and backwater charm make it distinctive in the Caribbean, and are the keys to its appeal. Most sightseeing here consists of poking around the enchanting capital, **Charlestown**, where well-preserved skirt-and-blouse homes and a couple of excellent history museums provide an easy afternoon's distraction.

Outside the capital, you can wander about the odd country church, go horseriding in the hinterlands, hike up Mount Nevis, snorkel off the coast or – as many visitors do – spend most of your time on one of the four white-sand **beaches**. The island is small enough that it can be experienced on a **day-trip** from St Kitts – a good option if you are watching your budget, as Nevis is a good deal pricier.

Accommodation

Despite its small size, there are plenty of **accommodation** options on Nevis, ranging from luxury five-star resorts to restored plantation inns, plus villas and guest houses. The five historic **plantation inns** on the island are all east of Fig Tree within a few miles of one another, and are accessed off the main road.

Four Seasons Resort Pinney's Beach ☎ 869/469-6238, ⊛ www.fourseasons.com/nevis. Set on its own stretch of golden sand, this is the country's most luxurious resort – and, unlike many mammoth resorts in the Caribbean, the *Four Seasons* has been attractively designed to blend in with its surroundings. Sporting facilities include ten tennis courts and an award-winning championship golf course. ❾

Golden Rock Gingerland ☎ 869/469-3346, ⊛ www.golden-rock.com. The relaxed *Golden Rock* has a number of homey rooms scattered about an 1815 plantation, with cosy communal areas, a tropical courtyard and a swimming pool perched 1000ft above sea level. A bell is rung to call guests to dinner. ⑨

The Hermitage Gingerland ☎869/469-3477, ⓦwww.hermitagenevis.com. The island's oldest inn, the *Hermitage* is a 1740 estate with antique-furnished colonial style cottages around the Great House; it offers packages that include horseriding trips, hiking and jeep rental, weddings or scuba diving. ⑨

Inn at Cades Bay Cades Bay ☎869/469-8139, ⓦwww.cadesbayinn.com. Amiable inn where sixteen spacious waterfront bungalows are fronted by hammock-strung porches. You can eat home-cooked beach fare and hearty Sunday brunches at the inn's restaurant, *Tequila Sheila's*, while listening to live jazz by local artists – or simply enjoy Nevis's longest stretch of beach. ⑦

Montpelier Plantation Inn and Beach Club Charlestown ☎869/469-3462, ⓦwww.montpeliernevis.com. Spread over sixty acres including beautifully landscaped gardens, with seventeen recently refurbished rooms at this exclusive and luxurious private hideaway; it hosted the wedding of Admiral Lord Nelson. Considered one of the best inns on the island, its facilities include swimming pool, gourmet restaurant and private beach. ⑨

Mount Nevis Hotel and Beach Club Newcastle ☎869/469-9373, ⓦwww.mountnevishotel.com. Perched on a plateau and blessed with awesome panoramic views of St Kitts, this hotel has 32 spacious rooms, an excellent pool and a terrace area. The hotel itself is not located on the beach but a free shuttle bus can transport you there. ⑨

Nisbet Plantation Beach Club St James ☎869/469 9325, ⓦwww.nisbetplantation.com. Occupying thirty acres backing a fine beach, accommodation options range from small cottage rooms to one-bedroom suites. There are several good restaurants, including one overlooking the immaculate lawn. ⑨

Oualie Beach Hotel Oualie Beach ☎869/469-9735, ⓦwww.oualie.com. Thirty-four casual, pretty gingerbread cottages right on the beach. Each has a mahogany four-poster bed and screened-in verandahs. Very convenient for watersports including snorkelling, scuba diving and ocean kayaks, which can be rented nearby. ⑧

Charlestown and around

Nevis's small capital, captivating **CHARLESTOWN**, boasts an impeccable assemblage of skirt-and-blouse houses, in keeping with residents' resolutely old-fashioned attitudes. There are a few scruffier, more modern buildings around, though the town is still more attractive than its neighbour's capital, Basseterre.

Charlestown's traditional attitudes can be seen in the 1825 **courthouse** on a day that someone is being tried for swearing in public; you will see the cusser in question sitting in a draconian crib-like prisoner's box. The upstairs **library**, with its heavy-set ceiling braced by mahogany gunwales, is equally devoid of modernity. The 1778 Bath House – once the Caribbean's most happening spa – closed its shutters for good in the 1950s, though recent efforts have taken place to renovate the structure. The **hot springs**, however, at the south end of town, remain as invigorating as ever, and Nevisians and visitors alike are still fond of immersion. To partake of them yourself, you will have to bring a towel and don your suit in advance, as there are no facilities. The hot **outdoor springs** in the village of Bath near Charlestown are fed by volcanic sulphur. The water temperature is kept at a constant 40°C so it is not the place to go if you want to cool off. Many believe that the sulphurous content has therapeutic properties and this is what bought many of the first tourists to the island in the eighteenth century.

The best place to garner some island background is at the quaint **Museum of Nevis History** on Main St (Mon–Fri 8am–4pm, Sat 9am–noon; US$2). Its informative collection of odds and sods occupies the main floor of a Georgian-style building on the grounds where Alexander Hamilton was born in 1757. Although the Hamilton house was devastated by a mid-1800s earthquake, sovereign state-making is still being discussed above the museum in chambers used by Nevis's pro-independence House of Assembly. Near the hot springs at the opposite end of town, the **Horatio Nelson Museum**, on Building Hill Rd (Mon–Fri 8am–4pm, Sat 9am–noon; US$2), focuses on Lord Nelson, who came ashore in 1785 and wound up marrying the governor's niece, Fanny Nisbet. While the collection consists mainly of kitsch and some pilaster copies of Nelson's Column, it gives a captivating overview of Nelson's Caribbean adventures. Along Government Road lies a remnant of another chapter in Nevisian history, a **Jewish cemetery** whose oldest stone dates from 1684. It is thought that a nearby grey-stone building served as a **synagogue**.

Just a fifteen-minute walk from the Charlestown pier, you'll find by far the most popular beach on Nevis, **Pinney's Beach**. There are some areas open to the public, though the best-manicured area belongs to the *Four Seasons* resort. At the four-mile-long stretch's northern end, there's a smattering of rusty cannons and crumbling bastions belonging to **Fort Ashby**, one of eight fortifications that defended the coast in the 1700s.

Oualie and Nisbet beaches

Further up the west coast from Charlestown, **OUALIE BEACH** graces a calm cove with the island's greatest concentration of watersports outfits right on the sand. You can rent snorkelling gear and organize half-day outings from these operators. After Oualie Beach, the island road wraps around the northern slopes of Mount Nevis and passes the airport before reaching **NISBET BEACH**, Nevis's nicest, although a substantial portion of it has been damaged by erosion. Its deep white sand, facing the Atlantic, is scattered with elegant coconut trees strung with hammocks.

Along the Atlantic coast to Gingerland

Nevis's **Atlantic coast**, a scenic haven of rustic settlements with evocative names like Brick Kiln, is completely devoid of resorts and beachfront but nonetheless worth the detour for its historic remnants. Centuries-old stone ovens still line the road and some houses rest on piled rocks, holdouts from the days when landless squatters had to move from plantation to plantation.

Rambling **GINGERLAND** begins south of the crumbling ruins of the reputedly haunted Eden Brown Estate and stretches along the southern coast to the outskirts of Charlestown. Known for the island's largest concentration of sugar plantations, which have since been transformed into inviting inns, the region's otherworldy charm and lush vegetation make it idyllic. Lord Nelson and Fanny Nisbet obviously thought so – they opted to hold their nuptials in Fig Tree village's picturesque 1680 **St John's Anglican Church**. The only other sight is a **botanical garden** near *Montpelier Inn* (Mon–Sat 10am–4pm; ☎869/469-3509), worth an hour or so of your time, where stepped terraces burgeon with violet orchids and Spanish-moss-draped trees. Be sure to visit the rainforest conservatory showcasing Nevis's inland flora; the resident speaking parrots are a lark.

Note that while there are no beaches to speak of in Gingerland, the region's plantation inns provide **shuttle services** to and from Pinney's Beach.

Eating, drinking and nightlife

The best **dining** on Nevis is at the plantation inns, where you'll dine on delicious West Indian curries and Nevisian seafood; **reservations** are nearly always required. On the beaches you will find less sophisticated surroundings, though boasting tasty options nonetheless. Nevis has a small number of **nightlife** options and musical diversions on offer, and many inns and hotels host their own nightly entertainment.

Bananas Bistro Cotton Ground ☎869/469-1891. Pleasant bistro on a panoramic terrace, with an imaginative menu including Thai curries, crab quesadillas and French onion soup. Dinner only, closed Sun.

Café des Arts Charlestown ☎869/469-7098. A delightful place serving up sandwiches, quiche and strong coffee on the ground floor and gardens of Hamilton House, across from the Museum of Nevis History. Breakfast and lunch only. Closed Sun.

Eddy's Bar and Restaurant Charlestown ☎869/469-5958. South of the pier, *Eddy's* dishes up fish 'n' chips and the like on a second-floor verandah; Wednesday's happy hour is popular with locals and there's a darts competition on Fridays.

Miss June's Cuisine Jones Bay ☎869/469-5330. Nevis's best restaurant, where thirty different Caribbean dishes are served dinner-party-style, allowing you to meet fellow visitors and locals alike. Typically only one dinner per week, so call ahead to check. Drinks are included in the price.

Montpelier Plantation Inn ☎869/469-3462. *Montpelier* has an original and celebrated menu that consistently wins international awards – speciality dishes include the five-spice duck and breadfruit and leek soup – as well as an enchanting atmosphere, with dinner served on the verandah.

Sunshine's Beach Bar and Grill Pinney's Beach ☎869/469-5817 Grilled seafood and lobster at Nevis's liveliest bar, famous for its Killer Bee, a potent rum and passion fruit concoction.

Unella's By The Sea Charlestown ☎869/469-5574. Close to the pier, the seaside terrace at *Unella's* is an appropriate backdrop for the fine seafood on offer; red snapper and lobster make star appearances.

Montserrat

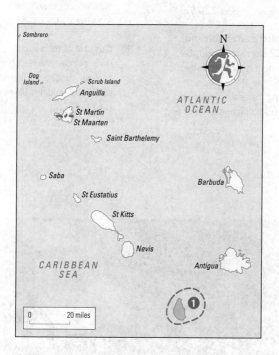

Montserrat highlights

✳ **Plymouth** Buried in places under 40ft of volcanic ash, Plymouth is an extraordinary testament to the destructive power of the Soufrière Hills Volcano. See p.576

✳ **Montserrat Volcano Observatory** Visit the observatory for fantastic views of the astonishing natural wonder and meet scientists living and working in its shadow. See p.576

✳ **Centre Hills hiking trails** A number of trails may be hard work, but the magnificent views repay the effort. See p.577

✳ **Coastal cliffs** Scuba diving under these cliffs reveals pristine reefs and abundant wildlife. See p.577

△ Plymouth after the volcano

Introduction and basics

Once famous for celebrity residents like Sting and Eric Clapton, **Montserrat** is now best known for its active volcano, **Soufrière Hills**, which began its current smouldering in 1995 and subsequently buried much of the southern half of the tiny island, including the former capital of **Plymouth**. One of the few places on the planet where you can witness the impact of a volcano on modern buildings and structures, the island landmass is composed largely of volcanic debris from three million years of eruptions. The result is a country of lush mountainous topography and beaches of black sand. Montserrat suits a range of tastes, from those looking to laze about in a private villa to the more adventurous eco-tourist seeking an escape from more crowded destinations.

Having seen the majority of its population depart after the destruction wrought by the most recent series of eruptions, Montserrat is slowly beginning to rebuild, offering attractions centred on eco-interests including a **volcano observatory**, trips to nearby **coral reefs**, and unusual rock formations of interest to scuba divers. There are also several **hiking** trails through rich and fertile landscape that hosts several rare species of birds. The delights that nature offers in Montserrat make a truly unforgettable visit, whether just for a day-trip or on a longer stay.

Where to go

With its smoking plume visible from across the island – and the devastation caused in the island's former capital **Plymouth** on display – the **volcano** is the highlight of any trip to Montserrat. There are no major towns or resorts on the island but there are a handful of quiet **beaches**.

When to go

The **climate** on Montserrat is usually sunny and warm year-round, with some cooling from trade winds between mid-December and mid-April, also the peak **tourist season**. Outside of this period the temperatures are only a few degrees higher, though the humidity increases dramatically, resulting in heavy afternoon downpours. Between June and November is the **hurricane season** in the Caribbean.

Arrival

The loss of the airport and deepwater harbour in Montserrat severely hampers those trying to reach the island directly. Most visitors will have to enter via nearby Antigua on a ferry or helicopter. Coming by helicopter, which makes the inter-island run a couple of times a day, you'll land at **Gerald's Heliport** in Montserrat. Contact Montserrat Aviation Services (☎664/491-2362, ⓔmonair@candw.ag) or Carib Aviation (☎268/480-2980) for prices and schedules.

A **new airport** is scheduled to open in the second half of 2005 at Gerald's (where the heliport is now), which should see options for getting to Montserrat improve. However, the airport's completion has been delayed on previous occasions; contact the Montserrat Tourist Board (see overleaf) for up-to-date information.

On the northern fringes of the island, **Little Bay** is the main port of entry for private boats and for the *Opale Express*, a high-speed ferry from Antigua. The prices, schedules, trip duration and Antiguan port for this ferry regularly change without notice; check for details with Carib World Travel (☎268/480-2980) or Montserrat Aviation Services (as above).

One way of seeing the island without touching down is a 45-minute **helicopter tour**, taking passengers from Antigua on dramatic flights over the boiling volcano peak. These trips are organized by Caribbean Helicopters (☎268/460-5900, ⓦwww.caribbeanhelicopters.com). If you'd like to visit Montserrat on a day-trip, Antiguan **tour operators to Montserrat** include Jenny's Tours (☎ 268/461-9361,

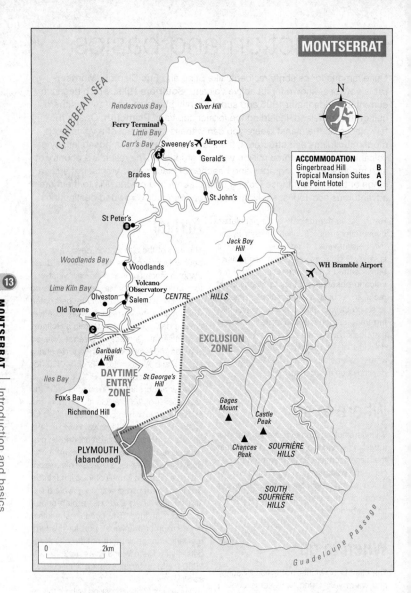

MONTSERRAT

N

ACCOMMODATION
Gingerbread Hill B
Tropical Mansion Suites A
Vue Point Hotel C

CARIBBEAN SEA

Rendezvous Bay
Silver Hill
Ferry Terminal
Little Bay
Carr's Bay
Sweeney's ✈ Airport
Ⓐ
Gerald's
Brades
St John's
St Peter's
Ⓑ
Jack Boy Hill
Woodlands Bay
Woodlands
WH Bramble Airport ✈
Volcano Observatory
Lime Kiln Bay
Olveston
Salem CENTRE HILLS
Old Towne
Ⓒ
EXCLUSION ZONE
Garibaldi Hill
DAYTIME ENTRY ZONE
St George's Hill
Iles Bay
Fox's Bay
Gages Mount
Castle Peak
Richmond Hill
Chances Peak SOUFRIÈRE HILLS
PLYMOUTH (abandoned)
SOUTH SOUFRIÈRE HILLS
Guadeloupe Passage

0   2km

Ⓔburkeb@candw.ag) and D&J Forwarders and Tours (☎268/773-9766).

Information

The **Montserrat Tourist Board** office is located on the main road in Brades

(Mon–Fri 8am–4pm; ☎664/491-2230, ⓦvisitmontserrat.com), and produces a comprehensive **tourist guide** with detailed listings of shops, accommodation and taxis. The guide can be picked up at the tourist office and at ports and hotels. Getting hold of detailed current maps can prove difficult, though the tourist board can provide a simple **map** outlining the major points of interest.

Money and costs

The island's unit of currency is the **Eastern Caribbean dollar (EC$)**, divided into 100 cents. Notes come in denominations of 5, 10, 20, 50 and 100 EC dollars; coins in 1, 2, 5, 10 and 25 cents. Prices are often listed in both EC$ and US$ and both currencies are accepted universally. The rate of exchange is fixed to the US dollar at EC$2.70 for each US dollar, although vendors will vary conversion rates for cash payments between 2.60 and 2.70.

Credit cards are taken in some restaurants and in hotels, though authorization is not automated in many locations and can take up to 40 minutes to finalize. **Travellers' cheques** are also accepted island-wide.

The Royal Bank of Canada in Brades (Mon–Thurs 9am–2pm, Fri 9am–3pm) is the only bank with a 24hr **ATM**, which dispenses EC$. The Bank of Montserrat (Mon, Tues & Thurs 8am–2pm, Wed 8am–1pm, Fri 8am–3pm) is located in St Peters, though they have plans to relocate to new offices in Brades.

A **service charge** of 10 percent is added to most restaurant and all hotel bills, and so tipping is discretionary. A government tax of 10 percent is added to bills as well.

Costs on Montserrat are reasonable in comparison to some other Caribbean islands. The modest hotels rarely charge more than US$100 per night for accommodation while meals will cost no more than US$20. Getting to Montserrat currently can only be done via Antigua so costs of trips there must be factored in. **Day-trips** from Antigua including meals, transport and guides can cost between US$50 and $100 depending on the day of the week and time of year.

There is a **departure tax**, payable in cash only of US$17/EC$45. Children under 12 years of age and transit passengers who continue their journey within 24 hours are exempt. If you are returning to Antigua, a further passenger charge for that island is required for entry.

Getting around

For visitors not on an organized tour there are a few options available to get around. There are several **taxis** that can be hired cheaply in Gerald's Airport or Little Bay; you can ask these drivers to take you on a personalized **sightseeing tour** of the island. The best of these organized tours is from Thomas Lee (℡664/491-2347); alternatively, try Slym Tours and Taxi Service (℡664/491-4479). There are no metered taxis so agree on a currency and fare before setting off.

The cheapest and most efficient way of getting around the island during the day is by **minibus**, which can be waved down on most roads. They only travel in the north but the cost is set at EC$2. There is no fixed schedule, stops or route, but you will often find locals queuing which will be happy to advise. At night it's best to arrange another form of transport as the frequency of minibuses becomes even more erratic after the sun goes down.

In order to drive on the island a temporary Montserrat **licence** is required. This costs EC$50, is valid for three months and can be purchased from the police station in Brades or at the ports. The island has only one **petrol station**, in Sweeney's. Cars and jeeps can be rented from BeeBeep Taxi Service and Auto Rentals (℡664/491-3787) or from Grant Enterprise and Trading (℡664/491-9654). Driving is on the left. **Scooters** can be rented at the *Tropical Mansion Suites* (℡664/491-8767).

Accommodation

Montserrat's small size means that the big tourist hotel chains found in many of its Caribbean neighbours are absent here. Despite this there are still a variety of **accommodation** choices on the island for those travellers who prefer to stay locally rather than make the short journey from nearby Antigua. Options include modestly sized **hotels**, **guesthouses** and a host of self-catered **rental properties** that often include private swimming pools. Rental properties are listed on the tourist board website. **Costs** for rooms typically range between US$50 and $100 per night. **Prices** do not vary widely between peak and off-peak season.

Food and drink

Dining options in Montserrat are basic and unpretentious. The island has a few speciality dishes, including goat water (which is a brown, soup-like dish comparable to Irish stew) and mountain chicken (actually the legs from a species of frog only found locally and in Dominica). **Seafood** and dishes accompanied with abundant local **fruits** are also widely available, though choices for **vegetarians** are pretty limited. Most bars serve imported **beers**, **spirits** and **wines**. The **local liquor** is a cocktail known as Montserrat Rum Punch.

Post, phones and Internet

Telephone kiosks are scattered around the island and take EC$ 25-cent coins, dollar coins and phone cards, sold at many shops and hotels or at the Cable and Wireless office in Sweeney's (Mon–Fri 8am–4pm, ☎664/491-2112). Credit card calls can be made via the operator.

To **place a call** within Montserrat, simply dial the seven-digit number; the 664 prefix is not required. Toll-free numbers use the 1800 prefix.

Mobile phone coverage for TDMA handsets exists in the northern parts of the island. This network is not compatible with GSM handsets. Handsets can be hired from the network provider, C&W Caribbean Cellular in Sweeney's (☎664/491-1000). The main **post office** is in Brades (Mon–Fri 8.15am–3.15pm, ☎664/491-2457).

Internet access is available for a fee at some hotels, and at Jim Lee's Computer Services in St Peter's (☎664/491-8499). Access is free at the public library in Brades (Mon–Fri 9am–4pm, Sat 10am–1pm). The library closes for lunch for a couple of hours each day but this time often varies from that published on the entrance.

Opening hours, holidays and festivals

Opening hours on the island are erratic – businesses normally open when the proprietor arrives in the morning or returns from lunch so it is worth checking with your hotel or locals if you're interested in the opening hours of a specific establishment.

In addition to the **public holidays** listed on

Public holidays and events

March 17 St Patrick's Day. This day's celebrations commemorate the Patron Saint of Ireland and are extended into a whole week of activities, which highlights Irish heritage as well as honouring those who lost their lives in the 1768 slave rebellion. Activities include a "Slave Feast" and "Freedom Run", accompanied by calypso and soca band music.
May 5 Labour Day
Second Saturday in June Queen's Birthday Parade
Early July Look Out Day
Late July Cudjoe Head Day celebrates the abolition of slavery in 1834. Highlights include a bazaar that takes place at the village rectory.
August 30 Roman Catholic Fete
Septempter Tourism Week. Often features a street fair with arts, crafts and local produce, along with cultural shows.
October Police, Fire and Search & Rescue Week
December Festival One of the year's highlights, showcasing the island's culture and performing talent. It's held during the last two weeks in December, and then climaxes on New Year's Day with a street parade.

The ash-laden air after an ash-fall or on windy days may cause **breathing difficulties** for people suffering from respiratory problems such as asthma or bronchitis; sufferers should take appropriate medications and precautions. Wearers of contact lenses should also consider using spectacles during any visit to the island to avoid irritation to the eyes.

To warn of volcanic activity an island-wide **siren system** will sound. If the siren does sound, advice and safety-related messages can be heard on Radio Montserrat (ZJB), FM 88.3.

p.60, Montserrat observes the holidays and events in the box opposite.

Outdoor activities

Scuba diving and **hiking** are Montserrat's two principal outdoor activities. Some locals also have boats that they will charter out for **sailing** or **fishing** trips. With its rugged terrain Montserrat is also ideal for **mountain biking**; Imagine Peace Bicycle Shop in Brades does rentals (☎664/491-1520).

The volcano has had a number of surprising benefits for scuba divers in the waters around Montserrat. While many believed that the **reefs** would be destroyed by a covering of ash and lava, the ash in fact was swept away by tidal currents and the deposits that remained created interesting new attractions in the dive sites. Instead of destruction the pyroclastic flows brought massive new **boulders** into the sea, onto which new reefs are growing. What's more, the island's sparse population is too small to dangerously pollute the sea and cause disease amongst the coral as has happened in some parts of the Caribbean.

Away from the violence of the volcano the island of Montserrat offers lush vegetation and tropical rainforests that exude peace and tranquillity. The Montserrat Forest Rangers, reachable through the tourist board, can help organize a range of hikes to several **trails** on the island, varying from the mountainous volcanic spine of the island, to fields of mango and banana or through picturesque colonial-style villages. Acquiring maps of the trails is difficult and signposting is inconsistent so a **guide** is highly recommended.

History

Montserrat was first occupied by **Amerindians**, who colonized the chain of Lesser Antilles from the area now known as Venezuela. Arawak artefacts have been found in several sites around the island dating from 500BC. When the **Caribs** arrived, they depopulated the island, though how they did this is uncertain. Precisely when this transpired is also not known, but it must have been within living memory of Columbus, since a native he had on board in his 1493 voyages reported it to him.

There are five coastal locations on the island that have been identified as former Amerindian **encampments**. While it's not clear whether they are Arawak, Carib or both, the artefacts and debris found indicate they were **farming communities**. The Caribs named the island Alliouagana, which means "land of the prickly bush". (This will seem particularly apt if you explore some of the island's trails.)

Columbus's ships sailed along the lee-ward side of the island on 11 November, 1493 but did not go ashore. He named the island **Santa Maria de Montserrat**, as it reminded him of the location of the abbey of Montserrat near Barcelona in Spain. Spain claimed all of the West Indies at the time, though eventually other European powers began to explore and settle.

By 1632 the population on nearby British-owned St Christopher (now St Kitts) included a number of **Irish indentured workers** who hoped to settle themselves once their indenture was over. Concerned that, in the event of war, the Irish might side with the Catholic French who shared St Kitts, the authorities sent them to form new colonies on Montserrat and Antigua. Although Montserrat was uninhabited when it was initially settled, the Caribs made their presence felt for five decades, launching regular raids on the island and the European colonists.

While the island has remained a **British territory** since that first settlement, it is unusual in that the first European settlers were predominately Irish. Montserrat soon became known as an asylum for **Roman Catholics** in search of religious freedom, a unique motive for settlement in the Caribbean. Signs of the Irish influence are evident in the celebration of **St Patrick's Day**, the faint Irish inflections that can be detected in many local voices, the heavy use of the shamrock emblem to illustrate the doctrine of the Holy Trinity and Montserrat's nickname, the **Emerald Isle**. Place names like Cork Hill and St Patrick's (not to mention Potato Hill) also bear witness to the Irish influence.

Between the mid-1600s and the mid-nineteenth century, thousands of enslaved Africans were transported to the West Indies to work on the booming sugar plantations. As with elsewhere in the Caribbean, **slaves** on Montserrat's sugar estates endured harsh conditions while making the "mother country" rich. Although slavery was **abolished** in 1834, it was many years before the island's population was able to shake off the legacy of poverty and the deprivation it brought.

In the late twentieth century, **residential tourism** developed, and people from all over the world built their luxurious retreats, including Beatles producer George Martin, who established his famous Air Studio, in which music has been recorded by Sting, Phil Collins, Elton John, the Rolling Stones and Stevie Wonder, among many others. The Air Studio, along with several other facilities, closed in 1989 when **Hurricane Hugo** devastated the island. After recovering from that natural disaster, the island experienced a **volcano eruption** in 1995. Nineteen people lost their lives, and, in the aftermath, locals left the island in droves; the population shrank from 11,000 to about 4000. Volcanic activity has continued ever since, and while it represents a simmering threat over the island, it is of great appeal to tourists.

13.1

Montserrat

P art of **MONTSERRAT**'s attraction is the seclusion brought on by the challenge of getting to this unique, pear-shaped island. The place is not visited by many tourists and thus, unlike many of its Caribbean neighbours, is never crowded. The only way to reach Montserrat is via Antigua: you can either stay overnight in one of the small hotels here, or make day-trips using Antiguan tour operators (see p.583) who will arrange meals, transport and local guides.

The main attractions on the island are the active **volcano** and the otherworldly vestiges of the **devastation** caused by its 1995 eruption. After Plymouth was completely buried in ash, it was abandoned, and the capital was moved to **Brades**, in the northwest of the island, which features a small collection of shops and government offices. There are a few good **beaches** around Montserrat, though these, unlike other Caribbean islands, aren't what draw visitors.

Accommodation

Montserrat has very few **hotels** and no resorts. To augment the island's meagre options, a number of residents offer **rooms** in their homes; the tourist board maintains a list of these.

Gingerbread Hill St Peters ☎664/491-8767, ⓦwww.volcano-island.com. Set on three tropical hillside acres that overlook the sea, this guesthouse has accommodation including both a private villa and an apartment, each of which has a patio, fridge, microwave and cable TV. ❷
Tropical Mansion Suites Sweeney's ☎664/491-8767, ⓦwww.tropicalmansion.com. Built with eighteen comfortable rooms in 1999, this was the first and currently only hotel erected after the volcano eruption. Conveniently located for both Gerald's and Little Bay, it has a restaurant and a

small swimming pool. All the rooms have balconies, and include a kingsize or double bed in addition to cable TV and ceiling fans. Some suites have kitchenettes. ❹
Vue Pointe Hotel Old Towne ☎664/491-5210, ⓦwww.vuepointe.com. Overlooking a beach and with terrific views of the smouldering volcano, *Vue Pointe Hotel* offers guests a number of self-contained cottages equipped with kitchenettes, ceiling fans and cable TV. Facilities include a swimming pool and lighted tennis courts, though sadly the golf course has been destroyed. ❹

Brades

After the destruction of Plymouth, small, nondescript **BRADES**, near the island's northwest coast, became the temporary capital. The government relocated many of its buildings here, and the town also has the greatest concentration of shops and businesses on Montserrat; these are spread at irregular intervals along Brades' steep **main road**. In addition to this, here you'll find the tourist board office (see p.570), the island's bank and a small number of restaurants (see "Eating, drinking and nightlife"). Besides these amenities, there's little to detain you in this tiny town, whose entire length can be walked in a just a few minutes.

The volcano and around

The exclusion zone around the volcano keeps people away from the many unsafe parts of Montserrat. The boundary for this zone begins in the devastated former capital of Plymouth and runs eastwards over **St George's Hill** to the site of the old airport. That said, you can get close to the volcano – aka **Soufrière Hills** (derived from the French word for sulphur, deposits of which can be found across the island) – via the **Daytime Entry Zone**, a portion of the off-limits area that's open to the public between 6am and 6pm, volcanic inactivity permitting. Though Soufrière Hills is expected to remain active for the next few decades, island authorities anticipate being able to expand the safe zones in the coming years.

Located within the Daytime Entry Zone, the former capital of **Plymouth**, now abandoned, was covered in pyroclastic ash from the volcano's eruption and provides some spectacularly eerie scenes, not least the **buried clock tower**. The ash has set as hard as concrete in places but in others it is a fine dust that can be collected, saving you a purchase at the gift shops. Entering some of Plymouth's ruined homes, you can see remnants of what residents left behind during the evacuation, including furniture, decade-old newspapers and even a poster of teenage pop stars New Kids on the Block. The most striking aspect of the town, though, is the complete silence that reigns over the many buildings, giving the place an utterly ghostly feeling. Note that while you can visit Plymouth independently, there are parts of the abandoned town that are off-limits and unsafe, though not always signposted – so for your own safety it is recommended you go with a **guide**.

To see the volcano in its full glory head-on visit the **Montserrat Volcano Observatory** in Fleming's (Mon–Fri 8.30am–4.30pm; ☎664/491-5647, ⓦwww.mvo.ms). At time of writing, tours have been suspended due to construction work, though these are expected to resume in 2006; visit the website to check on the progress. A two-day island **field trip** organized by the observatory is available to students, professionals and interested amateurs, allowing you to explore the effects of the volcano in greater detail. The **lectures** given by scientists with first-hand experience of the volcano's might are particularly informative.

A few other good observation points can be found at **Richmond**, **Garibaldi** and **Jack Boy hills**. The first two points stand in the Daytime Entry Zone and provide good panoramic vistas of Plymouth, while the latter has excellent views over the damaged eastern side of the island, including the old WH Bramble Airport and the lava dome itself. Note that if you're coming here on a day-trip, and the volcano is your primary reason for visiting, you should choose a day when the **weather** will be fair, as low clouds can obscure its steaming peak.

The beaches

With a population of only 5000, and just 15,000 visitors a year, the deserted **beaches** on Montserrat are a welcome change from those on its more overcrowded and commercialized neighbours. In the north, **Rendezvous Bay** is the only white-sand beach and has something for everyone, with quality snorkelling, swimming and walking. All of the other beaches are of the black volcanic sand variety. Of these, **Old Road Bay**, conveniently located for guests at the *Vue Pointe Hotel*, is a haven for sailboats and watersports with its small pier, and provides terrific views of Soufrière Hills. A short walk inland reveals further devastation caused by the volcanic flows. Lastly, **Woodlands Beach** and **Lime Kiln Bay** are also worth visiting for their isolation, with the former near an upmarket residential area.

Eating, drinking and nightlife

Especially during the week, many **restaurants** on Montserrat close before 9pm, so for dinner it's best to call ahead and make reservations. **Brades** has a number of choices for breakfast, lunch and dinner, while around Little Bay next to the Customs Office there are a few **vendors** selling drinks and snacks. As for **nightlife**, various locations occasionally feature bands or disco music, particularly on Friday and Saturday nights; these are usually listed on hotel and restaurant notice boards.

Bitter End Beach Bar Little Bay ☎664/491-3146. Popular with locals, expats and visitors alike, *Bitter End Beach Bar* serves up snacks at its lively bar as you wait for the ferry.

Jumpin' Jack's Bar and Restaurant Olveston ☎664/491-5645. A vibrant spot bar that's popular with the expat community and serves informal seafood lunch – the speciality is fresh tuna sandwiches. It's also possible to charter a four-man fishing boat with Danny "Jumpin' Jack" Sweeney and then return to have your catch prepared for your meal. Closed Mon & Tues.

Oriole Café Bar and Restaurant Brades ☎664/491-7144. Situated conveniently next to the tourist board office, this restaurant serves up a small selection of good-quality Caribbean and local dishes. Not much on offer for vegetarians.

Tina's Brades ☎664/491-3538. An attractive wooden building with verandah that serves a variety of tasty dishes, as good as anything you'll find on the island. These include lunches for tour parties and a menu with international as well as Caribbean cuisine on offer. Open late Fri & Sat, closed Sun.

Tropical Mansion Suites Sweeney's ☎664/491-8767. This hotel restaurant serves up a simple à la carte menu of reasonable quality, with a small selection of Caribbean and international dishes with vegetables, rice and salad. There's a daily happy hour at the well-stocked bar, while Sunday sees a barbecue lunch beside the small pool.

Vue Pointe Hotel Old Towne ☎664/491-5210. Poolside hotel restaurant that overlooks the beach and enjoys terrific views of the volcano, with one of the island's larger and more varied menus. There's a family buffet lunch on Sun, while on Wed at 7pm there's a chicken, fish and ribs barbecue, with a local steel band. Serves up a variety of cocktails as well, including the Vue Pointe Volcano, featuring three varieties of Caribbean rum.

Diving

The most active dive sites on Montserrat are around the island's northern portion, the lion's share of which are between **Old Road Bluff** and the **Northwest Bluff**. Some of the most impressive diving is under the **coastal cliffs**. In the shallowest areas neighbouring the cliffs many scattered rocks and ledges can be found, covered with sponges, sea plumes and sea fans. Plenty of fish and the sporadic octopus can be seen as well. In deeper areas, rocky ledges take the place of the boulders; these are separated by valleys that local divers compare to aisles in a supermarket. Here divers can find schools of flying fish that leap out of the water, barrel sponges and a wide variety of other species such as sea turtles.

Montserrat has only one PADI-approved **dive centre**, the Sea Wolf Diving School (☎664/491-6859, ⊛www.seawolfdivingschool.com), which offers professional training and equipment rental. Dive sites can be reached by their boat or directly just by swimming out from many beaches.

Hiking

Situated on the western side of the island, **Runaway Ghaut** provides a gentle stroll ideal for birdwatching and picnicking, with tables available en route and a drinking fountain that, if quaffed from, is said to bring visitors back to the island. In the northerly reaches, the **Silver Hills** trail leads hikers through open fields and forest up a 1000ft defunct volcano. Once again this trail is suited to bird-spotters with a variety of land and sea birds making their homes along it, including a breeding colony of frigate birds.

The **Centre Hills** trails leads visitors through the island's rainforest, where the majority of the 34 local bird species can be found, including rare and threatened Montserrat orioles, mangrove cuckoos and bridled quail doves. Several varieties of reptile and amphibian are also to be found on this, the premier of the island's hikes. Another good hike is the **Cot trail**, a picturesque tramp that climbs 1000ft, leading you through abundant flora and affording views of ruined buildings and the exclusion zone. Lastly, the trail from **Little Bay to Rendezvous Bay**, along a steep mountain path, is one of the most challenging hikes, though it rewards at the end with a combination of black-and-white-sand beaches, giving you an opportunity to cool off with a spot of swimming or snorkelling.

14

Antigua

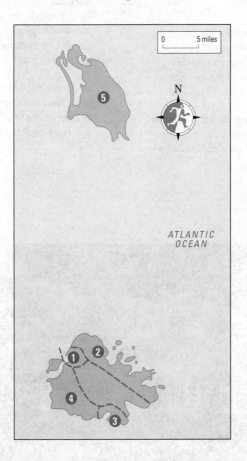

0   5 miles

N

*ATLANTIC
OCEAN*

Antigua highlights

* **Nelson's Dockyard**
Once a busy Georgian
dockyard, now an intrigu-
ing living museum. See
p.598

* **Long Bay** An appealing
stretch of white sand
with good snorkelling
around the reef just
offshore. See p.596

* **Long Street, St John's**
The place to view some
colourful old buildings

and catch an entertaining
game of cricket as well.
See p.591

* **Barbuda** Spectacular
Palm Beach is just one
of the highlights of this
delightfully secluded
island. See p.605

* **St John's** You'll find
great West Indian food
at local places like *Home*
and *Papa Zouk*. See
p.593

△ Nelson's Dockyard, Antigua

Introduction and basics

Famous for its beaches and its cricket players, tiny **Antigua**, including the even smaller island of **Barbuda**, is now one of the Caribbean's most popular destinations. The country has taken full advantage of the publicity gained from its independence in 1981 – and the remarkable success of its cricketers since then – to push its name into the big league of West Indian tourism alongside Barbados and Jamaica.

For centuries after the **British** settled the island in the 1600s, it was little more than a giant factory producing sugar and rum to send home. The tall brick chimneys of a hundred deserted and decaying sugar mills scattered around Antigua bear witness to that long colonial era. Today, though, it is **tourism** that drives the country's economy; dozens of hotels and restaurants have sprung up around the coastline, there's a smart airport and a number of outfits run boat and catamaran cruises and scuba diving and snorkelling trips to the island's fabulous **coral reefs**. A short flight away, Antigua's sister island of Barbuda is much less visited, but quite a delight in its own right.

Where to go

If all you want to do is crash out on a **beach** for a week or two, you'll find Antigua hard to beat. The island is dotted with superb patches of sand – look out for **Dickenson Bay** in the northwest, **Half Moon Bay** in the east and **Rendezvous Beach** in the south – and, while the nightlife is generally pretty quiet, there are plenty of great places to eat and drink. But, however lazy and beach-bound you're feeling, it's worth making the effort to get out and see some of the country. The superbly restored naval dockyard and the crumbling forts around **English Harbour** and **Shirley Heights** are as impressive as any historic site in the West Indies, and there are lots of other little nuggets to explore, including the capital, **St John's**, with its tiny museum and colourful quayside, and the old sugar estate at **Betty's Hope**. If you're prepared to do a bit of walking, you'll find some superb **hikes** that will take you out to completely deserted parts of the island.

Barbuda feels a world apart from its increasingly developed neighbour, even though it's just fifteen minutes away by plane. Despite its spectacular beaches and coral reefs, tourism is very low-key. Even if you can only manage a day-trip, you'll find Barbuda thoroughly repays the effort involved in organizing a tour to get there.

When to go

Antigua's tropical **climate** makes it a year-round destination. The weather is best during the high season, from mid-December to mid-April, with low rainfall and the heat tempered by cooling trade winds. As you'd expect, prices and crowds are at their peak during high season.

Things can get noticeably hotter during the summer and, particularly in September and October, the humidity can be oppressive. September is also the most threatening month for the annual **hurricane season**, which runs officially from June 1 to October 31.

Arrival

All flights to Antigua touch down at **V.C. Bird International Airport**, on the island's north coast. There is **no bus service** from the airport, though there are numerous **car rental** outlets at the terminal. **Taxis** – arranged through the dispatch desk – cost around US$6 to Dickenson or Runaway bays, US$7 to St John's or US$25 to English Harbour.

If you arrive on Antigua by cruise ship, you'll dock at either **Redcliffe or Heritage quay**, in St John's. From there, you can either take a taxi to anywhere on the island; take a bus to English Harbour, Parham or Willikies; or rent a car.

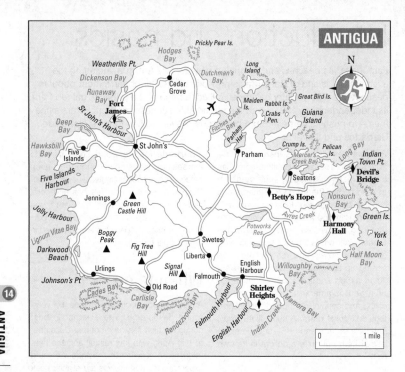

Information, websites and maps

The government **tourist office**, at the Government Complex on Queen Elizabeth Highway in St John's (☎268/462-0480), has a smattering of brochures and **maps**. The **Internet** is also a good source of information; see the box below for a few of the more helpful general sites.

Money and costs

The island's unit of currency is the **Eastern Caribbean dollar (EC$)**, divided into 100 cents. It comes in notes of $100, $50, $20, $10 and $5 and coins of $1, $0.50, $0.25, $0.10, $0.05 and $0.01. The rate of exchange is fixed at EC$2.70 to US$1.

In most tourist-related businesses – especially hotels, restaurants and car rental – the **US dollar** is used as an unofficial parallel currency, and you'll often find prices quoted in US dollars (a policy we have adopted in this guide). Bear in mind, though, that you

Websites

ⓦ **www.antigua-barbuda.org** The national tourism authority's official site has information on forthcoming events, places to stay, car rental outfits and more.
ⓦ **www.antiguacarnival.com** The summer schedule is set out in detail, and there's a "scrapbook" of last year's Carnival as well as details of this year's bands.
ⓦ **www.antiguanice.com** Masses of information, from hotels and restaurant reviews to details of travel agents and links to the island's news.

can always insist on paying in EC$ (and the exchange rate usually works out slightly in your favour). Changing money into EC$ is best left until you're in the country.

If you are using US dollars or travellers' cheques to pay a bill, ask in advance whether your change will be given in the same currency (it usually won't).

Banking hours are generally Monday to Thursday 8am–2pm and Friday 8am–4pm. Most of the banks are in St John's and include Antigua Commercial Bank, Barclays, ABIB and Bank of Antigua. The latter has a branch in Nelson's Dockyard and Bank of Antigua and ABIB in St John's are also open on Saturday morning.

Most hotels and restaurants automatically add a **service charge** of 10 percent and government tax of 8.5 percent. It's always worth asking if this charge is included in the quoted price or will be added on later.

Getting around

Antigua is not a big place, and it's easy to drive right round the island in less than a day. Buses are useful, but a car will help you see places you wouldn't otherwise reach.

See p.604 for how to get from Antigua to **Barbuda**.

By bus

Speedy and inexpensive **buses and minibuses** run to certain parts of the island, particularly between St John's and English Harbour on the south coast and along the west coast between St John's and Old Road, although none go to the big tourist area of Dickenson Bay and Runaway Bay.

By car

If you want to tour around, you're invariably better off **renting a car** for a couple of days, though prices are fairly high, starting at around US$40 per day, US$250 per week. You'll have to buy a **local driving licence** for US$20 (valid for three months and sold by all of the car rental firms). Reliable firms include Avis (☏268/462-2840), Budget (☏268/462-3009), Dollar (☏268/462-0362), Hertz (☏268/462-4114), Oakland (☏268/462-3021), Steads (☏268/462-9970) and Thrifty

(☏268/462-9532). Bear in mind that driving on Antigua and Barbuda is on the left.

By taxi

If you just want to make the odd excursion or short trip, it can be cheaper to hire **taxis**, identifiable by the H on their number plates and easy to find in St John's, Nelson's Dockyard or at the airport. Elsewhere you'll often need to call or ask your hotel to arrange one. Try West Bus Station Taxis (☏268/462-5190) or Antigua Reliable (☏268/460-5353). Fares are regulated but there are no meters, so be sure to agree on a price before you get into the car.

By bike and motorcycle

Since Antigua is so small, and there are few steep inclines, it is ideal cycling territory, and **bikes** can be rented for around US$15 per day, US$70 a week. Hiring a scooter or **motorcycle** is just as much fun – prices normally start at around US$30 per day, US$150 a week (plus US$20 for the local driving permit) – and can be a fantastic way of touring around, though you'll need to watch out for madcap drivers on the main roads. Rental agents for both bikes and motorcycles include Cycle Krazy, on St Mary's St in St John's (☏268/462-9253), and Paradise Boat Sales at Jolly Harbour (☏268/460-7125).

Tours

If you don't fancy driving, there are a few local companies who offer islandwide **sightseeing tours**, either to a set itinerary or customized to your needs. Remember to check whether the price includes entrance fees to the various attractions. If you can't get a good price from any of the companies below, check the taxi operators listed above about guided taxi tours.

Tropikelly Trails (☏268/461-0383, ⓦwww.tropikellytrails.com) offer five- to six-hour tours from US$65, including a picnic lunch, with trips to Great George Fort, Boggy Peak and a pineapple farm, or a half-day tour for US$35. Estate Safari Jeep Tours (☏268/463-4713) organizes similar tours that include Betty's Hope sugar plantation, Great George Fort and lunch on the beach, while Antours

(☎268/462-4788) and Bo Tours (☎268/462-6632) also take in the island's main sights, including English Harbour and Betty's Hope, at a similar cost.

Accommodation

While most visitors stay on **Antigua's north-west coast**, there are a handful of good places on the much more isolated east coast and around Falmouth and English Harbour (where the beaches are less impressive), and a wider range of options on the west coast. Accommodations on the quiet and undeveloped island of **Barbuda** range from the rustic to the luxurious, but all of them, whatever the price bracket, offer decent value. Always call ahead to book, and remember to bring mosquito repellent.

During the low season, rates can fall by as much as forty percent (though this is rare at the cheapest places), and proprietors are far more amenable to bargaining. Many of the all-inclusive hotels have a minimum-stay requirement, though this varies from place to place. Keep in mind that every place adds **government tax** of 8.5 percent to the bill and almost all add a **service charge** of 10 percent. Some places include those extras in the quoted price; always ask. All places listed are on the beach unless mentioned otherwise.

Food and drink

There are plenty of good **eating** options on Antigua and, though prices are generally on the high side, there's usually something to suit most budgets. Most hotel and restaurant menus aimed at tourists tend to offer familiar variations on Euro-American-style food, shunning local specialities – a real shame, as the latter are invariably excellent and well worth trying if you get the chance.

Antiguan specialities include the fabulous ducana (a solid hunk of grated sweet potato mixed with coconut and spices and steamed in a banana leaf), pepperpot stew with salt beef, pumpkin and okra, often served with a cornmeal pudding known as *fungi*, various types of curry, salted codfish and souse – cuts of pork marinated in lime juice, onions, hot and sweet peppers and spices.

There are few **bars** aimed specifically at drinkers; even though the island offers a good local beer in Wadadli and fine West Indian rums, most drinking is done at restaurants or hotel bars.

During the winter season (Dec–April) it's best to make **reservations** at many of the places recommended – and, if you've got your heart set on a special place, arrange it a couple of days in advance if you can. As for **prices**, some restaurants quote their prices in EC$, others in US$, and some in both. We've followed each restaurant's practice, using whichever currency a particular place quotes. As with accommodation, **government tax** of 8.5 percent is always added to the bill and, particularly at the pricier places, a 10 percent **service charge** is also automatic. As such, **tipping** is at your discretion.

On **Barbuda**, restaurants are low-key places with quiet trade. If you're coming on a day-trip package your meal will normally be arranged for you, but if you're making your own arrangements give as much advance notice as you can so that they can get the ingredients in.

Post, phones and the Internet

Post offices are located in English Harbour (Mon–Fri 8.30am–4pm), in St John's on Long St (Mon–Fri 8.15am–4pm) and in Woods Centre (Mon–Thurs 8.30am–4pm, Fri 8.30am–5pm).

Most hotels provide a **telephone** in each room and local calls are normally inexpensive. You'll also see phone booths all over the island, and these can be used for local and international calls. Most of the booths take phonecards only, available at hotels, post offices and some shops and supermarkets.

The **country code** for Antigua is ☎268. For fire, ambulance or police emergencies, dial ☎911 or 999.

There are a handful of **Internet cafés**,

Festivals and events

January
Official start of West Indian cricket season ☏268/462-9090, ⊛www.windiescricket.com.

February
Valentine's Day Regatta, Jolly Harbour ☏268/461-6324.

March–April
Test cricket ☏268/462-9090, ⊛www.windiescricket.com.

April
Classic Regatta ☏268/460-1799, ⊛www.antiguaclassics.com.
Sailing Week ☏268/460-8872, ⊛www.sailingweek.com.

May
Pro-Am Tennis Classic, Curtain Bluff Hotel ☏268/462-8400, ⊛www.curtainbluff.com.

July/August
Carnival ☏268/462-4707, ⊛www.antiguacarnival.com.

September
Bridge Championship ☏268/462-1459.

October
National Warri Championship ☏268/462-6317.

November
Antiguan Craft Fair, Harmony Hall ☏268/460-4120, ⊛www.harmonyhall.com.

---

mostly in St John's. The best rate is at Comnett, 14 Redcliff St, where it's US$3 for 15 minutes.

Public holidays and festivals

The main events in Antigua are the summertime **Carnival** and the April **Sailing Week**, but there are other events to distract you from the beach, including international cricket and windsurfing tournaments and a jazz festival. The tourist boards have full details of all activities.

As well as the public holidays listed on p.60, Antigua celebrates **Caricom Day** in early July, **Carnival** on the first Monday and Tuesday of August, **Independence Day** on November 1 and **United Nations Day** in October. See also the box above.

Outdoor activities

Antigua and, to a lesser extent, Barbuda – facilities are less built up on the smaller island – are both great for **outdoor activities**. There's something for everyone on these two islands, from more-active diving and snorkelling to laid-back boat tours and cruises.

Watersports

Diving is excellent on the coral reefs around Antigua and Barbuda, with most of the good sites – places like Sunken Rock and Cape Shirley – on the south side of the larger island and many of them very close to shore, rarely more than a fifteen-minute boat ride away. Expect to see a wealth of fabulously colourful reef fish, including parrot fish, angelfish, wrasse and barracuda, as well as the occasional harmless nurse shark and, if you're lucky, dolphins and turtles. The reefs for the most part are still in pristine, unspoiled condition, and, though there is no wall diving and most dives are fairly shallow, there are some good cliffs and canyons, and a handful of wrecks.

Antigua has plenty of reputable **dive operators** scattered conveniently around the island, so you should always be able to find a boat going out from near where you're staying. Rates are pretty uniform: reckon on around US$50–60 for a single-tank dive, US$70–80 for a two-tank dive and US$60–70 for a night dive. **Beginners** can get a feel for diving by taking a half-day resort course for around US$90–100. Full open-water certification ranges from US$300 to US$500. Call around for the best deal.

Serious divers should consider a **package deal**, either involving a simple package with three or five two-tank dives (roughly US$180–200 and US$265–300, respectively) or a deal that includes accommodation and diving. Prices for these can be pretty good value, particularly outside the winter season, and it's worth contacting the dive operators direct to find out the latest offers.

Barbuda's diving is at least as good as Antigua's, with countless wrecks dotted around the nearby reefs, but, sadly, there is no established dive outfit on the island.

Snorkelling around the islands is excellent, too, and several of the dive operators take snorkellers on their dive trips, mooring near some good, relatively shallow coralheads. Reckon on around US$15–20 for an outing, including equipment.

Dive operators

Deep Bay Divers Redcliffe Quay, St John's ☏ 268/463-8000, ⊕ www.deepbaydivers.com. New outfit with a 34ft dive boat offering trips, among others, down to Cades Reef in the southwest (a 50min ride) and straight out to Sandy Island (15min away). Snorkellers welcome if there's room.
Dive Antigua *Rex Halcyon Cove Hotel*, Dickenson Bay ☏ 268/462-3483, ⊕ www.diveantigua.com. The longest-established and best-known dive operation on the island, based on the northwest coast, though prices are normally a little higher than most of the others. They offer a glass-bottom boat to take snorkellers out to the reef.
Dockyard Divers Nelson's Dockyard ☏ 268/460-1178, ⓕ 460-1179. Decent-sized dive shop (and the only outfit in the English Harbour area offering snorkelling tours) that lays on diving trips around

the south and west coasts.
Jolly Dive Jolly Harbour Marina ☏ 268/462-8305, ⊕ www.jollydive.com. Second-oldest dive shop in Antigua and very popular with guests at the big, local hotels; look elsewhere if you want to go out in a small group.

Boat tours

There is no shortage of **boat** and **catamaran trips** to be made around Antigua, with the emphasis – not, it must be said, everyone's cup of tea – normally on being part of a big crowd all having a fun time together. Most of the cruises charge a single price, including a meal and all the drinks you want, and the two main cruise companies, Kokomo and Wadadli Cats, offer virtually identical trips, travelling on large and comfortable catamarans. A more interesting and unusual eco-tour is offered by Adventure Antigua.

The most popular **cruise** sails right round Antigua, taking in some snorkelling and lunch at Green Island off the east coast. There is also a superb snorkelling trip to Cades Reef on the south coast, stopping off for lunch on one of the west coast beaches, and another to uninhabited Great Bird Island – where there's plenty of birdlife – off the northeast. Finally, there's a "triple destination" cruise on Sundays to English Harbour via Green Island, ending with a taxi ride up to the steelband party on Shirley Heights and another taxi home.

Each of the trips is offered by Kokomo and Wadadli, and both will pick up passengers from a number of locations on the west coast. All are out from around 9am until 4pm, apart from the triple-destination tour (roughly 10am–sunset). The circumnavigation cruise costs US$75 per person, Cades Reef US$60 and the triple-destination cruise US$90, all prices including snorkelling gear, a buffet lunch and an open bar. Children under 12 are half-price.

Boat operators

Adventure Antigua ☏ 268/727-3261 or 560-4672, ⊕ www.adventureantigua.com. Owner Eli Fuller takes passengers by motorboat on a seven-hour eco-tour of the northeast coast of the island, showing where the endangered hawksbill turtles lay their eggs, and through the mangrove swamps to spot rays, frigate birds, osprey and turtles. There are several snorkelling opportunities, and lunch is served on a deserted beach. Cost is US$90 per person, and the trip goes out between two and five times a week, depending on demand.

Jolly Roger Pirate Cruises ☎ 268/462-2064, ⓦ www.jollyrogercruises.com. Hearty party cruises, with rope-swinging and walking the plank for would-be pirates and limbo competitions and calypso dance classes for the rest. Around US$50 per person.

Kokomo Cats ☎ 268/462-7245, ⓦ www. kokomocat.com. Round-the-island trips (Tues, Thurs & Sat), Cades Reef (Fri), Great Bird Island (Wed) and a triple-destination cruise (Sun) on

fast and comfortable catamarans. Kokomo also offers sunset cruises (Tues, Thurs & Sat) from Jolly Harbour on the west coast, out from 6.30pm to 9pm (US$40).

"Paddles" Kayak & Snorkel Club ☎ 268/463-1944, ⓦ www.antiguapaddles.com. Based in the village of Seatons on the northeast coast, this outfit offers half-day eco-tours of mangroves, reefs and the local coast via motorboat, kayak, snorkelling and a nature walk.

Wadadli Cats ☎ 268/462-4792, ⓦ www. wadadlicats.com. Offers circumnavigation cruises (Thurs & Sat; US$85), a sunset cruise (Sat; US$40), and a triple-destination cruise (Sun; US$100).

History

Antigua's **first people** were the nomadic Ciboney, originally from present-day Venezuela, whose earliest traces on the island date from around 3100 BC. By the early years of the first millenium AD the Ciboney had been replaced by Arawak-speaking **Amerindians** from the same region.

The first European sighting of Antigua came in 1493 when **Columbus** sailed close by, naming the island Santa Maria la Antigua. The island remained uninhabited for over a century until, in 1624, the first **British settlement** in the West Indies was established on the island of St Kitts, and the British laid claim to nearby Antigua and Barbuda. Within a decade, settlers at Falmouth on the south coast had experimented with a number of crops before settling on **sugar**, which was to guarantee the island its future wealth. For the next two hundred years, sugar remained the country's dominant industry, bringing enormous wealth to the **planters**.

Unlike most of Britain's West Indian colonies, Antigua remained British throughout the colonial era. This was due, in large part, to the massive fortifications built around it, the major ones at places like Shirley Heights on the south coast.

As the centuries passed, conditions for the **slaves** who worked the plantations improved very slowly. Even after the abolition of slavery in 1834, many

were obliged to continue to labour at the sugar estates, for wages that were insufficient to provide even the miserly levels of food, housing and care formerly offered under slavery.

Gradually, though, **free villages** began to emerge at places like Liberta, Jennings and Bendals, often based around Moravian or Methodist churches or on land reluctantly sold by the planters to a group of former slaves. Slowly a few Antiguans scratched together sufficient money to set up their own businesses – shops, taverns and tiny cottage industries. An embryonic black middle class was in the making. Nonetheless, economic progress on the island was extremely slow. By World War II, life for the vast majority of Antiguans was still extremely tough, with widespread poverty across the island.

After the war, Antigua continued to be administered by Britain, but gradually the island's politicians were given authority for the running of their country. Slowly, the national economy began to take strides forward, assisted by the development of **tourism**. By the elections of 1980 all parties considered that, politically and economically, the country was sufficiently mature for full independence and the flag of an **independent Antigua and Barbuda** was finally raised in November 1981. Since then, politics has been completely dominated by the political dynasty of the Bird family – father V.C and son Lester – but recent allegations of corruption took their toll and a new government of Baldwin Spencer's United Progressive Party was swept into power in elections in March 2004.

14.1

St John's and around

With a population of around 30,000 – nearly half the island's total – bustling **ST JOHN'S** is Antigua's capital and only city. No one could accuse it of being the prettiest city in the West Indies, but it does have a certain immediate charm and, in the centre, there are plenty of attractive old wooden and stone buildings – some of them superbly renovated, others in a perilous state of near-collapse – among the less appealing modern development. It'll only take you a couple of hours to see everything, but you'll probably want to come back for at least one evening to take advantage of some excellent **restaurants** and **bars**.

Arrival, getting around and accommodation

Flights touch down at **V.C. Bird International Airport** on the northeast coast. There is no bus service to and from the airport, though you will find numerous **car rental outlets**, as well as **taxis**: from the airport, expect to pay US$8 to St John's, US$7 to Dickenson Bay or Runaway Bay and US$25 to English Harbour. Renting a taxi for a day's sightseeing comes to around US$70.

There's little reason **to stay** in St John's as it's a fair distance from a decent beach, but if you need to spend the night here, *Joe Mike's Hotel* on Nevis Street (☎268/462-1142, ℱ462-6056; ❸) is a friendly place with just a dozen rooms, right in the centre of town.

The City

As all of the main places of interest in St John's are close together, the easiest way to see the place is **on foot**. You should certainly make your way to **Redcliffe Quay** – where the waterfront and its colonial buildings have been attractively restored – as well as the tiny **National Museum**, which offers a well-presented rundown on the country's history and culture. If you've got time, take a stroll through some of the city's old streets, and check out the twin-towered **cathedral** perched on top of Newgate Street. Redcliffe Quay and nearby **Heritage Quay** are the best places to eat, drink and shop for souvenirs, though you'll probably want to avoid them if the cruise ships are in, when the steel drums come out to play *Hot, Hot, Hot* and the area almost disappears beneath a scrum of duty-free shoppers.

Around Redcliffe Quay

Spread over several acres by the waterside, **Redcliffe Quay** is probably the best place to start your tour of the city. Named in honour of the church of St Mary Redcliffe in the English port city of Bristol, this is one of the oldest parts of St John's, and incorporates many old warehouses – now attractively restored as small boutiques, restaurants and bars – and a wooden boardwalk that runs alongside the water. There's not a huge amount to see, but it's a pleasant place to wander and soak up some of the city's history.

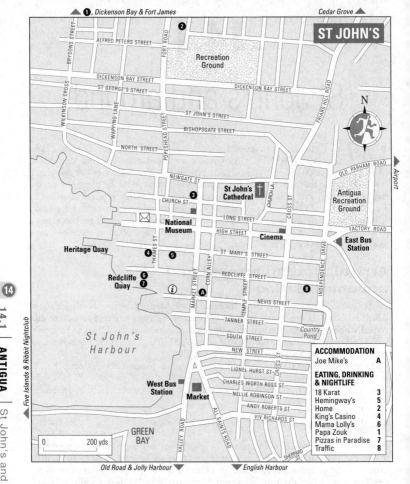

ST JOHN'S

BRYSONS STREET

ALFRED PETERS STREET

FORT ROAD

❷

Recreation Ground

DICKENSON BAY STREET

ST GEORGE'S STREET

WILKINSON CROSS

WAPPING LANE

POPESHEAD STREET

DICKENSON BAY STREET

ST JOHN'S STREET

BISHOPSGATE STREET

NORTH STREET

FRIARS HILL ROAD

N

OLD PARHAM ROAD

▶ Airport

NEWGATE ST

CHURCH ST

❸

St John's Cathedral

CHURCH LA.

CROSS ST

Antigua Recreation Ground

LONG STREET

National Museum

HIGH STREET

ST MARY'S STREET

Cinema

FACTORY ROAD

East Bus Station

Heritage Quay

❹ THAMES STREET ❺

MARKET STREET

CORN ALLEY

REDCLIFFE STREET

TEMPLE STREET

INDEPENDENCE DRIVE

Redcliffe Quay

❻
❼

(i)

Ⓐ

NEVIS STREET

❽

TANNER STREET

St John's Harbour

SOUTH STREET

Country Pond

NEW STREET

LIONEL HURST ST

CROSS ST

West Bus Station

Market

CHARLES WORTH ROSS ST

NELLIE ROBINSON ST

ANDY ROBERTS ST

VIV RICHARDS ST

ACCOMMODATION
Joe Mike's   **A**

EATING, DRINKING & NIGHTLIFE
18 Karat   **3**
Hemingway's   **5**
Home   **2**
King's Casino   **4**
Mama Lolly's   **6**
Papa Zouk   **1**
Pizzas in Paradise **7**
Traffic   **8**

GREEN BAY

VALLEY ROAD

ALL SAINTS ROAD

SHEPPARD ST

0   200 yds

14 | 14.1 | **ANTIGUA** | St John's and around

Many of the waterfront warehouses once housed supplies – barrels of sugar and rum, lumber for ship repairs, cotton and sheepskins – for the British navy and local merchant ships that traded between Antigua and the mother country during the eighteenth century. Behind the quay around the western end of Nevis Street there once stood a number of *barracoons*, compounds where slaves were held upon their arrival in the island, before they were sent to the plantations or shipped to other Caribbean islands.

Back at the front of the quay, a short stroll north takes you up to **Heritage Quay** at the foot of High Street. This modern concrete quay is given over to cruise ship arrivals and dozens of duty-free shops designed to catch their tourist dollars, along with a few roadside stalls where local vendors flog T-shirts and distinctive Haitian art. Take a quick look at the **cenotaph**, which is a memorial to Antiguans who died during World War I, a **monument to V.C. Bird**, first prime minister of the independent country, and the **Westerby Memorial**, which commemorates a Moravian missionary who dedicated his life to helping Antiguans in the decades after emancipation from slavery in 1834. Also worthy of note is the Island Arts Gallery (Mon–Sat 10am–6pm, free), which is crammed with interesting and exuberant paintings and prints, some by the British owner Nick Maley, who was a make-up artist on movies such as *Star Wars*.

Long Street and around

From the water, Long Street runs east as far as the **Antigua Recreation Ground**, the country's main cricket venue and home to most of the action during the ten-day Carnival each July and August (see box overleaf). Many of St John's finest old buildings line this street, including a couple of fabulously colourful liquor stores, still in operation more than a century after first opening.

The National Museum

Housed in a 1747 Neoclassical courthouse on the corner of Long and Market streets, the **National Museum of Antigua and Barbuda** (Mon–Fri 8.30am–4pm, Sat 10am–2pm; free) occupies just one large room, but given the almost palpable enthusiasm with which the collection has been assembled and displayed, it's indisputably worth thirty minutes of your time while you're exploring the capital. The exhibits start by showing off the islands' early geological history, backed up by fossils and coral skeletons, and move on to more extensive coverage of its first, Amerindian inhabitants. Jewellery, primitive tools, pottery shards and religious figures used by these early settlers are well laid out and explained.

Continuing chronologically, the museum touches on Columbus, the European invasion and sugar production – the country's *raison d'etre* from the mid-seventeenth century. Among the highlights are an interesting 1750 map of Antigua showing the plantations, as well as all the reefs that threatened shipping around the island, and an intriguing exhibit on the emancipation of the slaves.

St John's Cathedral

A few blocks east of the museum, on Church Lane between Long and Newgate streets, the imposing twin towers of the **Cathedral Church of St John the Divine** (daily 9am–5pm; free) are the capital's dominant landmark. A simple wooden church was first built on this hilltop site in 1681 and, after heavy destruction was wrought by a number of earthquakes and hurricanes, the present cathedral was put up in 1847.

From the outside, the grey-stone Baroque building is not particularly prepossessing – squat and bulky with the two towers capped by slightly awkward cupolas. More attractively, the airy interior of the cathedral is almost entirely encased in dark pine, designed to hold the building together in the event of earthquake or hurricane, and the walls are dotted with marble tablets commemorating distinguished figures from the island's history, some of them rescued from the wreckage of earlier churches here and incorporated into the new cathedral. In the grounds of the cathedral, the whitewashed and equally Baroque **lead figures** on the south gate – taken from a French ship near Martinique in the 1750s during the Seven Years' War between France and Britain – represent St John the Baptist and St John the Divine, draped in flowing robes.

Fort Bay

A short drive or taxi ride from town, heading north from St John's on Fort Road, a left turn at the old pink *Barrymore Hotel* (just north of the Texaco station) takes you out to the capital city's most popular beach and some of the best-preserved **military ruins** on the island. The road winds its way around to the coast at **Fort Bay**, where a long, wide strand of grainy white sand – packed with city-dwellers at weekends and holidays – offers the nearest quality beach to town. At its northern end, you can hire beach chairs from *Millers* (see p.593), and there's a vendors' mall nearby if you want to hunt for souvenirs.

At the other end of the strip, half a kilometre further on, a host of food and drink stalls open up at busy times, when a crowd descends from town, transforming the

Carnival

The highlight of Antigua's entertainment calendar is its **Carnival**, a colourful, exuberant party held for ten days, from late July until the first Tuesday in August. Warm-ups start in early July, with steel bands, calypsonians and DJs in action across the island, and Carnival proper gets cracking with the opening of Carnival City at the Antigua Recreation Ground in St John's. This is where all of the scheduled events take place – though you'll often find spontaneous outbreaks of partying across the city – and a festival village is set up nearby to provide space for the masses of food and drink vendors who emerge each year seemingly out of nowhere.

The major Carnival events take place over the last weekend, during which you'll have to forgo sleep for a few days of frantic action. The **Panorama** steel-band contest (Friday night) and the Calypso Monarch competition (Sunday night) are both packed and definitely worth catching, while on the Monday morning – the day on which the islands celebrate slave emancipation in 1834 – **Jouvert** (pronounced "jouvay", and meaning daybreak) is a huge jump-up party starting at 4am. The Judging of the Troupes and Groups competition in the afternoon sees ranks of brightly costumed marching bands and floats parading through the city streets, being judged for colour, sound and general party attitude.

Tuesday has a final costumed parade through the streets, finishing with the announcement of all of the winners and a roughly 6pm–midnight last lap from Carnival City – "the bacchanal" – as the exhausted partygoers stream through St John's, led by the steel bands. All in all, it's a great event – certainly one of the Caribbean's best summer carnivals – and a great chance to catch the Antiguans in a nonstop party mood.

place into a lively outdoor venue. If you want to swim, there's a protected, marked area at the top of the beach; elsewhere, the water is normally fine but you'll need to watch out for occasional undercurrents.

Fort James

At the far end of Fort Bay stands eighteenth-century **Fort James** (always open; free), built above the cliffs that overlook the entrance to St John's Harbour. You can walk or drive around to the south side of the fort, where the main gate is still in place. Together with St John's Fort on Rat Island – still visible down the channel – and Fort Barrington, on the opposite side of the channel (see p.602), this fort was designed to deter ships from attacking the capital, which had been sacked by French raiders in 1668. Earthworks were first raised in the 1680s, but the bulk of the fort was put up in 1739, when the long enclosing wall was added.

Today, Fort James is pretty dilapidated but offers plenty of atmosphere: unkempt, often windswept and providing great views across the channel and back down to St John's Harbour. Rusting British cannons from the early 1800s point out to sea and down the channel, their threat long gone but still a dramatic symbol of their era. Elsewhere, the old powder magazine is still intact, though leaning precariously, and the stone buildings on the fort's upper level – the oldest part of the structure, dating from 1705 – include the master gunner's house, the canteen and the barracks.

Eating and drinking

St John's is well served for **restaurants**, with several good longstanding places down near the quay and a couple of top-notch options just north of town in the Gambles.

Big Banana - Pizzas in Paradise Redcliffe Quay ☎ 268/480-6985. Pub-like restaurant, popular with tourists for lunch and dinner, serving reasonable-quality food inside or outdoors under the trees at decent prices – pizzas, salads and baked potatoes as well as more typical Antiguan fish and chicken meals at EC$15–35. Closed Sun.

George Market and Redcliffe streets ☎ 268 562-4866. Right in the heart of the city, this lively restaurant serves top-notch West Indian food on a large, airy upstairs gallery decked out in bright colours. The regular menu includes fire-roasted jerk shrimp and "chicken on a wire" (EC$35), while the weekend adds a number of Antiguan specialities, including goat water (a sort of soup) and souse (EC$30–50).

Hemingway's St Mary's Street ☎ 268/462-2763. Atmospheric, early nineteenth-century green-and-white wooden building with a balcony overlooking the street and Heritage Quay. Can be overwhelmingly crowded when the cruise ships are in; at other times it's a great place to be, serving a range of excellent food from sandwiches and burgers to fish and steak dinners, with prices for a main course between EC$25 and EC$50. Closed Sun.

Home Restaurant Gambles Terrace, just north of town ☎ 268/461-7651. Attractive restaurant in a converted home, a little way from the centre of town, serving great, adventurous West Indian food. Look for starters like fish cakes or lobster cakes (EC$26–34), main courses of fillet of snapper stuffed with shrimps with lobster sauce (EC$65) or blackened jackfish in chilli garlic sauce (EC$55). Mon–Fri dinner only; lunch and dinner on Sat; closed Sun.

Mama Lolly's Vegetarian Cafe Redcliffe Quay ☎ 268/562-1552. Small, friendly café serving fresh-pressed juices and smoothies for EC$10–15. Also has a good vegetarian lunch menu, including lasagne, roti and red bean stew, costing no more than EC$23 for a large portion with salads. Daily 8.30am–4.30pm.

Papa Zouk Hilda Davis Drive, Gambles ☎ 268/464 6044. Imaginative Antiguan food served on a tiny patio festooned with flowers. The menu is small but interesting, with local produce thrown into dishes like creole bouillabaisse or a seafood medley (EC$35–65). Dinner only, closed Sun.

Entertainment and nightlife

18 Karat Church Street ☎ 268/562-1858. Mainly frequented by young Antiguans, this clubbing hotspot plays a wide variety of Caribbean and international music. Thurs–Sun 10pm–late. Cover EC$10.

King's Casino Heritage Quay ☎ 268/462-1727. The city's main casino, packed with slot machines and offering blackjack, roulette and Caribbean stud poker tables for the more serious players. Live bands and karaoke give the place a bit of atmosphere after 10pm. The casino will normally lay on one-way shuttle services to St John's for those coming to gamble for the night. It'll pick you up anywhere on the island, but you'll have to get a taxi back. Mon–Sat 10am–4am, Sun 6pm–4am.

Millers by the Sea Fort James ☎ 268/462-9414. One of the best venues on the island, this large and often lively restaurant and bar has live music every night varying from local jazz and soca bands to guitarists and karaoke. Look out, too, for special events here on the big outdoor sets, which normally charge a cover between EC$30 and EC$50.

Traffic Independence Avenue and Redcliffe Street ☎ 268/562-2949. A popular new nightclub, which often features live jazz or blues; call ahead for info on bands.

Listings

All services listed are in **St John's** unless otherwise stated.

Airlines American Airlines (☎ 268/462-0950); British Airways (☎ 268/462-0876); BWIA (☎ 268/480-2942); Carib Aviation (☎ 268/462-3147); Caribbean Star (☎ 268/480-2591), LIAT (☎ 268/480-5600); and Virgin (☎ 268/560-2079).

American Express Corner of Long and Thames streets (Mon–Thurs 8.30am–4.30pm, Fri 8.30am–5pm; ☎ 268/462-4788).

Bookshops First Edition, Woods Centre (Mon–Sat 9am–9pm). Excellent place, with the best range of books – including fiction and local interest – in Antigua.

Embassies British High Commission, 11 Old Parham Rd (☎ 268/462-0008); US Consular Agent, Pigeon Point, English Harbour (☎ 268/463-6531).

Film Island Photo, Redcliffe and Market streets, sells film and does one-hour photo development; Benjie's, Heritage Quay, offers the same service and has various camera accessories at duty-free prices.

Pharmacies Full-service pharmacies in St John's: Benjies, Redcliffe and Market streets (Mon–Wed 8.30am–5pm, Thurs & Sat 8.30am–4pm, Fri 8.30am–5.30pm; ☎ 268/462-0733); and Woods, Woods Centre (Mon–Sat 9am–10pm, Sun 11am–6pm; ☎ 268/462-9287).

Police The main police station is on Newgate Street ☎ 268/462-0045. Emergency ☎ 268/462-0125 or ☎ 999 or 911.

14.2

From Runaway Bay
to Half Moon Bay

North of St John's, **Runaway Bay** and adjoining **Dickenson Bay** constitute the island's main tourist strip, with a couple of excellent beaches, a host of good hotels and restaurants, the chance to swim with dolphins, and plenty of action. Continuing clockwise around the island brings you to its Atlantic side, where the jagged coastline offers plenty of inlets, bays and swamps but, with a couple of noteworthy exceptions, rather less impressive beaches. Tourist facilities on this side of the island are much less developed, but there are several places of interest. **Betty's Hope** is a restored sugar plantation; **Devil's Bridge** offers one of the most dramatic landscapes on the island; at the delightful **Harmony Hall** you can relax from your exertions with an excellent lunch and a boat ride to Green Island; and at picturesque **Half Moon Bay** you can scramble along a vertiginous clifftop path above the pounding Atlantic.

Accommodation

Antigua's **northwest coast** is the most popular destination for visitors, with a series of large and small hotels dotted along the lovely beaches, and plenty of restaurants, watersports and beach life. The east coast is less visited, but there are two very good hotels there (and an excellent beach bar).

Dickenson Bay Cottages Dickenson Bay ☎268/462-4940, ⓦwww.dickensonbaycottages.com. Thirteen spacious, airy and attractively furnished cottages strewn around a well-landscaped garden and medium-sized pool, up on a hillside overlooking the bay. Just a short walk from the beach and from the much busier *Rex Halcyon Cove*, where *Dickenson Bay* guests have subsidized use of the facilities, including tennis courts and sun loungers. ➐

Harmony Hall Brown's Bay ☎268/460-4120, ⓦwww.harmonyhall.com. A delightfully classy but laid-back place in the middle of nowhere. The six simple but stylish rooms have large bathrooms, comfortable beds and small patios. The beach isn't up to much, but a small free boat regularly ferries guests out to the clean, white sand at Green Island (see p.596). The splendid restaurant is normally busy; when it's closed (as it is most evenings) the hotel lays on separate food for guests. Nov to mid-May only. ➏

Long Bay Hotel Long Bay ☎268/463-2005, ⓦwww.longbay-antigua.com. Small, friendly

and secluded all-inclusive choice located by a tiny turquoise bay, with twenty cosy rooms and cottages. Guests enjoy use of a few sailboats and windsurfers, plus there's a good tennis court, a big library and a game room. The chef is excellent and the bartender makes the best rum punch on the island. Closed September and October. Rates include breakfast and dinner. ➑

Rex Halcyon Cove Dickenson Bay ☎268/462-0256, ⓦwww.rexcaribbean.com. Sprawling low-rise resort, rather faded but with good-sized rooms, a decent pool and tennis courts, as well as a pleasant restaurant on the Warri pier. ➍–➏

Sandals Antigua Dickenson Bay ☎268/462-0267, ⓦwww.sandals.com. Part of the popular, all-inclusive Caribbean chain, this resort has 189 luxury rooms cleverly spread throughout the resort to reduce the sense of being part of a crowd. Four restaurants offer excellent Italian, Japanese, southern US and international food, and all watersports are included in the daily rate. Only couples (heterosexual) are allowed. ➒

Sunsail Club Colonna Hodges Bay ☎268/462-

6263, ⓦ www.sunsail.com. Attractive north-coast resort, Mediterranean in design, well-landscaped and with the most spectacular pool on the island. The beach is pretty ordinary, but most guests are on all-inclusive packages that include windsurfing and/or sailing. Very child-friendly, with kids' clubs for all ages. ❽

Sunset Cove Resort Runaway Bay ⓣ 268/462-3762, ⓕ 462-2684. This hotel has lost its beach entirely in heavy sea swells, and you have to walk five minutes around the headland to swim comfortably. That aside, it's a very pleasant place and great value. There's a small freshwater pool, and the rooms are sizeable and all have kitchen facilities and cable TV. Standard room ❹, one-bedroom villas (four to six people) ❻

Trade Winds Hotel Dickenson Bay ⓣ 268/462-1223, ⓦ www.antiguatradewindshotel.com. Lovely place in the hills above the bay, with big, comfortable a/c rooms. Guests can chill out by the lagoon pool on a wide verandah overlooking the ocean or take the regular shuttle down to the beach, a kilometre away. The hotel's restaurant (see overleaf) has good-quality food and great views. ❺–❼

Runaway Bay and Dickenson Bay

A few miles north of St John's, a series of attractive white-sand beaches runs around the island's northwest coast. Most of the tourist development is concentrated along Runaway Bay and Dickenson Bay, where the gleaming beaches slope gently down into the turquoise sea, offering calm swimming and, at the northern end of Dickenson Bay, a host of watersports. **Runaway Bay** is the quieter of the two and, because there are fewer hotels to tidy up their "patch", is strewn with more seaweed and rocks. It's still a great place to wander in the gentle surf, despite the northern end's erosion by heavy swells.

At the northern end of the Bay, **Dolphin Fantaseas** (ⓣ 268/562-7946; ⓦ www. dolphinfantaseas.com; US$140 per half-hour session) lets you swim with three dolphins in a man-made lagoon. It's not cheap, but the experience gets rave reviews from visitors. Others are less enthusiastic, concerned about the impact of captivity on the dolphins, although there is an active local education programme on marine life and conservation. There is also a mini-zoo, with parrots, tortoises and stingrays.

Trapped between two imposing sandstone bluffs not far to the north, **Dickenson Bay** is fringed by another wide, white-sand beach, which stretches for almost a mile between Corbison Point and the more thickly vegetated woodland of Weatherill's Hill at its northern end. It's a lovely bay, shelving gently into the sea and with a protected swimming zone dividing swimmers from the jet skiers, windsurfers, water-skiers and parasailers offshore. The northern half of the beach fronts some of Antigua's largest hotels, thus the area can get pretty busy, with a string of bars, hair braiders and T-shirt sellers doing a brisk trade, but it's still an easy-going place, with minimal hassle.

Betty's Hope to Long Bay

Heading southeast, the partly restored **Betty's Hope** (Tues–Sat 10am–4pm; EC$5) is the island's very first sugar estate. Built in 1650, the place was owned by the Codrington family for nearly two centuries until the end of World War II; by that time its lack of profitability had brought it to the edge of closure, which followed soon after. Although most of the estate still lies in ruins, one of the windmills has been restored to working condition, and a small and interesting museum at the visitor centre traces the history of sugar on Antigua as well as the development and restoration of the estate.

North of Betty's Hope, the village of Seatons is the starting point for two very enjoyable, informative and well-organized **eco-tour** attractions. The first, offered by Stingray City Antigua (ⓣ 268/562-7297, ⓦ www.stingraycityantigua.com), allows you to swim with stingrays in their "natural" environment, a large penned area of ocean not far offshore (US$50 per person, US$35 for children). The second, offered by "Paddles" Kayak and Snorkel Club (ⓣ 268/463-1944, ⓦ www.antiguapaddles. com) is a half-day kayak tour of the nearby islands, inlets and mangroves, with an option to hike to sunken caves and snorkel in the North South Marine Park (US$50, US$35 for children under 12).

East of Betty's Hope and approaching Long Bay, a track signposted off to the right takes you out for half a mile to **Devil's Bridge**, on a rocky outcrop edged by patches of grassy land, tall century plants and sunbathing cattle. Wander round the promontory to the "bridge", a narrow piece of rock whose underside has been washed away by thousands of years of relentless surf action. The hot, windswept spot offers some of the most fetching views on the island, back across a quiet cove and out over the lashing ocean and dark reefs to a series of small islands just offshore. En route back to the main road, a dirt track on your right after 30 yards leads down to a tiny but gorgeous bay – the perfect place for a picnic.

Past the turn-off for Devil's Bridge, at the end of the main road, **Long Bay** is home to a couple of rather exclusive all-inclusives, which doesn't stop you from getting access to a great, wide bay, enormously popular with local schoolkids, who are often splashing around or playing cricket at one end of the beach. The lengthy spread of white sand is protected by an extensive reef a few hundred yards offshore (bring your snorkelling gear) and there's a great little beach bar for shelter and refreshment.

Harmony Hall to Half Moon Bay

Tucked away on the east coast overlooking Nonsuch Bay, the restored plantation house at **Harmony Hall** (closed May–Oct) is now home to a tiny, chic hotel and one of the island's best restaurants (see below), as well as a free art gallery that showcases monthly exhibitions of local and Caribbean art from November to April.

From the jetty, boats regularly make the five-minute run out to deserted **Green Island**, where the beaches are powdery and the snorkelling excellent. If you're not a guest, there's a small charge for the boat service – ask at the bar of the hotel.

One of the prettiest spots on Antigua, **Half Moon Bay** has a half-mile semicircle of white-sand beach partially enclosing a deep-blue bay, where the Atlantic surf normally offers top-class body-surfing opportunities. Since the closure in 1995 of the hurricane-damaged hotel at the southern end, however, the beach is often pretty empty.

Eating and drinking

With a wide range of hotels scattered about the **north coast**, there is a steady stream of punters looking for good places to eat, and plenty of decent **restaurants** have popped up as a result, though there are few options in the low-budget range. **Dickenson Bay** has the widest choice. In the east, there's a great beach bar handy for those loafing on Long Bay, and one of Antigua's finest at Harmony Hall.

Bay House *Trade Winds Hotel*, Dickenson Bay ☎ 268/462-1223. Smart restaurant overlooking Dickenson Bay, and a romantic place for a drink at sunset followed by top-class food. Tasty and creative starters, plus main courses that might include tuna with breadfruit and pineapple salsa (EC$65) or fillet of beef marinated in soy sauce with Chinese cabbage (EC$70). Daily 7am–11pm.

The Beach Dickenson Bay ☎ 268/480-6940. Brightly painted restaurant on the beach serving good food all day. Lunches include sushi, satay, burgers and salads for EC$35–50; dinner specials might be sesame-crusted tuna, meaty pasta or seafood stew for EC$40–75. Daily 8.30am–midnight.

Beach Bar Long Bay. Completely chilled-out bar serving tasty local cooking for breakfast and lunch. Look out for inexpensive dishes of chicken curry, fish and chips or sandwiches. Daily 9am–5pm.

Coconut Grove *Siboney Beach Club*, Dickenson Bay ☎ 268/462-1538. Great cooking and friendly service combine at this delightful open-air beach-side location. Mouthwatering starters include deep-fried jumbo shrimp in a coconut dip (EC$32.50), while main courses feature dishes like mahi mahi in a mango salsa (EC$62) and rock lobster in creole sauce (EC$80). The coconut cream pie is magnificent. Daily for lunch and dinner.

Harmony Hall Browns Bay ☎ 268/460-4120. Run by a charming Italian couple, this is one of the island's best restaurants, even if it is set nowhere near anywhere else of note. Built around an old sugar mill, the elegant but simple food is served on a terrace overlooking the bay. The menu includes pumpkin soup (EC$20), home-made mozzarella with beetroots (EC$26), lobster tortellini (EC$35) and red snapper in white wine sauce (EC$65). Daily 10am–6pm; Fri & Sat dinner also. Closed May–Nov. **Julian's Alfresco** *Barrymore Beach Club*, Runaway Bay ⊤ 268/562-1545 or 770-3233. One of the top food choices on the island, with an appealing blend of Asian, European and West Indian cooking styles and a lovely open-air location in tropical gardens just yards from the beach. Menu highlights include starters of seafood chowder for EC$16 and "fusion of fish" for EC$34, while mains of Cajun-style mahi mahi and marinated tenderloin of beef cost EC$62 and EC$75 respectively. Tues–Sun for lunch and dinner.

14.3

Falmouth and English Harbour

An essential stop on any visit to Antigua, the picturesque area around **Falmouth** and **English Harbour** on the island's south coast not only holds some of the most important and interesting historical remains in the Caribbean, but is also now the region's leading yachting centre. The chief attraction is the eighteenth-century **Nelson's Dockyard**, which was the key facility for the British navy that once ruled the waves in the area. Today it's a living museum where visiting yachts are still cleaned, supplied and chartered. Nearby are several ruined forts as well as an abundance of attractive colonial buildings on the waterfront, several of which have been converted into hotels and restaurants.

Across the harbour from the dockyard, there is further evidence of the area's colonial past at **Shirley Heights**, where more ruined forts, gun batteries and an old cemetery hold a commanding position over the water.

The area also has a handful of spots off the beaten path that repay a trip, including the massive military complex at **Great Fort George**, high in the hills above **Falmouth**.

A car is invaluable for touring around this area of the south coast. There are frequent **buses** between St John's and English Harbour, handy if you just want to explore Nelson's Dockyard, but to get up to Shirley Heights you'll certainly need your own transport or a taxi.

Accommodation

Plenty of good restaurants and nightlife and the proximity to **Nelson's Dockyard** make this an attractive area in which to stay, though if you're after serious beaches you'll want to look elsewhere on the island.

Admiral's Inn Nelson's Dockyard, English Harbour ⓣ268/460-1027, ⓦwww.admiralsantigua.com. Built in 1788 as the dockyard's supply store and now attractively restored, this is one of the best accommodation options in Antigua, with a great colonial atmosphere, welcoming staff, a romantic setting by the harbour and sensible prices. An occasional free boat ferries guests to a nearby beach. ⑤

Catamaran Hotel Falmouth ⓣ268/460-1036, ⓦwww.catamaran-antigua.com. Friendly little place on the north side of the harbour in Falmouth, adjacent to a small marina. The beach is not great for swimming and it's a bit of a hike to the action at the dockyard, but the rooms are comfortable and good value. ④

The Inn at English Harbour English Harbour ⓣ268/460-1014, ⓦwww.theinn.ag. Attractive old hotel, popular with repeat guests and spread over a large site beside the harbour next to a pleasant white-sand beach. There are 22 rooms in a two-storey building bedecked in bougainvillea. ⑨

Ocean Inn English Harbour ⓣ268/463-7950, ⓦwww.theoceaninn.com. Small, friendly inn perched on a hillside above English Harbour, with six doubles and four cottages. It's some distance from a good beach, but there's a tiny pool and you're just five minutes' walk from Nelson's Dockyard. ④

Falmouth and around

The main road south from St John's, cutting through the very centre of Antigua, first hits the coast at **Falmouth Harbour**. This large and beautiful natural harbour has been used as a safe anchorage since the days of the earliest colonists, and the town that sprang up beside it was the first major settlement on the island. Today, though the harbour is still often busy with yachts, the town of Falmouth itself is a quiet place, most of the activity in the area having moved east to **English Harbour** and Nelson's Dockyard, divided from Falmouth Harbour by a small peninsula known as the **Middle Ground**.

Great Fort George

High above Falmouth, and offering terrific panoramic views over the harbour and surrounding countryside, are the ruins of **Great Fort George** (also known as **Monk's Hill**), one of Antigua's oldest defences, built in the 1690s as a secure retreat for Antigua's tiny population.

These days the fort is in a very dilapidated state, but it's well worth the effort to get there for the fabulous views and a quiet but evocative sense of the island's past. Much of the enormous stone perimeter wall is intact while, inside the main gate and to the right, the west gunpowder magazine (built in 1731) has been well restored.

To get to the fort you'll need to rent a 4WD vehicle; the alternative is a thirty-minute hike. A precipitous but passable track leads up from the village of Cobbs Cross, east of Falmouth; alternatively, from Liberta (north of Falmouth) take the inland road to Table Hill Gordon, from where another track winds up to the fort.

English Harbour and around

The road east from Falmouth leads to the tiny village of Cobb's Cross, where a right turn takes you down to the small village of **ENGLISH HARBOUR**, which today consists of little more than a handful of homes, shops and restaurants. Another right turn leads down to **Nelson's Dockyard**, to the excellent **Pigeon Beach** and to the Middle Ground peninsula. Alternatively, head straight on for the road that climbs up into the hills to the military ruins at **Shirley Heights**.

Nelson's Dockyard

One of Antigua's definite highlights, the eighteenth-century **Nelson's Dockyard** (daily 8am–6pm; EC$13, includes admission to Shirley Heights), is the only surviving Georgian-era dockyard in the world. Adjacent to a fine natural harbour, the place developed primarily as a careening station – where British ships had barnacles scraped from their bottoms and were generally put back into shape. It also provided the military with a local base to repair, water and supply the navy that patrolled the West Indies and protected Britain's prized colonies against enemy incursion.

The dockyard was begun in 1743, with most of the present buildings dating from 1785 and 1792, many built from the ballast of bricks and stones brought to the island by British trading ships, which sailed empty from home en route to loading up with sugar and rum.

During the nineteenth century, however, the advent of steam-powered ships which needed less attention coincided with a decline in British interest in the region, and the dockyard fell into disuse, finally closing in 1889. The 1950s saw a major restoration project, and in 1961 the dockyard was officially reopened as both a working harbour and a tourist attraction.

Entering the dockyard, the first building on your left is the **Admiral's Inn**, built in 1788 and originally used as a store for pitch, lead and turpentine. Today the place houses a hotel and restaurant, and is one of the most atmospheric spots on the south coast. Adjoining the hotel, a dozen thick, capped **stone pillars** – looking like the relics of an ancient Greek temple – are all that is left of a large boathouse, where ships were once pulled in along a narrow channel to have their sails repaired in the sail loft on the upper floor.

From the hotel, a lane leads down to the harbour itself, passing various restored colonial buildings, including the remains of a guardhouse, a blacksmith's workshop and an old canvas and clothing store that provided supplies for the ships. Just beyond is the Admiral's House (a local residence that never actually housed an admiral), which was built in 1855 and today serves as the dockyard's **museum** (daily 8am–6pm; free), good for a quick tour through its small but diverse collection, which focuses on the dockyard's history and the island's shipping tradition, aided by models and photographs of old schooners and battleships.

Fort Berkeley

The narrow path that leads from near the museum (behind the adjacent *Copper and Lumber Store Hotel*) to **Fort Berkeley** is easily overlooked, but a stroll around these dramatic military ruins should be an integral part of your visit. Perched above the crashing surf on a narrow spit of land that commands the entrance to English Harbour, the fort was the harbour's earliest defensive point and retains essentially the same long, thin shape today that it had in 1745.

Pigeon Beach

There's not much in the way of beach around Nelson's Dockyard but a good place to head for after some sightseeing is **Pigeon Beach**, five minutes' drive or twenty minutes' walk west of the dockyard. As you head out of the dockyard, turn left just before the harbour and follow the road past a series of restaurants and the Antigua yacht club. Keep going past the *Falmouth Harbour Apartments*, take the uphill track that goes sharply left and follow the road down to the right, where you'll find a wide expanse of white sand and a welcoming **beach bar** (though the bar is sometimes closed during the summer).

Shirley Heights

Spread over an extensive area of the hills to the east of English Harbour, numerous military ruins offer further evidence of the strategic importance of this part of southern Antigua. Collectively known as **Shirley Heights** (although technically this is only the name for the area around Fort Shirley), it's an interesting area to explore, with a couple of hiking opportunities for the adventurous who want to escape the crowds completely (daily; from 9am to 5pm there's an EC$13 entry charge which includes admission to Nelson's Dockyard).

Follow the road uphill from the tiny village of English Harbour and you'll pass the late eighteenth-century **Clarence House**, an attractive Georgian home built in 1787 for Prince William, Duke of Clarence (later King William IV), who was then serving in the Royal Navy. (At publication time, the house was undergoing renovation.) Past here, a right-hand turn-off leads down to the *Inn at English Harbour* (see p598) and the attractive crescent of Galleon Beach, where numerous yachts are normally moored just offshore.

Ignoring the turn-off and carrying straight on you'll pass the free **Dow's Hill Interpretation Centre** which has a fine collection of shells but, frankly, virtually nothing to do with the history of the area and is pretty missable. Beyond the centre, the road runs along the top of a ridge before dividing where a large cannon has been upended in the centre of the road. Fork left for the cliff known as **Cape Shirley**, where you'll find a cluster of ruined stone buildings – including barracks, officers' quarters and an arms storeroom – known collectively as the **Blockhouse**. On the eastern side a wide gun platform looks downhill to a narrow inlet at **Indian Creek**, beyond that to the **Standfast Point** peninsula and Eric Clapton's enormous house and gatehouse, and beyond that over the vast sweep of Willoughby Bay. Every year, stories leak out about Clapton and friends like Elton John and Keith Richards turning up for a jam at one of the island's nightclubs.

If you take the right-hand fork at the half-buried cannon, the road will lead you up to the ruins of **Fort Shirley**. On the right as you approach are the officers' quarters, still grandly arcaded though now roofless, overgrown with grass and grazed by the ubiquitous goats. To the left, across a bare patch of ground, are the remains of the military hospital and, in a small valley just below the surgeon's quarters, the **military cemetery** with its barely legible tombstones dating mostly from the 1850s and reflecting the prevalence of disease, particularly yellow fever.

The road ends at the fort itself, where a restored guardhouse now serves as an excellent little bar and restaurant, *The Lookout* (see below). The courtyard – where a battery of cannons once pointed out across the sea – now sees a battery of cameras snapping up the fabulous views over English Harbour, particularly on Sundays when the tourists descend in droves for the reggae and steel bands.

Eating, drinking and nightlife

Most of the good south coast **restaurants** are concentrated around Nelson's Dockyard and nearby Falmouth Harbour. Two others to look out for are *Alberto's* – a five-minute drive or taxi ride to the northeast – and the *Lookout*, high up on Shirley Heights.

Alberto's Willoughby Bay ☏ 268/460-3007. Probably the best food on the south coast, hosted by the eponymous long-time proprietor in an out-of-the-way spot. Recurring evening meals include thin slices of breadfruit roasted in a garlic and parsley sauce (EC$25) and pan-fried tuna or wahoo with wasabi and ginger (EC$60). Top-notch desserts send you happily on your way. Tues–Sun dinner only; closed July–Oct.

Cactus Main Road, Falmouth Harbour ☏ 268/460-6575. Well-positioned restaurant on a big verandah with spectacular views over Falmouth Harbour and the Middle Ground. Inside, there's a lively bar area with two darts boards and three pool tables. Food is served in tapas-style portions, with nachos at EC$15, fish dishes at EC$20.

Caribbean Taste Behind Dockyard Drive, English Harbour ☏ 268/562-3049. Authentic Antiguan eats in this small restaurant tucked away among local residences just before the entrance to the dockyard. Servings include large portions of ducana and salt cod, *fungi* and conch stew or curried goat, all for around EC$25–35.

HQ Nelson's Dockyard, English Harbour

☏ 268/562-2563. Excellent place in the heart of the dockyard serving well-prepared seafood, salads and chicken (EC$30–50). Daily for lunch and dinner, closed Sun evening.

The Last Lemming Falmouth Harbour ☏ 268/460-6910. Tasty food at this frequently crowded harbourside spot, though the service can be dreadfully slow. Pan-fried catch of the day and grilled steaks (EC$25–35) are typical of the daily offerings. Daily for lunch and dinner.

Life English Harbour ☏ 268/562-2353. In the evenings this bar and restaurant often becomes a vibrant party scene, playing 60s and 70s music. Popular with both the sailing crowd and locals. Daily except Tues. No cover charge.

The Lookout Shirley Heights ☏ 268/460-1785. The only place for a refreshment break while you're up on the Heights, offering up simple meals from US$5 on a large patio with superb views over the harbour and the dockyard (daily for lunch and dinner). The Sunday (and, to a lesser extent, Thursday) barbecues have a great party atmosphere, pulling a huge crowd for the reggae and steel-band performances (from 4pm, no cover charge).

14.4

The west coast

Tourism makes a firm impression on Antigua's **west coast**, with hotels dotted at regular intervals between the little fishing village of **Old Road** in the south and the capital, St John's. Two features dominate this area: a series of lovely beaches – with **Darkwood** probably the pick of the bunch for swimming, snorkelling and beachcombing – and a glowering range of hills known as the **Shekerley Mountains** in the southwest, offering the chance for a climb and some panoramic views. The lush and thickly wooded **Fig Tree Hill** on the edge of the range is as scenic a spot as you'll find, and you can take a variety of **hikes** inland to see a side of Antigua overlooked by the vast majority of tourists. Due west of St John's, the **Five Islands** peninsula holds several hotels, some good beaches and the substantial ruins of the eighteenth-century **Fort Barrington**.

Accommodation

Antigua's **west coast** has more rooms than any other part of the island, covering a wide range of options. The Five Islands peninsula has a handful of good hotels, though these feel a little more isolated than the rest of the coast's offerings.

Hawksbill Beach Five Islands ☎268/462-0301, ⓦwww.hawksbill.com. Attractive, sprawling hotel on the Five Islands peninsula, overlooking the bay and the jagged rock – shaped like the beak of a hawksbill turtle – that pokes up from the sea and gives the place its name. Four beaches, dramatic views, lovely landscaped gardens and a restored sugar mill converted into a store all add to the atmosphere. ❾
Jolly Harbour Villas Jolly Harbour ☎268/462-6166, ⓦwww.jollyharbour-marina.com. Fifty waterfront villas, mostly two-bedroom with a full kitchen and a balcony overlooking the harbour. Plenty of shops, restaurants and sports facilities (including a golf course and large, communal

swimming pool) are nearby, but the place feels somewhat bland and unimaginative. ❼
Rex Blue Heron Johnson's Point ☎268/462-8564, ⓦwww.rexcaribbean.com. Medium-sized and very popular all-inclusive on one of the best west coast beaches, with 64 comfortable and brightly decorated rooms and a small pool a stone's throw from the sea. ❾
Royal Antiguan Five Islands ☎268/462-3733. Located on Deep Bay, this is probably the ugliest hotel in Antigua, but the facilities are excellent, particularly for tennis and watersports, the rooms are comfortable and the beach busy but pleasant. Package deals can offer excellent rates. ❻

Fig Tree Hill

Heading east from Falmouth to the town of Swetes, you can then follow the main road through the most densely forested part of the island, **Fig Tree Hill**. You won't actually see any fig trees – the road is lined with bananas (known locally as figs) and mango trees as it carves its way through some gorgeous scenery down to the south coast at Old Road. About halfway along the drive, you can stop at a small roadside shack which calls itself the **Cultural Centre**, where you can get a drink and some fruit from local farms.

A dirt track leads south from the shack to a **reservoir** – the island's first – where you'll find picnic tables set up around the edge of the water. Those interested in a more serious hike can take the **Rendezvous Trail**, which starts on your left just before you reach the steps of the reservoir and crosses the **Wallings Woodlands** to the nearly always empty beach a two-hour walk away at Rendezvous Bay. Even a short stroll down this trail repays the effort; the woodlands are the best remaining example of the evergreen secondary forest that covered the island before the British settlers arrived, and are home to more than thirty species of shrubs and trees, including giant mahogany trees, and masses of noisy birdlife. Bear in mind that, though it's pretty hard to get lost, the main path is little used and in places can quickly become overgrown and hard to make out.

Boggy Peak

West of the small town of Old Road, the road follows the coast past a series of banana groves and pineapple plantations, and around **Cades Bay**, with delightful views out to sea over Cades Reef. On the right, half a mile from Old Road, a track leads up into the Shekerley Mountains to **Boggy Peak**, at 1312m the highest point on the island. The panoramic view from the top – on clear days you can even make out St Kitts, Guadeloupe and Montserrat – repays the effort of making the steep drive or the one-hour climb. Unfortunately, the peak is occupied by a communications station, safely tucked away behind a high-security fence, but the views from outside the perimeter fence are pretty good.

Darkwood Beach and around

Continuing west along the coast through the village of **Urlings**, the road runs alongside a number of excellent beaches. First up is **Turner's Beach** and **Johnson's Point**, where the sand shelves down to the sea beside a couple of good beach bars, including *Turner's* (see opposite), which rents snorkelling gear. The snorkelling is better just north of here at **Darkwood Beach**, a wide stretch of beach running right alongside the main road and a great spot for a swim. Look out for small underwater canyons just offshore, and schools of squid and colourful reef fish. Beachcombers will find this one of the best places on the island to look for shells and driftwood.

Just north of Darkwood Beach lies **Jolly Harbour**, where a marina complex includes rental apartments, a golf course, restaurants and a small shopping mall. It's a world apart from the "real Antigua" – like a small piece of America transplanted in the Caribbean.

Five Islands

To the west of St John's the highway leads out through a narrow isthmus onto the large **Five Islands** peninsula, named after five small rocks that jut from the sea just offshore. There are several hotels on the peninsula's northern coast, a few more on its west coast, though the interior is largely barren and scrubby, and there's not a huge amount to see. A half-mile offshore from **Hawksbill Bay** is a large rock in the shape of the head of a hawksbill turtle that gives the place its name. To reach the bay, and some excellent beaches, follow the main road straight through the peninsula.

On Goat Hill, at the northern point of the peninsula close to the *Royal Antiguan* hotel, the circular stone ruins of **Fort Barrington** overlook gorgeous Deep Bay. The British first built a simple fort here in the 1650s, to protect the southern entrance to St John's Harbour, though it was captured by the French when they took the city in 1666. Take the twenty-minute walk around the beach to the fort for the dramatic sense of isolation as you look out to sea or back over the tourists sunning themselves far below on the bay.

Eating, drinking and nightlife

There is a series of eateries lined up along the marina at **Jolly Harbour**, as well as the excellent *Sheer* further north and a couple of delightful little beach bars.

Dogwatch Tavern Jolly Harbour ☎ 268/462-6550. English-style pub, right beside the marina, with pool tables and dartboards, and an inexpensive outdoor snack bar and grill that sells burgers (EC$20), hot dogs (EC$10), red snapper with peas and rice (EC$28) and steak with fries (EC$45). Bar open Mon–Fri 11am–10pm, Sat & Sun 5–10pm, restaurant daily from 6pm.

OJ's Crabbe Hill Beach ☎ 268/460-0184. Simple beach bar and restaurant right on the water's edge between Darkwood Beach and Turner's Beach. The food is excellent (sandwiches and burgers from EC$15 and fish from EC$30) and the setting is wonderful; sand under your feet and fishing nets and driftwood strewn around. Daily 10am–11pm.

Rush Nightclub Grand Princess Casino, Jolly Harbour ☎ 268/562-7874. This new, nicely air-conditioned club has quickly become one of the most popular spots on the island for late-night partying. The music is a mix of Latin, disco, R&B, reggae and calypso, while the people getting down to it are a mix of young Antiguans and visitors to the island. Wed–Sun 10.30pm–late. Cover EC$15.

Sheer CocoBay Resort ☎ 268/562-2563. Wonderfully imaginative and eclectic food at this beautiful cliff-side restaurant, with only 12 tables and one sitting. The menu is Asian and South American, with fabulous starters from EC$36–46 and mains such as spiced rabbit and quail or "sugar-cane tuna" from EC$65–76. Tues–Sat for dinner.

Turner's Beach Bar and Grill Johnson's Point ☎ 268/462-9133. Charming little restaurant on one of the best west coast beaches. It's an unpretentious place, with plastic furniture right on the sand, but the cooking is good and the atmosphere mellow. The menu includes chicken curry (US$11), grilled red snapper (US$14) and grilled lobster (US$22), as well as rotis (US$7). Call ahead for a reservation at night. Daily 11am–9pm.

14.5

Barbuda

Taking a day-trip to the nation's other inhabited island, **Barbuda** – 48km to the north of Antigua – with its magnificent and often deserted beaches, spectacular coral reefs and rare colony of frigate birds, is a definite highlight of any visit to the country. Don't expect the same facilities as on Antigua; **accommodation** options are limited, you'll need to bring your own snorkelling or diving gear, and you'll find that schedules – whether for taxis, boats or meals – tend to drift.

Half the size of its better-known neighbour, **Barbuda** developed quite separately from Antigua and was only reluctantly coerced into joining the nation during the run-up to independence in 1981. The island is very much the poor neighbour in terms of financial resources, and its development has been slow; tourism has had only a minor impact, and fishing and farming remain the principal occupations of the tiny population of 1500, most of whom live in the small capital, **Codrington**.

Away from the beaches, the island is less fetching, mostly low-level scrub of cacti, bush, small trees and the distinctive century plants; for most of the year it is extremely arid and unwelcoming. There are a couple of exceptions: in the **southwest** the island suddenly bursts to life, with a fabulous grove of coconut palms

△ Pineapple farm at Cades Bay

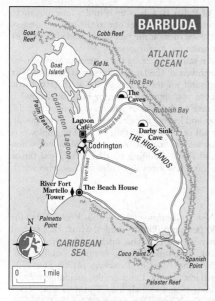

Map: BARBUDA — Goat Reef, Cobb Reef, ATLANTIC OCEAN, Goat Island, Kid Is., Hog Bay, The Caves, Rubbish Bay, Codrington Lagoon, Palm Beach, Lagoon Café, Highland Road, Darby Sink Cave, THE HIGHLANDS, Codrington, River Road, River Fort Martello Tower, The Beach House, Palmetto Point, N, CARIBBEAN SEA, Coco Point, Spanish Point, Palaster Reef, 0 — 1 mile

springing out of the sandy soil (and providing a useful source of export revenue), while in parts of the interior, government projects are reclaiming land from the bush to grow peanuts and sweet potatoes, also for the export market. For the most part, though, the island is left to the scrub, the elusive wild boar and deer and a multitude of birds – 170 species at last count.

Getting there

The only scheduled **flights** to Barbuda are from Antigua to Codrington on Carib Aviation (℡268/462-3147 or 481-2403; UK ℡01895 /450710, US ℡646/336-7600). They offer two flights a day from the main airport in Antigua (leaving at 8am and 5pm, returning thirty minutes later in each case) and charge US$74 round-trip. The planes take twenty minutes. A taxi can be arranged through Bryon Askie (℡268/460-0164 or 773-6082) or Lynton Thomas (℡268/460-0081 or 725-5023); they charge around US$50 per day.

A new **ferry service** began in January 2005, taking 90 minutes and costing EC$135 return. It leaves from Heritage Quay in St John's on Wed, Thurs, Sat and Sun at 8.30am, heading to River Dock in Barbuda, and returning the same days at 3.15pm. On Tues and Fri the service leaves Antigua at 4.45pm, returning the following day at 6.30am. For reservations call ℡268/464-9453.

Taking a **day tour** to the island is the best way to guarantee getting both a driver and a boat operator to take you to the bird sanctuary. Both D&J Forwarders (℡268/773-9766) and Jenny's Tours (℡268/461-9361) will organize a carefully packaged day-tour for US$160, including flights, pick-up at Barbuda airport, a jeep tour of the island, lunch and a boat visit to the bird sanctuary. Your driver will also leave you on the beach for as long as you want – just remember to take a bottle of water. Occasional day-tours by boat are run by Adventure Antigua (℡268/727-3261, ⓦwww.adventureantigua.com), who run fast boats to the Barbudan beaches in an hour and a half for snorkelling and beach cruising. Costs are around US$120 per person.

Codrington

CODRINGTON, the island's capital and only settlement, holds almost the entire population within its grid of narrow streets. It's a well-spread-out place, with plenty of brightly painted single-storey clapboard or concrete buildings. There are a couple of guesthouses, a handful of restaurants, bars and supermarkets, but, for the most part, people here keep to themselves, and there is little sign of life apart from a few curious schoolchildren, dogs and the occasional goat. On Sundays the capital livens up with a cricket match at the Holy Trinity School.

Codrington Lagoon

To the west of town, **Codrington Lagoon** is an expansive area of green, brackish water, fringed by mangroves. The lagoon is completely enclosed on its western side by the narrow but magnificent strip of **Palm Beach**, over 13 miles long, but there is a narrow cut to the north where fishing boats can get out to the ocean. Lobsters breed in the lagoon and you'll probably see them at the pier being loaded for export to Antigua – an important contribution to the local economy.

Equally significant – for this is what is starting to bring the tourists to Barbuda – a series of mangrove clumps to the northwest of the lagoon, known as **Man of War Island**, is the home and breeding ground for the largest group of **frigate birds** anywhere in the Caribbean. The sight as you approach them by boat (see below) is quite spectacular – the mothers will take to the skies as you draw near, joining the multitude of birds wheeling above you, and leaving their babies standing imperiously on the nest but watching you closely out of the corner of their eyes. The display gets even more dramatic during the mating season, from late August to December, when hundreds of the males put on a grand show – puffing up their bright-red throat pouches as they soar through the air just a few yards above the females, who watch admiringly from the bushes.

Practicalities

If you want to stay in Codrington, *Nedd's Guesthouse* (☎268/460-0059) offers four comfortable double rooms for US$60 per night (US$35 single), with a kitchen and grocery store downstairs, and the owners will pick you up from the airport. The *Carriage House* (✉lnedd@hotmail.co.uk; no phone) has two rooms at a similar rate.

Dining and **nightlife** are limited. At the *Palm Tree Restaurant* (☎268/560-2723 or 460-0517), Cerene Deazle serves Barbudan food and drinks, including conchs, lobster, fish and chicken as well as burgers and French fries. The restaurant serves alcohol and meals cost from US$10. The *Green Door Tavern* (☎268/562-3134) is open daily from 7am to midnight for tasty and inexpensive island food.

To see the frigate birds, you'll need to hire one of the small **boats** (for around US$50) that leave for the sanctuary from the main pier just outside Codrington. It's advisable, though, to visit as part of a Barbuda tour or to make arrangements through your hotel or taxi.

The rest of the island

Apart from any beach or snorkelling stops, a tour of the island is a pretty brief affair. Away from the lagoon, there are few sights and they're all pretty missable unless you're determined to get your money's worth.

North of Codrington a series of dirt roads fans out across the upper part of the island. One of these leads into the heart of Barbuda, to the scant remains of **Highlands House**, the castle the first Codringtons – early colonists – built on the island in the seventeenth century. The views across the island from here are as panoramic as you'll find. Another dirt road heads to the northeastern side of the island, where a series of **caves** has been naturally carved into the low cliffs. These are thought to have sheltered Taíno and possibly Carib Indians in the centuries preceding the arrival of Europeans. Scant evidence of their presence has been found here, however, except for some unusual **petroglyphs**. The entrance to the main cave is opposite a large boulder, with the ruins of an old **watchtower** built up alongside. You'll need to scramble up the rocks for five minutes, then make a short, stooped walk inside the cave to reach the petroglyphs – a couple of barely distinguishable and very amateurish faces carved into the rockface.

River Fort

You can clamber around some more substantial remains at the **River Fort** in the southwest of the island, just beyond the coconut grove. The fort provides a surprisingly large defence structure for an island of Barbuda's size and importance. The island was attacked by Carib Indians in the 1680s and by the French navy in 1710, but there was too little valuable property here to tempt any further assailants into braving the dangerous surrounding reefs. As a result, the fort never saw any action, and its main role has been as a lookout and a landmark for ships approaching the island from the south.

The remains are dominated by a **Martello tower**, one of the many such small, round fortifications built throughout the British Empire during the Napoleonic Wars. Right below the tower, the **River Landing** is the main point for access to Barbuda by boat and is always busy with trucks stockpiling and loading sand onto barges to be taken to replenish beaches in Antigua – a controversial but lucrative industry for the Barbudans.

Practicalities

If you need a **place to stay** outside Codrington, bring your credit cards. Least pricey of the three luxury resorts is the *Beach House Barbuda* (T268/725-4042, Wwww.thebeachhousebarbuda.com; ❽, all-inclusive, excluding drinks), where prices start at US$565 for bed and breakfast. The place is on a fantastic stretch of south coast beach, with 20 beachfront suites that all feature a/c and a private verandah. The rooms are big, comfortable and stylishly decorated.

15

The French West Indies

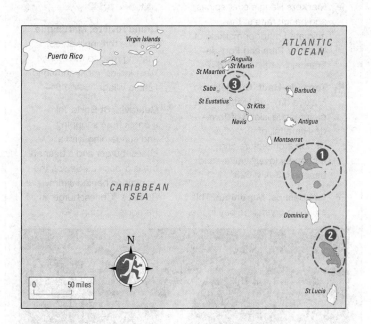

The French West Indies highlights

* **Parc National de Guadeloupe** Hike to thundering waterfalls, ascend cloud-capped mountain peaks, and explore lush rainforest at this outstanding reserve. See p.624

* **Markets** Haggle over spices and handicrafts at the animated outdoor markets of Pointe-à-Pitre and Fort-de-France. See pp.620 & 637

* **Terre-de-Haut, Guadeloupe** Make a day-trip to the picturesque island of Terre-de-Haut, full of attractive Breton architecture and fringed by lovely white-sand beaches. See p.628

* **Les Salines, Martinique** This stunning crystalline bay in the island's southern region is a perfect spot for watching the sunset. See p.641

* **St-Pierre, Martinique** The blackened, lava-ravaged ruins of the island's first capital make for a compelling visit. See p.642

* **Grand'Rivière, Martinique** Follow a thrillingly steep, winding road to the French West Indies' most authentic fishing village. See p.644

* **Gustavia, St Barts** Take a break from shopping and sunbathing with a cheeseburger and a beer at the laid-back *Le Select*, the inspiration behind Jimmy Buffett's "Cheeseburger in Paradise". See p.648

△ Parc National de la Guadeloupe

Introduction and basics

Beaten by the Atlantic on one side and caressed by the Caribbean on the other, the four volcanic islands that comprise the **French West Indies** boast some of the Caribbean's most varied scenery. Extending almost 650km across the Eastern Caribbean, the islands of **Guadeloupe**, **Martinique**, **St Barthélemy (St Barts)** and French **St Martin** (covered in its own chapter, p.511), are an exotic blend of long sandy beaches, lush rainforests, craggy mountain peaks, dazzling turquoise waters and dramatic limestone coasts.

The larger islands are crowned by dormant volcanoes, including the Eastern Caribbean's highest summit, Guadeloupe's **La Soufrière**, and its most renowned, Martinique's historic **Mont-Pelée**. The thundering waterfalls that course their flanks feed dense interior rainforests before flowing out to sea, where gorgeous **beaches** in hues ranging from white to gold and midnight-black drop off to a brilliant technicolour world of fish and coral that delights divers and snorkellers alike. The smallest island, St Barts, lacks the lush greenery of its southern siblings but compensates with spectacular secluded beaches and an unparalleled ambience of luxury and exclusivity.

Despite their setting amidst predominantly English islands, the French West Indies have remained remarkably French, especially so St Barts, a veritable Mediterranean outpost cast away on the Caribbean Sea. In contrast, Guadeloupe and Martinique have merged the hallmarks of **French** culture – vices like wine, sweets, coffee and cigarettes – with the best Creole traditions, from spicy food to atmospheric architecture and languid attitudes. The two meet head-on most noticeably in the major cities, like Guadeloupe's **Pointe-à-Pitre** and Martinique's **Fort-de-France**, where Caribbean marketplaces join smoke-filled cafés, narrow streets jammed with honking cars, and fading wooden colonial houses.

Where to go

Guadeloupe has the most to offer one-stop island visitors, from a massive Parc National with impressive rainforest flora, hiking trails and ample beaches to a phenomenal dive site and four remarkable offshore islands, including the charming Terre-de-Haut.

In contrast, **Martinique** is geared more toward package-oriented travellers, with resort towns like touristy Pointe-du-Bout. Still, visitors who search out less developed areas like the Presqu'île de la Caravelle will be rewarded with thrilling scenery and quiet, pristine beaches. Visitors can also visit authentically Martinican pockets like the charred ruins at St-Pierre and the superb Habitation Clément rum distillery, or escape the sun-worshipping throngs by hiking on Mont-Pelée.

For those who can afford it, tiny **St-Barthélemy** (St Barts) is the ultimate getaway – a decadent, beach-trimmed isle with a luxurious, self-pampering mindset, and little to do but shop and lie on the sand by day and eat sumptuously at night. While you may go home broke, you'll be completely rejuvenated.

When to go

Most of the year, puffy white clouds parade through a clear blue sky, and warm balmy breezes gently ruffle hair and sway palm fronds: T-shirt, shorts and sandals kind of weather, interrupted now and then by a tropical shower.

From July to November, however, this idyllic scene may be interrupted by the **hurricane season**, the wettest time of the year and also the most humid. The best time to visit is between mid-December and mid-April, when the weather is dry and the heat is tempered by cooling trade winds.

Arrival

Whichever island you happen to be visiting, you will most likely fly through Guadeloupe's **Pôle-Caraïbes airport** in the commercial hub of Pointe-à-Pitre, which also serves as a transport hub for this region of the Caribbean. From there, both ferries and flights are available to Martinique and St Barts.

Information

Each island has its own **tourism office** and **official website** with links to information and hotels and services that you can book yourself (see pp.620, 636 and 648).

Money and costs

Since the islands of the French West Indies are overseas extensions of France, the prices for food and lodging are considerably more expensive than elsewhere in the Caribbean. Thanks to its celeb status, St Barts is in a class all its own when it comes to budgetary considerations.

The **euro (€) is the official currency** on all three islands. Euro notes are issued in denominations of 5, 10, 20, 50, 100, 200 and 500 euros and coin denominations of 1, 2, 5, 10, 20 and 50 cents and 1 and 2 euros. The **US dollar** is also widely used on St Barts.

You'll find major **banks** in all island capitals and resort areas, usually equipped with ATMs. Tellers exchange **travellers' cheques** and cash Monday to Friday 8am–noon and 2.30–5pm. Moneychangers don't charge commission; they can be found near the main island tourist offices.

Even at two people sharing a room, it will be a challenge to get by on less than $75/day, particularly in St Barts. The simplest double room costs around $60; the same room near a beach costs $80–90. Rates include all tax and service charges, and many also include breakfast. **Camping** is the cheapest option, but it's allowed only on Martinique, with sites for around $15/night. Otherwise, consider going in **low season** (May to Nov), when rates go down by almost half.

The best restaurant deals are the three-course **prix-fixe menus** offered in most establishments. On Guadeloupe and Martinique they're commonly priced around $15–20 for dinner, while St Barts charges closer to $30 a head; they're usually modestly cheaper at lunchtime. The best lunch bargains are hefty ham and cheese baguettes and sodas from the beachside trucks that cost about $5. Wine can actually be less expensive than soda, at about $2 a glass in some bars.

Getting around

You'll be hard-pressed to make it to all French islands in one trip, as travelling between them is far from straightforward. Certainly, checking out two islands per visit is feasible – Guadeloupe and Martinique both have regular ferry crossings between them, as do St Martin and St Barts.

The best way to get around each island is with your own wheels; what **public transportation** exists in Martinique and Guadeloupe is far from efficient, while St Barts – which happens to have the worst roads of the lot – has none whatsoever.

By bus

While getting around Martinique and Guadeloupe by bus is the most reasonably priced mode of transportation (€1–3.50), the service is not for those in a hurry. Known as *taxis collectifs* (or "TC"), they're actually cramped minivans that generally run from 6am to 6pm weekdays, with scant service after 2pm on Saturdays and none on Sundays. There's no real schedule to speak of – they leave from the capitals when they're full. To board one outside the capitals, simply flag it down along the road; keep in mind, however, that TCs are often packed in the hinterlands. Tell the driver where you're going when you board and pay him when you get off.

By taxi

Taxis in the French West Indies are expensive, charging a minimum of €5 even if you're just going down the street, and doubling their rates Monday to Friday 8pm–6am and all day Sundays and holidays. Fortunately, the only time you're really likely to need one is to get yourself to and from your hotel and the respective islands' ferry docks or airport.

By car and hitching

Driving requires a good dose of fearlessness. The locals are very aggressive on the roads – especially in Martinique, where drivers will pass each other even on winding turns. Guadeloupe is slightly less harried, but it's still important to be alert at all times, especially when driving in the heavy traffic of Pointe-à-Pitre. St Barts has grown increasingly dangerous in recent years as the cars plying its narrow, mottled-cement roads have become both bigger and faster. Most car rentals start around $50/day; see individual islands for details.

Hitchhiking is a way of life on Martinique and Guadeloupe due to the irregular bus service (the usual precautions apply), though you won't see many hitchhikers on St Barts, since just about everyone seems to drive.

By boat

The most common **passenger boats** are twin-hulled catamarans with a covered upper deck and an enclosed, air-conditioned lower one. Note that the trip from Guadeloupe to Martinique can be choppy. Unlike the buses here, ferries do attempt to follow a schedule of sorts, especially those making the 40min–1hr 30min crossings to Guadeloupe's offshore islands (see p.629). The boats making the 1.5–3hr trips between Guadeloupe, Dominica and Martinique (see "Ferries", p.52), however, rarely leave on time as passengers must acquire a boarding pass and go through customs beforehand – it's a good idea to arrive 30–45 minutes before your departure. Even if you've bought your ticket in advance (which is recommended for all sea passages) you'll still have to join the crowd in front of the quayside ticket window to procure your boarding pass.

By plane

There are several **flights** daily between the three islands, but service is often erratic. Much of the air traffic consists of twenty-passenger aircraft that rarely leave on time and have low cargo weight restrictions. The fifteen-minute island hops between mainland Guadeloupe and its offshore isles are done by nine-seater planes with similar weight restrictions; more importantly, they may be cancelled if they're under-booked.

Accommodation

While Guadeloupe and St Barts have a wide range of **independent hotel** options, Martinique is heavily geared to **package-tour travellers**, with the result that most hotels are chains. To get the best rates, you should consult a travel agent.

Bungalow-style lodging is extremely popular on Guadeloupe and Martinique – basically a fully equipped studio or one-bedroom apartment with your own kitchen. If you're concerned about costs, it's an effective way to save money since you're not paying for hotel services, and you can make your own meals. A growing **bed-and-breakfast industry** is also starting to make a dent in the hotel scene thanks to lower prices and familial service; the best are part of the *Gîtes de France* network (☎ 01 49 70 75 75, ⓦ www.gites-de-france.fr). There are no B&Bs on St Barts, though there are plenty of luxurious villas to rent if you have the cash.

Camping is forbidden on St Barts, and Guadeloupe's only site closed after it was flooded in 2004. Martinique has a maintained campsite in Ste-Anne, and visitors are allowed to pitch their tents for free on the island's beaches during French school holidays (July & August and the March break).

Food and drink

As St Barts has grown ever more popular among an international crowd of jetsetters, the island's dining scene has become just as cosmopolitan. **French-Creole** cuisine still rules, but you'll also find great Italian, sushi, and other global fare – not to mention the killer burger that inspired Jimmy Buffett's "Cheeseburger in Paradise." Guadeloupe and Martinique's restaurants are less flashy and tend to stick to more traditional Creole seafood plates. The French influence shows most with breakfast here, which usually consists of a small espresso, croissant and fruit juice, and beach fare, mostly filling ham and cheese baguettes, crepes and pastries.

Lunch is the meal of the day – things pretty much shut down all over the islands noon–2pm, even in the touristy shopping districts of St Barts. Prix-fixe menus are the best deal, usually including at least a starter and a main course, plus a good selection of French wines to wash down the spicy Creole food. Dishes like *crabes farçi* (stuffed land crabs), *boudin* (blood pudding), *accras* (cod fritters) and the various *colombos*, a curry using *cabri* (goat), *poulet* (chicken), *lambi* (conch) and *ouassous* (crayfish), are the spiciest of all, though some resort areas tend to tone them down. Most main courses come with rice or beans.

The most expensive item on any menu is *langoustine*, a lobster-like delicacy served grilled, fricasseed, or in pasta. Other dishes, like *féroce d'avocat* (a zesty avocado and cod purée), *calalou* (a spinach-like soup), and grilled fish like *vivanneau* (red snapper), marlin and *requin* (shark) are less pricey and often equally tasty.

Individual islands have their speciailties too. Guadeloupe's offshore Marie-Galante is known for a hearty **bébélé**, a thick "everything in the pot" soup of African origin made only on Saturdays, while Martinican chefs make **coq colombo**, a rich rooster curry.

French wine availability notwithstanding, the most popular drink on Martinique and Guadeloupe is **rum** – no surprise, since the rum-making industry thrives on both islands. **Ti-punch**, a potent rum, sugar and lime concoction, is popular as an apéritif; a diluted version, **Planter's Punch**, mixes the booze with fruit juice. Both islands also produce their own **local beers**: Guadeloupe's Corsair is a light brew that goes down nicely with rich Creole fare; ditto for Martinique's Lorraine. On St Barts, most meals finish with a few sips of vanilla rum, a smooth, mellow digestif sold in souvenir bottles all over the island.

The **tap water** on Martinique and Guadeloupe is safe to drink; St Barts is more touch-and-go, as the island lacks a fresh-water source. The finer hotels all provide potable water, but the budget places may get theirs from unreliable rain-catchment systems; if you're staying at the latter, you're better off buying bottled water, which is widely available on all islands.

Mail and communications

There are **public telephones** on almost every square and many street corners, all of which accept only plastic *télécartes* (phone cards), available in units of 50 (about €7) and 100 (about €14) from any post office and most *tabacs* (tobacco shops). International phone cards are also available (€3–10) and offer good rates, particularly after 7pm. Many payphones list a 1-800 AT&T phone number to dial for collect calls.

Telephone numbers on all three islands are ten digits long, starting with 0. To make local calls on any of the islands, just dial the ten-digit number. International calls to Martinique and Guadeloupe do not require the 0 – simply dial the international access code of the country you're calling from, followed by the digits after the 0. To make an international call to St Barts, however, dial the international access code, followed by ☎590, then the ten-digit number.

Sending letters home using the French **postal system** is straightforward – postcards and airmail letters cost €0.75 to North America, Europe, Australia and New Zealand.

The **Internet** is still relatively new here, available mostly in the more resorty areas. Consequently, checking your email can be difficult and expensive. Until the islands catch up with the wired world, the **fax** remains the preferred mode of written communication.

Opening hours, holidays and festivals

As a general rule, **opening hours** run 8am–noon and 2–7pm during the week and 8am–noon on Saturdays. On Sundays little is open, and some shops take Wednesday afternoons off, too. In addition to closures on national holidays (see box opposite) the islands also shut down to celebrate local holidays, the most notable being the abolition of slavery, celebrated on May 22 (Martinique)

January 1 New Year's Day
March/April Easter Sunday, Easter
Monday
May 1 Labour Day
Fortieth day after Easter Ascension
Thursday
Seventh Monday after Easter Pente-
cost Monday
July 14 Bastille Day
August 15 Assumption
November 1 All Saints Day
November 2 All Souls Day
November 11 Armistice Day
December 25 Christmas Day

and May 27 (Guadeloupe); the man responsible for this feat, Victor Schoelcher, is
honoured on July 21.

Holidays aside, some big **festivals** add
spice to the region, the largest of all being
Carnival, which runs yearly from January
to Ash Wednesday in both Guadeloupe
and Martinique, with dancing and music
performances culminating in the election of
the year's beauty queen. The **Christmas
season** dovetails with the biannual Jazz Fest
in Martinique, a weeklong music festival in
Fort-de-France at the beginning of December showcasing acts from France and former
French colonies. The only other notable
event is a spiritual one, **La Toussaint** (All
Souls Day), when red votive candles are lit
throughout the cemeteries.

The major annual event in St Barts is its own
celebration on **August 24**, complete with
watersports and music. Earlier in the year,

the Cinéma Caraïbes **film festival** in late April
showcases Caribbean films over five days,
and a two-week international **music festival**
takes place in January, which includes ballet
and other dance performances.

Crime and safety

St Barts has so little **crime** that people leave
their car doors unlocked. The same isn't true
of Martinique, where break-ins at the parking lot near Mont-Pelée's hiking trails have
been reported. Even so, the most common
crime in Martinique and Guadeloupe is **pickpocketing** – as long as you don't flash your
money around, you're unlikely to have problems. Their major cities, however, are sketchy
at night, with **prostitutes** and **drug dealers**
hanging out in squares; they're significantly
less trouble, however, than the Creole men
who commonly **harass** white **women travellers**. While most is harmless catcalling, the
worst offenders will grope you in the street.
You can avoid harassment by covering up in
town and avoiding eye contact.

Guadeloupe ☎0590/82 00 89
(gendarmerie); ☎0590/82 08 81
(police).
Martinique ☎0596/60 60 44 (medical);
☎17 or ☎59 40 00 (police).
St Barts ☎18 or ☎0590/27 60 35
(medical); ☎0590/27 66 66 (police).

15

THE FRENCH WEST INDIES | Introduction and basics

History

Though the islands of Guadeloupe, Martinique and St Barts were each discovered by **Columbus** on his voyages to the New World in the late 15th and early 16th centuries, it is the **French** who have most impacted the three islands, having ruled over them as protected departments for the better part of 400 years. Peace has, for the most part, been the rule, and the islands have benefited from French trade and support; in recent years, though, the desire for a greater sense of **independence and autonomy** among the citizens of all three islands has become one of the region's most pressing issues.

Guadeloupe

Unlike the other islands under the French crown, the **Spanish** actually attempted to colonize Guadeloupe – twice – in the 1500s, after Columbus discovered its fertile soil during his second New World voyage. They were assailed both times by menacing Caribs, and it took the **French**, who arrived in 1635, to establish the French West Indies' first capital a few years later, at **Basse-Terre**. Their successful implementation of slavery by the 1670s caught British attention, who strove to take over the island several times in the mid-1700s, and succeeded in occupying it from 1759 to 1763, when they built up the harbour at Pointe-à-Pitre and expanded sugar cane trade markets to North America. The 1763 **Paris Treaty** returned Guadeloupe to France but the British invaded again in 1794. The French responded by sending in troops led by black nationalist **Victor Hugues**, who launched a reign of terror by freeing and arming local slaves, killing hundreds of royalists and attacking American ships; not surprisingly, the US declared war on France.

Napoleon reinstituted order by appointing a governing general who restored slavery in 1802. Peace was not to endure for long, however, as the British were still keen on controlling the fiefdom, and they continued to manage parts of the island between 1810 and 1816, when the **Vienna Treaty** ended their attempts for good.

Slavery wasn't actually abolished in the French West Indies until 1848,

after a dogged anti-slavery campaign mounted by French cabinet minister **Victor Schoelcher**. Since then, the only real issue has been Guadeloupe's status within the French government. The promise of political decentralization in the late 1900s gave birth to **pro-independence** uprisings, some occurring as recently as 1999, when Guadeloupe, Martinique and French Guiana (in South America) joined forces to sign the **Basse-Terre Declaration** seeking greater autonomy from the French government. More recently, though, the independence movement has lost some momentum; in late 2003, after two years of severe drought, residents of Guadeloupe voted to uphold the status quo, rejecting a referendum that would have allowed for greater autonomy from France.

Martinique

Though discovered by Columbus on his last New World voyage in 1502, the Lesser Antilles' third largest island wound up being settled in 1635 by French colonizers instead. Starting from a small encampment on the northwest side that would later become **St-Pierre**, the French made their way to **Fort-de-France** and completed their island take-over eight years later by massacring the remaining Caribs.

By this time, the French had begun importing slaves and sugar cane, and their efforts drew British interest near the end of the 1700s. An almost two-century power struggle ensued, with French losing Martinique to the British over a century later, then getting it back as part of the **Paris Treaty** in 1763, only to lose it again 1794. The tug-of-war ended for good in 1815, when the British returned the island on **Vienna Treaty** orders.

Martinique's return to the motherland was bittersweet, as France continued to endorse slavery well after neighbouring British islands had abolished the practice in 1833. It didn't help matters that Emperor Napoleon had married the daughter of a local plantation-owner, **Joséphine Beauharnais** (see p.638) – it's said he continued to endorse slavery as a favour to his in-laws. As on Guadeloupe, the determined efforts of French cabinet minister **Victor Schoelcher** led to the practice's end in 1848.

The twentieth century began tragically on the island; on May 8, 1902, a sudden eruption of **Mont-Pelée**, the volcano at its northern reaches, destroyed the bustling town of St-Pierre and all its inhabitants. The latter part of the century was marked by sometimes violent social unrest caused by pro-independence factions seeking **sovereignty** from France. In an effort to quell the movement, the French government granted Martinique greater overseas department status and powers in 1982–83. In recent years, the island has struggled with record unemployment rates, resulting in demand for greater trade with France and neighboring islands, plus a renewed support for the Martinique Independence Movement (MIM).

St Barts

St Barthélemy was spotted by **Columbus** in 1493 and named after his younger brother, Bartolomeo. The first **French** delegation to settle the island, in 1648, came from nearby St Kitts. Their effort was disastrous, however, as native **Caribs** massacred the lot in 1665. It was almost a decade later before a second attempt, this one by Norman and Breton Huguenots, was made. Under their reign, Gustavia's hurricane-proof harbour became a popular mooring port for **buccaneers**, who carried plunder from Spanish galleons in their holds; one legendary pirate, Montbars the Exterminator, even set up headquarters here.

Over a century later, in 1784, France's Marie-Antoinette ceded ownership to Sweden's King Gustaf II in exchange for free-port rights in Gothenburg. But after serving as an American-friendly port during the Revolution and, later, the War of 1812, Gustavia suffered a devastating fire in 1852 that proved too costly for the Swedes. They sold it back to France in 1878, for 320,000FF ($45,700 today), with the French condition that it remain a duty-free port. The island's administrative status changed in 1974, when it came under neighbouring Guadeloupe's jurisdiction. In 2003, however, the residents of St Barts voted overwhelmingly to separate from Guadeloupe and become their own **French overseas collectivity**, allowing for greater autonomy in its economic, political and social programmes. This status change is scheduled to take effect by the end of 2005.

15.1

Guadeloupe

T he largest French West Indian island, **GUADELOUPE** encompasses a massive 1704 square kilometres, the majority of which is taken up by its two adjoining mainland islands, Basse-Terre and Grande-Terre, whose outline resembles a greenbacked butterfly in flight. Its two "wings" have entirely different personas and equally misrepresentative names: the western **Basse-Terre**, or "low-land", is anything but, given that its central core is dominated by mountain ranges, including the Lesser Antilles' highest peak, **La Soufrière**. These surround the island's bountiful **rainforest** and descend to meet twinkling black-sand beaches like **Plage Malendure** that extend to protected underwater **dive** sites abounding with aqualife.

The eastern "wing", the furled **Grande-Terre**, or "large-land", is slightly smaller than Basse-Terre, utterly flat by contrast, and predominantly rural. Most of the action happens along its southern coast, where one white-sand beach after another seems to merge endlessly along the coast, with the stunning **Plage Caravelle** forming the centrepiece. Its outer reaches are pounded by the savage **Atlantic Ocean** to produce jagged limestone outcroppings like the windswept **Pointe-des-Châteaux**, and the exquisite **Lagon de la Porte d'Enfer** natural swimming pool.

Guadeloupe's offshore islands are equally diverse. **Marie-Galante**, with its rural landscape of sugar cane, hearkens back to a Guadeloupe of thirty years ago, while **La Désirade**, the most desolate of the lot, is quite possibly the Caribbean's least developed island. The most visited offshore isle, tiny **Terre-de-Haut**, is the prettiest of all, with quaint architecture and fabulous bays and beaches.

Arrival, information and getting around

Guadeloupe is served by numerous airlines, including Air Canada, Air Caraïbes, Air France, Cubana, Air Guadeloupe (☎0590/21 12 90), Air Martinique (☎0590/ 21 13 40), Air St-Martin (☎0590/21 12 88), American Airlines, Air La Liberté (☎0590/21 14 68), Air Calypso (☎0590/89 27 77) and Corsair (☎0590/21 12 50). Flights arrive daily from Antigua, Dominica, Paris, San Juan and St Martin, and weekly from Montreal. Ferries also link the island with Dominica and St Lucia. For information about travelling by boat between Guadeloupe, Martinique and St Barts see "Ferries", p.52.

Passengers arriving by **plane** land at one of mainland Guadeloupe's two airports: modern **Pôle-Caraïbes** or, less frequently, **Le Raizet**, a run-down nearby terminal used by **charter** flights. Both lie about 6km outside of Pointe-à-Pitre and are well served by metered **taxis** that cost between €25 and €60 to southern points (SOS ☎0590/83 63 94; Taxigua ☎0590/83 90 00).

If you're planning to explore the island, renting a **car** at the airport is the best way to do it, since the only other island transport, **minibuses**, is irregular and patience-wearing. Both terminals have numerous rental agencies, including Europcar (☎0590/21 13 52, ☏21 13 53); Avis (☎0590/21 13 54, ☏21 13 55); Budget (☎0590/21 13 48, ☏21 13 63); Hertz (☎0590/84 57 94, ☏84 57 90); and Jumbo Car (☎0590/91 55 66, ☏91 22 88, ☒www.jumbocar.com).

Passengers arriving by **ferry** disembark at the westernmost of Pointe-à-Pitre's quays, the **Gare Maritime** (or Quai Gatine), just west of the city centre. From here,

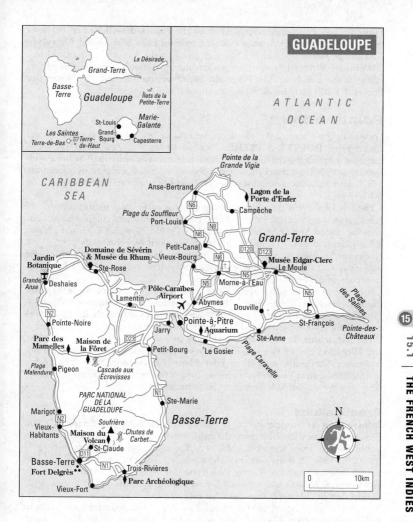

you can catch a taxi to Le Gosier (€20) or St-François (€50); while there are no car rental agencies near the docks, plenty are on hand at the bigger resort towns.

The airport has a tourism **information** booth near customs with flex-hours depending on plane arrival times. Should it be closed, the main office in downtown Pointe-à-Pitre keeps regular hours (see overleaf).

Grande-Terre

Remarkably flat **Grande-Terre** is skirted by beaches and studded with resort towns so glossy that the highway connecting them bears the nickname "Riviera Road". The busiest enclave, **Le Gosier**, has the most amenities and nightlife of the lot, making it the definitive one-stop destination for those seeking nothing but sun and fun. The crowds thin out further east, around bohemian **Ste-Anne** and swanky **St-**

François, and are almost nonexistent along the **Pointe-des-Châteaux**, the sliver of land that juts into the Atlantic at the easternmost point of the island. No visit to Guadeloupe would be complete without a visit to the colourful commercial hub of **Pointe-à-Pitre**, while northern pockets like **Port-Louis**, a picturesque fishing village at the mouth of calm **Plage du Souffleur**, and the dramatic **Lagon des Portes d'Enfer** combine to make a terrific day out.

Pointe-à-Pitre

Located in the centre of the island, on the isthmus that connects Basse-Terre and Grand-Terre, **POINTE-À-PITRE** is liveliest around the **Quai de la Darse**, an extensive pier edging the length of the waterfront. The quay itself is lined with Guadeloupe's liveliest **markets**, where a colourful, sensual jamboree of spices, fruit, fish, T-shirts and various island sundries are hawked from dawn until mid-afternoon (Mon–Sat).

The few local sights are within walking distance of the quay, starting a couple of blocks west, at no. 9 rue Nozières, where a handsome, renovated colonial house contains the modest **Musée St-Jean Perse** (Mon–Fri 9am–5pm, Sat 8.30am–12.30pm; €2.50), devoted to the life of the island's native-born Nobel laureate poet. A few blocks further west, at no. 24 rue Peynier, the **Musée Schoelcher** (Mon–Fri 9am–5pm; €2) showcases abolitionist Victor Schoelcher's assorted bric-a-brac – his own copy of the Venus de Milo among them.

A couple of blocks north of the Quai, behind the gritty **Place de la Victoire** that commemorates Victor Hugues' (see p.612) victory over the British, is Pointe-à-Pitre's major landmark, the Gustav Eiffel-designed steel **Cathédrale de St-Pierre-et-St-Paul**. Look for screws and bolts protruding from the columns in the apse.

The **Aquarium de la Guadeloupe** (daily 9am–7pm; €7.50, €3.50 under-12s), five kilometres east of Pointe-à-Pitre, is a kid-pleaser with open turtle and shark aquariums. The nearby remains of **Fort Fleur-d'Épée** (daily 9am–5pm; free), a seventeenth-century Vauban-style military base, have commanding views of Grande-Terre and the sea, but little remaining infrastructure.

Practicalities

Information on Guadeloupe and its outer islands, including free, detailed Chemin Bleu road **maps**, is available from the main tourism office, 5 square de la Banque, across from la Darse's markets (Mon–Fri 8am–5pm, Sat 8am–noon; ☎0590/82 09 30, ℻83 89 22; ⊛www.lesilesguadeloupe.com). You can check **email** and buy phone cards at *Arospeed*, 50 Centre John-Perse (Mon–Fri 9am–6pm, Sat 10am–3pm; €3/15min, €9/hour) and send regular mail from the **post office** on place de l'Hôtel de Ville (Mon–Fri 8am–6pm, Sat 8am–noon).

There's no good reason to **stay** in Pointe-à-Pitre – the downtown area starts to feel dodgy after 6pm – but for those getting on or off boats in the dead of night, the small but appealing rooms at the portside *Hôtel Saint-John*, Quai des Croisières (☎0590/82 51 57, ℻82 52 61, ⊛www.saint-john-perse.com; ❺ including breakfast) are your best option. Otherwise, the spartan *Victoria Palace*, 9bis place de la Victoire (☎0590/83 12 15; ❷), will do only if you need a transit stay; the cheapest rooms are cramped and fan-only with common shower and toilet.

The city doesn't have much of a **restaurant** scene, but there are a few gems to be found. Friendly *Le Petit Palais*, 4 place de l'Église (daily 7am–5pm), has pastries and coffee, plus traditional couscous on Thursdays and crayfish in coconut sauce on Fridays; *Maharaja Monty*, 43 rue Achille René-Boisneuf, serves up reasonably priced Indian curries (€12–16.50) in a French colonial-meets-Taj Mahal setting (Mon–Sat noon–3pm and 7–11pm); and nearby, *Le Jardin des Délices*, 26 rue Peynier, offers fine French-Creole fare in an elegant tearoom atmosphere (dishes between €13–25).

Le Gosier

Guadeloupe's premier resort area, **LE GOSIER**, lies 7km east of Pointe-à-Pitre; its pleasant beaches and convenient location adjacent to the island's major city have spurred major resort development that has given the small town a dual personality. The area known as **Pointe de la Verdure** resembles a gated community, with slick resort hotels enclosed by electric gates, and has private, man-made white-sand beaches dotted with canopied chairs and watersports huts that rent **snorkelling** gear, **windsurfers** and **body-boards**. Further east along the main road, **boulevard Général-de-Gaulle**, you'll find an authentic Caribbean village of rustic colonial houses and tight-knit streets perched above a small public **beach**.

Le Gosier's best beach is its trickiest to reach (and therefore most secluded), the lovely **Îlet du Gosier**, a minuscule, undeveloped isle located 100m offshore. There's good **snorkelling** to be had in its surrounding waters, as a capsized tug lies near the landing dock and there's an active coral reef to the rear - bring a mask and flippers with you, as you won't be able to rent them on site. Local fishermen ferry sunbathers back and forth daily from 8.30am–5pm in small motorboats from the pier at the east end of the town beach, closest to the islet (€3 return). Bring a picnic lunch, or grab a bite from the dockside **snack** shacks.

Accommodation

Auberge de la Vieille Tour 5 Montauban ☎0590/84 23 23, ⊛www.sofitel.com. This posh Sofitel property has English-speaking staff, two tennis courts, and 180 spacious, stylish rooms with minibar and satellite TV. ❾

Canella Beach Hotel Pointe de la Verdure ☎0590/90 44 00, ⊛www.canellabeach.fr. At the end of the Pointe, with clean, comfortable a/c rooms with balconies and kitchenette. ❼

Créole Beach Pointe de la Verdure ☎0590/90 46 46, ⑆90 46 66, ⊛www.leader-hotels.gp. Le Gosier's classiest resort hotel boasts over 150 comfortable, well-equipped doubles with sea or garden views; there's also a private beach and a three-tiered swimming pool. ❾

Formule Économique 112-120 Lot Gisors ☎0590/84 54 91, ⓔlaformule. economique@wanadoo.fr. Friendly, bargain-basement lodging down a residential street north of the town beach. ❸

Îlet de la Plage Plage Gosier ☎0590/84 20 73, ⑆84 25 71, ⓔdolhen@wanadoo.fr. The best budget lodgings in town. Pleasant, spacious fan-only or a/c studios overlooking the town beach with balconies and kitchenettes. Book months ahead for rooms in high season. ❸

Eating, drinking and nightlife

L'Affirmatif 17 blvd Général-de-Gaulle ☎0590/88 66 03. A cosy locals' hangout serving reasonably priced wood-oven pizzas along with the odd Creole dish. Daily lunch and dinner.

Au P'ti Paris 25 Montée Périnet ☎0590/84 56 65. Lovely, Paris-themed spot just east of town with delicious thin-crust pizzas and light salads, plus entertaining theme nights like café-theatre (Wed) and live music (Sat). Open Mon–Sat 7.15pm–12.30am, Sun 7.15pm–midnight.

Casino du Gosier 43 Pointe de la Verdure ☎0590/84 99 50. Flashy neon nightspot draws tourists and locals alike with jazz concerts, movies (€7), slot machines, and even Chippendale dance shows.

Loolapalooza 122 rue Montauban ☎0590/84 58 58. Gimmicky Cuban-style nightspot where bartenders dressed like Che Guevara periodically set the bar on fire – mind your fingers – while the clientele sweats to salsa 'til the wee hours.

Le Napoli Rue Montauban ☎0590/84 30 53. Cosy, open-air Italian place with filling Niçoise salads, pastas, and thin, crispy three-cheese pizzas (mains around €16). Open daily for dinner only.

Le Tam-Tam boulevard du Gosier ☎0590/84 07 08. Popular with locals, this restaurant serves up *boudin créole*, fricassee, and ribs *frites* (€10–13) along with ti-punch and *planteur* (a punch made with rum and tropical fruit juice). Lunch and dinner daily.

Plage Caravelle and Ste-Anne

As pleasant as they are, Le Gosier's beaches are nothing compared to **PLAGE CARAVELLE**, a sensational, palm-dotted swath of sand 13km eastwards, whose picture-postcard turquoise bay has been colonized by Club Med. If you're not a paying guest, you can still hit the beach by following the signs to *Le Rotabas* hotel (see overleaf), where a dirt path ends at a turnstile. You won't be allowed to play with

Club Med's water toys, though – for those, head to casual **STE-ANNE**, a small village another kilometre eastwards, with its own adequate stretch of sand. A beachfront **watersports** centre here rents kayaks, body-boards, windsurfers and canoes.

Practicalities

Aside from Club Med there are only a few places to **stay** in the immediate vicinity. The closest to Plage Caravelle, *Le Rotabas* (☎0590/88 25 60, ✆www.lerotobas. com; ➏ including breakfast) offers appealing, if cramped, garden-view bungalows (most with TV and fridge) just a short stroll from the sand. In Ste-Anne, *Auberge du Grand Large* (☎0590/85 48 28, ✆www.aubergelegrandlarge.com; ➌) has several small bungalows and doubles with a/c 50m from the beach. Nearby, the new *Le Diwali* (☎0590/85 39 70, ✆www.lediwali.fr; ➑) has stylishly spa-like, well-appointed rooms, some with sea views, plus direct access to the beach. A handful of open-air **restaurants** line Ste-Anne's beach; try *Kon-Tiki*, which serves omelettes, pastas and steak at covered picnic tables. Beach trucks also dish out merguez-stuffed **baguettes**, burgers and fries. *Américano Cafe*, a Western-style **bar** popular with locals and tourists alike, pulls pints of Leffe and Stella Artois, and features live acts on Friday.

St-François

Fashionable **ST-FRANÇOIS**, a posh harbour town another 20km due east of Ste-Anne, doesn't have much beachfront but makes up for it with its mast-filled **marina**, where a boardwalk lined with chic boutiques, cafés and restaurants draws affluent mainlanders for people-watching over drinks. The port is also a convenient departure point for **ferries** to Guadeloupe's offshore islands (see p.629), as well as for **dive boats** carting scuba and snorkelling enthusiasts to explore nearby waters. The major land activity happens next door to the marina, at the eighteen-hole **golf course**, Guadeloupe's only greens; the closest **beaches** are a few kilometres east of town, along the Pointe-des-Châteaux (see below).

The town centre has none of the marina's polish, but can be a fun place to wander about. Radiating from the **Place du Marché**, a roundabout circled by an active covered **market**, the tapered one-way streets are so disjointed it's easy to get lost here. You'll find some atmospheric, albeit downtrodden, **wooden colonial houses**; there used to be more before the town was hit by hurricane Hugo. You can pick up a **map** at the Office du Tourisme (Mon, Tue, Thurs & Fri 8am–noon & 2–5pm, Wed 8am–12.30pm, Sat 8am–noon; ☎0590/88 48 74) on the right-hand side of avenue de l'Europe as you head towards the marina.

Practicalities

The only **budget** hotels are located in the town centre, across from the market – expect to be woken up early. *Le Kali* (☎0590/88 40 10, ✆85 04 63; ➌) has simple doubles, most with fans and shared baths. **Resorts** are clustered around the marina. The recently renovated *Kayé La* (☎0590/88 10 10, ✆88 74 67; ➎) has standard doubles with a/c, TV and full bath. If they're booked, as they often are with tour groups, try the **studios** with TV and a/c next door at *Hôtel Résidence Port Marina* (☎0590/88 76 47; ➍). The classiest option, *Kalenda*, is on the north side (☎0590/48 05 00, ✆www.kalendaresort-hotels.com; ➒), with balconied rooms, pool, two tennis courts and a lovely **beach**.

Most of St-François' **dining** options frame the marina: *Le Navy*, on the marina's south side, has heaping bowls of mussels; on the north side, *La Terrasse* has reasonably priced Creole prix-fixe options at €17–24. In town, local favourite *Jerco Chez Nise*, on rue Paul-Thilby, serves up a nine-course menu that makes a great island sampler, with dishes like *lambi au jus* (marinated conch) and *langouste grillée* (grilled spiny lobster).

Towards Pointe-des-Châteaux

Guadeloupe's outermost tip, a needle-shaped isthmus that pokes into the Atlantic, culminates 11km east of St-François in the majestic **POINTE-DES-CHÂTEAUX**, where several barren limestone rock formations leap from the ocean, the tallest crowned by a wooden **cross**. Take in the view from the colourful *La Paillote* café, which serves cheap sandwiches and reasonable prix-fixe Creole menus, or indulge in just-made coconut sorbet from a local vendor. If you fancy a dip, the nearby **Plage des Salines**, with its natural breakwater, is a fine spot; shacks serve drinks and grilled fish on picnic tables perched above the water on stilts. Back towards St-François, the small cove of **Plage Anse Tarare** is popular with nudists - indeed, it's the island's only official nude beach.

Le Moule

Guadeloupe's original capital, **LE MOULE**, a short drive north of St-François on the N5, doesn't have much to offer visitors aside from a couple of decent beaches. You'll pass one of them, the sea-grape shaded **L'Autre Bord**, on your way in; the other, **Plage des Baies**, about 1km north of town, fronts a shallow bay ideal for young swimmers. The only other attraction in the area is the modest displays of Amerindian archeology at the **Musée Edgar-Clerc** (Wed–Mon 9am–5pm; €2), located past Plage des Baies on the right of the D123 towards Gros-Cap.

North to Anse-Bertrand

North from Le Moule on the D120 is Guadeloupe's most enchanting swimming hole, the **LAGON DE LA PORTE D'ENFER** (Gates of Hell). Despite the ominous name, the two salt-ravaged bluffs create a heavenly setting by funnelling the raging Atlantic into a calm lagoon. A ten-minute hike from the road reaches the top of the eastern barrier cliff for stupendous coastal **views**. A terrific **restaurant**, *Chez Coco*, cooks up tasty barbecued fish and chicken dishes (€10–15) at the water's edge.

Another 2km further on, **POINTE-DE-LA-GRANDE-VIGIE** is Grande-Terre's northernmost point and a **lookout** onto nearby islands. When you leave the Pointe, the road switches to the southern D122, passing **ANSE LABORDE**, a slim Atlantic-facing beach subject to large swells, before hitting sleepy **ANSE-BERTRAND**, with its ramshackle wooden houses and aluminium shacks.

Port-Louis and south to Morne-à-l'Eau

Grande-Terre's standout village, **PORT-LOUIS**, is a fishing hamlet with immaculate **wooden colonial houses**. The ambience alone is sufficient cause to stop here, but most people come for its magnificent beach, **Plage Du Souffleur**, a long golden band with a boardwalk hustled by locals selling divine, fresh-churned coconut sorbet. At the southern end, *Siwo Evasion*, on rue de la Liberté (☎0590/22 08 11, ✆www.actipages.com/siwo), rents **jet skis** and arranges guided outings to hard-to-reach beaches starting at €90 per person. Be sure to save some euros for *La Paillote*, a hacienda-style **café** serving traditional Creole lunch fare nearby. A few blocks away on rue Charles Caignet, **Le Petit Musée des Poupées Renovées** is an eccentric little spot run out of a local's home that features a collection of 360 dolls, plus traditional Creole dolls for sale at €20 apiece (daily 2–6pm; €1).

Heading south from Port-Louis, the N6 courses through quiet **Petit Canal** on its way to the **cemetery** at **MORNE-À-L'EAU**, 7km south. Hundreds of black-and-white-tiled mausoleums cover a hillside at the entrance of town with a recurring diamond motif that feels like something out of Alice in Wonderland. From here, the N6 meets up with the N5 to reach Pointe-à-Pitre (see p.620) 15km later.

Basse-Terre

Undulating with mountain ranges, gushing with waterfalls and packed with rainforests, **BASSE-TERRE** provides a rugged antidote to Grande-Terre's glossy resorts.

Scenic **hikes** in the inland **Parc National de la Guadeloupe** descend to the base of the **Chutes de Carbet** and ascend the slopes of **La Soufrière**. Outlying **beaches**, ranging from golden pockets like **Grande Anse** to sparkling black stretches like **Plage Malendure**, extend underwater to one of the world's top **dive** sites.

Despite everything it has to offer, Basse-Terre isn't a big resort area; instead you'll find bungalows and small hotels. Even if Grande-Terre is your base, you should still make time for a day-trip here – you can easily explore some of the rainforest in the morning, hit Grande Anse for lunch and go diving in the afternoon.

Parc National de la Guadeloupe

The most accessible parts of the **PARC NATIONAL DE LA GUADELOUPE**, a tremendous 17,300ha rainforest that encompasses the volcanic La Soufrière (see p.627) and the thundering Chutes de Carbet (see p.627), branch off from the Route de la Traversée (D23), Basse-Terre's cross-island road. Recently designated a UNESCO Biosphere Reserve, the park has numerous **hiking** trails, the easiest of which, the stroll to the **Cascade aux Écrevisses** and the meandering **Bras David**, can be done in a morning. The former is signposted to the left about 7km inland on the Route de la Traversée; it's a pleasant site with picnic tables and a straightforward 100m walk along a jungly pathway that culminates at the modest teal cascade. The latter begins another two kilometres westwards along the same route, behind the small information hut that is the **Maison de la Fôret** (Wed–Mon 9am–1.15pm & 2–4.30pm; closed Tues), which has free English trail **maps** for three nearby walks. The **Découverte de Bras David** is the shortest of these, consisting of a twenty-minute loop through lush, moss-covered white gum trees, tangled roots, and gurgling streams. Be sure to wear sturdy shoes, as things can get muddy and slippery, especially just after the rainy season. The park's fauna is showcased 3km further west, at the entertaining **Parc des Mamelles** (daily 9am–5pm; €11.50), where native endangered species including iguanas, green monkeys and raccoons are bred. Admission includes the thrilling Visite de la Canopie, a 25- to 40-minute trek atop the rainforest canopy up to 30m above the ground. From the park, the Route de la Traversée makes a steep descent to end at the southern outskirts of Pointe-Noire and the coastal N2 (see below).

Practicalities

A couple of mountain **lodges** are situated near the park. Facing the Parc des Mamelles, *Couleur Caraïbes* (℡/℻0590/98 89 59; closed Sat in low season & June 15–30 annually; ❸) has six basic garden bungalows in a tranquil hillside setting, plus a **restaurant** serving traditional French-Creole fare (mains for around €16). At the park's eastern end, in Petit-Bourg, the welcoming *Auberge de la Distillerie* (℡0590/94 25 91, ℮auberge.distillerie@wanadoo.fr; ❹ with breakfast) has a/c rooms (some with hammock-strung balconies), a pool, and on-site spa services. Another dining option midway along the Route de la Traversée, *Gîte des Mamelles* serves Creole fare along with stellar park views (lunch only; mains €10–15).

Northern Basse-Terre

The N2 north of the Route de la Traversée makes a roller-coaster drive up the Caribbean coast with picture-postcard scenes at every descent. Though this coast is rocky in spots, there are a couple of soft sand beaches, including Basse-Terre's finest, **Grande Anse**. The scenery changes dramatically the further northeast you go, as fields of sugar cane dominate the landscape around **Ste-Rose**. A couple of **rum distilleries** and a phenomenal **botanical garden** are the main draws this far north.

Pointe-Noire

The first settlement north of La Traversée, quiet **POINTE-NOIRE** owes its name to the dark volcanic highlands that encircle – and shade – its tangled streets. Some rays filter through to **Plage Caraïbe**, a laid-back locals' beach just south of town where friendly **dive** outfit Dédé & Jazz (☎0590/99 90 95, ℻99 92 69) rents snorkelling gear and organizes outings to the depths around Îlets Pigeon (see overleaf). Grab a bite on the beach at *Délice Caraïbe*, which whips up €15 menus of *fricassee de lambis* and *colombo poulet* (closed Wed).

The locals are renowned for their Arabica coffee beans, which perfume the grounds of the magnificently restored **Caféière Beauséjour** (Tues–Sun 10am–5pm; closed Sept 1–Oct 15; ⊛www.cafeierebeausejour.com; €6), a plantation house and café high on a hill with stunning sea views. Also in the area is the homespun **Maison du Cacao** (Mon–Sat 9am–5pm, Sun 9am–1pm; €5), an eco-museum that traces the path from cacao tree to chocolate. Admission includes a cup of hot chocolate made from pure cacao, and a boutique offers candies, cakes, liqueurs and other goodies made on site. Ponti-Néris are adept carpenters, and you can check out the tools of their trade and exquisite mahogany furnishings at the **Maison du Bois** (Tues–Sun 9.30am–5pm; €7), near the southern outskirts. Opposite is the hospitable *Camping de la Traversée* (☎0590/98 21 23, ℻98 25 23; ❷). Camping is no longer offered here, but the site does feature several fan-only bungalows with kitchenettes and access to a pebble beach; the place is set to undergo extensive renovations in 2005 and 2006, but will remain open throughout.

Deshaies and Grande Anse

Quaint **DESHAIES**, Basse-Terre's most inviting village, lies a few kilometres up the coast, its wooden Creole houses clasped around a deep harbour. So relaxed is the tempo here that the toughest part of your day may well involve deciding from which waterfront terrace to watch the sunset after lounging on **GRANDE ANSE**, Basse-Terre's longest beach, a peaceful 1.5km stretch of golden sand 2km north of town. To get there, follow the signs to *Le Karacoli* (see below); do not take the road signposted to Grande Anse – it's rocky and unpaved.

Practicalities

You can **stay** at *Habitation Grande-Anse* (☎0590/28 45 36, ⊛www.hotelhga.com; ❼), which has spacious kitchen-equipped doubles, studios and apartments in a lush, landscaped hillside setting 300m from the beach. Closer to the sand, the *Fleurs des Îles* (☎0590/28 54 44, ⊛www.fleursdesiles.com; ❼) rents by the week, with comfortable poolside bungalows and direct access to the beach. Budget rooms can be found at the friendly *Ti-Paradis* (☎0590/28 25 15, ⊛www.ti-paradis.com; ❹), just up from the beach on Allée du Coeur (turn at the Total petrol station). The seven bungalows are clean and comfortable, with kitchenette and a/c; the site has a grill and small pool.

Beachside **restaurants** range from shacks frying up inexpensive crispy chicken *boucané* (smoked chicken) and fresh red snapper, to terraced affairs with three-course Creole menus. The best of the lot is *Le Karacoli*, an atmospheric lunch place serving spicy *crabe farçi* (stuffed land crabs) and delicious *conch fricassé* on a tree-shaded beach terrace. Deshaies's rue Principale has several fine options for eating and sunset-watching, including comfortable Italian spot *Piano Piano* (lunch and dinner; closed Sun), on the back terrace of a restored colonial house, and traditional Creole joint *Le Kaz* (dinner only; closed Wed) down the block.

North to Ste-Rose

The one can't-miss spot along Basse-Terre's north coast is the **Jardin Botanique de Deshaies** (daily 9am–5pm; €10.50; ⊛www.jardin-botanique.com), about 1km past Grande Anse. A path leads through the expansive, immaculately tended gardens, which feature waterfalls, orchid-covered trellises and lily ponds and are home to pink flamingos and loriquets and parrots.

Past the gardens, the N2 heads into a region dominated by sugar cane and bamboo with not much worth stopping for until you hit the east coast **STE-ROSE**, an important agricultural town near two inland **rum** establishments. Closest is the

Domaine de Sévérin (Mon–Sat 8.30am–1pm & 2.30–5.30pm; free), Guadeloupe's last waterwheel-operated distillery; to see the 200-year-old wheel in motion, you'll have to get there before 12.30pm.

Further inland, the multifaceted **Musée du Rhum** (Mon–Sat 9am–5pm; €6) counts an impressive scythe collection among its rum-related equipment, and a spectacular insect collection upstairs, donated by a local writer; another chamber houses forty-odd model ships.

Southern Basse-Terre

Southern Basse-Terre is significantly more developed than the north, with sizeable coastal towns merging into one other along the N2, culminating with Guadeloupe's capital, also named **Basse-Terre**. Dominated by the island's highest point, the sulphuric **La Soufrière**, the region's other draws are the **Chutes de Carbet** waterfalls and the abundant underwater marine life around **Îlets Pigeon**.

Plage Malendure and Îlets Pigeon

The French West Indies' top dive site lies 4km south of La Traversée on the N2, off **Plage Malendure**, a sliver of dark volcanic sand that can get brutally crowded in high season as busloads arrive for the thrice-daily **diving** outings offered by numerous beachside outfits. Dives take place around two uninhabited offshore islands, **Îlets Pigeon**, in a 400ha reserve brought to international acclaim in the 1960s when Jacques Cousteau declared it one of the best dive sites he'd ever visited. Since then, upwards of 60,000 dives have taken place here yearly; even so, the marine life still thrives with coral and multicoloured fish. Visit in the late morning, when the sun hits the water directly and the colours are most vibrant.

Practicalities

For **information**, hit the tourism bureau right on the beach (Mon–Fri 8am–7pm, Sat & Sun 8.30am–4.30pm). Some local hotels (see below) have partnerships with dive outfits that give their guests a **discount**; day-trippers can try the top-notch Guy et Christian (T0590/98 82 43, F95 83 25 three dives daily €34–43), across from the beach car park. You can also explore the underwater action aboard *Nautilus*, a boat with a glass hull that makes hour-plus voyages with snorkelling pit-stops (€20; 10.30am; noon; 2.30pm & 4pm; T0590/98 89 08, F98 85 66).

Despite its popularity, the area is low-key with scarce accommodation and restaurant options. The poshest **lodging**, the *Domaine de la Malendure* (T0590/98 92 12, F98 92 10, Wwww.leader-hotels.gp; ❻ with breakfast), has Caribbean views, well-appointed doubles and villas and a pool – plus a 20 percent discount off dives with Guy et Christian (see above). The appealing *Rocher de la Malendure* (T0590/98 70 84, F98 89 92, Elerocher@outremer.com; ❹) is right on the water, and has a/c bungalows with balconies and kitchenettes. While beach trucks sell sandwiches and crepes by day, your best night-time **dining** options are the terraces at the *Rocher de la Malendure*, which serves up plates of locally caught seafood (€12–20), and *La Touna*, on the N2, with Creole and French lunch and dinner menus at €13–16 (closed Mon, Tues eve). Should you simply fancy a pint, *Le Ranch*, 2km south of the beach, has a good **bar** as well as pizzas, salads and fish.

South to Basse-Terre

The N2 hugs the coastline as it makes its way south, passing a slew of charming fishing villages with deep bays. A couple coffee-related sites provide entertaining diversions before Basse-Terre: **La Maison du Café** (hour-long guided tours daily 10am–5pm; €6.10) is a majestic former coffee plantation up a winding road several kilometres from the N2 in Vieux-Habitants. Not as picturesque but much more accessible is the **Musée du Café** (daily 8am–5pm; €6) on the outskirts of Vieux-Habitants, a working coffee mill that produces some seriously strong Arabica beans – you can get a buzz on a complimentary cup at the end of the visit.

You'll know you've reached the outskirts of the French West Indies' first settlement, **BASSE-TERRE**, when traffic comes to a halt. There's not much pay-off once you reach the centre, as Guadeloupe's administrative capital is a hot, downtrodden place without much to recommend it. The main public square, **Place du Champs d'Arbaud**, is a concrete eyesore, and many of the surrounding buildings are modern structures more suitable to a busy French suburb than a Caribbean island.

While the town core is pretty unappealing, two sights at Basse-Terre's southern outskirts are worth checking out if you've come this far. **Notre-Dame-du-Mont-Carmel**, a church fronted by Art Nouveau lamps, is reputed to have curative powers – look for marble thank-you plaques along the apse. Nearby loom the commanding ruins of the 1643 **Fort Delgrès** (daily 8am–5.30pm; free). The fort never saw battle, but its military cemetery contains the tomb of one of Guadeloupe's first governors, Admiral Gourbeyre. To get there, follow the signs for Fort St-Charles – the fort has gone through several name changes and the latest has yet to make it on signage.

La Soufrière

The easiest way to reach the Lesser Antilles' highest peak, the 1467-metre **LA SOUFRIÈRE**, is by heading north on Basse-Terre's main north–south artery, avenue du Général Félix-Éboué. North of town, it changes to the D11 and cuts a steep path to **St-Claude** – the last place en route for water and food supplies. Worth a stop in St-Claude is **La Boniferie** (Tues–Sun 9am–5pm), a restaurant and working coffee mill that also houses an orienteering maze and the self-guided adventure park **Mangofil** (€20), where participants glide across fields via high wires attached to a harness.

You'll need good walking shoes to make the 1.5hr ascent to La Soufrière's often cloud-covered summit, as the path that winds up its western flank gets rockier, tighter and more slippery as it nears the top. The trailhead starts about 8km past St-Claude, at **Savane à Mulets**, a car park at an elevation of 1142m. You'll pass deep gorges and panoramic vistas of the surrounding countryside before arriving on a moonscape plateau of boiling sulphuric cauldrons. Though you're officially not allowed to hike to the very top nowadays, most people ignore the sign and continue the ascent at their own risk. The adventurous can commit to a four-hour hike from Savane à Mulets to the Chutes du Carbet (see below).

Trois-Rivières

Lying at the confluence of three rivers a few kilometres east of the capital, **TROIS-RIVIÈRES** was a significant Amerindian settlement before French colonizers arrived and ousted the natives. What traces remain of its original tenants can be seen at the intriguing **Parc Archéologique des Roches Gravées** (daily 8.30am–5pm; €2), a park scattered with blackened boulders engraved with cartoonish human **petroglyphs** dating from circa 300 AD. A helpful pamphlet available at the entrance details the location of the markings along the park's winding stone path.

While the park is the star attraction here, Trois-Rivières also acts as a **ferry** departure point for Les Saintes (see overleaf), which lie a short 10km offshore, making for a shorter voyage than from Pointe-à-Pitre (see box p.629 for times). The pier is at the end of a well-marked spur road 2km south of the town centre and has a couple of decent **cafés** alongside the nearby car park: L'Etoile de Mer is a relaxed sit-down joint with ocean views and Creole specialities, while Chez Ako does chicken and sausage sandwiches on the cheap (€2).

Les Chutes de Carbet

Praised by Christopher Columbus in 1493 and marvelled at by thousands of tourists since, the magnificent **CHUTES DE CARBET** originate 1300m up La Soufrière's flanks and plummet down 10km inland from the N1 north of Trois-Rivières. While

Columbus only referred to one chute in his diary, there are in fact three **waterfalls** here; the middle one, a mighty 110-metre cascade, gets the greatest attention as it's the most accessible. To reach it, follow the signs (and the crowds); a stairwell descends to a dirt path that hits the fall's basin in twenty minutes.

The secondary trails for the **first** and **third falls** branch off from the same path – the former is the highest, at 115m, and reached by a 4.5hr round-trip hike along an occasionally muddy, but otherwise decent, trail. The third waterfall, a mere 20m high, is the least dramatic, and the hardest to reach; the 5.5hr circuit cuts through some narrow and slippery patches. An easier way to get to it is via Capesterre, a couple of kilometres north on the N1; a well-signposted turn-off in the centre of town ends at the start of a 2hr round-trip trail. Be warned that the paths will occasionally be closed after heavy rains.

North to La Traversée and Pointe-à-Pitre

Little happens along the stretch of N1 that connects the falls with the Route de la Traversée and Pointe-à-Pitre. The only commendable stop is the **Domaine de Valombreuse** (daily 8am–6pm; ⊛www.valombreuse.com; €8), a botanical garden and animal reserve in the hinterlands of Petit-Bourg. Here, you can see blooming red alpinia, porcelain roses and heliconia in the shade of papyrus and oleander trees, plus iguanas, raccoons and tropical birds. Another twenty minutes along the N1 lands you back in Pointe-à-Pitre (see p.620).

Offshore islands

Guadeloupe's **OFFSHORE ISLANDS** make for delightful day or overnight trips from the mainland. The closest, Mediterranean-like **Terre-de-Haut**, is one of two inhabited islands that form **Les Saintes**. Its much drier and rockier sibling, **Terre-de-Bas**, is an inviting escape from the crowds next door. Further out lies **Marie-Galante**, a laid-back island with graceful beaches that are just starting to get touristy. In the far distance looms sparsely populated **La Désirade** and its tiny, uninhabited neighbour **La Petite Terre**, each with shores so undeveloped that visitors may just feel like castaways.

Terre-de-Haut

Terrific beaches and attractive architecture make tiny **TERRE-DE-HAUT** the most striking of Guadeloupe's outer islands. Since its dry climate prevented the introduction of sugar cane, it was instead settled by white Breton and Poitevin fishermen whose descendants are today touted as the Antilles' best – their unique fishing boats, light and rapid wooden outboards called **Saintoises**, are famous in the trade.

Measuring a mere 5km from end to end, the craggy spit is capped by the 309-metre **Chameau** and anchored by a darling village simply called **Le Bourg** – The Town – which borders the **Baie des Saintes**, a glorious harbour enclosed by hilly outcroppings.

Arrival and information

Ferries to Les Saintes depart from Pointe-à-Pitre, St-François, Marie-Galante and Trois-Rivières; you can also **fly** with Air Caraïbes (℡0590/82 47 00, ℻82 47 48; 4 flights Mon–Fri; 2 flights Sat & Sun; €104). Most hotels will arrange to pick you up from the airport, ten minutes outside the town centre, or the pier; you can get around on **foot**, though **scooter** is the favoured means for island-roaming. Several pier-side outfits rent them for €25–30/day. The only island **bank**, the Crédit Agricole (Tues, Thurs & Fri 9.15am–2.30pm), is on rue Jean-Calot, left of the pier; its **ATM**, beside the *mairie* (town hall), a couple of blocks right of the pier, has been known to be empty, so bring some cash just in case. For island **information**, includ-

Several **ferries** make crossings to Guadeloupe's outer islands from Pointe-à-Pitre, St-François and Trois-Rivières, and a couple of companies run passengers between the outer islands as well. The largest operators – Brudey Frères and Express des Îles – are more reliable than the smaller outfits and tend to leave on time. Keep in mind that schedules are subject to change, and that boats often leave late.

Ferry operators

Brudey Frères (Guadeloupe ☏0590/90 04 48; Martinique ☏0596/70 08 50; ⊛www. brudey-freres.fr)

Express des Îles (Martinique ☏0596/63 12 11; Guadeloupe ☏0590/83 12 45; ⊛www. express-des-iles.com)

Comatril (Guadeloupe ☏0590/91 02 45, ☏82 57 73)

Iguana (Guadeloupe ☏0590/50 05 09, ☏22 26 31)

Deher (Guadeloupe ☏0590/99 50 68, ☏99 56 83)

Routes

Pointe-à-Pitre to: **Grand-Bourg**, Marie-Galante (3 daily; 45min; €33 round-trip); **St-Louis**, Marie-Galante (1–3 daily; 45min; €33 round-trip); **Terre-de-Haut** (1 daily; 1hr; €33.50 round-trip).

St-François to: **La Désirade** (1 daily; 45min; €22 round-trip); **St-Louis**, Marie-Galante (1–2 daily, except Sat; 45min; €31 round-trip); **Terre-de-Haut** (1–2 daily, except Sat; 1h 30min; €39 round-trip); **La Petite Terre** (2 weekly; 45 min; €39 round-trip).

Trois-Rivières to **Terre-de-Haut** (2 daily; 20min; €18 round-trip).

Terre-de-Haut to: **Pointe-à-Pitre** (1 daily; 1hr; €33.50 round-trip); **St-François** (1 daily, except Sat; 1h 30min; €33 round-trip); **St-Louis**, Marie-Galante (1 daily, except Sat; 45min; €31 round-trip).

Terre-de-Bas to **Terre-de-Haut** (3–5 daily; 20min; €6 round-trip).

St-Louis, Marie-Galante to: **Pointe-à-Pitre** (1–2 daily; 45min; €33 round-trip); **St-François** (1 daily, except Sun; 45min; €31 round-trip); **Terre-de-Haut** (1 daily, except Sat; 45min; €33 round-trip); **Terre-de-Bas** (4–5 daily; 20min; €6 round-trip); **Trois-Rivières** (2 daily; 20min; €18 round-trip).

Grand-Bourg, Marie-Galante to: **Pointe-à-Pitre** (3 daily; 45min; €33 round-trip).

La Désirade to **St-François** (2 daily; 45min; €22 round-trip).

ing **maps**, head to the helpful Office du Tourisme at 39 rue de la Grande Anse, behind the *mairie* (Mon–Sat 8am–noon & 2–5pm, Sun 8–11am; ☏0590/99 58 60; ⊛www.terredehaut-lessaintes.com).

The island

Most of the action happens around the **pier**, which drops arriving boat passengers off onto a miniature square where elderly women sell bittersweet coconut and guava *tourment d'amour* (agony of love) cakes, a tradition started by fishwives mourning their husbands' absence at sea.

East of the pier, atop a steep incline, you can get a bird's-eye **view** of Les Saintes from the 1867 **Fort Napoléon** (Mon–Fri 9am–12.30pm; €3; ⊛www.fort-napoleon. com), an outpost that got more use as a penitentiary than a defensive camp. The restored barracks now host the small **Musée d'histoire et traditions populaires**, showcasing traditional *Saintoise* crafts and full-scale fishing boats. Outside, sections of the parapets have been transformed into a prickly, iguana-inhabited **cactus garden**.

The island's best beach, **Plage de Pompierre**, lies southeast of the fort, along an almost perfectly enclosed bay. Free-roaming goats and roosters lie right down beside you here; they usually want some of your **food**, acquired from women selling baguettes and sodas near the entrance. To get to the beach, turn left when you reach the T-junction at the base of the hill from the fort, or take the road behind Le Bourg's church. Terre-de-Haut's other good beaches are on the south-west coast: **Pain du Sucre** – a modest nod to Rio's Sugar Loaf – wades into a deep cove, while nearby **Anse Crawen** is foregrounded by a sign proclaiming "Attention: Nudisme"; its waters, not surprisingly, are busy with stripped-down snorkellers.

Hundreds of white sand crabs scuttle the headland of the island's longest beach, **Grande Anse**. Unfortunately, its location, on Terre-de-Haut's Atlantic-facing coast, makes swimming impossible due to strong currents. Still, it's the best spot for sunrise, and you can take a plunge a few minutes east, off narrow **Anse Rodriguez**.

Accommodation

Terre-de-Haut's **accommodations** are plentiful, from posh bungalows to budget options; many boast English-speaking staff.

Auberge des Petits Saints ☎0590/99 50 99, ⓦwww.petitssaints.com. This inn near Grande Anse is chock-full of antiques – all of which are for sale – and its dozen tastefully decorated doubles have balconies with views of the pool and sea. ⑥ including breakfast.
Bois Jolie ☎0590/99 50 38, ⓦwww.hotel-boisjoli.com. The only hotel near Anse Crawen and Pain du Sucre; bungalow-style doubles have a/c, porches

and private beach and pool access. ⑦ including breakfast.
Coco Playa Rue B-Cassin ☎0590/92 40 00, ⓦwww.im-caraibes.com/cocoplaya. Refurbished hotel on Le Bourg's western outskirts; some rooms have terrific harbour views. ⑤ including breakfast.
La Saintoise Rue B-Cassin ☎0590/99 52 50. Ten straightforward budget doubles with private bath and a/c right in the centre of Le Bourg. ③

Eating and drinking

There are more than a dozen **restaurants** scattered across the island, with several close to the ferry dock offering day-tripper-friendly menus of salad and pizza. Seafood is obviously a speciality, with many spots serving up delectable plates of *blaff de poissons* and *thon fumé* (smoked tuna).

Auberge les Petits Saints (see above). The place to splurge; the decadent seafood prix-fixe menu offers dishes like *tarte à la langouste* (lobster pie) and *filet de dorade aux fruits de la passion* (dorado with passionfruit) and is served on an antique-furnished terrace.
Jardin Créole Ferry dock. Wave goodbye to all the day-trippers from this funky, chummy second-floor

pier-side bar; there's plenty of cheap beer, email access, pizzas and other items to distract you.
La Paillote Plage Marigot. Wood-oven-fired fish and chicken are the hallmarks of this popular seaside terrace eatery; *zouk* nights (Wed & Sat) get their share of raves too. Closed mid-Sept–mid-Oct; lunch only.

Terre-de-Bas

TERRE-DE-BAS, twenty minutes west of Terre-de-Haut by **ferry** (see p.629), needn't rank high on your must-see list, unless you're looking for isolation. There's only one easily accessible beach at **Grande Anse**, a small community ten minutes' walk from the pier, and a handful of rugged **hiking** circuits through the arid inland foothills. Few forge on to quaint **Petite-Anse**, at the island's western end, only really of note for its pretty conch-decorated **cemetery**.

Marie-Galante

Although Columbus baptized round **Marie-Galante** after his ship, Guadeloupe's largest offshore island is colloquially known nowadays as Grande-Galette, after its flat-stone shape. Overgrown with **sugar cane** and scattered with crumbling **wind-mills**, the 158-square-kilometre island 25km south of Pointe-à-Pitre has remained a rural, unhurried place that produces Guadeloupe's best and strongest **rum** – a woozy 59 percent alcohol – by adhering to customs that have altogether disappeared elsewhere. You'll likely see sugar cane cut by **scythe** and hauled on oxen-pulled **cabrouets** – the wooden chariots typically found in museums nowadays. The island's other main draw is its lovely **beaches**, which remain mostly uncrowded even during high season.

Marie-Galante's 12,400 inhabitants are split up between three towns: the capital of **Grand-Bourg** and smaller **St-Louis** and **Capesterre**. The island's flatness – its highest point is a mere 150m – makes it ideal **walking** and **biking** terrain. There's also some good **diving** off the southern coast.

Arrival, information and getting there

While you can **fly** to Marie-Galante with Air Caraïbes (℡0590/82 47 00, ℻82 47 48; 3 flights daily; €104), most visitors arrive by boat (see p.629 for details). Depending on where you've caught the **ferry** - Pointe-à-Pitre, St-François or Les Saintes - you'll arrive either at Grand-Bourg or St-Louis. Both quays have nearby **car** rental booths with rates around €35-40/day. For **automatic** cars, try the reliable Aïchi Location (℡0590/97 88 02) or Hertz (℡ & ℻0590/97 59 80). Regardless of the company, booking ahead is always advisable. **Minibuses** and **taxis** also service the island and can be reserved or picked up anywhere on the island; a few euros will get you just about anywhere you need to go. **Bike** rental is available at either pier for about €15 per day.

For **information**, the friendly Office du Tourisme, on rue du Fort in Grand-Bourg (Mon-Fri 9am-4pm; ℡0590/97 56 51; ⓦwww.ot-mariegalante.com), has activity brochures and an excellent **map**, plus a **trail guide** to the island's network of hiking paths - *Les sentiers de randonnée pédestre* (€3.50, in French only).

Grand-Bourg

Largely destroyed by fire in the early 1900s, and hit by a brutal hurricane in 1928, the island capital of **GRAND-BOURG** was rebuilt with a lot of two-storey cement structures, but has enough surviving wooden Creole houses to remind visitors of its roots. It's a compact place, with a few narrow streets heading north of the harbour, where the peeling **Notre-Dame-de-Marie-Galante** church overlooks the town **market**, which brims with spices, fruit and produce (Mon–Sat 6am–1pm). There's little to do here by day except wander about and peruse the market goods, and even less to do by night. The main attraction is the ruins of the island's one-time richest sugar plantation, **Château Murat** (free), 1.5km east of town. At its acme, in 1839, over 300 slaves worked the surrounding fields; three examples of the shacks they lived in are behind the former kitchen.

Practicalities

Hotels are scarce in Grand-Bourg, but there are plenty of *gîtes* (B&Bs) to choose from, like *Le Cerisier Créole*, on Grande Savane (℡0590/97 93 54; ❸), which features two comfortable, clean apartments with high ceilings, a/c, TV and kitchenette on a residential street. For **food**, there's a pleasant bakery, *Le Soleil Levant*, on Petite Place du Marché close to the church. More substantial fare can be had at *Le Papayer Club*, on rue Beaurenon, with delicious, moderately priced home-cooked Creole options. For quick eats, *Le Moana* on rue du Dr-Selbonne serves up good pizza, as does the colourful yellow walk-up stand *Le King Pizza* on rue de Savane.

St-Louis

Marie-Galante's oldest hamlet, quiet **ST-LOUIS**, is mostly visited as a debarkation point from inter-island ferries (see p.629) and for its nearby **beaches**. Starting 3km north of town, the lovely sands of **Plage Moustique**, **Anse Canot** and **Anse de Vieux-Fort** are rarely crowded; Canot is the most secluded and picturesque. None has facilities, so be sure to bring **food and drink** with you from St-Louis. You can stock

Marie-Galante's major sights are the **distilleries** that ferment some of the region's strongest rum, which you can taste liberally and free of charge most mornings before lunch. All three – Bellevue in Capesterre (daily 9.30am–1pm; closed Sept–Oct), Bielle (Mon–Sat 9.30am–1pm, Sun 10.30–11.30am; closed Sun in Sept) and Père Labat (Mon–Sat 7am–noon, Sun 9am–noon), both in Grand Bourg – maintain morning hours only. If you have time to visit only one, make it Bielle – it's the most bustling of the three. Just be sure to eat something for breakfast first.

up on pastries and sandwiches at *Délice Saint Louisiennes* (daily 6am–7pm), a corner bakery facing the pier. *Katimini Pub*, a hole-in-the-wall restaurant and bar to the left of the pier on rue de l'Église, has filling *boudin* (blood sausage), *accras* (fritters), and *crabe farçi* (stuffed land crabs), and is popular with young locals, especially at weekends when the tables often get pushed aside for *zouk*-style **dancing**. Next door, *Le Coin Tranquille* scores with lovingly made, fresh-from-the-pier seafood specials in a laid-back beach location (daily lunch and dinner). *Le Refuge*, another restaurant 2km south of town via the N9, doubles as a *gite* (B&B) with comfortable a/c **rooms** and individual apartments (☎ & ℻ 0590/97 02 95; ⊛www.im-caraibes.com/refuge; ❸). The island's only resort, *Cohoba* (☎0590/97 50 50, ⊛www.leader-hotels.gp; ❼), is nearby, offering tennis courts, swimming pool, and spacious, fully equipped doubles or bungalow-style chambers by a small, private beach. Just off the D205 several km east of St-Louis, the charming stone *Habitation Grand Bassin* (☎ & ℻0590/97 31 27; ❸) features mosquito-netted poster beds, kitchenette, and easy access to Les Falaises, a 20km round-trip hiking trail that skirts the island's northwestern coast.

Capesterre

A popular spot for scuba diving, laid-back **CAPESTERRE** occupies scenic lowlands near Marie-Galante's best beach, **Plage de la Feuillère**. Dive enthusiasts can check out a couple of island outfits: Man'Balaou, 22, avenue des Caraïbes in St-Louis (☎0590/97 75 24; ⊛www.manbalaou.com), and Ti'Bulles (☎0590/97 54 98; ⊛www.tibulles-plongee.com), on rue Beaurenon on the eastern outskirts of Grand Bourg; both offer daily dives for €38. The best overview of the local flora and fauna is at **Marée Sucré**, a shallow bay busy with rays, tiny baby fish, angelfish and trumpetfish.

Back on land, Capesterre's other draw is the mint-condition **Moulin de Bézard** (daily 10am–3pm; free), a functioning windmill 6km north of town, located behind some superbly restored slave shacks where local artisans sell handmade jewellery and carved bowls.

Practicalities

Capesterre's **lodging** options include the relaxed, hacienda-styled *Hôtel Hajo* (☎0590/97 32 76; ❸) between the two beaches on the N9; its appealing fan-only rooms have ocean views, and most have private bath. On a hillside over town, *Le Soleil Levant* (☎0590/97 31 55; ⊛www.multimania.com/residsoleil; ❸) has impeccable a/c rooms, some of which open onto a communal terrace. Capesterre's **dining** scene is mostly limited to beach kiosks selling snackish fare; for a sit-down meal, *Hajo's* on-site restaurant serves up salads, grilled *langouste*, and other traditional Creole fare in a great beachside setting (entrees €13–15).

La Désirade

Sighted by Columbus during his second New World voyage in 1493, **LA DÉSIRADE** appeared an oasis to his sailors, whose yearning for land earned the hump-backed isle its name – "the desired one". It ultimately proved anything but, as it's the most arid and rocky of Guadeloupe's outer islands. The lack of agricultural options gave it only one use to later French colonizers – ironically as a dumping ground for their "undesirables". From the early 1700s to the late 1950s, it served as a leper colony, a legacy it has deservedly now shed, as ever-greater numbers of visitors and day-tripping crowds are drawn by its peaceful, off-the-beaten-track charm.

Lying 11km off Guadeloupe's Pointe-des-Châteaux (see p.622), and measuring 11km from end to end, the two-kilometre-wide island is cut by mountain peaks topped with wind turbines. While the north coast is marked by rough seas, the south side has some pleasant beaches within easy access of the ferry dock and the main settlement, **Beauséjour**, a wee village with a cute little wooden church, fading wooden houses and a conch-shell-decorated sailor's cemetery. Two smaller communities, **Le Souffleur** and **Baie-Mahault**, are a few kilometres eastwards along the only island road; the latter hosted the leprosarium, whose only vestiges, the chapel walls, lie in ruins on the outskirts of town. Both villages front the island's nicest beaches; the best of them, the two-kilometre long **Le Souffleur**, is shaded by coconut trees.

Practicalities

The island's small size makes it an ideal day-trip. **Ferries** make the forty-minute crossing from St-François, or you can **fly** with Air Caraïbes (℡0590/82 47 00, ℻82 47 48; 1 or 2 flights weekly; €104). Regular **mini-buses** are the most convenient and inexpensive way to get around: A few euros will get you from one end of the island to the other, and for €8 per person drivers will offer an entertaining, 90-minute historical tour. If you prefer your own wheels, you can rent **bikes** and **scooters** from a handful of outfits facing the pier for €15–40/day. Note that, unlike the rest of Guadeloupe (and indeed, the Caribbean), La Désirade's **high season** runs from July to September, when the rain actually enhances the countryside.

Accommodation options are plentiful, with a few hotels and nearly 20 cosy *gites* - stop in at the friendly town hall in Beauséjour (Mon, Tue, Thurs & Fri 8am–noon & 2–5pm; Wed & Sat 8am–noon; ✉otladesirade@wanadoo.fr) for a list. *Oualiri Beach* (℡0590/20 20 08, ⊕www.multimania.com/fwi; ➎) is a cheerful new hotel with six small, pleasant rooms with TV, a/c and fridge plus beach access a stone's throw from the pier. Another island hotel, *L'Oasis* (℡0590/20 02 12; ➌) is across the road 300m from the pier, with basic fan-only rooms with shared or private bath. The best of the *gites* is *Alizea* (℡ & ℻0590/20 06 14, ⊕gite-alizea.web.ool.fr; ➌), with stellar ocean views from four clean, cheerful bungalows. The few **restaurants** that serve the island are mostly concentrated near the pier; *La Payotte* whips up fab seafood plates on a terrace (menus €14–19). There is no island **bank**, but there is an **ATM** at the post office in Beauséjour.

La Petite Terre

For true isolation, nothing compares to the gorgeous, uninhabited slivers of **LA PETITE TERRE**, two tiny islands that sit 12km north of La Désirade and 7.5km east of Pointe des Châteaux. The larger of the two, called **Terre-de-Bas** (not to be confused with Les Saintes' isle of the same name), is a draw for day-tripping cruises on the way to La Désirade. There's no pier or facilities to speak of, so boats simply drop anchor offshore, and visitors wade through waist-high water to the **beach** to relax, sunbathe and **snorkel** at a small offshore reef. The rocky island was once inhabited by 28 people, including a lighthouse keeper who finally left in 1974. Today the old lighthouse is solar-powered, and the only inhabitants of note are its many Antillian iguanas, which lurk timidly in the low shrubbery that covers much of the island and can be discovered on a fascinating, signposted 20-minute walking loop of the island's eastern end. The aptly named Iguana Sun (℡0590/22 26 31) does two weekly day-trips from St-François, with a combined visit to La Désirade starting at €39 (lunch included).

15.2

Martinique

Columbus once lauded **MARTINIQUE** as the "…most charming country there is in the world," and the 1100-square-kilometre island is indeed breathtaking, a tropical mix of lush forests, towering mountains, and some of the loveliest beaches in the region. Solitude can be hard to come by, though, as rapid development has resulted in built-up resort towns complete with artificial

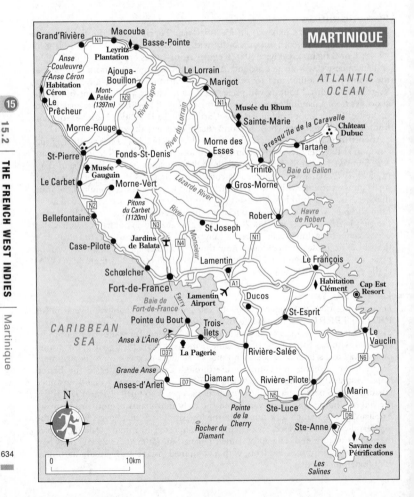

MARTINIQUE

Grand'Rivière
Macouba
Basse-Pointe
Leyritz Plantation
N1
Anse Couleuvre
Anse Céron
Habitation Céron
Ajoupa-Bouillon
Le Lorrain
Marigot
ATLANTIC OCEAN
Mont-Pelée (1397m)
N3
Musée du Rhum
Le Prêcheur
Sainte-Marie
Presqu'île de la Caravelle
Château Dubuc
Morne-Rouge
River Capot
River du Lorrain
Morne des Esses
Tartane
St-Pierre
Fonds-St-Denis
Musée Gauguin
Morne-Vert
Lézarde River
Trinité
Baie du Galion
Le Carbet
Gros-Morne
Pitons du Carbet (1120m)
Bellefontaine
N2
N3
River Monsieur
St Joseph
Robert
Havre de Robert
Case-Pilote
Jardins de Balata
N4
Lamentin
N1
Le François
Schœlcher
A1
Habitation Clément
Cap Est Resort
Fort-de-France
Lamentin Airport
Ducos
Baie de Fort-de-France
Ferry
Pointe du Bout
Trois-Îlets
St-Esprit
CARIBBEAN SEA
Anse à L'Âne
La Pagerie
Rivière-Salée
Le Vauclin
D37
Grande Anse
Anses-d'Arlet
D7
Diamant
Rivière-Pilote
N6
Marin
N
Pointe de la Cherry
N5
Ste-Luce
D9
Rocher du Diamant
Ste-Anne
Savane des Pétrifications
0   10km
Les Salines

beaches and pastel-hued cement hotels. That said, Martinique's resort emphasis makes the island ideal for all-inclusive travel, and most resorts organize optional day-trips to the spots that give an idea of what brought the developers here in the first place.

The second largest holding in the French West Indian empire, Martinique's terrain is topped by a series of mountain peaks. The most imposing, the dormant **Mont-Pelée** volcano, utterly destroyed **St-Pierre** in 1902; though the city has done much to rebuild itself, it's still an eerie experience to walk through the charred ruins of the fabled city and visit its fascinating museum, which is dedicated to the devastating effects of the eruption. **Botanical gardens** teeming with indigenous flora evoke Martinique's original designation as Madinina (island of flowers), while the stupendous **Habitation Clément** distillery hosts a fascinating anti-Columbus exhibit. In between these sights, villages like isolated **Grand'Rivière** and Atlantic-facing **Tartane** steadfastly retain the customs emblematic of traditional Caribbean fishing villages; the latter, on the **Presqu'île de la Caravelle**, is also the island's most laid-back destination, a wonderfully underdeveloped stretch that boasts some of Martinique's finest beaches.

Most **package tours** head straight to Martinique's southern edges, where the island's spectacular **Les Salines** beach is located, along with a host of smaller white-sand stretches and hamlets like **Ste-Anne** and **Diamant**, which have escaped the build-up elsewhere. The island's beaches get increasingly black as you head north, culminating in the breathtaking **Anse Couleuvre** at the island's furthest reaches – the place to go for total isolation.

Arrival, information and getting around

Airlines serving Martinique include Air Canada, Air Caraïbes, Air France, Cubana, Air Guadeloupe (℡0590/21 12 90), Air Martinique (℡0590/ 21 13 40), Air St-Martin (℡0590/21 12 88), American Airlines and LIAT. Ferries link the island with Dominica and St Lucia. For information about travelling by boat between Martinique, Guadeloupe, and St Barts see "Ferries", p.52.

Passengers arriving by **plane** land at Martinique's **Aéroport du Lamentin**, a snazzy terminal about 9km from Fort-de-France and 11km from the nearest southern resort town. Taxis from the airport charge €20 to the capital and €30 and up to the southern coast; there are no public buses from the airport. If you intend to do any additional island exploring, your best bet is to rent a **car** on the spot; several agencies (see below) are located to the left of the airport exit, with rates starting around €50/day. The airport's tourism counter stocks **information**, and staff can make on-the-spot reservations for you; the main tourism office is in downtown Fort-de-France (see overleaf). You can also check out ⓦwww.martinique.org.

Passengers arriving by **ferry** disembark at the **terminal inter-îles** on the southern outskirts of Fort-de-France. The fastest way to reach resort areas south of the capital is by taking a **taxi** (Madinina Taxi ℡0596/70 40 10 or Martinique Taxi ℡0596/63 63 62) straight to the **débarcadère** in downtown Fort-de-France, and hopping aboard a cross-bay **vedette** (see p.638), to avoid the brutal traffic jams on the southern highways. You can still rent a car in southern resorts, and most agencies will let you drop it off at the airport when you leave. Agencies with outlets at the airport and most main resort towns are: Avis (℡0596/42 11 00); Budget (℡0596/70 22 75); Europcar (℡0596/42 42 42, ⓦwww.europcar.com); Hertz (℡0596/42 16 90); Jumbo Car (℡0596/42 16 99, ⓦwww.jumbocar.com); and Rent-a-Car (℡0596/42 16 15, ⓦwww.rentacar-caraibes.com).

Fort-de-France

Often likened to a miniature Paris, **FORT-DE-FRANCE** is stunning to behold particularly when arriving by sea, with its panorama of colonial houses and multiple church steeples wrapping around the **Baie des Flamands** and ascending into the surrounding mountainside. And though traffic is often stifling, the city still charms with the high-fashion boutiques of **rue Victor Hugo** and the wide, bustling pedestrian walkway **rue de la République**. The best day to visit is Saturday before lunch, when the streets fill with locals and tourists alike, and the sounds of tam tam and steel drums resonate throughout the main core.

Information and orientation

Fort-de-France-specific **information** can be obtained at the small Office de Tourisme, conveniently close to the ferry docks at rue Schoelcher and rue Antoine Siger (Mon–Fri 9am–1pm, 2–5pm, Sat 9am–1pm; ☎ 0596/70 23 36, ⓦ www. ot-fortdefrance.fr/), which has loads of maps and brochures, will hold bags for up to an hour, and organizes half-day minibus tours (€10). Another office is located at 76 rue Lazare Carnot (Mon–Fri 8am–5pm).

Most of the city's action centres around **La Savane**, a park planted with royal palms and bamboo along the harbourfront facing **Fort St-Louis**, an imposing 1640 Vauban-style military base set on a promontory above the bay that is now closed to the public.

Accommodation

There's not much reason to **stay** in Fort-de-France, since it all but dies out at night and there's no beach nearby. Still, if you're catching an early flight or are using the city as a base to explore northern Martinique, there are some fine options; the best is actually outside of the town centre.

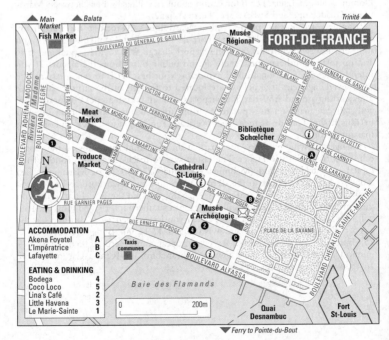

Akena Foyatel 68 av des Caraïbes, ☎0596/72
46 46, ⊛www.akena-foyatel.com. By far the
centre ville's best lodging; 38 comfortable rooms
overlook La Savane, and include a/c, satellite TV
and breakfast. ❺

L'Impératrice 15 rue de la Liberté ☎0596/63 06
82, ₱72 06 30. This *grande dame* has definitely
seen better days, but its location, smack dab in
front of La Savane, and the occasional room with
four-poster bed and balcony, make it a reasonable

mid-range option. ❹

Lafayette 5 rue de la Liberté ☎0596/73 80 50, ₱60
97 75. The 22 budget rooms boast TV and a/c and
are steps from the ferry docks and La Savane. ❸

Squash Hotel 3 blvd de la Marne ☎0596/72 80
80, ⊛www.karibea.com. The most upscale hotel
around, situated on a hill west of the city centre;
the 108 small doubles with a/c and TV are on
grounds with an infinity pool, fitness centre and
three squash courts. ❻

The Town

The city's most striking landmark, the unusual Byzantine and Beaux-Arts styled
Bibliothèque Schoelcher, overlooks La Savane from the west, on rue de la Liberté
(Mon 1–5.30pm, Tues–Thurs 8.30am–5.30pm, Fri 8.30am–5pm, Sat 8.30am–noon).
Designed to house abolitionist Victor Schoelcher's personal book collection, the
ornate library was shown at the Paris 1889 World's Fair before being dismantled
and shipped piecemeal to Martinique's capital. Still in use today, its shelves are filled
with everything from dusty old texts to modern *romans policiers* (crime novels).
Just down the street, at 9 rue de la Liberté, the engaging **Musée Départemen-
tal d'Archéologie et de Préhistoire** (Mon 1–5pm, Tue–Fri 8am–5pm, Sat
9am–noon, closed Sun; €3.05; www.cg972.fr/mdap/) has a two-storey exhibit
devoted to Amerindian artefacts from Martinique and the surrounding islands dating from 100 BC to 1400–1600 AD. Check out the 100-odd *adornos*, miniature clay
figureheads used by Arawaks to decorate bowls and vases. The **post office** is nearby
on rue de la Liberté, across from La Savane (Mon–Tues, Thurs & Fri 7am–6pm,
Wed 7am–5pm, Sat 7am–noon); for **Internet access**, try *Cyber Club Caraïbe*, 16
rue François Arago (Mon 8am–8pm, Tues–Sat 8am–10pm; 30min/€4, 60 min/€7).
Change **money** around the corner at *Change Point*, 14 rue Victor Hugo (daily
7.30am–5pm).

North of La Savane, at 10 blvd Général-de-Gaulle, the **Musée Régional
d'Histoire et d'Éthnographie** (Mon, Wed–Fri 8.30am–5pm, Tues 2–5pm, Sat
8.30am–noon; €3) occupies a Neoclassical 1887 villa. The main interest is upstairs,
where four rooms are decorated with mahogany furniture, gold candelabra, and fine
latticework to evoke a late 1800s bourgeois home. Look for the display of dolls in
ornate period dress, complete with lace and gold jewellery.

Fort-de-France's other landmark, the rust-coloured **Cathédrale St-Louis**, on rue
Schoelcher, boasts a 57-metre steeple and an apse inset with Martiniquan-themed
stained-glass windows. On the northwest outskirts, you can barter for meat, fish and
produce at the busy **markets** (daily 6am–5pm) across the street from the run-down
Parc Floral. Prime **shopping** can be done on rue Victor Hugo, where duty-free
shops like **Roger Albert** (nos. 7–9) offer great deals on perfume, jewellery and
more.

Eating and drinking

Bodega 28 rue Ernest d'Eproge. Set on a second-
floor verandah with bay views, the Italian-Creole
menu consists of simple and inexpensive dishes
such as spaghetti Bolognese and *moules frites*,
with nightly three-course menus at €12.50. Open
daily for dinner.

Coco Loco Rue Ernest d'Eproge. This happening
waterfront restaurant-bar serves up salads, *magret
de canard* (duck breast) (€14.50) and *maxi-
brochettes* (oversize skewers of meat) (€18.50),
plus speciality drinks like mojitos and daiquiris and

live music on weekend nights. Open daily for lunch
and dinner.

Lina's Café 15 rue Victor Hugo. Stellar two-storey
gourmet café with delicious, fresh-made sandwiches, pâtés, quiches and the best coffee in town,
all in a soothing, cosmopolitan atmosphere. Closed
Sunday and evenings on Monday.

Little Havana rue Joseph Compère. Dressed-up
local hipsters hit the town at this convivial Cuban-
themed restaurant and piano bar, where minty,
fresh mojitos are served up alongside fillet of
kangaroo (€18) and tournedos of bison (€20). Live

From Fort-de-France, the fastest and easiest way to reach Martinique's southern beaches is by vedette (ferry boat) run by Madinina (☏0596/63 06 46, ⦿www.vedettes-madinina) or Somatour (☏0596/73 05 53, ⦿www.somatour.com). A regular ferry service connects the capital to Pointe-du-Bout, with service on the half-hour from the quai Ouest near the main tourism office (6.30am–8.45pm; €6 return) and a couple of late night crossings at 11.15pm and 12.10am. Ferries for Anse Mitan and Anse à l'Âne have a similar schedule between 6am and 6.30pm, but are unreliable afterwards. For points elsewhere in Martinique, you can catch one of the minibuses that cover the island, from Pointe-Simon, southwest of the tourism office.

jazz Wed, karaoke Thurs. Dinner nightly.
Le Marie-Sainte 160 rue Victor Hugo. The town's best Creole food, with spicy concoctions

like *accras* (fritters of cod or vegetables) and rich *coq fricassé* (chicken fricassee). Open Mon–Sat 8am–4pm.

Southern Martinique

Most sun-worshippers head directly to **SOUTHERN MARTINIQUE**, where the Caribbean is bordered by the island's only white-sand **beaches**, including **Les Salines**, at the southernmost tip. Built up in recent years, many of the towns have lost much of their Martiniquan character; **Pointe-du-Bout** is the blandest and, thanks to its proximity to Fort-de-France, the busiest. Further south, **Diamant** and **Ste-Anne** are both more authentic and less crowded.

Trois-Îlets to Pointe-du-Bout

You won't have much reason to stop at **TROIS-ÎLETS**, the first hamlet along the southern coast, unless you want **information** on nearby Pointe-du-Bout, which falls under its jurisdiction; the tourism office is on place de l'Église (Mon–Fri 8am–5pm, Sat 9am–1pm, Sun 9am–noon). On the town's outskirts, **Le Village de la Poterie** hosts a handful of potters, artists and other craftsmen that sell their wares at the end of a red-clay road. More pottery can be found nearby at the recently built **Domaine Château Gaillard**, a complex that also hosts the charming **Musée Café & Cacao** (daily 9am–5.30pm; €5 includes coffee tasting) and, for the more adventurous, *Héli Blue* (☏0596/66 10 80; ⦿www.heliblue.com), which offers helicopter tours of the island by English-speaking guides (€28–185). Across the road is the outdoor adventure park *Mangofil* (daily 9am–5pm), where adrenaline junkies slide across high wires while attached to a harness. Further west is the engaging **Maison de la Canne** (Mon, Wed & Thurs 8.30am–5.30pm, Fri & Sat 8.30am–5pm, Sun 9am–5pm; €3), a sugar cane museum that presents a thorough history of slavery on the island.

Past Trois-Îlets in the direction of Anse à l'Âne, the main road branches off to the right and left around Martinique's **golf course**. The right leads to Pointe-du-Bout (see opposite), the left to **La Pagerie**, Empress Joséphine's homestead until the age of 16. While the main house was destroyed by a hurricane in 1766, the stone kitchen now hosts an engaging **museum** (Tues–Fri 9am–1pm & 2–5.30pm, Sat & Sun 9.30am–12.30pm & 3–5pm; €5) dedicated to the empress's torrid relationship with Napoleon. You'll find some intriguing pieces, like the doctored wedding certificate stating their mutual ages as 28, and a falsified coronation scene depicting Napoleon's mother among the guests – if fact, she didn't attend because she disliked Joséphine.

Pointe-du-Bout

Anchored around an almost perfectly square harbour, **POINTE-DU-BOUT** gets most of its traffic from upper-class French tourists with money to burn; the costs of staying in this glitzy area are the highest on Martinique. Still, there are bargains to be found, and the area makes a great base for exploring the wonders of the island's south. You can escape the scene with *Lychee Plongée* (ⓣ0596/66 05 26 ⓕ68 30 13, ⓔanthineaplongee@fr.st; €40–50), a friendly **diving** outfit on the Pointe's outskirts that heads up to St-Pierre and hits the grottoes around the Rocher du Diamant (see overleaf). Or rent a **boat** on the harbour's western side; *Turquoise Yachting* (ⓣ0596/66 10 74) offers small motorboats by the hour (e30) or the day (€130).

Accommodation

There are at least a dozen places to **stay** in Pointe-du-Bout, but you can save money by checking into one of the hotels clustered to the west of Anse Mitan, the natural white-sand beach at the mouth of the Pointe.

Auberge de l'Anse Mitan ⓣ0596/66 01 12, ⓦwww.aubergeansemitan.com. In a quiet location at Anse Mitan's westernmost edge, this recently renovated, family-run inn has twenty rooms with sea or garden views. ④ with breakfast.

L'Impératrice Village ⓣ0596/66 08 09, ⓕ66 07 10. Furthest from Anse Mitan, 59 comfortable kitchenette- and a/c- equipped studios share pleasant grounds with a pool and offer easy beach access. ⑤ with breakfast.

Novotel Carayou ⓣ0596/66 04 04, ⓕ66 00 57. Secluded Pointe-du-Bout option has a private beach, ample water toys and 201 comfortable rooms, many with sea views. ⑨

La Pagerie ⓣ0596/66 05 30, ⓔhpagerie@cgit.com. Smack dab in the heart of the Pointe, this hotel features 98 spacious rooms with a/c, TV and phone. ⑥

Sofitel Bakoua ⓣ0596/66 02 02, ⓦwww.accorhotels.com. The area's most exclusive hotel boasts 137 spacious, well-appointed rooms, an alluring bar and a terrific infinity pool with lovely bay views. ⑨

Village Créole ⓣ0596/66 03 19, ⓦwww.villagecreole.com. Upscale studios and one- to two-bedroom apartments in the hub of Pointe-du-Bout with full kitchen, TV, a/c and parking (reception desk located in *La Pagerie*). ⑤

Eating and drinking

Scads of **restaurants** on the Pointe serve international cuisine ranging from Chinese to Cuban; authentic local restaurants can be found near Anse-Mitan.

Au Poisson d'Or Anse Mitan. Generous portions of Creole fare are served up for lunch and dinner at this relaxed spot on the road leading to the beach (entrees €11–15). Closed Mon.

Chez Fanny Anse Mitan. This cheap, canteen-style restaurant across from the beach has an agreeable daily prix-fixe menu (€13) with an extensive selection of pizza and ice cream dishes. Closed Tues night, Wed & mid-Aug–Sept.

Manureva 25 rue des Anthuriums. Stylish, upscale Anse Mitan restaurant boasts specialties like house-made foie gras, filet mignon, and grilled *langouste* (most plates €16–25).

Le Yacht Pointe-du-Bout. Great central marina location and reasonably priced seafood options (€12–23) make this a convenient spot for plates like *filet de loup de mer* and *steak de thon*.

Anse à l'Âne

The crescent-shaped **ANSE À L'ÂNE**, just 2km east of Pointe-du-Bout, fell within developers' viewfinders recently, and earned its very own all-inclusive resort, the *Club des Trois-Îlets* (ⓣ0596/68 31 67, ⓦwww.hotel-club3ilets.com; ⑨). Popular **dive** shop Corail Club Caraïbes is on site (ⓣ0596/68 36 36, ⓦwww.corail.fr.st; half-day dives to Rocher du Diamant €40–50) and clients can use the hotel's pool. There are few places to **stay** otherwise; your best budget option is *Le Courbaril* (ⓣ0596/68 32 30, ⓦwww.courbarillocation.com; ③), which offers 40 cheerful fan-only bungalows with kitchenettes and terraces right on the beach. To **eat,** there's the convivial *Le*

Nid Tropical, a casual beachside lunch and dinner terrace with tasty *salade Niçoise* (€7) and a superlative *confit de canard* (€15).

South to Diamant

The D37 south of Anse à l'Âne skirts Grande Anse, a gorgeous harbour packed with colourful fishing boats, followed by Anse d'Arlet and Petite Anse, both quiet seaside villages with their own agreeable sandy stretches, before climbing 477-metre Morne Larcher, southern Martinique's highest point. The road here can get pretty tight, with a number of hairpin turns, but it's worth the grinding gear-shifting to reach the south side, where the road plunges down to the sea and the rocky outcropping known as **Rocher du Diamant** leaps into view. This volcanic islet 3km off the coast of Martinique is popular with scuba divers, as its depths are loaded with violet coral, multicoloured sponges and finely carved grottoes. A bit of history: In 1804, the British claimed the rough-cut-diamond outcropping as a battleship, the HMS Diamond Rock, and established unsinkable barracks on her cliffs. After using it to fend off French vessels for seventeen months, the British were outsmarted by the French, who sent over a rum-loaded ship – the isolated mariners drank the stuff, weakening their defences, and enabling the French to recapture the island.

The town of **DIAMANT** itself, which lies a few kilometres east of the eponymous Rocher, is a picturesque place, with pretty blue and coral houses overlooking a fine bay bounded to the east by the cloistered Pointe de la Cherry. The four-kilometre beach here is one of Martinique's nicest, but the swell can be rough; even so, it's still worth checking out for the awesome vista of the Rocher huddled below Morne Larcher. **Diving** around the rock is stellar; find out more from the friendly folks at Sub Diamond Rock (☎0596/76 10 65, ✉sub.diamond.rock@wanadoo.fr) in the compound-like *Hotel Diamond Rock*; they take groups out twice daily (€40–50).

Practicalities

Diamant's hotels are located outside of the town centre. About five kilometres west, *L'Anse Bleue* (☎0596/76 21 91, ⊛www.anse-bleue.mq/; ❹ including breakfast) has attractive wooden cottages and a handful of balconied doubles. If you've got the cash, check out the *Mercure Diamant*, on Pointe de la Cherry (☎0596/76 46 00, ⊛www. accorhotels.com; ❼ with breakfast), whose 149 rooms feature a/c, satellite TV, fridge and phone – all with sea views.

Diamant's best **restaurants** have terraces right over the sand. *Snack 82*, behind the town pharmacy, has cheap beach fare, such as burgers and *croquet-monsieur* sandwiches. Down the street, local favourite *Chez Lucie* has a wide-ranging choice of Creole dishes on their prix-fixe menu, including *poulet boucané* (smoked chicken) and *colombo de crevettes* (shrimp curry) Near L'Anse Bleue (see above), *Cap 110* serves up seafood specialities for lunch and dinner in a charming beachside location (closed Tues).

Ste-Anne

Delightful **STE-ANNE**, Martinique's southernmost village, seems almost blissfully unaware of the *Club Med* and hopping beaches nearby. The town itself revolves around two miniature squares: place Abbé Morland, at the north end, fronts a charming sandstone church, while place 22-Mé to the south hosts the bus depot. The two narrow roads that run between them are lined with lovely two-storey houses that overlook a deep emerald-blue bay.

The friendly **tourism office** on the left side of the road as you head into town (Mon–Fri 8.30am–6pm, Sat until 3.30pm) has information on what's doing in the area. Across the street, quality **dive** outfit Kalinago (☎0596/76 92 98, ✉kalinago@wanadoo.fr) offers trips to Rocher Diamant, night dives and more with English-speaking instructors (€41–48). You can also check out the underwater action on the glass-bottomed *Aquabulle*, which leaves the pier in nearby Marin three times daily; the last trip makes time for snorkelling (1.5–2hrs; €22–26).

Accommodation

Domaine de l'Anse Caritan Route des Caraïbes ☎0596/76 74 12, ⊛www.anse-caritan.com. Ritzy hotel with an exceptional beachfront location and 240 well-appointed and spacious rooms; there's also a gorgeous pool and lush, landscaped grounds. ❽

La Dunette Rue JM Tjibaou ☎0596/76 73 90, ⊛www.ladunette.com. Great location right on the main drag with eighteen straightforward a/c and TV-equipped rooms. Ask for one overlooking the water – there's no extra charge. ❺ with breakfast.

Manoir de Beauregard Av Nelson Mandela ☎0596/76 73 40, ⊛www.manoirdebeauregard. com. Stately 18th-century former plantation house boasts several grand, antique-filled rooms, plus standard bungalows with a/c, fridge and TV. ❻ with breakfast.

Vivre & Camper Pointe Marin ☎0596/76 72 79, ℻76 96 24. Reservations are a must at this beachfront campsite, where you can either bring your own gear or rent the whole kit and kaboodle

– a six-man tent with table, chair, mattresses, stove and dishes. ❶

Eating and drinking

Le Coco Nèg 4 rue Abbé Huard. A cosy restaurant run by a Martiniquan couple who emphasize simple but flavourful local dishes like *fricassée de langoustes* (lobster fricassee), *crabe farçis* (stuffed land crabs), and pig stew (most plates €10–16). Dinner only.

L'Épi Soleil Rue JM Tjibaou. Small counter with a few tables out back on a beach terrace serves pastries, sandwiches (€3–5) and other picnic staples.

Les Tamariniers Place de L'Église. A wonderful diner with superlative service and delicious Creole dishes like red snapper, avocado and lobster, and grouper. Basic menu €13; Creole menu with *langouste* €40. Closed Wed.

La Terrasse Place du 22-Mé. Alfresco restaurant with rustic furnishings, good people-watching from a covered terrace and straightforward, inexpensive home-cooked Creole plates (€10–15). Closed Wed.

Les Salines

The stupendous **GRANDE ANSE DES SALINES**, 5km south of Ste-Anne, is considered Martinique's best beach, and with good reason: its pristine white sands trim an azure bay framed by swaying palm trees. The one danger is the toxic manchineel trees, especially common at the southernmost end; they're marked with bands of red paint. Should you get bored with sun-worshipping, the sand is backed by a natural **salt pond**, after which the beach is named, and borders a desolate petrified forest, **La Savane des Petrifications** (also rife with manchineel trees); both make good side-explorations.

While the beach has countless **snack** trucks selling baguettes, crepes and drinks, **facilities** are minimal – if possible, don your suit in advance. **Camping** (free; see p.613) is permitted on the beach during school holidays. If you don't have your own wheels, you can catch a *taxi-commune* to Les Salines from the **bus** station in Ste-Anne; make sure to confirm return times.

Northern Martinique

The blend of ruins, botanical gardens, rainforests and mountainous areas common to **NORTHERN MARTINIQUE** offers a sharp counterpoint to its southern resort towns. One route here, the roller-coaster Route de la Trace, cuts through the lush valleys of cloud-shrouded **Mont-Pelée** and **Morne-Rouge**, while the Caribbean-hugging N2 is lined by silvery-blue-tinted black beaches. The most remarkable sight in this region is **St-Pierre**, the town destroyed by Mont-Pelée in 1902, while **Anse Couleuvre**, at the northernmost tip, is Martinique's most secluded beach.

Up the Caribbean coast

Once past the suburban communities outlying the capital, the N2 passes through a series of fishing villages before reaching **Le Carbet**, the spot Columbus claimed for Spain in 1502. North of here, two roadside black-sand beaches blend into one another, the first of which, **Anse Turin**, appeared in some of Paul Gauguin's works. He and his friend Charles Laval stayed in a nearby slave cottage during a brief, unhappy stint in Martinique in 1887, when the two were recovering from malaria. While the shack is long gone, the eclectic **Musée Paul Gauguin** (daily 9am–5.30pm; €4), off to the right before the tunnel to St-Pierre, commemorates Gauguin's short residency with everything from reproductions of his works and copies of letters to his wife to stamps, pottery, and other handicrafts from the era.

Immediately north on the N2 are the superb ruins and grounds of the pre-1643 **Habitation Anse Latouche** (daily 9.30am–5pm, closed Sept; €5.50), the island's largest sugar plantation in its heyday. The grounds and buildings were destroyed by Mont-Pelée's 1902 eruption, but vestiges of a 1716 aqueduct and dam are still visible – the only examples of their kind on Martinique. Just as fascinating are the immaculately tended cactus gardens that are now cultivated on the grounds.

St-Pierre

Little Pompeii, as Martinique's former capital, **ST-PIERRE**, is now known, begins due north of the Habitation Anse Latouche. On May 8, 1902, a sudden eruption of Mont-Pelée devastated the then 250-year-old town along with its nearly 28,000 inhabitants – all in a few seconds. The lone survivor, **Louis Cyparis**, was in prison and made it out alive only because his cell was sufficiently ballasted to withstand the heat. The grim effects of the lava's path are evident throughout the compact town, where blackened **ruins** dominate the landscape.

The best place to start your explorations is the **Musée Vulcanologique** on rue Victor Hugo (daily 9am–5pm; €2.50), a small museum that houses contorted glass and soot-streaked porcelain salvaged from the rubble; the centrepiece is a squashed church bell that once sounded Mass.

Facing the museum are St-Pierre's most impressive ruins, those belonging to the 1831–32 Bordeaux-inspired **theatre**: all that remain are the twin entrance staircases and the archway-encircled oval auditorium, but they evoke something of its former splendour. Connected one level below the theatre's northeast corner is what's left of the town jail – Cyparis's life-saving thick-walled cell is among the foundations. South towards the waterfront finds the **Quartier du Figuier**, the extensive ruins of several eighteenth-century portside storehouses.

After exploring the ruins of St-Pierre, the **Centre de Découverte des Sciences de la Terre** on the northern outskirts of town (Wed–Sun 9am–5pm; €5) is a fascinating follow-up. Built on the green flanks of Mont-Pélee, the multi-level centre opened in late 2004 with hands-on exhibits that demonstrate the physics of soil and the history of natural tragedies. Made of neoprene and cement, the boxy, ultra-modern structure is an attraction in itself, designed to withstand level 5 hurricanes and earthquakes of up to 8.0 on the Richter scale.

Practicalities

While St-Pierre is easily walkable, the rubber-wheeled Cyparis Express train covers the town with a narrated tour starting opposite the Quartier du Figuier (Mon–Fri 11am & 2.30pm; €8). For **information**, drop into the helpful Office de Tourisme on Victor Hugo facing the theatre ruins (Mon–Fri 9am–1pm & 2–5pm; ☎0596/78 15 41). They share space with the Bureau de la Randonnée (☎0596/78 30 77), an outfit that arranges **canyoning** trips – combination white-water and rainforest expeditions – and gives out **hiking** information. Tropicasub, on the southern outskirts (☎0596/78 38 03, ✆www.multimania.com/tropicasub), takes **divers** out to explore shipwrecks off the coast (€45–50).

There are a handful of places to **stay** in the area. Above town, *Le Fromager*, Route des Fonds, St-Denis (☎0596/78 19 07; ❸), has sea views from four terraced mountain-edge bungalows. North of the centre, the family-run *Résidence Surcouf* (☎0596/78 32 73, ✆www.residencesurcouf.com; ❸) offers basic bungalows and a pool; the on-site *Surcouf Dive* (☎0596/78 33 58, ✉surcouf-dive@residencesurcouf.com) offers dive packages starting at €39. **Dining** options include a handful of bakeries; *Habitation Joséphine*, a waterfront restaurant with good-value three-course Creole menus and fishermen's specials; and *La Vague*, with a lovely beachside terrace and an €19.85 lunch menu with grilled *langouste*.

Beyond St-Pierre

North of St-Pierre, the coastal road rims the Caribbean after passing the **Tombeau des Caraïbes**, the limestone cliff from which the last of the Carib chieftains committed suicide in 1658 after swallowing poison rather than submit to colonization. The villages along this quiet northern stretch, **Le Prêcheur** and **Anse Belleville**, are among the island's oldest, and their harbours make a picturesque prelude to the **Habitation Céron** (daily 9.30am–5pm; €6), a secluded seventeenth-century sugar plantation. The forested grounds here feature a towering zamana tree, whose branches spread out over 5,000 square metres. Ninety-minute tours on horseback (€35) or four-wheeler (€39) are available; if you're hungry, the on-site **restaurant** specializes in lunch dishes featuring locally farmed crayfish.

As you leave the plantation, turn right to reach **Anse Céron**, a relatively secluded black-sand beach equipped with changing facilities and a snack bar. For total isolation, forge onwards on the N2 as it ascends a jungly mountain road before descending to **Anse Couleuvre**, a magnificent emerald bay with a volcanic sand beach. A path to the left of the car park hits the sand in short order; a longer one to the right passes the ruins of a chocolate plantation, the aroma of which still pervades the air. The latter trail is also the start of a grinding eighteen-kilometre (6hr), walk to Grand'Rivière (see overleaf).

Route de la Trace

Opened by the Jesuits in the early 1700s, the snaking **ROUTE DE LA TRACE**, or N3, rises into the foggy altitudes of **Mont-Pelée** and the **Pitons du Carbet** northwest of Fort-de-France before heading to the Atlantic coast.

At the start of the N3 just outside Fort-de-France, the Byzantine **Sacré-Coeur-de-Balata** overlooks the capital from a hillside plateau; built in 1928, the domed church is a miniature replica of the one in Montmartre in Paris. Several km further northwest is the route's major tourist stop, the botanical **Jardin de Balata** (daily 9am–5pm; €6.50; ⊛www.jardindebalata.com), where buses deposit cruise ship day-trippers to check out the flowers. The landscaped gardens are lush with lily ponds and hundreds of palms and fruit trees, and afford awesome vistas of the Pitons de Carbet.

Heading another 10km inland from the gardens, the N3 reaches the **Site de l'Alma**, a cascading river with shallow pools in a dark rainforest, then moves onward to Martinique's highest settlement, **Morne-Rouge**, located 450m above sea level. The town's proximity to **Mont-Pelée**, the 1397-metre-high volcano that dominates northern Martinique, is the main reason to stop here; the **Maison du Volcan** (☎0596/52 45 45), on the rue Principale in the middle of town, organizes hikes to the summit. Nearby (look for the green gate), the island's modest **youth hostel**, *Auberge de Jeunesse*, on rue Jean-Jaurès (☎ & ☎0596/52 39 81, ⊛www.fuaj.org; ❶ with breakfast), has beds in dormitory, single or double rooms.

A junction at the northern outskirts of Morne-Rouge marks the end of the Route de la Trace; the eastern N2 hits St-Pierre (see opposite) in 8km while the westward N3 carries on past the access road to Mont-Pelée, signposted to Aileron 2km after the turn-off.

Onward to the Atlantic coast

The most notable stop along the stretch of N3 that heads towards the Atlantic is the **Gorges de la Falaise** (daily 9am–4pm, closed on rainy days; €7), on the southern outskirts of Ajoupa-Bouillon. With the help of a guide, visitors meander through the rainforest before descending into rushing cascades for some invigorating swimming. While the one-hour hike is not difficult, the stone pathways can be slippery, so bring good shoes.

A few kms further towards the coast is the circa-1700 **Plantation Leyritz** in Basse-Pointe, where the N3 meets the N1. This charming sugar-plantation-turned-**hotel** (☏0596/78 53 92, ⓦwww.plantationleyritz.com; ⓖ) is among Martinique's best-preserved colonial holdovers, with handsome grounds and a water mill; guests sleep in attractive terracotta-roofed cottages once home to married slaves.

North to Grand'Rivière

You can't visit northern Martinique without spending some time in secluded **GRAND'RIVIÈRE**, a jewel of a fishing village huddled on lowlands framed dramatically by Mont-Pelée. The drive from Basse-Pointe alone makes a visit worthwhile – the thirty-minute route is the island's most thrilling, with tight hairpin turns, overgrown hillsides and bridges suspended over gorges. The roller coaster ends at the village's black-sand beach, and it's literally the end of the road - the only way to go further from here is by foot or sea. A **syndicat d'initiative** facing the town church (Mon–Fri 8am–5pm, Sat & Sun 9am–1pm or in high season 4pm; ☏0596/55 72 74) organizes outings for around €30. Grab a bite nearby at friendly Creole **restaurant** *Chez Tante Arlette*, 3 rue Lucy de Fossarieu (Tues–Sun noon–4pm), where Arlette herself cooks up generous three-course prix-fixe menus of crayfish (€16–30). There's also a handful of recently renovated **rooms** upstairs (☏0596/55 75 75, ⓕ55 74 77; ❷).

Central Martinique

CENTRAL MARTINIQUE extends south from the capital to Trois-Îlets and north to Ste-Marie. Though the region is mostly suburban, it does boast the show-stopping **Presqu'île de la Caravelle**, a verdant peninsula that juts into the mighty Atlantic. Also worth a side trip is the **Habitation Clément**, a remote rum distillery that came to international fame when it hosted the 1991 Gulf War summit between then French President François Mitterand and US President George Bush Sr.

Presqu'île de la Caravelle and around

Despite flaunting some of Martinique's most beautiful beaches, the twelve-kilometre long **Presqu'île de la Caravelle** has remained delightfully underdeveloped. Sweeps of sugar cane and bamboo crush up against the access road before opening onto dramatic ocean vistas and arriving at the peninsula's solitary village, quaint **Tartane**, where a glorious Atlantic-facing beach is busy with fishing boats and red-throated pelicans angling for dinner.

Aside from Anse Tartane, there are five other Atlantic-facing **beaches** nearby, the best of which, **Anse l'Étang**, is 1km east of town. Another km further is **Anse Bonneville**, with prime windsurfing conditions. The peninsula's other draw, the protected **nature reserve** at its tip, has several **hiking** trails and contains what's left of the 1740 **Château Dubuc** (daily 8am–6pm; €3), a homestead with ruins of several slave *cachots*, small solitary-confinement units.

A couple of sights within easy driving distance combine to make a good half-day outing. The vicinity of Ste-Marie finds the engaging **Musée du Rhum** (daily 9am–5pm; free entry and tasting), where a mint collection of rum-related paraphernalia is complemented by hilariously outdated advertising campaigns. The area's main attraction, however, is the stellar **Habitation Clément**, 10km south of the

△ Picnic table near Pointe-de-la-Grande-Vigie, Guadeloupe

peninsula, at the western outskirts of Le François (daily 8.30am–5.30pm; closed Sept; €7, rum-tasting included; ⊛www.rhum-clement.com). The graceful property sits on eighteen hectares of grounds; the highlight is its unusual anti-Christopher Columbus exhibit in the rum-ageing room.

Practicalities

The best **hotel** value near Anse l'Étang is the charming, family-run run *La Caravelle* (☎0596/58 07 32, ⊛www.hotel-la-caravelle-martinique.com; ④), east of the beach on a commanding hillside perch on route du Chateau Dubuc. The 15 quaint studios and apartments – all with kitchenette, TV, a/c and easy beach access – were all completely renovated in early 2005. Closer to the beach is the kid-friendly *Vacances Familles Martinique* (☎0596/58 04 54 ✉vvf-martinique@wanadoo.fr; ③), whose simple, kitchenette- and a/c-equipped rooms are so close to the water that you can hear the crashing surf. The peninsula's poshest lodgings are at *Baie du Galion* (☎0596/58 76 10, ⊛www.karibea.com; ⑦), with spacious balconied suites and kitchenettes. For true luxury, head south from the peninsula to the decadent new *Cap Est Lagoon Resort* on the coast between Le François and Le Vauclin (☎0596/54 80 80, ⊛www.capest.com; ⑨); the 50 stylish, deluxe suites feature private terrace, king-size bed, and 32-inch plasma-screen TV.

Most of the **restaurants** in the area are casual spots near Anse Tartane, typically offering daily seafood specials and traditional Creole fare. The peninsula's standout dining destination is *La Table de Mamy Nounou* at La Caravelle (see above), which serves creative regional fare on a romantic enclosed terrace overlooking the ocean (mains €15–27). For something more laid-back, the *Mini-Golf Beach Club* by Anse l'Étang serves pizzas until 1am most nights, and transforms into a disco on Saturdays.

15.3

St Barthélemy

The Caribbean playground of the rich, famous and fashionable, diminutive 25-square-kilometre **ST BARTHÉLEMY (St Barts)** looks and feels like it's been plucked from the Côte d'Azur and dropped into the Antilles. Situated 25km south of St Martin and 175km north of Guadeloupe, the boomerang-shaped island is sprinkled with picturesque red-roofed **villas** and edged by some of the Caribbean's loveliest **beaches** and **bays**. Many of the beaches are only accessible by sea, giving the island a rare sense of **seclusion**. Indeed, even the most beautiful stretches of sand – **Grande Saline**, **Anse Colombier** and **Anse du Gouverneur** – never get crowded and, thanks to building laws forbidding big resort developments, everything is small-scale, including the capital, **Gustavia**, whose tallest buildings are shorter than the highest palm trees.

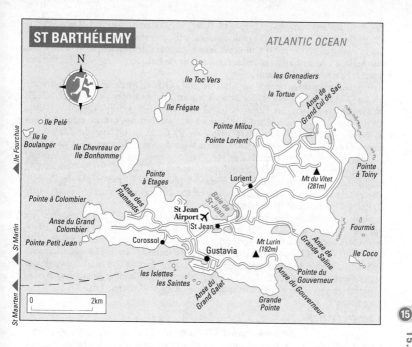

ST BARTHÉLEMY

ATLANTIC OCEAN

N

Ile Toc Vers
les Grenadiers
la Tortue
Anse de Grand Cul de Sac
Ile Frégate
Pointe Milou
Pointe Lorient
Ile Pelé
Ile le Boulanger
Ile Chevreau or Ile Bonhomme
Pointe à Etages
Lorient
Mt du Vitet (281m)
Pointe à Toiny
Pointe à Colombier
Anse des Flamands
Baie de St Jean
St Jean Airport
St Jean
Anse du Grand Colombier
Pointe Petit Jean
Corossol
Gustavia
Mt Lurin (192m)
Anse de Grande Saline
Fourmis
Ile Coco
les Islettes
les Saintes
Anse du Grand Galet
Pointe du Gouverneur
Anse du Gouverneur
Grande Pointe

Ile Fourchue
St Martin
St Maarten

0   2km

St Barts' privacy doesn't come cheaply, but considering the throngs that crowd the island's neighbours in high season, paying a little more for some personal space can make all the difference.

Arrival, information and island transport

Airlines that fly to St Barts are Air Caraïbes, Air St Thomas, St Barth Commuter and Winward. St Martin is the major hub; flights also arrive daily from San Juan and St Thomas. Ferries run daily between St Barts and both French St Martin and Dutch St Maarten. For information about travelling by boat between Guadeloupe, Martinique and St Barts see "Ferries", p.52.

Most overnight visitors arrive by twenty-seater **planes**, on a miniature runway that essentially ends in the water – making for a spectacular, if daunting, arrival. The terminal is also a modest affair. There's an **ATM** across the street at the St-Jean Centre Commercial, where you can also **exchange** currency. There's another currency exchange in Gustavia on rue de la République across from the Christian Dior boutique (Mon–Fri 8am–12.30pm, Sat 8.30am–noon).

Day-trippers from St Martin usually come by **ferry**, on a one-hour trip that ends in the centre of Gustavia, at the Quai Général-de-Gaulle.

Many hotels meet flights or ferries on request. While there are two **taxi** stands – one at the airport, the other at Gustavia's Quai Général-de-Gaulle – there are no public **buses**. (Call ahead for a taxi on ☎0590/27 66 31 in Gustavia, or 27 75 81 in St-Jean.) Consequently, most visitors rent a **car** – several agencies are located a few metres to the right as you exit the airport. Your best bet is a jeep, as the island's roads are notoriously steep and get quite slick when it rains – you'll be thankful for the four-wheel drive. Reservations are a must. Outfits include reliable local Turbé (☎0590/27 71 42, ✉sbbh@saint-barths.com); Budget (☎0590/27 66 30); Europcar (☎0590/27 74 34, ⊛www.europcar.com); Island Car (☎0590/27 70 01, ✉islandcr@wanadoo.fr); and Soleil Caraïbe (☎0590/27 67 18,

©soleil.caraibe@wanadoo). Tropic'all Rent, on Gustavia's rue du Roi Oscar II (℡0590/27 64 76, ©tropic'all.rent@wanadoo.fr), also rents small two-seaters similar to oversize golf carts. If you don't rent a car, consider staying in St-Jean; it has the highest concentration of restaurants and shops outside the capital, plus the two busiest beaches on the island.

For **information**, head to the helpful Office Municipal de Tourisme (Mon–Thurs 8.30am–12.30pm & 2–5.30pm; Fri until 5pm; ℡0590/27 87 27, ©odtsb@wanadoo.fr) in Gustavia on Quai Général-de-Gaulle, on the east side of the marina. Advance island web surfing and reservations can be done through ⓦwww.st-barths.com. The **post office** is in Gustavia on rue du Centenaire (Mon, Tue, Thurs & Fri 7.30am–3pm, Wed & Sat 7.30am–noon). **Internet access** is available in Gustavia at *ANT Informatique*, on rue Jeanne-d'Arc and Centre Alizés on rue de la République (Mon-Sat 8.30am-6.30pm; 30min/€5), which has 30 computers and also rents cell phones (€50 per week). In St-Jean, there's a stylish web-café-with-a-view at the hilltop restaurant *Terrazza* (daily 7.30am–11pm, closed Wed; 60min/€8).

Most of the island's **watersports operators** are based on La Pointe, on the west side of Gustavia's port. The highly recommended Marine Service (℡0590/27 70 34, ⓦwww.st-barths.com/marine.service), runs sunset cruises plus half- and full-day sails (€59–98) on a 42-foot catamaran and 44-foot sailboat. Nearby, Plongée Caraïbes (℡0590/27 55 94, ⓦwww.plongee-caraibes.com) focuses on scuba diving and snorkelling, with multilingual, PADI-certified instructors leading excursions to Anse Colombier and other prime dive spots (snorkelling €40, diving €55–110).

⑮ Gustavia

St Barts' capital, doll's house-quaint **GUSTAVIA**, is an appealing blend of red-roofed villas and heavy-set grey-stone buildings that hug a deep, U-shaped harbour, where yacht-watching over a glass of wine at a waterfront **café** ranks as the unofficial town pastime. A close runner-up for that title is **shopping**, as dozens of duty-free boutiques – from Gucci and Hermès to Louis Vuitton and Lacoste – line the main drag, **Rue de la République**.

The town's historical sights can all be seen in under an hour. The architectural highlight, the boxy, circa-1800 Swedish **Wall House**, anchors the west side of the harbour from **Place Vanadis**, named after the last Swedish military vessel to leave the island after the 1878 French repossession ceremony. The former storehouse now hosts the **Musée de St Barthélemy** (Mon 2.30–6pm, Tues–Fri 8.30am–12.30pm & 2.30–6pm, Sat 9am–noon; €2), a modest collection of tools, maps, model ships and other oddities. On the south side of the port, the intimate 1855 **St Bartholomew** Anglican church, with its sandstone façade, original marble floor and wood-shingled belfry, contrasts strikingly with the more sober stone arches and high altar of the Hispanic-influenced **Notre-Dame de l'Assumption** nearby. Across the street from the Anglican church, a 10-ton **anchor** juts skyward; found in 1981 when a tugboat accidentally got stuck on it, the iron anchor is thought to have come from an 18th-century American warship. A short walk west from both churches along rue de l'Église is Gustavia's small quiet beach, the pinkish seashell-covered **Anse du Grand Galet** (aka **Shell Beach**), not surprisingly a boon for beachcombers. At the other end of town, a red-topped lighthouse graces a promontory once home to **Fort Gustaf**, though scant evidence of its military origins remains save the odd cannon and sentinel; the main attraction today is the magnificent **view** of Gustavia and surrounding islands.

Accommodation
Most of St Barts' **hotels** are located outside the capital, close to the better beaches. Still, a couple of in-town options are the island's best **bargains**.

Carl Gustaf Rue des Normands ☎0590/29 79 00,
ⓦwww.carlgustaf.com. A decadent fourteen-suite
hideout on a hill above the town with gym, sauna,
and easy access to Shell Beach. Each room boasts
a private "plunge" pool and prime sunset views. ❾
Presqu'île La Pointe ☎0590/27 64 60,
ⓔapa@wanadoo.fr. The cheapest lodgings on the
island. These ten basic rooms on the west side of
the port have a/c and private bath; request one
with a balcony (there's no extra charge). ❸
Sunset Rue de la République ☎0590/27 77 21,
ⓔsunset-hotel@wanadoo.fr. A cosy option with ten
comfortable rooms right on the waterfront, plus a
sunny verandah with a lovely harbour view. ❻

Eating and drinking

Gustavia's **dining** scene is as cosmopolitan as its clientele, with sushi, Italian and
tapas menus nearly as plentiful as traditional French fare. Despite the jet-set atmosphere, however, the town doesn't have much of a **late-night scene**, though a couple
small dance clubs keep things going till the wee hours.

Baz Bar Rue Samuel Fahlberg. Hip, friendly sushi
hangout right on the water with English-
speaking staff, live music every night till midnight,
and excellent maki (€7–13) like the Baz Roll, with
eel, asparagus, avocado and *masago* wrapped in
egg crepe.
Carl Gustaf (see above). The terrace bar and
lounge at this luxury hotel offer Gustavia's best
views – perfect for a cocktail at sunset.
Casa Nikki Rue Courbet. DJs spin dance tunes
nightly from midnight till 3–4am at this unpretentious locals' spot, one of the island's only late-night
hangouts.
Chez Maya Public Beach ☎0590/27 75 73.
Popular, pricey beachfront restaurant with a daily-
changing menu of clean, simple plates like grilled
mahi-mahi (€26) and chicken sautéed with garlic
and ginger (€29). Reservations required. Dinner
only; closed Sun.
La Crêperie Rue Auguste Nyman. Locals pack this
cheerful cheap-eats nook for crepes both sweet
(chocolate-banana) and savoury (lobster, shrimp
and mushroom), plus salads, panini and ice cream.
Daily 8am–10pm.
Do Brazil Shell Beach (☎0590/29 06 66). Stylish,
global spot with a lovely terrace location overlooking the beach (mains €16–27). For a more relaxed
vibe, check out Zen Bar downstairs on the sand,
a relaxed hangout for cheap drinks, salads and
sandwiches.
La Saladerie Quai du Yacht Club. On the quiet
western side of the marina, this low-key lunch and
dinner destination offers an extensive list of salads
(€9–23) and pizzas (€9–15), plus tuna tartare,
carpaccio de boeuf (beef carpaccio), and pasta
plates. Closed Wed, Sun afternoon.
Le Sapotillier Rue du Centenaire ☎0590/27 60
28. A superlative setting in a handsome waterfront
house with an expensive but delicious menu
including frogs' legs fricassee and snail lasagne.
Reservations advised. Dinner only.
Le Select Rue de la France. This quirky, inexpensive outdoor pub serves the best cheeseburger
and fries on the island; no surprise that it was the
inspiration behind Jimmy Buffett's classic tune
"Cheeseburger in Paradise". Closed Sun.
Yacht Club 6 rue Jeanne d'Arc. Done up in white
leather, this stylish *boîte* attracts a chic, moneyed
crowd with thumping house music and pricey
cocktails. Open nightly till 4am.

St-Jean

St Barts' other main village, the twin-beached **ST-JEAN**, lies so close to the airport
that incoming planes practically land on the longer of the two white-sand crescents.
This hasn't prevented the area from becoming the island's premier resort, though; its
first hotel, the spectacular *Eden Rock* (see overleaf), was established here in the 1950s
atop the quartzite promontory that divides the two stretches. Since then, St-Jean has
become the most happening spot on the island after the capital, with plenty of shops,
restaurants and bars, both on and off the sand. The bay itself, protected by coral reefs,
has good **windsurfing** conditions.

Accommodation

Hotels are plentiful and conveniently located in St-Jean, with several properties
scoring points for "feet-in-the-sand" location right on the beach. There is no budget
lodging to be found, but hotels on the hillside overlooking the water are more
reasonably priced.

Eden Rock ☎0590/29 79 99 or 1-877/563-7105, ⓦwww.edenrockhotel.com. Completely rebuilt and expanded in late 2004, this cushy palace features 33 deluxe cottages, cabins, suites and villas, all with ocean views. ❾

Emeraude Plage ☎0590/27 64 78, ⓦwww.emeraudeplage.com. Thirty clean, whitewashed bungalows and cottages with terraces, kitchenettes, a/c and TV, just steps from the beach and a private bar. ❾

Tom Beach ☎0590/27 53 13, ⓦwww.tombeach.com. The island's coolest, most colourful hotel, this hip beachfront property boasts 12 stylish cottages with private patio, four-poster beds, hammocks, VCR and stereo. ❾

Tropical ☎0590/27 64 87, ⓦwww.tropicalhotel.net. Pleasant, peach-coloured boutique hotel with friendly staff, swimming pool, a lush garden, and 20 garden- and bay-view rooms up a steep hill from the beach. Closed June–mid-July. ❽ with breakfast.

Le Village St Jean ☎0590/27 61 39, ⓦwww.villagestjeanhotel.com. Good value family-run hotel on a hill above the beach with Internet café, English-speaking staff and 27 comfortable, spacious rooms with impressive bay views. ❽ including breakfast.

Eating and drinking

Most of the action in St-Jean takes place along the village's main drag, Route de Saline, which is dotted with upscale boutiques, **restaurants** and hotels.

Chez Ginette Anse des Cayes. Locals' hangout northwest of town serves up great value Creole dishes, but Ginette is even more popular for her 63 different flavoured rums (€8.50–12.50/bottle), perfect for souvenirs. Closed Sun.

The Hideaway The menu reads "Corked wine, warm beer and lousy food," but don't buy it – this casual joint packs 'em in for some of the tastiest pizzas, salads and pastas in town. Closed Sun lunch & Mon.

KiKi-é Mo Route de Saline. Busy roadside shop dishes out reasonably priced panini, pizza and pasta salads, plus gourmet goodies like Champagne and antipasto.

La Plage At Tom Beach (see above). St-Jean's best beach hangout, this breezy restaurant features casual fare and cocktails by day, creative, upscale seafood plates (€24–37) by night, all in a laid-back setting of cushy pillows, couches, and billowy curtains.

Maya's to Go Gourmet take-out place close to the airport with fancy salads, sandwiches, cookies, and other upscale nibbles for the flight home.

Nikki Beach Route de Saline. Everyone's a supermodel or a wannabe at this loud beachfront sushi restaurant and lounge, where DJs pump house music, bartenders mix up mean mojitos (€10), and servers with attitude drop off platters of maki (€8–16).

On-the-Rocks Restaurant & Tapas Bar At Eden Rock (see above). The best views in St-Jean. This lofty, newly rebuilt terrace bar jutting out into the bay is open for service only at night but is accessible all day long – feel free to grab a cocktail from the beach-level Sand Bar and stroll up.

Le Piment Route de Saline. Casual, reasonably priced restaurant open for breakfast, lunch and dinner serves up simple, standout burgers and panini (€6–9) and ice cream creations (€2–10).

Terrazza At Le Village St Jean. Contemporary Italian plates (€16–24) like perfectly al dente risotto with speck and artichokes star at this sophisticated restaurant on a hilltop terrace. Closed Wed.

Lorient

From St-Jean, the road makes a short climb before descending into quiet **LORIENT**, the site of the first French settlement in 1648. Today, its smallish bay is popular with **windsurfing** aficionados. Otherwise, the town's main appeal is its proximity to St-Jean. The most charming local **accommodation** is, hands down, Le Manoir de Marie, on route de Salines (☎0590/27 79 27, ⓦwww.lemanoirstbarth.com; ❼), a stunning 17th-century French Norman mansion brought over from France and rebuilt in 1984. The surrounding eight cottages – all in the same comfortable, rustic style – feature antiques, stone floors, TV, a/c and minibar. More posh is the modern, minimalist La Banane, on the way into the village (☎0590/52 03 00, ⓦwww.labanane.com; ❾ including breakfast and airport transfers), with two Zen-like swimming pools and nine ultra-stylish bungalows with bathrooms that open onto a private terrace or garden. La Normandie, also on route des Salines (☎0590/27 61 66, ☏27 98 83; ❹), is a much simpler affair, but rooms do have a/c and it's good value even in high season. Lorient's only upscale **restaurant**, *K'Fé Massaï* (☏0590/29 76 78; dinner only; closed Tues), is a sophisticated French-Creole spot at the entrance to town that serves seafood plates like mahi-mahi and shrimp stew with curry sauce (€29–39). Nearby, divey walk-up *Jojo Burger* keeps locals happy with a cheap-eats lunch menu of burgers and sandwiches (closed Sun). Pick up salads, sweets and more for the beach at patisserie/teahouse *La Petite Colombe*, also on the main drag (open daily for breakfast and lunch).

Anse de Grande Saline and Anse du Gouverneur

Two of St Barts' best beaches are approached from well-marked secondary roads south of St-Jean and Lorient. The local favourite is the white-sanded **Grande Saline**, which backs a salt pond at the island's core. The other, the facility-less **Anse du Gouverneur**, lies around another headland, at the end of a steep descent that passes hidden villas and marvellous views of St-Jean. You can **eat** near Grande Saline at *Le Grain du Sel*, a relaxing lunch spot with tempting goat-cheese burgers (€14) and house-made coconut tarte (€7). The best restaurant in the area is the comfortably upscale *Le Gommier*, an excellent white-tablecloth eatery with clean, creative dishes like refreshing tuna tartare with gazpacho sauce and linguine with *langouste*.

Pointe Milou to Grand Cul-de-Sac

A couple of kilometres past Lorient, the main road passes the island's swankiest neighbourhood, **POINTE MILOU**, a collection of stunning villas on a rocky cliff. The lone **hotel** here, *Christopher* (☏0590/27 63 63, ☏0590/27 92 92, ☏www.accor-hotels.com; ☻ with breakfast), is tucked along the base of the point, with 42 well-appointed rooms with private patios and ocean views, plus the island's largest swimming pool. The sexy, red-velvet-festooned *Ti St-Barth* (☏0590/27 97 71; dinner only) scores with a hipster bar scene and an Asian-inflected menu with Thai beef salad (€15) and grilled tuna steak with Chinese noodles (€29).

Grand Cul-de-Sac

From Pointe Milou, the road slopes down to reach the golden beach at **GRAND CUL-DE-SAC**, a tranquil lagoon ideal for families with small children. There's not much privacy to be had here since virtually every grain of sand has been colonized by major **hotels**. Of these, the best value is at *St-Barth's Beach* (☏0590/27 60 70, saintbarthbeachhotel.com; ☻), whose comfortable rooms all feature ocean views just steps from the sand (closed Sept). Close by, the just-renovated *Guanahani* (☏0590/27 66 60, ☏www.leguanahani.com; ☻) is St Barts' largest hotel and one of its poshest, with expansive grounds that feature tennis courts, two restaurants, and a full-service Clarins spa with eight treatment rooms. The 69 rooms are stylish, with terraces and high-pitched roofs, plus free wireless connectivity, a rarity on the island.

You need never leave the enclave to **eat**, given that each hotel hosts up to three restaurants. *Le Rivage*, at *St Barth's Beach*, serves giant salads (€14–23) and traditional, moderately priced French-Creole plates like prawn fricassee and excellent tagliatelle with langoustine. Nearby *La Gloriette* offers a €25 menu with *crabe farçi* and octopus-and-conch stew on a rustic seaside terrace (closed Wed & Sept–Oct). Even more tempting is the adjacent *Cocoloba Beach*, a mellow beachside hangout and bar with shaded picnic tables in the sand and a menu of cheap salads (€5–9), panini (€7), weekend barbecues and occasional live music.

West of Gustavia

Tiny **COROSSOL**, a charming fisherman's village 4km west of Gustavia, evokes an Antillian flavour altogether absent elsewhere on St Barts. The local women wear white, shoulder-length sunbonnets, and weave *latanier* leaves into baskets and hats, which they sell from their front porches. The main sight here is the red-roofed, quaint **Inter-Oceans Museum** (Tues–Sun 9am–12.30pm & 2–5pm; closed Mon; €3) along the waterfront, which showcases a fascinating collection of thousands of seashells from around the world, from giant conch shells to spiny sea urchins.

On the opposite coast, **FLAMANDS** village tumbles down quietly onto a long stretch of golden sand at Anse des Flamands, a broad bay backed by *latanier* and banana trees. Close by is another secluded beach, **Anse Colombier**, reached by a twenty-minute hike around a headland at the island's westernmost tip. The narrow path gets rocky and slick in parts – wearing sturdy sandals or trail shoes is advised – but the challenging trek is worth it; you just might have the gorgeous stretch of sand to yourself. There are several appealing places to **stay** on this side of the island. At the start of the trail to Anse Colombier, the charming *Auberge de la Petite Anse* (℡0590/27 64 89, ✉apa@wanadoo.fr; ➐) offers 16 small, simple bungalows with kitchenettes and stellar ocean views. *Baie des Anges* (℡0590/27 63 61, ⊕www. hotelbaiedesanges.com; ➒) has spacious rooms with terrace-kitchenettes right on Anse des Flamands, plus the excellent pool-side **restaurant** *La Langouste*, where the lobster-like critters displayed in a tank star in French-Creole dishes like *gratinée de langoustes* with champagne sauce (€26). Nearby, the four-star *Isle de France* (℡0590/27 61 81 or 1-800/810-4691, ⊕www.isle-de-france.com; ➒) has 33 well-appointed doubles, bungalows and suites, two swimming pools and a carpeted tennis court. For true seclusion, there's friendly *Le P'tit Morne*, (℡0590/52 95 50, ⊕www. timorne.com; ➑), one of the best deals on St Barts. Set on a hilltop in Colombier, this boutique hotel's cottages boast contemporary furnishings, private terraces, and gorgeous views of the rocky offshore islands.

16

Dominica

Dominica highlights

✳ **Scotts Head** Watch out for migrating whales on the Atlantic side, and swim in the calm Caribbean bay just feet away from this picturesque southern village. See p.665

✳ **Boeri Lake Hike** This accessible hike takes under two hours and leads past bright flowers and wild orchids though the highest and most colourful part of the rainforest. See p. 668

✳ **Titou Gorge** Swim against the cold current to reach the warm waters of the hidden waterfall. See p.668

✳ **Boiling Lake** Hike inland through the eerie Valley of Desolation to reach the perimeter of this natural cauldron. See p.668

✳ **Indian River** Take a colourful slow boat ride upstream into Dominica's swampy interior. See p.670

✳ **Escalier Tête Chien** A breathtaking natural "staircase" leads from Carib Territory to a vista over the rough Atlantic. See p.671

✳ **Eco-Tourism** Dominica is one of the Caribbean's best destinations for tourism that's low-impact on the environment but good for the local economy. See p.658

△ Fishing Boats in Scotts Head Bay

Introduction and basics

No past trips to the Caribbean can prepare you for the view of **Dominica** (pronounced Dah-min-EE-ka) as you fly over it – instead of the lush, bright green and rolling hills of other Caribbean islands, Dominica is an island of tall, sharp peaks, covered with the dark green of a deep **rainforest**. The steep-sided peaks rear up 4700 feet to meet cloud-capped summits that receive enough heavy rainfall to feed hundreds of mountain streams. These in turn nourish the majestic rainforest vegetation that covers over sixty percent of Dominica's centre.

Lying halfway between Guadeloupe and Martinique, Dominica's appeal has nothing to do with beaches – what few exist are paltry – or idle days spent under a palm tree. Rather, its abundant nature invites rigorous **hiking** to deep emerald pools, waterfalls and bubbling lakes. Offshore are superb drop-offs, volcanic arches and caves busy with stingrays, barracuda and parrotfish, making for some of the Caribbean's best **diving**, while **whales** and **dolphins** often play off the southern coast, near Champagne, a unique effervescent bay.

Despite all that Dominica has to offer in terms of **eco-tourism**, it's still vastly under-visited, in no small part because it's not easy to reach. There are no direct flights from the US or Europe, and ferries from surrounding islands don't stop daily. In addition, the island lacks luxury resorts. This means that a vacation here will necessarily involve travelling around to see the island, and Dominica is a great place to explore.

Where to go

Most hikers head directly to **Morne Trois Pitons National Park**, the expansive rainforest that covers most of Dominica's southern reaches. Its centrepiece, Boiling Lake, requires a full-day trek, but hitting the park's numerous waterfalls, like Emerald Pool, is easily achieved, even by novice hikers. Divers, in contrast, head to the waterfront south of Roseau where several outfits run trips to impressive underwater craters around **Scotts Head** and the northern **Cabrits National Park**'s drop-offs.

When to go

The **best time to visit** is between January or February and June, when the weather is at its driest; during August and October, the wettest months, rainfall ranges from thirty inches in Roseau to ten times that in the interior. As elsewhere in the Caribbean, **hurricane season** lasts from June 1 to November 30.

Arrival

The island has two small **airports**, Canefield and Melville Hall, neither with the capacity to accept an international jet. Canefield is close to Roseau and on the Caribbean side of the

---

The 2004 hurricane season

Hurricane Ivan, which ravaged some Caribbean islands in September 2004, skipped Dominica completely. However, the island was not entirely spared that year from natural disasters – just months after the hurricane, a small earthquake shook the island, and flooding in its wake damaged many roads, including the runway for the Canefield Airstrip (see overleaf). The damage here was nothing compared to that of a major hurricane, however, so cruise ships that were otherwise headed for Grenada (which suffered unprecedented damage, see p.782) for the 2004–05 winter season re-routed to Dominica, providing a welcomed boost to the island's economy.

Guadaloupe Channel

Capucin Cape
Carib Point
Pennville
Clifton
Morne aux Diables (2824ft)
Douglas Bay
CABRITS NATIONAL PARK
Fort Shirley
Portsmouth
Prince Rupert Bay
Indian River

ATLANTIC OCEAN

Calibishie
Wesley
Londonderry Bay
Marigot
Melville Hall Airfield

Hampstead River

Morne Diablotins (4697ft)
NORTHERN FOREST RESERVE

Salibia
Sineku

Carib Territory

Escalier Tête Chien

Colihaut

CENTRAL FOREST RESERVE

Castle Bruce

Salisbury
Méro
Macoucherie Rum Factory

Bells

Emerald Pool

Saint Joseph
Layou
Layou River

Rosalie
Rosalie Bay

Morne Trois Pitons (4546ft)
Middleham Falls
Boeri Lake
Morne Macaque
Freshwater Lake

Mahaut
Massacre
Pringles Bay
Canefield Airport

Laudat

MORNE TROIS PITONS NATIONAL PARK

Boiling Lake

CARIBBEAN SEA

Trafalgar Falls

La Plaine

Roseau
Botanical Gardens

Victoria Falls

Castle Comfort
Loubiere

Delices

Pointe Michel

Soufrière Sulphur Springs

Fond Saint John

Champagne Beach
Soufrière
Soufrière Bay
Berekua
Grand Bay

Scotts Head
Fort Cachacrou

Martinique Channel

N

0   2 miles

island, but Melville Hall, which is further afield on the north Atlantic side of the island is larger, and most flights go there.

At time of writing, Canefield Airport was closed due to damage to the runway from the 2004 earthquake and its stormy aftermath. All flights had been re-routed to Melville Hall. Canefield is scheduled to re-open sometime in 2005. Any airline or travel agent should be able to let you know if it has reopened, and it's worth asking since most attractions on the island are a long and expensive cab ride from Melville Hall.

Ferries arrive at the northern edge of Roseau, within walking distance of most guesthouses and hotels. If you're staying in the Castle Comfort area, a mile south of Roseau, grabbing a taxi or a bus (EC$1.50) is an inexpensive option.

Information, websites and maps

In addition to representation abroad, Dominica has **information kiosks** at both airports, the ferry docks and on the Bay Front (see p.622). The main island **tourist office** is in Roseau, on the Bay Front (Mon–Fri 8am–4pm, Sat 9am–2pm; ☎767/448-2401). All have detailed island **maps**.

The island's **official website**, ⓦwww.domi-nica.dm, has links to hotels and services that you can book yourself, though the glossier, corporate-sponsored ⓦwww.avirtualdomi-nica.com is more user-friendly.

Money and costs

The official currency is the **Eastern Carib-bean dollar** (EC$), although US dollars are widely accepted and used to quote hotel and service rates. The EC$ is divided into 100 cents. Notes come in denominations of 5, 10, 20, 50 and 100 EC dollars; coins in 1, 2, 5, 10 and 25 cents. At the time of writing, the **exchange rate** was EC$2.70 to US$1.

Roseau **banks** have ATMs dispensing local currency. Tellers here will also change money for transactions (Mon–Thurs 8am–3pm, Fri 8am–5pm). When paying for goods with US dollars in cash, the rate is usually lower, at EC$2.60/US$1. Hotels almost universally list their prices in American dollars, while food prices are listed in EC – often on the same brochure.

Even though Dominica is poor by Carib-bean standards, it's not necessarily a cheap place to visit. Additional costs for guides and activities have a way of increasing your bill, as do incidentals like the US$20 **departure tax** levied at the airport when you leave. A whale-watching outing costs US$50/four-hour trip; the rainforest tram (see p.667 also costs US$50, a guide to the Boiling Lake is set at US$40, not including transportation to the trailhead, and diving prices are compara-ble at US$45/single-tank dive.

At the bottom of the scale, you could man-age on a **daily budget** of US$45, if you split the cost of a fan-only double in a Roseau guesthouse, travel by bus, hike without a guide, and skip diving and whale-watching altogether. A budget of US$75/day will allow you to stay in a rainforest guesthouse and hire a guide.

Getting around

The best and most economical way to **get around** the island is by car. The driving is not for the faint of heart (or stomach), however, but a car will take you where buses rarely or never go, and will be far less expensive than taxis or a guide. The coast roads are especially manageable, and for hikes to the furthest regions you'll usually be taking a guide along to direct you (guides will walk you to the Boiling Lake or Victoria Falls, but they won't drive you to the trailhead). You can arrange a guide either through your guesthouse or hotel; each hotel has its own list of guides whom they use consistently.

By bus

Dominica's **public buses** are run by pri-vate, individual carriers who own 15-seat vans that careen around the island with various degrees of reliability. Buses are easy to find during the weekdays around Roseau – heading towards Scott's Head (see p.665), Trafalgar falls (see p.668), or Castle Comfort (see p.662) for example.

You can flag them down on the road or meet one in Roseau before it leaves on King George V Street, the main drag heading out of town. Buses run while the sun shines – from 6am to 6pm, and are less reliable on Saturday (officially 6am–2pm) and non-existent on Sundays. On days when cruise ships come into port there are also fewer buses because many of the drivers also act as expensive taxis, ferrying groups of off-island passengers to island sights. Similarly, it's not a great idea to take a bus to dinner, as you won't be able to get home once the sun goes down.

Buses cost EC$1.50–5; flag them down on the road, tell the driver your destination, and pay when you get off. You can have your hotel call a bus for you (make sure to state that you'd like the van to serve as a bus, not a taxi, and work out a fare in advance, usually EC$5–10.

By car

Driving is on the left on narrow, **badly paved roads**. In the mountains you'll be hard-pressed to exceed the 20mph speed limit as certain spots have no guardrails whatsoever, even on deadly mountain switchbacks, and many have deep rain gutters alongside. Other routes are nothing more than mud-covered rock (be aware that local car insurance does not cover damage to tyres). The **coastal roads** are better, widening enough to approximate two lanes

at some points. None of the roads are lit at night, making it unwise for first-time visitors to cruise around after dark.

If you intend to do a lot of island driving, renting a **four-wheel-drive vehicle** is your best option, even though they cost more (from US$45/day). Aside from a Budget rental office near Canefield Airport, and a courtesy phone inside the terminal that rings to Valley Car Rentals, Dominica's **car rental agencies** are based in Roseau; they'll meet you at the airport if you've made advance reservations. See p.664 for car rental details. To drive on the island, you'll need to buy a one-month local driver's licence (US$12) from the car rental provider. Renters must be over 25 and under 65, though the upper age limit is less strictly monitored than the lower one.

By taxi

A **taxi** is usually just a bus which agrees not to pick up other passengers when they're driving you. If your driver picks up locals along the way, you should demand to pay the shuttle, instead of taxi, rate. In theory, taxi rates are regulated by the government and are not supposed to vary based on the number of passengers, but in practice prices vary wildly, so stand up for yourself and try to negotiate before you agree on a price. Prices are usually in US dollars – a ride from Roseau to Portsmouth will cost anywhere from US$45 to $75. Taxis congregate at the

---

Eco-tourism in Dominica

Eco-tourism allows visitors the choice of having a lighter impact on the environment when they travel – and this can mean any number of things. Eco-friendly lodges use less **water** than the typical resort, they may also have solar powered heat, but the idea of "environmental impact" goes beyond tourism's impact on nature and includes its impact on the community. Eco-lodges aim to hire **locals** instead of importing staff from more affluent countries, they farm **food** without using pesticides and sometimes they've chosen to build on land that was already in use before so that they will not have to clear a new area.

Dominica has been promoting itself for several years as the foremost eco-friendly location in the Caribbean, and recently more and more of the hotels on the island have become **Green Globe certified** (see ⓦ www.greenglobe21.com). Several accommodations on the island, however, go beyond the tasks of getting certified as environmentally friendly and really do an excellent job of having a philosophy and atmosphere that fits in with the landscape; we especially recommend the 3 Rivers Eco Lodge, Crescent Moon Cabins, and Cocoa Cottages (all p.668).

airport and at the cruise ship docks, you're not likely to see one otherwise unless you call.

Accommodation

Dominica's **accommodation** options are nowhere near as fancy as elsewhere in the Caribbean, but that's a large part of the island's appeal. Hikers will find a clutch of rainforest **guesthouses** nestled amidst the greenery offering terrific packages that include guides, hearty food, and casual lodging in a convivial atmosphere. The disadvantages of these places are that they're often far from civilization and social opportunities of any sort. What modern **hotels** exist are mostly concentrated in Roseau and the Castle Comfort area and cater predominantly to divers with packages and well-equipped, if impersonal, rooms. Even the best of these hotels cannot match the luxury of other large resorts or boutique retreats in the Caribbean, but then you'll be hard-pressed to find a room that costs over US$150. Note that most hotels apply a 10 percent tax and 5 percent service charge to the bill, so ask whether it's included when booking.

Food and drink

Dominica's **cuisine** is simple, with a Creole flavour. Your best bets will often be a chicken or goat curry – both locally raised animals. Fish at all but the best restaurants usually comes straight from the freezer and is then overcooked. Additionally, the island has trouble retaining its fisheries' best specimens, which are often sold to wealthier neighbouring islands. Other island specialities include callaloo soup (similar to creamed spinach), and Caribbean staples like roti (curry-filled flat bread). Meals all come with rice and several sides, which could include fried plantains, mashed cooked green bananas, turnips, and beans. The food is hardly cheap, however. **Dinner** in most restaurants ranges EC$35–75 for an entree, **lunch** is less expensive and ranges EC$12–30, while **breakfast** can often cost more than lunch, usually starting at EC$20. Restaurants that are not geared towards tourists are slightly less expensive, but very few are open for dinner regularly. Similarly, because most manufactured food is imported, groceries are not a bargain, but can be found at the Whitchurch IGA on Old Street in Roseau.

At the time of writing the *crapaud* (toad) that supplied its legs to make the island's national dish, mountain chicken, had a year-round hunting ban due to its dwindling numbers.

Fruit juices and fresh fruit are ubiquitous for breakfast, and at dinner can be mixed with one of the island's two local rums, Soca or Macoucherie. But the island's best drink is its tasty local lager, Kubuli.

Due to the countless freshwater sources, the tap water here is often superb. Your hotel should let you know if they have a good water source. Bottled water is also readily available for hikes.

Mail and communications

There are public **telephones** at every square and many street corners, many of which take coins; those that don't take phone cards, which you can buy from the post office, Cable & Wireless outlets and some convenience stores. For the best rates, call after 7pm. There are a couple of places to check your **email** in Roseau (see p.664), with surprisingly reasonable rates, and many hotels have a computer with email as well – prices range from free to US$14/hr.

The sluggish Dominican **postal service** is headquartered at the corner of Roseau's Hillsborough and Bay streets on the waterfront (Mon–Wed & Fri 8am–3pm, Thurs & Sat 8am–noon). Sending a postcard anywhere in the world costs EC$1, while it costs EC$0.90 for letters to North America and EC$1.20 for those to Europe, Australia and New Zealand.

> The **country code** for Dominica is ☏767. For **directory assistance** once there, dial ☏411.

Opening hours, holidays and festivals

Generally, **opening hours** are Monday to Friday 8am–1pm and 2–4pm. Banks tend to keep shorter hours (Mon–Thurs 8am–3pm, Fri until 5pm). Shops and services close altogether on Sunday, when the only establishments open are hotel restaurants. In addition to closures on holidays (see box), Dominica often shuts down during lively festivals, the biggest of which, **Carnival**, takes place during the last two weeks of Lent, with calypso performances, costumed street dancing to *lapo kabwit* (goat-skin drum) bands, beauty pageants and such. The first week of June is the **Dive Fest**, with waterfront parties and cruises, while October showcases the three-day **Creole Music Festival**, a jamboree of Caribbean rock, African *soukous* and Louisiana *zydeco*. One of the biggest parties around happens the week prior to **Independence Day** (Nov 3), with colourful celebrations and traditional Creole food and music.

Public holidays

January 1 New Year's Day
First Monday in March Carnival Monday
March/April Good Friday, Easter Monday
May 1 May Day
Eighth Monday after Easter Whit Monday
First Monday in August August Monday
November 3 Independence Day
November 4 Community Service Day
December 25 Christmas Day
December 26 Boxing Day

History

In a rare imaginative lapse, Columbus simply named **Dominica** after the day he discovered it in 1493: Sunday. He didn't stick around long and, for over two centuries, interest in Dominica was virtually nonexistent, so much so that a 1660 treaty between the British and French declared the island a neutral territory, leaving it to the resident **Caribs**. The French rescinded the deal when they colonized Dominica in the 1720s, starting a near-century-long tug-of-war with the British. In 1763 the island went to the British in the treaty ending the Seven Years War, but when the British had their resources elsewhere during the Revolutionary War, the French successfully invaded. A second Treaty of Paris returned the island to Britain, and two subsequent invasions by the French were unsuccessful. The island was of little interest to the superpowers for its resources, but its strategic location between **Martinique** and **Guadeloupe,** both solidly French colonies, made it desirable to both nations.

After **slavery** ended in the British colonies in 1834, there was little reason for colonizers to remain on Dominica. The British ceded so much power, in fact, that Dominica was the only island to have a black-controlled legislature in the nineteenth century. However, by 1865 the British had taken back control of the legislature, and Dominica's history continued much like the other British Caribbean colonies, until it received its **independence** in 1978. Just six months later, in 1979, the island was ravaged by **Hurricane David**, a natural disaster that ruined the country's infrastructure and left its citizens on the verge of starvation. The political instability that began with the waves of that storm continues, arguably, to this day. The island's first prime minister, Patrick John, was forced to resign in 1979 after making a questionable land deal with US developers. After the hurricane, building was left to his successor, Eugenia Charles, the Caribbean's first woman prime minister, who remained so while surviving two coups against her. Subsequent leadership has been dogged by embezzlement and corruption charges, and though a beloved politician, Roosevelt "Rosie" Douglas, was elected prime minister in 2000, he died suddenly just eight months later. His successor, Pierre Charles, died, again suddenly, in 2004, and was replaced by the current prime minister, Roosevelt Skerrit.

Dominica's history is perhaps most notable for the uninterrupted presence of the **Carib Indian tribe** on its soil. While the Caribs were killed or "exported", often to Venezuela, from other Caribbean islands, Dominica's mountainous and difficult landscape made the island more difficult for the British and French to conquer. The result was that when the island was eventually colonized, the Caribs did not leave, but merely retreated to the Atlantic side of the island where their territory remains today (see p.670).

The island is also the birthplace of two important English-language authors: **Jean Rhys**, whose most famous novel, *Wide Sargasso Sea*, a reinvention of *Jane Eyre* from the point of view of Bertha, takes place largely on Dominica, and **Phyllis Shand Allfrey**, whose novel *The Orchid House* is well known in Britain. More recently, Antiguan-born Jamaica Kincaid's novel *The Autobiography of my Mother* takes place on Dominica and features a young woman of Carib, African and Scottish origin.

16.1

Roseau

The only trace of modernity in Dominica's capital, **ROSEAU** (pronounced rose-oh), is its lengthy, tidy waterfront promenade, **Bay Front**. Otherwise, the compact town is a colourful assortment of ramshackle West Indian **colonial houses** with louvred windows, intricate fretwork, and sagging second-floor French-style balconies held up over narrow streets by stilts. Despite the town's obvious poverty, it's a remarkably atmospheric place to stomp about: the roads get narrower as you head in from the harbourside area, passing covered **markets** and distinctive **cornerhouses**.

Accommodation

Aside from a couple of snazzy options near the Bay Front, most of Roseau's **accommodation** is in low-key guesthouses. The Castle Comfort area, a strip of road one mile south, has a handful of waterfront hotels that cater mostly to divers and offer a less noisy night's sleep than what you're likely to find in Roseau.

Roseau

Continental Inn 37 Independence St ☎767/448-2214 or 2215, ✉continental@cwdom.dm. A clean budget option with little else to offer: simple undecorated rooms, most with twin beds and some with private baths. Cable TV and a/c in all but two of the rooms. **②**

Fort Young Hotel Victoria Street ☎767/448-5000 or ☎800/766-6016, ⊛www.fortyounghotel.com. An attractive waterfront hotel incorporating the walls of the eighteenth-century fort, and offering standard doubles, spacious suites, a seaside pool and Jacuzzis, and a true activities desk. It's about as close to a luxury resort as you'll come on this island, though despite its prime waterfront location it's nowhere near a beach. **④**

Garraway 1 Dame Eugenia Charles Blvd ☎767/449-8800, ⊛www.garrawayhotel.com. A sterile upmarket option with 31 commodious doubles, picture windows overlooking the sea or the town, but no balconies. **⑤**

Ma Bass Central Guesthouse 44 Fields Lane ☎767/448-2999. The most appealing of the inexpensive guesthouses in the centre of town, with eight spotless fan-only rooms, a comfortable common room, shared or private bath, and a shared balcony with pleasant views. **②**

Sutton Place 25 Old St ☎767/449-8700 or 4313, ⊛www.avirtualdominica.com/sutton.htm. The best place to stay in the centre of town, but it's on a noisy street and above a bar that has live music once a week, so not for insomniacs. That said, it's a beautiful eight-room boutique hotel with appealing touches like wrought-iron gates, antique-furnished rooms trimmed with damask and chintz flounces, and a courtyard. **④**

Castle Comfort

Anchorage ☎767/448-2638, ⊛www.anchoragehotel.dm. A great deal – inexpensive waterfront rooms with pool, dive centre, and a waterfront bar next to an enormous whale skeleton. Motel-style rooms are clean with balconies, a/c, TV, and phone, most with water views. **③**

Castle Comfort Lodge ☎767/448-2188, ⊛www.castlecomfortdivelodge.com. The place to stay if you plan to spend most of your Dominican vacation underwater. The rooms aren't any nicer than its neighbour *Anchorage*, and half have no water view, but you're paying for the dive lodge; visits are priced by the number of dives per stay. There's a hot tub and a small pool in the garden for post-diving relaxation; breakfast, dinner, unlimited shore dives, tax, and airport transfer are included in rates. **⑤** with breakfast and dinner.

Sea World Guesthouse ☎767/448-5068, ✉seaworlddominica@yahoo.com. Eight bright, clean rooms with fan, TV and telephone in a cheery yellow building with a ground-floor grocery store. $US30 per person, with water view rooms the same price as those facing the road. **③**

The Town

Roseau is small enough that it is easy to navigate on foot, and all of its sights can be explored in under an hour. Among these, the **Dominica Museum** on the Bay Front (Mon–Fri 9am–4pm, Sat 9am–noon; US$3) does a bare bones job of tracing the island's history and culture through artifacts and short historical explanations. It includes Amerindian artifacts, a full-scale replica of a thatched Carib house, and King George III's silver mace, given to Dominica in 1770, but it won't satisfy a real desire for information about the island. For that it's best to head south along the Bay Front, up a small hill past the *Fort Young Hotel* (see opposite) to the **Free Library**, built from funds donated by American philanthropist Andrew Carnegie in 1905 (Mon–Fri 9am–6pm, Sat 9am–noon; free). Across from the library sits the **New Parliament Building**, a whitewashed two-storey mansion surrounded by landscaped grounds (closed to the public).

In the cobblestoned square behind the museum, and filling the alleyway alongside, is the **Old Market** (Mon–Sat), formerly the site of the island's slave market, now filled with vendors selling handicrafts. Fresh produce is sold at the **New Market**, at the end of Mary E. Charles Boulevard past the ferry docks. It's open every day, but most busy on Saturday, when vendors and buyers flock here from all over the island.

Heading northeast on Church Street away from the Old Market and taking a left turn onto Virgin Lane leads to the colourful **Methodist Church** (closed to public except for services), and the staid Gothic **Roman Catholic Church**. This church has an involved history – it was built between 1790 and 1916, and varied groups from French estate owners to Carib volunteers took part in its creation (open daily 8am–4pm).

Past the churches, a right turn on Queen Mary Street leads to the entrance to the fanciful forty-acre **Botanical Gardens** (daily 6am–10pm; free), below Morne Bruce hill, home to a variety of local flora and enormous trees, as well as an old yellow school bus crushed by a massive baobab commemorating Hurricane David's destructive powers. The gardens also contain a parrot aviary and research centre which are closed to the public, but from the surrounding fence you can spy the caged Sisserou and Jaco parrots. From just behind the aviary a steep fifteen-minute trail ascends **Morne Bruce** for stellar summit views of the town and sea below.

Eating, drinking and nightlife

Dining out in Roseau is a casual affair, with meals primarily consisting of hearty local dishes served in cosy rather than classy surroundings. The smaller local restaurants are mostly open for lunch only. What **nightlife** exists is moderately dressier.

Balas Bar and Lounge *Fort Young Hotel*, Victoria Street. This hotel bar, backed by the fort's original wall, offers a lively cocktail hour on Friday nights with happy hour prices 6–8pm.

Cartwheel Café Dame Eugenia Charles Boulevard ☎767/448-5353. Light, tropical breakfasts and flavourful curry lunch fare in a handsome stone house on the waterfront. Curry from EC$12 and a variety of sandwiches from EC$6. Closed Sunday and dinner.

Cornerhouse Café 11 King George V St ☎767/449-9000. Atmospheric café on a second-floor verandah with comfy indoor sofas, a small book exchange and Internet access. The menu has a range of sandwiches (from EC$15) and Creole specials, and it's a good place to meet up with other travellers.

Green Flash Grille Loubière, just beyond Castle Comfort ☎767/448-2145. This establishment, run by the owners of the *Cornerhouse Café*, has reasonable dinner (around EC$27), but the food's not the main attraction here. Instead, Americans and Europeans gather here to watch the sunset, quaff tropical drinks, and swim off the dock (there's a freshwater shower for customers). Quiz night on Wednesdays at 8.30, and it's one of the few restaurants not associated with a hotel open Sunday. Open Wed–Sun 5–10pm.

Guiyave Restaurant and Patisserie 15 Cork St ☎767/448-2930. This bright green and yellow local café serves tasty breakfast and lunch upstairs (sandwiches from EC$10), and inexpensive pastries downstairs (meat pies from EC$1.50). Closed Sunday and dinner.

La Robe Creole 3 Victoria St ☎767/448-2896. An intimate masonry-walled pub with an extensive wine list and good, mid-priced Creole dishes like curried conch (EC$65) and coconut shrimp (EC$35). The prices here do reflect quality, while the drinks remain inexpensive. Reservations recommended;

closed Sun. Downstairs is *Mousehole*, a take-out joint offering inexpensive rotis, meat pies, sandwiches and pastries.

Sutton Grill *Sutton Place Hotel*, 25 Old St ☎767/449-8700. One of Dominica's few expensive restaurants does grilled chicken and tuna fillet sandwiches at lunch, and juicy steak for dinner, in an outdoor courtyard. On Wednesday night there's live music at *The Cellar* bar downstairs.

Listings

Airlines American Airlines ☎767/448-0628; Air Guadeloupe (via HHV Whitchurch & Co) ☎767/448-2181; Caribbean Star ☎767/445-8936 or 8940; LIAT ☎767/448-3980. Canefield Airstrip ☎767/449-1199, Melville Hall Airport ☎767445-7100.

Banks Royal Bank, Bay Front; Scotiabank, 28 Hillsborough.

Car rental Budget, Canefield Airport (☎767/449-2080, 🌐www.avirtualdominica.com/budget); Best Deal, 15 Hanover St (☎767/449-9204, 🌐www.bestdealrentacar.com); Courtesy, 10 Winston Lane (☎767/448-7763, 🌐www.avirtualdominica.com/courtesycarrental); Valley Rent-a-Car, Goodwill Road (☎767/448-3233, Portsmouth ☎767/445-5252, 🌐www.valleydominica.com). Links to car rental websites are available at 🌐www.avirtualdominica.com.

Diving Anchorage Dive Centre (☎767/448-2638, 🌐www.anchoragehotel.dm); Cabrits Dive Centre (Portsmouth; ☎767/445-3010, 🌐www.cabritsdive.com); Dive Dominica (☎767/448-2188, 🌐www.castlecomfortdivelodge.com); Fort Young Hotel Dive Center (☎767/448-5000 ext#333, ✉fyhdivecenter@cwdom.dm) Nature Island Dive

(☎767/449-8181, 🌐www.natureislanddive.com).

Emergencies ☎999.

Internet Cyberland, in the small Woodstone Shopping Mall on the corner of Great George St and Cork St (Mon–Fri 8am–10pm, Sat 10am–7pm, Sun 1–8pm; US$1/30min); *Cornerhouse Café*, 6 King George V St (Mon–Fri 8.30am–4.30pm; US$3/30min).

Post office Bay Front ☎767/448-2601.

Taxis Choice Taxi ☎767/235-2012; Island Tours and Taxi ☎767/440-0944; Mally's Taxi ☎767/448-3114.

Tours Tour guides are most easily scheduled through hotels, who use the same, more reliable guides regularly. Barring that, almost every taxi driver on the island considers himself a tour guide, or can direct you to one. Another way to find a guide is through the tourist office on the Bay Front. From Portsmouth call Cobra Tours (☎767/445-3333, 🌐www.cobratours.dm).

Whale-watching Anchorage Whale Watch and Dive Centre (☎767/448-2638, 🌐www.anchoragehotel.dm); Nature Island Dive (☎767/449-8181, 📠449-8182, 🌐www.natureislanddive.dm).

Southward to Scotts Head

Heading south from Roseau, the coastal road winds past green hillsides on the way to the pretty fishing village of **SOUFRIÈRE**. The main attraction here is **Champagne Beach**, marked by a small sign just before the town. The spot is so named because of bubbles in the offshore waters, created by hot springs in the depths of nearby **Soufrière Bay**. The beach is a rocky affair – walk from the wooden steps near the sign to the end of the beach (about 100 yards). All you need is a snorkel mask or a pair of goggles to find the bubbles, which are just are on the close side of the point; the reef is more developed and beautiful (though not bubbly) just around the point. On days when cruise ships come in guides will hang around the entrance to the beach, offering to name the local fish for a small fee, but one advantage of snorkelling here is that you can do so without a boat or a guide.

The road continues to Soufrière Bay, where the Atlantic and Caribbean meet. The bay itself has a calm cove with good snorkelling, and you can rent diving, kayaking and snorkelling gear on the village outskirts at top-notch Nature Island Dive (☎767/449-8181, 🌐www.natureislanddive.dm). The dive shop also rents out two units in a beachfront **cottage** nearby – it's the only place to stay in the area

Diving and snorkelling off Dominica

The waters off Dominica are ideal for **diving**: the sites are plentiful and rarely crowded, and provide some of the best opportunities in the Caribbean to see seahorses. Most guides leave from around Roseau and head to the impressive sites off **Scotts Head**, where submerged volcanic craters are covered with seafans and busy with schools of fish and lobster. Easily accessible for snorkellers as well as divers are nearby **Soufrière Bay** and **Champagne Beach** – while the bubbles from the subaquatic hot spring that creates the champagne reef are fun to swim in, the reef around the point towards Soufrière holds more to see, including bright parrotfish and clownfish.

The best dive sites in the north on the Caribbean coast are around **Cabrits National Park** where reefs drop off to sandy bottoms over 100ft below the surface. Nearby **Douglas Point** has three sites worth exploring, including a coral-and-sponge-covered canyon and a 50ft wall teeming with lobster, barracuda and mackerels. For **wreck** diving, Pringles Bay near Canefield Airport holds the remains of a tug and barge. Dive outfits will rarely take tourists to the Atlantic side of the island, though if you're very experienced you might get there once in a week-long dive itinerary.

In the south, the Anchorage Dive Centre (☎767/448-2638, ⊛www.anchoragehotel. dm) and Castle Comfort Dive Lodge (☎767/448-2188, ⊛www.castlecomfortdivelodge. com) have the largest assortment of boats and equipment, though Nature Island Dive (☎767/449-8181, ⊛www.natureislanddive.com) is closer to most sights and will provide more personalized service. In the north, near **Portsmouth**, head to Cabrits Dive Centre (☎767/445-3010, ⊛www.cabritsdive.com); while the centre of the Caribbean side is home to East Carib Dive (☎767/449-6575, ⊛www.east-carib-dive.com).

(**⑤**). Back in town you can grab **lunch** at the petite and lovely restaurant *Tony's*, in one of the small cottages on the left side of the main drag as you head towards Scotts Head (☎767/440-3380, open for three meals Mon–Sat, baked chicken lunch EC$12).

You can check out the source of the hot springs one mile inland from Soufrière, at **Sulphur Springs** (daily 9am–5pm; EC$2). There's a small sulphur pool for bathing near the parking lot, and a ten-minute hike uphill will take you to the hot rocks from which the springs originate. Its barren landscape – white rocks, warmed by the lava below, and the overwhelming smell of rotten eggs – is similar to that of the Valley of Desolation for those who don't have a day (or the leg muscles) to spare for the hike to the Boiling Lake (see p.667).

Beyond Soufrière, the road curves around the bay to delightful **SCOTTS HEAD**, a village of brightly painted tin shacks and equally colourful fishing boats moored below a teardrop-shaped peninsula. A stroll to the tip of the headland reveals vestiges of **Fort Cachacrou**, a defense post dating from the early 1700s, and awesome coastal views. The surrounding waters shelter Dominica's best **diving** (see box above), and are visited by migrating **whales** from November to April, often visible from land.

16.2

Morne Trois Pitons
National Park

Dominica's best hiking trails are found in the magnificent, 16,000-acre **MORNE TROIS PITONS NATIONAL PARK**, which spreads over the island's southern region and rises to the 4550ft **Morne Trois Pitons**. Packed with primordial rainforest and sparse elfin woodland, and broken up by volcanic fumaroles and piping hot springs, the UNESCO World Heritage Site is an astonishing wilderness, likely to surpass any you'll find in the Caribbean.

Hikes run from the easy five- to ten-minute walks to beautiful **Emerald Pool** and stunning **Trafalgar Falls**, to the more arduous treks to **Boeri Lake** and **Middleham Falls**. The latter two start from the town of **Laudat**, 3.5 miles northeast of Roseau, also the location of the trailhead to **Boiling Lake**, a fascinating geological wonder buried deep inside the forest.

Around Laudat

The park's major hikes begin at **LAUDAT**, a village 1970ft above sea level with stupendous views of the undulating countryside (for details on how to get here, see opposite). The trail to one of Dominica's tallest waterfalls, the refreshing 275ft **Middleham Falls**, begins just south of town off the road into Laudat, and is a straightforward 45-minute walk through yanga palms, wild anthurium and leafy bromeliads to one of the largest waterfalls on the island. Thirty minutes past the falls lies **Tou Santi**, a collapsed lava tube emitting warm, smelly gases, and whose crevices shelter bats and the occasional boa constrictor.

At the entrance to Laudat proper, a well-marked and groomed path heads off to the largest of Dominica's four lakes, **Freshwater Lake**, 2500ft above sea level at the

---

Park practicalities

Trail **maps** are available (EC$1) at the **Forestry Division** offices in Roseau's Botanical Gardens (℡767/448-2401, ext 417; see p.663). Of all the treks, only those for Boiling Lake definitely require a **guide**; conveniently, all of Dominica's guesthouses can arrange one as part of your package. Otherwise, unaffiliated guides charge EC$20–50 depending on the hike's length and difficulty. You'll find these guides hanging out at the trailheads, where **park fees** must be paid (individual hikes US$2, day-pass US$5, multiple weeklong access US$10). All of the trails can be done in a day: the longest, the hike to Boiling Lake (see opposite), is a seven-hour round-trip affair. In general the trails are well kept, meaning that once you've found the trailhead off one of the poorly marked roads, you're unlikely to lose your way. That said, if there's been rain the rivers crossing the trails can get high, and the absence of footbridges means that wading is sometimes necessary. In all cases, bring sturdy shoes and rain gear; for longer hikes, make sure you have enough water and food.

end of a gradual 2.5-mile trail north of the town centre. There's not much to see here, aside from sulphurous jets that leave rust marks on nearby rocks and greenery. Fifteen minutes beyond Laudat the road ends in a cul-de-sac where you'll find the trailhead for the **Boeri Lake** hike. Though it's not far from the hike to Middleham Falls, this trail is on higher ground and goes through the mountain rainforest. A much more colourful area than the central rainforest, it's full of bright flowers, wild orchids, and large ferns. The forty-five minute hike leads to the beautiful crater lake, enclosed by jagged boulders.

At Laudat's eastern outskirts, an unsightly centipede-like contraption funnels a forceful mountain current into the island's main hydroelectric plant. Before reaching the plant, the water rushes below the unusual **Titou Gorge**, a dark passageway sheltered by solidified lava formations, about ten minutes' walk from the plant alongside the pipe. If the current isn't too rough, you can swim beneath the formations to a small waterfall at the back; if you see brown water sputtering in the access pool it means that the current is strong and you should not go in. You can warm up afterwards by leaning against a hot spring that feeds the pool.

Just past Titou Gorge is the trailhead to Dominica's ultimate hike, a full-day outing to **Boiling Lake**, an eerie 207ft-wide cauldron of bubbling greyish-blue water shrouded in vaporous cloud. A six-mile, seven-hour round-trip undertaking, the trek should only be attempted by fit hikers and with the help of a guide. Thought to be a flooded fumarole through which gases escape from molten lava below, Boiling Lake is the second largest of its kind in the world. On clear days, the hike includes vistas of both the Caribbean and the Atlantic from atop one of the highest points on the island. Traipse through thick forests of canopied chatannyé and bwa bandé trees on your way to the **Valley of Desolation** – a moonscape of white-hot sulphuric rocks, steam vents, and boiling puddles: you could fry an egg in the vents, and guides often do. On the final leg of the trip, bathe in secluded turquoise hot springs and explore a landscape of colourful minerals. This area is also the most treacherous of the hike; your guide can help keep you out of hot water as you climb up and down steep, scree-covered slopes. The standard, government-set fee for a guide for this hike is US$40, but make sure to negotiate fees beforehand.

For those not ready to tackle a full or even partial day-hike, the new **Rainforest Aerial Tram** also leaves from Laudat. For US$55, an eight-person gondola will take you for a ninety-minute ride over the rainforest canopy (☎767/440-3267, ⓦwww.rainforesttram.com; open on days the cruise ships come in and weekends 12-3.30pm).

Practicalities

The only guesthouse this high up is the very accommodating *Roxy's Mountain Lodge* (☎ & ☎767/448-4845, eroxys@cwdom.dm; ❸), where bright and simple doubles feature attractive woodwork and some have stunning views over the valley. Its small **restaurant** packs hearty picnic lunches and serves organic Creole cuisine at night if you plan with the staff in the morning.

Although Laudat is only eight miles from Roseau it's a good 35-minute drive up brutally tight hairpin turns, some with potholes and no guardrails – honk to signal your presence. To **reach** Laudat, take King George V Street 2.5 miles inland from Roseau, until you reach a fork with signs pointing left. From here the road begins its real ascent. There is also a sporadic **bus** (EC$5) which departs across from central Roseau every two hours after 6.30am; buses leave Laudat for the return trip starting about 45 minutes later. A **taxi** ride to Laudat costs around EC$70.

Trafalgar Falls

At the park's southwestern edges, the twin waterfalls known as **Trafalgar Falls** crash down a sheer 200ft rockface. The upper falls flow from the roiling currents at Titou Gorge while the lower are fed by the Trois Pitons River, which itself originates in the Boiling Lake region. The falls are easily accessed via a short trail, shaded by flowering bowers and canopied trees, that starts from the visitors' centre at the end of the road. While most visitors are content to enjoy the falls from a raised viewing platform at the end of an easy walk, the more adventurous can forge ahead over rocks to the lower falls' base for a dip in the sizeable pool.

You can **stay** near the falls at the upscale *Papillote Wilderness Retreat* (☎767/448-2287, ⓦwww.papillote.dm; ❺), a lovely inn with simply decorated doubles, commodious suites and a botanical garden with hot spa pools that work wonders on sore muscles. Nearby, the smaller and equally beautiful *Cocoa Cottages* (☎767/448-0412, ⓦwww.cocoacottages.com; ❹) has cheerful, colourful, creatively decorated and homey rooms, and intimate dining and living areas. Both are highly recommended.

The terrific *River Rock Café* (☎767/448-3472) below the falls offers local **food** on a splendid terrace overlooking the rainforest. Lunch is served à la carte, but dinner must be ordered in advance. The *Papillote Wilderness Retreat* (see above; reservations required) is also a good dinner spot with island staples like goat curry and fried fish and shrimp (*prix fixe* US$25).

To reach the falls **by car**, take the road heading east from Roseau, taking a right fork 2.5 miles inland and following the signs to the village of Trafalgar. **Buses** are fairly regular; ask for ones for Trafalgar at the stop facing the Botanical Gardens on Trafalgar Road (EC$5). **Taxis** from Roseau cost EC$50.

Emerald Pool

Dominica's most-visited natural wonder, the deep **Emerald Pool** at the base of a 40ft waterfall, is midway between Canefield and Castle Bruce and reached by an easy five-minute walk along a well-maintained jungly pathway whose paved sections date from its original use as a Carib trail. The pool itself is a wonderful spot for a swim, though it can get overly crowded on mornings when cruise ships dock.

The Emerald Pool is a 45-minute drive northeast of Canefield Airport along a steep road with hairpin turns. You can also hop aboard one of the infrequent **buses** beside Roseau's New Market (EC$2.50). **Taxis** from Roseau cost EC$50. It's an isolated road to **stay** on, but Dominica's best eco-friendly lodging is located down long dirt roads off it. Twenty minutes uphill from Canefield is the turn-off for the *Crescent Moon Cabins*, a secluded and beautiful place to stay, run by an American chef and his family who cultivate an extensive organic garden on the property, full of exotic spices (☎767/449-3449, ⓦwww.crescentmooncabins.com; ❺; call in advance to reserve for dinner). Beyond the Emerald Pool along the same road is the turn-off for the *3 Rivers Eco Lodge* (☎767/446-1886, ⓦwww.3riversdominica.com), aptly named as it is a reclaimed banana farm with at least three rivers on the premises. Maintaining an atmosphere that makes tourism seem not just sustainable, but great for the environment, *3 Rivers* is the only place on the island that permits camping (US$15 for a site, US$15 to rent a tent – less for hammocks), or has hostel accommodation (US$25), in addition to renting cottages (❸) and cabins (❷).

16.3

The rest of the island

Dotted with impoverished fishing villages and graced with a couple of hiking trails around the island's highest peak, rocky northern Dominica isn't nearly as compelling as the rest of the island and needn't be a priority if you're on a short visit. The Caribbean coast to the north has some decent black-sand **beaches** around the towns of **Mero** and **Portsmouth**. They're the best places to go if you can't leave the Caribbean without basking on some sand. In addition, the extensive ruins of **Fort Shirley** in **Cabrits National Park** and a trip up the **Indian River** are good reasons to take a day-trip to the north of the island. Though it's dangerous to swim on the Atlantic side of the island, the views are stunning, and the Atlantic-facing **Carib Territory**, the Caribbean's only modern-day Carib homeland, is another worthwhile day-trip from Roseau.

North to Portsmouth

The drive to Portsmouth from Roseau along the coastal "highway," a winding two-lane road, is longer than one might expect – at least an hour and a half along some of the island's best roads. North of Roseau, the coastal road passes the Layou River, then climbs through **St Joseph**, a rickety fishing hamlet perched on extremely steep roads, before hitting the village of **Mero**. There's little of interest here, save for the black-sand beach, where there's good **snorkelling** to be found in front of *Castaways Beach Hotel* (℡767/449-6245, ⓦwww.castaways-dominica.com; ❻); they hold Sunday afternoon beach barbecues, and you don't have to be a resident to stop by for a snorkel. Heading inland immediately north of Mero you'll arrive at Dominica's finest rum distillery, **Macoucherie** (Mon–Fri 7am–3pm), which produces rum from sugar cane grown on its estate. They don't have much in the way of touring facilities, but they'll sell you inexpensive rum, and if you're lucky they'll let you munch on some of the fresh sugarcane grown on the premises. There are two good **hotels** in the vicinity, just north of the distillery. Both are far from either Portsmouth or Roseau but offer proximity to the beach and all-inclusive amenities. The first, heading north is the small and lovely *Tamarind Tree Hotel*, on a cliff overlooking the Caribbean. The rooms are simple and new, and there's a small swimming pool and the restaurant serves great Swiss–German food (℡767/449-7395, ⓦwww.tamarindtreedominica.com; $88, ❹ includes breakfast, tax and gratuity). It's just uphill from a dive shop, East Carib Dive, so it's not hard to make good use of the beautiful Caribbean below. Further north is the *Sunset Bay Club* (℡767/446-6522, ⓦwww.sunsetbayclub.com; ❺ including breakfast and all fees), which is on the beach and very much in the style of an all-inclusive resort – though it's quite small it has its own dive shop, restaurant and bar, pool and sauna, and in addition to being on the beach, is also next to a small river. The simple rooms have neither TV or a/c.

Still further up the coast is the **Northern Forest Reserve**, a 22,000-acre parkland and home to the island's highest peak, the 4747ft **Morne Diablotin**. Despite the reserve's gargantuan size, only two **hiking** trails have been created here, both of which begin four miles inland along a well-signposted access road hedged by banana and pineapple plantations. The easier **Syndicate Nature Trail** is a straightforward 1.6km loop past a couple of **parrot**-viewing platforms; two endangered species – the imperial (or Sisserou) parrot and the red-necked parrot make their home here, and sightings often occur during early morning and late afternoon. The second of the hikes, a rugged day-long outing to the summit of Morne Diablotin, should only be attempted with a guide, which can be arranged through your hotel for about US$40.

Portsmouth and the North

Dominica's second largest town, down-at-heel **PORTSMOUTH**, has a picturesque location along Prince Rupert's Bay but is mostly residential. It also functions as a university centre for Ross Medical School, which is attended almost exclusively by Americans. Portsmouth was originally envisioned as the island's capital but plans went awry when the swampy, mosquito-infested environs couldn't be tamed. While there's not much to keep you in town, the **Indian River** on the southern outskirts is worth a visit for the boat trips upriver through a breathtaking mile of the forest that stymied developers. The river is the deepest on the island, and tours (from 8am daily, 1hr; US$10 per person, US$12 per person for fewer than 4 passengers) are given by knowledgeable Rasta guides whose boats are painted with their adopted names, such as Hurricane, Macaroni, and Ravioli. Sightings of blue herons, large iguanas and crabs are common, and you'll stop for some of the freshest drinks on the island at an alfresco jungle bar.

Portsmouth's other noteworthy attraction is the twin-peaked **Cabrits National Park** (daily 8.30am–5pm; US$2), a grassy headland jutting out into the Caribbean Sea 1.5 miles north of town. While the park encompasses the island's largest swamp and the shoals and coral reefs of nearby **Douglas Bay** (see box p.665), the main point of interest is the ruins of **Fort Shirley**. Built between 1770 and 1815 mostly by the British to defend against the French, and completed by the latter when they took control of the island, the fort became a mammoth complex that ultimately was abandoned in 1854. The ruins closest to the entrance have since been restored and are surrounded by manicured lawns and trees, while those further afield remain cloaked in jungle overgrowth. Stop by the visitor centre at the entrance for maps.

Practicalities

Portsmouth is not a town designed to cater to tourists, and recently even the nicer inns on the outskirts of town have been adjusting their accommodations to suit those most likely to stay there: medical students. That said, some true beachfront **lodging** can be found here, just south of Ross Medical School at the *Picard Beach Cottages* (☎767/445-5131, ⓦwww.avirtualdominica.dm/picard.htm; ⑤); its picturesque Creole cottages couldn't be closer to the water, and come with verandahs and kitchenettes. Another accommodation option is further out – beyond Portsmouth, on the north coast of the island is the tiny town of Calibishie, where the eight units in four cabins of the Calibishie Lodges (☎767/445-8537, ⓦcalibishie-lodges.com; ③) overlook a sand beach and the Guadeloupe Channel.

Portsmouth's limited **dining** options include the pink-roofed *Cabin*, on Bay Road, the main drag, for fish and chips; *Big Mama's* (☎767/445-5883), in the town centre two blocks inland, with fried chicken and curry shark; and the slightly more refined beachfront *Blue Bay* (☎767/445-4985), for tasty chicken and *columbos*. Just across from the entrance to Ross Medical School is *Brothers*, which serves acceptable and reasonably priced Chinese and Thai food. A hundred metres up and across the street is a small outdoor market known to the students as "the shacks;" most of the stands have local and inexpensive food to take away for lunch. The *Purple Turtle Beach Club* is just north of the centre of town along the bay front – it's a great place to stop for a drink or a swim, and is frequented by locals, students, and visitors alike.

Carib Territory

From Portsmouth, a road heads east across the island, passing towering royal palms and seemingly endless banana plantations, to the Atlantic coast where you'll encounter dramatic vistas of the ocean pounding against unusual **red rock** outcroppings, and roadsides bursting with red-hued hibiscus, poinsettia and malvina.

There's little to keep you in the string of villages clinging precariously to the rugged cliffs here, though they do offer some picture-postcard views before reaching **Bataka**, the northernmost village of the **CARIB TERRITORY**. This 3700-acre reserve is home to the only remaining tribe of Carib Indians in the Caribbean; a modern community, its traditions are nonetheless still evident in the intricate, handcrafted woodcarvings and baskets sold in huts along the 7.5-mile coastal road south of Bataka. The community's centre, the longhouse-shaped **Ste Marie of the Caribs Church**, overlooks the sea from **Salybia**, the main settlement, its dug-out canoe altar framed by colourful frescoes of Carib life. It's not obviously marked from town, though, so you're best to ask a local for directions.

Southwards, at the village of **Sineku**, a sign points seawards to the serpentine **Escalier Tête Chien** (or "dog's head stairs"), a peculiar lava formation that resembles steps climbing out of the sea. In Carib legend the outcrop is the tracks left from the bottom of an enormous snake, the "tête chien."

The friendly *Carib Territory Guesthouse* at Crayfish River (☎767/445-7256, ⊛www. avirtualdominica.com/ctgh.htm; ❷) has basic **doubles** and a communal verandah with ocean views. Just beyond Carib Territory if you're heading south is a friendly and more luxurious new inn, *Beau Rive*. The six rooms are furnished in an old-plantation style; all have sweeping ocean views, there's a swimming pool and welcoming common room as well (☎767/445-8992, ⊛www.BeauRive.com; ❺). Downhill towards Castle Bruce is the *Islet View Creole Park* **restaurant** (☎767/446-03780; open daily, call in advance for dinner), decorated with palm weavings and serving local food in thoughtful and creative ways (from EC$20).

St Lucia

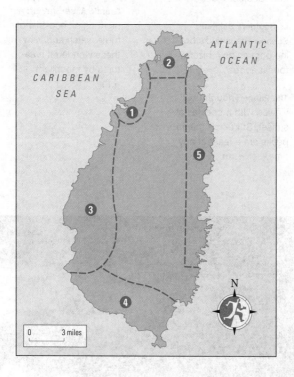

ATLANTIC
OCEAN

CARIBBEAN
SEA

0   3 miles

N

St Lucia highlights

* **Jungle Biking, Anse Mamin** Take a top-notch mountain bike through acres of trails in a private rainforest, just minutes from Soufrière. See p.682

* **La Soufrière Sulphur Springs** The island's boiling pool holds a bizarre tourist appeal. See p.700

* **The Pitons** Though best viewed with a cocktail at sunset, St Lucia's magic peaks are a feast at any time. See p.701

* **Eastern Nature Trail** Hike along St Lucia's wild and underexplored Atlantic coast. See p.708

* **Marine Turtle Watch, Grande Anse** Stay up all night on an eco-friendly turtle watch and view these wonderful creatures by moonlight. See p.709

△ Sulphur Springs, La Soufrière

Introduction and basics

St Lucia more than lives up to the paradisiacal Caribbean stereotype: a glorious mix of honey- and volcanic sand beaches, translucent waters, sheltering reefs swarming with tropical fish, lush interior rainforests, and a thriving culture that encompasses literature and theatre as well as music and dance. However, in contrast to other islands in the region, where the tourism infrastructure has been steadily expanding since the 1960s, St Lucia has only recently begun to attract visitors in any number. As a result, tourism has a much lower profile here, and this low-key feel is one of the island's biggest assets.

Despite the lack of hype, St Lucia's tourist facilities are top-notch, and cater to all tastes – you can stay at luxury hotels or intimate guesthouses, dine in world-class restaurants or at roadside kiosks, and shop in duty-free malls or at open-air village markets. With little of the jaded hustle that can mar more established Caribbean destinations, St Lucia makes for a relaxed, informal and incredibly friendly place to visit.

Where to go

If it's **shopping** and **nightlife** you prefer, then you'll probably head to the tourism strongholds of St Lucia's resort towns in the north; **Rodney Bay** is the main centre in this area, and it has the lovely **Reduit Beach** as its prime lure. More **beaches** and peaceful fishing villages line the west coast, especially once south of the mostly missable capital, **Castries**. Further south, near the inviting town of **Soufrière**, are the monolithic twin peaks of the **Pitons**, St Lucia's most famous sight. In the interior, the rainforest-smothered mountains of the **forest reserves** are strikingly beautiful and rich in flora and fauna, while the wild and windswept east coast offers the chance for a glimpse of some unusual wildlife, from one of the **rarest lizards** in the world to **leatherback turtles** nesting in the sand.

When to go

St Lucia's tropical climate is classically Caribbean. During **high season** (December to April), the island is pleasantly hot, with little rain and constant northeasterly trade winds keeping the nights cool. Temperatures rise even further during the **summer months**, which can also be wet: the rainy season lasts from June to October, with the **hurricane season** at the tail end, roughly from late August to October.

Arrival

Most visitors arrive at **Hewanorra Airport** in the south, but some connecting flights within the Caribbean land at **George F.L. Charles Airport** in the north (about an hour's drive from Hewanorra).

From October to May, **cruise lines** such as Norwegian, Celebrity, and Radisson Seven Seas, dock almost daily at Port Castries. Smaller lines like Sea Cloud and Star Clipper dock infrequently at Soufrière.

Money and costs

St Lucia is not cheap, and you'll pay US and European prices for restaurants and accommodation. St Lucia's official currency is the **Eastern Caribbean dollar** (EC$), which trades against the US dollar at an official rate of EC$2.68 to US$1 for travellers' cheque exchanges and EC$2.67 for cash conversions. In the case of hotels, car rental, restaurants and practically everything related to tourism, most **prices** in St Lucia are quoted in both EC and US dollars, and both currencies are accepted virtually island-wide. On the street, though, the exchange rate will likely be EC$2.50 to US$1, in the vendor's favour.

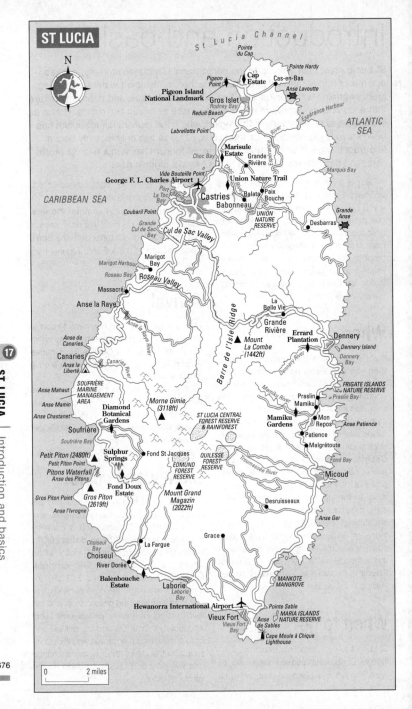

ST LUCIA

N

St Lucia Channel

Pointe
du Cap

Pigeon
Point
Pigeon Island
National Landmark
Gros Islet
Rodney Bay
Reduit Beach

Cap
Estate
Cas-en-Bas

Pointe Hardy

Anse Lavoutte

Espérance Harbour

ATLANTIC
SEA

Labrellotte Point

Marisule
Estate
Grande
Rivière

Choc Bay

Marquis Bay

Vide Bouteille Point
George F. L. Charles Airport

Union Nature Trail

CARIBBEAN SEA

Port
La Toc
Bay

Castries

Balata
Paix
Bouche

Babonneau

Coubaril Point

Grande
Cul de Sac Bay

Cul de Sac Valley

UNION
NATURE
RESERVE

Grande
Anse

Desbarras

Marigot Harbour

Marigot
Bay

Roseau Bay

Roseau Valley

Massacré

Anse la Raye

La
Belle Vie

Anse de
Canaries

Anse la Raye River

Grande
Rivière

Mount
La Combe
(1442ft)

Errard
Plantation

Dennery

Dennery Island

Canaries

Anse la
Liberté

Canaries River

SOUFRIÈRE
MARINE
MANAGEMENT
AREA

Morne Gimie
(3118ft)

ST LUCIA CENTRAL
FOREST RESERVE
& RAINFOREST

Dennery River

Dennery
Bay

Anse Mahaut

Anse Mamin

Anse Chastanet

Diamond
Botanical
Gardens

Soufrière

Soufrière Bay

Petit Piton (2480ft)
Petit Piton Point

Pitons Waterfall
Anse des Pitons

Gros Piton Point

Sulphur
Springs

Fond St Jacques

Fond Doux
Estate

Gros Piton
(2619ft)

Anse l'Ivrogne

Choiseul
Bay

Choiseul

River Dorée

Balenbouche
Estate

EDMUND
FOREST
RESERVE

QUILESSE
FOREST
RESERVE

Mount Grand
Magazin
(2022ft)

Grace

La Fargue

Barre de l'Isle Ridge

Mamiku River

Praslin
Mamiku

FRIGATE ISLANDS
NATURE RESERVE

Praslin Bay

Mamiku
Gardens

Mon
Repos

Anse Patience

Patience

Malgrétoute

Fond Bay

Micoud

Troumassée River

Desruisseaux

Anse Ger

MANKOTE
MANGROVE

Laborie

Laborie
Bay

Hewanorra International Airport

Vieux Fort

Vieux Fort
Bay

Pointe Sable

Anse
de Sables

MARIA ISLANDS
NATURE RESERVE

Cape Moule à Chique
Lighthouse

0   2 miles

Major **credit cards** are widely accepted for payment, and **cash machines** are readily available, especially at the airport and downtown Castries, dispensing EC dollars. US dollar **travellers' cheques** are accepted by many businesses, but it's always wise to carry some cash with you, as taxi drivers, market stalls and many smaller restaurants or guesthouses won't accept credit cards or travellers' cheques.

Standard **bank hours** are Monday to Thursday 8am–3pm, and Friday 8am–5pm. The Bank of St Lucia at Hewanorra airport keeps somewhat later hours (Mon 1–5pm, Tues 1–6.30pm, Wed 1–6pm, Thurs & Fri & Sat 1–5pm, Sun 1–7pm), and most bank branches at the Rodney Bay Marina are open Saturday mornings. Banks always offer the most favourable exchange rate.

Note that you must pay a **departure tax** of EC$54 when leaving St Lucia by air and EC$30 when departing by ferry.

Information and maps

The **St Lucia Tourist Board** maintains several offices abroad, while **on island**, the main office is in the Sureline Building, just after the roundabout on your way north from Castries (PO Box 221, Castries, St Lucia; ☎758/452-4094, ⊛www.stlucia.org). Generally, though, you'll find all the **maps** and brochures you might need at any of the more convenient **tourist board kiosks** – these are scattered around the island at George F.L. Charles Airport, the La Place Carenage and Pointe Seraphine shopping complexes in Castries, Hewanorra Airport in Vieux Fort, and the waterfront in Soufrière. Pick up a copy of *Visions* magazine, published yearly by the St Lucia Hotel and Tourism Association, which includes hotel and restaurant **listings** along with articles on island history and culture.

Getting around

How easy you'll find it to **get around** St Lucia depends very much on where you want to go. While the more populated regions are decently connected by **buses**, much of the interior is only accessible to those with their own **car**.

By bus

If you're laid-back enough to cope with both waiting an unknown period of time to be picked up and frequent stops along the route, travelling by **bus** is the most economical way to get around. Identifiable by an "M" on the licence plate, St Lucia's buses are minivans of various hues, many with windscreens emblazoned with colourful phrases like "Tempt Me" or "Redemption". Of the five main routes, route 1 links Castries and the north, route 2 Castries and Vieux Fort, route 3 Castries and Soufrière. Route 4 runs in and around Vieux Fort and route 5 serves Castries environs.

Though all the island's buses are privately owned, the inexpensive **fares** are set by the government: you'll pay no more than EC$10 to travel between any two points on a given bus line. From Castries, a ride to the north should cost less than EC$2, while a trip to Vieux Fort runs around EC$8.50. Schedules are nonexistent, with most drivers waiting until the bus is full before setting off; as a general rule, services between major towns run every thirty to sixty minutes from about 5am until 10pm on weekdays, with an extended timetable on Fridays for the Gros Islet street party and a reduced timetable on Saturdays – practically no buses run on Sundays. Brightly coloured pavilions serve as **bus stops**, but they are few and far between; it's more common to flag a bus down anywhere along a route – it will stop if it isn't jammed full.

By taxi

Taxis are an expensive but more convenient alternative. Identifiable by a "TX" on the licence plate, they are in plentiful supply: you'll see them cruising for fares on the streets of the main towns and at obvious tourist locations, and most hotels and restaurants can arrange for one to fetch you. All taxis are unmetered, and while the **fares** are set by the government and drivers theoretically carry rate sheets in their cars, it's always best to confirm the fare before getting in. Taxis also offer **guided tours**; rates are negotiable, but hover around US$25 per hour or US$150 per day and may depend on the number of passengers.

In and around Rodney Bay, Castries, Soufrière and Marigot Bay, it's possible to take advantage of the convenient **water-taxi** system, mostly used by tourists and handy for getting to nearby beaches.

By car and motorbike

The ideal way to get around is to rent a **car**, although it can be pricey. Rates start at US$45 per day for a compact, manual-shift vehicle without air conditioning, and go as high as US$75 for a luxury model. Jeeps and other 4WD vehicles, which you'll need to explore some parts of the island, range from US$65 to US$105. You'll generally pay less during low season, or if you rent for three or more days. While mileage is often unlimited, rates don't include **petrol**, which at the time of writing costs around EC$8.50 per imperial gallon; note that most petrol stations are cash-only.

To drive a car or ride a motorbike on the island, visitors must purchase a temporary St Lucian **licence** (EC$30 or US$12 for one day; EC$54 or US$21 for three months). These are issued by rental companies, the airport immigration departments, and the Gros Islet Police Station on production of a valid licence (or an international permit) from your own country of origin. Remember that in St Lucia drivers stick to the **left side** of the road. Note that road signs are rare, so finding your way can be tricky even with a map, and most interior roads are unpaved and difficult to navigate.

If a car is beyond your budget, renting a **motorbike** is worth considering, though this isn't exactly the safest way to get around. Wayne's Motorcycle Centre (☎ 758/452-2059), and Scottie's Scooter Rentals (☎758/450-1404), both just north of Castries, are the island's only motorbike rental outlets.

Car rental companies

Alto Gros Islet ☎ 758/452-0233, Hewanorra Airport ☎758/454-5311, ⊛ www.altorentacar.com.
Avis Castries ☎ 758/452-2202, Hewanorra Airport ☎758/454-6325, George F.L. Charles Airport ☎758/452-2046, ⓔ avisslu@candw.lc.
Budget Castries ☎ 758/452-9887, Hewanorra

Airport ☎ 758/454-7470, ⊛ www.budgetstlucia.net.
Candida's Rodney Bay Marina ☎758/452-9076, ⊛www.candysrentacar.com.
Cool Breeze Soufrière, Rodney Bay, and both airports ☎758/459-7729, ⊛www.coolbreezecarrental.com.
Courtesy Gros Islet ☎758/452-8140, ⊛www.courtesycarrentals.com.
Guy's George F.L. Charles Airport ☎758/451-7885.
Hertz Hewanorra Airport ☎758/454-9636, George F.L. Charles Airport ☎758/451-7351, ⓔhertz@candw.lc.

Tours

Several local companies offer extensive **guided tours** of St Lucia's sights. Most are all-day, **all-inclusive expeditions** averaging a hefty US$90 per person, with stops at waterfalls, high mountain viewing areas, and banana plantations; some involve hikes of up to three hours. Visit the central mountains aboard 4WD trucks with Jungle Tours in Castries (☎ 758/450-0434, ⊛ www.jungletoursstlucia.com), or choose from a slew of activities (from deep sea fishing to sampling rums at the local distillery) with SunLink Tours in Rodney Bay Village (☎758/456-9100, ⊛www.sunlinktours.com).

A comparatively staid but perhaps more informative option is the inland and coastal **guided walks** offered by the St Lucia National Trust (☎ 758/452-5005, ⊛ www.slunatrust.org), Heritage Tours (☎758/451-6058, ⊛ www.heritagetoursstlucia.com), and the Forestry Department (☎ 758/450-2231 or 2375, ⊛ www.slumaffe.org). **Helicopter tours** and airport transfers are available with SunLink and St Lucia Helicopters (☎ 758/453-6950, ⊛www.stluciahelicopters.com), costing around US$100 per person for the fifteen-minute transfer from Hewanorra to Castries and from US$55 per person for a ten–minute jaunt around the north.

Accommodation

While thankfully not as all-inclusive-ridden as many Caribbean islands, tourist facilities on St Lucia have much improved over the last two decades, and **accommodation** runs the full range, from spa and sushi all-inclusives and medium-sized family hotels to reasonable local bed and breakfasts and guesthouses. Many of these are bunched together in the northern region of **Rodney Bay**, but for more character, charm and seclusion seek out one of the spots strung along the less-touristy **west coast**. With the exception of a single campsite, nowhere is truly inexpensive, especially in the high season when you can expect to pay US$40 for even the most basic room. The 18 percent service charge and accommodation tax doesn't help, either.

Another accommodation option is renting a **villa**, which are available mainly in the northern Cap Estate area, with a handful of options in more remote locations. Rates generally include maid and cooking services; count on spending US$900–4000 per week in high season. For rentals, contact Tropical Villas (PO Box 189, Castries ☎ 758/450-8240, ⊛ www.tropicalvillas.net) or Lucian Leisure (PO Box 1538, Castries ☎758/452-8898, ⊛www.lucian-leisure.com).

Food, drink and entertainment

Though St Lucia's **restaurant scene** – clustered for the most part around the tourist areas – is dominated by small, unpretentious and reasonably priced eateries, there are a few upmarket restaurants offering *haute cuisine*, which rarely disappoint. Overall, service tends to be incredibly friendly, if sometimes rather slow.

The most common culinary style is **Creole**, with chicken, seafood, or meat cooked in a spicy tomato-based sauce (traditionally prepared in a clay "coal pot") and served with filling sides of rice, beans and local vegetables like dasheen, breadfruit and paw-paw (papaya). For a truly local experience, don't miss one of the island's weekend **fish fries** – Anse La Raye on Friday nights and Dennery on Saturdays are the most rewarding.

Piña coladas and the like are fixtures at resort bars, but the local drink of choice is **Piton lager**, brewed in Vieux Fort and best enjoyed in view of its namesake peaks. There's also a nonalcoholic version made with molasses, the Piton Malta, but it's an acquired taste.

Though St Lucia isn't exactly the **nightlife** capital of the Caribbean, there's plenty to do after dark. Many hotels and restaurants in the west coast resort areas offer some sort of **live music** or **dancing** most nights of the week, and at Rodney Bay there are numerous bars and restaurants where you can have a drink or a meal while listening to anything from a traditional *chak-chak* group to the hotter licks of a reggae, calypso or steel-pan band. The best sources of current **entertainment information** are local newspapers and the tourist publication *Tropical Traveller* (⊛www.tropicaltraveller.com).

Post, phones and Internet

Public **phone** booths are located all around St Lucia and take either coins (EC$0.25 or EC$1) or the phone cards available from Cable & Wireless offices, post offices, pharmacies and convenience shops.

All major towns and villages have a **post office**; major ones are open Monday to Friday 8.15am–4.30pm; sub-offices are open 1–5pm. The General Post Office on Bridge Street in Castries (☎758/452-5157) is the island's largest and also has a philatelic bureau. Although sending postcards to the US, Canada or Europe costs less than EC$1, it can take up to two weeks, so for more urgent items try the **courier** services in Castries: FedEx is on Derek Walcott Square (☎758/452-1320), and DHL (☎758/453-1538) and UPS (☎758/452-7211) are both on Bridge Street.

> The **country code** for St Lucia is
> ☎758.

Many larger hotels have a business centre with **Internet** access, and even some smaller guesthouses have a computer available for guest use. For public access, visit ClickCom at La Place Carenage in Castries, the Marine Management Office on Bay Street in Soufrière, Wegosite just before the town roundabout in Vieux Fort, or the Cable & Wireless office at the Rodney Bay Marina; prices range EC$8–20/hr.

Opening hours, holidays and festivals

Store **opening hours** in St Lucia are generally Mon–Fri 8.30am–4.30pm and Sat 8am–12.30pm. Stores in Rodney Bay and the Gablewoods Mall in Castries keep extended hours, generally to 7pm. Most shops are closed on Sundays, but Julian's and J.Q's Supermarkets in Rodney Bay are open seven days a week.

In early or mid-May, the island plays host to the two-week **St Lucia Jazz Festival** (✆www.stluciajazz.org), which has attracted some of the biggest names in jazz and R&B – including Herbie Hancock, Wynton Marsalis and Luther Vandross – who usually perform during the last four days of the fest. It takes place at several venues, the main ones being Pigeon Island, Derek Walcott Square in Castries, and Balenbouche Estate in the southwest. Some shows are free, but for most you'll need to pay an entrance fee (US$38–50).

A round of dancing, street masquerading and general partying, St Lucia's July **Carnival** is one of the true showcases of the island's culture, with storytelling, folk dancing and traditional music afforded as much prominence as the more contemporary Carnival melee of sequinned bikinis and thumping soca music. Carnival **information** is available from the St Lucia tourist board.

Two competing **flower festivals**, La Rose in August and La Marguerite in October, hearken back to the political rivalry

between the British and French during St Lucia's tumultuous colonial history. Costume parades and traditional song and dance performances take place throughout the island, although Micoud is the focal point.

In addition to the holidays listed on p.60, St Lucia also observes the following **public holidays** listed in the box above.

Watersports and outdoor activities

With miles of easily accessible sandy beaches, St Lucia is perfect for **watersports**. Larger resort hotels often have their own facilities, usually including snorkelling, scuba diving, sea kayaking, windsurfing and even sailing on small Sunfish boats; except at all-inclusives, non-guests can usually use in-hotel facilities – for a fee, of course. To enjoy the water and explore the island at the same time, consider booking a trip along the west coast on one of the popular **boat cruises**. St Lucia's mountainous terrain also offers plenty of opportunities for adventurous **hiking** and **jungle biking**; a nice alternative to soaking in the sun at the beach.

Diving and snorkelling

St Lucia's **diving** is not as highly regarded as the region's more pristine scuba environments, such as Saba or Bonaire. Still, many of the reefs are excellent dive sites, and there are several submerged wrecks to explore. The island also offers plenty of good certification programmes. If you're a serious enthusiast, it might be worth looking into packages offered by hotels such as *Anse Chastanet* (see p.697), which bundle accommodation, meals, and a specified number of dives at ostensibly discounted rates.

Both diving and **snorkelling** are particularly good around the island's southwestern fringes, where the Soufrière Marine Management Area (☎758/459-5500, ⓦwww.smma.org.lc) hugs the shoreline for nearly seven miles. As the area is protected for fishing and recreational use, the reefs here are pristine by most standards. At specially designated reserves (including sites around Anse Chastenet and both Pitons), permits are required for use and available through authorized dive/snorkel operators; the nominal fee (diving: EC$10.50/day or EC$40.50/year; snorkelling: EC$2.50/day) goes towards the park's upkeep.

Watersports operators

Action Adventures Divers *The Still Beach Resort*, Soufrière ☎758/459-5599, ⓦwww.aadivers.net. Scuba, snorkelling.
Buddies Scuba Rodney Bay Marina ☎758/450-8406, ⓦwww.buddiesscuba.com. Scuba and snorkelling.
Dive Fair Helen Vigie Marina, Choc Bay, and Marigot Bay ☎758/451-7716, ⓦwww.divefairhelen.com. Scuba, snorkelling, and kayaking.

Scuba St Lucia Anse Chastanet ☎758/459-7755, ⓦwww.scubastlucia.com. Scuba and snorkelling.
The Wharf Restaurant and Bar Choc Bay ☎758/450-4844. Snorkelling, kayaking, sailing, body-boarding, and paddle boating.
Tornado Anse de Sables, Vieux Fort ☎758/454-7579, ⓦwww.tornado-surf.com. Windsurfing and kitesurfing. Open Oct–June.

Boat trips

Gliding up and down St Lucia's accessible and calm west coast, **sightseeing** and **party boats** (usually customized catamarans) offer an alternative way to see the bays and interior mountain peaks. Most outings include stops for snorkelling and swimming, or a visit to a coastal village (probably Soufrière or Marigot Bay) as well as lunch and drinks; prices range from US$35 for a half-day (no lunch) to US$90 for a full day. Just bear in mind that as the boats are often crowded with rowdy revellers taking advantage of the free-flowing rum, the trip may not be the quiet cruise you might anticipate; if you're looking for a more sedate excursion, say so when you book.

Endless Summer Cruises (☎758/450-8651, ⓦwww.stluciaboattours.com) run

Local culture and language

In typical Caribbean fashion, the heart and soul of St Lucian **culture** is a syncretic amalgamation of the customs, languages, religions and societal norms of the island's French and British colonizers, and of the Africans that they brought with them. Today's population of 156,000 is of predominantly African origin, and some seventy percent of them are Roman Catholic, with the remainder largely made up of Protestants and Anglicans, as well as a small number of Rastafarians. However, though Christian hymns are sung lustily enough to raise the church roofs each Sunday, St Lucia is a society in which esoteric African traditions of magic and spiritualism still survive. Carnival is the best example of this fusion of Christianity and ancient belief: even though the festival originated as a pre-Lenten celebration (it's now held in July), one of the costume parades' stock characters is the distinctly non-Christian moko jumbie, a wildly attired figure on stilts representing the spirit world. **Language** is another aspect of St Lucian culture that shows African influence. Though African languages were suppressed as soon as slaves arrived on the island, French planters still needed to communicate with their workers, and gradually the common language of **St Lucian Creole** (Kwéyòl) – also called Patois, although this is seen as somewhat derogatory – evolved, heavily laced with French as well as West African grammar and vocabulary, and more recently, with smatterings of English. Though **English** became St Lucia's official language in 1842, Creole is still spoken widely throughout the island, on the radio, and in parliament, and many St Lucians speak only Creole until they start primary school, learning English there for the first time.

full-day tours out of Rodney Bay, as well as half-day **sunset cruises** complete with a half-bottle of champagne per person. The *Brig Unicorn*, a yacht featured in the recent film *Pirates of the Caribbean*, offers a popular family-friendly **pirate adventure** (contact SunLink, see p.702). **Whale and dolphin watching** excursions are available with Mystic Man Tours (☎758/459-7783, ✆www.mysticmantours.com) and Hackshaw's Boat Charters (☎758/453-0553, ✆www.hackshaws.com) – there's a good chance you'll spot a pod of dolphins or pilot, sperm, or humpback whales, many of which are resident in St Lucia waters year-round.

Jungle biking

Jungle biking is one of St Lucia's newer and more exciting adventure sports, accessible only by boat from the beach at *Anse Chastanet Resort*. Set in an old sugar plantation just inland from Anse Mamin, there are some 12 miles of trails suitable for all abilities, and you can expect to see anything from eighteenth-century colonial ruins and a swimming hole to hundreds of fruit trees along your chosen trail. Operated by Bike St Lucia (☎758/459-BIKE, ✆www.bikestlucia.com); from US$39 per day.

Hiking

Hiking through St Lucia's central rainforests and preserves is the best way to experience the island's fabulously beautiful **interior**; despite being laced by walkable trails, the mountains often go unexplored by beach devotees. You don't necessarily need guides for many of the hikes (though hiring one will help to identify local flora and fauna), but you do need advance permission and an inexpensive permit from the **Forestry Department** to enter protected areas such as the Edmund Forest Reserve and the Barre de L'Isle area (see p.702 for more information).

History

The first inhabitants of St Lucia were the **Ciboney** people, Amerindians who settled about 2500 years ago in caves along the coast, fishing and hunting with stone tools. The agrarian **Arawaks** arrived from the northeast regions of South America 700 years later, farming cassava, sweet potatoes, corn, and cotton, and building thatched-roof houses using a technique still seen today in small St Lucian villages. After a further 700 years of peace came the warlike **Caribs**, who ruled the island until being driven away by European settlers in the seventeenth century.

Unlike most other Caribbean islands, the European "discovery" of St Lucia is an ambiguous matter, though it's most likely that the first European to sight the island was a **Spaniard**. Cartographer Juan de la Cosa had sailed with Christopher Columbus on his first three voyages, and he listed the island as El Falcón on a map he prepared in 1500. In 1511, it appeared on a Spanish Royal Cedula of Population as St Lucia, and was included on a Vatican map of 1520. The Spanish, however, made no great efforts to colonize St Lucia, and the first European settler was a French pirate, François Leclerc. Also known as Jambe de Bois (Wooden Leg), Leclerc made Pigeon Island his hideout around 1550 and from there terrorized Spanish ships in the neighbouring seas. The next Europeans to arrive did so by accident: in 1605, a **British** ship called the *Oliphe Blossome* (or Olive Branch) was blown off course on its way to Guyana and forced to land on St Lucia's south coast. Tired of being at sea, 67 passengers decided to try their luck at settling where they were, but they would have been better off staying with their ship: not long after negotiating with the Caribs for food, they were attacked. After five weeks, just nineteen surviving settlers escaped in a Carib canoe.

While similar clashes between the Caribs and small bands of settlers continued over the next few decades, the **French** claimed St Lucia and several neighbouring islands with little opposition. They continued to battle with the Caribs until a **peace agreement** was signed in 1660, but the war for St Lucia was far from won. Over the next 150 years, prolonged and bloody Anglo-French **hostilities** saw the "Helen of the West Indies" change hands between the two nations at least fourteen times. Despite the fighting, the French tried to turn St Lucia into a money-making colony, settling along the fertile southwest coast and establishing the island's first official **town** in 1746, called Soufrière. By 1765, they had introduced **sugar cane**, setting up vast plantations and bringing in **slaves** from West Africa to tend the crops that they hoped would earn them huge profits.

When war broke out in 1778 between Britain and France, the British once again tried to conquer the island, desiring the strategic bays in the north – all with views of the French depot Fort Royal in Martinique. After four years of fighting, Britain's **Admiral George Rodney** decimated the French navy off the coast of Guadeloupe. The British victory in what became known as the **Battle of the Saints** signified that French domination of the Caribbean was soon to end.

However, French control of St Lucia was not immediately relinquished. The 1783 Treaty of Versailles put St Lucia into French hands once again, and during the 1789–99 **French Revolution** all the towns were renamed, French nobles were executed by guillotine, and, in a radical move of solidarity, the Republicans **freed the slaves**. Sensing that the British would soon regain power, the Africans justly feared for their new-found freedom. Many joined with Republicans to form a freedom-fighting group known as the **Brigands**

that launched attacks against the British, levelling plantations and terrorizing the island until finally surrendering in 1797. In 1814, the **Treaty of Paris** brought Anglo-French conflicts in the Caribbean to a long-overdue conclusion, with France ceding St Lucia to the British. English commercial law was introduced in 1827, and slavery was finally **abolished** on August 1, 1834 – a date recognized today by the Emancipation Day holiday.

After the First World War, the question of independence from Britain came to the forefront, and in 1958 St Lucia joined other British colonies in the **West Indies Federation**, formed with the aim of winning self-rule. Britain granted St Lucia full self-government in 1967 and, after years of lobbying by successive Caribbean autonomy movements, **independence** on February 22, 1979. However, the island remains a Commonwealth country and a constitutional monarchy, with the British sovereign as the titular head of state, represented on the island by a governor general.

Sugar was the staple crop for the St Lucian economy until the mid-twentieth century, when the market price plummeted. By 1965, the last stalk had been cut and **bananas** had become sugar's replacement, comprising a majority of the island's exports. Although appealing for their year-round fruit production, bananas were far from a profit guarantee: **competition** with Latin American farmers was fierce, and like other Caribbean islands, St Lucia's banana industry rested heavily on preferential trade agreements with the European market. But in 1997, the WTO ruled that these agreements were discriminatory, and today St Lucia is taking great strides to avoid a potentially grim economic future. **Tourism** has become a necessary alternative source of income, and organizations like the National Trust and Heritage Tours are working to ensure that the benefits of tourism extend to the local population.

17.1

Castries and around

H ome to some 62,000 people (more than a third of the island's total population), St Lucia's capital of **CASTRIES** on the northwest coast is a metaphor for contemporary West Indian urban culture: at times busy and congested, other times somnolent and peaceful, the town feels stuck between a centuries-old island lifestyle and a desperate push to modernize. Though Castries is easy to navigate on foot, the town is not particularly blessed with museums, theatres or historical sights, and you'll find that it's primarily a place where people go to conduct business or do some shopping rather than take sightseeing trips.

Thanks to extensive damage by fires between 1796 and 1948, only a few examples of colonial and Victorian architecture remain, and today's city is chiefly composed of unadorned modern concrete buildings. But despite its contemporary feel, Castries retains a certain unaffected charm, due more to its setting than anything else. The town is wrapped around the deep harbour of **Port Castries**, where hundreds of cruise ships dock each year to unload tourists for a day of duty-free shopping at the city's malls. Spreading back from the harbour is **downtown** Castries, a dozen or so blocks of noisy streets, shops, bus stands and general congestion.

Meanwhile, the area **around Castries** is well worth exploring, and many sights are reachable without a car, although it takes a little effort to learn the bus system. Hills surround the capital to the east and south: the southern Morne Fortune range once provided a natural defence for the island's various occupiers, and the remains of several **forts** and **batteries** scattered throughout the area are worth a quick look. North of downtown and across the harbour is **Vigie Peninsula**, host to the island's largest duty-free complex, as well as the small **George F.L. Charles Airport** and a few waterfront restaurants.

Arrival, information and getting around

St Lucia's regional airport lies just over half a mile from downtown Castries, the island's public transport hub: several informal bus depots are scattered around town. Formerly known as Vigie Airport, Castries' **George F.L. Charles Airport** (☎758/452-1156) on Vigie Peninsula mostly handles small aircraft arriving from neighbouring Caribbean islands. There's a **tourist information** booth (daily 7am–9pm; ☎758/452-2596) as well as a row of **car rental** kiosks at the arrival area, while just outside is a **taxi** stand. If you've arrived from Guadeloupe, Dominica or Martinique via the high-speed **L'Express des Iles** ferry, you'll disembark at the St Lucia Air and Sea Ports Authority ferry complex in Bananes Bay; downtown is a short walk east.

The administrative office of the **St Lucia Tourist Board** (☎758/452-4094, ⓦwww.stlucia.org) is on the second floor of the Sureline Building complex in Vide Bouteille, about a mile northeast of Castries. However, visitors are better served by the knowledgeable and helpful staff of the **tourist information kiosks** in the Pointe Seraphine (Mon–Fri 8am–4.30pm; ☎758/452-4094) and La Place Carenage (Mon–Fri 9am–5pm, Sat 9am–12.30pm; ☎758/458-7194) shopping complexes.

Castries is not an easy city to navigate by **car**. On weekdays in particular, the narrow streets are congested and choked with randomly parked cars and trucks. At least **parking** is easy, thanks to the municipal multistorey garage (EC$1.50/hr) behind

Castries market, just off the John Compton Highway as you come into town from the north.

All the main **bus** stops are located in the downtown area. Buses to **Soufrière** (route #3D) leave from Jeremie Street in front of Castries Market. Services north to **Gros Islet** and **Cap Estate** (route #1A) leave from the Anglican School on Darling Road east of the Market, and buses to **Vieux Fort** and the south via the east coast (route #2H) leave from just up the street at the junction of Darling Road and Jean Baptiste Street. Also in the neighbourhood, buses to **Praslin** and **Mon Repos** (route #2D) head out from Julian's Supermarket off Jean Baptiste Street. Further downtown, buses to **Dennery** (route #2C) leave from the Mongiraud and Micoud Street junction, while **Marigot** and **Anse la Raye** buses (route #3C) depart from Victoria Street between Chausée Road and Chisel Street.

Accommodation

Unless you have a yearning for busy streets and traffic, there's no compelling reason to stay in **downtown Castries**, and you'll find that most of the more pleasant hotels are located in the hills or on the bays around town.

East Winds Inn Labrellotte Bay ☎758/452-8212, ⓦwww.eastwinds.com. At this small, understated and peaceful all-inclusive, rooms are spacious and well appointed, the beach is private and the pool with swim-up bar generous. There are no staff variety shows here, nor group activities; what sets *East Winds* above the rest are the quality rooms and restaurant and the handsome gardens. ❾ **Seascape** Marisule ☎758/450-1645, ⓦwww.seascape-stlucia.com. Two wonderfully homey self-contained wooden cottages with large balconies, set in acres of beautiful gardens sweeping down

to a small secluded beach below. One cottage is for a private romantic getaway, the other has three bedrooms for large parties or shares. The well-ventilated rooms have great coastal views, while the pool is large and deep. Only the sound of the area's extensive birdlife ever intrudes on the serenity of it all. ❹ **Sundale Guesthouse** Sunny Acres ☎758/452-4120. Paul Kingshott's small, tightly run guesthouse on a side road near the Gablewoods Mall is bland but scrupulously clean, inexpensive and within walking distance of Choc Bay's beaches. Rooms

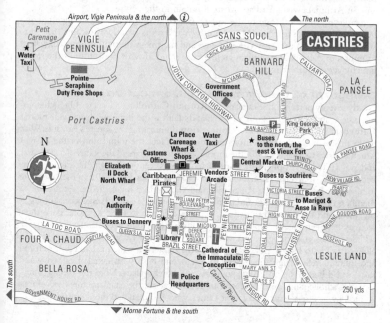

have fans and private bath with hot water; two one-bedroom cottages and one two-bedroom apartment are also on site, all plain but serviceable. There's a communal lounge with TV and VCR, and breakfast is included in the rates. No credit cards. ❷

Top o' The Morne Apartments The Morne ☎758/452-3603, ⓦwww.topothemorne.com. Once housing officers of the British army, this 150-year-old building has nine apartments available nightly or long-term for civilians. While the bricks show their age, the spacious apartments (thirteen-foot-high ceilings) are newly decorated with comfortable furnishings and equipped with high-speed Internet access. With spectacular harbour views, the pool and large verandahs offer a chance to wallow in the cool breezes drifting up the hills. Studio ❹, one-bedroom ❺

Windjammer Landing Labrellotte Bay ☎758/456-9000, US 800/743-9609, UK 0800/587-2308; ⓦwww.windjammer-landing.com. Sprawled over 55 hillside acres on and above Labrellotte Bay, with accommodation ranging from well-appointed rooms to self-contained villas – some with private pools, some with private chefs, all with lovely ocean views. Getting around is a hassle since walking is not really an option; instead, minivans shuttle you along treacherously windy roads from your room to the site's five restaurants (three are beachside), four pools and the beach, which offers watersports. Perhaps accustomed to being chauffeured, celebrity guests are not unusual. ❾

Downtown Castries

Named after St Lucia's famous poet and Nobel Prize-winner, **Derek Walcott Square** is southeast of Castries Market and bordered by Brazil, Micoud, Bourbon and Laborie streets. This small urban centrepiece is a landscaped oasis in an otherwise congested town, and its fine architecture and central location make it an ideal place to start any city tour. Though a peaceful place today, the square has had a turbulent history: in the late eighteenth century following the French Revolution, the square was known as the Place d'Armes, and legend has it a **guillotine** was set up by Republicans anxious to do away with selected nobles. It was later labelled Columbus Square (1893) in honour of the explorer, once thought to be the first European discoverer of the island; in light of recent evidence to the contrary, the square was renamed in 1993. Its east side is shaded by an immense **saman tree**, thought to be more than 400 years old, and busts of St Lucia's two Nobel Prize winners (Walcott and Sir Arthur Lewis) guard an ornate fountain in the centre.

Bordering the south side of the square, **Brazil Street** is the city's congested and busy architectural showcase. Miraculously, many of its structures escaped the hurricanes and fires of the early colonial days and the mid-twentieth century. Excellent examples of colonial West Indian architecture stand towards the centre of the street, directly across from the square.

Cathedral of the Immaculate Conception

Nearly seventy percent of St Lucians are **Roman Catholic** – a legacy of French colonial rule – and the cornerstone of the island's faith is the imposing brick-and-mortar **Cathedral of the Immaculate Conception** dominating the square's east side. With room to seat more than two thousand communicants, the foundation of the current structure dates to 1894. In 1957, the former church was granted the status of a cathedral, and was visited by **Pope John Paul II** in 1986. Recently, though, the cathedral has been home to much less illustrious visitors. On December 31, 2000, two men claiming to align themselves with the Rastafarian faith barged into the cathedral, setting fire to members of the congregation and killing both a priest and a nun. Rastafarians throughout the island condemned the attack, denying any link to their religion. Since then, security has been greatly improved, and no further problems have arisen.

Unless Mass is in progress (in which case you are welcome to worship), you're allowed inside to have a look around the ornate interior, which is bathed in rich red and diffused yellow light from ceiling portals, and busy with detailed carved wood inlay, wood benches, iron ceiling supports and stately pillars. Note the ceiling paintings of Catholic saints and apostles, with St Lucie above the altar, and the vivid murals painted by St Lucia artist Dunstan St Omer, who also designed the country's flag.

The Central Market and around

Vividly colourful and often loud, **Central Market** (Mon–Sat 9am–5pm, Sun cruise ship days only) on Jeremie Street at the northern perimeter of downtown is one of the busiest parts of Castries, especially on Saturday mornings. Inside are rows of craft booths, with vendors selling baskets, spices, carvings, T-shirts, straw hats and tacky souvenirs. At the northeast corner of the complex is the colourful and busy fruit and vegetable market, where you can find a wealth of fresh produce.

Across the John Compton Highway from the Central Market, and easily identifiable by the rust-coloured roof, is the **Vendor's Arcade** (Mon–Sat 9am–5pm, Sun cruise ship days only), another set of craft stalls selling the same rather tacky wares at slightly higher prices. For standard duty-free items like jewellery, perfume, and rum, visit **La Place Carenage** (Mon–Fri 9am–4pm, Sat 9am–1pm, Sun cruise ship days only) a couple blocks further west on Jeremie Street. Bring your airline tickets and identification for tax-free purchases.

Vigie Peninsula

Framing the northern half of Port Castries, the heavily developed **Vigie Peninsula** was the original site of the Castries town settlement. Then largely swampland, the area was afflicted by rampant disease, so by 1768 the town had relocated to drier land across the harbour. In the twentieth century, successive government reclamation projects created the flat spit of land where the airport now sits. At the peninsula's southern end, overlooking the bay, is **Pointe Seraphine** (Mon–Fri 9am–5pm, Sat 9am–2pm, Sun cruise ship days only), the island's biggest duty-free shopping complex. Two adjacent cruise-ship berths deliver disembarking tourists directly to the stores, while the **taxi stand** (☎758/451-6737) and the **water taxi** to downtown Castries (every 10min when cruise ships are docked, on demand otherwise; US$1) stand by to cater for the day-trippers.

From Pointe Seraphine, the main highway runs north to Rodney Bay. Parallel to it, between the airport runway and the sea, is the more picturesque Nelson Mandela Drive, listed on maps as **Peninsular Road** – to reach it from Castries, take the first exit off the Vigie Roundabout to double back around the landing strip. Flanking the road is **Vigie Beach**, which, despite the occasional roar of an engine and the proximity of the town cemetery, is appealing for its uncrowded two-kilometre stretch of smooth sand, ample shade and generally calm and inviting surf.

Once clear of the airport, Nelson Mandela Drive winds uphill towards Vigie Lighthouse at the apex. The entire peninsula was once a fortification, and many buildings here are restored military quarters, built from red brick (now painted yellow) in the late nineteenth century. At the corner of Nelson Mandela and Clarke Avenue, St Lucia's **National Archives** (Mon–Thurs 9am–4pm, Fri 9am–2pm; ☎758/452-1654, ⊛www.stluciaarchives.org) are housed in a circa-1890 building: inside, you can browse through hundreds of old photos, lithographs, postcards and maps, which provide a good historical perspective of the island. Next door are the offices of the St Lucia **National Trust** (Mon–Fri 9am–4.30pm; ☎758/452-5005, ⊛www.slunatrust.org), through which you can arrange tours of island highlights.

North and east of Castries

The busy Castries–Gros Islet Highway runs north passing Vigie Peninsula and a string of unappealing industrial sites, shops, restaurants, hotels and schools before swinging to the coast to run parallel to sweeping **Choc Bay**. Fringed to the north by **Labrellotte Point**, a sheltered bay hosting a couple of luxury resorts, and to the south by **Vide Bouteille Point**, Choc Bay is a handsome two-mile stretch of often secluded sand.

From Vide Bouteille Point the Castries–Gros Islet Highway swings into the suburban **Sunny Acres** area, home to one of the island's larger shopping complexes,

Gablewoods Mall, particularly good for groceries. Just past the mall, the winding but relatively smooth **Allan Bousquet Highway** strikes into the interior. Ten minutes' drive from the coast is the village of **Babonneau**, a small farming community huddled into the central hills of the island's northern half and worth visiting for both the sweeping hill views and for a taste of rural St Lucia. Several rivers flow through the hills around the settlement, and some say that Babonneau is a Patois version of the old French phrase *barre bon eau*, meaning, roughly, "mountain ridge, good water".

Set high in the hills east of Castries at Morne Pleasant, the **Folk Research Centre** (Mon–Fri 8.30am–4.30pm; donations accepted; ☎758/453-1477) – or *Plas Wichès Foklò*, to give it its Patois name – is a museum and cultural centre set in an old estate house once owned by the eminent Devaux family. Dedicated to preserving the culture and language of St Lucian **Creole**, the centre houses a small **museum** whose exhibits include a reproduction of a traditional Amerindian *ti-kay* hut (still built in rural villages today) and examples of indigenous musical instruments. The diminutive **research library** downstairs, accessible during opening hours, holds one of the island's best collections of books, research papers and photographs relating to St Lucia's folklore and history.

South and west of Castries

The La Toc Road leads west from downtown Castries along the south side of the harbour. Towards the western outskirts of town, as the road begins to climb, is the sizeable **Victoria Hospital**, the island's largest; a mile or so beyond is **La Toc Battery**, one of the island's best-preserved examples of British military bastions. The 2.5-acre, nineteenth-century cement fortification features mounted cannons and dim underground bunkers, tunnels and cartridge storage rooms; one of the bunkers holds a large exhibit of antique bottles. To visit the Battery, call ahead to schedule a tour (by appointment only Mon–Fri 9am–3pm; EC$13.25; ☎758/452-6039) with **Bagshaw's** silkscreening studio and shop, located about halfway between the hospital and the battery.

Regardless what road you take from Castries to get to the south of the island, you will inevitably end up winding through the loosely demarcated suburb of **Morne Fortune**. Comprising a series of hills that flank the capital to the south, the area's high elevation provides striking views of the city and the north coast – on a clear day you can see the island of Martinique – and to the south, glimpses of the conical Pitons at Soufrière. The area is reachable via Manoel Street in downtown Castries, which becomes Government House Road as it begins its snakelike ascent towards **Government House** (by appointment only Tues & Thurs 10am–noon & 2–4pm; US$10; ☎758/452-2481, ⊛www.stluciagovernmenthouse.com), an imposing structure dating from 1895 which houses the offices of St Lucia's governor general, the Queen's appointed representative. At the small adjoining **Le Pavillon Royal Museum**, you can see a collection of artefacts and documents relating to the history of the house as well as modern St Lucian pieces of significance.

A few winds and turns beyond Government House, Morne Road takes you into the heart of the neighbourhood to the top of the 852-foot Morne Fortune itself (also known as "The Morne"), named "Good Luck Hill" by the French. These hills were first fortified by the French in 1768, then recaptured (and renamed **Fort Charlotte**) by the British in 1803. Several of the existing military encampments, cemeteries, barracks and batteries have been slated to be restored and opened to the public for quite some time; however, the process is incomplete and many are still in a state of disrepair. The best-preserved remnants are part of a multipurpose government complex as well as the **Sir Arthur Lewis Community College** (☎758/452-5507, ⊛www.salcc.edu.lc), named after the St Lucian 1979 Nobel Prize-winner for economics who is buried in the grounds. The college itself comprises several larger, nineteenth-century yellow-brick structures with weathered white columns, all of military origin. You're free to amble about and visit the buildings and the **Inniskilling monument**, which honours British soldiers who battled the French here in 1796, located on the south side of the college complex behind the Combermere Barracks.

Eating and drinking

There are only a few places to **eat** in the Castries area, and many visitors make the drive north to Rodney Bay for a meal. That being said, the eateries downtown are good for grabbing a quick bite while shopping or sightseeing – by far the best of these are the stalls at Castries Central Market. For a more formal meal, there are a handful of excellent options in the surrounding areas – head across Port Castries or into the hills, where stunning views accentuate the experience.

Castries

Caribbean Pirates La Place Carenage ☎758/452-2543. On the Port Castries waterfront and popular with locals and the cruise ship crowd alike, *Caribbean Pirates* serves moderately priced nouvelle Creole cuisine with a menu that changes weekly. Seafood is the speciality – if you're feeling adventurous, try the curried turtle. Mon–Thurs 8am–7pm, Fri & Sat 8am–11pm, Sun cruise ship days only.

Castries Central Market Jeremie Street ☎758/453-1019. Market vendors, shoppers and local business people flock to eat breakfast or lunch at these dozen or so restaurant stalls in a small, crowded alleyway behind the market. Taken at unadorned plastic tables, the servings of seafood, rotis, rice and beans or meat and dumplings are hearty and delicious. Most stalls don't accept credit cards. Daily 6am–evening.

Around Castries

Bon Appétit Red Tape Lane, Morne Fortune ☎758/452-2757. A rather unique dining experience at a small guesthouse in the Castries hills, open by reservation only – it's much like you're eating in a private home. The brief menu includes (green-skinned) pumpkin soup and crab thermidor – smallish servings tastefully arranged and embellished with minimal amounts of heavy sauces.

Hand-painted pastels on the walls are as soothing as the views of the harbour below. Prices range EC$25–$55. Daily breakfast, lunch & dinner.

Coal Pot Vigie Marina ☎758/452-5566. One of the island's busiest and best restaurants – dinner reservations are essential. The cuisine is a fusion of French and St Lucian cultures, with choices like lobster bisque flavoured with cognac or St Lucian callaloo soup to start. Main courses are design-your-own: pair your choice of fresh local seafood or meat with your favourite sauce. Directly on the water's edge, with a dark interior embellished with local artwork, this is a perfect place for a special night out. Mon–Fri lunch & dinner, Sat dinner.

Froggie Jacques Tropical Bistro Vigie Marina ☎758/458-1900. A warm and personal bar and restaurant that's big on excellent food and small on overdressed pomp. Emphasis is on hearty dishes and home-smoked fish, but vegetarians are well catered to and special requests are welcome. Mains from EC$48. Mon–Sat lunch & dinner.

The Wharf Restaurant and Bar Castries–Gros Islet Highway, Choc Bay ☎758/450-4844. This roadside/beachside joint serves decent American and Caribbean dishes at moderate prices, but the beach is the main draw. Watersports, lounge chairs, and volleyball are all available, making it a popular spot for visitors without hotel beach facilities, especially cruise ship passengers. Daily 9am–6pm.

17.2

Rodney Bay and the north

St Lucia's compact northern tip encompasses not just a bustling strip of coastal resorts but also the remote and arid northern shoreline between Pointe du Cap and Pointe Hardy, the lavish vacation villas of Cap Estate and quiet **Cas-en-Bas** on the rugged northeast coast. On the west coast, the sweeping, two-mile-long horseshoe of **Rodney Bay** is where most of the region's tourist trappings are concentrated, with more planned for the future. As part of the push to develop the area, it's officially been renamed Rodney Bay Village, but that's not especially evident yet. And as St Lucia will be one of eight hosts of the 2007 Cricket World Cup, with four teams playing matches at the Beausejour Cricket Ground in Gros Islet, plans to increase room capacity in the area and capitalize on the event are already under way.

Rodney Bay opens into a deep-water yacht harbour, with a marina complex to the east housing a handful of water-side eateries and rather shabby shops. Most of the area activity, though, is focused around the restaurant-and-hotel-lined **Reduit Beach** on the sea side, one of St Lucia's most popular strips of sand. Across the harbour channel to the north is the quiet fishing village of **Gros Islet**, a place to soak up some local flavour at small, unpretentious Creole restaurants. Just about the entire village is overtaken each Friday night for the raucous **street party**, or Jump Up, when the streets are blocked off and revellers pour in for a rowdy night of roadside foodstuffs, music and alcohol.

Rodney Bay's northern half is framed by the heavily visited **Pigeon Island National Landmark**, an outcrop attached to the mainland by a causeway in the 1970s. Heavily fortified by the British in the eighteenth century, the island has been transformed into a recreation park holding the restored remains of military buildings, a string of beaches and some walking trails.

Arrival and getting around

Getting to and around St Lucia's northern point is relatively easy, since frequent **buses** run the length of the coast between Castries, Gros Islet and Cap Estate near the island's northern tip. Marked route #1A, they leave near the Anglican school on Darling Road. Schedules are theoretical, for buses leave when they are so inclined, but count on at least one departure every hour from 6.30am until 10pm, with more services for the Jump Up on Friday night. You'll pay around EC$2 to travel from Castries to Reduit Beach, Rodney Bay Marina or Gros Islet. If you're travelling from farther afield, you'll have to change buses at Castries. If you don't have a car and would rather avoid public transport, **taxis** are readily available at hotels and along the main tourist strips. From downtown Castries to any of the resorts along the northeast coast, expect to pay around EC$40–60.

Accommodation

As St Lucia's main tourist heartland, the island's northern tip is plentifully supplied with large **resorts**, medium-sized **hotels** and inexpensive **guesthouses**, the majority located within walking distance from Reduit Beach.

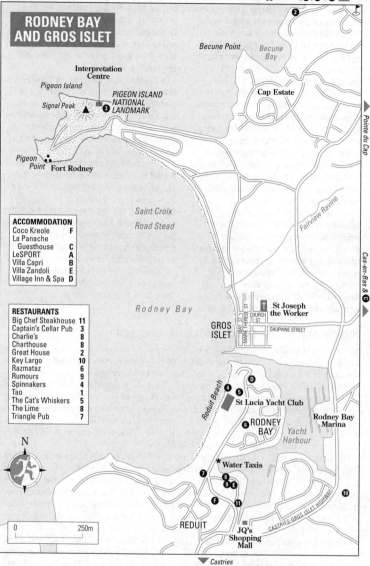

RODNEY BAY AND GROS ISLET

Smuggler's Cove, **1**, **A** & **B** ▲

2

Becune Point

Becune Bay

Cap Estate

Pigeon Island

Interpretation Centre

Signal Peak

PIGEON ISLAND NATIONAL LANDMARK

3

Pigeon Point **Fort Rodney**

Pointe du Cap ▶

Saint Croix Road Stead

Fairview Ravine

Cas-en-Bas & **C** ▶

ACCOMMODATION

Coco Kreole	**F**
La Panache Guesthouse	**C**
LeSPORT	**A**
Villa Capri	**B**
Villa Zandoli	**E**
Village Inn & Spa	**D**

Rodney Bay

St Joseph the Worker

GROS ISLET

BAY ST / MARIE THERESE ST / CHURCH ST

DAUPHINE STREET

RESTAURANTS

Big Chef Steakhouse	**11**
Captain's Cellar Pub	**3**
Charlie's	**8**
Charthouse	**8**
Great House	**2**
Key Largo	**10**
Razmataz	**6**
Rumours	**9**
Spinnakers	**4**
Tao	**1**
The Cat's Whiskers	**5**
The Lime	**8**
Triangle Pub	**7**

Reduit Beach

D

4 **5**

St Lucia Yacht Club

6 RODNEY BAY

Rodney Bay Marina

Yacht Harbour

★ Water Taxis

7

8

9 **E**

F

11

10

REDUIT

JQ's Shopping Mall

CASTRIES–GROS ISLET HIGHWAY

N

0 ——— 250m

▼ Castries

17

17.2 | **ST LUCIA** | Rodney Bay and the north

Coco Kreole Rodney Bay Village ☎ 758/452-0712, ⓦ www.cocokreole.com. Recently renovated, this compact 20-room boutique hotel is clean and crisp, but still manages to convey some character with a bright yellow exterior, attentive staff, cosy bar, and (very) small garden pool. Rooms have cable TV, a/c, fridges, and wireless Internet access. At the time of writing, plans for an additional 83 rooms were

under way at the adjacent and co-owned *Coco Palm*, where the large pool will be open to guests of *Coco Kreole*. **4**

La Panache Guesthouse Cas-en-Bas Road, Gros Islet ☎ 758/450-0765, ⓦ www.lapanache.com. Tucked into a hillside with views west to Gros Islet, *La Panache*'s three colourful rooms (one of which sleeps four at a push) all have private baths,

691

kitchenettes, and cable TV. There's a homey photo-graph-festooned dining area with a twice-weekly Creole buffet and a gazebo-style lounge with TV/VCR and books to borrow. Better for couples looking for an inexpensive and peaceful retreat than for singles seeking nightlife in Rodney Bay. ②

LeSPORT Cap Estate ☎758/457-7800, in US 800/544-2883; ⓦwww.thebodyholiday.com. One of the island's few all-inclusive resorts that manages to make non-predatory singles feel comfortable. Usually full of stressed-out city types who perhaps don't notice the cold, impersonal rooms and instead indulge in the (included) spa treatments, exercise classes, hikes, watersports, golf lessons and t'ai chi. However, the food is plentiful, healthful and well prepared, especially at the superlative *Tao* (see p.696). ⑨

Villa Capri Smuggler's Cove, Cap Estate ☎758/450-0009, ⓦwww.capristlucia.com. A delightful nine-room guesthouse nestled in the hills above Smuggler's Cove, this is the perfect getaway for independent travellers and those who like a touch of home and camaraderie; also an ideal spot for an intimate wedding retreat. The simply decorated rooms all have lovely views of the bay, some with hammocked balconies, and there's an open-air honour bar. Spa treatments are offered in a hillside "relaxation pyramid," and yoga, t'ai chi and meditation classes are held on an outdoor wooden deck overlooking the pool and herb garden below. Rates include breakfast, and other meals are cooked on demand. ④

Villa Zandoli Rodney Bay Village ☎758/452-8898, ⓦwww.saintelucie.com. A truly special, brightly painted guesthouse with five cheery and comfortable rooms; the owner also has three one-bedroom apartments across the way. It's all beautifully maintained, and the small but lush gardens are a welcome oasis in the otherwise developed Rodney Bay complex. There's an inviting communal area, Internet access and a well-equipped kitchen (rates include breakfast). All rooms have cable TV, some share baths. Single ②, double ③

Village Inn & Spa Reduit Beach ☎758/458-3300, ⓦwww.villageinnstlucia.com. Recently refurbished, the *Inn's* 76 rooms, all of which overlook the hot tub and waterfall pool, are well equipped but devoid of character. There's a spa, restaurant, bar, and rather worn tennis court all packed into the small property, and Reduit Beach is just across the street. Rates include breakfast. ⑤

Rodney Bay and Reduit Beach

Named **RODNEY BAY** after eighteenth-century British commander George Brydges Rodney, the current incarnation of this former American army base is a compact but fully fledged tourist resort, sandwiched between the glorious if over-crowded Reduit Beach and the shops and yachting facilities of Rodney Bay Marina. The mangrove swamp that once separated the villages of Rodney Bay and Gros Islet has been replaced by a man-made harbour channel, which opens out into a deep-water lagoon dotted with bobbing yachts. From the Castries–Gros Islet Highway, the main road into town (look for the sign to Rodney Bay) is on the west side at JQ's shopping mall just before the harbour and marina.

The settlement itself is quite small, and most of the action takes place on the strip of land between the beach and the **yacht harbour**, considered by many to be among the finest in the Caribbean. The harbour is served by the small **Rodney Bay Marina** complex, which has full services for boaters as well as a few waterside restaurants, banks, and somewhat unappealing gift shops. But **Rodney Bay Village**, at the southwest end of the harbour, is where landlubbers are likely to be found, soaking up the sun at one of any number of resorts or sipping a cocktail at one of the popular bars.

Lined by private villas, the harbour is rarely visible from the village itself, but along its western coast lies the original reason for Rodney Bay's growth into a tourism epicentre: the inviting, easily accessible **Reduit** (REH-doo-ee) **Beach**. This is the most popular beach on the island, around a mile long, with a wide swath of golden sand, generally calm surf, and views of Pigeon Island to the north and the coastal hills to the south. Don't be fooled into thinking you've found a Caribbean haven, though: the beach is generally packed with the well-oiled bodies of visiting sun-worshippers and is not exactly a secluded hideaway. Unsurprisingly, it's also lined with places to stay, many of them large-scale but low-lying concrete blocks sitting directly (and intrusively) on the beach, their proximity adding to the general crowded feel. The beach hotels provide chairs and umbrellas for their guests, and many will rent them to visitors staying elsewhere for about US$10/day.

△ The pool at the *Ladera Resort*

Gros Islet

Just north across the channel from Rodney Bay lies **GROS ISLET** (GROZ-i-lay), a small fishing village of rickety, rust-roofed wooden homes and narrow streets lined with fruit and vegetable vendors. The beach is somewhat dirty, and generally the town holds little of interest for the visitor. Come Friday nights, though, Lucians and visitors alike pour in for the **Jump Up** street party, when everyone lets loose and parties. Much of the town is blocked off, and armies of snack vendors peddling barbecue, fried fish, hot cakes and cold beers arrive to feed the hungry masses. Bars open their doors onto the street, street corners are festooned with speakers and the music is loud. Things get going around 10pm and last till late, and it's generally good-natured affair – though there can be a bit of an edge. Single women should be prepared for unwanted attention and should not attend alone. You're also best off leaving your valuables at home and being extra cautious if walking back to your guesthouse late at night.

Cas-en-Bas

Across from the turn-off for Gros Islet just pass the Shell petrol station, the Cas-en-Bas Road strikes east off the coastal highway towards a small settlement on the remote east coast called **CAS-EN-BAS** (CAZ-en-bah), worth visiting for its string of secluded **beaches** and rugged coast. A villa development is in the works for 2006, at which point the road here will be paved and the appeal perhaps diminished. For now, though, you can walk the dirt track in an hour, much better than negotiating the endless mucky potholes by 4WD – don't even attempt it after rain, or in a normal car. Perhaps the best option is to go on horseback; riders can wade through the water bareback when they reach the beach – Trim's Stables (℡758/450-8273) offers trail rides. Hand-painted signs mark a fork in the road: left for Cas-en-Bas and right for the beach at **Anse Lavoutte**, favoured by **leatherback turtles** as a secluded spot for egg-laying between March and August. If you want to witness this spectacle for yourself, you must join a turtle watch further south at Grande Anse.

The ocean marks the end of the Cas-en-Bas Road, and here you'll find a quiet, soft-sand beach with some shady spots and an outlying reef taming the rougher waters of the Atlantic. A wooden-hut beach **bar** named *Marjorie's* serves up cold drinks and BBQ. There's a truly isolated spot – **Donkey Beach** – fifteen minutes' walk **north**, along a trail that hugs the rocky, cactus-strewn coastline – look out for a track that goes back down to the water atop the hillside. Thirty minutes' walk **south** of Cas-en-Bas along the unmarked coastal path brings you to the beach at Anse Lavoutte. Visitors to these shores, particularly Donkey Beach, should take the utmost care in the water due to the powerful Atlantic undercurrents; more than a few people have drowned here. Much of the area is deserted, so tell someone where you are going before you set off.

Pigeon Island National Landmark

The 44-acre **Pigeon Island National Landmark** (daily 9am–5pm; EC$13.35 or US$5; ℡758/450-0603, ⊛www.slunatrust.org/pisland.htm) is a handsome promontory of land striking into the ocean just north of Gros Islet – and no longer an island at all, having been linked to the mainland via a causeway during the 1970s. It's one of St Lucia's most popular recreation spots, a combination of easy hiking trail, concert venue, historic site and pleasant lunch stop with the added bonus of several excellent beaches and a fine pub. In the hotter months, it's best to visit Pigeon Island early in the day, as the hills provide excellent views and are well worth the climb, which is more than pleasant before it gets too hot.

The island has served as a base for several notable inhabitants, from the Arawaks, who are alleged to have left behind clay pottery, to the infamous pirate François Leclerc. In 1778, Pigeon Island was fortified by the newly arrived British colonials, and it was from here that Admiral Rodney launched the attack against the French that effectively ended their domination of the Caribbean. When African slaves were given their freedom following the French Revolution, imminent British repossession caused them to fear re-enslavement and spurred them into action. Tagged as the "**Brigands**", the Africans banded together to create a minor rebellion, razing plantations and even taking brief possession of Pigeon Island, before signing a peace treaty in 1797. Since then, the island has been at various times a camp for indentured East Indian labourers, a quarantine station for patients afflicted with tropical disease, and a whaling station. Declared a national landmark in the 1970s, and afforded the protection of the St Lucia National Trust, the island's buildings were restored, the causeway was constructed, and Britain's Princess Alexandra opened the park to the public on February 23, 1979, St Lucia's first day of independence.

Visiting the park

To get to the park by car, turn west from the Castries–Gros Islet Highway at the sign for the *Jambe de Bois* café and continue along the causeway. You can also hop on a ferry at the southwest side of the Rodney Bay harbour (daily except Sat 10am–1pm, hourly departures, returns at 12.30, 2 and 4pm; EC$26 round-trip; ☎758/452-8079), which drops you off at a small dock on the south side of the park fortifications. Once you've passed the main gate, paid your entrance fee and collected a map of the area, the **Pigeon Island Interpretation Centre** is on your right, located on the foundation of an old officers' mess. A mini-museum of the island's chequered past, the one-room centre is worth a brief look for its displays of Amerindian axes, clay bowls, flint and shell tools and a discussion of the infamous Battle of the Saints (see p.683); some video displays are now defunct but plans for an upgrade are in the works. Just below the centre is the wonderfully cavernous *Captain's Cellar Pub*, housed in an old barracks and well worth visiting for an ice-cold Piton after tackling the park's hills.

Past the Interpretation Centre, the south side of the island is peppered with the remains of the **military barracks** and **encampments**, including gun batteries, a powder magazine, a lime kiln and the ruins of the British admiral's Fort Rodney. Some structures are more intact than others, such as the thick-walled powder magazine to the left of the entrance and the old cooperage near the beach on the south side of the island – now home to the park's toilets. Nearby is the *Jambe de Bois* waterside cafe, sufficient for sandwiches, snacks and a 2-for-1 drink special.

Several prominent hillocks dominate the island north of the military buildings; of these, 319-foot **Signal Peak** is the highest. A marked trail leads right to its base, from which it takes about fifteen minutes to reach the summit, affording panoramic views south to Gros Islet and the outskirts of Castries, and north over the expanse of the St Lucia Channel to the island of Martinique.

Eating and drinking

Back-to-back **restaurants** in the busy tourist stronghold north of Castries provide an array of choices from tandoori to steak and kidney pie, and Rodney Bay as a whole seems to have more restaurants per square mile than anywhere else on the island. Nightlife generally consists of bar hopping and a few dance spots, with *The Lime* serving as a common meeting point. During the Friday night **street party** in Gros Islet, restaurateurs and vendors set up roadside barbecues and sell roasted chicken, fish or meats, as well as cold beers to wash it down.

Restaurants

Rodney Bay

Big Chef Steakhouse Rodney Bay Village ☎758/450-0210. Popular local TV chef caters for those who like their meal meaty (and pricey). From an 8oz tenderloin to "as big as you can handle"

(65oz is the latest record), these meats are not for the faint at heart – or the gourmet. Pasta and seafood are also available, if you must. Mon–Sat 6pm–10pm.

The Cat's Whiskers Reduit Beach Road ☎758/452-8880. Unassuming pub-restaurant once known as *Mel & H's Old English Pub*, serving hearty traditional English fare from full breakfasts to ploughman's lunches, bangers and mash, hand-cut chips and steak and kidney pies (all between EC$30 and $40), as well as cider (EC$8) and reasonable brews on tap (EC$10). The popular Sunday brunch is a feast: roast beef, Yorkshire pudding and all the trimmings for EC$45. Tues–Sun 8am–late.

Charthouse Rodney Bay Village ☎758/452-8115. At this dark-wood, marina-side restaurant (reserve seats on the waterside deck), steaks, hickory-smoked ribs and lobster are the specialities, with large portions and hearty sides. Vegetarians take note: there's little to nothing of interest on offer here. Top off your meal with a Cuban cigar, on sale at the restaurant. Expensive. Daily 6–10:30pm.

The Lime Rodney Bay Village ☎758/452-0761. "Liming" is West Indian slang for "hanging out", and this is one of Rodney Bay's more popular spots to do just that. The food is consistently good Caribbean fare, with the best rotis on the island (EC$10), although most dishes start at EC$35). Dining is indoor and alfresco (on the patio next to the road) with an in-house DJ nightly. Also open late on Fri and Sat for dancing to a wide range of live music, making for one of the island's hottest nightlife venues. 11am–midnight, closed Tues.

Razmataz Reduit Beach Road, Rodney Bay ☎758/452-9800. If you're craving curry, then this popular Reduit Beach restaurant is your best bet. Specialities are spicy vindaloo, korma and tikka masala, all prepared with tandoori (grilled) chicken, lamb, beef or shrimp, from EC$28 – there are plenty of non-meat options as well, plus occasional live music. 4pm–late, closed Tues.

Spinnakers Reduit Beach, Rodney Bay ☎758/452-8491. Hopping beach bar and restaurant serving an international mix of steaks and grilled seafood with a family-friendly kids menu; most prices hover around EC$20. Local lobster is the most popular and expensive item at EC$85, but the ribs are tangy, tender and 1/3 the price. Come for the steel band on Sundays from noon to 3pm. Daily 9am–11pm.

North of Rodney Bay

Great House Cap Estate ☎758/450-0450. Expensive fine dining – afternoon tea and dinner only – in a 250-year-old stone plantation house overlooking Bécune Bay, with seating on the covered stone patio. The cuisine is French with a touch of Creole – try the fillet of dorado Creole. Tues–Sun 4.30–9.45pm.

Key Largo Castries–Gros Islet Highway ☎758/452-0282. Casual pizza place on the east side of the Castries–Gros Islet Highway, across from the marina, serving by far the best pizza on the island, freshly cooked in a wood-fired brick oven; excellent pasta dishes also available. Be warned, though – meals may be accompanied by pumping music from the sports gym upstairs. Daily 9am–11pm.

Tao *LeSPORT*, Cap Estate ☎758/457-7821. Superlative East/West fusion cuisine, impeccable service and a gorgeous setting overlooking the bay make this one of the island's finest dining experiences. Booking is essential: request a table on the edge of the balcony, choose from sushi, tofu dishes and wonderful seafood and don't forget to leave room for dessert. Dinner daily.

Bars and clubs

Charlie's Rodney Bay Village ☎758/458-0565. *Charlie's* is the place to be any night of the week (take Monday to recover), with a piano bar Tues, Wed, and Sun, a DJ the rest of the week, and dancing to a wide variety of music at the adjoining nightclub Wed–Sat (EC$20 Fri & Sat). Tues is karaoke night as well, led by a local whose strong vocals weed out the weak among the crowd. Tues–Sun from 6pm.

Rumours Rodney Bay Village ☎758/452-9249. Across the street from Charlie's and popular with an upmarket crowd, *Rumours* has live music or a DJ on Fri and Sat (EC$10 after 11pm), plus retro Tuesdays, *salsa* Wednesdays, and karaoke Thursdays. No nightclub here, but there's dancing on a backyard wooden deck under the stars. Daily from 9pm.

Triangle Pub Rodney Bay Village ☎758/458-0699. Small barbecue next to *The Lime* (see left column) which puts on live music on occasion, from reggae and steel bands to jazz. The main entertainment, though, is karaoke on Mon, Thurs, Sat, and Sun. Good fun, good mix of people and good cheap food, too. Daily until late.

17.3

Soufrière and the west coast

The beautiful **west coast** of St Lucia is notable for its rich and varied attractions, pretty beaches and, in parts, its decided lack of tourist traffic. You can search out isolated waterfalls, hike through astounding rainforest, swim, snorkel and scuba dive in secluded bays and visit peaceful fishing villages, all without the commercial feel of the northwest coast. However, the area is not without its more blatant tourist draws, and these are centred around **Soufrière**, which dwells in the shadows of the imposing **Pitons**, and the deep and lush **Marigot Bay**. Traditionally, Marigot Bay has been little more than a quiet shelter for yachts and their crews, but it's currently in the midst of development, suggesting that it's likely to become a busier and more manicured destination for the high-end tourist market. Soufrière, despite some popular attractions and a few upmarket hotels, remains quite rustic and rural, and in 2004, the region's Pitons Management Area, including the Pitons and the malodorous **Sulphur Springs**, was named a UNESCO World Heritage Site.

Arrival and getting around

A treacherously steep and twisted – if well-paved – road snakes along the southwest coast, making the trip from Castries to Soufrière an entertaining drive. Once in town, **buses** returning north to Castries (route #3D) and heading south to Vieux Fort (route #4F) cluster around the town square; **taxis** can be found there and also by the waterfront piers. The waterfront is also the place to hop aboard convenient **water taxis**, which traverse the area servicing all of the nearby bays, many of which are difficult or impossible to access from the land. Official rides (along with tours up the west coast) can be organized with Mystic Man Tours (☎758/459-7783) at the end of the waterfront promenade. Roundtrip to Anse Chastenet is EC$25; just arrange with your driver a good time for him to pick you up. Local boat owners also provide rides and can be found at the same spot or at the north end of town by Hummingbird Beach, as it's known locally; negotiate a fee before you set off.

Accommodation

Staying along the west coast between Castries and Soufrière is ideal if you want to get away from heavily trafficked tourist areas and relax in some of the finest resorts and guesthouses on the island. The beaches are inviting and relatively uncrowded, and the limited number of accommodation choices (the vast majority in Marigot Bay or Soufrière) tend to be less resort-like and more distinctive than those further north.

Anse Chastanet Anse Chastanet ☎758/459-7000, in US ☎ 1-800/223-1108, in UK ☎0800/894057; ⊛www.ansechastenet.com. Most rooms at this pricey resort are hillside, spacious, and airy, like very luxurious treehouses (some with trees growing through them), with lovely ocean or mountain views; twelve rooms are at beach level. Guests are encouraged to enjoy watersports, tennis and a great in-house jungle biking outfit, or to opt to "simply do nothing", but with a steep climb to your room and more than 100 steps from reception down to the beach, you're guaranteed some exercise. Guests say the biggest draw is the escape from modern conveniences (no TVs, radios, or telephones), not to mention the attentive staff. ❾

Anse La Liberté Campsite one mile south of Canaries off West Coast Highway ☎758/452-5005 or 453-1495, ⓦ www.slunatrust.org/ans_la_liberte. htm. Maintained by the National Trust, this campsite is set around four miles of hiking trails, a fifteen-minute walk from the beach or a half-hour from the main road. Although tents may be on offer in the future, currently only bare sites are available, with picnic tables, fireplaces, shower blocks, and a communal solar-powered pavilion. Bookings essential, as the site is not staffed. Single ❶, double ❷

La Haut Plantation West Coast Rd, Soufrière ☎758/459-7008, ⓦ www.lahaut.com. Set high in the hills north of Soufrière with a spectacular and sweeping view of all the area attractions, this tranquil 52-acre working plantation is a real treat. The half-dozen guesthouse rooms are spacious and airy, there's a cliffside pool with adjacent restaurant and bar, plus a cosy lounge with library, pool table and TV. Shuttles to town and beaches are complimentary. ❺

Ladera Resort Soufrière–Vieux Fort Rd ☎758/459-7323, in US 800/738-4752, ⓦ www. ladera.com. Exquisite views are key in this unusual hillside resort, which looks down 1000ft to the bay framed by the Pitons on either side. All 25 villas and suites are deliberately open to the elements and entirely without a back wall in order to maximize both the vista and the sense of being at one with nature. The effect is spectacular, and soothing dark polished wood interiors, outdoor cliffside showers, and plunge pools may mean you never leave your room. ❾

Marigot Beach Club Marigot Bay ☎758/451-4974, ⓦ www.marigotbeachclubhotel.com. Ensconced on the north side of the bay just a minute or two from the road's end by ferry, the Marigot Beach Club's location has long been its main draw. All rooms (villas and studios) come with kitchen/ettes, and the pool, beach, watersports and shops manage to keep guests plenty busy; the open-air restaurant is named *Dolittle*'s after the Rex Harrison movie filmed here in the 1960s. Studios ❺, villas ❼

Still Beach Resort Soufrière ☎758/459-5049, ⓦ www.thestillresort.com. Five rather plain apartments on the coast with shared balcony and views of Soufrière Bay and Petit Piton; Creole restaurant on site. The beach is not one of the island's best, but nice enough for a stroll or a quick dip, and the view of Petit Piton is stunning. For a change of scenery, spend a few days at the co-owned *Still Plantation Resort*, set on a serene 400-acre working cocoa plantation just outside of town. Dive packages available. ❺, ❻ with kitchen and a/c.

Stonefield Estate Soufrière ☎758/459-7037, ⓦ www.stonefieldvillas.com. These sixteen spacious villas (with plans for more) on the well-manicured grounds of an old 26-acre plantation may be Soufrière's best-kept secret: designed and decorated with nature in mind, they rival the aesthetic of any of the area's luxury hotels at a fraction of the cost. Each airy villa has slatted wooden windows and large hammocked wooden balconies; most have separate kitchens and wonderfully spacious and private open-air showers, with flowers trailing all around. A pool, restaurant and bar are situated to maximize the views of Petit Piton, and beach shuttles are free. ❼

Talk to Me Cool Spot West Coast Road, Soufrière ☎758/459-7437, ⓦ www.talk-2me.com. Owners Michael and Andrea Abraham make guests of this inexpensive guesthouse feel like family, especially when eating Andrea's tasty traditional Caribbean cooking. Studio rooms are small and rustic (curtained in-room toilets and showers), but doubles are spacious and decorated with hand-painted murals. Unique views of Petit Piton and Soufrière, colourful by day and sparkling by night, make up for noises wafting up the hill from town. Single ❷, double ❸

Ti Kaye Village Anse Cochon ☎758/456-8101, ⓦ www.tikaye.com. Remote, secluded and special, *Ti Kaye*'s cottages all have garden showers, hammocked balconies, and ocean views, some with private plunge pools. Perfect for a romantic retreat, but also good for families, who can opt for rooms adjoined by a balcony door. The black sand beach is gloriously unspoiled by the hotel's presence, with an unobtrusive beachside bar, and well worth the 167 steps to reach, but if you can't face the climb there's also a small ocean-view pool. ❼

Marigot Bay and around

From Castries, the West Coast Highway scoots through winding, hilly terrain and passes the signposted turn-off for **MARIGOT BAY** about three miles south, an exquisite oasis of mangroves and palm trees lined by quiet wooden walkways. Marigot Bay's sheltered inner lagoon, one of the island's best-protected natural yacht harbours, is permanently dotted with boats and their crews, but the small community has always been a sleepy spot, with just a fistful of reclusive hotels and waterside cafés. Encroaching development may signal a change, with the completion of a large, upscale apartment/hotel complex known as *Discovery at Marigot Bay*, and plans for a new marina village, which currently consists only of the jetty of **The Moorings Yacht Charters**, a small **police station**, a **customs office** (☎758/458-3318, VHF 16) for incoming yachts, and a **taxi stand** (☎758/453-4406).

Across the Bay, the *Marigot Beach Club* (see opposite) and its **beach** (open to non-guests and the bay's best swimming spot) are accessible 24 hours a day via a small ferry boat (EC$5 per person return). The beach is spacious but compact (although there are plans to expand it), with calm surf, plenty of shade and good snorkelling to its west side. Unfortunately, several drug dealers hang around here and will inevitably try to sell you some of their wares, although the Marigot Bay Business Association is doing its best to curb their presence, and the opening of *Discovery* will likely change the clientele dramatically. Legal refreshments are available from *Dolittle's*, and the hotel also runs a watersports concession.

South of Marigot Bay, the highway dips through the sharp west coast hills to the next settled area, **Roseau** (ruh-ZOH), a valley extensively planted with fields of bananas, dotted with small settlements and home to the St Lucia rum distillery.

Soufrière and around

Officially established in 1746, **SOUFRIÈRE** (pronounced sou-FRAY) is the oldest town in St Lucia. Still the largest settlement of the southwest coast, it is nonetheless a quiet place, charming in its lack of polish and filled with a melange of architectural styles ranging from slapped-together wooden huts to modern cement blocks. Naturally framed by rainforest-smothered hills and dominated by the looming **Petit Piton** – one of the twin volcanic peaks thrusting straight out of the sea south of the town – Soufrière's valley and deep **bay** is extremely picturesque, particularly when viewed from the hilly coastal roads as you enter town from the north or south. This unspoiled allure has often drawn the attention of film producers: scenes from *Superman II* and the Michael Caine film *Water* were shot in and around town. Most visitors just come for a quick tour of the beaches, the Sulphur Springs and the mineral baths, all fine attractions in themselves, but very touristy and devoid of local presence or a true taste of St Lucia's southwest coast. Save an afternoon to explore the town itself so you don't make the same mistake.

The Town

Soufrière is small enough to explore on foot, with the abundance of jammed and narrow streets rendering driving here inadvisable. A good place to start your tour is the pretty **waterfront** walkway, decorated with ornate streetlamps, benches, and poinciana trees, and framed by the two town piers where local craft and tourist party boats dock. Across the street is Soufrière's **tourist office** (Mon–Fri 8am–4pm, Sat 8.30am–noon; ☎758/459-7200), a handy source of information on local sights and attractions.

A block inland, hemmed in by Bridge and Church streets, is the grassy **town square**, laid out by Soufrière's settlers in the eighteenth century and, during the French Revolution, the scene of numerous **executions** by guillotine. It's a local hangout today, bordered by businesses and homes built in the classic French colonial style with second-floor balconies and intricate decorative woodwork. Dominating the east end of the square is the **Lady of Assumption Church**, built in 1953 as an expansion of the original (of which only the belfry was kept, although two years later that too had to be rebuilt after a fire that razed half the town to the ground); while it looks a bit derelict from the outside, the inside is charming. At the time of writing, a multistorey development on Bridge Street was in the works; when complete, it will be home to more than a dozen shops and offices.

Just across the Soufrière River at the northern end of town (and, a bit unsettlingly, next to the town cemetery), a fruit and vegetable **market** is in full effect on Saturdays, with a much smaller version there on weekdays.

Nearby beaches

To the immediate north of Soufrière is the popular **Anse Chastanet Beach**, presided over by the resort of the same name (see p.697). Although long and wide, it's heavily dotted with thatched huts for use by resort guests only, making it difficult for others to find a place to lay a towel. But due to the proximity of the reef to the shore, the spot makes for one of the best shore dives in the Caribbean and is perfect for snorkelling – visibility ranges from 60 to 120ft year-round. Scuba St Lucia (see p.681) is an excellent dive operation by the water, renting both snorkelling and scuba gear. Anse Chastanet is reachable via a deplorably bad, pothole-filled road, jutting right from the main road just before you enter Soufrière from the north. The two-mile track takes about fifteen minutes by car or 45 minutes on foot. A much more pleasant option is to catch a water taxi from Soufrière (EC$25 return).

For a little more privacy, head north to one of a string of other volcanic sand beaches accessible only by boat. Just around the corner from Anse Chastenet is **Anse Mamin**, the starting point for a jungle biking adventure with Bike St Lucia (see p.682). Also on resort property, Anse Mamin is a slightly smaller but much less crowded version of Anse Chastanet, with more room for non-guests to spread out. Further along, spots like **Anse Jambon** and **Anse Mahaut** tend to be rocky but are secluded and untouched – be sure to secure a return trip with your water taxi, though, because there's no other way back to town.

To the south of Soufrière and edging the bay between the Pitons is **Anse des Pitons**, also known as Hilton beach – originally rocky and volcanic, it's now a stretch of soft golden sand imported from Guyana by the property's *Jalousie Hilton* resort. Like Anse Chastenet, the beach is crowded with hotel paraphernalia, but the setting between the Pitons is stunning.

Diamond Botanical Gardens

The **Diamond Botanical Gardens** (Mon–Sat 10am–5pm, Sun 10am–3pm; EC$10; ☎758/459-7565, ⊛www.diamondstlucia.com), about a ten-minute walk from the town square, are the main attraction at Soufrière Estate, a former sugar plantation dating from 1713 that was originally part of a 2000-acre land grant bestowed by Louis XIV to the Devaux family (who settled widely in the West Indies at that time). The popular tours (guides can be found at the main entrance gate; tips of EC$15–20 are expected) include trips to the gardens themselves, some small **mineral baths** and a **waterfall**; come very early or in late afternoon to avoid the crowds. You can't swim by the falls, but for EC$10 you can splash about in the slightly pungent depths of three small, rather uninviting outdoor pools fed directly by volcanic hot springs. For an additional EC$5, you can disappear into a private room with two bath-size tubs (recently renovated but originally dating to 1784) where the water reaches 106°F. The setting is not especially pristine, but the waters, comparable to Aix-les-Bains in France, are said to relieve stress and arthritis and nourish the skin.

Also on the property is a pleasant nature trail, once used to transport harvested coconuts, now leading to an old sugar mill housing a **restaurant** that serves lunch 3–4 times a week (call for days); adjoining is a still-churning waterwheel which once provided the town of Soufrière with its first electricity.

La Soufrière Sulphur Springs

Misleadingly billed as the world's only drive-in volcano, **La Soufrière Sulphur Springs** (daily 9am–5pm; EC$7; ☎758/459-7686), a short drive south of town off the road to Vieux Fort, is only a small fraction of a 4.5 square-mile volcano that also includes the town of Soufrière itself. There's no crater to peer into here; instead, La Soufrière is known as a caldera, having erupted and collapsed into itself some 40,000 years ago. Nonetheless, it remains active to this day – theoretically, it could erupt anywhere, anytime. As La Soufrière is now classified as a **solfatara**, meaning it emits gases and vapours rather than lava and hot ash, a molten shower is extremely unlikely.

The Springs themselves are a small collection of steaming, bubbling pools of sulphur-dense water and green- and yellow-tinged rocks. Turn in at the signed road and it's quickly apparent that you're in the midst of a volcano – killed off by sulphuric emissions, the vegetation becomes sparse and an eggy odour hangs in the air. The services of an official (and very informative) **guide** are included in the entrance fee, and they will walk you up from the car park to the viewing platforms that overlook the boiling pools. Some years ago, visitors were allowed to walk across the field, but this practice was stopped when one of the guides fell through a fissure – though sustaining severe burns, he lived to tell the tale. Now only goats occasionally hop among the rocks, cheerfully oblivious of how close they are to becoming stew. You can, however, for no extra fee, take a **dip** in the cooler pools of a river that flows through the area so bring along a bathing suit if you wish, but note that the hydrogen sulphide in the air can be irritating.

An **information centre**, reached by a steep hike up the hill from the viewing points (so steep your guide won't take you there), has a nice exhibit on Caribbean volcanic activity and a short video on the springs.

The Pitons

Also of volcanic origin, the anomalous and majestic peaks of the **Pitons** dominate the southwest coast, towering more than half a mile above sea level. Visible on a clear day from as far north as the hills of Castries, these breathtaking cones are undoubtedly St Lucia's most photographed feature. Overlooking the south side of Soufrière's harbour, the northern peak is Petit Piton; south of Petit is Gros Piton, wider at the base but similar in height. Maps and publications give various elevations for each of the peaks, some even claiming that Petit is taller than Gros Piton, but the St Lucian government figures of 2480ft and 2619ft respectively are generally accepted. Although from certain vantage points the peaks appear to be next to each other, they are actually nearly three miles apart.

Beyond their aesthetic appeal, the Pitons offer an opportunity – literally – for high adventure. Though climbing up **Petit Piton** is discouraged by island authorities due to the inherent difficulty and danger of climbing a near-vertical slab of rock, some still seem willing to clamber up. This is not, however, to be advised. **Gros Piton**, while still a challenge, is much more manageable, largely thanks to the work of the **Gros Piton Tour Guides Association** (☎758/489-0136), which maintains the trail. Managed by descendents of the freedom-fighting Brigands from the community of Fond Gens Libre at the peak's southern base (considered the first settlement of freed black people in St Lucia), this group conducts hikes of the peak and also works to promote the area's historical and ecological value. It's about a four-hour hike round-trip; the EC$65 trail fee includes a guide (call ahead to ensure guides are available), which you'll need: self-guided hikes are not allowed since the path branches off in several places, making it easy to get lost. Getting to the trail independently currently requires a 4WD vehicle (although plans to pave the access road are in the works), but package tours including transportation, lunch, and refreshments are also available.

Eating and drinking

Soufrière and Marigot Bay hold their own against the tourism strongholds of the northwest, with a wealth of **eating** establishments ranging from small cafés to more elegant restaurants for relaxed evening dining. While many spots offer wide-ranging menus, don't miss out on the local Creole fare. Note that closing times are often just an estimate.

Dasheene *Ladera Resort*, Soufrière ☎758/459-7323. An eclectic mix of West Indian, Oriental, Italian and vegetarian cuisine, the majority of it creative and artful. Dinner is pricey, and usually excellent, but the buffets can be mediocre and lunch is hit-or-miss. Try the pool/bar menu for a simpler and less expensive option. The views of the Pitons and bay below are astonishing – come up for drinks before sunset. Daily 7–10am, noon–2.30pm & 6.30–9pm.

Stretching across the island's central and north-central interior, the vast, uninhabited and irregularly shaped **St Lucia Forest Reserve** comprises the 19,000 acres of rainforest and dry forest which are maintained by the government's forestry department. Though many of the trails within the reserve were used as transportation routes in the early colonial days, today most people who venture in do so for pleasure rather than necessity. Arrestingly beautiful and teeming with exotic flora and wildlife, the forests offer an absorbing alternative to the sun-and-beach culture of coastal resorts.

St Lucia's protected forest reserves (and all of the hiking trails within them) are maintained by the **Forestry Department** (☎758/450-2231 or 2375, ⓦwww.slumaffe. org). The department also determines public access (some parts of the interior are restricted) and provides trained **hiking guides**. For most trails, a flat fee of EC$25 covers both access and the services of a guide. It's best to call ahead to ensure guides will be on site, as ranger stations will often close early if no one has come by.

Note that in addition to the routes described below, it's also possible to reach the trails on a tour with a Castries-based operator such as Jungle Tours (☎758/450-0434) or SunLink Tours (☎758/456-9100).

Union Nature Trail

The short, easy **Union Nature Trail** (Mon–Fri 8.30am–4pm; EC$5) starts about ten minutes' drive from Castries, in the Forestry Department's headquarters, which also contains a medicinal herb garden, a depressing **mini-zoo** and an interpretive centre where you can learn about endangered species. The easy 1.6km **trail** loops through dry forest that was once planted as a tree nursery, returning after about an hour of walking if you don't make too many stops.

To get there, turn off the Castries–Gros Islet Highway onto the Allan Bousquet Highway (not marked; if you pass a sign denoting the boundary of Castries, you've gone too far). Along a winding 1.5km, you'll pass three large fences on your right; turn right at the end of the third to reach the centre. Bus route #1B will bring you from Castries.

Barre de L'Isle Trail

The "island ridge" **Barre de L'Isle Trail** (Mon–Fri 8.30am–3pm; EC$25) bisects the Central Forest Reserve and the island itself. It's a worthwhile, mildly challenging adventure that provides a good look at St Lucia's richly diverse topography and mountain flora and fauna: throughout, the trail alternates between a thick overhead cover of trees and wide-open areas with expansive vistas in all directions. The two-hour hike – three if you extend the trek and climb the ridge of Mount La Combe – is marked well enough to go it alone, though a guide will be able to identify bird, tree and plant species along the way.

The signposted start of the Barre de L'Isle trail strikes into the forest directly from the central Castries–Dennery highway, opposite the **rangers' hut** and a twenty- to thirty-minute drive or bus journey from downtown Castries. Route #2B buses leave from Manoel Street in Castries.

Enbas Saut Waterfalls Trail

Located in the **Edmund Forest Reserve** which spreads over the southwestern interior, the **Enbas Saut Waterfalls Trail** (Mon–Fri 8.30am–3pm, Sat mornings only; EC$25) offers a fairly strenuous 5km (2.5hr), guided loop down to the base of two cascading waterfalls on the Troumassée river. Bathing in the pools of rainforest water is encouraged and will rejuvenate you for the return hike back up.

The eight-kilometre drive to the Edmund Reserve takes about an hour from the west coast. From Soufrière take the inland road to Fond St Jacques, bypassing the turn-off to Morne Coubaril Estate and the south. The road to the trails is signposted off the main road, and after a very rough thirty-minute drive (requiring 4WD), a wooden forestry department **ranger station** marks the start of the trail. Relying on public transport to get here is not really a viable option.

Fedo's New Venture New Development, Soufrière ☎758/459-5220. A local joint at the back of town with a rather bland interior but a very inexpensive menu. A sizeable portion of fish Creole (usually tuna) is delicious – but watch for bones – and sandwiches are only EC$4–6. Mon–Sat 10am–9pm.

The Green Room Soufrière ☎758/457-1324. An informal neighbourhood restaurant serving Creole dishes with large sides of local fruits and vegetables like dasheen, plantain, and breadfruit. The chalkboard menu changes on occasion; ask for prices, which range EC$20–45. Daily 9am–11pm.

Hummingbird Beach Resort Anse Chastanet Road, Soufrière ☎758/459-7232. A popular hangout for visitors at guesthouses all over town, especially for drinks at sunset by the beachside pool. It's hard to see what you're eating at the dark restaurant tables and the service is exasperatingly slow, but the seafood comes recommended, with conch, king crab, and octopus available seasonally. Daily 6.30am–11pm.

JJ's Paradise Resort Marigot Bay ☎758/451-4076. Choose between an inland nightly buffet or an à la carte menu at the waterfront, reached by a short stroll along a wooden boardwalk through the Marigot mangrove forest. Lively Wednesday Creole crab nights are popular with locals, and Saturday BBQs feature pork, ribs, chicken, and fish. Pizzas are available Tues–Sun. At adjoining Club Johnnie

Walker (from 10pm on Wed & Fri–Sun), Wednesday is ladies' night. Daily 8am–midnight.

La Marie 16 Bay Street, Soufrière ☎758/459-5002. A bright second-floor restaurant with large windows overlooking the waterfront and cheerful, hand-painted masks decorating the walls. The moderately priced cuisine is Caribbean with Indian twists – and although billed as a "light meal", the rotis are filling, delicious, and a great buy at EC$12–15. Daily 8.30am–11pm.

Rainforest Hideaway Marigot Bay ☎758/286-0511. Geared to please discriminating residents of the imminent five-star development across the bay, this intimate floating champagne bar and fusion restaurant features a menu that changes daily and live entertainment 3–4 nights a week. Children are not allowed after 6pm at the dinners by candle-light; reservations are strongly recommended. Priced accordingly: dinner mains EC$75–90. Sun noon–10pm, Mon & Wed–Sat noon–3pm & 6–10pm.

The Shack Marigot Bay ☎758/451-4145. Cheap, filling and tasty American-style fare (think burgers, chicken fingers, and fries) with a Caribbean twist – the Kingfish burger is excellent – and plentiful seafood in a lovely floating café-restaurant looking out to sea from the bay. Happy hour is 5–7pm; come for the sunset. Daily 9am–11pm; breakfast items on request.

17.4

The south coast

S t Lucia's **southern coast** boasts some striking scenery: south of Soufrière, the mountain road whirls and dips inland before swinging towards the ocean to reveal a string of coastal villages and, ultimately, the island's second largest town, **Vieux Fort**, all framed by the towering ranges of the Central Forest Reserve. This southwest corner was once an **Amerindian** stronghold, and petroglyphs have been found throughout the area, suggesting a long and fruitful habitation by the Arawaks and Caribs. After Europeans arrived, the area was home to large **plantations** producing coconuts, sugar cane and, more recently, bananas, though today these have mostly been replaced by smaller farms and fishing enterprises.

Arrival, information and getting around

Most visitors arrive in St Lucia at **Hewanorra International Airport** in Vieux Fort, and onward transportation throughout the island is readily available from here. Once through customs, your first stop should be the **tourist booth** (Mon–Fri 8am–last flight, Sat & Sun 10am–last flight; ☏758/454-6644), where you can pick up brochures and maps and get the low-down on the latest official taxi rates. Also lining the arrival area are a half-dozen **car rental** booths which keep limited hours (most from noon–6pm) and may not stay open for late flights, so be sure to make prearrangements as necessary. The dispatcher at the **taxi** stand across from the rental booths can arrange official taxi rides. Taxis to Castries from the airport or anywhere in Vieux Fort travel the wide but pot-holed East Coast Highway and turn inland towards the capital at Dennery. The **fare** to Castries is EC$150 (or US$55) and the 33-mile trip takes a little over an hour. Vieux Fort to Soufrière is the same price, and the 29-mile ride takes around 45 minutes now that the road has been predominantly paved. To travel by **bus**, you'll first need to get to Vieux Fort by taxi – about EC$6 (or, if you're patient, you can try flagging down a bus from the main road). Buses to Castries (route #2H) leave from New Dock Road and those to Soufrière (route #4F) leave from Clarke Street, next to the town traffic light and a Shell service station.

Accommodation

The area **south of Soufrière**, through the fishing villages of Choiseul and Laborie to Vieux Fort, is more residential than tourist-oriented and offers a relaxed alternative to the relentless activity of the northwest coast.

Balenbouche Estate Balenbouche Bay ☏758/455-1244, ⊛ www.balenbouche.com. Scattered with fruit trees, sugar factory remains and even a few Amerindian rock carvings, this charming, slightly dilapidated seventy-acre plantation just south of Choiseul is most welcoming. Furnished with eclectic antiques, rooms in the estate house are clean and cosy (shared bath); nearby cottages have fun, unique features like swinging couches and outdoor (covered) kitchens. Meals are available on request, and a string of secluded beaches are just a short walk away. Single ❷, double share ❸, private cottage ❺

Coconut Bay Resort and Spa Vieux Fort ☏758/456-9999, ⊛ www.coconutbayresortandspa.com. The only resort of its kind in the south, Coconut Bay is a sprawling 85-acre all-inclusive on the beach less than ten minutes from the airport. Three pools, a waterpark, and an activities centre will keep kids happy; tennis courts, spa, and jogging trails appeal to adults. ❾

Juliette's Lodge Beanfield, Vieux Fort ☏758/454-5300, ⊛ www.julietteslodge.com. Conveniently close to Hewanorra International Airport and Anse de Sables beach, *Juliette's* is popular amongst both airline crews and the windsurfer crowd. The 24 rooms and three apartments are comfortable and clean with a/c, cable TV, and balconies with views of the Maria Islands. There are mountain bikes for hire, a small pool, and a lively restaurant serving basic but hearty fare. Rooms ❹, apartments ❻

Mirage Beach Resort Laborie Bay, Laborie ☏758/455-9763, ⊛ www.cavip.com/mirage. Located right on the bay in the serene, beautiful fishing village of Laborie, this divine spot offers five comfortable rooms on the beach, all with kitchenette and terrace; the intimate beachside setting is a rarity on the island. A pristine reef not far from shore makes for excellent snorkelling. The friendly owners also have a relaxing French/Creole open-air restaurant and bar on site. ❸

The southwest coast

South of Soufrière, the west coast road meanders through hilly inland terrain, passing several small settlements before descending abruptly towards the coast and the community of Choiseul. Named after the compact village of **CHOISEUL** (shwa-ZEL) itself, a quiet place with little to do or see, especially now that the waterfront is dominated by a concrete fishing complex built by the Japanese in 2003, the area is best known for being the origin of most of St Lucia's crafts. Each village within the community has its own speciality – like pottery, khuskhus grass floormats, wicker baskets, or white cedar chairs – depending on the available raw materials. The **Choiseul Arts and Craft Development Centre** (open Mon–Fri 9am–4.30pm; ☎758/459-3226), about half a mile south of the village centre in **La Fargue**, and **Crafty Creations** (open Mon–Fri 8am–6pm, Sat 9am–5pm, Sun noon–3pm, ☎758/717-1917), just down the road, have the best selection.

Between Choiseul and the friendly fishing village of **Laborie**, a few miles southeast, is **Balenbouche Estate**, an eighteenth-century plantation well worth a visit even if you're not staying there (daily 9am–6pm; EC$5, or EC$15 with guide – call ahead; see opposite for accommodation). Dotting the serene grounds are some spectacular sugar factory ruins, including a massive sunken waterwheel.

Vieux Fort and around

Jammed with traffic, **VIEUX FORT** is St Lucia's second largest town and its most southerly settlement, a busy commercial centre and the base for businesses that service **Hewanorra International Airport**, just north of downtown. Both the town and the airport lie on a relatively flat plain that slopes gently towards the north and the south-central mountains, and as the southern tip of St Lucia comes to a point around Vieux Fort, the runway stretches almost entirely from the east to the west coast of the island.

Vieux Fort itself is more a place of business than a place to explore; most visitors only glimpse it on their journey to and from the airport. However, just south of town – in fact, it's St Lucia's most southerly point – lies **Moule à Chique Lighthouse**, actually intended for Saint Lucia Cape in South Africa but brought to the Caribbean by mistake. It's one of the finest viewpoints on the island, reached by bearing left onto New Dock Road at the town roundabout and then left again into the hills. The **Anse de Sables Beach** stretches a little over a mile from the foot of the cliffs here to Pointe Sable, and is the only place to swim near Vieux Fort. It's also a favoured spot for wind- and kitesurfers thanks to mild surf and the presence of watersports operator Tornado (Oct–June 9am–5pm; ☎758/454-7579, ⊛www.tornado-surf.com). At its southern end, the expansive seashore is usually windy, with virtually no trees for shade; nor are there toilet facilities except for those at the oceanside bars and restaurants. Also at the south end of the beach is the **Maria Islands Interpretation Centre**, the meeting point for all visits to the Maria Islands.

Maria Islands Nature Reserve

Just over half a mile off the Anse de Sables shore are the two scrubby, windswept cays that comprise the **Maria Islands Nature Reserve**. Both islands are breeding areas for numerous **sea birds**, including the frigate and various terns, and are home to two rare reptiles, one of which – the **kouwés snake** – is found nowhere else in the world. About a yard long with blue eyes and dark green and brown markings, the harmless *kouwés* (cou-RESS) once thrived on the mainland but was eradicated by the mongooses introduced by sugar cane planters; today, they number a mere one hundred or so. The other reptile is St Lucia's *zandoli tè*, or ground lizard, found only on the Maria Islands and nearby Praslin Island on the east coast, where some of their number were transferred to ensure a second habitat. At around 14 inches long with a bright blue tail, a yellow belly, and a black back with white spots, the male vividly displays all the colours of the St Lucian flag; females, brown with darker vertical stripes, are harder to spot.

Only the larger of the two islands, Maria **Major**, can be visited (with only 4 acres, there's not much to see of Maria **Minor**), and no one is allowed there without an **authorized guide** from the St Lucia National Trust. To arrange one, contact the Trust head office in Castries (℡758/452-5005) in advance. Costing EC$80 per person for groups of two or more (or a whopping EC$225 for one person), the trips (9am–4.30pm except Sat) begin at the Interpretation Centre, a one-room **museum** open only for tours with small displays on mangroves, marine life and Amerindian culture (including a skull found in the area). Trips take about three hours and consist of walking tours of the island and stops for swimming and snorkelling (bring your own gear). Several unchallenging trails loop around the island and there's a short but comely **beach** of golden sand with a **reef** a few yards offshore.

Eating and drinking

Though there are fewer choices than along the north and west coasts, the south has its share of good places to **eat** nonetheless. There are some reliable hotel restaurants near Hewanorra airport, and for snacks, try the beach bars along the Anse de Sables shoreline.

Debbie's Soufrière-Vieux Fort Road, Laborie ℡758/455-1625. Aunty Debbie, as she's known around town, cooks up feasts of seafood, lamb, pork, and chicken with large portions of creamed pumpkin, mashed potatoes, fried plantains, and corn cakes. Leave room for dessert and choose anything from profiteroles to passionfruit cake, all home made. Mon–Sat breakfast, lunch & dinner.
Old Plantation Yard Commercial Street, Vieux Fort ℡758/454-7969. Very local food prepared in an old residence dating to 1890 and served in a casual backyard patio of picnic tables. Stewed meats and fish broths are the specialities, with a selection of local juices. Come for a traditional Creole breakfast of roast bakes (bread), cocoa

tea, saltfish, and smoked herring on a Saturday morning, all for only EC$10; stop by the fruit and vegetable market across the street on your way home. Mon–Sat 7am–5pm; dinner by request.
The Reef Beach Café Anse de Sables ℡758/454-3418. A busy beachside restaurant and bar serving just edible fare of burgers, pizza and some West Indian dishes. The location is the main draw for a predominantly young crowd of tourists, windsurfers from adjacent Tornado, locals and students from a nearby medical school. Four basic and inexpensive rooms are also available, mostly for the surfer crew (②). Tues–Sun 8am–10pm; Mon high season only 8am–6pm.

17.5

The east coast

Churned up by the Caribbean trade winds, the pounding waters of the Atlantic have carved out a rough and jagged **east coast** on St Lucia, one that's mainly ignored by visitors – to their loss. Characterized by lively surf smashing against rocky and cliff-lined shores and a verdant blanket of banana plants, the area provides a visual as well as an atmospheric contrast to the more populated and more visited north and west.

St Lucia's **coastal highway** parallels the eastern shoreline from Vieux Fort to Dennery, where it cuts inland, heading northwest up and over the inland rainforest to Castries. It's the preferred route for buses and taxis travelling the 33 miles between Vieux Fort and the capital, but rains in recent years have created a slew of potholes, making it a rather disconcerting drive. Along the way, east-coast **bus** stops include Micoud, Desruisseaux (in the hills south of Micoud), Mon Repos, Praslin and Dennery, but due to erratic scheduling, exploring the coastline by bus is not particularly efficient.

Micoud

Named in honour of the French Governor de Micoud, who ruled St Lucia from 1768 to 1771, the relatively sizeable town of **MICOUD** spreads back from the sheltered bay of Port Micoud. The suitability of the harbour to fishing (a rarity on the rough coast), and the ready availability of fresh water from the **Troumassée River**, which borders the town to the south, are the principal factors cited by archeologists as evidence of intense **Amerindian** presence in the area. Some nine settlements are believed to have existed in the Micoud Quarter, all rapidly abandoned after the arrival of European settlers in the eighteenth century.

Aside from the quiet bay, dotted with fishing boats and churches, Micoud is best known for being a particularly enthusiastic focal point for two island-wide Carnivalesque religious **festivals**: **La Rose** in August and **La Marguerite** in October; see p.680 for more on these.

Mamiku Gardens and The Fox Grove Inn

Just a few minutes north of Micoud by car lies one of the most serene places in St Lucia, the beautifully landscaped fifteen-acre **Mamiku Gardens** (daily 9am–5pm; EC$15, or $20 with guide – call ahead to arrange a tour; ☎758/455-3729, ⊛www.mamiku.com). The gardens are teeming with brightly coloured exotic blooms such as orchids, ginger and heliconia, and you can explore the former plantation site via a simple network of short **walking trails**, each with resting spots at suitably beautiful points.

A ten-minute walk southwest of the gardens is the east coast's finest **dining** and **accommodation** option, the *Fox Grove Inn* (☎758/455-3800, ⊛www.foxgroveinn.com; single ❷, double ❸). The rooms are basic but charming, most with gorgeous seaviews, and all have full breakfast included; two spacious two-bedroom apartments are available weekly. A pool table and a large, inviting swimming pool are on site. By special arrangement, unguided entry to the Eastern Nature Trail (see below) is available to guests on request for a small fee. The reasonably priced restaurant, open to

Three tours in and around the northern section of **Praslin** (PRAW-lay) **Bay** present the best opportunity to explore the rugged Atlantic Coast; each is interesting in its own right, and they're also easily combined. You can see the birds of the Fregate Islands, or spend time on the small beach at Praslin Island or along the Eastern Nature Trail. All must be booked in advance through Eastern Tours (daily except Sat flexible hours, ☎758/455-3163 or 384-7056), which strives to ensure tourism directly benefits the local population, critical in the especially economically depressed east coast; another excellent reason to make your way here.

non-guests as well, features delicately presented fresh seafood and lobster (seasonally) – and a famous garlic soup – all prepared by a chef with three decades' experience at five-star hotels in Europe. Portions are generous, the salads excellent (try the smoked king fish) and, as from the rooms, the views over acres of banana plantation to Praslin Bay and the Fregates are second to none.

Fregate Islands Nature Reserve

A haven for birdwatchers, the **Fregate Islands Nature Reserve** is centred around two tiny **cays** just a few yards offshore and named after the seagoing **frigate** (or fregate) **bird** that nests here between late March and early August (making that the best time to visit). Glossy jet-black birds with forked tail feathers, male frigates have distinctive red or bright orange throat pouches which are expanded during mating time to attract females. The islands themselves are not accessible, but instead, an easy, mile-long **walking trail** heads out along a peninsula to a lookout point where you can rest on a bench and observe the birds (easily spotted with a six-foot wingspan) almost as well as if you were on the islands themselves. One-hour **tours** are US$5 per person plus a US$15 guide fee per group.

Praslin Island and the Eastern Nature Trail

Unlike the Fregates, you *are* able to visit nearby **Praslin Island**, which has a small beach perfect for swimming and wading; a great picnic spot. Your only company is likely to be a few *zandoli tè* (see p.705), and you can arrange trips for as long as an hour or an afternoon, as you wish. Guides are necessary only for the boat trip across; US$8 per person.

The beautifully maintained **Eastern Nature Trail** offers a more active adventure: a 1- to 3.5-mile (your preference) guided stroll along the coastline just north of the nature reserve, where you may see any of 38 bird species, 116 plant species and – if you're really lucky – a St Lucia boa constrictor, not to mention a gorgeous stretch of craggy coastline. Cost is US$12 per person, plus an additional shared US$16 guide fee for groups fewer than four.

Dennery and Grande Anse

Previously known as Anse Canot (in reference to the carved canoes that once lined the bay), **DENNERY** was given its current name in the eighteenth century by the French, in honour of Count D'Ennery, governor general of the Windward Islands 1766–70. The village extends back from a deep and protected **bay**, with uninhabited **Dennery Island** at its northern tip. Although once a major export centre for agricultural produce, Dennery has become one of St Lucia's busiest **fishing** centres since the addition of the large, Japanese-funded Daito Complex and Pier processing facility; much of the local fish served in the major restaurants around the island comes from here. The **town** itself is a jumble of compact streets with a few bars

Turtle watching

In conjunction with the Department of Fisheries, Heritage Tours organizes an annual programme of **turtle watches** at Grande Anse, allowing around 1000 visitors each season to experience the stirring spectacle of leatherback turtles laying their eggs. The all-night watches take place Mon–Sat in leatherback season (late-March to late-August) and cost US$85, which covers transport from your hotel and tent expenses, dinner, breakfast and sleeping mats; you'll have to bring your own flashlight, insect repellent, and warm clothing, as nights can be cool and breezy. Once at the beach, you settle into a rustic tent village and take turns at patrolling the beach. Whenever a turtle is spotted, you'll be called to have a look. The watches are becoming very popular, so to ensure a place, it's best to contact Heritage Tours well in advance (PO Box GM868, Sans Souci, Castries, St Lucia, WI; ☏758/451-6058, 458-1587 or 452-5067, ⓦwww.heritagetoursstlucia.com)

but nothing much of interest save the Saturday night **fish fry** on the seafront. A pleasant and low-key affair, it's much less developed or touristy than the similar but overpriced affairs at Anse La Raye and Gros Islet.

Around six miles north of Dennery, the wide, windswept **Grande Anse beach** boasts more than a mile of blond sand set against a backdrop of cliffs and hills covered with dry vegetation. Once part of a plantation estate, the bay sits in the middle of an area slated to become a new **national park** comprising several other nearby beaches, including Anse Lavoutte to the north. As with Anse Lavoutte, the beach here is a favoured nesting spot of the giant **leatherback turtles**, and turtle-watching tours are given throughout the egg-laying season (see box, above). National park or not, most of the roads to Grande Anse remain dirt and gravel tracks that become impassable after rains. A sedan car might make it, but a 4WD is a safer bet, and it's a good idea to ask locals about current conditions. Access is usually easiest from the west coast at Choc Bay, via the paved Allan Bousquet Highway. At Babonneau, turn off onto the gravel and dirt track that leads to the village of Desbarras, from where a single track leads down to Grande Anse. The seven-mile ride from Choc Bay can take up to ninety minutes.

18

Barbados

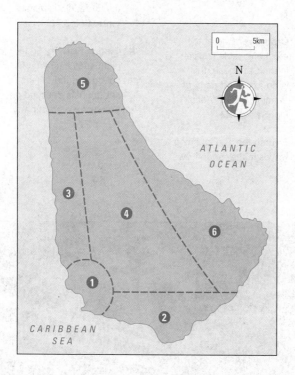

Barbados highlights

* **Andromeda Botanical Gardens** Probably the finest gardens in the Caribbean, packed with fabulous species like the bearded fig tree. See p.742

* **Crop Over** One of the most enjoyable festivals in the Caribbean, this is an extended party of dancing and rum-drinking. See p.722

* **Bathsheba** The crashing waves in the "soup bowl" make this an ideal spot for surfing year-round. See p.742

* **Holetown** Sample from the town's varied selection of fabulous restaurants. See p.735

* **Oistins Fish Fry** Friday night sees a crowd of young and old Bajans and tourists descend on Oistins for a great party. See p.728

△ Mount Gay Rum Factory

Introduction and basics

Pulling in Caribbean first-timers and experienced travellers in equal measure, **Barbados** is justifiably one of the most popular islands in the region. Certain pleasures are quite obvious – the delightful climate, the big blue sea and brilliant white sandy beaches – but an engaging blend of cultures and a balanced approach to development help set it apart from neighbouring sun-drenched destinations. And while many visitors rarely stray from their hotels and guesthouses, those who make an effort find a proud island scattered with an impressive range of colonial sites and, away from the mostly gently rolling landscape, dramatic scenery in hidden caves, cliffs and gullies.

A **British colony** for over three centuries, Barbados retains something of a British feel: the place names, the cricket, horse-racing and polo, Anglican parish churches and even a hilly district known as Scotland. But despite the Britishness, this is a distinctly **West Indian country**, covered by a patchwork of sugar cane fields and dotted with rum shops, where calypso is the music of choice and flying fish the favoured food.

The people of Barbados, known as **Bajans**, take great pride in their tiny island of 430 square kilometres and 250,000 people, which has produced writers like George Lamming, calypsonians like the Mighty Gabby and cricket players including the great Sir Gary Sobers, who have for decades held an influence way out of proportion to the size of their home country.

While **tourism** plays a major part in the country's economy, revenues have been put to good use. The infrastructure and public transport are first-rate and there is no sign of the poverty that continues to bedevil some Caribbean islands. Development has mostly been pretty discreet, and many of the facilities are Bajan-owned; there are no private beaches and no sign of fast-food franchises.

Where to go

Chief among the island's attractions are its **old plantation houses**, like St Nicholas Abbey and Francia; superb **botanical gardens** at Andromeda and the Flower Forest; and the **military forts** and signal stations at Gun Hill and Grenade Hall. The capital, **Bridgetown**, is a lively place to visit, with an excellent national museum and great nightlife in its bars and clubs. Small and largely untouristed **Speightstown** – once a thriving and wealthy port – is a good place to wander for a couple of hours then grab a drink on a terrace overlooking the sea. And, of course, there are the beaches, from the often crowded strips such as **Accra Beach** and **Mullins Bay** to tiny but superb patches of palm-fringed sand in the southeast.

Diving is excellent on the coral reefs around Barbados, with the good sites all off the calm west and southwest coasts, from Maycocks Bay in the north right round to Castle Bank near St Lawrence Gap.

When to go

For many visitors, Barbados's tropical climate is its leading attraction – hot and sunny year-round. The weather is best, however, during the **high season**, from mid-December to mid-April, with rainfall low and the heat tempered by cooling trade winds. The peak season also brings the biggest crowds and the highest prices.

Things can get a good bit hotter in the **summer**, and, particularly in September and October, the humidity can become oppressive. September is also the most threatening month for **hurricanes**. The season officially runs from early June to late October, but big blows only hit about once a decade.

Arrival

All flights arrive at **Grantley Adams International Airport**, located on the south

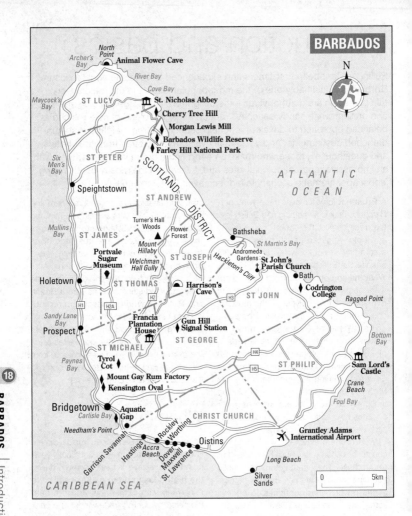

BARBADOS

Archer's Bay · North Point · **Animal Flower Cave**
River Bay
Cove Bay
Maycock's Bay
ST LUCY · **St. Nicholas Abbey**
· **Cherry Tree Hill**
· **Morgan Lewis Mill**
· **Barbados Wildlife Reserve**
· **Farley Hill National Park**
Six Men's Bay
ST PETER
SCOTLAND DISTRICT
ATLANTIC OCEAN
· Speightstown
ST ANDREW
Mullins Bay
ST JAMES · Turner's Hall Woods · Flower Forest · Bathsheba
· St Martin's Bay
Andromeda Gardens · **St John's Parish Church**
Portvale Sugar Museum · Mount Hillaby · Welchman Hall Gully
ST JOSEPH · Hackleton's Cliff
· Bath
Holetown · **ST THOMAS** · **Harrison's Cave** · **Codrington College**
Ragged Point
Sandy Lane Bay · H1 · H2A · H2 · H3 · **ST JOHN**
Prospect · **Francia Plantation House** · **Gun Hill Signal Station** · Bottom Bay
ST MICHAEL · **ST GEORGE**
Paynes Bay · **Tyrol Cot** · H4 · H5 · **ST PHILIP** · **Sam Lord's Castle**
· **Mount Gay Rum Factory**
· **Kensington Oval** · Crane Beach
Bridgetown · Carlisle Bay · **Aquatic Gap** · Foul Bay
Needham's Point · Garrison Savannah · Hastings · Rockley · Worthing · Oistins · **CHRIST CHURCH** · **Grantley Adams International Airport**
Accra Beach · Dover · Maxwell · St.Lawrence · Long Beach
Silver Sands
CARIBBEAN SEA

0   5km

coast about eight miles east of Bridgetown, and within easy striking distance of all the main south coast resorts. **Buses** (B$1.50) between the airport and Bridgetown run every half-hour, stopping at or near most of the south coast resorts en route; services to the resorts on the west coast are less frequent. From the airport, expect to pay around B$40 for a **taxi** to the hotels in St James on the west coast, B$50 to Speightstown, B$20 to Crane Bay and B$25 to the resorts in the southwest.

Cruise ships arrive at Deep Water Harbour just north of Bridgetwon, from where taxis are always available to ferry passengers around the island.

Information, websites and maps

Brochures on the main attractions and events, and a good road map, are available from the **Barbados Tourism Authority** (BTA), which has an office at Harbour Road in Bridgetown (℡ 246/427-2623, ℻ 426-4080) and a desk at the airport.

While there is no detailed listings publication, the free fortnightly **magazine** Sunseeker – available from the tourist office and some hotels – carries information on many of the events. Keep an eye also on the daily papers and flyers posted up around the island.

Money and costs

The island's unit of currency is the **Barbados dollar (B$)**, divided into 100 cents. It comes in notes of B$100, B$50, B$20, B$10, B$5 and B$2 and coins of B$1, B$0.25, B$0.10, B$0.05 and B$0.01. The **rate of exchange** is fixed roughly at B$2 to US$1; the US dollar is also widely accepted. Prices are normally quoted in B$, with the exception of accommodation which is almost universally quoted in US$, and we have followed this practice in this chapter.

Banking hours are generally Monday to Thursday 8am–3pm and Friday 8am–5pm. Bridgetown, Holetown and Speightstown have numerous banks, and there are branches at most of the south coast resorts; most have **ATMs**. Many hotels will also exchange money. Major credit cards are widely accepted, though not always at the smaller establishments.

Barbados is not a particularly cheap place to visit, and **prices** for many items are at least what you'd expect to pay at home. Bargaining is usually frowned upon, but during the off-season, it's worth asking for reduced rates. Many hotels and restaurants automatically add a **service charge** of 10 percent.

An **airport departure tax** of B$25 is payable at the airport, in local currency only.

Getting around

While the **roads** in Barbados are mostly good and the distances small, car rental prices are fairly high, starting at around B$80 per day, B$500 per week, for the mini mokes (open-sided buggies) that you'll see all over the island (you'll pay a little more for a regular car). As **car rental** companies here are all local, it can be easier to arrange rentals once you've arrived. Reliable firms include: Coconut (☎246/437-0297), Jones (☎246/426-5030), Mangera (☎246/436-0562) and National (☎246/422-0603). Prices for **scooters and motorbikes** normally start at around B$80 per day; try Caribbean Scooters, Waterfront Marina, Bridgetown (☎246/436-8522).

The **bus system** in Barbados is excellent, with blue government buses and yellow, privately owned minibuses running all over the island. Fares are a flat rate of B$1.50. Buses run roughly every half-hour between Grantley Adams International Airport and Bridgetown, stopping at or near most of the south coast resorts en route. Services to the resorts on the west coast are less frequent. White **minivans** known as "route taxis" also operate like minibuses, packing in passengers and stopping anywhere en route. They're particularly numerous on the south coast and the fare is B$1.50.

Finding a **taxi** – identifiable by the Z on their licence plates – is rarely a problem. Fares are regulated but there are no meters, so be sure to agree on the fare beforehand.

Tours and boat trips

Various local companies offer island-wide **sightseeing tours**, and the following are just a selection of what's available:

EL Scenic Tours ⊕246/424-9108. Daily tours taking in one or more of the following: Harrison's Cave, the Flower Forest, Bathsheba and St John's Parish Church.

Island Safari ⊕246/429-5337. Informative and off-the-beaten-track Land Rover trips.

Johnston Stables ⊕246/426-5181. Day- and half-day trips to Speightstown, Farley Hill Park, Bathsheba and Sunbury Plantation House.

Boat trips

All these boats sail out of Bridgetown's Shallow Harbour, but most will pick up guests from any of the major resorts:

Atlantis Submarine ⊕246/436-8929. A boat takes you out of the Bridgetown harbour to board the sub, which then submerges to 30–45m, cruising slowly above the seabed for the thirty-minute trip. Everyone has a seat by a porthole, and there's a commentary from the co-pilot. B$165 per person.

Harbour Master ⊕246/430-0900. Four-decker boat runs day-tours, taking you up the coast to a beach, with a buffet lunch and free drinks (Tues & Thurs 11am–4pm; B$95). It also runs evening trips (Tues & Thurs 6–10pm), with a floor show, live band, dinner and drinks all included in the price, and a cheaper option (Sun 5–9pm; B$35), where you pay for your food and drinks and there's a DJ.

Jolly Roger ⊕246/427-7245. Sleek, two-sailed "pirate ship" running west coast lunch cruises (Tues, Thurs & Sat 10am–2pm; B$125), with the emphasis on drinking and dancing up on the top deck, walking the plank and swinging from the yardarm into the sea.

Accommodation

With hotels stringing out virtually back-to-back both north and east of Bridgetown, there is no shortage of **accommodation** in Barbados. Heading up the west coast you'll find most of the pricier (and swankier) options, many of them concentrated around the lovely Paynes Bay or on either side of Holetown, but thinning out considerably as you continue north towards Speightstown.

On the south coast, where the beaches are just as good (or better), accommodation is much more reasonably priced, with plenty of affordable guesthouses, particularly around Worthing and St Lawrence Gap. There are very few options elsewhere on the island, though a handful of small, long-established hotels still do a light trade on the wild east coast, around Bathsheba and Cattlewash.

Food and drink

Despite the island's small size, the tourist market has produced a staggering variety of places to eat. Although most of Barbados's restaurants have a vague international flavour, it's well worth sampling traditional Bajan cuisine.

Unsurprisingly, **fresh seafood** is the island's speciality: snapper, barracuda and dolphin fish, as well as fresh prawns and lobster. Most popular of all is the flying fish – virtually the Bajan national emblem.

Look out, too, for other traditional Bajan dishes: the national dish is **cou-cou** (a cornmeal and okra pudding) and **saltfish**, and you'll occasionally find the fabulous pudding and **souse** – steamed sweet potato served with cuts of pork pickled in onion, lime and hot peppers. **Cohobblopot** (also known as pepperpot) is a spicy meat and okra stew.

For snacks, you'll find **cutters** (bread rolls with a meat or cheese filling), coconut bread, and more substantial **rotis** (flat, unleavened bread wrapped around a filling of curried meat or vegetables); all are widely available.

Rum is the liquor of choice for many Bajans. Hundreds of tiny rum bars dot the island, which are an integral part of Bajan social life. On the coast, you'll find fewer places that cater specifically to drinkers but, all-inclusives apart, most hotels and restaurants will welcome you for a drink even if you're not staying or eating.

Holidays and festivals

Mid-January Barbados Jazz Festival
☎246/429-2084
January 21 Errol Barrow Day
Mid-February Holetown Festival
☎246/430-7300
First two weeks in March Holder's
Classical Music Festival
Last weekend in March Oistins Fish
Festival ☎246/428-6738
April 28 National Heroes Day
Last week in April Congaline Carnival
☎246/424-0909
Mid-May to end July Crop Over
Festival
August 1 Emancipation Day
First Monday in August Kadooment
Day
November 30 Independence Day

Post, phones and the Internet

Barbados's **postal service** is extremely efficient. The GPO is located in Bridgetown and there are branches across the island, in the larger towns and villages and at the airport.

Calling within Barbados is simple – most hotels provide a telephone in each room and local calls are usually free. You'll also see **Bartel** phone booths all over the island, and these can be used for local and international calls. Most of the booths take phone cards only, available from hotels, post offices and shops.

If you want to use **the Internet**, many hotels will let you use their computers for free or for a nominal charge. Alternatively, in St Lawrence Gap, *Bean & Bagel* (see p.730) offers Internet access, as does Global Business Centre, a stall in the West Coast Mall in Holetown.

Opening hours, holidays and festivals

Shops and businesses are typically **open** Monday to Friday 9am–5pm, with some open at the weekend, too. In addition to the **public holidays** listed on p.60, Barbados observes the holidays and festivals listed in the box above.

Sports and outdoor activities

While Barbados features some of the finest **diving and snorkelling** in the Caribbean, the island is also renowned for more leisurely pursuits, from golfing to watching the local passion of cricket.

Diving and watersports

With excellent **diving** opportunities, the island has plenty of reputable dive operators (see box, overleaf), most of whom will provide transport to and from your hotel. Prices can vary dramatically between dive shops – but expect around B$100 for a single-tank dive, B$150 for a two-tank dive and B$120 for a night dive, including use of equipment. For full open-water certification, budget around B$750. Serious divers should consider a **package deal**; these may simply cover three or five two-tank dives (roughly B$400 and B$600 respectively), or may also include accommodation.

There's good **snorkelling**, too, again especially off the west coast, where there are plenty of good coralheads just offshore and sea turtles in the turtle grass near the *Lone Star*. Several of the dive operators also take snorkellers out on their dive trips for around B$20–30, including equipment. Many top hotels provide guests with free snorkelling gear.

18

BARBADOS | Introduction and basics

Watersports operators

Dive Barbados next to *Lone Star* (see p.731) ⓣ246/422-3133, ⓦwww.divebarbados.net.

The Dive Shop Aquatic Gap ⓣ246/426-9947, ⓦwww.divebds.com.

Hightide Watersports *Sandy Lane Hotel*, St James ⓣ246/432-0931, ⓦwww.divehightide.com.

A number of the hotels in the southeast cater mainly or exclusively for windsurfers; boards can be rented beside the *Silver Rock Hotel* (ⓣ246/428-2866) or at the *Silver Sands Hotel* (ⓣ246/428-6001), and cost around B$40 per hour, B$70 for half a day, or from the windsurfing schools, whose prices for coaching border on the extortionate. Surfing is also superb, notably on the east coast at the Bathsheba "soup bowl", and boards can be rented from the *Round House Inn* in Bathsheba (see p.743).

If you're after water-skiing, jet-ski rides or a speedy tow on an inflatable banana, most hotels can find a reputable operator for you; Hightide Watersports is one of the most trustworthy. Kayaks can be rented from Kayaker's Point (ⓣ246/428-6747) near Oistins.

Other activities

Alongside Jamaica and Trinidad, Barbados is one of the Big Three Caribbean cricketing nations, but while success in other sports has diverted attention from the game in the other two countries, Bajans remain largely focused on **cricket**. More perhaps than anywhere else on earth, the game is *the* national passion. If you get the chance, go and catch a day of international cricket at the Kensington Oval in Bridgetown.

The island also has a lively **equestrian tradition**, with races every other Saturday (except during April) at the Garrison Savannah racecourse, and at Sandy Lane in March. There are several **polo fields** as well, the most famous at Holder's House (see p.732).

For **golfers**, there are two eighteen-hole public golf courses: at the Barbados Golf Club in Durants (ⓣ 246/428-8463) and Sandy Lane (ⓣ246/432-4563). Greens fees are around B$150. There is also a decent nine-hole course at the *Club Rockley* resort (ⓣ246/435-7873) on the south coast.

Some of the best and most scenic **hiking** on Barbados is along the beaches, particularly between Martin's Bay and Bath and between Bathsheba and Cattlewash. Hikes are arranged by the Barbados National Trust (ⓣ246/436-9033).

History

The earliest settlers in Barbados were **Amerindians**, who came to the island in dug-out canoes from the Guianas in South America. Christopher Columbus, the first European visitor to the West Indies, never stopped at Barbados, but in the early sixteenth century, Spanish **slave-traders** arrived to collect Amerindians to work in the gold and silver mines of New Spain.

In 1625, a party of **British sailors** landed in Barbados, claiming the island for their king, and in February 1627 eighty colonists landed at present-day Holetown. They quickly found that sugar grew well in the island soil, and the industry brought almost instantaneous prosperity; by the 1650s, Barbados was considered the wealthiest place in the New World.

As Barbados developed, a workforce was needed for the **sugar plantations**. At first, the main source of workers was indentured labourers, escaping poverty in England and Scotland. In return for their passage to Barbados, these men and women signed contracts to work on the plantations without wages for up to seven years. Later, large numbers of West African **slaves** were brought to Barbados, and the island slowly began to take on its present-day ethnic composition.

By 1700, the glory days of Barbados sugar had passed. Huge fortunes had been made, but increased competition from Jamaica and the Leeward Islands had reduced profits. Many of the small planters were squeezed out of business, handing even more economic power to the large plantation owners. In 1807, the British government abolished the slave trade, yet far more threatening to the planters was the movement for the abolition of slavery itself.

In April 1816, Barbados faced its only serious slave uprising. Named after its alleged leader, **Bussa's Rebellion** began in the southeast with attacks on property and widespread burning of the sugar fields, and quickly spread to all of the island's southern and central parishes. Within three days, however, the rebellion was crushed; just a handful of whites were killed, but over a thousand slaves were either killed in battle or executed afterwards.

Nonetheless, by the early 1830s the reformers in London had won the argument for the abolition of slavery and **full emancipation** took place on August 1, 1838. Some former slaves headed to the towns, particularly Bridgetown, but most had little choice but to continue work on the sugar estates. The white planters still ran Barbados; they owned almost all of the farmland, and controlled the Assembly that made the island's laws.

The US digging of the **Panama Canal** in 1904 had a huge impact on the island, which supplied at least 20,000 workers by the outbreak of World War I. Many of this huge percentage of the local workforce – which was virtually all black – returned to Barbados with sizeable savings, which they were able to invest in new businesses and in land. The white planters, who had previously refused to sell land to blacks, were now obliged to do so by economic circumstances. Even if much of the land bought by blacks was marginal, by the 1930s the pattern of land ownership had changed dramatically.

Alongside economic change, the island saw significant political development. Black political parties were formed in the 1930s and 1940s to fight elections and, although executive power remained with the British-appointed governor, black politicians were appointed to the highly influential Executive Committee. During the 1960s, **foreign investment** and tourism were actively encouraged to reduce the island's dependence on sugar. The British government finally recognized the capability of the Bajans to govern themselves and, in 1966, Barbados attained **independence**.

Development has been fast since independence and the economy has boomed. Tourism remains the main money-earner, but success in manufacturing and other service industries means that not all of the island's eggs are in the tourism basket.

18.1

Bridgetown and around

Giving off the air of a well-to-do and self-contented city, **Bridgetown** is the nation's busy but easy-going capital. One of the oldest cities in the Caribbean, its architecture today is a blend of attractive, balconied colonial buildings, warehouses and brash modern office blocks. The centre of activity is the Careenage, parking place for numerous sleek yachts overlooked by the **Barbadian parliament**. A number of the island's major religious buildings stand within five minutes' walk of here, including **St Michael's Cathedral** and the **synagogue**, both on the sites of their mid-seventeenth-century originals.

Just north of the city, a couple of **rum factories** are open for tours, while **Tyrol Cot** is an unusual nineteenth-century house that was home to two of the island's leading post-war politicians, Sir Grantley Adams and his son Tom Adams. Southeast is the historic **Garrison area**, where the British Empire maintained its Caribbean military headquarters from 1780 to 1905; the huge grassy savannah, today a racecourse and public park, was once the army's parade ground. The ranks of brightly coloured military buildings around its edge include the excellent **Barbados Museum**.

The City

The best place to start your tour of Bridgetown is beside the **Careenage**, a long, thin finger of water that pushes right into the city centre. There are always plenty of expensive yachts and fishing boats moored at its western end. The **parliament buildings** (open to visitors during parliamentary debates), as well as bustling shops and a couple of smart restaurants, can all be found in the immediate vicinity, some of the latter housed in restored warehouses.

Seeing the central sights is easiest **on foot**. Bridgetown is an extremely **safe** city, even at night, though you may want to avoid the seedy area southeast of the Fairchild Street bus station, particularly around Nelson Street and Jordan's Lane, where the red-light district is located.

National Heroes Square and St Michael's Cathedral

On the north side of the Careenage lies the tiny **National Heroes Square**, formerly known for over a century as Trafalgar Square. In 1999, the square was renamed, though a bronze statue of the British Admiral Horatio Nelson, surrounded by the whirlwind of Bridgetown traffic, still stands. The square is dominated by the **parliament buildings** (open to visitors during parliamentary debates). Established in 1639, Barbados's parliament is one of the oldest in the world, though it was not until the 1870s that it settled in its current Greek Revival home.

About 200m east of the square, along St Michael's Row, the large, red-roofed **St Michael's Cathedral** (daily 9am–4pm; free) is the country's principal Anglican place of worship. A stone church was first erected here in 1665, although the present building mostly dates from 1786. It's a spacious, airy place, with a large barrel

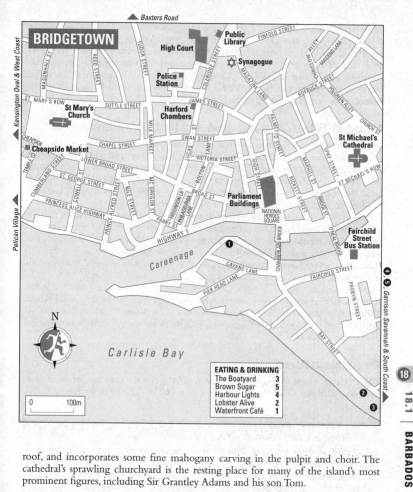

◀ Kensington Oval & West Coast

◀ Pelican Village

▲ Baxters Road

BRIDGETOWN

High Court

Public Library

Synagogue

PINFOLD STREET

Police Station

St Mary's Church

SUTTLE STREET

JAMES STREET

Harford Chambers

MAGAZINE LANE

ROEBUCK STREET

POLGREEN ALLEY

MAIDENS LANE

CHAPELTOWN ALLEY

CHURCH ST

TUDOR STREET

COLERIDGE STREET

ST MARY'S ROW

MASONHALL ST

REED STREET

CHEAPSIDE

Cheapside Market

CHAPEL STREET

SWAN STREET

MILK MARKET

LUCAS ST

PALMETTO STREET

St Michael's Cathedral

ST MICHAEL'S ROW

VICTORIA STREET

LOWER BROAD STREET

TEMPLE ST

CUMBERLAND STREET

ST GEORGE STREET

COWELL ST

NILE STREET

MC GREGOR ST

BOLTON LANE

HIGGINSON LA

PHILADELPHIA LANE

BROAD ST

HIGH STREET

MARHILL ST

SPRY STREET

BICKETT STREET

BRIDGE ST

Parliament Buildings

NATIONAL HEROES SQUARE

PRINCESS ALICE HIGHWAY

PRINCE ALFRED STREET

PARRI ST

HIGHWAY 1

CHAMBERLAIN BRIDGE

Fairchild Street Bus Station

O'NEAL ROAD

Careenage

CAVANS LANE

PIER HEAD LANE

FAIRCHILD STREET

PROBYN STREET

BAY STREET

N

Carlisle Bay

4, 5, Garrison Savannah & South Coast ▶

0   100m

EATING & DRINKING

The Boatyard	3
Brown Sugar	5
Harbour Lights	4
Lobster Alive	2
Waterfront Café	1

18.1 | BARBADOS | Bridgetown and around

roof, and incorporates some fine mahogany carving in the pulpit and choir. The cathedral's sprawling churchyard is the resting place for many of the island's most prominent figures, including Sir Grantley Adams and his son Tom.

The old city

Retrace your steps to the town centre, where a network of narrow lanes links the main roads above the parliament buildings, marking the parts of the city that were first developed. Bridgetown's oldest surviving building is probably the attorney's office, **Harford Chambers**, on the corner of Lucas and James streets, with its irregular brickwork and classic Dutch gables.

Heading up Coleridge Street, and across the road from the public library, you'll find the elaborate **drinking fountain** that was a gift to the city from John Montefiore, one of its leading Jewish traders, in 1865. Though not as jauntily painted as in its heyday, the fountain still has stone reliefs of Prudence, Justice, Fortitude and Temperance and exhortations to the thirsty citizens of Bridgetown to "Be sober minded" and "Look to the end".

Just south of the fountain, the pink and white **synagogue** (daily 10am–4pm; free) was first erected in 1655 and rebuilt after hurricane damage in 1833. Jews were among the earliest settlers in Barbados; many of them arrived in the 1650s to escape the

Inquisition in Brazil, bringing a knowledge of sugar cane cultivation that was to prove crucial in boosting the island's fledgling agriculture. Although the country's Jewish population declined over the centuries, a revitalized community – boosted during the 1930s and 1940s by refugees from Europe – persuaded the government to let them take the building back after World War II. Extensive restoration has returned it to something like its original shape, and the interior has been attractively restored. Outside, the Jewish **cemetery** is one of the oldest in the Western Hemisphere.

Broad Street and the Pelican Village

Much of central Bridgetown is given over to shopping, with dozens of duty-free stores competing for the cruise ship dollar. The main drag is **Broad Street**, which runs northwest from National Heroes Square. This has been the city's market centre since the mid-seventeenth century, and still retains some splendid colonial buildings amid the modern chaos of clothes and jewellery shops, fast-food joints and fruit vendors. It merits a stroll, even if you're not planning to shop.

Beyond St Mary's Church, Broad Street runs into **Cheapside**, where you'll find the station for buses and minibuses heading north, as well as the **GPO** and one of the city's larger **public markets**. On your left, Temple Street runs down to the waterfront past a row of wooden stalls that mark the edge of **Temple Yard**, where many of the city's Rastas have set up small businesses, selling sandals and other handcrafted leather goods, as well as their distinctive red, gold and green jewellery and headgear.

At the bottom end of Temple Yard, the main artery running east–west is the Princess Alice Highway. Five minutes' walk along the highway to the west, **Pelican Village** is an excellent shopping complex built on reclaimed land, with a small art gallery, a dozen or so stores selling batiks, T-shirts, paintings and other souvenirs, and a couple of snack bars.

Practicalties

There is little reason to stay in Bridgetown, and the city has only one **hotel** of note: the *Grand Barbados Beach Resort* at Aquatic Gap (☎246/426-4000, ⊛www.barbados.

Crop Over and Congaline Carnival

Held every summer, the **Crop Over Festival**, traditionally celebrated the completion of the sugar harvest and the end of months of exhausting work for the labourers on the sugar estates. As with carnival in many countries (which immediately precedes a period of fasting), Crop Over carried a frenzied sense of "enjoy-yourself-while-you-may", as workers knew that earnings would now be minimal until the next crop. Alongside the flags, dances and rum-drinking, the symbol of the festival was "Mr Harding" – a scarecrow-like figure stuffed with the dried leaves of the sugar cane – who was paraded around and introduced to the manager of the sugar plantation.

Though Crop Over has lost some of its significance since the 1960s, with tourism replacing sugar as the country's main industry, it's still the island's main festival and an excuse for an extended party. Things start slowly in early July, with craft exhibitions and band rehearsals, heating up in late July and early August with street parades, concerts and competitions between the *tuk* bands, steel bands and – most importantly – the battle for the title of **calypso monarch**, dominated in recent decades by the Mighty Gabby and Red Plastic Bag.

The **Congaline Carnival** is held during the last week in April, with a varied package of mostly local music that includes soca, reggae, steel pan and calypso. Daily shows are held from mid-afternoon to late evening, usually at Dover pasture near St Lawrence Gap, and other events around the island conclude with a May Day parade through Bridgetown from the Garrison savannah to the Spring Garden Highway.

org; ⓖ), which caters mainly to visitors on business.

Some of the best **food** in town can be had at *The Waterfront Café* Careenage (☎246/427-0093), whose authentic Caribbean dishes – try the creole snapper (B\$35) – are served indoors or out beside the water. There's live music most evenings, and a buffet dinner on Tues. Right by the beach, *Lobster Alive* (☎246/435-0305) features excellent seafood, including live lobsters cooked fresh from the tank, conch stew, lobster salad and fresh fish from around B\$30; dinner is served daily, lunch Mon–Sat. Offering the best seafood in the Garrison area, *Brown Sugar*, at Aquatic Gap (☎246/426-7684), is housed in an attractive building with iron fretwork and an interior draped with greenery; prices start around B\$25.

While few make the trip into Bridgetown specifically to eat, there are a couple of excellent restaurants open in the evening, and the city boasts the island's best venues for **nightlife** – several of them with stages right on the beach. At *The Boatyard*, on Bay St (☎246/436-2622), live bands play by the beach on Tues, Fri and Sun (B\$10–25) and DJs spin records on Sat; a B\$35 cover gets you in and all you can drink. Another nightclub right on the beach that's open nightly till 1am, *Harbour Lights* (☎246/436-7225) gets crowded during the all-you-can-drink beach parties on Mon, Wed and Fri (B\$25 entry).

Listings

Airlines Air Canada (☎246/428-1635); Air Jamaica (☎246/228-6625); American Airlines (☎246/428-4170); British Airways (☎246/436-6413); BWIA (☎246/426-2111); LIAT (☎246/434-5428 and 428-0986); Virgin (☎246/228-4886).

Embassies Australian High Commission, Bishop's Court Hill, St Michael (☎246/435-2834); British High Commission, Lower Collymore Rock Street, St Michael (☎246/430-7800); Canadian High Commission, Bishop's Court Hill, St Michael (☎246/429-3550); United States Embassy, Broad Street, Bridgetown (☎246/436-4950).

Pharmacies Cheapside Pharmacy, Cheapside (Mon–Fri 7.30am–5.30pm, Sat 7.30am–1.30pm; ☎246/437-2004), Knight's, Lower Broad Street (daily 8am–1pm; ☎246/426-5196).

Post office Bridgetown's main post office is on Cheapside (Mon 7.30am–noon & 1–3pm, Tues–Fri 8am–noon & 1–3.15pm; ☎246/43-4800).

Taxis Nelson's (☎246/429-4421); Independence (☎246/426-0090).

North of the city

North of the city, and just above the Kensington Oval cricket ground, the Spring Garden Highway heads up along the west coast, skirting the beach almost all the way to historic Speightstown (see p.733) in the far northwest. Much of the area immediately north of Bridgetown is given over to industrial production, including a couple of **rum factories** that are open for tours. To the northeast is **Tyrol Cot**, the former home of Sir Grantley Adams.

The Mount Gay Rum Factory and Tyrol Cot

The **Mount Gay Rum Factory**, a five-minute drive north of town on the Spring Garden Highway (Mon–Fri 9am–4pm, 45min tours every half-hour; B\$10; ☎246/425-8757), offers marginally the better of the rum tours. It starts with a short **film** giving the history of the company, which first distilled rum on the island in 1703 and is reckoned to be the world's oldest surviving producer of the spirit. The tour covers all stages of production, including refining, ageing, blending and bottling. Afterwards, head to the **bar**, where the bartender demonstrates how to be a rum-taster, and you're given a complimentary cocktail.

Five minutes' northeast of Bridgetown's city centre, the exquisite little house at **Tyrol Cot** (Mon–Fri 9am–5pm; B\$11.50) was the launching pad for two of the island's most illustrious political careers. From 1929, it served as the home of Sir Grantley Adams, the first elected leader of pre-independence Barbados, and it was the birthplace of his son, Tom Adams, the nation's prime minister from 1976 until his death in 1985. The family's memorabilia is scattered about the building, which has some unusual architectural features, combining European and vernacular Caribbean styles. Note, for instance, the Demerara windows, framed by Roman arches but containing adjustable double-jalousied shutters, with sloping slates to keep the rain and sun out while letting in light and allowing circulation,

Outside the house, a tiny **heritage village** has been built, featuring half a dozen old-fashioned chattel houses built to various designs; several showcase traditional handicrafts, with local artists selling (and occasionally demonstrating) their crafts, and there's a typical rum shop where you can get a drink and a bite to eat.

The Garrison area

By the late seventeenth century, sugar-rich Barbados had become one of the most important of Britain's overseas possessions. To protect against possible invasion, defensive forts were erected along the calm south and west coasts, with the biggest of them protecting Carlisle Bay and the capital. In 1705, work was begun on a major land fort near the capital, known as **St Ann's Fort** and designed to offer back-up protection. By 1780, as Barbados developed, the British decided to make the island the regional centre for their West Indian troops, and more and more army buildings were put up around the fort.

Today, this part of the city's outer zone, just a couple of kilometres south of the centre, is known as the **Garrison area**. Chock-full of superb Georgian architecture, it remains one of Bridgetown's most evocative districts. It retains the most attractive of the island's colonial **military buildings** including, in a restored jail, the **Barbados Museum**.

The savannah and the Barbados Museum

The centre of the Garrison area is the **savannah**, a huge grassy space that served as the army's parade ground. The military buildings – barracks, quartermaster's store and hospitals, as well as the fort itself – stand in a rough square around its outer edges, flanked by coconut palms and large mango trees. The savannah is still active, with sports grounds and play areas bounded by the city's **racetrack**.

To the south, you can still see the thick eighteenth-century walls of **St Ann's Fort** (now used by the Barbadian defence force and closed to visitors) while, just north of here, the spectacular **Main Guard** – with its tall, bright-red tower and green cupola – is the area's most striking construction. This was the guardhouse, built in 1803, where courts martial and subsequent punishments were carried out; you're normally free to wander around the building, though there's little to see. Outside, ranks of cannon point menacingly across the savannah towards some superbly restored **barrack buildings**, which now serve as government offices.

Housed in the Garrison's old military prison on the east side of the savannah, the **Barbados Museum** (Mon–Sat 9am–5pm, Sun 2–6pm; B\$11.50) is a treat. A series of galleries run clockwise around an airy central courtyard that once rang with the sound of prisoners breaking stones. Don't try to rush through – the place is stuffed with interesting and informative exhibits on the island's history, culture, flora and fauna, and also showcases **prints and paintings** of old Barbados, **African crafts**, and **decorative arts** from around the world. **Period rooms** show what a typical bedroom, living room and dining room would have looked like in one of the plantation houses.

△ Green monkeys, Barbados Wildlife Reserve

18.2

The south coast

The southwest of Barbados was the birthplace of tourism on the island and it remains dominated by the holiday industry. On the whole, the area is not as beautiful as the west coast, but the beaches are just as fine, there are plenty of good eateries, and prices are much more reasonable.

As you head east from Bridgetown towards the airport, several of the coastal towns bear the names (and some of the atmosphere) of British seaside resorts. Each has its speciality, however: you'll find the best beaches at **Rockley** and **Worthing**, the liveliest restaurants and nightlife at **St Lawrence Gap**, and a bustling local scene at **Oistins**, while the quieter beaches at **Silver Sands** attract windsurfers and those who want to spend their holiday strolling on relatively deserted stretches of sand. On the other side of the airport, in the southeast of the island, you enter the far less developed parish of **St Philip**. There's just a handful of hotels here, but the scenery is spectacular, with the Atlantic waves lashing the rocky coast.

If you're driving, **Highway 7** runs along the coast between Bridgetown and Oistins, from where it doglegs up past the airport and on to Crane Bay. **Buses and minibuses** run from Bridgetown as far as the currently defunct hotel at *Sam Lord's Castle* (see p.729), passing through most of the tourist zones on the coast, while route taxis go as far as Silver Sands. Service stops around midnight, so you'll need a car or a private taxi after that. Getting here from the west coast is a little harder – buses run between Speightstown and Oistins, usually bypassing Bridgetown, though they're less frequent than the ones that ply the south coast.

Accommodation

Rockley and Worthing

Abbeville Hotel Rockley ☎246/435-7924, ⓔabbeville@sunbeach.net. Friendly and relaxed little place, motel-like in design, with a small pool. The rooms are simple and somewhat tired, but the setting, around a courtyard and huge bar, gives the place a welcoming feel. ❷

Accra Beach Hotel Rockley ☎246/435-8920, ⓦwww.accrabeachhotel.com. Attractive hotel with fifty elegantly furnished rooms right on the island's busiest beach, balconies overlooking the sea, palm trees strewn around the gardens and a giant swimming pool. For the evenings there's a Polynesian restaurant and an outdoor dancefloor. ❻

Cleverdale Guesthouse Worthing ☎246/428-1035, ⓦwww.barbados-rentals.com. German-managed guesthouse with a communal kitchen, breakfast room, living room and spacious verandah. ❷

Club Rockley Rockley ☎246/435-7880, ⓦwww.clubrockley.com. Popular all-inclusive, ten minutes' walk (or a free shuttle ride) from the beach, with good facilities including its own nine-hole golf course and a nightclub. ❼

Dover

Casuarina Beach Club Dover ☎246/428-3600, ⓦwww.barbados.org. Big, popular and beautifully landscaped hotel on an excellent beach, with tennis courts, pool, and one of the finest collections of local art in the country. All rooms have self-catering facilities, and the front desk arranges tours, including cycle excursions with the hotel's enthusiastic owner. ❼

Dover Beach Hotel Dover ☎246/428-8076, ⓦwww.doverbeach.com. Comfortable, laid-back place located beside a superb beach. All rooms have a/c, some have kitchenettes, and there's a good-size pool. Ask for a room with a beach or pool view. ❹

Maraval Guesthouse Dover ☎246/435-7437, ⓦwww.maravalbarbados.com. Funky little place, popular with European backpackers, is a stone's throw from the beach. ❷

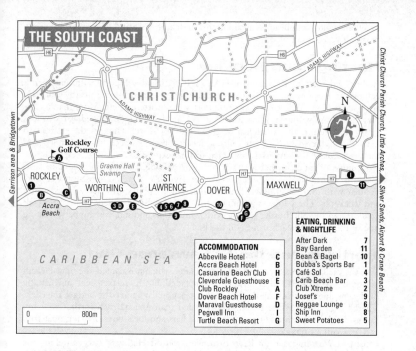

THE SOUTH COAST

CHRIST CHURCH

Rockley
Golf Course

Graeme Hall
Swamp

ROCKLEY
WORTHING
ST LAWRENCE
DOVER
MAXWELL

Accra
Beach

CARIBBEAN SEA

0 — 800m

Garrison area & Bridgetown

Christ Church Parish Church, Little Arches, Silver Sands, Airport & Crane Beach

ACCOMMODATION

Abbeville Hotel	C
Accra Beach Hotel	B
Casuarina Beach Club	H
Cleverdale Guesthouse	E
Club Rockley	A
Dover Beach Hotel	F
Maraval Guesthouse	D
Pegwell Inn	I
Turtle Beach Resort	G

EATING, DRINKING & NIGHTLIFE

After Dark	7
Bay Garden	11
Bean & Bagel	10
Bubba's Sports Bar	1
Café Sol	4
Carib Beach Bar	3
Club Xtreme	2
Josef's	9
Reggae Lounge	6
Ship Inn	8
Sweet Potatoes	5

Turtle Beach Resort Dover ☎246/428-7131, ⓦwww.eleganthotels.com. Top-notch all-inclusive, with 160 rooms, fine restaurants, good watersports facilities and a kids' club. Delightful beach outside can get a bit crowded with the hotel's guests, but it's a short walk to find a quiet space. ❼

Oistins and Silver Sands

Little Arches Miami Beach (just east of Oistins) ☎246/420-4689, ⓦwww.barbados.org. Smart new place, a short walk from delightful Miami Beach. The rooms are good sized, there's a tiny pool and hammocks on the deck area, and a good outdoors restaurant on the top floor. ❻

Pegwell Inn Welchs (just west of Oistins) ☎246/428-6150. This tiny guesthouse is the cheapest place to stay in Barbados, and though it's beside the main road and can be a little noisy,

it's only a five-minute walk to the beach. The four rooms all have fans and private bath. ❷

Silver Sands Resort Silver Sands ☎246/428-6001, ⓔsilvsnd@sunbeach.net. The only full-blown resort in the area, elegantly furnished with two restaurants, tennis courts, a large swimming pool and over a hundred a/c rooms spread across a large area of landscaped grounds. ❺

The southeast

Crane Beach Hotel ☎246/423-6220, ⓦwww.thecrane.com. Small, beautifully designed hotel, in a stunning setting high above Crane Bay. The main hotel is supplemented by superbly comfortable apartments in the adjoining timeshare blocks, though they do detract from the beauty of the place. The beach is lovely, and there are two terrific restaurants. ❻

Christ Church

Most of the island's "lower end" tourism is concentrated in the parish of **CHRIST CHURCH** in the southwest of Barbados, between Bridgetown and the airport, with several small villages offering a variety of lodgings and places to eat. There are

18

18.2 | **BARBADOS** | The south coast

excellent white-sand beaches all along this stretch of coast, and the sea is calm pretty much all year round.

Hastings and Rockley

A short ride east of Bridgetown, **HASTINGS** first developed in the eighteenth century as a by-product of Britain's military development of the nearby Garrison area (see p.724); soldiers from St Ann's Fort were quartered here. More than a century later, its proximity to the capital led to Hastings being developed as Barbados's first tourist resort, and a handful of grand old hotels still stand on the seafront to mark those glory days. Sadly, the once attractive beach has been heavily eroded, and the whole place now wears a somewhat forlorn expression.

A couple of miles further along Highway 7, **ROCKLEY**'s main attraction is its magnificent beach, known locally as **Accra Beach** – a great white swath of sand, popular with tourists and local families, that can get pretty crowded at peak season and weekends. The people-watching is top-notch, as hair-braiders, T-shirt and craft vendors and the odd hustler mingle with windsurfers and sun-worshippers, creating one of the liveliest beach scenes on the island.

Worthing and the St Lawrence Gap

Like the Victorian seaside resort in England after which it is named, the once elegant village of **WORTHING** is now tatty and faded, but its relaxed feel and handful of decent, inexpensive guesthouses make it a popular target for budget travellers. There's a gleaming white beach, less crowded than Accra Beach further west but just as enjoyable, with a couple of laid-back bars and local guys offering boat trips and waverunner rentals.

Just past Worthing, a right-hand turn takes you off Highway 7 to run along the coast for a kilometre or so, passing through the heavily touristed **ST LAWRENCE GAP** and **Dover** before rejoining the main road near Maxwell. As the most developed area of the south coast – with hotels, restaurants, tourist shops and vendors strung out along virtually the entire road – this is something of a tourist enclave; you'll see few Bajans here, other than those who work in the industry. Still, it's a laid-back place with more great beaches, particularly towards the eastern end of St Lawrence Gap, although erosion has taken its toll in a few spots. Most south coast buses and minibuses run through the area.

Oistins and Miami Beach

Continuing east brings you into **OISTINS**, the main town along the south coast and one of its less touristed parts. A couple of **buses** run here from Bridgetown, as does route taxi 11, which continues to Silver Sands. The unusual name is a corruption of Austin, one of the first landowners in the area, described by an early historian as "a wild, mad drunken fellow, whose lewd and extravagant carriage made him infamous in the island". Austin is long gone, but it's still a busy little town, dominated by a fish market, that retains an authentic sense of Barbados before the tourist boom. The best time to visit is in the evening, when a dozen shacks in the central Bay Garden sell fried fish straight from the boats, and on Friday nights hundreds of people descend for a "lime", the local term for a social gathering.

As you head east of Oistins, the Enterprise Coast Road offers a fabulous drive beside the sea and leads to **MIAMI BEACH** – a lovely stretch dotted with casuarina trees that marks the last protected beach before you round the headland for the exposed central and eastern beaches. You'll often find local Bajans exercising here; children playing cricket on the beach and elderly folk taking a refreshing morning swim.

Silver Sands and Long Beach

Famous for windsurfing, **SILVER SANDS** attracts enthusiasts from all over the world, though non-surfers come here too for the quiet, easy-going vibe. Fantastic waves roll in for most of the year and there are a handful of (pretty expensive) places where you can rent a windsurfer if you haven't brought your own. The beaches are less busy than further west – mainly because of the often choppy seas – but equally attractive; true to its name, **LONG BEACH**, just beyond the *Ocean Spray Apartments*, is the longest beach on the island – a huge stretch of crunchy white sand strewn with driftwood – and is often completely deserted.

St Philip

The largest parish on the island, but with less than half the population of busy Christ Church, **ST PHILIP** exudes a different feel from its more touristed neighbour, with no crowds, far less development and a general sense of isolation. The coastline here is rugged, with only a handful of white-sand beaches divided from each other by long cliffs and rocky outcrops. The sea is rough, too, with pounding Atlantic waves.

If you're relying on **public transport**, buses run along the south coast road as far as the hotel known as *Sam Lord's Castle*, passing the *Crane Beach Hotel* (see below), though if you're heading for any of the beaches, you'll need to walk down to them from the main road – usually around 500m.

Foul Bay and Crane Bay

Three or four kilometres beyond the airport, **FOUL BAY** is the largest beach on this section of the coast. Access isn't signposted – look out for the large Methodist Church beside the road in the small village of Rice and a right turn 100m further on takes you right down to the beach. It's a long, wide white-sand beach with a handful of fishing boats normally pulled up on its eastern side and few tourists (and no food and drink facilities). The long cliffs give the place a rugged feel but it's not particularly pretty.

Back on the main road, the **Crane Beach Hotel** lies half a kilometre beyond Foul Bay, commanding a superb site above **CRANE BAY**. A house was first erected here in 1790 and today forms the east wing; during the 1880s the place was converted into a hotel, whose early guests included "Wild Bill" Hickock. More recently, developers have decided that a timeshare development is the best way of reaping tourist dollars from the site, and the hotel is now backed by a couple of large and brightly coloured apartment blocks. In spite of the development it's a fetching place and worth a look even if you're not staying. A long Roman-style swimming pool runs alongside the main hotel building at the top of the cliff and, beside the restaurant with a panoramic view, two hundred steps lead down to a pretty beach.

Eating, drinking and nightlife

You'll find the widest variety of **places to eat** on the south coast, particularly at the crowded **St Lawrence Gap**, where street vendors flogging jerk chicken jostle with punters heading for the classy oceanfront restaurants. St Lawrence Gap is also the heart of south coast **nightlife**, with plenty of options, whether you want to see a band or hit the dancefloor.

Rockley and Worthing

Bubba's Sports Bar Across from the *Accra Beach Hotel* ☎ 246/435-6217. The food is secondary to the entertainment here, with large and small TV screens dotted around the place showing sport from around the world, but the burgers, chicken and sandwiches are decent and well priced. Daily 10am–10pm.

Carib Beach Bar next to the *Crystal Waters* guesthouse. A lively place for a drink, especially during happy hour from 5pm to 6pm, when you'll also get reasonably priced snacks including spicy chicken wings, shrimp kebabs and fishcakes. Daily 11.30am–10pm.

St Lawrence Gap and Dover

After Dark St Lawrence Gap ☎246/435-6547. The late-night zone – a huge and cleverly laid-out place with a dark disco and a massive stage and dancefloor out the back for the live bands who play a couple of times a week. The bar – nearly 30m long – claims to stock every liquor you can name, and the crowd is a good mix of Bajans and tourists, all dressed to the nines. Cover charge varies. 10pm–3am.

Bean & Bagel Dover ☎246/420-4604. Great coffee, all-day breakfasts of bagels, pancakes and omelettes, muffins and tasty lunch options (lasagne, crab backs and the like) have made this Internet café something of an institution for those staying at the eastern end of the Gap. Daily 7am–5.30pm.

Café Sol St Lawrence Gap ☎246/435-9531. Lively, often crowded Mexican place doing a roaring trade in margaritas and Mexican beers, particularly during the 6–7pm and 10–11pm happy hours; decent and sensibly priced burritos, tacos and enchiladas are available. Daily 6–11pm.

Club Xtreme Dover ☎246/228 2582. New, cavernous and high-energy club, with a superb sound system banging out the latest techno and dance, as well as a big games area. Wed, Fri & Sun from 9pm.

Josef's St Lawrence Gap ☎246/435-6541. Both the food and the service at this elegant coral-stone restaurant are as good as you'll find on the south coast, with candelit tables both indoors and (more romantically) down by the water's edge. Starters run B$8–22 and include soups, char-grilled shrimp and beef *carpaccio*; main courses of blackened dolphin, roast chicken or rack of lamb start at B$35. Daily 6–10pm, Dec–April also noon–2pm.

Reggae Lounge St Lawrence Gap ☎246/435-6462. Intimate, unpretentious club with a small bar up top and steps down to the open-air dancefloor under the palm trees. The DJs love to play the latest Jamaican dancehall, but you'll also get "oldies" nights – Bob Marley, Jimmy Cliff, Peter Tosh – and live bands several times a week, usually Thurs and Sun. Cover charge varies. 9pm–late.

Ship Inn St Lawrence Gap ☎246/435-6961. Several bars and a small, sweaty dancefloor, with the most tourist-friendly bands – reggae meets hip-hop meets Marvin Gaye. There's music every night around 10.30pm–12.30am and bands, and a big crowd, on Tues and Sat 9pm–1am.

Sweet Potatoes St Lawrence Gap ☎246/428 7143. Lively, fun place with colourful decking and a long wooden bar. Sells itself as "good old-fashioned Bajan cooking" and dishes up pretty good food – marinated codfish, pumpkin and spinach fritters (B$10–12) and mains of jerk pork and mango chicken (B$32–35), all with tasty side dishes. Mon–Sat, dinner only.

Oistins

The Bay Garden Oistins Market. One of the most distinctive places on the island, with a dozen stalls offering a variety of seafood from conch fritters to fried kingfish to dolphin. Prices are low: you'll be hard-pressed to pay more than B$12 a head, and if you go into the covered *Fish Net* area you'll find plenty of Bajans tucking into equally good barbecued fish straight off the grill. Daily 5.30–10pm.

The southeast

Crane Beach Hotel ☎246/423-6220. The best food in the southeast, with a restaurant that overlooks the bay and serves excellent and innovative seafood dishes. A good lunch stop if you're making a day-trip to the area. Bear in mind, though, that prices are on the high side, and that the place tends to lack atmosphere out of season. Daily 11.30am–2pm & 5.30–9.30pm.

18.3

The west coast

Barbados's **west coast** is a fringe of idyllic bays and coves along the sheltered, Caribbean side of the island. Its sandy beaches and warm blue waters have made it the island's prime resort area. As a result, the coastline has been heavily built up; it holds the island's top golf courses and priciest hotels, and its sought-after private homes change hands at formidable prices.

You don't, however, need to win the lottery to visit. There's a smattering of reasonably priced places to stay and, as everywhere on Barbados, all of the beaches are public. Admittedly, it's a bit of a tramp to reach a few of them, but there are many that are well worth a visit, particularly those at **Prospect**, **Sandy Lane** and **Mullins Bay**. If you're into some serious exercise it's even possible to walk most of the way along the coast at low tide.

Drag yourself away from the beach for a while, though, as the region has other attractions. Lively, modern **Holetown** has a fine old church and a legion of shopping opportunities, while further north, **Speightstown** repays a visit with its colonial relics and picturesque old streets that recall its vanished heyday as a major port.

Highway 1 runs up the coast, rarely straying more than 100m from the shoreline. Highway 2A runs parallel to it, some way inland, and offers a speedier way of getting to the north of the island. **Buses** and **minibuses** ply the coast road between Bridgetown and Speightstown all day, and there are bus stops every couple of hundred metres. Services normally stop at around midnight, after which you'll need a car or private taxi. If you're coming from the south coast, look for buses marked "Speightstown" – these usually bypass Bridgetown and save you having to change buses (and terminals) in the city.

Accommodation

Although the west coast of Barbados is renowned for **luxury hotels**, several of which are ranked among the best in the Caribbean, there are a handful of cheaper places sandwiched in between.

From Prospect to Paynes Bay

Angler Apartments Derricks ☎246/432-0817, ⓦwww.barbadosahoy.com. A dozen self-catering apartments in three small blocks shaded by mango and breadfruit trees and set back 200m from the highway. The fan-cooled rooms are comfortable, the atmosphere relaxed and friendly, and you're five minutes' walk from a good beach. The restaurant is excellent. ❹

Beachcomber Apartments Paynes Bay ☎246/432-0489, ⓦwww.beachcombersuites.com. Small apartment block popular with families, offering large, luxurious balconied apartments or studios with smaller balconies. All rooms have kitchen facilities. ❼

Crystal Cove ☎246/424-2683, ⓦwww.eleganthotels.com. One of the best of the island's

all-inclusives, with comfortable rooms, excellent food, good watersports and several pools, one with a swim-up bar under a waterfall. It's one of four west coast hotels owned by *Elegant Hotels* (all connected by a free boat taxi), and you're welcome to use the facilities at the sister hotels. ❼

Smugglers' Cove ☎246/432-1741, ⓦwww.Barbados.org. Small, friendly but slightly cramped hotel complete with gardens colourfully decked out with crotons. The rooms all have tiny kitchenettes, and there's a bar/restaurant and small swimming pool, ten metres from the beach. ❺

Around Holetown

Lone Star Mount Standfast ☎246/422-1617, ⓦwww.thelonestar.com. Fabulous little boutique

hotel in an old house converted into four spectacular rooms right over the beach. Also home to one of the island's trendiest restaurants (see p.735).
Sandy Lane ☏246/432-1311, ⊛www.sandylane.com. The jewel of the west coast, a magnificent place in every way, offering spectacular luxury in the rooms, restaurants, bars and other communal areas. Rather popular with the nouveaux riches.
Sunset Crest Resort ☏246/432-6750, ℱ432-7229. Ten minutes' walk from the beach, with several swimming pools, restaurants and bars, and over a hundred one-, two- and three-bedroom apartments scattered around the complex.

Around Speightstown

Cobblers Cove Hotel ☏246/422-2291, ⊛www.cobblerscove.com. Spacious rooms are hidden around a beautifully landscaped garden. The main building – bright pink in colour but very English country house in design – holds a splendid bar and restaurant (as well as two spectacular suites) and

fronts onto a relatively empty beach. Overall, one of the most delightful hotels on the island.
Little Good Harbour ☏246/439-3000, ⊛www.littlegoodharbourbarbados.com. Friendly little place in a quiet spot just north of Speightstown, *Little Good Harbour* is less outrageously priced than many of its west coast competitors. Wooden gingerbread cottages house one- and two-bedroom suites.
Mango Lane Apartments ☏246/422-3146, ℮clemlau@sunbeach.net. An assortment of colourful and lightly furnished chattel houses and apartments dotted around the local area, rented out by the friendly owners of the *Fisherman's Pub* in Speightstown (see p.736).
Sandridge Hotel ☏246/422-2361, ℮bernmar@caribsurf.com. This three-storey hotel on a lovely strip of beach is as good for your money as you'll find on the west coast. It's not fancy, but the sizeable rooms are brightly decorated, there are two restaurants, a large pool, and great snorkelling offshore.

North to Prospect

There is little sign of the hotel extravaganza to come as Highway 1 begins to carve its way up the west coast through the tiny village of **PROSPECT**. Most of the area here is residential and the beaches – largely bereft of tourists – are popular at weekends and holidays with families up from Bridgetown. A good bet, if you want to swim, is **Prospect Beach** – a narrow crescent of sand, backed by manchineel trees and palms, and a calm turquoise bay. Public access is via a path just north of the all-inclusive *Escape Hotel*, and at busy times the beach can get crowded with the hotel's guests.

Continuing north, there isn't much to distinguish this area of coast other than a series of superlative bays and beaches, many of them tucked away behind an increasingly grand row of hotels and private mansions, themselves often hidden by security fences. A right turn opposite the *Tamarind Cove Hotel* winds upwards into the island's interior, past the grand polo field at **Holder's House** – an old Great House and the venue for a prestigious classical music festival every March.

Sandy Lane

Back on the coast, the road through the area of Sandy Lane Bay is overhung with lush vegetation and reeks of wealth. In Barbados, the name **SANDY LANE** is synonymous with the grandest of the island's hotels (see above), whose list of repeat celebrity guests is impressive. The place guards its guests jealously behind high walls and security guards. Nevertheless, as part of its deal with the government to get permission for the hotel (and the rerouting of the coastal road that it involved), the owners promised to provide a ten-metre right of way to the south of the property, giving public access to the shore. If you've got the energy, you can wander down to the bay past the tall casuarinas and manchineel trees. The sweep of gently shelving sand, backed by the elegant hotel (completely rebuilt by its new Irish owners between 1998 and 2001), is magnificent.

Holetown and around

The third-largest town in Barbados. **HOLETOWN** is a busy, modern hub for the local tourist industry, if somewhat lacking in character. All west coast buses run through it, and the main highway is lined with fast-food restaurants, souvenir shops, banks and grocery stores. Just before you reach the centre, **Sunset Crest** shopping centre on the east side of the highway has plenty of places where you can pick up souvenirs. There are more shopping options once you reach Holetown itself, with a dozen reproduction chattel houses in the **chattel house village** (also alongside the highway) selling gifts and the like, and the nearby **West Coast Mall** offering equally good spending opportunities. On the northern edge of town, 1st and 2nd streets, lined with trendy restaurants, lead down to the sea.

Ten minutes' walk north of the centre of Holetown, **St James's Parish Church** is one of the most attractive on the island. It is also the oldest religious site in Barbados – the original wooden church was built here in 1628. The present church is a small, graceful building, with thick stone walls and two columns supporting the stone chancel arch that divides the nave from the choir. There are the usual marble funerary monuments on the walls, while more modern works of art include a colourful biblical triptych by Ethiopian painter Alemayehu Bizumeh and bronze bas-reliefs of St James and St Mary by Czech sculptor George Kveton.

A couple of miles inland from Holetown. the informative **Sir Frank Hutson Sugar Museum** is signposted off Highway 2A just north of the main roundabout (Mon–Sat 9am–5pm; B$15). The small museum is the brainchild of Frank Hutson, a former sugar worker who rescued a load of rusting sugar-mill machinery, cleaned it up and incorporated it into the museum, adding captions, maps and photos explaining the role of sugar on the island since its introduction in the 1640s. Between February and June, you can tour the adjacent sugar factory and view the full production process, from the loading and grinding of the cane to the crystallization of the brown sugar; it's a heady experience for the smell alone.

North to Mullins Bay

Once you've passed Holetown there is little of particular interest to hold you en route north to Speightstown. A series of exclusive hotels and grand private houses, fenced in behind security gates, is interspersed with small villages of shops, fishing shacks and chattel houses, keeping a typically Bajan toehold on the increasingly developed west coast. Access to many of the small bays along the coast is difficult, but good snorkeling can be found offshore from the *Lone Star* hotel (see p.731) where endangered hawksbill turtles can often be spotted – look out for the buoys and other snorkellers about 200m out. Further north, **MULLINS BAY** – a strip of sugary sand with a lively beach bar (see p.736) – is a good place to stop for a swim. Buses stop here and there's a car park across from the bay.

Speightstown

Small, run-down, yet utterly charming, **SPEIGHTSTOWN** (pronounced "Spikestown") is the second town of Barbados, though it remains largely untouched by tourist development. It was once a thriving port, famous for its tough-talking, uncompromising inhabitants – "Speightstown flattery" is an old Bajan term for a backhanded compliment – the place has declined precipitately over the last century, and there is little to do today but stroll around and soak up the remnants of the local fishing industry, a few stylish old buildings and a handful of excellent restaurants that cater for day visitors and the guests of nearby hotels. A mark of Speightstown's former importance is that three major forts were erected to protect it, with several additional gun emplacements scattered along the coast to add to the barrage of any enemy ships (though the only invasion was by the British in 1651). Little remains of the military hardware, but some of the old iron cannon from Fort Orange point out to sea from **the Esplanade**, to the north of town.

Across from the Esplanade, **St Peter's Parish Church**, on Church Street, was first built in the 1630s, making it one of the oldest churches in Barbados. Destroyed by the 1831 hurricane, the Georgian building was rebuilt in a graceful Greek Revival

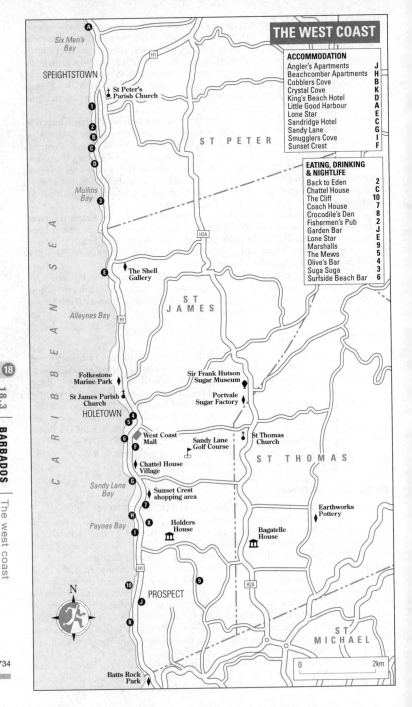

THE WEST COAST

ACCOMMODATION

Angler's Apartments	J
Beachcomber Apartments	H
Cobblers Cove	B
Crystal Cove	K
King's Beach Hotel	D
Little Good Harbour	A
Lone Star	E
Sandridge Hotel	C
Sandy Lane	G
Smugglers Cove	I
Sunset Crest	F

EATING, DRINKING & NIGHTLIFE

Back to Eden	2
Chattel House	C
The Cliff	10
Coach House	7
Crocodile's Den	8
Fishermen's Pub	2
Garden Bar	J
Lone Star	E
Marshalls	9
The Mews	5
Olive's Bar	4
Suga Suga	3
Surfside Beach Bar	6

Six Men's Bay

SPEIGHTSTOWN

St Peter's Parish Church

ST PETER

Mullins Bay

C A R I B B E A N   S E A

The Shell Gallery

ST JAMES

Alleynes Bay

Folkestone Marine Park

St James Parish Church

HOLETOWN

West Coast Mall

Chattel House Village

Sandy Lane Bay

Sunset Crest shopping area

Paynes Bay

Holders House

Sir Frank Hutson Sugar Museum

Portvale Sugar Factory

St Thomas Church

Sandy Lane Golf Course

ST THOMAS

Earthworks Pottery

Bagatelle House

PROSPECT

ST MICHAEL

N

Batts Rock Park

0   2km

style – though with the standard tower tacked on for good measure – and the present incarnation is the result of superb restoration after the place was gutted by fire in 1980.

Back on the main road, head south across the bridge and past the fish market, always humming with vendors in the early morning. **Queen Street** is the main drag and has several grand old buildings that have survived the town's decline. Almost medieval in design, **Arlington** is a classic example of the island's early townhouses – narrow, tall and gabled, with a sharply sloping roof. While you're here, cross the road and check out the **Gallery of Caribbean Art** (Mon–Fri 9.30am–4.30pm), where there are three rooms of sculpture, paintings and metalwork by artists from Barbados and the wider Caribbean.

Buses running up the west coast normally terminate at Speightstown, stopping at the eastern end of Church Street – from here, head down towards the sea, passing the parish church on your right. Queen Street has an unofficial tourist information office in the *Fisherman's Pub* (see overleaf).

Eating and drinking

Plenty of top-notch **restaurants** line the "platinum coast", some as good as anything you'll find anywhere in the Caribbean, though prices tend to be high. You'll have to look a bit harder to find interesting low-priced options, but they do exist, and several – including the *Fisherman's Pub* in Speightstown and the *Garden Bar* at *Angler Apartments* – are worth checking out, whatever your budget.

From Prospect to Paynes Bay

The Cliff Fitts ☎ 246/432-1922. This long-standing west coast favourite is in a pillared coral-stone building on a clifftop, with a small army of waiters and exquisite food. Expect some of the island's most innovative cooking and prices of B$80–100 for two courses not including drinks. Daily 6–10.30pm.

Crocodile's Den Paynes Bay ☎ 246/432-7625. Funky bar, with pool table, darts and board games, canned and occasional live music, satellite sports and a great late-night atmosphere. Daily from 5pm.

Garden Bar at *Angler Apartments* ☎ 246/432-0817. Small, laid-back, no-frills place offering traditional inexpensive West Indian meals like pepperpot, cook-up rice (rice and peas with salt beef and lamb, cooked in coconut milk) and Guyanese specialities like *metagee* (a root vegetable stew of plantains). Worth calling ahead, as some of the dishes take a while to prepare. Daily 6–8.30pm.

Marshalls Holders Hill. One-and-a-half kilometres inland, this relaxed local bar serves a wide selection of dishes for around B$15 – try the flying fish or stewed beef. An essential stop for cricket fans: the owner is mad about the game, and the walls are papered with cricket memorabilia. Head uphill, past Holder's Great House, and the restaurant is on your left, opposite the playing field. Daily noon–2pm & 5–9pm.

Holetown

Lone Star at the *Lone Star* hotel ☎ 246/419-0598. Spectacular seaside location, and the trendiest place on the west coast. Expect to find fish soup,

sushi or crabcakes as starters (B$20–40). Main courses range from jerk chicken to *piri piri* shrimp (B$50–90). There's also a first-class chilled seafood selection – a platter for two costs B$220. Daily 11.30am–5.30pm & 6.30–10.30pm.

The Mews ☎ 246/432-1122. Top-notch food is served at this Holetown townhouse – ask for a table on one of the terraces. The seafood is imaginative – try the baked snapper in a parmesan crust – and the place is often packed with local bigwigs. B$15–25 for starters, B$45–65 for mains. Daily 5.30–11pm.

Olive's Bar and Bistro ☎ 246/432-2112. Popular eatery, simple in design with its wooden floor and white tablecloths, but offering a wide choice of excellent meals. Starters include beef *carpaccio* or warm shrimp salad for B$19–22, with main courses like jerk pork with roasted garlic mash (B$40) or seared sea scallops (B$56). The relaxed upstairs bar is one of the best places for a drink. Daily 6–10pm.

Surfside Beach Bar, behind the Holetown police station ☎ 246/432-2105. A buzzing beach bar that's popular from breakfast to late evening, with lunches of sandwiches, pasta or fish and chips (B$20) and dinner options like lasagne, fresh fish or a seafood platter (B$27–35). There's a daily happy hour 4.30–5.30pm and sports on satellite TV. Daily 9am–midnight.

From Mullins Bay to Speightstown

Back to Eden Jordan's Plaza, Queen Street, Speightstown. One of very few vegetarian places on Barbados, serving tasty and inexpensive island stews and other dishes. The fresh fruit juices and home-baked cakes are worth stopping for on their own. Mon–Fri 11am–4pm.

Chattel House at *Sandridge Hotel* (see p.731). Slightly sanitized but hugely engaging version of a typical Bajan rum shop with enthusiastic service and good, inexpensive cutters, burgers and pies. Don't miss the delicious weekend special of pudding and souse. Daily 11am–9pm.

Fisherman's Pub Queen Street ☎246/422-2703. Delightful place, with a large verandah jutting out over the ocean, and the best-value food in town. You can munch on a sizeable roti or flying fish cutters at lunch for around B$5; at night, typical Bajan dinners cost around B$20. Daily 11am–10pm.

Suga Suga Beach Bar Mullins Beach ☎246/422-1878. One of the busiest bars on the west coast, with good if rather pricey all-day dining at tables on a wide ocean-view verandah. The Bajan fish soup and conch salads (B$25–35) are excellent, as are the grilled steaks, pigs' tails and fried pork chops (B$30 upwards). Mon–Sat 8.30am–10.30pm; Sun 8.30am–7pm.

Entertainment and nightlife

Nightlife on the west coast is generally pretty quiet, mostly limited to steel bands and floor shows put on by the more exclusive hotels. There's not much in the way of local entertainment, but a couple of places occasionally feature a Bajan band.

The Coach House Paynes Bay ☎246/432-1163. Live music most nights, with the island's top soca and steel bands as well as a Latin Fiesta night on Fri and the occasional karaoke evening. 8pm–2am.

Crocodile's Den Paynes Bay ☎246/432-7625. Bar with pool tables and darts that usually features live music on Fri and Sat with local bands, DJs and occasional Latin nights. 8pm–3am; happy hour 9–10pm.

Fisherman's Pub Speightstown ☎246/422-2703. Often the liveliest place in town, with a steel band on Wed nights, and occasional floor shows on the oceanfront verandah. 6–11pm.

18.4

Central Barbados

Don't expect a dramatic change of scenery as you head into the **interior of Barbados**; the landscape of the central parishes of **St George** and **St Thomas** is almost uniformly flat or gently rolling – perfect for the sugar crop that's been under cultivation here for almost four centuries. As you head north towards the parish of **St Andrew**, however, the land rises in a short series of peaks to the island's highest point, **Mount Hillaby**.

Despite its small area, central Barbados offers a considerable number of attractions to lure you away from the beach. The parish of St George has some rewarding historic sights, including the military signal station at **Gun Hill** and the beautiful plantation house at **Francia**. To the north in St Thomas – slap-bang in the middle of the island – is **Harrison's Cave**, a series of weirdly beautiful subterranean chambers. The narrow strip of jungle at nearby **Welchman Hall Gully**, hemmed in by cliffs and densely covered with the island's most attractive plants and trees, offers a unique glimpse of the island in its primal state, while the gardens at **Flower Forest** offer a more carefully managed look at local flora.

Getting to and around the interior of Barbados is straightforward – **buses** from Bridgetown run to the main attractions, though services are less frequent than on the coasts. You'll save a lot of time if you rent a car for a day or two – a network of country lanes crisscross the centre, offering easy access from the coast.

Gun Hill Signal Station

Sitting among pretty landscaped gardens that belie its turbulent origins, **GUN HILL SIGNAL STATION** (Mon–Sat 9am–5pm; B$10) was built in 1818 and restored by the Barbados National Trust. The watchtower offers fabulous panoramic views across the green, gently rolling hills of central Barbados and out to the ocean beyond Bridgetown. Guides give an expert introduction to the local history, and there is a small but immaculate display of military memorabilia, including flags of the various army regiments that were stationed here, maps of the island's many forts – 23 of them had been built as early as 1728 – and the cannon (never fired) that would have alerted the population to enemy invasion. Below the station, and visible from the tower, is a giant **white lion** – a British military emblem carved from a single block of limestone by soldiers stationed here in 1868.

Francia

Just south of Gun Hill, signposted off to the west, **FRANCIA** (Mon–Fri 10am–4pm; B$10), is a working plantation growing sweet potatoes and yams for export. The plantation house is one of the most attractive in Barbados; it was also one of the last of the island's great houses, built at the end of the nineteenth century, when the plantations were already in decline as the value of sugar fell on world markets. The sweeping stone staircase, triple-arched entrance and enclosed upper balcony are unusual features, reflecting the influence of the original French owner. The double-jalousied windows are also rare on Barbados, though they are also found at the nineteenth-century Tyrol Cot in Bridgetown (see p.723).

The pride of the house – and what really distinguishes it from the other great houses you can tour – is its superb **collection of antique maps** of Barbados and the Caribbean, collected from dusty bookshops and grand auction rooms around the world and dating back to the early sixteenth century, only decades after Columbus first "discovered" the region. Outside, the huge terraced garden feels very English in style, despite the abundance of tropical flora, including a gigantic mammee apple tree, mangoes, frangipani, hibiscus and the ubiquitous bougainvillea.

Harrison's Cave and the Springvale Eco-Heritage Museum

Fifteen minutes' drive north of the Francia plantation, **HARRISON'S CAVE** (40min tours daily 9am–4pm; B$25) is an enormous subterranean labyrinth, where underground streams and dripping water have carved huge limestone caverns with stalactites hanging like teeth from the ceilings and weirdly shaped stalagmites pushing up from the cave floor. The existence of caves here has been known for over two hundred years, though it was only by accident that the ones you'll see on your tour were discovered in 1970, and subsequently opened up to the public.

No serious potholing is expected of you – you're taken underground and around the various chambers on an electric tram, which, with the guide's mechanized voice-over, rather spoils the eerie, otherwise soundless atmosphere of the place. However, it can't completely detract from the beauty – you'll be hard put to find more spectacular cave scenery anywhere in the world.

A small folk collection, the **SPRINGVALE ECO-HERITAGE MUSEUM** (Mon–Sat 10am–4pm; B$5), 5km north of the caves, provides a glimpse of some of the disappearing ways of Bajan life. Besides a collection of locally made furniture, there are traditional cooking pots and exhibits on the mining of manjak, known as "Barbados tar". Browse the extensive library or take a pleasant stroll through the grounds, which used to be part of a sugar plantation and now have a diverting nature trail that leads to an old manjak mine. The café serves cake and soft drinks, including the traditional mauby, made from boiling up bitter tree bark with spices.

Welchman Hall Gully

Signposted off Highway 2, a kilometre or so north of Harrison's Cave, the dramatic **WELCHMAN HALL GULLY** (Mon–Sat 9am–5pm; B$11.50) is a long, deep corridor of jungle, hemmed in by steep cliffs and abounding with local flora and fauna. Though a handful of non-indigenous plants have been planted here over the years, the vegetation is not dissimilar to that which covered the whole island when the British first arrived here. The gully itself was created aeons ago by a fissure in the limestone cap that covers this part of Barbados, and is named after a Welshman, General Williams, an early settler on the island and the first owner of the surrounding land. There are two entrances – one at either end of the gully and both with parking spaces – and buses from Bridgetown stop outside each one, where a National Trust representative will give you a brochure describing the walk and the plants and trees.

A **footpath** leads down into the gully, and it's a short walk from one end of the marked trail to the other, along which prolific fruit and spice trees dangling with lianas offer protection from the sun. Keep your eyes out for green monkeys cavorting in the undergrowth.

Flower Forest

As you head across the parish boundary into St Joseph, the meticulously landscaped **FLOWER FOREST** (daily 9am–5pm; B$15) is signposted just south of Highway 2. There is a great variety of indigenous and imported plants and trees here, all labelled with their Latin and English names and country of origin, and some fabulous views over the hills of the Scotland district, but overall the place feels just a little bit too neat and ordered. If you only have time to visit one of the island's botanical gardens, you're probably better off making for the more rugged Andromeda Botanical Gardens on the east coast (see p.742) but Flower Forest certainly warrants a look if you're in the area.

The seemingly endless variety of trees include breadfruit, coffee, Barbados cherry, avocado and a single African baobab tree, and there is a fine collection of orchids, hibiscus and the "lobster claw" heliconias. Other highlights include Palm Walk, where dozens of different types of palm are scattered around.

18.5

The north

The **north of Barbados** is the most rugged and least visited part of the island; for the adventurous, though, the area offers an excellent variety of places to explore. The most popular target is the **Barbados Wildlife Reserve**, home to hundreds of green monkeys and a host of other animals; nearby, there's an old signal station and a nature trail through the forest at **Grenade Hall**, while the lovely park and desolate ruins at **Farley Hill** make a good place to stop for a picnic. Just north of here there is a working **sugar mill** at Morgan Lewis and a superb Jacobean Great House, **St Nicholas Abbey**.

Buses run through the northern parishes from both Speightstown and Bridgetown, though services are less regular than along the south and west coasts. If you're planning on visiting more than one of the main attractions – and you could comfortably see all of them in a day – renting a car will make getting around a lot less hassle.

The Barbados Wildlife Reserve

Green monkeys are the chief attraction at the **BARBADOS WILDLIFE RESERVE** (daily 10am–5pm; B$25, including access to Grenade Hall), just off Highway 1 in the parish of St Peter and directly accessible by bus from Speightstown or Bridgetown. The nonprofit reserve was first established as the island's leading centre for conservation of the monkeys, and – more controversially – to look at the possibility of exporting them for medical research, particularly the production and testing of vaccines. As the idea of making it into a tourist attraction developed, other creatures were gradually introduced, including brocket deer, otters, armadillos, racoons and caiman alligators, as well as plenty of caged parrots, macaws and other fabulously coloured tropical birds.

Paths meander through the lush mahogany woods and, in a thirty-minute stroll, you'll see pretty much everything on offer, including the aviary, fishponds and bird-cages. Monkeys swarm freely around the reserve in playful mood. The **information centre**, at the reserve's northeast corner, has excellent displays on the monkeys.

Grenade Hall Signal Station

The **GRENADE HALL SIGNAL STATION** (daily 10am–5pm; B$25, including access to the Barbados Wildlife Reserve), was one of the chain of communication stations built in the years immediately after Barbados faced its first and only major slave revolt in 1816 (see p.719). The stations, which communicated by semaphore flags and lanterns, were designed to get news of any trouble afoot rapidly to the garrison in Bridgetown.

Grenade Hall is not as attractively situated as Gun Hill (see p.737), though the watchtower offers great views of the surrounding countryside, and the place is certainly worth a quick tour if you're in the area. Prints of the British military hang downstairs, alongside various bits and pieces belonging to the signalmen – medallions, clay pipes, coins and pottery shards. Upstairs, the old semaphore signals are on display – though most of them postdate the era of possible slave revolts, and relate to shipping movements.

Below Grenade Hall, a large tract of **native forest** (same hours and ticket) has been preserved, and several kilometres of pathways loop down through the woods and under whitewood, dogwood, mahogany and magnificent silk cotton trees. Walking down from the signal station you can feel yourself entering a different ecosystem – shaded, damp, humid and sticky.

Farley Hill National Park and Morgan Lewis Sugar Mill

Just south of the wildlife reserve, **FARLEY HILL NATIOANL PARK** (daily 8am–6pm; free; with car B$3.50) is a small, pleasant park at the top of a 300-metre cliff, with commanding views over the Scotland district. It's a good place to retreat with a picnic once you've finished looking around Grenade Hall. The park is the site of what was once a spectacular Great House, built for a sugar baron in 1857 but destroyed in a fire a century later. Today, the charred coral-block walls of the rather ghostly mansion form the park's focus, surrounded by landscaped lawns and masses of fruit trees.

Set in the midst of the crumbling ruins of an old sugar factory, a short drive northeast of Farley Hill, with a tall chimney poking defiantly from the overgrown grass, **MORGAN LEWIS SUGAR MILL** (Mon–Sat 9am–5pm; B$10) is the only windmill in Barbados still in operation. The island once boasted more than five hundred mills, all grinding juice from the sugar cane that covered the island like a blanket, but twentieth-century mechanization has all but eliminated them from the countryside. If not an essential object of pilgrimage during your stay on Barbados, the mill affords a poignant testament to this part of the island's history.

Though it's no longer in commercial use, the mill – first built in the nineteenth century – is still in perfect working order. The sails, wheelhouse and British-made machinery have been thoroughly restored over the last few years, and you'll get a demonstration of how the thick bamboo-like stems were pushed through mechanical grinders to extract cane juice, subsequently used for making sugar.

Cherry Tree Hill and St Nicholas Abbey

Heading north uphill from the sugar mill the main road sweeps past sugar fields before reaching a magnificent canopy of mahogany trees at **CHERRY TREE HILL**. Stop to look behind you across the east coast and out to the Atlantic Ocean – this is one of the most spectacular views on the island. There is actually no record of cherry trees having existed here; the local legend that they were all chopped down because passers-by kept stealing the fruit sounds a little unlikely.

Over the brow of the hill, a signposted right turn takes you to the Great House of **ST NICHOLAS ABBEY** (Mon–Fri 10am–3.30pm; B$10) – the oldest house on Barbados. Built during the 1650s, the white-painted structure was originally owned by two of the largest sugar growers in the north of the island. How the place came to be called an abbey is unclear. So too is the reason for the fireplaces – completely unnecessary in view of the island's tropical weather – in the upstairs bedrooms. Presumably they are the result of the builders slavishly following the drawings of a British architect, regardless of the Caribbean climate.

Your entrance fee entitles you to a rather lacklustre guided tour of the ground floor of the house (the upstairs, still in use, is closed to visitors), crammed with eighteenth-century furniture, Wedgwood porcelain and other traditional accoutrements of the old Barbadian aristocracy. The outbuildings at the back of the house are rather more rustic, and include the original bathhouse and a four-seater toilet.

While the tour of the house may be a little unexciting, there is an evocative twenty-minute black-and-white **film** shown on request. Made in 1934 by a previous owner of the abbey, it shows the family making a visit by sea from England to their West Indian home. There is some great footage of the boats arriving at Bridgetown harbour and of the prewar capital, followed by loving shots of the sugar plantation in action. After the film you can take a short stroll through the woods behind the house or grab a drink in the small café.

18.6

The east coast

For many the rugged, little-explored **east coast** is the most beautiful part of Barbados. Almost all year round, the Atlantic waves crash in against this wild coastline, making for superb surfing but difficult and sometimes dangerous swimming. It's certainly worth making the effort to explore since this is a very different side of the island from the heavily touristed south and west; if possible, try to spend a night or two up here. If you can't stay, do at least check out one of the excellent restaurants around the laid-back old resort of **Bathsheba** for lunch.

Although the coastal scenery is the main attraction, there are a few specific places that merit a visit, most notably the delightful **Andromeda Botanical Gardens**. Specific sightseeing apart, this is a lovely area to drive through, particularly under the steep-sided **Hackleton's Cliff** that runs parallel to the coast, where the road weaves through lush tropical forest, offering stunning views over the ocean. You can also walk along the beaches at **Bath** and **Martin's Bay**, watching the surf ride in.

Accommodation

A handful of small but cosy **accommodation** options on the east coast offers a change from the built-up south and west of the island. It's a great, quiet area to unwind for a couple of days, away from the crowds. In Bathsheba try the *Atlantis Hotel* (☎246/433-9445, ⊛www.atlantisbarbados.com ❸), an ancient, faded and extremely welcoming place overlooking Tent Bay with good food and eight modest rooms – ask for one with a balcony. Just above the *Atlantis* and surrounded by an acre of tropical garden is *Sea-U Guest House* (☎246/433-9030, ⊛www.seaubarbados. com; ❹), a friendly little German-managed guesthouse offering four studios with kitchenettes and one guest-room, and food is laid on if you don't want to cook.

Codrington College

Signposted on your right as you head up the east coast, Skeete Bay and Consett Bay are a couple of quiet, pretty coves, each with a strip of sand backed by palm trees and with fishing boats pulled up on the beach as they have been for centuries. Just north of Consett Bay, on the clifftop, stand the handsome buildings of **CODRINGTON COLLEGE** (daily 10am–4pm; B$5). The first degree-level institution in the English-speaking West Indies, it continues to teach theology to budding Anglican vicars, and is now affiliated to the University of the West Indies.

The approach to the college is dramatic, along a long avenue lined on either side with a graceful row of tall cabbage palms and ending beside a large ornamental lake covered in waterlilies. The buildings are arranged around an unfinished quadrangle, with an arched central portico that opens onto large, elegant gardens offering panoramic views over the coast.

St John's Parish Church and Hackleton's Cliff

From Martin's Bay, a steep road climbs dramatically up through Hackleton's Cliff. Turn left at the top of the hill, past more sweeping fields of sugar cane, for the Gothic **ST JOHN'S PARISH CHURCH** (daily 9am–5pm; free), probably the most elegant of the island's churches. Like many of the parish churches, St John's – typically English with its arched doors and windows and attractive tower – was first built in the mid-seventeenth century but, following severe hurricane damage in the great storm of 1831, now dates from around 1836.

The floor of the church is paved with ancient memorial tablets, rescued from earlier versions of the building, and a Madonna and Child sculpture by Richard Westmacott stands to the left of the main entrance. Most attractive of all is the reddish-brown **pulpit**, superbly hand-carved from four local woods and imported oak and pine. Outside, the expansive **graveyard** is perched on top of the cliff, looking down over miles of jagged coastline and crammed with moss-covered tombs, family vaults and a wide array of tropical flora.

From the church, follow the road north where, after a kilometre or so, a sign diverts you to **HACKLETON'S CLIFF**. This steep 300-metre limestone escarpment marks the edge of the Scotland district to the west and, to the east, the rugged east coast whose limestone cap was eroded by sea action many centuries ago. At the end of a short track, you can park right by the edge of the cliff for fabulous views across the craggy hills of **Scotland**, nostalgically named by early settlers for its supposed resemblance to the land of Robert Burns, and up the sandy northeast coastline.

The Andromeda Botanical Gardens

Back on the main highway, a bit further north, the colourful, sprawling **Andromeda Botanical Gardens** (daily 9am–5pm; B$12) make up one of the most attractive spots on the island, spread over a hillside strewn with coral boulders and with vistas over the Bathsheba coastline. Created by a local botanist, the gardens feature masses of local and imported shrubs and plants, landscaped around a trail that incorporates several ponds and a giant, ancient bearded fig tree.

The colourful hibiscus garden, on your left as you enter, is the best place to see the tiny hummingbirds that frequent the place. The trail then takes you past some old traveller's trees and a small clump of papyrus before turning uphill past a series of heliconia – including the bizarrely shaped "beefsteak" heliconia – and a Panama hat tree. The bearded fig tree is the real star of the gardens, but there are plenty of other highlights, including a bank of frangipani, rose of Sharon trees, superb cycads and a *Bombax ellipticum*, also known as the shaving brush tree for the large pink-bristled flower it produces. At the lower end of the trail is the Queen Ingrid Palm Garden.

Beyond the gardens the road continues to the seafront and the *Atlantis Hotel* (see p.741), a slightly faded and very easy-going place overlooking **Tent Bay**. Built in the 1880s, this was one of the first hotels to be put up outside Bridgetown and, though there's not a great deal to do, the place offers an excellent buffet lunch.

Bathsheba

A kilometre or so north of Andromeda you'll reach a crossroads; the east coast road continues straight on, a left takes you towards Hackleton's Cliff (see above), while a right drops you down into **BATHSHEBA**. Picturesque, easy-going and washed by Atlantic breezes, this has long been a favoured resort for Bajans, though surprisingly few tourists make it up here. Small holiday homes and the odd rum shop line the roadside as it runs along beside the sea.

If the bay here looks familiar, it's because this is one of the most painted landscapes in Barbados. Also known as the "**soup bowl**", because of the crashing surf that comes racing in here pretty much all year round, the area is popular with surfers who stage annual tournaments. Unfortunately, the currents mean that it's not a good place to swim, but the wide brown beach is attractive here and an old pathway runs north and south if you fancy a walk.

Eating

For lunch or dinner, you can't go wrong at the *Round House Inn* (daily 11.30am–2.30pm & 6–10pm; ☎246/433-9678), which offers **top-quality cooking** and a casual, family atmosphere, halfway down the steep hill that plunges to Bathsheba Bay. The lunch and dinner menus are similar – offering dishes like blackened snapper for around B$35 – but you can also get sandwiches and salads at lunchtime for B$14 and up. There's an ocean view and you can sit indoors or on the verandah. It's also pretty much the only place to find regular live music in the area, with a decent jazz or reggae band on Tuesday and Saturday nights. The other top-notch restaurant in the area is slightly harder to find but well worth the effort; *Naniki* (☎246/433-1300, Tues–Sun lunch noon–3pm), in the nearby village of Suriname, is a delightful place offering starters like grilled chicken salad with curry and mango dressing and mains like grilled snapper or mock duck with lentils (B$28–32).

St Vincent and the Grenadines

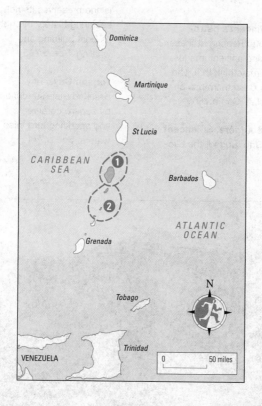

St Vincent and the Grenadines highlights

✳ **Inter-island ferries** A great way to see all the islands and surrounding ocean – although only recommended when the seas are calm. See p.751

✳ **St Vincent's petroglyphs** Peering at these striking ancient images, you may think that whoever drew them has only just left. See p.760

✳ **La Soufrière, St Vincent** Though rugged, the two-hour strenuous trek up to the peak of this active volcano is well worth the effort. See p.761

✳ **Bequia** Besides glorious beaches, this laid-back island preserves its rich seafaring history through its boat building and whaling. See p.765

✳ **Tobago Cays** Tiny deserted islets surrounded by superb coral reefs and sparkling turquoise waters. See p.771

△ La Soufrière, St Vincent

Introduction and basics

Situated about one hundred miles west of Barbados, and nestled between St Lucia to the north and Grenada to the south, the string of islands known collectively as **St Vincent and the Grenadines** may be physically close together, but vary enormously in character, terrain and appeal.

The northernmost of the islands is the mountainous St Vincent, which, although far less visited than other large Caribbean islands, is the main centre of the area's activity. As well as exploring St Vincent's two distinct coastlines – the rugged windward side and the gentle leeward side – and lush, interior hiking trails, don't miss the opportunity to spend time on the tiny isle of Bequia. Just a short ferry ride away, this yachters' haven is also an increasingly popular holiday destination that boasts shimmering beaches and a fascinating seafaring history. The less developed and less populated islands of Canouan, Mayreau and Union are all easily reachable by ferry and, despite the growing dominance of large resorts, still offer a taste of the unspoiled Caribbean, while Mustique, an island hideaway of the rich and famous, makes for an affordable day-trip of swimming and snorkelling, though expect to part with a good deal of money if you plan to stay overnight.

The uninhabited national park of the Tobago Cays, a cluster of islets which form the eastern point of a triangle between Union Island and Mayreau, are surrounded by coral reefs and unbelievably aquamarine waters, and collectively make an excellent excursion from nearby islands.

Where to go

No doubt the highlight of any trip to St Vincent and the Grenadines is making the strenuous trek through **St Vincent's lush rainforest** and volcanic ridges to the rim of **La Soufrière**, St Vincent's active volcano in the north of the island. Beyond St Vincent, although the more than thirty islands that make up St Vincent and the Grenadines are becoming increasingly affected by tourism, they are still a superb destination for adventurous sun-seekers, snorkellers, divers and yachters. Particularly worthwhile destinations include the turquoise waters of the **Tobago Cays**, offering superb diving, snorkelling and windsurfing, and the delightful island of **Bequia**, whose relaxed pace of life and seafaring ways warrant a longer stay than the size of the island might suggest.

When to go

As in much of the Caribbean the best time to visit St Vincent and the Grenadines is during the **winter** – roughly January to May – when the tropical heat is tempered by cooling trade winds and rainfall is minimal. August to October is **hurricane season**, also the island's wettest season, and although the region was badly affected by Hurricane Ivan in 2004, such occurrences are rare, and the threat of hurricanes need not be a deterrent from visiting at this time of year.

Arrival

Flights touch down on St Vincent at E.T. Joshua Airport in Arnos Vale, roughly 1.5 miles southeast of the capital of Kingstown. The airport does not receive international flights from outside the Caribbean, so you'll need to fly first to Barbados, Grenada, Martinique, St Lucia, Puerto Rico or Trinidad and make a connection there. It's also possible to travel to Union Island from Carriacou (one of Grenada's islands) by **boat** – see box on p.749 for details.

Information, websites and maps

There are four **tourist information centres** in the country. The main one is situated at

ST VINCENT AND THE GRENADINES

St Vincent

Port
Elizabeth
Bequia

CARIBBEAN
SEA

Mustique

Canouan

Union
Island

Mayreau

Tobago Cays

THE GRENADINES

Fancy
Commantawana Bay

Owia Salt
Pond
Sandy Bay

Falls of
Baleine

Soufrière
(1219m)

La Soufrière

Larikai Bay

Richmond
Beach
Richmond

Chateaubelair
Troumaka

Georgetown

Black
Point
Tunnel

St Vincent

Colonarie

Wallilabou Bay

Wallia Bou Falls

Barrouallie

Vermont
Nature Trails

Colonarie
Bay

Montreal
Gardens

Biabou

Grant's Bay

Layou

Layou Bay

Emerald Valley
Hotel & Casino

Buccament
Bay

Mesopotamia

Campden Park Bay

Kingstown

Argyle

Fort Charlotte

E T Joshua
Airport

Vigie Hwy

Indian Bay
Villa Beach
Young Island
Fort Duvernette Island

Milligan Cay

ACCOMMODATION

Beachcombers	H
The Cobblestone Inn	C
New Haddon Hotel	D
The New Montrose Hotel	B
Paradise Inn	G
Petit Byahaut	A
Rosewood Apartment Hotel	F
Roy's Inn	E
Young Island Resort	I

N

0   2 miles

the cruise ship terminal in Kingstown, St Vincent; to access the terminal you will be required to show photo identification at a security check-point. There is also an information desk inside E.T. Joshua Airport and tourist centres on Bequia (see p.762) and Union Island (see p.770).

You can pick up **maps** of St Vincent and most of the Grenadines at the main tourist information centre in Kingstown. A detailed Ordnance Survey map of St Vincent is also available from tourist information and some tourist-oriented shops.

Money and costs

The official currency of St Vincent and the Grenadines is the **Eastern Caribbean dollar** (EC$), although the US dollar is also widely accepted, as are major credit cards,

Emergency numbers

Police, fire and **coastguard** ☎999
Police stations Kingstown ☎784/457-1211, Bequia ☎784/458-3350

The Jasper

An economical way to travel between Union Island and Grenada's Carriacou is via **The Jasper**, a passenger and cargo boat that operates on Mondays and Thursdays, leaving from the jetty at Ashton village on Union Island for Carriacou at 6.30am and departing Hillsborough on Carriacou for the return journey to Union Island at 12.30pm. The trip takes approximately **one hour** and the **fare** is EC$15 one-way. To travel between the two islands you must go through **immigration**, either on Carriacou at the end of the Hillsborough jetty or on Union Island at the airport. It is important to keep in mind that immigration on Union Island will not be open when *The Jasper* leaves at 6.30am and you will need to clear immigration before 4.00pm on the previous day.

On Union Island the **bus fare** from Ashton to the airport is EC$3 and a bus will be waiting when *The Jasper* docks to transfer passengers to the airport in order to go through immigration. If you are leaving on the 6.30am boat, it is a good idea to book a taxi to Ashton rather than rely on the bus service at this time.

Be aware that *The Jasper* is sometimes a fairly large motor-powered vessel and on other occasions a small, wooden boat that has seen better days and which runs on both motor power and under sail, so expect an exhilarating ride even when the sea looks calm. As well, departure can be delayed if the boat is waiting for cargo. If you're adventurous and have good sea legs, *The Jasper* can be fun – if not take a plane.

---

at hotels and restaurants and by car rental agencies and dive and tour companies. The EC$ is divided into 100 cents. Notes come in denominations of 5, 10, 20, 50 and 100 EC dollars; coins in 1, 2, 5, 10 and 25 cents. At the time of writing, the **exchange rate** was roughly EC$2.70 to US$1.

There are plenty of **banks** on St Vincent, including Barclays Bank and Scotiabank on Halifax Street in Kingstown, both of which have ATMs. E.T. Joshua Airport has an **exchange bureau** which is open 8am–noon and 3–5pm on weekdays. There are also two banks on Bequia and a branch of the National Commercial Bank on Canouan and Union Island; all have ATMs. **Banking hours** are generally Monday to Thursday 9am–3pm and Friday 9am–5pm; however, some banks close at 1pm.

Hotels and restaurants will automatically add a 7 percent **government tax** and 10 percent **service charge** to your bill. Tipping is at your discretion, but not expected.

In St Vincent and the Grenadines a **departure tax** of EC$40 applies to stays longer than 24 hours.

Getting around

Details on **transport** to specific islands is covered in the individual island sections. Islands without bus services however are small enough to walk around.

19

By bus

Buses are small minivans that operate on the larger islands. On St Vincent, buses run from the bus terminal in Kingstown, next to the New Tokyo Fishmarket, from 6am to 8pm, although service is much less frequent on Sundays than during the rest of the week. The terminal is organized into sections marked Leeward, Windward or Kingstown. Ask any driver if you're not sure which one you want.

Although buses pack in as many people as possible, play loud music and drive very fast around the steep mountain roads, they are safe, fun and heavily used by locals. Though there are frequent **bus stops**, buses can be flagged down anywhere along the route – you'll always know when one is around by their incessant use of the horn. Let the conductor know when you want to get off and pay as you leave. Fares from Kingstown work out to around EC$1 to the airport, EC$1.50 to Villa Beach, EC$3 to Argyle and

Websites

⊛ **www.grenadines.net**
This regularly updated, comprehensive site features summaries of each island, articles, travel tips and promotions.

⊛ **www.heraldsvg.com**
Check this site for the online version of St Vincent and the Grenadine's daily newspaper, *The Herald*.

⊛ **www.svghotels.com**
Full of practical information on accommodation, transport, holidays and festivals, this site of the SVG Hotel and Tourism Association is a useful place to research the region before a visit.

⊛ **www.nbcsvg.com**
Listen to local news and sports programmes on the website of the National Broadcasting Corporation for St Vincent and the Grenadines.

⊛ **www.svgtourism.com**
This official site of the SVG Ministry of Tourism and Culture contains a wealth of information on each island, things to do, year-round events and the country's history.

EC$2 to Buccament. Similar bus services run on Bequia (see p.762) and Union Island (see p.770).

By car

To **rent a car** you'll need a local driving permit, available for EC$75 in Kingstown, either from the police station on Bay Street or from the Licensing Authority on Halifax Street (Mon–Fri 9am–3pm). If you have an International Driving Licence, you must get it stamped at the police station.

Avis (☏ 784/457-2929) is the only international car rental company on the islands and has offices at E.T. Joshua Airport, but there are plenty of local agencies, including Rent & Drive (☏ 784/457-5601, ⓔ rentanddrive@vincysurf.com), which also rents scooters; Ben's Auto Rentals (☏ 784/456-2907), who rent jeeps; and David's Auto Clinic (☏ 784/456-4026, ⓔ dacl761@hotmail.com). Remember that driving is on the left-hand side.

Prices range from EC$130–170 per day and there is little difference between local and international firms.

By taxi

Taxis are plentiful on St Vincent and tout aggressively for business around the jetty and waterfront area of Kingstown. Fares are regulated but there are no meters, so be sure to agree on a price before you get into the

car. Fares are raised for early morning and late night journeys.

There are taxi ranks in Kingstown on the corner of Upper Bay Street and South River Road and opposite the *Courts* store on Upper Bay Street, while main taxi companies include Sam's Taxi and Tours (☏ 784/456-4338) or Belford Taxis (☏ 784/457-9190). Fares from Kingstown to the airport cost about EC$20 and from the airport to Villa Beach EC$20.

By scooter and bike

Scooters can be rented from Trotmans Dept (☏ 784/482-9498) for EC$80 per day or EC$470 per week or Rent & Drive (see above). Sailor Cycles on Middle Street in Kingstown (☏ 784/457-1274) rents **bikes** for around EC$20 per day.

By boat

A **ferry** ride is a wonderful way to see the islands – especially if you don't want to stay at them all – and makes for the cheapest "cruise" by far. The MV *Barracuda* and MV *Gem Star* both ply the glorious waters of the Caribbean between St Vincent, Canouan, Mayreau and Union Island. (Be sure to keep your eyes peeled for flying fish, whales and dolphins.) From St Vincent expect to pay, EC$20 to Canouan, EC$25 to Mayreau and EC$30 to Union Island. Ferries also run frequently between Kingstown and Bequia

MVs Barracuda and Gem Star ferry schedule

MV Barracuda
St Vincent to Canouan, Mayreau and Union Island
Monday, Thursday and Saturday
Departs   St Vincent at 10.30am
              Canouan 2pm
              Mayreau 3.25pm
Arrives at Union Island at 3.45pm.
From Union Island to St Vincent
Tuesdays and Fridays
Departs   Union Island 6.30am
              Mayreau 7.30am
              Canouan 8.45am
Arrives at St Vincent at noon.

MV Gem Star
St Vincent to Canouan and Union Island
Tuesdays and Fridays
Departs St Vincent 11.00am
              Canouan, 2.30pm
Arrives at Union Island at 4.15pm
From Union Island to Canouan and St Vincent
Wednesdays and Saturdays
Departs Union Island 7.30am
              Canouan 8.30am
Arrives at St Vincent at noon.

As both of these ferry services are susceptible to delays, alterations and cancellations, always check with either a tourist information centre or the port authority before travel, or call the ferry service directly on ☎784/526-1158.

19

– see p.762 for details – and less frequently to Mustique (see p.768).

To reach some of the smaller, uninhabited islands, yacht charters are the only option – see individual island sections for details.

By plane

Planes are a fast, convenient and relatively inexpensive option for travelling between islands. Sample one-way fares from St Vincent are EC$65 to Mustique, EC$80 to Canouan, and EC$85 to Union Island. Caribbean Star (ⓦwww.flycaribbeanstar. com), LIAT (ⓦwww.liatairline.com), SVG Airways (ⓦwww.svgair.com), and Mustique Airways (ⓦwww.mustique.com) all provide frequent services. Tickets can be purchased at any of the island's airports, and LIAT and Caribbean Star both have agents on Halifax Street, Kingstown, while Universal Travel on Upper Bay Street, Kingstown (☎784/457-

2779), is efficient in at organizing inter-island flights.

Accommodation

St Vincent and the Grenadines offer a wide range of **accommodation**, from small hotels, guesthouses and self-catering apartments to large and at times luxurious beach resorts. **Prices** vary almost as much as the type of accommodation. Most hotels, especially those that cater for business travellers, have year-round rates, while others drop their prices during summer months (mid-April to mid-December), though not by a lot. Finding a place to stay usually isn't hard, but during the winter months it's wise to **book ahead**.

Camping isn't an option here as there are no campsites in St Vincent and the Grenadines and camping itself is not encouraged.

Food and drink

St Vincent grows a variety of fruit and vegetables, among them oranges, breadfruit and avocado. The island also produces 90 percent of the world's supply of **arrowroot**, a plant whose starch is used in cooking and in making glossy computer paper. Fresh **seafood** is abundant on the islands, ranging from lobster to flying fish, with conch being particularly common.

While larger restaurants generally serve a mix of West Indian and international cuisine, you will almost always find **rotis**, curries and saltfish on offer. Vegetarians are well catered for at most large cafés and restaurants, although smaller towns and islands may not be as amenable.

The beer of choice is **Hairoun** (the Carib name for St Vincent), brewed at the St Vincent Brewery in Kingstown, along with Guinness and a selection of popular soft drinks, such as ginger beer, tonic and soda water.

When dining out, bear in mind that **prices** generally increase after 7pm when most establishments switch to their more expensive dinner menus, and the number of inexpensive dining options dwindles significantly.

Mail and communications

The main **post office** is situated on Halifax Street in Kingstown (Mon–Fri 8.30am–3pm, Sat 8.30–11.30am). There are also branches in smaller communities on St Vincent, as well as on the other islands; in addition many hotels will sell stamps and post letters.

Coin- and card-operated **phones** can be found on all the islands, and you can buy cards from Cable & Wireless on Halifax Street in St Vincent, as well as from tourist information centres and shops.

Kingstown has numerous **Internet cafés**, and others can be found throughout the Grenadines.

The **country code** for St Vincent and the Grenadines is ☎784.

Opening hours, holidays and festivals

Business hours are generally Monday to Friday 8am–noon and 1–4pm and Saturday 8am–noon, although times can vary from store to store.

Aside from the public holidays listed on p.60, St Vincent and the Grenadines celebrate **National Heroes' Day** on March 14, **Caricom Day** on the second Monday in July, **August Monday** on the first Monday in August and **Independence Day** on October 27.

The following are a selection of the major festivals on the islands. St Vincent's **Carnival**, known as Vincy Mas, is usually held on the second Tuesday of July, although festivities begin at the end of June. Like other carnivals, Vincy Mas brings the whole island onto the streets to party with parades, vibrant costumes and calypso and steelband music. At the end of January there is also a **Blues Festival** that attracts international entertainers to St Vincent, Bequia and Mustique. Bequia hosts an **Easter Regatta**, while Union Island annually celebrates **Easterval**, a three-day festival of boat races, sports games and calypso music. Canouan's **Regatta** occurs at the end of May.

Outdoor activities

St Vincent and the Grenadines' **volcanic features** and **coral reefs** make their underwater topography ideal for diving. Breathtaking walls and spectacular drop-offs combined with large reefs and shallow coral gardens provide first-class day and night dives. Top sites include those around the coastlines of the larger islands, or the spectacular coral reefs of the Tobago Cays, reached on day-trips.

A large network of **hiking trails** weaves through St Vincent's rugged, mountainous interior; though you can follow them on your own, you'll be better off hiring a guide. The other islands are so small that walking is the easiest way to get around, but be wary of walking in the midday sun and take plenty of water.

19

History

Prior to European contact, the history of St Vincent and the Grenadines is hard to distinguish from that of the rest of the Eastern Caribbean. The first known inhabitants, the **Ciboneys**, were displaced by the **Arawaks** about 2000 years ago, who were in turn swept out of the territory by the **Caribs** a thousand years later. It is only when the history of the Caribs collides with that of the later arrivals (both European and African) that the history of these islands becomes distinct.

St Vincent was once densely populated, especially after it became a refuge for Caribs fleeing European control of other islands. Their numbers, combined with their ferocity, helped to repulse all European attempts to establish a foothold on the island. While all Europeans were resisted, the most virulent hatred was saved for the British, who were presumptuous enough to grant the rights to St Vincent lands to their subjects. In the end, it was Britain's rival, France, who was allowed to form the first settlement in the early eighteenth century. By this time, the Grenadines (called Los Pajaros, or The Birds, by early Spanish sailors) had all been colonized and converted into plantation economies worked by slaves, while the native populations were eliminated, removed or marginalized.

In 1675, some years before the French settlement was established, a Dutch slave ship sank in the channel between Bequia and St Vincent. The crew and a large number of slaves perished, but many slaves managed to swim ashore and were accepted by the Caribs, forming one large community. However, within a couple generations, division emerged and the Caribs divided along racial lines: the Black Caribs, descendants of the slave-ship survivors, and Yellow Caribs, who were of strictly native heritage. European influence increased and plantations flourished, and in 1783 Britain was granted sole control of St Vincent as part of the Treaty of Paris, which officially ended the American Revolutionary War.

In 1795 French radical **Victor Hugues** instigated a revolt that resulted in the Yellow Caribs, led by **Chief Duvallier**, and the Black Caribs, led by **Joseph Chatoyer**, sweeping across the island, burning plantations and killing settlers in their wake. Chatoyer, convinced he could not be killed by another mortal, challenged the British commander, Alexander Leith, to a duel and was killed (though under mysterious circumstances).

A year later, Carib resistance was finally crushed. Most of the surviving Caribs, some 5000, were shipped to the island of Roaton, off the coast of Honduras, and the few that were allowed to remain were settled in the northeast tip of the island at Sandy Bay. The British soon set up a plantation economy and imported 18,000 African slaves to support it. When **slavery** was abolished in 1834, the freed slaves turned to small-plot farming, and European immigrant labour was brought in to replace them on the plantations.

However, this more expensive workforce, combined with the fact that cane was being replaced by **beet** as a main source of sugar, led to the decline of the plantation system throughout the region. What economy and politics had started, nature finished. In 1812, **La Soufrière**, a volcano in the north of St Vincent, erupted producing major explosions which destroyed coffee and cotton crops. Another major eruption in 1902 killed 2000 people, devastated much of the northern end of the island and was the final death knell of the island's plantation economy. Nature has played its part ever since. An eruption in 1979 (the year St Vincent and the Grenadines gained independence) led to the evacuation of 20,000 people and destroyed crops and land, and hurricanes in 1980, 1986 and the notorious Hurricane Ivan in 2004 all damaged the agricultural industry.

Following anti-government protests in 2000, general elections were brought forward from 2003 to 2001. The long-time opposition Unity Labour Party won in a landslide victory ending almost 17 years of New Democratic Party rule under James Mitchell.

Known to many Vincentians as 'Comrade Ralph', the current prime minister Ralph Gonsalves has started to implement an ambitious programme of social reform aimed at reducing poverty and the county's high unemployment rate.

19.1

St Vincent

Although some typical golden Caribbean beaches are to be found in **ST VINCENT**, the island is famous for its black stretches of volcanic sand, dotted along its entire coastline. The Leeward (western) side of the island is characterized by secluded coastal valleys and fishing villages, while the dramatic Windward (eastern) side, lined with windswept beaches, is pounded by the waves of the Atlantic Ocean.

Despite these enviable assets, the main reason to visit lies more in the mountainous interior, which rises to an impressive 4048ft at **La Soufrière,** an active volcano that last erupted in 1979. Running through the region is a network of tranquil hiking trails rich with wildlife.

Whether you choose to lie on the beach, exert yourself outdoors, or try a mixture of both, the island is small enough to take in the full range of activities over just a few days. The best place to start is **Kingstown**, the charming capital, which also makes a good starting if you plan to hop around St Vincent's Grenadine islands or don't want to stay in expensive resort accommodation. The main tourist areas of **Villa Beach** and **Indian Bay** and the luxury resort of **Young Island** have the most popular beaches, though more appealing beaches lie in the more remote parts of the island.

Kingstown and the beach resorts

Situated in a sheltered bay on the southwest tip of St Vincent, the hardworking harbour town of **Kingstown** is the island's commercial hub. On weekdays the town moves at a frantic pace, especially around the bustling jetty, bus station and fish market. The heat here can be fierce as sea breezes barely penetrate the compact, one-way streets, lined with warehouses and dense with human and commercial traffic. Though breathtaking from a distance, Kingstown's harbour reveals the grubbiness of an active port city on closer inspection. There's not much to see along the industrial waterfront, but this matters little as the town's main appeal lies in its entertaining **streets**. Dressed in pristine white shirts and gloves, traffic officers direct vehicles through the narrow roads lending an unexpected air of formality to this energetic, but laid-back town where tourists are barely noticed by the busy locals. Things slow down considerably in the evenings, however, when Kingstown is a shadow of its busy weekday self, and on Saturday afternoons and Sundays when the town lies in slumber.

Not far away are the major beach resort options on the island, **Villa Beach** and **Indian Bay**, though neither are as good a choice as the **Grenadine islands** which are within easy reach of Kingstown.

Accommodation

Kingstown and the Villa Beach area hold St Vincent's highest concentration of **accommodation** options, and may well be where you stay regardless of what area on the island you decide to visit – the options are better here than anywhere else. If you're looking for a real splurge, you can try the lone resort on **Young Island**, just offshore.

Kingstown

The Cobblestone Inn Upper Bay Street ☎784/456-1937, ⓦwww.thecobblestoneinn.com. Housed in a restored sugar warehouse, this gem of a hotel, with its cobblestone walkways and arches, is a tranquil haven. The comfortable rooms are individually decorated and come with all the amenities. ❸

New Haddon Hotel McKies Hill ☎784/456-1897, ⓦwww.newhaddonhotel.com. This charming, rambling hotel on the outskirts of Kingstown offers pleasant rooms and self-contained apartments, both with modern amenities. The on-site *Mango Tree* restaurant, resplendent in polished oak and local stone, serves fine food and fantastic cocktails. ❺–❼

The New Montrose Hotel New Montrose ☎784/457-0172, ⓦwww.newmontrosehotel.com. Modern apartment-hotel on the Leeward Highway bus route, near the botanical gardens. All rooms have cable TV, private balcony and kitchenette; there is also a bar and restaurant on site. ❹

Roy's Inn PO Box 2500 ☎784/456-2100, ⓦwww.roysinnsvg.com. Situated between Kingstown and the airport, this modern elegant hotel boasts fabulous views of the city and Caribbean Sea beyond. The rooms and suites are spacious and all have their own private verandahs. Additional facilities include a swimming pool, fitness centre, beauty salon and good restaurant and bar. ❺–❻

Villa Beach

Beachcombers ☎784/458-4283, ⓦwww.beachcombershotel.com. Lovely, family-run place set in attractive gardens on the edge of Villa Beach and made up of colourfully decorated little villas with en-suite bathrooms and patios. There's a health and beauty spa on site, as well as a pool, and a bar and restaurant overlooking the beach. Rates include Continental breakfast. ❹–❻

Paradise Inn ☎784/457-4795, ⓕ457-4221, ⓦwww.paradiseinnsvg.com. Attractive, budget hotel near Villa and Indian beaches with self-catering apartments or rooms with private, ocean-facing balconies and air conditioning. ❹

Rosewood Apartment Hotel ☎784/457-5051, ⓦwww.rosewoodsvg.com. Friendly new hotel, overlooking Villa Bay and just a few minutes from the beach, with a bus stop for Kingstown at the end of the drive. The colourful rooms come with private patios, and most have full kitchenette – a few cheaper rooms (❸) only have a fridge and kettle. ❹

Young Island

Young Island Resort ☎784/458-4826, ⓕ457-4567, ⓦwww.youngisland.com. The most romantic and expensive place to stay on the island, consisting of luxury cottages each with ocean view, private terrace and fresh fruit and flowers. There's also a pool, tennis courts and a white-sand beach outfitted with sun loungers and hammocks. Meals at the on-site restaurant are inventive and elegantly served. ❾

The Town

Starting at the cruise ship terminal adjacent to the port on the east side of town you'll find the **tourist information centre** (Mon–Fri 8am–4pm; ☎784/457-1502, ⓦwww.svgtourism.com). There's little to see in this area, and the best way to start exploring the town is to head west to Upper Bay Street, which runs parallel to the sea, where you'll find the vibrant two-storey **market** (Mon–Sat 8am–4pm), crammed with stalls selling everything from fresh produce and local arts and crafts to toiletries and souvenirs. Just as busy, but twice as smelly, is the **Little Tokyo Fish Market** on the waterfront side of the road next to the bus station. This distinctive landmark is however, in the process of being replaced by a new fish market, funded by Japanese aid money, which, at the time of writing, is under construction next door.

Heading west from the market's north end, Grenville Street turns into Tyrrel Street at North River Road, where you will find the **St George's Anglican Cathedral**, a traditional Georgian design with airy vaulted ceilings and exquisite stained glass. A window depicting an angel dressed in red robes was originally commissioned by Queen Victoria for London's St Paul's Cathedral; it was later bestowed as a gift to the church's bishop after the queen deemed it inappropriate for angels to wear anything but white. No visit to Kingstown is complete without a visit to the striking **St Mary's Roman Catholic Cathedral**, which stands across the street from its Anglican counterpart. Built in 1823, the cathedral was designed by local Belgian Benedictine Dom Charles Verbeke, and constructed from dark volcanic sand bricks in an eclectic mix of architectural styles including Romanesque, Moorish and Georgian.

A ten-minute walk or a short bus ride northwest along the main road towards the Leeward Highway brings you to Kingstown's superb **Botanical Gardens** (daily dawn to dusk; free), an immaculately kept twenty-acre oasis and delightful place to wander or simply relax on a bench. Founded in 1765, the gardens are the oldest of their kind in the western hemisphere, and even include a 50ft breadfruit tree grown from one of the original plants introduced here by Captain Bligh in 1793. Signs posted along an educational trail near the entrance explain how to identify various species of plant, and along the trail you'll spy the usual palm, bamboo, coconut and cashew trees, as well as more unusual flora such as custard apple and miraculous trees. There's also a small aviary on the grounds where St Vincent parrots are bred to help keep them from extinction. Though the gardens are free, expect to be stopped by a "guide" at the entrance who will ask you to pay an EC$3 entrance fee, plus a tip, for showing you around.

A recent addition to the gardens is a small **museum** dedicated to the life and work of local master surgeon Dr Cecil Cyrus, (Mon–Fri 9.30am–5pm, Sat 9am–1pm; EC$10). A working hospital until 2000, this lovingly created museum also features some items of local historical interest such as photographs of La Soufrière's eruptions in 1902 and 1979, some Carib artefacts, and photos and specimens collected by the doctor, including some of his medical innovations and squash exploits.

If you fancy a panoramic view of Kingstown and the south Grenadines, head for **Fort Charlotte**, situated on a 636ft-high ridge to the west of the town. Built by the British to protect the harbour from the French and completed in 1806, the fort holds a collection of colourful Lindsay Prescott paintings depicting scenes from Black Carib history. Exhibited in the small museum inside the old barracks, they are reason alone to visit this beautiful historic building. Fort Charlotte is about an hour's walk from Kingstown – head west along Tyrrell Street which then becomes the Fort Charlotte road, or for the less energetic, hop on a bus at any point along the route that connects it with Kingstown and ask the bus conductor for directions.

Villa Beach and Indian Bay

Four miles east of Kingstown is St Vincent's main resort area, a two-mile stretch of coast encompassing Villa Beach and Indian Bay and frequented by yachters, tourists and locals alike.

As Caribbean beaches go, **Villa Beach** is disappointingly shabby and dominated by a handful of average resorts and punctuated by the jetty that serves the far more

Young and Fort Duvernette islands

The two islands off Villa Beach – **Young Island** and **Fort Duvernette Island** – make for an interesting excursion. The private, 35-acre Young Island is an exclusive resort, (see opposite) once hired in its entirety by Bill Gates, and its gardens are a national wildlife reserve. The long golden beach offers a stark contrast to the rest of the island's lush, green foliage, and the whole place seems to float above the waters of the bay. If you want to visit the island without staying overnight, you will need to phone the resort for permission – dial 210 on the phone situated at the end of the jetty on Villa Beach. Water taxis to Young Island leave from the jetty and cost EC$2 one-way.

Tiny Fort Duvernette Island, whose steep cliffs rise to 250ft above sea level, offers splendid views of the Grenadines, as well as a crumbling fort, complete with original 24-pound guns and an eight-inch mortar. Built at the beginning of the nineteenth century to defend Calliaqua Bay from European rivals, the fort is unsafe and caution is advised when exploring its remains. Catch a water taxi from Young Island to Fort Duvernette Island and arrange a pick-up time with the driver for the return trip. The round-trip fare is approximately EC$20.

attractive **Young Island** which sits just offshore. Although well used, the beach is not up to the quality of other, more remote beaches on the island; its thin strip of sand is ruined by two storm drains that continuously pour water into the sea. Equally unsightly are the graffiti-covered rocks separating the beach from adjacent **Indian Bay**; the latter is cleaner, more popular with locals and excellent for snorkelling. This beach is also frequented by local vendors selling drinks and snacks at a fraction of the price of anything you'll find at Villa.

Buses from Kingstown drop passengers off at the end of the short road leading down to the jetty on Villa Beach. To reach Indian Bay ask to be dropped off at the narrow path that leads down to this beach just before the Villa Beach stop.

Eating and drinking

Eating options on the island are surprisingly limited, with again the most variety around Kingstown and Villa Beach. Prices tend to be lower in Kingstown than in Villa Beach, where you can expect to pay at least twice as much for food and drink as anywhere else on the island. In addition, many Villa Beach establishments add a 15 percent service charge, instead of the usual 10 percent. Bear in mind that most restaurants in Kingstown close on Sunday. Bars in Kingstown are mainly stalls frequented by locals.

Kingstown

Basil's Bar and Restaurant Upper Bay Street ☎784/457-2713. One of the most popular bars in Kingstown, *Basil's* has a tasty menu including a buffet lunch Mon–Fri for around EC$16, while the dinner menu features a range of local and international cuisine such as lobster in mornay sauce (EC$65). Closed Sun.

Bounty Restaurant Egmont Street ☎784/456-1776. This pleasant café overlooking the bustling heart of Kingstown doubles as a small art gallery and secondhand bookshop. It serves numerous breakfast options including saltfish and bake and fresh local fruit juices (from EC$8), and there are various rotis and curries for lunch.

Rainbow Palace Tyrrell Street (no phone). Very popular with the locals, this excellent eat-in or take-away restaurant and bar serves the best and cheapest rotis in town as well as a good selection of burgers, sandwiches and saltfish for EC$3–13.

The Roof Bar *The Cobblestones Inn* Upper Bay Street ☎784/456-1937. Open 7am–3pm this excellent, laid-back hotel bar and restaurant serves a good range of breakfast and lunch options including toasted sandwiches, salads, burgers and daily specials at reasonable prices.

Tony's Original Pizza Halifax Street and Grenville Street ☎784/457-2430. These two branches of the same pizza and burger joint with accompanying bar are very friendly, with upbeat music, and are among the few places for cheap food in the evening as their menus and prices remain the same all day (pizzas start from EC$30, burgers EC$6). Open daily though hours vary.

Villa Beach

Beachcombers Restaurant and Bar ☎784/458-4283. Open from 7am for breakfast and taking the last dinner order at 10pm, this attractive beachfront restaurant commands beautiful views of Young Island and the ocean beyond. Serving a varied range of local and international dishes, lunch prices range from EC$6 for soup to EC$12 for sandwiches and the dinner menu features main courses for around EC$40. A programme of special events spice up the atmosphere throughout the year including Halloween, Christmas and Carnival parties.

Lime Restaurant and Pub Villa Beach ☎784/458-4227. With a wall made up of lobster traps, fishing nets draped around the ceiling and even a mechanical singing fish in the ladies' toilet, the feel of the sea permeates this waterfront restaurant. The food is excellent and the pub menu at lunch features curries from EC$40. Reservations are required for dinner, when prices range from EC$62 for dolphin fillet to EC$86 for African black pepper steak. There is also a long cocktail and cigar menu.

The airport

Pizza Party Opposite the airport, Arnos Vale ☎784/456-4939. Located between Kingstown and Villa Beach, this popular fast-food restaurant has a menu of pizza, barbecued chicken and local dishes from EC$19. Cash only. Open daily 9am–11pm.

Nightlife and entertainment

Kingstown is the centre for island **nightlife**, such as it is. For official establishments, try *The Attic*, at Melville and Grenville streets (11am until late; EC$10–15 cover charge; ☎784/457-2559), which features a wide variety of music – live at weekends – and karaoke; it's also a decent and popular place to watch sports on the multi-screen TVs. Popular with yachters, *The Aquatic Club* (☎784/458-4205) at Villa Beach is loud and lively while, also at Villa, the open air *Chewee's Chill 'n' Grill* (☎784/456-6329) offers pool tables and a big-screen TV. The hotels in this area also often feature live entertainment in the evenings. Outside of these popular areas, *Buccama On the Bay* restaurant and bar (see p.761), is a favourite night out for both locals and visitors and host venue for the St Vincent Blues Festival at the end of January.

For more nightlife information, pick up the small weekly *What's On* guide produced by The SVG Hotel & Tourism Association and available at the tourist information centre.

Diving, sailing and island tours

Due to its volcanic origins, the underwater topography of St Vincent is breathtaking, and there is no shortage of **dive operators** on the island to help you explore it. Dive St Vincent, next to the Young Island jetty at Villa Beach (☎784/457-4928, ⓦwww.divestvincent.com), offers numerous dives, courses and packages, some of which include accommodation. Packages for seven days' accommodation and diving range from US$773 to US$2477 (the latter covers a stay at Young Island), depending on where you stay and the number of dives you make. They also organize an excellent snorkelling trip to the stunning 60ft Falls of Baleine (see p.761). Dive Fantasea, also based in Villa Beach (☎784/457-5560, ⓦwww.divefantasea.com), offer dive packages and run day and night dives for both beginners and experienced divers. They also operate Fantasea Tours, arranging one-day sailing and snorkelling trips to some of the Grenadine Islands, including Mustique and the Tobago Cays, for prices starting from US$70. In addition to diving packages starting at US$1170, Caribbean Fun Tours (☎784/456-5600, ⓦwww.caribbeanfuntours.com) organize luxury sailing packages around the Grenadines from US$2900 to US$4480 depending on time of year and length of trip, as well as one-day sailing tours and sunset cruises from US$20 per person.

One of the best ways to explore the island is on an organized tour, and most companies offer similar choices. For challenging, day-long hikes to La Soufrière, expect to pay US$65–125 (including lunch) depending on how extensive the tour is. For hikes to places like Trinity Falls, expect to pay US$65–70 including lunch, and about the same for a trip and swim at Owia Salt Lake. A light hike on the Vermont Nature Trails will cost $40–45, as will a scenic or historic tour of the island, again including lunch. Good options include the ecologically aware HazEco Tours (☎784/457-8634, ⓦwww.hazecotours.com) who offer a wide range of boat, jeep and hiking tours, and Baleine Tours (☎784/457-4089, ✉prosec@caribsurf.com) who organize various hiking and sightseeing trips.

The rest of the island

Most of the island's sights outside Kingstown and the main resort areas are accessible from the coastal highway that runs up both the island's **Leeward** and **Windward** coasts. However, except for St Vincent's southwest corner, where a few roads penetrate inland, St Vincent's mountainous **interior** can be reached only via walking trails, and in one case only by boat.

The Leeward coast

On the Leeward coast the road clings to the mountainside, with little to protect you from the steep drops, and runs as far as **Richmond Beach**. The drive will take you past lush valleys formerly the site of vast plantations but now dotted with small farms, black-sand beaches ideal for swimming and snorkelling, and peaceful communities many with beautiful old stone, sea-facing churches.

A half-hour drive or bus ride from Kingstown, **Buccament Bay** is reached by a short walk from the main road down a dirt track – marked by a signpost to *Buccama on the Bay* restaurant (see opposite). Small and secluded, this horseshoe beach is used more by local villagers than tourists. Gazing inland from the beach, past the fishing nets hung out to dry, is a stunning vista of rugged mountain peaks. The valley here is the site of a former sugar plantation; the cliffs that frame it feature some of St Vincent's ancient **petroglyphs**. As you walk along the dirt track towards the beach, you'll come across a sign on the left-hand side announcing the "Petroglyphs of Buccament". Although some of the fields in the area are fenced off and look like private land, visitors can walk up to the cliff face (watch out for the grazing cows along the way) to view a collection of evocative white etchings in the rock.

Less than a mile north of the pretty village of **Barrouallie**, with its quaint, ornately trimmed houses, is the tranquil beach of **Wallilabou**, famous for being transformed into the set of Jamaica's seventeenth-century Port Royal for the Hollywood swashbuckler *Pirates of the Caribbean*. Here you can explore the remains of the set and hang out at the *Waillilabou Anchorage*, a sea-facing bar and restaurant decked out in rusting suites of armour and maritime paraphernalia and home to models of the film's complete set. A number of local "guides", some of whom were extras in the film, hang around the bay and are happy to show you round and share their experiences. Expect to pay for their time, or be diplomatically firm if you want to explore alone. The idyllic surrounds here are also perfect for sunbathing and a dip in the ocean. While you are in the area, continue north for a mile on the inland side of the road to reach **Wallilabou Falls**, an attractive 13ft cascade of water where you can escape the heat by taking a refreshing swim.

Practicalities

If you are not staying in the main beach resorts or Kingstown, the Leeward coast offers the only other major facilities around. Situated about four miles north of Kingstown in a secluded bay reachable only by sea (transport provided), is the private and unique *Petit Byahaut* (℡784/457-7008, ✆www.petitbyahaut.com; ⑨). **Accommodation** comes in the form of five luxury huts, with screened bedrooms, decks and solar lighting, nestled into 50 acres of gardens and set against surrounding

The petroglyphs of St Vincent

The word **petroglyph** literally means drawings on stone, and although these striking white inscriptions on St Vincent have been attributed to the Ciboneys, Arawaks and Caribs, the identity of the people who created them is still disputed. Most petroglyphs, such as those at Layou, are deeply cut into hard andesite rock, but some are carved onto agglomerate, rock made from a mass of volcanic fragments such as those near Argyle and Buccament.

Although efforts are being made to make access easier, petroglyphs take a bit of hunting out. The most popular sites are at Buccament (see above), Layou, and Barrouallie on the Leeward coast. At Layou a cluster of them can be found near the river by the Bible Camp, on the main road to the north of the town; however, they are on private land and you'll need permission from the owner to see them (EC$5 per person; ℡784/458-7243). At Barrouallie, petroglyphs can be found in the yard of the local secondary school.

forested peaks. This is an excellent spot to hike, swim, dive, snorkel, sail and kayak, or simply sunbathe, and rates include some of these activities, plus day-trips, all meals and airport transfer. There is also a bar, games and library on site and five- and seven-night packages can be arranged.

Buccament Bay is where you'll find the best **place to eat** in all of St Vincent, *Buccama on the Bay* (☎784/456-7855, ⍟www.buccama.com). Reservations are required for dinner, when a three-course meal – fresh and delicious, prepared with produce from local farms – includes delicacies such as river lobster, crayfish and the best cheesecake in the Caribbean and costs just EC$70–80. The restaurant can be reached by bus from Kingstown; just ask to be dropped off at Buccament's main road and follow the signposted dirt track for about ten minutes down to the sea. A return taxi to Kingstown costs about EC$40.

The Windward coast

The highway on the Windward coast leads all the way up to the village of **Fancy**, at St Vincent's northern tip, and offers startling views of rugged coastline and sweeping beaches. Ten miles from Kingstown, along the Windward side, you will find the very antithesis of the expected Caribbean shoreline — the windswept beach of **Argyle**, a bleak and rocky stretch reminiscent of northern Scotland (no swimming is allowed here). To the west of Argyle spreads the rich fertile valley of **Mesopotamia**, where bananas, nutmeg, cocoa, coconuts and breadfruit all grow in abundance. Here and further north in the colourful **Montreal Gardens** (Dec–Aug Mon–Fri 9am–5pm; EC$5), the views of the river valleys and ocean are hard to match anywhere in the Caribbean.

Most buses travel only as far as **Georgetown**, halfway up the coast – check with the drivers and conductors at the bus station in Kingstown if you want to travel further up. To get to Georgetown you'll have to pass through the **Black Point Tunnel**, which was drilled by slave labour in 1815 to create a direct route for transporting sugar from the northern plantations to Kingstown. The 350ft tunnel was considered an engineering feat in its time and remains impressive today, especially as you can still see the old blast holes in the volcanic rock. The only other point of interest on this highway is the **Owia Salt Pond**, a short distance south of Fancy, near the village of Owia – home to the remaining descendants of the Black Caribs. The tidal pools, a popular spot with sightseeing tours, are sheltered from the rolling Atlantic by a huge wall of rock, and the cool, clean salt waters here are used by locals and visitors alike.

The interior

St Vincent's **interior** can only be explored by walking trails, which are not always well marked. The **Vermont Nature Trails** on the Leeward side, signposted about five miles from Kingstown, are one of the few places where you are likely to spot the endangered St Vincent parrot, a colourful bird recognizable by its pale head, blue tail and wing-tip feathers, and russet wings. Here the **Parrot Lookout trail** threads its way through lush rainforest, rising approximately 500ft, and you also stand a good chance of seeing hummingbirds, black hawks and green heron along the way. The trails begin near the top of Buccament Valley and pass picnic areas along the way.

Hiking is also excellent in the north of the island around the stunning peak of **La Soufrière**. The trail to the summit leads through fertile rainforest, banana plantations and volcanic ridges, and is a rigorous one: the ascent to the crater is approximately three miles and takes around two hours. The best way to explore this area is on an organized tour as the trail is not clearly marked, and guides can also point out features along the way (see p.759).

In the remote northwest tip, beyond the reach of the coastal highway, lie the breathtaking 60ft **Falls of Baleine**, where a swim in the large rock-lined pool is unforgettable and time spent in this stunning spot is well worth the trip. The falls are only reachable by organized tour (see p.759).

19

19.2

The Grenadines

T HE GRENADINES consist of 32 islands and cays, some of which are reachable by plane, but most only by boat. Each island has its own distinct character, whether its the exclusive decadence of **Mustique**, the rustic appeal of **Union**, the laid-back vibe of **Bequia** or the idyllic isolation of **Mayreau**.

Bequia

Though separated from St Vincent by a mere nine miles, **BEQUIA** (pronounced "beck-way"), the largest of the Grenadine islands with its aura of tranquillity and relaxed pace, feels light years away from frantic Kingstown. No visit to St Vincent and the Grenadines is complete without a visit to this seven-square-mile island, where the beaches are breathtaking and the inhabitants friendly. However, don't be fooled into thinking that there's little here to experience except a laid-back attitude and stunning scenery. Bequia also has a rich seafaring history from which time-honoured traditions, such as whaling and boat building, are still practised; it was the island's proximity to the migration path of the **humpback whale** that made it the most important whaling station in the area during the nineteenth and twentieth centuries.

Arrival, information and getting around

James F. Mitchell Airport, near the village of Paget Farm, is situated in the southwest of the island, approximately three miles from the capital of Port Elizabeth. **Ferries** run frequently, often three to four times daily, from Kingstown on St Vincent to Port Elizabeth, operated by *The Admiral* (☎784/458-3348) and *The Bequia Express* (☎784/458-3472). Journey time is an hour; cost is EC$15 one-way, EC$25 return if you travel with the same ferry line.

Brochures, leaflets and maps are available from the **tourist office** at the end of the ferry jetty in Port Elizabeth (Mon–Fri 8.30am–6pm, Sat 8.30am–2pm & Sun 8.30am-noon, closed on public holidays; ☎784/458-3286, ⊛www.bequiatourism.com).

Buses, or "dollar vans" as they are known, depart from the end of the ferry jetty in Port Elizabeth for points around the island. Service is frequent and efficient, but the island is so small and scenic that walking is the best way to explore most of it. Fares are EC$1–3 depending on how far you travel. **Taxis** are plentiful and wait under the almond trees of Port Elizabeth's waterfront. The fare from Port Elizabeth to the airport is EC$30 and to Friendship Bay EC$20. If you need to call for one ahead of time, try Bequia Car Rentals and Taxi Service (☎784/458-3349). **Water taxis** ply the waters around Port Elizabeth's Belmont Walkway and the nearby beaches. They are popular, easy to hail and a quick way to travel to the beach. A one-way fare from Port Elizabeth to Princess Margaret or Lower Bay beach is EC$15.

Accommodation

There is no shortage of **places to stay** on Bequia, where options vary from basic to luxury. The more expensive choices tend to be small hotels, full of character and

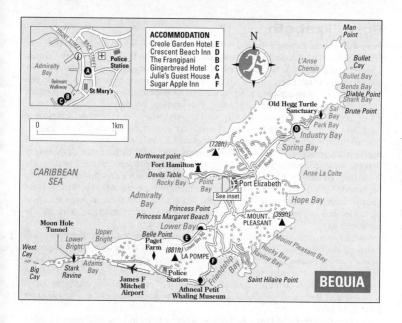

very comfortable. That said, most of the accommodation here is of a high quality and even the more budget options are excellent value for money. Although you'll find much of the accommodation concentrated around Port Elizabeth and Friendship Bay, there's also plenty throughout the island.

Creole Garden Hotel Lower Bay ☎784/458-3154 ⒲www.creolegarden.com. Nestled in tropical gardens on a hillside surrounding Lower Bay beach, this small family-run hotel offers basic rooms with ceiling fans, mosquito nets, private bathrooms and verandahs – all with sea views. Some rooms have fully equipped kitchenettes, and all are cheaper if booked by the week. There is also a good on-site bar, restaurant and beachside café. ❸–❹

Crescent Beach Inn Crescent Beach, near Industry Bay ☎784/458-3400. Situated in the northeast of the island near the Turtle Sanctuary, this secluded inn has pleasant rooms, and a bar and restaurant next door. Breakfast is included, and the beachside bar has table tennis and darts. Cash only. ❸

The Frangipani Belmont Walkway, Port Elizabeth ☎784/458-3255, ⒲www.frangipani.net. This old family home has been converted into a hotel and is a truly special place to stay, for both location and atmosphere. The five basic rooms in the main house have mosquito nets over the beds and shared showers, toilets and balcony, while the cottage-like units in the back come with king-size beds and private bathrooms. An excellent and

popular waterfront bar and restaurant is on site, as well as a tennis court for guests. ❸–❻

Gingerbread Hotel Belmont Walkway, Port Elizabeth ☎784/458-3800, ⒲www.gingerbreadhotel.com. This hotel, with its ornate trimmings does look like it should be made out of gingerbread. Luxurious suites, some with four-poster beds, include kitchen, private bathroom, and a large porch overlooking Admiralty Bay. The hotel arranges tennis, kayaking, windsurfing and scuba diving for guests as well as excursions to nearby islands. ❺–❼

Julie's Guest House Port Elizabeth ☎784/458-3304, ⒠julies@caribsurf.com. Situated on the main street near the jetty, an old wooden boarding house with simple, comfortable rooms with showers, toilets and fans. A bar, restaurant and laundry service is on the first floor. ❸

Sugar Apple Inn Friendship Bay ☎784/457-3148, ⒲www.sugarappleinn.com. Located on the opposite side of the island from Port Elizabeth, near the little village of La Pompe, and set in private gardens, these spacious, individually decorated apartments come with full kitchen and panoramic views of the beach – just a five-minute walk away. ❹

Port Elizabeth

Port Elizabeth, Bequia's main town, is nestled deep inside **Admiralty Bay**, the island's large natural harbour and favourite stop for yachters from all over the world. This relaxed little town has lost none of its lively Caribbean character, despite cosmopolitan influences brought by settlers and sailors of many nationalities. While the few hours it takes to explore the town are time well spent, most will find it a pleasant distraction from Bequia's main attraction – its fabulous beaches.

The centre of the town's activity is the jetty, where ferries from Kingstown dock and sailboats depart for other Grenadine islands. At the end of the jetty is a small market selling fresh produce, spices and a plethora of tourist fare, including T-shirts, jewellery and locally made jams. Port Elizabeth's main drag, **Front Street**, with its collection of souvenir shops, yacht provisioners and restaurants, leads into **Belmont Walkway**, where most of the town's accommodation is to be found. Among the shops, top ones to check out are the Mauvin Model Boat Shop, which sells handmade model boats, Bequia Bookshop, for its large selection of Caribbean literature, maps and prints, and the Garden Boutique, with locally produced batik.

Across the road from the Garden Boutique, just before the main street becomes Belmont Walkway, you'll find the understated **St Mary's Church**. With its profusion of wood beams painted pale blue, its pristine white, wooden pews and tall doors letting in the salty sea breeze, the church feels very much a part of the ocean it faces. Two striking paintings hang on either side of the altar, one of St Vincent and the other of Our Lady of the Seas, both painted by English artist John Constable.

Head northwest out of Port Elizabeth for about a mile, and the road turns uphill to the site of **Fort Hamilton**. All that remains of the fort are a few British and French cannons pointing out over the harbour they once protected; however, the real reason to come here is to enjoy the panoramic views over Admiralty Bay below.

The beaches

While Bequia's beaches fulfil every expectation of a Caribbean paradise – with sparkling sands and crystal-clear waters – what makes them unforgettable is their appealing roughness. Expect to find rocky headlands, and dense palm woodland that extends to the edge of the beaches, and an aura of castaway isolation. Although the swimming is fantastic, the sea is not tame, at times unleashing large, wild waves which pound the beach to create a dramatic (though not dangerous) setting.

The crown jewel of Bequia's beaches is the stunning **Princess Margaret Beach**, a few minutes' walk over the Princess Point headland from the end of Belmont Walkway, or a quick jaunt by road or water taxi from Port Elizabeth. Here, the waves froth onto golden sands and the beautiful sunlight bouncing off the waters is perfectly framed by shady palm fronds and stark rocky outcrops. Swimming, sunbathing and snorkelling along this large horseshoe bay are excellent and the beach is never crowded. It has, however, few facilities, apart from local vendors selling trinkets, beer or soft drinks and snacks.

To the south of Princess Margaret Beach, reached either via a rough trail over the headland, short walk from Port Elizabeth along the road to the interior, or water taxi, lies the lively **Lower Bay**, where you'll find another striking beach with more in the way of tourist amenities, including restaurants, bars and toilets.

Friendship Bay in the southwest is within easy walking distance and also served by frequent buses. Despite its clutch of hotels and restaurants, this broad sweep of Atlantic shoreline remains unspoiled. The picture-perfect beach is ideal for swimming, snorkelling and diving, and a climb up the steep hillside behind it may afford a rare glimpse of a breaching whale.

Whaling on Bequia

Whaling was once big business in Bequia as the island used to be one of the most important whaling stations in the Caribbean, reaching its peak in the 1920s when 20 percent of the island's working men were employed in this seasonal industry. In recognition of this longstanding cultural tradition, which dates to the early nineteenth century when American whalers would hire locals to man their ships, the International Whaling Commission allows Bequia's whalers to kill up to two animals per year. Humpback whales, which appear in the waters around the island between February and April, are the whalers' prime target. In preparation for the hunt, the whaling boats are blessed in Friendship Bay at the end of January. The traditional methods still practised here include hand-held harpoons and wooden boats, which at 25ft long, are less than half the size of most humpback whales. The whalers aren't successful every year, but when they are all of Bequia celebrates.

Not all locals or visitors agree with the maintenance of this tradition, however. Hand-held harpoon attacks rarely equate to quick mortal strikes, which means that a whale usually takes between 30 minutes and two hours to die from its wounds. The one exception was the year that local whaling legend Athneal Ollivierre harpooned a humpback directly in the heart killing it instantly.

Whatever your feelings are about whaling, the small museum dedicated to preserving its history (see above), which is lovingly looked after by Athneal's nephew Harold, provides an insight into this important aspect of the island's history and a fantastic view of the waters where the whales roam. In addition, in Port Elizabeth three old whaling boats can be viewed through the wire mesh sides of a shed at the end of the jetty.

The rest of the island

On the northeast tip of the island at the end of Industry Bay is the **Oldhegg Turtle Sanctuary** (daily; EC$10; ☏784/458-3245), which endeavours to save the endangered Hawksbill turtle, distinguished by its pointed bill and sleek shell. In the winter months, baby turtles are collected from the beach soon after they are hatched and released two years later when they are fully capable of looking after themselves and have a vastly increased chance of survival.

On the southwest tip of the island near the village of La Pompe is the **Athneal Petit Museum** (open daily, no set hours; EC$5; ☏784/458-3322), dedicated to local hero and whaler Athneal Ollivierre in addition to the island's long history of whaling (see box, above). The tiny, shrine-like collection is full of fascinating whaling artefacts as well as the odd inclusion like signed photos of Clint Eastwood and Tom Cruise, both said to have been inspired by Ollivierre's exploits.

The museum also holds various artworks by local professor Sam McDowell, whose home and **studio** in Page Farm is not far away (by appointment; ☏784/458-3865), if you can't get enough of it at the museum.

Eating and drinking

Bequia has a fine selection of character-filled **restaurants** and **bars** dotted around the island and concentrated along Port Elizabeth's waterfront. The Belmont Walkway has a particularly excellent selection, but it's worth trying options further afield.

Coco's Place Lower Bay, ☏784/458-3463. Situated on a hillside at the south end of Lower Bay, this lively bar and restaurant, surrounded by lush foliage and with superb sea views, opens for lunch and dinner, and serves a good range of local and international cuisine – especially local fish.

Lunch menu includes tuna sandwiches for EC$13 or a West Indian buffet for EC$34, while dinner dishes include curried goat for EC$26.
Crescent Beach Inn Crescent Beach, near Industry Bay ☏784/458-3400. This large shady bar by the ocean is a unique and unpretentious place,

making for a perfect refreshment stop on the way to the Turtle Sanctuary, or a memorable night out, especially at full moon when the owners organize a beach barbecue. At lunchtime, sandwiches start from EC$8 and starters at dinner include pumpkin soup (EC$10) with main courses such as curried shrimp (EC$44).

The Frangipani Belmont Walkway, Port Elizabeth ☎784/458-3255. The food and the view is first class. This restaurant is popular with yachters, especially those crewing larger vessels, which makes for a friendly and lively atmosphere. Breakfast starts at 7am, the lunch menu features numerous sandwiches, burgers and omelettes from EC$26 and seafood is a speciality in the evening, when main courses average EC$80. Thursday night is barbecue night; reservations are required.

Green Boley Belmont Walkway, Port Elizabeth ☎784/458-3041. This laid-back, welcoming bar is one of the few places where prices remain the same all day. Here you'll find budget-conscious travellers and family groups munching on tasty rotis and substantial sandwiches (from EC$8), fish and chips (EC$16) and conch curry (EC$20). There

is often live music and always a good crowd.

Lina's Bayshore Mall, Port Elizabeth ☎784/457-3388. This small, but popular take-away bakery and delicatessen caters primarily to yachters, selling a selection of fresh-baked breads and pastries, great for beach picnics.

Mac's Pizzeria Belmont Walkway, Port Elizabeth ☎784/458-3474. It's easy to see why dinner reservations are recommended at this bustling and trendy Italian restaurant. Diners eat on a large, sea-facing terrace, decorated with fairy lights and set to a funky sound system. Lobster pizza is a speciality, but many cheaper and unusual options are also available, as are pastas, salads and quiches. Pizzas EC$20–80.

Port Hole Belmont Walkway, Port Elizabeth ☎784/458-3458. This basic but very popular restaurant has a reasonable lunch menu featuring tasty rotis from EC$10 and sandwiches from EC$8. The evening menu includes Caribbean and international dishes starting at EC$60. There's also a small supermarket and a large book exchange on the premises.

Nightlife

For a small island Bequia has plenty of **nightlife**. In Port Elizabeth most bars and restaurants along Belmont Walkway feature **live music** on alternate nights – *The Whaleboner* (☎784/458-3233) is a popular option, while above Court's furniture shop near the jetty, *Club Cinnamon* (☎784/457-3688) is a great place for live music, as is *The Salty Dog* bar, where Front Street meets the Belmont Walkway (☎784/457-3443). While at weekends an open-air party with local DJs centres around the *Penthouse Bar*. In Lower Bay both *Coco's Place* (see p.765) and *Keegan's* beachfront bar (☎784/458-3530) host live music nights which are usually popular and fun. Detailed information on what's on where can be found listed in *Bequia This Week* – a free paper that can picked up at the tourist information centre.

Diving and sailing

Diving in the pristine waters around Bequia is excellent. Most sites are on the Leeward side of the island and include everything from colourful reefs to dramatic walls. Most local **dive companies** organize similar packages – some including accommodation. Bequia Dive Adventures (☎784/458-3826, ⦾www.bequiadiveadventures.com) offer a range of dive packages from US$47 for a single dive to US$400 for ten, while Dive Bequia (☎784/458-3504, ⦾www.dive-bequia.com) operate from the *Gingerbread Hotel* (see p.763) and charge US$56 for single dives and US$46 per dive for seven or more.

Given the island's long seafaring history, it's no surprise that Bequia is one of the best places in the Grenadines to take a **sailing** excursion to one of the other nearby islands. Highly recommended is the romantic 80ft sailing schooner *The Friendship Rose* (☎784/495-0886, ⦾www.friendshiprose.com). The ship makes frequent trips from Port Elizabeth's jetty to Mustique, the Tobago Cays and St Vincent. Trips start at US$70 and include gourmet local cuisine and all drinks. The *Passion* (☎784/458-3884,

△ Signpost, Union Island

⊕www.vincy.com/passion) offers day-trips on a 60ft catamaran to Mustique (US$60), the Tobago Cays (US$75) and St Vincent's Falls of Baleine (US$75); all rates include drinks and the use of sport fishing and snorkelling equipment.

Mustique

Situated just seven miles southeast of Bequia, beautiful **MUSTIQUE** is a fantasy island for the ultra-rich. Most visitors to the island are day-trippers drawn by the island's air of exclusivity, though their explorations are fairly restricted as much of place is privately owned and curious visitors are discouraged. Those who do spend some time here can enjoy the island's hilly terrain, its large plain to the north and seven lush valleys leading to the white-sand beaches along its coast.

Mustique's first inhabitants were European planters who arrived in the 1740s. The decline of the West Indian sugar cane industry in later years led to the closing of the plantations, and prospects for the island faded. Mustique didn't regain its footing until 1958 when Scottish landowner Colin Tennant bought the 1400-acre island for £45,000 and transformed it into a holiday hotspot for the rich and famous. Now under the management of a private corporation, the island is a haven for pop stars and celebrities of the likes of Mick Jagger, David Bowie and Elton John, all of whom own properties on the island.

Practicalities

Mustique's **airport** is situated in the north of the island and receives daily flights from St Vincent and other Grenadine islands. The Mustique Company (see below) operate a scheduled Mustique Shuttle flight service which departs St Vincent two or three times a day Mon–Sat. For details on sailing tour operators on other islands who organize day-trips to Mustique, see Fantasea Tours on St Vincent (p.759), *The Friendship Rose* and *Passion* on Bequia (see p.766). *The Glenconner* ferry operates on Mondays, Tuesdays, Thursdays and Fridays (except public holidays), departing Mustique's Britannia Bay jetty for St Vincent at 7.30am and leaving St Vincent for the return journey at 2pm. The one-way fare is EC$20 and tickets can be bought at the Mustique Company offices in Kingstown or Mustique Marine, Britannia Bay on Mustique.

Accommodation and **eating** options are limited but luxurious and must be booked in advance. The two hotels, *Cotton House*, between Endeavour and L'Ansecoy Bays (☎784/456-4777, ⊕www.cottonhouseresort.com; US$700–2300 including breakfast), and *The Firefly*, overlooking Britannia Bay (☎784/456-3414, ⊕www.mustiquefirefly.com; US$725–825, including all meals and vehicle hire), have every amenity imaginable; other than the two hotels, the only other way to stay on the island is to rent one of the numerous decadent villas through the Mustique Company (☎784/458-4621, ⊕www.mustique-island.com; US$3000–30,000 weekly). To see who's who in town, head to *Basil's Bar and Restaurant* (☎784/458-4621, ⊕www.basilsmustique.com), a bamboo and thatch bar extending off the beach – and on stilts in the ocean. Main courses for dinner start at EC$70.

Canouan

In the middle of the Grenadine island chain, tiny, crescent-shaped **CANOUAN** – the Carib word for turtle – consists of five square miles of lush green hills and beautiful reef-protected white-sand beaches. It is these beaches that draw a growing number of visitors and an increasing amount of development. The construction of a large new luxury resort, 18-hole golf course, casino and holiday villas, has not been without local resentment as many islanders feel increasingly squeezed out. Its growing popularity as a luxury Caribbean holiday destination means that Canouan is largely set up to cater for the needs of its visitors. The ferry docks at **Charlestown**, the island's main town, situated on one of the island's longest beaches at Charlestown Bay (also known as Grand Bay), while the airport is situated just to the west of the town.

There is, however, more to the island than luxury resorts. The low, undulating hills are pleasant for walking, and you'll meet more goats than people along its peaceful pathways. Also, there's no beating the beaches, and the sunbathing, swimming, snorkelling and diving here are all first class. There are coral reefs just offshore, which means the beaches are well protected and snorkellers needn't be daring to investigate them – though care should be taken to preserve these delicate organisms. The local dive company, Dive Canouan (☎784/458-8044, ☏458-8875), is located at the *Tamarind Beach Hotel* (see below) and can arrange dives for beginners and experienced divers.

Practicalities

There are few restaurants independent of **accommodation** on Canouan, and each hotel has its own facilities, with menus ranging from French cuisine and West Indian fare to pizza. The top choices include *Anchor Inn Guest House* (☎ & ☏784/458-8568; ❹), a tiny guesthouse in a two-storey home near the beach at Grand Bay, with three simple rooms, and breakfast and dinner included in the room rate. Also at Grand Bay, *Casa del Mar* (☎784/482-0639, ⊛www.adonalfoyle.com/AFE_casa_del_mar.shtml; ❼), owned by Golden State Warriors basketball player and local hero Adonal Foyes, offers luxurious master suites and guest rooms in this sea-facing villa and the use of a large kitchen, spacious living room and private bar. Another Grand Bay option, the *Tamarind Beach Hotel* (☎784/458-8044, ⊛tamarindbeachotel.com; ❾), and the 156-room *Raffles Resort* (☎784/458-8000, ⊛www.raffles-canouanisland.com; ❾), in the north of the island, both offer every luxury imaginable for those who can afford it.

Mayreau

With a population of a mere 300 residents, and covering only one and half square miles, **MAYREAU** is the smallest of the inhabited Grenadine islands. It almost goes without saying that the beaches, watersports and views are wonderful, but unless you want to splash out for a stay at an exclusive resort, there is little to warrant anything more than a day's exploration – a water taxi from Union Island costs EC$130 one-way if you don't want to stay on the island (see p.771).

As with most of the small Grenadines, visitors come for the immaculate beaches, of which Saline Bay and Salt Whistle Bay are justly popular. The sands of **Saline Bay** in the south are nearly a mile long and completely undeveloped, though when a cruise ship visits the island this beach can get very busy. With dazzling white sand and pale-blue waters **Salt Whistle Bay**, home of a small resort (see overleaf), is both stunning and a favourite anchorage for yachts. Good hiking can be found on the island in the form of a long trail that winds its way from Salt Whistle Bay to Salt Whistle village where most islanders live and a number of local bars and restaurants can be found. The village is also home to a striking, tiny stone Catholic Church whose windows and grounds provide incredible views of the Caribbean and neighbouring islands. If you visit the church during a local wedding, you'll be fortunate, as these are very well celebrated on Mayreau; flags are flown from relatives' houses and rum is sprinkled over graves to encourage ancestors to bless the union. To get married on the island you'll need to stay more than 72 hours, and a more romantic setting would be hard to find.

Practicalities

If you're planning to stay over here, an excellent choice for a bed and fine food is *Dennis' Hideaway*, Saline Bay (☎ & ℱ784/458-8594, ⊛www.dennis-hideaway.com; ❹), a peaceful guesthouse consisting of five rooms, each with a private bathroom and balcony facing the sea. Downstairs, the bar and restaurant opens at 7am for breakfast (included in the room rate). Lunch starts at EC$10 and evening meals include locally caught seafood and mouthwatering spare ribs (EC$40–80). More expensive is *Saltwhistle Bay Club* (☎784/458-8444, ⊛www.saltwhistlebay.com; ❾), a quiet beachside resort whose charming, airy bungalows made of local stone each have private patios. There's an open-air restaurant too, serving standard Caribbean dishes.

Other **eating** options include the beachside *Island Paradise* (☎784/458-8941), with local favourites like callaloo soup, conch stew and red snapper; expect to pay about EC$40 for a main course at dinner. Similar dishes can be had at *J & C Restaurant and Bar* (☎784/458-8558), such as curried conch, snapper and West Indian cake. Transport by boat is included in their reasonable prices. Situated on top of a hill, just a few minutes walk from Saline Bay, *Combination Café* (☎784/458-8561) serves Caribbean and international fare at prices upwards of EC$20, from its rooftop dining area with panoramic views of the harbour below.

Union Island

Rustic **UNION ISLAND**, the southernmost of the Grenadines, is primarily a stopoff for visitors to the Tobago Cays and a point of entry for yachters into St Vincent and the Grenadines. The terrain of this roughly three-miles-long and one-mile-wide island is not as picture-postcard perfect as some of its fellow Grenadines, but the jagged volcanic peaks rising from low scrubby hills to a height of 1000ft at Mount Taboi – the tallest peak in the Grenadines – have earned the island the nickname "little Tahiti". Less built up than many of its neighbours, Union's unpolished atmosphere comes as a welcome relief from the pretentiousness of many Caribbean resorts.

The commercial centre, **Clifton**, has whatever **tourist information** you might need (daily 9am–4pm), as well as the airport, ferry jetty, banks, and numerous bars, restaurants and shops. Situated at the edge of the colourful local market, where you will find every kind of Caribbean fruit and vegetables and a tiny Internet café, is a 9lb cannon, which once protected Clifton Harbour from American privateers during the American War of Independence.

Set in tropical gardens on the waterfront, east towards the airport, the **Bougainville Centre**, a complex catering for tourists and yatchers, is the most tourist-oriented it gets on Union Island. Even here the luxury gift shop and first class restaurant (see opposite) is well within most budgets. Also located here are the offices of Wind and Sea Ltd (☎784/458-8678, ⊛www.grenadines.net/union/windandsea.html), who organize numerous sailing, snorkelling, diving and sightseeing tours around the Grenadines.

Above the small village of **Ashton**, a short bus ride (EC$3 fare) or half an hour's walk from Clifton, towards the centre of the island, a few hiking trails wend their way through the hills, offering good walking terrain and excellent views of the surrounding Grenadines, while the remote beaches of **Richmond** and **Big Sand Beach** on the northern end of the island can be reached by road from Clifton. The best snorkelling to be had is at **Lagoon Reef**, which protects the southern coast of the island. Teeming with colourful marine life and rarely visited, the reef provides excellent conditions, especially around **Frigate Island**.

If you want to venture beyond Union Island, Captain Yannis (☎784/458-8513, ℮yannis@caribsurf.com), based at the *Clifton Beach Hotel* (see opposite), operates day-trips on 60ft **catamarans** to the neighbouring islands of the Tobago Cays and

Palm Island for EC\$140; a filling lunch, drinks and the use of snorkelling equipment are included in the price. In addition to a water taxi service to neighbouring islands at reasonable prices Seckie's (☎784/530-5913, ✉seckietours@hotmail.com) organize "sun, beach, eat" tours which include snorkelling and a beach BBQ for EC\$130–180. **Diving** can be arranged through Grenadines Dive (☎784/458-8138, ⓦwww.grenadinesdive.com), based at *The West Indies Restaurant* in Clifton (see below), which offers easy to adventurous dives; among the latter is a dive to a 90ft volcanic valley complete with a bubbling seabed.

Practicalities

Stay at *Anchorage Yacht Club* (☎784/458-8221, ⓦwww.ayc-hotel-grenadines.com; ❺), right on the waterfront in Clifton, with comfortable rooms that have good views from private patios. Otherwise, the relaxed *Clifton Beach Hotel* (☎784/458-8235, ⓦwww.cliftonbeachhotel.com; ❷/❹) has basic rooms and cottages, plus an excellent restaurant and bar on the premises. On the north side of the island at Richmond Bay, the tranquil and isolated *Bigsand Hotel* (☎784/485-8447, ⓦwww.bigsandhotel.com; ❺), rent spacious and airy apartment-style rooms complete with living area, kitchen, bathroom and beachfront balcony, and the beachside restaurant is ideal for a peaceful lunch or dinner. The lunch menu includes rotis from EC\$18 and dinner options feature a mix of French and local cuisine starting at EC\$34. Other **eating** options include *The Seaquarium* (☎784/458-8678) located at the Bougainville Centre. Complete with its own large aquarium, and wonderful sea views, this is the perfect spot to enjoy a cocktail, or one of their reasonably priced and excellent fish and pasta dishes from EC\$23. Located in Clifton, *The West Indies Restaurant* (☎784/458-8911) serve tasty salads, burgers and omelettes for lunch from EC\$18 and pasta, fish and meat dishes for dinner, EC\$30–57.

Tobago Cays

Accessible only by boat, the numerous tiny deserted islets and spectacular coral reefs of the lovely **TOBAGO CAYS** are justifiably famous for their superb snorkelling, diving, windsurfing and birdwatching opportunities. During high season, the translucent waters of this major tourist attraction are busy with visiting yachts and local vendors touting everything from food to jewellery from their boats. The cays' popularity, however, is leading to their destruction as anchoring boats and over-fishing have caused considerable damage to the coral reefs. The islands are now a National Marine Park, and fishing, jet skis and anchoring dinghies are all prohibited to preserve the endangered coral.

    Sailing day-trips to the Tobago Cays can be organized from other Grenadine islands; try The Friendship Rose on Bequia (see p.766) and Captain Yannis on Union Island (see opposite). Resorts also offer packages that include similar trips.

Grenada

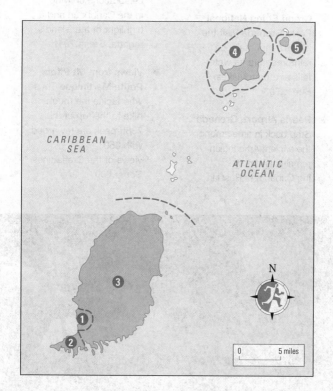

Grenada highlights

* **Grand Anse Beach, Grenada** Sunbathe on the magnificent white sands or take advantage of the many watersports options. See p.787

* **Grand Etang National Park, Grenada** Visit the island's mountainous rainforest and its waterfalls and crater lakes. See p.793

* **Pearls Airport, Grenada** Step back in time among the ancient Amerindian remains and rusting Cuban and Russian planes abandoned on the runway. See p.792

* **Carriacou's Big Drum Dances** The only remaining pre-Christian African celebration surviving in the Caribbean and a highlight of the island's regatta. See p.794

* **Views from Mt Piton, Petite Martinique** Those who tackle the tough hike to the top of this 738ft peak are rewarded with 360° views of the Grenadines. See p.800

△ Old airplane at Pearls Airport

Introduction and basics

The southernmost of the Windward Islands, **Grenada** is known as "The Isle of Spice", due to its production of nutmeg along with quantities of cinnamon, cloves, ginger, turmeric and mace. However, all of these crops were devastated, along with much of the island, by a direct hit from Hurricane Ivan on September 7 2004. Ivan's 125mph winds wreaked havoc on Grenada, damaging many of the island's buildings, destroying its agriculture and laying waste to its lush rainforest.

While largely dependent on its recovering agriculture, the tiny nation of Grenada – which includes neighbouring **Carriacou** and **Petite Martinique**, both of which suffered far less damage from Ivan, as well as other smaller Grenadine islands – has been building a reputation as a top holiday destination. Though Ivan seriously damaged this reputation, along with many of the hotels that housed an increasing number of visitors, anyone planning to visit Grenada should be assured that many repairs have been achieved in a remarkably short period of time. While there is still a lot of rebuilding to complete, there is no reason to stay away from the country, which remains relatively unspoiled compared to many other top Caribbean destinations and can still reward any visitor with the best that the region has to offer.

All three of the main islands offer excellent **watersports** opportunities, while Grenada in particular has its share of stunning white-sand beaches, ranging from the resort-lined **Grand Anse Beach** on the southwest tip to the ruggedly spectacular **Bathway Beach** in the northeast.

Ringing the island are a variety of communities, chief among them the elegant capital of **St George's**, as well as the charming fishing village of **Goyave** on the west coast and, on the east coast, **Grenville**, the country's agricultural heart. The country's inhabitants, 90 percent of whom live on the island of Grenada, are descended from British, French, African and West Indian settlers, and their inviting and friendly nature belies the country's turbulent history.

Much smaller and far less visited are the islands of **Carriacou** and **Petite Martinique**, appealing for their slow pace and a welcome respite from the more tourist-oriented Grenada.

Where to go

Of Grenada's many attractions a few stand apart. The mountainous interior of the rainforest of **Grand Etang National Park** was a lush walkers' paradise before Hurricane Ivan struck. While nature is bouncing back at a remarkable rate, at the time of writing the forest still has a great deal of recovery to go through before it is restored to its former glory, and its network of trails leading to spectacular waterfalls, fascinating crater lakes and mist-shrouded mountain peaks are all in the process of being cleared and repaired. Among the country's numerous white-sand beaches, by far the most stunning is Grenada's **Grand Anse**, whose long horseshoe bay is the focus of the island's tourist trade. For a taste of laid-back island life, as well as quieter beaches and secluded sunbathing, there's the smaller island of **Carriacou** just a short ferry ride away.

When to go

Grenada's climate is warm and humid, with a **rainy season** from June to December – it rarely rains for more than an hour and lets up on some days. The coolest time of the year is November to February, also the island's **high season**, with average temperatures in the high twenties Celsius (around the low eighties Fahrenheit). The official **hurricane season** lasts from June to November with September being the peak month, though, in theory, Grenada lies outside of the hurricane belt.

> When leaving, you'll be required to pay a **departure tax** of EC$50.

Arrival

Flights arrive at Point Salines International Airport, located on the southwest tip of Grenada, approximately five miles from the capital, St George's.

Although flying is the quickest and easiest option for travelling between neighbouring islands, it is possible to travel by **boat** to Carriacou from Union Island, the most southerly of the Grenadine islands and under the jurisdiction of St Vincent (covered in Chapter 19, starting p.745). This journey, however, is only recommended for the adventurous as the one-hour trip, which ends at the Hillsborough jetty, can sometimes be quite rough.

Information, websites and maps

The main visitor centre is the **Grenada Board of Tourism**, located on the cruise ship terminal in St George's Carenage (℡473/440-2279, ⊛www.grenadagrenadines.com); you'll find it well stocked with brochures and maps. There is also an **information booth** at the airport, just before immigration, and one at the Craft and Spice Market on Grand Anse Beach (see p.788). The Grenada Hotel and Tourism Association in St George's (PO Box 440, ℡473/444-1353, ⊛www.grenadahotelsinfo.com) can help book accommodation. On **Carriacou** the main tourist office is in Hillsborough on Main Street.

Adequate, free **maps** – including one that details a historic walking tour of St George's – are available at tourist offices and many hotels. A detailed Ordnance Survey map can be purchased for EC$15 from hotels and tourist shops.

Money and costs

Grenada's official currency is the **Eastern Caribbean dollar (EC$)**, although the US dollar is widely accepted at hotels, restaurants and shops, and by car rental and taxi companies. The EC dollar is divided into 100 cents. Notes come in denominations of 5, 10, 20, 50 and 100 EC dollars; coins in 1, 2, 5, 10 and 25 cents. At the time of writing, the

---

Grenada websites

⊛**www.grenadaexplorer.com** From accommodation to eco-tourism, this large site contains detailed travel information and features an excellent search option.

⊛**www.grenada.org** An attractive and easy-to-navigate site, crammed with information on the island's history, as well as where to stay and what to do.

⊛**www.grenadaguide.com** Comprehensive site covering accommodation, restaurants, airlines, car rentals, tours and dive operators.

⊛**www.grenadianvoice.com** This online edition of the local weekly contains all the latest Grenadian news, weather and entertainment listings.

⊛**www.travelgrenada.com** Filled with travel information and tips, as well as maps, a currency calculator and even local recipes.

Hurricane Ivan update and information sites

⊛**www.grenadaemergency.com** Grenada's official information site on the progress of relief efforts in the aftermath of Ivan. It includes regular updates on hotels, attractions and events, and numerous photographs of the island just after the hurricane struck.

⊛**www.grenadaexplorer.net** Site dedicated to providing information and updates on Grenada's rebuilding and recovery post Hurricane Ivan, and ways in which you can help.

⊛**www.spiceisland.info** Another useful disaster relief information site detailing the progress of rebuilding accommodation.

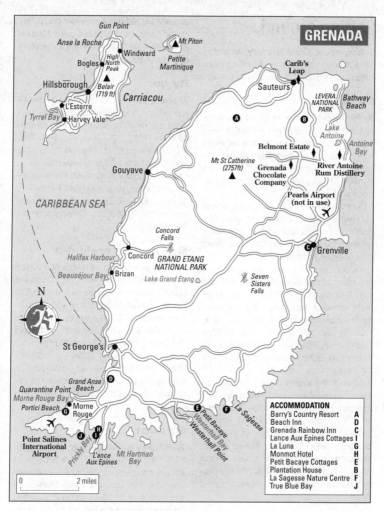

ACCOMMODATION

Barry's Country Resort	A
Beach Inn	D
Grenada Rainbow Inn	C
Lance Aux Epines Cottages	I
La Luna	G
Monmot Hotel	H
Petit Bacaye Cottages	E
Plantation House	B
La Sagesse Nature Centre	F
True Blue Bay	J

rate of exchange was roughly EC$2.70 to US$1.

Credit cards and major **travellers' cheques** are accepted at most hotels, restaurants and larger shops. In this chapter prices such as bus fares and admission fees have been quoted in EC$; all other prices are given in US$.

Banking hours are generally Monday to Thursday 8am–3pm, Friday 8am–5pm, with some variations. Barclays Bank, Scotiabank, Grenada Bank of Commerce and National Commercial Bank all have branches in St George's and the Grand Anse area. Most have an **ATM**, and there's also one at Point Salines Airport. Banks with ATMs can be found in Hillsborough on Carriacou, and Petit Martinique's one bank opens Tuesdays and Thursdays 9am–12 noon and has no ATM.

An 8 percent **government tax** is added at hotels and restaurants on top of a 10 percent **service charge**. Tipping is at your discretion, but not necessary.

Getting around

Getting around Grenada is fairly straightforward, though you'll end up travelling more miles than you expect due to the hilly terrain.

By bus

By far the cheapest way to get around is by **bus**. These privately owned, but government-regulated minivans cram in as many people as possible, drive very fast and play loud reggae, ragga and soca. Don't be intimidated, however, as they're also great fun, friendly and safe.

Buses run 6am–8pm daily, with a less frequent service on only the most popular routes on Sundays and holidays, and routes run from the main terminal on Bruce Street in St George's to cover the entire island. Bus stops punctuate all routes, you can also flag one down at any point along the way, and with their constant honking, you'll always know when they are around. To get off simply rap the side of the van and pay as you leave. From St George's, expect to pay EC$2 to Grand Anse, EC$3 to Grand Etang, EC$5 to Grenville, EC$6 to Sauteurs and EC$4 to Gouyave.

Although the **airport** is not on a main bus route, it is possible to take a bus there; stop any bus going to Grand Anse Beach and ask if it will take you to the airport, which is just a few miles further on. Expect to pay the **off-route fare** of EC$10 for this service. It's sometimes possible to pick up one of these off-route buses at the airport on its way back to the main route to St George's or Grand Anse.

By taxi

Taxis are plentiful and you will be constantly hassled by drivers seeking business. Fares from the airport to Grand Anse are around EC$25 and to St George's EC$40; expect to pay about EC$4 per mile for journeys from St George's to the rest of the island. A **surcharge** of EC$10 is added between 6pm and 6am. Taxi companies to try in St George's are the National Taxi Association (T 440 6850) situated next door to tourist information and The Carenage Taxi Co-operative (T 473/444-9223), which has a stand opposite the *Nutmeg Restaurant* (see p.786) on the Carenage. Local tour guide Mandoo (T 473/407-0024) also provides an excellent and reliable taxi service.

By car

To **rent a car** you will need a valid driver's licence and a local permit, available from most car rental agencies and police stations for US$30. Dollar (T 473/444-4786, E callistena@caribsurf.com) and David's Car Rental (T 473/444-3399, W www.davidscars.com) have offices at the Point Salines International Airport, while Avis (T 473/440-3936) operates out of St George's. Cars and jeeps cost US$50–70 per day. **Driving** is on the left-hand side.

By scooter and bike

To drive a **scooter** you will need a local licence available from police stations for around US$30. Scooters can be rented from Eze Rentals (T 473/444-3263, E vicwill@caribsurf.com) and cost US$20 a day or US$120 per week. **Bikes** can be hired from Trailblazers (T 473/444-5337, W www.adventuregrenada.com); expect to pay US$15 per day or US$90 per week. Be warned – cycling can be tough-going on Grenada as roads are mostly hilly and the smaller ones are not always well maintained.

By boat

The **Osprey passenger ferry** (T 473/440-8126, W www.ospreylines.com) is the most efficient and cheapest way to travel between Grenada, Carriacou and Petite Martinique. It departs from the Carenage in St George's (opposite the red fire station) for Carriacou Monday to Friday 9am and 5.30pm, Saturday 9am only and Sunday 8am and 5.30pm. It then departs Carriacou for Petite Martinique Monday to Friday 10.30am and 7pm and Sunday 9.30am and 7pm. The **return trip** leaves Petite Martinique for Carriacou Monday to Saturday 5.30am and 3pm and Sunday 3pm, and departs Carriacou to Grenada Monday to Saturday 6am and 3.30pm and Sunday 3.30pm only. The journey takes ninety minutes between Grenada and Carriacou and twenty minutes from Carriacou to Petite Martinique. The fare from Grenada to Carriacou and Petite Martinique is EC$50 one-way, EC$100 round-trip and from Carriacou to Petite Martinique EC$15 one-way, EC$30 round-trip.

There is also a cheaper but slower and less frequent mailboat service which departs Grenada for Carriacou Tues, Wed, Fri and Sat at 10am and leaves Carriacou for Grenada Mon, Wed & Thurs 10am and Sun 12 noon. Journey time is 3–4 hours and the one-way fare is EC$25.

By plane

St Vincent and the Grenadines Airways (☎473/444-3549m, ✆www.svgair.com) flies daily from Grenada, Barbados, and St Vincent and the Grenadine islands to **Lauriston Airstrip**, one mile south of Hillsborough on Carriacou (see p.795).

There is no airport on Petite Martinique, and the only way to get there is by boat or ferry (see above).

Tours

Most of the island can easily be explored by bus, but, if you're short on time, **organized tours** are an excellent way to see the island in a day and learn about its history and culture along the way. Local tour guide Mandoo (☎473/407-0024, ✆www.grenadatours.com) has an encyclopedic knowledge of Grenada's history, politics and nature, and his selection of full- and half-day bus and trekking tours cost US$40–90 per person. His full-day bus tours covering Halifax Bay, Gouyave, Carib's Leap, Grenville and Grand Etang National Park cost US$55 (this includes entrance fees, lunch and even impromptu stops for fruit along the way); and half-day tours to St George's open-air market at US$15 include a visit to the downtown area of the island's capital.

Sunsation Tours (☎ 473/444-1594, ✆ www.grenadasunsation.com) also run full- and part-day tours. At US$60 the "Tutti Frutti" tour passes through the island's major sites, while more specialized tours, such as a visit to the outstanding private gardens on the island, can also be organized for US$35.

Another option is Adventure Jeep Tours (☎473/444-5337, ✆grenadajeeptours.com) whose all-terrain jeeps will take you all over the island, with some trips including a swim and snorkel. Full-day tours cost US$65.

If you fancy **biking** around the island, Trailblazers (☎473/444-5337, ✆www.adventuregrenada.com) runs full-day cycling tours for US$60, which will take you along the island's off-road trails and include lunch and time on the beach.

Accommodation

A considerable proportion of Grenada's **accommodation** was damaged or destroyed by Hurricane Ivan. All of the listings in this guide were open at the time of writing; however, if you are planning to trip, check the Hurricane Ivan Information and Updates websites (see p.776) for details on accommodation as it reopens. Most places to stay on Grenada are clustered around the tourist-saturated southwest, but there are some interesting and unusual options outside this area. A variety of lodging is available, ranging from self-catering apartments to modern resort complexes. Villas are an excellent, and often economical, option if you are travelling in a large group. Villas of Grenada (☎473/444-1896, ✆ www.villasofgrenada.com) rent a large selection of villas around Grenada, while Down Island Ltd (☎473/443-8182, ✆www.islandvillas.com), offer the same service on Carriacou.

Prices are much lower during the summer months – April to December – which is also the rainy season. Furthermore, accommodation rates on Carriacou and Petite Martinique are significantly lower than on Grenada, ranging from US$35 to US$125 per night; on Grenada prices vary between US$45 and US$500.

There are no **youth hostels** on the island, but the numerous **guesthouses** are aimed at more budget-minded travellers and locals. **Camping**, though permitted in Grand Etang National Park, is not encouraged and there are no facilities.

Food and drink

As Grenada's agriculture industry gets back on its feet after Hurricane Ivan, an increasing number of the island's many home-grown fruits, vegetables and spices are reappearing in the colourful market in St George's (see p.783). Seafood is plentiful, ranging from conch – known locally as *lambie* – to flying fish. Also widely available and unmissable are delicious rotis, fine layers of pastry folded around various fillings. Favourite starters include *callaloo* soup and **nutmeg ice cream** is an island speciality.

The beer of choice is **Carib**, brewed on the island and available in all bars. Likewise rum produced in Grenada's distilleries is used in a wide variety of punches and cocktails. Be sure to sample the locally produced **fruit juice**. Bursting with flavour, what's on offer depends on the season; those made from passionfruit and sorrel are both delicious and well worth trying.

Hurricane Ivan considerably reduced Grenada's range of **places to eat** and while all options listed were open at the time of writing, many others are in the process of repair. Vegetarians will find generally that most restaurants do not cater for them. A large number of dining options outside of St George's on Grenada are limited to **hotel restaurants and bars**. Most establishments serve a dinner menu after 7pm that is considerably more expensive than meals served during the day, and the choice of inexpensive restaurants dwindles after this time.

Mail and communications

Payphones can be found throughout the island. Some accept only phone cards, which you can buy from the main visitor centre, at the airport, in shops and from the Cable & Wireless office on the Carenage in Grenada or Patterson Street, Hillsborough on Carriacou.

The general **post office** (Mon–Fri 8am–3.30pm) is on Lagoon Road in St George's and there are smaller offices in towns and villages on Grenada and Carriacou and one on Petite Martinique (Mon–Fri 10am–noon & 2–4pm)

The country code for Grenada is ☏473.

Emergency numbers

Police and fire ☏911
Ambulance in St George's ☏434, in St Andrews ☏724 and on Carriacou ☏774
Coastguard ☏399

You'll find several **Internet cafés** in St George's and at numerous other places on Grenada and Carriacou, and one on Petite Martinique in Matthew's Shopping Centre.

Opening hours, holidays and festivals

Business hours are generally Monday to Friday 8am–4pm and Saturday 8am–1pm. When a cruise ship is in harbour some tourist shops in St George's will stay open later and on Sundays.

As well as the **public holidays** listed on p.60, Grenada celebrates Independence Day on February 7, Corpus Christi on the ninth Thursday after Easter, Emancipation Days on the first Monday and Tuesday in August and Thanksgiving on October 25.

The biggest event on Grenada's **festival** calendar is its lively and colourful **Carnival**, held every year on the second weekend in August. Although Carriacou's Carnival is in early March, the island's main event is the **Carriacou Regatta**, which takes place in late July/early August and brings boats of all kinds from all over the Caribbean. Petite Martinique also hosts an annual **regatta** over Easter. Jazz festivals are held on Grenada and Carriacou in May and mid-June respectively.

Outdoor activities

Grenada's underwater terrain is as beautiful as the dramatic landscape rising above it, and there's no shortage of **dive operators** to help you explore it. Most dive shops operate from resorts on Grand Anse Beach in Grenada and out of Tyrrel Bay in Carriacou, and cater for all levels of experience. Though shallow reef, wall and drift dives are all on offer, the most popular site is the wreck of the *Bianca C* (see p.785) on Grenada, known locally as the "Titanic of the Caribbean".

For those who prefer to explore on dry land the **hiking trails** throughout Grenada's Grand Etang National Park, are, at the time of writing, undergoing repairs and Carricou's High North National Park has a good range of trails to explore.

History

Long before Columbus espied Grenada and named it **Concepción** (the name Grenada was given by homesick Spanish sailors and adopted by the British) on his third voyage to the Americas in 1498, Grenada had been settled by a series of migrating Amerindian peoples. Its first known residents were the **Ciboney**, who populated much of the Eastern Caribbean and left little but a few artefacts and petroglyphs behind. The Ciboney were replaced or absorbed by **Arawaks**, who came to the island by way of Venezuela and the outflow of the Orinoco River. In turn, the Arawaks were invaded and enslaved by the **Caribs**, who were making their way up through the islands from Guyana.

The **British**, in 1609, were the first Europeans to attempt to settle the island, followed in 1650 by the **French**, whose first town sank into the mouth of St George's Lagoon. These efforts were fiercely resisted by the Caribs. In 1651, the French took decisive action against the Caribs, pushing them north to **Sauteurs** where, rather than surrender to French control, they threw themselves off a cliff, now known as Caribs' Leap and, ironically, marked by a Catholic church.

Control of Grenada passed between France and Britain as part of the settlements of various treaties, and both countries established **plantations** of indigo, tobacco, coffee, cocoa and sugar, worked by African slaves, until the French ceded the island to Britain in the Treaty of Paris in 1783, the French-brokered agreement which formally ended the American War of Independence.

In 1795 **Julian Fedon**, a mulatto planter, led a peasant rebellion based on the principles of the French Revolution and controlled most of the island for fourteen months before the rebels were crushed by British reinforcements. British rule was stable throughout the nineteenth century, a peace that culminated in 1877 with Grenada being granted crown colony status and a measure of independence.

In 1967, Grenada became a semi-independent state within the British Commonwealth and seven years later an independent country. By that time, control of the government was firmly in the hands of **Eric Gairy**, a union leader who had led the resistance to British rule since the 1950s. During the 1970s, Gairy's rule became increasingly dictatorial and his secret police (**the Mongoose Gang**) more notorious for their corruption and suppression of the opposition. Gairy was ousted from power on March 13, 1979, by a bloodless coup led by Maurice Bishop, the charismatic leader of the left-wing New Jewel Movement whose father had been killed during demonstrations against Gairy's rule.

Bishop's **Revolutionary Government** became a pawn of the Cold War, supported by Cuba, Nicaragua and the Soviet Union but reviled by the United States. The period of Revolutionary Government came to an end in 1983 with Bishop's imprisonment by enemies within his own government and an American-led invasion – on the pretext of evacuating American medical students from the island, but having more to do with the fear of increased Soviet influence in the Caribbean. Bishop and his wife were killed, but mystery remains about when, how and where.

Grenada's first post-revolution elections were held in 1985 and won by **Herbert Blaize**, Gairy's political opponent from the 1950s and 1960s. Elections in 1995 brought **Dr Keith Mitchell** and the New National Party (NNP) to power, who, despite the shadow cast over his leadership by the investigation of alleged links to the collapse of a bank that supported him during his election campaign, is currently in his third term in office after winning the 2003 elections by a very narrow majority.

Grenada was dealt a severe blow on September 7, 2004 when it suffered a direct hit from the mighty **Hurricane Ivan**, which devastated ninety percent of the island as well as the tourism and agriculture strands to the country's economy. Prime Minister Mitchell optimistically hopes that Grenada will recover from the damage caused by Ivan within five years.

20.1

St George's

Grenada's capital, **ST GEORGE'S**, an attractive colonial town nestled in the hillside above a horseshoe-shaped harbour, received the full brunt of Hurricane Ivan's high winds. Many of the low, whitewashed buildings that follow the sweep of the bay had roofs torn off, and are currently patched up with bright blue tarpaulin, and the town's beautiful churches all suffered considerable damage. Ivan however, was not the first disaster to strike this picturesque town dominated by **British colonial architecture** but with a distinctly Mediterranean feel. During the eighteenth century, the town was partly gutted by three devastating fires, leading to legislation that restricted the height of buildings and banned the use of timber.

St George's won't take more than a day to explore, and it's worth taking time away from the beach to do so. Though the **market** is at its liveliest on Saturday morning, most shops close on Saturday afternoons, Sundays and public holidays, making the town a quiet place during those times – except when a **cruise ship** docks, in which case the town explodes into a frenzy of activity, market stalls spring up on shore, restaurants and bars fill up, street vendors and local guides come out in force, and all visitors – whether they're cruise-ship passengers or not – become the focus of a barrage of offers from taxi drivers and spice sellers.

Bear in mind, though, that although St George's is a laid-back town, attitudes veer towards the conservative, and it is considered rude to wear **swimwear or high-cut shorts** in the streets and in shops and restaurants.

Accommodation

Most of the few **accommodation** options in St George's are in the process of being repaired following Hurricane Ivan. Open at the time of writing is *Bailey's Inn* in Springs (☎473/440-2912, ✉otwaybailey@caribsurf.com; ❷), situated on a hillside outside St George's, a charming inn with several attractive rooms with private bathrooms, and one self-contained apartment. Facing the Lagoon on Lagoon Road, the *Tropicana Inn* (☎473/440-1586, ⊛www.tropicanainn.com; ❸), one of the most economical options on Grenada, makes a convenient base from which to explore the island. It has a variety of rooms, all with private bathroom and cable TV, and a few with balconies. The bar and restaurant on site are excellent and the full Grenadian breakfast – a plateful of saltfish stir-fry, fish cakes, savoury bakes and seasonal fruits – will keep you going until dinner-time.

The Town

The core of the town is a maze of streets surrounding the harbour – the **Carenage** – and leading away to the west where they concentrate around the lively **market square**, the heart of town.

The market square and around

Once the site of the town's slave exchange until the trade was made illegal in 1807, the colourful **market square** on Halifax Street is now the bustling and aromatic centre of St George's, where stalls crammed with local spices and seasonal fresh

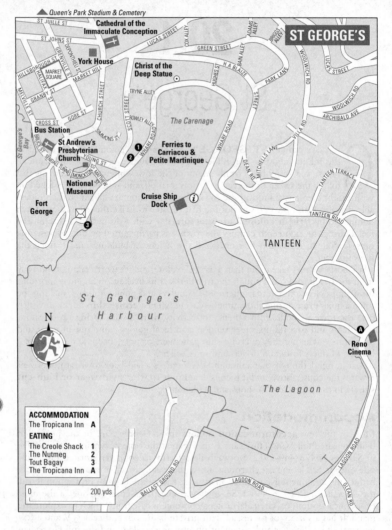

▲ Queen's Park Stadium & Cemetery

ST GEORGE'S

ST JUILLE ST
ST JOHNS ST
Cathedral of the Immaculate Conception
LUCAS STREET
COX ALLEY
GREEN STREET
ADAMS ALLEY
BRIGGS ALLEY
WOOLWICH RD
LUCAS STREET
HILLSBOROUGH ST
DEPONTHIEU ST
GRENVILLE ST
York House
HAIFA ST
MARKET SQUARE
MEVILLE'S ST
GRANBY ST
GORE ST
MARKET HILL
CHURCH STREET
Christ of the Deep Statue
H A BLAIZE
HUGHES ST
PARK LANE
WOOLWICH RD
WOOLWICH AVE
ARCHIBALD AVE
CROSS ST
SCOTT STREET
ROWLEY ALLEY
TRYNE ALLEY
The Carenage
WHARF ROAD
VILLA RD
MITCHELLS LANE
DEAN RD
Bus Station
St Andrew's Presbyterian Church
BRUCE ST
SIMMONS ST
YOUNG ST
❶
❷
Ferries to Carriacou & Petite Martinique
TANTEEN TERRACE
St George's Bay
TUNNEL
MONCKTON ST
MATTHEW ST
National Museum
Cruise Ship Dock
ⓘ
TANTEEN ROAD
Fort George
✉
❸
TANTEEN

St George's Harbour

N

Ⓐ
Reno Cinema

The Lagoon

ACCOMMODATION
The Tropicana Inn   A
EATING
The Creole Shack   1
The Nutmeg   2
Tout Bagay   3
The Tropicana Inn   A

0   200 yds

LAGOON ROAD
BALLAST GROUND RD
GLEAN RD

St George's

20.1 | GRENADA | St George's

20

produce vie for your senses alongside vendors selling barbecued corn cobs (Mon–Sat). Clothes, shoes, music and much more are traded here, and the numerous buses that pick up and drop off around its confined perimeter add to the market's sense of contained mayhem.

The streets around the market are worth exploring as they contain many architectural treasures and will give you a feel for local life – not to mention numerous stunning views. Just inland, above the market square on Upper Church Street is the **Cathedral of the Immaculate Conception**. Completed in 1820, the statuesque grey-stone building houses a number of impressive stained-glass windows. Despite being severely damaged by Hurricane Ivan, including the loss of the wood trussed roof, three of the windows and the nineteenth-century pipe organ, the cathedral still commands an impressive panoramic view of the harbour.

Opposite the cathedral and home to the Houses of Parliament, the **York House**, although similarly damaged, remains a fine example of the town's Georgian architecture. The mace belonging to the House of Representatives is reputed to be the largest in the world.

One block south of the market on Bruce Street is the main **bus terminal** for the island. Here buses leave from clearly marked stops and arrive via the Carenage and **Sendall Tunnel**, built in 1895 to stop horse carts from having to scramble over the headland and allowing their safe passage to the market.

Fort George

On a hilltop at the western end of the Carenage presides **Fort George**. To reach the entrance from the market, follow Halifax Street towards the Carenage before turning right onto the steep Grand Etang Road, which climbs up to the fort. On the way you'll pass the ruins of **St Andrew's Presbyterian Church**, once a dark, imposing structure also known as Scot's Kirk. Built in 1831, the church is famous for its bell, cast in Glasgow in 1833 and now housed in the damaged four-spired clock tower whose clock stopped at twenty to four on the day Ivan struck. Fort George itself has splendid panoramic views of the Carenage and beyond towards Grand Anse. Built by the French in 1705 (who originally named it Fort Royal) to protect the harbour, the fort had additional defences added by the British who took control of the fort in 1763 and made it a part of their defence of the Caribbean (both the British and French used the Windward Islands as a base to raid Spanish ships). The fort has played an integral role in Grenada's history, being the focal point of every armed intervention and military coup, the most recent of which were the events surrounding the end of the Revolutionary Government in 1983.

The Carenage

The inner harbour, known as the **Carenage**, was once the meeting point for ships from all over the Caribbean prior to their journey across the Atlantic to Britain. A perfect horseshoe, the Carenage is where a number of working boats and smaller cruise liners dock – larger vessels use the newer cruise ship terminal situated on the waterfront to the west of the Fort George headland. The waterfront area of the Carenage was the focus of the town's tourism but, at the time of writing, the duty-free stores, high-end souvenir shops, cafés and restaurants are largely still repairing themselves post Ivan. Ringing the Carenage is a paved walkway dotted with old cannons removed from the island's forts and now used as bollards to tie up ships. Halfway around the harbour, the walkway opens out to accommodate some sea-facing benches, a favourite meeting point for locals. This is also where you'll attract the attention of the local **"guides"**, who often approach visitors by starting to chat about the history of the island. Be warned, they expect payment for their time (about EC$20 per hour), so if you don't want them to take you on a guided tour of the town, be firm and extract yourself as soon as you can.

It is also here that you will find the striking statue of the **Christ of the Deep** looking out to sea, arms outstretched to commemorate the events of October 22, 1961, when the Carenage was the scene of the largest shipwreck in the Caribbean. The **Bianca C**, a 600ft-long Italian ocean liner, was anchored in St George's when an explosion occurred in its engine room. The whole ship soon caught fire and a fleet of local boats, yachts and swimmers raced to the rescue, managing to save everyone aboard – except a single crewman who later died of severe burns. As the still-burning ship was being towed to the shallow waters around Point Saline, the towrope broke and the *Bianca C* sank a mile and a half offshore. The bronze statue was donated by the ship's owners in recognition of local rescue efforts.

Towards the western end of the Carenage, take a right turn on narrow Young Street to Monckton Street where Grenada's **National Museum** (Mon–Fri 9am–4.30pm, Sat 10am–2pm; EC$5) is housed in a building constructed by the French in 1704 as a prison and army barracks, and subsequently used by the British as the island's first hotel. Exhibits include Amerindian artifacts and information on the revolutionary events of 1979 that led to the US invasion in 1983.

The Lagoon

Not strictly part of St George's, the **Lagoon**, a ten-minute walk south of the town past the docks, is the site of the first town in Grenada. Fort Louis, established by the governor of Martinique in 1650, has since sunk into the Lagoon, and today this naturally protected circle of water is a popular anchorage for yachts. While the waterfront is largely parkland, the rest of the area is home to a cinema, hotel, restaurants and stores, and residential properties higher in the hills.

Eating and drinking

In St George's most **places to eat** can be found around the Carenage, where options range from cafés to restaurants. Dining here is inexpensive, laid-back and a bit more authentic than at the beaches.

The Creole Shack The Carenage ☎ 473/435-7422. An attractive street-level restaurant and bar overlooking the waterfront, serving a mix of Creole and other Caribbean dishes at reasonable prices. The popular lunch menu, including saltfish pie and oildown, starts at EC$8 while dinner prices average at EC$40.

The Nutmeg The Carenage ☎ 473/440-2539. Famous for its Grenadian-style seafood dinners and nutmeg rum punch, this very popular restaurant also has sweeping views of the Carenage and beyond. Burgers and rotis (from EC$8) make up the lunch menu, while typical dinner dishes include Caribbean shrimp cocktails (EC$27) and a delicious seafood platter (EC$54).

Tout Bagay The Carenage ☎ 473/440-1500. Reservations are recommended for dinner at this colourfully decorated restaurant at the far west end of the Carenage, where the menu has everything from seafood, curried goat, steaks and vegetarian options. Main courses start at EC$40.

The Tropicana Inn Lagoon Road ☎ 473/440-1586. Besides the mouthwatering full Grenadian breakfast (EC$16), this restaurant serves a consistently tasty and reasonably priced daily menu, including options such as curried shrimp (EC$35), stewed fish (EC$25) and T-bone steak (EC$50). Order food to go at the take-away annexe next door where large portions of fish with vegetables and rice cost EC$11.

Shopping and entertainment

Throughout St George's you will find plenty of **arts and crafts shops**, many aimed at cruise ship passengers and varying in price and quality. Among the better ones is Art Fabrick (☎ 473/440-0568) on Young Street, where local **batik** artists can usually be seen at work. Fedon Books (☎ 473/435-2665) on H.A. Blaize Street has an extensive range of Caribbean literature and history books and Turbo Charge record (☎ 473/440-0586) on St John's Street is recommended for recordings of local reggae, soca and ragga music.

The town has a smattering of **entertainment** options, including *The Creole Shack* (see above) a popular evening bar with large-screen TV, open until 10pm Mon–Thurs, while Fridays and Saturdays are karaoke night and the bar remains open until after midnight. Just out of town on Lagoon Road the *Tropicana Inn* (see above), has a lively bar, which sometimes offers **live steel-band** and **calypso music** in the evenings. Opposite the *Tropicana Inn,* the Reno Cinema on Lagoon Road (☎ 473/440-2403) screens current mainstream films and charges EC$7–15.

Unfortunately for **cricket** fans the Queens Park National Stadium, a five- to ten-minute walk north of St George's, was severely damaged by Hurricane Ivan. Although the government has announced plans to rebuild the stadium in time for the 2007 World Cup, with financial assistance from mainland China, this decision is a controversial one while so many locals remain homeless.

20.2

The southwest

The southwest corner of the island is home to Grenada's most popular beaches. Only two miles from St George's is the king of them all, **Grand Anse**, whose long curve of immaculate white sands is frequented by locals and visitors alike. Further south and separated by the headland of Quarantine Point, formerly a leper colony, is the secluded **Morne Rouge Bay**. A favourite among wealthy tourists, the beach is excellent for swimming and it's also a popular place to snorkel. Continuing south beyond the airport are several smaller beaches and **Lance Aux Épines**, a peninsula at Grenada's southernmost point dotted with many luxury homes. **Prickly Bay** on the peninsula's west side is a popular anchorage for yachts and home to a good-sized palm-fringed beach where watersports are abundant. **Mount Hartman Bay** on the eastern side may lack beaches, but has no shortage of stunning views over the island's south coast. Be aware that, while some visitors to these beaches do sunbathe topless, this practice is not permitted anywhere on the island.

Accommodation

A considerable portion of **accommodation** options in Grand Anse was severely damaged by Hurricane Ivan. Check the Hurricane Ivan Information and Update websites or the Grenada Tourist Board for the latest details on what has reopened in this area.

Beach Inn Grand Anse ☎473/444-4216, 🌐www.beachinngrenada.com. This small, colourful inn, located in Grand Anse, which has a communal verandah, is the perfect place to watch sunsets. All rooms have a refrigerator and ceiling fans. ❸

Lance Aux Epines Cottages L'Anse Aux Epines ☎473/444-4565, 🌐www.laecottages.com. A ten-minute drive from the airport and situated on the edge of a shady beach, these basic but fully equipped cottages come with maid service and TV. A supermarket, restaurant and pub are all close by. ❻

La Luna Portici Beach ☎473/439-0001, 🌐www.laluna.com. The sixteen beach cottages of this hideaway resort are the most exclusive places to stay on the island. Each pastel-coloured cottage has a plunge pool, TV, video and CD player, and there's also a stunning beachfront swimming pool

and free watersports, which is just as well as a night here can set you back as much as US$500.

Monmot Hotel L'Anse Aux Epines ☎473/439-3408, 🌐www.monmothotel.com. This small, locally run hotel, is two minutes' walk away from the nearest beach. Clustered around the hotel pool, all the comfortable rooms come with a/c or ceiling fans and cable TV. There is an excellent bar and restaurant on site. ❻

True Blue Bay True Blue ☎473/443-8783, 🌐www.truebluebay.com. Nestled around the waters of True Blue Bay, this friendly resort displays a certain quirkiness amidst its luxury. All of its rooms, apartments and villas are colourfully decorated and come with a/c, cable TV, Internet connection and balconies with views over the bay. The on-site, waterfront restaurant and bar are both lively and feature live music some nights. ❻–❽

Grand Anse Beach and around

Most people's experience of Grenada begins and ends with the stunning **Grand Anse Beach**, a 1.3-mile stretch of white sand with a perfect view of St George's and the surrounding hills. Even on busy days large pockets of peace and quiet can be found amidst the gaggles of tourists that congregate on the sands. The sea is exquisite and there is no shortage of opportunities to water-ski, windsurf or be pulled around the bay in an inflated inner tube by speedboat. The Craft and Spice Market selling jewellery, clothes and the ubiquitous spices (daily 8am–6pm) is situated at the north end of the beach, which also has a number of small refreshment bars, as well as showers and toilets. Many vendors wander the beach touting their wares and you're likely to get some hassle from them, though not much.

Just south of Grand Anse on the other side of Quarantine Point lies **Morne Rouge Beach**. Having fewer resort complexes and being slightly harder to reach, this smaller and shadeless beach has an air of exclusivity and is excellent for swimming, snorkelling and private sunbathing.

The next beach along the coast, just past Petit Cabrits Point, is the even more isolated **Portici Beach**, which is accessible from the main road to the airport – just take the turn marked "Beach House Bar and Restaurant" and follow the dirt track down to the shore. The walk from the airport takes about twenty minutes, so if your plane is delayed you can while away your time on the sands rather than in the departure lounge. Here, if anywhere, you'll bump into the rich and famous who visit Grenada – the beach backs onto the exclusive resort of *La Luna* (see p.787).

Diving

Many of the island's **dive companies** operate out of hotels or resorts in the southwest. Scuba World Grenada based at, and sharing the same contact details as, the *Beach Inn* on Grand Anse (see p.787) offers a variety of dive packages from US$36 for a single dive to US$280 for ten. They also organize a range of PADI. courses from Discover Scuba at US$80 for beginners to Advanced Open Water at US$340 for the experienced diver. Dive sites they visit include the *Bianca C* shipwreck and the Molinere Reef where a wide variety of tropical fish can be found. In addition, Scuba World Grenada organizes snorkelling trips and a range of watersports including water- and jet skiing and windsurfing. Operating from *True Blue Bay Resort* (see p.787) and with an additional store on Grand Anse beach, Aquanauts (☎473/444-1126, ⊕www.aquanautsgrenada.com), offer free trial dives and a range of courses from US$79 for beginners to advanced courses for US$299, as well as trips to the near by Isle de Rhonde for US$40. Another reliable and long-established dive outfit is Dive Grenada (☎473/444-1092, ⊕www.divegrenada.com) which organizes dives from US$40 and night dives for US$50 as well as snorkel trips from US$20.

Eating and drinking

The southwest is where you'll find the island's more upmarket **restaurants**, most of which are connected to hotels and resorts; however, at the time of writing options are restricted due to ongoing repairs following Hurricane Ivan. A number of takeaway and fast food options can be found around the Spiceland Mall area of Grand Anse.

The Aquarium Restaurant Pink Gin Beach ☎473/444-1410, ⊕www.aquarium-grenada.com. Popular with locals and visitors alike, this beachfront restaurant and bar set in tropical gardens is one of the best places on the island to enjoy gourmet local and international cuisine, including coconut-cilantro Thai chicken and *callaloo* canneloni, or simply sip a cocktail. Be sure to stop for the Sunday BBQ which is consistently popular with locals. Closed Mondays.
Bananas True Blue ☎473/444-4662. This laid-back and reasonably priced restaurant and bar has an extensive lunch menu including sandwiches,

burgers, soup and rotis from EC$8. There's also a good range of seafood and a couple of vegetarian options on the dinner menu, with prices averaging EC$40.
Da Big Fish Prickly Bay Marina ☎473/439-5265. Overlooking the marina and waters of Prickly Bay, this relaxed open-air bar and restaurant is a popular spot with yachters and non-yachters alike. Lunch options range from fish burgers at EC$10 and bean burritos for EC$16, while dinner dishes include grilled fish for EC$34. There is also a lively daily happy hour 5–6pm. Open Mon–Sat 8am–11pm & Sun 1–8pm.

20

Red Crab L'Anse Aux Epines ☎473/444-4424. This popular local restaurant has a choice of indoor or outdoor seating and an extensive menu featuring especially good fish and seafood options. There's live music Monday and Friday evenings. Closed Sundays.

True Blue Bay True Blue ☎473/443-8783. This popular resort restaurant serves a range of Creole, Mexican and Thai food from its fairy-light-strewn terrace on the water's edge. Lunch dishes include nachos for EC$20 and salads from EC$15, and the dinner menu starts at EC$40.

Nightlife

There are a variety of **nightlife** options dotted around the southwest of the island. Many hotel bars and restaurants feature live entertainment including steel bands and calypso music, and *La Sirena* (☎473/444–1410), the beach bar at the Aquarium restaurant (see opposite), has regular live music nights (closed Mondays). For late-night bars and clubs try *Bananas* in True Blue which has a large screen TV and stays open until 2am most nights, while Grenada's newest club *The Music Room* (☎473/4444–4687) on Maurice Bishop Highway has a cover charge of EC$20 and features live music of all genres at the weekends. The island's best-known and busiest nightclub is *Fantazia 2001* in Morne Rouge (☎473/444–2288) where you can bop until the small hours of the morning for a small cover charge.

20.3

The rest of the island

There is much more to Grenada than its tourist beaches and the bustle of St George's. Travelling around the island you will encounter the variety of its terrain – from the mountainous rainforest of the interior to the rugged shoreline of the northeast. There are three main areas to be explored: the sheltered and gentle **Leeward Coast**, the weather-beaten **Windward Coast**, and the dramatic, largely uninhabited **interior**.

Accommodation

Barry's Country Resort Castlehill ☎473/442-0330, ⓦwww.barrysresort.com. Situated close to Bathway Beach in the northeast of the island, this large new hotel's rooms all have a/c and cable TV. There's also a pool, tennis court and restaurant on site. ❹

Grenada Rainbow Inn Grenville ☎473/442-7714, ⓦwww.grenadarainbowinn.com. The rooms at this delightful inn near Grand Etang National Park are clean and comfortable and come with private bathrooms, balconies and cable TV. Organic food is available at the hotel restaurant. ❷

Petit Bacaye Cottages Westerhall ☎473/443-2902, ⓦwww.petitbacaye.com. These palm-thatched cottages on the edge of a small bay are the place to stay if you're seeking solitude. The rooms are simple and tastefully decorated, but don't expect to find a TV or radio. If you feel the need for company there is a small restaurant and bar on the premises, and buses to St George's pass close by. ❻

Plantation House Morne Fendue ☎473/442-9330, ⓦwww.caribbean-connexion.com/hotels/

fendue.htm. Built from colourful stones from a nearby river, this authentic Victorian plantation house has simple rooms, some with private bath. ❸

La Sagesse Nature Centre La Sagesse ☎473/444-6458, ⊛www.lasagesse.com. Easily accessible by public transport, yet also one of the most secluded places to stay on the island, this sedate old manor house on the edge of a quiet beach has a number of elegant rooms all of which have retained their original grandeur. There are also a number of stylish new beachfront rooms and the food at the beachfront restaurant and bar is delicious. ❺

Leeward Coast

Heading north from St George's the **Leeward Highway** is a scenic road that twists and turns in on itself until finally reaching Sauteurs and the famous Caribs' Leap.

As the highway winds along it passes through a number of colourful fishing and former plantation communities such as **Beauséjour Bay**, centre of radio communication for the Revolutionary Government from 1979, and the small town of **Brizan**, once a safe haven for escaped slaves and now home to a recording studio built by pop star Billy Ocean, a native Grenadian.

After passing through **Halifax Harbour**, where you'll find the Grenada Dove Sanctuary, a reserve for the national bird of Grenada (also known as the invisible bird because sightings are rare), the road leads through the tiny village of **Concord**, birthplace of calypso legend the "Mighty Sparrow" and on to **Gouyave**, a lovely old sea-weathered town, whose long main street overhung with balconies and strings of lights belongs more to the Wild West than the Caribbean. Famous for its fishing, the town celebrates Fisherman's Birthday (June 29), the Feast Day of SS Peter and Paul, during which residents of Gouyave head down to the beaches in the morning to bless the fishing boats and then party the rest of the day away. Gouyave is also one of the main centres of the **nutmeg industry**, and a worthwhile stop is the town's nutmeg processing station (Mon–Fri 8am–4pm), where employees lead tours through the various stages of nutmeg and mace production for EC$2. Both the building and the supplies of nutmeg and mace it processes were damaged by Ivan, and despite the short-term decline in this industry due to reduced harvest, you can still experience something of the island's working culture here – a slice of Grenada that the resorts in the southwest gloss over.

Situated at the end of the road is the exposed and windswept village of **Sauteurs**, dominated by both a Roman Catholic and an Anglican church – symbols of the conflicts in Grenada's colonial past. The main attraction is **Caribs' Leap**, a steep cliff rising more than 100 feet out of the ocean, from which the last of the island's Carib Indians threw themselves in an effort to resist French rule. From up here you'll have a stunning view of the channel where the Atlantic Ocean and the Caribbean Sea meet, which is punctuated by an arch of rock known as London Bridge, and other Grenadine islands, including Carriacou.

Windward Coast

Travelling south from St George's, veer left at the Spiceland Mall on Grand Anse Main Road. A sharp left at the next junction will put you on Grand Anse Valley Road, which heads east towards the affluent **Westerhall Bay**. The road clings to the island's east coast, passing the secluded and pretty beach of **Petit Bacaye**, before heading on to **La Sagesse Bay**. A signposted dirt track leads down to the sheltered beach with its straggling palm trees and small mangrove swamp, and to **La Sagesse Nature Centre** (see also above), formerly the home of the late Lord Brownlow, Queen Elizabeth II's cousin, who in the early 1970s built the infamous Brownlow's Gate, which blocked public access to the beach. Protestors removed the gate to regain access to the beach and the Revolutionary Government nationalized the estate in 1979. A map of the walking trails in the area can be obtained from the Nature Centre, which also organizes special day-packages (EC$75) that cover transportation from your hotel, a guided nature walk, lunch and a little time on the beach.

△ St George's market square

Continuing north around the eastern side of the island, the endlessly twisting Windward Highway, in various states of repair, leads on to Grenada's second largest town, **Grenville**. Established by the French in 1763, the town is the backbone of the country's agricultural sector and home to Grenada's largest nutmeg processing station. There is little of interest in this sprawling and busy, working town and harbour, and the best day to visit is a Saturday when a large colourful market selling fresh fish, fruit, vegetables and spices becomes a lively attraction. The market square is also the focus of the **Rainbow City Festival** held every year in late July and early August. Celebrating emancipation, this vibrant festival features street dancing and calypso bands.

Regardless of the time of year, the eerie **Pearls Airport**, two miles north of Grenville, is reason enough to visit the area. With a duty-free store whose specials are still posted in the window and a café that looks as if it will open at any minute, it is as if time stopped the moment the airport was abandoned in 1984 after the opening of the Cuban-built Point Salines Airport in the southwest. Two rusting Cold War relics – a Russian Aeroflot plane and a Cubana aircraft – lie just off the runway, and are slowly being dismantled by weather and vandals. The area was once a large Amerindian settlement and burial ground, and a large number of artefacts have been recovered, and though it is illegal to remove artefacts, this doesn't stop local children from attempting to sell them to visitors.

Situated a couple of miles north of Pearl's Airport, and a short detour inland at the small village of Tivoli, is Grenada's newest tourist attraction, **Belmont Estate** (Sun–Fri 8am–4pm; EC$10; ☎473/442-9524; ⊛www.belmontestate.net). This lovingly restored seventeenth-century plantation had only been open two years when the fury of Ivan destroyed a large part of the estate, including its lively restaurant. At the time of writing, although the museum, cocoa fermentary, sugar cane garden and old cemetery are undergoing extensive repairs, Belmont remains a fascinating place to explore as it gives the visitor a real insight into agricultural history of the Caribbean and cocoa production in a beautiful setting. A further mile inland, and fully operational, is the factory of the famous **Grenada Chocolate Company** (open daily; no set hours; ☎473/442-0050; ⊛www.grenadachocolate.com) where high-quality rich organic dark chocolate is produced using environmentally friendly methods and locally grown cocoa. Free tours of this tiny and delightful factory are available if the staff are not too busy.

Back on the Windward Highway and just a short distance from Tivoli, is the **River Antoine Rum Distillery** (Mon–Fri 8am–4pm; EC$14; ☎473/442-7109), the oldest functioning water powered distillery in the Caribbean whose water wheel has been crushing juice from locally grown sugar cane since 1785. Tours led by workers take you through the fragrant factory, which still uses traditional distilling methods to produce its powerful 150-proof rum.

Another not-to-be-missed detour from the highway north is **Lake Antoine**. Surrounded by lush agricultural land, this spectacular sixteen-acre lake inside the crater of an extinct volcano has been known to bubble when eruptions have occurred elsewhere in the region, prompting speculation that it is linked to a volcanic chain. Looking towards the coast from the lake's edge you can see rugged **Antoine Bay**, originally called Conception by Columbus when he first sighted it in 1498.

From Antoine Bay the road leads to the far northeast and **Levera National Park**. It's not hard to understand why this remote part of the coastline attracts so many visitors; the undulating hills of this volcanic landscape are threaded with scenic hiking trails. On the easternmost tip of the island **Bathway Beach** is a striking, windswept beach shaded by palm trees and popular for picnics, although swimming past the reef is not permitted due to dangerous undercurrents. Visitors can buy refreshments at a roadside bar and learn more about the area at the visitor centre, situated at Bathway Beach, which has small displays explaining the region's geology, and showers and rest rooms and even an outdoor amphitheatre.

The interior

Grenada may be famous for its beaches, but no visit to the island is complete without a trip to its dramatic rainforest. One of the worst casualties of Ivan, the lush, tropical vegetation that characterized the 3860 acres of **Grand Etang National Park** was torn to shreds by the hurricane's ferocious winds. Although re-growing at a rapid rate, the dense rainforest canopy, which at its highest point rises to the majestic 2757ft peak at **Mount St Catherine**, and network of **walking trails** which thread through it, are currently in the early stages of repair. Anyone wanting to explore the rainforest, reached by a fifteen-minute drive or bus ride from St George's, should contact either tourist information or one of the island's tour guides (see p.779) in order to obtain up-to-date information.

Situated 1700ft above sea level and one rainforest sight that remains accessible within the Grand Etang Forest Reserve, although often shrouded in mist, is **Lake Grand Etang**. Grenada's water reservoir and an essential stop, its shores offer striking views of Mount Qua Qua and other peaks, and the rainforest which surrounds it, on the road through the interior.

Although some of Grenada's spectacular waterfalls are currently inaccessible, those that can be reached should not be missed. Easily accessed by road – just turn inland from the Leeward Highway at Concord – are the famous **Concord Falls**. These three waterfalls, one of which is 65ft high and has a freshwater pool large enough for swimming at its base, are one of the highlights of the Grand Etang National Park.

Eating, drinking and entertainment

If you are looking for a place to eat in the south, highly recommended is the beach-front restaurant and bar at La Sagesse Nature Centre (see p.790). A range of delicious and simple meals such as grilled flying fish (EC$30) are served in stylish dark-wood surrounds – one of the most romantic spots for dinner on the island.

If you need a break from beaches, Grenville's Deluxe Cinema (☎473/442-6200) screens current mainstream **films** and charges EC$7–15 admission.

20.4

Carriacou

The most southerly of the Grenadine islands, **CARRIACOU** (an Arawak name meaning "island of reefs") is, at thirteen square miles, the largest of the island chain that lies between Grenada and St Vincent. Although just a short ferry hop from Grenada, the seven thousand inhabitants of Carriacou, fondly nicknamed "Kayaks" by Grenadians, enjoy a more relaxed pace of life and suffered far less damage from Hurricane Ivan than their neighbours. The main town of **Hillsborough**, surrounded by low, forested hills, won't detain you for long, but the

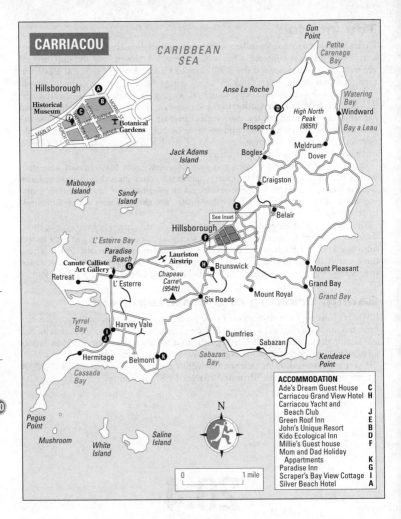

CARRIACOU

CARIBBEAN SEA

Gun Point
Petite Carenage Bay
Anse La Roche
Watering Bay
Windward
High North Peak (985ft)
Prospect
Bay a Leau
Bogles
Meldrum
Dover
Craigston
Hillsborough
See Inset
Belair
Jack Adams Island
Mabouya Island
Sandy Island
L' Esterre Bay
Paradise Beach
Canute Calliste Art Gallery
Retreat
L' Esterre
Lauriston Airstrip
Chapeau Carré (954ft)
Brunswick
Mount Pleasant
Grand Bay
Mount Royal
Grand Bay
Six Roads
Tyrrel Bay
Harvey Vale
Dumfries
Sabazan
Hermitage
Belmont
Sabazan Bay
Kendeace Point
Cassada Bay
Pegus Point
Mushroom
White Island
Saline Island

Hillsborough
Historical Museum
Botanical Gardens
MORRIS ST
MAIN ST
CHURCH ST
PATTERSON ST
2ND AVENUE
3RD AVENUE

N

0   1 mile

ACCOMMODATION
Ade's Dream Guest House   C
Carriacou Grand View Hotel   H
Carriacou Yacht and
  Beach Club   J
Green Roof Inn   E
John's Unique Resort   B
Kido Ecological Inn   D
Millie's Guest house   F
Mom and Dad Holiday
  Appartments   K
Paradise Inn   G
Scraper's Bay View Cottage   I
Silver Beach Hotel   A

rest of the island, with its excellent watersports and unspoiled beaches in the south and good walking trails in the north, is well worth exploring. Diving is also first class on the island, with a range of sites for all levels of experience, including the wreck of a small World War I gunboat.

Carriacou also has no shortage of **culture**. Belief systems of the African slaves remain strong on Carriacou and are preserved in rituals such as the powerful **Big Drum Dance**, a pre-Christian ceremony in which ancestors communicate with their descendants (see box on p.797). The Big Drum Dances, along with street parties and calypso, are the highlights of the **Carriacou Regatta** held every August, during which descendants of the island's Scottish boat-builders show off their hand-built schooners. Other festive times to visit are **Carnival**, celebrated before the start of Lent, **May Day** and the **Parang festival** prior to Christmas – all are opportunities to hit the streets, dance and eat, and there is never any shortage of calypso.

Kick'em Jenny

Directly under the waters of the published ferry route from Grenada to Carriacou, although in practice slightly bypassed due to a mile-wide exclusion zone, lies a growing underwater volcano known as **Kick'em Jenny**, whose peak is now approximately 180 metres from the surface of the water. Kick'em Jenny's first known eruption, which lasted 24 hours, occurred on July 24, 1939. This produced a column of water and debris over 900ft high and tsunamis in Grenada and the south Grenadines. Twelve smaller eruptions have occurred since, the most recent in December 2001.

Kick'em Jenny is continually monitored by the Seismic Research Unit at the University of the West Indies in Trinidad, which issues warnings if there are signs of over-activity.

For details and a sonar image of the volcano, visit ⊛www.uwiseismic.com/KeJ/Kejhome.html.

Arrival and information

Carriacou is easily accessible by **air**, with daily connecting flights from Barbados, Grenada, St Vincent and other Grenadine islands; flights touch down at **Lauriston Airstrip** one mile south of Hillsborough. However, by far the most scenic and economical way to get here from Grenada is the regular *Osprey Express* **passenger ferry** (see p.778), which arrives and departs from the Hillsborough jetty. Monday–Saturday tickets for the Osprey should be bought from their office on Patterson Street in Hillsborough (Mon–Fri 5.30–6.30am & 10.30am–4.30pm, Sat 5.30–6.30am, 10am–noon & 3–4pm; ☎473/443-8126), while on Sundays they can be bought on board. A passenger and cargo boat (*The Jasper* – see p.749) also runs between Carriacou and **Union Island** in St Vincent and the Grenadines; passengers from Union Island must pass through immigration at the small office across the main road, opposite the foot of the jetty.

The **tourist office** (Mon–Fri 8am–noon & 1–4pm; ☎473/443-6014) on Patterson Street is where you can pick up accommodation information and a map of the island. Both Barclays Bank and National Commercial Bank have branches in Hillsborough; the latter has an **ATM**. The lone **post office** (Mon–Fri 8am–noon & 1–4pm) is in front of the pier, while payphones can be found in front of the Cable & Wireless office on Patterson Street (Mon–Fri 7.30am–6pm, Sat 7.30am–1pm). Phone-cards can be bought inside. The Internet Café on Main Street is open Mon & Fri 9am–4pm and Tues–Thurs 9am–noon and the EC$10 per half-hour charge includes a free cold drink.

Getting around

Buses operate from the jetty in Hillsborough and typical fares are EC$1.50 for trips up to one mile and EC$2.50 for those over one mile. A service also runs from Lauriston Airport, Tyrrel Bay and Belmont to south of Hillsborough and north to the town of Windward. **Taxis** run from the airport to Hillsborough for around EC$15 and to Belair for roughly EC$20. **Water taxis** from the jetty are the easiest way to get to the beaches. **Car rental agencies** include Sunkey's Auto Rentals in Hillsborough (☎473/443-8382); Martin Bullen (☎473/443-7204), who is based at the island's only petrol station on Patterson Street in Hillsborough; and John Gabriel (☎473/443-7454) in Tyrrel Bay. All charge around EC$110–135 per day. **Bikes** can be hired from Wild Track Cycles in Tyrrel Bay (☎473/443-6472; ✉wildtrackcycles@grenadines.net), for EC$50 per day or EC$25 for a half-day.

Accommodation

Despite its small size, Carriacou has a varied selection of good-value **accommodation** options.

Hillsborough

Ade's Dream Guest House Main Street ☎473/443-7317, ⊕www.grenadines.net /carriacou/ade.htm. Claiming that "your best dream awaits you", this charming guesthouse with ornate balconies has a range of rooms from small with shared bathroom to larger, new rooms with kitchenettes and private bathrooms. A grocery store is on the ground floor and the well-reviewed *Sea Wave Restaurant* is right across the street. ❷

Green Roof Inn Hillsborough 473/443-6399, ⊕www.greenroofinn.com. A ten-minute walk north of Hillsborough (or an EC$1.25 bus ride), this highly recommended small, family-run inn is a peaceful haven with breathtaking views. The rooms are simple but stylish and all have mosquito nets and fans. Bikes and snorkel equipment are available for rent and an excellent Continental breakfast and airport/jetty transfer are included in the rates. ❸

John's Unique Resort Upper Main Street ☎473/443-8345 ⓔjunique@caribsurf.com. All of the spacious rooms and apartments of this private hotel, located five minutes' walk from the centre of Hillsborough, are en suite and come with private balconies and cable TV; some also have kitchens. There is also an on-site restaurant and bar. ❶–❸

Millie's Guest House Main Street ☎473/443-7310 ⓔmillies@caribsurf.com. On the beachfront side of Main Street, this rambling hotel with covered wooden balconies is good-value budget accommodation. One room has a private bathroom and the rest share bathrooms and kitchens. ❷

Silver Beach Hotel ☎473/443-7337, ⓔsilverbeach@caribsurf.com. Nestled by the water's edge in a secluded bay, this small resort has a range of one-bedroom suites, some of which are self-catering. Free transport is available from the airport and bus tours and sailing excursions can be arranged. One free night is offered for every seven-night stay. ❸

The rest of the island

Carriacou Grand View Hotel Beauséjour ☎473/443-6348, ⊕www.carriacougrandview.com.
Perched above Hillsborough harbour, this large hotel with its own pool and on-site restaurant and piano bar, commands magnificent views over the sea and surrounding countryside. All of the simple, but comfortable en-suite rooms come with private balconies, TV and a/c or ceiling fans. Apartments with kitchenettes are also available. ❸–❹

Carriacou Yacht and Beach Club Tyrrel Bay ☎473/443-6123, ⓔcarriyacht@caribsurf.com. Surrounded by palm trees, this self-contained complex at the water's edge is a popular haunt for yachters. The rooms are neat and comfortable and all have private bathrooms, refrigerators and coffeemakers. The resort also has its own bar and restaurant. ❷

Kido Ecological Inn Prospect ☎473/443-7936, ⊕www.kido-projects.com. Eco-tourism is high on *Kido*'s list of priorities due to its location on a forested ridge on the northwestern coast. The inn is also a research station, and birdwatching, hiking, cycling, sailing and diving are all available, as is the chance to volunteer for one of their ongoing ecological projects. Accommodation includes a two-bedroom villa and large pagoda, and there's a well-stocked library. ❺

Mom and Dad Holiday Apartments Belmont ☎473/443-8056. Five minutes from lovely Harvey Vale Beach, this gleaming white apartment block are fitted with mahogany furniture and all come with a well-equipped kitchen and verandah. ❸

Paradise Inn L'Esterre Bay ☎473/443-8406, ⊕www.paradise-inn-carriacou.com. Right on the edge of the secluded Paradise Beach, this small, attractive inn has spacious rooms, each with private shower and toilet and ceiling fans. *Ali's* restaurant on site has a varied menu. ❷

Scraper's Bay View Cottages Tyrrel Bay ☎473/443-7403. Appealing Caribbean-style apartments whose modest rooms all have private kitchens and bathrooms. The adjoining bar and restaurant serves a range of fish and pasta dishes as well as sandwiches and burgers. ❸

Hillsborough

A small cluster of weather-worn buildings overlooking the sea, Hillsborough may be the main point of entry to the island, but has little to warrant a long stay and is easily explored in an hour or two. The town stretches along its at times tatty Main Street, which runs parallel to the beach. Here most of the town's **places to stay and eat** as well as banks and public services are to be found. The beach around the

The Big Drum Dance

The **Big Drum Dance** is an integral part of all festivities in Carriacou. Rooted in ancestral worship and tribal identity, the tradition has survived the centuries since it came to the Caribbean with the West African slaves. The drums are made from old rum kegs and goatskin and, until independence, were banned by the British who saw them as a threat to Christianity and feared they would incite rebellion. The ritual has survived, thanks to the lack of attention of absentee European landowners and the people's determination to preserve their culture. Once reserved for special occasions, such as the launching of a boat or a funeral ceremony, the vibrant drumming and dancing is now also performed for tourists.

jetty is narrow and a heavily used part of the working harbour – though not for recreation.

The main focus of Hillsborough is its **jetty**, which punctuates the middle of the town and offers a view of nearby Union Island (see p.770). On Mondays the jetty is the site for a small and lively **market** where local fruit and vegetable vendors display their produce in a haphazard collection of stalls. Throughout the town old stone merchant houses serve as a reminder of the island's colonial, sugar-producing past, as does its small but interesting **Historical Museum** on Patterson Street (Mon–Fri 9.30am–4pm, Sat 10am–4pm; EC$5). Housed in the restored ruins of an old cotton gin mill, the museum features a varied collection of Amerindian utensils and pottery, and has sections devoted to the island's European and African heritage. The only other place of interest in Hillsborough is its small **Botanical Gardens** nestled a block inland from Main Street on First Avenue. The small collection of tropical plants, flowers and trees won't detain you for long, but this is a peaceful and shady spot in which to escape the hot sun.

The rest of the island

Approximately one and half miles southwest of Hillsborough past the airport, is the appropriately named **Paradise Beach**, a sweeping expanse of golden sand protected by two small islands and an ideal spot for safe swimming and snorkelling. In addition to a beachfront hotel (see opposite), facilities here include a couple of bars serving snacks and hot meals and a gift shack. A short distance west from Paradise Beach, is the small village of **L'Esterre**, home of local artist Canute Calliste, who claims a mermaid visited him when he was a small boy and blessed him with the gift of painting and music. So productive is his gift that Canute, now in his nineties, has been known to finish sixteen paintings in one day. You can view his cheerful and vibrant paintings at the artist's shop and studio in the village.

The main road then leads south away from L'Esterre, and on to one of the most popular beaches in the area, **Tyrrel Bay**, also known as Hurricane Bay because it is a favourite anchorage for yachts during storms. The three-mile journey to this large horseshoe bay on Carriacou's western side is serviced by a frequent bus service from Hillsborough. Here the waters are well protected and the beaches golden, especially at the southern end of the bay around the yacht club (see opposite), after the string of bars and shops that line the road peters out.

Tyrrel Bay is also famous for its oysters, and here protected tree oysters grow amongst mangrove roots which you can reach by boat. All of the bay's tranquillity is, however, under threat by a planned new marina development. Just yards inland from the bay is the pretty village of **Harvey Vale**. There's not much here to explore, but do take time to visit an old Amerindian well, whose waters are thought to have therapeutic qualities.

Looming over Hillsborough about a mile to the north is **Belair**, a peak 719ft above sea level that commands sweeping views of the Grenadines – especially Sandy Island

and Grenada. Here you will find scenic walking trails and the ruins of old French and British plantations nestled amongst white immortelle trees.

Further north is the small village of **Bogles,** the terminus of a bus route from the capital, and after which the road north becomes a track. A fifteen-minute walk, or two-minute drive if you're in a jeep, along the track leads to the **Kido Ecological Research Station** (for contact information, see *Kido Ecological Inn* p.796) and a short walk further along, or a water taxi ride from Hillsborough, leads to **Anse La Roche,** a peaceful beach on the northwest coast of the island where a variety of species of turtles, including green sea turtles and hawksbill turtles, swim ashore to lay their eggs at night. With its sea life-infested coral reefs lying just offshore, this crescent-shaped gem of a beach is one of the best places to snorkel in Grenada. It's also a pleasant spot to simply lie back and watch the yachts sail by, but make sure to bring food and drink as there are currently no facilities. However, the unspoiled seclusion of Anse La Roche is set to change as the area is earmarked for the construction of a new hotel complex.

A short walk from Anse La Roche, the northernmost tip of the island is known as **Gun Point,** so named for the cannons that used to contribute to the region's defences and which falls under the jurisdiction of the island of St Vincent. On the east side of the headland is the 955ft **High North Peak**, the highest point on the island and a protected national park. Details on the network of trails that thread through this region's dry deciduous forest, and the wildlife you might encounter along the way, can be found at a small interpretive centre in Bogles, managed by Kido Research Station. However, to fully appreciate the region a guide is recommended, and Kido organize hiking tours in the High North Park with local guides for EC$50 per person.

Nestled on the eastern edge of the High North National Park is the tiny and picturesque fishing village of **Windward**. The windswept community's occupants are boat-builders and descendants of Scottish immigrants who brought the craft here from Glasgow, back when the island was still under British colonial rule, and a small nautical museum in the village celebrates its seafaring history. Claiming to use plans passed down through the generations, many of these craftspeople now work at Tyrrel Bay. **Petite Carenage Bay** is also nestled in the northeast corner of the island, between Gun Point and Windward, and is home to a mangrove restoration project managed by Kido Research Station. You can explore a unique and ancient ecosystem whose dense vegetation and shallow waters are home to numerous fish, insects and birds. Kido organizes guided tours of the mangrove swamp, as well as turtle watching tours, both of which are recommended.

Ocean activities

Carriacou is especially good for **reef diving**, and is quieter than Grenada for practising other **watersports**. Diving, snorkelling, water-skiing and windsurfing are popular on the island and can be arranged through Carriacou Silver Diving Ltd (☎473/443-7882, ☜www.scubamax.com), whose office is in Hillsborough. Offering a range of day and night dives, this company caters for all levels of experience and will also arrange accommodation, island tours and even barbecues. Single dives start at US$38 and diving courses start at US$70 for a half-day Discover Scuba Diving trip. Arawak Divers in Tyrrel Bay (☎473/443-6906, ☜www.arawak.de) offers a similar range of dives and runs day excursions to the Isle of Rhonde and the Tobago Cays. Also based in Tyrrel Bay, *Lumbadive* (☎473/443-8566, ☜www.lumbadive.com) offer a range of dive courses including accommodation packages with *Paradise Inn* (see p.796). A six-night, ten-dive package costs US$490.

One of the most popular places to dive is **Sandy Island**, just off the coast from Hillsborough, whose stunning beaches and vibrant coral reefs have made it a popular location for television commercials. Sadly, its popularity has also been its undoing as dropped anchors have damaged the coral and are eroding the reef.

Turtle-watching tours, snorkelling trips and sailing excursions from a one-day whale- and dolphin-watching trip for US$160 to a two-day overnight sailing trip for US$340 can all be arranged by the Kido Research Station (see opposite).

Eating, drinking and nightlife

When it comes to **dining** and **nightlife** on Carriacou the main options are hotel bars and restaurants. There are a few independent establishments, but don't expect a lively nightlife or too much choice when it comes to finding something to eat.

Callaloo by the Sea Main Street, Hillsborough ☎473/443-8004. A quaint restaurant with fine views of Hillsborough Bay. Seafood is a speciality, and the menu also has a range of chicken dishes, as well as chips and a selection of salads. Open Mon–Sat 10am–10pm and the same time on Sundays in season. Prices range EC$36–130.

The Green Roof Inn Hillsborough ☎473/443-6399. Reservations are recommended at this superb second-floor verandah restaurant, whose food is as good as the views it commands. The menu varies depending on what's in season and typical dishes include smoked swordfish EC$47 and filet mignon EC$65.

Scraper's Restaurant Tyrrel Bay ☎473/443-7403. Reasonably priced burgers, sandwiches and pasta dishes, among others, are on the menu at this seaside spot. Prices start from EC$18 a head for dinner.

Sea Wave Restaurant Main Street, Hillsborough ☎473/443-7317. Across the road from *Ade's Dream Guest House* (see p.796), this no-frills restaurant cooks up a combination of Caribbean and international dishes starting from EC$18. Open daily 7am–9pm. The upstairs bar is a popular late-night drinking spot with a dress code.

Turtle Dove Pizzeria Tyrrel Bay ☎473/443-8322. This attractive blue and white restaurant next door to Lumbadive serves a good range of home-made Italian pizza and pasta dishes priced EC$15–36. Open daily noon–2pm and dinner from 6pm when reservations are recommended.

Twilight Restaurant & Bar Tyrrel Bay (no phone). This charming and friendly beachfront restaurant and bar serves a good range of local dishes such as curried lamb (EC$26) and grilled lobster (EC$47). Desserts include a range of delicious ice creams and live steel bands play into the night on Wednesdays and Sundays.

20.5

Petite Martinique

Situated approximately three miles northeast of Carriacou, **PETITE MARTINIQUE** is a large, mile-wide hill of unspoilt forestland whose 486 acres were first settled by the French in the seventeenth century and its nearly one thousand inhabitants are mainly their descendants. The sea has long been the main source of income for locals, who continue the tradition of seafaring, fishing and boat-building – and some say, smuggling – to this day.

As the island is tiny, don't expect to find a lot to do or see, especially if the weather is bad. This is in fact a great place to do nothing at all, and most people visit on a day-trip from Grenada or Carriacou. If the ferry is too slow for you (see p.778), the tourist office in Carriacou can book a speedboat which will whiz you across the water in a matter of minutes for EC$160 round-trip. Once there, you can easily walk around Petite Martinique via its one road, which stretches along the west coast and is dotted with houses, shops, bars and small family graveyards. At its southern end when the road stops it becomes a grassy headland with great views of the surrounding Grenadine islands. However, even greater panoramic views are rewarded to those who follow the, at times tough, trail which leads from the headland to the island's 738ft peak of **Mt Piton** – a walk which requires good shoes and plenty of water.

For those who prefer to lounge on the beach, the stretch of sand leading south away from the ferry jetty is your best bet. This is both a working and a tourist beach with rocky headlands at both ends, and a small boatyard with a number of traditional wooden boats in various states of repair at the far southern end.

Petite Martinique's **Carnival** is held in the two days before Lent, and at Easter the island holds its two-day **regatta**, which features the famous greasy-pole contest, in which competitors inch their way out over the water along a slippery pole to reach the prize hanging at the end.

Practicalities

As most visitors come here on a day-trip, **accommodation** and **dining options** are limited. Try *Melodies Guest House* (☎473/443-9052, ✆www.spiceisle.com/melodies; ❷), a family-run beachside guesthouse just three minutes' walk from the main jetty, where the basic rooms come with private showers and some with verandahs. The restaurant and bar serves a variety of local food and you can choose to eat either inside or under shady trees on the edge of the sea. Overlooking the harbour is *Seaside View Holiday Cottages* (☎473/443-9007; ❸), an attractive collection of one- and two-bedroom self-catering beachfront cottages, all of them well maintained, whose owners also run the Sea View supermarket and gift shop, and will arrange pick-up charters from Carriacou.

The friendly *Palm Beach Restaurant* (daily 10am–10pm; ☎473/443-9103) is a pleasant alternative to **eating** where you are staying. Tables are under outdoor gazebos in sea-facing gardens, and the stunning harbour view makes this a fine place to enjoy a cocktail or two as well as a meal. The lunch menu features rotis, burgers and grilled fish dishes for EC$18–47 and main courses on the dinner menu include grilled fish for EC$47 and BBQ chicken for EC$47. Vegetarian options are available on request.

Other than the local bars strung out along the main road, the only other place for an evening drink and occasional live music is the bar at *Melodies Guest House*.

For those wanting to **dive** around the island, Seaside Diving, on the beach near Melodies Guesthouse, (☎473/443-9007) provide equipment rental only; those seeking courses and organized dives should try one of the dive shops on Grenada or Carriacou.

Trinidad and Tobago

CARIBBEAN SEA

ATLANTIC OCEAN

N

0   20km

Trinidad and Tobago highlights

* **Trinidad street food** Better than most restaurant fare, Trinidad's delicious street food includes curry-filled rotis, corn soup and doubles. See p.807

* **Carnival, Trinidad** The original West Indian carnival – now exported worldwide – features spectacular costumes and fabulous music. See p.808

* **Northern Range, Trinidad** The densely forested peaks are home to over 100 species of mammal, 430 types of birds and stunning waterfalls. See p.825

* **Leatherback turtles** During laying season these huge creatures nest nightly on Trinidad and Tobago's north coasts, providing a rare and moving sight. See pp.828, 831, 832 & 848

* **Caroni Swamp, Trinidad** Visit the nesting grounds of the stunning scarlet ibis on a boat trip through eerie mangrove swamps. See p.833

* **Diving and snorkelling on Tobago** Challenging drift dives and easily accessible coral reefs make Tobago a superb destination for these watersports. See p.842

* **Sunday School, Tobago** Check out the live pan performances and "lime" with the locals at the biggest weekly party on Tobago. See p.847

△ Street party steel band, Tobago

21

Introduction and basics

Just off the coast of the South American mainland they were once part of, **Trinidad and Tobago** (usually shortened to "T&T") form the southernmost islands of the Lesser Antilles chain and the most influential republic in the Eastern Caribbean. They are the most exciting, underexplored and un-contrived of the Caribbean islands, rich in indigenous culture. A cultural pacemaker best known as the home and heart of West Indian **Carnival**, the nation can also boast of having the most diverse and absorbing society in the region.

T&T remain relatively **inexpensive** as natural gas and oil reserves have ensured economic independence and freedom from the tourist trade. Regionally, they are the richest destinations for **eco-tourism**, combining the flora and fauna of the Caribbean with the wilder aspect of the South American mainland. In Trinidad, you can hike through undisturbed tropical rainforest, take a boat ride through mangrove swamps and watch leatherback turtles nest on remote beaches. **Birdwatching**, with more than 430 species in an area of 4830 square kilometres, is among the world's best. Meanwhile, **Tobago** (300sq km) has glorious beaches and stunning coral reefs. Declared the "Disneyland of diving", Tobago has the largest brain coral in the world and sightings of manta rays are common.

Equally absorbing are T&T's dynamic **towns** and **cities**, showcases for the architectural, religious and cultural traditions of their cosmopolitan populations. The 1.3 million inhabitants hail from India, China, Portugal and Syria as well as Africa, England, France and Spain, and though racial tensions are inevitably present, Trinbagonians (as they're collectively known) co-exist with good humour, and are proud of their **multiculturalism**. The result is a highly creative culture with a lively **music scene** that rivals even Jamaica.

Unlike its Caribbean neighbours, Trinidad experienced full-scale **slavery** for a relatively short fifty years, while the Dutch, French and British were too busy fighting over Tobago to dedicate it to the demands of King Sugar. Consequently, the national psyche is characterized by a strong sense of identity and a laid-back enjoyment of the good things in life, best displayed in the local propensity for "**liming**" – meeting friends for a drink

and a chat. With more than a dozen public holidays, local festivals and the pre-Lenten **Carnival**, a no-holds-barred two days of dancing in the street, the islands' reputation of knowing how to party is well deserved.

Where to go

A visit to Trinidad inevitably begins in the capital, **Port of Spain**, home to most of the island's accommodation and the centre of its transport system. The most accessible **beaches** are on the north coast, while the **Northern Range** offers excellent hiking and superb birdwatching. In contrast to the north, central Trinidad is dominated by flat agricultural plains with a population of primarily Indian descent. The island's greatest natural assets are located here: **Caroni swamp**, nesting area of the scarlet ibis, and the protected **wetlands of Nariva**, home of manatees and anacondas. The burgeoning city of **San Fernando** is a friendly base to explore Trinidad's "deep south", an area largely unvisited by tourists, where modern oil towns contrast with the picturesque fishing villages and deserted beaches.

In **Tobago**, the majority of visitors stay in the hotel-dominated **western tip**. A more genuine picture of local life can be seen in the capital, **Scarborough**, and along the northern coast in friendly **Castara** or at the fishing village of **Charlotteville**.

When to go

Most travellers come to T&T between January and March, during the **Carnival** season when the **climate** is at its most forgiving (25–30°C/72–87°F). By May, the **dry sea-**

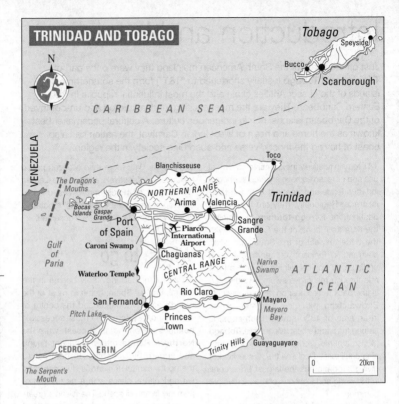

son parches the lush landscape and bush fires often rage through the hills. The **rainy season** starts in June and lasts till December, but in September there's a dry spell known as the *petit carem*, an Indian summer of two to four weeks; it's an excellent time to visit, with flights at low-season rates. Tobago hoteliers hike rates during high season (mid-Dec to mid-April), as do Trinidad hotels during Carnival, but smaller hotels on both islands charge the same all year round.

Arrival

In Trinidad flights touch down at **Piarco International Airport**, a large, relatively new complex with numerous facilities situated approximately 32km southeast of Port of Spain on Golden Grove Road in Piarco. For details of travelling between the airport and Port of Spain see p.813. Flights into

Tobago arrive at **Crown Point International Airport**, a small open-plan complex with limited facilities situated on the southeast tip of the island. For details of transport around Tobago from the airport see p.841.

Those that arrive via **cruise ship**, any other form of boat or travel between the islands by ferry will in Trinidad dock at the **King's Wharf** in Port of Spain or, if you're arriving by ferry from Venezuela, at **Williams Bay** in Chaguaramas on the northwest tip, while in Tobago all ships and ferries dock at the cruise ship and ferry terminal in **Scarborough**.

Money and costs

The local currency is the **Trinidad and Tobago dollar (TT$)**, divided into one hundred cents. Coins come in 1, 5, 10 and 25-cent pieces, while notes come in denominations of 1, 5, 10, 20 and 100. Keep some cash in small denominations as supermarkets and bars may exchange TT$100 but taxis and street vendors often can't, and should be paid with TT$20 or less.

Travellers' cheques and **credit cards** are accepted in most restaurants, high-class shops and hotels, though in smaller establishments and rural areas they are unlikely to take anything but local currency. Personal cheques are not usually accepted in hotels, and most host homes do not have credit card facilities.

As the **exchange rate** is much more favourable on the islands it is best to buy local currency once you have arrived in T&T. At the time of publication the rate of exchange was around TT$6.27 to US$1. For **Trinidad**, Piarco Airport Exchange Bureau (daily 24hr) has reasonable rates, although it is not as competitive as the banks in Port of Spain, including Republic (Independence Square), Royal (Park St) and Scotiabank (Frederick St). In San Fernando try Republic (Coffee St) and in Arima the Republic (Broadway) or the Royal (corner of Queen and Devenish streets).

Travellers flying into **Tobago** can change money at the bureau de change in Crown Point Airport or the Republic Bank opposite the terminal (Mon–Thurs 8–11am & noon–2pm, Fri 8am–noon & 3–5pm). Most banks on the island are located in Scarborough; Republic is on Carrington Street, while Scotiabank is on Milford Road and First Citizen on Lower Milford Road. The TIDCO map of the islands marks the locations of **ATMs** on both Trinidad and Tobago.

Banking hours vary slightly, but are usually Monday to Thursday 8am–2pm and Fridays 8am–noon and 3–5pm. Most banks in Trinidad's larger malls open and close later (9am–6pm) with no break. Outside banking hours money can be exchanged in the larger hotels in Port of Spain. Most shops and vendors will accept American dollars – pay in small denominations and be prepared to receive your change in local currency.

Trinidad and Tobago are undoubtedly one of the **cheapest** Caribbean destinations due to their low profile on the tourist market. It is possible to survive on £25/US$35 a day if you're prepared to take the least expensive accommodation, eat at low-cost cafés

and travel by public transport. If you stay at tourist accommodation and eat at finer restaurants, you will need at least £65/US$95 a day. A rental car will add around £30–40/US$45–60 per day.

During **Carnival** season, all accommodation rates in Port of Spain rise by 10 to 70 percent, as do other prices, including entrance fees, drinks and taxi fares. If you want to enjoy yourself during Carnival, plan on a budget of at least £100/US$140 a day.

Upon leaving T&T, you'll be required to pay a TT$100 (US$17) **departure tax** in local currency.

Information, maps and websites

Offices of the T&T tourist board, TIDCO (Tourism and Industrial Development Company of Trinidad and Tobago, ⊛www.visittnt.com), located in the US, Canada, UK and T&T, send out **information packets** on request, which include useful accommodation and calendar of events booklets, as well as glossy promotional pamphlets and sometimes a **road map**. On the islands their information booths at Crown Point and Piarco airports have friendly, helpful staff. Tobago's main tourist advice centre is at the Tobago House of Assembly (THA) in Scarborough (⊕868/639-2125 or 4636, ⊛www.visittobago.gov.tt).

With some of the best writers of the Caribbean, the local **media** are an excellent introduction to T&T. The main newspapers include the broadsheet *Trinidad Guardian* (⊛ www.guardian.co.tt), the tabloid *Express* (⊛ www.trinidadexpress.com) and *Newsday* (⊛ www.newsday.co.tt); Tobago has only one paper, *Tobago News* (⊛www.thetobagonews.com), published on Fridays. Though the islands have two terrestrial **TV stations** – the main local news slot is at 7pm on TV6 – cable TV is predominant. **Radio** is hugely popular, with the best stations for contemporary local music being Yes FM (98.9), POWER 102 (102.5 FM), The Vibe (Comedy Tempo, 105.1 FM), WE FM (96.1) and Tobago's local station, Radio Tambrin (92.1 FM).

Websites

There are hundreds of T&T-oriented **websites**, which differ hugely in style and content. The listings below are for sites with good general content and lots of links to get you started.

ⓦ**www.carnaval.com** The best T&T Carnival site, with features on everything from *mas* camps and panyards to music, accommodation and restaurants. Pretty good for visits to Port of Spain, too.

ⓦ**www.homeviewtnt.com** Slick site with extensive content, from live feeds to radio stations, sports, news, music, Carnival, history, listings and loads of Trini titbits. A good place to start.

ⓦ**www.lanic.utexas.edu/la/cb/tt** Huge directory of T&T-related links, organized by category, from academic research and arts and culture to business, economy and the environment.

ⓦ**www.search.co.tt** Exhaustive directory of T&T-related sites.

ⓦ**www.visittnt.com** Maintained by TIDCO, this is the best all-rounder, with country details, attraction listings, flight information and feature pages on Carnival, soca and calypso, with links to lots of other pertinent sites.

Getting around

Travelling around Trinidad and Tobago takes ingenuity and patience. **Public transport** is minimal, so an unofficial, private system of route taxis, maxi taxis and private taxis fill the gaps. If you wish to see more than the urban areas, however, it is advisable to **rent a car**.

By bus

Though the small network of **public buses** has improved in recent years through the introduction of rural buses in Trinidad and an expansion of Tobago's services, public transport remains erratic, with most buses clustered around peak hours. **Tickets** cost around TT$2–10 and must be bought in advance from the Port of Spain and Scarborough bus terminals or from small general stores around the country. All buses in Trinidad leave and terminate at City Gate/South Quay in Port of Spain. In Tobago, all buses depart from the terminal on Greenside Street in Scarborough.

By car

Tobago's roads are much quieter than Trinidad's; the main hazards are blind corners and potholes in the road. Road signs are based on the English system (although distances and speed limits are in kilometres) and you must drive on the left. **Petrol stations** are scarce outside urban areas, so it's wise

to keep the tank full. **Car rental** starts at US$35 per day in Trinidad and US$45 in Tobago. Thrifty is the only major international chain on both islands, though there are many local firms. Econo Cars (191–193 Western Main Rd, Cocorite; ☎ 868/669-1119, ⓦ www.trinidad.net/econocar) is the least expensive in Trinidad, while in Tobago, Sherman's (Lambeau ☎ 868/639-2292, ⓦ www.shermansrental.com) is the most reliable; Sheppy's (Crown Point ☎ 868/639-1543) rents jeeps and motorbikes. All companies require you to be 25 or over and to have held a driving licence for a minimum of two years, and require a credit card imprint.

By taxi

Maxi taxis are private minibuses taking ten to twenty people, with set routes and standardized fares (TT$2–10) but no set timetables. An entertaining experience for the decor, the music and the conversation, maxis are organized by region and have colour-coded stripes relating to the area in which they work. Yellow (Port of Spain to the Western Tip), red (the east) and green (central and south) commute between Port of Spain and outlying towns, while black (Princes Town), brown (San Fernando to the southwest peninsula) and blue (Tobago) work within their own areas. Routes radiate from main centres; you can board anywhere – just stick out your hand to be picked up. **Route taxis** follow similar rules, but take a maximum of five passengers and are slightly more expensive. **Private taxis** take you directly to your destination alone, but are as expensive as a British or US cab; always agree on the price beforehand.

Inter-island transport

For those wishing to travel **between** Trinidad and Tobago, there are two options: by **ferry**, slow and inexpensive, and sometimes on rough seas (TT$50–60 return; ☎ 868/625-4906 or 639-2416), and by **plane**, which is quick but pricier. The boat leaves twice daily Mon–Fri and once on Saturdays and Sundays from Port of Spain and Scarborough and takes five to six hours. The Tobago Express, a BWIA affiliate, operates twelve flights per day, with the trip lasting 25 minutes (US$16/TT$100 one-way and US$32/TT$200 round-trip; ☎ 868/627-2942, ⊛ www. bwee.com).

Accommodation

Most **accommodation** in Trinidad is located in Port of Spain and the larger towns, while in tourist-oriented Tobago most hotels are found in the Crown Point area on the island's western tip. Expect to pay US$30–80 for a room in Port of Spain and slightly more in Tobago. There are no high and low seasons in Trinidad, but rates may rise by up to 70 percent during Carnival. In Tobago high-season rates (quoted throughout the guide) operate between December and mid-April, dropping by 25 percent in low season. We have taken room tax (10–15 percent) and service charge (10 percent) into account, but it's worth checking each time you rent a room whether these have been included.

One time of year you simply cannot count on getting a room in Trinidad is the three weeks before and after **Carnival**. Rooms must be booked months in advance. Most hotels, guesthouses and host homes (see below) offer special Carnival packages for the Friday before Carnival to Ash Wednesday; expect to pay US$70–90 per night for a basic room, and anything up to US$200 in the smarter hotels.

For those looking for an alternative to standard hotels, **guesthouses** are small-scale properties with fewer facilities (expect a shared bathroom and fan instead of a/c), while private **host homes** are an excellent and inexpensive option giving you greater insight into the local lifestyle. They normally cost around US$35 per person. For host homes in Trinidad contact the Bed and Breakfast Co-operative Society (☎868/663-4413, ⊜ la-belle@tstt.net.tt); in Tobago contact Tourist Information at Crown Point Airport (☎868/639-0509). Those travelling in a group may prefer holiday **villas**: in Tobago prices range from US$150 to US$4000 per week. A recommended agency is Villas of Tobago Ltd (☎ 868/639-9600, ⊛ www. villasoftobago.com) while ⊛www.seetobago. com is a good source for all types of Tobago accommodation.

Alternatively, **beach houses** and **furnished apartments** are advertised in local newspapers.

Food and drink

One of the highlights of Trinidad and Tobago is the fantastic **cuisine**, a unique blend of African, Indian, Chinese and European influences. Although you may be offered insipid tourist-oriented fare in larger hotels, local cooking – meaning anything from Indian curry to Creole oil-down or Spanish-style *pastelles* – still reigns supreme.

The national dish is the Creole staple **callaloo** – dasheen leaves cooked with okra and coconut. Other Creole favourites are oil-down, vegetables stewed in coconut milk, cowheel soup and fish broth. Wild meat, such as agouti, lappe, manicou and even iguana are a staple of Tobago's harvest festivals, while no trip to that island would be complete without tasting the delicious **coconut curried crab and dumpling**. Indian influences have created the unofficial national dish: invented in Trinidad, the **roti** is a stretchy flat bread (called a skin) containing curried meat, vegetables or fish.

In **Trinidad**, where tourism is minimal and most people prefer to eat at home, restaurant culture is only just developing. There are stylish places to eat but the majority are no-nonsense venues where the food is invariably inexpensive and delicious. The

21

best option is **street food**; doubles (runny *channa* sandwiched between soft, fried *bara* bread), oysters, corn soup and a variety of pies – fish, vegetable and meat. The St James district of Port of Spain offers particularly rich pickings, and with food subject to stringent hygiene checks, eating on the hop rarely constitutes a health risk. The ubiquitous **shark and bake** is best consumed on Maracas beach, where vendors compete to produce the tastiest version of fried bread filled with shark meat. **Tobago** has more tourist-oriented restaurants, some with prices to match. Local seafood and Creole dishes feature, but you'll encounter plenty of imported US steak and chips as well. Remember tax (up to 15 percent) and a service charge (usually 10 percent) will be added to your bill.

Carib and Stag are the light, locally produced **lagers**, while Royal Extra or Mackeson **stouts** are excellent local alternatives to Guinness – also brewed in Trinidad and iced in the local Guinness-flavoured ice cream. The best **rum** is produced by the Trinidadian Angostura/Fernandes manufacturers, makers of the world-famous Angostura Bitters; their Black Label red rum is considered sublime.

A recommended nonalcoholic thirst quencher is the vitamin- and mineral-packed **coconut water**, fresh from street vendors. Mauby, made from tree bark, cloves and aniseed, is delicious but an acquired taste, while **fuchsia sorrel**, made from a flower of the hibiscus family, is a sweet drink enjoyed at Christmas.

Phones, post and email

Public telephones take 25¢ coins, but if you're making international calls it's easier to use the Companion **phone cards** (TT$10, $30, $60 and $100 + VAT) issued by Telecommunication Service of T&T (TSTT) and available in newsagents, pharmacies and supermarkets. You can rent a **cellular phone** from Caribel (☎ 868/652-4982, ⓦ www.caribel.com) for around US$35 per week plus call charges. Only tri-band units work in T&T, and as TSTT has a monopoly

> The **country code** for Trinidad and Tobago is ☎ 868.

your mobile phone will not work unless you register with them first – call ☎ 868/824-8788 (toll-free) for more information. Phones must be TDMA and digital compatible.

The local **TT Post** is reliable if a little slow. A normal letter takes one to two weeks to Europe and the US, three to Australia. Most towns and villages have a **post office** (Mon–Fri 8am–4.15pm). Letters and postcards cost TT$3.75 to the US and Canada, TT$4.50 to Europe and TT$5.25 to the rest of the world, and decorated aerogrammes can be sent worldwide for TT$2. Postboxes are small, red, rare and easily missed.

You'll find **Internet services** mainly at cyber-cafés, computer shops and some hotels in Port of Spain, San Fernando, Crown Point and Scarborough. Prices range from TT$5–12 per hour.

Festivals and public holidays

Trinbagonians have a well-deserved reputation for partying. With thirteen **public holidays** embodying T&T's cultural and ethnic diversity, there are plenty of occasions to celebrate.

Carnival, held on the Monday and Tuesday before Ash Wednesday, is the most famous – a hedonistic two days of drinking and dancing in ornate and revealing costumes. In Trinidad, especially in Port of Spain, everything shuts down for two days, and increasingly three, as people use Ash Wednesday to recover. Other popular Trinidadian celebrations are the Islamic **Hosay** (see p.820) during May and June and the Hindu **Phagwa** festival (see p.834). The festival of **Diwali**, celebrated nationwide in late October, honours the Hindu goddess of light. *Deyas* – small oil-wick candles – are lit in every house.

For music lovers, October's **World Steel Band Festival**, known as "Pan is Beautiful", features music ranging from classical to the latest calypso tunes. In May, the month-long

Public holidays

January 1 New Year's Day
March/April Good Friday, Easter Monday
March 30 Spiritual Baptist (Shouter) Liberation Day
June 10 Corpus Christi
May 30 Indian Arrival Day
June 19 Labour Day
August 1 Emancipation Day
August 31 Independence Day
October Diwali
November/December Eid-ul-Fitr (celebration at the end of Ramadan)
December 25 Christmas Day
December 26 Boxing Day

---

steel-band festival **Pan Ramajay** is held, and December is the season of **parang** – Nativity songs sung in Spanish, sounding more Latin American than Caribbean.

In Tobago the eagerly awaited **Tobago Heritage Festival** occurs in the last two weeks of July and features traditional customs, storytelling and festivities. The Charlotteville **Fisherman's Fete**, held on Man O' War Bay in the middle of July, is a wild beach party. On the Tuesday after Easter in Buccoo, crab and goat races are held. These bizarre spectacles are entertaining to watch – though for those betting they're no laughing matter. For the latest information on events and a festival calendar, contact TIDCO at ☎868/623-6022.

Outdoor activities

Unique in the Caribbean for its **environmental diversity**, a visit to T&T would not be complete without seeing the wildlife in its natural habitat. The islands rank among the world's top ten **birding** sites, with more than 430 recorded bird species per square kilometre. The most accessible places to see birdlife in Trinidad are the Asa Wright Nature Centre and the Caroni Bird Sanctuary – nesting place of the scarlet ibis. In Tobago,

head for Little Tobago, also known as Bird of Paradise Island, and the protected Tobago Forest Reserve.

There is excellent **hiking** to be had in the Trinidad forests of the Northern Range and the Chaguaramas hills – though make sure you go with a group as it is easy to get lost in the jungle. **Snorkelling** and **scuba diving** are extremely popular; both are best in Tobago, where the water is clear and the coral reef spectacular. The best dive spots are Speyside, Charlotteville and around the Sister's Rocks. If you prefer to stick to **swimming**, bear in mind that undertows and strong currents make many of Trinidad's (and some of Tobago's) beaches downright risky. If in doubt, check with a local. Maracas is Trinidad's most popular beach, though most agree that the best beaches are in Tobago, where the water is cleaner and the facilities more developed. The increasingly commercial Pigeon Point is queen here, though the undeveloped Castara, Parlatuvier, Englishman's Bay and Pirate's Bay are far more stunning. Lush **waterfalls** such as Argyll in Tobago and Blue Basin, Maracas and La Laja in Trinidad offer great freshwater swimming, while big breakers around Mount Irvine in Tobago and Toco in Trinidad make ideal conditions for **surfing**.

The main **yachting** centre is Chaguaramas, a haven especially during hurricane season. For more information contact the Trinidad and Tobago Yachting Association (☎868/634-4210) or consult the *Boaters' Directory*, available from marinas and the tourist board.

There are hundreds of **tour companies** in T&T offering everything from hiking, bird-watching and kayaking to more conventional driving tours. The average cost is US$50–100 per day, though the Chaguaramas Development Authority (☎868/634-4364 or 4349, ☜www.chagdev.com) provides excellent hiking from US$25. Wildways (☎868/623-7332, ☜www.wildways.org) operates out of both Trinidad and Tobago and is one of the best, ploughing profits back into eco-educational programmes for local schools. Island Experiences (☎868/625-2410, ☜gunda@wow.net) provides tailor-made cultural tours including *mas* camps and panyards, while Caribbean Discovery Tours (☎868/624-7281, ☜www.

For the **police** dial ☎999, and for fire and **ambulance** dial ☎990.

21

caribbeandiscoverytours.com) gives informative hikes and safaris with a birdwatching, animal-spotting slant.

Music

Trinbagonian **music** is some of the most exciting and thought-provoking in the Caribbean. The heart of T&T's music scene is **calypso**, which comments on shifting attitudes towards love, gender, race and religion. Its most eloquent proponent is **David Rudder** (📶www.davidrudder.com), Trinidad's answer to Bob Marley. The best place to hear calypso is in the "tents" at Carnival, such as Calypso Revue, Kaiso House, Maljo Kaiso, Yangatang and Spektakula Forum.

Equally popular nowadays is **soca**. Most attribute the birth of this musical style to the late calypsonian Lord Shorty (Ras Shorty I), whose souped-up rhythm created a more danceable form reflecting the then-popular disco. Soca dominates Carnival, with more than 400 new songs released per year. The Road March title – given to the song played most often during Carnival – is almost wholly soca's domain, often won by singers such as Super Blue and Machel Montano and the loose collective he heads, Xtatik.

East Indians have given soca their own slant through **chutney**, mixing soca beats with sitars, dholak drums and Hindi and English lyrics. Vocalists to look out for include Rikki Jai, Sonny Mann and Drupatee Ramgoonai. Chutney has also influenced the conventional soca industry; white calypsonian Denise Plummer continues to flirt with the form, as does Machel Montano.

In the poor Port of Spain suburb of Laventille, oil drums brought by US troops in World War II were hammered into concave sections that produced rough notes, creating the **steel drum**, or **pan**, as it's known locally. Though panyards were initially seen as dens of iniquity, the movement gained respectability as the music became more complex. These days, the panyard calendar revolves around **Panorama**, the nationwide competition held during Carnival. Other places to listen to the sweet pan music are local panyards and national events such as Pan Ramajay (see overleaf).

All that said, T&T's musical spectrum is wider than just these styles: at Christmas, you'll hear the Spanish-sounding **parang**, while East Indian festivals such as Hosay (see box on p.820) and Phagwa (see box on p.834) take place to **tassa drumming**, and Jamaican **dancehall reggae** is popular all year round.

History of Trinidad

For a history of **Tobago**, see p.839.

Trinidad was the first inhabited island of the Caribbean, settled by **Amerindians** from South America as early as 5000 BC. They called it "Ieri", the land of the hummingbird. When **Christopher Columbus** "discovered" the island in 1498 – naming it **Trinidad** after the three peaks of the Trinity Hills – there was a population of 35,000, who had trade links to South America. Within three hundred years, the indigenous people were all but wiped out through exposure to European diseases and Spanish massacres. **Spanish settlers** arrived in 1592 but the Spanish empire had neither the desire nor the resources to develop the island. Governors of Trinidad did as they pleased and **pirate** attacks were commonplace. In 1783 Spain issued the **Cedula of Population**, to encourage fellow Catholics – **French planters** – to settle; the land allocated depended on the number of **slaves** they brought with them. Unusually for the region, immigrants of mixed European/African race could also receive land, thus opening the way for a property-owning coloured middle class.

Though Spanish-run, the island's culture became increasingly **French**: it was during this period that **Carnival** was introduced. Things heated up politically when the British, led by **Sir Ralph Abercromby**, invaded in 1797. The Spanish surrendered with hardly a shot fired and **Thomas Picton** became governor, ruling with a reign of terror. By 1802, Picton's activities had become an embarrassment even to the British government and he was demoted.

The island became a British experiment, a **Crown colony** ruled directly from London but governed by French and Spanish law. Planters, forced to look for alternative sources of labour after the Act of Emancipation, introduced indentured **Indian labourers** to the island in 1845. By 1917, when the system finally ended, some 145,000 Indians, mainly from Calcutta, had arrived. Though better regulated than slavery, the working and living conditions of the labourers were indistinguishable from those of slaves. Many never returned to India, accepting land in lieu of their passage home. Known still as "East Indians", they have contributed greatly to the island's culture, especially with their food. Further adding to the ethnic mix in T&T were **immigrants** from other parts of the world, among them Africans, Portuguese labourers, Chinese, a handful of Jews and Syrians.

Several components – including the **oil industry**, an **anti-indentureship movement**, and the establishment of the *Beacon* (1931–34), a stridently anti-colonial, anti-government magazine – meant Britain faced an increasingly unruly population. **World War II** brought economic improvements as large areas, such as the Chaguaramas peninsula, were leased to the US military to establish their Caribbean base. In return, the Americans improved Trinidad's infrastructure and brought oil drums to the island, inspiring the invention of the **steel drum**.

Though universal **suffrage** was granted in 1945, Britain did not hand over control until 1956, when the **People's National Movement** (PNM), under the leadership of the Oxford-educated historian Dr Eric Williams, took power. **Independence** was granted in 1962 but the colonial structure of society remained. Disillusionment led to the **Black Power** movement in the late Sixties, resulting in jobs being given to locals rather than expatriates. By 1970, Trinidad was **bankrupt** – though vast **oil reserves**, discovered just as the world was sliding into the 1974 oil crisis, meant the country found itself swimming in money overnight. When oil prices fell in the 1980s, the economy went into recession. As the population became increasingly dissatisfied, the political opposition unified, and in 1986 PNM was ousted for the first time in favour of the **National Alliance for Reconstruction** (NAR), led by the Tobagonian A.N.R. Robinson. Within a year the government was breaking up under the pressure of harsh economic measures imposed by the IMF. In 1990, the **Jamaat-al-Muslimeen** – a revolutionary Muslim organization – attempted to overthrow the government (see p.817). Though the coup was crushed, the government's authority was undermined, and the following year the PNM returned to power.

Over the next five years, the PNM stabilized the economy and paid off the IMF. The 1995 election split the country down the middle, with the PNM and the **Indo-Trinidadian United National Congress** (UNC) both winning exactly seventeen seats. The first Indo-Trinidadian prime minister, **Basdeo Panday**, took power in 1995, and although the 2000 election returned the UNC to power with nineteen seats, Panday's government was to last only ten months, as the following October three UNC parliamentarians defected to the opposition. After much political squabbling, new elections in 2002 returned the PNM to power, with **Patrick Manning** confirmed as prime minister.

Trinidad and Tobago can boast the most **stable economy** in the Caribbean, thanks mainly to the oil's continuing source of revenue. However, rising crime rates, drug trafficking, high

21

rates of domestic violence and HIV infection, not to mention political **corruption**, have ensured that locals have more to worry about than what to wear to next year's Carnival.

21.1

Port of Spain and the Western Tip

PORT OF SPAIN is the hub of Trinidad's booming economy, and the main port of arrival for many immigrants from other Caribbean islands. It's also the centre of Trinidad's rich **cultural life**, with countless *mas* camps (see p.819), art galleries, panyards and theatres. The city is bordered by the Gulf of Paria on one side and the Northern Range on the other, providing its 51,000 inhabitants with both mountain and sea views. The mish-mash of the city's architectural styles can seem rather ugly at first sight, especially **downtown**, but look closely and you'll spot many fine nineteenth-century buildings along with quaint "gingerbread" houses, so named because of their intricate fretted woodwork.

Thanks in large part to its fine natural harbour, Port of Spain was made Trinidad's capital in 1757. The downtown area is the oldest section of the city, and despite its run-down appearance is the **shopping** and **finance centre** of the capital. Within the compact grid of streets surrounding broad Brian Lara Promenade/Independence Square and bustling Frederick Street, internationally known shops jostle for space with old Spanish warehouses, offices, shops and the paraphernalia of the docks, while the thoroughfares are jammed with traffic, pedestrians and pavement vendors. The discovery of offshore oil in the 1970s left the city with a sleek **financial district**, dominated by the imposing twin towers of the Central Bank and the futuristic Nicholas Tower on the western side of the promenade.

Tumbling down the hills to the east of the city are the poor suburbs of **Laventille** and **Belmont**, established by freed slaves after **emancipation** in 1834. West of the city centre lies Woodbrook, an elegant middle-class suburb settled in the early twentieth century. Established by Indian immigrants in the nineteenth century, the St James district further west still has streets named after the settlers' home towns. North of the city at the base of the Northern Range are the districts of St Ann's and Maraval, which have fast become the centre of the city's expanding hotel trade. In addition, **settlers** from China, Portugal, Venezuela and Syria have all come to Trinidad to try their luck. Descendants of these groups, and those of the French, Spanish, British, African and Indian communities, ensure that Port of Spain retains its cosmopolitan mix of peoples and cultures.

Arrival and getting around

Port of Spain is about 20km northwest of **Piarco International Airport**. Official **airport taxis** wait outside the main entrance and will take you to the capital for US$20 (30min, 1hr during rush hour, 6-8am and 4-6pm). Alternatively, take a shared **route taxi** (they pass in front of the main entrance at regular intervals during the day; less frequently during the night) to Arouca Junction on the Eastern Main Road (TT$3). From there, catch an eastbound **red-band maxi taxi** to **City Gate**, the

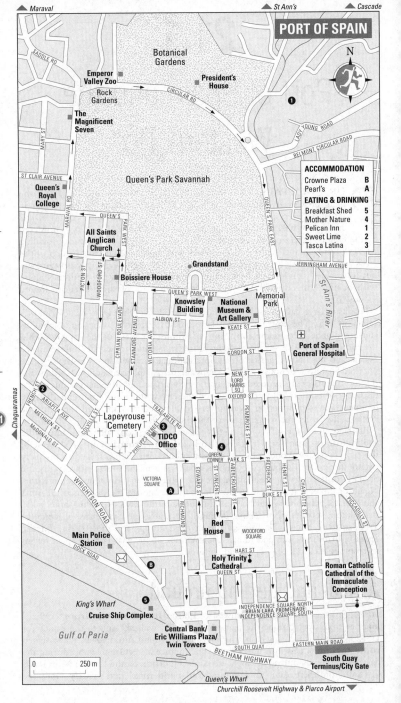

PORT OF SPAIN

N

ACCOMMODATION	
Crowne Plaza	**B**
Pearl's	**A**
EATING & DRINKING	
Breakfast Shed	5
Mother Nature	4
Pelican Inn	1
Sweet Lime	2
Tasca Latina	3

Maraval

St Ann's

Cascade

SADDLE RD

Botanical Gardens

Emperor Valley Zoo

President's House

Rock Gardens

CIRCULAR RD

The Magnificent Seven

MARY ST

Queen's Park Savannah

LADY YOUNG ROAD

BELMONT CIRCULAR ROAD

ST CLAIR AVENUE

Queen's Royal College

MARAVAL RD

QUEEN'S PARK WEST

All Saints Anglican Church

PICTON ST

WOODFORD ST

QUEEN'S PARK EAST

JERNINGHAM AVENUE

Grandstand

Boissiere House

Queen's Park West

St Ann's River

CIPRIANI BOULEVARD

Knowsley Building

National Museum & Art Gallery

Memorial Park

ALBION ST

KEATE ST

Port of Spain General Hospital

STANMORE AVENUE

VICTORIA AVE

GORDON ST

Chaguaramas

FRENCH ST

ARIAPITA AVE

CHARLOTTE ST

METHUEN ST

McDONALD ST

COLVILLE ST

Lapeyrouse Cemetery

PHILIPPS STREET

TRAGARETE RD

NEW ST

LORD HARRIS SQ

OXFORD ST

PEMBROKE ST

PICCADILLY ST

TIDCO Office

GREEN CORNER

PARK ST

ST VINCENT ST

ABERCROMBY ST

FREDERICK ST

HENRY ST

EDWARD ST

WRIGHTSON ROAD

VICTORIA SQUARE

A

RICHMOND ST

DUKE ST

Red House

WOODFORD SQUARE

Main Police Station

DOCK ROAD

B

HART ST

Holy Trinity Cathedral

QUEEN ST

Roman Catholic Cathedral of the Immaculate Conception

King's Wharf

Cruise Ship Complex

5

Central Bank/ Eric Williams Plaza/ Twin Towers

INDEPENDENCE SQUARE NORTH

BRIAN LARA PROMENADE

INDEPENDENCE SQUARE SOUTH

Gulf of Paria

SOUTH QUAY

EASTERN MAIN ROAD

BEETHAM HIGHWAY

South Quay Terminus/City Gate

0   250 m

Queen's Wharf

Churchill Roosevelt Highway & Piarco Airport

main transport terminus downtown (TT$4). **Route taxis** to Arouca Junction are open to negotiation to take you directly to Port of Spain for TT$60–80, though you may share the car with others.

If **arriving by ship**, you'll pull into Port of Spain's docks. Private taxis tout for passengers coming off the boat from Tobago, but unless you arrive late at night, it's much cheaper to use the route and maxi taxis that run along the Wrightson Road.

Port of Spain has a compact, grid-based city centre. **City Gate**, located east of the docks, is the main transport terminal, and many route taxi ranks are also located in the city centre. Most of the sights are within walking distance of each other, but bear in mind that under the hot sun energy fades fast.

Maxi taxis operating in Port of Spain and the west – recognizable by their yellow stripes – can be caught in three locations. For **Diego Martin/Petit Valley**, the maxi rank is at the junction of South Quay and Abercromby Street. Maxis bound for **Maraval** (and sometimes **Diego Martin**) go via **St James** and start at the corner of Charlotte and Oxford streets. Maxis for **Carenage** and **Chaguaramas** go via **Ariapita Avenue** in **Woodbrook** and start at Green Corner (corner of St Vincent and Park streets).

Route taxis, which are usually old but functional cars, are distinguishable by the "H" numberplate. Starting points are dotted around Port of Spain, so it is best to ask a local to find the appropriate stand. From 7pm until 5am, many taxi stands relocate to Brian Lara Promenade/Independence Square. Private taxis can be hired by phone (try Independence Square Taxi Service, ☎868/625-3032, or Ice House Taxi Service, ☎868/627-6984) or by going to their ranks at Brian Lara Promenade/Independence Square, but be warned they're as expensive as any in the US or Europe. There are a variety of **car rental firms** in Port of Spain if you prefer to have your own transport. Singh's, 7–9 Wrightson Rd (☎868/623-0150), and Econo Cars, 191–193 Western Main Rd, Cocorite (☎868/622-8072), are reputable.

Accommodation

The main areas for **accommodation** in Port of Spain are the city centre, **Woodbrook** and **St Ann's-Cascade**. The **city centre** is obviously convenient, though Woodbrook has the most inexpensive accommodation and the lion's share of the **guesthouses**; it's also excellent for Carnival activities. St Ann's-Cascade is greener and less urbanized, but slightly less accessible. Another alternative is the suburb of **Maraval** outside of the city limits to the north. If you're planning to come for the festival, make sure you book well in advance; the higher price codes given below correspond to prices during Carnival season.

Hotels

Crowne Plaza Wrightson Rd ☎868/625-3366, ⓦwww.crowneplaza.com. Glitzy corporate hotel with all mod cons, pool, three restaurants, bar and gym. Rooms are equipped with hairdryer, iron, coffeemaker, a/c, cable TV and great views over the Gulf of Paria and the capital. Breakfast is included in the rates. ⑨

Kapok 16–18 Cotton Hill, St Clair ☎868/622-5765, ⓦwww.kapok.co.tt. Stylish, spacious rooms decorated with rattan furniture and batik. All have a/c, satellite TV, dataport and an en-suite bathroom. There's a good restaurant and bar, along with a swimming pool, gym and sundeck on site, and breakfast is included in the Carnival rate. ⑦–⑧

Normandie 10 Nook Ave, St Ann's ☎868/624-1181, ⓦwww.normandie.com. One of the city's more atmospheric hotels, with an on-site theatre, art gallery and boutiques as well as a popular restaurant and café. All rooms have a/c, cable TV, phone with voicemail and en-suite bathroom, and there's a lovely pool. Breakfast included in the room rate. ⑤–⑧

Guesthouses

Alicia's House 7 Coblentz Gardens, St Ann's ☎868/623-2802, ⓦwww.aliciashouse.com. Located on a quiet road close to the Queen's Park Savannah, all the rooms of this little hotel, with pool, Jacuzzi and sundeck, have wicker furniture,

21

a/c, phone and most are en-suite. Breakfast is included with the Carnival rate. **3**–**7**

Fondes Amandes 9b Fondes Amandes Rd, St Ann's ☎868/624-7281, ⊛www.caribbeandiscoverytours.com. Charming family home with a pool and flower-filled garden. Rooms are eclectic; some have a private bathroom, and one accommodates four to six people. Breakfast is included. **3**–**6**

Par-May-La's Inn 53 Picton St, Newtown ☎868/628-2008, ⊛www.parmaylas.com. On a quiet street (though very convenient for downtown), with helpful hosts and a communal verandah where breakfast – included in the rates – is served. Very spacious a/c rooms with phone, TV and en-suite bathroom. **3**–**6**

Pavilion Inn 149 Tragarete Rd ☎868/633-8167, ⊛www.pavilioninn.com. Opposite the Queen's Park Oval, the *Pavilion* is convenient for cricket matches and for Carnival. All rooms are appealing, with a/c, cable TV and private bathrooms; rates include breakfast. **3**–**5**

Pearl's 3–4 Victoria Square East ☎868/625-2158. This old colonial mansion, with a verandah overlooking picturesque Victoria Square, is the best bargain in Port of Spain. The basic rooms have fans, sinks and 1960s furniture. Perfectly situated for Carnival and downtown sightseeing. **1**–**2**

Sundeck Suites 42–44 Picton St, Newtown ☎868/622-9560, ⊛sundeck.co.tt. Bright, modern self-catering apartments with kitchenette, ceiling fans, a/c, en-suite bathroom and TV; some have a small balcony. There's a sundeck on the roof, and facilities for the disabled. Ten-night minimum stay for Carnival. **3**–**5**

Trinbago 37 Ariapita Ave, Woodbrook ☎868/627-7114, ⓔtourist@tstt.net.tt. This guesthouse has a tiny pool and a balcony overlooking Ariapita Avenue – perfect for watching Carnival. Rooms vary; some have a/c, some a fan, a few share bathrooms. **2**–**5**

Ville de French 5 French St, Woodbrook ☎868/625-4776, ⓔschultzi2000@hotmail.com. Large rooms in a well-located colonial house, all with fans and sinks, some en-suite; there are a couple of self-contained units with kitchen as well. Excellent value, and breakfast is included in the Carnival rate. **2**–**5**

Downtown Port of Spain

Dating back to the 1780s, Port of Spain's **downtown** area is the oldest part of the city as well as the capital's **shopping** and **financial centre**. With its busy docks, vast warehouses and jagged, industrialized skyline of cranes, gantries and containers, the first sight of the capital for anyone arriving by boat is also the city's most un-attractive area, **King's Wharf** – the hub of Trinidad's booming import–export trade and also the place to catch a ferry to Tobago. Nearby, the **Cruise Ship Complex** caters to cruise passengers during their few hours on dry land with an overpriced craft market. Commonly referred to as **City Gate**, the grand Victorian stone building on South Quay – originally Port of Spain's **train station** – just east of the docks is the hub of Trinidad's transport system. This is the terminus for all buses and maxi taxis running to all parts of the island.

The heart of downtown, just north of the docks, is **Brian Lara Promenade/ Independence Square**. Consisting of two parallel streets, divided by a paved area furnished with benches and chess tables, this promenade runs the width of the city centre. It is a popular after-work hangout; stalls are set up against closed offices and street food vendors do a brisk trade. During the festival season, the promenade hosts **free concerts** and performances, advertised in the local press and radio. The western end is dominated by the **Nicholas Tower**, a new, futuristic 21-storey blue-and-silver office block, and the twin towers of the **Central Bank of Trinidad and Tobago** – the first and second tallest buildings on the island respectively – while the eastern end is marked by the imposing **Roman Catholic Cathedral**, completed in 1836 after sixteen years of construction. Near the cathedral on the southern side of the square, the **UCW Drag Brothers Mall** (Mon–Sat 9am–6pm) is a great place to buy handmade leather sandals and local crafts.

Frederick Street, which bisects the promenade, is Port of Spain's main shopping drag, crammed with clothes and souvenir shops as well as street vendors selling

The Red House and the 1990 coup

The imposing neo-Renaissance **Red House**, at the edge of Woodford Square, derives its name from an earlier building on the site which was painted bright red to celebrate Queen Victoria's diamond jubilee in 1897. The present structure, completed four years after its predecessor was destroyed in the 1903 water riots, was itself attacked in a **coup** in 1990, and bullet holes still scar the stonework.

The coup, led by **Yasin Abu Bakr**, leader of the fundamentalist revolutionary group **Jamaat-al-Muslimeen**, occurred on July 27, 1990. The group stormed the Red House and took the prime minister and other government officials hostage. A **state of emergency** was declared.

Though many Trinidadians were discontented with the government at the time due to harsh fiscal measures, few supported its violent overthrow. With little public support, the rebels surrendered, on condition of amnesty, after a six-day siege. Bakr and 113 other Jamaat members were jailed for two years while the courts debated the amnesty's validity, and eventually set them free after a ruling by the UK Privy Council.

Many Trinidadians found it hard to believe that such events could take place in stable, democratic, fun-loving Trinidad. With characteristic humour, though, the crisis was turned into amusing stories, such as those told of wild **"curfew parties"**, riffing on the common conception of Trinidadians always being keen for a good time.

home-made jewellery, belts, cassettes and arts and crafts. Halfway up, the pretty, tree-shaded **Woodford Square** provides a pleasant space to escape the crowds and listen to local orators at the equivalent of London's Speakers' Corner in Hyde Park. Anyone can join in – if they can get a word in edgeways. On the western side of the square is the grand, though bullet-scarred, **Red House**, seat of Trinidad and Tobago's parliament and site of the 1990 coup (see box above); on the square's southern side stands the city's **Anglican Cathedral**.

Uptown Port of Spain

Ranged around the broad, grassy expanse of the Queen's Park Savannah and framed by the foothills of the Northern Range, Port of Spain's **uptown** district oozes prosperity. Along the wide boulevards that ring the Savannah, the palatial mansions of the colonial plantocracy compete with the residences of the republic's president and prime minister – and the glitzy modern headquarters of insurance companies. This part of town also boasts Port of Spain's main tourist attractions: a comprehensive **museum**, an above-average **zoo** and beautiful **botanical gardens**.

The **Queen's Park Savannah** is Port of Spain's largest open space. Within the 3.7km circuit of its perimeter roads, its grassy expanse is crisscrossed by paths and shaded by the spreading branches of old samaan trees. Often deserted during the hot daylight hours, the Savannah comes to life after 4pm, with football games, joggers, couples and families taking an early evening stroll. At this time, food stalls, serving tasty snacks such as roasted corn, bake and shark, *pholouri* and rotis are set up.

All Carnival competitions, including **Panorama**, **Dimanche Gras**, **Parade of the Bands** and **Champs in Concert**, are held in the grandstands on the southern side of the park. Many other events take place here, including performances by visiting international artists. Though the seats are numbingly hard, the setting is incomparably atmospheric, with performances taking place against a backdrop of the mountains and the starry Caribbean sky.

At the top end of Frederick Street, as the Savannah comes into view, stands the imposing, gabled **National Museum and Art Gallery** (Tues–Sat 10am–6pm,

21

Sun 2–6pm; free) at the corner of Keate Street. The museum's collection is extensive and wide-ranging, covering everything from early **Amerindian history** and the technology of the **oil industry** to an excellent collection of works by **local artists**. Worth a couple hours of browsing, the museum provides an essential overview of the history, economy and culture of Trinidad and Tobago.

One of the finest of the many mansions surrounding the Queen's Park Savannah is the ornately decorated **Knowsley Building**, home to the Ministry of Foreign Affairs, on the corner of Queen's Park West and Chancery Lane. Resembling a fantasy doll's house, it's one of numerous examples of the work of Glaswegian architect George Brown, who introduced the mass production of fretted woodwork to the islands. **Boissiere House**, on the corner of Cipriani Boulevard and Queen's Park West, is perhaps the best example of the style, with a whimsical concoction of fretted wooden finials and bargeboards, stained glass depicting meandering strawberry vines and a small pagoda-like roof over one room.

North of Queen's Park West on Maraval Road stands a bizarre group of mansions affectionately known as the **Magnificent Seven**, a magical-realist parade of European architectural styles with a tropical slant. Constructed between 1904 and 1910, the remarkable buildings are the result of the competing egos of rival plantation owners, each of whom tried to outdo their neighbours in grandeur. Standouts among them are **Queen's Royal College**, first of the seven, built in Germanic Renaissance style, and now Trinidad's most prestigious school (former pupils include authors V.S. and Shiva Naipaul and the country's first prime minister, Eric Williams); **Whitehall**, a Venetian-style palazzo whose gleaming white paint gives it the air of a freshly iced birthday cake; and **Killarney**, or Stollmeyer's Castle, as it is sometimes known, which stands at the northern end. This fairy-tale castle, bristling with turrets and spires, was modelled on Queen Victoria's residence at Balmoral. Unfortunately none of these buildings is open to the public.

On the northern side of the Savannah is the **Emperor Valley Zoo** (daily 9.30am–6pm, last tickets sold at 5.30pm; TT$4, children 3–12 years TT$2; ⊕www.trinizoo.com). A magnet for local kids, it's worth a wander to get a close-up look at Trinidadian species that you're unlikely to see in the wild. Its collection of relatively well-kept animals is reputedly the most extensive in the Caribbean, including **brocket deer**, **quenk**, a large selection of **monkeys**, aquarium fish and snakes, as well as **ocelots**, **spectacled caiman** and numerous **birds**, including parrots, toucans and scarlet ibis.

Next door to the zoo, and spreading back from the Savannah towards the President's House, are the exquisite **Botanical Gardens** (daily 6am–6pm; free), home to one of the oldest collections of exotic plants and trees in the western hemisphere. There are no official guides, though for a small fee unofficial guides will take you round – a good idea as most of the labels have disappeared. A small **cemetery** within the gardens contains the crumbling gravestones of many of the island's governors. Behind the Botanical Gardens stands the **President's House**, a stately villa built in 1876, while behind it, hidden from view, is the **Prime Minister's Residence**. Both buildings are closed to the public.

The suburbs of Port of Spain

Behind the residential fretworked facades of the suburbs of Port of Spain lies the engine room of T&T's cultural life. The creative energy of **Carnival production** is concentrated in the western suburb of **Woodbrook**, while further west still, the streets of **St James** come alive with revellers at night throughout the year. In the east, **Laventille** is the home of the Caribbean's favourite instrument, the **steel drum**, while the suburb of **Belmont** is home to the fascinating Rada community. All the suburbs are a ten- to twenty-minute walk from the city centre, but as the heat can quickly sap your energy, you might like to take a taxi to your destination.

Mas camps

Mas camps are the headquarters of the Carnival bands where the costumes are produced. Often converted private houses, the camps provide a focus for the whole Trinidadian art community, and you can usually watch costumes being made if you ring in advance – during the Carnival season some are open 24 hours a day. All the bands choose to portray a theme and create a number of different costumes that link to their theme, which can be purchased; prices start at about US$130. You can also join a band and take part in Carnival or **"play mas"** for around US$320. Contemporary costumes are increasingly revealing, catering to the mainly female participants' desire to show off their assets, though a few carnival artists such as Peter Minshall still make more elaborate, artistic and traditional creations. For an idea of traditional family-run camps visit the **Mas Factory** (15 Buller St, Woodbrook ☎868/628-1178) – known for their skilful wire-bending – and **D'Midas Associates** (15–17 Kitchener St, Woodbrook ☎868/622-8233), famous for their feathers. Those interested in more modern factory-style production and minimal costumes should visit **Masquerade** (49–51 Cipriani Blvd, Newtown ☎868/623-2161). For more information contact the National Carnival Band's Association, Queen's Park Savannah (☎868/627-1422, ⓦwww.carnaval.com).

The elegant old district of **Woodbrook** – between Philipps Street to the east and the Maraval River to the west – was originally a sugar cane estate owned by the Siegert family, creators of Trinidad's famous **Angostura Bitters**, and many of the streets still bear their names. The suburb has traditionally been a middle-class residential area, and its streets are still graced by old houses with wonderful fretwork bargeboards, delicate balustrades and finials. Though it has become increasingly commercialized in recent decades, it is a safe and pleasant area to stay, with several good restaurants and a handful of lively nightspots. Woodbrook is also home to numerous **mas camps**, which burst into life during Carnival season, from November to February (see box).

At the edge of Woodbrook, on Philipps Street, is the entrance to the **Lapeyrouse Cemetery** (daily 6am–6pm), a walled burial ground dating back to 1813 and filled with Victorian – as well as more modern – tombs. At the western end of Tragarete Road is the **Queen's Park Oval** (daily 8am-4pm; ☎868/622-4325), Trinidad's premier **cricket ground**. Hosting national and international matches between February and April, you'll pay TT$40–200 for a seat in the stands, or TT$250–300 for an all-inclusive ticket to the Trini Posse stand (food and drink included).

St James

It was in the western suburb of **St James** that the British landed in 1797. Legend has it that they fortified themselves with rum punch they found here, giving themselves the courage to capture Port of Spain. The area was settled by **Indian** indentured labourers after emancipation, and local street names – Calcutta, Delhi and Madras – bear witness to their homesickness.

Today, St James is one of the capital's most cosmopolitan districts, with residents from all the country's ethnic groups. It's a bustling place, especially at night when it becomes the prime liming spot in Port of Spain. Music blasts from cars, bars and clubs; locals dressed in clubbing gear lime alongside old men in jeans and T-shirts; and street stalls sell roti, oysters, corn soup, halal sandwiches and jerk chicken. **Western Main Road**, which runs through the centre of St James, is a broad thoroughfare lined with shops, bars and take-aways. It's most known, though, as the scene of the annual Muslim **Hosay** processions (see box overleaf), which take place in May or June.

Hosay

The Islamic festival of **Hosay**, commemorating the martyrdom of Mohammed's grand-sons Hussein and Hassan during the *jihad* (holy war) in Persia, has been celebrated in Trinidad ever since the first Indian Muslims arrived in 1845. Its exposure to the island's other cultures has turned it into something carnivalesque, with lewd dancing and loud music, but local Shi'a Muslims have recently taken great pains to restore the occasion's solemnity.

Hosay is celebrated in Curepe, Tunapuna, Couva and Cedros, but the best place to see it is undoubtedly in St James. The celebrations take place over four days (occurring in May or June depending on the moon). All the parades start at 11pm and continue into the early hours of the morning. The third night is the most spectacular. Large *tadjahs* more than two metres high are paraded through the streets accompanied by loud *tassa* drumming, while dancers carry two large sickle moons representing the two brothers. At midnight there is the ritual "kissing of the moons", as the dancers symbolically enact a brotherly embrace. The following night the exquisite *tadjahs* are thrown into the sea, a sacrifice to ensure that prayers for recovery from sickness and adversity will be answered.

In the weeks running up to Hosay, it is possible to watch craftsmen build the ornate minareted tombs from bamboo and coloured paper (**tadjahs**); the houses where they work have large flags planted in their yards. The task involves great financial, physical and spiritual sacrifice; the materials can cost up to TT$30,000, and the builders have to fast during daylight hours and refrain from alcohol and sexual activity for the duration. Understandably, perhaps, not many of the younger generation find the prospect appealing, and as the years pass fewer and fewer *tadjahs* are being built.

The eastern suburbs: Belmont and Laventille

Port of Spain's eastern suburbs are rarely visited by tourists, but **Belmont** – the city's first suburb – has a close-knit community famous for its continuance of African traditions and the celebration of feasts and festivals of the Orisha religion, a Yoruban faith with a somewhat clandestine presence in Trinidad and Tobago. Neighbouring **Laventille**, with its steep alleys lined with ramshackle houses made from salvaged boards and galvanized roofing, perches on the hillside in defiance of gravity. The area has spawned many a great pan player and calypsonian; it was the birthplace of the **steel drum**; and was celebrated by the Nobel laureate **Derek Walcott** in his poem *The Hills of Laventille*. Many visitors are put off the area by scare stories, but much of this is exaggerated. Exploring with a local resident will certainly help you to get more out of the area; Elwyn Francis (☎868/627-3377), a trained tour guide with the Chaguaramas Development Authority, conducts excellent walking tours of the area for TT$50.

Panyards

The best way to hear **pan** is live, in the open air on a warm starry night. Though there are many official events organized, an often more enjoyable time can be had by going to a local **panyard** when they practise – you may even be given the chance to play yourself. The most accessible panyards to visit in Port of Spain are BWIA Invaders (Tragarete Rd, opposite the Queen's Park Oval, Woodbrook), Petrotrin Phase II Pan Grove (13 Hamilton St, Woodbrook) and BPTT Renegades (138 Charlotte St, Port of Spain).

Eating

Port of Spain's **restaurant** scene has boomed in recent years. Ariapita Avenue is best for upscale establishments, and you'll most likely need to reserve a table here. For something more casual, there are scores of **cafés** in the downtown area, while the best **street food** is located in St James and, to a lesser extent, Independence Square.

Battimamzelle *Coblentz Inn*, 44 Coblentz Ave, Cascade ☎868/621-0591. This Caribbean-flavoured gourmet spot is one of Trinidad's top restaurants. Dishes include barbecue kingfish, oxtail pepperpot and crab gallette, served amidst decor that's in keeping with the hotel's hip-yet-coy ambience. Closed Sun, no lunch on Sat.

Breakfast Shed Wrightson Rd, downtown Port of Spain, next to the Cruise Ship Complex. Hearty, inexpensive and excellent local food, served at long communal trestle tables mainly for local workers; expect to pay under TT$25. The traditional breakfast of bake and shark and cocoa for TT$15 is delicious. Breakfast and lunch only.

Irie Bites 68 Ariapita Ave, Woodbrook. Jamaican jerk shack painted red, gold and green that's the best of the cluster on this stretch of Ariapita Avenue. Seasoned with Jamaican spices and cooked over pimento wood, the jerk chicken, pork and fish are served with festival (a sweetish fried dumpling) for under TT$25. Lunch and dinner Mon–Sat, closed Sun.

Mélange 40 Ariapita Ave, Woodbrook ☎868/628-

8687. Genteel, colonial-style decor and sophisticated international cuisine at this fine dining restaurant. Choose from seafood, steak, pork, lamb or chicken dishes or go for a mix at the lunch buffet. Lunch only Mon, lunch and dinner Tues–Sat, closed Sun.

Mother Nature Vegetarian Restaurant St Vincent St, central Port of Spain. Creative vegetarian meals and wonderfully filling fruit punches, everything from beetroot to papaya for under TT$25. Breakfast and lunch only, closed Sun.

Sweet Lime Ariapita Ave, at French St, Woodbrook. A great spot for people-watching and moderate prices (between TT$70–150). Satay chicken, crab backs, mussels and shrimp for starters, seafood, ribs and steaks for mains. Good kids' meals available as well. Open late.

Syps 3a Cipriani Blvd, Newtown. Intimate coffee bar and restaurant serving light lunches and dinners of crepes, quiche, crab backs, burritos and tacos. The coffees are delicious, too. A great spot for an afternoon lime, a meal will set you back between TT$75–100.

Drinking, nightlife and entertainment

Trinidadians seem to live to party, so it's no surprise that Port of Spain boasts excellent **nightclubs**, though **fetes** – large outdoor parties advertised by posters – are a better option if you want to immerse yourself in the local lifestyle. Most bars and nightclubs come alive after 10pm and are busiest from Thursday to Sunday.

The capital also boasts a number of good **theatre** companies, including the **Trinidad Theatre Workshop** (TTW), which specializes in the work of Derek Walcott. During **Carnival** time a hectic schedule of fetes, competitions and calypso tents makes excellent entertainment. Check ❺www.carnaval.com and ❺www.visittnt. com for updated calendars of events.

Liquid ground floor, Maritime Plaza, Barataria ☎868/675-9958. One of the newest clubs in Trinidad, where a bit of rock, pop and Latin is mixed in with the soca and reggae. Try and talk your way into the lavishly decorated VIP area and the Champagne Lounge with its black leather sofas. Entrance fee varies.

Martin's 13 Cipriani Blvd, Newtown ☎868/623-7632. Friendly, intimate bar with a plant-bedecked open-air seating area out back, where you can

hear the music from the adjacent panyard. A good place to meet people, especially on Friday evenings.

Pelican Inn 2–4 Coblentz Ave, St Ann's ☎868/624-7486. This Caribbean version of an English pub, popular with locals and tourists alike, is quiet on weekdays, but comes to life at weekends with a packed dancefloor and DJs. Open till 2am.

Smokey and Bunty's 97 Western Main Rd, at

Dengue St, St James, ☎868/623-3850. This local institution draws a mixed crowd – young, old, arty, gay and straight. The bar clientele spills onto the pavement, making for some excellent people-watching. Open till 3am on weekdays, 6am at the weekends.

Tasca Latina 16 Philipps St, Woodbrook

☎868/625-3497. Spanish taverna-style bar and restaurant with a dancefloor and friendly atmosphere. Varied live entertainment, often with a Latin feel and local bands, makes it popular at weekends, attracting a mature crowd. Entrance TT$20 when there's a band. Open till 2am, closed Sun.

Listings

Embassies and high commissions British High Commission, 19 St Clair Ave, St Clair ☎868/622-2748, ⊕www.britain-in-trinidad.org; US Embassy, 15 Queen's Park West ☎868/622-6371, ⊕628-5462.

Hospital The Community Hospital, 767 Western Main Rd, Cocorite (☎868/622-1191) and the St Clair Medical Centre, 18 Elizabeth St, St Clair (☎868/628-1451).

Internet In downtown Port of Spain, Inet Café, upstairs at Town Centre Mall (Mon–Thurs 8am–5pm, Fri 8am–6pm, Sat 8.30am–3pm, TT$10/hour); at Woodford Sq, Port of Spain Adult

Library, Hart St (Mon–Fri 8.30am–6pm, Sat 8.30am–noon; free for members); in Maraval, Rikmer Technologies, 36 Saddle Rd (Mon–Fri 10am–4pm; TT$10 per hr).

Laundry Simply Clean Laundromat, 99 Saddle Rd, Maraval ☎868/628-1060. Costs TT$7–12 to do your own or TT$40 for a service wash.

Police Report crimes at the Central Police Station, St Vincent St, at Hart St (☎868/625-1261); in an emergency dial ☎999.

Post office TT Post, 177 Tragarete Rd, next to Roxy Roundabout, Woodbrook (Mon–Fri 7am–5pm, Sat 8am–noon).

The Western Tip

The **Western Tip** encompasses satellite suburbs of Port of Spain, friendly fishing villages, the island's largest national park and local playground and an extensive marina hosting international yachters escaping the hurricane belt. Easy and accessible to explore from Port of Spain, the furthest point is thirty minutes' drive from the city centre.

Travelling west from the capital you pass the ever-expanding residential suburbs of Diego Martin, Petit Valley, West Moorings, West Mall and Glencoe. There's little of interest here for the visitor, apart from **River Estate** (daily 9am–4pm; free, but donations are appreciated) at the northern end of Diego Martin Main Road. Set amidst lush scenery a restored wooden estate house, the small **museum** of local history includes a rather bizarre but engaging diorama called "The River", depicting a random history of the estate with the help of floor-pad triggered sound effects. A ten-minute drive northeast of the estate is the **Blue Basin Waterfall**, one of the most accessible falls in Trinidad, though also one of the smallest. The rainforest setting is beautiful, however, and blue emperor butterflies and exotic birds flutter through the undergrowth. The small pool at the base is good for bathing and is popular with children at weekends. To get there, stay on the main Diego Martin Road past the River Estate, then turn right onto Blue Basin Road. Go up the steep hill till you reach a sign pointing to the waterfall and follow the track on foot for five minutes.

Back on the Western Main Road, a few kilometres from the Diego Martin junction is the small fishing village of **Carenage**. On leaving the village you enter the area of **Chaguaramas** (pronounced Shag-ger-*rarm*-ms), with its wide expanses of grassland and virgin forests – much of which have been set aside to form the Chaguaramas National Park. More rainforest than park, the protected area spans the low-lying mountains of the western end of the Northern Range. Tracks into the

△ Waterloo Temple, Trinidad

forest take you along rivers to waterfalls and spectacular mountain views. On the flatlands opposite the Chagville Beach are a series of buildings remaining from the US occupation of the area in World War II – now the location of the **Callaloo mas camp**, the Carnival workshop of one of Trinidad's most famous Carnival designers, Peter Minshall – and the **Chaguaramas Military History and Aviation Museum** (daily 9am–5pm; TT$20; ☎868/634-4391). The museum exhibits chronicle the military history of Trinidad and Tobago from 1498 to the present and though the presentation is somewhat haphazard, it is interesting in contrast to the typical beaches-and-palms image of the Caribbean.

Despite being the nation's playground, leisure development in Chaguaramas has, for the most part, been sensitive and unobtrusive. The protected Chaguaramas National Park is pristine rainforest, popular with hikers and birdwatchers, whilst the strip of flatland along the south coast is the only built-up area, shelter to a scattering of restaurants and nightclubs. At weekends the area becomes busy with locals going kayaking, hiking and cycling. There is a string of **beaches** along the south coast, though the sea can be dirty and polluted here; better swimming can be had on the north coast at **Macqueripe Beach** (daily 7am-6pm; TT$10 parking fee), a delightful cove that's easily accessible by road. To get there take the Tucker Valley Road, by *The Base* nightclub in the built-up stretch of Chaguaramas.

You can rent a kayak from the **Kayak Centre**, located immediately after the sign welcoming you to Chaguaramas (daily 6am–6pm; ☎868/633-7871), for TT$25 for a single and TT$35 for a double; both rates are per hour. Another energetic option is to rent a **mountain bike** from Bay Sports next door (Sat, Sun and public holidays 6am–6pm; ☎868/687-0566), costing TT$20 per hour; you can pay an extra TT$10 for a **guided ride** into the interior of the National Park. The **Chaguaramas Development Authority** (Mon–Fri 8am–4pm; ☎868/634-4227, ⊛www.chagdev. com) offers well-informed tours of the local area and the Bocas (see below) for anywhere between US$8 and $25. The Chaguaramas **Golf** Course (daily 7am–6pm; ☎868/634-4227) is TT$60 for nine holes, TT$10–65 to use the driving range and TT$40 to rent clubs.

Beyond the cluster of former military buildings and newly built restaurants, a plethora of **yachting** facilities draw some three thousand vessels each month. Past the **marinas** with their extensive facilities – supermarket, ATM, a doctor's service, shops, Internet café and a bank – lies **the Cove** (daily 7am–6pm; TT$10), a beach with well-maintained facilities. From here you can go no further, unless you take a boat to the **Bocas**, or as locals refer to them "down de islands". These rocky islets are separated from the mainland by the **Bocas del Dragon (Dragon's Mouth)**, a series of rocky channels connecting the Gulf of Paria with the Caribbean. Difficult to access, there is little tourist traffic to the islands. For those who do persevere, either by hiring a boat or booking a tour, **Gaspar Grande** is the most accessible, with caves – filled with bats and glittering stalactites and stalagmites – to visit and the *Bayview* resort (☎868/678-9001) – consisting of a restaurant, café, beach with facilities, swimming pool, hotel and self-catering apartments – making the trip most worthwhile. The fare to Gaspar Grande is TT$50 one-way by boat from the Island Property Owners' Association marina (on Western Main Road, just before the Cove). Before disembarking, arrange a pick-up time to ensure that you're not stranded.

21.2

The north

The north of Trinidad is an eighty-odd-kilometre stretch dominated by the **Northern Range**, a rugged spine boasting the island's highest peaks, El Cerro del Aripo and El Tucuche. Trinidad's most splendid **beaches** line the coast to the north of the range, with the enduringly popular Maracas Bay melting into the quieter, undeveloped beaches of Blanchisseuse and beyond. The Arima–Blanchisseuse Road, the location of the Asa Wright Nature Centre – a birdwatcher's paradise – cuts across the mountainous spine, connecting the coast with the Eastern Main Road: an amazing drive through lush **rainforest**.

Away from the jungle-smothered hills, along the traffic-choked **Eastern Main Road** (EMR), known locally as the "East–West Corridor", are some of Trinidad's most **densely populated** areas outside of Port of Spain. Towns such as the historic **St Joseph** and **Arima** are home to the majority of the island's **African** population and Indian culture is far less visible here than in the south. Creole cooking reigns supreme and the soundtrack that blares from shops, bars and maxis is **soca** and Jamaican **dancehall**. Inland of the EMR, river valleys cut into the Northern Range to a host of interior attractions such as the island's two most spectacular **waterfalls**, La Laja and Sombasson, and **river swimming** at Maracas Valley, Caura and Guanapo Gorge. The EMR ends abruptly just east of Arima, replaced by the winding minor roads spanning the weather-beaten northeast coast and tip. This wild and rugged peninsula, jutting some 20km into the Atlantic Ocean, is Trinidad's best-kept secret. The populace is overwhelmingly friendly, and along the **Toco coast** on its northern side, **leatherback turtles** clamber up the wave-battered sandy beaches to lay their eggs.

Though parts of the north are well served by **public transport** – especially the East–West Corridor – a **car** is useful to visit the more remote north coast. Surprisingly, there is not a huge amount of **accommodation** in the region, though there are clusters of guesthouses at Blanchisseuse and Grande Riviere. However, all the East–West Corridor is within an hour's drive from Port of Spain and there are a few excellent options for those wishing to stay in the interior. As the northwest tip is more than three hours' drive from the capital, it's better to arrange accommodation at one of the lovely hotels and guesthouses found in the region. Apart from unmissable bake and shark at Maracas Beach and the hundreds of roti parlours, cafés and fast-food joints along the Eastern Main Road, there are few established **restaurants** in the area. Those that do exist are usually joined to hotels and welcome non-guests – recommended establishments are listed throughout the text.

The Saddle to Maracas Bay

Saddle Road (usually called "the Saddle") makes one of the island's best scenic journeys, climbing the Northern Range and joining the **North Coast Road**. Bordered by the glittering Caribbean sea on one side and cliffs smothered with tangled jungle on the other, its destination is Maracas, where predominantly local devotees soak up the sun. If you're going by **public transport**, route taxis make the trip to Maracas from Port of Spain's City Gate (TT$8). The area hasn't yet succumbed to leisure development, and most villages here still rely on **fishing** or **farming**, and hotels are few and far between.

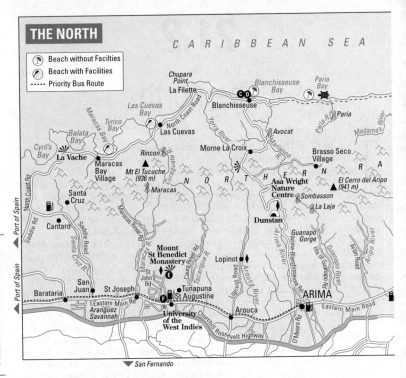

THE NORTH

🌴 Beach without Facilities
🌴 Beach with Facilities
----- Priority Bus Route

CARIBBEAN SEA

Chupara Point
La Filette
Blanchisseuse Bay
Paria Bay
Blanchisseuse
Las Cuevas Bay
North Coast Road
Yarra River
Paria
Tyrico Bay
Las Cuevas
Avocat
Madamas River
Maracas Bay
Balata Bay
Morne La Croix
Cyril's Bay
La Vache
Rincon
Brasso Seco Village
Maracas Bay Village
Mt El Tucuche (936 m)
NORTHERN RANGE
El Cerro del Aripo (941 m)
Maracas
Asa Wright Nature Centre
Santa Cruz
Sombasson
La Laja
Cantaro
Maracas Royal Rd.
Dunstan
Guanapo Gorge
Saddle Rd
Santa Cruz Rd
Saddle Road
Maracas Rd.
Arima River
Arima-Blanchisseuse Rd.
Rio de Guanapo Rd.
Guanapo River
Aripo River
Aripo Road
Mount St Benedict Monastery
Lopinot
Caura Royal Rd.
Tacarigua R.
Port of Spain
Port of Spain
San Juan
St Joseph
John's Rd
Tunapuna
Lopinot Road
Arouca River
ARIMA
Barataria
Aranguez Savannah
Eastern Main Rd
St Augustine
Churchill Roosevelt Highway
Arouca
Eastern Main Road
Oropouche Rd.
University of the West Indies

San Fernando

Gliding by St Andrew's Golf Course and the last of Maraval's grand residences, Saddle Road begins its serpentine ascent into the Northern Range. After a succession of hairpin bends, two four-metre-high stone pillars mark a **junction**. To the right, **Saddle Road** squeezes through a narrow gorge of rock (if driving through, beep your horn and approach with caution) before meandering downhill through the pastoral Santa Cruz Valley, a half-hour scenic jaunt through cattle pastures and farmland to the urban bedlam of San Juan. Cricket supremo **Brian Lara** spent his childhood in Cantaro Village, the valley's largest community. The left of the junction is the North Coast Road, one of the smoothest on the island, built by US Army engineers in 1944 as a recompense for the American occupation of the Chaguaramas peninsula (see p.822). The brightly painted *Hot Bamboo Hut* (open for snacks and souvenirs, weekends only) is a sign you've nearly reached **La Vache Scenic Area**, where the coastal views are marvellous.

Maracas Bay

Maracas Bay, a 45-minute drive from Port of Spain, is more than just a beach, it's an institution. Hundreds make the traditional Sunday pilgrimage from Port of Spain to see and be seen here. It's also the island's main Ash Wednesday chill-out spot, where revellers come to relax after the mayhem of Carnival, and sound systems keep the prostrated bodies twitching to the beat. On weekdays it's much quieter – the sand is almost empty and the extensive facilities look a bit out of place.

A generous 1850-metre curve of fine off-white sand fringed with groves of palm trees is bordered by **Maracas Bay Village**, a fishing hamlet, on the west, and *Uncle Sam and Son's* bar – pumping out reggae and soca – on the east. Swimming out to sea, you'll get a sublime view of the beach and the cloud-tipped peaks of the Northern Range.

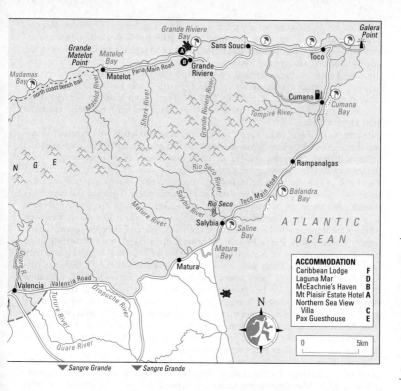

Grande Riviere Bay · Sans Souci · Toco · Galera Point · Grande Matelot Point · Matelot Bay · Paria Main Road · Grande Riviere · Madamas Bay · Matelot · north coast bench trail · Matelot River · Shark River · Grande Riviere River · Cumana · Cumana Bay · Tompire River · Rio Seco River · Rampanalgas · N G E · Salybia River · Toco Main Road · Balandra Bay · Rio Seco · Salybia · Saline Bay · ATLANTIC OCEAN · Matura River · Matura Bay · Matura · Quare R. · Valencia · Valencia Road · Oropuche River · Turure River · Quare River · N

ACCOMMODATION
Caribbean Lodge   F
Laguna Mar   D
McEachnie's Haven   B
Mt Plaisir Estate Hotel   A
Northern Sea View
  Villa   C
Pax Guesthouse   E

0   5km

▼ Sangre Grande   ▼ Sangre Grande

The water is usually clear, though the tides and undercurrents are often dangerously strong; stick to the areas between red and yellow flags and listen to the lifeguards (daily 10am–6pm). The extensive **facilities** include numerous tasty bake and shark vendors (*Richard's* and *Natalie's* are the best), a huge car park (TT$10; you'll get a ticket if you park anywhere else at weekends) and changing facilities (daily 10am–6pm; TT$1). The petrol station on the eastern edge of Maracas Bay is now closed, so it's wise to fill up at Port of Spain because there are now no places to buy petrol along this coast.

Further east of Maracas is the smaller **Tyrico Bay**, popular with the Indian community, and with slightly less wave action, a better choice for those travelling with children. Lifeguards are on duty daily 10am–6pm. Even quieter is the isolated beach at **Diamier Bay**, just a few minutes' drive east.

Las Cuevas Bay and around

After an inland curve that provides impressive views of the jagged double apex of Mount El Tucuche, Trinidad's second highest mountain, the North Coast Road turns back to the sea at **Las Cuevas Bay**, the north coast's second most popular strip of sand. Headlands enclose the bay in a tight horseshoe, affording protection from the wind and a relatively gentle surf – lifeguards put out yellow and red flags to mark safe bathing spots. There's a car park above the bay (free), as well as changing rooms, showers and toilets (10am–6pm; TT$1) and a bar serving budget-priced Creole food. The only drawback to the beach is the legendary **sandfly** population – take repellent and try to cover up as the day wears on.

On the eastern outskirts of Las Cuevas, the secluded **One Thousand Steps Beach** is ideal for a secluded swim, but keep to a depth you can stand in – the tides can be strong even on apparently calm days. The beach is opposite Rincon Trace, which is the route to the spectacular **Rincon Waterfall**, a two-and-a-half-hour uphill walk through the bush. You'll need a guide to find this and the nearby **Angel Falls**; guides have to be arranged in advance as few tourists trek this way. Laurence Pierre (☎868/634-4284, ⊛www.hikeseekers.com) is recommended. For those taking public transport, North Coast Road maxis and route taxis from Port of Spain (City Gate, TT$9–13) travel this route to Blanchisseuse, as does the rural bus service (also from City Gate), but all tend to be clustered around peak hours.

Past the tiny villages of La Filette and Yarra is **Blanchisseuse** (pronounced "blaan-she-shers"), the last village before the road tails off into the bush. With a population of around three thousand and an attractive assortment of weather-beaten board houses wreathed by rambling bougainvillea, Blanchisseuse isn't exactly a hamlet, and the clutch of ever-growing flashy holiday homes on the western outskirts are testament to its growing popularity as a retreat. The atmosphere is relaxed and supremely friendly, and there are as many local holiday-makers as there are foreign. Tourists divide their time between enjoying the succession of marvellous sandy **beaches**, hiring a local guide and hiking through the rainforest, and river-swimming in the nearby **Three Pools**, **Paria Beach** and **waterfall**, or the **Avocat Waterfall**. Local Eric Blackman, owner of *Northern Sea View Villa* (see below), is a good guide with tours including Three Pools with kayaking, hiking and swimming (TT$80 per person), Avocat Waterfall (TT$50) and a four-hour walk to Paria (TT$50). Take note that Blanchisseuse's three beaches have a reputation for rough and **treacherous waters**, particularly between November and February, so keep to a depth you can stand in (the large waves are popular with local **surfers**, though). **Marianne** is the main beach stretching around 2km. At the eastern end the Marianne river **lagoon** is an inviting place to swim and you can also rent kayaks (TT$20 for 30min) from here. It's also an excellent place for birdwatching.

Beyond Blanchisseuse, the North Coast Road gives way to the only remaining piece of **undeveloped coastline** in Trinidad. The next piece of tarmac is some 30km away in Matelot, leaving intact a sanctuary for bird and animal life, with gorgeous waterfalls and stunning beaches that are the favourite nesting sites for **leatherback turtles**. Through all this cuts the **north coast bench trail**, a two-day hike that requires camping in the bush along the way, though shorter options are available. If you prefer a solitary walk, go during the week; Saturdays, Sundays and public holidays are prime times for local hiking groups. A good local guide is Carl Fitz-James Jr (☎868/667-5968).

Practicalities

The best **accommodation** options for the north coast are located in Blanchisseuse, where there are a rash of guesthouses and host homes. *Laguna Mar*, c/o Zollna House, 12 Ramlogan Development, La Seiva, Maraval (☎868/669-2963, reservations also taken on ☎868/628-3731, ⊛www.lagunamar.com; ❸), is the largest and most professional of the bunch. Tucked away at the end of the road, this comfy hotel has rooms housed in blocks of six sits with a communal balcony; each has two double beds, fans and bathroom. There is also a three-bedroom villa to rent, and Marianne Beach is two minutes' walk away. The hotel restaurant, *Cocos Hut*, is in a converted cocoa-drying house and serves lunch and dinners consisting of tasty, local-style fish, chicken and meat. Expect to pay TT$70–100 for a meal. Vegetarians are catered for – ask in advance. For those on a budget, *Northern Sea View Villa*, North Coast Rd and Wilson Trace (☎868/669-3995, ⊜elope@tstt. net.tt; ❷), is an excellent choice. These two basic apartments offer little in the way of luxury, but they are directly opposite Marianne Beach and the owners are extremely friendly. Both apartments have two bedrooms with a fan, a kitchen, verandah and living room.

The Arima–Blanchisseuse Road

Inland from Blanchisseuse, the **Arima–Blanchisseuse Road** cuts south through the Northern Range, climbing high into misty peaks and through a tunnel-like road of green with overhanging canopies of mahogany, teak, poui, cedar and immortelle. There are impressive mountain views throughout the drive and you're more or less guaranteed to see **birdlife** wherever you stop; crested oropendola, hummingbirds and hawk-eagles are commonplace. For those wanting greater insight into the rainforest, naturalist Courtenay Rooks (☎868/622-8826, ⊛www.pariasprings.com) does excellent **nature hikes** and **birdwatching trips** starting from US$35. He can also sort you out local accommodation if necessary.

Seven miles north of Arima lies a birdwatcher's paradise, the **Asa Wright Nature Centre** (PO Box 4710, Arima, Trinidad; ☎868/667-4655, bookings in US via Caligo Ventures ☎1-800/426-7781, ⊛www.asawright.org; ❺–❻). The 800,000-square-metre estate was established as a **conservation area** in 1967 and today is Trinidad's most popular birdwatching retreat, with hummingbirds, honeycreepers, tanagers and manakins among the forty species making frequent visits to the verandah feeders. The centre offers luxurious accommodation, with rates including three meals and afternoon tea. However, if you're not staying, it's a good idea to get there before 10am to avoid the rush – the centre's on many a tour-bus route and the excited squeals of an unusual sighting and the whirr and click of paparazzi-standard zoom lenses can spoil the peaceful setting. Open daily 9am–5pm, the entrance fee (US$10) includes an hour-and-a-half tour and access to the verandah. Residents of more than three nights get a tour of **Dunston Cave**, which houses the world's most accessible colony of **oilbirds**.

The East-West Corridor

Running along the southern flank of the Northern Range, the **East–West Corridor** is traversed by the **Eastern Main Road** (EMR), a driver's nightmare; the **Priority Bus Route**, a fast-track commuter thoroughfare that's accessible only to public transport; and the **Churchill Roosevelt Highway**, a quick route connecting Port of Spain with the northeast tip. Hot and dusty as it is, the slow pace of the EMR allows you to absorb the commercial chaos, passing through the old Spanish capital of **St Joseph** and ending at **Arima**, the corridor's largest town and home to what's left of Trinidad's **Carib** community. The road is also the gateway to many a day-trip from Port of Spain, including the **Maracas Waterfall** and the **Mount St Benedict Monastery**. Beyond Arima, the buildings let up, but a few country lanes lead to the two most impressive waterfalls on the island, **La Laja** and **Sombasson**.

St Joseph

The imposing **Mohammed Al Jinnah Memorial Mosque**, resplendent with a crescent- and star-topped main dome, signals your arrival into **ST JOSEPH**, Trinidad's oldest European town and first official **capital**. Lined with fretworked French and Spanish architecture, it's one of the better places along the EMR to get a flavour of the East–West Corridor. Striking uphill into Abercromby Street takes you through the town to the Maracas Royal Road, continuing north into the lush Maracas–St Joseph Valley. Eight kilometres from the EMR is the signposted Waterfall Road – the appropriately named route to **Maracas Waterfall**. A spectacular ninety-metre fall best seen during the rainy season (June–Dec), it's an excellent place for a quick dip after the sweaty twenty-minute walk it takes to get there. Route taxis run from Curepe junction, a busy public transport exchange two kilometres east of St Joseph, to Maracas Valley between 7am and 6pm; the fare is around TT$4, though you'll pay more if you go off-route along Waterfall Road.

Mount St Benedict

Back on the EMR, past the busy town of Curepe, lies the crucifix-lined, serpentine St John's Road, the route to **Mount St Benedict Monastery**. Visible from the central plains, the white-walled, red-roofed buildings dominate the hillside. Established in 1912 by Benedictine monks fleeing religious persecution in Brazil, it's a great place to go for spectacular views, peace and quiet and a spot of afternoon tea at the neighbouring *Pax Guesthouse* (daily 3–6pm). Taxis for Mount St Benedict leave from the corner of St John's Road and the EMR (TT$4).

Past the junction with the Churchill Roosevelt Highway and the entrance to the **University of the West Indies St Augustine Campus** lies Caura Royal Road, the turn-off for **Caura Valley** – one of the most popular **picnic** and **hiking spots** in the East–West Corridor.

Practicalities

Though this area is within thirty minutes' drive of Port of Spain, if you wish to find accommodation outside the hustle of the capital, there are two excellent options for those seeking a more peaceful base from which to explore. The highly recommended **Pax Guesthouse**, Mount St Benedict (☎868/662-4084, ⊛www.paxguesthouse. com; ❹), is perched adjacent to the monastary and commands magnificent views across central Trinidad. Along with an atmosphere of complete peace, the spacious rooms are furnished with antiques, some have private bathrooms and nos. 1 to 7 have great views across the central plains. The rates include breakfast, a pre-dinner rum punch and a delicious three-course evening meal (TT$100 for non-guests). Surrounded by rainforest, the guesthouse is a popular spot with bird-lovers – hummingbirds are seen frequently on the verandah – and is an excellent, if not better alternative, to the Asa Wright Centre, for it is far less busy. The **Caribbean Lodge**, 32 St Augustine Circular Rd (☎868/645-2937, ⊛thecaribbeanlodge@hotmail.com; ❶), is a supremely friendly and attractive place adjacent to the UWI campus. Their rooms are not fancy, catering mainly for visiting students, but they are functional and very clean, with shared or private shower; some have a/c and kitchenette. There's an area for washing clothes, and meals are available. It's the best bargain to be found in the East–West Corridor. Both accommodation options are convenient for the **airport**, which is just a ten- to fifteen-minute drive away.

Lopinot

Further east and easily missed is Arouca, notable only as the point where you turn off the EMR onto snaking Lopinot Road for an eight-kilometre drive to **LOPINOT**. This pretty hamlet is best known for the **Lopinot complex**, a former cocoa estate that has been transformed into a beautiful, secluded picnic spot (daily 6am–6pm; free). Settled by the **Comte de Lopinot**, a planter who fled Haiti following the 1791 revolution, the estate house has been carefully restored, complete with a small **museum** dedicated to the culture of local residents. The community – mainly of Spanish, African and Amerindian descent – has spawned some of Trinidad's finest parang players; they can be heard at Christmas and the annual harvest festival on May 17. The route taxi fare from Arouca to Lopinot is TT$3; cars are fairly frequent (Mon–Sat 5am–6pm), but the service is reduced on Sundays.

Arima

Past Arouca, the EMR takes on a more rural aspect, wreathing through Cleaver Woods up to **ARIMA**. Named Naparima by the Amerindians who were the first to settle in the area, it has a far deeper history than its commercial facade would suggest. The town is home to what's left of Trinidad's **Carib** community – most of whom live around the crucifix-strewn **Calvary Hill**. The Santa Rosa Carib Community Association, formed in 1974 to look after their interests, has its headquarters on Paul Mitchell Street, behind the cemetery, and sells good-quality traditional Amerindian craft such as woven baskets or carved calabashes. Apart from the **Santa Rosa** festival

– a combination of Catholic and Carib celebration, held during the last week in August – the only other compelling reason to stop in Arima is the fabulous open-air **market**, which is liveliest on Fridays and is a great opportunity to view local life and vegetables. As the region's **main transport hub**, maxis to Sangre Grande (TT$4), Manzanilla (TT$3), Toco (TT$7), Mayaro (TT$7) and Grande Riviere (TT$15) leave from Raglan Street and Broadway, whilst maxis to Port of Spain (TT$4) leave from the northern end of St Joseph Street. **Taxis** to Sangre Grande (TT$4) and Valencia (TT$2) leave from the roundabout, and taxis to Port of Spain (TT$5) can be caught on Broadway. Alternatively, catch the ECS **bus** to the capital (TT$4 outside the courthouse on Hollis Avenue.

Once past the outskirts of Arima, a turn-off at the WASA Guanapo Waterworks sign leads to the **Heights of Guanapo Road**. This is a fantastic hiking area, but not a place to explore without a **guide**; Laurence Pierre is recommended (☎868/634-4284, ⊛www.hikeseekers.com). The breathtaking **Guanapo Gorge**, the **La Laja** and **Sombasson waterfalls** are here – a vine-wreathed deep channel, a twenty-metre and a three-tiered fifty-metre cascade respectively – and you can see them all in a day, though you'll need to be in fairly good shape.

The Northeast Tip

Stretching from **Matura** in the east to **Matelot** in the north, the rugged coastline of Trinidad's **Northeast Tip** is a perfect escape from the bustle of the capital and the northwest corridor. At least a three-hour drive from Port of Spain to Matelot, the region seems suspended in a time warp; people and houses are few and far between and an air of hypnotic quiet pervades. The residents have the only community radio station on the island – Radio Toco 106.7 FM – which is great for giving you a taste of local life. **Farming** and **fishing** are the mainstays of the economy, and you'll lose count of the signs advertising shark oil, saltfish and sea moss for sale.

To explore the Northeast Tip easily you'll need your own car. Though there is a rural **bus** service (TT$9) – with buses concentrated at peak periods – and the occasional **maxi** and **taxi** (TT$6–20), service is somewhat sporadic; all options leave from Sangre Grande, fifteen kilometres southeast of Valencia and accessible by public transport from Port of Spain and Arima. The quickest way by **car** from Port of Spain is to take the Churchill Roosevelt Highway, turn left when it ends, and then right onto the quiet portion of the EMR to Valencia, from where the Valencia Road swings north to the Toco coast.

After passing through the quiet town of Valencia and the one-street town of **Matura**, you reach the prime nesting sites of **leatherback turtles**. If you want to visit the beach you'll need a permit (TT$5) and a guide (TT$10) – restrictions imposed in order to protect the turtles – and both can be obtained from **Nature Seekers Incorporated** on the main road (☎868/668-7337, ⊛natseek@tstt.net.tt), a local conservation project who also arrange night visits to the beach to watch female leatherbacks nest during season (March–Aug). Past Matura, the Toco Road meets the east coast for the first time. The first safe place to swim is a beach just past the tiny village of **Salybia**. Opposite the entrance to the beach is the clearly signposted **Rio Seco waterfall trail**, a pleasant one-hour walk and the route to one of the area's more spectacular **waterfalls** (known locally as Salybia Waterfall), an eight-metre cascade surrounded by bathing pools. Approximately fifteen kilometres past Salybia is the village of Cumana, home to the last **petrol station** on this stretch of coast (Mon–Sat 8.30am–6pm, Sun 8.30am–noon).

Toco and Galera Point

The largest town in the area, **TOCO** is an attractive, quiet fishing village which retains a distinctly antiquated air and contains the highest concentration of Baptists in the Caribbean. As you enter the town, Galera Road strikes off to the right; this is where the **Toco Folk Museum** (open during school hours 8am–3.30pm, or ring

868/670-8261; TT$3, TT$2 children), located in the Toco Composite School, is based. A fascinating local project highlighting local history, the small museum houses Amerindian artefacts, snakeskins, butterflies and household items, including a gramophone and some rare 78rpm calypso records, which can be played if especially requested. The road continues to a good **beach** and **Galera Point**, the island's extreme eastern tip. Adjacent to the lighthouse is a windblown, rocky bluff, known as Fishing Rock, an atmospheric place where the Caribbean Sea and Atlantic collide in a swirl of aquamarine and shimmering slate froth. Standing on the rock you feel as if you are on the edge of the world, which is how a group of rebellious Amerindians must have felt in 1699 when they leapt to their deaths here rather than be killed by their Spanish slave-masters.

Past Toco, the road becomes **Paria Main Road**, running perilously close to the cliffs, where huge waves crash onto a wild and rugged coast. At the next village, **Sans Souci**, is a safe beach and the island's **surfing** capital – a regular venue for competitions.

Grande Riviere

One of the most appealing villages on the Toco coast, **Grande Riviere** is also the only place in the area with any kind of tourist infrastructure. The beautiful beachside *Mount Plaisir Estate Hotel* (see below) has spurred some local residents to open up **guesthouses**, but development has remained low-key. Local people are incredibly welcoming, often throwing parties for leaving guests.

The village boasts a superlative **beach**, famous for nesting **leatherback turtles** – it's common for 150 or more to lay simultaneously here in season. Local residents have formed the Grande Riviere Environmental Awareness Trust, to guard against poachers and provide guides, most of which work either through *Mount Plaisir Estate Hotel* or the Grande Riviere Nature Tours Guide Association (868/670-8381), housed in a small hut next to the hotel. As well as the beach there are hosts of **waterfalls** and **river walks**, and also excellent **birdwatching** – including the rare piping guan; local guides (see above) can be hired to help you explore the surrounding hiking trails. As for village life and entertainment, most of the action occurs at the *Mount Plaisir Estate*, where the **bar** is a favourite liming spot. Other friendly options include the *First and Last Bar* and *Jamesy's Stone Wall Bar* on the main road.

Apart from the popular swimming spot, **Shark River**, there's little reason to continue along the road past Grande Riviere, which soon ends at the tiny fishing hamlet of Matelot.

Practicalities

Grande Riviere may be small but it has one of the best **hotels** in Trinidad: *Mount Plaisir Estate Hotel* (868/670-8381, www.mtplaisir.com; ❹), a fantastic place to stay if you can afford it. The *Estate* overflows with easy style – the wooden rooms, decorated with hand-crafted furniture, beautiful paintings and wall hangings, sleep four to six people; ask for one that opens directly onto the beach. The excellent on-site *Ylang Ylang* **restaurant** equals the best in Port of Spain. Food served includes home-made bread, local-style meat, fish and imaginative vegetarian options, as well as an extensive wine list; expect to pay in excess of TT$150 for a three-course meal. The hotel will also collect you from the airport (US$85). For those on a more limited budget, *McEachnie's Haven*, at Bristol and Thomas streets (868/670-1014, www.mchaventt; ❸), makes up in friendliness for what it lacks in style. This yellow guesthouse has homey, basic rooms sleeping up to four, with fans, mosquito nets and en-suite bathroom. The owner, Ingrid, cooks delicious meals on request for both guests and non-guests (TT$50–70), and as her children are tour guides and her husband, Eric, is a well-known local musician, a stay here makes for a great opportunity to get to know a local family. The beach is just five minutes away, too.

21.3

Central and south Trinidad

Central and south Trinidad encompasses an astonishing variety of land-scapes. The **west coast** is gritty and industrialized, punctuated by the odd oasis of calm such as the **Caroni Swamp** – home of the scarlet ibis – and Trinidad's busy second city, **San Fernando**. On the **east coast**, there are the stunning **Manzanilla** and **Mayaro beaches**, both lined with coconut palms and still undiscovered by the tourist trade, while inland sits the protected **Nariva Swamp**, home of endangered species such as the **manatee** (sea cows). In contrast to the northern East–West Corridor, the central and southern regions of Trinidad are populated predominantly by people of Indian descent; look out for Hindu temples, flags and Indian delicacies along the roadside.

Transport is no problem along the west coast; most towns are easily accessible from the **Uriah Butler–Solomon Hochoy Highway**, which runs from Port of Spain to San Fernando. Rural areas inland and the south and southwest coast can be more of a problem, however – **maxis** and **taxis** take long circular routes and the absence of road signs can make driving confusing.

Accommodation in the region is minimal, with most hotels geared more towards oil-industry personnel than to tourists. **Host homes** are your best bet, and an excellent way of meeting local people; contact the Bed and Breakfast Co-operative Society (see p.807). Most of the region, however, can be reached from Port of Spain in a day-trip, unless you plan to spend time on the south and southeastern coast. **Restaurants** and **nightlife** are very limited in the region, though there are plenty of **fast-food places** serving cheap, filling meals, especially Indian and Chinese food, while the many small **bars** and **rum shops** provide friendly conversation and a good night out. In central Trinidad there are a few high-class **restaurants** at the **Grand Bazaar Mall**, at the junction of the Uriah Butler–Solomon Hochway and Churchill Roosevelt Highways: *Rasam* (☎868/645-0994) is especially good, serving excellent southern Indian dishes, and *Botticelli's* (☎868/645-8733; closed Sun), opposite the Imperial Garden, is another first-class option; expect to pay at least TT$100 for a main course at both establishments. In the south, restaurants, hotels and entertainment are clustered in San Fernando; recommended establishments are listed in the text.

Central Trinidad

While busy, industrial **Chaguanas** is Central Trinidad's main town, the region is predominantly rural, typified by the agricultural **Caroni Plains**, which are bracketed between the woody Montserrat Hills and the stunning Manzanilla Beach. The dominance of **Indian** culture is immediately noticeable upon joining the Uriah Butler–Solomon Hochoy Highway, as the twelve-metre statue of Swami Vivekananda, which presides over the **National Council of Indian Culture** complex, looms into view on the eastern side of the road. Meanwhile, at the **Waterloo Temple** west of Chaguanas you may be forgiven if you think you are in southern Asia, not the Caribbean.

Caroni Swamp and Bird Sanctuary

Less than an hour's drive from Port of Spain is Trinidad's most heavily promoted environmental attraction, the **Caroni Swamp and Bird Sanctuary**. This is the

Phagwa

A lighthearted celebration of the arrival of spring, the Hindu Holi festival – known in Trinidad as Phagwa (pronounced "pag-wah") – is held in March. Upbeat and carniva-lesque, Phagwa celebrations are massive outdoor parties that represent a symbolic triumph of light over darkness. The festivities include the singing of devotional folk songs called **chowtals**, but the main focus is an intense fuchsia-pink dye known as **abir**, which is squirted from plastic bottles over participants wearing white. Games add to the fun; adults participate in **makhan chor**, where teams form a human pyramid in order to grab a suspended flag, while children compete in roti-eating contests. **Chaguanas** hosts one of the largest celebrations in Trinidad, in an open space off Longdenville Old Road. There are other gatherings at Aranguez Savannah in San Juan and at Couva, but none is widely publicized – contact TIDCO for the exact dates (☎868/623-1932).

only roosting place on the island of the **scarlet ibis**, the national bird, sporting an amazingly bright red plumage. The swamp is home to 157 species of birds, and caimans, snakes and silky anteaters all can be observed in the water and the surrounding mangroves. It's a quiet, mysteriously beautiful place, and well worth a visit. Tours, taken at dusk on small wooden boats, are available (TT$60/US$10), leaving daily at 4pm and lasting two and a half hours; advance booking is advisable. Contact Nanan (☎868/645-1305) or James (☎868/662-7356) for more information and to make bookings.

It is not possible to get close to the birds' roosting spot without disturbing them, so bring binoculars or a powerful zoom lens, or you'll see little more than red specks against the dark green foliage. Leave Port of Spain at 3pm if you're driving, and if catching public transport take **maxis** or **route taxis** bound for Chaguanas; ask them to drop you at the Caroni Swamp exit, from where it's a five-minute walk. Lashings of insect repellent are a must during the rainy season, when mosquitoes go on the offensive.

The Waterloo Temple

Past the sprawling settlement of **Chaguanas** – the birthplace of the Nobel Prize winner **V.S. Naipaul** and site of the annual Phagwa celebration (see box) – and onto the Southern Main Road, you'll pass a selection of small settlements and grandiose, crumbling estate houses. About a kilometre south of Chase Village, Orange Field Road cuts west off the Southern Main Road through the **Orange Valley Estate** to join the signposted Waterloo Road down to the sea. This superb drive through sugar cane plantations culminates half a kilometre down the road where, as you emerge at the sea, you'll be greeted by a remarkable scene. The gleaming white, onion-domed **Waterloo Temple** stands on a pier overlooking the waters of the Gulf of Paria at high tide, or extensive mud flats at low tide. The funeral pyres at the water's edge and the flags (*jhandes*) flapping in the breeze all contribute to the impression that you are standing by the River Ganges rather than on a Caribbean island.

Built in 1947 by **Seedas Sadhu**, an Indian labourer, the temple is a testament to one man's struggle against colonial bureaucracy; refused planning permission on land, he decided to build in the sea, using his bicycle to carry the foundation rocks into the water. Anyone can enter the temple, provided they remove their shoes first. Opening hours are Tues, Wed, Sat & Sun 8am–3pm, though these times depend on when the caretaker arrives; the grounds are open daily between 6am and 6pm. To get to the temple by **public transport**, take a route taxi from Chaguanas to the start of Orange Field Road (TT$2–3), where you pick up another taxi (TT$3) to the temple.

Pointe-a-Pierre Wildfowl Trust

After Waterloo the Southern Main Road winds its way through Trinidad's economic heartland, an area of smoke-belching sugar and oil refineries. Past Claxton Bay, an industrial suburb cloaked in dust from the nearby cement factory, stands a stunning oasis of nature, located on the extensive grounds of the Petrotrin Oil Refinery. The **Pointe-a-Pierre Wildfowl Trust** (Mon–Fri 8am–5pm, Sat & Sun 10am–4pm; TT$8; ☎868/658-4200 ext 2512, ⊛www.trinwetlands.org) consists of 250,000 square metres of attractively landscaped grounds that are home to many **rare species of bird**, including the wild Muscovy duck, the red-billed whistling duck and white-cheeked pintail. Some of the rarer birds, including scarlet ibis, are caged to allow breeding programmes to continue. The well-maintained **learning centre** has good photographic displays, collections of shells, insects and Amerindian artifacts and an informative account of Trinidad's original inhabitants. To **drive** to the Trust from Port of Spain or San Fernando, leave the Uriah Butler–Solomon Hochoy Highway at the Gasparillo exit and follow the signs to the Petrotrin Oil Refinery. On **public transport**, take a Port of Spain–San Fernando maxi, route taxi or bus, and get out at the Gasparillo exit, from where the refinery is a two-minute walk. Once inside, it's another fifteen-minute walk to the Trust. The best time to visit is before 11am or after 3pm.

Manzanilla

In refreshing contrast to the smoggy, industrialized central west coast, central Trinidad's east coast features nothing more than miles of sand and endless coconut palms. South of Sangre Grande, the largest town in the east, the **coast** is dominated by the **Cocal**, 24km of unbroken sand, lined by grove upon grove of swaying coconut palms. The air is raucous with the calls of the **red-chested macaws**, and street vendors line the road selling the shellfish known as chip-chip, crabs, black conch, fish and watermelon, when in season. So far, the owners of the east coast coconut estates have declined to sell the property to hotel developers, and Manzanilla beach and the protected Nariva Swamp retain their idyllic seclusion. Deserted during the week, but popular at weekends, take care while swimming as the undercurrents can be dangerous. There are changing facilities at the northern end (daily 10am–6pm; TT$1). If you're planning to visit Manzanilla for the Ash Wednesday or Easter beach parties, try to get there early – it's not unknown for the traffic jams to start as far back as Valencia, some twenty kilometres to the northwest. The only hotel directly on the beach along this stretch of coast is the well-signposted **Calypso Inn** (☎868/691 5939 or 868/671-7369; ④). Beautifully located on the sands between Manzanilla and Matura, their smart double rooms have a/c, TV and a balcony overlooking the sea. There is also a bar and restaurant on site.

Nariva Swamp

The internationally recognized wetland of **Nariva Swamp** covers 15 square kilometres behind the coconut estates along the east coast. The area is made up of agricultural land as well as reed-fringed marshes, mangroves and **Bush Bush Island**, bordered by palmiste and moriche palms and covered in hardwood forest. The swamp's unique freshwater ecosystem harbours large concentrations of rare **wildlife**, with some 58 species of mammals, 37 species of reptiles, and 171 species of birds. The swamp is also home to 92 species of mosquito, so remember to bring your insect repellent.

Nariva is the only place in Trinidad to see the threatened **manatee** or sea cow, a peculiar elephantine mammal that can grow up to three metres in length and weigh over 900 kilograms, and which feeds off water hyacinth, moss and waterlilies. The swamp is also an excellent place to view caimans, freshwater turtles, red howler monkeys, white-fronted capuchin monkeys, silky anteaters, opossums, porcupines and a wide variety of birds including savannah hawks, dicksissels, orange-winged parrots and the yellow-capped Amazon parrot. Its most alarming inhabitants must be the **anacondas**, capable of growing up to ten metres long; they're the heaviest reptiles in the world, and the largest in the Americas.

To visit the sanctuary, you must first obtain a free permit from the Wildlife Division of the Forestry Department on Farm Road in St Joseph (Mon–Fri 8am–4pm; ☎868/662-5114); the division will also advise you about which guides to contact. Caribbean Discovery Tours (☎868/624-7281) offer a marvellous Nariva trip, with a walk through Bush Bush, kayaking if water levels permit and an excellent Indian lunch cooked by residents of Kernaham Village (US$50–100). If you're a serious ornithologist, opt for the excellent birding tours offered by Paria Springs that start at US$35 (☎868/622-8826, ⊛www.pariasprings.com).

The south

Geographically, Trinidad's south presents a mirror image of the north, with the low ridge of the forested **Southern Range** as its spine and a peninsula jutting out towards Venezuela. That's as far as the comparison goes, though, as apart from Trinidad's second city, **San Fernando**, the region is the most sparsely populated area of the island. Although many of the inhabitants still earn a living from agriculture, the economy is based around **oil**. Ironically, this is what has left the region so unspoilt; the petroleum business leases large expanses of forest from the government that remain largely undeveloped, providing homes for wildlife reserves and endangered species such as the ocelot. Tourists rarely venture this far south – those who do make a beeline for the **Pitch Lake**, the only potted attraction in these parts. Still, **Cedros** and **Erin** are picturesque areas, and **Mayaro** offers up a gorgeous swath of sand on the southeast coast – a popular holiday resort with Trinidadians. Consequently there are few facilities for visitors, but all of the towns and villages in the south, along with many of the beaches, are accessible by **public transport**. **Beaches** in the south are best visited during the dry season (Dec–May), as from June to November they are polluted by brackish water and litter swept downstream.

San Fernando

Nestled against the base of the bizarrely shaped **San Fernando Hill**, the city of **SAN FERNANDO** enjoys the most striking location of any in Trinidad. Usually referred to as the industrial capital of T&T, it has an old-fashioned charm helped in large part by the old winding lanes studded with charming gingerbread buildings. It is also the best place in the region to find **accommodation**, good **restaurants** and lively **entertainment**. Far quieter than Port of Spain, San Fernando is essentially a friendly place, and getting to know the people here is easy enough provided you make an effort – and often the first move. There are no buses or maxis travelling within San Fernando, and **route taxis** charge a flat fare of TT$3 for most journeys, with an added dollar or two for off-route drops; a good place to hail one is Library Corner next to the *KFC*.

Most of the historical sights and shops are located on and around the **Harris Promenade**, a broad, elegant boulevard running west from the foot of San Fernando Hill. At 200 metres high, the hill – flattened with steep protruding points, the result of quarrying activity – overshadows the town centre and makes for a pleasant recreation area with picnic tables, a childrens' playground and panoramic views.

High Street is San Fernando's main shopping street, lined with clothes stores and street vendors. At its southern end is **Happy Corner**, location of a few renovated colonial buildings and **King's Wharf**, where you can buy fresh snapper, kingfish and shark at the local fish market. On **Carib Street** stands the city's oldest building, the **Carib House** – an eighteenth-century Spanish colonial building – while neighbouring **Coffee Street** is home to many of the south's **steel bands**, including the highly acclaimed **Fonclaire**. San Fernando is the hub of the south's transport system; from here you can catch maxis, buses and taxis to Port of Spain, La Brea, Princes Town and Point Fortin.

Accommodation

Most **accommodation** in San Fernando caters for visiting oil-industry personnel, so expect a more business than holiday atmosphere.

Royal Hotel 46–54 Royal Rd ☎868/652-3924, ⓦwww.royalhoteltt.com. Recently renovated after a fire, but comfortable and reasonably priced for facilities: bright rooms have a/c, cable TV, phone, fridge, jacks for Internet access and en-suite bathrooms. There's a breezy open-air restaurant on site and a pool. ❹

Tradewinds Hotel 38 London St ☎868/652-9463, ⓦwww.tradewindshotel.net. The best-equipped hotel in the south and a friendly place in a quiet suburb. The best rooms are in the renovated building next to the pool, but all have a/c, cable TV, fridge, minibar, kettle and en-suite bathrooms. There's a popular restaurant/bar on site, and breakfast is included in the rates. ❹

Eating and entertainment

While there are numerous **fast food** outlets in San Fernando, finding a more formal **restaurant** is less straightforward: choices are restricted to a couple of Chinese places, hotel restaurants and a handful of other eateries. If you're looking for a little more **entertainment** than the local rum shops, which nevertheless are ideal places to meet locals, you will have to make your way to the city, where bar/restaurants are the best bet for **live music**.

Belle Bagai 20 Gransaul St. Elegant bar/restaurant in a wooden gingerbread house, all creaky floorboards and polished mahogany. The open-air verandah on a quiet street is perfect for a low-key lime or game of pool. Closed Sun.

Club Celebs top level, Gulf City Shopping Complex ☎868/652-7641. The most popular nightspot in the south – a modern club and sports bar playing a wide variety of music to a young crowd. Entrance fee varies. Wed, Fri & Sat 10pm–4am.

Kolumbo Restaurant 34 Sutton St ☎868/653-7684. Set in a restored colonial building, this stylish restaurant on two levels is very romantic at night, serving a menu of international cuisine with gourmet burgers and pâtés. Dinner only, closed Sun & Mon.

Nam Fong Lotus Restaurant 91–93 Cipero St ☎868/652-3356. Serves huge Chinese lunches

and dinners at inexpensive prices. A relaxing, comfy and more upmarket atmosphere than the usual plastic tables. Closed Sun.

Naparima Bowl 19 Paradise Pasture ☎868/657-8770. Comfy theatre and outdoor amphitheatre hosting plays, touring from Port of Spain, as well as big calypso and steel-band events. Ticket prices vary.

Tree House 38 London St ☎868/653-8733. Lively place inside the *Tradewinds Hotel* – a popular local haunt on a plant-bedecked balcony overlooking the city. Food is reliably good and the menu varied, from crab backs and shrimp bruschetta to seafood, steaks and Mexican and Cajun dishes (although portions are disappointingly small for the high prices). Open very early for local and international breakfasts; reservations recommended for dinner.

Around San Fernando

Trinidad's **southwest peninsula**, known locally as the "deep south", offers a mix of gritty oil towns and marvellous drives through sleepy backwaters, forested hills, and teak and coconut plantations, down to beaches of soft brown sand backed by red-earth cliffs and lapped by calm seas. The larger towns, such as **Point Fortin** and the **Siparia-Fyzabad** conurbation, revolve around the oil industry and provide little interest to the passing visitor. The south coast, though, has a variety of excellent, deserted beaches at **Cedros** and **Erin**, while in the southeast, **Guayaguayare** and **Mayaro** beaches are popular with Trinidadian holiday-makers – quiet during the week but busy at weekends and public holidays. If you're **driving** to Mayaro from Port of Spain, the quickest route is via the Churchill Roosevelt Highway to Valencia, through Sangre Grande and down the east coast via Manzanilla. This is also the quickest way by **public transport** – take a maxi to Arima, then one to Sangre Grande and then one down to Mayaro. If you're coming from San Fernando and the west coast, drive east along the Manahambre, Naparima and Mayaro roads. Maxis go from San Fernando to Princes Town; change here for a maxi to Mayaro. There

21

are few places to stay on the south coast – most are basic beach houses advertised in the local press. **Azee's Guest House**, at the 3.5-mile marker on Guayaguayare Rd (☎868/630-4619, ✆azees@tstt.net.tt; ❷), is a small, friendly hotel just two minutes' walk from Guayaguayare Beach. All rooms have a/c, cable TV, telephone, fridge and en-suite bathrooms, and there's a homey bar on site as well as a restaurant, good for meals even if you're not a guest. Popular with Trinidadian holiday-makers during school holidays, so it is best to book ahead.

The Pitch Lake

Roughly 25km southwest of San Fernando lies the **Pitch Lake** (daily 9am–5pm; ☎868/623-6022), location of some of the world's finest-quality **asphalt**. The popular tourist attraction is well signposted 1.5km south of La Brea on the Southern Main Road. Locals may claim it as the eighth wonder of the world, but to the sightseer it bears a remarkable resemblance to the wrinkly hide of an elephant. It is a genuine curiosity, however, as there are only a few such lakes in the world; the others are in Los Angeles, Norway and Lake Maracaibo, Venezuela, which is connected to La Brea by veins that run under the sea. Five to six million years ago, asphaltic oil flowed into a huge mud volcano, developing over time into the asphalt that is now extracted from the lake. The material is used to pave roads all over the world, including Pall Mall leading to Buckingham Palace in London – though the poor local village has yet to profit from this resource on their doorstep. Although **free** to enter it's worth visiting with a **guide**. Authorized guides operate from the main booth (TT$30), and if you plan on touring wear shoes with low heels and be careful not to let the pitch touch your clothes – it's a nightmare to clean.

21.4

Tobago

An elongated oval just 41 by 14 kilometres, **TOBAGO** features astonishing riches including deserted beaches, pristine coral reefs and a wealth of lush rainforest – the island really does feel as if it's the last of the "unspoilt Caribbean". Though tourism has taken root with breathtaking speed, Tobago is hardly the typically jaded resort island. There are few all-inclusives, celebrations such as the Easter **goat races** are attended by more Tobagonians than tourists, and local culture is honoured at the annual **Heritage Festival** each August. Nevertheless, tourism *is* changing Tobago. Helping hands sharing the labour of pulling in seine fishing nets are still called by a resonant toot on a conch shell, but nowadays the fishermen often wait until they've captured an audience before hauling the catch onto the sand. And the African drumming that forms a major part of local **Orisha** and **Spiritual Baptist** ceremonies is now the soundtrack of many a hotel floor-show.

Physically, Tobago is breathtaking; heavy industry is confined to Trinidad, so the beaches are clean and the landscape left largely to its own devices. The flat coral and limestone plateau of the southwest – the **Lowlands** – is the island's most heavily developed region, with hotels clustered around powder-sand beaches such as **Pigeon Point** and **Mount Irvine**, home to excellent **surfing** (best during November to February). The tourist clamour is kept in check by the capital, **Scarborough**, a picturesque port town tumbling down a lighthouse-topped hillside.

The island's rugged **windward** (south) **coast** is lined with appealing fishing villages; **Speyside** and **Charlotteville** in the remote eastern reaches have some of the finest **coral reefs** in the southern Caribbean and **scuba diving** is a burgeoning industry. Tobago is an excellent and inexpensive place to learn to dive, and there's plenty of challenging drift diving for the more experienced, while the many reefs within swimming distance of the beaches make for fantastic **snorkelling**. The **leeward** (north) **coast** has Tobago's finest beaches; some, like **Englishman's Bay**, are regularly deserted, while at **Castara**, **Parlatuvier** and **Bloody Bay**, you'll share the sand with local fishermen.

The landscape of the eastern interior rises steeply, forming the **Main Ridge**, mountains which shelter the **Forest Reserve**, the oldest protected rainforest in the western hemisphere. Ornithologists and naturalists flock in for the **bird** and **animal** life that flourishes here; David Attenborough filmed parts of his celebrated *Trials of Life* series at **Little Tobago**, a solitary sea bird sanctuary off the coast of Speyside. For more casual visitors, the squawking, chirruping forest offers plenty of opportunities for birdwatching or a splash in the icy **waterfalls**.

One point worth making is that Tobago's close-knit community keeps the island very **safe** – especially outside the Crown Point area. Ignore the warnings of all-inclusive hotels, which encourage tourists to stay on-site by claiming that Tobago is dangerous; the best food, entertainment and scenic areas are outside the hotel complexes, so be adventurous, explore and keep the locals in business.

Some history

Tobago has been hotly contested over the centuries. The original **Carib** population fiercely defended their *Tavaco* (the name derived from the Indian word for tobacco), driving off several attempts by European colonists throughout the late 1500s and early 1600s. English sailors staked England's claim in 1580, but in 1658 the Dutch took over, calling it "Nieuw Vlissingen".

Declared a no-man's-land in 1684 under the treaty of Aix La Chapelle, French, British and Dutch colonists lived fairly peaceably alongside free Africans, slaves and the remnants of the Caribs for the next eighty-odd years. But a French attempt to seize control in 1648 shook the neutral status and worried Britain enough for them to send a powerful fleet in 1672, taking possession of the island with swift precision. **Plantation culture** began in earnest soon after and the island rapidly became a highly efficient sugar, cotton and indigo factory. Africans were imported to work as slaves, and by 1772, three thousand-odd of them were sweating it out under less than three hundred whites. The economy flourished, and by 1777, the island's eighty or so estates had exported 160,000 gallons of rum, 1.5 million pounds of cotton, 5000lbs of indigo and 24,000 hundredweight of sugar. The numerical might of the slave population led to many bloody **uprisings**, with planters doling out amputations and death by burning and hanging to the dissenters.

From 1781 to 1814, the island changed hands four times in a tit for tat struggle between the French and the British, ending in British control, after which another phase of successful sugar production ensued. In 1899, Tobago was made a **ward** of Trinidad, effectively becoming the bigger island's poor relation with little control over her own destiny. With the collapse of the sugar industry, the black population, including **free Africans** who arrived in the mid-1800s, clubbed together to farm the land – the **"Len-Hand" system** – still celebrated in the annual harvest festivals.

In 1963, **Hurricane Flora** ravaged Tobago. In the restructuring programme that followed, attempts were made to diversify the economy, tentatively developing a tourist industry. By 1980, the island had her sovereignty partially restored when the

21

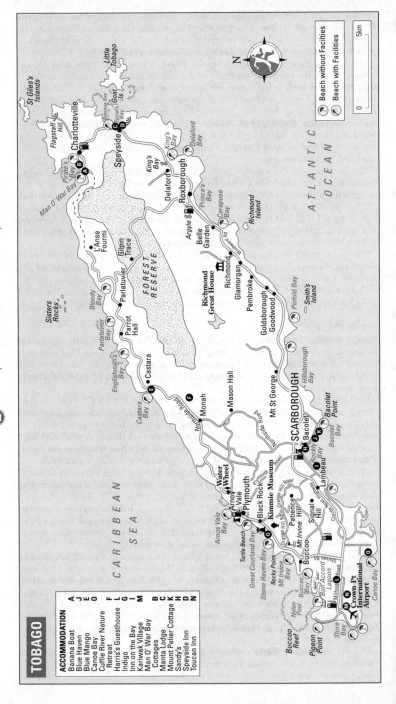

TOBAGO

ACCOMMODATION

Banana Boat	A
Blue Haven	J
Blue Mango	E
Canoe Bay	O
Cuffie River Nature Retreat	F
Harris's Guesthouse	G
Indigo	I
Inn on the Bay	M
Kariwak Village	B
Man O' War Bay Cottages	C
Manta Lodge	K
Mount Pelier Cottage	H
Sandy's	D
Speyside Inn	N
Toucan Inn	

Tobago House of Assembly (THA) was reconvened, with authority over the island's more mundane affairs. Nevertheless, with agriculture on the decline, Tobago's economy now revolves around **tourism**. That said, the island has largely resisted the most ruinous aspects of the industry it depends on, and the majority of residents remain proud of the place they rightly consider to be paradise.

Arrival and information

Most people arrive via **Crown Point International Airport**, small enough to feel overwhelmed by the arrival of a single jet. There is a row of shops in the airport complex, among them a branch of the Republic Bank (Mon–Thurs 8am–3pm, Fri 8am–1pm & 3–5pm) with an ATM, and useful for **currency exchange**. The tourist board office (daily 6am–10pm; ☎868/639-0509) is here too, a useful source of **information**. There's also a small newsagent where local and Companion phone **cards** are sold.

Official **private taxis** advertise their rates on the taxi price list on the wall of the arrivals lounge. The rates are high, but not wildly so. If you're on a budget, cross the street and haggle with the drivers who are not part of the authorized system. There's an hourly **shuttle bus** between Crown Point (the stop's just outside the airport complex) and Scarborough (half past the hour from Crown Point and on the hour from Scarborough); you can buy bus **tickets** from newsagents. If you're heading towards Charlotteville or Speyside, check with the tourist board, as chartering a taxi is quite expensive and many hotels throw in free airport collection. Remember, on your return journey all visitors must pay a TT$100 **departure tax**, in local currency.

If you're arriving by **boat**, you'll land in Scarborough docks; private and route taxi ranks are located at the docks' entrance.

Getting around

Although Tobago's **public transport** system is improving all the time, **renting a car** is the best option if you're only on the island for a few days. Most of the international and local **car rental operators** are clustered around the airport; local operators tend to be cheaper but are less likely to offer 24hr assistance. Sherman's (☎868/639-2292, ⊛www.shermansrental.com) is a recommended local operator, and amongst the internationals, Thrifty (☎868/639-8507, ⊛www.thrifty.com) is reliable. Expect to leave a **deposit**, usually a credit card imprint; a notable exception is Auto Rentals (☎868/639-0644, ✉mail@autorentals.co.tt), which has one of the largest fleets in Tobago. **Scooters** are available from some beach outlets and cost approximately US$20–25 a day. **Motorbikes** are catching on fast and there are several places offering dirt bikes for about US$30 per day.

The blue-banded **maxi taxis** run between Scarborough and various places on the island, but offer an infrequent service to the more remote areas and at weekends. However, the **route taxi** network is extensive and convenient for short hops in the western portion of the island. If you're heading further afield, you'll need to travel into Scarborough, where the main route taxi departure points are to be found as well as a taxi rank located by the docks.

Tobago's grey **buses** have greatly improved in recent years. From Scarborough, buses run along the windward coast to Charlotteville (seven buses Mon–Fri, four on Sat & Sun, running 4.30am–6.30pm at variable times). The leeward coast route extends from Scarborough to L'Anse Fourmi via Moriah, Castara, Englishman's Bay, Parlatuvier and Bloody Bay (seven Mon–Fri, four on Sat & Sun, running 4.30am–6.30pm at variable times). In the Lowlands, buses run from Scarborough to Mount Thomas via Les Coteaux and Golden Lane (five Mon–Fri, running 5.30am–6pm at variable times); they also go from Scarborough to Plymouth via Mount Irvine and Black Rock (Mon–Fri, 4–8am at variable times and then hourly until 8pm). All tickets must be **pre-purchased** (fares range TT$2–8) and are available from shops in the airport complex and throughout the island.

For information on travel **between** Tobago and Trinidad, see p.807.

Organized tours

A multitude of **tour companies** offer rather sterile itineraries of Tobago's main sights costing US$55–70 per person; Frankie's Tours (☎868/639-4527, ⓦwww.frankietourstobago.com) and Classic Tours (☎868/639-9891, ⓦwww.classictoursltd.com) are the best of the bunch. For custom-designed **hiking** and **wildlife tours**, certified tour guide Harris McDonald (☎868/639-0513, ⓦwww.harris-jungle-tours.com) runs half-day rainforest and birdwatching walks (US$45) as well as full-day excursions and night trips to the rainforest and turtle watching in season. Renowned naturalist David Rooks (☎868/639-4276, ⓦwww.rooks-tobago.com) leads informed and professional tours to **Little Tobago** (US$65); Mark Puddy (☎868/639-4931) does fabulous offbeat **hiking trips** to deserted beaches and waterfalls (US$25–40); and Margaret Hinkson's thoughtful Educatours (☎868/639-7422, ⓔmagintob@hotmail.com) organizes excursions with local guides, custom-designed to suit your interests (from US$65). Adventurous **sea safaris** aboard mini-catamarans are available from Cool Runnings (from US$50; ☎868/639-6363, ⓦwww.outdoor-tobago.com), while popular boat **cruises** are offered by several operators; prices range from US$35 for a two-hour sunset trip to US$70 per person for a six- to eight-hour cruise. Atmosphere varies from racy booze cruises to sedate sightseeing. Natural Mystic (☎868/639-7245, ⓔmystic@tstt.net.tt) is the best boat operator. **Glass-bottom boat** tours of Buccoo Reef (US$20) leave from Store Bay, Pigeon Point and Buccoo.

Scuba diving and watersports

Tobago is one of the best **diving** spots in the southeastern Caribbean, internationally recognized for its exciting, though difficult, drift dives, where you essentially let yourself be carried along by the current. The island's aquamarine seas are home to three hundred species of South Atlantic coral and a variety of spectacular multicoloured tropical fish. Tobago is best known for the enormous number of **manta rays** that are frequently encountered and the largest **brain coral** in the world. Speyside is known as "the Disneyland of diving", while Goat Island is popular for drift dives and Little Tobago is where many of the manta ray encounters occur. The island's **diving industry** was established in the 1980s but since then scuba diving operations have multiplied, with many hotels, beaches and guesthouses sporting their own centres. Prices for one to three dives are US$30–35 each; one-day resort courses US$55–65; five-day PADI open-water certification courses US$375–425; and advanced open-water from US$225. Reliable operators include SubLime (☎868/639-9642, ⓦwww.sublimescuba.com), Proscuba (☎868/639-7424, ⓦwww.diveguide.com/proscuba) and Manta Dive Centre (☎868/639-9969 or 9209, ⓦwww.mantadive.com). Much of the exotic plant and fish life in Tobago's waters can also be seen **snorkelling**. Recommended sites include Pirate's Bay in Charlotteville, Arnos Vale and Englishman's and Great Courland bays. Most dive operators rent out snorkelling equipment for US$10 a day, so note that if you plan to do plenty it's cheaper to bring your own.

Jet skis have yet to become a regular feature amid the surf (though you can rent them from R & Sea Divers Den on Pigeon Point (US$25 for 20min), while **kayaking** costs about US$10 an hour at Pigeon Point. Wild Turtle (☎868/639-7936, ⓦwww.wildturtledive.com) and World of Watersports (☎868/660-7234, ⓦwww.worldofwatersports.com) offer a variety of watersports including **water-skiing** and **inflatable bananas** (TT$80 for 15min), as well as **jet skiing** (TT$200 for 20min) and **windsurfing** (TT$200 for 60min). The most popular local **surfing** site is Mount Irvine beach – a well-kept secret, and local surfers are trying to keep it that way; keen surfers should bring their own equipment as it's difficult to rent. Note that the water here is shallow and directly over coral reef, so surf fins can be badly damaged and no protective footwear is allowed to protect the reef from overeager surfers jumping in and damaging the coral.

△ Turtle Beach, Tobago

Accommodation

Most of the island's **hotels** and **guesthouses** are concentrated in the tourist-oriented lowlands, meaning this is where you'll find the greatest choice and variety – from basic, locally run budget rooms to lavish, luxurious hotel complexes. The upmarket hotels are clustered along the beaches between Buccoo and Plymouth, as are exclusive villas (costing US$110–600 per day). There are a few excellent alternatives in the capital, especially around Lambeau and Little Rockly Bay, while those wishing to spend time further afield – Castara, Speyside and Charlotteville – will find a growing number of excellent options which should be booked in advance during high season. The tourist board recommends a number of **host homes** in their standard accommodation listings booklet (available from offices worldwide;) – most rent at around US$35–55 per person, but you can often get a room for less than this, particularly in the off-season. The best way to find a good **B&B** is also through tourist information.

Banana Boat 6 Mac's Lane, Charlotteville ☎868/660-6176, ⊛www.banana-boat-tobago. com. Quirky hotel and great budget option set on the edge of the beach. The basic en-suite rooms come with a/c or fan and banana-related decor. There's a great bar and restaurant on site, and vehicle hire, diving and trips can all be arranged by the owner. ❷

Blue Haven Bacolet Bay ☎868/660-7400, ⊛www.bluehavenhotel.com. This recently restored historic hotel – former guests include Rita Hayworth – is the best luxury accommodation on the island. The lavish rooms have four-poster or sleigh beds, a/c, TV, minibar, phone and modern artwork, along with spacious bathrooms and a balcony overlooking stunning Bacolet Bay. There's a pool, mini-gym, spa and tennis court, and an excellent – though expensive – restaurant on site. Scarborough's a ten-minute walk away. ❽–❾

Canoe Bay Beach Resort Cove Estate ☎868/631-0367, ⊛www.find-us.net/canoebay. Set in 44 acres of beautiful landscaped gardens, each self-contained apartment at this secluded resort on the edge of a quiet beach consists of a bedroom, kitchen, bathroom and private balcony, with TV and a/c. ❸

Cuffie River Nature Retreat Runnemede, near Moriah ☎868/660-0505, ⊛www.cuffie-river.com. Nestled in the forest of an old plantation, peaceful hideaways don't come better than this. All the large, airy, comfortable en-suite rooms have a/c, radio and private balconies. There's a pool, beautiful shared lounge areas and excellent restaurant on site. ❹

Harris's Guesthouse Golden Grove Rd, Canaan ☎868/639-0513, ⊛www.harris-jungle-tours.com. This fabulous guesthouse, situated on a quiet road, has two spotless double rooms with private patios and one family room, all en-suite with fans. Freshly cooked local breakfast included in the rates. ❷

Inn on the Bay Old Milford Rd, Lambeau ☎868/639-7173, ⊛www.innbay.de. Set in tropical gardens across from a small beach, all the en-suite rooms at this supremely friendly hotel are spacious and come with private balconies with sea views, a/c, phone and TV on request. There's also a pool, sundeck and excellent on-site restaurant and bar. A collection of brand-new villas are also available to rent. Rooms ❺, villas ❻

Kariwak Village Store Bay Local Rd, Crown Point ☎868/639-8442, ⊛www.kariwak.co.tt. A jewel in the middle of bustling Crown Point, accommodation is in thatched-roof cabanas furnished using local wood crafted on the premises; each has a/c and phone. Facilities include a pool, Jacuzzi and fabulous restaurant/bar. The only downside is intermittent airport noise. ❼

Man O' War Bay Cottages Man O' War Bay, Charlotteville ☎868/660-4327, ⊛www.man-o-warbaycottages.com. Situated right on the bay in pretty landscaped gardens, the cottages are different shapes and sizes, with one to four bedrooms. All have fan, bathroom, hot water and kitchen, simple but attractive decor, books on the shelves, driftwood ornaments and an overwhelming feeling of peace. There's a small commissary on site and the maid/cook service, which costs extra, is optional. ❹

Manta Lodge Main Rd, Speyside ☎868/660-5268, in US ☎1-800/544-7631, ⊛www.mantalodge.com. Located opposite the bay, this hotel is colonial-style luxury catering for scuba enthusiasts. Standard rooms are small but stylish with ceiling fan and balcony; "superior" rooms provide more space and a/c, while the quirky attics have the lot plus a private sundeck on the roof. There's a good restaurant (breakfast included in the rates), pool and dive shop on site. ❺–❻

Mount Pelier Cottage Mount Pelier Crown Trace, Scarborough ☎868/639-4931, ℮puddy@tstt.net.tt. Unique and utterly fabulous home away from home

21

in the host's self-built wooden house perched on Scarborough's hillside. These airy rooms (double, twin or single) have lattice windows, creative hand-carved decor and shared bathroom. Meals are served on a balcony overlooking the forest in the company of mot-mots, blue jays and bananaquits. Rates include excellent home-cooked breakfast, huge evening meals and the owner as personal guide and driver. ❸

Sandy's Robinson St, Scarborough, ☏868/639-2737, ⊛www.tobagobluecrab.com. Run by the hospitable owner of the Blue Crab restaurant, this

wonderful guesthouse has four pretty and spotless rooms with a/c and private bathrooms. Breakfast included. ❸

Toucan Inn Store Bay Local Rd, Crown Point ☏868/639-7173, ⊛www.toucan-inn.com. This welcoming hotel is a haven of tranquillity in the middle of Crown Point's bustle. The unusual, octagonal cabana rooms are set in attractive gardens around a pool; all have a/c and fittings made from local teak and pine. *Bonkers* – the on-site restaurant – is a local institution. ❹

The Lowlands: Crown Point to Arnos Vale

Tobago's flattest, most accessible portion is focused around a crowded five-kilometre stretch of **Milford Road** from the airport and Store Bay Beach – a tiny area known as **Crown Point** – through Bon Accord, Canaan and Mount Pleasant, and 10km north along **Shirvan Road** to **Buccoo**, **Mount Irvine** and **Plymouth**. Usually lumped together as "**the Lowlands**", this is home to most of Tobago's residents as well as the vast majority of hotels, restaurants, nightclubs and the most popular beaches; you'll inevitably spend a lot of time here.

Tobago's most popular **beaches** are within shouting distance of the airport – **Store Bay** is a couple of minutes on foot, and **Pigeon Point** is about ten minutes further. **Buccoo** harbours two main attractions: an abundant **reef**, trawled by fleets of glass-bottom boats carrying snorkellers out to the coral, and the **Nylon Pool**, a metre-deep bathing spot on a sand bar in the middle of the bay. **Sunday School**, Tobago's biggest, brashest open-air party, is held in Buccoo as well. Attractions like the **Arnos Vale water wheel** and the **Kimme art exhibition**, as well as plenty of restaurants and the fabulous prospect of watching a **turtle** lay eggs metres from your hotel room, draw enthusiastic crowds of locals and tourists alike.

Store Bay to Pigeon Point

A two-minute walk from the airport brings you to one of the most popular places to swim in Crown Point, **Store Bay Beach** (lifeguards 10am–6pm). Close to the main hotels and with excellent, inexpensive food and crafts available, the fine, off-white sand is a favourite with many people (including the notoriously unadventurous Trinidadian holiday-makers). Though the cove is fairly small, the crystal calm waters and family atmosphere make it excellent for children and for those with a keen interest in people-watching. Facilities include a car park, showers and changing facilities (daily 10am–6pm; TT$1) with lockers (TT$10 per day), as well as a couple of bars blasting reggae and soca. Not to be missed are the row of cream-brick take-aways housing a number of famed cookshops (8.30am–8.30pm) including local institutions *Miss Jean's* and *Miss Esmie's*; any trip to Tobago would be incomplete without a plate of their **crab and dumplin'**. The purpose-built **craft shops** (8am–8pm) at Store Bay are some of the more popular but also more expensive places to buy souvenirs, including carved calabashes, leather sandals and batiks.

Running north from the airport past the entrance to Store Bay, Airport Road becomes Milford Road. Here, a left-hand turn (marked by the neon constellation of the *Golden Star* bar and restaurant) leads to **Pigeon Point Beach** (daily 8am–7pm; TT$18). This picture-postcard Caribbean beach increasingly dominated by foreign sun-worshippers. The shoreline here – unlike the majority of Tobago's rugged beaches – is definitively Caribbean, with powdery white sand and a turquoise sea lined with coconut palms. As an immensely popular strip that includes Tobago's most photo-graphed pier – a weathered wooden boardwalk with a thatched roof hut at the end – it is one of the few places in the island to suffer from overdevelopment. A series of shops selling beachwear, clothes and upmarket souvenirs nestle into the landscaped area around the busy bar, and the road leading to the beach is also lined with craft stalls and watersports outlets.

The groynes constructed to curtail beach erosion have reduced the water circulation, and this – along with general pollution – has allowed **algae** to flourish on the sea floor, making local people question the sagacity of swimming in what on a bad day resembles a rather milky soup. Though water quality is monitored by local environmental groups, and the chance of getting sick is pretty scant, try to shower off as soon as you leave the water and avoid immersing your head. During the rainy season, mosquitoes from the nearby marsh have a field day – insect repellent is essential. If you're driving into Pigeon Point, avoid parking under a coconut-laden palm – a single fallen nut can cause a lot of damage.

Bon Accord to Buccoo

Bisecting Tobago's low-lying southwest tip, ruler-straight **Milford Road** is the artery of the area, a busy main road traversing the Bon Accord, Tyson Hall, Canaan and Friendship communities. One community melts seamlessly into another, but as this is probably the most well-travelled thoroughfare on the island, the strip rapidly becomes familiar.

North of the road is **Bon Accord Lagoon**, a sweeping oval of mangrove swamp and reef-sheltered shallow water which forms one of the most important fish nurseries on the island. The lagoon, despite suffering pollution in the past, is a sanctuary for conch, snails, shrimp, oysters, crab, urchins and sponges – though the thick sea grass makes them difficult to spot. The land is difficult to access, so it's best to go with a guide; Adolphus James (☎868/639-2231) is recommended. Adjoining the lagoon, **No Man's Land** is a beautiful deserted beach, often featured on boat cruises and an idyllic place to swim; it's a good spot to escape the hotel-dominated area – for a budget place to stay check *Harris's Guesthouse* (see "Accommodation," p.844).

A kilometre or so before Milford Road widens into Claude Noel Highway, **Shirvan Road** strikes off to the left. This is the route to Buccoo Bay and its famous **reef** as well as several wide yellow-sand **beaches** and the neat coastal town of Plymouth. The first stretch is bordered to the left by a plantation of towering coconut palms and to the right by thick hedges masking what was once the Shirvan Park **horse-racing track**; it's now *The Lush* nightclub.

Studded with swanky restaurants, upmarket hotels, fruit stalls and simple board shacks, Shirvan Road continues north, passing turn-offs to quietly residential Mount Pleasant and Carnbee Village – the latter has a supermarket and petrol station.

Buccoo

There's a cluster of tourist-oriented signposts at the next crossroads, the intersection of Auchenskeoch (pronounced "or-kins-styor")/Buccoo Bay Road and Shirvan Road, known as **Buccoo Junction**. A right turn climbs into one of Tobago's smartest residential districts, where opulent villas nestle next to tiny villages, while the left takes you to **BUCCOO**, a small village haphazardly built around a calm and beautiful bay. Fishing remains a major industry here, but since the nearby reef has become a premier attraction, the community has embraced tourism. The annual **goat races**, established back in 1925, are held here each Easter and the event is taken very seriously by competitors – jockeys train the belligerent animals, who continue to refuse to obey any orders, and the result is a joy to watch. **Crab races** also take place but are taken less seriously. The quiet village atmosphere disappears every Sunday when the masses descend for **Sunday School** (see box opposite). The combined effect of a muddy sea bed and its Sunday job as a urinal make Buccoo a terrible place to swim, though the palm-lined western fringe of the bay is more appealing with cleaner water and plenty of shells and coral fragments to collect.

Covering around twelve square kilometres of Caribbean seabed, **Buccoo Reef** is the largest and most heavily visited reef in Tobago. Home to forty-odd species of

Sunday School

A Tobago institution, **Sunday School** is most definitely not for the pious. A massive beach party that the whole island seems to attend, Sunday School is the highlight of the week's nightlife. The action begins at 8pm, when the Buccooneers Steel Orchestra play pan for a couple of hours. The crowd begins to thicken at around 10–11pm, when the sound system at the covered beach facilities begins to play. Music policy is inevitably Jamaican dancehall with the most popular soca tunes thrown in alongside hip-hop and R&B. Experienced winers – "wining" being the locally practised art of gyrating hips in a provocative manner – display their skills, foreigners relax and the gigolos (and tourists) scout for a partner – it's a well-known pick-up joint. The largest Sunday School of the year takes place each Easter Monday, when several more sound systems add to the cacophony and parked cars back up all the way to the Mount Irvine golf course. To avoid car parking hassles it's a good idea to book a taxi to collect you at a prearranged time, or a place on an organized trip which costs about US$17.

hard and soft coral, the reef has taken around ten thousand years to grow. The corals make good feeding for the brilliantly coloured trigger, butterfly, surgeon and parrot fish. To the south of the reef is **Nylon Pool**, a gleaming coralline sand bar forming an appealing metre-deep swimming pool smack in the middle of the sea. It's said to have been named by Princess Margaret in the 1950s; she remarked that the water was as clear as her nylon stockings.

Sadly, carelessly placed anchors and removal of coral souvenirs mean many parts bear more resemblance to a coral graveyard than a living reef. Overfishing has reduced fish and crustacean populations, and misplaced spear guns have ripped chunks from the coral. Declared a protected **national park** in 1973, scant resources have failed to enforce the law and the damage continues unabated. Today, glass-bottom boat operators are more conscientious, anchoring only on dead reef and warning visitors that touching or removing reef matter and shells is illegal, but they still hand out the plastic shoes, making it possible for a single footstep to damage or kill hundreds of years' growth. Do your bit by standing on seabed only and refusing to buy any coral trinkets. **Glass-bottom boat** tours cost around US$20. The best leave from Buccoo and include snorkelling and a dip in Nylon Pool; the most reliable operator is Buccoo-based Johnson and Sons (☎868/639-8519). Trips taken at low tide are best for snorkelling.

Mount Irvine to Turtle Beach

The shaven greens of Tobago's first **golf course** herald the outskirts of **MOUNT IRVINE**, the next coastal village past Buccoo. The challenging course plays host to the Tobago Pro-Am tournament every January, and greens fees are US$30 for nine holes, US$48 for eighteen – there's also a weekly rate of US$264 (☎868/639-8871). Around the next bend is **Mount Irvine Bay Beach**, a busy slip of fine yellow sand with just enough room for beach tennis and volleyball, surrounded by gazebos and the ubiquitous palm and sea grape trees. The facilities (daylight hours; TT$1) are adequate and there's a bar/restaurant on site doling out mountains of fried shark and bake. During summer months, the water is calm enough to make exploration of the ornate offshore **reef** a joy, but Mount Irvine becomes one of the island's best **surfing** beaches between December and March, when huge breakers crash against the sand all morning. Boards can be rented from Mt Irvine Watersports, right next to the beach complex (☎868/639-9379).

Past Mount Irvine is the sublime **Stone Haven Bay**, a good beach, though dominated by an all-inclusive hotel, expanding villa complexes and the inevitable beach vendors. A friendly and less commercial option for accommodation is a few minutes' walk away, *Indigo*.

Nestled in the hills behind the beach along Orange Hill Road (take the right turn just past the Mount Irvine golf course then follow the signposts) is the **Kimme Museum** (open Sun only, 10am–2pm, appointments taken for other days; TT$20; ☎868/639-0257, ⌨www.kimme.de). Here you'll find the private gallery of eccentric German sculptor Luise Kimme, who settled in Tobago in 1979. Her eerily beguiling wood and bronze sculptures are dotted around the artist's quirky, mural-decorated fretworked home, and a tour makes for a pleasant break from beach-related activities.

Back on the Shirvan Road, a few minutes' drive beyond a grating section of potholes marking the end of the small village of Black Rock, is another fine beach, **Turtle Beach**, a good kilometre of picturesque, coarse yellow sand. A uninspiring two-storey hotel dominates the sand – only its package tourist guests are allowed to use the purpose-built sun shelters – and the constant presence of unadventurous guests has generated an ideal market for itinerant beach vendors. Though the beach is officially called **Great Courland Bay**, it acquired its colloquial title on account of the **turtles** that still lay eggs here in the dark of night. All of the hotels along this stretch organize a turtle watch during the laying and hatching seasons, but if you're not staying in the area, contact Nick Hardwicke at the small *Seahorse Inn* (☎868/639-0686) or Save Our Sea Turtles Tobago (☎868/639-9669) for turtle-watching expeditions.

Plymouth and Arnos Vale

A mile or so beyond Turtle Beach, Grafton Road meets a junction; here a left turn leads to **PLYMOUTH**, Tobago's first European community, settled first by Latvians, then the Dutch and finally by the British. An attractive little town, its main attraction is **Fort James**, the oldest stockade in Tobago, built in 1811 by the British. The coral-stone structure and four cannons preside over an excellent view of Turtle Beach. If you're driving up the coast, it's wise to fill your tank at Plymouth's petrol station (Mon–Sat 6.30am–9pm, Sun 5.30am–9pm), as it's the only one for miles.

From the centre of Plymouth, a well-signposted but narrow road meanders through the greenery towards **Arnos Vale**, one of the few sugar estates to keep its land. The main point of access is at the old estate **water wheel** (daily 9am–10.30pm; TT$12), where new buildings constructed from natural materials house a modest **museum**, gift shop, bar and restaurant. The wheel, pump and fermenting house that once worked the sugar cane have been restored and can be viewed via a system of wooden walkways. The estate is a pretty and atmospheric spot, lavish with flowering plants and lush foliage and nice for a relaxing drink. The local bay – overlooked by one of Tobago's oldest hotels – is great for **snorkelling**. Road improvements have finally linked Arnos Vale with the rest of the leeward coast, though you can also get there via the Northside Road from Scarborough, which in turn is accessible from Plymouth by travelling south along the Plymouth Road.

Scarborough

SCARBOROUGH, Tobago's raucous, hot and dusty capital (population 18,000), spills higgledy-piggledy down the hillside. The island's administrative centre and its main **port**, the flourishing town is devoid of touristic pretensions. Don't expect a very cosmopolitan atmosphere, though; the docking of the **ferry** from Trinidad is spectacle enough to draw crowds of onlookers.

As the commercial centre of the island, one of the town's main attractions is the shopping. The town's **market**, located opposite the docks, with its fruit and vegetables display, bargain crafts and excellent fast food, is a must; main trading days are Friday and Saturday. The **Fort King George** complex, perched on the lighthouse-topped hill, also contains a local craft centre (Mon–Fri 9am–1pm) with more unusual items. This complex, at the top of the well-signposted Fort Street, is free to enter and contains a landscaped **park,** the largest fortification in Tobago,

21

Fort King George, and at 140m above sea level, excellent views. It is also the site of the unmissable **Tobago Museum** (Mon–Fri 9am–4.30pm; TT$5, children TT$1). Curated by the Tobago Trust, the small but fascinating collection includes Amerindian artefacts, satirical colonial prints from slavery days, African drums and notes on local culture.

Away from the commercial clamour, the peaceful **botanical gardens** (daily during daylight hours; free), opposite the bus station on Gardenside St, offer respite from the traffic and steep climbs that can make Scarborough a bit of an ordeal; visiting on an overcast day makes sightseeing more comfortable. The nearby **orchid house** displays most of T&T's indigenous orchids as well as a few imported species.

As Scarborough is so small, there are no bus services within the town, but you can easily see all the sights by foot. For **information**, head to the tourism offices of the Tobago House of Assembly, Division of Tourism, 197 Doretta's Court, Mt Marie (Mon–Fri 8am–4pm; ☎868/639-2125, ⌨www.visittobago.gov.tt). Free **parking** is available at the wharf car park on the corner of Carrington and Castries streets. Scarborough is the departure point for **route taxis** serving the whole of the island; ask a local to find the appropriate stand. **Maxis** to Charlotteville leave two or three times a day from outside James Park on Burnett Street (TT$12). Three good **accommodation** options, for Scarborough as well as a base for the rest of the island, are the *Blue Haven* hotel (for the well-heeled), *Sandy's* and *Mount Pelier Cottage* (for those who like the personal eccentric touch; see "Accommodation" p.844, for all three).

The leeward coast

Beyond Arnos Vale, the leeward coast feels more remote than any other part of the island; tourist development is minimal, leaving the ravishing beaches at **Castara**, **Englishman's Bay**, **Parlatuvier** and **Bloody Bay** much the same as they were twenty years ago. **Fishing** is the main industry of the area, and you'll often see machete-wielding men walking the route to small-scale plantations or meandering along with a pack of hunting dogs.

Though the area is accessible from Crown Point along the coast road via Plymouth, the twists and turns in the route make for a long drive. In fact, the quickest way to the leeward coast is along the **Northside Road**, which begins on the outskirts of Scarborough at Calder Hall, off the Claude Noel Highway. The road then works its way across the island to the leeward coast where it follows the coastline, passing through all of the settlements on this side.

Castara is an attractive fishing village that's slowly developing a nonchalant tourist-friendliness; low-key guesthouses are scattered on a hillside, while visitors dribble in to swim at the marvellous **beach** or splash in the nearby waterfall. Fishing remains the main earner, though, and the beach is one of the best places to participate in the pulling of a **seine net**, still in constant use by the supremely friendly posse of Rasta fishermen. The village abandons its languid air each August, when the beach is packed with revellers attending the **Castara Fishermen's Fete**, one of Tobago's biggest. It's also the only place along this stretch of coast that has **accommodation** for the foreign visitor; the *Blue Mango* cottages are a good option.

Past Castara, houses and shops melt away and the road is flanked by enormous bamboo. The next worthy beach, **Englishman's Bay** (look out for the blue and white sign), is utterly beautiful and completely undeveloped save for a stall near the entrance serving hot meals (including roti on Sundays), soft drinks and bamboo craft.

East of Englishman's Bay, the coast road climbs upwards and inland, passing through the diminutive community of **Parrot Hall** before descending to reveal one of the most arresting views on the island: **Parlatuvier Bay**, flanked by an absurdly pretty hillside scattered with palms, terraced provision grounds and the odd house. Another crescent of pearly sand, the bay makes **swimming** a vigorous experience: waves are usually quite strong and the water deepens sharply from the sand. The last accessible beach on the coast is **Bloody Bay**, another deserted shoreline; the right turn at the Bloody Bay junction takes you to the **Tobago Forest Reserve**.

Tobago Forest Reserve

The road swinging inland through the protected **forest reserve** is known as the Roxborough–Parlatuvier Road. The route makes for a steep but beautifully quiet drive through the seemingly impenetrable rainforest canopy which in fact contains a number of managed **trails** that even the most confirmed city-dweller should find easy to explore.

The oldest protected rainforest in the western hemisphere, the Tobago Reserve is easily accessed at **Gilpin Trace**, marked by a huge slab of rock by the road in front of a forestry division hut. A trail strikes straight into the forest from here, but unless you only plan to go a few hundred yards, it's advisable to hire a **guide**; he or she will understand a lot more about forest dynamics, and you won't need to worry about getting lost. Guides are often found hanging around at Gilpin Trace, but the best bet is to book on an organized trip before you get here. Both Harris McDonald and David Rooks are recommended (see p.842 for contact info).

The windward coast

Rugged and continually breathtaking, Tobago's southern shoreline is usually referred to as the **windward coast**. Narrow and peppered with blind corners and potholes, the Windward Road spans its length and sticks close to the sea, providing fantastic views of choppy Atlantic waters and tiny spray-shrouded islands. The parade of languid coastal villages is a complete contrast to the developed west. Though rip tides and strong undercurrents make some of the most attractive-looking beaches unsafe for swimming, there are plenty of sheltered bays to take a dip in the cool Atlantic. Some – such as **King's Bay** – have changing facilities, but at most you'll share the sand only with fishermen. Tour buses make regular rounds, but most of the windward traffic heads for the tiny village of **Speyside** and its smattering of guesthouses and small hotels. Fifteen minutes' drive from Speyside and directly opposite on the Caribbean coast, picturesque **Charlotteville**, with its attractive hillside houses and perfect twin beaches, is the last point of call on the windward route. The tarmac ends here, replaced by a treacherous and often impassable stretch of coastal track that divides the town from the rest of the leeward coast.

The Windward Road

From Scarborough the Windward Road leads northeast through numerous tiny villages, including **Mount St George** (the island's first British capital), Goodwood, Goldsborough, Pembroke and Glamorgan. Worth a stop en route is the *First Historical Café* at Studley Park, 3km past Mount St George, where local history and anecdotes make for a fascinating visit, even if you're not hungry.

Shortly after Glamorgan is a signposted left turn for the **Richmond Great House**, a hotel, restaurant and essential point of call for almost all tour buses. Built of solid brick and whitewashed board in the eighteenth century, this was the estate house of the old Richmond sugar estate, and it offers fantastic views over the jungle-smothered interior hills. It also contains an extensive collection of African art and textiles; tours are available (daily 10am–4pm; TT$15).

Past Richmond and the tiny village of Belle Garden is Argyll, the location of the **Argyll Waterfall** (daily 7.30am–5pm; TT$30), signalled by the cache of guides waiting by the roadside. Official guides (carrying ID and wearing khaki; additional TT$30, plus tip) are located in the car park, where you pay the entrance fee. The falls, a pleasant fifteen-minute walk away, are the island's highest (54m) and comprise three main cascades – the different tiers are great for a dip.

Turning inland past the small village of Roxborough, the Windward Road swings through the hilltop village of **Delaford**, making one almighty bend at the outskirts to reveal a breathtaking view of the spiky coconut plantation surrounding beautiful, deep-blue **King's Bay** below. The **beach** (open daylight hours; free) here is one of the few along the windward coast to provide changing facilities (TT$1).

Speyside

Past King's Bay, the coast swings out of view as the road turns inland. Constant hair-pin bends and a steep incline make the going pretty treacherous, so if you're driving, don't let your surroundings become too much of a distraction. Luckily, a designated **lookout** point has been built before the descent into **SPEYSIDE** – be sure to stop, as there's an amazing view of the horseshoe **Tyrrel's Bay**, along with **Little Tobago** and **Goat Island** and an expanse of aquamarine coral reef-strewn water.

Speyside feels as remote as it is; just over ten years ago the road was little more than a dirt track. Though the town is slowly adjusting to its latest role as a **scuba-diving** destination, it still retains its fishing village atmosphere and small-town attitude. The main strip consists of several dive shops, a couple of restaurants, including the well-known *Jemma's*, and a few hotels and guesthouses; *Speyside Inn* and the *Manta Lodge* are two of the better ones.

As you descend into the village, a cluster of candy floss-coloured grocery shops and snack bars surround a large playing field – the venue for local football matches – to the right. A dirt track running between the playing field and the sea takes you to the **beach** facilities, basic changing rooms and toilets (daylight hours; TT$1). The sand here is slightly wider than in the central part of the bay, and the famous **reefs**, Speyside's main attraction, are within swimming distance. Generally pristine with little sign of bleaching or human damage, the reefs boast one of the world's largest **brain corals**, an awesome four metres high and six metres across. Apart from the regular shoals of small fish – butterfly, grunt, angel, parrot and damsel – the currents also attract a number of deep-water dwellers, including **nurse sharks**, **dolphins** and, most notably, **manta rays**. For those who wish to see more than small fish and lim-ited portions of reef, scuba diving is excellent in this area. The most popular Speyside dive sites include Japanese Gardens, Angel Reef, Bookends and Blackjack Hole, and most dives are of the drift variety (for reliable operators see p.842). **Glass-bottom boats** are a good way to see the reefs if you don't want to get wet, though you can always jump overboard for a spot of snorkelling as well. Frank's (☎868/660-5438), based at *Blue Waters Inn*, offers a basic tour with snorkelling at Angel Reef, as does local operator Fear Not (☎868/660-4654) for around US$15.

On leaving Speyside, just past the *Manta Lodge* hotel, the road forks; left takes you across the interior and into Charlotteville, while the right turn is the route to the astonishingly blue waters and rich reefs of **Bateaux Bay**, site of another luxurious hotel. Beyond Bateaux Bay are the picturesque Belmont and Starwood bays, but the road is often impassable; if so, ask a local fisherman to take you aboard a pirogue. Both bays offer great snorkelling and diving.

Little Tobago and Goat Island

Of the two misshapen islets sitting five kilometres or so out of Tyrrel's Bay, **Goat Island** is the closer, though it's privately owned and closed to the public. However, birdwatchers and hikers flock to the larger island, **Little Tobago**, a kilometre fur-ther out to sea. Known as "Bird of Paradise Island", it has been a bird sanctuary since 1924. Uninhabited, it's home to one of the largest sea bird colonies in the Caribbean, including flocks of frigates, boobies, terns and the spectacular red-billed tropic bird, the latter especially prevalent between October and June. Make sure you take drinking water with you, as there are no refreshments available on the island. To get the most from your visit, hire an experienced guide such as David Rooks (☎868/639-4276, ◉www.rooks-tobago.com; US$60), the man who persuaded David Attenborough to include Little Tobago in his famous BBC documentary

21

Trials of Life. Local fishermen will be happy to take you to Little Tobago as well for around TT$75, though if you're interested in birdwatching, it's better to go in more expert company.

Charlotteville

From Speyside, the Windward Road strikes inland, climbing steeply upwards through jungle-like mountain foliage before plummeting down to the opposite shoreline. Just before the descent, there's a stunning perspective of **CHARLOTTE-VILLE**; houses tumble down a hillside to be met by calm Caribbean waters. Snugly situated under the protective cover of the two-kilometre-wide **Man O' War Bay**, Charlotteville is Tobago's foremost **fishing** community – more than 60 percent of the island's total catch is brought in by local fishermen. The town has an isolated feel, and though the tourist dollar is steadily encroaching upon this self-contained community, the atmosphere is so friendly that it's hard not to relax.

Charlotteville is actually one of Tobago's oldest communities, first settled by Caribs and then by the Dutch in 1633. Increasingly popular as a retreat, accommodation gets booked up quickly; the *Banana Boat* and *Man O' War Bay Cottages* are two good options (see "Accommodation", p.844), though a number of locals will rent you a room in their house if the situation's desperate. There's little to do but arrange a **fishing** trip, while away the hours on the fine brown sand of **Man O' War Bay Beach** (open during daylight hours; changing facilities TT$1) or enjoy the excellent snorkelling in the sublime **Pirate's Bay**. Benches along the sea wall, the fishing pier and a covered pavilion are popular liming spots, great for soaking up the village scene. In July, Man O' War Bay is the site of Tobago's most popular fisherman's fete, held to celebrate **St Peter's Day**. Charlotteville's petrol station is open Monday to Saturday 6am–8pm and Sunday 6–11am & 8.15–8.30pm.

Eating, drinking and entertainment

Unlike Trinidad – where fetes and street food are a daily staple – Tobago is far more low-key. The best budget **food** options – including the sublime curry crab and dumpling and fantastic rotis – are available from the stalls on Store Bay. Most **restaurants** cater for the tourist trade, as most locals eat at home, and are therefore located in the Lowlands area, but options are expanding further afield. If you're here in the slow season (mid-April to mid-Dec), bear in mind that many kitchens close at around 9pm. Apart from occasional concerts – look out for posters – most **entertainment** on the island revolves around bars, rum shops, a limited number of clubs and the infamous Sunday School in Buccoo (see box, p.847).

Bonkers *Toucan Inn*, Store Bay Local Rd, Crown Point ☎868/639-7173. This excellent and popular restaurant serves tasty Tobagonian food at moderate prices under a shady pavilion or at poolside tables. There's a good and varied wine list and a regular "limetable" of live music.

Blue Crab Robinson St, at Main, Scarborough ☎868/639-2737. This friendly restaurant with a lovely shady terrace serves decently priced, excellent Creole food. Lunch weekdays, dinner by reservation only.

Café Iguana Store Bay Local Rd, at Airport Rd, Crown Point ☎868/631 8205. This lively bar and restaurant serves great, decently priced Caribbean cuisine, with a range of cocktails, with live jazz and *salsa* on Fri & Sat. Daily from 6pm.

Cat & Fiddle Old Milford Rd, Lambeau ☎868/639-4347. An excellent and popular bar, especially on

Fridays when live music, a barbecue and late-night DJ are the perfect way to kick-start the weekend for locals and tourists alike.

Ciao Café King's Well, Scarborough ☎868/639-3001. This fantastic, popular Italian café and bar with outside terrace serves authentic cappuccino, over twenty different flavours of delicious homemade ice cream, fine Italian wine, good beer and colourful cocktails.

First Historical Café Windward Rd, Studley Park. This eccentric, brightly painted café is a shrine to the island's history, every inch of wall being covered with handwritten accounts of Tobago's turbulent past alongside local anecdotes (which the owner charges visitors TT$5 to read). The budget-priced food is good; breakfast is served from 9am, and you can have inexpensive salads, burgers and sandwiches for lunch.

Jemma's Treehouse Main Rd, Speyside
☎868/660-4066. Popular with every island tour
bus, this place lurches crazily in the boughs of a
tree, and the sea view is fantastic. Serves tasty
Creole-style food for reasonable prices; expect to
pay $TT70–150. No alcohol. Closes Fri at 4pm,
closed Sat.

Kariwak Village Store Bay Local Rd, Crown
Point ☎868/639-8442. Fresh herbs and spices,
inventive slants on local staples and genuine love
in the kitchen makes this an excellent place to eat
on the island. It's also one of the most expensive,
with meals costing TT$150 and up. Breakfast and
dinner menus are set – usually with a meat, fish
or vegetarian option – and vegan food is available.
Accompanied by live music, the Saturday night
buffet is particularly good.

La Tartaruga Bucco Bay ☎868/639-0940. Tobago's
best Italian restaurant, with open-air patio near the
sea. The select menu features top-class cuisine,
including a selection of authentic regional Italian
specialities, plus an extensive wine list. Closed Sun.

Salsa Kitchen 8 Pumpmill Rd, Scarborough
☎868/639-1522. This fabulous but pricey
restaurant has a great atmosphere and an enticing
menu of pizza, pasta, tapas and grilled food, along
with fresh fruit juices and locally grown coffee. At
weekends the café livens up with Latin music and
dancing. Closed Mon. Dinner only.

Shore Things Old Milford Rd, Lambeau
☎868/635-1072. A delightful café in a brightly
painted old house with verandah overlooking
the sea. Serves delicious light lunches, pizzas,
pastelles, quiches and salads plus fresh pastries
and fruit juices (TT$10–50). High-quality regional
crafts and furniture are also on sale. Closed Sun.

Under the Mango Tree Black Rock ☎868/639-
8964. Lovely yellow-and-green café on the
roadside serving sandwiches, pizza, salads and
hot meals inside or under the shady mango tree.
Delicious fruit juices and amusing signs complete
the atmosphere. Lunch and dinner only.

22

The ABC Islands

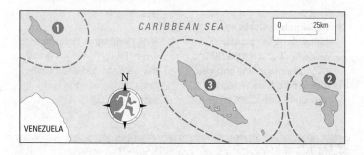

The ABC Islands highlights

✳ **Aruba's beach strip** Seven kilometres of unspoilt white-sand beaches line the turquoise waters of the island's west coast. See p.868

✳ **Bonaire Marine Park, Bonaire** Magnificent coral gardens harbour vast schools of tropical fish just off the leeward coast. See p.881

✳ **Willemstad, Curaçao** Stroll along the picturesque waterfront of this UNESCO World Heritage Site and visit the superb Kura Hulanda museum. See p.886

✳ **Arikok National Park, Aruba** Explore the Martian-like interior, home to towering stands of cacti, divi divi trees, iguanas and herds of wandering goats. See p.871

✳ **Hato Caves, Curaçao** A guided tour through these mystical caves and their incredible flowstone formations will leave you breathless. See p.889

✳ **Pink flamingos, Bonaire** Over 10,000 flamingos grace the saltpans and lakes scattered throughout this tiny island. See p.878

△ Tree on Bonaire Dutch Antilles

Introduction and basics

Tucked away from the main Caribbean chain of islands, just north of Venezuela, lie **Aruba**, **Bonaire** and **Curaçao**, collectively known as the "ABC islands". Part of the Netherlands Antilles, these tiny islands share a similar heritage, all having been originally inhabited by the Caiquitios Indians before the arrival of the Spanish, and later the Dutch, to whom they have been tied ever since.

Over the centuries, however, each island has developed its own distinct identity. Aruba is the **priciest and most touristed** of the three islands, attracting mostly American holiday-makers on package vacations as well as cruise-ship passengers to its glamorous (some would say tacky) beachfront resort complexes, flashy casinos, upscale boutiques and duty-free shops. Laid-back Bonaire, renowned for its phenomenal **diving and snorkelling**, draws a select group of visitors from around the world in search of an outdoors-oriented vacation. Much less known than its smaller neighbours, Curaçao lags behind Aruba and Bonaire in terms of tourism. But still it attracts its share of travellers who come for its beaches and to experience the charms of the capital city of Willemstad, home to some of the most attractive **colonial architecture** and one of the best museums in all of the Caribbean.

Where to go

Most travellers to Aruba spend their time in the resort areas between **Eagle and Palm beaches** or in the capital of **Oranjestad**, where the casinos and shop-filled streets are the main diversions. Those interested in natural attractions head to **Arikok National Park** to explore its arid landscape and rugged coastline. West of the park finds interesting rock formations at **Casibari** and **Ayó** along with the nearby **Bushiribana Gold Ruins** and much-photographed **Natural Bridge**.

Divers and snorkellers come to Bonaire to surround themselves with colourful marine life at the **Bonaire Marine Park** and **Klein Bonaire** on the western side of the island. Unique in the ABCs, the island is also home to a large number of pink flamingos that are mostly concentrated around the colourful saltpans in the south. In the far north, hiking enthusiasts should make for **Washington-Slagbaai National Park**.

Not to be missed on Curaçao is lively **Willemstad**, whose pristine Dutch colonial architecture has earned it the designation of a UNESCO World Heritage Site, and whose cultural and historical attractions hold much of interest. Put simply, it is has some of the prettiest buildings in the whole Caribbean. Away from Willemstad, most of the best **beaches** are in the northwest, not far from **Christoffel National Park**, which boasts a variety of flora and fauna and good hiking trails. For something different, take a guided tour of the limestone **Hato Caves** or visit the **plantation houses** scattered about the island.

When to go

The ABC islands are a year-round destination, though **peak tourist season** is mid-December to mid-April when the weather is at its best. Sitting outside of the **hurricane belt**, the islands generally enjoy warm weather year-round. The average daytime temperature is 28°C (82°F) and steady trade winds keep the humidity down.

All three islands receive very little **rainfall**, which usually comes in the form of gentle showers between October and March.

Arrival

The majority of visitors to Aruba **fly** to the state-of-the-art **Queen Beatrix International Airport** (☎297/582-4800), a few kilometres south of Oranjestad. Numerous **taxis** wait for passengers outside the arrival terminal. If you are staying at one of the smaller hotels or guesthouses in town, the ride will set you

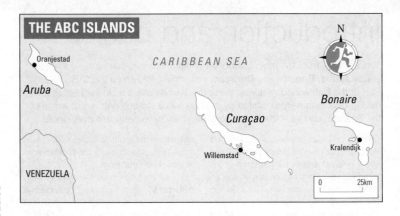

THE ABC ISLANDS

Oranjestad

Aruba

CARIBBEAN SEA

N

Bonaire

Curaçao

Kralendijk

Willemstad

VENEZUELA

0   25km

back US$10–12; fares to the hotels along the beach are US$16–20. Alternatively, De Palm Tours (☎297/582-4400) operates an efficient network of air-conditioned **motor coaches** that take visitors to the major beachfront hotels. Round-trip tickets ($20; about 30 min) can be purchased from the booth at the terminal's baggage claim. **Cruise ships** dock at the pier in downtown Oranjestad. Taxis are on hand to take you around the island.

Bonaire's principal gateway, **Flamingo International Airport**, lies 5km south of Kralendijk. The easiest way to reach the capital or your hotel is to take a taxi from outside the terminal; expect to pay around US$10–15. Several **cruise ships** also visit the island twice a week and usually spend most of the day in port, just long enough for passengers to take in some sightseeing and shopping.

On Curaçao, **Hato International Airport** (☎5999/868-1719), 12km northwest of Willemstad, is where most visitors to the island arrive. Numerous car rental agencies, taxis and buses wait for passengers outside the arrivals terminal. A taxi to downtown Willemstad usually costs US$20, while a ride to most hotels outside the city will set you back US$15–25; ask for the price in advance. Alternatively, many hotels provide a shuttle **bus** to and from the airport. There are two **cruise terminals** in the capital, both of them in Willemstad's Otrobanda district. The mega-pier is located near the Riffort by the harbour entrance, a ten-minute walk from

downtown. The smaller terminal is closer to downtown in Santa Anna Bay.

Information and maps

All three islands have **tourism information** offices, where friendly staff can provide maps, brochures and free magazines, as well as arrange tours or lodging.

The **Aruba Tourism Authority** (ATA) operates a tourist information office near Eagle Beach on L.G. Smith Blvd 172 (Mon–Fri 7.30am–noon & 1–4.30pm; ☎297/582-3777, ☞www.aruba.com). Grab a copy of *Aruba Nights* and *Aruba Experience*, both of which have maps and useful tips on accommodation, restaurants, activities, nightlife and beaches. A decent road map to the island (B&B Map to Aruba, 1:50,000) is available for US$4 at bookstores in Oranjestad.

Tourism Corporation Bonaire has a tourist information office in the centre of Kralendijk on Kaya Grandi 2 (Mon–Fri 7.30am–noon & 1.30–5pm; ☎599/717-8322, ☞www. InfoBonaire.com), where you can pick up *Bonaire Nights* and *Bonaire Affair*, two useful free magazines. A tiny visitors' information stand with a handful of brochures and maps is also at the airport.

The **Curaçao Tourism Development** Bureau (CTDB) operates a tourist information office just outside central Punda in Willemstad on Pietermaaiweg 19 (Mon–Fri 8am–5pm & Sat 9am–noon; ☎5999/616-0000, ☞www. Curaçao-tourism.com) and manages booths at the airport and at the cruise terminal in Otrobanda. They distribute *Curaçao Nights, Curaçao Explorer* and *Curaçao Holiday* as well as a free guide to the beaches and diving sites of Curaçao. The informative weekly dining and entertainment guide, *K-Pasa* (⊛www.k-pasa.com), can also be picked up at tourist offices and most hotels and cafes.

Money and costs

The **official currency** of Aruba, Bonaire and Curaçao is the **Netherlands Antillean Florin (NAf)**, also known as the **guilder**, which is divided into 100 cents. In Aruba it's known as the Aruban Florin and abbreviated as **AFl**. Florin notes come in denominations of 10, 25, 50, 100, 250 and 500, and coins come as 5, 10, 25 and 50 cents, one florin and five florins. The florin is fixed to the US dollar and is very stable, with the rate of exchange roughly US$1 to NAf1.785 at the time of publication. US dollars in cash are widely accepted at most hotels, restaurants and shops, as are most major credit cards. Banks are found throughout all three islands, with most ATMs located in the capital cities.

Aruba is an **expensive** destination, but it is possible to get by on US$100 a day if you're very conscientious. Bus travel is cheap, most beaches are free and there are a few rooms (mostly in the outskirts of Oranjestad) to be found for around US$70 a night. Lodging at the major beachside resorts starts at about US$175 per night, and many require a minimum stay of at least three nights. All-inclusive holiday packages from tour operators and charter companies usually offer the best value for your stay in Aruba.

Apart from your flight, **accommodation** is likely to be your greatest expense in Bonaire, particularly if you stay at one of the many **dive resorts** during peak season. If you want to do much exploring on and off the island, count on spending around US$150–200 a day, twice that if you're looking for a more luxurious vacation.

With a **wide range** of accommodation and eating options in and around Willemstad on Curaçao, it's possible to squeak by on a daily budget of less than US$60 a day, though you'll pay closer to double that if you want to take part in any tours or land- and water-based activities.

Getting around

Getting around on all of the islands is fairly straightforward, thanks to their small size. In most cases, however, you'll need to rent a car or taxi if you want to explore beyond the capitals and resort areas.

By bus

Aruba has an inexpensive and reliable daily **bus** service linking Oranjestad with all the major areas. The main **bus terminal** is located in town across from the Port of Call Shopping Centre, and buses depart frequently for the hotels; route #10 services downtown Oranjestad and the hotel strip between Eagle Beach and Palm Beach. Tickets can be purchased directly from the driver (US$1.15 one-way; US$2 round-trip).

On Curaçao, buses run to all the major towns and districts, but the system is very slow and may require several **transfers** before you reach your destination. Bus terminals are located outside the post office in Punda and near the highway overpass in Otrobanda.

Bonaire has no public bus system.

By car

By far the easiest way to get around all three islands is with a **rented vehicle**, and all of the major rental agencies operate booths at the airports as well as at most hotel chains (see individual island sections for specific details).

While many of the major roads in Aruba are in excellent condition, you'd be wise to rent a **four-wheel-drive** vehicle (US$450/week) if you're planning to explore the interior or Arikok National Park, as the winding roads on this part of the island become rugged. Bear in mind that many of the **main highways** are labelled according to the direction you are travelling (you may be driving east on 7A, but as soon as you turn back the same road is referred to as 7B).

Most visitors to Bonaire rent **pick-up trucks** (US$40–60/day) to haul their bulky scuba equipment and tanks between their hotels and the dive sites. Rentals are handled at the airport (see p.883) and they will usually deliver the car to your hotel. For Washington-Slagbaai National Park you'll need a four-wheel-drive vehicle if you're not visiting on a tour.

By taxi

Taxis on the ABC islands are very safe and reliable, and can be hired from hotels, hailed from the street or requested by calling the central dispatch. **Rates** are fixed according to zones (there are no meters). Sightseeing tours around each island average US$30/hour on Aruba and Curaçao, and US$30 for a half-day on Bonaire; in all cases prices cover up to four passengers.

On Aruba, a ride from the capital to Eagle Beach costs US$6 and US$8 to Palm Beach for up to four people. Add an extra US$1 if you're travelling after midnight and US$3 on Sundays and holidays. For pick-up call the central dispatch (☏ 297/582-2116 or 582-1604).

On Bonaire, expect to pay anywhere from US$5 to US$12 to travel from downtown to most area hotels; US$16 to Lac Bay. A **surcharge** applies for more than four passengers and fares increase by 25 percent after 6pm and by another 50 percent after midnight. Call the central dispatch (☏ 599/717-8100) to arrange for pick-up from anywhere on the island.

On Curaçao a ride from most hotels to downtown costs US$8–12 and close to US$20 to the beaches south of Willemstad; fares increase by 25 percent after 11pm. Call the central dispatch (☏ 5999/869-0752) to arrange a pick-up.

By bike or scooter

Renting a **mountain bike** or **scooter** is a good option on islands like Bonaire, whose more than 300km of unpaved roads make this a pleasant way to see some of the island's unspoiled beauty. Bike and scooter rental agencies are found in Kralendijk (see "Listings", p.883). Plan on spending US$10–20 per day for a bike or US$18–25 per day for a scooter.

Accommodation

The vast majority of rooms in Aruba are in **expensive resorts** along the narrow beach strip between Eagle and Palm beaches. Expect to pay at least US$125 a night for a room, keeping in mind that many require a **minimum stay** of at least three nights during peak season. More reasonably priced apartment-style accommodation (less than US$100 per day) is available on the outskirts of downtown Oranjestad and away from the beaches. In addition, a 6 percent **tax** and 11 percent **service charge** will be added to your bill.

Bonaire is also pricey and offers very little in the way of budget accommodation. Most hotels and resorts are geared towards divers and as such have on-site dive centres that offer underwater certification courses, fill stations and gear rental, often as part of **package deals**. Most places are located a few minutes' drive outside of Kralendijk along the coast. Rooms typically start around US$150–200 per night during high season. There is a hotel **service charge** of 10–20 percent and a government room **tax** of US$6.50 per person per night.

Curaçao's options are more varied, and travellers can choose from budget-style apartments to exclusive hotels and dive resorts. Many of the more luxurious places are found along the coast just north and south of town, while most budget choices are in Punda and Otrobanda in downtown Willemstad. Be prepared to pay a **room service charge** of 6–15 percent.

While prohibited on Bonaire and Curaçao, **camping** is permitted in Aruba on parts of Eagle and Arashi beaches during Easter week and in early July when local schools are on holiday. Permits (US$15) must be obtained from local police officials who will tell you where you can set up camp.

Food and drink

You'll find ample **dining options** on all three islands, spanning a wide range of international and local cuisines and concentrated in the capitals and major tourist areas. On Aruba dining out tends to be an elegant and

Local dishes

Aros bruin	brown rice
Funchi	cornmeal
Galina	chicken
Giambo	okra soup
Hobi duchi	cactus soup with pork, fish and/or shrimp
Kabritu	goat meat
Karni stoba	beef stew
Moro	rice and peas
Papaja stoba	papaya stew with pig's tail and corn beef
Piska kora	red snapper, usually deep-fried whole
Piska mula	wahoo, usually deep-fried
Snijboonchi	green beans
Sopi karni-piska	meat or fish soup

expensive affair, and you'll find a crop of top-class restaurants, though a number of good, reasonably priced options are also to be found. Dining on Bonaire and Curaçao is less expensive than on Aruba and caters to all tastes and budgets. The best bargains on both islands are at snack stands and bars, busiest at lunchtime and serving scrumptious **local meals** (goat or conch stew, iguana soup, fried fish), cooked on an open grill that can cost less than US$6.

You'll find imported brands of beer and wine at most restaurants and bars, as well as the locally produced beers – Aruba's **Balashi** and Curaçao's **Amstel Bright**. The islands' popular cocktails include the local liqueur **Curaçao Blue**, made from the peels of the Valencia orange. You'll also find delicious fruit drinks and smoothies sold at many snack stands.

Popular dishes on all three islands usually include **goat**, **chicken** and **beef**, as well as local **fish** such as red snapper, wahoo and barracuda. Not-to-be-missed **Aruban specialities** include *stoba*, goat stew with vegetables; *soppi di pisca*, a fish soup made with coconut milk; freshly caught red snapper or wahoo served with plantain or *funchi* (cornmeal); and *keshi yena*, a baked mixture of Gouda cheese stuffed with beef, fish or chicken and seasoned with spices, raisins, tomatoes and olives. For dessert or for a snack try the mildly sweet *pan bati*, which is similar to a thick pancake. You'll find similar local dishes on Bonaire and Curaçao, though slight local differences in their names.

Prices at dinner will on average set you back US$20–25, though you'll pay twice that at the finer restaurants on Aruba. On all three islands a 10–15 percent **service charge** is normally added to your bill; while the service is included it's not uncommon to add a little extra at your discretion (especially on Aruba where this is customary).

On all the islands **reservations** are recommended, especially during high season. Be aware that some restaurants open only for dinner, so it pays to check ahead if possible.

Post, phones and Internet

Payphones are located all over Aruba and Curaçao and many require **phone cards**, which can be purchased from shops or vendors throughout the islands. On Bonaire you're likely to be stuck calling from hotels – which charge exorbitant rates as they do on the other islands – unless you use the island's few payphones (see below).

On Aruba, international calls are best made from the **SETAR telephone office** in the Royal Plaza in downtown Oranjestad (daily 8am–10.30pm). There are also a few specially marked telephone booths where you can reach the international operator, at the cruise terminal, airport and scattered throughout the downtown area.

On Bonaire local and international phone calls can be made from payphones outside the **TELBO office** near the tourist information

22

office on Kaya Libertador S. Bolivar; phone-cards can be purchased from a vending machine located near the front door of the office. There are also a few phones at the airport and in town where you can reach the international operator.

If you want to make an international call from Curaçao, it's best to call from the capital where there are a couple of **privately run businesses** that charge reasonable rates for international calls.

A few specially designated telephone **booths** in Willemstad and at the airport also have direct access to the international operator, allowing you to use your calling card or credit card.

The **postal systems** in all three islands are relatively efficient, and **Internet access** is available at hotels and a handful of locations in the capitals (see "Listings" sections for individual islands for details).

Opening hours, holidays, and festivals

On all three islands, most shops and business are normally **open** Monday to Saturday 8am–noon and 2–6pm, with a few places on Curaçao opening on Sunday mornings if cruise ships are in port. **Banks** are generally open Monday to Friday 8am–3.30pm, and some close for lunch; the bank at Curaçao's airport is open Monday to Saturday 8am–8pm and on Sundays 9am–4pm.

Of the many festivals and celebrations on the islands, the one that all three share is **Carnival**, which on Aruba and Bonaire officially begins forty days before Lent, and is celebrated with parades, steel bands, costumes and colourful floats, though Bonaire's Carnival is smaller than those on the other islands. Curaçao has a month-long Carnival

season, which kicks off on New Year's Day and culminates with a grand parade on the day before Ash Wednesday. Emotions run high during the four-day **Tumba festival**, a preamble to Carnival, when local musicians compete to have their piece (*tumba*) selected as the official road song.

During the rest of the year, Aruba's calendar includes **One Cool Summer**, a festival from May to October that features concerts, traditional food, and cultural and sporting events; the **Hi Winds Pro-Am Windsurfing competition** in June, which draws international competitors of all ages and skill levels; **Dera Gai** on June 24, a folkloric celebration commemorating the harvest; and the annual **Festival de las Americas** in October, a music celebration showcasing the unique rhythms of the Americas.

Outside Carnival, Bonaireans have a number of events to look forward to: the **Simadan harvest festival** in Rincon in April, when locals pay tribute to the farmers with traditional music and costumes; the week-long **Bonaire Dive Festival** in June, when activities and games focus on raising awareness of the importance of the coral reefs; and the **International Sailing Regatta** in October. The events of the preceding twelve months are recapped in song and dance during the colourful **Bari Festival** held in December.

Curaçao has a number of international events, including its **regatta** (late Jan or early Feb), when sailors from around the world compete in races near Willemstad; the **Jazz**

22

The following holidays are observed on all three islands, unless specified otherwise.

January 1 New Year's Day
January 25 G.F. Croes Day (Aruba)
Monday before Ash Wednesday Carnival Monday (Aruba)
March 18 National Anthem and Flag Day (Aruba)
March/April Good Friday and Easter Monday
April 30 Queen's Birthday and Rincon Day (Bonaire)
May 1 Labour Day
May 24 Ascension Day
July 2 Curaçao Flag Day
September 6 Bonaire Flag Day
December 25 and 26 Christmas
December 31 New Year's Eve

Festival in May; and the **Salsa Festival** (dates vary in summer), which attracts popular international stars.

Language

The **official language** of the Netherlands Antilles is **Dutch**, although English and Spanish are also widely spoken, as is **Papiamentu**, a Creole language that developed in Curaçao in the 1500s between the African slaves and their owners. The colourful language quickly spread to Aruba and Bonaire and evolved over time as Portuguese and Spanish missionaries, Dutch merchants and South American traders each added their own vocabulary.

While you're more likely to hear English spoken in Aruba (due largely to the influx of US visitors) and Dutch in Curaçao, Papiamentu is the dominant language in Bonaire. Why not try a few of the phrases listed in the box below?

Welcome	Bon bini
Good morning	Bon dia
Good afternoon	Bon tardi
Good evening	Bon nochi
How are you?	Con ta bai?
I am fine	Mi ta bon
Have a good day	Pasa bon dia
Thank you	Masha danki
Goodbye	Ayo
You're welcome	Di nada
Very good!	Hopi bon
See you later	Te aworo

Watersports

All of the ABC islands offer good **watersports** opportunities, though each has its own particular strengths. For diving, Bonaire is unmatched by its neighbours: pristine coral reefs dot the waters around the island, most of them on the sheltered western coast and around **Klein Bonaire**, a 1500-acre cay just offshore from Kralendijk. Diving is virtually nonexistent on the east coast due to rough waters and a rugged coastline. The majority of sites are so close at hand, all you need to do is park your truck, grab your gear and swim a few metres to the reef. There's also good windsurfing to be had at **Lac Bay** on the island's east coast.

Though Aruba is known more for its beaches than its diving, it does have some exciting **dives** at sites scattered along the northwestern coast of the island, including a few shipwrecks. Dive centres located at many of the hotels arrange charter boat tours to these spots. There are also excellent **windsurfing** conditions on the island just a few metres north at Hadicurari, while the best **snorkelling** is found still further north at Malmok and Arashi.

Curaçao has plenty of watersports to choose from. The island has some decent dive sites scattered on its leeward side along the southern coast in the twenty-kilometre **Curaçao Underwater Park** and around **Klein Curaçao**, a small deserted volcanic island to the southeast (an hour-and-a-half boat ride from Willemstad). Most sites are rich in coral formations while others have sunken ships and submerged artefacts. Some sites are easily accessible from shore but most require getting there by **boat**. Good snorkelling exists at most of these locations.

22

History

The first inhabitants of the ABC islands were the **Caiquitìos Indians**, an Arawak-speaking tribe from South America who established themselves on all three of the islands centuries before the arrival of the **Spanish** in 1499. In the years that followed, more Spaniards settled here in search of precious metals and drinking water. Not finding any gold or silver, they quickly dubbed the ABCs "las islas inutiles" or the "useless islands". (In fact, they should have looked harder on Aruba where over three million pounds of gold were discovered in the nineteenth century.)

Disappointed by the lack of natural resources, the Spanish **enslaved** many of the Amerindians and shipped them to Hispaniola to labour in the mines and plantations there. Returning in the mid-1520s to colonize the ABCs, the Spaniards introduced cattle and other livestock, and brought back many of the original slaves to work in agriculture.

During the early 1630s the **Dutch**, on a quest for a suitable Caribbean base from which to launch attacks against the Spanish, took control of Aruba, Bonaire and Curaçao, and the next century saw a drastic increase in commerce on all three islands.

Prized for its naturally deep harbour, its strategic location and its **saltpans** (salt was an important commodity for preserving fish and meat shipped back to Europe), Curaçao quickly developed into an important Dutch naval base. Bonaire was also valued for its vast quantities of salt and tracts of agricultural land left behind by the Spaniards. The **Dutch West India Company** began exporting large amounts of salt, along with sorghum, maize, divi divi pods (used in the tanning process) and meat to Europe and to the rest of the world. They also imported livestock to Aruba for the sole purpose of feeding the many slaves and colonists living on Curaçao.

More slaves from Africa and the Caribbean were brought in to work the salt fields and the **plantations**. Curaçao, in fact, became the Caribbean's busiest **slave depot** during the seventeenth century when the Dutch West India Company shipped tens of thousands of slaves to Curaçao and Brazil where they were sold to plantation owners from across the Caribbean and the Americas. Slavery wouldn't be abolished in the ABCs until 1863, after which the Dutch West India Company closed many of the plantations.

Economic prospects were bleak until the discovery of rich **oilfields** off the coast of Venezuela at the beginning of the twentieth century, which proved to be a boon for all three of the islands. Aruba and Curaçao both built refineries, attracting workers from Bonaire and around the world. These refineries flourished until they were forced to close in the mid-1980s. While the oil and salt industries remain important today, it was the **tourism initiatives** of the 1990s that revived the islands' economies, providing jobs for a substantial number of their populations and increasing the ABC islands' profile as a holiday destination, particularly for Aruba and Bonaire, the more well known of the islands.

22.1

Aruba

With its seemingly endless supply of white sandy beaches and turquoise blue waters, **ARUBA** is one of the more popular Caribbean destinations for many (especially American) sun-worshippers and cruise ship passengers. The smallest of the ABC islands, Aruba is 25km north of Venezuela and only 30km wide. Over one million visitors a year come to this tiny island of 90,000 to indulge in the glitz associated with its luxurious beachside resorts, elegant restaurants, 24-hour casinos, shops and boutiques. As a result, it can feel rather crowded and, at times, a little lacking in soul.

The harbourside capital **Oranjestad** attracts many of the visitors, as do resort-filled **Eagle** and **Palm beaches** just north of town. In stark contrast to these glamorous areas, the rugged interior is dotted with stands of cacti, twisted divi divi trees and herds of wandering goats. In the Mars-like landscape of **Arikok National Park**, mysterious boulders painted with ancient petroglyphs and limestone caves are sights worth catching.

Gold was discovered here in 1824, but the real economic boom began in the early 1900s when **oil** was discovered off the coast of Venezuela and a refinery was built here in **San Nicolas**. After the oil supply's decline in the 1980s, the Aruban government launched a new initiative, focusing its attention on large-scale **tourism**. Seeking more independence and greater control of its finances, Aruba gained *status aparte* in 1986, thus allowing Arubans to have their own parliament, flag, currency and more freedom in their internal affairs than their counterparts in the Netherlands Antilles. Today more than half of the population is employed by the flourishing tourism industry and Arubans enjoy a higher standard of living than those on many other Caribbean islands.

Accommodation

Aruba is small enough that you can pretty much base yourself anywhere and be close to all activities and attractions. In downtown Oranjestad, there is really not much in the way of **accommodation**; most of the affordable guesthouses and apartments are located just outside the capital, while the majority of the more expensive resorts and hotels are along the main **seafront strip** between Eagle and Palm beaches.

Oranjestad

Renaissance Aruba Resort & Casino L.G. Smith Blvd 82 ☎297/583-6000, ⊛www.marriott.com. There is no lack of activity at this enormous, all-new village-like resort in the heart of downtown. With over 500 rooms, the complex also has multiple restaurants, bars, pools, boutiques, fitness centres and a casino. Rooms are spacious and have balconies affording spectacular views of the coast or city. The real treat here, though, is free access to a private island just a fifteen-minute boat ride away. ❾

The beach strip and northwest tip

Amsterdam Manor Hotel Eagle Beach ☎297/587-1492, ⊛www.amsterdammanor.com. Dutch colonial-style architecture at this friendly 72-room hotel on excellent Eagle Beach, with its own swimming pool, sports facilities and beach bar. Popular, good food and many repeat visitors. ❼

Aruba Beach Villas across from Hadicurari Beach on L.G. Smith Blvd 462 ☎297/586-1072, ⊛www.arubabeachvillas.com. Rooms range from one- to two-bedroom apartments with kitchenettes to large private villas with ocean and sunset views. The

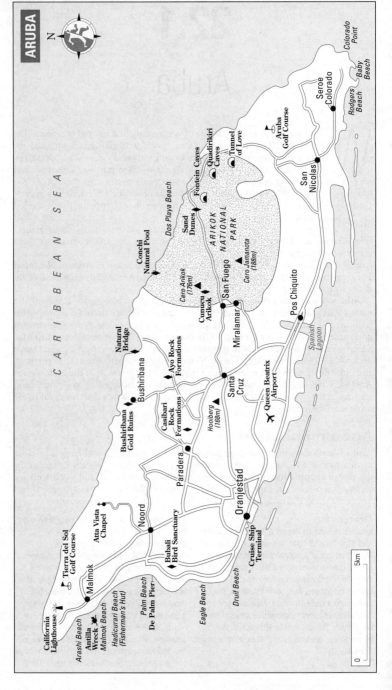

ARUBA

N

CARIBBEAN SEA

Colorado Point

Baby Beach
Rodgers Beach
Seroe Colorado

San Nicolas

Aruba Golf Course

Tunnel of Love
Quadirikiri Caves
Fontein Caves

Dos Playa Beach

Sand Dunes

ARIKOK NATIONAL PARK

Cero Arikok (176m)

Cero Jamanota (188m)

San Fuego

Cunucu Arikok

Conchi Natural Pool

Pos Chiquito

Spanish Lagoon

Miralamar

Natural Bridge

Ayo Rock Formations

Bushiribana

Bushiribana Gold Ruins

Casibari Rock Formations

Santa Cruz

Hooiberg (168m)

Queen Beatrix Airport

Paradera

Noord

Atta Vista Chapel

Bubali Bird Sanctuary

Oranjestad

Cruise Ship Terminal

Druif Beach

Eagle Beach

Palm Beach
De Palm Pier

Hadicurari Beach (Fisherman's Hut)

Tierra del Sol Golf Course

Malmok

Malmok Beach
Antilla Wreck
Arashi Beach

California Lighthouse

0   5km

location makes this hotel popular with windsurfers. ❸

Bucuti Beach Resort Eagle Beach on L.G. Smith Blvd 55B ☎ 297/583-1100, ⊛ www.bucuti.com. The sixty comfortable one-bedroom units, popular with Europeans, all have a/c, phone, private bath, TV and a large terrace or balcony overlooking the water. There's a fitness centre on the premises, and meal plans are available. ❽

Divi Aruba Beach Resort Druif Beach on J.E. Irausquin Blvd 45 ☎ 297/582-3300, ⊛ www. diviaruba.com. This all-inclusive mega-resort, popular with young families and couples, features two restaurants, beachside bars, a pool and 200 spacious one-bedroom units with Spanish decor. All rooms adjoin a small outside patio or balcony, and end-units offer stunning ocean views. Daily fitness activities and nightly entertainment are on offer, and guests can use restaurant or beach facilities at the neighbouring *Tamarijn Aruba Resort*. ❾

Radisson Aruba Resort J.E. Irausquin Blvd 81 ☎ 297/586-6555, ⊛ www.radisson.com/aruba.

Extremely popular resort, covering a vast and well-landscaped area with 350 rooms surrounded by pretty gardens, swimming pools and other interesting features. The place can feel a little impersonal, but the facilities – watersports, restaurants and casino particularly – are undeniably excellent. ❾

The rest of the island

Cactus Apartments Matadera 5, Noord ☎ 297/582-2903, ⊛ www.cactusaruba.com. A basic hotel with thirteen apartments in the small town of Noord, just east of Palm Beach. Rooms have kitchenettes, a/c and TV. Laundry service, which is hard to come by and expensive on the island, is available here for a modest fee. ❸

Turibana Plaza Apartments Noord 124, Noord ☎ 297/586-7292, ⊕ 586-2658. This excellent-value small apartment complex with eighteen two-bedroom units has spacious, clean rooms with a/c, kitchenettes and daily service. It is located next to several restaurants, and is close to beaches and the capital. ❸

Oranjestad

Named in honour of the Dutch Royal House of Orange, **ORANJESTAD** has been Aruba's capital since 1797 and has served as the island's main port ever since. Today, the small harbour continues to attract schooners, fishing boats and cruise ships from all over the world. The tiny capital on the southwest shore bustles with activity as thousands of visitors descend upon it each day to shop, dine or try their luck at one of the many casinos. The streets that make up the downtown core are lined with modern imitations of pastel-coloured Dutch colonial houses adorned with ornate gabled roofs; a good number of them have been renovated into shopping complexes, administrative buildings, museums and restaurants. A handful of older buildings, including Fort Zoutman and the lofty King Willem III Tower, offer reminders of Aruba's past. Just a hop and a skip away from the city is the island's main **beach strip** and resort area.

The City

For many tourists, the first glimpse of Oranjestad is along the busy palm-fringed thoroughfare of **L.G. Smith Boulevard**, the island's main artery, connecting the capital with the hotel district and the northwest and with San Nicholas in the southeast. Running parallel to the harbour, the downtown stretch of the road is lined with shopping malls, boutiques, casinos, government offices and parliament buildings. Unless you plan to shop till you drop or while away the hours gambling, the city's sights won't occupy too much of your time. There are, however, a number of interesting cultural attractions best explored, like the city itself, on foot, as everything you'll want to see is concentrated in a small area.

The picturesque harbour is a good place to begin your wanderings. Starting from the white **tourist information booth** adjacent to the Atlantis Pier, head east for five minutes past the yellow parliament building. Turning left onto Oranjestraat, you'll reach the beautifully preserved **Fort Zoutman**, the oldest building on the island and perhaps the town's most important landmark. The fort was built in 1796 and played a vital role in securing Dutch interests on the island. Armed with four cannons, it was originally sited along the coast; centuries of shifting currents have changed the coastline so that today the fort now sits some 300m away from the

Shopping

Duty-free **shopping** is an irresistible draw for many visitors to Aruba. Bargain-hunters crowd the heart of the shopping district in downtown Oranjestad, where malls, duty-free stores, boutiques and craft shops line the main streets of L.G. Smith Boulevard, Havenstraat and Caya G.F. Betico Croes. Most stores are full of imported goods such as fragrances, linens, liquors, gold jewellery, watches, cameras, name-brand fashions and Dutch porcelain figurines. Malls of note are the large **Seaport Mall** within the luxurious *Sonesta Beach Resort and Casino* complex, the nearby two-storey **Royal Plaza Mall**, at the corner of Weststraat and L.G. Smith Blvd, and the open-air **Seaport Marketplace Mall**, on the east side of the harbour and across L.G. Smith Blvd. Shops are open Monday to Saturday 8am–6.30pm; many close for lunch between noon and 2pm. A small cluster of craft stalls selling typical souvenirs and wooden handicrafts can also be found at the Wharfside Market on L.G. Smith Blvd.

water. The adjoining **Willem III Tower** was added in 1868 to serve as a lighthouse and the town's first public clock. The fort houses a small **historical museum** (Mon–Fri 8.30am–4.15pm; US$6) displaying an interesting collection of artefacts that trace Aruba's history. Its open-air courtyard also hosts the weekly folkloric **Bon Bini Festival** (Tues 6.30–8.30pm; US$3), which features traditional music and dance, and is the best place to try local dishes.

One block east, on Zuidstraat 27, is the fascinating **Numismatic Museum** (Mon–Fri 7.30am–noon & 1–4pm; free), home to over 30,000 historical coins from Aruba and around the world dating back to 220 BC. Some of the many highlights include a display of Aruban Indian shells used for barter, beads used as money by North American Indians and notes made of silk and linen.

At the north end of the city the tiny **Archeological Museum**, J.E. Irausquin Blvd 2-A (Mon–Fri 8am–noon & 1–4pm; free), has an impressive array of local artefacts and pottery. The most important exhibits include stone tools from 2000 BC, pottery from the ceramic period (500 AD) and skeletal remains excavated from an Indian burial site.

Back near the harbour, around the corner from the Seaport Casino, is the quiet **Wilhelmina Park**, honouring the 1955 visit of Queen Juliana of the Netherlands, a white marble statue of whom dominates the plaza. The park is especially striking when tropical plants are in bloom between June and October. Benches set amongst the shady grove of trees makes this an ideal place to rest after sightseeing or a long day of shopping.

The beach strip and the northwest tip

Easily reached from J.E. Irausquin Boulevard, which intersects the main L.G. Smith Boulevard, the best **beaches**, **watersports facilities** and **hotels** are found along the famous gold coast on the leeward side (northwest) of the island. Here, Aruba's best 7km of fine white sand stretches between Eagle Beach and Palm Beach, meeting up with the turquoise waters of the Caribbean. Further northwest, good conditions coupled with a handful of colourful coral reefs and sunken ships attract **windsurfers**, **divers** and **snorkellers**.

Eagle Beach and Palm Beach

Eagle Beach is the largest and most popular sandy stretch along this excellent strand, offering plenty of shade and watersports activities. Several low-rise hotels nearby allow beach-goers to eat and drink at their restaurants and bars. Divi Winds (see box opposite) offers windsurfing and sailing lessons, and rents boards, kayaks and snorkelling gear. A few kilometres north on J.E. Irausquin Boulevard is **Palm**

Watersports and activities

Aruba offers a wide selection of watersports and related activities, many of which are based on the stretch between Eagle Beach and Palm Beach.

Snorkelling excursions to nearby coral reefs and shipwrecks can be arranged with Fun Factory Sailing Adventure (℡297/586-2017), departing daily from the De Palm Pier behind the *Radisson Hotel* at 9.30am. The four-hour trip on board the catamaran (US$60) includes an open bar, hot buffet lunch, snorkelling gear and visits to a couple of reefs and to the *Antilla*, a sunken World War II German freighter off the coast of Malmok. **Diving** lessons and packages to area dive sites can be arranged with Pelican Watersports (℡297/587-2302, ℗www.pelican-aruba.com), located next to De Palm Pier. One and two-tank dives cost US$40/$60; a fully certified Open Water Certification course will set you back US$350. Red Sail Sports (℡297/586-1603), behind the *Hyatt Hotel* and *Allegro Resort* on Palm Beach, also have a series of dive courses, charter tours to area reefs and night dives.

Aruba's only **kayak** company, Aruba Kayak Adventure (℡297/582-5520, ℗www. arubawavedancer.com), offers a four-hour guided kayaking trip along the southern coast of the island near Spanish Lagoon, a legendary hiding place for pirates. The fee of US$77 includes hotel pick-up and delivery, use of kayak and brief instructions, lunch and snorkelling gear. They depart every morning at 9.30am.

Deep-sea fishing with Teaser Charters and Pair-a-dice Charters can be arranged by calling ℡297/582-5088 and ℡297/592-9586 respectively. The crews usually fish for marlin, wahoo, kingfish or barracuda. Half-day charters run from US$250.

A variety of **sailing** trips and sunset tours can be arranged with several agencies. Jolly Pirates (℡297/583-7355) operates a 70-ton schooner and organizes sailing and snorkelling trips departing from De Palm Pier (tours start at US$50), while Mi Dushi Sailing Adventures (℡297/586-2010) sets sail Monday to Saturday on a sunset cruise (US$30).

Divi Winds (℡297/583-7841), between the *Divi* and *Tamarijn* resorts on Druif Beach, offers **windsurfing** lessons (US$45), sailing lessons (US$50) and board rental (US$15/ hr). At Hadicurari Beach, Aruba Boardsailing Productions (℡297/586-0989) rents windsurfers at US$20 per hour or US$55 for the day; lessons are prohibitively expensive at US$135/day. Kitesurfing Aruba (℡297/733-1515, ℗www.kitesurfingaruba.com) offer, surprisingly, **kitesurfing** in the same area; it's US$100 for a two-and-a-half-hour lesson.

A different and exciting way to explore Aruba's underwater realm is on board the island's only passenger **submarine**. The *Atlantis Submarine* (℡297/588-6881) descends to 150ft, where passengers can view schools of tropical fish, coral reefs and the remains of the *Mi Dushi* shipwreck. It leaves from the Atlantis Pier located across from the *Sonesta Resort* in downtown Oranjestad at a cost of US$74 for adults and US$35 for children.

Beach, known for its luxurious high-rise resorts and more superb watersports. De Palm Tours operates a pier here from which many of their water-based tours and activities originate (see box above). The surrounding shallow waters and long stretches of clean sand are very popular with families. It gets crowded at weekends and holidays, during which time food stalls selling local dishes are set up.

There are a couple of diversions in the area if you're looking to take a break from the beach. Naturalists will delight in exploring the tropical enclosures of the nearby **Butterfly Farm** (daily 9am–4pm; US$10, US$5 children) located on J.E. Irausquin Boulevard across from the *Aruba Phoenix Beach Resort*. The small garden is home to many different types of plants and over forty species of butterflies, including the large-winged blue morpho. Interesting guided tours along the path provide insights into the life cycle and ecological importance of the butterfly. Around the corner, bird enthusiasts will enjoy the **Bubali Bird Sanctuary**, a small oasis of marshland on this dry island, sheltering hundreds of species of migratory waterfowl. A viewing platform atop a tower provides the only vantage point from which to observe the birds, which include grebes, terns, herons, cormorants and coots.

The northwest tip

Further north along L.G. Smith Boulevard is **Hadicurari**, locally referred to as Fisherman's Hut Beach, a popular **windsurfing** and **kitesurfing** destination and host to the Hi Winds Pro-Am Windsurfing Challenge held each year in June. A couple of boardsailing companies offer windsurfing lessons and board rentals (see box p.869).

Superb snorkelling, diving and swimming can be had near the northern tip of the island at **Malmok** and **Arashi beaches**. Several coral reefs and offshore shipwrecks are worth checking out – you'll need a boat to get to them.

Overlooking the northwestern tip of the island is the towering yellow **California Lighthouse**, a favourite place to enjoy sunsets. Built on top of a small hill and sandwiched between sand dunes, this 125-foot lighthouse was named in honour of a British steamship, the *California*, shipwrecked off the coast in 1891. Though nearly all of the ship's crew were able to make it safely to land, the Arubans were prompted to build the lighthouse in 1914 to warn other sailors of possible offshore dangers. Today the lighthouse is still operational and remains closed to the public. Nearby, in a building which once housed the lighthouse keeper, is an elegant Italian restaurant, *La Trattoria el Faro Blanco*.

The north coast and around

Leaving the beach district behind, Highway 4A heads east to Aruba's rugged north coast and its barren interior. Past the small community of Paradera, a series of road signs direct you to the mysterious **rock formations** of **Casibari** and nearby **Ayû**. Resembling something out of *The Flintstones*, nobody knows for sure how these smooth, monolithic diorite boulders came to be dropped here, particularly because their geology is so different from that of the rest of the island. Also a mystery is the origin of the ancient **petroglyphs** found on the surface of a few of these boulders; the weathered vestiges of these paintings can be seen through protective steel bars. Both Casibari and Ayû offer well-groomed trails through the rock gardens lined with cacti, aloe and other species of plants, while steps carved into the boulders allow you to climb up for a panoramic view of the island and nearby **Hooiberg**, a 168-metre hill resembling a haystack.

Continuing north from Ayû, a gravel road leads to the **Bushiribana Gold Ruins**, the site of a gold smelter on the coast that was operational for most of the nineteenth century. Constructed with natural rock in 1825, a year after the discovery of gold triggered a economic mini-boom, the smelter processed over three million tons of raw material from the nearby mines before it was abandoned some ninety years later. Today the crumbling ruins stand as a testament to Aruba's rich gold history; unfortunately there are no guides on hand.

A short distance away, the road turns east and follows the coast for 2.5km until it ends at the **Natural Bridge**, perhaps the most photographed attraction on the island. Rising 25 feet above sea level and spanning a hundred feet across a small bay, this natural coral archway was carved by centuries of raging surf, strong winds and tectonic processes that continue to shape it today. A sandy beach, accessible by a set of stairs from the parking lot, allows visitors to take close-up pictures. The more adventurous can walk the entire length of the bridge and experience first-hand the powerful force of the pounding surf. A small "thirst-aid station" and café sells refreshments and snacks at the car park, which is often crowded with tour buses and hundreds of visitors.

Finally, sitting on top of a hill overlooking the north coast, the charming **Alto Vista Chapel**, 5km west of the gold ruins, was the first Catholic chapel on the island. It was originally built by Spanish missionaries in 1750 and renovated two hundred years later. A necklace with a Spanish cross on display in the chapel dates back to the time of the original missionaries and is believed to be the oldest of its kind in the Netherlands Antilles. Getting there is relatively easy: head west along the coastal gravel road from the gold ruins or take Highway 2B north from the town of **Noord** for 0.5km and turn right at the narrow road which winds uphill to the chapel (3.3km).

Arikok National Park

The untamed beauty of Aruba is best experienced in **Arikok National Park**, a large protected area encompassing almost twenty percent of the island's landmass, stretching from the coast inland. Located on the eastern side of the island, the park preserves many of the natural, geological and cultural features that have shaped Aruba's past and present.

The park's desert landscape looks more like the Australian outback than a tropical Caribbean island, and is interspersed with bizarre patches of reddish-orange rock and soil formations. The hilly interior also reveals several abandoned gold mines and traditional country homes, while the park's rugged coastline is littered with sand dunes, grottoes and secluded bays. Growing throughout are groves of towering cacti, contorted divi divi trees and other thorny plants. Typical animals found here include burrowing owls, fruit-eating bats, lizards and herds of wandering goats.

A potholed dirt road and 34km of well-marked **hiking trails** allow visitors to see the park at their own pace. Access is via Highway 7A, which leads to the **park gate** near the town of San Fuego. Past the entrance, the highway turns into a very narrow dirt road and continues to the coast before it heads south towards San Nicolas. A sturdy 4WD vehicle is highly recommended, as is sunscreen, drinking water and a hat. Guidebooks with **trail maps** can be purchased for US$15 at the gate.

Exploring the park

A sign posted shortly beyond the entrance will direct you to a **fork** in the road. Straight ahead leads to the coast, dunes and caves; heading right will bring you uphill to **Cunucu Arikok**, a small rocky garden surrounded by a stone and cactus-lined wall. Inside the enclosure a 1.5km trail guides visitors past several species of native and introduced plants as well as **rock formations** similar to those found in Ayû and Casibari. A **petroglyph** of an ancient bird is painted on one of these boulders. Close to the centre of the garden is a recently renovated **cas di torta**, a traditional nineteenth-century country home used by farmers who attempted to cultivate this relatively infertile land. This type of structure was typically constructed with rocks and dried cactus husks and held together with layers of mud and grass.

A short drive uphill from the garden will take you to the top of **Cero Arikok** (176m), where you'll be rewarded with a spectacular panoramic view of the park. If you want to explore the coastline and its many caves, head back to the fork in the road at the main gate. Once there, take the road heading east for 5km. Along the way there is a 4km hiking trail (watch for signs shortly after the fork) that leads to the gold pits of **Miralamar** and the foot of **Cero Jamanota**, Aruba's highest peak (188m). Hiking conditions are relatively easy and involve navigating some small slopes.

Gently rolling white **sand dunes** mark the beginning of the coastline. The secluded **Dos Playa** beach can be reached by turning left at the dunes for 1.5km. Swimming is not recommended here – the surf is too dangerous – but it's an ideal place to stop for a picnic. Past the dunes the main road heads southeast along the coast; after 200m there's a small open-air **snack bar** (daily 10am–6pm) serving a good selection of burgers, chicken and seafood dishes for US$10–15. Film, drinks and a variety of munchies can also be purchased.

Turning right at the snack bar the road leads to the **Fontein Caves**, a collection of small grottoes that were once occupied by native peoples. Centuries of graffiti, brownish-red Indian rock paintings and beautiful flowstone formations adorn the walls and ceilings of these limestone caves. Fruit-eating bats roost during the day and fly out at night in search of food. Free tours are offered every fifteen minutes by the park rangers; flash photography is not permitted.

Adjacent to the caves is the **Fontein Garden** (Place Hofi Fontein), the site of a nineteenth-century **plantation** run by the Gravenhorst-Croes family. This was the only place on the north coast where permanent running fresh water was available throughout the year; this feature allowed for the plantation's development. The house has been restored and now houses a small **museum** displaying a scant collection of photos, tools and animal specimens.

San Nicolas and the southeast tip

Up until the late nineteenth century, **SAN NICOLAS**, the oldest and largest city in Aruba, existed as a peaceful settlement of a few fishermen and their families living in small huts scattered along the southeast coast. All that changed in 1879 when the Aruba Phosphate Company began exporting locally mined **phosphate** in large quantities to the US. Subsequent demand, combined with the need for a larger workforce, prompted officials to build houses for their employees, and the makings of the town began. In addition, after vast oilfields were discovered off the coast of Venezuela during the early part of the twentieth century, the Largo Oil and Transport Company announced plans to build an **oil refinery** near town. By 1951, the once-quiet village had a population of just over 20,000 residents, almost twice the size of Oranjestad – and twice the size of the town's current population. Social clubs, golf courses and luxurious homes in the new suburbs of Largo Heights and Cero Colorado were built for the hordes of workers – from the island and beyond – who flocked to this boom town. When the refinery closed in 1985, the city was left in a shambles until it was reopened in 1991 by Coastal Aruba Refining.

Although there is some hotel **development** out here, few tourists head this way as – to be honest - the town hasn't got much to offer, other than a few abandoned ruins of old buildings that give a glimpse of the British-Caribbean charm of the town's former glory days. A handful of restaurants, snack stalls and shops selling local crafts and souvenirs can be found alongside the picturesque promenade on Zeppenfeldstraat. A requisite stop is the legendary *Charlie's Bar and Restaurant*, which dates back to 1941. Over sixty years' worth of mementos left by seamen, refinery workers, scuba divers and other visitors adorn its walls and ceilings.

Nearby, about 6km east of San Nicolas, are two small popular public **beaches**. To reach them, take Fortheuvelstraat out of town until you come to a huge cement anchor at the end of the road. Turn right on the main road and follow the signs to Rodger's Beach and Baby Beach. You'll first hit **Rodger's Beach**, which, despite a view of the nearby oil refinery, is a good spot with decent swimming conditions and the *Coco Bar and Grill Restaurant*. Just east of here, the sheltered waters of **Baby Beach** offer ideal swimming conditions, especially, as the name might suggest, for families with small children; there's also good snorkelling to be had. JADS Beach Store (℗297/584-6070) rents beach and snorkelling gear.

Eating and drinking

The majority of the island's finer **eateries** are in the capital along Wilhelminastraat, serving everything from prime Argentine beef to local seafood dishes, although an increasing number of good places are opening around Palm Beach. Many are only open for lunch and dinner and some close on Sundays or Mondays; it's usually wise to make reservations. Most of the resorts also have their own restaurants.

Oranjestad

Cuba's Cookin' Wilhelminastraat 27 ℡ 297/588-0627. Genuine Cuban cuisine and lively entertainment are on offer at this traditional nineteenth-century country house. Try the lobster enchilada. Entrees US$20–30. Dinner only.

Don Carlos L.G. Smith Blvd ℡ 297/583-6246. You can't get any closer to the water than this place, serving reasonably priced authentic Italian cuisine directly on the waterfront in the heart of town. Very popular with young families, it can get rather busy.

Iguana Joe's Royal Plaza Mall, second floor ℡ 297/583-9373. Long one of Aruba's most popular restaurants. Delicious dishes include quesadillas and crispy calamari; vegetarian options also available. Don't miss out on their enormous tropical drinks like the famous Pink Iguana, a smooth, refreshing strawberry colada. Mains under US$20.

Jamaica Me Krazy Certified Mega Mall, 150 LG Smith Blvd ℡ 297/583-4692. Excellent little Jamaican restaurant, with all the usual options like brown fish stew, ackee and saltfish and curried goat. Closed Sun.

Taj Mahal Wilhelminastraat 4A ℡ 297/588-4494. The oldest and best Indian restaurant in town. Delicious authentic dishes, averaging US$7–8, all prepared to order.

Villa Germania Seaport Marketplace Mall ℡ 297/583-0078. One of the few places in town open for breakfast ($5–8), *Villa Germania* also has home-made European cuisine like schnitzel and sauerkraut and desserts for lunch and dinner (mains US$12–20). Open terrace faces the harbour.

The Waterfront Seaport Marketplace Mall ℡ 297/583-5858. Specializing in seafood dishes as well as burgers and chicken dishes. Open for breakfast ($6–10), lunch and dinner (mains US$7–15).

The beach strip and the northwest tip

La Trattoria el Faro Blanco at the California Lighthouse ℡ 297/586-0786. Fine Italian dining in a small restaurant belonging to the former lighthouse keeper. The food is expensive but excellent, and the views of the ocean and sunset are stunning. Reservations recommended.

Madame Janette near the mini-golf course on Cunucu Abao 37 ℡ 297/587-0184. This very popular, friendly restaurant attracts both locals and tourists, and a varied menu features international and seafood dishes. Closed Tues.

Smokey Joes Playa Linda, Palm Beach ℡ 297/586-1000. Popular outdoor restaurant serving excellent ribs, slathered in a variety of sauces, as well as jerk chicken and fish dishes for US$12–18. Dinner only.

Texas de Brazil 382 J.E. Irausquin Blvd, Palm Beach ℡ 297/586-4686. Authentic Brazilian steakhouse, with superb grilled meats passed around the restaurant by a small army of waiters; take your pick from chicken, pork, beef and lamb, and help yourself from the excellent salad bar. Daily from 6pm.

San Nicolas area

Charlie's Bar and Restaurant downtown on Zeppenfeldstraat 56 ℡ 297/584-5086. This popular hangout has become something of a legend in Aruba. Over sixty years of mementos left here by seamen, refinery workers and scores of visitors cover the interior – including everything from sport shirts to licence plates, business cards to photographs. Don't be turned off by all the "reserved" signs on the tables: the owners are keeping the table for you. Be sure to try the mouthwatering jumbo shrimp and *pasapalo* (delicious local-style tenderloin) served with their famous hot honeymoon sauce.

Yuwana Crijnssenstraat ℡ 297/584-8283. Sports bar and restaurant with twenty screens showing the latest sports from around the world and a decent menu of Caribbean food. Closed Tues.

Nightlife

At night, the dazzling lights of Oranjestad attract party buses and scores of revellers who visit as many **bars**, **nightclubs** and **casinos** as possible before daybreak. Many of the restaurants and bars have live local **bands** at weekends, and most hotels and resorts offer theme nights and activities for their guests. If your heart is set on spending an elegant evening, the glitzy Las Vegas-style **dance shows** at the Crystal Theater in the *Sonesta Resort* are well worth the price of admission.

Blue L.G. Smith Blvd 82 ℡ 297/583-6000. Elegance is the watchword at this grand and pricey venue, with no expense spared on an excellent sound and light system, with the latest music interspersed with golden oldies.

Carlos'n Charlie's Weststraat 3A ℡ 297/582-0355. A popular bar with tourists who dance to tunes from the 1960s to the 1980s. The music gets going after 11pm. US$3 cover charge.

Crystal Theater downtown at the *Aruba Sonesta*

Beach Resort on L.G. Smith Blvd ☎297/583-6000. An impressive heart-thumping "Let's Go Latin" dance show (US$37) with live music and dancers. Show times are from Mon to Sat beginning at 9pm. The resort also has a 24-hour casino.

La Fiesta Adventura Mall, second floor, on Klipstraat ☎297/588-9982. This trendy terrace bar attracts both locals and tourists. Latin beats are mixed with European and American tunes.

Mambo Jambos Royal Plaza Mall, second floor ☎297/583-3632. Tables are removed on Fri and Sat for dancing; other nights this place is great for hanging out and listening to Latin music, especially *salsa* and *merengue*. It's also a restaurant serving sandwiches and snacks.

Radisson Aruba Caribbean Resort Casino at the *Radisson Caribbean Resort* on Palm Beach ☎297/586-4045. Casino surrounded by lavish drapery and Caribbean palms. The lounge and sports bar are also popular.

Stellaris Casino at the *Aruba Marriott* on Palm Beach ☎297/586-9000. One of the island's most popular casinos.

Listings

Banks Many banks are located on Caya G.F. Betico Croes, including ABN/AMRO (☎297/582-1515); Aruba Bank (☎297/582-1550); Caribbean Mercantile Bank (☎297/582-3118); and Interbank Aruba (☎297/583-1080). Many ATMs are also found in shopping centres. Opening hours are normally weekdays 8 or 9am–4pm.

Car rental Alamo (☎297/583-3244); Amigo (☎297/586-0502); Bon Bini (☎297/583-4471); Budget (☎297/582-8600); Caribbean (☎297/582-2515); Hertz (☎297/582-1845); Thrifty (☎297/583-5335).

Internet access Cyber Café, Royal Plaza Mall, second floor (Mon–Sat 8.30am–9.30pm & Sun 10am–6pm; US$5 for 1hr); Cyberzone Internet Café, Seaport Marketplace Mall (Mon–Sat 9am–11pm, Sun 2–10pm; US$6 for 1hr).

Laundry Aruba Laundry & Cleaning, Hendrikstraat 30 (☎297/582-3627); Oranjestad Laundry, Arendstraat 107 (☎297/582-1638).

Pharmacies Called *boticas* in Aruba, pharmacies are open Mon–Sat 7.30am–7.30pm. A few good ones are Botica Eagle, near the hospital (☎297/587-6103); Botica del Pueblo, Caya G.F. Betico Croes 48 (☎297/582-2154); and Kibrahacha Botica, across from the SETAR telephone office on Havenstraat (☎297/583-4908).

Post office The main post office is located across from the St Franciscus Church (Mon–Fri 7.30am–noon & 1–4.30pm). A small postal outlet is also located on the ground floor of the Royal Plaza Mall (Mon–Fri 8am–3.30pm).

22.2

Bonaire

Regarded as one of the world's premier sites for shore diving, the tiny boomerang-shaped island of **BONAIRE**, located 80km north of Venezuela, has much to offer those seeking an active tropical holiday. Beneath the clear blue waters, divers and snorkellers are treated to a stunning spectacle: schools of fish of every imaginable shape, size and colour swim with sea turtles and other marine creatures in and around the delicate coral and sponge gardens. All this and more can be found in the waters of the **Bonaire Marine Park**, which surrounds the entire island and its neighbouring offshore cay, the uninhabited **Klein Bonaire**.

As rugged and barren as the land may seem, the island has a different character to it depending on where you are. In the hilly north, the cactus-strewn landscape of **Washington-Slagbaai National Park** preserves remnants of the island's history along with a host of local flora and fauna. To the south, the land opens up and becomes flatter, and vast multicoloured **saltpans** attract the largest colony of **pink flamingos** in the Caribbean. If you're after more adventure, there's windsurfing at **Lac Cai**, on the island's east coast, and kayaking in the nearby mangrove swamps.

Outside of its natural attractions, Bonaire's appeal is low-key. In the evening you can enjoy the sunset while dining in one of the many restaurants found in **Kralendijk**, the island's tidy capital, also home to a few cultural attractions and numerous shops.

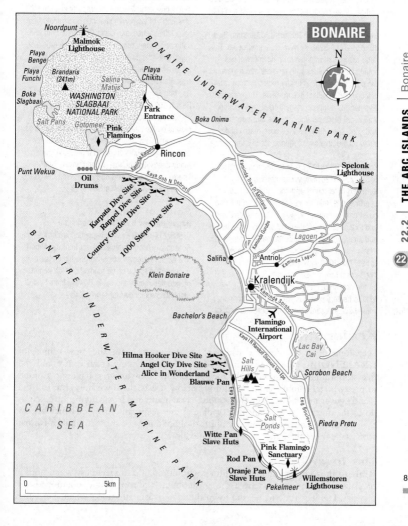

Accommodation

The largest concentration of Bonaire's **hotels** and **dive resorts** is along the coast just north and south of downtown Kralendijk. Most dive resorts will have a dive centre on the premises and many will have a house **reef** just offshore.

Kralendijk

Caribbean Court J.A. Abraham Blvd ☎599/717-5353, ⊛www.caribbeancourt.com. Located close to the airport and only five minutes from the beach, this hotel is built in the style of the charming houses that line the canals of Amsterdam; a small canal provides access to the oceanfront, perfect for those arriving by sailboat. Rooms are spacious with fully equipped kitchenettes, a/c and cable TV, and the small restaurant serves breakfast and light lunches. **❼**

Divi Flamingo Beach Resort J.A. Abraham Blvd 40 ☎599/717-8285, ⊛www.divibonaire.com. This large resort, just minutes from downtown, has small standard rooms with terraces and a view of the pool, and spacious luxury rooms with private balcony and excellent ocean views. There's also a dive centre, tennis court, mini-mart, spa, casino, waterfront restaurant/bar, on-site tour operator and good snorkelling on the house reef. A slide show on the diversity of marine life is shown once a week. **❻**

Eden Beach Kaya Gobernador Nicolaas Debrot ☎599/717-6720, ⊛www.edenbeach.com. Standard hotel rooms and one- and two-bed apartments at this friendly little place on the north coast east of Kralendijk, with an on-site dive shop and lounge chairs scattered along the small beach and around the excellent beach bar/restaurant. **❺**

Plaza Resort Bonaire J.A. Abraham Blvd 80 ☎599/717-2500, ⊛www.plazaresortbonaire.com. The largest luxury resort on the island, located on the only stretch of beach downtown. Rooms tend to be very spacious with huge bathrooms; some have a decent view of the ocean. Excellent restaurants, a lively beachside bar, fitness centre, spa, pool, casino and dive centre are all on site. There's also decent snorkelling offshore, and gear (US$11/day) is available for rent to both guests and non-guests. **❼**

North of Kralendijk

Buddy Beach and Dive Resort Kaya Gobenador Nicolaas Debrot 85 ☎599/717-5080, ⊛www.buddydive.com. Oceanfront property just ten minutes north of town with spacious apartments that have kitchenettes, a/c, cable TV, private bath and patio or balcony; request an ocean view (upstairs, building #4). Popular dive-and-drive packages are available, and there's also a pool and decent restaurant/bar on site. **❺**

Captain Don's Habitat Kaya Gobernador Nicolaas Debrot 103 ☎599/717-8290, ⊛www.habitatdiveresorts.com. One of the first dive resorts on the island, this laid-back place remains a favourite with divers. Simple but comfortable cottage-style rooms surround a pool and garden; many have kitchenettes, a/c and private bath. There's a fully equipped dive centre and the gorgeous house reef is just offshore. **❻**

South of Kralendijk

Happy Holiday Homes Punt Vierkant 9 ☎599/717-8405, ⊛www.happyholidayhomes.com. Reasonably priced bungalows south of the airport in a quiet residential neighbourhood, minutes from popular dive spots. Large rooms have kitchenettes, private bathrooms and cable TV. Very friendly staff; highly recommended for families. **❸**

Kralendijk

Set alongside a picturesque harbour on the west coast, the tiny capital of **KRALENDIJK** ("coral dike" in Dutch) is Bonaire's commercial centre and the first stop for anyone visiting the island. Marked by a few low-rise buildings painted in pretty pastel colours and a handful of narrow streets, the town holds most of the island's government buildings, shops, hotels, restaurants and bars. There's not much to do or see in town other than shop or dine at the restaurants, many of which are on the waterfront. The town's couple of historical buildings and small cultural **museum** won't take more than an hour or two to explore.

The Town

Kralendijk is a quiet and pleasant little town, although it can feel busy when hordes of cruise ship passengers crowd the small streets and zip around on mopeds or bicycles. The best time to see the town therefore is late afternoon when the cruise ships have departed. Due to the many one-way streets the town is easiest to explore on **foot**, and you won't need a map to see the few attractions, many of which are found close to the coast on the main roads of Kaya Charles E.B. Helimund and Kaya Grandi.

Perhaps the best way to get your bearings is to follow the colourful **waterfront** thoroughfare known as Kaya Jan N.E Craane, which merges with Kaya Charles E.B. Helimund toward the south end of town. Along this route you'll find several government buildings, shops, restaurants and bars, as well as the occasional Dutch Caribbean-style building painted yellow and gold. Benches and a few palm trees en route make this stretch a popular place to take in the tropical surroundings or catch the sunset.

On the north end of the route, **Karel's Pier** is home to a favourite watering hole for locals and tourists, as well as Pirate Cruises and Seacow Watertaxi. Across the way, you can also browse through the shops, boutiques and restaurants of the **Harbourside Mall**.

Further south and closer to the centre of Kralendijk is the Town Pier, often referred to as the **North Pier**; it's a superb spot for night diving. Its underwater pillars are encrusted with sponges, corals and other sea creatures, all of which come to life after sundown. The pier can be extremely busy at times with heavy cruise ship and boat traffic, and you must obtain permission from the harbourmaster if you wish to dive here. The harbourmaster's office is located in Fort Oranje, a few metres to the south and across from the smaller Ro-Ro Pier.

Next door to the North Pier is a small open-air **market** where vendors peddle fresh produce and fish from Venezuela. Several souvenir stands selling locally made wooden handicrafts and artwork are usually set up inland across the avenue in **Wilhelminaplein**, a courtyard near the Protestant church. Here you'll find a monument honouring Eleanor Roosevelt's 1944 visit to American troops stationed on the island, as well as the **Van Walbeck Monument**, commemorating the landing in 1634 of the director of the Dutch West India Company.

At the southern end of the route sits the **South Pier**, which receives a fair amount of marine traffic. On the way you'll pass small, mustard-coloured **Fort Oranje** with its four cannons and stone lighthouse. The fort was built by the Dutch in 1817 to protect the island's flourishing salt industry, and has since served as a prison and a storage depot. Today, the fort is home to the city hall and a few government offices. There's really not much to see inside the buildings, and most people are content with taking a few snapshots and moving on.

Running parallel to the waterfront a block inland from Kaya Jan N.E. Craane is another main road, the short stretch of **Kaya Grandi**, where you'll find the **tourist information centre** and many of the island's shops, boutiques and restaurants.

The town's only other noteworthy sight is a ten-minute walk east of town. The quaint **Bonaire Museum**, Kaya J. van de Ree 7 (Mon–Fri 8am–noon & 1–5pm; US$1.50, children US$1), is worth a visit for its tiny but interesting collection of old photographs, artefacts and exhibits of folkloric costumes.

South of Kralendijk

You could easily spend a half-day exploring this flat and somewhat bleak part of the island, longer if you want to dive or snorkel the many sites found offshore. From Kralendijk head south along Boulevard L.A. Abraham for 5km until you reach the airport, where the coastal road Eeg Boulevard begins a 32km loop around the island's southern end, taking in numerous dive sites, glistening mountains of salt, slave huts dating back to Bonaire's darker days and a flamingo sanctuary hidden among the saltpans. Facilities are very limited in the area, so be sure to bring plenty of water and something to eat.

Shortly beyond the airport you'll see several dive and snorkelling sites just a stone's throw from the narrow beaches of washed-up coral; the most popular are the **shipwreck** at Hilma Hooker and the double **reef** at Angel City and Alice in Wonderland. Simply park your car near the site and swim the short distance to the site. Watch out too for the pink **Dive Bus**, which sells refreshments and has locker space for valuables. Stopping at different dive locations on this road, the bus has become a meeting place of sorts for divers. More importantly it serves as an emergency centre if divers run into trouble – it has a first aid kit and a mobile phone to call for medical help.

The road continues southwards alongside numerous dive sites as well as the expansive pink and turquoise **saltpans** belonging to Cargill Salt – one of the largest businesses on Bonaire. Ocean water pumped into the pools gradually evaporates under the heat of the sun, leaving behind a briny solution from which salt crystals are eventually grown and harvested for export. The cement **obelisks** that remain standing today at Blauwe Pan and Rod Pan were used until 1863 as flagpoles signalling to trade boats that the salt was ready for export.

At Whitte Pan and 2km further south near Oranje Pan, you'll find clusters of small white and reddish-brown former **slave huts** atop a bluff overlooking the exposed coastline. Built in 1850, these tiny cement buildings housed slaves from the nearby salt fields, each building just waist high with a steep roof and a tiny opening for a door and window. If you look carefully in the salt fields you can still see the trails once used by these slaves.

As the road winds its way to the southern tip keep your eyes peeled for the pink haze over the salt fields in the far distance. With binoculars it's possible to distinguish this haze as the thousands of **pink flamingos** that inhabit Pekelmeer Sanctuary, the largest breeding ground of flamingos in the western hemisphere. These tall, graceful birds are shy by nature and easily disturbed by noise; to protect them the government has declared the entire area off limits – even the airspace overhead is closed to all air traffic. Each night many of these birds make their way to Venezuela and return to feed at dawn. Across from Pekelmeer stands the battered remains of the **Willemstoren Lighthouse**, the first lighthouse built on the island in 1837.

From the lighthouse the road turns north and follows a more rugged coastline, passing **Piedra Pretu** (black stone), worth a brief stop for a wander among the large chunks of sun-bleached coral and piles of twisted driftwood, and to experience first-hand the awesome force of the waves that have shaped this side of the island.

At the north end of the road, just before it turns back towards Kralendijk, is **Lac Bay**, a shallow stretch of water on the east coast with the best **windsurfing** and **kayaking** conditions on the island. Shortly after *Sorobon Beach Resort* (clothing optional), you'll come upon a couple of locally run businesses renting boards and kayaks and offering windsurfing lessons, the most popular of which is Jibe City (daily 9am–5pm, closed Sept; ☏599/717-5233), whose lively snack bar is a hangout for surfers. You can also rent kayaks (from US$35/day) and windsurfing boards (US$60/day) and take windsurfing lessons (US$45 for beginners and advanced; board included for beginners only). The bay's sheltered waters and steady trade winds draw surfers of all levels and ages, and each October serve as the site of Bonaire's international windsurfing regatta.

Beyond Lac Bay the road heads inland for 500m before splitting into two roads. The left fork, Kaya I.R. Randolf Statuuis Van Eps, will take you to the hotels close to the airport, while the right, Kaminda Sorobon, leads back to downtown Kralendijk. Both roads pass through desert terrain littered with cacti and scrubby vegetation; watch out for the roaming wild donkeys and goats.

If you take Kaminda Sorobon, follow the signs to the dirt road leading east to **Cai**, a small point on the northern tip of Lac Bay. Every Sunday afternoon the place comes to life as scores of locals and surfers gather to listen to live music, dance, drink beer and eat local food. *Lac Suid*, a small restaurant at the end of the road, is also a good place for a meal. You can stop for snacks en route to the bay at *Maiky*, which is signposted off Kaminda Sorobon. This area is also the starting point for **kayaking** trips to nearby mangrove swamps (Bonaire Boating organizes tours; see box p.881).

△ Longsnout seahorse, Bonaire Marine Park

Rincon and Washington-Slagbaai National Park

Bonaire's oldest settlement, **RINCON**, is nestled in a valley northwest of Kralendijk – a cluster of red-roofed houses, a petrol station and one phone booth shared by all of its residents. Originally established as a Spanish settlement in the sixteenth century, Rincon eventually became home to many slave families who laboured in the nearby plantations and salt fields of the southern peninsula. The town is best visited during the annual **Rincon Day festival** (April 30), when visitors from all over the Caribbean come here for traditional music and dancing, as well as local food such as goat stew served with *funchi* (cornmeal). During the rest of the year Rincon is worth seeking out for its laid-back atmosphere and rural setting; before leaving be sure to stop at popular *Prisca's Ice Cream* on Kaya Komkomber for a taste of her famous concoctions.

Washington-Slagbaai National Park

From Rincon follow the main road northwest for 3.5km to **Washington-Slagbaai National Park** (8am–5pm, no entrance after 2.45pm; US$10), which occupies most of the island's northwestern tip. The land, which once belonged to two plantation owners who produced and exported vast quantities of aloe, goat meat and charcoal, is now a protected reserve for fascinating flora and fauna, including the towering cacti (known locally as *kadushi*, a staple of soups), pink flamingos and numerous species of parrot, bats, iguanas and lizards. Other highlights include salt ponds, rocky coves, plantation houses, snorkelling spots and **Brandaris Hill**, the highest point on the island at 241m.

Once past the gate you can choose to drive along two routes that will take you through the park: the shorter 24km **green route** (2hr), traversing the hilly interior, or the longer 40km **yellow route** (4hr), which winds around the coast before venturing inland and joining up with the green route. Stick to the coloured trail markers and follow the map, keeping in mind that once you start your journey you cannot backtrack – all roads lead in one direction. Feel free to venture out of your car to explore the landscape at any of the stops marked on the map.

Both routes start by taking you past the saltpans of **Salina Matijs**, which can be dry for most of the year, though between December and March hundreds of flamingos arrive here as soon as the saltpan fills with rainwater. From here the road forks into the separate coloured routes. Taking the yellow route will bring you to **Playa Chikitu**, a popular sunbathing spot with a few umbrellas on the beach, though swimming is not advisable because of the strong outgoing current. Continuing along this route, you'll pass many rugged coves (*bokas*) and stunning vistas of the park; the green route, meanwhile, cuts west across the park, skipping the park's northern reaches.

At Brandaris Hill the yellow route joins the green route, and nearby you'll find decent snorkelling at playas Funchi and Bengé. The best place for swimming, however, is at **Boka Slagbaai**, 1.5km south of Playa Funchi. From there both routes make their way inland; the yellow route offers the option of seeing more flamingos at the larger saltpan of Gotomeer before joining the green route for the final stretch back to the park entrance.

It is worth bearing in mind that you can also get to see Gotomeer without having to enter the park; simply follow the coast road as far west as you can go (dodging the hordes of bright green lizards that zip across the road), then cut north past the eastern side of the park, and you should see a flock of flamingos at the lake. Continuing along the road brings you around to Rincon.

Park practicalities

To navigate the park's bumpy and narrow dirt roads, a rugged **4WD** vehicle is necessary, especially after a rainstorm; mountain bikes, scooters and camping are all strictly

Dive centres and tour operators

There's no shortage of **dive centres** on Bonaire, many of them located in hotels or resorts. All offer rentals and equipment repair and can organize boat tours to many of the dive sites, including those on Klein Bonaire. Expect to pay around US$15–20 for a shore dive, US$25–30 for a one-tank boat tour and around US$300–350 for a five-day underwater certification course, plus equipment rentals (US$8/day for regulators; US$10/day for snorkel, fin and mask; and US$12/day for tanks, including weights). Your best bet is to arrange a package deal with a resort, which usually covers accommodation, equipment rental and a specified number of dives. The following dive centres are recommended: *Buddy Beach and Dive Resort*, north of Kralendijk, offers an eight-day drive-and-dive package for US$984–1119 (based on two sharing), including accommodation, a rental vehicle and unlimited air fills for shore diving, plus six boat dives. Also north of Kralendijk is *Captain Don's*, which has a range of underwater certification and photography courses taught by highly qualified instructors. For **underwater camera** rentals (US$25–45/day), visit Photo Tours Divers, *Caribbean Court*, J.A. Abraham Blvd (☏599/777-3460, ⊛www.bonphototours.com). Diving packages and instruction are also available here, as are inexpensive and unlimited air fills (US$77/week).

Bonaire also has many **tour operators** offering a range of land- and water-based activities; most will pick you up and deliver you back to your hotel. Look in the free tourist newspapers for details (they're in most hotels) and call ahead for reservations, especially when there's a cruise ship in town. Two worth trying are Pirate Cruises on Karel's Pier in Kralendijk (☏599/790-8330), which offers guided snorkelling trips to Klein Bonaire for US$25, departing daily at 9.30am and 1.30pm; and Bonaire Boating, based at *Divi Flamingo Beach Resort* (☏599/790-5353). The latter offers diving, snorkelling and sailing trips, in addition to activities like kayaking in the mangroves at Lac Bay (daily 9am; $40 for 3hr) and touring Washington-Slagbaai National Park (Tues & Fri 9am; US$65 for 6hr, including lunch).

forbidden inside the park. The alternative is taking a **tour** led by Bonaire Boating, highly recommended for its coverage of the park's natural and cultural history (see box above).

Before venturing in, stock up on refreshments and snacks at the small **plantation house** where you pay your fee, as there are no facilities past the park gate. You can also view a small collection of Arawak artefacts and tools at the nearby **museum**. Proper footwear and a pair of binoculars are recommended if you plan to leave your car for a bit of hiking.

Bonaire Marine Park and Klein Bonaire

Bonaire's pristine coral reefs and abundant marine life have been protected from development since 1979, when the government established the **Bonaire Marine Park** (⊛www.bmp.org) as a means of regulating diving and its impact on the marine environment. Comprising the entire coastline of the island – and that of the neighbouring uninhabited cay of **Klein Bonaire** – from the high-water mark down to 60m, the park is widely recognized as a model of marine conservation.

Bonaire has 86 **dive and snorkel sites**, the majority of which are on the leeward side of the island. All sites are marked with yellow stone markers or a buoy and come with colourful names such as Country Garden, Forest, Yellow Man's Reef, Ol' Blue and Bloodlet. **Boats** are not permitted to drop anchor and must instead use the mooring site. The majority of sites can be reached directly from shore, while Klein Bonaire is accessible only by boat (many operators schedule charter trips to the island; see box above). Popular dive and snorkelling spots include 1000 Steps, Karpata, Rappel, Pink Beach, the aforementioned Country Garden and, on Klein Bonaire, No Name. Most sites harbour magnificent stands of elkhorn and brain coral as well as sponges surrounded by an array of tropical fish and marine invertebrates. Many resorts have an on-site house reef and offer a variety of underwater certification and photography courses. A **map** available on the island (including from the tourist office) describes which of the marked sites are for divers and which for snorkellers. Bear in mind that most of the entry points to the sea are rather rocky (the pretty site at 1000 Steps is a notable exception), so it helps to have good footwear.

The shallow and clear waters provide excellent visibility for **snorkelling**, and though a major storm in 1999 damaged many beaches and shallow-water corals, signs of recovery are visible; snorkellers can still enjoy schools of parrotfish, trumpet fish, barracuda, moray eels and angel fish swimming around the sponges and numerous species of soft and hard coral.

Park practicalities

Rangers patrol the 6400-acre park to enforce the strict rules that govern the use of this facility. Divers and snorkellers will be asked to show their **Marine Park Tag** (US$10, valid for one calendar year), available from island dive operators or from the Marine Park's office at Barcardera. They'll also need to attend a warm-up dive session with a qualified instructor, which can be arranged through any dive centre. Diving gloves and kneepads are not permitted, nor is disturbing or removing any coral, fish or marine invertebrate, whether dead or alive.

Eating, drinking and nightlife

Surprisingly, for its small size there are plenty of good **eating opportunities** in and around Kralendijk, many of them within walking distance of downtown. It's possible to sample a variety of cuisines, among them Italian, Indonesian, Dutch and local fare. While **hotel restaurants** are generally more expensive than dining in town, Kralendijk also has a couple of grocery stores and bakeries offering a wide selection of fresh produce and imported goods. The many **snack stands** scattered throughout the island are the best place to try delicious local favourites, including goat, fish or conch stews. Most meals cost under US$8.

While Bonaire is not known for its **nightlife**, there are a few fun spots where you can unwind at the end of the day, and many of the **bars** at hotels and resorts have **live music** at weekends; check *Bonaire Update*, a free bimonthly publication, for upcoming events and activities.

Kralendijk

Capriccio Kaya Isla Riba 1 ☎599/717-7230. Classy Italian place, serving pizzas (US$10–17), pasta dishes (US$15–25) and mains like duck breast in a red wine sauce or fresh catch of the day (US$20–25). The wine list is superb. Closed Sun.

City Cafe Kaya Grandi 7 ☎599/717-8286. A great place to grab a light snack and have a pint or two as the sun goes down. Happy hour 5.30–6.30pm; live bands at weekends.

Cozzoli's Pizzeria Harbourside Mall ☎599/717-5195. Open all day, serving bacon and eggs for breakfast as well as some fruit plates. For lunch and dinner they offer a variety of tasty pizzas and grill items starting at NAf$20. The outdoor covered terrace has harbour views.

Karel's Beach Bar on a small pier across from Harbourside Mall. A favourite watering hole for locals and tourists alike, and a great place to start a tour of the town, with good views of the busy

harbour. Happy hour 5.30–8pm. Local bands play at weekends.

Mona Lisa Bar and Restaurant Kaya Grandi 15 ☎599/717-8718. Located on the main street in town, this cosy Dutch-owned establishment serves scrumptious seafood and smoked chicken dishes. Expect to pay NAf$35 for the catch of the day. Mon–Fri: restaurant 6–10pm, bar 4pm–2am.

Imperial Harbourside Mall. Good Japanese restaurant opposite *Karel's Beach Bar*, offering fresh sushi and sashimi (US$21 for a large combo platter) as well as teppanyaki.

North of Kralendijk

Bongos Beach at the *Eden Beach Resort* on Kaya Gobernador Nicolaas Debrot 73 ☎599/717-7238. Popular beachside hangout offering tasty snacks and speciality drinks. Especially lively on Friday nights. Happy hour 5.30–6.30pm.

Giby's Terrace Kaya Andres A. Emerenciana ☎599/567-0655. Just minutes from downtown,

Giby's is a well-known snack stand serving delicious conch and goat stews. Enjoy your meal outside on the small terrace or take it back to your hotel. Closed Tues.

It Rains Fishes Kaya Jan N.E. Craane 24 ☎599/717-8780. This popular, friendly restaurant on a covered outdoor terrace facing the water offers delicious and affordable local seafood dishes for NAf$27.50. Also available are chicken, beef tenderloin and a selection of salads. Dinner only, closed Sun.

Rendez-Vous Kaya L.D. Gerharts 3 ☎599/717-8454. One of Bonaire's oldest restaurants, with pictures of famous diners adorning its walls.

Delicious home-made meals include mixed catch of the day and shrimp in a tropical sauce; lamb and beef dishes are also available. Entrees about NAf$25. Dinner only, closed Sat & Sun.

East of Kralendijk

Lac Suid Lac Bay. A small restaurant right on the coast, with an open-air dance patio, that serves a wonderful conch meal for less than US$10. Sun 11am–8pm.

Maiky ☎599/565-3804. Snack stand offering traditional Bonairean food; try the huge portions of chicken or goat served with rice or *funchi* (cornmeal). Daily 11am–3pm, closed Thurs.

Listings

Banks Banco di Caribe, Kaya Grandi 22 (☎599/717-8295); Maduro & Curiel's Bank, Kaya L.D. Gerharts 1 (☎599/717-5520).

Bicycle rental Cycle Bonaire, Kaya L.D. Gerharts 11D (☎599/717-7558), and De Freewieler, Kaya Grandi 61 (☎599/717- 8545). Both rent mountain and touring bikes for about US$10–20 per day.

Bookshops Bonaire Boekhandel, Kaya Grandi 50 (☎599/717-8499), has a small selection of paperback books, maps and stationery supplies.

Car and scooter rental AB Car Rental, located at the airport (☎599/717-8980, ℮info@abcarrental.com).

Internet access De Tuin Eetcafé, Kaya L.D. Gerharts 9 (Mon–Fri 11am–midnight, Sat &

Sun 2pm–midnight), and Bonaire Access, in the Harbourside Mall on Kaya L.D. Gerharts 10 (Mon–Fri 9am–noon & 1.30–6pm, Sat 9am–noon & 2–5pm), offer access for around US$4 for 30min.

Pharmacies Botica Bonaire, Kaya Grandi 27 (☎599/717-8905).

Post office Bonaire's main post office is located on Kaya Simón Bolívar near the tourist information office (Mon–Thurs 7.30am–noon & 1.30–5pm, Fri 7.30am–noon & 1.30–4.30pm).

Supermarkets Cultimara Supermarket, close to De Tuin Eetcafé, Kaya L.D. Gerharts 13 (☎599/717-8278), has a large selection of fresh produce, meat and other grocery items.

22.3

Curaçao

C URAÇAO (population 130,000), the largest of the ABC islands, and the administrative centre of the Netherlands Antilles, remains relatively unknown outside of the Netherlands and the Caribbean. Originally discovered by the Spaniards in 1499 and taken over by the Dutch in 1634, Curaçao has been slower to develop the kind of tourist industry its neighbours are known

Curaçao dive centres

Though nowhere near as renowned as Bonaire, Curaçao is home to some decent **diving** and **snorkelling**. There are several reputable dive centres on the island, most of them offering a variety of services including open-water dive courses, equipment rental and charter boat services. The following are highly recommended: *Habitat Curaçao Resort*, north of Willemstad, offers a wide selection of courses, underwater camera rental, offshore diving and chartered boat dives to surrounding reefs; the friendly Dutch owners of Scuba Do, at Jan Thiel Beach (℡5999/767-9300), who have unlimited air fills and weights at US$85, numerous underwater courses beginning at US$200 and charters to Klein Curaçao for US$55; and the modern PADI five-star Seascapes Dive and Watersports Centre (℡5999/462-5905) on a private beach at the *Sheraton Curaçao*, who offer equipment rental and storage, a host of courses and an introduction to snorkelling/diving programme for kids.

for, though its capital city – and recently designated UNESCO World Heritage Site – **Willemstad**, rivals any in the Caribbean for picturesque charm. The island also offers decent diving and swimming possibilities, especially on the leeward side, with its secluded coves. More active pursuits can be had in the rugged and hilly interior: **Christoffel National Park**, in the north, is overgrown with towering cacti, scrubby vegetation and gnarled divi divi trees, well worthy of a hike around it. Besides such flora, island inhabitants include goats, bats, lizards, iguanas and countless species of colourful birds. The various **plantation houses** that dot the island are remnants from Curaçao's history as the Caribbean's busiest slave depot in the seventeenth century; the trade was finally abolished here in 1863.

Accommodation

You'll have no problem finding a **place to stay** in Curaçao. The largest concentration of **hotels** and **dive resorts** is within fifteen minutes of downtown Willemstad, many of them to the south along the coast. The larger hotel chains are a five-minute drive northwest of the capital on the coast near Piscadera Bay. There are some budget-style options to be found in Willemstad's **Punda** and **Otrobanda** districts.

Willemstad

Estoril Hotel Breedestraat 181, Otrobanda ℡5999/462-5244, ℮edgar@banderaportuguesa. com. Set on the main street in Otrobanda, this hotel offers twenty basic but clean rooms with private bathrooms, public telephone and a/c. ❷

Hotel Mira Punda Van de Brandhofstraat 12, Scharloo ℡5999/461-3995, ℮joserosales@cura. net. Good location, next to the Maritime Museum and the ferry to Bonaire. Ten simple rooms with fans, some with shared bath. Look for a green building; entrance is on the east-side gate. ❶

Hotel Otrobanda next to the cruise terminal on Breedestraat, Otrobanda ℡5999/462-7400, ℗www.otrobandahotel.com. Located in the heart of Willemstad, the *Otrobanda*'s rooms are cramped but afford terrific views of the city; price includes breakfast and the use of the pool. There's also a lively casino on the premises. ❺

Kura Hulanda Langestraat 8, Otrobanda ℡5999/434-7700, ℗www.kurahulanda.com. Fabulous 80-room hotel, near the Queen Emma

Bridge. The restored architecture is a mix of eighteenth- and nineteenth-century styles, and the rooms are luxurious and welcoming. Four great restaurants on site. ❾

Pelikaan Hotel and Casino Langestraat 78, Otrobanda ℡5999/462-3555, ℗www.hotelpelikaan. com. Popular with budget travellers; small and simple rooms with a/c and televisions, and a casino on site. ❷

Pietersz Guesthouse and Apartments Roodeweg 1, Otrobanda ℡5999/462-5222, ℮germain@interneeds.net. A few metres from the *Estoril*, this is one of the top budget places to stay, its twelve pleasant rooms coming with fully furnished kitchenettes, TV and private baths. Tucked in below is the *Pietersz Coffeeshop*, serving home-made snacks, cold drinks and ice cream. Recommended. If it's full, a second *Pietersz* guesthouse is just down the street. ❸

San Marco Hotel Columbusstraat 7, Punda ℡5999/461-2988, ℗www.sanmarcocuracao.com. Located in the heart of Punda atop a casino, the

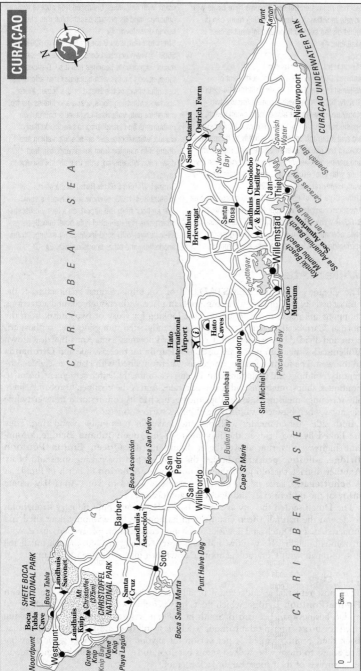

CURAÇAO

CARIBBEAN SEA

Noordpunt
Westpunt
SHETE BOCA NATIONAL PARK
Boca Tabla
Boca Tabla Cave
Landhuis Savonet
Grote Knip
Knip Bay
Kleine Knip
Playa Lagún
Landhuis Knip
Mt Christoffel (375m)
CHRISTOFFEL NATIONAL PARK
Santa Cruz
Barber
Landhuis Ascención
Soto
Punt Halve Dag
San Willibrordo
Cape St Marie
San Pedro
Boca Ascención
Boca San Pedro
Boca Santa Marta

Sint Michiel
Bullen Bay
Bullenbaai
Julianadorp
Piscadera Bay

Hato International Airport ✈ ⓘ
Hato Caves

Schottegat
Willemstad
Kon̄iki Beach
Mambo Beach
Sea Aquarium Beach
Sea Aquarium
Curaçao Museum

Landhuis Brievengat
Santa Rosa
Landhuis Chobolobo & Rum Distillery
Jan Thiel
"Jan Thiel Bay"
Caracas Bay
Spanish Water
Spanish Bay

St Joris Bay
Santa Catarina
Ostrich Farm

Nieuwpoort
Punt Kanon
CURAÇAO UNDERWATER PARK

N

0   5km

885

22.3 │ **THE ABC ISLANDS** │ Curaçao

22

recently renovated but small rooms here come with private facilities. A relaxing reading room can be found on the second floor, and Internet access is available. ❸

Around the island

Habitat Curaçao 30 minutes' northwest of Willemstad near Rif. St Marie ☎5999/864-8800, ⓦwww.habitatdiveresorts.com. Attractive two-storey apartments set alongside a small beach. Spacious rooms come complete with kitchenettes, a/c and a terrace or balcony – many of them over-looking the ocean. There's also a pool, restaurant and bar on site, as well as a professionally run dive shop with boat excursions to nearby reefs. Friendly staff. Highly recommended. ❻

Lions Dive Hotel south of Willemstad near the Sea Aquarium complex on Bapor Kibra ☎5999/461-8100, ⓦwww.lionsdive.com. Dutch-Caribbean-style accommodation with ocean-facing rooms surrounded by a tropical garden. Clean rooms,

many with balconies. Unlimited free access to Sea Aquarium and its private beach, plus free shuttle bus to downtown. ❾

Sheraton Curaçao Resort JFK Blvd ☎5999/462-5000, ⓦwww.ccresort.com. This deluxe beachfront resort with private beaches has it all. Besides the spacious rooms with balconies that afford beautiful views of the island or the ocean, there are two swimming pools, a spa and fitness centre, miniature golf, volleyball and tennis courts, two restaurants and snack bars, a beachside bar, casino, watersports and on-site snorkelling and diving. Ten minutes from the airport, five from downtown Willemstad, with free shuttle service to town. ❽

Sunset Waters Beach Hotel Santa Marta Bay ☎5999/864-1233, ⓦwww.sunsetwaters.com. Half an hour from the airport, on a lovely crescent beach, this is a delightful little hotel (mostly all-Inclusive) with good facilities for sailing, diving, snorkelling and other sports on-site. ❼–❽

Willemstad

The vibrant city of **WILLEMSTAD**, full of colourful colonial architecture, is the hub of activity in Curaçao. It's a cosmopolitan place, with enough cultural attractions, shopping and places to eat to satisfy those looking for a day or two's break from the normal Caribbean beach vacation. Magnificently sited alongside the southeastern coast and divided by a narrow, but deep, channel known as Santa Anna Bay, downtown Willemstad is split into two main districts – **Punda** on the east side and **Otrobanda** to the west. The former, with its gorgeous waterfront lined with elaborate eighteenth-century buildings and gingerbread mansions, is a distinctly Dutch settlement, home to boutiques, shops, museums and street-side cafes. Across the channel, Otrobanda, liter-ally meaning "the other side" in Papiamentu, has had its core restored to its erstwhile elegance, when business was thriving along its narrow streets.

Both sides are eminently walkable, and make for memorable wandering. They are linked by two bridges: the fifty-metre-high **Queen Juliana Bridge**, a four-lane highway towering above the harbour, and the **Queen Emma Pontoon Bridge**, a floating pedestrian bridge that swings open for passing ships and boats. Another district, the old Jewish neighbourhood of **Scharloo**, is north of Punda, as is **Schottegat**, a large inland body of water connected to Santa Anna Bay, where many of the oil refineries and dockyards are located.

The Dutch settled the city as a naval base in 1643, and built military strongholds to defend the naturally deep channel and harbour. As the economy flourished and attracted many Dutch and Jewish merchants, construction proceeded apace, with mansions built for the wealthy and new districts being created, though much fell into disrepair with Curaçao's economic downturn in the nineteenth century.

The City

The most remarkable and central of all landmarks in Willemstad is the **Queen Emma Pontoon Bridge**, which floats between the two central districts. Designed by US businessman Leonard B. Smith in 1888, it was designed to be able to swing open for boats entering the harbour – which it still does around thirty times a day. Back then, Smith charged 2¢ per person for anyone wearing shoes while allowing free access to those who walked across barefoot; today crossing the bridge is free to all regardless of their footwear, or lack thereof.

Across the pontoon bridge to the east, the scenic waterfront along the bustling street of **Handelskade** in Punda is the most photographed spot in all of Curaçao. Lined with centuries-old pastel-coloured buildings and a string of cafés, this is the best place in the city to start a walking tour. Many of the buildings found along here have been renovated into government offices, banks, shops and restaurants (the red tiles seen on the roofs of these buildings originally came from Europe as ships' ballast). One of the best examples of traditional architecture is right across from the pontoon bridge at the multilevel **Penha & Sons**, a canary-yellow shop decorated with elaborate white gables, built in 1708. Close at hand is Punda's main **shopping district**, bounded by Handelskade, Madurostraat and Breedestraat.

Just south of the busy main street of Breedestraat is the large **Fort Amsterdam** complex, one of the first military strongholds; it was built in 1635 by the Dutch West Indies Company. Today, the restored fort seats the government of the Netherlands Antilles and other government offices. If you look closely you can still see a British cannonball embedded in one of its walls (the result of a brief skirmish between the Dutch and British in the early 1800s). Around the corner is the renovated Protestant **Fort Church**, the oldest church in Curaçao (built in 1769).

The remains of the island's original fort, **Waterfort**, are located near the mouth of Santa Anna Bay, a block south of Fort Amsterdam. Built in 1634 and renovated two hundred years later, this fort was used by the US army as a military base during World War II (a steel net was dragged across the mouth of the bay to prevent German submarines from entering the deep harbour). A series of stone **waterfront arches**, once used to store gunpowder, are located east of the fort along the waterfront and today house a string of seaside restaurants.

Situated in the heart of Punda, the **Mikvé Israel-Emanuel Synagogue**, on Hanchi Snoa at Columbusstraat (Mon–Fri 9am–4.30pm; US$5), is one of the Caribbean's most important landmarks and possibly the oldest synagogue still in use in the western hemisphere. Members of the original Jewish community who came here from Europe dedicated the synagogue in 1732. The white sand sprinkled on the floor is said to honour Moses' leading of his people through the desert. Tucked inside is the **Jewish Cultural Museum** where you can view an impressive array of Torah scrolls, Hanukah lamps and other religious artefacts.

In the northern corner of Punda, it's worth a visit to the very colourful **floating market**, which lines the canal beside Sha Carpileskade. Every morning small wooden boats loaded with fish, fresh tropical fruits and vegetables make their way from Venezuela to sell their produce in Willemstad; they typically leave by noon. A few other sights exist nearby, including the popular **Marshe Bieu** (old market) behind the post office, where you can sample inexpensive local cuisine off open charcoal grills.

Directly across the water from the market, in the former Jewish district of Scharloo, you'll find the **Maritime Museum** (Mon–Sat 9am–4pm; US$5.50), which pays homage to Curaçao's rich seafaring history. Ship models, maps and coins from sunken treasures are on display.

Across the channel and west of the pontoon bridge, Otrobanda has a couple of attractions worth looking into. Right beside the bridge is the main square, **Brionplein**, where a statue of Pedro Brion holds sway. Brion is one of the island's most famous men, born in 1782 and a right hand man to Simón Bolívar as they fought for the independence of South American countries from the Spanish.

Otrabanda's main street, **Breedestraat** (not to be confused with the street of the same name in Punda) runs perpendicular from the channel and is chock-full of small shops selling bargain clothing and souvenirs. Be sure to visit the magnificent **Kura Hulanda Museum**, just off Breedestraat to the north on Klipstraat 9 (Mon–Sun 10am–5pm; US$6), built in a restored nineteenth-century mansion. The museum boasts a splendid selection of original art and artefacts from all over Africa, as well as a superb collection of gold pre-Columbian figures from South America. Several permanent exhibits, including one on the slave trade and one on human evolution, are

22

also among the museum's highlights. Across town on the western outskirts of Otrobanda, the smaller **Curaçao Museum**, V. Leeuwenhoekstraat (Mon–Fri 9am–noon & 2–5pm, Sun 10am–4pm; US$3), is home to a scant collection of traditional and contemporary local art and artefacts.

South of Willemstad

One of the more popular attractions outside of Willemstad is the **Sea Aquarium** (daily 8.30am–5.30pm; US$15, children 5–12 US$7.50; ☎5999/461-6666, ⊛www.curacao-sea-aquarium.com), a twenty-minute drive south of the capital. Touch tanks, aquariums, an underwater shark-feeding observatory and a 3D movie theatre all provide a good preface to perhaps getting underwater yourself: you can swim, snorkel or dive with dolphins or sea lions (from an additional US$64 per person) or offshore at the entrance to the twenty-kilometre **Curaçao Underwater Park**, which is actually a preserve protecting the delicate marine environment.

A short stroll from the Sea Aquarium leads to a rather large stretch of man-made sandy **beach** fringed with palm trees. An entrance fee of US$3.50 will get you into Kontiki and Mambo beaches as well as the nearby Sea Aquarium Beach. All three are safe for swimming and have bars, restaurants, changing room facilities and plenty of parking.

Located 4km east of the Sea Aquarium, another smaller but quieter beach can be found at *Zanzibar Beach Resort* on **Jan Thiel Bay** (US$3); this also offers snorkelling, diving and swimming possibilities. Beach chairs and mountain bikes are available for rent (US$20/day).

Many **watersports** activities, including jet-skiing, kayaking and windsurfing, are offered at nearby **Caracas Bay Island**, a recreation park near the town of Jan Thiel (☎5999/747-0666 or 567-6654).

East of Willemstad

Free tours and liqueur sampling are available at the **Senior & Company Liqueur Distillery** (Mon–Fri 8am–noon & 1–5pm), a few minutes' drive east of Punda at the Landhuis Chobolobo in Saliòa. Known for producing the sweet-tasting **Curaçao Blue**, a liqueur made from the peel of the bitter Valencia orange, this small factory bottles more than 20,000 gallons per week. The plant has been in operation since 1896; pick up any of the four varieties – orange, coffee, chocolate or rum raisin – in the on-site gift shop.

Christoffel National Park and the northern tip

Tucked in the northwest corner of the island is the spectacular **Christoffel National Park**, a 4600-acre wilderness preserve protecting a diverse array of plants and animals. Located 45 minutes from Willemstad and centred around **Mount Christoffel** (375m), the highest point on Curaçao, this former plantation is home to the tiny Curaçao deer as well as numerous species of bats, birds, non-poisonous snakes, iguanas, orchids and cacti. Several well-marked walking and driving routes allow you to explore the rugged and hilly interior at your own pace.

The **main entrance** (Mon–Sat 8am–4pm, Sun 6am–3pm; NAf$25) is located at the mustard-coloured **Savonet** plantation house, on the right-hand side of the main road leading to Westpunt. A local restaurant and small museum can also be found here. From the main gate it's possible to access any of eight well-marked colour-coded **hiking trails**, which vary in difficulty and can take anywhere from twenty minutes to around five hours to complete. The most strenuous is a steep ascent up Mount Christoffel, which rewards with breathtaking views of the entire island, not to mention the numerous delicate orchids visible along the path. It's also possible to drive through the interior on any one of three well-maintained dirt roads. **Trail maps** are available at the main entrance, as is a highly recommended guidebook outlining the trails and history of the park.

Various **tours** of the park are also on offer, including a two-and-a-half-hour one with park rangers from the main gate on Friday mornings at 10am (US$8.50), and horse-riding and mountain-biking tours; call Rancho Alfin (℡5999/864-0535) for details.

Two kilometres north of Christoffel's main gate, the rugged north coast is best viewed from the tiny **Shete Boka National Park** (US$2). A series of walking trails on exposed sharp coral wind their way along the coast to several limestone **grottoes**, including **Boka Tabla**, where you can climb inside and watch the waves come crashing in. Keep an eye out for ancient coral formations and fossils along the path, as well as sea turtles swimming in the rough waters – the park was established as a sanctuary for breeding these animals. Swimming is not advisable here; the currents are far too dangerous.

A few kilometres further north, you can easily give **Westpunt** a miss, though you may want to dine at *Jaanchie's* if you've come up to one of the parks or nearby beaches for the day. Ten minutes south of Westpunt along a winding and hilly coastal road is **Landhuis Knip**, the island's best example of a restored colonial plantation house. Built in the early 1700s and rebuilt in 1830 after a fire, this was one of Curaçao's largest and most prosperous plantations, producing wool, indigo, sorghum, beans and divi divi pods (used in tanning leather). Antique furniture and period pieces decorate the large rooms inside.

Some of the island's best **beaches**, **diving** and **snorkelling sites** are found along this northwest stretch of Curaçao. If you're coming directly from Willemstad (instead of from the park) head north on the main road to Westpunt and turn left on the road to Santa Cruz at the town of San Pedro; otherwise follow the signs from Westpunt or from Landhuis Knip. The most popular spots, both on Knip Bay, are **Grote Knip** with its calm, turquoise-blue waters and beautiful sandy beach nestled in a protected cove, and the smaller **Kleine Knip**, a few kilometres south of Grote Knip. Both beaches offer superb swimming and snorkelling opportunities and are crowded at weekends and holidays; a small snack bar and changing facilities are available at Grote Knip. Watch out for the poisonous manchineel trees growing by the beach.

As you're making your way back to Willemstad stop by **Landhuis Ascension**, the oldest plantation house on the island, dating back to 1672. Some 5km north of the highway intersection to the beaches, this beautifully restored plantation house is used as a recreation centre for the Dutch marines. There's an open house on the first Sunday of every month, with local music, handicrafts and food.

The rest of the island

The rest of the island has some scattered attractions, most along the lines of **plantation houses** (known as *landhuizen*), though many of these are in fact in disrepair. Ones that have been transformed into restaurants or museums include the lovely **Landhuis Brievengat** (Mon–Fri 9.15am–noon & 3–6pm), north of Willemstad close to the coast and east of the airport, which has a wide selection of local crafts on view, as well as occasional live *salsa* music.

Just a half-kilometre south of the airport are the mysterious limestone **Hato Caves** (daily 10am–5pm; US$6.50), where stunning flowstone formations, stalagmites and stalactites grow in humid chambers. These can be viewed, alongside ancient rock drawings, on the 45-minute guided tours that depart every hour on the hour.

Quite the sight to see as well are the eight hundred ostriches penned in at the **Curaçao Ostrich Farm** (Tues–Sun 8am–5pm; US$13; ℡5999/747-2777), situated in the remote eastern corner of the island. Tours (call to be picked up from your hotel) offer the chance to feed these flightless creatures, hold one of the large eggs (equivalent to twenty chicken eggs) and learn a bit about their life cycle.

Eating and drinking

Willemstad

Astrolab Observatory in the *Hotel Kura Hulanda*, Langestraat 8, Otrabanda ☎5999/434-7700. Superb new restaurant, with starters such as lobster salad or crab cakes for US$8–15 and entrees such as home-made duck ravioli or sesame-crusted tuna US$23–36. Daily 7–11pm.

Iguana Cafe on the waterfront at Handelskade (next to Queen Emma Bridge), Punda ☎5999/461-9866. One of the few places in Punda where you can enjoy a light dinner at a reasonable price. The menu includes sandwiches and Dutch specialities, and it's a great place to watch the cruise ships and tankers pass by. Closed Sun.

Il Barile Hanchi Snoa 12, Punda ☎5999/461-3025. Don't let appearances fool you; this small street-side restaurant is the best place in Willemstad for home-made Italian food (mains US$10–15), sandwiches and cappuccinos. Sit outside on the small patio or dine upstairs. Closed Sun.

Jaipur in the *Hotel Kura Hulanda*, Langestraat 8, Otrabanda ☎5999/434-7700. Fine Indian food, with chicken, fish and jumbo shrimp curries US$19–29. Dinner only, closed Sun.

Marshe Bieu on the open-air terrace behind the post office, Punda. A popular lunch spot, this market is a great place to sample local dishes such as deep-fried *kora* (red snapper); Chinese food is also available. Mains US$6. Lunch only, closed Sun.

Plein Cafe Wilhelmina Wilhelmina Park, Punda ☎5999/461-0461. A pleasant downtown setting for a cold beer from an excellent range, and a fresh baguette or "toastie" (toasted cheese). The chicken sate smothered in peanut sauce is also worth trying. Mains around US$10. Closed Sun.

Rasta Hut Columbusstraat 6A, Punda. Located across from the synagogue, a friendly and very reasonably priced place to enjoy wings, chicken and other fast-food dishes while listening to reggae. Mains around US$12.

Time Out Café Keukenplein 8, Punda. Tucked into a small courtyard in the heart of Punda's shopping district, this tiny café offers excellent sandwiches plus the catch of the day, and there are Internet facilities upstairs. Open daily except Sun, closes at 4pm on Sat.

Tu Tu Tango Plasa Mundo Merced, Scharloo ☎5999/465-4633. Hidden in a small alley behind the theatre, this is one of the few places in the city open for dinner seven days a week. Seafood dishes, steaks and sandwiches cost around US$15 and an excellent Indonesian buffet is offered every Wednesday night for NAf$39.50. You can also just munch on tapas, which cost US$3–8. Happy hour Fri 6–7pm. Dinner only.

The northern tip

Jaanchie's on main road in Westpunt ☎5999/864-0126. Delicious and inexpensive local dishes served by friendly staff. Their speciality is wahoo (a fish) served with rice, salad and plantains (US$13), but you can get soups (fish, iguana, goat or beef) for US$3 and fish, shrimp and conch sandwiches for US$6. Watch for the "I Love Jaanchie's" sign on the main road. Open daily for lunch and dinner.

Rijsttafel Mercuriusstraat 13–15, Salina, close to Chobolobo (home of Senior & Co.) ☎5999/461-2606. An elegant and pricey Indonesian restaurant decorated with shadow puppets, batiks and copper pots. Go with a group to enjoy a traditional Indonesian banquet; a vegetarian menu is also available. The banquet costs US$22 per person (minimum two people); other mains around US$25. Open for lunch and dinner; closed Sun. Reservations recommended.

The rest of the island

Sjalotte west of Willemstad at the *Floris Suite Hotel*, Piscadera Bay ☎5999/462-6111. Right on the bay, this is a fine restaurant, serving starters like snails or fried sweetbreads for US$8–11 and mains like bouillabaisse of local fish or vegetable lasagne for US$12–20. Open daily for lunch and dinner.

Zambezi Restaurant at the Curaçao Ostrich Farm, Groot St Joris West ☎5999/747-2777. Ostrich and other African dishes are their speciality, with most main courses around US$20. Reservations are recommended. Closed Mon, lunch only Tues, lunch and dinner Wed–Sun.

Nightlife

Most of the popular **bars** and **nightclubs** are located outside of downtown Willemstad. Cover charges apply only when a live band is playing.

De Heeren north of Punda next to a shopping centre, Zuikertuintje ☎5999/736-0491. Popular hangout on Monday and Thursday nights, attracting

a fairly young crowd of Dutch locals. Great place to dance, listen to music and have a beer.

De Tropen SBN Doormanweg 37. While there's

dancing on Friday and Saturday nights, most come to listen to European music and just relax.

Hooks Hut Piscaderabaai ☎5999/462-6575. Popular Willemstad bar, with live Caribbean music on Weds. Look out for the seventeen-piece Grupo Ritmiko Karabela, who play here from time to time.

The Living Room Saliòa 129. A popular nightspot on Friday and Saturday for listening to music from reggae to *salsa*.

Mambo Beach Sea Aquarium Beach, Bapor Kibra ☎5999/461-8999. Lively after-work bar offering something different every night of the week and dancing every Saturday until 4am. Happy hour 5–6pm.

Wet and Wild Beach Club next door to *Mambo Beach*, Bapor Kibra ☎5999/561-2477. Another beach bar full of weekend energy. On Sunday there's a live DJ and happy hour from 6pm.

Listings

Banks There are many banks located in the shopping district of Punda and Otrobanda. Most of the ATMs at the Maduro & Curiel's Bank dispense US cash or guilders.

Car rental Antillean (☎5999/461-3144); Casual (☎5999/737-4193); Hertz (☎5999/888-0088); and Noordstar (☎5999/737-5616).

Cinema There's an excellent seven-screen cinema in Scharloo, five minutes' walk from the centre (☎5999/465-1000).

Internet access Telecentre, Brionplein just across from the floating bridge (Mon–Sat 9am–5pm; US$3/hr; ☎5999/699-9515); in Punda upstairs at Time Out Café, Keukenplein 8 (Mon–Fri 9.30am–7pm, Sat 10am–4pm; US$5 for 30min); and at C@fe Internet in the Blue Marlin Building by the

Queen Emma Bridge, Handelskade 38 (Mon–Sat 9am–8pm; US$5 for 30min; ☎5999/465-5088). The Telecentre is also the best place to make international calls.

Pharmacies Botica Brion is across from the post office in Otrobanda (☎5999/462-7027); in Punda try the centrally located Botica Popular at Madurostraat 15 (☎5999/461-1269).

Post office In Punda, the post office is next to the main market on Waaigatplein 1 (Mon–Fri 7.30am–noon & 1.30–5pm; ☎5999/433-1100), while in Otrobanda the post office is located on the main floor of the large white Landskantoor building on Breedestraat (same hours as above).

Taxis Taxi Central ☎5999/869-0747.

Travel store

Rough Guides travel...

...music & reference

Mexico
Peru
St Lucia
South America
Trinidad & Tobago
Yúcatan

Africa & Middle East

Cape Town & the
    Garden Route
Egypt
The Gambia
Jordan
Kenya
Marrakesh
    DIRECTIONS
Morocco
South Africa, Lesotho
    & Swaziland
Syria
Tanzania
Tunisia
West Africa
Zanzibar

Travel Theme guides

First-Time Around the
    World
First-Time Asia
First-Time Europe
First-Time Latin
    America
Travel Online
Travel Health
Travel Survival
Walks in London & SE
    England
Women Travel

Maps

Algarve
Amsterdam
Andalucia & Costa
    del Sol
Argentina
Athens
Australia
Baja California
Barcelona
Berlin
Boston

Brittany
Brussels
California
Chicago
Corsica
Costa Rica & Panama
Crete
Croatia
Cuba
Cyprus
Czech Republic
Dominican Republic
Dubai & UAE
Dublin
Egypt
Florence & Siena
Florida
France
Frankfurt
Germany
Greece
Guatemala & Belize
Hong Kong
Iceland
Ireland
Kenya
Lisbon
London
Los Angeles
Madrid
Mallorca
Marrakesh
Mexico
Miami & Key West
Morocco
New England
New York City
New Zealand
Northern Spain
Paris
Peru
Portugal
Prague
Rome
San Francisco
Sicily
South Africa
South India
Sri Lanka
Tenerife
Thailand

Toronto
Trinidad & Tobago
Tuscany
Venice
Washington DC
Yucatán Peninsula

Dictionary Phrasebooks

Croatian
Czech
Dutch
Egyptian Arabic
European Languages
    (Czech, French,
    German, Greek,
    Italian, Portuguese,
    Spanish)
French
German
Greek
Hindi & Urdu
Hungarian
Indonesian
Italian
Japanese
Latin American
    Spanish
Mandarin Chinese
Mexican Spanish
Polish
Portuguese
Russian
Spanish
Swahili
Thai
Turkish
Vietnamese

Music Guides

The Beatles
Bob Dylan
Cult Pop
Classical Music
Elvis
Frank Sinatra
Heavy Metal
Hip-Hop
Jazz
Opera
Reggae

Rock
World Music (2 vols)

Reference Guides

Babies
Books for Teenagers
Children's Books, 0–5
Children's Books, 5–11
Comedy Movies
Conspiracy Theories
Cult Fiction
Cult Football
Cult Movies
Cult TV
The Da Vinci Code
Ethical Shopping
Gangster Movies
Horror Movies
iPods, iTunes & Music
    Online
The Internet
James Bond
Kids' Movies
Lord of the Rings
Macs & OS X
Muhammad Ali
Music Playlists
PCs and Windows
Poker
Pregnancy & Birth
Sci-Fi Movies
Shakespeare
Superheroes

Unexplained
    Phenomena
The Universe
Weather
Website Directory

Football

Arsenal 11s
Celtic 11s
Chelsea 11s
Liverpool 11s
Newcastle 11s
Rangers 11s
Tottenham 11s
Man United 11s

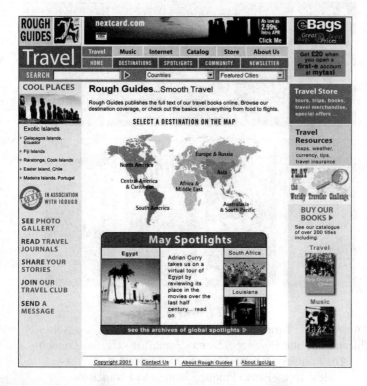

ROUGH GUIDES

not just travel

THE **ROUGH GUIDE** TO

Superheroes

THE COMICS ✹ THE COSTUMES ✹ THE CREATORS ✹ THE CATCHPHRASES

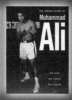

small print and
Index

A Rough Guide to Rough Guides

In the summer of 1981, Mark Ellingham, a recent graduate from Bristol University, was travelling round Greece and couldn't find a guidebook that really met his needs. On the one hand there were the student guides, insistent on saving every last cent, and on the other the heavyweight cultural tomes whose authors seemed to have spent more time in a research library than lounging away the afternoon at a taverna or on the beach.

In a bid to avoid getting a job, Mark and a small group of writers set about creating their own guidebook. It was a guide to Greece that aimed to combine a journalistic approach to description with a thoroughly practical approach to travellers' needs – a guide that would incorporate culture, history and contemporary insights with a critical edge, together with up-to-date, value-for-money listings. Back in London, Mark and the team finished their Rough Guide, as they called it, and talked Routledge into publishing the book.

That first *Rough Guide to Greece*, published in 1982, was a student scheme that became a publishing phenomenon. The immediate success of the book – with numerous reprints and a Thomas Cook prize shortlisting – spawned a series that rapidly covered dozens of destinations. Rough Guides had a ready market among low-budget backpackers, but soon also acquired a much broader and older readership that relished Rough Guides' wit and inquisitiveness as much as their enthusiastic, critical approach. Everyone wants value for money, but not at any price.

Rough Guides soon began supplementing the "rougher" information about hostels and low-budget listings with the kind of detail on restaurants and quality hotels that independent-minded visitors on any budget might expect, whether on business in New York or trekking in Thailand.

These days the guides – distributed worldwide by the Penguin Group – offer recommendations from shoestring to luxury and cover more than 200 destinations around the globe, including almost every country in the Americas and Europe, more than half of Africa and most of Asia and Australasia. Our ever-growing team of authors and photographers is spread all over the world, particularly in Europe, the USA and Australia.

In 1994, we published the *Rough Guide to World Music* and *Rough Guide to Classical Music*; and a year later the *Rough Guide to the Internet*. All three books have become benchmark titles in their fields – which encouraged us to expand into other areas of publishing, mainly around popular culture. Rough Guides now publish:

- Travel guides to more than 200 worldwide destinations
- Dictionary phrasebooks to 22 major languages
- History guides ranging from Ireland to Islam
- Maps printed on rip-proof and waterproof Polyart™ paper
- Music guides running the gamut from Opera to Elvis
- Restaurant guides to London, New York and San Francisco
- Reference books on topics as diverse as the Weather and Shakespeare
- Sports guides from Formula 1 to Man Utd
- Pop culture books from *Lord of the Rings* to Cult TV
- World Music CDs in association with World Music Network

Visit **www.roughguides.com** to see our latest publications.

Rough Guide credits

Text editor: Hunter Slaton
Layout: Dan May
Cartography: Katie Lloyd-Jones, Maxine Repath
Picture editor: Mark Thomas
Production: Katherine Owers
Proofreader: David Price
Cover design: Chloë Roberts
....

Editorial: London Kate Berens, Claire Saunders, Geoff Howard, Ruth Blackmore, Gavin Thomas, Polly Thomas, Richard Lim, Clifton Wilkinson, Alison Murchie, Sally Schafer, Karoline Densley, Andy Turner, Ella O'Donnell, Keith Drew, Edward Aves, Nikki Birrell, Helen Marsden, Joe Staines, Duncan Clark, Peter Buckley, Matthew Milton, Daniel Crewe; **New York** Andrew Rosenberg, Richard Koss, Steven Horak, AnneLise Sorensen, Amy Hegarty, Hunter Slaton, April Isaacs
Design & Pictures: London Simon Bracken, Dan May, Diana Jarvis, Mark Thomas, Jj Luck, Harriet Mills, Chloë Roberts; **Delhi** Madhulita Mohapatra, Umesh Aggarwal, Ajay Verma, Jessica Subramanian, Amit Verma, Ankur Guha

Production: Julia Bovis, Sophie Hewat, Katherine Owers
Cartography: London Maxine Repath, Ed Wright, Katie Lloyd-Jones; **Delhi** Manish Chandra, Rajesh Chhibber, Jai Prakash Mishra, Ashutosh Bharti, Rajesh Mishra, Animesh Pathak, Jasbir Sandhu, Karobi Gogoi
Online: New York Jennifer Gold, Suzanne Welles, Kristin Mingrone; **Delhi** Manik Chauhan, Narender Kumar, Shekhar Jha, Rakesh Kumar
Marketing & Publicity: London Richard Trillo, Niki Hanmer, David Wearn, Demelza Dallow, Louise Maher; **New York** Geoff Colquitt, Megan Kennedy, Katy Ball; **Delhi** Reem Khokhar
Custom publishing and foreign rights: Philippa Hopkins
Manager India: Punita Singh
Series editor: Mark Ellingham
Reference Director: Andrew Lockett
PA to Managing and Publishing Directors: Megan McIntyre
Publishing Director: Martin Dunford
Managing Director: Kevin Fitzgerald

Publishing information

This 2nd edition published October 2005 by
Rough Guides Ltd,
80 Strand, London WC2R 0RL
345 Hudson St, 4th Floor,
New York, NY 10014, USA
14 Local Shopping Centre, Panchsheel Park,
New Delhi 110017, India
Distributed by the Penguin Group
Penguin Books Ltd,
80 Strand, London WC2R 0RL
Penguin Putnam, Inc.
375 Hudson Street, NY 10014, USA
Penguin Group (Australia)
250 Camberwell Road, Camberwell
Victoria 3124, Australia
Penguin Books Canada Ltd,
10 Alcorn Avenue, Toronto, Ontario,
Canada M4V 1E4
Penguin Group (New Zealand)
Cnr Rosedale and Airborne Roads
Albany, Auckland, New Zealand

Typeset in Bembo and Helvetica to an original design by Henry Iles.

Printed in Italy at Legoprint

© Rough Guides 2005

920pp includes index

A catalogue record for this book is available from the British Library

ISBN 1-84353-514-9

1   3   5   7   9   8   6   4   2

SMALL PRINT

Help us update

We've gone to a lot of effort to ensure that the second edition of **The Rough Guide to the Caribbean** is accurate and up to date. However, things change – places get "discovered", opening hours are notoriously fickle, restaurants and rooms raise prices or lower standards. If you feel we've got it wrong or left something out, we'd like to know, and if you can remember the address, the price, the time, the phone number, so much the better.

We'll credit all contributions, and send a copy of the next edition (or any other Rough Guide if you prefer) for the best letters. Everyone who writes to us and isn't already a subscriber will receive a copy of our full-colour thrice-yearly newsletter. Please mark letters: "**Rough Guide Caribbean Update**" and send to: Rough Guides, 80 Strand, London WC2R 0RL, or Rough Guides, 4th Floor, 345 Hudson St, New York, NY 10014. Or send an email to **mail@roughguides.com**

Have your questions answered and tell others about your trip at
www.roughguides.atinfopop.com

Acknowledgements

J.P. Anderson Many, many thanks to miracle-worker Elise Magras at the St Barth's Tourist Office; Valerie Vulcain-Augustine at the Martinique Promotion Bureau, for invaluable last-minute assistance; and on Guadeloupe, the friendly folks at the tourist offices of Point-a-Pitre, La Desirade, and Marie-Galante.

Undeleeb Din Thanks to the Tourist Board and Lewyn Blake of Montserrat; Carolyn Brown, Bart van Deventer, Barbara "Miss B" Joyce, and Michael Abraham of Anguilla; Antoine Mignot and Indiana Broch of St Martin; Desiree Johnson and Glenn Holm of Saba; Glenn Faires, Michele Faires all the staff of STENAPA and the Statia Tourist Office, Nevis Tourism Authority; Randolph Hamilton of St Kitts.

S.E. Kramer Thanks to Dominica's NDC and their helpers John and Prosper Paris, Marie Rosa of Adams Unlimited, and Anne Jno Baptiste of Papillote. Thanks also to her patient editors Chris, Hunter, and Steve, and her inimitable traveling companion, Robbie.

Emma Lozman For great info and help in St Lucia, thanks to the Abrahams, Takashi Aoki, Peter Ernest, and Esther Louis-Fernand. Thanks to my friends around the globe, especially to Olive, Todd, and Evan for their incredible hospitality in Cayman; to Sabine, Holger, and Julia for their friendship in St Lucia; and to Zaidee and Carey for their encouragement. Much love to Melie, Mom, and Jay for their infinite support.
Benedict Mander Thanks to Taino Divers.

Fiona McAuslan Thanks to the editors and everyone else at Rough Guides for all their unstinting support and help. In Cuba Fiona would like to thank Aurora Ampudia and everyone at Sol Melía for all their advice and support.

Matt Norman Thanks to Sinai Sole Rodriguez, Miriam Rodriguez Dominguez and Ricardo Morales at the house in Havana.

Kevin Revolinski Enormous thanks to Renee Lajcak and Brian Babler for home base, Janeen Bittmann and Susan Curtis for my second home, Bruce and Mathilde Wilson for yet a third home, Louise Benjamin and Danielle Hylton at the USVI Tourism Board for outstanding assistance, Lumumba for the bush tour, Sue Ward and Carl Moore for dive help, and Cedric Bodet, Tom Huhti and Cruzan Rum for keeping me from panicking.

Lesley Anne Rose Many thanks to Martin Chester for being a patient travelling companion, research assistant and grammar geek, Mandoo for sharing Grenada, Lisa at Just Grenada for advice post Hurricane Ivan and Christine Horne for safe passage on troubled waters.

Polly Thomas Huge thanks to all those who once again made my trip such a pleasure, and who smoothed the path in countless ways. Particular thanks to Marjorie Morris and the Morris family for support and hospitality; thanks also to Ozzy Osman; Helmut Steiner; Andre McGann; Joel Goldfus; Bertram, Greer Ann and Scotty Saulter; Herbert "Super Herb" Kennedy; Jason Henzell; Rebecca Wiersma; Andree Edwards-Bowles; and Claire Barry.

Adam Vaitilingam Thanks to the CRAMs for sorting out Antigua.

Benedict Mander Thanks to Taino Divers.

Natalie Folster Thanks very much to Charity Armbrister, Carmeta Miller, Warden Ray, Evelyn Darville, David "Blue" Brown, District Administrator Cooper, Mike and Valerie Dudash, Peter and Betty Oxley, North Carolina Outward Bound, Peterina Hannah, the Goede family, Tommy Sands, Charlie Moore, Mrs. Eurene Nottage, Peter Kuska, Fred Welsford, Andrew Rosenberg, Hunter Slaton and Chris Barsanti.

The editor would like to thank all of the contributors for their hard work, Chris Barsanti for starting the guide, Richard Koss and Steve Horak for editorial assistance, Katie Lloyd-Jones and Maxine Repath for maps, Daniel May and Michelle Bhatia for typesetting, Mark Thomas for tireless photo research, and Simon Bracken, Julia Bovis and Diana Jarvis for other essential bits and pieces.

Readers' letters

Thanks to all the readers who have taken the time to write in with comments and suggestions (and apologies if we've inadvertently omitted or misspelt anyone's name):

Takashi Aoki, James Pash, Tania Denesiuk, Natasha White, Mrs. M.E. Leggett.

Photo credits

SMALL PRINT

Index

Map entries are in colour.

P

U

V

W

Y

Map symbols

maps are listed in the full index using coloured text

------	International boundary	♟	Museum
▬▬▬	Motorway	🏛	Stately home
═══	Major paved road	🏛	Monument
══	Minor paved road	⊙	Statue/memorial
▬▬	Pedestrianised road	🏛	Windmill
∙∙∙∙∙∙	Unpaved road	⬟	Observatory
- - - -	Footpath	⚲	Church (regional maps)
▬◆▬	Railway	✡	Synagogue
– – –	Ferry routes	⛳	Golf course
────	Waterway	⚘	Gardens
────	Wall	🌳	Tree
♦	Place of interest	⛽	Petrol station
✈	Airport	◉	Accommodation
✗	Airfield/airstrip	■	Restaurant/café
⌃⌃	Mountains	ⓘ	Information office
▲	Mountain peak	✉	Post office
⚡	Waterfall	☏	Telephone
⩘	Springs	@	Internet access
⸾	Reef	⊞	Hospital
⤸	Dive site	★	Transport stop
⚓	Shipwreck	🅿	Parking
⚘	Turtle nesting site	▮	Building
⚲	Lighthouse	⊞	Church (town maps)
⩙	Viewpoint	▭	Market
◴	Crater	⊞	Cemetery
◖	Cave	▦	Park
∴	Ruins	▦	Beach
⚑	Fortress	▦	Salt pond
▮	Tower	〰	Marshland